Wm. Ackley
Sept. 10, 1939

McGRAW-HILL PUBLICATIONS IN THE
AGRICULTURAL SCIENCES

LEON J. COLE, Consulting Editor

THE FUNDAMENTALS

OF

FRUIT PRODUCTION

THE FUNDAMENTALS

OF

FRUIT PRODUCTION

BY

VICTOR RAY GARDNER
Professor of Horticulture, Michigan State College

FREDERICK CHARLES BRADFORD
Formerly Associate Professor of Horticulture
Michigan State College

AND

HENRY DAGGETT HOOKER, Jr.
Late Associate Professor of Horticulture
University of Missouri

SECOND EDITION

McGRAW-HILL BOOK COMPANY, Inc.
NEW YORK AND LONDON
1939

PREFACE

If a tree is to live, it must constantly make new growth; failing in this, it begins to die. One of its vital conductive channels, the sapwood, is composed of cells that have a limited duration of life, and as they become senescent new cells must be formed to take over the conductive processes. Thus the trunk and the branches grow thicker and thicker; to maintain the conductive channels more and more food is required. A tree's nutrient and water requirements are therefore constantly increasing.

The present work attempts to focus attention on the tree's growth and its steadily increasing requirements and on the conditions that make it profitable as a producer of fruit. Practices are considered only as they affect these conditions, not as ends in themselves. Maintenance of this point of view has necessitated a rather wide departure from conventional arrangement of subject matter. The common orchard practices are not sacred in themselves; indeed, they are important only in so far as they help vegetative growth and especially fruit production. Fundamentally the plant's growth and functioning depend on the nature of the environment and the adjustment thereto and not directly on cultural practices, which only modify the relation of the plant to the environmental complex. Consequently these practices appear inconspicuous in the chapter and section headings.

Acquaintance with principles without the facts on which they rest is itself empirical. Particular attention, therefore, is given to the inclusion of sufficient illustrative matter to permit quantitative estimate of the validity and applicability of the principles enunciated. Comparatively little that is original is presented; much of the material that is novel to pomological texts is included because of its inaccessibility to the average student. Many significant observations which have been neglected because their ultimate bearing was not appreciated at the time they were recorded have been reviewed in the light of modern knowledge. Plant physiology, plant chemistry, soil science and physics have been requisitioned freely and advisedly, in no case, however, without an indication of applicability to pomology. Careful consideration has approved this course because special applications to fruit growing are rare in the general university courses in these subjects and because in the arrangement of many curricula pomology precedes some of the science courses that are needed as preparatory training. Exhaustive treatment was not attempted in the first edition, nor is it attempted here. Nevertheless, an effort has been made to include the results of the more significant researches and experiences as they lead to a better understanding of the tree's adjustment and reaction to its environment.

The solution of a problem arising outside the classroom depends on obtaining all the pertinent data, systematizing them to ascertain the factors involved and applying to the problem the knowledge so gained. This text is designed to prepare the student to undertake these steps. As with any text, much is necessarily left to the instructor, particularly matters of opinion and of local application.

Finally, it hardly need be said that this text is intended for students of college grade. It is not a manual on how to grow fruit; it does not attempt to enter fields best covered by classroom discussion, laboratory work or practical experience. It is intended, however, to be a supplement and guide to these.

In the preparation of this second edition, the authors have made use of many criticisms and suggestions that have come to them from those who have employed the first edition as a text or for reference, and to them grateful acknowledgment is made.

THE AUTHORS.

EAST LANSING, MICH.,
March, 1939.

CONTENTS

SECTION I

WATER RELATIONS

CHAPTER I

Water as a Plant Constituent—The Water Requirements of Plants in Terms of Dry Weight—The Water Requirements of Plants in Terms of Precipitation—Amounts Used by the Plants Themselves; Total Amounts Required for Plants and to Compensate for Evaporation, Runoff and Seepage—Planting Distances Related to Moisture Supply—Factors Influencing the Water Requirements of Plants—Nutrient Supply; Cultivation; Light; In General; Some Applications to Practice—The Wilting Point for Fruit Plants—Wilting Coefficients; Wilting under Field Conditions; Wilting Coefficients and Drought Resistance—Summary.

CHAPTER II

Water Absorption—The Water-absorbing Organs—The Handling and Transplanting of Nursery Stock—The Water-absorbing Process—Factors Enabling the Roots to Exploit the Soil; Adaptation of Roots to Moisture Conditions; Factors Influencing Rate of Absorption; Submergence and Root Killing—Transpiration—Cuticular and Stomatal Transpiration Compared; Variability in Number of Stomata in Accordance with External Conditions—Factors Influencing Rate of Transpiration—Kind of Plant; Character of Cuticle; Age of Leaf; Defoliation, Summer Pruning; Wind Velocity, Windbreaks; Light; Temperature, Slope of Ground; Soil Moisture—The Water-conducting System of the Tree—Summary.

CHAPTER III

Orchard Soil Management Methods Defined and Described—Orchard Soil Management Methods and Surface Run-off—Moisture under Tillage and Sod-mulch Systems of Management—Some New York and Pennsylvania Records; Some New Hampshire Records; English Experience; Some Kentucky and Kansas Records; In General; Practicability of Sod-mulch System Influenced by Depth of Rooting—Influence of Depth and Frequency of Cultivation upon Soil Moisture—Intercrops and the Soil Moisture Supply—Cover Crops and the Moisture Supply—Effects of Early and Late Seeding; Winter-killed and Winter-surviving Cover Crops—Wind Velocity and Evaporation, Windbreaks—Summary.

CONTENTS

PAGE

CHAPTER XXXV

THE FUNDAMENTALS OF FRUIT PRODUCTION

SECTION I

WATER RELATIONS

The importance of moisture as a factor in the production of fruit is appreciated only in part. In arid sections the lack is obvious; in many regions certain lands are recognized as too moist for fruit plants. In the majority of the so-called humid sections, however, there is a tacit assumption that nature provides satisfactorily for the requirements of fruit plants. Drought may diminish or destroy other crops, but as long as trees survive there is considered to be sufficient moisture.

The forest trees, relied on as evidence of this sufficiency, show, even in a limited area, striking differences in vigor, according to their locations. One of the most important factors recognized by the forester, as affecting tree growth is moisture. Certain spots even in humid regions, are chronically dry, some are nearly always wet; others, favorable in some seasons, are subject rather frequently to excess or deficiency of moisture.

Much of the complacence concerning the water supply of trees is based on the supposedly great range of their roots and the consequent great amount of soil from which they can draw water. For this reason a statement of the extent to which forest trees actually deplete the soil moisture is pertinent. Zon[204] cites data showing moisture contents in June of 4.5 and 4.8 per cent. respectively at 4 and 8 inches in soil through which forest tree roots were ranging, while adjacent spots within the forest, exactly similar except that the roots had been excluded contained, at the same depths, 13.8 and 11.0 per cent. respectively. At 16 inches the root free soil had over twice as much moisture as that to which the roots had access. Evidence is cited to the effect that the water level is lowered under forest and that with the removal of the forest the water level rises. Zon considers that the inability of many species to grow under an established cover of trees, commonly called shade intolerance, is in reality due to the low supply of moisture in the soil. When the roots of the top growth are excluded from an area, the intolerant species grow there with considerable vigor.

1

Deficient and excessive moisture are admittedly each a limiting factor in crop production. Table 1, based on estimates by crop reporters of the United States Department of Agriculture, shows the damage caused by injurious moisture conditions in comparison with other factors. The figures on apples and berries are averages for the period 1912–1919 and on other crops selected in comparison for the period 1909–1919. According to these estimates small fruits suffer more from drought than from any other single factor, while apples are injured more only by cold weather.

TABLE 1.—DAMAGE TO CROPS FROM DIFFERENT CAUSES
(*After Smith*[168])

	Deficient moisture, per cent.	Excessive moisture, per cent.	Floods, per cent.	Frost or freeze, per cent.	Hail, per cent.	Hot winds, per cent.	Storms, per cent.	Total weather, per cent.	Plant disease, per cent.	Insect pests, per cent.	Animal pests, per cent.	Defective seed, per cent.	Total, per cent.
Wheat	12.4	2.0	0.3	4.5	1.1	2.0	0.3	22.9	2.7	2.1	0.2	0.2	28.8
Corn	16.3	4.0	0.9	2.9	0.4	2.2	0.5	27.7	0.2	2.7	0.2	0.7	31.1
Rice	6.7	3.1	1.5	0.3	...	0.4	1.8	14.1	1.2	0.8	0.3	0.1	19.0
Potatoes	14.4	3.1	0.2	1.6	0.1	0.7	0.1	20.7	4.4	3.2	0.1	0.3	30.0
Tobacco	8.7	3.7	0.6	1.1	0.8	0.2	0.3	15.8	0.4	2.6	...	0.1	20.5
Cotton	12.3	4.3	1.0	1.4	0.5	1.6	0.7	22.3	2.0	9.7	...	0.2	35.5
Apples	5.4	1.6	0.2	14.6	0.8	0.5	0.9	24.9	3.7	3.6	0.1	...	39.6
Berries	9.3	1.7	0.2	7.3	0.5	0.6	0.2	20.3	1.1	0.6	0.1	...	24.9

Precipitation cannot be controlled. Soil moisture, however, is susceptible more or less to modification by various practices and adjustments of fruits or of stocks for fruits can be made in some cases to the moisture conditions of the soil. For these reasons recognition of soil conditions, understanding of the water requirements of the various fruit plants and knowledge of the relation of various cultural practices to moisture control are of fundamental importance to the fruit grower.

CHAPTER I

THE WATER REQUIREMENTS OF FRUIT PLANTS

There is more or less acknowledgment of a difference in adaptability of different fruits to varying moisture conditions in the soil; this is, however, expressed in terms of tolerance more often than in terms of requirements. It is stated frequently that sour cherries will stand a dry soil or that pears will endure a wet soil; there is very little exact information on what the various fruits actually require. Table 2 gives some interesting results of investigation in California on the requirements of fruit and other crops under conditions common in that section. The requirements of the several fruits, stated in terms of the amounts of free water in the soil, exhibit a considerable difference. Other data to be introduced later (Tables 10 and 11) show that the same fruit may have different moisture requirements in different localities.

TABLE 2.—RELATIVE WATER REQUIREMENTS OF DIFFERENT PLANTS
(*After Loughridge*[121])

Free water in 4 feet of soil		Plants for which the soil moisture is just above the minimum; cultures did well	Plants for which the soil moisture is just below the minimum; cultures suffered
Percentage	Tons per acre		
0.0 to 1.0	80	Apricots, olives, peaches, soy bean	Citrus, pears, plums, acacia
1.0 to 1.5	120	Citrus, figs	Almonds, apples
1.5 to 2.0	160	Almonds, plums, saltbush	Barley
2.0 to 2.5	200	Walnuts, grapes, eucalyptus	
2.5 to 3.0	240	Apples, prunes	Prunes
3.0 to 4.0	320	Pears, hairy vetch	Wheat
4.0 to 5.0	400	Wheat, corn	
5.0 to 6.0	480	Sugar beets, sorghum	Sugar beets

Water as a Plant Constituent.—Water is a normal constituent of all plant tissues, comprising from 50 to 75 per cent. of the leaves and twigs, from 60 to 85 per cent. of the roots, and 85 per cent. or more of most fleshy fruits (Table 3).

Table 4 shows the moisture content of bearing, non-bearing and barren spurs of the apple at various periods. All spurs have a maximum water

3

content during or directly after the time of blossoming, but blossoming spurs contain much more water than spurs in the off year and these more than barren spurs.

TABLE 3.—TYPICAL WATER CONTENT OF FRUIT PLANTS IN THE FALL[186]

	Fruit	Flesh	Skin	Core or stone	Stem	Leaves	New growth	Old growth
Apple...............	85.64	89.74	85.81	85.71	....	53.00	49.40	....
Pear...............	86.78	86.07	78.32	83.62	....	38.20	50.33	....
Peach..............	....	88.78	....	32.67	....	63.78	49.52	....
Plum..............	....	88.06	....	32.83	59.52	61.10	49.59	....
Cherry.............	....	89.98	....	46.81	68.76	65.10	49.51	....
Currant............	87.13	....	....	....	75.18	65.97	50.36	45.74
Blackberry.........	85.10	....	....	....	....	48.14	38.15	38.26
Gooseberry.........	89.42	....	....	....	....	66.25	44.20	39.77
Raspberry..........	84.35	....	....	....	....	33.28	41.33	33.52
Grape..............	78.44	....	....	....	....	69.00	54.33	....

Besides being a plant constituent, water is a plant nutrient and as such is indispensable for the manufacture of plant material, particularly in the photosynthetic production of carbohydrates. Finally, water is the medium in which all the nutrients essential to green plants, except carbon, occur in solution.

TABLE 4.—VARIATIONS IN THE WATER CONTENT OF APPLE SPURS[97]

	Feb. 4	Mar. 11	Mar. 26	May 13	June 26	Sept. 2	Nov. 19	Jan. 24
Bearing Spurs:								
Wealthy...........	49.9	....	....	65.5	61.1	53.2	50.5	45.7
Ben Davis.........	....	....	60.0	64.6	61.8	55.2	51.6	51.1
Jonathan..........	....	47.5	....	63.2	60.2	54.8	51.6	47.7
Non-bearing Spurs:								
Jonathan........	....	47.1	....	54.8	53.0	51.4	48.6	49.6
Ben Davis.........	....	....	50.8	59.8	55.1	48.6	48.5	48.9
Barren Spurs:								
Ben Davis.........	....	....	45.6	52.7	47.8	47.6	44.6	45.5
Nixonite..........	47.4	....	....	56.2	51.4	47.6	48.6	43.1

The Water Requirements of Plants in Terms of Dry Weight.—The water requirement of any plant is defined as the amount of water used while a unit weight of dry matter is produced. The weights may be measured in grams or in pounds, but the ratio obtained is the same in any case. Table 5 brings together data that have a bearing on this point, as reported by several investigators.

TABLE 5.—WATER EVAPORATED BY GROWING PLANTS FOR 1 PART OF DRY MATTER PRODUCED[123]

Lawes and Gilbert (England)		Hellriegel (Germany)		Wollny (Germany)		King (Wisconsin)	
Peas	235	Peas	292	Peas	479	Peas	447
Barley	262	Barley	310	Barley	774	Barley	393
Red clover	249	Red clover	330			Red clover	453
Beans	214	Beans	262	Maize	233	Maize	272
Wheat	225	Wheat	354	Millet	416	Potatoes	423
		Oats	402	Oats	665	Oats	557
		Buckwheat	374	Buckwheat	664		
		Lupin	373	Rape	912		
		Rye	377	Sunflower	490		
				Mustard	843		

Though Table 5 does not include figures for fruit plants, as a class they do not differ materially from herbaceous plants in this respect. Experiments conducted by one of the authors in 1927 in Michigan with peach trees grown from seeds showed a range in water requirement of from 115 to 268, expressed in terms of units of water per unit of fresh weight of wood and roots.

Hilgard[92] states that oaks require from 200 to 300 pounds of water for each pound of dry matter produced, while birches and lindens use from 600 to 700 pounds in producing 1 pound of dry leaves; the figures for beech and maple are intermediate. Hilgard estimates from 30 to 70 units of water needed for the production of one unit of dry matter in spruce, fir and pine trees. Thus the range in water requirement for at least some of the ordinary deciduous trees is similar to that of herbaceous crops grown under similar conditions.

Two striking points are shown by these figures on water requirements: (1) the great differences in the water requirements of different species and (2) the variation shown by the same plant in different sections, according to the determinations of different investigators.

These differences carry two suggestions of practical import in fruit production; first, that certain species or certain fruits can do more than others with a given amount of water, second, that the same species of fruit plant will produce more vegetative growth with a given supply of water under certain conditions than under others.

The Water Requirements of Plants in Terms of Precipitation.— Figures have been given showing the approximate water requirements of plants in terms of the number of units of water used while one unit of dry matter is produced. It is interesting to speculate as to what these figures mean in terms of rainfall or amounts of irrigation water.

Amounts Used by the Plants Themselves.—Thompson[182] has calculated the average weight of wood, roots and leaves produced by a normal healthy peach tree up to the time it has attained the age of 9 years as approximately 215 pounds. This represents an average annual dry weight production of wood, leaves and roots of approximately 25 pounds. With increasing age the amount would be somewhat greater. If a 300 bushel per acre yield is assumed, it means the production of approximately 20 pounds of dry matter per tree to be taken away in the form of fruit. In other words, the mature peach tree would be expected to produce about 45 pounds of dry matter per year. Assuming a stand of 100 trees to the acre this would mean a production of 4,500 pounds of dry matter per acre. If it takes 500 parts of water to produce one part of dry weight, it would require 22,500 pounds, over 11 tons or nearly 3,000 gallons per tree to mature the crop properly. This estimate considers only the amount actually taken up by the roots and for the most part transpired through the leaves and does not make any allowance for run-off from the surface, or for seepage and evaporation. It means 300,000 gallons per acre, equivalent to a rainfall of approximately 11 inches, or an equivalent amount of irrigation water. For each additional 100 bushels of fruit per acre approximately 2 acre-inches more would be required by the plant. Looking at the matter from another angle, for every acre-inch under the 11 that is denied the trees, there would be a decrease in yield of approximately 50 bushels. Of course, if the water requirement of this fruit is only 300 instead of 500 under a given set of conditions, 7 acre-inches actually available to the trees would mature as large a crop as the 11 acre-inches in the first instance.

That the first presented figures are probably representative for many tree fruits is suggested by their close agreement with the 9 acre-inches estimate of Hilgard[92] as the water requirement of 15-year old orange trees in southern California and the 4,500 gallons per tree estimate of Duggar[57] as the requirement of a 30-year old apple tree, though recent studies in Arizona have shown that mature Washington navel orange trees remove from the soil as much as 30 acre-inches of water in the course of a year, and Marsh grapefruit trees as much as 42 acre-inches.[79] It is interesting to note that a 12-inch summer rainfall has been estimated as sufficient for the actual water consumption of 100-year-old beech trees standing about 200 to the acre.[149] Data presented in Table 5 show that the variation in the water requirements of individual crops often exceeds the difference of 200 assumed in the case of the peach orchard. This emphasizes the point that it is frequently a matter of much practical importance to provide the tree with as nearly optimum nutritive conditions as possible, to secure the economical use of water if for no other reason.

Total Amounts Required for Plants and to Compensate for Evaporation Run-off and Seepage.—It should be noted that in the last paragraph when 7 to 11 acre-inches of water was mentioned, as approximately the amount required to mature a peach crop of a certain size, reference was made only to the water actually taken up and used by the plant. As is well known, a considerable percentage of the water that reaches the land as rain or snow or through the irrigation channel is made unavailable by run-off, evaporation and seepage.

The exact percentages removed in these ways vary greatly, depending on the seasonal distribution of the rainfall, the rate of any precipitation, the topography, the character of soil and subsoil, the atmospheric humidity and other factors. The measurements made by Shantz[165] in the Great Plains area indicate that approximately one-half of the total rainfall reaching either the short-grass sod or cultivated plats in that section was lost by run-off. With respect to the water taken in by the soil, considerably more than 50 per cent. of it disappeared through transpiration from the short-grass cover of vegetation and the remainder by evaporation from the soil surface. It has been estimated that in the forest, where conditions are more favorable than in most fruit plantations for the reduction of run-off and evaporation, probably not more than 35 per cent. of the precipitation actually becomes available for tree growth.[26] In orchard practice then, it is doubtful if much more than one-third of the natural precipitation or irrigation water can be considered to be utilized by the trees, and under poor methods of soil management or in soils of poor water-absorbing and water-holding capacity the percentage may be much lower.

In the light of what has been said it obviously would be impracticable to attempt the construction of a table showing the rainfall requirements of different fruit crops, such as strawberries, cherries, apples and olives, for there are too many contributing factors to be evaluated, but the general principles that have been given should be capable of interpretation and intelligent application to many concrete practical problems as they arise in orchard management. For instance, with a fairly accurate knowledge of the mean and minimum rainfall of a particular location and its seasonal distribution, and after a first-hand study of soil conditions as they relate to moisture, it should not be difficult to determine more or less accurately the practicability of growing a certain fruit crop without irrigation facilities, or to determine the relative importance of certain moisture conserving practices. Experience may be a still better guide but only to the extent that it gives ability to judge local conditions and so permits a more accurate interpretation and application of general principles.

Some measure of the way these principles apply to concrete cases may be obtained from the statement that it has been found practicable to use irrigation water amounting to about 30 acre-inches for mature peach trees on some of the gravelly loams of Utah and 40 acre-inches on full bearing apple orchards on sandy loam in Idaho where rainfall averaged 10 or less inches per year.   On the other hand, heavy crops of sweet cherries, prunes and apricots are obtained without irrigation from orchards on a light sandy loam at The Dalles, Ore., with an average annual rainfall of 16 or 17 inches.

Some years ago 16 or 18 inches of rainfall annually was generally considered sufficient for the production of deciduous fruits in California, but experience has demonstrated that the percentage of this amount that is actually left for the trees after run-off, seepage and evaporation is not adequate for the average orchard with the trees spaced the usual distances.   As a matter of fact there is a growing belief that even a rainfall of 30 inches in California should be supplemented by provision for irrigation to take care of occasional emergencies.[184]

Planting Distances Related to Moisture Supply.—Application of the principles just pointed out to particular fruits and particular locations should be the main deciding factor in determining distance of planting for orchard fruits, for water supply is most frequently the limiting factor in this connection even though the grower seldom realizes it at the time of setting.   This is contrary, in the way it often works out, to the frequently repeated statement that trees can be planted more closely in a "poor" than in a "good" soil.   If the soil is "poor" because it is shallow or of poor water-holding capacity unproductiveness will only be increased by closer spacing.   In soils that are both fertile and well-watered, planting distance should be governed by the size of the plants and the growing habit.   If they are infertile and well-watered, again planting distance should be determined by size of plant and growing habit, and the fertility question solved through the proper use of fertilizers.   If moisture is the limiting factor, regardless of the relative productivity of the land, spacing should be determined largely by moisture requirements, though due attention should be given to growth characteristics.

A notable instance of the intelligent and successful application of these principles to the question of planting distance is found in some of the olive orchards of northern Africa.   Though the usual planting distance for this fruit in irrigated sections, or in regions of ample rainfall is 18 to 22 feet, near Sfax in Tunis the trees are planted 60 to 80 feet apart, making only 7 or 8 to the acre. This arrangement makes possible a profitable dry-land industry without irrigation, though the mean annual rainfall is only 9.3 inches and though there are often several successive years in which the total precipitation does not exceed 6 inches.[106]

Another interesting application of the same principle has been recorded in South Dakota. Cottonwoods planted rather close together for windbreak or shelter belt purposes, thrive for a number of years, but eventually a stage is reached when they begin to die from crowding. If wider spacing or thinning is practiced their longevity is increased correspondingly.[46]

Factors Influencing the Water Requirements of Plants.—It is advisable at this point to review some of the data available on the economy with which the plant uses water. From what has been said regarding the total water requirements of the plant it is evident that only an extremely small percentage is finally held by the plant as a constituent of the protoplasm or is used in the manufacture of chemical compounds. The greater portion of the water has been required to meet evaporation. Since the water requirement is a ratio between the water used and the plant material produced, it is evident that all other factors favoring the nutrition of land plants will tend to decrease their water requirement and that all factors tending to increase water loss through transpiration will increase it.

Nutrient Supply.—It is a reasonable assumption that when the soil solution is poor in any indispensable element more water must be taken up by the plant to obtain an ample amount of this element. However, this is true only within certain limits, because of the ability of plants to withdraw from the soil nutrient materials in proportions quite different from those in which they occur there. Nevertheless, experimental evidence indicates that water requirements are considerably lower on fertile than on infertile soils and that manuring increases the efficiency with which water is utilized by the plant, though this increase in efficiency is not proportional to the increase in vigor induced by the treatment.[145]

Table 6 shows the mean water requirements of oats and wheat as influenced by fertilizer treatments and Table 7 presents data showing the effects of various amounts of nitrogen upon the water requirement of the plant.

Attention has been called to the considerably higher water requirement of plants in the very rainy climate of Munich, Germany, than in the drier portions of northern Germany or in Wisconsin. It is suggested that as the moisture approaches the extreme in a wet soil the soil solution is diluted; hence conditions are presented that at least in a way are comparable with those found in a "poor" soil. More water is required to absorb a given amount of nutrients. In this case the poor aeration attendant upon a soil-moisture content above the optimum may also affect the water requirement. Poor aeration means a relative dilution of the oxygen content of the soil, a condition which leads to unusual root respiration.

The immediate effect is the reduced absorption of both water and nutrient substances. Reduction of the latter exceeds considerably that of the former and consequently gives rise to a higher water requirement. The effect of a very dry soil, which likewise increases the water requirement, is attributed by Briggs and Shantz[29] to the restricted area which the active roots and root hairs occupy under these conditions. It seems a strange perversity of fate that the soil conditions and soil treatment which are most likely to result in a restricted root system, such as heavy soils, hardpan, waterlogging, puddling and baking, are those which lead to an increased water requirement of the plant.

TABLE 6.—MEAN WATER REQUIREMENTS OF OATS AND WHEAT WITH DIFFERENT FERTILIZER TREATMENTS
(*From determinations made by Liebacher, Von Seelhorst, Bunger and Ohlmer*[29])

FERTILIZER	MEAN WATER REQUIREMENTS FOR OATS AND WHEAT
K N P	238
N P	243
N K	246
N	259
P K	294
P	297
Check	308
K	314

TABLE 7.—EFFECTS OF VARIOUS AMOUNTS OF NITROGEN ON THE WATER REQUIREMENT OF PLANTS
(*After Hellriegel*[36])

$CaNO_3$ supplied (grams)	Dry matter produced (grams)	Water transpired (grams)	Water requirement
1.640	25.026	7451	292
1.312	23.026	6957	302
0.984	18.288	6317	345
0.656	13.936	4839	347
0.328	8.479	3386	399
0.000	1.103	956	867

Cultivation.—Bearing directly on this point are data obtained on the effects of cultivation in lessening the water requirements of plants. Some of these data are presented in Table 8. In every case the water requirement was materially reduced by cultivation; in one case it was more than cut in two. In certain soils the influence of cultivation was much more pronounced than in others. Presumably cultivation affects the water requirements of plants by effecting a better aeration of the soil, which leads in turn to a significant increase in the supply of available plant nutrients. It may also occasion an increase of soil-moisture content, but not to an extent equaling that for the nutrients.

TABLE 8.—THE INFLUENCE OF CULTIVATION UPON WATER REQUIREMENTS OF PLANTS IN DIFFERENT SOILS[198]

	Not cultivated	Cultivated
Sandy loam	603	252
Clay loam	535	428
Clay	753	582
Type not given	451	265

Light.—It should not be inferred from what has been said, that the plant's water requirement is entirely governed by its nutrition. Investigation has shown, for instance, that in tobacco the amount of water absorbed is quite independent of the amount of mineral constituents taken in.[82] Thus the average ratio of water to ash for six plants grown in the open was 2,548, while for six plants grown under shade it was 1,718. These data, however, apply only to the water-ash ratio of plants growing in full sunlight and in shade. For the water-dry-matter ratio in sunlight and shade a somewhat different condition holds, probably because of the influence of the sunlight in promoting photosynthetic activities and the storage of elaborated materials.

TABLE 9.—WATER REQUIREMENTS PER UNIT OF DRY WEIGHT OF LEAVES IN SUN AND SHADE
(*After Hönel*[149])
(Kilograms per 100 grams of dry leaves)

Species	Sun	Shade
Beech	76.18	107.80
Hornbeam	81.30	98.90
Sycamore	61.69	76.19
Scots pine	19.15	5.02
Silver fir	13.91	4.85
Black pine	8.76	5.25

Data presented in Table 9 show that in all the broad-leaved trees studied, the water-dry-matter ratio rose in the shade, though with the conifers it was greatly lowered. The data on tobacco alone might suggest that with the nutrition factor constant more water would be required in exposed than in protected situations and that shading and windbreaks might be expected to reduce materially the plant's water requirements. On the other hand, the data of Hasselbring and Hönel together lead to the inference that though the mineral requirements of the plant as related to water supply may be increased in exposed and decreased in protected situations, tissue building and the manufacture and storage of elaborated materials may be promoted by the opposite conditions.

In General.—Recent investigations by Briggs and Shantz[30] lead them to conclude that when a crop is thoroughly adapted to a certain environment it has its water requirement at the minimum and that its water requirement gradually increases as it is forced to grow in more and more uncongenial conditions, whatever they may be. Thus as a rule, cool weather crops have a lower water requirement in a cool than in a warm climate, the reverse being true of warm weather crops. In the latter instance, however, the difference is less pronounced, due to the effect of increase in temperature upon transpiration in general.

As will be shown later, however, plants are able to adapt themselves in certain ways to dry conditions, the result being a lowering of what otherwise would be a very high transpiration rate. Only limited data are available as to how these tendencies balance each other and as to what is the final resultant. Leather[115] has found that at Pusa, India, the water requirements of wheat, barley, oats and peas are nearly twice those of maize, though this ratio does not hold in most sections (see Table 5). Apparently this high water requirement of these cool season crops is associated with their maturing during the dry season, while in India maize matures during the more humid season of the monsoon. The greater water requirement of plants cropped by means of pasturing as compared with that of plants which are allowed to continue their growth uncropped,[191] may be taken as an indication that new growth has a higher water requirement than older growth. It would seem that the water requirements of different plants vary mainly because of differences in the economy of their nutrition and because of different physiological and structural modifications affecting their rate of transpiration.

Some Applications to Practice.—The influence of both the chemical and the physical conditions of the soil upon the water requirement of the plant is of practical importance to the grower, the influence of soil productivity being particularly significant. Few realize that, when the soil provides conditions for tree growth that are optimum from the standpoint of nutrient supply, actually less water is required for a given yield than when the plant is handicapped because of the lack of some nutrient as well. This difference in water requirement is not one of academic interest only; it is large enough frequently to account for crop failure or crop success under conditions of limited water supply.

A quotation from King[111] is to the point: "In the long series of studies made by the writer on the amounts of water required for a pound of dry matter, it was found true, almost without exception, that strong vigorous growth and high yields of dry matter are always associated with a small transpiration of water when measured by the dry matter produced."

Even more significant is the statement of Leather,[115] who made a careful study of this question in the dry climate of Pusa, India: "The effect of a suitable manure in aiding the plant to economize water is the most important factor which has yet been noticed in relation to transpiration."

It would probably be a mistake to advise watering or irrigating trees by fertilizing them, because the advice would be taken too literally. Nevertheless, the reduction of the water requirement of the plant by maintaining the soil in a condition as near as possible to the optimum with respect to nutrient supply should be a constant and conscious aim in scientific orchard management, though perhaps the water conservation influence of optimum growing conditions may be more or less masked by the increased requirements for the accompanying increased growth.

The Wilting Point for Fruit Plants.—There seems to be some difference of opinion as to how near to the hygroscopic coefficient plants can exhaust the water supply of the soil. Loughridge states that certain plants can remove enough of the hygroscopic moisture of the soil to maintain life though they cannot grow under these conditions; Hilgard states that soils of great hygroscopic power can withdraw from moist air enough moisture to be of material help in sustaining the life of vegetation in rainless summers or in time of drought, though only a few desert plants can maintain normal growth.[91] In most plants, however, wilting will occur before the moisture content of the soil has been reduced to its hygroscopic coefficient.

Wilting Coefficients.—The work of Briggs and Shantz[28] has led them to conclude that the wilting coefficients for most soils equal their $\dfrac{\text{hygroscopic coefficient}}{0.68 \pm 0.012}$. Thus a sandy loam with a hygroscopic coefficient of 3.5 per cent. would have a wilting coefficient of about 4.8 and a clay loam with a hygroscopic coefficient of 11.4 would have a wilting coefficient of 16.3 per cent. These investigators state, "The wilting coefficient is the same, within the limits of experimental error, for a plant in all stages of development. In other words, the soil-moisture content at the wilting point is not dependent to any material degree upon the age of the plant. . . . [It] is not materially influenced by the dryness of the air, by moderate changes in the solar intensity, or by differences in the amount of soil moisture available during the period of growth."[28] It ranges for different soils from less than 1 per cent. in the coarsest sands to as high as 30 per cent. in the heaviest clays. "The use of different plants as indicators of the wilting point produces only a relatively small change in the wilting coefficient of a given soil. Representing the mean value of the wilting coefficient of a given soil by 100, a range from 95 to 105 approximately, would result from the use of different plants as indicators. . . . The xerophytes tested gave a mean ratio intermediate between the hydrophytes and mesophytes. This would indicate that plants native to dry regions are unable to reduce the water content of the soil to a lower point at the time of wilting than is reached by other plants. . . . There is evidence that drought resistance in a plant is not due to an additional water supply made available for growth by virtue of a greater ability on the part of that plant to remove moisture from the soil."[28]

Wilting under Field Conditions.—The work of Briggs and Shantz on wilting coefficients of different soils was done, however, under fairly uniform conditions of temperature (about 70°F.) and humidity (about 85 per cent.), conditions under which the evaporating power of the air is low. In other words the plants exhausted the water supply of the soil slowly and because of favorable atmospheric conditions were actually able to use the last of the "available" moisture before transpiration demands overtook absorption. In the field, wilting does not usually occur under such favorable atmospheric conditions—favorable from the standpoint of soil moisture supply.

It has been found that when atmospheric conditions are such as to promote rapid evaporation, "the departure of observed from calculated soil moisture contents at permanent wilting is extremely marked for all soils; permanent wilting in the open occurs with a soil moisture content from 30 to 40 per cent. in excess of that present when the same or similar plants are wilted in a moist chamber. . . . Marked increase in the evaporating power of the air accelerates the outgo of water without producing a proportionate increase in its rate of entrance from the soil. With every increase in transpiration rate above a certain limit, this rate becomes, therefore, more and more significant as a factor determining the extent to which the soil water may be exhausted by the plant before the advent of permanent wilting. Thus, permanent wilting under high rates of evaporation does not at all indicate that the available soil moisture has been exhausted. Instead, it merely indicates the reduction of the soil moisture content to a magnitude which corresponds to the residue of water left in the soil at the time when excess of transpiration over absorption has brought the entire plant into the permanently wilted condition. Repeated determinations, under widely varying conditions but with relatively high evaporation rates, show that the magnitude of this residue is directly related to the intensity of the evaporating power of the air."[39]

Undoubtedly, one reason why plants under field conditions show signs of wilting some time before the wilting coefficient of the soil is reached or even closely approached is the greater resistance of the thin films of water surrounding the soil particles to the osmotic pull within the root hairs.

Of greater importance, however, is the fact that the soil mass is not uniformly penetrated by the roots, and these are able to extract the water only from the soil with which they are in almost immediate contact, while capillary action within the soil moves water from the unexploited areas to the exploited root zone only very slowly. Thus, although the soil mass as a whole may show a moisture content considerably above the wilting point, the soil actually consists temporarily of numerous small areas or volumes that are relatively moist intermingled with areas or volumes from which the water has been withdrawn by the roots nearly or quite to the wilting coefficient.[118,202]

It is these higher wilting coefficients under the comparatively high transpiration rates of midsummer which interest the deciduous fruit grower most frequently. Perhaps the wilting coefficient based upon soil texture and calculated for low transpiration rates is most important in determining whether the plant shall or shall not survive the period of drought, for before death occurs there usually will be a shedding of foliage and other protective measures will be taken to reduce moisture losses and lower the transpiration rate. Veihmeyer found that prune and peach trees are able actually to use about half of the water in the soil between the theoretical wilting coefficient and the hygroscopic coefficient.[187] Reduction of the soil-moisture content to the hygroscopic coefficient late in the season is apparently not harmful, provided this condition does not continue too far into the fall and winter.[17] On the other hand, the effects of drought upon the vegetative activities of the tree during the summer, upon the size of its fruit and upon the abscission

TABLE 10.—MINIMUM WATER REQUIREMENTS OF THE APRICOT IN DIFFERENT SOILS[121]
(Records made in early September)

Soils	Locality	Condition of trees	Moisture in 4 feet of soil (per cent.)			
			Total	Hygro-scopic	Free	Tons of free water per acre
Dark loam.....	Sisquoc Valley.	Good	5.5	3.1	2.4	192
Loam..........	East of Ventura (shallow cultivation)	Growth 6 inches	6.5	5.5	1.0	80
Loam..........	Ventura (shallow cultivation)	Growth 8 inches	5.6	4.2	1.4	112
Loam..........	Ventura (deep cultivation)	Growth 36 inches	9.3	5.5	3.8	304
Sand..........	Los Berrios Hill	Good	1.7	0.8	0.9	72
Loam..........	Experiment station	Good	6.1	5.0	1.1	88
Loam..........	Niles (no cultivation)	Very poor	4.4	4.4	0.0	0
Loam..........	Niles (cultivation 3 inches)	Fair	5.4	3.3	2.1	168
Loam..........	Niles (cultivation 6 inches)	Excellent	6.3	3.3	3.0	240
Black clay.....	Woodland	Excellent	18.8	9.6	9.2	736
Gravelly loam..	Woodland	Poor	6.9	5.0	1.9	152
Sand..........	East of Davisville	Good	4.8	3.6	1.2	96
Alluvial........	Davisville	Good	9.0	6.9	2.1	168

of its leaves, flowers and partially grown fruit are exercised during periods of very high transpiration rates. This means that the aim of the grower should be, as far as possible, to maintain the moisture supply of the soil well above these higher amounts.

Wilting Coefficients and Drought Resistance.—Tables 2, 10 and 11 compiled by Loughridge, showing the minimum water requirements of certain fruits in comparison with those of certain other plants, are particularly interesting in this connection.

In commenting upon these tables Loughridge states: "The apricot, olive and peach do well on less water than other orchard fruits, 1 per cent. of free water being sufficient if constantly present. With this amount the citrus fruits, pears and plums were found to suffer, though the citrus fruits were in good condition with a little more water. The almond seems to require about twice the water that the apricot does, while the prune was found to suffer with three times the water in which the apricot was flourishing.

"Emphasis should be placed on the fact that this free water should be present throughout the soil to the depth of 4 feet at least and especially around the feeding rootlets of the tree. The surface of the soil may be wet, and yet the tree may suffer if the ground below be so dry that the rootlets are not able to draw sufficient moisture. This drying-out of the under-soil is one of the evil effects of a severely dry season, and unless the rainfall of the succeeding winter be sufficient to penetrate to the depth of several feet and moisten the soil around the rootlets the trees will suffer almost as if no rain had fallen. The same is true with regard to irrigation; those who have to resort to the artificial application of water to their lands because of insufficient rainfall, should so apply it that it may reach the tree rootlets at the depth of several feet below the surface. This is too often not done, and examination will show that the water has, even after 2 days' irrigation with running water in furrows, not soaked down more than 10 or 12 inches, if that much."[121]

At first, it may seem that the field observations of Loughridge are not in agreement with the conclusion of Briggs and Shantz that the wilting coefficients are practically the same for all plants growing in the same soil. The greater tolerance of the apricot, olive and peach for drought probably is not due to a utilization of the soil water in contact with their roots greater than that of other plants, or in other words, to the reduction of the soil water content to a lower wilting coefficient. It is possibly associated with a greater ability of their roots to exploit every bit of soil within their range, to a wider range that their roots may possess, or more likely still, to a greater ability to reduce transpiration losses to correspond with water intake during periods when the soil-moisture content is approaching the wilting point. It is important that both factors be kept in mind, namely, the marked uniformity in the wilting coefficient for different plants and the marked difference in their ability

TABLE 11.—RELATIVE WATER REQUIREMENTS OF DIFFERENT FRUITS IN DIFFERENT SOILS
(*After Loughridge*[121])

Free water in 4 feet of soil		Plants for which the soil moisture is just above the minimum; cultures did well	Plants for which the soil moisture is just below the minimum; cultures suffered
Percentage	Tons per acre	Sandy soils—hygroscopic moisture 1 to 3	
2.0	160	Apricots, saltbush	Olives, peaches, plums, grapes
2.5	200	Olives, peaches, wheat	Cherries, pears
3.5	280	....	Citrus, prunes
		Sandy loam soils—hygroscopic moisture 3 to 5	
4 to 5	400	Saltbush	Apricots
5 to 6	480	Apricots	....
6 to 7	560	....	Prunes
7 to 8	640	Almonds, plums	....
8 to 9	720	Apples, olives, peaches, walnuts	....
		Loam soils—hygroscopic moisture 5	
4 to 5	400	Saltbush	Apricots, almonds
5 to 6	480	Apricots, citrus, figs, walnuts	....
6 to 7	560	Prunes, grapes	Prunes
7 to 8	640	Plums....................	....
8 to 9	720	Apples	Almonds
9 to 10	800	Almonds	....
		Clay loams—hygroscopic moisture 5 to 7	
6 to 7	560	....	Peaches, plums
7 to 8	640	....	Wheat
8 to 9	720	Peaches, grapes	Sugar beets
		Clay soils—hygroscopic moisture 7 to 10	
8 to 9	720	Apricots	Figs
9 to 10	800	Grapes	....
10 to 11	880	....	Wheat
11 to 12	960	....	Citrus
12 to 14	1120	Corn, sugar beets	....

to get along on a limited water supply, for both are factors that may alter materially cultural methods, the choice of stocks upon which the fruits are grown and planting plans.   As a rule it is not necessary to wait until wilting actually begins to determine when the danger point is at hand. Most plants will show signs of distress before the moisture supply of the soil reaches its wilting coefficient.   Many weeds or cover crop plants growing among the trees may wilt noticeably before the trees give visible evidence of moisture deficiency.   Temporary wilting at the middle of the day is quite likely to be an indication that the water supply of the soil is approaching a critical point and efforts should be made to deal with the situation promptly.

Summary.—Water is an important plant constituent, composing from 50 to 85 per cent. of most living tissue.   It is the solvent for all plant nutrients.   The intake of from less than 30 to more than 1,000 parts of water is required for each part of dry matter produced, the amount varying with the species and with the conditions under which the plant is grown.   When seepage, run-off and evaporation are included this means that for the average deciduous fruit crop a precipitation of something like 30 inches is required.   Inability to secure the requisite amount of water checks growth and reduces yield and often a relatively small amount of additional available moisture at a critical period will make possible material increases in the size of the crop.   Planting distances in the orchard should be determined largely by the available moisture supply and the growing habits of the particular species or variety.   The minimum water requirement of the plant, in terms of units of water per unit of dry matter, is correlated with thorough acclimatization and optimum growing conditions.   Favorable nutritive conditions in particular make for water economy.   The final wilting coefficient is practically the same for all plants in all soils, but it varies greatly for the same plant with different soils, being low for soils of coarse texture and very high for fine clays.   In the field, temporary wilting generally occurs before the wilting coefficient is reached, the evaporating power of the air being an important determining factor.   In practice it is therefore desirable to maintain the soil moisture supply well above the wilting coefficient. Different species and varieties show considerable variation in their ability to withstand drought.

CHAPTER II

THE INTAKE AND UTILIZATION OF WATER

Under favorable conditions the entrance of water into the plant, its translocation and its egress take care of themselves, without conscious manipulation by the grower. At times, however, one or another of these processes should be controlled to some degree and pathological symptoms or conditions may arise which can be understood only through a knowledge of these processes.

WATER ABSORPTION

Proper absorption, as the necessary prelude to the other processes, is of obvious importance. Furthermore, it is the process with which the grower is most frequently brought into contact.

The Water-absorbing Organs.—The root is the absorbing system and for practical purposes all the water which enters the plant is absorbed through the root. There are indeed other sources from which moisture can be obtained, such as, for example, the water resulting as an end product of the oxidation of carbohydrates, which has been termed metabolic water,[6] but such sources are significant only in extreme circumstances. The absorption of water by the root takes place chiefly through special structures, the root hairs, which are extensions from the epidermal cells of the root a short distance back of the growing point. The absorption power of the root depends upon the extent of its surface and it is increased to a marked degree by the presence of root hairs. The ratio of the surface of the root supplied with hairs to one from which the hairs have been removed has been calculated as 5.5:1 for maize and in the garden pea 12.4:1.[164] These figures give some idea of the efficiency of the root hairs for water absorption. Moisture can be absorbed by the root tip and also through the surface of the root for some distance above the zone of root hairs. In the older portions of the root the cortex and epidermis die and peel off as a result of the formation of deep seated cork; hence, this portion of the root is incapable of absorbing appreciable amounts of water.

The number of root hairs varies with different plants and, in the same plant, with the conditions under which it grows. Thus, the development of root hairs is reduced in wet soil, or in very dry soil and may be entirely prevented where the root is in contact with water.[77] This occurs in certain plants, such as the cranberry, which normally grow in bogs where the roots do not develop root hairs.

The Handling and Transplanting of Nursery Stock.—The practical bearing of the point just brought out upon the transplanting of fruit trees or other plants is important. The transplanting of most deciduous fruit trees and of many other plants is usually accompanied by the loss of a considerable part of the large and of the fibrous roots and by the destruction of practically all of the root hairs. New root hairs must be produced before active absorption can begin; these new root hairs will be formed only on new branch rootlets. This means that if the top of the plant has any considerable water requirement at the time of transplanting it will suffer for lack of moisture and perhaps wilt and die if new roots are not formed immediately. The grower is likely to place a rather high premium upon a large and extensive root system in nursery trees, thinking that they will surely absorb enough water to maintain the moisture supply of the tops until new roots are formed. A fairly extensive root system in the nursery tree may be an asset, but not because these roots devoid of root hairs are of any material aid in the direct absorption of water. This explains why tree roots pruned according to the so-called Stringfellow method at the time of setting are usually as sure to take root and grow as those pruned less severely, though the subsequent growth may not be so satisfactory. More important still, it explains also why it is desirable to prune back the tops of most plants at the time of transplanting so as to reduce transpiration to a minimum and prevent desiccation. It shows furthermore why in climates not too cold, fall transplanted trees are more likely to give a good stand than corresponding spring-set trees, for during the winter months new root formation is initiated and water can be absorbed in the spring as fast as the new shoots and leaves use it.[197] The spring-set trees, on the other hand, must wait until new roots are formed before they can take up moisture and if soil conditions remain unfavorable for this root formation and atmospheric conditions stimulate vegetative growth of the top, the pushing shoots will wilt and die, and the tree will be lost. In the autumn conditions are favorable for root growth for some time after good growing conditions for the top have passed; in the spring they frequently become favorable for top growth before or simultaneously with suitable growing conditions for the roots.

In the light of the facts presented it is not difficult to understand why the transplanting of trees after their buds have once started in the spring is attended with very uncertain results. It is simply a case of a demand for water for supplying the top, great in comparison with the demand while in the dormant stage, a demand that cannot be met by the roots because, temporarily, they are practically without absorbing organs. If it is necessary to plant trees late in the spring, after some vegetative growth may be expected to take place, it is well to remember that the transplanted tree will have practically no root hairs for several days or even weeks after the transplanting operation and that, therefore, the tree must be kept practically dormant until it is actually planted. This may be done by holding it at a low temperature in shade, or, if suitable storage facilities are not available, by repeatedly lifting and immediately heeling in again. The effect of the low temperature is to keep the tree dormant because no top growth will take place at a temperature approximating the freezing point. The effect of the repeated lifting and heeling in again is to check growth of the top by preventing the formation of new roots and root hairs though the temperature may be suitable for their development and thus cutting off the tree's water supply without which the shoots are retarded.

It is necessary to move evergreen trees of any considerable size, like the pine or the orange or the avocado, with a ball of earth so that at least a moderate portion of the real water-absorbing organs of the plants are retained and remain active; otherwise, the foliage wilts or falls off and the plant is likely to die. The facts that have been presented explain why excessive watering will not make up for the loss of roots, and particularly of root hairs, by trees transplanted during their growing season. Though their remaining roots may be surrounded by a nearly saturated soil they cannot take up appreciable quantities of this moisture.

The Water-absorbing Process.—The process by which water is absorbed by the root hairs is osmosis. A plant cell such as the epidermal cell of a root with a root hair attached has a cell wall lined with protoplasm surrounding a central vacuole. When the root hair comes in contact with the moisture of the soil an osmotic system is established and the protoplasm of the root hair becomes a semi-permeable membrane separating two solutions, the soil solution on the outside and the vacuole on the inside. These two solutions have different concentrations, that of the vacuole being greater than that of the soil solution; in other words there is less water in the vacuole than in a corresponding volume of soil solution. To equalize the concentrations of water on either side of the membrane water passes from the soil into the vacuole.

That the plant itself possesses in a marked degree the ability to change its sap concentration so as to conform more or less closely with that of the soil solution which surrounds its roots is indicated by studies of McCool and Millar.[139] Harris and Lawrence[78] have shown that some marine mangroves may have osmotic pressures as high as 50 atmospheres, whereas other mangroves growing in nearby fresh water may have osmotic pressures not more than half this amount. As the hygroscopic coefficient is approached, the water imbibitional forces of the root hair gradually come into more or less of a state of equilibrium with the water-retaining forces of the soil, and in extreme cases there may even be an exudation of small quantities of water from the root to the soil.[125]

The absorption of water in this way by the cell must increase the size of the vacuole and therefore induce a simultaneous distention of the cell wall. Eventually the elasticity of the cell wall will exert such a pressure on the vacuole that no more water can be absorbed and there is a balance between the elasticity of the cell wall and the osmotic pressure of the cell contents; the cell is in a state of turgidity. Under ordinary conditions all the living cells of a plant are turgid, but this turgidity may be lost, either by an increase in the plasticity of the cell wall or by the loss of water from the vacuole. Either process destroys the balance on which turgidity depends.

To a certain extent, the movement of water out of the root hairs into the adjoining cells of the cortex and, finally, into the conducting vessels of the fibrovascular bundles may be accounted for by a continuation of the osmotic process. Experimental evidence indicates, however, that the amount of water thus obtained by and transported through the plants by active root suction, which the osmotic process essentially amounts to, is small in comparison with that "sucked in passively by the roots, under the influence of the strong suction transmitted to the roots from the transpiring leaves."[136]   Thus leaf pull, coupled with the tensile strength of a column of water, to which further reference will be made shortly, rather than osmotic pressure, is principally responsible for water absorption as well as its translocation in the plant.

Factors Enabling the Root to Exploit the Soil.—Several factors cooperate in enabling the plant to exploit the moisture content of the soil. The root hairs are continuously formed anew at a certain distance from the tip of the growing root so that a new supply is produced as fast as the older root hairs die. As these extend into untouched portions of the soil, the roots are continually pushing into new soil throughout the growing season, leaving those regions from which they have already drawn their water and nutrient supply.

Furthermore, the absorbing capacity of the root hairs is not limited to that portion of the soil with which they come in immediate contact. As the root hair withdraws moisture from the water films about the soil particles, these films become thinner than those about neighboring soil particles. Since surface tension maintains an equilibrium between the amounts of water on contiguous surfaces, water tends to distribute itself evenly. As a result it flows toward those parts of the soil from which water has been withdrawn, hence, in the direction of the root hairs. In this way the individual root hair is capable of absorbing water which is a considerable distance away from it.

The movement of the roots, which their growth in length brings about, is likewise a movement in a definite direction, for the root tip is sensitive to differences in the amount of moisture present on opposite sides and responds to this difference by bending toward that side where there is more moisture.[96]   By this means roots grow toward those portions of the soil which have the optimum water content.

Adaptation of Roots to Moisture Conditions.—In addition to the factors already discussed the adaptability of the root system to the condition of the soil is important in enabling the plant to obtain a maximum supply of water. A small water content of the soil, within certain limits, stimulates the roots to greater development, resulting in a greatly increased absorbing surface. In spite of this greater surface, however, the supply of water is often restricted and the portion of the plant above ground is not capable of much development. In one investigation the ratio of roots to tops for oats, grown in dry soil, was found to be 1:7.4 and in wet soil 1:16.16.[183] In this second instance the roots remained small because the optimum conditions for moisture were exceeded. These figures give some indication of the correlation which exists between root and shoot development though the relation may be quite different in other plants and under other conditions. The accommodation of roots to soil conditions varies with different species. Thus Weaver[193] finds that 7 out of 10 species investigated by him respond to changed environmental conditions. Pulling[153] states that characteristically shallow rooted plants such as *Picea Mariana*, *Larix laricina* and *Betula alba papyrifera*, as well as the more deeply rooted *Pinus Strobus* and *P. Banksiana* do not adapt themselves, while the shallow rooted *Picea canadensis* and the deeply rooted *Populus balsamifera* exhibit considerable plasticity. In another place the root distribution of orchard trees is discussed in greater detail and some of its relations to water supply are mentioned in that connection.

Factors Influencing Rate of Absorption.—The ability of plants to absorb water depends upon the absorbing surface of their roots and on the following external factors: the power of the soil to deliver water, the temperature and aeration of the soil, its chemical properties and the concentration of the soil solution. Other things being equal the higher the temperature the greater the absorption until a certain optimum value is reached; temperatures above this optimum retard water absorption. The effect of gradually lowering soil temperature in the autumn on rate of water absorption is considered by some authorities as explaining a condition of internal drought that often develops slowly in the plant in the fall, and that may account in part for leaf abscission and other evidences of maturity of wood.[131] Though water absorption is greatly reduced at low temperatures many plants are able to take up water when the soil temperature is below 0°C., for even at −3 or −4°C., much of the soil water is not frozen and the soil is still capable of delivering water to the root surface.[114]

The amount of oxygen in the soil air has a marked effect on root absorption; if for any reason the supply of oxygen is inadequate, absorption ceases. Cannon[42] reports on the reaction of the roots of 30 species to a deficiency of oxygen and finds that absorption takes place and, likewise, that the roots of most species studied grow slowly in as little as 0.5 per cent. oxygen for a limited period of time, though the critical point rises as the temperature is raised.

It should be remembered, however, that oxygen dissolved in the soil water is available to the root system. In fact, the oxygen absorbed by the living cells of the root must be dissolved in water before it can be taken up. The susceptibility of the roots to differences in the oxygen supply varies markedly with different plants. Thus roots of *Coleus Blumei* and *Heliotropium peruvianum* showed injury after three days' exposure to a soil atmosphere mixed with 25 per cent. nitrogen gas, while roots of *Salix* sp. grew freely in pure nitrogen.[41] Probably in many instances where absorption is stopped and the roots are asphyxiated because of poor aeration, the injury is as much due to the poisonous effect of a high concentration of carbon dioxide in the soil atmosphere as to a lack of oxygen.[132] In either case, however, the remedy lies in making provision for better aeration of the soil. It has been found that injury to the foliage and fruit of cranberry plants submerged during the first half of the summer is due mainly to a deficiency of dissolved oxygen.[192] There is some indication that roots of deeper penetration are less responsive to changes in aeration and temperature than the more superficial roots.

The effect upon top growth of reduced absorption by the roots, occasioned by poor aeration incident to a condition of the soil approaching saturation, is strikingly illustrated by the behavior of established trees of certain kinds in portions of India. Howard and Howard[100] record that these trees naturally have a short resting period during midwinter, a period often accompanied or preceded by leaf fall. With a rise in temperature during February, new leaves, shoots and flowers are formed and rapid growth continues until hot weather checks it. A second period of rapid vegetative growth is inaugurated with the advent of the monsoon, but when the soil approaches saturation, growth slows down again or nearly ceases. There is a third period of vegetative activity at the end of the monsoon when, with the drying out of the soil, the attendant aeration makes increased root activity possible. This third period of growth is finally checked by the low temperature of the winter season.

Transpiration (and hence absorption) is decreased by the addition of small amounts of tartaric, oxalic, nitric, or carbonic acid to the soil and is increased by alkalies, such as potash, soda, or ammonia, though under field conditions these factors are likely to be of minor importance.[37] An increase in the concentration of the soil solution likewise decreases water absorption by its effect on the osmotic process. Such effects probably vary greatly with different plants.

Submergence and Root Killing.—The effects of submergence on deciduous fruit plants are due primarily to the diminished aeration of the roots which this ordinarily involves. It has been found that certain land plants with submerged roots absorb water more rapidly at first but that later the rate of absorption falls off to a marked degree, the plants wilt and after a few days the leaves become yellow and drop.[20] After prolonged submergence the roots below the surface die and no new roots develop;

eventually the entire plant succumbs. All of these effects, however, were alleviated or eliminated when the roots were submerged in aerated water. Under these conditions some plants have survived submergence for three weeks. The roots lived in this aerated water but grew more slowly and in some cases root hairs developed. Even the roots of the cocoanut, though often found in a practically saturated soil, are sensitive to a lack of aeration, for they thrive only if the water bathing them is continually moving and they die if it is stagnant.[1] It is not the water but the lack of air in standing water that is harmful. The submergence to which the roots of orchard trees are occasionally subject in certain locations is of a type that is generally accompanied by a lack of aeration. The result is a prompt killing of the root hairs, followed more or less closely by the death of the roots themselves. This is also likely to be the

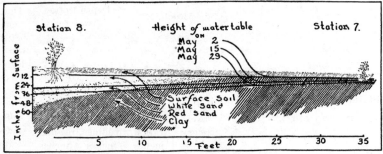

Fig. 1.—Influence of variations in height of water table on size of raspberry plants. (*After Hoffman and Schlubatis.*[94])

case when roots are submerged by the rise of the ground water in irrigated sections and in orchards planted in low-lying poorly drained ground. It is not so likely to be the case with trees planted on low but well-drained bottom lands, or alluvial soils subject to occasional overflow of short duration during periods of flood. Even in the latter instance, however, it is noteworthy that the trees are likely to be severely injured, or killed, if the roots are submerged for more than several days during the growing season or for a period of as many weeks during their dormant season. Striking evidence on the importance of height of water table in the raspberry plantation is furnished by data presented in Table 12 and is illustrated graphically in Fig. 1. Where the roots were confined to the surface 7 inches, the plants never reached an age or size adequate for profitable commercial production; where they ranged to an average depth of 14 inches, they were vigorous and productive. Drainage of low-lying forest areas in Belgium and Holland resulting in a lowering of the water table has been reported as resulting in an increase in growth rate from 1 inch in 14 years to 1 in 4 years.[105] Certain bog plants like the swamp blueberry and cranberry, however, will stand complete submergence of their root systems for a period of four or five months during the winter, though submergence of as many days during the growing season is attended with great risk.[47] It has been shown that during the growing season the water table should be held about 12 inches below the surface for the best growth of the cranberry. When it is permitted to rise higher both growth and yield are reduced.[56] Studies in Michigan[102] indicate that for the highbush blueberry a water table of from 12 to 24 inches from the surface permits maximum growth and production. A higher water table seriously limits growth and the plants likewise grow slowly if the water table does not come closer than 30 inches to the surface.

TABLE 12.—YIELD RECORDS AS RELATED TO ROOT DISTRIBUTION AND WATER LEVELS
AT VARIOUS STATIONS
(After Hoffman and Schlubatis[94])

Station	Yield per hill, ounces		Roots		Depth to free water		Difference between working level of roots and average of 3 lowest water-level readings, inches
	1924	1925	Working level, inches	Maximum penetration, inches	Average 3 highest readings, inches	Average 3 lowest readings, inches	
"Good" soils							
6	18.6	20.0	16	34	26	65	49
5	15.0	34.7	10	20	15	42	32
12	12.9	21.2	14	28	18	60	46
10	17.6	10.9	12	30	14	25	13
8	16.4	10.4	19	28	15	38	19
4	9.4	16.1	13	34	15	38	25
Average........	15.0	18.9	14	29	17	45	31
"Poor" soils							
3	4.2	4.8	9	15	14	45	36
2	0.9	0.8	8	14	10	25	17
1	0.7	0.5	7	10	8	30	23
7	0.3	Dead	5	11	8	33	28
9	Dead	Dead	6	10	10	25	19
13	Dead	Dead	7	17	13	48	41
Average........	1.5	2.0	7	13	11	34	27

There is good reason to believe that many of the troubles variously attributed to winter injury, drought and soil infertility may be end products of temporary root submergence that leads immediately to a kind of root pruning.   It should be realized that root systems may be submerged though no water stands on the surface of the soil.   More attention is devoted to this phase of the subject in a later chapter of this section and in the section on Temperature Relations.

TRANSPIRATION

Large quantities of water are lost by evaporation from the portions of the plant above ground and particularly from the leaves.   Duggar[57] estimates that an apple tree 30 years old might lose 250 pounds of water a day or possibly 36,000 pounds a season.   At this rate an acre of 40 trees would represent a water elimination of 600 tons a year.   This water loss from plants is not strictly a physical process of evaporation, because it is influenced by factors such as light and is subject to some degree of modification by the plant.   Since evaporation is not affected in the same way by these factors the water loss of plants must be considered a physiological process; hence it is designated transpiration. Whether transpiration performs any useful role in aiding the process of absorption of mineral constituents, or in lowering the temperature of the leaves, is an open question.   The generally accepted opinion is that transpiration is a necessary evil rather than an advantage to the plant.

Cuticular and Stomatal Transpiration Compared.—Transpiration is of two kinds; a small amount of water is lost from the cuticular surface of the leaf, but by far the greater proportion is lost through the stomata. Some measure of the proportion between these is furnished by the data presented in Table 13.

TABLE 13.—RELATION BETWEEN STOMATAL DISTRIBUTION AND TRANSPIRATION

	Stomata per square millimeter		Water transpired in 24 hours from 20 square centimeters	
	Upper surface	Lower surface	Upper surface (grams)	Lower surface (grams)
Pear............	0	253	...	...
Apple............	0	246	...	...
Red currant........	0	145	...	...
Canna	0	25	5	35
Linden...........	0	60	20	49

The amount of cuticular transpiration is relatively constant while the amount of stomatal transpiration can be regulated by the activity of the stomatal guard cells.   In sunlight these cells manufacture sugars by means of the chloroplasts which they contain and thereby increase their osmotic concentration so that they absorb water from the surrounding tissue and increase in turgidity.   The walls of the guard cells are peculiarly thickened so that when the cells are turgid, the stomatal aperture is open and when turgidity is lost the aperture is closed.   The guard cells are likewise sensitive to light stimuli, to which they respond by changes in turgidity more rapid than those produced in the manner just described.

The water lost by transpiration from the leaves first evaporates from the surface of the mesophyll cells in the interior and collects as water vapor in the intercellular spaces.   This water vapor then passes from the intercellular spaces of the leaf through the stomatal apertures to the outside.   This is largely a process of diffusion and follows Brown and Escombe's Law which states that diffusion through an aperture is proportional to the radius and not to the area of the aperture.   Thus the diffusion which might take place, through 10 small apertures with a radius of 1 millimeter, would be equal to the diffusion which could take place through one aperture with a radius of 1 centimeter.   It is evident that if the apertures are sufficiently small and are scattered over a surface in such a way that the diffusion through one does not interfere with that through another, then diffusion through such a perforated surface will take place as if no surface were present.   When the apertures are distributed over a surface so that they are about 10 diameters distant from one another, the maximum amount of diffusion is possible.   This proportion holds roughly for the distribution of the stomata in most leaves.   It is evident that when the stomata are opened the surface of the leaf offers little or no resistance to the diffusion of water vapor, but that when the stomata are closed transpiration practically ceases except for cuticular water loss.

Variability in Structure of Leaf in Accordance with External Conditions. The number of stomata on the leaf surface is not determined in the unopened bud, but varies with the conditions under which the leaf develops.

Table 14 presents data showing the reduction in the number of stomata per square millimeter when the available water supply in the soil is reduced. Though the reduction in the number of stomata per unit of leaf surface is not exactly proportional to the reduction in soil moisture, there is a very material decrease, indicating a marked ability on the part of the plant to adjust itself to its water supply.   Coincident with the reduction in the number of stomata there is likely to be an increase in the amount of vascular tissue per unit of leaf area,[137] thus providing for a more rapid transport of water to the points where it is required and doubly insuring against permanent wilting unless the supply gives out.

This flexibility is perhaps one of the reasons why many plants are able to thrive under wide ranges of soil moisture and atmospheric humidity.

However, the number of stomata cannot be modified after the leaf once attains full size.   This means that its ability to adapt itself in this way to extremes of soil or atmospheric moisture must be exercised early in the season. Foliage developing in the spring on a plant in a moisture-laden soil will probably transpire somewhat more per unit of area later in the season, than it would had it developed under drier conditions, though the increase will probably not be proportional to the increase in number of stomata. However, the extra amount of water required by such plants during the summer is due mainly to the increased leaf area. If trees are so handled early in the season as to develop large water requirements the cultivator should recognize the fact that this demand will be more or less continuous through the summer and shape his cultural practices accordingly. Conversely, in situations where relatively high transpiration may be expected in midseason under conditions of limited moisture supply, effort should be made early in the season through pruning, fertilizing and other practices so to develop the plant that it will be able to get along with such supplies as are likely to be available.

TABLE 14.—THE INFLUENCE OF SOIL MOISTURE UPON NUMBER OF STOMATA
(*After Duggar*[57])

Percentage of water in sand	Stomata per square millimeter	
	Corn	Wheat
38	181	103
30	130	85
20	129	82
15	124	81
11	107	59

Factors Influencing Rate of Transpiration.—The rate of transpiration is influenced by a number of factors, such as the character of the plant itself, its cuticle, the age of the leaf, defoliation, wind velocity, light and temperature.

Kind of Plant.—First in importance in determining rate of transpiration is the character of the plant itself. By definition xerophytes are plants that are able to adjust themselves to the conditions of an arid section, though many of these, as, for instance, many of the bulbs, are simply drought-escaping or drought-evading. That is, the portion of their life cycle which coincides with the dry season is confined to what amounts to resting-stage structures, such as tubers, bulbs or corms, while active vegetative growth takes place only during periods that are relatively humid. On the other hand, there are genuine drought-enduring plants, such as the cacti, sage brush and other desert shrubs that are able to reduce water losses from their transpiring organs to a minimum, even during periods of extreme heat. Even between common mesophytes that frequently are grown side by side there are marked differences in this respect.   Thus it has been determined that if the mean transpiration capacity during the daytime of the birch is 0.59, that of the oak is 0.006—a difference of 100:1.[133]   It is differences of this kind that should form the basis of selection of species and varieties for locations varying greatly in their humidity and soil moisture supply, though, as a matter of fact, few data are available on the drouth endurance of different kinds and varieties of fruit plants.[107]

Character of Cuticle.—The cuticular water loss of plants is affected materially by the thickness and character of the cuticle.   The presence of a waxy coating diminishes the amount of water loss.   The effectiveness of such a coating may be seen from data given by Boussingault[24] which show that an apple loses 0.05 grams of water per square centimeter per hour through its cuticle, but that when the cuticle is removed it loses 0.277 gram or 55 times as much from the same surface.   Cork is also an effective protection against water loss.   A peeled potato loses water 64 times as rapidly as an unpeeled potato.[163]

However, a corky surface does not afford the same degree of protection against water loss as one that is covered by unbroken cuticle or wax. Thus apples and pears having a more or less russeted surface are especially subject to wilting in storage and must be kept where atmospheric humidity is high if they are to be carried through their storage period in prime condition.

Age of Leaf.—The amount of transpiration from a leaf likewise varies with age.   The youngest leaves transpire most for the cuticle is thin and permeable; as the leaf grows older the cuticle thickens and permeability decreases, and with it the rate of transpiration.   Later this rate rises to a second maximum, lower than the first, as the result of the development and functioning of the stomata. Then as the leaf ages further there is another decline in the rate of transpiration due possibly to changes in the properties of the epidermis.

Defoliation.   Summer Pruning.—Data presented in Table 15 show that the rate of transpiration is also affected by defoliation.   This indicates that, though midsummer or late summer pruning to protect a plant and its fruit from drought injury will reduce its water requirements

TABLE 15.—THE INFLUENCE OF DEFOLIATION UPON RATE OF TRANSPIRATION IN A 5-YEAR OLD FIR TREE

(*After Hartig*[80])

PERCENTAGE OF FOLIAGE	EVAPORATION PER SQUARE METER OF SURFACE (GRAMS)
100	270
60	272
30	460
10	607

somewhat, the reduction will not be directly proportional to the percentage of the foliage that is removed.   If limitation of top is necessary in order to adjust a tree to its moisture supply, it is more practicable to do this by dormant season rather than summer pruning.

Wind Velocity.   Windbreaks.—The agencies thus far mentioned as affecting rate of transpiration have been internal to the plant.   Various external factors also have their effects.   The most important of these external factors are atmospheric humidity, wind, light, temperature and soil temperature, which together determine the evaporating power of the air.   It has been found that the rate of water loss is a simple linear function of the evaporating power of the air and that the leaf gives off water as if the water were at a temperature about 1°C. higher than the surrounding air.[52]

Water loss in wind is greater than in still air.   This is brought out by the data presented in Table 16.   Attention has been called already to the fact that one of the functions of the windbreak is to reduce the water requirement of the plants in its shelter.   Probably the decrease in the amount of water required for a given unit of dry matter is not directly proportional to the lessened rate of transpiration consequent upon decreased wind velocity, but in both cases the saving of water is great enough to be of real importance in plant production.

TABLE 16.—THE INFLUENCE OF WIND VELOCITY UPON RATE OF TRANSPIRATION
(*After Eberdt*[58])

Wind velocity (feet per second)	Evaporation in 5 minutes from free-moving sunflower leaf at constant temperature and humidity	Check in still air	
		Before (grams)	After (grams)
2	0.593	0.371	0.311
3	0.631	0.358	0.320
5	0.638	0.361	0.319

Light.—In its lower ranges increased illumination has been found to cause increased transpiration irrespective of the action of the guard cells already discussed.[52]   The effect of light may be due to absorption of radiant energy or to increased permeability of the membranes.   The heat set free by chemical processes or received by radiation may pass directly into the latent form without effecting a rise in the temperature of the leaf: that is, it may be used completely in vaporizing water.   Protoplasmic membranes are more permeable in light than in darkness and the same seems to hold for the non-cutinized cell wall.[116]

This increased rate of transpiration produced by exposure to light probably accounts for the characteristic action of illumination in retarding the rate of growth and the dependence of green plants upon light for the differentiation of tissues.[150]   The gradual reduction in the osmotic concentration of the stomatal guard cells found by Wiggins[199] may also be attributed to increased permeability after exposure to light. In the afternoon the manufacture of soluble carbohydrates is apparently more than offset by the increased permeability. Hence, the osmotically active substances in the guard cells diffuse into the adjoining cells, the guard cells lose their turgidity and the stomata close soon after darkness sets in.

Temperature.   Slope of Ground.—The rate of transpiration increases with rising temperature. It is one of the reasons, though probably not the main reason, why north slopes may be preferable to south slopes when moisture is a limiting factor. It likewise furnishes the explanation of most of the phenomena connected with the temporary wilting and later recovery of turgidity in plants. Of particular interest is the effect of temperatures below 0°C. on the transpiration from twigs. The data presented in Table 17 on the transpiration from a branch of *Taxus baccata* from which the leaves had been removed are interesting not only in showing the influence upon transpiration of an increase in temperature, but also in showing that transpiration takes place at temperatures considerably below the freezing point. Water loss under these conditions is associated with certain types of winter injury, a matter discussed in more detail in another section.

TABLE 17.—THE INFLUENCE OF TEMPERATURE UPON RATE OF TRANSPIRATION
(*After Burgerstein*[36])

AVERAGE TEMPERATURE (CENTIGRADE)	WATER TRANSPIRED PER HOUR (IN PER CENT. OF WEIGHT OF BRANCH)
− 2.0	0.288
− 2.8	0.227
− 5.2	0.131
− 5.7	0.127
− 6.2	0.093
− 6.8	0.028
−10.7	0.019

Soil Moisture.—The influence of varying soil-moisture supply on transpiration rate when atmospheric conditions remain uniform evidently varies considerably with different species and under different conditions. Thus it has been found that increasing from 10 to 20 per cent. the water content of a soil whose saturation point was 24.13 per cent. resulted in increasing the transpiration rate of white pine seedlings from two to seven times.[55]   Hendrickson[88] reports that the transpiration rate of fruit trees is greatly accelerated by irrigation, though this effect wears off after two or three days. On the other hand, studies with a number of other plants indicate that until the water content of a soil is reduced to a comparatively low point there is comparatively little difference in transpiration rate with rather large changes in soil moisture supply.[135] Differences are greater, too, when the evaporating power of the air is high, as for instance, in the latter part of the afternoon as compared with the forenoon.[134]   Experiments in California have shown that practically optimum moisture conditions for growth range from close to maximum field capacity to a point not far above the wilting coefficient.[67,187]

In another sense, however, transpiration is very sensitive to soil-moisture supply.   The stomata open in the morning in response to light and transpiration is greatly accelerated as compared with conditions while it is dark.   This water loss from the leaves at once creates a water deficit in the stems which is promptly transmitted to the roots.[89,135]   If the roots are unable to absorb water as fast as it is being transpired, the cells (first the stomatal guard cells) lose their turgidity, the stomata start to close and transpiration is reduced, though not proportionally. This, however, is more of an adjustment to the rate at which the roots are able to absorb water than to the supply that is available in the soil.

THE WATER CONDUCTING SYSTEM OF THE TREE

The conduction of water from the roots to the leaves has been investigated by Dixon,[54] from whom the following account is largely taken.   The water absorbed by the root hairs passes by osmosis from cell to cell through the cortex of the root and into the cavities of the wood cells.   It then passes through the younger layers of wood from the roots through the trunk to the branches and eventually to the tracheæ of the leaf.   From these cells it is abstracted by the endodermis and eventually finds its way by osmosis to the mesophyll cells from whose outer surfaces it evaporates.   Water passes into the cavities of the wood cells in the root by osmosis.   The osmotic system involved here consists of the water of the soil, the solution in the elements of the wood, and the cortical cells of the roots which constitute the semi-permeable membrane separating these two solutions.   These cortical cells have a higher osmotic pressure than the tracheæ but, being fully distended, they function merely as a complex membrane across which a flow of water takes place.   The concentration of the solution which fills the tracheæ is higher than that of the soil solution and is maintained by the secretion of sugars from the wood parenchyma cells with which they come in contact.[4]   This osmotic system may develop considerable pressure and result in the exudation of liquid from cut surfaces as in the well-known phenomenon of bleeding in the vine.

After the water has entered the wood cells in the root, it is carried up in the woody tissue in an unbroken column, which extends into the veinlets of the leaf.   The water in the conducting tracts of high trees hangs there by virtue of cohesion.   It must not enclose bubbles, which would break the column of water and permanently interfere with conduction.   The structure of woody tissue may be considered a special adaptation which confers stability on the transpiration stream and prevents bubbles which may develop from occupying more than an infinitesimal part of the cross section of the whole water current. The imbibitional properties of the walls of neighboring water-filled tracheæ render the water continuous between them.   If a bubble develops anywhere in the transpiration stream it will enlarge until it fills the cavity of the cell in which it originated, but the walls of the tracheæ limit the bubble and prevent its further expansion.   From these considerations it follows that the column of water will not be broken unless a very large number of the conducting tubes contain air. Despite its mobility the water, as it rises in the wood, behaves very much like a rigid body.

The vessels may be considered as the path of the most rapid portion of the transpiration stream.   The tracheids transmit water more slowly but continue to function when the water supply is limited.   Though the internal thickenings on the walls of the tracheæ are essential for the transmission and stability of a stream under tension, the whole wall is not uniformly thickened because the permeability of the thinner portions is necessary.   The flow of water is further facilitated by the presence of bordered pits, which are themselves remarkably adapted to permit a flow of water under proper conditions and to prevent the expansion of bubbles beyond the limits of a single cell.   The membrane and torus of each bordered pit is able to take up three positions, a median position when it is not acted upon by lateral forces and two lateral positions when the membrane is deflected against one dome or the other.   When adjacent cells are filled with water, the membrane assumes the median position and permits a flow of water through the delicate membrane which surrounds the torus.   When a bubble develops in the trachea and gradually distends until it fills it, the membranes of the pits in the walls of the trachea become deflected away from the bubble, until the torus lies over the perforation in the dome like a valve in its seat.   In this position the tension of the water on the one side and the pressure of the gas on the other are withstood.

The water after it reaches the tracheæ of the leaf is drawn into the leaf cells by osmosis.   Thus the entire transpiration stream is raised by the activity of the leaf cells.   According to Dixon[54] these cells actually secrete the water and it is removed by evaporation from their outer surfaces.   The resistance encountered by the current of water in passing through the wood at the velocity of the transpiration stream is probably equivalent to a head of water equal in length to the wood traversed.   Hence, the tension needed to raise the transpiration stream in a tree must equal the pressure of a head of water twice as high as the tree. In a tree 100 meters high, for example, a tension of 20 atmospheres is needed. Dixon finds the cohesion of sap to be at least 200 atmospheres, so that it is in no way taxed by the tension.   He also finds that the osmotic concentration of the mesophyll cells is adequate to resist the transpiration tension and is in many cases much in excess of that required.   Finally, he shows that the energy set free by respiration in the leaves is sufficient to do the work of secretion against the resistance of the transpiration stream.

In woody plants the older conducting vessels gradually become plugged with accumulations of both organic and inorganic materials, the color darkens and heartwood is formed.   There is no definite age at which this change takes place—indeed, it may commence at one side of an annual ring while the other side is still functioning.   Heartwood is physiologically inactive, water and nutrient transport taking place only through the sapwood.   Various factors influence the rate at which the change from sapwood to heartwood takes place.   Drought accelerates this change and extreme drought may result in so much heartwood being formed that the remaining sapwood is inadequate for the proper transport later of water and nutrients from roots to leaves, even when moisture supply is again abundant.[8]   This condition may be somewhat alleviated by the subsequent formation of new layers of sapwood, but in the mean-time the tree may show drought symptoms under conditions of ample soil moisture.   A similar change of sapwood to heartwood takes place in close proximity to pruning wounds; it is occasioned by a form of winter injury designated as "blackheart."

Summary.—The total system of water absorption, conduction and transpiration is more or less a unit.   As a rule water is absorbed only to replace water lost by transpiration and in the long run the amounts of each are equal.   For short periods, however, transpiration may slightly exceed absorption.   The chief factors determining the flow of water through the plant are the available water supply and transpiration.   If for any reason more water is transpired than is absorbed and this condi-tion continues for any length of time, the cells lose their turgidity and the plant wilts.   If the supply of water is renewed in time, the plant recovers its turgidity without ill effects, but prolonged wilting is attended by serious disturbances and eventually results in death.

Nursery stock loses its water-absorbing organs, the root hairs, upon digging and should be so handled until permanently planted that the buds cannot start.   Plants in leaf should be moved with a "ball of earth."   In most deciduous fruits aeration of soil is necessary for absorption and continued submergence leads to the death of root hairs and roots.   Plants developing in the spring, under circumstances such that they have large water requirements, continue to demand large amounts throughout the season and cultural operations should be shaped accordingly.   Summer pruning may reduce water requirements some-what, but the reduction is not proportional to the loss of foliage.   Some protection against water loss may be afforded by windbreaks and the choice of northern slopes.

In general, the grower can do comparatively little to aid his plants in economizing on their water supply.   His efforts, rather, should be directed toward irrigation or soil management practices that keep them adequately supplied.   Under conditions where water supply is likely to become a limiting factor, future difficulties often can be avoided or greatly reduced by the selection of types, species and varieties whose transpiration rate is relatively low.

CHAPTER III

ORCHARD SOIL MANAGEMENT METHODS
AND MOISTURE CONSERVATION

Most cultural practices which involve the orchard soil are for the purpose of influencing more or less directly its moisture supply or its productivity. It is well, therefore, at this point to examine somewhat carefully into the ways in which the several cultural practices commonly employed in the fruit plantation affect the water content of its soil, for though they must be considered also as they influence soil chemistry, they concern water supply even more directly. In general farm practice, certain soil treatments are given with the purpose of reducing, at least temporarily, the water content of the soil. In the orchard, however, excess moisture is taken care of by surface run-off and by natural or artificial underdrainage if the orchard has been well located. The efficiency of orchard soil management methods, therefore, is to be judged by the way in which they conserve moisture rather than by the way in which they dissipate it, though sometimes there may be occasion to dry out the soil in the fall for the purpose of hastening maturity.

Orchard Soil Management Methods Defined and Described.—The commonly recognized and more or less distinct methods of soil management in the orchard may be listed as follows: (1) clean culture, (2) clean culture with cover crop, (3) artificial mulch, (4) sod mulch, (5) sod, (6) intercropping. There are almost endless combinations and forms of treatments intermediate between each two of these methods; consequently it is nearly impossible to differentiate clearly between them. For instance, clean cultivation may be practiced in the orchard until the first of August. If the land remains fairly clean and free from weed growth during the fall and winter months, the orchard is said to be under the clean-culture method of management. If no cover crop were seeded, but a heavy growth of weeds comes in and serves as a fall and winter cover, the orchard is practically under a cover-crop method of management, though many growers would refer to it as a clean-culture orchard. Similarly, if the land were seeded down to bluegrass or alfalfa or some other pasture crop, the method of soil management would be classed as sod, sod mulch or intercrop, depending upon what disposition is made of the vegetation produced between the trees. If the vegetation were cut and removed from the land, the orchard would be said to be under an intercrop system of management, but if it were pastured off by sheep the management probably would be called a sod system, though if the vegetation were cut and allowed to remain on the ground as a mulch the treatment would be called a sod-mulch system. No attempt is made here to go into any detail regarding some of these systems of soil management that are very much alike or that are intermediate in character between those that stand out clearly as types. However, it is desirable to recognize how certain of the typical systems of soil management may be expected to influence the water content of the soil and, through it, the growth and behavior of the tree. With this information at hand, it will not be difficult, as a rule, to predict more or less accurately the results that may be expected from one of the intermediate or combination treatments.

Orchard Soil Management Methods and Surface Run-off.—A word may be said first regarding the influence of these several methods of soil treatment upon surface run-off. Much of course depends upon the lay of the land, the character of the soil itself and the way in which precipitation occurs. Most soils cannot take up the water that falls in a torrential rain lasting but an hour so completely as they can the same amount of rainfall distributed over a 12- or 24-hour period. There is much less run-off from sodded areas than from equal areas of similarly lying bare land. The covering of vegetation or of mulching material checks the flow of the water over the surface of the ground and gives it a greater opportunity to soak in. Furthermore, if there is any considerable amount of mulching on the ground it acts as a sponge, first absorbing the water as it falls and then permitting it slowly to seep into the soil. In this connection, mention should be made of the influence of mulching material or vegetation of any kind upon erosion. There are many orchards and parts of many others, planted on slopes so steep that there would be much loss of soil from washing, were the land to be cultivated and left bare any considerable portion of the year. Orchards of this type should be left in sod or artificially mulched, regardless of how these treatments may influence the water or nutrient supply available to the trees.

The effect of soil management methods on surface run-off through their influence on the humus content of the soil is likewise a matter of considerable importance. When the organic matter of loam or clay soils becomes seriously depleted as a result of long continued cultivation, the surface is inclined to pack and cement together; water is absorbed slowly and increasing percentages of the rainfall are carried away through surface drainage. One of the most beneficial effects of cover crops and of the application of animal manures, peat and other humus-forming materials is to loosen the surface soil and make it more sponge-like in character.

Moisture under Tillage and Sod-mulch Systems of Management.—
There is little reason to believe that there is much difference between
the methods of soil management in the amounts of seepage into the lower
layers of the soil. However, it is obvious that these several treatments
would have very different influences upon surface evaporation from the
soil and the evaporation that takes place through the plant itself. Fortunately, considerable data are available upon certain phases of this
question.

Some New York and Pennsylvania Records.—The New York data
presented in Table 18 show nearly 5 per cent. difference in soil moisture
between the surface soils of the tilled and of the sodded orchards and
nearly 4 per cent. difference in the respective subsoils. When it is considered that a part of the water in each case is unavailable for tree growth
because needed to supply the hygroscopic requirements of the soil, it is
evident that the tilled ground may contain many times as much available
moisture as the land in sod and that the difference between the two

TABLE 18.—SOIL MOISTURE DETERMINATIONS IN A MATURE APPLE ORCHARD IN
NEW YORK[33]

(Under different methods of soil management)

	1907					1908			
	1 to 6 inches		6 to 12 inches			1 to 6 inches		6 to 12 inches	
Date	Till-age	Sod	Till-age	Sod	Date	Till-age	Sod	Till-age	Sod
6–28	12.71	6.23	12.90	6.31	7– 7	12.77	11.59	11.56	10.70
7– 2	14.88	11.20	14.86	6.99	7–10	12.43	6.62	10.89	6.29
7– 5	12.07	5.87	10.96	3.37	7–14	12.69	9.00	10.58	6.03
7– 9	13.12	6.96	12.04	6.53	7–22	18.31	14.02	17.76	9.59
7–12	16.43	13.51	15.31	9.26	7–24	15.25	11.85	16.14	9.37
7–16	13.77	9.63	11.75	8.69	7–28	12.40	10.84	11.67	8.25
7–19	11.68	9.51	9.48	7.80	7–31	15.50	13.31	15.56	10.09
7–23	13.42	8.36	9.19	7.80	8– 4	14.00	12.97	12.84	10.87
7–26	11.93	6.81	8.84	5.21	8– 7	15.35	9.72	15.31	7.61
7–30	11.69	5.46	9.84	4.72	8–11	15.27	10.08	15.28	8.02
8– 2	13.20	7.82	10.92	5.75	8–14	14.72	11.70	12.47	8.10
8– 6	10.64	7.08	10.72	5.47	8–18	14.56	14.07	12.98	12.71
8– 8	10.02	4.82	10.15	3.80	8–21	12.33	8.70	11.21	7.81
8–14	11.79	4.38	9.62	4.07	8–25	10.98	6.39	9.39	6.08
8–17	9.37	5.21	9.07	3.58	....	.....	.....	.....	.....
8–20	8.56	3.99	8.18	2.68	....	.....	.....	.....	.....
Average for season.....	12.20	7.30	10.86	5.75	....	14.04	10.06	13.12	8.68

methods of culture in respect to the available water is actually much greater than the figures would suggest at first glance. The Pennsylvania data presented in Table 19 show clearly that artificial mulching may be, and indeed usually is, a most efficient means of reducing evaporation. They also throw some light on the effect of intercrops and cover crops upon the water content of the soil, though no information is available as to the season in which the determinations were made. Incidentally, Table 19 shows how the soil-water supply influences the growth and the yield of apple trees, though it should not be inferred that all the differences in growth and yield are due directly to the variations in water supply. It is significant, however, that there is a close correlation between the two.

TABLE 19.—INFLUENCE OF CULTURAL METHODS ON MOISTURE, GROWTH AND YIELD IN A YOUNG ORCHARD

(Results from Experiment 331, first 7 years, 1908–1914[179])

Treatment	Moisture content 1913, per cent.	Relation to optimum content, per cent.	Average gain in girth, inches	Gain over tillage, per cent.	Total yield 1914, pounds	General rank
Tillage................	10.6	53.0	6.84	....	1.5	8
Tillage and intercrop......	5.5	27.6	7.69	12.4	21.6	6
Tillage and cover crop....	8.5	42.7	6.84	....	7.0	7
Cover crop and manure...	9.2	45.9	8.31	21.5	135.4	3
Cover crop and fertilizer..	9.4	47.2	7.76	13.5	18.9	5
Mulch................	17.1	85.6	8.29	21.2	38.5	4
Mulch and manure.......	18.2	90.8	8.76	28.1	300.5	2
Mulch and fertilizer......	18.1	90.4	8.93	30.5	390.1	1

Some New Hampshire Records.—That the moisture supply in a tilled orchard is not invariably superior to that in one under a sod-mulch system of soil management is shown by the data presented in Table 20 from an orchard on light sandy loam in New Hampshire. In this instance measurements were taken of the percentage of moisture in the surface 7 to 9 inches of soil and in the subsoil (to a depth of 3 feet) at weekly intervals during the growing periods of four successive seasons. The figures represent seasonal averages.

Gourley, in reporting these observations, suggests that the lower moisture in the tilled plot may be due in part to the greater permeability of the subsoil and in part to the absence of a covering to shade the soil. Additional factors cited as possible explanations are a slight mulch in the sod plot, the slight demand made by the poor grass and finally, the increased drain on the soil in the tilled plot due to the larger growth and larger leaves on the apple trees growing there.

It should be stated that despite the higher moisture content in the sod plot the growth and yields there were inferior. Gourley, discussing a late summer drought accompanied by a severe dropping of fruit, states, "The dropping was just as severe in the heavier soil which showed 12 per cent. of moisture as in the lighter soil which showed about 7 per cent. which would agree with the findings of the soil physicists on the wilting point in light and heavy soils."[71]

English Experience.—Bedford and Pickering[19] report some interesting data showing that uniform results do not always follow similar treatments. "Pot experiments under glass indicated that, during the summer months, 30 per cent. more water was lost from the pots where there was a surface crop than from those where there was none; but when the pots were in the open, exposed to the sun and wind, the reverse was often—not always—the case, and the evaporation from the pots with the surface crop might, during the season, be even less than half of that from those without a surface crop."

TABLE 20.—MOISTURE DETERMINATIONS ON SOD, CULTIVATION AND COVER CROP PLOTS
(Light sandy loam in New Hampshire)
(*After Gourley*[71])
Surface soil

Year	Sod	Tillage	Tillage and cover crops
1913	16.02	13.69	14.20
1914	18.87	13.39	15.03
1915	25.63	19.29	20.82
1916	20.48	16.45	21.31
Average............	20.25	15.70	17.84

Subsoil

Year	Sod	Tillage	Tillage and cover crops
1913	10.98	9.06	8.93
1914	14.14	9.78	10.26
1915	14.26	14.03	13.33
1916	14.82	12.74	13.24
Average............	13.55	11.40	11.44

At Harpenden they found during May, June and July an average of 4 per cent. more moisture in tilled soil than in grass land; in Ridgmont soil, grassed land in August and September contained on the average 0.7 per cent. more water than tilled land. In no case did the amount of moisture appear to be the chief factor in tree growth. Irrigation increased the vigor of fruit trees growing in grass land, but did not make them as thrifty as those grown in tilled ground.

The New Hampshire and the English results agree in the superior growth made by trees in tilled ground, despite the absence of significant differences in moisture, or indeed, despite the frequent superiority of grass land in moisture content. In these cases there is evidence of the effect of other limiting factors, some of which are discussed in the section on nutrition.

Special cases deserve passing consideration. The Hitchings orchard in New York showed under test as good results in growth and yield under the sod-mulch system as under tillage.[84] This condition is explained as the result of seepage from the hill at the bottom of which the orchard is located, supplying so much water that moisture is eliminated as a limiting factor. Many orchards in the eastern United States are in just such locations.

Some Kentucky and Kansas Records.—Some of the findings of the United States Bureau of Soils on soil moisture conditions in grass land and in cultivated soil may be summarized here. Records were made during the months of May, June and July, 1895, of the water content of soils at a number of places in the United States and under different tillage conditions.[185] These records bring out a great difference between soils in the way their moisture content is influenced by treatment. For instance, at Greendale, Ky., during the last half of May, the moisture contents of uncultivated, bare land and of bluegrass sod were practically the same (about 18 per cent.); during June, however, the moisture content under the bluegrass gradually decreased to about 10 per cent. while that of the uncultivated bare land remained about 17 per cent. except for a period of about 5 days at the end of the month when it dropped practically to the figure shown by the sod land. During July the bare, uncultivated land averaged 2 to 3 per cent. higher moisture content than the grass land. At Lexington, Ky., a similar series of records showed an average moisture content about 5 per cent. higher during May, 8 to 10 per cent. during June, and 1 to 5 per cent. during July, in the bare, uncultivated land compared with that under bluegrass sod. During June the bluegrass made its very heavy draft upon the moisture supply of the soil, lowering it to the point where little water was available for plant growth and cultivated crops consequently suffered.

This suggests that if the sod-mulch system of orchard culture checks tree growth materially during the early part of the season or again after mid-season it is not on account of its lowering the water content of the soil, at least in those sections favored with summer rains. On the other hand, orchards in sections likely to have little rain between the middle of June and early fall probably would suffer materially from drought during that period. In any case, the growth of grass mulching material would take large amounts of water during June; during that month the trees may or may not be able to spare it. The question of the practicability, desirability or efficiency of the grass mulch method of culture so far as it concerns soil moisture therefore depends on what precipitation can be expected reasonably during July, August and September or what can be applied by irrigation—for orchards under these two methods of soil management are very likely to enter this period with material differences in the amount of available soil moisture. In Scott, Kan., on the other hand, the moisture content of prairie sod land has been found to average only about 8 per cent. during the last half of May, while cultivated land averaged about 17 per cent. Rains late in May and scattered through June and July, brought up the averages in both soils to well above the danger point for plant growth and the cultivated soil averaged only 2 to 5 per cent. more moisture during those months.

In General.—That the sod-mulch, or any other sod method of management, makes something of a draft upon the water supply of the soil, as compared with a tillage method of management, cannot be denied, though this draft is often less than is supposed. It would be a very good sod mulch indeed that would produce 1 dry-weight ton of mulching material per acre. More frequently the amount does not exceed half that figure. One-half ton of dry mulching material would require from 31,250 to 62,500 gallons of water, assuming from 250 to 500 parts of water for each part of dry matter. This would be the equivalent of $1\frac{1}{4}$ to $2\frac{1}{2}$ acre-inches of rainfall or irrigation. Furthermore, most of this water is used by the grass during the months of April, May and June, when the soil is most likely to be well supplied with moisture and best able to part with it. If the growing season of the grass is followed by moderate or heavy summer rains or irrigation the requirements of the trees will be well taken care of in this respect. On the other hand, if there should follow a period of drought, it is easy to understand why trees under sod treatment would suffer. An important factor, then, in determining the practicability of the sod-mulch method of management is the likelihood or certainty of summer precipitation, or, what amounts to the same thing, available irrigation supply during the summer months. In sections such as the Willamette valley of Oregon where winter and spring rains are abundant but the summer is dry, the sod-mulch method of management cannot be employed safely without irrigation. In such regions it is wise to use every means of conserving the natural water supply. On the other hand, there are many sections and many locations where summer rains can be counted on to supply the requirements of the trees during their growing season year after year; in other cases an orchard may be so located on a valley floor or a piece of bench land that it is sub-irrigated by means of seepage water.   Under these conditions the sod-mulch method of management is entirely practicable, though such orchards may need somewhat different treatment, so far as nutrition is concerned, than orchards in cultivation. A study of the records of the United States Weather Bureau showing monthly precipitation over a series of years will give important data as to the relative desirability or practicability of these several methods of soil management for any particular region or district.

Sometimes the choice of methods is influenced by considerations of the cost of the systems.   Hedrick[84] reports that the operations involved in the sod-mulch and tillage systems cost per acre respectively: for the Auchter orchard 80 cents and $7.39, for the Hitchings orchard 72 cents and $16.28.   In many cases the tillage method will more than return the extra labor cost; however, when results are equal, costs should be considered.

Practicability of the Sod-mulch System Influenced by Depth of Rooting.— Mention of depth of rooting, a subject considered in more detail later, is pertinent to this discussion.   A tree with a root system penetrating the soil to a depth of 8 or 10 feet can draw upon the moisture supply of a large volume of soil.   Such a tree is in a much better position to withstand temporary surface drying such as may be produced by evaporation from the surface or from weeds and grass, than a tree whose roots are limited to the upper foot or 18 inches of soil.   Consequently it will thrive under the sod-mulch method of culture when a shallow-rooted tree would suffer serious injury.   To keep an orchard in sod under conditions such that deep rooting is not possible and where there is not an abundant summer rainfall or plenty of irrigation water, is to invite trouble.   However, there are successful orchards in sod where the summers are long and dry and irrigation is not known.   The explanation lies in the deep root system of the trees that makes them independent, to a great degree, of surface soil conditions.

In passing it should be mentioned that the grass, both cut and uncut, of the sod systems of management affords some protection against surface evaporation, the exact degree depending on the thickness of the protective layer.   As this layer is frequently rather thin, its importance in checking evaporation is often exaggerated, for the stubble of the cut grass continues to evaporate moisture into the air, even after it has turned brown and has died down to the ground.   In some cases this water-dissipating action of the stubble during the summer months may even equal the protective action of the mulch against evaporation.

Influence of Depth and Frequency of Cultivation upon Soil Moisture. Since cultivation is in general a means of conserving soil moisture, the presumption is that the deeper the cultivation, within reasonable limits, the more effective it will be.   This idea is not borne out, however, by the data presented in Table 21.   More recent investigations indicate clearly that evaporation losses from uncultivated bare soil and cultivated soil are practically identical,[188] thus proving that cultivation is effective in reducing moisture losses principally through destruction of weeds.

Table 21 is interesting also because it shows the combined effects of depth and frequency of cultivation.   It is evident that increasing the frequency of the cultivations, at least up to a certain point, increased the effectiveness of the soil mulch under the conditions of the experiment. Probably under arid or semiarid conditions with few or no summer rains and less weed growth the more intensive tillage would not give materially increased protection against evaporation.

TABLE 21.—THE RELATIVE EFFECTIVENESS OF SOIL MULCHES OF DIFFERENT DEPTHS
AND DIFFERENT FREQUENCIES OF CULTIVATION[110]

Depth of soil mulch, inches	Loss of water per acre per 100 days	Cultivation			
		None	Once in 2 weeks	Once per week	Twice per week
1	Tons......................	724.1	551.2	545.0	527.8
	Inches....................	6.394	4.867	4.812	4.662
	Water saved, per cent.....	....	23.88	24.73	27.10
2	Tons......................	724.1	609.2	552.1	515.4
	Inches....................	6.394	5.380	4.875	4.552
	Water saved, per cent.....	....	15.88	23.76	28.81
3	Tons......................	724.1	612.0	531.5	495.0
	Inches....................	6.394	5.402	4.694	4.371
	Water saved, per cent.....	....	15.49	26.60	31.64

Intercrops and the Soil Moisture Supply.—The influence of various intercrops upon soil moisture conditions in the young orchard has been studied by Emerson.[59]   Results of these studies, covering two successive seasons, 1901 and 1902, are presented graphically in Fig. 2.   These two seasons afforded more or less extreme conditions of precipitation.   The summer of 1901 was characterized by very light rainfall, so light in fact that the trees would have to depend largely upon stored moisture during the period of their most active growth.   On the other hand, the summer of 1902 was a season of abundant rainfall.   The crops grown in the vegetable plot included watermelons, bush beans, pole beans and turnips.

In commenting upon the results of this investigation Emerson says: "The vegetables dried the soil but little more than clean cultivation.   In neither case did the percentage of moisture become dangerously low, even during the protracted drought of 1901, when only a little over 7 inches of rain fell during the 4 months from May to August inclusive. The crops of rye dried the ground much more than any other method of culture tried. Not only was the rye ground somewhat drier, but it became dry earlier, and moreover, since no rains occurred to thoroughly moisten the ground after it had once become dry, the rye plot

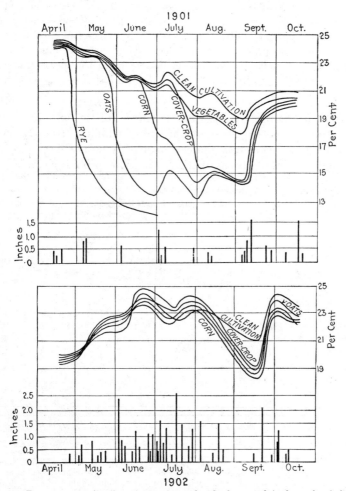

FIG. 2.—Percentages of soil moisture in orchard plots and inches of rainfall during summers of 1901 and 1902. The curved lines indicate the fluctuations in soil moisture content. The vertical bars show dates and amounts of rainfall. (*After Emerson.*[59])

remained dry nearly a month longer than any of the other plots. Next to rye, the oat crop dried the soil most seriously during the dry season of 1901, though it did not make the soil much drier than corn or cover crops. Its effect, however, was noticeable much earlier in summer and lasted much longer. By the middle of July, when the corn plot was becoming dry, many trees have completed their greatest length growth and do not need so large a supply of moisture as they do earlier in the season. The corn plot was very dry, therefore, only about half as long as the oats plot. The important difference between the cover crop and the corn, just as between the corn and the oats, is that the soil in the cover crop plot did not become dry for a week or two after the corn ground had become dry. The great difference, as regards soil moisture between the clean cultivation on the one hand and the rye and oats on the other is fully appreciated only when it is remembered that the moisture in excess of 8 or 10 per cent. (in this particular soil) is available to plants. . . . In 1902, the plots did not vary greatly as regards soil moisture. Naturally, no method of culture dried the ground seriously at any time during this very wet season, when over 28 inches of rain fell during the 4 months from May to August inclusive."[59]

Table 22 presents data showing the effects of the various intercrops in this Nebraska experiment upon the drought killing of newly set trees. The data for the cover crops indicate relatively more injury than would occur in older orchards because the cover crops probably made a much

TABLE 22.—EFFECT OF VARIOUS INTERCROPS ON DROUGHT KILLING OF YOUNG TREES (After Emerson[59])

Intercrop	Apple			Cherry			Peach		
	Number set	Number died	Per cent. died	Number set	Number died	Per cent. died	Number set	Number died	Per cent. died
Watermelon crop...............	30	2	7	12	1	9	10	0	0
Watermelon crop...............	30	2	7	12	2	17	10	0	0
Corn crop.....................	30	2	7	12	1	9	10	2	20
Clean cultivation..............	30	1	3	12	0	0	10	0	0
Oats crop.....................	30	14	47	12	6	50	10	8	80
Cover crop, millet.............	30	4	13	12	2	17	10	1	10
Cover crop, oats..............	30	4	13	12	4	33	10	0	0
Cover crop, weeds.............	30	7	23	12	6	50	10	0	0

Intercrop	Pear			Plum			Total		
	Number set	Number died	Per cent. died	Number set	Number died	Per cent. died	Number set	Number died	Per cent. died
Watermelon crop...............	10	0	0	14	1	7	76	4	5.4
Watermelon crop...............	10	2	20	14	0	0	76	6	7.9
Corn crop.....................	10	2	20	14	0	0	76	7	9.2
Clean cultivation..............	10	1	10	14	0	0	76	2	2.6
Oats crop.....................	10	6	60	14	5	36	76	39	51.3
Cover crop, millet.............	10	2	20	14	0	0	76	9	11.8
Cover crop, oats..............	10	1	10	14	1	7	76	10	12.2
Cover crop, weeds.............	10	0	0	14	2	14	76	15	19.7

more vigorous growth than they would in competition with well established trees. The suggestion is made, however, that cover crops should be selected and used with considerable care in recently established orchards. The danger from the use of the small grains as orchard intercrops is indicated plainly. On the other hand, little loss is occasioned by the growing of tilled or hoed intercrops.

Cover Crops and the Moisture Supply.—Orchard cover crops are not generally considered in relation to soil moisture, but rather as means of adding organic matter to the soil and increasing productivity. Nevertheless they do influence water content in several ways and some data on this question have already been presented in connection with the discussion of intercrops. As this influence is, in many cases, important it seems desirable that further consideration be given the matter.

Effects of Early and Late Seeding.—Cover crops use considerable water in their growth. A good cover crop probably produces at least ½ ton of dry matter per acre involving the transpiration of from 2 to 4 acre-inches of water. However, the cover crop makes its demand for water upon the soil during the fall, winter and spring months—a time when there is most likelihood of an abundant water supply and consequently when the trees are not so likely to be injured by the draft of the cover crops. It is true that cover crops are usually seeded in late July or in August, but their growth is so limited before the middle or end of September that they compete but little with the trees for either nutrients

TABLE 23.—PERCENTAGE OF SOIL MOISTURE IN BARE GROUND AND UNDER COVER CROPS IN EARLY NOVEMBER AFTER A DROUGHT[48]

Depth in inches	Bare ground	Hairy vetch	Cowpea
1 to 12	6.48	12.15	9.30
12 to 18	8.52	10.30	12.27
18 to 24	7.60	11.65	9.80

or water. Furthermore, the protective action of the cover crop through checking wind velocity close to the ground and through shading the soil, thus lowering its temperature, may fully compensate for its use of water during the late summer and early fall. The data presented in Tables 23 and 24 show that later in the season, cover crops may actually contribute indirectly to the soil moisture content. The examinations recorded in Table 23 were made at Ithaca, N. Y., in November, 1901, at the close of an extended drought. Those recorded in Table 24 were made at intervals during the winter of 1905–1906 in Wisconsin. The report upon this

TABLE 24.—PERCENTAGE OF SOIL MOISTURE FOR EACH COVER CROP FROM NOV. 1, 1905, TO FEB. 17, 1906, AND THE AVERAGE FOR THREE DETERMINATIONS[53]

Crop	Percentage of moisture in soil to depth of 30 inches			
	Nov. 21–22, 1905	Jan. 2–3, 1906	Feb. 16–17, 1906	Average
Cowpeas	17.7	24.5	21.9	21.7
Soy beans...............	18.9	23.2	23.4	21.9
Crimson clover...........	18.6	23.7	23.4	21.9
Hairy vetch.............	17.4	24.6	20.5	20.8
Oats....................	17.0	22.7	21.2	20.3
Canada peas.............	17.7	21.4	18.8	19.3
Oats and Canada peas.....	16.7	25.5	22.0	21.1
Rye....................	16.5	22.5	21.7	20.2
Check..................	16.2	22.4	20.4	19.7
Millet..................	16.1	23.4	20.6	20.0
Rape...................	16.5	24.0	21.7	20.7
Turnip	16.3	....	19.3	....
Turnip and rye...........	15.5	....	22.5	....
Hairy vetch and Canada peas	17.3	....	19.2	....
Oats and crimson clover...	17.6	....	20.0	....
Cowpeas and crimson clover	18.1	....	26.7	....
Average...............	17.1	23.5	21.5	20.7

latter investigation states that the moisture determination taken in the spring on the soil under these cover crops confirms the results obtained in the fall and winter "in that it shows the average moisture content of the covered ground to be considerably more than that of the bare ground."[53] There are distinct differences between various cover crops in their influence upon the water content of the soil.

However, if cover crops are started so early in the season that a considerable amount of growth is made during July and August, or even early September, they are likely to make serious drafts upon the water supply of the surface soil, which might check the vegetative growth of the trees prematurely and reduce the size of the fruit. Striking evidence on this point is furnished by an experiment in which cylindrical cans were filled with heavy soil from an orange grove.[31] One was left undisturbed as a check, in one a surface soil mulch was maintained and one was seeded to barley. The experiment was started June 25, at which time the soil contained 19.2 per cent. moisture. At the end of 38 days the soil in the check cylinder contained 10.1 per cent., the mulched soil 14 per cent. and the soil seeded to barley 3.1 per cent. moisture. The soil seeded to barley had reached its wilting coefficient 21 days after seeding.

In certain cultural experiments in Pennsylvania the beneficial effects of cover crops registered in vegetative growth and yield have been most apparent during the moist seasons, and little or no benefit has been derived from their use during dry years.[130] The rapid drying effect of oats, when used as a cover crop for peaches in Delaware, has prevented "the best growth of new wood to produce the maximum number of fruit buds."[140] The rate of growth of cover crops as the season advances is an important factor in determining their draft upon the water supply of the soil from week to week. From this point of view, the ideal cover crop is one which grows slowly at first but rapidly late in the season when the trees do not require so much moisture and when the supply is more abundant. Figures on the rates of growth, under Wisconsin conditions, of some of the more common crops of the northern states are given in Table 25. The indirect influence of cover crops upon soil moisture in adding organic matter to the soil and thereby increasing its water-holding capacity is more difficult to estimate accurately.

Another indirect effect of a vegetative cover in the orchard is brought out by data obtained by Morris in Washington.[147] He found that when an afternoon temperature of 95°F. and humidity of 20 per cent. were registered in a block of clean cultivated trees, corresponding temperature and humidity in an adjoining block of alfalfa were 90°F. and 35 per cent. Transpiration was considerably more rapid in the clean cultivated trees.

TABLE 25.—RATE OF GROWTH OF DIFFERENT CROPS FROM AUG. 25 TO OCT. 2[53]
(Height in inches)

	Aug. 25	Sept. 3	Sept. 15	Sept. 23	Oct. 2
Cowpeas	4.5	10.0	12.0	14.0	20.0
Soy beans	4.5	8.0	13.0	14.5	22.0
Crimson clover	2.5	3.0	3.5	4.0	6.0
Hairy vetch	4.0	4.5	5.0	5.5	8.0
Oats	6.0	11.0	16.0	18.0	24.0
Canada peas	5.0	8.0	13.0	20.0	24.0
Rye	5.5	8.0	9.0	10.0	12.0
Rape	2.5	4.0	10.0	14.0	16.0
Turnip	2.5	4.0	7.0	8.0	12.0
Millet	3.0	5.0	11.0	12.0	18.0

Winter-killed and Winter-surviving Cover Crops.—Cover crops are generally classed as leguminous and non-leguminous when considered in relation to their influence upon soil productivity. Emerson suggests that when they are being considered as they influence soil moisture a better classification would be winter-killed and winter-surviving.[60] The degree of cold actually experienced in a particular section determines whether a given crop is killed by or survives the winter. Hence, a crop that belongs in the one class in one place may fall in the other in some other section. Any cover crop that survives the winter and resumes active growth draws upon the moisture supply of the soil in the spring and will continue to do so until plowed under or until cultivation of some kind is begun. Since it is generally considered inadvisable to plow or cultivate deeply while trees are in bloom or the fruit is setting and since soil moisture conditions and the press of other work often make the plowing of the orchard before blossoming impracticable, cultivation is often not begun until late in May or early in June. This gives a winter-surviving cover crop an opportunity to make considerable growth in the spring, often more than it was able to make the previous fall. The general effect of this growth upon soil moisture is shown by the figures in Table 26 and is presented graphically in Fig. 3. By June 3 the winter-surviving cover crop had reduced the soil moisture to approximately half the amount in the soil protected by a winter-killed crop. In fact it had used up practically all of the available moisture, leaving the water content of the soil but little above its wilting coefficient. In regions of comparatively high rainfall during the spring months, this water loss due to the growth of winter-surviving cover crops would be of secondary importance and it would likewise be unimportant in sections with abundant and cheap irrigation water, but in those sections or in those seasons with a light late spring and summer rainfall it could easily occasion much more financial loss than would be compensated by the advantages accruing from the use of the cover crops. A certain quantity of organic material produced in the autumn is just as valuable for soil improvement purposes as an equal amount grown in the spring.

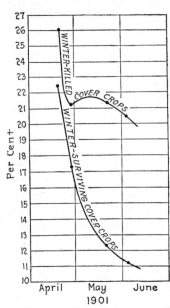

Fig. 3.—Percentages of soil moisture in plots of winter-killed and winter-surviving cover crops, spring of 1901. The dots show the dates of making the moisture determinations and the exact percentages of moisture found. The curved lines indicate the probable fluctuations in moisture between these dates. (*After Emerson.*[59])

Wind Velocity and Evaporation: Windbreaks.—Attention has been called to the almost continual evaporation of water from the soil. In regions of low precipitation this amounts to a much larger percentage of the total supply than in regions of frequent and abundant rains. Assuming uniform soil management methods, evaporation may be expected to

TABLE 26.—EFFECT OF VARIOUS COVER CROPS ON SOIL MOISTURE DURING THE SPRING OF 1901[60]

Kind of crop	Percentage of soil moisture			
	Apr. 19	Apr. 27	May 20	June 3
Winter-killed crops:				
Oats..........................	28.7	20.2	20.5	20.1
Millet.........................	26.0	21.8	21.9	20.7
Cane..........................	24.0	22.1	21.7	20.7
Average.....................	26.2	21.4	21.4	20.5
Winter-surviving crops:				
Rye..........................	22.6	17.4	12.2	11.2

rise with an increase in wind velocity and to vary with temperature of the soil water, with temperature of the air close to the evaporating surface, with vapor pressure in the air near the water and with atmospheric humidity. Air temperature is probably the factor of greatest importance in this connection. Experiments in Kansas have shown a correlation coefficient of 0.69 between evaporation rate from tanks of water and air temperature, while the correlation coefficient between evaporation rate and air movement was only 0.29.[167] However, the only one of these factors at present under the control of the grower to any considerable extent is wind velocity. Consequently it is discussed at this time. In one series of determinations when the relative humidity was 50 per cent. and the air temperature 84°F. evaporation was found to be 2.2 times as rapid with a wind velocity of 5 miles per hour as in a calm atmosphere; 3.8, at 10 miles per hour; 4.9, at 15 miles per hour; 5.7 at 20 miles per hour; 6.1, at 25 miles per hour and 6.3 at 30 miles per hour.[162] The influence of windbreaks upon wind velocity varies with their height and density and much depends also on the topography. Card[43] measured the evaporation in Nebraska at varying distances from the protected side of a windbreak of forest trees some 30 feet high, during the period July 15 to Sept. 15, and for those portions of the period when the wind was from the south, southeast and southwest, these being the most drying winds. Expressing the evaporation at a point 300 feet south of the windbreak as 100, evaporation 200 feet north was 83 and 50 feet north, 55. During a 12-hour period on Aug. 3, when the weather was hot and dry with a high wind, evaporation 50 feet north of the windbreak was 29 and 200 feet north it was 67, compared with 100 at a point 300 feet south. It is thus evident that wind barriers of one kind or another reduce evaporation very materially. However, the moisture required for the growth of the windbreak materially reduces their total moisture-conserving effect, though deep plowing or subsoiling close to the windbreak reduces its injurious influence in this direction.   In connection with the discussion of windbreaks, attention should be called to the fact that wind often apparently exercises an influence on tree growth and productivity far ‘greater than can be accounted for through its effect on water losses from surface evaporation and leaf transpiration.   In some of the young coastal citrus orchards of California, protection from wind has enabled the trees to attain the same size in 3 years that has required 5 when fully exposed, and, in orchards that have reached bearing age, the yields of those trees protected from the wind have been 3 times as great as those from trees fully exposed to its force.[23]

Summary.—There are six fairly distinct methods of soil management commonly used in the deciduous fruit plantation: (1) clean cultivation, (2) clean culture with cover crop, (3) artificial mulch, (4) sod mulch, (5) sod, (6) intercropping.   The sod and sod-mulch systems are most effective in reducing run-off and in preventing erosion; in certain situations their use is to be recommended for these reasons if for no other. The various systems of soil management employing tillage generally conserve a larger percentage of the water that enters the soil and consequently they are more effective in preventing injury from drought.   The sod-mulch method has its place where abundant summer rainfall, deep rooting or availability of irrigation water largely removes the trees from competition with the surface cultures for water.   The moisture-conserving effects of tillage increase somewhat with its frequency and depth, but when cost is considered there is a decreasing margin of profit with the deeper and more frequent cultivation.   Cultivated intercrops may be used safely in the orchard, but the small grains are likely to make too serious a draft on moisture at a period when the trees should be abundantly supplied.   Cover crops consume considerable moisture but unless planted too early they are not likely to injure the trees seriously by their growth in the fall.   In fact they may actually conserve moisture for the trees by cutting down surface evaporation and holding snow.   In some sections winter-surviving cover crops should not be used because of their draft on the moisture supply in the spring when the trees require it.   This is particularly true in sections with only moderate rainfall and long dry summers.   Evaporation increases rapidly with temperature and wind velocity and moisture losses from this latter cause can be lessened materially in many cases by choice of sites and use of windbreaks.   It should be pointed out, however, that losses in the orchard from seepage, run-off and surface evaporation are greatly influenced by the trees themselves, as well as by soil management methods.   Thus, the effect of their shade is to reduce air temperature close to the soil and reduce evaporation rate accordingly.   Similarly, the effect of the transpiration of water from their leaves is to reduce soil-moisture losses through increasing atmospheric humidity.   Indeed, the fact that in some sections bare soil fully exposed to the evaporating power of the air dries out much more rapidly and completely than that of adjoining areas covered with forest[205] indicates that their influence may be even greater than the differences between soil management methods.

CHAPTER IV

SOIL MOISTURE: ITS CLASSIFICATION, MOVEMENT AND INFLUENCE ON ROOT DISTRIBUTION

Within certain limits the size and general character of top growth are influenced by the root system that supports it. Similarly the size and distribution of the root system depend to an important degree on the moisture content of the soil.

CLASSIFICATION OF THE WATER IN SOILS AND PLANT TISSUES

The physicist finds it desirable to distinguish between water in the solid, liquid and vapor form; the chemist distinguishes between free water, water of crystallization and water of constitution. Similarly it is convenient for the student of soils and plant physiology to classify water according to the form in which it is held in the soil or in plant tissue and the consequent uses to which it may be put. No one classification has proven most satisfactory for all purposes. Attention is here directed to those that seem more useful in explaining the response of the plant to varying water content.

The Response of Water to the Force of Gravity and the Evaporating Power of the Air.—The water of the soil is held in three conditions: (1) free or gravitational water, (2) capillary water and (3) hygroscopic water. The free or gravitational water is that which moves down through the soil under the influence of gravity. It is the surplus water that drains away after heavy rains or heavy irrigation, finding its way eventually through underground channels to streams or springs or to the so-called ground-water level. Capillary water, on the other hand, does not move downward in response to the force of gravity, but adheres to the soil particles in the form of films of varying thicknesses. It does not drain away freely with the seepage water, though there is some reduction in its amount within a given soil depth if there is a material lowering of the water table of the soil. However, it may be lost through evaporation from the surface soil. Hygroscopic water is the moisture that is to be found in air-dry soil exposed to a moist or saturated atmosphere. Like capillary water it exists in the form of thin films adhering to the surface of the particles. The films, however, are much thinner than those of capillary moisture and the soil retains this hygroscopic water with great tenacity. The capillary and hygroscopic moisture together may be regarded as a

54

product of what the soil particle can hold against the pull of gravity on the one hand and the evaporating power of the air on the other.

The maximum amount of water that a given soil may contain depends on the volume of its pore space. Both may range from about 32 to a little over 52 per cent.[109] This amount of water is equivalent to a 4 to 6 acre-inch precipitation and would weigh from 20 to 32 pounds per cubic foot of soil. Naturally these large amounts of water are not found in any soil except below the water table line or immediately after heavy precipitation or irrigation and before drainage has had an opportunity to carry away the surplus moisture. It is the amounts of capillary and hygroscopic water that a soil will retain rather than its total water-holding capacity as determined by pore space that are of interest in fruit growing, for the reason that little or none of the free or gravitational water is utilized by the plants. For most purposes and under most conditions it is only the capillary moisture that they use, though Loughridge[120] is responsible for the statement that in some instances plants are able to remain alive, even though they cannot grow, in soils whose water supply is reduced to the point where only hygroscopic moisture is present. The total amount of capillary water that a soil will retain depends not so much on the pore space as on the size of the soil particles and the distance from the level of the ground water below. Tables 27 and 28 show the percentage of water that certain typical soils will hold as capillary moisture against the force of gravity. These figures were obtained from soils of undisturbed field texture several days after heavy rains so that gravitational water had had ample opportunity to drain away. It should be stated in connection with these tables, that in each case the soil became somewhat more sandy at greater depths.

TABLE 27.—AMOUNTS OF CAPILLARY MOISTURE HELD AGAINST THE FORCE OF GRAVITY IN CERTAIN TYPICAL SOILS[109]

Depth	Sandy loam, per cent.	Clay loam, per cent.	Humus soil, per cent.
First foot....................	17.65	22.67	44.72
Second foot..................	14.59	19.78	31.24
Third foot...................	10.67	18.16	21.29

TABLE 28.—MAXIMUM CAPILLARY CAPACITY OF SOILS FOR WATER

	Percentage of water	Pounds of water per cubic foot	Inches of water
Surface foot of clay loam...............	32.2	23.9	4.59
Second foot of reddish clay..............	23.8	22.2	4.26
Third foot of reddish clay...............	24.5	22.7	4.37
Fourth foot of clay and sand............	22.6	22.1	4.25
Fifth foot of fine sand..................	17.5	19.6	3.77

Though it has been thought that the optimum condition for the growth of most mesophytic plants is afforded by a soil when the capillary water amounts to between 40 and 60 per cent. of the total water-holding capacity of the soil, recent investigations in California[67,187] lead to the conclusion that practically optimum conditions are provided by a considerably wider range. Desert plants or plants coming from dry climates are more tolerant of deficiency in soil moisture and the optimum capillary moisture content for these plants is lower. The reverse is true of certain other plants that thrive under moist conditions. The almond is mentioned by Hilgard and Loughridge[93] as suffering from excess moisture when approximately three-fourths of the pore space was filled with water.

The hygroscopic moisture of the soil varies greatly with the composition. In sandy soils it may be as low as 2 or 3 per cent. and in coarse sands even lower. In ordinary loams it ranges from 4 to 5 per cent. and in heavy clays and adobes it may be as high as 8 or 10 per cent.[120]

The Relative Saturation.—Brown[35] suggested that a more useful way of expressing the water content of the soil would be in terms of its relative saturation. This would take into account the maximum water capacity as well as the actual water content and would afford a more accurate index of the biological or physiological wetness of the soil than the standards of measurement now employed. In commenting upon this question of relative saturation he says:

"The water content alone is . . . but an imperfect index of the soil conditions. Since soils of different mechanical composition have different capacities for water, the same quantity of water produces different changes in humidity in these different soils. For example, the quantity of moisture sufficient to saturate a given mass of sandy soil is insufficient to saturate a like mass of humous soil. The degree of wetness or dryness, of a soil, therefore, really depends on the amount of water which the soil can still take in before being saturated. Consequently, a more perfect index to the 'wetness' or 'dryness' of a soil is to be had by expressing the water content of the soil in terms of its maximum water capacity, the ratio $\dfrac{\text{Water content}}{\text{Maximum water capacity}}$, being termed the Relative Saturation of the soil . . . This value, and not the actual water content itself, will be the index to the 'biological wetness' of the soil . . . in comparing two soils whose actual moisture contents are different, say, the ratios may indicate that both soils, however, have the same degree of wetness, and so, in relation to the physiological action of the plant are of similar conditions."

Resistance to Freezing.—Another classification of the soil water is made by Bouyoucos.[25] This classification is based upon freezing point determinations with the dilatometer. Water which freezes at or slightly below 0°C. is termed free water, that which freezes between 0°C. or a little below and −78°C. is termed capillary or capillary-adsorbed water and that which does not freeze except at temperatures below −78°C. is termed combined water. These classes do not coincide exactly with those of the classification used before and they serve to bring out some of the features of the water supply of the soil that are of significance to the physiologist and that investigations indicate are intimately associated with the question of winter injury.

Bouyoucos[25] points out that the relative amounts of these forms of water vary greatly in different soils. He says: "In some soils only one or two forms predominate, while in others all three are about equally represented. In the sands and fine sandy loams, it is the free water that predominates, which amounts, in some cases, to about 95 per cent. of the total water present; the other 5 per cent. consists as a rule, of combined water; capillary adsorbed water is apparently not present in these classes of soil. In the loams and silt loams, it is the free and combined water which predominates. Here, again the capillary-adsorbed water is present in small amounts. In some of the heavy loams all three forms are about equally distributed. In clay loams and humus loams and clay, it is the combined water which predominates followed by capillary-adsorbed and free. Although the amount of free water tends to decrease and the amount of the capillary-adsorbed and combined water tends to increase correspondingly as the soils ascend from the simple and non-colloidal to the complex and colloidal classes. There are many exceptions to this rule."[25]

Of equal importance are the differences in the amounts of free or easily frozen water in plant cells, as determined by McCool and Millar,[138] using the dilatometer. The differences found suggest corresponding differences in the amounts of adsorbed water in plant cells.

The different water-absorbing capacity of plant cells is attributed by Spoehr[178] to their pentosan content. This is confirmed by the work of Hooker.[98] It seems probable, therefore, that the chemical composition of plant tissue, as of soils, has a most important bearing on the condition in which its water is held. This in turn has a direct relation to the susceptibility of plant tissue to environmental changes, a subject that is discussed in greater detail in the section on Temperature Relations.

McCool and Millar[138] measured the amounts of easily-frozen water in plants grown in soils of high, medium and low water content. They found that the plants grown in soils of high water content contained more easily-frozen water. Rosa[160] has shown that with lower moisture content of the soil there is an increase in the pentosan content of the plants grown in it. This amplifies the discovery that pentosans are produced under xerophytic conditions and that the water-retaining capacity of the cells is thereby increased.[178] The greater amount of adsorbed water that such plants contain would mean the presence of smaller amounts of free or easily frozen water, such as McCool and Millar found. These investigators have also shown a correlation between the depression of the freezing point of plant sap and the amount of easily frozen water it contains; the lower the freezing point the less easily frozen water is present.[138]   This suggests that differences in the concentration of cell sap may be due in part to the relative amounts of free and adsorbed water.   It is obvious that with a given amount of soluble material, the concentration of the sap will depend on the amount of free water available for its solution.   The less the proportion of free water and the greater the proportion of adsorbed water the higher the concentration of the solution.

These differences in condition of the water present are important in practical ways.   They explain the increased moisture requirement of a plant grown in moist surroundings; their application in cold resistance is shown elsewhere; it is possible that the greater adaptability of some plants to varied environments is related to their capacity to form water-retaining substances.   These water-retaining substances represent a mechanism for the retention of moisture by living plant cells, a mechanism which is entirely distinct from that represented by the anatomical modifications characteristic of xerophytic or semi-xerophytic plants.   The former has to do with the loss of water from the cells to the intercellular spaces; the latter with the loss of water from the plant tissue to the outside.   The two means of protection against water loss may occur together in which case the effectiveness of each would be increased, but they may be quite independent of each other.

MOVEMENT OF WATER IN THE SOIL

After water once reaches the soil, either following natural precipitation or irrigation, it becomes subject to the forces of gravity and surface tension and in a general way these may be said to control its movement. Percolation downward represents the result of the two forces working together.   Lateral movement and rise by capillarity represent what the force of surface tension is able to do in opposition to the force of gravity.

Percolation.—It has been pointed out that optimum growing conditions for most crop plants are found when from 40 to 60 per cent. of the total pore space of the soil is filled with capillary water.   Immediately after heavy rains the soil moisture occupies a larger percentage of pore space in the soil.   Therefore, the movement of water through the soil must be considered.   In humid regions its vertical movement is of chief interest; in irrigated sections both its vertical and its lateral movement are important.   Few realize the rate at which water percolates through the soil and the percentage of the total precipitation or of the total amount applied by irrigation that is lost in this way.   Table 29 averages the percolation data obtained during a period of 34 years at the Rothamsted Experiment Station on a rather heavy loam, or clay loam soil.   It shows the amounts of water percolating through the soil columns 20, 40 and 60 inches deep.

Attention is directed particularly to the great difference between the proportions of rainfall removed by seepage in years of light and years of heavy rainfall. The figures also show a much higher percentage of percolation during winter months when there is comparatively little evaporation than during the summer months when the evaporation rate is high. As a rule, the lighter the soil, the larger is the percentage of percolation water. Consequently in the irrigation of light soils it is

TABLE 29.—RATE OF PERCOLATION OF WATER THROUGH CLAY LOAM SOIL[124]

	Inches of rain-fall	Inches of water drained through soil columns			Per cent. of rainfall percolating through soil column		
		20 inches deep	40 inches deep	60 inches deep	20 inches deep	40 inches deep	60 inches deep
January...............	2.32	1.82	2.05	1.96	78.5	88.4	84.5
February.............	1.97	1.42	1.57	1.48	72.2	80.0	75.2
March...............	1.85	0.87	1.02	0.95	47.6	55.6	52.0
April...............	1.89	0.50	0.57	0.53	26.5	30.0	28.0
May...............	2.11	0.49	0.55	0.50	23.2	26.1	23.6
June...............	2.36	0.63	0.65	0.62	24.0	27.6	26.3
July...............	2.73	0.69	0.70	0.65	25.3	25.6	23.8
August...............	2.67	0.62	0.62	0.58	23.2	23.2	21.7
September............	2.52	0.88	0.83	0.76	35.0	32.8	30.0
October.............	3.20	1.85	1.84	1.68	57.8	57.5	52.3
November............	2.86	2.11	2.18	2.04	76.7	76.3	72.4
December............	2.52	2.02	2.15	2.04	80.3	85.4	81.0
Mean total per year....	28.98	13.90	14.73	13.79	48.2	51.0	48.0
Results for:							
Maximum rainfall. ...	38.70	23.50	23.60	24.30	60.7	61.0	63.0
Minimum rainfall.....	20.50	7.32	7.90	7.70	35.7	38.5	37.6

generally necessary to use more water than in heavy soils under similar climatic conditions and with the same fruits. The extra amount of water required by such soils may be reduced somewhat by lighter and more frequent applications, but this too may be carried to an extreme and result in an unnecessary waste through evaporation. An illustration of this principle is furnished by certain orchards on the Umatilla Irrigation Project in eastern Oregon. Many orchards on this project have required 7 or 8 acre-feet of water in order to bring a crop of fruit to maturity, though the trees themselves probably used only 9 or 10 inches. Evaporation rates in the climate of that section are very high, but the main reason for applying 9 to 10 times more than the trees actually use is the extremely high percolation through light porous sandy soils and subsoils.

The Rise of Water by Capillarity.—It is often thought that much of the water that percolates through the soil again rises by capillary action and becomes available to the trees later in the season. Investigations

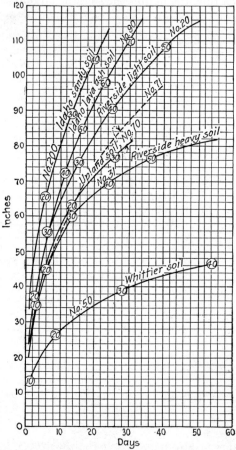

FIG. 4.—Rate of movement of moisture in soil in horizontal open flumes. Figures in circles indicate points at which that number of liters of water had been taken up. The dotted line for flume No. 71 (covered) is for comparison with flume No. 70 (open). (*After McLaughlin.*[141])

of recent years tend to minimize the importance of this upward movement of soil moisture. The generally accepted opinion of the present may be summarized in the following statement by Rotmistrov.[161] "As regards the mechanical raising of water, however, by capillary action it may be assumed that the limit from which water can make its way upward lies much higher than the limit accessible to the roots. All the data at my command regarding moisture in the soil of the Odessa Experimental field point only to one conclusion, namely, that water percolating beyond the depth of 40 to 50 centimeters (16 to 20 inches) does not return to the surface except by way of the roots." Briggs, Jensen and McLane,[31] in reporting upon the results of irrigation experiments in citrus groves in California state that available soil moisture below the third foot did not prevent orange trees from wilting when the moisture content in the first 3 feet of soil fell below its wilting coefficient and the roots of the trees were limited to the first 3 feet. This is a point that must be kept in mind in irrigation practice for it means that trees can utilize the moisture supply in the volume of the soil that the roots occupy, but very little that percolates to or stands at a lower level. In other words, the tree can make use of the water supply at 3 or 4 or 5 or 10 feet in depth only to the extent that it can develop a root system that penetrates to these depths.

Lateral Movement of Water in the Soil.—The lateral movement of water in soils is likewise dependent largely upon texture, though the amount and kinds of soluble mineral salts, the soil colloids, the organic material and other factors have their influences. In open, porous soils, water spreads laterally to a considerable distance and with comparative rapidity. In heavy, compact soils, its lateral spread is slight and slow. For instance, in one experiment on a heavy soil in California, after an irrigation considered sufficient to last about four weeks, the moisture was found to have penetrated laterally only about 18 inches from the irrigation furrow.[31] Figure 4 shows graphically the rate of this lateral spread as it takes place through the force of capillarity and unaided by gravity. The spacing of irrigation furrows must be made accordingly, if the entire volume of the soil is to be wetted. It is for this reason that basin irrigation or flooding is sometimes preferred to furrow irrigation in comparatively heavy land. Slow lateral and vertical movement of water in soils accounts in large part for the temporary wilting of plants whose roots do not fully explore the soil—all the available water being absorbed from the areas immediately surrounding the roots while areas a little distance away remain comparatively moist.[118,202]

THE DISTRIBUTION OF FRUIT-TREE ROOTS AS INFLUENCED BY SOIL MOISTURE

The size and distribution of the root system depend upon the operation of many factors, such as the moisture supply, aeration of the soil and nutrient supply. In most cases it is impossible to assign to each factor the part it has played, but as they are more or less interdependent they may be discussed together.

The Ideal Root System.—Deep rooting is desirable, for the purpose of making the water (and nutrient) supply contained in a large volume of soil available to the plant.   For the same reason there should be at least a moderate lateral spread.   In other words the tree, or other fruit-producing plant, that is equipped with an extensive root system will be able better to endure extremes of drought or temperature or exceptional demands for a supply of nutrients, than one with a limited root system.   Plants grown in a comparatively concentrated nutrient solution or in rich soil have roots that are shorter, more branched and more compact than those grown in a weak nutrient solution or in a poor soil.   Changing fertility is one explanation of the marked contrasts in the degree of ramification of roots as they penetrate different strata.[27] The ideal root system is, therefore, not the one with branches that reach out or down the farthest, but the one that more or less fully explores and occupies the soil to a reasonable depth and within a reasonable radius.   Otherwise, it would be necessary to regard the root system produced only in an infertile soil as the ideal.

Specific and Varietal Differences in Root Distribution.—Depth of rooting and lateral spread of roots depend in the first place on the species or variety of plant.   Some, like the walnut and pecan, are characteristically deep rooted; others like the spruces and hemlocks and the river bank grape (*Vitis riparia*) are characteristically shallow-rooted.   The roots of certain fruit varieties, like the Wealthy apple, are strong, stocky and far ranging; those of other varieties, like certain strains of the Doucin, are short, slender, compact and much branched.   These characteristics should be borne in mind when selecting fruits or fruit stocks for particular soils and when considering the influence of various environmental factors and cultural practices upon root distribution, for though root distribution is influenced profoundly there are limits to the plasticity of any species; nothing stated in this connection should be construed as implying that these usual limits for the species or variety may be exceeded.

The Distribution of Tree Roots under Varying Conditions.—Tree roots often range deep, but such investigations as have been reported show a surprisingly shallow root system in most of our orchard plantations at least in the humid regions.

In the Hood River Valley, Oregon, and in Ohio.—For instance a report upon the condition of the root system of apple trees in the Hood River valley states:

"It was found that the majority of the feeding roots of fruit trees of bearing age were located from 3 to 10 inches below the surface of the soil."[3]   A discussion of the root systems of apple trees in Ohio includes the following statement: "The main root systems, of apple trees, under the different methods of culture (clean culture with cover crops, sod culture, and sod mulch), were found to be at a surprisingly uniform depth—the greater portion of the roots, both large and minute, being removed with the upper 6 inches of soil. . . .   The fibrous or feeding-root

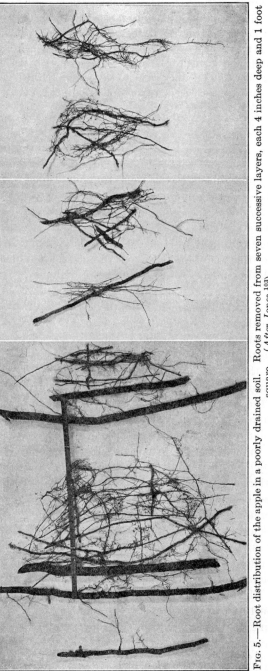

Fig. 5.—Root distribution of the apple in a poorly drained soil. Roots removed from seven successive layers, each 4 inches deep and 1 foot square. (*After Jones.*[103])

system of a tree under annual plowing and clean culture with cover crops, practically renews itself annually—pushing up thousands of succulent, fibrous rootlets to the very surface of the soil where they actually meet with the steel hoes or spikes of the cultivator or harrow, especially in seasons when moisture is abundant.   Apparently but a small percentage of these rootlets penetrate the lower, more compact colder soil, but they come to feed where warmth and air and moisture combine to provide the necessary conditions for root pasturage.   As a matter of fact, these feeding rootlets are cleanly pruned away by the plowshare each succeeding year, and without apparent injury to the trees or crops."[73]

The writers then go on to state that the destruction of the roots in the upper 2 or 3 inches of soil by summer drought or by winter cold results in no serious injury to the tree, as those ranging deeper, 4 to 6 inches, can take care of the tree's requirements.

In a Gravelly Loam, Underlaid by Hardpan, in Maine.—Some valuable data on the root distribution of apple trees growing under different soil conditions were obtained by Jones[103] in Maine.   Figures 5 and 6 show photographs of the tree roots obtained from a square foot of soil midway between two Baldwin trees set 27 feet apart and about 28 years old.   The photographs show the roots in successive layers of soil 4 inches thick. This soil was a gravelly loam to a depth of 2 or 2½ feet where a rather impervious hardpan was encountered.   Figure 5 shows roots growing in a rather wet portion of the orchard; those in Fig. 6 were from a drier portion.   The tops of these trees were not meeting, yet in both the wet and dry areas their roots were interlacing and the soil to a depth of over 2 feet was more or less thoroughly exploited.   Though the greatest expansion of the root system was in the 4- to 8-inch layer, there was a fairly large number of roots 20 inches deeper.   There was also much better expansion of the root system at both upper and lower levels in the drier soil than in the one classed by Jones as a little too wet for the best growth of the apple tree.   The question is raised by Jones as to whether interlacing of roots is not evidence that for a number of years these trees had been suffering from lack of room, a suggestion supported by the indifferent performance of the orchard for some time previous.

Table 30 shows the length of the roots, in feet, found in each cubic foot of soil at successive distances from the tree trunk.   These measurements were taken for a Milding apple tree 9.33 inches in diameter 2 feet from the ground, with an 11-foot spread of branches, and growing in a stony loam.   The last column shows the computed length of roots for the cylinder of soil 1 foot in thickness surrounding the tree at a given distance from the trunk, assuming that the section examined is typical for the entire area of which the tree is the center.   Figure 7 shows graphically the data presented in Table 30.   They afford some idea of the relatively extensive development of a tree's root system under conditions that are

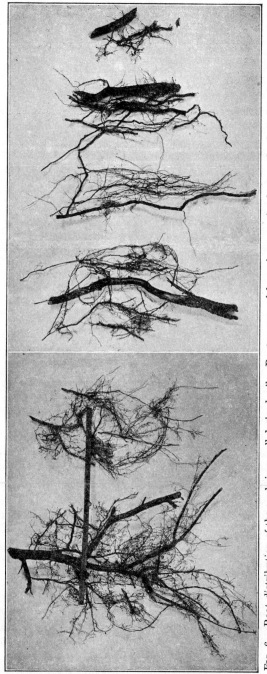

FIG. 6.—Root distribution of the apple in a well drained soil. Roots removed from six successive layers; the first, 8 inches deep, and the others 4 inches deep, and each 1 foot square. (*After Jones.*[103])

TABLE 30.—ROOT DISTRIBUTION OF A 25-YEAR OLD APPLE TREE, MEASURED BY
SECTIONS
(After Jones[103])

Distance of section in feet from tree trunk	Length of roots in first 6-inch layer of soil, feet	Length of roots in second 6-inch layer of soil, feet	Total length of root in cubic foot of soil, feet	Computed length for cylinder about trunk, feet
1	112	32	144	144
2	66	109	175	1650
3	19	74	93	1460
4	3	72	75	1650
5	0	28	28	792
6	3	48	51	1712
7	0	48	48	2008
8	0	32	32	1508
9	4	72	76	4059
10	0	35	35	2089
11	5	37	42	2771
12	4	16	20	1445
13	3	26	29	2278
14	0	18	18	1527
15	0	12	12	1093
16	0	8	8	779
17	6	2	8	829
18	0	8	8	880
19	0	7	7	814
20	0	$\frac{1}{2}$	$\frac{1}{2}$	61

presumably more or less common.   In this case plowing and cultivating
to a depth of 6 inches would have destroyed a little less than one-tenth
of the conducting roots.   The percentage of the very small absorbing
and feeding roots would not necessarily be the same.   Over 19,000 of
the total of 29,547 feet of conducting roots, in other words about 65 per
cent., lie beyond the spread of its branches.   Probably the proportion
of feeding roots is still greater.   Irrigation water and fertilizers should be
distributed accordingly; the treatment of the small area of soil immediately surrounding a large bearing tree which is difficult of access with the
tools of cultivation would seem to be of small importance so far as either
water or nutrient supply is concerned.

In a Thin Gravelly Loam, Underlaid by Rock, in Maine.—The data
given in Table 31 represent extreme conditions.   They are for an undersized, stunted seedling apple tree probably 40 years old, on level ground
at the top of a hill thinly covered with a rocky, gravelly clay loam.   The
soil was less than a foot deep and was underlaid by rock or ledge or with a
heavy clay mixed with gravel.   For many years the orchard had been in

pasture and the trees, having received practically no care, had experienced a hard struggle for existence and many had died.

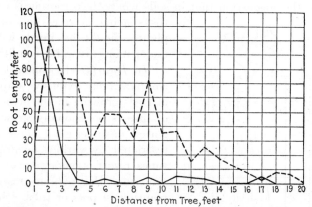

Fig. 7.—Distribution of apple roots in surface 6 inches and second 6 inches in a soil section 1 foot wide in rather heavy loam. Solid line shows surface layer; broken line shows second layer. (*After Jones.*[103])

Without doubt, limited nutrient as well as limited moisture supply had been an important factor in forcing this tree to extend its root system so far and wide in order to hold on in its struggle for existence. Whatever

TABLE 31.—ROOT DISTRIBUTION OF A 40-YEAR OLD APPLE TREE IN A THIN ROCKY SOIL UNDER SOD FOR MANY YEARS

(*After Jones*[103])

Distance of section from trunk, feet	Length of roots in top 6 inches, feet	Length of roots in next 6 inches, feet	Total length, feet	Distance of section from trunk, feet	Length of roots in top 6 inches, feet	Length of roots in next 6 inches, feet	Total length, feet
1	64	96	160	16	32	2	34
2	98	22	120	17	10	0	10
3	20	50	70	18	6	7	13
4	34	80	104	19	6	14	20
5	54	34	88	20	8	12	20
6	22	4	26	21	8	0	8
7	14	7	21	22	11	3	14
8	17	18	35	23	3	8	11
9	16	26	42	24	3	5	8
10	0	0	0	25	0	7	7
11	0	10	10	26	2	0	2
12	6	9	15	27	5	7	12
13	12	12	24	28	0	2	2
14	28	23	51	29	0	2	2
15	0	18	18	..	.	.	.

may have been the exact combination of factors leading to this development it shows a marked power of adaptation on the part of the plant.   It also carries the suggestion that in soils where deep rooting is impossible the spacing of trees and other fruit plants should be much wider than under more favorable conditions.

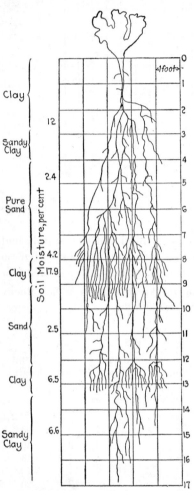

FIG. 8.—Influence of soil moisture upon root distribution of *Kuhnia glutinosa.* (*After Weaver.*[193])

In Dwarfs.—In contrast with the comparatively extensive root systems of trees growing in the field are those of dwarfs occasionally grown in the garden or under glass whose growth is restricted by various means.   Sometimes resort is made to root pruning; sometimes the roots are restricted by planting in pots or tubs.   Such trees develop very compact and much branched root systems that exploit very completely the soil within their range.   Dwarf trees with such restricted root systems are much more subject to injury from extremes of moisture than standards with unrestricted root systems.   Consequently their successful culture necessitates much greater care in watering, fertilization, pruning, exposure to light and management in general.

The Influence of Soil-moisture Content.—Within the ranges possible for the different species, depth of rooting depends to a very important extent on soil moisture and the correlated factor, aeration.   Roots do not grow and branch freely in a very dry soil, or in one that is approaching a water-logged condition.   The water-logged soil probably inhibits root growth and activity through a lack of aeration; the dry soil through a lack of the stimulating effect of the water itself.   Figure 8 gives some idea of the influence exerted by the percentage of soil moisture on root formation and root distribution when other factors are as uniform as it is possible to make them.   In this case, however, the soil moisture did not approach sufficiently near the saturation point to check root formation.

When roots find an abundance of water close to the surface they branch freely through the surface soil and show little tendency to go deeper, particularly if conditions are more and more unfavorable for root development at greater depths. These two factors together probably explain the comparatively shallow rooting of most tree, bush and vine fruits in a large portion of the humid region. Compact, water-logged subsoils or a high water table prevent the roots from penetrating deeply. The surface inch or so is too dry during a major portion of the growing season to encourage root growth; the result is a distribution of most of the roots between the depths of 3 to 10 or 15 inches.

When, however, moisture and aeration conditions are favorable for root development at considerable depths, deep penetration occurs. Thus Hilgard and Loughridge[93] state that on some of the silty "low mesa" soils of California the roots of cherry and prune trees are frequently found at depths of 20 to 25 feet. Such deep rooting is also characteristic of fruit trees in the loess soils along the Mississippi and Missouri rivers. These are soils, however, with no hardpan or plowsole and with the water table many feet below the surface. In them soil grades insensibly into subsoil. Indeed, subsoil in the sense in which the term is generally used does not exist except below the region of this exceptional root penetration. Investigations in the prairie states indicate that deep rooting characterizes many native shrubs and trees that are markedly drought resistant, though fully 95 per cent. of the roots are found in the upper 4 feet of soil, more or less regardless of its texture.[203] Apparently water absorption from the different soil horizons is more or less closely proportional to the relative amount of roots occupying them.[2]

When plants, accustomed to growing in a soil where shallow rooting is necessary, are transplanted to one in which deep penetration is possible, they first send out shallow lateral roots, their distribution being much like that of the same plant in the region or soil from which it came. They probably encounter in the surface layers, shortly after the time of setting, those conditions of air and moisture approaching the optimum for growth. Then as the season progresses and the surface soil dries, the roots in many cases turn down and send branches into deeper layers and a distribution is effected resembling that of native plants.[90] This may be looked upon as a kind of adaptation, an accommodative change, to meet new conditions of environment. That this change in rooting habit is very largely a response to moisture and aeration conditions is indicated by the fact that with a rise in the ground-water table from heavy irrigation the roots are again forced to occupy only a shallow layer of soil. This condition is found in some of the orange groves of California.[90] Three or four feet beneath the surface the soil is so water-logged that roots will not penetrate and the top 6 or 8 inches are so filled with feeding rootlets that each cultivation results in more or less serious root pruning.   Trees under such conditions require heavier irrigation and more fertilization than those with deeper roots and, what is perhaps more important, they are more sensitive to extremes of any kind affecting the roots either directly or indirectly.   Consequently they are more exacting in their cultural demands.   The same danger from heavy irrigation is met in deciduous fruit production.   Thus it has been found in Utah that raising the water table even temporarily by irrigation causes the death of the deeper roots and results in a kind of root pruning or root training and that the general shape of the root system of the tree may be controlled more or less by the distribution of the irrigation water.[9]   One of the most difficult problems in many irrigated sections is to apply the water in such a way that plants are not made surface feeders and the natural advantages of a deep soil lost.

The Influence of Cultivation.—Allen[3] found that tillage methods influenced root distribution in the Hood River district. He reports that where clean culture had been practiced without the use of the plow but with disk and other cultivators "a thick mat of fibrous roots was found immediately below the soil mulch. . . . In the few restricted areas that received neither cultivation nor irrigation, the roots were found to be distributed from near the surface to 1 foot and 16 inches in depth.   Under sod and irrigation conditions the roots were quite uniformly distributed from near the surface to $2\frac{1}{2}$ feet in depth."   Immediately under the loose surface soil of the cultivated areas he found an impervious hardpan or plowsole had developed, which was dry at the time of this examination.   The untilled and irrigated land did not have this hardpan layer.

Different tillage methods had resulted in great variation in the physical character and moisture content of the soil between the depths of 6 and 30 inches, and in corresponding variations in root distribution.   Evidently the varying tillage methods used in certain Ohio orchards[73] did not change materially the character of the soil below a depth of 6 or 10 inches and since few roots developed in it below this depth, root distribution was influenced but little in this particular case.   Cultivation is mentioned often as a means of forcing deeper rooting of fruit trees and sod culture and mulching as encouraging shallower rooting.   These practices often have these effects, but they may have no such effect, as in the Ohio investigation cited, or they may have the opposite effects, as in Hood River.   This brings out the point that tillage methods as such are not to be regarded as direct means of influencing root distribution, but as means of altering the physical and chemical condition of the soil and thus indirectly leading to shallow or deep penetration.   Root growth and distribution are a response to these physical and chemical conditions.   It is noteworthy that in the Hood River orchards many of the symptoms of drought injury were associated with extreme shallow rooting—premature dropping of the foliage, dieback and fruit-pit.

Interesting data concerning the effect of cultivation on root distribution are afforded by the figures in Table 32. Cultivation along one or both sides of the tree row reduced the absolute lateral spread and the ratio between the lateral spread and height of the trees. The greater reduction accompanied cultivation along both sides. In the cultivated soil the tree roots did not have to range so wide to meet the actually increased water requirements of the trees as in the uncultivated land.

Incidentally the figures in Table 32 throw some light on the lateral spread of tree roots as compared with the spread of their branches. Though spread of top is not given it is reasonable to assume that in this species it is less than tree height. It is often said that the lateral spread of the roots is about equal to the lateral spread of the branches. In uncultivated ground it was in this instance more than twice as great.

TABLE 32.—EFFECT OF CULTIVATION UPON ROOT SPREAD OF THE OSAGE ORANGE[18]

Amount of cultivation	Cases measured	Average height of trees	Average root extent	Average root extent; proportion to height
None............	8	20.0	43.7	218.7
One side of trees..	25	17.2	28.9	167.8
Both sides........	35	21.7	29.2	134.5

Mason[129] cites an instance in which the olive grown in an extremely dry soil and climate had a root system radiating 10 to 11 feet in nearly all directions when the top was only 6 feet in height, had a spread of only 7 feet and a trunk diameter of 3¾ inches. In this case there was a total of 185 feet of roots ⅛ inch or more in diameter and the area occupied by roots of this size was about nine times that of the spread of the branches. This fruit as it grows in the Sfax region of Northern Africa furnishes a good illustration of the adaptation of the root system to moisture conditions. There it sends out numerous roots which run for long distances comparatively close to the surface where they can make use of the moisture that penetrates only a few inches into the ground at the time of the infrequent light rains.

The Influence of Soil "Alkali."—It should not be inferred from the emphasis that has been placed upon moisture and aeration in determining root distribution that other factors are of little significance. Other factors are often controlling.

For instance in reporting upon an investigation of the effects of alkali on citrus trees Kelley and Thomas[108] state: "It is especially interesting that the roots of the lemon trees have not penetrated deeply in this soil, more than 95 per cent. of them being within 18 inches of the surface. There is probably some connection between this fact and the higher concentration of alkali salts found in the third and fourth feet."

Applications to Orchard Practice.—The whole subject of the distribution of the root system of orchard plants may be summarized in this way: though different species of plants and different varieties of the same species have characteristic habits of root growth, the extent and the distribution of their root systems are profoundly influenced by environment. Root development, as to both amount and direction, may be regarded as a response of the plant to this environment. The functioning of that part of the plant above ground is conditioned to a very important degree by the functioning of the part of the plant below ground, and therefore by the distribution of the roots in the soil. Root distribution is under control to the extent that soil conditions—texture, moisture, aeration and nutrient supply—are under control and to a certain extent by the pruning that is afforded the top, a matter discussed in detail later. If the soil is one in which these conditions are not favorable for a suitable root distribution or in which they cannot be made favorable, it should not be devoted to fruit culture, because fruit culture cannot be successful on it. As soon as the orchard is planted, or before if possible, and as long as the orchard remains, it is well to study from year to year the way in which various soil treatments influence those factors determining root distribution and then employ those practices that lead indirectly toward ideal root systems. Orchards do not die out or become unprofitable only because of fungi, bacteria, summer drought or winter cold. These are always possible contributing factors and often determining factors, but in many cases the fundamental cause of distress is a root system inadequate for requirements of the tree in an emergency—inadequate perhaps because too shallow, or in too severe competition with the roots of other plants or because it is not exploiting enough soil. Sometimes, though the contributing causes to the death or failure of the trees may be unavoidable, the fundamental factor may be completely under control.

Summary.—In terms of response to gravity and the evaporating power of the air, soil moisture may be classified as gravitational or free, capillary and hygroscopic. Only the capillary moisture is available to the plant in any considerable amount. The capillary supply is derived from precipitation and irrigation or to a limited extent from the gravitational water that reaches the ground-water level. The optimum water content for the growth of plants is reached when its relative saturation is approximately 50 per cent. A certain percentage of the soil moisture is held in a capillary adsorbed or colloidal form and is not frozen at the ordinary freezing point of water. This portion of the water supply is of great importance to the plant. The evidence indicates that a part of the water of plant tissues is held in a similar manner and that this moisture is significant in determining drought and frost resistant qualities of the tissue in question. The percentage of the rainfall that percolates beyond the range of the tree roots varies greatly with many factors, total precipitation being one of the most important. Comparatively little water that percolates beyond the range of the roots becomes available for later use through capillary rise. The lateral movement of soil moisture depends principally upon soil texture and the method by which irrigation water is applied to the soil should be determined accordingly.

Root distribution is governed first of all by the growth characteristic of the species or variety in question. To an important extent, however, it is influenced by soil conditions, particularly soil moisture and soil aeration. A deep, moderately wide-ranging root system is preferable to one that is shallow, wide spreading or narrow. Though the great majority of the roots of most orchard trees are in the upper foot or fifteen inches of soil, there is little evidence that ordinary tillage results in an injurious root pruning. Shallow soils, soils underlaid by hardpan or with a high water table, should be avoided for fruit culture because of the restricted root range that they necessitate and the consequent susceptibility to drought injury of one kind or another. Depth of rooting can be controlled to a considerable extent by cultural practices, such as tillage, the use of cover crops or intercrops of different kinds, irrigation and drainage.

CHAPTER V

THE RESPONSE OF FRUIT PLANTS TO VARYING CONDITIONS OF SOIL MOISTURE AND HUMIDITY

Water as a factor in growth thus far has been discussed only in its general importance in the development of the plant as a whole. There are, in addition, certain specific responses made by the plant to a varying water supply.

Influence of Soil Moisture on Vegetative Growth.—One of the most important of these specific responses is in new tissue formation, an increase in size or bulk. Data have been presented in Table 19 showing the influence that various methods of culture, such as tillage, tillage and cover crops and artificial mulches, have upon vegetative growth measured by trunk circumference.

New Shoots and Their Leaves.—Table 33 gives certain averages found by Hedrick in sod-mulched and cultivated plots in a New York apple orchard. Every phase of vegetative growth measured showed a gain from tillage. Moreover the tillage plot averaged considerably higher in moisture during the growing season. Probably much of the influence of tillage was due to the increased moisture available in the soil, yet it is difficult to say how much is to be attributed to this factor and how much to the influence of the tillage on plant nutrients, particularly nitrates.

TABLE 33.—INFLUENCE OF TILLAGE METHODS UPON VEGETATIVE GROWTH IN APPLES[83]

	Sod	Cultivated
Average length of new laterals in inches	3.40	6.70
Average number of new laterals per year	1.90	4.40
Average weight of leaves in grams	0.87	1.15
Average gain in trunk diameter in inches in 4 years	1.10	2.10

More direct evidence of the effect of water on vegetative growth is furnished by certain orchard irrigation experiments. The following quotations from a report on an investigation in Utah bear on this point. "Frequent applications of irrigation water applied to peaches on a gravel loam (about 15 feet deep) at intervals of 7 or 8 days produced a more continuous and greater total twig growth than the same total amount of water applied with larger applications at intervals of every

10 to 12 days.   The more porous the soil the more frequently the trees should be watered. . . .   With varying times of application of irrigation water the season of most rapid twig growth is during the season of watering."[14]   Barss,[10] reporting upon the results of some pot irrigation experiments with pears, states: "The most noticeable variation in response to the application of different amounts of water, was found in the development of the new wood.   All the lots started vegetative growth at about the same time . . .   but terminal bud formation took place early on the poorly watered trees and much later on the trees of the other lots. Furthermore there were great differences in the rate of wood growth in these different lots while they were actually growing. . . .   The spurs on the better-watered trees were larger and more vigorous. . . .   From leaf samples, collected and weighed in order to bring out any existing differences in weight, it is apparent that, on the average, the leaves

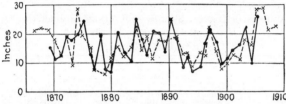

Fig. 9.—Actual rainfall compared with rainfall calculated from growth of trees, Arizona. Solid line equals calculated rainfall. Broken line equals observed rainfall. (*After Douglass.*[101])

in the lots receiving most water were far heavier than those in the lots receiving less water."   He also found the leaves on the trees receiving the smallest water supply were variable in both size and shape, their petioles were slender, their lower surfaces were markedly pubescent and their color was dark green.   Callus tissue formed much more frequently on the well-watered trees.

Annual Rings and Trunk Circumference.—The results of study on the relation between tree growth and total yearly rainfall in Arizona are interesting in this connection.   Under the comparatively arid conditions of that region the correlation between the two was found to be so close that with a knowledge of the total rainfall of any one year the average increase in diameter of trees could be estimated with an average accuracy of 82 per cent.; conversely, knowing the average diameter increment of a small group of forest trees for any one year it was possible to estimate with equal accuracy the total precipitation of that year.   Figure 9 shows graphically the closeness of this correlation.   Huntington[101] employed this method of estimating annual rainfall for the study of climatic variations during the last 1,000 years, obtaining growth records from the giant Sequoias of California.   Hartig,[81] however, found that in parts of

Germany where low moisture content of the soil apparently is not the limiting factor to growth, the beech makes a smaller annual ring during seasons that are cold and wet than during years of more nearly average temperature and humidity. The decreased growth during the wet season may be correlated with poorer aeration in the soil.

Moisture Supply and the Growth Period in Early Spring.—Most deciduous fruits have a short period of very rapid vegetative growth in the spring, followed by a longer period of comparatively slow growth that precedes the resting stage. That this is a characteristic of most deciduous woody plants is brought out by data condensed in Table 34. Of the 70 species of trees, shrubs and vines considered hardy enough for outdoor culture in central Michigan approximately one-fourth had completed their shoot growth and formed their terminal buds by June 1, and over two-thirds had reached a similar stage by June 20. In no case was there appreciable shoot growth before May 1. Gourley[72] states that this

TABLE 34.—NUMBERS OF TREES, SHRUBS AND VINES COMPLETING SHOOT GROWTH AT DIFFERENT DATES

(After Bailey[7])

	Date of terminal bud formation					
	June 1 or earlier	June 1 to 10	June 10 to 20	June 20 to July 1	July 1 to 15	After July 15
Number..............	16	8	24	14	5	3
Per cent..............	23	11	34	20	7	4

period of rapid growth in the apple lasts only about 25 days in New Hampshire and that it is during this period that external factors, such as moisture, have their greatest influence upon new tissue formation. In his work approximately 43,000 measurements were taken and his data point to the conclusion that there was no very close correlation between the humidity and rainfall curves and the growth curve during this period, though it was not possible to control all factors under field conditions. The growth curve showed a closer correlation with temperature than with any other factors studied. In Idaho, irrigation of apple trees after July 15 had no effect upon shoot growth but as a rule the more irrigation water applied before July 1, the greater was the shoot growth.[181] A similar correlation between growth and soil moisture during the months of May, June and July has been observed in Indiana[201] and it was in the plots with the lowest water content that there was the closest correlation between growth and soil moisture. With moisture conditions approaching the optimum, an increased rainfall or surplus irrigation water has comparatively little influence in forcing growth.

Pearson[152] has made a valuable contribution to the knowledge of the importance of an adequate soil moisture supply during the comparatively short period of rapid vegetative growth. Figure 10 presents graphically the results of his series of observations upon yellow pine seedlings near Flagstaff, Ariz.

In commenting upon the data presented in this figure he says: "Contrary to what might be expected, there is no apparent relation between height growth and annual precipitation, summer precipitation or winter precipitation, in fact, the growth from year to year often varies inversely with the precipitation for any of these periods. When it is considered that of the total annual precipitation at Fort Valley, the mean amounting to about 23 inches, approximately 40 per cent. comes during the winter months (December to March), 30 per cent.

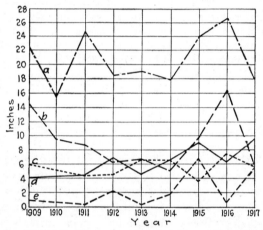

Fig. 10.—Seasonal precipitation and annual height growth of western yellow pine saplings from 1909 to 1917. *a*, annual precipitation; *b*, winter precipitation (December-March preceding the corresponding year's growth); *c*, summer (July-August) precipitation; *d*, annual height growth; *e*, spring (April-May) precipitation. (*After Pearson.*[152])

during July and August, and less than 10 per cent. during the spring months (April and May), the foregoing statements are startling. In order to clarify the problem, it is necessary to analyze the growth habits of Western yellow pine as well as the climatic and soil conditions under which it grows in this locality. The terminal shoots begin to elongate about the middle of May, and by July 1 they have practically completed their growth. Thus it appears that the entire height growth occurs during the period of lowest precipitation of the year. From the middle of May to the middle of July the rainfall is normally less than one half inch, and comes in such small showers as to be of no benefit to deep-rooted plants. It is evident, therefore, that the moisture utilized in making this growth is drawn almost entirely from a stored supply. It is also evident that the midsummer rainfall, since it does not begin until July, when height growth has practically ceased, is of little or no consequence, as far as the current year's height growth is concerned. The water storage which makes growth possible is mainly the

result of the preceding winter's precipitation; but it is the supplementary supply in April and May which determines whether the growth is to be above or
below normal. . . . It is evident from the precipitation figures for 1913 that
the pines in that year depended entirely upon winter precipitation for their height
growth. Since the total precipitation in April, May, and June was only 0.25
inch, it may be readily seen that an addition of 2 or 3 inches during this period
would have resulted in an appreciable increase in soil moisture and presumably
in height growth. Such was the case in 1914 and in a more marked degree in 1915
and 1917. If, as is often the case, the first of April marks the end of the season's
storms, a dry period of 3 months prior to the beginning of the summer rains may
be expected. Since yellow pine, on account of the low temperature, does not
begin growth until about the middle of May, a dry period of 6 weeks intervenes
between the last storm or the disappearance of snow and the beginning of growth.
During this period a large portion of the stored moisture supply is dissipated
without benefit to the tree. If, on the other hand, belated storms continue
through April and into May, the stored water supply is not only conserved, but
may be actually augmented. A typical example of the first type of spring was in
1916. Despite a winter precipitation of over 16 inches, the highest on record in
9 years, soil moisture conditions, after it became warm enough for growth, were
decidedly below normal. . . . The years 1915 and 1917 are examples of the
second type of spring. The winter precipitation was only 9.4 inches in 1914–15
and 6.1 inches in 1916–17, but in both years the precipitation between April
1 and May 15 was around 6 inches."

The "Second Growth" of Midsummer or Late Summer.—A second
period of rapid vegetative growth frequently occurs in late summer or
fall. Usually it takes place after terminal bud formation on both spurs
and shoots in the case of spur bearing species. Sometimes the terminal
buds on the shoots "break" and a new shoot growth is pushed out;
sometimes terminal buds on many of the spurs "break" and a secondary
spur growth takes place and sometimes the lateral buds, rather than
the terminals, initiate this new shoot growth. In some instances terminal
bud formation has not yet occurred in the primary shoots of the season,
though growth has slowed down very materially, so there is a sudden
flush of rapid vegetative development. Occasionally this "second
growth," as it is generally called, is as extensive in amount as that made
early in the season, though this is not usually the case. Without doubt
nutritive conditions within the plant and in the soil have something to
do in determining "second growth" but the fact that it occurs almost
invariably after heavy rains or irrigation following a drought, leads to
the conclusion that it is due at least in part to changed moisture conditions. It is to be regarded as a phenomenon likely to accompany irregularity in moisture supply late in the season, and is a response of the
plant to disturbed moisture relations. This second growth is sometimes
accompanied by fall blooming in some of the tree fruits. Without

doubt the "flush" of certain evergreen plants of tropical countries is a related phenomenon. It sometimes gives rise to two "annual" rings in one season in the trunks and limbs of trees and other woody plants. If this second growth comes fairly early so that the new tissues have time to harden and mature properly before winter freezing, little harm may result, but often when it comes late in the season the tissues do not mature thoroughly and serious winter killing or winter injury follows. It is doubtful if, irrespective of susceptibility to winter injury, much "second growth" is desirable in sections with more or less severe winter weather, for there is reason to believe that the tissues are formed at the expense of stored materials that could be used perhaps to better advantage the following spring and summer.

Influence of Water Supply on the Development of Fruit.—The influence of soil moisture on the development of the fruit is no less important than its influence on vegetative growth.

Size.—The largest fruits are found on the best watered trees and there is abundant experimental data to show the effect of soil moisture upon fruit size. Thus Hedrick,[83] who found his tillage plots to contain more soil moisture than his sod-mulch plots reports the average weight of apples from the cultivated trees to be 7.04 ounces while the average weight of those growing in sod was only 5.01 ounces. This difference of 40 per cent. was presumably due mainly to the difference in moisture supply and accounts in large part for the difference in yield between the two plots, which averaged 36 barrels per acre.

In the discussion of the influence of soil moisture upon vegetative growth it is pointed out that new shoot growth and new leaves are made early in the season and it may be only during a comparatively short period in spring and early summer that this growth is influenced in amount by soil moisture. On the other hand, most of the growth of the fruit tissues takes place after midseason and therefore it is reasonable to believe that soil moisture exerts its greatest influence on their development during the last half of the summer and during the autumn. That this is actually the case is indicated clearly by a number of irrigation experiments. In Idaho, irrigation of winter apples before July 10 had very little influence on their size, though irrigation after that date had a very decided influence.[181] Batchelor,[14] in reporting upon the results of irrigation experiments with peaches, states: "No amount of water applied early in the season to a crop of peaches on a gravelly soil will compensate for the lack of water during the month before harvest. . . . A larger amount of water is evidently required if the irrigation is deferred until late in the season than in case the water is applied throughout a longer period of growth." There is ample evidence to show that for the production of fruits of large size the trees should be well supplied with available soil moisture throughout their growing season.   Through measurements of apples made at intervals of two weeks throughout the season it has been found that size increased steadily from the time of setting to maturity.[195]   This suggests the advisability of cultural treatments to promote a steady growth, and irrigation experiments show that, if growth is temporarily checked because of drought, the size of the fruit at the end of the season will be reduced more or less in proportion to its duration and severity.   That there is a limit, however, to the increase in fruit size that can be effected through increased moisture supply is shown by many irrigation experiments.   For instance, with peaches on a deep gravelly loam in Utah, it was found that 31 acre-inches of irrigation water gave as large size and as large yields as 62 acre-inches under the same conditions.[14]   On the other hand, the size of walnut, pecan and certain other nuts is determined comparatively early in the growing season, and an abundant soil-moisture supply is necessary during this period if they are to attain large size.[16]   Drought late in the season may result in poor filling.

An interesting moisture relation within the plant itself that often affects fruit size is pointed out by Chandler.[44]   He shows that the concentration of the sap within the leaves of the tree is higher than that within its developing fruits.   Consequently in times of drought, when the roots are unable to supply the amounts transpired, the leaves actually withdraw moisture from the fruits, even to the point of causing wilting while the leaves themselves remain turgid.   This not only checks temporarily all increase in fruit size but may result in a reduction.   Chandler cites several instances in which, under these extreme conditions, more disastrous results occurred in cultivated than in uncultivated orchards. Cultivation had been given largely for the purpose of conserving moisture; nevertheless toward the end of a long drought when the moisture supply of both cultivated and uncultivated orchards was approaching the wilting coefficient, the trees in the cultivated orchard suffered more because they had larger leaf systems and required more water to support them.   Had summer pruning to reduce the leaf systems been done promptly in these cases, evaporation would have been reduced and wilting of the fruit prevented.   Chandler states, however, that summer pruning for the purpose of *increasing* fruit size through reducing leaf area has not been successful.

Another, perhaps less direct, but none the less interesting and important, influence of moisture supply on fruit size has been reported from Michigan.[154]   Cherries from trees that have been sprayed with Bordeaux mixture or certain other copper-containing compounds are much smaller in size than those from unsprayed trees or trees sprayed with sulphur-containing compounds, owing to water deficits within the trees occasioned by higher transpiration rates caused by the copper compounds. Such effects are intensified during ripening seasons of high temperature and low humidity. To what extent similar influences of spray materials on transpiration rates are important with other fruits has not been established, but they are of commercial importance with the cherry.

Yield.—The increases in yield from an increased moisture supply, up to the optimum, are in general still more striking than the increases in size because of the indirect effects of moisture through better fruit setting and the formation of more fruit buds.

A striking illustration of the influence of rainfall upon yield is recorded for the palm oil tree (*Elaeis guineensis*) in the British Colony of Lagos. Data showing the yearly rainfall and the yearly exports of palm oil and of palm kernels are condensed in Table 35. The following quotation furnishes comment on these data:

"The yield of fruit from the palm oil tree (Elaeis guineensis) varies according to rainfall. With a sufficiency of moisture the tree flowers every five or six weeks, and bears eight or nine mature bunches of fruit in the year, but if the rain supply is scanty the tree flowers only every ninth or tenth week, and the annual yield is reduced to about five bunches. In normal times the Elaeis bears eight heads (so-called nuts) in the year, but it follows a similar habit to the cocoanut, the heads being formed spirally in the axils of the leaves at regular intervals, which are long or short, according as the season is favorable. The mischief arising from insufficient rainfall does not finish with the number of heads, for the oil is extracted from the fiber of the thin outside layers of the fruit, which are either red, ripe,

TABLE 35.—YEARLY RAINFALL AND EXPORTS OF PALM OIL FROM LAGOS[38]

Year	Rainfall, inches	Palm oil, gallons	Palm kernels, tons
1887	70.80	. . . .	. . . . . .
1888	49.87	2,446,705	42,525
1889	61.61	3,349,011	32,715
1890	90.88	3,200,824	38,829
1891	64.26	4,204,835	42,342
1892	69.68	2,458,260	32,180
1893	82.55	4,073,055	51,456
1894	70.10	3,393,533	53,534
1895	80.62	3,826,392	46,501
1896	74.23	3,154,333	47,649
1897	51.10	1,858,968	41,299
1898	80.20	1,889,939	42,775
1899	83.46	3,292,881	49,501
1900	72.82	2,977,926	48,514
1901	112.59	3,304,055	57,176
1902	47.82	5,240,137	75,416
1903	70.08	3,174,060	63,568

succulent and rich with oil, or starved, yellow, and destitute wholly or partially of oil, according to the amount of moisture afforded to the tree during the time the fruit has been maturing."[38]   Three things are of particular interest in connection with the behavior of the palm oil tree in Lagos: (1) Moisture affects yield mainly through influencing the frequency of flowering and fruiting.   (2) The chemical composition of the fruit is greatly modified.   (3) Variations in rainfall are as likely to influence fruit production the succeeding season as during the current year.   This is explained by the existence of two seasons of heavy rainfall—one early and one late.   If the excess or the deficiency is mainly in the latter period, its influence is more evident in production the following calendar year.   More attention is devoted to this phase of the question under Residual Effects of Soil Moisture.

Shape and Color.—The influence of soil moisture on the color and shape of fruit is of little importance relatively but it is none the less of interest.   In Oregon it was found that with the use of increasing amounts of irrigation water apples tended to become more angular and elongated[117] and the same phenomenon has been noted in irrigated orchards in Idaho.[181] Many observations have indicated that apples in a very dry soil are flatter than those of the same variety grown near by but in a somewhat better watered medium.   In irrigation experiments with peaches in Utah, poor color was associated with a small amount of water and high coloration with abundant and particularly with late, watering.[14]   A brighter red color was found on Esopus apples that were well irrigated, as compared with a darker and duller red on fruit of the unirrigated or lightly irrigated plots in Oregon.[117]   Barss[10] observes that Bartlett pears from trees well supplied with moisture are a clear green at picking time; those from trees suffering for lack of moisture he describes as bluish-gray green.   Possibly the explanation of all these instances of the association of drought with poor coloration lies in the reduction in carbohydrate manufacture that is caused by closing of the stomata during periods of water deficit.[127]

Increased moisture may lead indirectly to poorer color of varieties of apples, pears and peaches that have more or less red coloring matter in their skin by producing a larger wood and leaf growth and thus more shade, the formation of the red pigment in these cases being dependent upon sunlight reaching the fruit itself.   Though this effect of soil moisture is noted only late in the season as the fruit is maturing, it is not an effect of surplus moisture at that time or just previous, but is rather to be attributed to surplus moisture during the spring months when most of the shoots and leaves are developed.   Thus trees with fruits showing the effects of drought in poor size and quality may at the same time show the effects of too much moisture during the spring months in poor color.   Such a condition suggests the contrasting extreme, namely high color from good exposure to the light incident to proper foliage and shoot development early in the season and good size and quality incident to abundant moisture late in the season. Either extreme can be produced or at least approximated by skillful culture, particularly in irrigated sections where water supply is under control.

Composition.—That the composition of fruit is influenced materially by water supply is suggested by the large percentage of water in the tissues of the fruit. It is probable, however, that the most important influence of soil moisture upon quality and composition is not in modifying its water content, but rather in its effect upon other constituents. Thus the poor quality of strawberries ripening during or immediately after a rainy period is due more to a low sugar than to a high water content. Exact figures are not available to show how chemical composition of fruits varies with definite changes or variations in soil moisture, conditions being otherwise the same, but it is presumable that such figures would show material differences. Developing oranges may contain 25 to 30 per cent. less moisture during the middle of the day, when transpiration is at its highest, than at night when it is at its minimum,[45] but the moisture content of apple leaves has been found to vary only from 62.8 per cent. to 64.8 per cent. when the soil moisture in the plots in which the trees were growing ranged from 11 to 24 per cent.[181] This suggests that such extreme variations as have been found in the orange are only temporary and that the plant possesses a marked ability to construct its tissues along a chemical pattern independent of available soil moisture to a considerable degree. However, comparatively slight differences in chemical composition are often responsible for large differences in flavor or quality. In addition, differences in soil moisture may cause slight differences in texture and in the size and cohesion of individual cells or groups of cells, resulting in great differences in quality. The comparative crispness of fruit grown where there is an abundance of soil moisture is a matter of common knowledge. Bartlett pears grown with an extremely limited water supply are distinctly and unpleasantly astringent, though fruit of that variety under usual conditions is without astringency.[10] Peaches supplied early with abundant irrigation water but suffering because of its lack late in the season, may be especially sweet and of high quality but somewhat shriveled and of little commercial value.[14]

Many claims are made for and against fruits grown in irrigated sections. The discussion is based on the assumption that there is some more or less direct influence of irrigation water on the composition and consequently on flavor and quality. If this were the case the evidence would not be conclusive, for fruit raised either in an irrigated or in an unirrigated section is a product of the many factors constituting environment and not solely of differences in soil moisture. Chemical analyses of many hundreds of fruits of different kinds, grown with and without the use of irrigation water, have led to the conclusion that in most deciduous fruits differences between those irrigated and those not irrigated are negligible.[104]   Only in the strawberry were important differences found. In that fruit the irrigated berries were lower in dry matter, sugar, acid and crude protein and these differences were accompanied by a marked difference in keeping quality.   There appears to be little reason for the popular belief that irrigated fruits as a rule are softer and more watery than those not irrigated.   It seems to make no difference whether the soil receives its water from rains or through an irrigation flume.

Disease Resistance and Susceptibility.—Correlated with the influence of soil moisture on the texture and composition of the tissues of shoot, leaf and fruit is its influence on resistance and susceptibility to certain diseases.   This has been noted many times in the common bacterial fireblight of apples and pears.   This disease works much more freely in soft succulent tissues, slowing up or ceasing entirely as it reaches older and harder wood.   Thus high moisture content of the soil, forcing a more succulent and vigorous growth, favors the development of the disease and there are sections where the most practicable method of controlling it on certain varieties is such culture as will maintain the soil moisture at a point somewhat below the optimum for growth though well above the wilting coefficient.   An investigation of the relation between water content of soil and the prevalence of fireblight in Idaho showed that the soil moisture averaged 3 to 8 per cent. higher in badly blighted orchards than in nearby orchards having little of the disease.[181]   Similar differences were found in the soil moisture content of slightly blighted and badly blighted parts of the same orchard and in the soil under diseased and disease-free trees.   It is reported that the sal-root fungus *Polyporus shoraae*, which is widely distributed throughout the sal forests of India, causes serious damage only in the wet forests of Bengal and Assam in which conditions of soil aeration are known to be particularly unfavorable.[95]   A series of dry seasons is almost certain to be accompanied by an increase in the virulence of the Illinois blister canker in those regions where that disease is prevalent.[69]   The influence of soil moisture on certain physiological disturbances is discussed later.

Residual Effects of Soil Moisture.—The influence of precipitation or of irrigation early during the growing season is more or less immediate. On the other hand water falling or applied late during the growing season may have less of an immediate effect on the plant and a correspondingly greater effect at a later period, or even the following year.   Particularly is this true of late fall or early winter rains or irrigation.   This is due partly to the fact that some of the water is stored in the soil for later use and partly to the fact that the benefit that the plant derives from absorbing some of it immediately may not be apparent until considerably later. It is thus proper to speak of the residual effects of soil moisture.

On Vegetative Growth.—It is a common observation that trees suffering from drought in late summer and early fall shed their foliage early. This is particularly true of species and varieties ripening their fruit comparatively early. The function of the foliage during late summer and fall is to manufacture food materials which, for the most part, are stored through the winter for use in tissue building in the spring. A large part of the new growth (roots, shoots, leaves and flowers) in early spring is at the expense of stored foods. Premature defoliation, from drought or any other cause, therefore, is likely to result in a check to growth the following spring through cutting down the available reserves. Though exact experimental data in support of this line of reasoning are not available there is abundant circumstantial evidence and the record of numerous observations is very suggestive.

Whitten[196] has assembled some data bearing on this question for the years 1894–1898 (see Table 36). In commenting on these he says: "It will be observed that the last part of the years 1894 and 1897 were marked by severe drouths, and that the average growth of uncultivated trees fell off to a marked degree during the next year or two after each of these dry seasons. Where trees were well cultivated, to conserve the moisture in the soil, this falling off of growth was not noticeable. . . . The unfavorable effects of drouth upon uncultivated trees may not be so apparent during the dry year itself as it is 1 or even 2 years later." Though unfortunately data are not available as to the exact moisture content of the soils in these plots during the 5-year period in question, there is little doubt about soil moisture being mainly responsible for the differences in growth recorded.

An even more serious, though usually more insidious, residual effect of drought that is associated with premature dropping of the leaves is in making the wood less resistant to winter injury, especially of the black-heart type. When this occurs, the effects of the drought on subsequent vegetative growth are likely to be more or less permanent throughout the life of the tree. Furthermore, as has already been pointed out, drought stimulates heartwood formation and thus decreases the amount of physiologically active sapwood.[8]

On Yields.—The residual effects of soil moisture are not limited to vegetative growth. In all probability they have rather general influence and affect yield. This is indicated by investigation of the olive industry near Sfax in Northern Africa.[166]

The following quotation illustrates the point:

"Although the records do not cover a sufficiently long period to establish a definite relation, it would appear that there is some connection between the size

TABLE 36.—SHOWING CERTAIN RESIDUAL EFFECTS OF SOIL MOISTURE
(*After Whitten*[196])

Variety	Age	Growth (in inches)				Kind of cultivation
		1895	1896	1897	1898	
Ben Davis........	7	17.6	21.7	23.2	24.5	Clean cultivation.
Ben Davis........	11	12.1	12.4	16.6	14.5	Clean cultivation; cover crops.
Ben Davis........	14	17.0	9.5	16.2	10.8	Seeded to clover.
Jonathan.........	9	17.2	9.3	13.6	11.0	In clover; cultivated under each tree.
Jonathan.........	10	7.3	6.6	11.4	9.6	Clean cultivation; cover crops.
Genet...........	30	4.2	6.1	10.4	6.6	In bluegrass and clover; some cultivation around each tree.
Genet...........	30	3.6	5.5	8.9	4.4	In bluegrass pasture.
Genet...........	14	13.0	9.3	11.2	7.4	In clover.

RAINFALL IN INCHES DURING THE GROWING SEASON FOR EACH OF THE 5 YEARS

Month	1894	1895	1896	1897	1898
April............................	2.02	1.04	3.08	4.83	2.76
May.............................	4.33	6.09	5.61	3.19	8.39
June............................	3.04	5.78	4.33	6.59	9.02
July............................	1.20	4.93	3.79	4.28	4.60
August..........................	1.29	2.30	1.85	1.89	0.47
September.......................	7.57	1.48	3.61	0.51	5.43
October.........................	0.98	0.25	2.45	0.69	2.61

of the crop and the amount of rainfall of the preceding year or years, but not that of the spring preceding the ripening of the crop. Thus, the comparatively heavy rainfall (3.6 inches above the normal) in 1897 doubtless had something to do with the large crop of 1898, although the total rainfall of the first 5 months of the latter year was less than half of the normal. Again in 1901, when the crop was less than half the average of 9 years, the rainfall for the first 5 months was not greatly below the normal, but that of the previous year was less than half the normal, and during the 3 years previous the annual rainfall was only a little more than half the normal. It is noteworthy that in 1900, after 2 years of rainfall much below the normal, the crop was about an average one. This was probably due to the heavy rainfall of November, 1899, which was more than three times the normal for that month, while the precipitation during the first 5 months of the year in which the crop was made was less than 40 per cent. of the normal."

Still further evidence is furnished by a report on the relation of certain climatological factors to fruit production in California:

"The character of the autumn, particularly with reference to rainfall, determines in large measure the size and the quality of the fruit crop of the following year. An interesting example of this relation is apparent in the 1919 deciduous fruit crop, which is the largest of this kind ever grown in California. During September, 1918, the heaviest rains recorded in a month of September in California during 69 years of record were general throughout the central portions of the State."[151]

Regularity of bearing, as is pointed out later, is probably more closely associated with and dependent upon, natural flowering habit and the nutritive conditions within the plant than upon soil moisture. However, the following quotation from a report on a series of orchard soil experiments in Pennsylvania suggests the wisdom of looking after the moisture supply when it is more or less under control: "In two treatments, the yields of Baldwin and Spy have remained almost constantly between 400 and 700 bushels per acre annually for the past 7 years, while marked fluctuations in yield were occurring in adjacent plots under other treatments. The essential features of the former treatments have been an ample food and moisture supply, the absence of excessive yields in any one year, and undisturbed root system."[180]

In most of the cases cited it is impossible to differentiate between the direct influence upon the plant of water from the rains of the preceding summer and fall stored over winter in the soil and what has been termed indirect effects through immediately influencing leaf fall and food storage. To the grower it is the combined effect that is important. The facts presented carry a particularly significant lesson for the grower in an irrigated section where fall and winter rains cannot be depended on, but irrigation water is available. They suggest also that the tree that matures its crop early in the season, whether a cherry, apricot, peach or summer apple, has as real, though perhaps not so great a need of late summer, fall and winter irrigation as one maturing its crop in October.

Influence of Atmospheric Moisture on Growth.—It is difficult in many cases to distinguish clearly between the effects of soil moisture and of atmospheric humidity on the plant. Atmospheric humidity has an influence on plant development independent and distinct from that of soil moisture, though it often happens that both influences tend in the same general direction.

In General.—Under average outdoor growing conditions abundant soil moisture is likely to be accompanied by relatively high humidity and low soil moisture by a dry atmosphere. In practice, therefore, these two factors of environment are more or less interdependent. The relation of the two is brought out by data presented in Table 37. In a general way it may be stated that extreme moisture, either of soil or of air, hinders the differentiation of tissues while dryness accentuates the development of strengthening and conducting tissues. Examples of these results are to be found in aquatic plants on the one hand and in desert

TABLE 37.—THE INFLUENCE OF MOIST AND DRY SOIL AND AIR ON SIZE OF LEAF
OF TROPAEOLUM MAJUS
(*After Kohl*[112])

Soil	Air	Relative size of leaf blade
Moist	Moist	5
Moist	Dry	4
Dry	Moist	3
Dry	Dry	1

plants on the other.   In the former the cuticle is usually thin and permeable, the stomata are numerous and exposed, frequently the surface of the epidermis is enlarged and woody tissue, sclerenchyma and collenchyma are poorly developed.   In xerophytic plants, growing under very dry conditions, the cuticle is thickened and rendered impermeable by waxy impregnations; the surface of the entire plant is reduced to a minimum, the stomata are few in number and frequently situated at the base of depressions in the surface of the leaf.   Wood and fibers are developed to a marked degree and specially differentiated water storage tissue is of frequent occurrence.

When cacti are grown under humid conditions they make a greatly increased vegetative growth and become much more subject to decay.[74] Even minor changes in atmospheric humidity from hour to hour have been found to be closely paralleled by changes in rate of growth of the culms of the giant bamboo.[119]   Presumably these changes in growth rate are not direct responses to differences in humidity, but rather to differences in turgidity of the growing cells caused by varying rates of water loss from adult members of the same clump.

The variations in the susceptibility of the foliage of citrus trees to hydrocyanic acid gas due to differences in atmospheric humidity are great enough to be of considerable importance in their fumigation.   In general, the more humid the atmosphere the greater is the danger of fumigation injury.[200]

Apparently atmospheric humidity, rather than soil moisture, soil, or temperature, is the factor determining the limits for the production of certain varieties of dates.   Those of the Deglet Noor type thrive only in the driest climates, like that of the desert oasis with a mean humidity of 35 to 40 per cent.   Dates of a different type are grown in the vicinity of Alexandria, Egypt, with a mean annual humidity of 68 per cent.[130]

Russeting of Fruit.—In addition to the more general influences of atmospheric humidity and soil moisture on plant development there are certain more or less specific influences on fruits and fruit plants. One of the most conspicuous and frequently observed is the effect on the russeting of the skin of certain pomaceous fruits, particularly the apple and the pear. This results from a cracking and weathering off of the epidermis and an increased development of the corky parenchyma beneath. It occurs especially in humid climates or during rainy seasons. For instance the Bosc and Winter Nelis pears as grown in the dry atmosphere of the Rogue River valley of southern Oregon are practically smooth-skinned fruits. Grown in the more humid Willamette valley a hundred miles farther north their surface is almost completely russeted. The Cox Orange apple is a half russet variety as grown in England; it is a smooth-skinned fruit as grown in the Okanogan region in British Columbia. The fruit trade generally considers that fruit produced in irrigated sections has a higher "finish" than fruit of the same varieties produced in non-irrigated orchards. The reason lies in the lower atmospheric humidity of the sections where irrigation is practiced and is in no way directly connected with the irrigation.

This russeting of the skin is often attributed to the action of certain spray materials and without doubt is sometimes partly or even entirely caused by them. In most cases, however, atmospheric humidity is an important contributing factor. The following quotation from a report by Morse,[146] who has made a study of the subject particularly as it relates to spray injury, is instructive:

"One of the most prominent facts shown by the tabulated results of 1916 is the relatively high per cent. of russeted fruit on each plot, even on the unsprayed check which showed 20.57 per cent. This duplicated a condition which prevailed in 1913 when over 31 per cent. of russeted fruit was obtained on the plot upon which no insecticide or fungicide was applied, and the different sprays produced a corresponding increase in amount. Although this russeting was materially increased by different sprays it is evident that much of it must be attributed to natural causes. The weather conditions of 1913 and 1916 were remarkably similar in many ways, and differed from previous seasons in which abnormal fruit russeting did not occur. In 1913 the first spray application was followed by a month of unseasonably, cold weather, with frosts and cold, northwest winds, associated with much cloudiness and heavy rainfall. In 1916, similar conditions prevailed previous to and following the first application. This was also followed in 1916 by heavy rains and continuous cloudy weather in June after the second application, which was not the case in 1913."

Sorauer[176] notes that in the grape similar atmospheric conditions may lead to the development of cork pustules on the peduncles or pedicels as well as on the fruit. The cork generally starts to develop under the stomata and the disorder is likely to make its initial appearance comparatively early. The enlargement of the lenticels of the apple when rain and cloudy weather follow a prolonged drought apparently is a related phenomenon,[22] and in extreme cases this may be accompanied by cracking and malformation of the fruit, resulting in considerable loss.

Some of the effects of high humidity previously mentioned, for example increased leaf surface and the russeting of fruit, are phenomena that likewise accompany a decreased light supply. This raises the question as to whether a part of the apparent direct influence of atmospheric humidity may not be due in reality to its action in intercepting light.

Fruit Setting.—Inquiry shows that atmospheric humidity is often of greater importance in the setting of fruit than is generally realized. Hot drying winds at blossoming time may evaporate the moisture from the stigmatic secretions and thus prevent the germination of the pollen. Extreme atmospheric humidity may interfere with the work of insects in carrying pollen or it may encourage the development of certain fungi such as brown rot and apple and pear scab that work on the flowers and destroy or injure them. The well known effects of rain during the blossoming season in preventing pollination, in washing away and destroying pollen and in diluting stigmatic secretions may be mentioned. A study of the "June drop" of the Washington Navel orange in California indicates that a large part of this drop is due to abnormal water relations during that part of the day when transpiration is at its highest.[45]

"During the day the fruits (of the Washington Navel orange) decrease in water content as much as 25 to 30 per cent. It has been definitely established that under severe conditions when the atmospheric pull is high the leaves actually draw water back out of the young fruits to maintain themselves. But this supply is not sufficient and they decrease in moisture content also. The combined effect of this tremendous loss from leaves and fruits results in tensions in the water-conducting systems of the tree. These tensions as well as the water deficits have been found to be at their maxima when environmental conditions are most severe, that is, between 10 a.m. and 3 p.m.

"Meteorological records show that the atmospheric humidity of the interior valleys is quite low during the growing months, relative humidities of 15 per cent. being not uncommon. Such humidities may and do occur without marked increase in air temperature. In other words, it is possible for extremely dry weather to occur without the characteristic hot-norther.

"Experiments have been performed in the laboratories at Berkeley in which this process of abscission of leaves on cut branches has been induced by artificial means. The process itself has been studied and found to consist in the gelatinization and dissolution of the cell walls resulting in complete separation of the cells. . . .

"The major part of the June drop occurs early in the season and has to do with blossoms and small fruits. It is caused by a stimulus to abscission arising from abnormal water relations within the plant due to peculiar climatic conditions.

"Further evidence that the cause as indicated is substantially correct lies in the fact that in certain orchards which are provided with efficient windbreaks and interplanted with alfalfa and heavily irrigated, the water deficits in leaves and fruits have been found to be much reduced.   Such orchards have less drop and are notable for their comparatively large yields.   The Kellogg orchard at Bakersfield is planted to alfalfa and is shielded by a fairly efficient windbreak. Meteorological measurements made in this orchard and on the desert to windward show that the climatic complex is greatly ameliorated. . . .   The alfalfa tran-spires at a tremendous rate and literally bathes the trees in a moist atmosphere. The windbreak retards the movement of this relatively moist air away from the vicinity.   The vaporization of water from soil and plants tends to lower the temperature of the air.   As the soil is largely shaded, the high soil temperatures are reduced, which temperatures operate to cut down root absorption at the time of day when water loss from the leaves is greatest. . . .

"It thus seems probable that under the prevalent practice of clean cultivation, during the middle of the day when transpiration is greatest the root absorption is actually reduced, resulting in water deficits in all parts of the tree.

"Not only are clean cultivated orchards subjected to higher soil temperatures, but inasmuch as the root system tends constantly toward the surface layers, it is much reduced by the annual spring plowing which shears off many of the fibrous feeders, thus reducing the root area just before blooming and at the very time the trees are under the greatest strain."[45]

To what extent a very high transpiration may lead to the formation of abscission layers and the dropping of fruit in other varieties and in other species is not known, but presumably the phenomenon is not limited to the Washington Navel orange.   On the other hand there is a limited amount of experimental evidence showing that very high atmos-pheric humidity tends to cause the abscission of partly developed apples from the spur[85] and the irrigation of olives during blossoming is likely to cause their dropping.[51]   It is stated that in California heavy irrigation of citrus groves when the soil moisture has been reduced to nearly the wilting point is likely to cause many leaves and partly developed fruits to drop.[13]

Summary.—Evidence from both tillage and irrigation experiments shows increased vegetative growth, as measured by length of new shoots, leaf area and increment in trunk circumference, with increasing moisture supply up to a certain limit (the optimum for growth).   The amount of soil moisture available during the short period of rapid growth in early spring is particularly important.   When the optimum moisture supply is exceeded the correlation becomes negative.   Second growth of mid-summer and the late summer months is generally associated with an irregular moisture supply.   An increased moisture supply late in the sea-son results in an increase in size of fruit and in larger yields.   Regularity of bearing is encouraged by an adequate and continuous moisture supply. There is a limit, however, to what can be accomplished in this direction through increasing soil moisture.   In certain species, as the apple, dry soil conditions tend to promote an oblate form of fruit. There is no very direct relation between moisture supply and fruit color, though good moisture conditions tend to yield fruits with brighter colors than are obtained from soils that are too dry for best growth and development of tree and fruit. The higher colors of fruit from irrigated sections may be attributed to more nearly cloudless skies, in comparison with those of more humid regions. Fruits that develop where the soil moisture is either deficient or in excess are inferior in quality to those developing where soil moisture conditions are more nearly normal. Disease suscepti- bility is often modified materially by the rate of growth, as influenced by soil moisture conditions. The injurious effects of deficient moisture supply may be more evident the season following the drought than during its occurrence, taking the form of decreased vegetative growth and lowered yields. The effects of variations in atmospheric humidity are hardly less pronounced than those in soil moisture supply. Russeting of fruit is common in many species when the humidity is high. Water deficiencies at the time of fruit setting are likely to result in an undue amount of dropping.

CHAPTER VI

PATHOLOGICAL CONDITIONS ASSOCIATED WITH EXCESSES OR DEFICIENCIES IN MOISTURE

Not only is water a limiting factor to growth, but when there is a deficiency or when it is present in excess well defined pathological conditions may arise. Some of the most difficult disorders with which the fruit grower has to deal are to be regarded as drought or as excess moisture diseases.

DISTURBANCES DUE TO MOISTURE EXCESSES

Excessive moisture conditions are likely to be accompanied by a disproportionate development of certain tissues, usually parenchyma and this is at the expense of conductive tissue.

The Cracking and Splitting of Fruit.—One of the most frequent troubles incident to too high atmospheric humidity or to the presence of too much moisture in the soil at certain seasons of the year is checking, cracking or splitting of the fruit. These disorders are most likely to occur shortly before maturity when rains follow a period of drought during which the fruit has been checked in its growth. Apparently the checking of growth is accompanied by changes in the fruit skin which render it less elastic so that when growth processes are accelerated during and following a rain it is unable to expand rapidly enough to make provision for the developing tissues within. Many fruits are susceptible to these forms of injury.

In the date two forms of injury are recognized: (1) checking, which consists in small, linear, concentric breaks in the skin, and (2) severe splitting or tearing of the skin. Which form of injury is occasioned by wet weather depends on the stage of development of the fruit at the time that it occurs. Checking occurs in the late green and in the khalal stages, while tearing occurs mainly in the late khalal or in the rutab stages.[76] Severely checked fruits often turn dark in color and shrivel, in which condition they are said to be "blacknosed."

In the fig, splitting may accompany high atmospheric humidity during the ripening period even though there be no rain or no sudden changes in water content of the soil. However, they are much less likely to split under such conditions than when rain accompanies a humid atmosphere so that the trees can take up an increased amount of moisture.[158] Should dry, warm weather follow

93

the splitting of this fruit the fissures may close and partially heal over without fermentation setting in.

It has been demonstrated that in the case of the sweet cherry there may be an increase of 10 per cent. in volume, because of the osmotic intake of water through the epidermis at the time of a rain, and this is enough in the case of certain varieties to result in practically all of the fruits cracking.[189] Similarly, the cracking of apples has been shown to be associated usually with periods of rainfall or high humidity either when water could be absorbed through the epidermis or when the transpiration rate was greatly depressed.[190] Apparently in neither the sweet cherry nor apple is cracking due directly to variations in soil-moisture supply. On the other hand, splitting of the stones of the peach and plum seems to be due to periods of rapid growth following a check in development occasioned by drought.

Related to the splitting of the skin and fleshy tissues of many fruits and the splitting of the stones of drupaceous fruits is the cracking of carpels and seed coats frequently found in apples and occasionally in pears and other pomaceous fruits. This is often accompanied by the development of a whitish mold-like growth along the edges of the cracks, giving rise to a condition spoken of as "tufted" carpels or "tufted" seeds. According to Sorauer[173] this condition is due to an excessive moisture supply and the consequent disproportionate growth of certain cells and tissues. The "tufting" itself is hardly to be regarded as a diseased condition, for it is more or less common in certain varieties, but apparently an excess of moisture greatly accentuates the condition. It in no way injures the quality or value of the apple, except as it provides a favorable place for the work of certain fungi which may gain entrance to the seed cavity through a broken calyx tube.

Œdema.—Œdema may be described as a swelling of certain parts of a plant caused by a great enlargement of the component cells. In extreme cases the cell walls break and the cells collapse, resulting in the death of the affected tissues. This condition is due frequently to an excess of moisture. It is favored in the case of the tomato by insufficient light, too much soil moisture or a soil temperature too high in comparison with the air temperature so that transpiration cannot take care of water absorption.[5] Sorauer[175] states that in fruit trees these swellings are usually covered by cork but that sometimes they break open. He notes that the trouble is fairly common when either currants or gooseberries are grafted upon the Golden Currant (*Ribes aureum*). The swellings develop just below the union and the cion does not make a satisfactory growth. In this case the excess of water is to be regarded as a local rather than a general condition.

A similar disorder, in which the bark develops at the expense of the wood, has been described in the pear, under the name "parenchymatosis."[175] The swellings may be on one side only of the limb or trunk or they may extend around it, giving rise to a barrel shaped or cylindrical enlargement, which may be accompanied by a splitting of the bark.

There has been described a disorder of the grape also, more or less closely related to œdema, due to excessive atmospheric humidity. It is most frequently found in grapes grown under glass. On the leaves and peduncles intumescences develop which are characterized by great turgidity, a high oxalic acid and low starch content.[177]

Fasciation and Phyllody.—Fasciation, or the production of a flat branch which resembles several branches grown together, is regarded generally as a malformation belonging in the field of teratology rather than as a pathological or diseased condition induced by agencies more or less under control. Sorauer,[174] however, places it among the disturbances due to overfeeding and associated with excessive water supply.

A form of phyllody, known as "false-blossom" or "Wisconsin false-blossom," apparently caused by an excessive water supply, has been observed in some of the cranberry bogs of the northern states. It is characterized by more or less leaf-like calyx lobes and petals, aborted or malformed pistils and stamens, the production of little or no fruit and an appearance of the plant suggestive of witches' broom. The trouble "is usually associated with extreme wet or dry conditions of the bog, but most frequently with an excessive water supply. In most of the localities in which it has been observed the affected plants were growing in a deep, coarse peat soil having an excessive water supply during the greater part of the growing season."[166] What is evidently a very similar disorder, often caused by disturbed water relations, has been described under the name "virescence" as affecting the coffee tree in Indo-China.[49]

Chlorosis.—Chlorosis in plants is generally associated with some form of malnutrition and some attention is devoted to it in that connection. However, Taylor and Downing[181] found it accompanying over-irrigation in a number of Idaho apple orchards. Indeed they came to regard it as one of the evidences of excessive applications of irrigation water. It is possible that the chlorotic condition of the trees was induced through some influence of the excess water supply on the plant nutrients in the soil or the foods in the plant, but directly or indirectly the surplus moisture was responsible for it. A chlorotic condition of the peach induced by over-irrigation has been reported in Baluchistan.[99] Its early symptoms were much like those of the "peach yellows" of the eastern United States and at one time it was thought to be that disease. It was accompanied often by much gumming and unless promptly treated the tree died. The use of less irrigation water and the employment of cultural practices leading to a better aeration of the soil were efficient correctives. Chlorosis has been found in heavily watered seed beds of the western pine in Nebraska while check plots showed none.[113]

Rough Bark or Scaly Bark Disease.—This disease according to Sorauer results in a scaling off of the bark from the roots and to a less extent from the stem. It has been described as affecting the apple, cherry and plum when growing on low, wet ground. When appearing on the roots it is likely to cause the death of the tree; when it attacks the trunk it is less serious. Histologically what takes place is an excessive lengthening of some of the bark cells. This process may continue deep into the bark layer and interfere with normal functions at the diseased spot.

Watercore.—Curiously enough it is sometimes difficult to decide whether a certain disturbance is due to drought or to an excess of moisture. The temporary rising of the ground-water table may result in the death of a considerable part of the root system. Later, with lowering of the water table the soil dries out and if there is a prolonged dry period, the tree with its reduced root system may suffer for lack of water and drought injury ensue. It is a case of drought injury but in the last analysis excess soil moisture at another season is the real determining factor. It is likewise a paradox that some forms of watercore must be regarded as due to drought. Though many cases are to be attributed to other factors, Sorauer[172] describes at least one form as associated with a deficient soil moisture supply. In this form, water fills the intercellular spaces and the affected tissues become hard and glassy. The outer portion of the fruit is involved more directly than the tissues immediately surrounding the core. The seeds remain white and do not ripen and the affected fleshy tissues turn dark upon exposure to air more rapidly than normal tissues. They have less dry matter, less ash and less acid. Zurich Transparent, Gloria Mundi, White Astrachan and Virginia Summer Rose are mentioned as varieties particularly susceptible to this disease.

The watercore more frequently occurring in the United States is found in the core of the fruit and in the region of the main vascular bundles, though it not infrequently extends to the surface or may be limited even to the surface layers. This form of watercore is particularly virulent in regions of intense sunlight. Tompkins King, Fall Pippin, Yellow Transparent, Early Harvest, Rambo and Winesap are mentioned as particularly susceptible varieties.[34] It is found to be more common in the fruits borne on the freely exposed branches of the top and south side of the tree than in those borne on the shaded lower branches. Delayed picking accentuates the trouble.[63] There is a tendency for watercore to disappear in storage.[128]

Gummosis and Sour Sap.—Gummosis is a term applied to a diseased condition of trees, more especially of stone and citrus fruits, characterized by the formation of gum-filled pockets within or beneath the bark and by the exudation of gum from breaks in the bark or skin of trunk, limb or fruit. In many instances, the underlying cause is the attack of some bacterial or fungous disease; in others, gum formation seems to be due to disturbed moisture relations. A high or extreme fluctuating water table is often associated with the trouble.[64,65] It is found principally in low spots in the orchard, in heavy, poorly drained soils or in orchards subject to overflow. Both prevention and remedy lie in providing suitable drainage.

A related disorder, apparently similarly due to poor drainage and a high water table during the early part of the growing season, is known as "sour sap."[70] Trees that may have entered the winter in excellent condition either fail to start in the spring or start feebly and soon die. The sap is characterized by a distinctly sour, fermented odor. There is some reason to believe that early resumption of cambial activity in late winter and early spring, followed by cold weather, is a contributing cause of the disorder. It may affect many different kinds of fruit trees.

DISTURBANCES DUE TO MOISTURE DEFICIENCIES

A deficiency in the water supply is likely to be accompanied by disturbances in the conductive system and an excessive development of stone cells and strengthening tissue.

Tip-burn and Windburn.—Tip-burn of certain plants occurs during periods of very high transpiration. Even a few hours of very rapid transpiration in intense sunlight, high temperature and low atmospheric humidity may lead to so great a reduction of the water content in the edges of the leaves of the potato that recovery of turgidity is impossible.[122] The affected tissues die, a condition known as tip-burn.

It is said that fully 50 per cent. of the citrus acreage in California is subjected at times to windburning of foliage and shoots,[143] one form of which, characterized by brown cork-like areas on the under side of the leaves and associated with a collapse of the mesophyll, is known as "blasting."[75] Indeed, orchard enterprises in whole areas where conditions have otherwise been favorable for fruit production and which have been set to fruit have had to be abandoned later because of the desiccating effects of high wind.[148] The free use of irrigation water to supply the roots of cover crops to increase atmospheric humidity[50] and of windbreaks to reduce air flow are the best known protective measures.

Apparently a form of wilt, defoliation, dieback and decline often referred to as "blight" and attacking citrus trees in Florida is a related

disorder of a more chronic type.[157] It is said to attack trees after they
have attained an age of 12 to 14 years and to occur most frequently on the
lighter, droughtier types of high-hammock soils closely underlaid with
rock, though sometimes it is found on poorly drained soils with a high
water table.

Defoliation. Premature Ripening of Wood.—Summer drought often
leads to premature ripening of the fruit, early leaf fall and premature
entrance into the winter rest period. Frequently the attacks of certain
fungi hasten these processes so that distinction between their influence
and that of drought is difficult; nevertheless there can be no doubt that a
lack of available moisture has an important influence of this kind. These
effects of drought are manifest in various ways in the different fruits.
For instance, the leaves of the peach and cherry turn yellow and fall,
those of the grape turn yellow or red at the edges or between the veins
and those of the pear do not become yellow but appear brown or burned
in spots and remain clinging to the trees.[171] When yellowing is due to
drought injury it is as a rule those parts of the leaf farthest removed from
the veins that yellow first. A somewhat unusual form of defoliation due
to a drought has been mentioned as a pectin disease.[171] It has been
observed on the grape and consists in the formation of an abscission layer
between the leaf blade and petiole, resulting in the premature falling of
the blade. The loss of leaves from drought robs the plant of essential
mineral matter, particularly nitrogen, and may interfere in this way with
its nutrition as well as through reducing the manufacture and storage of
elaborated organic materials. Table 38 shows the mineral constituents
of Syringa leaves at the time of defoliation from drought and at the time
of normal abscission. The yellowing and dropping of the leaves of
dwarf pear trees in times of drought while those of standard trees remain
normal are clear evidence that the trouble is due mainly to a lack of
moisture, the limited root system of the quince being unable to supply
the requirements of the cion in such emergencies.[171]

TABLE 38.—MINERAL CONSTITUENTS OF SYRINGA LEAVES AT DIFFERENT PERIODS
IN PERCENTAGES OF DRY WEIGHT
(After Sorauer[171])

	When defoliated by summer drought	When normally dropping in the fall
Nitrogen	1.847	1.370
Phosphoric acid	0.522	0.373
Potash	2.998	3.831
Calcium oxid	1.878	2.416
Ash	8.028	9.636

Closely related forms of drought injury have been described as affecting grapes in New York,[68] California[21] and Florida,[156] though in all three cases they are attributed almost as much to irregularity in moisture supply as to drought. The New York disorder is described as follows in the original report:

"Vines affected with the trouble first show a streaked pallidness of the leaves in the intervascular spaces. Later these streaked areas become yellow. The discoloration is more marked near the margins and eventually the pallid areas coalesce and form a yellowed band extending around the margin. As the season advances this band dies and becomes functionless. Isolated areas of the leaf blade deaden and when these join, a considerable part of the leaf tissue may become functionless. When the entire leaf is affected the outer margin often curls upward. The injury is cumulative unless favorable conditions are established in the succeeding years, *i.e.*, optimum rainfall, etc. As a result of the injury to the foliage, growth is materially checked and the wood usually fails to mature well. The fruit does not color nor is the normal amount of sugar fixed. 'Shelling' may result.

"Considering the facts at hand it would seem that a lack of available soil moisture, at critical periods in the vine's growth, or a lack of root aeration as a result of the impervious subsoil together with the shallow depth of surface soil, are the principal contributing factors to the affection. With this soil type the sickness is at its height in seasons of drought as well as in those of excessive rainfall. Soils such as the yellow silt are generally deficient in organic matter, and hence in their water-holding capacity. With them the affection is worst in seasons of drouth and least in those of normal rainfall. During early summer the vine makes a rapid growth of succulent shoots and leaves which require large amounts of water to develop."[68] Newly planted vineyards, where the vines do not yet have extensive root systems, are more likely to be affected.

The grape disorders in California that apparently are due to a combination of drought and overbearing have been described under a number of names: black measles, Spanish measles, black mildew, blight, Anaheim disease, California disease, Santa Clara disease, top disease, water berries, grape shrivel.[21] Apparently a similar trouble in Algeria has been described under the name of "brunissure."[155]

Regarding the symptoms and contributing causes of the California vine disorders associated with drought, Bioletti has the following to say:[21]

"Between 1884 and 1893 most of the vineyards of Los Angeles and Orange counties, estimated at over 20,000 acres, were completely destroyed. Vineyards covering an equally large area were destroyed between 1898 and 1900 in the Santa Clara valley. In addition to the vines destroyed in great epidemics, numerous sporadic cases of destruction occur in most of the vineyard areas every year. . . .

"The chief symptoms to be observed are various spots, patches, and dead areas on the leaves, with various brown, red and yellow colorations; spotting, softening, and premature drying of the fruit, with lack of sugar, acid, color, and flavor; dying back of the tips of the shoots; uneven or imperfect ripening of the canes, which are deficient in starch; dark spots and streaks in the wood; short growth and dying of arms, branches, and in the worst cases death of whole vines and whole vineyards.

"The terms California vine disease, Santa Clara disease and Anaheim disease are applied when it appears in epidemic form, destroying whole vineyards. Black measles, Spanish measles and black mildew are names descriptive of certain of the symptoms and are applied when the occurrence of the disease is of a more sporadic character, being confined to certain parts of the vineyard, certain vines or even parts of a single vine. The terms water berries and grape shrivel indicate still other symptoms. They are more commonly employed when it seems that the fruit alone is affected. The berries are soft, watery, and more or less tasteless and may finally dry up without maturing. In Water Berries the vine has been overtaxed only enough to prevent the proper nourishment and complete development of the fruit. . . . In Black Measles and in the California Disease any or all of the symptoms listed may occur. . . . Overbearing for one year produces Water Berries. Overbearing for two years or more produces Black Measles or California Disease. . . .

"When the incidence of these diseases is compared with the coinciding variations in rainfall and in crop, it appears that a close relationship exists between the three factors. . . . In these three great epidemics, therefore, we find similar conditions: (1) a series of years of abundant rainfall; (2) a year of very low rainfall immediately following this series of years; (3) very heavy crops immediately preceding the year of drought and rapid dying of the vines in the year immediately following the drought."

Dieback.—One of the symptoms of the so-called California disease of the grape that has just been described is a dying back of the vine, and in extreme cases the entire vine succumbs. Dieback due to drought, however, is not limited to the grape. It may occur in trees of almost any kind, the symptoms varying somewhat in different species. However, there is no mistaking the disease when it is present. Without doubt dieback may be due to any one of a number of factors. Chief among these is an inadequate water supply, not necessarily at the time the symptoms are first noticed, but perhaps many months earlier. Batchelor and Reed[15] have described dieback as it occurs on the English walnut. Since its appearance there is fairly typical of its occurrence on many other fruit trees the following account is taken from their report:

"We have very convincing evidence to show that trees which enter the dormant period in the fall in a perfectly normal and healthy condition may suffer from dieback due primarily to a lack of sufficient soil moisture during the winter months. During the winter, trees give off moisture through the limbs and twigs. If for a prolonged period there is not enough soil moisture available to the roots, the trees are unable to obtain sufficient water to offset the loss by evaporation from the branches. In that case young branches, the thin bark of which permits rapid loss of water from the wood, may die as a result of desiccation. This injury is first evident when such branches fail to produce new growth the following spring. . . . Frost injury is usually confined to 1- or 2-year old wood, but winter drought may kill back limbs 8 years old.

"Another condition which is equally critical and apt to injure bearing trees, as well as young ones, is the occurrence of a fluctuating water-table. The sudden rise of a fluctuating water-table kills that portion of the root system which is located in the saturated stratum. In severe cases where the major portion of the root system is killed the twigs and young limbs of the tree later exhibit typical cases of 'dieback.' It might seem paradoxical that the top of the tree should dry out and die when the roots stand in an excessively wet soil, but there is nothing contradictory in the situation when it is seen that the death of the major portion of the roots makes it impossible for the top to receive the necessary moisture to sustain life."

Though much of the dieback or exanthema found in citrus trees is due to disturbed conditions of nutrition there seems to be no doubt that the disease is generally associated with abnormal moisture conditions. Trees subject to poor drainage, underlaid with hardpan or subject during the previous season to extreme drought or to an irregular water supply are most subject to the disease.[66] Drought, therefore, must be regarded as an important contributing factor. Other than the dying back of the limbs, this disease presents a number of well defined symptoms in citrus trees that may be mentioned as further illustrations of the disturbed and pathological conditions which may arise from, or be end products of, an abnormal water supply. Among them are: the production of gum pockets, stained terminal branches, ammoniated fruits, bark excrescences, multiple buds, exceptionally deep green color of the foliage, the production of S-shaped terminal shoots and of coarse leaves somewhat like those of the peach in shape.[66]

Cork, Drought Spot and Related Diseases.—Under these names have been described numerous disorders of fruit trees that are apparently related. Indeed differentiation between them is frequently difficult, if not impossible. This is understood easily because they are in fact closely related and are perhaps only different symptoms of the same fundamental disturbance in the physiology of the plant. The following descriptions are from the reports of those who have made a close study of them.

Fruit-pit.—"In the early stages of fruit-pit one finds numerous sunken areas from 2 to 6 millimeters in diameter on the surface of the apple. These depressions are somewhat hemispherical in shape and have the appearance of bruises. At this stage the spots are not brown and often show no difference in color from the surrounding surface of the apple. . . . Later they begin to take on a brown tint, but at first this seems to show through from rather deeply seated tissue and not to arise from any discoloration of the epidermal or immediately underlying cells. Sections of such spots show that this is the case, and that the browning and shrinking of the cells occur in the pulp of the fruit and in the tissue that is transitional between it and the hypodermal parenchyma. . . . Later the surface cells also become dark brown. . . . As the disease advances spots situated near each other often become confluent, developing into one large spot.   In all such cases examined it was found that the *original spots were closely connected with one vascular branch.* . . .   The surface spotting is often accompanied by browning of the tissue immediately surrounding the vascular bundles. Upon cutting such an apple one sees numerous apparently isolated brown spots. Further study shows that these are not isolated but are in reality continuous strands of brown tissue surrounding the vascular bundles.   The portion of the vascular system that is most commonly affected is that lying within fifteen millimeters of the surface of the apple.   The surface spots often occur without the internal browning and also the internal browning may occur unaccompanied by any surface derangement."[32]

Cork.—Cork is most commonly observed when the apple is anywhere from half grown to nearly mature.   It may be briefly characterized as internal browning, described by Brooks in the preceding paragraph, but without external pits and with the surface of the apple thrown into a series of elevations and depressions.   A large number of brown corky areas occur throughout the flesh, following closely the course of the vascular bundles.   In no case do these extend outward as far as the skin, consequently there are no external brown pits characteristic of true fruit-pit or stippen.   A further difference from the usual type of fruit-pit is that the spots are not more abundant in the peripheral zone, but are scattered throughout the flesh of the fruit.   There is no bitter taste connected with this disease in Fameuse apples.[144]

"Under the microscope the internal brown spots of cork appear as aggregations of cells with brown shrunken contents.   A number of the cells, though not all, are shrunken and collapsed.   Around the corky portion the healthy cortex cells form a ladder-like arrangement of smaller, more nearly rectangular cells. It is as though they had been stimulated to rapid division in response to the decreased pressure from the direction of the diseased area.   Outside of this zone the pulp cells are normal in size and form.   The *close relation of the dead spots to the vascular system* is very evident under the microscope."[144]

Surface Drought Spot.—"An early stage of the disease is manifested by an irregular light-brown area in the skin.   When the fruits affected are large, two or three centimeters in transverse diameter, the surface of the fruit is usually smooth and regular, there is no shrinkage or sinking in, nor any abnormality in the flesh beneath. . . .   When the spot first appears tiny drops of a clear or yellowish gummy exudate may occur on its surface.   Under the microscope this exudate shows as a clear gum. . . .   It is considered to be merely an expression of cell sap from the diseased hypodermal cells. . . .   Most of the fruits affected when young drop from the tree.   Some of them . . . persist, and as they grow the affected areas become roughened and cracked."[144]

Deep-seated Drought Spot.—"This type of lesion is characterized by the presence of brown, corky areas in the flesh of the apple and by a sinking in of portions of the epidermis. On young fruits, from 1 to 2 or 2½ centimeters in transverse diameter, the disease appears as a large brownish area in the skin of the fruit, usually near the blossom end, which is irregularly sunken and wrinkled, indicating shrinkage of the tissues beneath. Cross-sections show brown areas in the flesh near the periphery. *These are opposite the main vasculars, and often in the center of one of them there is a large cavity, the apex of which reaches one of these vessels.* (Occasionally, apples are found in which there is one of these corky areas or cavities opposite each of the 10 main vasculars.) These internal spots are often connected by a narrow brown streak running close to the periphery of the apple. Sometimes these streaks do not connect, but extend only a short distance in either direction from the central spot. The shrinkage of the skin over a considerable area, and the presence of these brown corky spots and streaks in the periphery, suggest the type of fruit-pit described by McAlpine as 'confluent bitter-pit' or 'crinkle.' . . . Microscopically, sections of the diseased spots show that the trouble is confined to two or three layers of the hypodermal parenchyma, usually the inner layers, though sometimes the entire hypodermis is affected and a few dead cells are also found in the flesh. The diseased cells retain their normal outline, but their contents have become brown and amorphous."[144]

Dieback and Rosette.—Dieback in its early stages appears usually in the spring. Some or all of the buds toward the ends of the shoots remain dormant, while lower buds start. The shoot ends that do not vegetate may remain alive all season or they may dry out and die earlier. "The appearance of one of these dieback shoots the following summer was that of a completely dead tip from 6 inches to 1 foot long, often with a distinct marginal crack between it and the living part below. From some point back of this tip a healthy lateral developed to renew the branch."[144]

The early stages of dieback may be observed in cross sections of dieback twigs of the current season's growth. "Such a twig usually shows entirely dead tissue near its tip and a discoloration in the cambial area running back for a variable distance. Under the microscope this discolored zone shows, if the sections are taken near the tip, a large number of cells with browned contents in the cambium, phloem and pericycle. If sections are made from parts of the twig a short distance below, it will be seen that growth has been made subsequent to the injury. The injured cambium has produced a quantity of the so-called parenchyma wood, the browned cells of the phloem and pericycle being pushed outward. Finally, the parenchyma zone becomes buried by a layer of new xylem, outside of which are found normal bark and cambium." . . . Often some of the buds on the lower part of such dieback shoots "developed clusters of very small, lanceolate leaves with shortened petioles. In some cases the twigs made a very short terminal growth, resulting in a thickened, shortened axis an inch or so long, bearing a cluster of leaves, some normal and some short lanceolate, the general effect being that of a long bare twig capped by a rosette of leaves."[144]

In commenting on these diseases Mix remarks: "It is evident that we have under consideration, not two distinct apple diseases, but at the most, two types of the same disease: (a) Drouth spot, with which are associated abnormalities of the foliage, called drouth dieback and drouth rosette; and (b) cork, which may occur in association with drouth spot, but which often occurs independently, and is then not associated, except rarely, with any disease of the foliage.

"The writer's observations show that these diseases may occur in both wet and dry seasons. There is, however, a marked relation of weather conditions to the disease. They tend to disappear during wet weather and are much more serious during a dry period, especially dry weather occurring early in the season.

"Since, however, in a wet season, and under conditions where there seems to be no deficiency of moisture, these diseases may occur in trees that have been previously diseased year after year, insufficient soil moisture cannot be looked upon as the sole cause. . . .

"It is suggested that the exact manner of occurrence of the injury may be by the leaves robbing the fruit of water during a critical period of low root supply and high transpiration. Rapid wilting of the fruits can be brought about by excessive transpiration from the leaves. It has been seen that this wilting may result in the death of certain cells near the vascular bundles, forming lesions resembling those of drouth spot, and occasionally, of cork. Chandler has presented evidence that transpiration from the leaves may bring about a scarcity of water in the fruit under field conditions. It is not impossible that this is at least one of the ways in which the disease may be caused.

"This seems more likely than that injury is due to an excessive transpiration from the fruit itself, or, as suggested by McAlpine for 'crinkle,' to the failure of the vascular network over large areas. The striking thing about these diseases is the presence, not the absence, of meshes of this vascular network in close proximity to the dead cell areas.

"In making the above suggestion as to the cause of cork and drouth spot, the writer realizes that the small amount of experimental work done does not warrant a definite conclusion. There is, undoubtedly, much yet to be learned of the real nature of these diseases.

"Furthermore, it is not intended to advance this theory to explain the cause of true fruit-pit, or stippen, which occurs in a late stage of the fruit's growth and is said to develop in storage."

The findings of Brooks and Fisher,[33] who also made an extended study of drought spot and cork in apples, in the main corroborate the conclusions of Mix just quoted. They succeeded in producing drought spot experimentally by subjecting Winesap trees to a sudden and severe drought when the fruit was about 1 inch in diameter. Furthermore, trees of other varieties accidentally receiving similar treatment through mishaps to the irrigation system produced fruits exhibiting the same condition. It was noted in the course of the investigation that many trees after once producing drought spot fruits continued to bear them in later years, even though suitable soil moisture conditions were provided. This the investigators believed to be due to the loss of many roots when the drought occurred. They found cork, or troubles very similar to it, in many of the apple producing sections of the Pacific Northwest and in New York, Virginia and West Virginia. In summarizing their findings they state:

"In nearly every case where the disease has been observed either in the East or West, its occurrence in the orchard has been closely correlated with certain peculiar soil conditions; sometimes an excess of alkali or an out-cropping of slate, but more often a shallowness or openness of the soil. In most sections cork has been most serious when there was a shortage in soil-water supply, either resulting from light rainfall or a lack of irrigation.

"The observations reported above seem to indicate that cork is a form of drouth injury; yet the disease appears to differ from typical drouth spot, both in characteristics and conditions of occurrences. With certain varieties of apples drouth spot can apparently be produced on any soil under conditions of sudden and extreme drouth. Cork seems to be the result of a less severe but more chronic drouth on trees located on certain peculiar soils, especially on soils that are lacking in humus and are not retentive of moisture. Blister is closely associated with cork and is probably produced by the same agencies.

"It should be noted in this connection that the harmful effects of drouth are not always in proportion to the degree of desiccation. Other factors must be considered in a study of drouth troubles, and among these are the percentage of harmful substances in the soil water and the general growth condition of the plant."[33]

In the pecan there is a related disorder, though its most conspicuous symptom is the appearance of rosetted branches. This is associated with a deficiency of humus as well as an insufficient moisture supply in the soil but destruction of roots through drought or an extreme depletion of the soil moisture is an important contributing factor.[142]

Bitter-pit.—In bitter-pit "the diseased tissue is dry and spongy, the cells are collapsed but still full of starch, and the cell walls show no sign of thickening or disintegration. . . . The pits *are usually associated with the terminal branches of the vascular bundles,* and the surface spotting is often accompanied by a browning of the vascular tissue deeper in the fruit, giving the appearance of numerous brown spots in the flesh when the apple is cut. . . .

"The results of the various experiments have been uniformly consistent in showing that heavy irrigation favors the development of bitter-pit. Heavy irrigation throughout the season has given less of the disease than medium irrigation followed by heavy, and light irrigation throughout the season has resulted in more bitter-pit than heavy irrigation followed by light. Heavy irrigation the first half of the season caused the trees to develop a more luxuriant foliage and probably produced a lower concentration of cell sap in the apples, both of which facts would tend to make the fruit less susceptible to the forcing effects of late irrigation. The amount of irrigation in August and September has apparently largely determined the amount of disease.

"Sudden changes in the amount of soil water do not appear to have had any effect upon the amount of disease. No evidence has been found that bitter-pit is brought about by a rupture or bursting of the cells.

"Large apples have been more susceptible to bitter-pit than small ones, but the increase in the disease from heavy irrigation has been almost as great on the small and medium sized fruits as on the large. . . . Apparently apples are not susceptible to bitter-pit merely because they are large, but rather because of conditions that may sometimes accompany an increased growth.

"The results as a whole point to the harmful effects of heavy late irrigation regardless of the size of the fruit. In looking for the final cause of the disease not only the direct growth-forcing effects of the water should be considered but also the effects of the excess water upon the soil flora and soil solutes."[33]

Jonathan-spot.—' Jonathan-spot' is the term applied to superficial black or brown spots that are especially common on Jonathan apples. . . . In the early stages of the disease only the surface color-bearing cells are involved and the spots are seldom more than 2 mm. in diameter, but later the spots may enlarge to a diameter of 3 to 5 mm., become slightly sunken and spread down into the tissue of the apple to a considerable depth. . . . The results of both years gave some evidence that heavy irrigation was more favorable to the disease than light irrigation, but there was nothing to indicate that the amount of soil moisture was an important factor in determining the amount of Jonathan spot."[33]

Barss[11] records "cork" as of frequent occurrence in pears in Oregon and a "drought spot" or "gum-spot" as not uncommon in prunes. Both are attributed to disturbed water relations. In speaking of the gum-spot of prunes he says: "It comes on just about in midseason and appears first as watery-looking spots on the fruit. These usually swell and burst open by a crescent-shaped slit, from which there is an exudation of transparent gum that hardens on the surface. In the flesh of such prunes small brown flecks always appear, beneath the gum-spot. These usually consist of a few dead pulp cells situated in the region of the outer network of veins. Such injury is often slight and the prunes mature with very little evidence of the trouble. More severe injury, however, may result in the death of larger areas of the pulp. The resulting collapse of the tissues and cessation of growth produces an irregular or corrugated surface. Such affected prunes usually color up prematurely and drop off.

"In some years, as the prunes approach maturity great losses to growers result from an internal breaking down of the flesh, with brown discoloration and disagreeable odor, which has sometimes been erroneously mistaken for brown rot. This internal browning usually starts immediately around the pit, but often extends outward until in some cases it reaches the skin and involves the whole flesh. The trouble is . . . presumably due to disturbed water balance in the tree and perhaps is similar in origin to 'punk' in the apple."

Black-end.—Under the name black-end has been described a physiological disease of pears in which the skin around the apical end of the fruit turns black while the flesh immediately underneath becomes hard and dry and may crack.[11] Such fruits are likely to be rounded at the apical end instead of depressed in the usual manner. The blackened area often blends gradually into healthy tissue. This disease is found most frequently in the hotter and drier portions of Oregon, and "all the circumstantial evidence points to the probability that excessive evaporation in hot weather or insufficient soil moisture are responsible for its development, since it appears usually on soils either unfavorable for root growth or unretentive of moisture or both."

There is a very closely related disorder of the apricot described by Roger under the name "drought spot." This trouble "is characterized by the appearance, on the skin of maturing fruit, of small reddish brown, scale-like markings. The spots are irregular in shape and vary in size from minute specks to blemishes which sometimes involve the whole side of the fruit. In severe cases the fruit cracks and shrivels, but usually the small marks are only skin deep. . . . It has been observed that the disease may appear on the whole tree, or it may be confined to some branches only."[159] Both field surveys and irrigation experiments in the Okanagan region of British Columbia indicate this disease is due to the death of many small absorbing rootlets, presumably caused by too long a submergence from a high-water table.

Endoxerosis.—A form of internal decline in lemons has been described under the name "endoxerosis."[12,40] It is associated with clogging of the water-conducting vessels in the twigs and branches with gum and apparently is due to water deficits in the fruits during periods of high evaporation.

The assumption should not be made, however, that all these diseases described and discussed here under the names of cork, fruit-pit, bitter-pit, Jonathan-spot, dieback, rosette, etc., are always due exclusively to disturbed water relations. Though without doubt they often are caused directly or indirectly by excessive moisture or by drought, there are other contributing factors and in some instances their occurrence may be due to these other factors alone. For instance, White[194] and Ewert[61,62] present evidence that in Australia some of the bitter-pit in the apple is due to localized poisoning caused by the presence of minute quantities of certain mineral toxins absorbed either from the soil or from the coating of certain spray materials on the fruit itself.

Silver Leaf.—Sorauer[171] describes one type of silver leaf occurring on apricots, plums, cherries and apples. The immediate cause of the silvery or milky appearance of the leaves is the partial separation of the epidermal cells from one another and from the palisade cells, the intercellular spaces becoming greatly enlarged. The older leaves are more subject than the younger. This disease is usually associated with some gummosis of the limbs and in aggravated cases the affected branches die. Aderhold suggests that the failure of the middle lamella to cement adjoining cells is due to a lack of calcium, which permits the pectin to become soluble. As the disease generally occurs locally in the plant, the lack of calcium is not the result of a deficiency in the soil but is due to a local disturbance in the conducting system.

Some other forms of silver leaf occasionally appearing in the orchard and affecting entire trees or entire orchards may be due to quite different causes.

Lithiasis.—Drought at or shortly before the maturing season of pears has been noted often to cause increased grittiness of the flesh, the stony aggregations around the core becoming larger. Sorauer[169] describes an aggravated form of this trouble under the name lithiasis. In this drought disease sclerotic tissue develops near the surface of the fruit, particularly on the sunny side. Ordinarily it is found only in cases of extreme drought.

Summary.—Either an excess or a deficiency in soil moisture is likely to be accompanied by a disturbed condition within the plant and often by the appearance of some pathological symptom. Among those brought on by excesses in the moisture supply are fruit splitting, fasciation, phyllody, œdema, chlorosis, scaly bark and water core. High atmospheric humidity is an important contributing factor in œdema and fruit splitting. Measures against all of these troubles should be preventive rather than remedial. They include provision for adequate drainage and caution in the use of irrigation water. Premature defoliation and the attendant ripening of the wood are among the more serious results of a moisture deficiency. They are likely to be followed by decreased vegetative growth, lessened yields and in extreme cases, dieback. The earlier entrance into the rest period and the poorer maturity of the wood both tend toward susceptibility to winter injury. Dieback, rosette and little-leaf are closely related disorders of the tree due in many cases to summer drought. Often associated with these tree diseases, but sometimes more or less independent of them, are a number of closely related diseases of the fruit itself that have been described under the names: fruit-pit, cork, drought spot, bitter-pit, Baldwin-spot, Jonathan-spot, black-end and water berries. It is probable that some of these terms as commonly used refer to one and the same trouble, or at least they overlap. This group of disorders, though directly due to drought, frequently may be a result of too much moisture, or a water table too high at some other season, resulting in a restricted root system. Here again, protection lies more in preventive than in remedial treatments.

Suggested Collateral Readings

1. Schimper, A. F. W. Plant Geography. (English Translation) Oxford, 1903. (Particularly pp. 159–173, 81–85.)
2. Bowman, I. Forest Physiography. New York, 1914. (Chapter 3 on Water Supply of Soils; Relation to Plant Growth and Distribution, pp. 41–54.)
3. Weaver, J. E. The Ecological Relations of Roots. Pub. 286 Carnegie Inst. of Washington. 1919. (Particularly pp. 27–28 100–108, 121–127.)

4. Curtis, O. F.   The Translocation of Solutes in Plants.   New York.   1935. (Particularly Chapter 6.)
5. Dixon, H. H.   Transpiration and the Ascent of Sap in Plants.   London.   1914. (Particularly Chapters 1–4.)
6. Maximov, N. A., and Yapp, R. H.   The Plant in Relation to Water.   London. 1929.   (Particularly Chapters 1–8.)
7. Huntington, E., and others.   The Climatic Factor as Illustrated in Arid America. Pub. Carnegie Inst. of Washington, pp. 101–174.   1914.
8. Bates, C. G.   Windbreaks; Their Influence and Use.   U. S. D. A., Forest Service Bul. 86.   1911.
9. Briggs, L. J., and Shantz, H. L.   The Water Requirement of Plants.   A Review of Literature.   U. S. D. A., Bur. Pl. Ind. Bul. 285.   1913.

Literature Cited

1. Agr. Jour. India.   13: 150.   1918.
2. Aldrich, W. W., Work, R. A., and Lewis, M. R.   Jour. Agr. Res.   50 (12): 975–988.   1935.
3. Allen, R. W.   Ore. Agr. Exp. Sta. Rept. of the Hood River Branch Exp. Sta. Pp. 20–24.   1914–15.
4. Atkins, W. R. G.   Some Recent Researches in Plant Physiology.   P. 201. London, 1916.
5. Atkinson, G. F.   Cornell Univ. Agr. Exp. Sta. Bul. 53.   1893.
6. Babcock, S. M.   Wisc. Agr. Exp. Sta. Research Bul. 22.   1912.
7. Bailey, L. H.   Mich. Agr. Exp. Sta. Bul. 31.   1887.
8. Baker, C. E.   Thesis on file in library of Univ. of Ill.   1933.
9. Ballantyne, A. B.   Utah Agr. Exp. Sta. Bul. 143.   1916.
10. Barss, A. F.   Bienn. Crop Pest and Hort. Rept.   Ore. Agr. Exp. Sta.   1: 38–49. 1913–14.
11. Barss, H. P.   Bienn. Crop Pest and Hort. Rept.   Ore. Agr. Exp. Sta.   3: 159–166.   1921.
12. Bartholomew, E. T.   Cal. Agr. Exp. Sta. Bul. 296.   1936.
13. Bartholomew, E. T.   Letter to one of the authors, dated Dec. 20, 1937.
14. Batchelor, L. D.   Utah Agr. Exp. Sta. Bul. 142.   1916.
15. Batchelor, L. D., and Reed, H. S.   Cal. Agr. Exp. Sta. Circ. 216.   1919.
16. Batchelor, L. D.   Cal. Agr. Exp. Sta. Bul. 379.   1924.
17. Batchelor, L. D., and Reed, H. S.   Univ. Cal. Agr. Exp. Sta. Tech. Pap. 10. 1923.
18. Bates, C. G.   U. S. D. A., Forest Service Bul. 86.   1911.
19. Bedford, H. A. R., and Pickering, S. U.   Science and Fruit Growing.   P. 283. London, 1919.
20. Bergman, H. F.   Ann. Bot.   34: 13–33.   1920.
21. Bioletti, F. T.   Cal. Agr. Exp. Sta. Bul. 358.   1923.
22. Blake, M. A.   N. J. Hort. Soc. News.   11: 351.   1930.
23. Blanchard, V. F.   Calif. Citrogr.   19: 206.   1934.
24. Boussingault, J.   Agronomie.   6: 349.   1878.
25. Bouyoucos, G. J.   Mich. Agr. Exp. Sta. Tech. Bul. 36.   1917.
26. Bowman, I.   Forest Physiography.   P. 42.   New York, 1914.
27. Ibid.   P. 66.
28. Briggs, L. J., and Shantz, H. L.   U. S. D. A., Bur. Pl. Ind. Bul. 230.   1912.
29. Ibid.   Bul. 285.   1913.

30. Briggs, L. J., and Shantz, H. L.   Proc. Pan.-Amer. Sci. Cong.   3: 95–107. 1915–16.   (Reviewed in Exp. Sta. Rec.   41: 632.   1919.)
31. Briggs, L. J., Jensen, C. A., and McLane, J. W.   U. S. D. A. Bul. 499.   1917.
32. Brooks, C.   Torrey Bul.   35: 423–456.   1908.
33. Brooks, C., and Fisher, D. F.   Jour. Agr. Research.   13: 109–137.   1918.
34. Brooks, C., Cooley, J. S., and Fisher, D. F.   U. S. D. A., Farmers' Bul. 1160. 1920.
35. Brown, G.   Jour. Ecology.   3: 30–31.   1915.
36. Burgerstein, A.   Oester. bot. Zeitsch.   25: 6.   1875.
37. Burgerstein, A.   Sitzungsb. d. Wien. Akad.   73: abt. 1 Riehe 2; 78.   1876.
38. Buttenshaw, W. R.   Mo. Weather Rev.   32: 470.   1904.
39. Caldwell, J. S.   Physiological Researches.   1.   1913.
40. Cal. Agr. Exp. Sta. Ann. Rept.   1926.   p. 42.
41. Cannon, W. A.   Carnegie Inst. Wash. Yearbook.   17: 83–85.   1919.
42. Cannon, W. A.   Carnegie Inst. Wash. Pub. 368.   1925.
43. Card, F. W.   Neb. Agr. Exp. Sta. Bul. 48.   1897.
44. Chandler, W. H.   Mo. Agr. Exp. Sta. Research Bul. 14.   1914.
45. Coit, J. E., and Hodgson, R. W.   Cal. Agr. Exp. Sta. Bul. 290.   1918.
46. Corbett, L. C.   S. D. Agr. Exp. Sta. Bul. 44.   1895.
47. Coville, F. V.   U. S. D. A., Bur. Pl. Ind. Bul. 193.   1910.
48. Craig, J.   Cornell Univ. Agr. Exp. Sta. Bul. 198.   1902.
49. Cramer, P. J. S.   Philippine Agr. Rev.   3: 94–100.   1910.
50. Crider, F. J.   Ariz. Agr. Exp. Sta. Ann. Rept.   52: 589.   1921.
51. Crider, F. J.   Ariz. Agr. Exp. Sta. Bul. 94.   1922.
52. Darwin, F.   Proc. Roy. Soc.   B87: 281–299.   1914.
53. Delwiche, E. J., and Moore, J. G.   Wis. Agr. Exp. Sta. Rept.   P. 382.   1907.
54. Dixon, H. H.   Transpiration and the Ascent of Sap in Plants.   London, 1914.
55. Dole, E. J.   Vt. Agr. Exp. Sta. Bul. 238.   1924.
56. Driggers, B. F.   N. J. Agr. Exp. Sta. Ann. Rept.   Pp. 365–372.   1926.
57. Duggar, B. M.   Plant Physiology.   P. 87.   New York, 1912.
58. Eberdt, O.   Die Transpiration der Pflanze und ihre Abhängigkeit von aüsseren Bedingungen.   P. 88.   Marburg, 1889.
59. Emerson, R. A.   Neb. Agr. Exp. Sta. Bul. 79.   1903.
60. Ibid.   Bul. 92.   1906.
61. Ewert, A. J.   Proc. Roy. Soc. Victoria.   24 (N. S.): 367–419.   1911.
62. Ibid.   26 (N. S.): 2–44, 226–242.   1914.
63. Fisher, D. F.   Proc. Wash. St. Hort. Assoc.   19: 98–104.   1923.
64. Firky, A.   Minist. Agric. Egypt.   Bul. 141.   1934.
65. Ibid.   Bul. 154.   1936.
66. Floyd, B. F.   Fla. Agr. Exp. Sta. Bul. 140.   1917.
67. Fowler, L. W., and Lipman, C. B.   Cal. Pub. in Agr. Sci.   3: 25–26.   1917.
68. Gladwin, F. E.   N. Y. Agr. Exp. Sta. Bul. 499.   1918.
69. Gloyer, W. O.   N. Y. Agr. Exp. Sta. Bul. 485.   1921.
70. Goldsworthy, M. C., and Smith, R. E.   Science.   71: 506–507.   1930.
71. Gourley, J. H., and Shunk, V. D.   N. H. Agr. Exp. Sta. Tech. Bul. 11.   1916.
72. Gourley, J. H.   N. H. Agr. Exp. Sta. Tech. Bul. 12.   1917.
73. Green, W. J., and Ballou, F. H.   Ohio Agr. Exp. Sta. Bul. 171.   1906.
74. Griffiths, D.   U. S. D. A. Bul. 31.   1913.
75. Haas, A. R. C.   Calif. Citrogr.   22 (3): 114.   1937.
76. Haas, A. R. C., and Bliss, D. E.   Hilgardia.   9 (6): 338–339.   1935.
77. Haberlandt, G.   Physiological Plant Anatomy.   English translation.   P. 219. London, 1914.

78. Harris, J. A., and Lawrence, J. V. Carnegie Inst. Yearbook. 131–132. 1917.
79. Harris, K., Kinnison, A. F., and Albert, D. W. Ariz. Agr. Exp. Sta. Bul. 153. 1936.
80. Hartig, T. Allg. Forst u. Jagdzeit. N. F. 54. 1878.
81. Hartig, T. Bot. Centralblatt. 36: 388–391. 1888.
82. Hasselbring, H. Bot. Gaz. 57: 72–73. 1914.
83. Hedrick, U. P. N. Y. Agr. Exp. Sta. Bul. 314. 1909.
84. Ibid. Bul. 375. 1914.
85. Heinicke, A. J. Cornell Univ. Agr. Exp. Sta. Bul. 393. 1917.
86. Hellriegel, F. H. Beiträge zu den Natur wissenschaftlichen Grundlagen des Ackerbaus. Pp. 662–664. Braunschweig, 1883.
88. Hendrickson, A. H. Cal. Agr. Exp. Sta. Ann. Rept. P. 51. 1922.
89. Hendrickson, A. H. Hilgardia. 1: 503. 1926.
90. Hilgard, E. W. Soils, 6th Edition. Pp. 168–171, 245. New York, 1914.
91. Ibid. P. 200.
92. Ibid. P. 263.
93. Hilgard, E. W., and Loughridge, R. H. Cal. Agr. Exp. Sta. Rept. Pp. 41, 56. 1897–8.
94. Hoffman, M. B., and Schlubatis, G. R. Mich. Agr. Exp. Sta. Sp. Bul. 177. 1928.
95. Hole, R. S. Jour. Agr. India. 13: 430–440. 1918.
96. Hooker, H. D., Jr. Ann. of Bot. 29: 265–283. 1915.
97. Hooker, H. D., Jr. Mo. Agr. Exp. Sta. Research Bul. 40. 1920.
98. Hooker, H. D., Jr. Proc. Am. Soc. Hort. Sci. 17: 204–207. 1920.
99. Howard, A. Rept. Agr. Research Inst. Pusa. P. 43. 1913–14.
100. Howard, A., and Howard, G. L. C. Agr. Research Inst. Pusa. Buls. 52 and 61. 1915–16. (Abs. in Plant World. 20: 260–262. 1917.)
101. Huntington, E. The Climatic Factor as Illustrated in Arid America. Pp. 101–174. Carnegie Inst. Washington, 1914.
102. Johnston, S. Mich. Agr. Exp. Sta. Sp. Bul. 252. 1934.
103. Jones, F. R. A Study of the Development and Extent of the Roots of Apple Trees. 1912. Unpublished Thesis on file in the Library of the University of Maine.
104. Jones, J. S., and Colver, C. W. Ida. Agr. Exp. Sta. Bul. 75. 1912.
105. Jones, E. R., and Wilson, F. G. Wis. Agr. Exp. Sta. Bul. 388. 1926.
106. Kearney, T. H. U. S. D. A., Bur. Pl. Ind. Bul. 125. 1908.
107. Kelley, V. W. Ill. Agr. Exp. Sta. Bul. 341. 1930.
108. Kelley, W. P., and Thomas, E. E. Cal. Agr. Exp. Sta. Bul. 318. 1920.
109. King, F. H. Physics of Agriculture. 2d Edition. P. 131. Madison, Wis. 1901.
110. Ibid. P. 189.
111. King, F. H. U. S. D. A., Bur. Soils Bul. 26. 1905.
112. Kohl, F. G. Die Transpiration der Pflanzen. Brunswick, 1886.
113. Korstian, C. F., Hartley, C., Watts, L. F., and Hahn, G. G. Jour. Agr. Research. 21: 153–169. 1921.
114. Kosaroff, P. Einfluss verschiedenen äusseren Faktoren auf die Wasseraufnahme der Pflanzen. Dissertation. Leipzig, 1897.
115. Leather, J. W. Cited by J. W. Patterson. Jour. Agr. Victoria. 10: 353. 1912.
116. Lepeschkin, W. W. Beih. Botan. Centralbl. 19: 409–452. 1906.
117. Lewis, C. I., Kraus, E. J., and Rees, R. W. Ore. Agr. Exp. Sta. Bul. 113. 1912.
118. Lewis, M. R., and others. Plant Physiology. 10: 309–323. 1935.
119. Loch, R. H. Peradenia Roy. Bot. Gard. Ann. Rept. 2: 211–266. 1904.

120. Loughridge, R. H.   Cal. Agr. Exp. Sta. Rept.   Pp. 61, 64, 66.   1897–98.
121. Ibid.   Pp. 82, 94, 95, 96.
122. Lutman, B. F.   Vt. Agr. Exp. Sta. Bul. 214.   1919.
123. Lyon, T. L., and Fippin, E. O.   The Principles of Soil Management.   4th Edition.   New York, 1911.
124. Ibid.   P. 192.
125. Magistad, O. C., and Breazeale, J. F.   Ariz. Agr. Exp. Sta. Tech. Bul. 25. 1929.
126. Magness, J. R., Degman, E. G., and Furr, J. R.   U. S. D. A. Tech. Bul. 491. 1935.
127. Magness, J. R., and Overley, F. L.   Proc. Am. Soc. Hort. Sci.   26: 160–162, 1929.
128. Marshall, R. E.   Mich. Agr. Exp. Sta. Quart. Bul.   13 (1): 22–24.   1930.
129. Mason, S. C.   U. S. D. A., Bur. Pl. Ind. Bul. 192.   1911.
130. Mason, S. C.   U. S. D. A. Bul. 271.   1915.
131. Maximov, N. A., and Yapp, R. H.   The Plant in Relation to Water.   London. 1929.   Pp. 85–86.
132. Ibid.   Pp. 91–92.
133. Ibid.   P. 209.
134. Ibid.   Pp. 210–211.
135. Ibid.   Pp. 214–215.
136. Ibid.   Pp. 245–246.
137. Ibid.   Pp. 366–369.
138. McCool, M. M., and Millar, C. E.   Soil Sci.   9: 217–223.   1920.
139. Ibid.   9 (4): 217–222.   1920.
140. McCue, C. A.   Del. Agr. Exp. Sta. Bul. 120.   1918.
141. McLaughlin, W. W.   U. S. D. A. Bul. 835.   1920.
142. McMurran, S. M.   U. S. D. A. Bul. 756.   1919.
143. Mertz, W. M.   Cal. Dept. Agr. Mo. Bul.   13: 46–53.   1924.
144. Mix, A. J.   N. Y. Agr. Exp. Sta. Bul. 426.   1916.
145. Montgomery, E. G., and Kiesselbach, T. A.   Nebr. Agr. Exp. Sta. Bul. 128. 1912.
146. Morse, W. J.   Me. Agr. Exp. Sta. Bul. 271.   1918.
147. Morris, O. M.   Wash. Agr. Exp. Sta. Bul. 217.   1927.
148. Nichol, A. A.   Ariz. Agr. Exp. Sta. Tech. Bul. 68.   1937.
149. Nisbit, J.   Studies in Forestry.   P. 77.   Oxford, 1894.
150. Palladin, W.   Ber. deutsch. Bot. Ges.   8: 364–371.   1890.
151. Palmer, A. H.   U. S. D. A., Mo. Weather Rev.   48: 151–154.   1920.
152. Pearson, G. A.   Jour. Forestry.   16: 677–683.   1918.
153. Pulling, H. E.   Plant World.   21: 223–233.   1918.
154. Rasmussen, E. J.   Mich. Agr. Exp. Sta. Quart. Bul.   19 (3): 135.   1937.
155. Ravaz, L.   Influence de la surproduction sur la végétation de la vigne.   Montpellier.   1906.
156. Rhoads, A. S.   Fla. Agr. Exp. Sta. Bul. 178.   1926.
157. Ibid.   Bul. 296.   1936.
158. Rixford, G. P.   U. S. D. A. Bul. 732.   1918.
159. Roger, J. C.   Rept. Dom. Botanist.   Can. Dept. Agr. for 1929, p. 129.   1931.
160. Rosa, J. T., Jr.   Proc. Am. Soc. Hort. Sci.   17: 207–210.   1920.
161. Rotmistrov, V. G.   Nature of Drought According to the Evidence of the Odessa Experiment Station, Russia.   Eng. Edition.   P. 20.   Odessa, 1913.
162. Russell, T.   Cited by S. B. Green.   Minn. Agr. Exp. Sta. Bul. 32.   1893.

163. Schnee, F.   Über den Lebenszustand allseitig verkorkter Zellen.   Dissertation. Leipzig, 1907.
164. Schwartz, F.   Unters. a. d. Bot. Inst. zu Tübingen.   1: 140.   1883.
165. Shantz, H. L.   U. S. D. A.   B. P. I.   Bul. 201.   1911.
166. Shear, C. L.   U. S. D. A., Farmers' Bul. 1081.   1920.
167. Shull, C. A.   Plant World.   22: 210–215.   1919.
168. Smith, J. W.   U. S. D. A., Mo. Weather Rev.   48: 446.   1920.
169. Sorauer, P.   Pflanzenkrankheiten.   3te Auflage.   1: 169–170.   Berlin, 1909.
170. Ibid.   P. 210.
171. Ibid.   P. 275, 284–285.
172. Ibid.   P. 286.
173. Ibid.   P. 324.
174. Ibid.   P. 332.
175. Ibid.   P. 335.
176. Ibid.   P. 422.
177. Ibid.   P. 435.
178. Spoehr, H. A.   Carnegie Inst. Wash. Pub. 287.   1919.
179. Stewart, J. P.   Pa. Agr. Exp. Sta. Bul. 134.   1915.
180. Ibid.   Bul. 141.   1916.
181. Taylor, E. P., and Downing, G. J.   Ida. Agr. Exp. Sta. Bul. 99.   1917.
182. Thompson, R. C.   Ark. Agr. Exp. Sta. Bul. 123.   1916.
183. Tucker, M., and von Seelhorst, C.   Journ. f. Landw.   46: 52–63.   1898.
184. Tufts, W. P.   Letter to one of the authors, dated March 21, 1921.
185. U. S. D. A., Div. Agr. Soils Buls. 1, 2 and 3.   1895.
186. Van Slyke, L. L., Taylor, O. M., and Andrews, W. H.   Geneva Agr. Exp. Sta. · Bul. 265.   1905.
187. Veihmeyer, F. J.   Hilgardia.   2: 228.   1927.
188. Ibid.   2: 240.   1927.
189. Verner, L.   Ida. Agr. Exp. Sta. Bul. 164.   1929.
190. Verner, L.   Jour. Agr. Res.   51 (3): 191–222.   1936.
191. Von Seelhorst, C.   Journ. f. Landw.   58: 83–88.   1910.
192. Wakaboyashi, S.   N. J. Agr. Exp. Sta. Bul. 420.   1925.
193. Weaver, J. E.   Carn. Inst. Wash. Pub. 286.   1919.
194. White, J.   Proc. Roy. Soc. Victoria.   24 (N. S.): 2–16.   1911.
195. Whitehouse, W. E.   Ore. Agr. Exp. Sta. Bul. 134.   1916.
196. Whitten, J. C.   Mo. Agr. Exp. Sta. Bul. 49.   1900.
197. Whitten, J. C.   Mo. Agr. Exp. Sta. Research Bul. 33.   1919.
198. Widtsoe, J. A.   Dry Farming.   P. 185.   New York, 1911.
199. Wiggins, P. G.   Am. Jour. Bot.   8: 30–40.   1921.
200. Woglum, R. S.   U. S. D. A., Farmers' Bul. 1321.   1923.
201. Woodbury, C. G., Noyes, H. A., and Oskamp, J.   Purdue Univ. Agr. Exp. Sta. Bul. 205.   1917.
202. Work, R. A., and Lewis, M. R.   Jour. Am. Soc. Agron.   28 (2): 124–134.   1936.
203. Yeager, A. F.   Jour. Agr. Res.   51 (12): 1085–1092.   1936.
204. Zon, R.   Proc. Soc. Amer. Foresters.   2: 79.   1907.
205. Zon, R.   Forests and Water in the Light of Scientific Investigations.   U. S. D. A. Forest Service Pub.   P. 32.   1927.

SECTION II
NUTRITION

Nutrient supply is generally considered the most important of the factors limiting growth and productiveness. Certainly it ranks second to no other in determining the success or failure of the orchard enterprise within those sections or areas where climatic conditions make possible a fruit industry and where economic conditions make practicable its development. Though there are many single cases in which the water supply, the prevalence of pests or some other factor assumes paramount importance, the most common limiting influence is associated with nutritive conditions. Much of the effort of the careful grower is directed toward relieving his plants from unnecessary competition and struggle for a nutrient supply.

Few general questions pertaining to fruit growing have been less thoroughly understood than soil productivity as it relates to tree growth. This condition has existed mainly because of the assumption by analogy that the requirements of trees, vines or other fruit producing plants are practically identical with those of annual crops and because until comparatively recently experimental evidence upon which to base reliable interpretations and conclusions has been lacking. Trees, shrubs and vines have life histories, even seasonal life histories, different from those of annuals. It is to be expected, therefore, that they possess somewhat different nutrient requirements or, at least, somewhat different feeding habits. These nutrient requirements and feeding habits must be studied thoroughly before there can be a proper appreciation of the orchard soil productivity problem.

CHAPTER VII

PLANT NUTRIENTS AND THEIR ABSORPTION

Plants require for their nutriment water, carbon dioxide, oxygen, nitrates (or other nitrogen-carrying compounds), sulphates, phosphates, salts of iron, magnesium, potassium and calcium. Though chemical analysis of plant tissue shows that almost every element may be found in one plant or another, carbon, hydrogen, oxygen, nitrogen, phosphorus, sulphur, potassium, magnesium, iron, calcium, chlorine, silicon, sodium, aluminum and manganese are found in practically all plants. The first ten of these have long been regarded as necessary for all the higher plants and recent studies indicate that small quantities of several of the elements formerly considered as non-essential are required for normal growth and production. In no case does any single mineral element, or all of them put together for that matter, constitute a major part of the tissue of the plant. Furthermore, certain tissues may show no traces of them, and in any tissue the total mineral content, as well as the amount of any single element, may vary greatly from season to season. Water, nitrogen and all the mineral elements are absorbed by the roots from the soil. Absorption by the leaves also occurs under certain circumstances but ordinarily this process may be disregarded. The water relations of plants have been treated in the previous section; the other plant nutrients absorbed from the soil form the subject of this chapter.

DISTRIBUTION OF ELEMENTS FOUND IN ASH

The mineral constituents of plants, except a part of the sulfur, are left as ash after the tissue has been burned. Therefore, a fairly accurate picture of the distribution of mineral matter at any one time may be obtained by separating the parts or tissues, burning them and analyzing the resultant ash. Representative data on such analyses are presented in Tables 1, 2 and 3.

In Tissues of Different Kinds.—As between different tissues, there are striking variations not only in total mineral content but in the relative amounts of the different kinds that are present. Thus, bark shows several times as much total ash per unit of dry weight as does wood (Table 3) and roots and branches distinctly more than trunks (Table 1). Leaves have a higher mineral content than either roots or branches (Table 5), while fruits are relatively low in mineral matter (Table 6). In general, seeds show a higher ash content than fruits.[14]   The fact that there is considerable variation between the same tissues of different varieties in respect to total ash and relatively great variation in certain constituents (Table 1) leads to the inference that at least in many cases far more mineral matter is taken up by the plant than is actually required or utilized, as there is no suggestion that any of the trees furnishing material for these analyses functioned abnormally.   It is for this reason that

TABLE 1.—ASH ANALYSES OF APPLE VARIETIES[228]

	Ash in percentages of dry weight	SiO₂	P₂O₅	SO₃	CaO	MgO	Na₂O	K₂O
		(In percentages of ash)						
Branches:								
Haas............	3.93	1.81	7.35	3.02	43.68	10.02	2.51	8.59
Golden Sweet.....	3.04	2.49	5.89	2.96	40.60	8.07	7.09	3.37
Hurlburt.........	4.92	2.60	4.44	3.57	41.55	2.88	4.98	5.16
Trunks:								
Haas............	2.04	2.04	2.13	7.55	44.52	9.30	1.33	6.96
Golden Sweet.....	2.29	4.98	4.61	1.17	41.96	4.61	3.91	8.02
Hurlburt.........	2.89	3.93	4.08	3.85	44.80	5.22	2.48	1.31
Roots:								
Haas............	5.64	26.84	9.44	5.11	32.98	9.30	4.74	5.43
Golden Sweet.....	3.53	27.65	7.71	2.83	26.99	4.84	3.87	2.00
Hurlburt.........	4.34	25.72	4.17	6.19	25.20	10.37	7.22	9.86

TABLE 2.—ASH ANALYSES OF A 7-YEAR OLD APPLE TREE AT THE TIME OF LEAF-FALL[47]
(In percentages of dry weight)

Summer growth..	3.57
1-year old branches......................................	2.83
2-year old branches......................................	2.76
3-year old branches......................................	2.75
4-year old branches......................................	1.87
5-year old branches......................................	1.78
Trunk...	1.33
Large roots...	1.83
Small roots...	4.51

TABLE 3.—ASH CONTENT OF WOOD AND BARK[14]
(In percentages of dry weight)

	Bark	Wood
Mahaleb cherry.......................................	6.81	1.38
Sweet cherry...	9.76	0.23
Horse chestnut.......................................	6.78	2.58

analyses showing the mineral composition of fruit plants is not a reliable guide to their requirements.

In Tissues of Different Age.—Age is likewise an important factor influencing ash content.

In general, older wood contains more ash than younger wood (Table 4), that tissue which is the most inactive physiologically showing the highest percentages. This may be taken as still further evidence that surplus quantities of at least some of the minerals are absorbed by the plant only to be stored in the older tissues to get them out of the way. The figures presented in Table 2 showing the ash content of different parts of a 7-year old apple tree at the time of leaf-fall seem to contradict the statements that have just been made, as both the new shoot growth and the small roots contain percentages of mineral matter three times that of the trunk. These figures, however, are for bark and wood together and are explained by the fact that the smaller branches and roots consist of relatively much greater percentages of bark than of wood.

TABLE 4.—ASH CONTENT OF BEECH WOOD[327]
(In percentages of dry weight)

YEARS OF RINGS

1 to 15	1.162
15 to 25	0.825
25 to 35	0.645
35 to 45	0.612
45 to 60	0.555
60 to 83	0.458
83 to 94 (sapwood)	0.205

At Different Seasons.—An increase in the percentage ash content of apple, pear, cherry and plum leaves during the season is shown in Table 5. The absolute amount of ash present declines, however, before the leaves fall.[246] Developing fruits, on the other hand, show a very decided decrease in the percentage of ash and an equally pronounced increase in the absolute amount. The data in Table 6 illustrate these

TABLE 5.—ASH CONTENT OF LEAVES[246] (in percentages of dry weight)

	Apple	Pear	Cherry	Plum
May 9	8.304	6.908	......	......
May 14	......	....	9.006	......
May 18	......	....	......	7.369
June 22	8.017	7.157	10.510	15.031
Aug. 29	9.166	9.454	12.319	17.757
Sept. 30	......	....	......	20.987
Oct. 2	......	9.552	14.446	......
Oct. 15	10.889	....	......	......

changes.   The decrease in percentage when there is an increase in absolute amount is associated with an even more rapid increase in bulk that is due

TABLE 6.—ASH CONTENT OF FRUIT[237]

	Pear			Apple	
Date	Percentage of dry weight	Absolute amount, grams	Date	Percentage of dry weight	Absolute amount, grams
May 26	7.96	0.0017	June 2	8.88	0.0019
June 5	5.50	0.0068	June 12	5.09	0.0066
June 15	4.32	0.0198	June 22	3.44	0.011
June 25	2.87	0.0269	July 2	2.89	0.026
July 5	3.27	0.043	July 12	1.80	0.034
July 15	2.73	0.057	July 22	1.33	0.044
July 25	2.27	0.069	Aug. 1	1.78	0.070
Aug. 4	1.76	0.068	Aug. 11	1.43	0.075
Aug. 14	1.46	0.079	Aug. 21	1.33	0.076
Aug. 24	1.56	0.098	Aug. 31	1.07	0.079
Sept. 3	0.91	0.065	Sept. 10	0.80	0.066
Sept. 8	1.31	0.090	Sept. 20	1.67	0.160
			Sept. 30	1.58	0.150

principally to an accumulation of organic substances.   The large increase in the ash content of the fruit affects the ash content of the spur on which

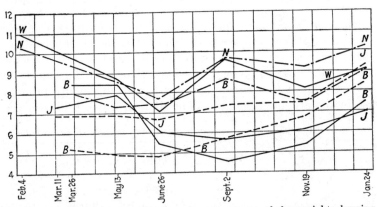

FIG. 11.—Ash content of apple spurs in percentages of dry weight; bearing spurs represented by continuous lines marked *W*, *B* and *J* for Wealthy, Ben Davis and Jonathan respectively; non-bearing spurs shown by broken lines marked *J* and *B*; barren spurs represented by dot-dash lines marked *B* and *N* for Ben Davis and Nixonite.   (*After Hooker.*[156])

the fruit is borne.   Figure 11 shows a rapid decrease in the percentage ash content of bearing spurs beginning the latter part of May or in June and continuing until the fruit is picked.[156]   In a summer apple like Wealthy, the curve rises in September, the fruit having been picked in August. In Ben Davis and Jonathan, the fruit of which is picked the beginning of October, the curve does not rise until November.   Spurs in the off year and barren spurs have no such characteristic decrease in ash content during June.   The seasonal fluctuation in the mineral content of other tissues or of the same tissues of other fruits is equally great, their direction and nature depending on the growing and fruiting habits of the plant. Furthermore, temporary changes in the ash content of certain tissues are brought about by changes in environmental conditions.   Thus it has been shown that desiccating winds lead to the accumulation of salts in the leaves of citrus trees, a condition that disappears through their translocation to other parts during subsequent colder weather.[130]

ABSORPTION

Mineral constituents and nitrogen are absorbed by the plant mostly through the roots.   They are present in the soil as salts in solution and are taken up in large part by osmosis along with the soil water, the osmotic system being the same as that involved in water absorption.

The Osmotic System.—The soil solution and the cell sap are separated by a semi-permeable membrane, through which the salts present in the soil solution are able to enter though the organic substances within the cell are, for the most part, incapable of passing in the opposite direction. Inorganic salts dissociate to a considerable degree, so that in a solution of sodium chloride, for example, there are present, besides molecules of salt, ions of sodium and ions of chlorine.   These separate ions have the same value in regard to osmotic concentration as entire molecules; consequently a solution of inorganic salts is capable of producing a higher osmotic pressure than a solution of organic compounds having the same number of molecules in a given volume.   In order that absorption of the various mineral constituents should take place by osmosis, the concentration of each salt within the plant must be less than its concentration in the soil solution.   Though, as previous analyses have shown, plant tissue contains considerable amounts of these mineral elements the plant is still able to absorb material from an exceedingly dilute soil solution which, in many cases, contains a lower percentage of a given constituent than the plant tissue itself.   This is possible because the constituents in the plant are insoluble or are combined in an organic form.   Since in either case they are removed from the osmotic system, the effective concentration of inorganic salts within the plant remains less than that of the soil solution.   It is evident, though, that a certain concentration of salts in the soil is necessary for osmotic absorption.   In other words, the plant is unable to avail itself of all the mineral matter of the soil solution. However, very dilute solutions are often sufficient for ordinary growth.

Thus "Birner and Lucanus many years ago found that mature crops of good yield could be grown in a well water containing about 18 parts potassium (K) and about 2 parts phosphoric acid (PO_4) per million of solution and very satisfactory growth of wheat has been obtained in the water from the Potomac River, which contained about 7 parts per million of potassium."[50]

When these facts are combined with the conclusions reached by Cameron and Bell,[50] that the concentration of the soil solution, with respect to the principal mineral plant nutrients, is sufficient for the growth and development of crops and that the magnitude of the concentration is the same for practically all soils, one might easily be led to the belief that fruit plants seldom suffer from lack of an adequate supply of mineral nutrients. However, this inference is hardly warranted for, as is shown later, mineral nutrients may be in solution and still be unavailable to the plant. In other words solubility and availability are not synonymous.

With some nutrient elements, the rapidity of absorption is largely a function of the concentration of the nutrient solution; with others this is not the case. Thus absorption of potassium and phosphorus increases in rate until a soil concentration of approximately 100 parts per million is reached, after which there is a sharp decline with increasing concentration.[192] On the other hand, the rate of nitrogen absorption is not so greatly influenced by its concentration. However, it may be noted that the 5 parts of water-soluble nitrates per million of dry soil found by Gourley and Shunk[119] in sod-mulched orchards during the growing season were apparently insufficient for satisfactory wood growth and fruit production, while a concentration of 15 to 40 parts per million under certain other systems of culture proved entirely adequate. In this case all the nitrogen measured was in an available form. Whether in the sodded area nitrogen could be absorbed by the trees only when the concentration in the soil reached a certain minimum, or whether a very limited amount was absorbed even at the lowest concentrations, cannot be stated from available data; they show clearly, however, that the trees were unable to remove nitrates completely from the soil and further, that a nutrient solution very dilute in respect to this element provides only for very slow growth.

There is reason to believe that plants can absorb nutrients from the soil solution in a soil whose water content has fallen below the wilting point and from which it cannot longer obtain moisture.[192] This means that a tree whose surface feeding roots may be in a very dry soil may not suffer from starvation even though the deeper layers from which it is obtaining its moisture are practically devoid of mineral nutrients.

Displacement.—The amounts of the various inorganic constituents in the soil are subject to variation and exchanges of bases may occur when they are present as silicates. Potassium, ammonium, magnesium, sodium and calcium form a series in which each member is capable of displacing any member following it in the series. One of two things may happen: an essential element may be lost to the plant by becoming soluble and being washed out of the soil, or it may be changed from an unavailable to an available compound and so placed at the disposal of the plant.

Of most common occurrence is the displacement of calcium by potassium or sodium, resulting in the calcium salts going into solution. However, large amounts of calcium are capable of displacing small amounts of potassium[274] or any other base standing ahead of it in the series. Hence, calcareous soils are likely to be deficient in potash and the application of calcium in great amounts tends to deplete the potassium supply. Grape-fruit seedlings have been observed to show injuries characterized by yellowing of the foliage due apparently to the presence of ground limestone; more injury was evident in sandy soils than in loams.[100] One type of this yellowing is "frenching," a lack of green color in the areas between the largest veins, which is shown later to be a characteristic symptom of potassium starvation. "Frenching" was produced also by sulphate of ammonia or organic fertilizers containing ammonia. This effect may be attributed to displacement of potassium in the soil by relatively large amounts of ammonia.

The effects on the plant of displacement of bases may be indirect rather than direct, for the displacement elements may combine to form more soluble salts and thus be rendered more available.

As an instance, according to Loew:[187] "Lime and gypsum can also in certain cases release such potash in the soil as is still unavailable. This, as well as the enhanced root-hair production under the influence of the increased amount of lime, accounts for the greater absorption of potash by the plant on soils rich in lime."

Displacement would of course be of little value to the plant if the elements released were washed from the soil as a result of the greater solubility of their salts.

Availability of Ash Constituents.—The soil constituents are of use to the plant only when combined in certain specific chemical compounds. Thus, sulphur must be present as sulphate, phosphorus as phosphate, and the various bases as relatively soluble salts.

Availability and Solubility Distinguished.—Solubility, however, is only the first prerequisite to availability and absorption; it is not an absolute criterion of the crop-producing power of soils, as is indicated by

studies on many soils in this country[50] and by investigations on the red
soils of the "djati" forests of Java.[26]   Nevertheless, "in general it can
be said that a very heavily fertilized or extremely rich soil gives a greater
solubility product than an unfertilized or poor soil."[35]   Conversely
"as a result of laboratory studies it appears that the constituents of
soils which have been cropped for a long period of years go into solution
at a somewhat slower rate than do those of the corresponding virgin
soils."[206]

Factors Influencing Solubility.—The solubility of soil ingredients is
affected by such factors as temperature, moisture content, chemical
composition of the soil and root activity.   According to McCool and
Millar[206] the rate of solution is more rapid at 25°C. than at 0°C.   The
concentration of the soil solution apparently depends also on the relative
masses of the soil and water.

"At the ratio of 1 of soil to 5 of water the rate of solubility of natural soils
is also slow and the extent of solubility extremely small.   In fact, the amount of
material that went into solution at this water content is only about half as much
as that at the water content of 1 of soil to .7 of water, and yet an apparent
equilibrium was attained. . . .   The amount of material that goes into solution
seems to increase as the ratio of soil to water is increased up to about the optimum
moisture content and then it decreases."[35]

The effect of chemical composition on solubility is discussed by
Bouyoucos.[35]

"As a whole it appears that the phosphates tend to depress solubility and that
they probably act as conservers of bases under field conditions."   Other salts,
however, tend to increase solubility.   "The result of solubility of these singly
salt treated soils goes to indicate that a salt or fertilizer treatment leaves a residual
effect upon the soil and this residual effect continues to be manifested in increased
solubility and in increased crop-producing power."

Availability of Phosphorus.—It has been stated that phosphorus is
available to the plant only when present as a phosphate and that sulphur is absorbed only as sulphate.   However, all phosphates and sulphates are not equally available; furthermore, a phosphate that is highly
available for the plants of one species may be much less available to those
of another.   This principle is well illustrated by the data presented in
Table 7 showing the percentage of normal growth made by plants grown
in nutrient solutions that were uniform except for the form in which
phosphorus was presented.

In commenting on these data Truog[295] remarks: "The great differences
exhibited by the various plants in their growths on the different phosphates
indicate that plant characteristics play an important role in this connection.
The fact that rape made a better growth on rock phosphate than on ferric

TABLE 7.—COMPARATIVE GROWTH OF VARIOUS PLANTS WITH DIFFERENT
PHOSPHATES
(*After Truog*[295])
(Growth on acid phosphate represented by 100)

Kind of plant	Kind of phosphate							
	Blank	Aluminum	Tricalcium	Ferric	Ferrous	Rock	Magnesium	Manganese
Oats........	6.8	96.4	70.5	79.9	82.9	9.1	....	....
Buckwheat..	3.6	88.0	70.1	32.5	63.3	70.0	....	....
Rape........	0.8	96.4	76.2	23.4	61.5	46.8	....	....
Corn........	8.6	56.3	26.8	40.3	19.3	10.0	21.3	76.4
Barley......	16.7	104.7	62.2	133.5	79.7	25.8	15.5	125.3
Alfalfa......	1.5	78.6	99.2	93.6	28.1	38.3	7.1	20.8
Clover......	1.0	84.2	64.5	68.9	23.6	6.1	26.7	4.2
Millet.......	0.7	86.7	34.8	103.8	31.0	4.1	16.0	73.8
Serradella...	0.6	78.7	90.4	111.7	28.2	3.2	49.9	51.7

phosphate, while in the case of oats the opposite was true, indicates that solubility alone is not the only factor involved in the utilization of these phosphates by plants. The remarkably vigorous growth of the barley with ferric phosphate is another indication that aside from solubility or availability, some phosphates seem to serve the needs of certain plants better than others. The remarkable adaptability of certain soils to certain crops may partly be due to causes of this nature."

In this connection attention should be called to the fact that salts of phosphorus and potassium applied to the soil as fertilizers are quickly fixed in the surface layers and for the most part are unavailable to the plants, partly because of insolubility and partly because those layers are not exploited by tree roots.[120] Under conditions where the desirability of phosphatic or potash-containing fertilizers to the fruit plantation is established, the necessity of working them into the soil to a depth where the feeding rootlets will reach them is evident.

Availability Varies According to Kind of Plant.—In general the availability of inorganic soil constituents is increased by the activity of the roots. Their solvent action is yet to be accounted for satisfactorily. Crocker suggests that the strong, insoluble pectic acids found in the walls of root hairs may be responsible for the absorption of bases and the setting free of mineral acids, which would have a localized and temporary solvent action on the soil. Various plants show great differences in the dissolving power of their roots, or at least in their ability to obtain required nutrients. Thus seedlings of *Pinus echinata* and *P. taeda* have been found to thrive in sand cultures containing one-fifth the concentration of nitrogen required for an equally vigorous growth of the apple[297] and red maple have been found to absorb (and presumably require) twice as much phosphorus as red oak seedlings under identical conditions and making comparable growth.[214]   Sassafras and white pine grow vigorously on light sandy or gravelly soils on which trees of the stone fruits die out from apparent starvation.

Hartwell[137] found that carrots secured all the phosphorus they required from a soil in which rutabagas and cabbage were practically unable to grow, while wheat, oats, white beans and soy beans ranged between these extremes.   Similarly, he found "an ability of the soy bean to obtain from the deficient [in available potassium] plots about two-thirds of their maximum requirements, whereas carrots obtained about half their needs, mangels about one-fourth and summer squash only about one-tenth."

It is not clear to what extent this characteristic feeding power of various plants may be due to a more extensive root system and therefore the exploitation of more soil, to varying ability to dissolve the materials they encounter in a solid or colloidal form, to varying ability to use nutrients combined in different forms (*e.g.*, potassium in the form of a chloride instead of sulphate), or what part may be due to varying ability to absorb from very dilute solutions.   This question needs careful investigation, particularly in its application to orchard and vineyard fruits of different kinds and to the stocks upon which they may be grown.   It is conceivable that the high feeding power of a certain stock in respect to some particular material may be of as great significance in the success of a fruit plantation in a certain soil as the question of "congeniality" of stock and cion.   Thus Bennett points out that pear trees grafted on Japanese pear (*Pyrus serotina*) or quince rootstocks develop chlorosis on high-lime soils much more quickly and severely than do those on French stocks and stone fruits on myrobolan stocks generally show little or no chlorosis, whereas peaches and apricots on peach stocks may suffer severely.[30]

From the data presented by Hartwell, the inference may be drawn that the potassium found in the soil and practically unavailable to mangels and summer squash would be made available to them were soy beans first grown upon the land and then plowed under, for, after the soy beans had dissolved and used it, other plants would find it in a different form.   There may be little occasion for special efforts to make potash more available to orchard trees by using intercultures, for evidence is presented later that for fruit trees potash is seldom a limiting factor. Nevertheless, the general principle involved may be important in relation to other elements.

Availability of Nitrogen.—Just as sulphur is available only in the form of sulphate and phosphorus in the form of phosphate, most nitrogen is absorbed in the form of nitrate.   However, nitrites and salts of ammonia can be utilized to a limited extent, different plants showing considerable variations in this respect.[291] For instance, there is evidence to indicate that ammonium is superior to nitrate as a source of nitrogen for the cranberry.[4]

Organic nitrogen also may be a substitute for nitrate, though inorganic nitrogen compounds are used in preference. It has been shown that such nitrogenous soil constituents as nucleic acid, hypoxanthine, xanthine, guanine, creatinine, creatine, histidine, arginine and choline serve as sources of nitrogen when nitrates are absent, but not to any great extent when large amounts of nitrate are present.[258,267] Moreover, the absorption of nitrate by plants grown in culture is always reduced when creatine or creatinine is present, though the total nitrogen intake remains fairly constant. These organic nitrogen compounds have no effect on potash or phosphorus absorption.

Bacteria are of great importance in making organic nitrogen compounds in the soil more available to the plant and incidentally in destroying toxic substances. Putrefying bacteria, for example, convert the nitrogen of organic compounds to ammonia and nitrogen gas.

Hart and Tottingham[134] have shown that "soluble phosphates increase enormously the number of soil organisms and the rate of ammonification and destruction of organic matter, while the sulphates activate but slightly in these directions. The processes mentioned are admitted to be of great importance to the plant's nutrition and environment, involving, as they must, not only a more rapid formation of readily soluble compounds of nitrogen and a possible destruction of harmful organic materials, but a greater saturation of the soil moisture with carbon dioxide, resulting in increased solution of mineral materials necessary for rapid growth." Work at the Utah Experiment Station[122] indicates that sulphates have a particularly stimulating effect on soil bacteria under certain conditions.

Nitrification.—The ammonia produced by bacterial action is in its turn converted to nitrites and these nitrites to nitrates by nitrifying bacteria, each of these changes being carried out by distinct organisms. These organisms require, for the process of nitrification, good aeration, involving both oxygen and carbon dioxide, a certain water supply, the presence of calcium or magnesium compounds, a medium temperature and freedom from an excess of soluble organic compounds or from free ammonia. It is evident that conditions favoring the action of nitrifying organisms will tend to increase the supply of available nitrogen.

Aided by Liming.—It has been found that applications of lime in many cases increase nitrification. Table 8 presents the results of one such experiment with orchard soils in New Hampshire. Obviously in this instance liming benefited the soil in at least this one direction and it is possible that at the same time it exerted no harmful influence.   However, data are presented later to show that it may have a very harmful effect through rendering iron unavailable.   Consequently a single fertilizer application may produce at the same time both beneficial and harmful

TABLE 8.—NITRATES IN LIMED AND UNLIMED PLOTS[119]
(In parts per million of dry soil)

Year	Limed plot		Unlimed plot	
	Surface soil	Subsoil	Surface soil	Subsoil
1913	82.33	19.60	57.46	6.16
1914	82.46	23.43	57.09	15.21
1915	29.98	13.78	24.26	17.24
1916	98.48	24.16	80.36	11.56
Average......	73.31	20.23	54.79	12.54

effects.   These may just about neutralize each other and leave the plants practically uninfluenced by the treatment, or the one influence may greatly outweigh the other.   Caution should be exercised, however, in making applications of lime to the orchard.

Influenced by Methods of Soil Management.—Moreover, different methods of soil management, particularly as they affect aeration and soil temperature, have a marked effect on nitrate production.

Gourley and Shunk[119] found that "the ratio of nitrates between sod, tillage and tillage with cover crops is as 1:5.4:10.6 in the surface soil and in the subsoil as 1:3.3:3.7.   At no time during the experiment have we obtained a sample under sod that showed more than 14.78 parts nitrates per million and the average for the 4 years is 3.18 p.p.m. with an average of 17.40 p.p.m. and for tillage plus a leguminous cover crop it has shown as high as 132 p.p.m. and the average is 33.91 p.p.m. for the 4 years."

The nitrate determinations showing the result of 4 years' experiments on orchard soils are summarized in Table 9.   Whether the small amount of nitrate under sod is the result of reduced nitrate production or merely the residue from a greater nitrate consumption by the plants constituting the sod, the effect on the orchard trees is the same.   Under sod there is but little available nitrate.   In Indiana also, it was found that in a young orchard most nitrates are formed under the clean culture-cover crop system of soil management, and the straw mulch ranked next.[323]   The heavier the mulch, the later in the spring does bacterial activity begin because of the lower temperature and the later in the fall does it persist as a result of the higher temperature of the soil.

It is probably because of their influence upon nitrate formation that various tillage methods have so generally proved superior to sod management methods in promoting both vegetative growth and fruit production. This is true particularly in areas that are more humid or have deeper soils. On the other hand, in sections having a long dry period during

TABLE 9.—WATER-SOLUBLE NITRATE IN PARTS PER MILLION OF DRY SOIL[119]
(Average per plot)

Year	Sod	Tillage	Tillage with cover crop
Surface soil			
1913	2.64	18.25	38.37
1914	4.41	14.01	37.27
1915	2.09	21.05	18.75
1916	3.59	16.29	41.26
Average...........	3.18	17.40	33.91
Subsoil			
1913	1.55	6.90	6.87
1914	3.56	6.62	10.81
1915	1.51	10.76	6.88
1916	2.18	5.05	8.05
Average...........	2.20	7.33	8.15

the summer, wherever the soils are of such nature that they encourage shallow rooting, the influence of these various systems of soil management upon moisture supply is probably a factor of equal or greater importance. However, it is neither difficult nor expensive to furnish trees growing in sod with an adequate supply of nitrates through the use of certain fertilizers. Indeed, it is in orchards of this kind that nitrogenous fertilizers have given some of the most striking results and the question may be raised whether some nitrogen-carrying fertilizer may not be a more or less constant requirement if orchards permanently under this method of soil management are to be kept growing and producing most efficiently.

Influenced by Temperature and Soil Moisture.—The effects of moisture and of temperature on the activity of nitrifying bacteria are shown by a seasonal variation in nitrate content. For example, in Illinois soils[158] the most active season of nitrate production and accumulation is late spring and early summer when optimum moisture and temperature conditions are approached. Early autumn is the next most active season, when these optimum conditions for nitrate production are frequently approached. During the summer little nitrate is produced unless the weather is cool and moisture plentiful; in winter there is no evidence of nitrate production.

Similar conditions are reported for orchard soils in Indiana[323] where very little nitrate was found in late fall and winter, though maxima were found in early summer and early fall. Orcharding, however, is carried on in many sections where seasonal and soil conditions are materially different from those of Illinois and Indiana and it is conceivable that under certain environmental conditions nitrate production, even under sod, might keep pace with the tree's requirements for nitrogen.

Losses of Nitrogen from the Soil.—Nitrates are very soluble in water and, unlike most of the mineral nutrients, are not adsorbed or otherwise fixed in the soil to any considerable degree. Heavy rains or heavy irrigation washes them out and carries them away in the drainage water. In one Florida experiment this loss from leaching was found to equal the nitrate content of over 800 pounds of nitrate of soda per acre during a 10-month period.[11] Not the least important function of cover crops is to take up the nitrates that are being formed in late summer and autumn, to store their nitrogen in organic form during the winter and to return it to the soil—thence to the trees—the following growing season, thus preventing a large loss through drainage. The advantage of a soil, and of orchard management methods, permitting deep rooting and the storage of large quantities of capillary water minimizing seepage losses, is evident.

Under some conditions considerable quantities of nitrates are made unavailable to the plant through the action of cellulose-destroying bacteria and other soil microorganisms. This becomes a matter of considerable importance when straw, strawy manure or other undecomposed crop residues are plowed under. Nitrates are used freely by these organisms in the decomposition of cellulose and related compounds, the result being that the growth rate is depressed and the plants show symptoms of nitrogen starvation. Some idea of the magnitude of this effect of cellulose-decomposing organisms is afforded by the results of some studies with a Massachusetts timothy sod soil. Nitrate nitrogen from a 3,000 pounds per acre application of nitrate of soda disappeared within two weeks after it had been added to the soil, though conditions were such that no leaching could take place.[287] The injury is not permanent, however, continuing only until the plant residues are well decayed, after which a large part of the nitrogen assimilated by the microorganisms gradually becomes available for the crop plants.[44,144] Though in this instance the nitrates are not lost to the soil or plant, they are locked up for the time being and the liberal application of nitrogen-carrying fertilizers may be required for satisfactory growth and production.

Maintaining the Nitrogen Supply of the Soil.—Despite the means that may be taken to prevent undue loss of soil nitrates, crop production alone removes considerable quantities and unless the supply of nitrogenous compounds from which they are derived is maintained the time will come when they cannot be formed in quantities sufficient for maximum crop production. The organic matter of the soil is the storehouse of these nitrogenous compounds and with its gradual depletion the nitrogen problem becomes acute. It is well known that constant tillage is one of the most effective means of reducing or "burning out" humus supply. Consequently the cultural methods in the orchard, which make nitrogen available most rapidly, deplete the total supply most rapidly. Indeed it may be questioned if, over a long period, the orchard under a strictly clean-culture method of management will not need heavier nitrogen fertilization than the one in sod.

Some measure of the cumulative effect of tillage as compared with a sod covering on total nitrogen supply is contained in the following statement: "Analysis of soil taken from this land at the time the experimental work was started indicated a nitrogen content of 5,000 pounds per acre. After this soil had been cropped and cultivated for 20 years, the nitrogen content was approximately 4,000 pounds per acre. Adjacent soil which was in grass during the 20-year period contained 5,600 pounds of nitrogen."[11] It is significant that, though there was a loss of 20 per cent. of the total nitrogen supply of the soil during the 20 years in the cultivated land, there was an actual increase of 12 per cent. in the sod land during the same period. This can be attributed to nitrogen fixation, particularly by leguminous plants in the sod, in addition to the nitric acid contributed by rain water.

The likelihood of trees under one of the two standard systems of orchard culture suffering from lack of available nitrogen and, on the other hand, the nearly absolute certainty that under the other system the soil will have its total nitrogen reserve seriously depleted, suggest that a combination of the two methods possibly might afford a means of maintaining permanently the nitrogen supply of the soil and at the same time obviate the necessity of supplying the trees artificially with readily available nitrates. Such a combination might consist in alternating sod and cultivation each in 2-year periods or, better still, in maintaining alternate tree rows, the "middles," under the two respective systems and then occasionally reversing the treatments on these alternate strips. The marked success that frequently has attended such a combination is evidence of its practicability under many conditions. Such a combination treatment is a compromise also in its influence upon soil moisture supply and soil erosion. In some instances it might prove undesirable because of the increased difficulty in controlling certain orchard pests which are best held in check by cultivation.

Few, if any, of the plant nutrients obtained from the soil are subject to such great variation from season to season and even from week to week as is nitrogen; likewise few are so completely under the control of the grower through methods of soil management. It is largely because of the first two facts that the problem of maintaining fertility in the orchard generally centers around the nitrogen supply. The discussion that has preceded serves also to bring out clearly the fact that proper treatment of the soil may reduce or altogether remove the necessity for nitrogen fertilization and that, on the other hand, there are instances where it may be true economy not to employ those practices that will lead to greatest nitrate formation but deliberately to limit this process and supply the deficiency by artificial means.

Nitrogen Fixation.—Nitrogen gas is not available to the higher plants, but it is acted upon by nitrogen-fixing bacteria which convert it either to nitrates or to other nitrogenous compounds that in due time are converted into nitrates. Some of these bacteria are able, independent of any association with the roots of higher plants, to fix this atmospheric nitrogen and thus effect the first step in rendering it available.[104,105] Indeed there are conditions under which their activity is so great that the resultant accumulation of nitrates renders the soil toxic to trees and other plants.[143] For the most part, however, nitrogen fixation by bacteria is effected by forms living in colonies on the roots of leguminous plants where they produce nodules or tubercles. The amount of nitrogen that is fixed by legumes naturally varies greatly with the kind of plant and with conditions. Amounts as high as 250 pounds per acre per year have been reported and an average of 122 pounds for all legumes from 16 state experiment stations where tests have been made.[11,44]

As very few of the species bearing edible fruits belong to the legume family, nitrogen-fixing bacteria are of comparatively little direct benefit except when they fix nitrogen in the absence of host plants. However, they become of great value indirectly when leguminous cover crops or a sod including legumes is maintained. There are conditions under which it is difficult or impracticable to grow legumes in the orchard; nevertheless their special value should not be overlooked, particularly where there is need of increasing the available nitrate supply. Their judicious use in place of some of the other cover or mulching crops or in the place of some other system of orchard management often obviates the necessity of supplying the trees with nitrogen through mineral or animal fertilizers.

An instance of the results that can be obtained by the use of leguminous plants as cover crops is described by Coville.[63] "The trees in one newly planted orchard of Grimes apples have been kept in a remarkable condition of growth by one initial application of manure in the year of their planting, succeeded by the following rotation: In May the ground is sowed to cowpeas. These are plowed under in September and followed immediately by the sowing of rye mixed with hairy vetch. In the following May the mixed crop is plowed under. The same 1-year rotation has been followed year after year. Under this treatment the soil, which has the appearance of almost pure sand, has become so fertile without the application of lime, commercial fertilizer or manure that an occasional crop of cowpeas has been cut for hay without serious interference with the progress of the orchard." The successful use of such a system would depend upon an abundant water supply.

Were it possible to maintain permanently a good stand of clover, vetch, alfalfa or some other leguminous crop in the orchard and to leave the growth that it produced on the ground for a mulch, it would afford an almost ideal sod system of management—from the standpoint of maintaining soil fertility—though water competition between the trees and the intercrop would make it entirely impracticable under many circumstances. Under average conditions, however, the maintenance of such a sod is next to impossible because bluegrass or other species crowd out the legumes. Where such a legume sod can be maintained and the competition for moisture can be largely eliminated by irrigation, a system of soil management is possible that affords the trees excellent nutritive conditions for vigorous growth and heavy production and is at the same time economical. Various fungi found in the roots of certain heaths (Ericaceæ), are likewise capable of fixing nitrogen. It is possible that the cranberry and blueberry obtain at least a portion of their nitrogen supply through similar agencies, though the role of these endotropic mycorhiza in the nutrition and culture of this group of plants is by no means settled.[21]

Soil Reaction: Acidity and Alkalinity.—The absorption of available inorganic salts by the root is affected to an important degree by acidity, concentration, toxicity, aeration and temperature of the soil and of the soil solution. The reaction of the soil solution is of great importance. Most plants thrive best when the soil is very weakly acid. Many water plants live better in a very weakly alkaline solution, while land plants show marked differences in the amount of acidity which they will endure. When the acidity of the soil increases beyond the low value which is most favorable to land plants, it becomes an important factor.

Soil Reaction and the Availability of Phosphorus.—The effect of soil acidity on the availability of phosphorus is shown by the following quotation from Harris:[133]

"In addition to the work that has been done on determining the degree of soil acidity, many investigations have been undertaken to determine the relation of soil acidity to the quantity of available phosphorus in the soil. As a result of the work of Wheeler, Thorne, Whitson and Stoddart, it has been shown that the content of this element is generally low in acid soils and largely unavailable for use by plants. Stoddart explains this by saying that acid soils convert any calcium phosphate that may be present into soluble compounds which are either washed out or are fixed in an insoluble form by the formation of iron and aluminum phosphates."

Soil Reaction and the Availability of Iron.—An excess of calcium salts affects the availability of iron in such a way that many plants grown on calcareous soils suffer from lack of iron, even though iron is present in considerable amounts. It is from this cause that grape vines and fruit trees become chlorotic on some of the calcareous soils of France and England, pineapples and sugar cane on Porto Rican soils containing large amounts of lime and citrus fruits in Florida when ground limestone is added to the soil.

"In Porto Rico the extension of the pineapple industry has been retarded by a disease known as chlorosis, the principal external mark of which is the yellowing of the foliage and the consequent poor nutrition of the plant. From investigations by Gile and by Loew it appears that the yellow color of the leaves and the accompanying weakness of the plant are due to the lack of iron, and that where the soil contains an excess of lime the organic acids which are needed to dissolve the iron of the soil are themselves neutralized and the iron, although present, is not available for absorption by the pineapple roots."[63]

According to Gile and Carrero,[109] sugar cane grown on the calcareous soils of Porto Rico suffers from chlorosis. Analysis shows that the ash of these chlorotic leaves has less iron than normal leaves.

Floyd[100] describes two types of injury to grape-fruit seedlings from the presence of ground limestone in the soil. In addition to frenching which has been discussed, chlorosis occurs. This type of injury may be attributed to iron deficiency and is probably quite distinct from frenching, since no case of the latter was observed to develop into complete chlorosis. The larger the amount of limestone in the soil the greater was the injury observed.

The unavailability of iron in calcareous soils is probably attributable to the alkaline reaction produced by an excess of calcium salts in solution. Colloidal iron hydroxide is formed in alkaline solutions and is for the most part unavailable to plants. Similar conditions prevailing in manganiferous soils confirm the idea that the basic reaction of the soil solution, rather than the presence of specific calcium or manganese compounds, is responsible for the formation of iron hydroxide.

Pineapples grown in Hawaii on the black manganese soils of the island of Oahu suffer from chlorosis. This condition is recognized by yellowing of the leaves, stunted red or pink fruits, many of which crack open and decay and other toxic effects.[314] Other crops grown on these manganese soils suffer similarly, especially corn, pigeon peas, cowpeas and rice.   On the other hand, sugar cane is less sensitive and certain weeds such as the sow thistle, *Waltheria americana* and *Crotalaria* sp., show no effects from manganese.[166]   The difference between these two types of plants was revealed by ash analyses.   Those to which the soil is toxic have less iron in their ash when grown on manganiferous soils than when grown on ordinary soils.   The ash of the weeds growing wild on the manganese soils without apparent ill effects showed no decrease in iron, containing even more than when grown on other soils.[314]

The other elements in the ash showed no such significant variation, though in practically every instance the absorption of manganese was increased on the manganese soil and with it the absorption of calcium.

The unhealthy growth on the manganese soil thus appears to be due to a lack of available iron.   The plants suffered from iron starvation in spite of the 10 to 30 per cent. of iron oxide in the manganese soils.

Applications of iron sulphate to the soil, at rates varying from 500 to 3,000 pounds to the acre, were unsuccessful in preventing chlorosis; but less than 50 pounds of iron sulphate per acre sprayed on the leaves effected a prompt cure.[141]   This is of particular interest for it shows that pineapple leaves can absorb enough iron to cure chlorosis, though the roots are not able to do so under the circumstances.   It has been found that the chlorosis of many coniferous seedlings growing on a calcareous soil can be remedied by spraying with a 1 per cent. solution of iron sulphate and this treatment has become a regular practice in certain nurseries.[173] An interesting treatment more or less generally and successfully used in France and Germany for the cure of chlorosis in grape vines[241] consists in brushing the cut surfaces of pruned vines with a concentrated solution of ferrous sulphate.   Filling, with a soluble iron salt, holes bored in chlorotic trees frequently has been tried in New Mexico and generally with satisfactory results.[227]

From this discussion of the effects of calcium and manganese on iron, it is evident that fertilization may be of value, not only for adding plant nutrients to the soil, but also under certain conditions, for rendering soluble and available to the plant, nutrients that though present are unavailable.   Conversely, ill advised fertilization may change mineral elements that are present from a soluble to an insoluble form and therefore make them unavailable to the plant.   Through this effect liming has led to chlorosis of the pineapple in Porto Rico.[110]   It would be of interest to know the results following direct attempts to change the reaction of the solution of calcareous or manganiferous soils where chlorosis is produced. Possibly the application of acid in some form would be as effective in preventing chlorosis as the application of iron salts to the leaves or cut surfaces.

An instance of rather extreme sensitivity to hydrogen-ion concentration is furnished by the hydrangea. Atkins, who has studied its response to soil reaction, summarizes the situation as follows:[20]

"The common garden hydrangea, *H. hortensis*, produces blue flowers when grown in soil at pH 5.7 to 6 or slightly over. In less acid habitats some flowers may be pink and others blue on the same plant, but above about pH 7.5, pink flowers only are the rule. Ferrous salts remain in solution after ferric salts have been precipitated or rendered completely insoluble as the hydroxid. The precipitation of ferrous hydroxid does not begin until about pH 5.1, and even at pH 7.1 an appreciable amount remains unprecipitated. Since plants grow at pH values beyond the limits for the complete precipitation of ferric salts, they must, under these conditions, utilize ferrous salts only. The difference between the pink and blue flowers of hydrangea is not due to acidity, since both kinds from the same plant were found to be at precisely the same H-ion concentration, pH 4.2.

"The . . . hæmotoxylin test shows that blue hydrangea flowers give the typical purple and brown reactions for 'inorganic' iron, whereas pink flowers have only minute traces of 'inorganic' iron. Colorimetric estimations with ammonium thiocyanate show that the ash of the pink flowers contains only six-tenths as much iron as that of the blue. Calculating on the dry weight of the flowers themselves, the blue contain about 140 parts per million of iron and the pink about 60 parts per million. Dilute solutions of alum and of aluminum sulphate give a reaction of about pH 4, ranging up to about pH 3.6 for more concentrated ones. These substances, therefore, are convenient reagents for increasing soil acidity without risk of attaining injuriously high H-ion concentrations by accident. To the increase in acidity, and consequent liberation of iron, is due the blue color of hydrangea found by Molisch to result from this treatment. . . . "

Acid Tolerance of Certain Crops.—Most orchard fruits are acid tolerant to a considerable degree. This is indicated both by the reaction of the soil where the wild forms from which they have been derived grow most luxuriantly[324] and by the results of numerous experiments in which the reaction of the nutrient medium has been controlled.[90,217,290,307] The strawberry prefers a soil with a pH range of 5.0 to 6.0, though it will do reasonably well within a considerably wider range[217,307]; the blueberry and its close relatives prefer one with a pH range of 4.0 to 5.5[62,162]; pome and stone fruits prefer one with a range between 5.5 and 6.5, and this likewise seems to be the best for citrus fruits.[58] Recent investigations indicate that in the peach, apple, strawberry, cranberry and presumably other fruits nitrates are more readily absorbed when the acidity of the soil is relatively high, while the ammonium ion is absorbed more readily when the soil solution is less acid.[5,90,290]

Apparently a hydrogen-ion concentration of about 5.0 is ideal for the pineapple plant, chlorosis appearing when it is 6.0 or less. It has also been shown that these lower concentrations favor the development of a number of species of

Fusarium that injure or destroy pineapple roots, while concentrations of 4.0 to 5.0 inhibit their development.[266]

Furthermore, practically all of the best orchard cover crops are distinctly acid tolerant. The following commonly used cover crops belong in this class; cowpeas, soy beans, hairy vetch, crimson clover, rye, oats, millet, buckwheat and turnip.[63]

Since deciduous fruit plants are predominantly acid tolerant, they should not be exposed to a markedly alkaline reaction of the soil as this is likely to lead to chlorosis and various other disorders. In Arizona an alkaline soil reaction has been reported as causing a decline of citrus trees and giving rise to a disorder sometimes designated as "crazy top."[208] Ash analyses of affected plants reveal a lower calcium content and a higher content of water-soluble alkalinity. Remedial treatment consists in neutralizing or acidifying the soil through adding small quantities of acid to the irrigation water or through incorporating sulphur in the soil.[208]

Ammonia in considerable amount depresses root growth and eventually kills the roots, because of its effect on the soil reaction. However, applications of ammonium sulphate usually result in making the soil more acid in reaction, the ammonium ion being taken up by the plant more freely than the sulphate that is left in the soil. Injuries resulting from an excess of "alkali," as the term is generally used in the arid and semiarid sections, are due not to any effect these salts may have on the reaction of the soil, but rather to the excessive concentration of the potassium and sodium salts that are present. The difference between the toxic

TABLE 10.—HIGHEST AMOUNT OF ALKALI IN WHICH FRUIT TREES WERE FOUND
UNAFFECTED
(*After Loughridge*[189])
(Pounds per acre in 4 feet depth)

Sulphates (Glauber salt)		Carbonates (Sal soda)		Chlorid (Common salt)		Total alkali	
Grapes....	40,800	Grapes.....	7,550	Grapes.....	9,640	Grapes....	45,760
Olives....	30,640	Oranges....	3,840	Olives......	6,640	Olives.....	40,160
Figs......	24,480	Olives....	2,880	Oranges....	3,360	Almonds...	26,400
Almonds..	22,720	Pears.......	1,760	Almonds....	2,400	Figs.......	26,400
Oranges...	18,600	Almonds....	1,440	Mulberry...	2,240	Oranges...	21,740
Pears.....	17,800	Prunes.....	1,360	Pears.......	1,360	Pears......	20,920
Apples....	14,240	Figs........	1,120	Apples......	1,240	Apples.....	16,120
Peaches...	9,600	Peaches.....	680	Prunes.....	1,200	Prunes....	11,800
Prunes....	9,240	Apples......	640	Peaches.....	1,000	Peaches...	11,280
Apricots..	8,640	Apricots....	480	Apricots....	960	Apricots...	10,080
Lemons...	4,480	Lemons.....	480	Lemons.....	800	Lemons....	5,750
Mulberry.	3,360	Mulberry...	160	Figs........	800	Mulberry..	5,740

symptoms attending an alkaline or basic soil reaction and those attending impregnation with "alkali" is well marked. A soil solution having an alkaline reaction affects the roots before the shoots; the toxic effects of a soil solution which is too concentrated are evident first in the shoots.

Concentration: Soil "Alkali."—As just pointed out, the term "soil alkali" does not refer to the soil reaction, but to an excessive concentration of certain salts. The carbonates, chlorides and sulfates of sodium and potassium are concerned chiefly, though occasionally other salts accumulate in such amounts as to be injurious.

Tolerance of Different Fruits.—The degree of tolerance of various fruit crops to salts of different kinds is indicated by data presented in Table 10.

Loughridge[189] makes the following comments on these data: "The amount tolerated depends largely upon the distribution of the several salts in the vertical soil column, the injury being most severe in the surface foot, where under the influence of the unfortunate practice of surface irrigation the feeding rootlets are usually found. It is therefore important that in alkali regions such methods of culture and irrigation should be followed as to encourage deep rooting on the part of crops.

"The amount tolerated varies with the variety of the same plant, as shown in the grape." For instance, Flame Tokay is reported as "not growing" with a total of 24,320 pounds of alkali in the surface 4 feet per acre while Trousseau is reported as thrifty in the presence of 31,360 pounds, though the sal soda content of the Flame Tokay soil was somewhat higher but still well within the general tolerance limit of the grape for this salt.

"The amount of alkali tolerated by the various cultures varies with the nature of the soil. It is lowest in heavy clay soils and fine-grained soils, in which the downward movement of plant roots is restricted; and highest in loam and sandy soils, in which the roots have freedom of penetration."

Injuries from Excessive Fertilization.—It is evident that continued application of fertilizer such as sodium nitrate may produce concentrations that are harmful.

In discussing experiments with citrus trees Kelly and Thomas[167] state: "While the growth of the trees was notably stimulated by sodium nitrate during the first few years of the experiment, and healthy, normal appearing trees were produced, since that time excessive mottle leaf has appeared on every tree in this plot. The mottling here became so severe during the past 2 or 3 years as to render the trees wholly unprofitable. No marketable fruit whatever is now produced by these trees."

Table 11 presents data showing the toxic limits of citrus seedlings for various nitrate salts and for ammonium sulphate and the toxic limits for these salts in the presence of lime. Their lesson in connection with the use of commercial fertilizers in the orchard is well summarized in the words of Breazeale:[37]

"It will be seen that marked differences occur in the toxic limits of the various salts, sodium nitrate being five times as toxic as calcium nitrate. The toxic limits for this group of salts are so high that the matter may appear to be of no practical import. But a simple calculation will show that the surface feeding roots of citrus trees are at times subjected to fertilizer concentrations in field practice so great as to approach toxic conditions. Application of 2 to 3 pounds of nitrate of soda per tree, or 200 to 300 pounds per acre, which is not an unusual practice for some citrus growers, would correspond approximately to a concentration of 70 to 100 parts per million in the soil of the surface foot. The fertilizer, moreover, is ordinarily applied to the open ground between the tree rows—that is not more than one-half the total soil area. If the moisture content of the soil were reduced to 10 per cent. of the weight of the soil, the concentration of the sodium nitrate in the soil solution would range from 1,400 to 2,000 parts per million—that is, it would approach the toxic limit. The surface crusts in citrus groves are often highly toxic to citrus seedlings."

TABLE 11.—TOXIC LIMITS OF NITRATES AND AMMONIUM SULPHATE FOR CITRUS SEEDLINGS[37]

SALT	TOXIC LIMIT PARTS PER MILLION
Sodium nitrate	1,800
Potassium nitrate	3,500
Calcium nitrate	10,000
Ammonium sulphate	1,000
Sodium nitrate and calcium carbonate (solid phase)	6,000
Ammonium sulphate and calcium carbonate (solid phase)	2,000

Some Effects of Soil Alkali.—The effects of excessive concentration produced by "alkali" on citrus trees are described by Kelly and Thomas.[167]

"Different varieties and species of citrus trees are affected differently by alkali. Lemon trees show the effects by a pronounced yellowing of the margins and burning of the tips of the leaves, followed by unusually heavy shedding of the leaves in the latter part of the winter and spring. The subsequent new growth may appear to be quite normal and vigorous for several months, but later a large portion of the leaves turn yellow in irregularly shaped areas around the margins and fall excessively. In the presence of excessive concentrations of salts, especially chlorides, complete defoliation may take place. Mottle leaf frequently occurs, and sometimes chlorosis. Both the quality and quantity of the fruit are impaired.

"It has been found that orange trees affected by alkali are unusually susceptible to injury from adverse climatic conditions. Hot winds burn the young leaves and frosts produce more serious injury than with normal trees. Alkali injury is also accentuated by the lack of care, such as improper tillage, the insufficient use of manure or other fertilizers, and withholding irrigation, thereby allowing the soil to become too dry. If the soil be allowed to dry out excessively, the concentration of alkali in the soil moisture may become harmful, while a more abundant supply of water would so dilute the salts present as to reduce the concentration to a point where normal growth could take place.

"In certain localities the dissolved salts are predominantly chlorides, in others sulphates and in still others bicarbonates. A few wells have been found to contain large amounts of nitrates."

Alkali in the soil may also have a marked effect on root distribution.

"It is especially interesting that the roots of the lemon trees have not penetrated deeply in this soil, more than 95 per cent. of them being within 18 inches of the surface. There is probably some connection between this fact and the higher concentration of alkali salts found in the third and fourth feet.

"Local areas occur in a Valencia orange grove near Garden Grove in Orange County where many of the trees have been severely injured by alkali brought up as a result of a temporarily high water table in the winter and spring of 1916. The water table receded within a few months but the alkali salts remained in the soil. A considerable number of trees have recently died, and all of them in certain areas became excessively chlorotic, following the rise of the alkali."

When irrigation is practiced, the composition of the irrigation water is an important factor. Kelly and Thomas found from their investigations, "a remarkably close relationship between the composition of the irrigation water, on the one hand, and the accumulation of alkali salts and the condition of the orange and the lemon trees, on the other. In every case we have studied, where saline irrigation water has been applied for a series of years, alkaline salts have accumulated in the soil and the citrus trees have been injured in consequence. The rates at which salts have actually accumulated vary, however, in different soils, depending on (1) the composition of the water, (2) the amounts applied, and (3) the freedom with which it penetrated into the subsoil."[167]

The injurious effects of high concentrations produced by excessive amounts of alkali or other salts in the soil are due largely to the inability of plants to absorb water by osmosis from a solution having a higher osmotic concentration than that of the plant itself. Hence, the harmful effects of alkali are partly those of starvation and drought. The concentration of the soil solution requires attention only under conditions where the salt content of the soil is naturally high, as in salt marshes and in regions near salt water generally, or where the moisture supply is restricted, as in arid or semiarid regions. However, summer drought may produce temporarily excessive concentrations in any soil and so bring about injury.

Remedial Measures.—When a soil once becomes impregnated with alkali about the only effective treatment is flooding the land with irrigation water to dissolve out the excessive amounts which are then either forced down to a depth where they will do no harm or carried away in the drainage water. Provision for thorough drainage is very important in places where there is danger from alkali, as the rise of the water table attending poor drainage may result in bringing salts from lower soil to the surface and thereby increase concentrations in the upper layers as evaporation takes place. Moderate, as opposed to excessive, irrigation is a preventive measure. Though there is not often a choice between two or more sources of irrigation water, the irrigation fruit grower should remember that certain water supplies are more or less saline and that special precautions must be taken to neutralize the injurious effect when such water alone is available. Much can be done to avoid the effects of soil alkali through the choice of alkali-tolerant fruit crops and particularly the selection of stocks having this characteristic, though the roots of the cion may be susceptible. The importance of caution in the use of fertilizers, particularly in irrigated sections, has been mentioned.

Finally, it should be pointed out that insufficient as well as excessive concentrations may exist. That extremely low concentrations permit growth has been emphasized but it is the insufficient concentration of particular salts that renders the use of fertilizers necessary.

Soil Toxicity.—In a broad way a toxin may be defined as any substance that exerts a deleterious influence on growth or on some of the other functions of the plant. In a sense then, straw or other plant residues, when incorporated with the soil, can be said to have toxic effects due simply to their interference with absorption through the utilization of nitrates by the bacteria and moulds engaged in their decomposition,[44,144,225] and the residues from certain crop plants, *e.g.*, timothy, have more of a toxic effect than those of certain other crops, *e.g.*, clover, because their own nitrogen content is lower and their decomposition consequently slower.[322] In a narrower sense, however, some of the specific decomposition products produced by these same bacteria or moulds acting on the plant residues, even when present in very small quantities, may have very toxic effects. These poisons are produced not only from plant residues artificially spread on and incorporated into the soil incident to the use of mulching materials, soiling crops and farm manures but from fragments of dead root hairs, roots and aerial portions of the plant that are washed down into the soil. They are not, as a rule, excreted as such from plant roots, though this occurs under exceptional conditions, as, for example, when the supply of oxygen is deficient. However, it must not be overlooked that bacterial activity may likewise result in the formation of compounds that have the opposite effect on the plant, serving as nutrients,[258] or even exerting an influence more or less comparable to that of vitamins in animal nutrition.[38]

General and Specific Effects.—The general effects of toxins are shown in decreased green weight and inhibited growth. The specific morphological effects vary considerably with different substances, some producing more marked effects on the roots than on the green parts of the plant. For instance, vanillin-affected plants show decreased growth of the top

and root growth is strongly inhibited. Dihydroxystearic acid affects
the tops but especially the roots, the root tips becoming darkened, their
growth stunted; the root ends are enlarged and often turned upward
like fishhooks and their oxidizing power is strongly inhibited. Pyridine
and picoline affect the green parts more than the roots. Cumarin-
affected plants have stunted tops and broad distorted leaves; quinone-
affected plants are tall and slender, with thin narrow leaves. Guanidine
has apparently no effect on the roots, but the green parts develop small
bleached spots which spread, the plant becomes weakened and the leaves
break at the stem, wilt and die.[256,259]

The manner in which these toxic substances check growth is shown
by a study of the absorption of mineral constituents. Though absorption is always decreased, the various toxins have more or less specific
effects. Cumarin and salicylic aldehyde depress potash and nitrate
absorption more than phosphate absorption; quinone depresses phosphate
and nitrate more than potash; dihydroxystearic acid and perhaps vanillin retard phosphate and potash more than nitrate absorption.

Protecting Against Toxins.—The harmful effects of these toxins may
be counteracted in numerous ways. Fertilizer treatment is efficacious; as
might be expected, various salts act differently in overcoming the respective effects of the toxic substances. Phosphatic fertilizers, for example,
are most efficient in overcoming the effects of cumarin, potassic fertilizers
in overcoming the effects of quinone and nitrogenous fertilizers in overcoming the effects of vanillin.

Another way of ameliorating the effects of toxic substances in the soil
is treatment with absorbing agents. Roots appear able to oxidize
organic materials in such a way that their toxic properties are lost. The
large amount of root surface which most plants have makes this oxidizing
power important in relation to the destruction of toxic substances through
crop rotation.

Schreiner, Reed and Skinner[260] found that toxic solutions lost much of their
toxicity after plants had been grown in them. They state: "The vanillin
solution, for example, was so reduced in toxicity that a solution originally containing 500 parts per million was no more toxic to the second set of plants than
a solution of 50 parts per million was to the first. It has been found that an
equal number of wheat plants can remove in a similar length of time not more
than 30 to 50 parts per million of nitrates from solution and there is no reason
to believe that toxic substances should be removed at a much more rapid rate."

Breazeale[37] reports that peat extract in dilute concentrations (20 parts
per million) and calcium carbonate protect citrus seedlings against the
toxicity of distilled water, usually associated with the presence of small
amounts of copper. Sodium carbonate on the other hand augments the
toxicity of soluble organic matter.

Thus, "When soluble organic matter which is acid in reaction and stimulating to citrus seedlings in concentrations up to 1,000 parts per million or more is added to a sodium carbonate solution of 400 parts per million which in itself is not toxic, a highly toxic solution is formed which will kill the root tips of citrus seedlings. This reaction appears to be of importance in connection with the toxicity of soils containing small amounts of sodium carbonate."[37]

Importance in the Fruit Plantation.—To just what extent organic soil toxins are important in the fruit plantation is not known. That they are of greater significance than is generally realized there can be no question. Most deciduous fruit crops occupy the same soil for a considerable number of years and consequently are subject to the influence of any toxins that arise from the disintegration of their own leaves, rootlets or other dead tissues. In addition they are subject to the action of toxins that may arise from the growth or decay of intercrops or cover crops that are grown between them.

It has been shown[139] that ordinary crop plants exert an important influence upon those which follow them and that this influence "seems not to be attributable, at least primarily, to differences in the amount of fertilizer nutrients removed by the crops grown before." Thus the yield of buckwheat following redtop, rye, buckwheat and onions was as 7:30: 45:88, in a nutrient medium deficient in nitrogen but well supplied with other plant nutrients, even though the nitrogen removal of the preceding redtop, rye and buckwheat crops was as 1.00:2.72:2.42.[139] The presumption is that the differences in the yields of the second crops were due to the effect of toxins.

Pickering[238] has been able by means of various field trials and pot experiments to eliminate the influence of one plant upon another through its effect on moisture and nutrient supply, soil temperature, soil reaction, texture, carbon dioxide and bacterial content and thus to determine both quantitatively and qualitatively their mutual influence through toxic substances.

He comments as follows on the results of his investigations:

"It has now been established with a reasonable amount of certainty that the deleterious effect of one growing plant on another is a general phenomenon. By means chiefly of pot experiments . . . the following plants have been found susceptible to such influence: apples, pears, plums, cherries, six kinds of forest trees, mustard, tobacco, tomatoes, barley, clover, and two varieties of grasses, whilst the plants exercising this baleful influence have been apple seedlings, mustard, tobacco, tomatoes, two varieties of clover, and 16 varieties of grasses. In no case have negative results been obtained. The extent of the effect varies very greatly: in pot experiments the maximum reduction in growth of the plants affected has been 97 per cent., the minimum 6 per cent., whilst in field experiments with trees the effect may vary from a small quantity up to that sufficient to cause the death of the tree. The average effect in pot experiments may be roughly placed at a reduction of one-half to two-thirds of the normal growth of the plant, but no sufficient evidence has yet been obtained to justify the conclusion that any particular kinds of plants are more susceptible than others, or any particular surface crop is more toxic than another; that such differences exist is highly probable, but all the variations observed so far may be explained by the greater or lesser vigour of the plants in the particular experiments in question. Similarly as regards the effect of grass on fruit trees, though the extent of it varies very greatly, and in many soils is certainly small, we must hesitate to attribute this to any specific properties of the soils in question; for when soils from different localities (including those from places where the grass effect is small) have been examined in pot experiments, they have all given very similar results; and this applies equally to cases where pure sand, with the addition of artificial nutrients, has been taken as the medium of growth."[238] Evidence which will serve partially to differentiate between the influence of a living plant and the disintegration products of its dying roots is afforded by the following: " . . . a quarter of an acre of land, over which some 15 apple trees, 20 years of age, were distributed, was planted uniformly with Brussels sprouts; those under the trees suffered to the extent of 48 per cent. in their growth; but there were patches in the ground where trees had been growing until the preceding winter, when they had been cut down, leaving the roots undisturbed in the soil, and in these patches the sprouts did better than elsewhere to the extent of 12 per cent. In other parts of the ground canvas screens had been erected, at a height of 6 feet above the surface, to simulate, and even exaggerate, the shading of the trees, and under these the sprouts gave exactly the same values as on the unshaded ground. Thus, the trees themselves materially injured the crop, though the soil under the trees was more fertile than elsewhere, and though the shading was inoperative."[238]

The degree of susceptibility of the apple tree to the toxic influence of some other plant is indicated by Pickering's[238] statement that the color of the fruit may be materially affected "in cases of trees weighing about 2 hundredweight when only 3 to 6 ounces of their roots extended into grassed ground." Walnut trees are known to exert a very harmful influence on crop plants of many kinds grown in their vicinity and instances are on record of where considerable numbers of apple trees have been killed by them.[253] It has been suggested that this influence is due largely to a specific chemical substance, juglone.[200] Many species of both deciduous and non-deciduous fruits have been found very sensitive to toxic effects of grass in India[160] and in this country rye used as a cover crop has been found to give off some kind of growth-inhibiting substance as it is approaching maturity.[64]

In commenting upon the investigations that have just been cited and on others of a similar character Alderman[8] remarks: "Do they not at least open to some question many of our preconceived ideas bearing upon plant growth and plant nutrition? . . . Do they not raise a question as to the arrangement of many crop rotations (*e.g.*, of cover crops or other intercultures) which were originally worked out with the economic convenience of the grower in view rather than the growth reactions of the plants under consideration? . . . If it is true in Rhode Island that onions will yield 412 bushels per acre following redtop and only 13 bushels following cabbages, it is probably true elsewhere and the place of the onion in the cropping system of the truck grower deserves the most serious study. If grass affords direct injury to apple trees growing in shallow soils underlaid with an impervious stratum of subsoil, it is probably as offensive in North America as in England. The writer and others interested in plant nutrition have repeatedly pointed out the difference in reaction to fertilizers between orchards in sod and those under cultivation. It has been generally believed that this difference was due to soil exhaustion of important plant food material or to an influence on moisture supply but the work of Pickering is a direct challenge to such a belief. Perhaps it is not important to the grower of fruit to know whether an application of nitrate of soda to a sod orchard is beneficial because it supplies some element of plant food material heretofore lacking or because it hastens the change of toxic substances to harmless or beneficial materials, but it is extremely important to the investigator for it strikes back to a fundamental problem in plant nutrition."

The whole question of the interrelationship of plants in the orchard still needs thorough investigation.

Antagonism.—Beside organic poisons, certain inorganic salts may have toxic effects; for example, magnesium compounds may become injurious to the higher plants. The toxic action of magnesium is modified, however, by calcium because of the antagonism between these two elements. Salts of either calcium or magnesium by themselves tend to increase the permeability of protoplasm more than a mixture of calcium and magnesium salts in proper proportion. Therefore, the action of calcium in offsetting the toxic effect of the magnesium probably is due to diminished magnesium absorption when both elements are present in suitable proportion. Similarly injurious concentrations of the sulphates may sometimes be counteracted by applications of nitrates and phosphates.[131]

Aeration.—In the absence of aeration roots are unable to function properly and toxic substances are secreted. Moreover poor aeration favors the formation of toxins by bacteria and in the absence of an adequate supply of oxygen, numerous soil bacteria reduce nitrates, utilize the oxygen and leave gaseous nitrogen which is not available to the higher plants.

The physical character of the soil has an important effect on aeration; stiff, retentive clays, for example, do not drain so well as sandy soils; consequently they are usually not so well aerated. The application of lime or organic fertilizers to such clays may render them mellow, better drained and more readily cultivated.

Selective Absorption.—Within certain limits, plants are able to absorb larger amounts of one mineral constituent at their disposal than of another and in this way to exert a selective action. This is strikingly shown by Table 12, which compares the percentage composition of the ash of duckweed with the water in which it grew.

Interesting as illustrating not only selective absorption but differences in the feeding habits of plants at different stages in their development is the following reported nutrient intake of the pineapple plant: "During the first six months only a small amount of potash (7.3 per cent. of the total amount) is absorbed, but thereafter the uptake is rapid and continuous. With nitrogen 100 per cent. of the total is absorbed during the first 6 months, none is taken up during the 3 months before flowering and there is a considerable uptake during the fruiting period. Phosphate uptake closely resembles that of nitrogen. Appreciable amounts of lime and magnesia are also absorbed but not until after the first 6 months."[102]

TABLE 12.—ANALYSES OF ASH OF DUCKWEED AND OF THE MINERAL MATTER CONTAINED IN THE WATER IN WHICH IT GREW[164]

	K_2O	Na_2O	CaO	MgO	Fe_2O_3	P_2O_5	SO_3	SiO_2	Cl
Duckweed........	18.29	4.05	21.86	6.60	9.57	11.35	7.91	16.05	5.55
Water..........	5.15	7.60	45.55	16.00	0.94	3.42	10.79	4.23	7.99

This selective ability of the plant may be explained by greater action on certain constituents which are thereby rendered osmotically inactive within the plant. This leads to further absorption of these particular constituents. However, selective action has definite limits and plants absorb a certain amount of any constituent which is present in an available form and to which the protoplasm is permeable. Thus, salt marsh plants contain relatively large amounts of sodium chloride which may raise the osmotic concentration of their cell sap, but is of no apparent nutritive value. Similarly plants grown in nutrient solutions absorb whatever salts are present in solution, though the rate is greatest and growth best when the nutrient substances are available to the plant in a ratio corresponding to that in which they are utilized.

Investigations by Schreiner and Skinner[256] bearing on this subject are very suggestive: "In this study the growth relationships and concentration differences were observed between solution cultures in which the phosphate, nitrate and potash varied from single constituents to mixtures of two and three in all possible ratios in 10 per cent. stages. The better growth occurred when all these nutrient elements were present and was best in those mixtures which contained between 10 and 30 per cent. phosphate; between 30 and 60 per cent. nitrate; and between 30 and 60 per cent. potash. The growth in the solutions containing all three constituents was much greater than in the solutions containing two constituents, the solutions containing the single constituents giving the least growth. The concentration differences noticed in the solutions were also very striking, the greater reduction in concentration occurring where the greatest growth occurred. The change in the ratios of the solutions and the ratios of the materials that were removed from the solutions showed that where greatest growth occurred, as above outlined, the solutions suffered the least change in ratio, although the greatest change in concentration occurred. The more the ratios in these solutions differed from the ratios in which the greatest growth occurred, the more were the solutions altered in the course of the experiment, the tendency in all cases seeming to be for the plant to remove from any and all of these solutions the ratio which normally existed where greatest growth occurred, but was hindered in doing so by the unbalanced condition of the solution. The results show that the higher the amount of any one constituent present in the solution, the more does the culture growing in that solution take up of this constituent, although it does not seem able to use this additional amount economically."

Similarly surpluses of lime in plants are not uncommon.[187] A part of the lime may be precipitated as calcium oxalate, or in some plants as calcium carbonate, of which cystoliths are largely composed.

Transpiration.—The ash content of plants varies considerably under different conditions of soil water, available salt supply and temperature. Data have been reported[168] indicating that increased transpiration does not increase the ash absorption of plants growing in soil, though it has been shown that there may sometimes be enough of a temporary accumulation of salts in the leaves of citrus trees as a result of desiccating winds to cause foliage injury.[130] Transpiration and the absorption of nutrient salts are largely independent of each other.

Schreiner and Skinner[258] discuss this subject as follows: "Many writers in agricultural literature seem to be under the impression that the only way that a plant can get the nutrients from a solution is to use all the water it can in building tissue and to lose the remainder by transpiration, so as to obtain the necessary nutrients dissolved in the soil water or nutrient solution. In other words, that the plant maintains a current of water entering at the root as the nutrient solution and leaving the plant as pure water at the leaf surfaces, that is, by transpiration or evaporation. From their arguments it follows that if a half strength solution is presented to the plant it will have to take up and transpire twice as much water to obtain the same nutrients. In other words, the plant is supposed to absorb the mineral constituents in the same concentration as the solution in which the roots bathe. This is, however, not in accordance with the facts. The plant has greater difficulty in obtaining the mineral elements from the weaker solution, but it does not accomplish this by expending the extra energy involved in transpiring double the amount of water.

"For instance, the loss of water from a 250-cubic centimeter [nutrient] solution during this 3-day period is only about 10 per cent., whereas the analysis of the solution after supplying this water showed the mineral nutrients to be reduced from 80 to as low as 23.8 parts per million, or a decrease of 70 per cent. It is obvious that the plants have taken the nutrients faster than the water, and this under conditions of good growth.

"Not only does the absorbing power of the root enable the plant to take more nutrients per cubic centimeter of water absorbed than is contained in the same volume of the soil solution, but it also enables the plant to obtain a different ratio of the mineral nutrients for its use than exist in the nutrient solution.

"These facts are extremely important, as they show that the absorbing power of the plant is not regulated by the amount of transpiration, but rather by the life processes within the plant and the requirements of these life processes."

THE NUTRIENT REQUIREMENTS OF CROP AND FRUIT PLANTS

Typical crop plants and typical deciduous fruits make distinctly different demands upon the soil. For most crops the soil should not be acid and the nitrogen requirement is relatively low. For most fruit trees, soil acidity, unless very high, is not a factor of concern and the demands for nitrogen are great. It is suggested that this more or less characteristic difference which requires agronomists and horticulturists to adopt correspondingly different attitudes on the problem of soil productivity is connected with the different ecological habits of these plants, together with the type of crop desired. Cereal crops in particular are adapted to an early stage in ecological succession which has not proceeded beyond an association where grasses are dominant. Humus has not yet collected in great amount; hence, crops flourish in soils of low acidity and require relatively little nitrogen (though they may do equally well or better in soils abundantly supplied with it). Fruit trees belong to a much later stage in an ecological succession which has reached an association of forest trees and in which the character of the soil has been affected by previous plant associations that have grown on it. Humus is therefore more abundant and the plants are adapted to soils of relatively high acidity and great nitrogen content. Hence, lime is most useful for crops and nitrogen the fertilizer most often required by fruit trees. It is more profitable to grow cereal and forage crops on the great plains, prairies, savannahs and pampas while fruit trees thrive best in the regions of coniferous and deciduous forests.

Summary.—The various mineral elements and nitrogen are absorbed by the plant from the soil solution. These mineral elements, except a portion of the sulphur, may be recovered in the ash of the plant. In addition to the necessary mineral elements, the ash generally includes small quantities of a number of non-essential elements occurring in the soil solution. The ash content of plants varies with the kind of plant and with the soil upon which it is grown. The ash content of different tissues also varies with the kind of tissue, its age and the season. Nutrient elements must not only be in solution but must be in an available form—that is, combined with certain other elements and in certain compounds. Nitrogen is absorbed mainly as nitrates. The nitrate supply in the soil is subject to great fluctuations, depending on temperature, moisture, aeration, bacterial activity, the supply of nitrogen-carrying materials from which nitrates can be formed and many other factors. An important part of the orchard soil fertility question consists in maintaining a liberal supply of nitrates in the soil during the growing season. Most crop plants prefer a soil practically neutral in reaction. Deciduous fruits are distinctly acid tolerant and certain of them thrive best in an acid soil. The best orchard cover crops are likewise acid tolerant. The chlorotic conditions frequently found in strongly calcareous and manganiferous soils apparently are due to iron starvation incident to an alkaline or near-alkaline reaction. Many organic disintegration products are known to be toxic to certain crop plants and there is evidence that they are often of considerable importance in determining the productivity of orchard soils. Some of the injurious effects of sod upon trees evidently are due to these toxins in the grass land. Excessive concentrations of certain salts, particularly of sodium and potassium, are toxic to orchard trees and give rise to the so-called "alkali" conditions. Treatment for disorders of this kind may be both remedial and preventive. Optimum conditions for absorption are provided when the various nutrient elements are found in the soil solution in certain rather definite proportions. Sometimes harmful influences result when these ratios do not obtain. Both transpiration and soil aeration influence somewhat the rate of absorption. Within certain limits plants are able to absorb from the soil solution the elements most necessary, taking them out in proportions sometimes very different from those in which they exist.

CHAPTER VIII

INDIVIDUAL ELEMENTS

The intake of nitrogen and mineral constituents in inorganic form has been described. Their incorporation into the plant is now considered with particular reference to orchard or fruit plants. In studies that have been made analyses have been expressed in percentages of fresh weight or of dry weight or in the absolute amounts present in a certain tissue, such as 100 leaves; ash analyses have been given in percentages of fresh weight or of dry weight, in percentages of total ash or in absolute amounts. Careful distinction should be made between determinations expressed in these different terms since they are not comparable. For example, during the development of a tissue—say the leaf—some ash constituent may decrease in terms of percentage of total ash, remain constant in percentage of dry weight and increase in absolute amount. Data on absolute amounts are particularly valuable and show the actual changes in the amount of substance present. Percentages of dry weight will indicate the same changes provided there is no increase or decrease in the absolute dry weight. If there is, then these changes must be taken into consideration. Expression of percentage in terms of fresh weight involves in addition changes in the water content. Percentages of total ash show the relative proportions of the various ash constituents. Each of these determinations has its value, but each expresses different relations.

NITROGEN

Nitrogen enters the roots from the soil solution as a salt of nitric acid, such as potassium or sodium nitrate, or sometimes as ammonia. The supply of nitrates in the soil varies with temperature and moisture, usually being greatest in late spring and early autumn, but persisting throughout the growing season.

Synthesis of Organic Nitrogenous Compounds.—Most of the inorganic nitrogen absorbed is carried up the trunk and branches to the leaves where it is elaborated into amino-acids and other nitrogenous organic compounds. The elaboration of nitrates to amino-acids takes place for the most part in the chloroplasts of the leaf mesophyll cells. Light has been shown[179] to increase nitrogen assimilation, blue-violet and ultra-violet light being particularly effective. Light from the blue end of the

148

solar spectrum is relatively stronger in cloudy weather; light from the other end of the spectrum, which is the more important for the photosynthetic process, predominates in direct sunlight. According to one investigator[301] the influence of light in favoring protein formation and the elaboration of inorganic to organic nitrogenous compounds becomes more pronounced as the stage of development advances. Nitrogen elaboration can take place in the absence of chlorophyll and light, in which case presumably carbohydrates are used.[326] The amino-acids which are the first products of elaboration are either used directly in the leaf or are conducted through the phloem to all parts of the plant where they are used in the building up of every nitrogen-containing organic compound found in plants as well as of certain nitrogen-free organic substances (essential oils, resins and polyterpenes). The amino-acids are combined to form the proteins which occur in all protoplasm. Other nitrogenous organic compounds are the purines and pyrimidines which enter into the composition of nucleic acids, nucleins and nucleoproteins, substances characteristic of the cell nucleus. Lecithins and chlorophyll contain nitrogen. Nitrogen-containing compounds which are not of universal occurrence are the alkaloids, ptomaines, amines, cyanogenetic glucosides and indican (natural indigo blue).

Translocation and Use of Elaborated Nitrogenous Compounds.—The elaboration of nitrates to amino-acids, beginning at the time the leaves are well developed, proceeds as long as they remain green, reaching a maximum when temperature, light and soil supply conditions are at an optimum. The elaborated nitrogen-containing compounds are constantly passing out of the leaves throughout the season of elaboration as fast as they are made. They are used for new tissue development, for shoot growth, new leaves, increments to branches, trunks and roots, new roots and especially for fruit and seed development. A considerable part of the remainder is stored in the phloem. Storage is particularly rapid in the fall when growth has ceased and before the leaves are separated from the plant by abscission layers.

New tissue growth in early spring is at the expense of stored foods, including stored nitrogen. This reserve supplies the developing shoots, leaves, flowers, rootlets, much of the new tissue in trunk, branches and roots and the fruit in its initial stages. Hence for good spring growth of tissues, especially shoots, leaves and spurs, abundant nitrogen storage the previous season is a prime requisite. This, in turn, depends on a good supply of available nitrogen in the soil between June 1 and Sept. 15 or Oct. 15, a supply more than sufficient for fruit and tissue development. Summer defoliation or a diseased condition of the leaves evidently checks growth the following year by cutting down the supply of stored and elaborated nitrogen.

Attention should be called to the apparent usefulness of unelaborated nitrogen to the apple and pear tree and probably to other fruits, through enabling them to set a larger crop.   It is a common experience to secure a good set of fruit when liberal applications of some readily available nitrogen-carrying fertilizer, such as nitrate of soda, are made to weak trees just before blossoming, though without such applications these same trees would bloom heavily but set little or no fruit.   This response by the tree is obtained within 2 or 3 weeks after application of the fertilizer and at a season when there is practically no leaf area to build up elaborated foods.   It would seem, therefore, that the synthesis of organic nitrogenous compounds can take place in tissues other than the leaves.

Seasonal Distribution of Nitrogen.—A study of the seasonal variation in nitrogen content of different parts of the plant gives a perspective of the processes of nitrogen elaboration, storage and utilization.

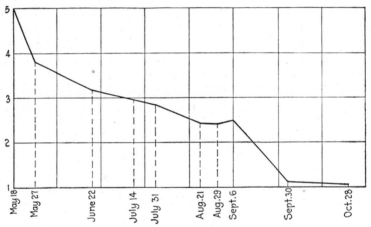

Fig. 12.—Nitrogen content of plum leaves in percentages of dry weight.   (*Plotted from data given by Richter.*[246])

In Leaves.—Leaf buds have a high percentage of nitrogen; certain analyses show 3.687 per cent. of the dry weight in the cherry and 3.779 per cent. in the plum.[246]   Fruit buds have a slightly higher percentage composition in nitrogen, corresponding analyses showing 3.771 per cent. in the cherry and 4.142 per cent. in the plum.[246]

As the leaf bud opens and the leaves unfold and start to grow, there is a steady decline in their percentage composition of nitrogen (Fig. 12), though the total amount that they contain actually increases.   There are two periods of rapid decrease, one in May and the other in September.   Between the periods of rapid decrease the percentage composition of the leaf is fairly constant.   The first period of decrease is at the time when the leaf is growing rapidly and the available nitrogen supply is limited, because of rapid and simultaneous shoot, wood and root development.   The period of relatively constant nitrogen content occurs when nitrogen intake is very nearly balanced by the demands for new vegetative tissue and for the development of the fruit and seed. The second period of decrease indicates withdrawal from the leaf shortly before its abscission. A curve showing the trend in the absolute amount of nitrogen in the leaf would be almost the reverse of that in Fig. 12 for the spring and summer months. At the time of nitrogen withdrawal in the fall, however, it would turn sharply downward. This simply means that in young leaves with their high percentage of nitrogen, growth and carbohydrate formation proceed at such a rate as to reduce the percentage composition of nitrogen even though the intake of nitrates during this period is greater than the outgo of elaborated nitrogen. During July and August and sometimes later, the leaf supplies the branches with an amount of elaborated nitrogen about equal to the amount of nitrates taken in. From September on, however, the leaves receive less nitrate in proportion to the elaborated nitrogen which passes back into the branches; consequently the percentage nitrogen content of the leaf is cut in half and only one-third the amount the leaves once contained remains in them when they fall.

In Branches, Trunks and Roots.—A study of the seasonal variation in the content of other parts of a tree shows what becomes of the nitrogen that passes out of the leaf. Table 13 shows the distribution of nitrogen in a 7-year old apple tree at different seasons. These figures bring out two important points—first, that the younger the tissue the greater is its nitrogen content and second, that practically all tissues have a minimum when active growth has ceased and a maximum at the time of bud swelling. The increase in all tissues, except leaves, during the fall indicates nitrogen storage. The nitrogen that is stored over the winter evidently comes from the leaves.

TABLE 13.—SEASONAL CHANGES IN THE NITROGEN CONTENT OF A 7-YEAR OLD APPLE TREE[47]
(Percentages of dry weight)

	Dormant, Dec. 3	Buds swelling, Apr. 20	In bloom, May 18	Active growth over, July 12	Leaves falling, Oct. 12
Summer's growth.......	....	....	....	0.64	0.61
1-year old branches.....	0.80	1.01	0.69	0.40	0.57
2-year old branches.....	0.63	0.68	0.38	0.32	0.50
3-year old branches.....	0.42	0.62	0.32	0.27	0.37
4-year old branches.....	0.40	0.41	0.29	0.24	0.30
5-year old branches.....	0.39	0.32	0.28	0.23	0.25
Trunk.................	0.23	0.32	0.27	0.22	0.24
Large roots............	0.41	0.47	0.46	0.28	0.31
Small roots............	0.79	0.78	0.70	0.48	0.77

Reference to the last table shows that in two places only is there a decrease in the percentage of nitrogen before bud swelling, namely, in the smaller roots and in the 5-year old branches. The decrease in the roots probably is due to their beginning to function and to renew growth earlier in the spring than do the tops.

In Spurs.—The seasonal changes in the nitrogen content of bearing, non-bearing and barren spurs from mature apple trees is shown in Fig. 13. The variations in non-bearing spurs, or more accurately productive spurs in the off year, are similar to those in the roots, trunks and branches with a maximum in March at the time of bud swelling and a minimum at the end of June when growth is over.[156] Barren spurs have a lower nitrogen content throughout the year and there is little evidence of accumulation in the fall; this may be associated with the absence of fruit bud differentiation in these spurs.

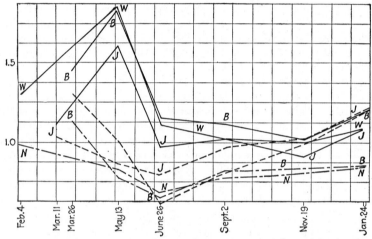

FIG. 13.—Nitrogen content of apple spurs in percentages of dry weight, bearing spurs represented by continuous lines marked *W*, *B* and *J* for Wealthy, Ben Davis and Jonathan respectively; non-bearing spurs shown by broken lines marked *B* and *J*; barren spurs represented by dot-dash lines marked *B* and *N* for Ben Davis and Nixonite. (*After Hooker.*[156])

Bearing spurs are peculiar, however, in that their nitrogen content increases after the buds have broken, though in all other tissues of spur-bearing trees it decreases when the plant is in bloom. This indicates that though the vegetative tissues use locally stored nitrogen with the result that their nitrogen content decreases, the blossoming spurs draw on a general supply and later upon the new supply of the current season with the result that their nitrogen content is augmented up to the time of fruit setting. This reserve supply is located probably in the phloem, for a marked decrease in the nitrogen content of bark has been found in many plants.[69] In *Rhus elegans* for example the bark at this season has been found to contain 1.52 per cent. of nitrogen in the winter and only 0.36 per cent. in the spring. Similarly in the bark of *Acer platanoides* 26 per cent. of the stored nitrogen disappeared from winter to spring; in the bark of the cherry 37.16 per cent. and in the red beech 30 to 50 per cent. disappeared during shoot growth.

The nitrogen that is moved from the bark into the blossoming spur passes on into the developing fruit, so that in the biennially bearing spur the nitrogen content decreases as long as the fruit is attached. Indeed, the maturing of a large fruit crop may bring about a condition of nitrogen starvation with its attendant manifestations in the vegetative parts of the plant.[220] Murneek[140] has shown that the total nitrogen content of apple spurs is proportional to the leaf area and that it decreases as a result of defoliation.

In Various Tissues of Trees of Different Age.—Table 14 shows the percentages of nitrogen in the leaves, new growth, trunk, roots and fruit of apple trees of ages ranging from 1 to 100. Since the material was collected from various sources, the analyses are not strictly comparable, though they are suggestive.

TABLE 14.—ANALYSES OF APPLE TREES

(1 *to* 9 *from Thompson,*[289] 13 *and* 100 *from Roberts,*[250] 30 *from Van Slyke*[300])

A, nitrogen in percentage of dry weight. *B*, absolute amounts of nitrogen in grams.

Age	Leaves		New growth		Trunks and branches		Roots		Fruit	
	A	*B*	*A*	*B*	*A*	*B*	*A*	*B*	*A*	*B*
1	1.71	0.44	....	......	0.30	0.29	0.39	0.20	....	......
2	2.09	1.51	....	......	0.57	1.36	0.88	1.14	....	......
3	2.36	2.08	....	......	0.52	4.00	0.73	3.29	....	......
4	1.66	2.24	....	......	0.45	6.35	0.59	2.99	....	......
5	1.76	7.84	0.89	1.93	0.48	17.20	0.64	9.85	....	......
6	1.74	10.50	0.94	2.41	0.39	16.60	0.62	17.70	....	......
7	1.45	13.60	0.84	3.66	0.45	30.55	0.64	26.10	0.35	4.34
8	1.74	41.00	0.93	6.06	0.36	45.30	0.62	47.70	0.43	5.93
9	1.70	61.50	0.82	9.08	0.35	85.50	0.58	81.00	0.31	10.55
13	1.85	131.50	....	......	....	....	....	......	....	......
30	2.09	394.00	0.95	13.60	....	....	....	......	0.31	258.00
100	1.04	435.00	1.04	390.00	0.27	2863.00	0.22	417.00	....	......

These figures, along with those presented in Table 13, show that the young tree is specially rich in nitrogen. The roots have a higher percentage content than the trunk, but a lower content than the new growth. The percentage nitrogen content of both roots and trunk falls to a very low level in the 100-year old tree, due to the great preponderance of woody tissue. That of the leaves was estimated from samples collected in the fall and consequently is probably too low, except in the case of the 100-year old tree, where the sample was taken in July.

The most striking observation to be made concerns the large proportion of the total nitrogen of the plant that is in the leaves, roughly about one-fourth in trees up to 9 years of age. Since these figures represent the amounts at leaf fall, even larger amounts must be present in the leaves during the summer.

From the data available it is impossible to say how much of the nitrogen of the trunk is stored and how much is a permanent part of its tissues. Hence any attempt to calculate the amount taken up yearly from the soil would be guess-work. However, it is interesting that in a 30-year old tree, two-thirds as much nitrogen goes into the crop as falls with the leaves and the amount used for new growth is insignificant in comparison.

In Fruit.—Though the nitrogen of the fruit, measured in percentages of dry weight, decreases throughout development on account of the increment in dry matter, the absolute amount present increases continuously. Table 15 shows the nitrogen content of apples in percentages of dry weight and in absolute amounts. The increase in the absolute nitrogen content is rapid at first; in August there is little or no change and in September there is a second period of increase. The periods of increasing nitrogen content correspond to those seasons when temperature and moisture conditions are such as to favor nitrification in the soil.

TABLE 15.—NITROGEN CONTENT OF DEVELOPING APPLES[237]

White Astrakan			Pleissner Rambour		
Date	Percentage of dry weight	Grams in 1,000 fruits	Date	Percentage of dry weight	Grams in 1,000 fruits
May 29	3.28	0.87	June 2	3.65	1.12
June 8	2.20	3.81	June 12	2.78	5.76
June 18	1.57	9.75	June 22	1.76	11.40
June 28	1.21	14.70	July 2	1.26	19.70
July 8	0.71	15.00	July 12	1.48	52.20
July 18	0.51	19.00	July 22	0.54	34.20
July 28	0.29	16.60	Aug. 1	0.65	56.00
Aug. 7	0.37	28.60	Aug. 11	0.63	73.60
Aug. 17	0.58	23.40	Aug. 21	0.56	59.20
Aug. 27	0.23	16.80	Aug. 31	0.39	62.40
			Sept. 10	0.61	91.20
			Sept. 20	0.66	114.00
			Sept. 30	0.47	86.40

Though the nitrogen content of most fruits when mature is not high, the data presented in Table 16 indicate, nevertheless, that large crops remove considerable quantities from the land. Thus, a 25-bushel apple crop contains a little over a pound of nitrogen, the equivalent of that provided by about 7 pounds of nitrate of soda.

TABLE 16.—POUNDS OF NITROGEN IN 1,000 POUNDS OF FRESH FRUIT[56]

Almonds	7.01	Lemons	1.51
Apricots	1.94	Olives	5.60
Apples	1.05	Oranges	1.83
Bananas	0.97	Peaches	1.20
Cherries	2.29	Pears	0.90
Chestnuts	6.40	French prunes	1.82
Figs	2.38	Plums	1.81
Grapes	1.26	Walnuts	5.41

Seeds are much richer in nitrogen. In terms of dry weight, the nitrogen content of apple seeds has been found to be 3.17 per cent.; of almonds 4 per cent.; of coffee (*Coffea arabica*) beans 1.96 per cent.; and of cocoanuts 1.65 per cent.[67] The absolute amounts removed by nut crops such as the almond and walnut, however, are less than those removed by crops of comparable size of most of the fleshy fruits (see Table 16).

PHOSPHORUS

It has been pointed out that the nitrates absorbed by the roots probably are carried to the leaves and there elaborated into organic nitrogen-containing compounds. Though there is no direct evidence to show where the elaboration of inorganic phosphates to organic phosphorus-containing compounds takes place, the remarkable similarity that exists between the variations in nitrogen and in phosphorus content of practically all tissues, suggests that phosphorus, like nitrogen, is elaborated for the most part in the leaf.

Synthesis of Phosphorus-containing Organic Compounds.—The amount of phosphorus assimilated is stated to be closely related to the amount of illumination[216] the plant receives and appears to be connected with photosynthetic activity. Red and yellow light have been found more effective than blue or violet in promoting phosphorus assimilation.[310]

Wherever phosphorus is found in organic combination it exists as phosphate. Thus it occurs in nucleic acids, nucleins and nucleo-proteins —substances always present in the cell nucleus—in lecithins, in hexose phosphoric acid which is essential to zymase activity in yeast and probably to the activity of similar enzymes in all plant tissues. The globoid in aleurone grains is composed of calcium-magnesium phosphate.

Translocation and Use of Phosphorus-containing Compounds.—The distribution of phosphorus in the fruit tree is very similar to that of nitrogen. Young tissue is richer in phosphorus than older tissue, young leaves and young bark being particularly rich in this element and much the same relations hold in regard to elaboration, storage and utilization of phosphorus as with nitrogen. Most tissues contain approximately six times as much nitrogen as phosphorus. This holds roughly for trunk and branches, new growth, buds and young leaves. The older leaves have less phosphorus, the fruit and the apple spur more. The general constancy of the phosphorus-nitrogen ratio indicates that the two elements may be combined in the same molecule. Nucleins, nucleo-proteins and lecithin contain both elements and are of universal occurrence in all living plant tissues. Table 17 shows the relative amounts of the various types of organic phosphorus in developing grape seeds. The bulk is nuclein phosphorus and should this be the case in most plant tissues the relative constancy of the nitrogen-phosphorus ratio would

TABLE 17.—THE PHOSPHORUS CONTENT OF GRAPE SEEDS[68]
(In percentages of fresh weight)

	Hard, Sept. 6	Softening, Sept. 30	Ripe, Oct. 30
Lecithin P.................	0.0017	0.0018	0.0021
Nuclein P.................	0.0159	0.0184	0.0197
HCl-soluble P............	0.0019	0.0016	0.0016
	0.0195	0.0218	0.0234

be explained. Nevertheless distinct differences exist between the variations in the nitrogen and in the phosphorus content of the same tissue and these show that phosphorus compounds do not play the same part in plant metabolism as nitrogen compounds.

If organic phosphorus-containing compounds are built up chiefly in the leaves, they pass out of the leaves as fast as they are made and are used by the developing fruit and in the growth of vegetative tissues. Before the leaves fall, a considerable amount of their phosphorus is withdrawn and stored in the phloem. The phosphorus used in the first stages of growth in the spring and in the initiation of fruit development is obtained from stored compounds.

Seasonal Distribution of Phosphorus.—Some measure of the close similarity between the seasonal distribution of phosphorus and that of nitrogen in many parts of the tree may be obtained by a comparison of Tables 18 and 19 with Tables 13 and 14 and of Figs. 14 and 15 with Figs. 12 and 13.

The young leaf has about the same high percentage of phosphorus as the bud, but this decreases rapidly with age as does the nitrogen, there being two periods of rapid decline, one in May, the other in September (see Fig. 14). The ratio of phosphorus to nitrogen in the young leaf is 1:6. Before leaf fall it is 1:10 or 1:15. This indicates that the plant uses its phosphorus supply more thoroughly than its nitrogen, withdrawing it more completely from tissues that are exfoliated and either using it immediately in tissue building or storing it.

As with nitrogen, the total amount of phosphorus in the leaf is low at first, despite the high percentage, because of the small size of the leaf. It then increases as the leaf grows, reaches a maximum and finally declines, the decline, however, coming only a short time before abscission. Le Clerc and Breazeale[183] have called attention to the possibility that plant tissue may lose considerable amounts of mineral constituents through the dissolving action of rain. In this way apple leaves attached to the branches lost 3 per cent. of their nitrogen, 25 per cent. of their phosphorus, 18 per cent. of their potash and 6 per cent. of their lime simply by washing in water. This indicates that considerable amounts of soluble substances exuded from the surface may be washed off the leaves during the period between the formation of the abscission layer and the time of actual leaf fall.

In Branches, Trunk and Roots.—The percentage of phosphoric acid (P_2O_5) in the ash of sap-wood is usually higher than in bark ash; for example, in the pear it has been recorded as 12.62 per cent. in the sap-wood, as 2.98 per cent. in the bark and in the grape 7.625 per cent. in the sap-wood and 4.705 per cent. in the bark.[96] This does not mean, however, that the bark contains less phosphorus than the sap-wood, for as has been pointed out, the total ash content of wood and especially

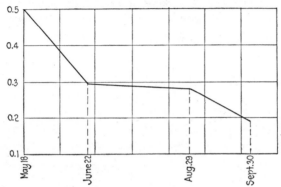

Fig. 14.—Phosphorus content of plum leaves in percentages of dry weight. (*Plotted from data given by Richter.*[246])

sap-wood is much less than that of bark.   The figures indicate that though the sap-wood contains relatively large percentages of phosphoric acid, in the pear and grape at least the bark contains larger absolute amounts.

TABLE 18.—THE PHOSPHORUS CONTENT OF A 7-YEAR OLD APPLE TREE[47]
(Expressed in percentages of dry weight)

	Dormant, Dec. 3, 1914	Buds swelling, April 20, 1915	In bloom, May 18, 1915	Growth over, July 12, 1915	Leaves falling, Oct. 12, 1915
Summer's growth.......	....	....	....	0.14	0.13
1-year old branches.....	0.14	0.16	0.10	0.10	0.10
2-year old branches.....	0.11	0.11	0.07	0.08	0.08
3-year old branches.....	0.08	0.10	0.06	0.07	0.07
4-year old branches.....	0.07	0.07	0.05	0.06	0.06
5-year old branches.....	0.05	0.06	0.04	0.05	0.05
Trunk................	0.04	0.06	0.04	0.06	0.06
Large roots............	0.10	0.12	0.09	0.11	0.12
Small roots............	0.16	0.17	0.14	0.14	0.17

Phosphorus, like nitrogen, is present in greatest amounts in the younger roots and branches and is at a maximum in nearly all tissues when the buds are swelling (see Table 18).   The chief difference between phosphorus and nitrogen is that phosphorus reaches a minimum in most tissues in May when the tree is in bloom, while nitrogen does not reach a minimum until July when active growth is over. In all woody tissues there is an accumulation of phosphorus, as of nitrogen, in the fall, indicating storage.

In Spurs.—Figure 15 shows the seasonal variations in the phosphorus content of apple spurs.[156] In non-bearing and in barren spurs, the variations are similar to those in other woody tissues, with a minimum in May. However, in June during the period of fruit bud differentiation there is a marked increase which is particularly pronounced in spurs differentiating fruit buds. Phosphorus accumulation in the fall is well marked, especially in productive spurs.

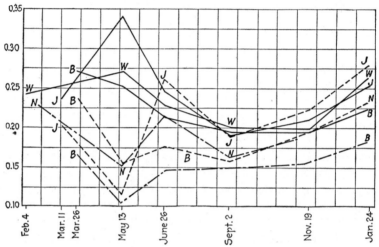

Fig. 15.—Phosphorus content of apple spurs in percentages of dry weight; bearing spurs represented by continuous lines, non-bearing spurs by broken lines and barren spurs by dot-dash lines. (*After Hooker.*[156])

In bearing spurs there is a considerable increase in phosphorus during blossoming, indicating that these organs draw upon a supply of stored phosphorus, which may be assumed, by analogy with nitrogen, to be in the bark. Moreover, the phosphorus content of bark is at a maximum in the spring.

In Various Tissues of Trees of Different Ages.—The percentages and absolute amounts of phosphorus in the tissues of apple trees of various ages are shown in Table 19. In general the new growth and the leaves, even at the time of leaf fall, are richest in phosphorus, the fruit next, then the roots; the trunk and older branches have the lowest percentages, though the absolute amount may be greater than that contained in either leaves or roots. Taken together the analyses indicate that the tree husbands its phosphorus supply carefully. Comparatively little is lost through the leaves at the time of their abscission, and relatively small amounts are locked up in the older parts of trunk, branches and roots where, of necessity, it must remain physiologically inactive. On the other hand, it is translocated freely from places where it has been temporarily accumulated to tissues that require it for growth processes.

TABLE 19.—PHOSPHORUS CONTENT OF APPLE TREES OF VARIOUS AGES
(1 *to* 9 *computed from Thompson,*[289] 13 *and* 100 *from Roberts,*[250] 30 *from Van Slyke*[300])

Age	Leaves		New Growth		Trunk and branches		Roots		Fruits, per cent. dry weight
	Per cent. dry weight	Grams	Per cent. dry weight	Grams	Per cent. dry weight	Grams	Per cent. dry weight	Grams	
1	0.12	0.03	....	.....	0.03	0.03	0.03	0.02	
2	0.13	0.10	....	.....	0.07	0.17	0.10	0.13	
3	0.14	0.13	....	.....	0.07	0.50	0.11	0.47	
4	0.10	0.13	....	.....	0.06	0.80	0.06	0.31	
5	0.11	0.51	0.11	0.24	0.05	1.96	0.06	1.00	
6	0.10	0.63	0.13	0.34	0.04	1.85	0.07	1.99	
7	0.10	0.90	0.11	0.47	0.06	4.14	0.06	2.48	0.08
8	0.11	2.68	0.13	0.82	0.05	6.03	0.07	5.33	0.08
9	0.15	5.33	0.15	1.64	0.08	19.15	0.09	12.62	0.07
13	0.21	15.83	....	.....	....	......	....	.....	....
30	0.13	27.70	0.13	2.00	....	......	....	.....	0.6
100	0.17	73.20	0.16	61.40	0.04	705.00	0.04	83.00	....

In Fruit.—As soon as the fruit begins to develop, the phosphorus content of the bearing spur decreases. At this time the spur probably is supplying the young fruit with phosphorus, which accumulates, to a considerable extent, in fruits and seeds.

A comparison of the figures in Table 20 with those in Table 16 shows that, in general, a fruit crop removes from the orchard only about 10 per cent. as much phosphorus as it does nitrogen, though the range is from 5 to 20.

TABLE 20.—POUNDS OF PHOSPHORUS IN 1,000 POUNDS OF FRESH FRUIT[56]

Almonds	0.45	Lemons	0.25
Apricots	0.29	Olives	0.55
Apples	0.14	Oranges	0.23
Bananas	0.07	Peaches	0.37
Cherries	0.31	Pears	0.15
Chestnuts	0.52	French prunes	0.30
Figs	0.38	Plums	0.33
Grapes	0.05	Walnuts	0.65

Amounts Used in Fruit Production.—Considering the limited amounts of phosphorus used by deciduous fruit trees, and the comparatively large amounts present in nearly all soils as well as the supply in the subsoil available to deep-rooted trees, it is evident that under average orchard conditions phosphorus is not likely to be a limiting factor and that phosphorus fertilizers are likely to be of little direct use in assisting tree growth or in promoting fruit production.   On the other hand it may be of great value in promoting the growth of grasses, legumes or other crops grown between the trees for mulching or other purposes.   This subject is discussed in some detail under the heading of indirect methods of fertilization.

POTASSIUM

Though the history of potassium in a fruit tree like the apple is in many respects similar to that of phosphorus, there are important differences.

Synthesis, Translocation and Use of Potassium-containing Compounds.—It is not known where potassium is elaborated and there is no evidence to show that the inorganic potassium taken from the soil by the roots is combined in organic form in the leaves to any greater extent than in any other part of the plant.   In just what form of organic combination potassium is necessary for the proper activity of the plant is also unknown.   However, certain proteins crystallize as potassium salts; sinigrin is myronate of potash.   Complex salts of calcium, magnesium and potassium are not uncommon.   Gum arabic contains a calcium-magnesium-potassium salt of arabic acid.

During the winter, potassium is stored in both the sapwood and bark and in older branches than nitrogen or phosphorus.   In the spring, it is translocated and used in the development of new tissue, but preeminently for fruit and then for leaves.   Heavy crops reduce the potassium content of the leaves and much more potassium goes into the fruit than is lost with the leaves.   In general wherever potassium is present in large amounts as in seeds and in young tissue, calcium is present in small quantities and wherever there is a small amount of potassium, calcium is present in large amounts.

Seasonal Distribution of Potassium.—Rather marked differences between potassium and the elements already considered, in translocation, storage and utilization are shown by the seasonal changes in its distribution within the plant.

In Leaves.—Fruit buds are much richer than leaf buds in potassium, contrasting with the condition presented by phosphorus.   Thus the potash content of fruit buds has been found to be 2.290 per cent. of the dry weight in the cherry and 2.344 per cent. in the plum, while that of leaf buds was 1.961 per cent. in the cherry and 2.213 per cent. in the plum.[246]

The variation in the percentage content of potash in leaves during the growing season is illustrated by the figures in Table 21.   As with phosphorus and nitrogen the percentage of potassium decreases as the leaf grows older and the absolute amount present in the leaf passes through a maximum.   However, the decrease in the potash content of leaves during the fall is slight in all fruits for which data are available.   The marked difference in this respect between potassium and

TABLE 21.—POTASH CONTENT OF LEAVES
(In percentage of dry weight[246])

	Apple	Pear	Cherry
May 9....................	3.150	2.460	
May 14....................	.....	.....	3.006
June 22....................	1.886	1.690	2.782
Aug. 29....................	1.927	1.770	2.637
Oct. 2....................	.....	1.320	3.080
Oct. 15....................	1.601		

phosphorus or nitrogen suggests a corresponding difference in their utilization by the plant.

Though the amounts of potassium removed from the leaves before they fall seem small in comparison with phosphorus, there is none the less evidence of potassium storage in the branches.

In Branches, Roots and Trunks.—The leaves lose more potassium than can be accounted for by the gain in the branches on which they were borne, indicating that considerable amounts of potash are washed from the leaves by rain. The relative amounts of potash in the ash of sap-wood and bark resemble those of phosphorus. In one series of determinations the ash of the sap-wood of the pear was 22.25 per cent. potash, of the bark 6.2 per cent.; the sap-wood ash of the apple was 16.19 per cent. potash, the bark ash 4.93 per cent. and the sap-wood ash of the grape was 20.84 per cent. potash, the bark ash 1.77 per cent.[96] In the sap-wood ash there is more potash than any other element except calcium; in the bark the potash content is lower and the calcium content higher, but the absolute amount in the bark is probably greater than in the sap-wood on account of the bark's higher ash content.

Table 22, showing seasonal variations in the potash content of the root, trunk and branches of a 7-year old apple tree, gives additional evidence of the storage of potassium in the branches. Apparently potassium is stored in old branches to a relatively greater extent than nitrogen or phosphorus, for in the 3-, 4- and 5-year old branches the potash content reaches a minimum in May though the 1- and 2-year old branches have a high content at that time and do not reach a minimum until later. The young roots and branches are richer in potassium, as in phosphorus and nitrogen, than the older parts of the tree.

Potassium is stored in both bark and sap-wood. The layers of bark nearest the cambium are richest in this element. Furthermore, the young bark of the oak, horse-chestnut and walnut contains more potash in percentage of total ash at the time of greatest vegetative activity in the spring than later in the season.[80] Similar seasonal differences occur in the potash content of the sap-wood of these trees, while the heart-wood not only contains considerably less but its content is subject to much smaller fluctuations.[75] Weber[311] found that in beeches producing many seeds, the sap-wood was particularly rich in potash while the phosphorus content was not materially greater than in trees bearing few seeds. Warren[308] found that in peach, apple, plum and pear trees the ash of

TABLE 22.—THE POTASH CONTENT OF A 7-YEAR OLD APPLE TREE
(Expressed in percentages of dry weight[47])

	Dormant, Dec. 3	Buds swelling, Apr. 20	In bloom, May 18	Growth over, July 12	Leaves falling, Oct. 12
Summer's growth.......	....	....	....	1.03	0.60
1-year old branches.....	0.46	0.49	0.62	0.52	0.47
2-year old branches.....	0.33	0.33	0.39	0.33	0.40
3-year old branches.....	0.30	0.27	0.28	0.31	0.33
4-year old branches.....	0.24	0.25	0.20	0.25	0.29
5-year old branches.....	0.20	0.22	0.17	0.20	0.28
Trunk................	0.15	0.21	0.20	0.18	0.25
Large roots............	0.42	0.40	0.39	0.43	0.40
Small roots............	0.57	0.45	0.45	0.54	0.65

the leaves contained less potash in years when the crop was large. This suggests that fruit trees usually take up more potassium from the soil than is actually required, when they are not bearing fruit.

In Spurs.—Figure 16 shows that the potassium content of bearing spurs rises to a very high maximum in May. This increment passes into the fruit and the potassium content of the spur falls to a minimum in September. The low figure for barren spurs throughout the year is noteworthy, as is also the increase in the

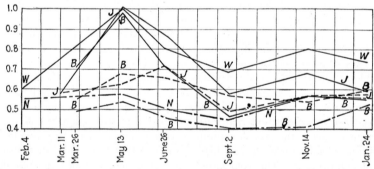

FIG. 16.—Potassium content of apple spurs in percentages of dry weight; bearing spurs represented by continuous lines, non-bearing spurs by broken lines and barren spurs by dot-dash lines. (*After Hooker.*[156])

potassium content of spurs in the off year at the time when fruit buds are being differentiated (June).

In Various Tissues of Trees of Different Age.—Table 23 shows the variations with age in the several parts of apple trees. It is noteworthy in connection with what has been said of the relations of potash content to bearing that the 30-year old trees have the lowest percentage of potash in the leaves. These trees were in full bearing, as reference to the last column of the table shows. Furthermore, there is no reduction in the percentage of potash in the leaves of the

100-year old trees which were not in bearing at the time the analyses were made. The leaves of a tree in full bearing contain much less potassium when they fall than its fruit.

TABLE 23.—POTASH CONTENT OF APPLE TREES OF VARIOUS AGES
(1 *to* 9 *from Thompson*,[289] 13 *and* 100 *from Roberts*,[250] 30 *from Van Slyke*[300])
A, percentage of dry weight.   *B*, grams

Age	Leaves		New growth		Trunk and branches		Roots		Fruit	
	A	*B*	*A*	*B*	*A*	*B*	*A*	*B*	*A*	*B*
1	1.25	0.33	....	....	0.21	0.20	0.30	0.18	....	......
2	1.22	0.88	....	....	0.34	0.81	0.55	0.71	....	......
3	1.35	1.22	....	....	0.30	2.31	0.53	2.39	....	......
4	1.13	1.53	....	....	0.31	4.37	0.48	2.43	....	......
5	1.65	7.79	0.72	1.56	0.47	16.84	0.57	9.34	....	......
6	1.00	6.04	0.61	1.56	0.35	14.87	0.50	16.30	....	......
7	1.24	11.64	0.55	2.40	0.36	24.45	0.46	18.70	1.12	13.87
8	1.42	33.50	0.64	4.17	0.31	39.00	0.48	36.95	1.20	16.56
9	2.08	75.20	0.61	6.76	0.33	80.60	0.49	68.40	1.17	39.83
13	1.76	127.00	....	....	....	......	....	......	....	......
30	0.59	122.00	0.60	9.00	....	......	....	......	0.70	589.00
100	1.43	598.00	0.80	4.00	0.41	2697.00	0.22	417.00	....	......

Comparison with Table 14 shows that the absolute amounts of potassium actually utilized and retained by the different vegetative tissues of the tree are not greatly different from those of nitrogen.

In Fruit.—In most edible fruits potash comprises 30 to 60 per cent. of the total ash and that of seeds is about the same as that of fruits.[70] Comparison of the figures in Table 24 with those in Tables 16 and 20 indicates that in general slightly larger amounts of potassium are removed with the crop than is true of nitrogen and from 10 to 20 times as much as of phosphorus.

TABLE 24.—POUNDS OF POTASH IN 1,000 POUNDS OF FRESH FRUIT[56]

Almonds	9.95	Lemons	2.54
Apricots	3.01	Olives	9.11
Apples	1.40	Oranges	2.11
Bananas	6.80	Peaches	3.94
Cherries	2.77	Pears	1.34
Chestnuts	3.67	French prunes	3.10
Figs	4.69	Plums	3.41
Grapes	2.55	Walnuts	8.18

The Demand and the Supply.—In one way or another the idea has gained credence that fruit trees make heavy demands on the soil for potash and consequently that potash is one of the most necessary ingredients in fertilizers for orchards. Indeed, so firmly has this idea become established that "Fertilize trees with nitrogen for wood growth and with potash for fruit production" is a time-honored recommendation in the literature of fruit growing. It has also been a rather general opinion that potash mainly is responsible for the red coloration of fruits and that consequently potash-carrying fertilizers are especially desirable for improving color. That this last idea is erroneous is shown by the results of many carefully conducted investigations of recent years, investigations that are reported in more detail later in this section. The data in this chapter afford some idea of the approximate amounts of potash that are required for usual tree growth and production. Though these are considerable in comparison with the amounts required by many farm crops, the enormous quantities of this element found within reach of tree roots in most soils make the application of potash-carrying fertilizers seem of doubtful promise, at least so far as supplying the plant with larger quantities of this element is concerned. This statement is supported by numerous experiments in which potash in different forms has been applied to orchard trees apparently without positive results, and also by soil investigations like those of Hopkins and Aumer,[158] showing that in 6 feet of soil covering an area of 1 square mile of the Illinois corn belt there is as much potash as is applied annually in fertilizers to all the farms of the United States. It is true that many orchard soils are not so liberally supplied with potash as those of the Illinois corn belt; nevertheless, so far as data are available, they indicate the presence of quantities much in excess of probable requirements for many years, if not for many generations. Beneficial results in greater vegetative growth and increased yields have been reported occasionally from the application of potash-carrying fertilizers to orchard soils. The question may be raised, whether this increase in growth or yield is due to indirect effects of the potash on some other factor, such as the availability of phosphorus, or to the influence of other elements with which potassium is combined in the fertilizer. This last suggestion receives some support from the fact that in most cases when the muriate and sulphate of potash have been used side by side, the sulphate has almost invariably given a much more pronounced response than the muriate and has often yielded positive results when the muriate has given entirely negative results.

SULPHUR

Data are not available to present such a detailed picture of what happens to sulphur in the fruit tree as has been attempted with nitrogen, phosphorus and potash. The inorganic sulphate taken from the soil is incorporated into organic compounds as both sulphate and sulphide sulphur. As sulphate, it occurs in some of the mustard oils, such as sinigrin; as sulphide, it occurs in cystin, one of the amino-acids used in the construction of most proteins.

Because considerable amounts of sulphur are lost in ashing, many of the determinations that have been reported are of doubtful value. The evidence indicates, however, that the tree absorbs and probably utilizes as much sulphur as it does phosphorus. In the apple the greatest amount has been found in the leaves (0.22 to 0.48 per cent.), with progressively smaller percentages in the spurs, the young bark and old bark.[201] In a number of tissues the seasonal trends of sulphur have been found to be the opposite to those of phosphorus. Furthermore, a more or less close parallelism of changes in sulphur content and hydrogen-ion concentration[201] of certain tissues suggests that sulphur may be important in determining their degree of acidity and the further fact that the initiation and the breaking of the rest period seem to be limited with high and low acidity, respectively,[2] links this element with that important process.

The data in Table 25 are representative of a few reliable analyses of sulphur in fruit plants. They show that fruit contains approximately as much sulphur as phosphorus.

TABLE 25.—POUNDS OF SULPHUR IN 1,000 POUNDS OF FRESH FRUITS[261]

Apples	0.43	Grapefruit	0.20
Raspberries	0.35	Peach pulp	0.14
Gooseberries	0.12	Oranges	0.26
Dewberries	0.37	Lemons	0.22
Cherries	1.08	Limes	0.47
Red currants	0.56	Pineapple	0.39
Blackberries	0.40		

Sulphur has been thought generally to be present in most soils in amounts sufficient to meet the requirements of crop plants and recent investigations would indicate that this condition holds for a great many soils. Thus the sulphur content of Illinois soils has been reported as ranging from 280 to 750 pounds per acre in the top $6\frac{2}{3}$ inches.[279] Since the average growing crop removes only 4 to 10 pounds of this element per acre and losses through seepage are likely to be nearly offset by additions through rainfall, it would appear that the application of sulphur as fertilizer to such soils does not offer much promise of increased crop returns. However alfalfa removes 40 pounds per acre per year and cabbage nearly as much. Moreover there are many soils not so well supplied with sulphur and Shull[265] is authority for the statement that "the normal sulphur content of soils is sufficient for from 15 to 70 crops, provided there are no additions from outside sources as from rainfall. Even if we count in the rainfall sulphur, it is probable that sulphur is just as often a limiting factor as is phosphorus, or nitrogen, or potassium." The soils of the Rogue River valley in southern Oregon have been found very poor in sulphur and applications of compounds containing this element have greatly increased yields of leguminous crops.[244]   In some instances these increases have amounted to 500 to 1,000 per cent.   Without doubt these conditions are very exceptional; nevertheless the results suggest that sulphur may be a much more important limiting factor in soil productivity than has been considered generally.   Recent investigations indicate that sulphates have a special influence on root development.[134] This is particularly marked with red clover and rape, where sulphate applications resulted in root elongation and consequently in an extension of the feeding area and a greater ability to withstand drought.   Little is known regarding the direct effect of sulphur-carrying fertilizers on deciduous fruits.   However, the application of 178 pounds of sulphur per acre to certain vineyard soils has resulted in increases in yield of 19.2 to 32.7 per cent. and in increases of 25.03 to 27.3 per cent. when applied with 14 tons of stable manure.[54]   Though no direct influence of sulphur-carrying fertilizers upon tree growth or production was reported in the Rogue River valley experiments the crops so greatly benefited by their application were those commonly grown as intercrops and cover crops in the orchard.   Through them the trees might be greatly benefited in later years.

Heavy applications of sulphur to the soil result in markedly increasing its acidity, a change, however, that is not permanent.   In some instances sulphur applications have been made to pineapple plantations to secure this effect, thereby increasing the availability of iron and reducing injury from mole crickets.[149]

These facts taken with the lack of data on the distribution of sulphur in plants accentuate the importance of more analytical and experimental work on this element.   Sulphur has been neglected because it was thought to occur in relatively small amounts, but the small amounts found were due to faulty methods of analysis and sulphur is just as essential to plants and as worthy of consideration as phosphorus.

IRON

Iron occurs in plants in even smaller amounts than sulphur.   It is found in organic combination in some nucleic acids.[236]

Iron usually constitutes 1 to 4 per cent. of the leaf ash.   Grape leaves have been known to have an exceptionally high figure, 10.20 per cent.[84]   The absolute iron content of leaves increases with age, though the percentage composition of the leaf remains fairly constant.   The ash of bark ranges from 0.2 to 3 per cent. of iron, the amount often increasing with age; for example 0.2 per cent. has been found in the apple and 2.545 per cent. in the grape.[96]   Wood ash has but little iron, usually from 0.1 to 0.8 per cent.—0.16 per cent. in the pear, 0.42 per cent. in the apple and 0.635 per cent. in the grape.[96]   Exceptionally high figures have been found in the olive, 2.11 per cent. of the ash, and in the orange, 3.08 per cent.[78]

TABLE 26.—THE IRON OXIDE CONTENT OF FRUITS[86] AND SEEDS[72]
(In percentages of total ash)

Fruits		Seeds	
Banana	1.46	Grape	0.37
Plum	2.54	Almond	0.55
Apple	1.40	Walnut	1.32
Pear	1.04	Coffee	0.65
Orange	0.46	Chestnut	0.14
Grape	1.04		
Olive	0.72		

Iron is a constituent of practically all soils; furthermore it is always found in quantities sufficient for the requirements of crop plants. However, in many cases it is held in the soil in a form unavailable to the plant; consequently the plants may suffer because of iron starvation. Reference has been made to this in connection with the discussion of soil reaction and more is said regarding the disturbances caused by a lack of iron and methods of dealing with them under the heading of Surpluses and Deficiencies.

MAGNESIUM

The most important organic compound containing magnesium is chlorophyll. This element also occurs in organic combination in salts of arabic acid and in the globoid of aleurone grains. Some proteins are thought to contain magnesium. Anthocyan pigments are complex compounds with salts of magnesium, calcium or other metals.[262]

The absolute amount of magnesia in leaves increases as they grow older. Thus 500 leaves of *Platanus* were found to contain 0.24 gram of magnesia on June 13, 0.85 gram at the end of August and 0.69 gram at leaf fall, showing a slight decline.[83] However, there is not much change in the percentage of magnesia in the total ash. On May 16, in beech leaves it was found to be 4.36 per cent.; on July 18, 5.63 per cent. and on Oct. 15, 4.12 per cent.[233] The magnesium, like the iron content, keeps pace with leaf development; this increase may be associated with the chlorophyll content of the leaf. However, there is some evidence that magnesium is withdrawn to the branches from the leaves late in the season. There are also indications of magnesium storage in the sap-wood, which is slightly richer in magnesium than the heart-wood. During the spring, there is more magnesium in the sap-wood than at other times. Weber found that in beeches producing many seeds, the sap-wood was especially rich in magnesia and potash, as compared with trees bearing few seeds.[311] The sap-wood ash of the pear has been found to contain 3 per cent. magnesia, of the grape 4.4 per cent. and of the apple 8.49 per cent.[96]

The magnesia content of bark ash decreases with age. In young bark it is 3 to 8 per cent., as in the leaves; in old bark 2 to 5 per cent. Thus the magnesia of pear bark has been found to be 9.4 per cent. of the ash, while in the apple bark it is 1.5 per cent. and in grape bark 0.8 per cent.[96] The sieve tubes sometimes contain magnesium phosphate; this may be a form of storage.

As a rule fat-storing seeds are richer in magnesia than starchy or reserve-cellulose seeds; in the almond, magnesia has been found to be 17.66 per cent. of the ash, in the walnut 13.03 per cent., while in coffee (*Coffea arabica*) beans it is 9.69 per cent. and in chestnuts 7.47 per cent.[71] The leaves of fruit trees contain much more magnesium than the fruit. In the apple the magnesia content of the fruit has been found to be 0.10 per cent. of the dry weight; of the leaves 1.03 per cent. and of the new growth 0.30 per cent.[300]

TABLE 27.—THE MAGNESIA CONTENT OF FRUITS[86]
(In percentages of total ash)

Pineapple	9.79	Pear	5.22
Banana	9.21	Orange	8.06
Strawberry	2.93	Grape	2.61
Plum	4.69	Olive	0.18
Apple	8.75		

Though magnesium is necessary for plant growth, it is not required in large quantities and so far as is known all soils contain sufficient amounts. Certainly no data are available showing the necessity of fertilizing fruit plantations with magnesium-carrying compounds.

CALCIUM

Calcium is for the most part absent from the growing points and from embryonic tissues generally and it accumulates in all tissues with age. This indicates that calcium is utilized in ways very different from the other essential elements, a surmise substantiated by the fact that it is not necessary for the growth of fungi.

It is found organically combined in calcium oxalate crystals, in calcium pectate of the middle lamella which holds adjoining cells together, in salts of arabic acid, in the globoid of aleurone grains and in the anthocyan pigments. It is prevalent also as calcium carbonate.

Seasonal Distribution of Calcium.—Calcium differs from the elements previously discussed in its seasonal history in the tree. Thus where potassium is present in large amounts, calcium is usually present in small amounts and *vice versa*.

In Buds and Leaves.—The calcium content of buds is not great as compared with that of other plant tissues. Leaf buds have more lime, but less potassium, than fruit buds. In percentages of dry weight, the lime content of leaf buds has been found to be 1.364 per cent. in the cherry and 2.365 per cent. in the plum; that of fruit buds was 1.113 per cent. in the cherry and 1.761 per cent. in the plum.[246] Very heavy deposits of calcium oxalate have been found in resting fruit buds, the amount decreasing after growth begins. As leaves grow older their percentage lime content increases. In most cases there is a reduction in the absolute calcium content before leaf fall, probably because of the dissolving action of rain. The lime content of full grown leaves is often very great, sometimes constituting 52.82 per cent. of the ash of the olive, 54.33 per cent. of the ash of the apple, 56.83 per cent. of the ash of the orange and 34 to 60.9 per cent. of the ash of the grape.[81]

The data in Table 28 showing the simultaneous changes in the calcium content of leaves and branches indicate that there is no removal of calcium from the leaves to the branches.

TABLE 28.—GRAMS OF LIME IN 100 BRANCHES OF HORSE-CHESTNUT AND THEIR LEAVES[13]

	Branches	Leaves
July 29.................	4.274	27.292
Sept. 11.................	6.549	39.785
Oct. 14.................	5.938	51.201
Nov. 16.................	5.804	......

In Bark and Wood.—Young bark contains considerable lime, about 40 per cent. of the ash, chiefly in the form of calcium carbonate. It increases with age to 70 or 80 per cent. of the ash, sometimes reaching 95 per cent. in oak bark.[82] Pear bark ash has been found to contain 33.88 per cent. lime, apple bark ash 51.84 per cent. and grape bark ash 42.05 per cent.[96] The seasonal variation is counter to that of potassium, there being proportionately less calcium in the bark in the spring than at other times. For example, in the walnut, bark ash was found to contain 8.37 per cent. calcium on May 31 and 70.08 per cent. on Aug. 27.[82] Calcium increases with age in the wood also and the heart-wood contains progressively more than the sap-wood, as Table 29 shows.

In general 60 to 78 per cent. of wood ash is lime. In the orange it has been known to rise to 68.88 per cent.[77] In the sap-wood there is less; in the pear there has been found 27.39 per cent., in the apple 18.65 per cent. and in the grape 25.67 per cent.[96] In the heart-wood, the vessels and sometimes the tracheids, wood fibers and parenchyma cells are filled with spherites of calcium carbonate. The older the wood, the more calcium there is in its ash.

In Fruits.—In fruit trees, the calcium required by the crop is insignificant compared with that lost with the leaves and sometimes it is less than that in the new growth. In one set of determinations the lime in apple leaves was 3.10 per cent. of their dry weight; in new growth 2.39 per cent. and in the fruit 0.06 per cent.[300]

TABLE 29.—ASH CONTENT OF HEART-WOOD IN A RED BEECH[327]
(In percentages of dry weight)

Rings	Ash	CaCO₃
1 to 15	1.162	0.579
15 to 25	0.825	0.251
25 to 35	0.645	Trace
35 to 45	0.612	Trace
45 to 60	0.555	.....
60 to 83	0.458	.....
83 to 94 (sap-wood)	0.205	.....

TABLE 30.—POUNDS OF LIME IN 1,000 POUNDS OF FRESH FRUIT[56]

Almonds	1.04	Lemons	1.55
Apricots	0.16	Olives	2.43
Apples	0.11	Oranges	0.97
Bananas	0.10	Peaches	0.14
Cherries	0.20	Pears	0.19
Chestnuts	1.20	French prunes	0.22
Figs	0.85	Plums	0.25
Grapes	0.25	Walnuts	1.55

According to Trabut, "a high lime content is a very favorable factor in growing olives for oil production, as olives produced in limestone regions are richer in oil and the oil is of better quality than where the soils are deficient in this component."[165]

The Demand and the Supply.—In general it may be said that the calcium requirements of fruit trees are insignificant compared with the amounts usually available in the soil. For instance, it has been shown that certain typical Illinois soils contain quantities sufficient in the surface layers to produce 5,000 to 55,000 heavy corn crops if the supply is not replenished and if it becomes available gradually.[280] All the chemical analyses of fruit soils given in the chapter on Orchard Soils indicate that the danger from calcium starvation in the orchard is very remote. In all probability the amounts of calcium found in plant tissues are often much in excess of their nutritive requirements. There is no doubt that calcium is of use in the elimination of poisonous products of catabolism, such as oxalic acid, but it seems not at all unlikely that in many cases the oxalic acid is produced as a means of rendering a surplus of calcium insoluble.

Many orchard fertilizer experiments have been conducted in which lime has been used, either alone or in combination. The results attending these experiments have been variable, but on the whole negative in character. Certainly there is no clear evidence available to show that liming the soil is of any direct benefit to the trees. It has been pointed out that applications of lime may aid nitrification in the soil and may be of use to other cultures that are being grown in the fruit plantation and thus indirectly to the trees; on the other hand, it has been shown also that they may have a very deleterious influence on tree or vine growth and these deleterious influences are of sufficiently frequent occurrence in actual field practice to suggest caution. It may be recalled that the purpose for which lime is generally used with field crops, namely the correction of soil acidity, needs but little consideration in deciduous fruit production.

OTHER MINERAL ELEMENTS

Besides the elements already discussed, there are others that are of almost universal occurrence in plants. They have been considered to be unessential but recent investigations have shown that some of them are apparently required in minute quantities for normal growth and reproduction,[10,129] and in some instances they become a limiting factor in crop production.

Silicon.—Silica is universally present in both soils and plants, though the amount is very variable. In leaves, for example, it may be present in mere traces or it may constitute 80 per cent. of the ash. In grape leaves amounts ranging from 1.61 per cent. to 39.44 per cent. have been found, the amount usually increasing with age.[85]

Bark ash usually contains less than 2 per cent. of silica; for example, 0.4 per cent. in the pear and 0.6 per cent. in the apple.[96] The ash of grape bark has been shown to contain 14.3 per cent. silica.[96] Wood ash usually contains less than 3 per cent. of silica; for example, 0.3 per cent. has been recorded for pear wood, 1.65 per cent. for apple wood and 2.8 per cent. for grape wood.[96] The ash of olive wood has been found to contain as much as 14.23 per cent. silica.[79] As a rule the heart-wood contains a higher percentage than the sap-wood.

Fruits contain silica in amounts shown in Table 31. The seed usually contains less, as the same table shows, though a trace at least is always present.

TABLE 31.—THE SILICA CONTENT OF FRUITS[86] AND SEEDS[72]
(In percentages of total ash)

Fruits		Seeds	
Pineapple	5.77	Chestnut	1.54
Banana	5.93	Grape	1.04
Fig	2.34	Coffee	0.54
Plum	3.15	Cocoanut	0.50
Apple	4.32	Walnut	Trace
Pear	1.49		
Orange	0.44		
Grape	1.00		
Olive	0.65		

Silicon usually is associated with the cell wall and sometimes confers strength and stability on a plant tissue. However, the strongest and hardest of plant materials are often of very nearly pure cellulose; hence, a lack of silicon does not necessarily involve mechanical weakness of mature tissues. So far as is known, silicon is not essential to plant growth.

Sodium.—Sodium also is of universal occurrence in plant tissues. Leaves usually contain 1 to 3 per cent. Bark and wood ash usually contain but little soda, 3.495 per cent. having been recorded in the ash of apple bark and 0.27 per cent. in that of grape bark.[96] The wood of the sweet cherry has been known to contain as much as 10.13 per cent.[76] As a rule there is less soda in the ash of heart-wood than in that of sap-wood, certain sap-wood records showing for the pear 1.84 per cent. soda; for the apple, 3.275 per cent. and for the grape, 2.06 per cent.[96] Fruits contain soda in the widely varying amounts shown in Table 32.

TABLE 32.—THE SODA CONTENT OF FRUITS[86]
(In percentages of total ash)

Pineapple	6.75	Apple	26.09
Banana	26.27	Pear	8.52
Fig	19.63	Orange	13.47
Plum	9.05	Olive	7.53

Seeds usually contain less than fruits, from 1 to 2 per cent., but walnuts have been recorded as having 2.25 per cent., cocoanuts 8.39 per cent. and dates 9.03 per cent.[70]

Though sodium is regarded as unessential for the growth of very many plants, investigations with turnips, radishes, beets, cucumbers, buckwheat, oats, potatoes and a number of other crop plants, indicate that this element can partially replace potassium when the latter is not present in amounts sufficient for good growth.[138] "In the field, however, more potassium was removed in the larger crops which usually resulted when sodium was increased in connection with an insufficient amount of potassium, and this was in spite of the fact that sodium frequently decreased the percentage of potassium in the crop. A portion of the benefits arising from the use of sodium in the field is, therefore, attributable to indirect action, but the solution work indicates that also direct beneficial effects were probably obtained in the field."[138]

Probably this function of sodium is of little direct importance in the deciduous fruit plantation, since it is very seldom that a lack of potassium is a limiting factor; however, it is at least a matter of interest.

Chlorine.—Chlorine occurs in many plants, but seldom in large amounts except in salt marsh plants. In leaves the amount varies from 25 per cent. of the total ash to mere traces. The chlorine content of bark ash is low, certain records in the pear showing 1.7 per cent., in the apple 0.33 per cent. and in the grape 0.4 per cent.[96] The chlorine content of wood ash is even less, being 0.31 per cent. in the pear, 0.255 per cent. in the apple and 0.02 per cent. in the grape.[96] The chlorine content of fruits is more variable, but never very great.

TABLE 33.—THE CHLORINE CONTENT OF FRUITS[86]
(In percentages of total ash)

Pineapple	Trace	Plum	0.38
Banana	2.69	Orange	2.35
Fig	0.83	Olive	0.16

Seeds usually have 0.5 to 1.5 per cent. of chlorine in the ash, but the amount present varies greatly. Walnuts and almonds have mere traces. Other records are: for chestnuts, 0.52 per cent. of the ash, for grape seeds, 0.27 per cent. and for the cocoanut, which grows on the seashore, 13.42 per cent.[73]

There is no definite relation between the amount of sodium and the amount of chlorine a tissue contains.

It would appear from the preceding statements that no benefit would be derived from the chlorine in fertilizers carrying this element. Common salt has often been suggested as having possible value as a fertilizer and has been tried in a limited way. So far as records are available they indicate that it is of no value for deciduous or for most other fruit trees. However, greatly increased yields of the mango have been reported in the province of Bombay, India, from applying 10 pounds to the tree and likewise marked increases in yield from its application to cocoanuts.[115] To what extent these increases were due to direct or indirect effects of the sodium or the direct or indirect effects of the chlorine is not known.

Aluminum.—Aluminum is not uncommon in seeds. It sometimes comprises 0.062 per cent. of the ash of fig seeds and 0.138 per cent. of the ash of almonds.[74] Aluminum is capable of forming complex salts with the anthocyan pigments.[101] The color of the pigment depends on the base which it contains, which accounts for the fact that the hydrangea (*H. hortensis*) develops blue instead of pink flowers when soluble aluminum compounds are applied to the soil in which it grows.[215]

Manganese.—Manganese is a common constituent of the bark of trees, where it may constitute as much as one per cent. of the ash. The other parts of the tree usually have less. So far as is known, a lack of manganese has not proven to be a limiting factor in fruit production, though a chlorotic condition of a number of other plants has been associated with manganese deficiency in the soil.[191] More frequently an excess of manganese in the soil has led to chlorosis through making the iron unavailable.[166]

Copper.—Small quantities of copper are taken up from the soil by the roots and considerable amounts may also be absorbed by the leaves following applications of Bordeaux mixture or other copper-containing sprays.[59] That these small quantities may be necessary for normal growth is indicated by investigations of Maquenne and Demoussey,[197] by fertilizer studies on some of the raw everglade soils in Florida[10] and by the fact that in both California[49] and New South Wales[203] citrus trees affected by "yellows" and exanthema have been cured by treating the soil with small amounts of copper sulphate.

Boron.—Boron has been shown to be essential to the growth of some plants, though in the case of others it apparently is either unnecessary or is required in such extremely small amounts that what is stored in the seeds will suffice for the life of the plant.[40]   Some of the soils and irrigation waters of California apparently carry such large amounts of this element that it is toxic to citrus trees and walnuts, whereas in other cases the amounts present are so small that the trees develop serious nutritional disorders because of its deficiency.

Zinc.—Another element that until recently has not been considered essential for the growth of plants is zinc.   Apparently this has been due to the fact that very small quantities suffice and most soils contain enough to supply all that is required.   With the discovery, however, that certain forms of yellows or mottle leaf in citrus fruits,[242,243] rosette and little leaf in the walnut, pecan and apple[98] and "bronzing" in the tung oil tree[218] are alleviated by treatment with certain zinc-containing salts, this element has come to assume a rather important role.

Summary.—Certain elements, especially nitrogen, phosphorus, potassium and sulphur are present in greatest amount in young tissues.   Certain amounts are stored in the bark over the winter and in the spring a supply is on hand for the rapid development of leaves and shoots, flowers, fruit and seeds.   Since the seeds themselves are storage organs and in addition contain embryonic tissue, they accumulate these elements in relatively large proportions.   Magnesium and iron likewise are stored in the bark and in the wood as well.   They are utilized in new growth, though they appear to be more equally distributed in mature and in embryonic tissues.   All of these elements show more or less mobility and are translocated to regions where they are more in demand.   The plant conserves its supply and withdraws at least a part of the amount contained in the leaves, after they have ceased to function.

Calcium and silicon are very nearly absent from embryonic tissues. They accumulate throughout the plant with age.   There are no indications that these elements are stored for future use and to a great degree they remain where they are deposited.

With respect to the other mineral elements found in plants, little can be said in generalization.   This is because no regularity has been observed in the amounts present or in their seasonal variation.   Nevertheless, it appears that manganese, copper, boron and zinc are essential in the nutrition of plants and that field soils may contain such small amounts of them in an available form that serious disorders arise.

CHAPTER IX

MANUFACTURE AND UTILIZATION OF CARBOHYDRATES

The essential elements discussed in the previous section are used ultimately in the construction of the plant's substance. They are indispensable because the plant cannot be constructed unless each one of them is present.

ASSIMILATION AND LIMITING FACTORS DEFINED

The term assimilation, in its broadest sense, is used to describe the process by which a plant builds up the substances that comprise it out of compounds obtained from its environment. To be sure any compound will not serve; certain specific materials are necessary. Assimilation depends on a supply of such materials and on a source of energy. The amount of assimilation and hence of growth is determined by the operation of the principle of limiting factors.

Most plants require at least seven elements in combined form from the soil, namely, S, P, N, K, Fe, Mg and Ca. If αS, βP, γN, δK, ϵFe, ζMg and ηCa combine exactly to produce a unit amount of growth in some particular plant, say an apple tree, and if aS, bP, cN, dK, eFe, fMg and gCa are present in a particular soil in available form, the maximum amount of apple tree tissue that can be grown in that soil will be the smallest of the fractions a/α, b/β, c/γ, d/δ, e/ϵ, f/ζ, g/η. That element which gives the smallest fraction is the limiting factor of growth.[155]

The principle of limiting factors applies not merely to nitrogen and the essential mineral elements, but also to water, to carbon dioxide and to oxygen which likewise are essential nutrients entering into the composition of the plant. Moreover the principle covers the effects of external factors such as temperature and light which also may be limiting factors of assimilation. All these possible limiting factors of assimilation and growth constitute the external stimuli to which the organism reacts and these reactions tend to overcome the limiting factors of assimilation and so bring the organism in the most favorable situation for assimilation that circumstances permit. In consequence of the reactivity of the plant and its apparent complete adjustment to its environment the principle of limiting factors sometimes may seem not to be operative. This, however, is not the case, for the principle of limiting factors is always effective. The principle is generally recognized in the saying that a chain is no stronger than its weakest link and it is so universally applied in everyday life that it is taken as a matter of course and consequently overlooked.

The principle of limiting factors is particularly important for an understanding of the process of carbon assimilation and it has a direct practical application in the use of fertilizers. These two subjects are discussed in the following pages.

CARBON ASSIMILATION

The synthesis of organic compounds in plants depends on the assimilation of an element which occurs in and is characteristic of all organic compounds, namely, carbon. This element is provided by the carbon dioxide of the air, which, together with water absorbed by the roots, furnishes the materials for the synthesis of carbohydrates. These compounds contain more potential energy than those from which they are formed; this energy is supplied by the sun, whose radiant energy is transformed into the potential energy of carbohydrates by means of the green pigments of the leaf, the chlorophylls. The reaction or reactions by which water and carbon dioxide in the presence of light and through the agency of chlorophyll form carbohydrates and oxygen depend on two other factors, namely, enzymes and temperature which affects the rate of all chemical reactions.

Factors Involved

The rate of carbon assimilation depends on six factors:
1. The supply of carbon dioxide.
2. The supply of water.
3. The intensity, duration and quality of light.
4. The amount of chlorophyll.
5. Temperature.
6. The amount of enzymes.

Carbon Dioxide.—The carbon dioxide content of the atmosphere is practically constant, varying little from 3 parts in each 10,000 of air. Carbon dioxide enters the leaf mainly through the stomata, though the epidermis with its cuticle is slightly permeable to it. Hence the diffusion of carbon dioxide into the leaf depends on about the same factors as the outward passage of water vapor, namely, the number of stomata, the rate at which carbon dioxide is utilized within the leaf and the condition of the air outside the leaf, whether it be moving or still.

The amount of carbon dioxide assimilated has been shown to depend on the number of stomata on the upper and the lower surfaces of the leaf. For example, Table 34 shows the relation in leaves illuminated on the upper surface. In leaves with stomata confined to one surface the correlation of assimilation to number of stomata holds, but with leaves bearing stomata on both surfaces there is more intake of carbon dioxide

TABLE 34.—THE RELATION OF CARBON DIOXIDE ASSIMILATED TO THE NUMBER OF STOMATA IN LEAVES ILLUMINATED ON THE UPPER SURFACE

(*After Brown and Escombe*[43])

	Stomatal ratio Upper surface Lower surface	CO₂ assimilated Upper surface Lower surface
Nuphar advena............................	$\frac{100}{0}$	$\frac{100}{0}$
Catalpa bignonioides......................	$\frac{0}{100}$	$\frac{0}{100}$
Colchicum speciosum......................	$\frac{100}{119}$	$\frac{100}{72}$
Rumex alpinus............................	$\frac{100}{269}$	$\frac{100}{144}$

than might be expected from the number of stomata on the upper side. This is because the leaves were illuminated from above, resulting probably in a greater degree of opening of the stomata and a more rapid utilization of carbon dioxide by this side of the leaf. Both of these factors would favor a more rapid intake of carbon dioxide.

The large amount absorbed by a leaf during active assimilation despite the low partial pressure of carbon dioxide in the atmosphere and the small fraction of the leaf surface occupied by stomata is explained by Brown and Escombe's law[42] which states that diffusion through a perforated membrane is proportional to the diameter of the apertures and not to their area. Because of the small size of the stomata, their great number and their distribution over the surface, the amount of carbon dioxide that theoretically could be taken in by the leaf under the most favorable circumstances is much greater than any observed quantity absorbed. Some idea of the amount used by leaves is given by an experiment of Brown and Escombe[43] on the sunflower, in which they found that approximately half a liter of carbon dioxide was used by each square meter of leaf surface in an hour.

The carbon dioxide content of the atmosphere is constant; therefore it is not a factor to be considered in fruit growing. However, when it is artificially changed, in the absence of other limiting factors, the rate of assimilation increases in proportion to an increase in the carbon dioxide supply until an atmospheric concentration of 30 to 50 per cent. is reached. Cummings and Jones[65] have obtained very marked results from aerial fertilization with carbon dioxide. Legumes fertilized in this way showed increased carbohydrate storage and an increased production of pods and beans. Potatoes produced better tubers and strawberries showed distinct effects. This probably holds until an atmospheric concentration of about 30 per cent. or more is reached. Atmospheric concentrations of 50 per cent. carbon dioxide have a narcotic effect and depress assimilation. Changes in the rate of assimilation in so far as they depend on carbon dioxide supply are affected only by those factors that determine the rate of intake. This is increased by movement of the air, by the degree of stomatal opening and by any factors increasing the rate of utilization.

Water.—The water supply of plants is treated in a preceding section and no further discussion need be added here. However, it must not be forgotten that water is one of the materials out of which carbohydrates are made. Furthermore, when there is a water deficit within the plant caused by a limited water supply in the soil and a high transpiration rate, the stomata close, thus cutting off the supply of carbon dioxide and materially retarding the photosynthetic process.[195] Herein probably lies the explanation of the fact, reported by Hartig,[135] that the leaves of trees often do not work to anywhere near their theoretical capacity and that sometimes fully 50 per cent. of their leaves and branches may be removed without decreasing their rate of growth. The defoliation simply permits the foliage that remains to carry more nearly a full load because it has available a more adequate moisture supply.

Light.—In the absence of other limiting factors and particularly of high temperatures and extremely high light intensities, carbon assimilation increases with the intensity of light. Though a limited amount of shading, such as would be provided by a single thickness of cheesecloth, has not been found to reduce leaf efficiency in the white pine, measurements made in the lower and interior portions of fairly thick topped apple trees indicate that the amount of light reaching a given unit of leaf area may be reduced to as little as 10, or in extreme cases, 1 per cent. of that reaching the same area of fully exposed leaf surface in the top of the tree.[148] Under such conditions photosynthesis is greatly reduced.[148] It is a reasonable assumption that the poor performance of the weak, slender branches in the heavily shaded, lower and interior portions of the tree[247] is due in part to an effect of the shading on the efficiency of the leaf. Data are not available to show how much leaf efficiency in those portions of the tree is increased by pruning to admit more light, though such an assumed influence has usually been offered as the principal reason for the thinning-out type of pruning commonly recommended and commonly employed. However, the marked differences in the results that attend thinning out the tops of trees to admit light to the lower branches as compared with leaving the tops unthinned and pruning away the lower, interior branches—the so-called thin-wood method of pruning[247]—

indicate that probably something more than the light factor is involved. The difference of 8:1 in photosynthetic rate that has been found sometimes to characterize "fine weather" and "bad weather" in the case of the beech and hornbeam[223] likewise is probably far greater than can be accounted for by differences in light intensity.

Evidence presented by Caldwell[48] indicates that the year-to-year differences in the chemical composition and quality of grapes from the same vineyard or from vineyards of the same variety located some distance apart are due in greater measure to differences in the amount of sunlight received during the growing season and, hence, in the accumulation of the products of photosynthesis than to similar responses to temperature variations.

There is evidence that at the intensities of the different wave lengths in the solar spectrum, red light is the most and green the least effective for photosynthesis.

Light acts indirectly on carbon assimilation by raising the temperature of the leaf and by stimulating the guard cells of the stomata to open, thus increasing the absorption of carbon dioxide.[123]

Leaf Pigments.—The chloroplasts of all green plants contain four pigments, two green and two yellow. They are:

1. Chlorophyll *a*, blue-black in the solid state, green-blue in solution.
2. Chlorophyll *b*, green-black in the solid state, pure green in solution.
3. Carotin, forming orange-red crystals.
4. Xanthophyll, forming yellow crystals.

In the fresh nettle leaf, these four pigments occur in the following quantities, chlorophyll *a*, 24 parts in 12,000; chlorophyll *b*, 9; carotin 2 and xanthophyll 4.[163]

In the chloroplast these pigments occur in a colloidal mixture with fats, waxes and salts of fatty acids. The chlorophyll content of leaves varies from 9.6 to 1.2 per cent. of the dry weight. Shade leaves have a higher chlorophyll content than sun leaves in terms of dry weight, but not in proportion to leaf surface. The yellow pigments comprise 0.1 to 1.2 per cent. of the dry weight and there is no higher percentage in shade leaves than in sun leaves. There is no diurnal fluctuation in the amounts of the pigments, the mean ratio of chlorophyll *a* to chlorophyll *b* being 2.85:1. On the whole, shade leaves contain less chlorophyll *a* than other leaves, their ratio of chlorophylls being 2.93:1. Less difference in this ratio is found in real shade plants like the beech than in plants that are ill adapted to growth in the shade. The mean ratio of carotin to xanthophyll for ordinary leaves is 0.603:1 and for shade leaves 0.421:1. Xanthophyll is relatively more abundant in shade leaves.

Variation with Age.—The chlorophyll content of leaves increases with age; so also the assimilatory power of the leaf, though not in the same degree. Hence, it appears that mature leaves contain an excess of chlorophyll and some other factor limits the rate of assimilation. In autumn the chlorophyll content decreases but as chlorophyll is not usually the limiting factor, assimilation does not decrease in proportion at first.   If leaves remain green, they maintain their assimilatory power until they fall—a matter of no small importance in food storage.

Variation with Light Supply.—The development of chlorophyll in most plants depends on the action of light in which the red rays seem the most effective.[61,296]   In all probability precursors of chlorophyll are present and exposure to light effects certain chemical reactions necessary for the complete development of the pigment.   Light is not always essential to chlorophyll development, however, for conifer seeds germinate and become green even in the dark.

Light not only aids in the development of chlorophyll but at higher intensities brings about its destruction, probably through oxidation.   The decomposition of chlorophyll occurs outside the plant as well as within its tissues.   This can be demonstrated by exposing a test tube containing a solution of chlorophyll to the light and comparing it with another kept in darkness.   Red and yellow light are most effective in destroying chlorophyll.   Consequently it is found that at low light intensities plants grown in yellow light contain the most chlorophyll but that at higher intensities plants grown in blue light contain the most, owing to the destructive effect of the yellow light at these higher intensities.[321] Similar effects from red light have been observed.[286]   The double effect of light in stimulating the development of chlorophyll and in bringing about its destruction, leads to noticeable differences in the chlorophyll content of plants growing in different latitudes and altitudes.   It has been found that the minimum amount of chlorophyll necessary for growth is approximately the same at all latitudes but that the maximum amount increases toward the equator.[190]   Hence, a plant may have twice as much chlorophyll in the tropics as at 60° north latitude. For a given species, however, the amount is less at both extremes of its range than at the center and it has been suggested that this may be due to greater oxidizing action at the limit on the equator side where the light would be more intense.   The significance of these discoveries lies in the relation of carbohydrate accumulation to fruitfulness.   Plants growing at high altitudes contain less chlorophyll than those growing in the lowlands.[150]   In Alpine plants carbon assimilation requires greater light intensities but lower temperatures.

Temperature.—At low and medium temperatures in the absence of other limiting factors, the rate of assimilation is a coefficient of the temperature.   Assimilation has been detected at −6°C. and from this point to 25°C. the rule stated above has been found to hold with the plants investigated.   Above 25°C., the rate of assimilation does not remain constant at any given temperature.   The higher the temperature, the more rapidly it decreases; at any given temperature the initial decrease is greatest.   This "time factor" that enters at higher temperatures probably is indicative of the interference of another factor, namely, enzymes.

Nutrient Supply.—Though none of the mineral nutrients enter into the composition of carbohydrates, the rate of carbohydrate manufacture depends on their presence in adequate amounts. Limitation of the nitrogen supply reduces the rate of photosynthesis more than is the case when there is a deficiency of either phosphorus or potassium.[55] On the other hand there is evidence that with an extremely liberal nutrient supply the rate of photosynthesis is reduced and that the leaves on closely or moderately spaced trees are more efficient carbohydrate-manufacturing organs than those on trees spaced more widely.[3]

Enzymes.—Assimilation is an enzyme reaction. Enzymes are organic catalytic substances that accelerate the rate of a reaction. Their chemical composition is unknown and their existence is shown only by their activity. They are not used up in a reaction, remaining after the process is completed. A minute amount of enzyme can effect the formation of a relatively large amount of end product; however, this is proportional to the amount of enzyme present. The effects of temperature described above are characteristic of enzyme reactions. The time factor manifesting itself at temperatures above 25°C. is not due to any direct effect of the temperatures on assimilation, but may be due to the permanent inactivation or decomposition of enzymes at high temperatures. Under these circumstances the rate of assimilation would decrease because the amount of enzyme diminished. The longer the temperature acted, the more enzyme would be decomposed. Similarly the narcotic effect of strong concentrations of carbon dioxide and the harmful influences of high light intensities are attributable in part to their effects on the assimilatory enzymes. Such adaptations as different species may show in their ability to assimilate best at higher or lower temperatures or light intensities probably are attributable to differences in their enzymes.

The principle of limiting factors applies to the six factors determining carbon assimilation.[33] If any one factor is limiting, the rate of assimilation cannot be increased by any other. The carbon assimilation of green plants is usually limited by the seasonal variation in temperature and the diurnal variation in light. When temperature and light are both favorable, the supply of carbon dioxide is probably the limiting factor.[65] Water may be a limiting factor either through a direct effect on assimilation or indirectly by closing the stomata and so shutting off the supply of carbon dioxide.

Products

The products of photosynthesis are oxygen and carbohydrates.

Oxygen.—The relation between the amount of oxygen evolved in the process of carbon assimilation and the amount of carbon dioxide taken in is not accurately known.   When the respiration of the assimilating tissue is evaluated, it appears that the volume of oxygen evolved is practically equal to, or very slightly greater than, the amount of carbon dioxide absorbed.   The path by which oxygen escapes from the leaf is the same as that by which carbon dioxide enters or water vapor is lost, namely, through the intercellular spaces and the stomata.   Oxygen is used in respiration, however, and when assimilation proceeds very slowly, the oxygen given off by assimilation may be entirely consumed by respiration.   Similarly the carbon dioxide evolved by respiration may just about equal that used in assimilation under these circumstances.

Carbohydrates.—What carbohydrate is the first product of carbon assimilation, is not known.   Assuming it to be glucose, the reaction may be written as follows: $6CO_2 + 6H_2O + light + chlorophyll = C_6H_{12}O_6 + 6O_2$.

Simple, naturally occurring carbohydrates may contain five or six carbon atoms and are called accordingly pentoses or hexoses.   There are two pentoses of common occurrence, arabinose and xylose; neither of these has been shown to be formed directly by assimilation.   Four naturally occurring hexoses are known: glucose, fructose, mannose and galactose.

Besides these simple sugars, there are compound sugars made up of two or more molecules of the simple, less one or more molecules of water. The disaccharides yield two molecules of simple sugars on hydrolysis. The two most common disaccharides are sucrose (cane sugar) which yields one molecule of glucose and one of fructose when hydrolyzed by dilute acids or inverted by an enzyme and maltose (malt sugar) which yields two molecules of glucose.

In addition to the sugars there are complex carbohydrates, called polysaccharides; these yield an indefinite number of molecules of simple sugars on hydrolysis.   They are for the most part less soluble in water than the sugars.   One kind of sugar or a mixture of different kinds may be formed on hydrolysis.   If the predominant sugar produced is a hexose, they are called hexosans; if a pentose, pentosans.

Hexosans are classified according to the nature of the predominating sugar produced on hydrolysis.   Thus there are glucosans which include starch, soluble starch, dextrin and cellulose; fructosans such as inulin; mannans, a constituent found in the wood and leaves of the lime, apple and chestnut, and galactans such as agar-agar.   Pentosans include gums, mucilages and pectins, on which the jelling properties of fruit depend, and presumably hemicellulose, one of the forms in which carbohydrates are stored, is derived at least in part from them.[277]   The relationships of the carbohydrates are shown diagrammatically in Fig. 17.

Daily and Seasonal Fluctuation in Leaves.—Though no reliable data are available on which to base a detailed picture of the carbohydrate

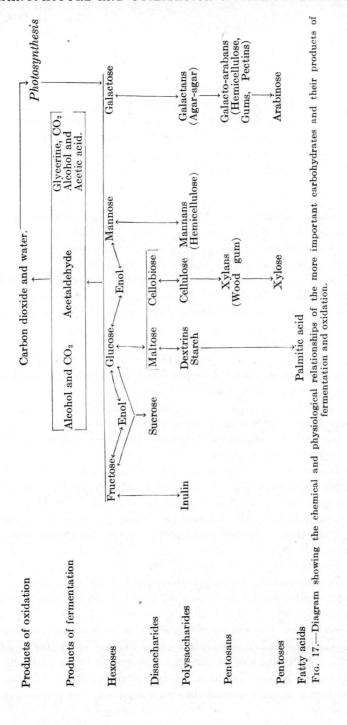

Fig. 17.—Diagram showing the chemical and physiological relationships of the more important carbohydrates and their products of fermentation and oxidation.

changes in the leaf, the following statements may be made.[163]   Hexose sugars and sucrose increase during the day, reach a maximum about mid-day, after which the quantity present decreases; these changes closely parallel the temperature variations and probably the variations in light intensity.   There is no diurnal fluctuation in the amount of pentoses or of pentosans.   As a result of the accumulation of sugars, starch is formed; the process occurs only in cell plastids, either in chloroplasts which are green or in leucoplasts which are colorless.   Species vary greatly in their capacity to form starch.   Many plants—the onion, for instance—form none at all.   Starch and sucrose formation in the leaf are only temporary. The carbohydrates are continuously conducted from the leaf as hexoses, which occur in greater amounts than other sugars in the conducting tissues.   The starch present in the leaf accumulates there only because the manufacture of sugars is proceeding more rapidly than their removal. During the night the starch is digested by enzymes to maltose and the maltose to glucose, which then passes out of the leaf.

The seasonal variation in the carbohydrate supply of leaves has been studied by Michel Durant.[213]   He distinguishes two stages in the life of a leaf: (1) a period of carbohydrate synthesis and polymerization, extending from the time the leaves begin to function until the end of summer or in annual plants until the seeds begin to develop, during which period carbohydrate assimilation is active and carbohydrates of all types increase in amount; (2) a period of hydrolysis and simplification beginning about the time when the leaves turn yellow.   This is marked by a decrease in the amount of compound carbohydrates and a further accumulation of simple sugars.   The development of the abscission layer at the base of the leaves of deciduous plants is correlated with this accumulation of simple sugars in the leaf blade, so that their removal to the branch is soon stopped.   The sugars increase until they are respired, fermented or washed out by rain.   In leaves of annual plants, a larger proportion of these sugars is removed to the developing seeds and fruits; consequently, accumulation of simple sugars is less pronounced than in tree leaves.   Nevertheless, at the end of this second period there are always appreciable amounts of carbohydrates left in the leaf.

In evergreen leaves, the accumulation of simple sugars in the fall and winter is accentuated by photosynthesis which continues and pro-duces appreciable effects because cold weather retards respiration more than photosynthesis.   Starch disappears or persists in small amounts and disaccharides containing fructose, such as sucrose, are prevalent. In the spring, starch is resynthesized at the expense of soluble sugars.   In June, the polysaccharides of the leaves decrease, being added to stores in the branches or used in the development of the fruit.   The carbohy-drate content remains low until the end of autumn.   In general, the older the leaf, the greater its carbohydrate content and a maximum in polysaccharides corresponds to a minimum in simple sugars.

It has been found that the pentosans form a larger and larger proportion of the matter insoluble in alcohol and that the pentoses increase as the season advances, the latter probably representing hydrolytic products of pentosans.[92]

The entire plant depends on the assimilating function of its leaves for its supply of carbohydrates and of those compounds manufactured from them. The carbohydrates synthesized in the leaves are translocated as hexoses through the phloem to all parts of the plant where they are either stored or utilized in ways specified later.

Forms of Storage.—Since starch is perhaps the most common form in which carbohydrates are stored, it is important to consider the structure of the starch molecule in order to gain some idea of the factors involved in its formation. When starch is hydrolyzed slowly, it yields maltose and dextrin. Both of these yield glucose on further hydrolysis. Corn starch contains palmitic acid, a fatty acid and a related unsaturated compound. These fatty substances are liberated only after hydrolysis and are probably attached to the carbohydrate of the starch molecule.[285] There is enough fatty acid in the corn starch molecule to make commercially profitable, in the manufacture of glucose from corn starch, the use of this residue as soap stock. Moreover, starch probably is not chemically homogeneous. At least two substances with distinct properties have been separated and called amylose and amylopectin.

When the concentration of hexoses is sufficiently great, starch is usually formed in the plastids. In fact, leaves of plants such as the onion which do not ordinarily form starch, will do so when floated on a 10 per cent. solution of fructose.

Starch will be formed, therefore, whenever the concentration of sugars reaches a certain point and other conditions such as temperature permit. In the summer and early autumn, starch is stored in the branches. In the peach, great amounts are found in the leaf gaps. In the younger apple shoots, it accumulates predominantly in the pith, being especially abundant at the nodes.

In woody plants, a considerable portion of the reserve carbohydrate is stored in the form of hemicellulose, which is apparently derived, at least in part, from the pentoses. Indeed, there is evidence that in some cases there may be 5 or 6 times as much hemicellulose present as of starch.[221] The work of Harvey[136] indicates that at least in the apple and pear other compounds, such as phloridzin, play a more or less important part in carbohydrate storage.

The association of fat with the starch molecule indicates that the latter is the starting point for fat formation in plants. Fatty oils therefore may be considered as a reserve food derived from carbohydrates especially in fruits like the avocado, in the seed of fruits like the apple and cocoanut and also over the winter in the younger roots and branches. Fats are esters which yield on hydrolysis one molecule of glycerine and three molecules of fatty acids.   The commonest fatty acids found in plant fats and oils are: (1) oleic acid, in olive oil, almond oil, quince oil, cherry-, plum-, peach- and apricot-kernel oil; (2) linolic acid, in the oils from pumpkin, watermelon, melon, apple, pear and orange seeds; (3) palmitic acid, in cocoanut oil and cocoa butter and (4) dihydroxystearic acid, in grape-seed oil.   Fats contain less oxygen in proportion to the carbon present in the molecule than carbohydrates.   They, therefore, yield more energy when oxidized and may be regarded as concentrated energy in chemical combination.

Sucrose and even glucose also must at times be considered forms of carbohydrate storage.

Seasonal Fluctuations of Stored Carbohydrates.—There is much seasonal variation in the carbohydrate content of the different tissues

TABLE 35.—EASILY HYDROLYZED CARBOHYDRATE IN PERCENTAGES OF DRY WEIGHT IN PEAR AND CHESTNUT TREES[184]

Pear

Date	Branches	Roots
Feb. 18.	23.0	39.3
Apr. 13.	21.3	22.4
June 16.	23.7	27.9
Aug. 4.	24.7	29.2
Sept. 24.	25.7	33.8
Dec. 1.	25.4	29.3

Chestnut

Date	Branches	Roots
Jan. 11.	24.7	27.2
Feb. 26.	24.7	25.7
Mar. 28.	21.5	24.7
May 20.	19.9	19.8
June 22.	20.4	21.8
July 27.	21.1	24.3
Sept. 12.	25.9	30.3
Oct. 19.	26.4	29.1
Nov. 22.	24.7	28.9
Dec. 12.	23.0	27.3

in which carbohydrates are stored.   There is also much variation between different tissues.   Thus, "on a dry weight basis, the total reserve carbohydrate content of the woody tissues is higher than that of the cortex-phloem at all times of the year, and that of the periderm is usually lower than that of the cortex-phloem."[294]

Easily Hydrolyzable Carbohydrates.—Leclerc du Sablon's[184] determina-tons of the easily hydrolyzable carbohydrate in the roots and branches of the pear and chestnut are given in Table 35. This type of carbohydrate which includes sugars, starch and other easily hydrolyzed polysaccharides, but not crude fiber, is at a maximum in September and at a minimum in May. Moreover there is a steady increase from May to September and a fairly steady decrease from September to May.

Similar data showing the variations in the easily hydrolyzed polysac-charide of 7-year-old apple trees are given in Table 36. Here also much

TABLE 36.—EASILY HYDROLYZED CARBOHYDRATE IN PERCENTAGES OF DRY WEIGHT
IN 7-YEAR-OLD APPLE TREES[47]
(Each figure is the average of analyses from two trees)

	Dormant, Dec. 3	Buds swelling, Apr. 20	In bloom, May 18	Growth over, July 12	Leaves falling, Oct. 12
New growth.....................	.....	.....	.....	30.54	27.34
1-year old branches..............	21.36	30.31	19.21	25.22	26.50
2-year old branches..............	22.13	29.38	13.24	26.59	26.72
3-year old branches..............	22.41	35.75	11.68	32.26	26.10
4-year old branches..............	20.44	31.58	18.48	30.03	27.88
5-year old branches..............	20.43	31.29	16.08	25.07	27.28
Trunk.........................	25.83	34.08	17.80	32.23	27.96
Large roots....................	29.90	38.38	21.77	28.90	32.02
Small roots....................	29.36	36.47	36.47	31.87	33.88

the same picture is presented except an increase from December to April, accounting for which is difficult. The minimum in May is apparent, but the maximum in September does not appear, as samples were not col-lected at that time.

In all the data presented, the roots have shown a higher percentage and a greater fluctuation in carbohydrate than the shoots. However, this does not indicate a greater absolute carbohydrate content. Esti-mates by Curtis[66] indicating the probable relationships at the time of bud swelling (April) are shown in Table 37. According to these figures the

TABLE 37.—ESTIMATED NUMBER OF POUNDS OF CARBOHYDRATE IN TOPS AND ROOTS
OF A 7-YEAR OLD APPLE TREE[66]

1 year twigs...................	1.10	Large roots.....................	5.71
Older branches.................	5.89	Small roots.....................	2.43
Trunk........................	5.25		
Total.....................	12.24	Total.....................	8.14

portions of a tree above ground contain half again as much as the roots. The conditions found in apple spurs are shown in Table 38. These figures evidently are comparable to the data of Le Clerc du Sablon on the pear and chestnut.

TABLE 38.—TOTAL CARBOHYDRATE (NOT INCLUDING CRUDE FIBER) OF APPLE SPURS[156]
(In percentages of dry weight)

	Bearing (average of three trees)	Non-bearing (average of two trees)
March	22.0	25.1
May 13	20.3	24.0
June 25	24.7	25.2
Sept. 2	35.1	30.1
Nov. 19	28.2	24.5
Jan. 24	24.7	23.9

The increase in carbohydrate from May to September is explained by the assimilatory activity of the leaves. The decrease from September to May must be attributed to several factors. The major part is due to

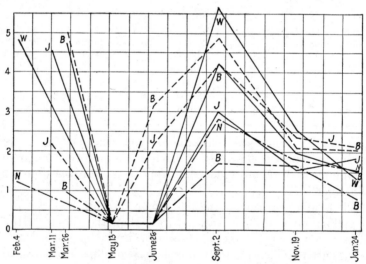

FIG. 18.—Starch content of apple spurs in percentages of dry weight; bearing spurs represented by continuous lines, non-bearing spurs by broken lines and barren spurs by dot-dash lines. (*After Hooker.*[156])

the use of carbohydrates for the formation of other substances—probably of nitrogenous compounds which increase in September and of fatty substances, which are discussed presently. The decrease in carbohydrate is also in part the result of consumption in respiration, which proceeds from September to May, but most actively after growth has begun and in part the result of translocation into the newly developing leaves, flowers and eventually fruits.   Hence the lower minimum in the carbohydrate content of bearing spurs in May may be associated with flowering.   The higher maximum in these same spurs in September is probably connected with the development of specialized tissues in the purse during fruit development.

The study of the various types of carbohydrate, particularly starch and sugars, shows similar seasonal fluctuations despite some variation.

Starch.—In woody tissues, starch is a relatively small fraction of the total polysaccharides, but probably a significant fraction of the available carbohydrates.   Figure 18 shows the starch variations in bearing, non-bearing and barren spurs of the apple.[156]   There are two maxima

TABLE 39.—ETHER EXTRACT IN PERCENTAGES OF DRY WEIGHT IN 7-YEAR OLD APPLE TREES[47]
(Each figure is the average of analyses from two trees)

	Dormant, Dec. 3	Buds swelling, Apr. 20	In bloom, May 18	Growth over, July 12	Leaves falling, Oct. 12
New growth	....	....	....	3.15	4.11
1-year branches	3.26	5.18	5.00	2.68	3.01
2-year branches	2.77	3.58	3.03	2.31	2.92
3-year branches	2.49	2.92	2.39	1.99	2.71
4-year branches	1.75	1.50	1.57	1.31	1.07
5-year branches	1.28	1.07	1.14	1.18	0.91
Trunk	0.85	0.96	0.79	0.72	0.70
Large roots	2.25	1.86	2.02	2.38	1.31
Small roots	6.79	5.03	4.06	5.85	6.55

for starch and two minima.   This was shown microchemically by Mer and d'Arbaumont.[211]   The maximum in September and the minimum in May correspond to the maximum and minimum for total carbohydrates.   The second minimum in January and the second maximum in March are due to conversion of starch to sugars and a resynthesis of starch in spring just before vegetation commences.   The second maximum is not, however, so high as the first—except in bearing spurs—which indicates that a certain amount of carbohydrate has been consumed in respiration or used for the formation of other substances.

Determinations of the ether extract permit an estimate of the fat and oil content and show that fats increase during the winter.   The previous discussion of the structure of starch indicates that this is the point of departure for fat formation.   Table 39 shows the seasonal variation in ether extract in 7-year old apple trees.   It is evident that the younger the tissue, the more fat it contains and that the fat content is at a maximum just before active growth begins and at a minimum after active growth is over.

Characteristic differences between the starch content of bearing and non-bearing spurs appear in Fig. 18.   In winter the spurs with fruit buds have more starch.   Moreover, starch accumulation commences in non-bearing spurs in May and in bearing spurs in June.   This difference is connected with carbohydrate utilization by the fruit.   The relation of this to fruit bud differentiation is discussed later.

Hemicellulose.—Less is known about seasonal changes in hemicellulose content than about those in starch or sugar.   However, like starch, it tends to accumulate in the woody storage tissues as the growing season

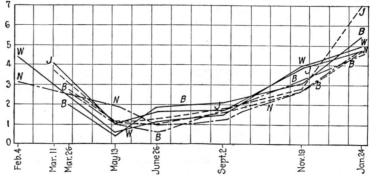

Fig. 19.—Total sugar content of apple spurs in percentages of dry weight; bearing spurs represented by continuous lines, non-bearing spurs by broken lines and barren spurs by dot-dash lines.   (*After Hooker.*[156])

advances and to disappear in the spring as it is utilized for new growth. It "appears to be formed in great quantity in the developing fruits (of the apple), which show a consistent increase to a maximum concentration by midsummer, followed by a rapid decrease later on.   The data suggest that hemicellulose is laid down in the flesh or cortex of the fruit as a reserve food in the form of accretions to cell walls which during the latter part of the development are hydrolyzed through enzymatic action.   Thus, in addition to starch, evidently it is a source of increasing sugar content for the maturing fruit."[221]

Sugars.—During the growing season the sugar content of most woody tissues is relatively low, even though sugar is being constantly translocated to them from the leaves.   This is because carbohydrates are stored at this season principally in other forms, such as starch or hemicellulose.   With the approach of cold weather, however, "there is a quantitative change of hexosans into sugar, beginning in September-October (in the apple, in Minnesota) for the periderm and cortex-phloem and in October for the xylem tissues."[294] A rapid drop in sugar which occurs during the spring is explained by respiration, translocation to the leaves and fruit and utilization in the formation of complex carbohydrates.

The seasonal variation in the sugar content of spurs is shown in Fig. 19. The assimilatory activity of the leaves soon restores the sugar content of the spurs, but a marked increase does not commence until September. This is due to continued demands for sugar by the developing fruit on bearing spurs and to starch accumulation in non-bearing spurs. The increase in sugars after September is associated with the decrease in starch during this period and represents a partial conversion of starch to sugars. Some of this sugar is sucrose, a form in which carbohydrate is stored during the winter, as the figures in Table 40 show.

TABLE 40.—AVERAGE NON-REDUCING SUGAR CONTENT OF SPURS IN PERCENTAGES OF DRY WEIGHT[156]

	Bearing spurs	Non-bearing spurs	Barren spurs
March..................................	0.59	0.47	0.97
May 13................................	0.44	0.27	0.45
June 26...............................	0.00	0.05	0.19
Sept. 2................................	0.09	0.45	0.35
Nov. 14...............................	1.27	0.77	0.91
Jan. 24...............................	0.56	2.40	1.66

The sugar used in the development of fruit is considerable, as Table 41 indicates. In the apple, the percentage and absolute amounts in the fruit increase steadily, the rate of increase becoming greater as maturity approaches. This holds for prunes also.[282] In pears the percentage decreases at first and then increases, while the absolute amounts increase steadily. In either case the increase in absolute amount extends to the end of August or the middle of September.

Michel Durant[213] points out that a period of carbohydrate synthesis followed by one of hydrolysis and simplification is found in fruits as well as in leaves. Ripe fruit therefore contains more sugar than unripe fruit. The increase in the sugar content may continue even after the fruit is picked. This occurs in drying prunes when sugar is formed by the hydrolysis of starch. If prunes after removal from the tree are exposed to the sunlight for 2 or 3 days, their sugar content increases, but after 5 days' exposure their sugar is rapidly consumed in respiration and fermentation.[282]

In recapitulation, it is emphasized that the carbohydrate supply of the plant is manufactured in the leaves and that the leaves supply the entire plant. In consequence, movement of carbohydrate is usually away from the leaves to the growing points, cambium and storage organs. Carbohydrate is stored mostly in the immediate vicinity of places where it may later be used.   Thus the work of Magness[194] and of Curtis[66] indi-

TABLE 41.—REDUCING SUGAR CONTENT OF DEVELOPING APPLES AND PEARS[237]

	Apples					Pears			
	Pleissner Rambour		Red Easter Calville			Salzburg		Liegel's Honey	
Date	Percentage of dry weight	Grams in 1,000 fruits	Percentage of dry weight	Grams in 1,000 fruits	Date	Percentage of dry weight	Grams in 1,000 fruits	Percentage of dry weight	Grams in 1,000 fruits
June 2........	3.05	0.9	3.28	0.7	May 26.......	4.98	1.0	5.03	0.8
June 12.......	10.70	22.0	6.75	8.8	June 5........	2.17	2.7	3.26	3.6
June 22.......	14.91	97.0	12.70	43.0	June 15.......	1.66	7.7	2.50	10.2
July 2........	22.90	368.0	16.51	150.0	June 25.......	1.92	18.0	4.56	32.0
July 12........	24.19	870.0	19.78	370.0	July 5........	2.78	36.0	6.74	68.0
July 22........	17.11	1,150.0	20.29	670.0	July 15.......	4.56	95.0	12.01	175.0
Aug. 1........	39.45	2,540.0	23.19	950.0	July 25.......	7.16	218.0	23.60	536.0
Aug. 11.......	34.65	4,260.0	26.42	1,400.0	Aug. 4.......	16.43	637.0	36.49	770.0
Aug. 21.......	39.69	4,250.0	30.17	1,740.0	Aug. 14.......	30.03	1,660.0	43.68	1,520.0
Aug. 31.......	43.07	6,600.0	31.47	2,400.0	Aug. 24.......	35.02	2,230.0	50.61	1,800.0
Sept. 10.......	51.28	7,530.0	35.41	3,040.0	Sept. 3........	51.35	3,590.0	.....	....
Sept. 20......	60.04	10,850.0	36.28	3,550.0	Sept. 8........	.....	4,180.0	.....	....
Sept. 30......	52.99	9,630.0	33.73	3,200.0	....	.....	....	.....	....
Dec. 12.......	.....	....	48.14	4,730.0					

cates that the carbohydrate stores in the roots do not return to the tops. They are used by the roots.   Cambial activity depends on the carbo-hydrate stored in the medullary rays and the starch sheath.   Bud development in the spring depends largely on the carbohydrate stored in the pith or leaf gap near the bud.

CARBOHYDRATE UTILIZATION

Carbohydrates are used in any one of the following ways:

1. For tissue building, that is for the construction of other carbo-hydrates, or of different substances manufactured from carbohydrates, which enter into the composition of plant cells.

2. For the retention of moisture.

3. To increase osmotic concentration.

4. As a source of energy.

In Tissue Building.—According to Czapek, glucose is a constituent of every living cell and therefore may be considered a necessary part of the chemical equipment of living matter.   The great value of glucose in metabolism is probably associated with the ease with which it is altered to a number of different but related compounds. Through its enolitic form it may be changed to fructose and mannose. Glucose, fructose and mannose exist in at least five forms each. Whenever glucose is present in solution, as in protoplasm, certain of these forms—depending on the prevailing conditions—tend to develop until a complex equilibrium is established. Since each form has different physical and chemical properties the multiplicity of ways in which glucose may become the basic material for a great diversity of physiological processes and for the synthesis of many diverse and complex chemical substances is evident. Besides the forms in which glucose may be stored temporarily, it is utilized for the construction of the permanent framework of the plant, being the substance from which many forms of carbohydrate as well as of other groups of organic compounds are made. The cellulose wall is secreted by each cell from its supply of hexose or pentose sugars. So also is the middle lamella, which is a pentosan, a salt of pectic acid. It has been suggested that fats probably are derived from carbohydrates and that starch is presumably an intermediate stage in fat formation. Glucosides give rise to one or more molecules of sugar on hydrolysis and it is shown presently that organic acids arise from the respiration of carbohydrates. The proteins and alkaloids likewise are at least in part built up out of carbohydrates. Indeed, they constitute the principal building blocks for most of the plant structure.

Little is known concerning the seasonal quantitative variation in many of these constituents. It may be said, however, that crude fiber, which is composed chiefly of cellulose and lignin, increases steadily with age in roots and branches and that seasonal variations are insignificant in comparison with this regular trend.

Complete vegetative development depends on an adequate carbohydrate supply and a plant is unable to attain its full size and ordinary shape in darkness or particularly in the absence of red light. This is true especially of leaves. If they are supplied with carbohydrates in a form in which they can be absorbed, the effect of the absence of light on the size of the leaf can largely be eliminated. However, different plants show more or less characteristic responses to an absence of light in this respect, which seems to be associated with the amount of carbohydrate that tends to accumulate when the leaves are kept in darkness. Bean leaves, for example, contain small amounts of carbohydrates when kept in the dark; consequently the leaves do not grow. This is the case with most of the fruit plants. In a certain number of plants such as wheat, starch is always present in the leaves and considerable amounts of carbohydrate accumulate even when the leaves are kept in darkness; these attain their usual size under such conditions, though they may be narrower than the leaves of illuminated plants.[234] There are, however, other peculiarities in the form and structure of plants grown in darkness which cannot be attributed in any way to the carbohydrate supply.

In Retaining Moisture.—Pentosans have, according to Spoehr,[277] the property of holding moisture. Certain pentosans develop under conditions where the moisture supply is limited and furnish the plant with a water-retaining mechanism which minimizes the effect of the water deficiency. The moisture held by pentosans seems to be in a colloidal mixture, where it is retained tenaciously and offers resistance to desiccating agencies. The same may be said for other classes of colloidal substances, such as the proteins, which presumably are derived principally from carbohydrates. This colloidally held water should be differentiated from free water since it is characterized by distinct physical properties.

Increasing Osmotic Concentration.—Sugars are important to the plant because they are osmotically active. Since the osmotic concentration depends on the number of molecules and not on their size, it is evident that the formation of disaccharides from simple sugars reduces the osmotic concentration. Conversely, the hydrolysis of compound sugars or polysaccharides to simple sugars increases the osmotic concentration. Thus the building up and splitting down of carbohydrates regulate the osmotic concentration. On the other hand, they unquestionably play an important part in controlling synthetic and hydrolytic processes. Thus compound sugars and especially starch are usually produced wherever the concentration of sugars is high, though other factors are involved, particularly enzymes. The hydrolysis of compound carbohydrates proceeds most rapidly when the concentration of sugars is low; therefore their consumption in respiration, their removal to other organs and their use in the formation of other compounds, particularly of substances like cellulose that are insoluble and consequently not involved in the osmotic system, accelerate the processes of hydrolysis.

As a Source of Energy.—One of the most important properties of carbohydrates is that of yielding energy in the process of respiration. In fact most of the energy used by plants and animals is the stored potential energy of fats and carbohydrates. By means of carbohydrates the roots are able to utilize the energy of sunlight. It has been estimated that upwards of 80 per cent. of the carbohydrates synthesized by plants is respired by them incident to their normal growth processes and that, consequently, less than 20 per cent. of the total is left for storage or tissue building. The proportion that is used in respiration depends on many factors, among the more important of which are the kind of plant and temperature. Thus it has been determined that the optimum temperature for maximum accumulation of the products of photosynthesis and tuber formation in the potato is 17°C., the respiration rate gains rapidly on photosynthesis above that point till at temperatures of 29°C. and above no tubers are formed.[46] Baldwin apple trees respire more rapidly than do Stayman and Delicious trees at high temperatures but function more efficiently in respect to carbohydrate manufacture and utilization at lower growing-season temperatures.[226]   In view of the fact that Baldwin is known to be suited to distinctly cooler growing seasons than are the Stayman and Delicious, we have here a suggested explanation of a number of known peculiarities of varietal adaptation.

Respiration involves several processes.   There are many theories, but according to the most suggestive, respiration consists of two main reactions; one is a process of cleavage, in which the simple carbohydrate molecule is split into carbon dioxide and certain intermediate substances,

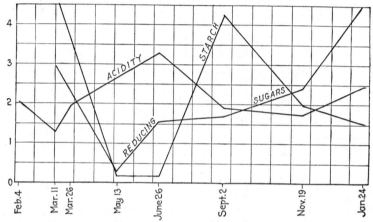

Fig. 20.—Starch, reducing-sugar content and titratable acidity of bearing apple spurs compared. (*After Hooker.*[156])

probably alcohols or acids; the other is a process of oxidation, in which these intermediate substances are oxidized to carbon dioxide and water. The first process is essentially a fermentation for which the enzyme, zymase, is essential.   The second process—of oxidation—depends on enzymes called peroxidases which act only in the presence of peroxides. Peroxidases supposedly transfer oxygen from organic peroxides to the products of cleavage formed during the first process in respiration, oxidizing them to carbon dioxide and water.   According to some investigators there are other enzymes involved but, if this be true, they play subsidiary parts and need not be considered here.

In general the amount of carbon dioxide given off is approximately equal to the amount of oxygen used in respiration so that the respiration of a hexose may be represented by the formula $C_6H_{12}O_6 + 6O_2 = 6H_2O + 6CO_2 +$ energy.   The two processes of respiration, cleavage and oxidation, are more or less independent of each other, so that an accumulation of acid may occur in plant tissues during periods of active respiration, through the incomplete oxidation of carbohydrates and other substances.   The inverse correlation existing between starch content and acidity in apple spurs is shown in Figs. 20 and 21.   In the spring, starch and sugar decreased rapidly in these spurs and acidity rose.   This may be interpreted as indicating the hydrolysis of starch to sugar and the incomplete oxidation of the sugar to acid.   Some of the decrease in sugar is explained by removal to the developing leaves and flowers.   The increase in acidity in the spring lasted longer and reached a higher maximum in bearing spurs.   At the same time the consumption of reducing sugars

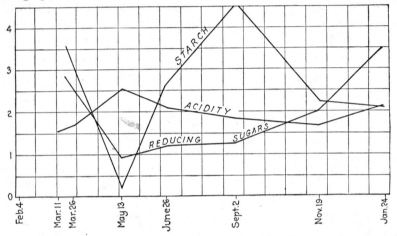

Fig. 21.—Starch, reducing-sugar content and titratable acidity of non-bearing apple spurs compared.   (*After Hooker.*[156])

was more complete.   This may be associated with greater respiratory activity in flowers.   Respiratory activity is particularly pronounced in floral parts, germinating seeds and growing parts in general.

Relation to Pigment Formation.—A supply of carbohydrates is necessary for the development of certain pigments in leaves, flowers and fruits.   Laurent[178] showed that fruit pigments are of two types; some develop only as a result of direct exposure to light; others do not require direct illumination of the fruit but for their development the leaves must be able to manufacture carbohydrates and the connection between the leaves and the fruit must not be interrupted. Kraus[174] suggests that pigments of both sorts occur in apples.   The effect of low temperature or parasitic attack in increasing the pigmentation of fruit or leaves is attributed to an attendant accumulation of sugars, especially glucose, fructose and sucrose.

Summary.—The elaborated plant foods used in tissue building are manufactured from the nutrient materials obtained from the soil and air at a rate depending principally on (1) the available supply of the several materials, including water, (2) the intensity, duration and quality of the light reaching the plant, (3) the amounts of the green leaf pigments, (4) temperature and (5) the presence of certain enzymes.   Any of these factors of the plant's environment or composition may become limiting in plant food synthesis, their degree of importance varying with conditions. The immediate products of photosynthetic activity of the plant are oxygen and carbohydrates. Oxygen for the most part is set free and is in effect a by-product. Glucose is assumed to be the first synthetic product of photosynthesis. Glucose may be considered a starting point for the formation of more complex substances, such as the other hexoses, disaccharides, polysaccharides, pentosans and pentoses. Starch and hemicellulose are the most common forms in which carbohydrates are stored. They are also stored frequently as sugars and sometimes they are transformed into fats. The seasonal distribution of the more important of these materials is discussed. Their storage is more common in or near the organs where they are later used. Carbohydrates are used principally for new tissue building, for the retention of moisture, for increasing osmotic concentration and as a source of energy. Glucose particularly is a basic material in the construction of plant tissues; for a great diversity of physiological processes, pentosans are particularly important because of their water-retaining capacity. Sugars are important in determining osmotic concentration. Carbohydrates supply energy in the process of respiration. The formation of certain pigments, of proteins, alkaloids and other compounds also depends on carbohydrates.

CHAPTER X

THE INITIATION OF THE REPRODUCTIVE PROCESSES

During their first few years in the orchard most of the tree fruits make vegetative growth only, forming no flower buds. As they become older, however, and their rate of growth diminishes, flower buds are differentiated, and they come into bearing. The length of time required for this change from a vegetative to a fruitful condition varies greatly with the species; it varies considerably between varieties of the same species, and it likewise varies with cultural treatments and environmental conditions. However, the change occurs naturally, and ordinarily little thought need be given to hastening or retarding the process. In the case of the vine and bush fruits the fruitful condition develops at an earlier age than in most tree fruits. With them it can be said that almost never is scanty or delayed flower-bud differentiation a factor of major importance in commercial production. There are, nevertheless, instances in which some of the fruits—notably the apple and pear and a number of species of nut-bearing trees—remain vegetative long after they should be in bearing, and throughout their lives trees of some of their varieties show a decided irregularity in their formation of flower buds, giving rise to a more or less distinct alternate bearing habit. This is true to a lesser degree with many other tree fruits. There is much evidence that conditions associated with reserve food supply have an important relation to fruitfulness in plants. The initiation of the reproductive processes of the plant should, therefore, be considered in the light of chemical conditions and the concurrent morphological changes.

THE DEVELOPMENT OF THE FRUITFUL CONDITION

As already pointed out, most tissues of the plant undergo rather marked seasonal changes in composition. These include changes in content in respect to the several mineral elements and likewise in respect to nitrogen, carbohydrates and food reserves of other kinds. Apparently both total and relative amounts of certain of the nitrogen and carbohydrate fractions are particularly important in connection with the process of flower-bud differentiation, though there is plenty of evidence that they are not the sole determining factors.

The Response of the Plant to Changes in Relative Amounts of Nitrogen and of Carbohydrates.—Kraus and Kraybill,[176] studying the effects on the tomato of various treatments, found that striking differences in chemical composition and in behavior with respect to fruitfulness and vegetative growth could be produced by controlling the environmental conditions. They summarize their work as follows:

"1. Plants grown with an abundant supply of available nitrogen and the opportunity for carbohydrate synthesis, are vigorously vegetative and unfruitful. Such plants are high in moisture, total nitrogen, nitrate nitrogen and low in total dry matter, free reducing substances, sucrose and polysaccharides.

"2. Plants grown with an abundant supply of nitrogen and then transferred and grown with a moderate supply of available nitrogen are less vegetative but fruitful. As compared with the vegetative plants, they are lower in moisture, total nitrogen, and nitrate nitrogen, and higher in total dry matter, free reducing substances, sucrose and polysaccharides.

"3. Plants grown with an abundant supply of nitrogen and then transferred and grown with a very low supply of available nitrogen are very weakly vegetative and unfruitful. As compared with the vegetative plants, they are very much lower in moisture and total nitrogen and are lacking in nitrate nitrogen; they are much higher in total dry matter, free reducing substances, sucrose, and polysaccharides."

Three typical effects, measured principally in terms of total nitrogen, carbohydrate and moisture, have been produced by these three distinct environments. The first is characteristic of vigorous vegetative growth. "An abundance of moisture and mineral nutrients, including nitrates, coupled with an available carbohydrate supply, makes for increased vegetation, barrenness and sterility."[176] The second condition represents a readjustment through which the plant must pass before it becomes fruitful. "A relative decrease in nitrates in proportion to the carbohydrates makes for an accumulation of the latter; and also for fruitfulness, fertility, and lessened vegetation."[176] The third condition, in which "a further reduction of nitrates without inhibiting a possible increase of carbohydrates, makes for a suppression both of vegetation and fruitfulness,"[176] is evidently the manifestation of the effect of a limiting factor, nitrate supply. In addition to these three, a fourth condition was found. "Though there be an abundance of moisture and mineral nutrients, including nitrates, yet without an available carbohydrate supply, vegetation is weakened and the plants are non-fruitful. . . . The available carbohydrate supply or the possibility for their manufacture or supply, constitutes as much a limiting factor in growth as the available nitrogen and moisture supply."[176]

Those instances (3 and 4), in which nitrogen or carbohydrate supply is a limiting factor of growth, reveal the necessity of a proper balance between carbohydrate and nitrate supply for the best vegetative development.

"In other words, this experiment indicates first, that the limitation of the nitrates resulted in the suppression of growth and the accumulation of the more complex carbohydrates; second, that the limitation of the carbohydrates, even with large quantities of available nitrates in the soil, results in a suppression of growth; third, that a rapid vegetative extension results from an adjustment of the carbohydrates and nitrates relative to one another so that both may be utilized in the formation and expansion of such structures; and fourth, that such a relationship can be secured either by increasing the nitrates without decreasing the carbohydrates, or by decreasing the carbohydrates without increasing the nitrates.   While it is apparent that the amounts of these compounds relative to one another would be the same in both the above cases, the total amounts would be greater in the former and less in the latter, a condition faithfully reflected in the amount of growth produced."[176]

In this passage Kraus and Kraybill show that there is a distinct nutritive relation between the supply of nitrates and of carbohydrates, for vegetative growth and development.   A carbohydrate supply is therefore not only just as essential for the manufacture of protoplasm as are nitrogen and the essential mineral elements, but it combines with them in definite proportion for the building up of the plant tissue.

The Significance of Carbohydrate Accumulation.   Manufacture in Excess of Utilization.—The differences between the conditions characteristic of vigorous vegetative growth which is unfruitful and vegetation accompanied by fruitfulness are of interest.   There is no evidence to show that the utilization of nutrient substances is any different in a plant showing fruit bud differentiation from that in one which does not, or that the nutritive relation between carbohydrate and nitrate supply in particular is altered.   Kraus and Kraybill's work shows that, in so far as the materials determined by them are concerned, the chief difference is associated with circumstances making for carbohydrate accumulation in fruitful plants rather than a difference in the method of carbohydrate utilization.   In other words, the carbohydrate supplied must be in excess of the amount used.

Carbohydrate accumulation depends primarily on light conditions.   Under experimental conditions carbohydrate assimilation varies with light intensity, in the absence of other limiting factors; however, other factors become limiting for plants grown in the open, so that carbohydrate assimilation and hence carbohydrate accumulation depends on the number of hours of sunlight rather than on the light intensity.[249]   Garner and Allard[108] have shown experimentally that an increase in the duration of light exposure determines fruitfulness in some plants and they suggest that the daily increase in duration of illumination which reaches a maximum on June 21, may have an important relation to the time at which these plants blossom.   It is interesting to observe that fruit bud differentiation in the apple usually occurs the latter part of June or early part of July, though it has been observed to occur at almost every season.   However, Garner and

Allard found that many plants do not blossom unless the duration of light exposure is short.

According to Darrow and Waldo,[89] "Everbearing varieties of strawberries are 'long-day' plants, forming fruit buds under the long days of summer in the northern states.   Ordinary varieties of strawberries are 'short-day' plants, rarely forming fruit buds under natural conditions except in the fall, when the days become short and the temperature low.   Runner formation does not occur with a 10-hour day in summer in ordinary varieties or in a few varieties with a 12-hour day. Branch crowns tend to form when the daily light periods become too short for runner formation.   Fruit buds tend to form when the daily light period becomes still shorter than for optimum branch-crown formation."   Just how closely these photoperiodic responses of the strawberry plant are due to, or associated with, changes in carbohydrate-nitrogen or other nutritive relationships is not known. Voechting[302] found that a decrease in light intensity reduced the number of blossoms and eventually prevented flowering altogether in some plants, while in others there was a tendency for the development of cleistogamous flowers.

Klebs[170] found that when blossoming depends on the intensity of illumination, red light which is the most effective in photosynthesis is essential, blue light having much the same effect as darkness.

Defoliation previous to the period of fruit bud differentiation obviously interferes with carbohydrate manufacture and the work of Harvey[140] shows that this is reflected in the chemical composition of defoliated apple spurs which contain less hydrolyzable polysaccharides and total carbohydrates than normal spurs.   This is particularly important in connection with the decreased fruit bud differentiation observed by Harvey on defoliated fruit spurs.

In Fruit Spurs.—Hooker[156] in a study of the seasonal changes in the chemical composition of apple spurs of certain varieties and bearing habits found that, when there was a relatively low total nitrogen content, starch accumulation occurred while fruit buds were being differentiated. When there was a relatively high total nitrogen content, starch accumulation did not occur at the same time, though it followed later, and the spurs remained vegetative for another year.   These conditions were found in spurs showing characteristically different behavior regardless of whether spurs of only one or of several different bearing habits were found on the same tree at one time.   Some of these results, shown graphically in Figs. 22 and 23, emphasize two principles involved in the development of the fruitful condition; (1) At certain critical periods in the life of the plant, its activities are directed into one channel or another, depending on the nature of the conditions affecting its equilibrium at that particular time.   This lends weight to Kraus and Kraybill's surmise that "the conditions for the initiation of floral primordia and even blooming are probably different from those accompanying fruit setting."   In fact, recent work by Murneek[140] shows that the conditions favoring fruit setting in apples are quite different from those determining fruit bud differentiation. (2) Different parts of a plant may act quite independently of one another, depending on the local factors affecting them.

Influence of the Nitrate Supply.—When the nitrate supply was varied in Kraus and Kraybill's experiments the amount of carbohydrate utiliza-

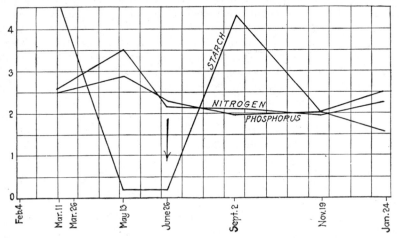

Fig. 22.—Nitrogen, phosphorus and starch contents of bearing apple spurs compared. The arrow indicates the season when fruit bud differentiation would occur in non-bearing spurs. (*After Hooker.*[156])

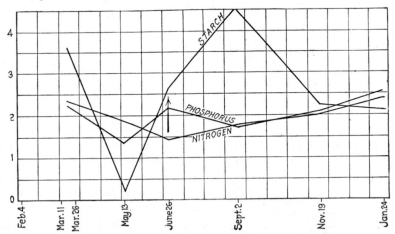

Fig. 23.—Nitrogen, phosphorus and starch contents of non-bearing apple spurs compared. The arrow indicates the season of fruit bud differentiation. (*After Hooker.*[156])

tion varied with it, in accordance with the nutritive relation between carbohydrates and nitrates. Hence, in the absence of any other limiting factors for vegetative development, the balance of carbohydrate manufacture over utilization depends on the nitrate supply. When this is kept high, though carbohydrates are manufactured in large quantities, they are immediately utilized for vegetative development and the plants are unfruitful and vigorously vegetative. If the nitrate supply is reduced moderately, carbohydrate utilization is checked and there is opportunity for carbohydrate accumulation; fruitfulness follows. To be sure carbohydrate accumulation occurs when the nitrate supply is still further reduced, but here the situation is complicated because nitrate then becomes a limiting factor to fruitfulness by inhibiting such vegetative development as appears necessary for fruit bud differentiation. Plants of this type are stunted and altogether lacking in nitrate nitrogen.

Influence of the Moisture Supply.—Nitrate supply is not the only factor which may determine the balance of carbohydrate manufacture over utilization. This may be accomplished also by a decrease in any other factor involved in the process of growth and development. For example, Kraus and Kraybill report that "withholding moisture from plants grown under conditions of relative abundance of available nitrogen results in much the same condition of fruitfulness and carbohydrate storage as the limiting of the supply of available nitrogen." A diminution of the water supply is well known to be frequently associated with fruitfulness. In this case, as in that of nitrate supply, there is probably a limit beyond which a further reduction of the water supply results in unfruitfulness and stunted growth.

Influence of Other Factors.—Klebs[171] concluded from numerous investigations that a reduction in the supply of nutritive salts leads to the fruitful condition, provided there be adequate facilities for photosynthesis and hence for carbohydrate accumulation. Recent work of Walster[306] has shown that heat may be a limiting factor to vegetative development as well as water or any of the essential nutrient and food materials and that diminished heat, even with a high nitrogen supply, leads to carbohydrate accumulation and culm formation in barley. These investigations indicate that any environmental factor may check growth and lead to carbohydrate accumulation and that fruitfulness may result provided vegetative development is not seriously retarded or altogether stopped.

Furthermore, it should not be assumed that whenever there is a surplus of carbohydrates or a certain proportion of carbohydrates to nitrogen within the plant or even in the tissues near the point where fruit bud formation theoretically can take place, it necessarily will take place. Apparently such conditions of carbohydrate surplus or of balance between carbohydrates and nitrogen can and do occur at seasons other than when the differentiating process normally takes place, yet there is no flower-bud differentiation.[188] Furthermore, the freedom with which the shoots or canes or crowns of many species (such as the raspberry, grape and strawberry) form flower buds at seasons characteristic for them, indicates that there is a comparatively wide range of nutritive conditions within which the process may go on.   These and other facts lead to the conclusion that there are other limiting factors, as yet undetermined, in flower-bud formation.   It is shown later in this section that vigorous vegetative growth is not inimical to fruitfulness.   On the contrary, the facts just presented indicate that fruitfulness and vegetative development are associated functions.   There is evidence that in the pecan a comparatively highly vegetative condition early in the season favors the maximum production of flowers, though filling of the nuts later in the season is favored by greatly lessened vegetative growth.[18]

FRUIT BUD FORMATION

Since carbohydrate accumulation seems associated with flower-bud differentiation and the conditions for carbohydrate accumulation vary with the growing and bearing habits of the plant and change during the season, it is evident that there must be considerable variation in the time when flower buds are formed.   A knowledge of the approximate time when their differentiation occurs is of fundamental importance, particularly in connection with possible means of influencing their number by cultural treatment.   Furthermore, the stage of advancement in which the fruit buds enter the winter is shown elsewhere to have an important relation to winter injury.

For many years flower buds of the ordinary deciduous fruit trees have been known, in a rather indefinite way, to have their inception in the summer previous to their opening; more exact knowledge is comparatively recent.

Investigation of the apple has been more extensive than is the case with the other fruits; there is, however, enough similarity between them to permit the use of the apple as the type.   One difference, however, between buds of apple and those of some of the other fruits, pointed out elsewhere, should be borne in mind.   The fruit bud of the apple is, with trivial exceptions, a mixed bud, containing leaves and blossoms; in the other type, as the peach, fruit buds contain no leaves.

Evidence of Differentiation.—The growing point of the apple shoot or spur presents a rounded surface surrounded by embryonic leaves and it is characterized by its relatively large amount of meristematic tissue. Sooner or later its aspect changes, taking one of two forms.

In one case the change consists principally in the greater breadth of the surface with a somewhat smaller degree of convexity and in the absence of the swellings at the periphery that in the actively growing shoot precede the formation of a rudimentary leaf.   The amount of meristematic tissue becomes relatively smaller.   The growing point is at the resting stage; surrounded by protective scales and embryonic leaves, it constitutes the leaf bud.

In the alternative case the growing point differentiates into structures that form the essential part of the flower or fruit bud. The first evidence of differentiation in this direction is the rapid elevation of the crown or surface of the growing point into a narrow conical form, rounded at the apex, with the fibro-vascular connections and pith areas advancing concurrently. In the axils of the young leaves within the bud appear other protuberances which soon become blunt at the top. At the same time other leaf primordia develop rapidly higher in the spiral in which they appear and in turn younger protuberances (the floral primordia) appear in their axils. The apical protuberance, destined to become the central (terminal) flower of the cluster, is differentiated last; however, when it does take shape it is already larger than those previously laid down. It soon takes and thenceforth maintains the lead in development over the other flower primordia (see Fig. 24).

Whether a bud which has entered the resting stage as a leaf bud, can, without a renewal of growth, develop into a fruit bud later the same season is a matter obviously difficult of determination. Indirect evidence, however, points to this possibility and suggests that fruit buds may be initiated at any time when conditions are favorable. It is certain that a spur after forming a leaf bud may start into second growth and then form a fruit bud, all during the same growing season.

Magness[193] has traced the development of axillary buds. He finds that: "axillary buds originate very close to the tip or apex of rapidly growing shoots. As the shoot elongates, the leaves are given off at the side of the growing point, and the young bud appears first as simply an undifferentiated mass of rapidly dividing cells in the axils of these leaves . . . no primordia were found developing in the axils of leaves that were not fairly well formed.

"The buds developed very rapidly and those subtended by half-grown leaves, 1 to 2 inches above the terminal, were well differentiated, with a growing point or apex, and bud scales being rapidly formed. The cells of the growing tip were not well differentiated and this, with the high staining reaction of this region, indicated that much growth was still taking place." By July 9 some of the older axial buds had nearly reached the condition in which they would pass the winter.

Time of Differentiation.—Drinkard[94] reported that fruit bud differentiation in the Oldenburg apple occurred about June 20 in Virginia. Goff[112] found the first clear evidence in the Hoadley apple on June 30 in Wisconsin. Bradford[36] in Oregon found similar stages during the first 10 days of July, though resting stages of leaf buds were apparent in May. The earliest differentiation observed by Kirby[169] in Iowa was about the first of July.

In the pear it was observed in Virginia in samples of Kieffer taken about the middle of July, somewhat later than the initial period for the apple.[94] In Wisconsin evidence was found in the Wilder Early on July

21.[112]   Albert first found differentiation in the pear early in August. In the Champion quince Goff found embryonic flowers in buds examined late in the autumn, but did not determine the exact period of their

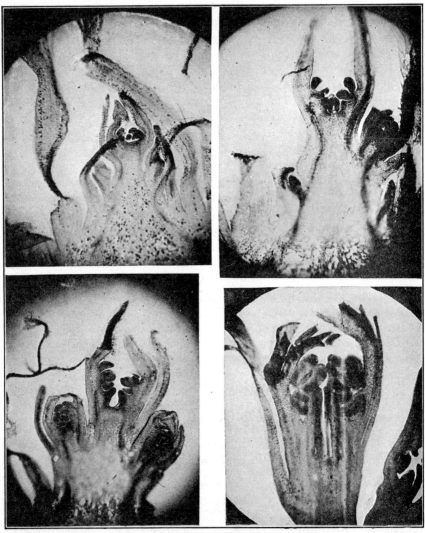

Fig. 24.—Stages in fruit bud development of the Yellow Newtown apple.   Above, to the left Sept. 10, to the right Nov. 25; below, to the left, Feb. 14, to the right, Mar. 6. (*After Bradford.*[36])

inception.   Albert found differentiation in the Japanese quince in August.   In the Luster peach initial stages of flower formation were observed in Virginia the first week in July;[94] Quaintance[240] in Georgia found no indication of differentiation in Demming's September peach on June 14, but on July 23 he reported: "the embryo flower is well under way and the calyx lobes are quite pronounced." Apparently, then, the initial stages must have occurred late in June. Goff,[113] working with a Bokhara peach, considered that "flowers began to form about the middle of September the past season." At Davis, California, the first evidence of differentiation in the almond has been reported as about Aug. 18.[284]

The plum as investigated by Drinkard shows some variation in the time of initiation of fruit buds. Whitaker, one of the Wildgoose group, gave no evidence until the first week in September; "observations on several varieties of Japanese plums showed that the initial formation of fruit buds occurred during the second week in July; and the individual fruit buds within the cluster were clear and distinct on August 7th."[94] In Wisconsin, flower formation has been found under way in the Aitken plum on Aug. 9 and some differentiation in the Rollingstone on July 8 in 1899 and on July 5 in the following year.[112]

In the Louis Philippe cherry of the Morello group, signs of differentiation have been noted on June 30 in Virginia. Goff, working with the King's Amarelle cherry, found the earliest indications of flowers on July 11[112] and in the following year on July 8. At Heidelberg, Germany, blossom primordia of the sweet cherry were visible during July.[132]

Investigations of flower-bud formation in the small fruits were made by Goff. In the strawberry Sept. 20 was the date of the first indication of flower buds in Wisconsin.[113] Later studies by Waldo,[303] Hill and Davis[151] and others indicate that this is the approximate time for the initiation of the process in many other sections. Waldo's work shows that in some varieties fruit bud differentiation is extended over a considerable period of time; in others, it occurs within a relatively short period. He found that "*Fragaria nilgerrensis*, a species native to northern India, did not differentiate fruit buds until November. Rapidity and uniformity of subsequent development were found to vary to a considerable degree between different varieties and species. There is no absolute correlation between early differentiation of fruit buds, early blooming, and early ripening, or between late differentiation, late blooming and late maturity. However, for many varieties this correlation actually existed."[303] In the case of the everbearing varieties, flower-bud differentiation proceeds throughout summer, though there is evidence of a short break in the process immediately following the maturity of the spring crop.[304] Apparently length of day is more closely correlated with time of flower-bud formation in the strawberry than is carbohydrate-nitrogen balance, ordinary varieties forming them during the short (10 to 12 hours) days of fall, and the everbearers during the longer days of summer.[89] Some of ormation by length of day.

Differentiation was found to occur in the Pomona currant about July 8 and in the Black Victoria currant about Aug. 3.[114] In the Downing gooseberry there was evidence on Aug. 30; in the cranberry no clear signs were found until Sept. 16. Less definite observations were made in raspberries and blackberries; nevertheless, unquestionable evidence shows that the flowers are formed the year previous to blossoming. "In the raspberry and blackberry," states Goff, "the buds that form in the axils of the leaves of the young shoots contain a whole branch in embryo—often several nodes, with a leaf at each node. The bud at the apex of this branch and the axillary buds along it, if they form, are flower-buds . . . embryo flowers in those buds are formed the season before their expansion, at least in part."

Fruit bud formation in the grape occurs during the summer previous to blossoming. A single bud contains in embryo a shoot with blossom primordia. General observations to this effect are recorded by Goff[114] and Bioletti[31] and have been followed by more detailed studies by Snyder[269] and Barnard and Thomas[24] indicating differentiation from very early in the growing season (when the new shoots are only a foot long) to relatively late as the shoots continue to grow. Tendril and inflorescence primordia differentiate from morphologically similar *anlagen*, hence the grape tendril may be regarded as a kind of vegetative flower cluster. "The development of *anlagen* as inflorescence primordia or as tendril primordia is correlated with the time of the season during which the growth of the *anlagen* occurs. Differentiation of *anlagen* into inflorescence takes place during late spring, summer, and autumn; whilst *anlagen* which are initiated after the winter rest become tendril primordia. . . . *Anlagen* which are initiated in late summer or autumn and have not developed before winter to acquire a definite habit of growth become tendril primordia during the following spring, whilst *anlagen* which have just begun to acquire the inflorescence mode of growth in autumn, develop into 'transition' forms when growth recommences. Differentiation of the flowers of the inflorescence occurs as the buds are opening in spring and prohibits further ramification of the inflorescence. . . . The potential size of the inflorescence is determined by the amount of growth made by the primordia prior to bud burst in the spring."[24]

In the filbert (*Corylus Avellana*) Albert[6] found signs of catkins on June 10, before embryonic leaves were laid down; female blossoms were not found until early in September. In the beech he was unable to find blossom buds until the beginning of leaf fall, but since the pollen mother cells in the anthers had already formed, differentiation must have occurred much earlier.

The pistillate flowers of the pecan are differentiated in late winter or early spring, as the hitherto vegetative buds begin to swell.[161,264] These "continue their development as the internodes of the vegetative shoot elongate until about ten or more leaves have unfolded, at which time the pistillate flowers become visible." The staminate flowers are differentiated a little later in the season in the lateral buds on the shoots, but they do not complete their development and shed their pollen until the following year.[161] Staminate flowers may be differentiated on secondary shoots comparatively late in the summer.

In citrus fruits differentiation of blossom buds takes place at or shortly after the beginning of growth in the spring (January to April in Florida) or at almost any other season when there is "a resumption of growth following a period of environmental conditions favorable and of sufficient duration for the accumulation of a reserve food supply."[1]

In Relation to Position.—Not all fruit buds are differentiated simultaneously, even on the same tree. Investigations by Goff[113] convinced him that in the apple and pear fruit-bud formation may occur after the first of September; he suggested as alternatives either (1) two periods of flower formation or (2) a continual differentiation through the season. Bradford, working with the Yellow Newtown apple, reports least variation in spurs which have borne previously but are not bearing in the current season (see Fig. 24); terminal fruit buds on long shoots obviously must be differentiated at a later period than is known to characterize formation on spurs. Considerable variation in the time of differentiation occurs also in young spurs which have never before formed fruit buds. Even in bearing spurs, when they form fruit buds, the formation may occur from early July to late August. Spurs which had blossomed during the current season but failed to set fruit varied still more; some of the earliest differentiation observed was found in spurs of this class and later differentiation also occurred.

Magness[193] in a careful study of axial buds found resting stages of leaf buds in several varieties as early as July 9 and early in September he recognized differentiation into flower buds. Some of his preparations taken in December suggest an initial differentiation into fruit buds, though he evidently did not regard them as such. In the Tetofski apple he considered some differentiation to have occurred about the first of August. He states that a spur bud of July 23 showed as much development as the most advanced axillary buds of Sept. 2. In the investigations of the following year the "main period of axillary fruit-bud formation in the varieties studied began after August 1, and a great many buds were apparently being differentiated on September 8. This was fully one month later than spur buds on the same trees."

Direct comparisons of the time of differentiation in buds of stone fruits in different positions are not available. Roberts,[251] however, found in September a difference in the development of buds on sour cherries according to their positions on the 4- or 5-inch shoot. This difference suggests that flower formation is initiated first both in the basal and in terminal regions. It is probable that a similar condition occurs in the peach.

Goff[113] found little or no difference in the comparative development of flower buds in rooted runners and parent plants in the strawberry. In the chestnut, which produces two sets of catkins, one subterminally on the growth of the past season and another laterally on the new shoots of the current season, the indications are that, though both sets open at approximately the same time, there is a period of 9 or 10 months between the times when they are differentiated.

Varietal Differences.—Bradford[36] found considerable difference between varieties of apple in the stage of development attained early in August, indicating a lack of uniformity in the time of differentiation. Of the varieties observed, Stark, Red Astrachan and Oldenburg seemed farther advanced than Jonathan, Northern Spy and Grimes. The season of ripening of the fruit appears to make little difference in the time of differentiation; there appears to be, however, some correspondence, though not absolute, between the order of blossoming and the order of differentiation. Magness[193] found White Pearmain, Tetofski and Yellow Transparent noticeably advanced in development in early July as compared with Lady and Jonathan.

Goff[114] found considerable difference between varieties in the time of fruit bud formation, some forming fruit buds before Aug. 1 while some were considered to form none until after the first of September. Differences between varieties of plums and strawberries have been mentioned earlier.

Differences Induced by Cultural Treatment.—Kirby[169] notes an earlier differentiation of fruit buds in apples growing in sod than in the same varieties in cultivated soil. Still finer distinctions were noted.

"The earliest time," he states, "at which flower buds were formed occurred on clover sod, with a low percentage of soil moisture. Flower buds formed earlier on a clover sod than on a blue grass sod having slightly less soil moisture. On the other hand, flower buds formed earlier on a blue grass sod than on a clover sod having about 2.5 per cent. more soil moisture. These facts indicate two things; *first*, that the addition of nitrates in the clover sod causes the flower buds to form earlier; and *second*, that the amount of soil moisture is a very important if not the chief external factor in determining the time at which flower buds form.

"The formation of flower buds began about the first of July on the plots where it occurred earliest and extended until the middle of September on the plots where it occurred latest, thus occupying a period of about 2½ months. The time occupied by each tree in forming flower buds was about 4 weeks."

The time of differentiation in the Baldwin apple in New Hampshire has been found somewhat variable, suggesting the effect of influences proceeding directly or indirectly from weather conditions.[32]

Goff[114] supplied water to a 9-year old Gideon apple tree in a dry season. Comparison on Aug. 9 with a similar unwatered tree showed very little difference in the stage of development reached at that time, though buds on the non-watered tree were somewhat more advanced.

In the sour cherry very strongly growing shoots and shoots partly defoliated by shot-hole fungus were retarded in their development.[251] Buds on younger trees were less advanced than those on older trees of the same variety. Since these studies were made at the approach of winter they do not furnish conclusive evidence as to the time of differentiation. However, they harmonize with the available direct evidence.

Abnormalities.—Finally, the occurrence of the so-called second bloom should be noted. Paddock and Whipple[231] mention a case of this kind. Similar teratological variations reported by Daniel were attributed by him to excessive pruning. This occurrence has been attributed at times to late frosts which destroyed the first blossoms and induced the formation of another set. This may be a correct explanation in some instances. The occurrence of blossoms on the vegetative shoots of several spurs bearing fruit in normal position was noted in an Oldenburg apple at Columbia, Mo., in 1920; the following year the same tree showed this phenomenon in about 20 per cent. of its spurs before any injurious frost occurred. Whether these buds were differentiated the preceding season cannot be stated positively. However, in the Rome Beauty apple vegetative shoots from fruiting spurs were observed to grow to a length of 4 to 6 inches, forming 6 to 7 leaves and then—still early in the season—to open solitary blossoms. In this case differentiation undoubtedly occurred in the spring. Hand pollination in some cases resulted in the formation of fruits with seeds of normal appearance and in Oldenburg without such assistance a considerable proportion of the crop actually harvested developed from secondary bloom.

Apple trees in tropical climates, though they blossom little, seem not to be restricted in the time of fruit bud formation. Certain bud sports of the Montmorency cherry have been described, in which flower-bud formation regularly takes place over a comparatively long period and beginning fully a month after the process is completed in the normal part of the same trees.[107]

The conclusion seems warranted that a fruit bud may be formed at any time, though ordinarily the period is rather restricted. The period evidently can be varied somewhat by cultural treatments, including perhaps any practice that modifies the rate of growth. In general the earlier the period of differentiation, the greater the number of fruit buds finally formed, but as shown elsewhere, with some qualifications, the less hardy those buds are.

Winter Stages.—Kraus[175] has described in detail the development of the individual flower within the bud. The sepals are differentiated first, followed closely by the primordia of the petals. Either simultaneously with, or directly after, their appearance those of the stamens are laid down; after these come the primordia of the carpels. The ovules do not appear until the resumption of growth in the spring.

During November and December in Virginia, Drinkard[94] found little development of the gross parts of the apple flower but noted some cytological changes. "During December," he states, "the pollen mother cells developed large, prominent nuclei. . . . Nearly all changes which occurred during the month of January took place in the stamens. . . . On February 19, there was some indication of renewed development in the anthers; these had enlarged appreciably on February 24. . . . Early in March there was a beginning of development of ovules in the cells of the ovary. These became very distinct by March 22. At the same time tetrad formation was going on in the pollen mother cells."

Drinkard found some development during the winter in buds of pear also. In the peach, growth during winter seemed more active. The ovule appeared late in December and tetrad formation in the pollen mother cells late in January, in both instances considerably in advance of the apple. Similarly the plum was found to show more or less development, practically throughout the winter. These observations are of interest in connection with the differences in hardiness of fruit buds discussed elsewhere.

However, it has been reported that in New York fruit buds do not develop from the middle of November until about the first of March[320] and in Wisconsin no evidences of activity were found from the beginning of freezing weather until after the middle of March.[112] In fact it was stated that there was no change in pear flowers from Dec. 1 to Mar. 30.[112] Albert reports pear blossoms to be unchanged until March, though he records development in the pistils of the filbert during November and December. In Japanese quince he found that development is arrested only during cold weather and is resumed whenever temperatures permit. Many of these blossoms are killed by cold.

Magness[193] noted a difference in the stage of development of buds on spurs in successive years. Buds of the Tetofski apple in November, 1914, showed ovules developed, while in December, 1915, they had not reached that stage.

"The blooming season during the spring of 1915 was fully one week earlier," he states, "than that of 1916. It is quite probable that factors operating during the late summer and fall to hasten or retard flower development, as well as factors operating during the spring, materially influence the time of blossoming in our orchard fruits." This statement is of particular interest when correlated with Sandsten's work, discussed under Temperature Relations.

Summary.—The available data do not permit a definite statement of the exact cause or causes of fruit bud differentiation or an exact description of the internal nutritive conditions associated with fruitfulness and unfruitfulness. However, there apparently must be at least two antecedents to an initiation of the reproductive processes: (1) There must be an excess of carbohydrates above the amount required for vegetative development. The rate of manufacture must exceed the rate of utilization. (2) There must not be any limiting factor that entirely stops vegetative growth which must continue within the bud even though there be no new shoots and leaves formed or even no visible indication of an increase in the size of the buds that are differentiating flower parts. In the orchard the supply of available nitrogen is probably the most common limiting factor. If nitrogen is present in large amounts it forces the rapid utilization of carbohydrates so that their accumulation cannot occur. If it is very limited in amount, growth is practically stopped before fruit bud differentiation can take place. Carbohydrate accumulation may not in itself be the cause of the fruitful condition in the plant as a whole or in its individual parts. It may simply be another result of the same factors that lead to fruitfulness; at least, however, the two are associated.

In practically all the deciduous fruits growing in temperate climates fruit bud differentiation occurs during the summer or fall previous to the opening of the buds. Every bud that is formed may be considered a potential fruit bud, but practically differentiation takes place only when suitable nutritive conditions are provided. Ordinarily each bud develops to a certain point and then comes to a comparative rest. Later development is as a vegetative bud or a flower bud, depending on whether conditions do or do not favor differentiation of flower parts in the slow growth that takes place during the period of comparative rest. The exact time of differentiation varies considerably with variety, seasonal conditions, moisture supply, method of culture, position on the plant and other factors. In cold climates there are practically no changes within the bud during the winter.

CHAPTER XI

SURPLUSES AND DEFICIENCIES

Though much has been written on the function of individual mineral constituents, it is questionable whether definite roles can be assigned to them, except in so far as they enter into the composition of specific organic compounds that have known functions. Thus magnesium is a component of the chlorophyll molecule, which is essential for photosynthesis. It is important, nevertheless, to know the effects attending a surplus or a deficiency of one or more mineral elements, so that the symptoms may be recognized and the condition corrected. However, pathological conditions found to follow an excess or deficiency of any one element do not necessarily indicate a direct relation of the element to the symptoms. Thus, though a deficiency of iron is known to produce chlorosis, a disordered condition in which chlorophyll does not develop, iron does not occur in the chlorophyll molecule.

From the considerations in the previous chapters, it follows that either a surplus or a deficiency of any soil element may affect the plant by disturbing the balance between its various constituents. A deficiency of an element may also affect the plant when that element is a limiting factor of growth. In all cases, a surplus or a deficiency must be understood to mean an amount greater or less than that which is utilized along with the other elements of the soil. The effect of a surplus of any essential soil constituent must be upon the balance or equilibrium of the plant. There may be no effect, since the plant may adjust itself to a surplus which is merely tolerated. There is much evidence that the quantities of potassium and calcium in plant tissues are often much in excess of the amounts used in metabolism. The same undoubtedly holds for other essential and many non-essential elements such as sodium, chlorine, aluminum and silicon. On the other hand, distinct pathological conditions may ensue which lead eventually to the death of the plant. Likewise elements which are not essential to the nutrition of the plant may be tolerated or they may produce disturbances, the effects of which may be either to stimulate assimilation or to induce pathological conditions and eventually death. As a general physiological theorem, it may be stated that any substance which is toxic in certain amounts is stimulating in smaller amounts.

214

SURPLUSES

The evidences for the existence of pathological conditions due to the absorption of a surplus of some soil nutrient are limited to a comparatively few elements.

Nitrogen.—The results of an excess of nitrogen usually appear the year following the actual surplus nitrogen absorption. They are shown[276] in trees by a tendency in the fruit to physiological decay. Dieback, or exanthema, and gummosis of citrus trees also are attributed to a surplus of nitrogen.[309] This causes a diseased condition in the growing tissues of the tree characterized primarily by gum pockets, stained terminal branches, "ammoniated" fruits, bark excrescences and multiple buds. The secondary symptoms are an unusually deep green color of the foliage, distorted growth of the terminal branches, frenching of the foliage and thick coarse leaves shaped like those of the peach. Mineral sources of nitrogen, even in great quantities, are not known to produce dieback though they may accentuate the symptoms in trees already affected,[101] but organic fertilizers containing nitrogen often lead to its development when they are applied in large amounts.

Magnesium.—The poisonous action of an excess of magnesium absorbed by the plant is attended by a browning of the roots and of vessels in the wood, cessation of growth in the roots and eventually death of the root hairs, the entire roots and leaves. These toxic effects may be counteracted in large part by calcium through its antagonistic action on magnesium, previously discussed. It should be pointed out that toxic effects similar to those following an excess of magnesium have been observed to develop from oxalic acid and that the toxic effects of other salts and salt mixtures, such as potassium nitrate with potassium phosphate, may be corrected by calcium.

Copper.—Though the evidence indicates that, at least in some plants, minute quantities of copper are necessary for normal growth[197] and that applications of copper-containing compounds may serve as soil correctives,[49,203] orchard disorders are likely to be occasioned by surpluses of this element. Copper salts are poisonous even in exceedingly small concentrations. Water distilled in copper receptacles is frequently toxic. Coupin[60] found that the lethal dose for grains grown in water culture was for each 100 cubic centimeters of nutrient solutions, 0.0049 gram copper bromide; 0.005 copper chloride; 0.0056 copper sulphate; 0.0057 copper acetate and 0.006 copper nitrate. Copper salts absorbed by the roots are likely to stop root growth. On the other hand, the stimulating effect of a mixture of copper sulphate and lime sprayed on leaves is well known. Leaf development is stimulated, the chlorophyll content increased, the palisade cells become longer and narrower and the spongy parenchyma has smaller intercellular spaces.[25]   Probably the amounts of copper absorbed by the sprayed leaves are less than those which produce toxic effects when absorbed by the roots.   Ewert,[97] however, has demonstrated that concentrations of 1 to 100,000,000 of copper sulphate are toxic to the pulp cells of the apple and that minute quantities entering through the stomata after spraying or taken up by the roots may result in one of the forms of bitter pit.   Fortunately the lime or other materials used with copper in spraying render the copper relatively insoluble and thus counteract or reduce its toxic effects on the plants and in the soil, though continued spraying with copper-containing compounds may result in toxic concentrations in the surface soil.[59]

Arsenic.—Arsenic is another mineral toxic to plants in exceedingly small amounts.   In many of the higher plants exposure to a concentration of 1 part in 1,000,000 is sufficient to inhibit growth.[229]   When arsenic is absorbed by the roots, they show its effects first.

The toxic effects of arsenic on fruit trees are described in an article in the Horticulturist.[159]   "When a little arsenic is introduced into the circulation of a fruit tree at that season (early spring) it first discolors the sap vessels of the inner bark, then the leaves suddenly flag, and droop; the branch shrivels and turns black; and finally if the dose is large enough, the whole tree dies."   Stimulating effects from arsenic have been observed, presumably when absorption was restricted to amounts smaller than that indicated above as toxic.

The question of the toxic action of arsenic is one of much interest since nearly all deciduous orchard fruits require one or more applications of arsenical sprays each year.   In old bearing orchards the total arsenic used per acre each year is likely to be as much as 6 pounds, figured as arsenic trioxide.   Though applied directly to the foliage and fruit, most of it reaches the ground in the course of the season.   It is generally applied in some very insoluble and chemically inactive form, such as arsenate of lead.   However, there is a considerable accumulation, especially in the surface soil, as spraying is continued.   Analyses of soils from certain Utah orchards have shown amounts of total arsenic in the surface foot of soil varying from 7.2 to 367.2 pounds per acre and of water-soluble arsenic from 0.7 to 31.9 pounds,[124] and in certain unproductive Washington orchard soils the concentration of readily soluble arsenic, calculated as arsenious trioxide, has been found to range from 4.5 to 12.5 p.p.m.[299]   This has led to considerable uneasiness among growers and much injury has been reported to be due to these accumulations in some of the irrigated sections.   The injury has taken the form of collar and root rot and in addition it has often been followed by premature ripening of the fruit and wood in the fall and the death of the tree the following year.   However, it is principally in irrigated sections and in soils with a rather high alkali content that this trouble has been encountered. This suggests that the injury is attributable to the action of various alkali salts reacting with the arsenic to make it soluble, to the combined action of alkali salts and arsenic, or possibly to alkali salts alone, since similar injuries are known to result from alkali poisoning. Results with Ben Davis apple trees sprayed in one season with as much arsenic as ordinarily would be applied in 10 to 40 years and under conditions where soil alkali was not a factor, have led to the conclusion that such arsenical poisoning as has been reported from certain sections is not attributable to the arsenic.[22] Some of these applications were so heavy that the trees not only remained whitened all summer, but the "ground under the entire head of the tree was so saturated with the arsenic as to appear moldy white to a depth of 3 or 4 inches." No injury appeared in the trees or even in the vegetation (including strawberries, alfalfa and a number of weeds) under some of them. This makes it evident that little is to be feared from the toxic effect of the arsenic used in spraying unless the soil has a fairly high alkali content and then the problem is one of dealing with the alkali rather than with the arsenic. Arsenic is, however, a contributing factor. More recently arsenic has been reported as leading to unproductivity in cranberry plantations that have been heavily sprayed[198] and even comparatively light applications are known to have a very injurious effect on citrus trees.

Manganese.—The relation of an excess of manganese to iron deficit and the method of curing the diseased condition have been discussed. In excess, this element produces interesting symptoms, illustrated by pineapples grown on manganese soils.

The root system is reduced by the death of a large percentage of the fine branched rootlets some months after their formation. The roots that remain alive have a superabundance of root hairs, almost every epidermal cell elongating into one, and also a blunt growing tip, about half as large as a lead pencil, frequently swollen into an enlarged fleshy end. The formation of these enlargements seems to mark the end of growth and death soon follows. The leaf has an irregular surface due to shrinkage from loss of water, producing prominences which become dark brown. The cells have brown walls and in some cases the protoplasm eventually disintegrates. The green cells thus lose their color, become plasmolyzed and in some cases the nuclei turn brown. Here also the protoplasm loses its granular structure and disintegrates. As a result of the lack of chlorophyll, the leaves contain limited amounts of starch, but at the base of the leaves, in the stalks and roots, starch is abundant, having been stored there before the decomposition of the chlorophyll. Frequently no fruit develops, but that which does is reddish pink, without a trace of green, undersized and excessively acid.[166]

Apparently manganese poisoning is rare in deciduous fruits. In very dilute amounts manganese has a stimulating effect.[39]

Sulphur.—Apparently sulphur is seldom or never found in soil that would be classed as generally suitable for orchard purposes in such quantities as to be toxic to fruit plants, and the sulphur added to the soil through the use of sulphur-containing sprays or fertilizers has not been proved to be directly harmful to the trees.   However, there is some evidence that such applications have resulted in changes in soil reaction great enough to influence considerably the growth of cover or mulching crops and to modify the response of the trees to fertilizer applications. Furthermore, applications of such sprays has been found to lead to yellowing and premature dropping of foliage and to a stunting of the fruit in the case of apricots[268] in California and apples[95] in Michigan.

Other Elements.—Compounds of many other elements such as lead, mercury, zinc, boron[39] and silver are toxic in certain concentrations, but toxic effects from them are rare.   However, these materials are known occasionally to be absorbed in considerable quantities—zinc for example up to 13 per cent. of the ash, mercury and copper up to 1 per cent.[97] Ewert[97] has shown that extremely minute quantities of these, in concentrations varying from 1 in 1,000,000 to 1 in 1,000,000,000, may cause local browning in the tissues of the fruit of the apple and induce the condition known as bitter pit.   Concentrations of boron sufficient to produce toxic effects on trees are found in some of the irrigation waters of southern California.

"Citrus trees show the toxic effect of boron by a yellowing of the older leaves around the margins and between the veins and a dying back of the tips and margins.   The new growth may not show the injury until it is several months old.   Many of the affected leaves fall off in the winter and early spring months. When walnut trees are injured by boron, the leaves turn brown around the margins and between the veins during August and September.   Earlier in the year the leaves may not show any evidence of boron injury.   Boron-affected walnut leaves tend to fall prematurely.[166a]

"Surpluses of chlorides in the irrigation water have led to chlorine absorption by avocado trees in California in excess of the amounts that they were able to tolerate, resulting in tip and marginal burning of the leaves, defoliation and the drying out and shriveling of surface areas on the fruit pedicels—a disorder known as 'ring neck.' "[126]

Mention may be made here of certain toxic gases such as hydrogen sulphide, sulphur dioxide, hydrogen cyanide and chlorine.   Sulphur dioxide injury is of considerable practical importance because the damage done to vegetation by smelter fumes is due largely to this compound.

The bulk of the evidence on the toxicity of inorganic mineral soil constituents, that has been discussed, suggests that the effects are largely local in the plant.   Amounts small enough to be stimulating are unquestionably absorbed by the roots, or in the case of spraying, by the leaves, but amounts large enough to poison the plant seem to induce injury chiefly by affecting the absorbing organs. Hence cessation of growth and eventually death of the roots are the primary symptoms. Disorders proceeding from the causes just outlined should be distinguished from the toxic effects produced by organic compounds or by excessive soil concentrations, discussed previously.

DEFICIENCIES

The lack of a sufficient amount of any essential soil constituent may lead to the development of distinct pathological conditions, or it may result simply in checking vegetative development and fruit production without producing obvious pathological symptoms. The use of fertilizers for correcting both of these conditions is discussed in the two following chapters in which particular emphasis is accorded the correction of conditions interfering with fruit production on a commercial scale. The discussion immediately following concerns the more important pathological symptoms which are associated with the presence of unduly small amounts or with the complete exhaustion of essential mineral elements.

Nitrogen.—A deficiency of nitrogen may become evident in several different ways. The plant may be dwarfed, though it develops completely and produces flowers, fruits and seeds. As a rule, however, the leaves are pale green because of the relatively small amounts of chlorophyll and the development of the mature fruit is affected in one way or another. In some instances more extreme types of chlorophyll deficiencies, such as chlorosis[212] and frenching,[298] have been shown to be due to a very limited supply of available nitrogen.

There may be an incomplete development of the sexual organs, and consequent unfruitfulness;[270] in case fruits develop they may be seedless, as in apples, pears and grapes,[271] or the fruit may develop somewhat but drop prematurely. This is a common result of nitrogen deficiency in apples and pears. The latter sometimes show excessive thorn development in connection with a lack of nitrogen.[272]

All these symptoms may be due to a number of other causes and therefore considerable care is necessary in the diagnosis of any particular case. In general, however, the symptoms exhibited by fruit trees that, together, most observers would be inclined to consider as those of starvation are the result of nitrogen deficiency, or, at least, nitrogen deficiency is likely to be a factor of major importance in causing them.

Phosphorus and Potassium.—As stated before, phosphorus deficiencies are not likely to be met with under field conditions. When brought about by treatment, the resulting symptoms are a dull green foliage without luster and purpling and bronzing and with premature fall.[91]   These same symptoms are more or less characteristic of the blackheart form of winter injury and of certain other disorders, and diagnosis, therefore, needs to be made with considerable care.   Peaches borne on phosphate-deficient trees mature early and keep poorly.[152]

A deficiency of potassium[272] is usually associated with a scarcity of carbohydrate reserves.   In trees, the terminal shoots show weak development and eventually dry out, or shoot formation may be suppressed wholly.   Dieback has been recorded as characterizing coffee trees in Hawaii[121,248] and prune trees in California[186] growing in potash-deficient soils.   Plants suffering from a lack of potassium often maintain a healthy appearance longer than those lacking nitrogen or phosphorus.   Whatever potassium is available apparently is used first for vegetative growth and development and, if there is no residuum, the plant does not blossom. Eventually the leaf blade becomes yellow on the edges and between the veins, then brown and finally white, while the veins and petiole remain green.   The leaf blades are likely to become brittle.   This condition is often classified as a type of chlorosis, though it is more accurately referred to as frenching.   Frenching due to potassium deficiency is characterized by the ash in the dry matter being relatively low, though the percentages of iron, calcium, magnesium and phosphorus in the ash are relatively high.[305]   This is in contrast with the condition that characterizes lime-induced chlorosis where the leaves show high ash in the dry matter and low calcium and high potassium in the ash.   Frenching due to potassium deficiencies have been reported in plums and certain other fruits in parts of England.[305]

Leaf scorch and bronzing are symptoms of potash deficiency in numerous instances,[152,153,177] though these conditions may be accentuated or perhaps be due entirely to other causes and therefore diagnosis is sometimes difficult.   Fischer[99] points out that leaf scorch caused by potassium deficiency is more gradual in its incidence than when caused by the desiccating effect of wind.   In citrus trees leaf scorch caused by potassium deficiency may be accompanied or followed by a marked tendency toward gum formation in wood and bark.[127]

A potassium deficiency renders the roots susceptible to rotting, and the plant eventually dies.   In Porto Rico it has been found that in soils deficient in potash, pineapple plants contain less of this element, are much more susceptible to certain diseases and produce few suckers.[239]   These symptoms can be relieved by suitable applications of potash-carrying fertilizers.   When nitrogen or phosphorus is deficient, plants are likely to remain alive longer in a stunted condition.

Sulphur.—As a result of sulphur deficiency, cell division is retarded and fruit development is suppressed,[275] but the plant is able to develop vegetatively to a limited extent. Sulphur deficiencies in the soil are more likely to react unfavorably on fruit plants through limiting the growth of certain leguminous cover or mulching crops than through any direct influence on fruit plants themselves. However, chlorotic conditions in the tea bush in Nyasaland, South Africa,[281] and in the strawberry in Texas[283] are known to be associated with sulphur deficiencies and have been alleviated with applications of elemental sulphur or of sulphur-containing compounds to the soil. Possibly in some of these instances the indirect effect of the sulphur applications, through changing soil reaction and thus rendering iron more available, has been more important than the direct supplying of sulphur as a nutrient, though in others there is definite experimental evidence that it serves primarily as a nutrient.

Iron.—A lack of iron produces the well-known condition of chlorosis or yellows. This is not characteristic solely of iron want, for it may result eventually from a lack of either nitrogen or magnesium, or from other deficiencies but the effects of iron deficiency in producing chlorosis are more rapid than those of nitrogen insufficiency and consequently more striking. When iron is deficient, developing leaves are at first able to avail themselves of iron in older tissues. Later the new leaves are green only at the tips and eventually the newly developed leaves are entirely yellow. Chloroplasts develop in them, but they contain no chlorophyll. Recent investigation[230] has shown that organic compounds containing the pyrrol ring, which appears in the structure of chlorophyll, correct the condition of chlorosis produced by iron want, suggesting that iron may have something to do with the formation of this ring. However, since iron is just as essential for fungi and other parasitic plants which have no chlorophyll as for green plants, its importance cannot be limited to the part it apparently plays in the synthesis of the pyrrol ring. The treatment that would at once be suggested for iron deficiencies, namely, the application of iron-containing salts to the soil, has afforded temporary relief in many instances, but most soils whose plants become chlorotic because of lack of iron promptly fix the iron that is applied and render it unavailable.[125] Such soil applications, if made, should be accompanied by treatments that tend to acidify the soil, thus making the iron more completely available. A procedure that promptly and effectively alleviates the chlorotic condition is to inject ferrous salts directly into holes bored in the trunk of the tree.[29,34] Such treatments are usually effective for a period of two or more years. Owing to the fact that iron salts in the concentration required to effect improvement discolor and kill the wood for a considerable distance up and down the trunk, new holes must be bored for each injection and eventually considerable damage results to the trunk.[288]

Magnesium and Calcium.—A deficiency of magnesium[273] reduces fruit formation and eventually produces chlorosis or frenching. This may develop as typical center blotch or brown patches or an early development of high yellowish orange tints, followed by severe premature defoliation.[91]

A lack of calcium interferes with carbohydrate transportation and utilization, but does not stop its manufacture. These disturbances may be associated with the formation by calcium of insoluble salts with substances which are products of carbohydrate utilization, as oxalic acid. A lack of calcium would result in an accumulation of oxalic acid, which is toxic in solution. This might be expected to interfere with the processes of carbohydrate utilization. Root growth is retarded or stopped, an effect already mentioned as resulting from an excess of magnesium. Hence some of the effects of calcium deficiency may be associated with the resultant effect on the calcium-magnesium ratio.[187] In reality, however, there is little evidence that calcium deficiency is a factor of importance in the fruit plantation.

Chlorine.—Though chlorine is not an essential element, some mention should be made here of the effects of an absence of chlorine. There are conditions in the field under which the best development occurs only when chlorides are added to the soil.[87] Recent investigations show that the effects of chlorides are markedly different on different plants, but that in many cases they serve directly or indirectly as a fertilizer.[292]

Boron.—As already stated, boron has been found to be essential to the growth of a number of plants. Symptoms of boron deficiency, as exhibited by citrus trees in California, have been given as follows:

"1. Boron deficiency is marked by a gradual reduction in the size of the shoots produced, which, in extreme cases, finally results in the formation of "multiple buds." Boron appears to be essential for cell division in the meristematic tissue of growing points, such as buds, but it is likewise essential for cambial activity.

"2. When boron is deficient the cambium and portions of the phloem disintegrate. The xylem tissue disintegrates to a much smaller degree, if at all. A copious amount of gum is formed, which finds its way to the exterior through a split in the cortex.

"3. Growth is related to the presence of boron. When growth has ceased and gum has formed as a result of a boron deficiency, the addition of boron to the culture solution has been the means of bringing about recovery.

"4. The abnormal accumulation of carbohydrates in the leaves of boron-deficient Citrus, coupled with the fact that the phloem tissues are destroyed, show that translocation is seriously interfered with.

"5. Reduction in the total sugar content of the leaves accompanies recovery of the tissues brought about by the addition of boron to the culture solution."[128]

The fact that the occurrence of corky core in apples has been prevented both in Canada[209] and in New Zealand[19] by treatment with boron indicates that at least in some instances this disorder may be due to boron deficiency. More recently a widespread dwarfing disease of apple twigs and branches, known as measles and especially serious on the Delicious, has been reported to be due to boron deficiency and to yield to treatments of certain chemicals containing that element.[325] In California it has been observed that strawberry plants provided with an ample supply of boron are relatively free from mildew and red spider attack as compared with those grown with a very limited supply.[153]

Copper.—Though minute quantities of copper have been shown to be essential for plant growth and the treatment of certain soils with copper-containing compounds is necessary for the profitable production of some of the vegetable crops, thus far there is little evidence that a lack of copper is a limiting factor in fruit production. Nevertheless the possibility that it sometimes may be a limiting factor is indicated by the results that have attended treating with copper sulphate citrus trees in New South Wales affected with exanthema,[203] walnut trees in California that were affected with "yellows" or rosette[49] and chlorotic deciduous trees of various kinds in Cape Province, South Africa.[12]

Zinc.—Some of the symptoms due to a deficiency of zinc have already been mentioned. Apparently most of them, such as bronzing of foliage,[218] mottling of leaves[242,243] and rosette,[198] may be due to other causes, but whenever they occur, there is at least the suspicion that they may be due to an insufficient supply of zinc in the soil or nutrient medium.

Organic Matter.—Besides the disorders due to a deficiency in the supply of one of the essential mineral elements, there are a number of disorders, almost equally serious, that are associated with a very low content of soil organic matter. These are disorders of such types as exanthema of citrus trees[202] and rosette of the pecan,[210] apple and other fruits. To what extent, if at all, the humus supplies organic compounds that are absorbed as such by the plants is not known, for fruit plants are grown successfully in water and sand cultures supplied only with inorganic nutrients. Nevertheless, the marked stimulating effect that has been reported from the addition of small quantities of humus to sand cultures and the well-known results that attend the addition of large amounts of organic matter to soils deficient in humus attest its value in the fruit plantation and indicate that from a practical standpoint deficiency in humus supply is almost as serious as a deficiency in one of the essential nutrients. The extent to which its beneficial influence in the orchard is brought about through its effect on soil texture and water-holding capacity, through promoting desirable bacterial activity or through still other influences probably varies greatly with conditions.

AN ANALYSIS OF THE FERTILIZER PROBLEM

The data that have been presented, on the factors affecting soil productivity on the one hand and the metabolic processes going on within the plant on the other, emphasize the incompleteness of the knowledge of plant nutrition. Much important information has been obtained regarding changes occurring in the soil and something is known of the synthesis, translocation, storage and utilization of organic materials. At best, however, this information is fragmentary and much generalization regarding the use of fertilizers in the orchard is unsafe. Some idea of the complexity of the problem is obtained when we consider the numerous ways in which fertilizers may act: (1) to change conditions in the soil and (2) to disturb or restore equilibria within the plant. Among the more important of these methods of action may be mentioned the following:

1. Altering the physical properties of the soil.
2. Affecting the displacement (lyotropic succession) of various elements.
3. Changing the solubility of other soil constituents.
4. Changing the availability of other soil constituents.
5. Changing the concentration of the soil solution.
6. Changing the reaction of the soil solution.
7. Influencing bacterial activity in the soil.
8. Correcting or disturbing the balance between certain soil constituents, *e.g.*, calcium and magnesium antagonism.
9. Stimulating or checking chemical reactions in the soil or absorption by the roots.
10. Acting as toxins or protecting against their influence.
11. Serving directly as nutrients for the plant.
12. Restoring or disturbing chemical equilibria within the plant after absorption.

The Fertilizer Requirements of the Orchard.—In the discussion that has preceded some attention has been devoted to each of these factors in the nutrition of the plant. There has been presented also a general résumé of some of the available information regarding synthesis, translocation and use of certain plant constituents. Incidentally the following facts have been brought out:

1. Many elements that evidently are not required are found in plants. Seldom are they harmful; they are merely tolerated. Among them may be mentioned silicon, aluminum, sodium, titanium and probably chlorine. These elements are not required in fertilizers. They may be combined with certain others that are of importance and they may have some indirect influence upon the physical condition of the soil or the chemical nature of the soil solution. They may often serve a useful purpose in

furnishing some of the so-called "indifferent" ash and occasionally some distinctly beneficial response attributable to their presence may be obtained when they are carried in fertilizers, but on the whole they need not be given serious consideration in the problem of orchard fertilization.

2. Certain elements are found universally in plants and are necessary constituents; however, except in very unusual cases, they exist in the soil in sufficient quantities and in forms sufficiently available to meet the requirements of orchard trees. The plant often takes up more than it uses. This surplus is merely tolerated and usually no harmful influence results. Among these elements may be mentioned potassium, calcium and magnesium. As with the preceding list, their application in fertilizers may indirectly benefit the plant through improving physical and chemical conditions within the soil, or restoring a proper ratio between them in the case of the last two.

It would seem that sufficient evidence to support these statements has been presented in the discussion of the individual elements that has preceded. It is realized, however, that they run counter to the opinions that have been expressed in a great number of published statements dealing with this question, to many recommendations that have been made for the fertilization of fruit trees, to what has in some instances become more or less well established practice and to the apparent results of certain plot experiments. This is true particularly in the cases of potassium and calcium. It seems desirable, therefore, to bring together the results of some of the orchard fertilizer experiments with potash and lime and examine them somewhat critically. Table 42 presents such data gathered from many sources. It does not include all the records that might be assembled, but it represents the results of American plot trials.

In some cases the application of potassium- or of calcium-carrying fertilizers has resulted in increased yields; in others in decreased yields. The increases outweigh the decreases in both number and amount; but in the Pennsylvania experiments alone, of those included in the table, are the increases striking or to be regarded as of considerable significance. These particular Pennsylvania records are extremes purposely chosen from a large number, the great majority of which show no such marked response from potash applications. Furthermore, the different check plots in these two orchards show such variation as to justify some hesitancy in drawing conclusions when comparing the results of one fertilizer treatment with those of another on a plot some distance removed from the first. For instance, it may be questioned if the plots treated with lime alone and with nitrogen alone were as good at the outset as those receiving nitrate of soda and muriate of potash. In nearly every case in which comparison is possible between potash or lime treated plots and those treated with nitrogen alone or in combination, nitrogen stands out as the element most needed, the one from the application of which the greatest response is obtained. The fact that in most cases the application of nitrogen alone resulted in yields exceeding those afforded by potash or lime is further evidence that there was an ample supply of these two elements in the soil for larger crop production, that they were present in an available form and that they were not the real limiting factors. Theoretically potassium and calcium are to be considered as possible limiting factors just as nitrogen or iron or phosphorus or sulfur. Here and there is to be found evidence that occasionally they actually are not present in an available form and in quantities sufficient for the trees' requirements, but in the great majority of cases there is no occasion to supplement the supply already present in the soil.

3. Certain elements, such as arsenic and lead, are occasionally found in plant tissues and when present in considerable amounts they have toxic effects. However, their presence is the result of spray applications or unusual conditions of one kind or another and the problems incident to their presence are hardly to be considered as belonging in the field of nutrition.

4. Two elements, phosphorus and sulphur, are found in all soils and in all plants. Though they are necessary for plant growth, deciduous fruits are able ordinarily to obtain all of them they require. However, their application in fertilizers is frequently warranted, mainly because of their indirect value to the trees through the effect they may have on intercrops or cover crops. Some attention is devoted to this phase of the orchard fertilizer problem. Perhaps the same statements should be extended to apply to boron, copper, zinc and manganese, though available evidence indicates that they are still less frequently limiting factors in the fruit plantation.

5. Two other essential elements, iron and nitrogen, though found in all soils, are often either deficient in quantity or present in forms unavailable to the plant. The result is arrested development or, in extreme cases, the appearance of pathological conditions. An excess of nitrogen also leads to disturbed nutritive relations and to pathological symptoms. Considerable attention has already been devoted to the question of iron deficiencies and to methods of dealing with them.

6. Elaborated organic compounds of many kinds have uses in growth processes equal in importance to those of the mineral constituents. Though for the most part they are synthesized within the plant, the materials for their manufacture are water, carbon dioxide and the nutrients just mentioned.

It is therefore evident that the question of fertilizers for deciduous fruits, in so far as such fertilizers serve more or less directly as nutrients for the plant, centers largely around the proper use of nitrogen. This is far from stating that fertilizers other than those carrying nitrogen are never of direct nutrient value. For instance, work with grapes and strawberries[51] suggests strongly that sulfur-carrying fertilizers in the one case and phosphorus-carrying compounds in the other supplied the plants directly with these nutrients, though it is possible that certain of their indirect influences may have been more important than their direct effects. Furthermore, there is reason to believe that many of the results obtained from the use of phosphorus-, potassium- and calcium-carrying fertilizers on deciduous fruits of different kinds and generally attributed to their direct nutrient value have in reality been due to their functioning

TABLE 42.—INFLUENCE OF POTASH-CARRYING FERTILIZERS UPON FRUIT YIELDS

Investigator	State	Crop	Fertilizer	Yield	Yield of check	Gain, per cent.
Alderman[7]	West Virginia	Peach	K + P	42.42	49.48	−14.2
Alderman[7]	West Virginia	Peach	K + N	71.93	49.48	45.3
Alderman[7]	West Virginia	Peach	Lime	60.82	49.48	22.9
Mc Cue[207]	Delaware	Peach	K	764.40	684.30	11.7
Mc Cue[207]	Delaware	Peach	K	1565.90	684.30	129.6
Mc Cue[207]	Delaware	Peach	N	2210.80	684.30	223.0
Gladwin[111]	New York	Grape	K_2SO_4	940.50	711.00	32.3
Gladwin[111]	New York	Grape	NaNO₃+ K_2SO_4	1185.50	711.00	66.7
Gladwin[111]	New York	Grape	N + K + P	1230.50	711.00	73.0
Gladwin[111]	New York	Grape	N + K + P+ Lime	1118.00	711.00	57.2
Ballou[23]	Ohio	Apple	KCl	96.00	69.90	27.2
Ballou[23]	Ohio	Apple	NaNO₃	315.60	69.90	351.2
Hedrick, et al[147]	New York	Apple	KCl	4877.00	4375.00	11.5
Hedrick, et al[147]	New York	Apple	KCl + P + N	4823.50	4375.00	10.2
Reimer[245]	Oregon	Apple	KCl	3.31	2.85	16.1
Reimer[245]	Oregon	Apple	N	14.50	2.85	408.5
Reimer[245]	Oregon	Peach	KCl	30.00	30.80	−2.6
Reimer[245]	Oregon	Peach	N	42.25	30.80	37.2
Collison[57]	New York	Apple	N + P + KCl	79.00	76.80	2.9
Collison[57]	New York	Apple	N + P	77.10	76.80	0.4
Collison[57]	New York	Cherry	N + P + KCl	122.70	111.60	9.9
Collison[57]	New York	Cherry	N + P	105.90	111.60	−4.9
Collison[57]	New York	Grape	Lime	280.00	220.00	27.2
Collison[57]	New York	Grape	Lime	261.00	443.00	−69.7
Chandler[51]	Missouri	Strawberries	KCl	11.10	14.20	−21.8
Brown[41]	Oregon	Strawberries	K_2SO_4	222.00	230.00	−3.5
Franklin[103]	Massachusetts	Cranberries	K	43.25	48.18	−10.3
Munson[219]	Maine	Apples	KCl	2.06	2.30	11.5
Munson[219]	Maine	Apples	K_2SO_4	2.28	2.30	−0.9
Stewart[278]	Pennsylvania	Apples	N + KCl	318.20	117.80	170.2
Stewart[278]	Pennsylvania	Apples	N	186.20	98.00	90.0
Stewart[278]	Pennsylvania	Apples	P + KCl	113.10	75.60	49.6
Stewart[278]	Pennsylvania	Apples	P + K_2SO_4	91.30	93.20	−2.4
Stewart[278]	Pennsylvania	Apples	Lime	73.70	67.70	8.0
Stewart[278]	Pennsylvania	Apples	N + KCl	350.40	230.30	52.1
Stewart[278]	Pennsylvania	Apples	N	236.80	208.40	13.1
Stewart[278]	Pennsylvania	Apples	Lime	61.00	53.80	13.4

in other ways. These statements are not made to minimize the possible effects or uses of fertilizing elements other than nitrogen. That they often are of value in the orchard there is no doubt. The point is that nitrogenous fertilizers act more or less directly as nutrient-carrying substances; others generally act rather indirectly through correction of unfavorable soil conditions or by protecting the orchard plants from harmful substances or only indirectly as nutrients through assisting the growth of intercrops or cover crops.   Clear differentiation between these different modes of operation is important, for only when there is a clear conception of how a fertilizer works can it be used intelligently and with certainty as to results.

CHAPTER XII

THE APPLICATION OF NITROGEN-CARRYING FERTILIZERS

The general purpose of fertilizer application is to increase yields. In the orchard this may result from larger tree growth, from increased fruit bud formation, from better setting of the fruit, from the production of fruit of larger size, or from a combination of two or more of these rather distinct responses.

The Influence of Nitrogenous Fertilizers on Vegetative Growth.— An abundant supply of available nitrogen in the soil has long been associated, by well informed gardeners, with strong, vigorous growth. So well is this connection recognized that gardeners and florists generally have become skilled in the art of using nitrogenous fertilizers for vegetables and ornamental plants. Fruit growers, however, though inclined to recognize the general value of such fertilizers, have, for one reason or

TABLE 43.—EFFECT OF FERTILIZATION ON VEGETATIVE GROWTH OF THE PEACH
(*After Alderman*[7])

Fertilizer treatment	Average shoot length, 4-year average (inches)	Average leaf area, 3-year average (square inches)	Number leaves per tree, 3-year average	Leaf area per tree, 3-year average (square feet)	Per cent. of fruit buds, 4-year average
Nitrogen and phosphoric acid.	16.10	4.28	25,424	755.6	80.6
Nitrogen and potash.........	14.47	4.26	24,808	734.4	75.5
Complete fertilizer...........	15.00	4.06	23,208	654.3	74.0
Potash and phosphoric acid...	8.16	2.63	8,768	160.1	58.0
Check.....................	7.28	2.89	10,596	212.6	57.9
Complete fertilizer...........	14.40	4.12	29,536	845.0	76.6
Complete with potash doubled	15.59	4.39	32,368	986.7	75.2
Complete with potash tripled..	15.00	4.26	22,648	670.0	76.2
Lime......................	7.84	3.26	14,172	320.8	64.4

another, not employed them to any considerable extent and it is not until recent years that much experimental evidence has been available as to their place in orchard practice.

In Peaches.—Alderman[7] reported the results of a series of fertilizer experiments with peaches in West Virginia. The trees were growing in a rather thin shale loam, a soil commonly used in that section for apples and peaches, though it would generally be classed as rather unproductive. Some of his data pertaining to shoot and leaf growth are assembled in Table 43. They show that wherever nitrogen was used, shoot growth was practically doubled; this increased shoot growth was accompanied by a corresponding increase in leaf number. Furthermore there was a great gain in leaf size; this increase coupled with the greater number of leaves multiplied the total leaf area by three or four. In commenting on this effect of nitrogen, Alderman[7] remarks: " . . . for every foot of bearing surface on the check tree the fertilized tree carried over 2½ feet of wood upon which fruit might be borne. This difference in size has been increasing so that the ratio would be much greater in favor of the nitrogen fertilized trees at the present time after 4 years of treatment." Incidentally the data presented in this table support earlier statements to the effect that few orchards require potash, phosphoric acid or lime.

In Apples.—Lewis and Allen[185] have reported practically the same influence on the shoot growth and foliage of apple trees in the Hood River valley, Ore., when nitrate of soda was applied to bearing apple trees in a rather weakened condition. They observed an even more striking change in the color of the foliage, which was pale yellowish green in the check plots and dark rich green in those that were fertilized. Still another effect noted many times is delayed leaf fall. This delay may vary from a few days to several weeks. Since the leaves late in the season can build elaborated foods for winter storage and spring utilization, this delayed maturity may bring about an accumulation of materials which might promote greater vegetative growth the following season and maintain the tree in a more vigorous condition. At the same time, however, danger from sharp fall frosts or early freezes is increased, especially if applications are heavy enough to force the formation of new vegetative tissues late in the season. Consequently considerable caution should be exercised to apply nitrogen so as to postpone leaf fall but not materially to delay maturity of wood.

In Strawberries.—Chandler[51] reports that nitrogen in either nitrate of soda or dried blood applied to strawberry plants in the spring before the crop is harvested causes excessive leaf growth and that when the latter material is applied even a year before the crop is to be harvested it causes considerably increased vegetative growth. This excessive leaf growth was found to be associated with decreased fruit production.

Negative Results. Nitrogen Not a Limiting Factor.—On the other hand, Hedrick and Anthony[147] in reporting the results of 20 years of experimentation with fertilizers in apple orchards in New York state: " . . . heavy applications of nitrogen in a complete fertilizer and in manure have not increased tree growth." The results obtained by

Stewart[278] in Pennsylvania from the use of nitrogen-carrying fertilizers in bearing apple orchards are for the most part in accord with those of Lewis and Allen; at least most of his applications of nitrogenous fertilizers resulted in increased vegetative growth. However, some of these increases were comparatively small and there were a few instances in which no increase was obtained. Gourley[116] found substantially the same general condition in his experimental plots in New Hampshire—particularly during the early years of the experimental treatments. Table 44 assembled from data presented by him and some of his associates, recapitulating the first 5-years results, explains some of the preceding statements that at first appear more or less conflicting. This table shows practically no increased vegetative growth accompanying the use of fertilizers, as compared with plots under clean cultivation or plots growing annual cover crops, even though one of the fertilizers contained

TABLE 44.—RESPONSE IN VEGETATIVE GROWTH FROM FERTILIZER APPLICATIONS
(*After Gourley[116]*)

Treatment	Nitrates in soil in parts per million, 4-year average	Yield of fruit, 5-year average	Shoot growth, 4-year average	Size of fruit, 4-year average	Leaf area, 1913	Fresh leaf weight, 1913
Sod...............................	3.18	100	100	100	100	100
Cultivation every odd year.........	.....	132	140	168	107	111
Cultivation every even year........	.....	176	163	165	113	117
Clean culture......................	17.40	213	190	142	119	123
Cultivation and cover crop.........	33.91	216	212	135	124	123
Cultivation, cover crop and complete fertilizer......................	.....	191	222	165	129	135
Cultivation, cover crop and complete fertilizer......................	.....	195	198	155	126	131
Cultivation, cover crop and excess P_2O_5............................	.....	166	200	168	126	131
Cultivation, cover crop and excess N.	.....	163	217	196	125	128
Cultivation, cover crop and excess K_2O...........................	.....	161	202	206	131	134

relatively large amounts of nitrogen. However, soil cultivation, particularly when coupled with cover crops, made available to the plants an abundant supply of nitrogen—a supply that obviously was present in the sod land, but unavailable. This abundant supply met the trees' nutritive requirements and the surplus resulting from applications of nitrate did not effect any consistently increased growth. In a report on the same series of experiments 5 years later Gourley[117] states that though there was no special or marked increase in yield in the fertilized plots over those not receiving fertilizer "the orchard is developing in that direction." In other words, the period of maximum production without applications of nitrogenous fertilizers had been reached. This period might last for a number of years, or be of short duration; in either case greater and greater increases in vegetative growth and fruit production could be expected from proper fertilization. As trees increase in age and size they require larger amounts of nutrients and with the actual reduction in the total nitrogen supply of cultivated soils taking place each year it is easy to see how the margin of safety may disappear entirely. Increased vegetative growth follows the application of nitrogen-carrying fertilizers only when the supply of available nitrates in the soil is less than the plant must have for its best growth and there is a limit to what the plant can use. Within limits, surplus amounts of available nitrogen, like surplus amounts of available potassium or calcium or other materials, are simply tolerated. Analyses are not at hand showing the exact amounts of available nitrates in the West Virginia and Oregon soils to which reference has just been made, but it may be presumed that they contained very small amounts or amounts smaller than those required by the trees for maximum growth and production.

Many orchards will not respond to nitrogenous fertilizers because the soils and the methods of soil management are of such a character that nitrogen is not a limiting factor. On the other hand experience shows that there are many orchards in which nitrogen is a limiting factor and in which, consequently, nitrogen-carrying fertilizers can be used profitably. To conclude from one experiment or a series of experiments giving negative results that orchard fertilization in general is not needed or that it does not pay is as erroneous as it is to conclude from striking returns on a nitrate deficient soil that orchards generally should be regularly fertilized with that element. Statements that have been made give some idea of the symptoms of nitrogen starvation. Short, slender shoot growth and small pale leaves are perhaps the most frequent indices of this condition, though there are many others. However, some of these symptoms likewise characterize injuries resulting from deficient water supply, borer attack or other troubles and care should be exercised to identify the real cause or causes of the trouble before deciding upon fertilization of any considerable area.

A given supply of available nitrogen in the soil though entirely adequate for the requirements of one fruit crop may not prove sufficient for the best growth of another. Thus Chandler[53] has found that in a certain clay loam in New York applications of nitrogen-carrying fertilizers resulted in greatly increased shoot and leaf growth in gooseberries and red raspberries, though currants and black raspberries showed but little response. Reimer[245] reports that in the Rogue River of southern Oregon the Yellow Newtown apple does not respond to fertilizer applications so readily as Esopus (Spitzenburg) and McClelland has found that in certain coffee plantations in Porto Rico applications of fertilizers containing nitrogen only have resulted in sparse foliage and decreased growth.[205] Much yet remains to be done toward determining the actual total yearly nitrate requirements of different fruit crops and also their varying requirements from season to season with increasing age. However, the amount and character of the vegetative growth probably provide the grower with a better index to his trees' fertilizer requirements than is afforded by any other of its features.

Influence of Nitrogen on Blossom Bud Formation.—It is not the intention at this point to discuss in detail the many factors influencing blossom bud formation. It is generally conceded, however, that fruit bud initiation is in a way a response to nutritive conditions within the plant and it has been shown that these nutritive conditions are modified by the nature of the soil solution. At least theoretically, then, it should be possible to influence fruit bud formation through the use of fertilizers.

In Peaches.—In a preceding paragraph Alderman[7] is quoted as reporting that in his fertilizer experiments with peaches in West Virginia the application of nitrogen-carrying fertilizers resulted in more than double the shoot growth and hence double the amount of possible fruit-bearing surface. Data on fruit bud formation on these shoots are presented in the last column of Table 43. If these figures for numbers of fruit buds per unit of shoot length were plotted, the curve would take the same general direction as one for figures on total shoot length, though the two would not be exactly parallel. In commenting on these data Alderman[7] says: the "table. . . shows during the first 3 years a uniformly high percentage of fruit buds formed on the nitrogen-fed plots and a correspondingly low percentage in plots 4, 5 and 9 (those receiving nothing, potash and phosphoric acid or lime only). By 100 per cent. set of buds we mean that practically all the new growth is filled with double buds from base to tip . . . while a 50 per cent. set would indicate that buds were found over only about one-half the twig and were single in many cases."

In Apples.—The situation is somewhat more complicated in fruits like the apple that bear mainly upon spurs. However, Roberts[252] has reported that there is a distinct correlation between the annual increase in length of spurs and their blossom bud formation. Both those spurs making a very short and those making a very long annual growth did not form many fruit buds, but, on the other hand, those that made a medium growth were highly fruitful. Length was in turn correlated directly with number of leaves and total leaf area and within certain limits (*i.e.*, for the shorter spurs) there was also a correlation between spur length and average leaf area. Experiments on the influence of nitrogenous fertilizers on spur length are reported by Roberts[252] as follows: "In 1918 the difference in spur growth of non-bearing Wealthy was as follows: check trees 4.89 mm.; nitrate of soda 11.98.   In 1919, when there was a larger growth on checks than usual, less difference was also noted.   The figures for different trees than those used in 1918 are: check 7.41; nitrate 9.25."   In general the influence of the nitrate was to increase the length of the spurs and consequently leaf numbers and total leaf areas.   In the trees with spurs too short for fruit bud formation the effect would be to encourage that process; in those trees with spurs averaging just long enough or a little too long for maximum fruit formation the effect would be to discourage it.   Roberts[252] also points out certain correlations between the amount of shoot growth and the number and character of fruit spurs.   This suggests a further indirect correlation between fertilizer applications and fruit bud formation, for the amount of shoot growth is greatly influenced by the available nitrate supply.   The work of Hooker[156] and others showing the importance of the synthesis and storage of organic compounds in late summer and fall in determining the amount and character of growth early the next season suggests still further indirect correlations—correlations no less important, though less easily recognized, than those first mentioned.

Influence of Nitrogen on the Setting of Fruit.—The influence of nitrogenous fertilizers on shoot and leaf growth and on the formation of fruit buds is not less striking than their effect on the setting of fruit, especially in rather weak trees that still bloom heavily.   This is well brought out by the data presented in Table 45, for apple trees in the Hood River valley.

TABLE 45.—INFLUENCE OF NITRATE OF SODA APPLICATIONS UPON SET OF FRUIT IN TWO HOOD RIVER, ORE., APPLE ORCHARDS

(*After Lewis and Allen*[185])

Treatment	Number of blossoming spurs	Percentage of fruit set June 4	Percentage of fruit set Sept. 30	Average yield per tree (bushels)
First orchard:				
Check (unfertilized).....	483	35.3	16.4	3.75
Fertilized with nitrate...	542	68.0	30.7	21.50
Second orchard:				
Check (unfertilized).....	386	9.0	4.6	1.33
Fertilized with nitrate...	620	58.0	15.1	9.50

The setting of fruit in the fertilized plots ranged from 100 to 300 per cent. higher than that in the check plots.   Furthermore this influence was evident right after blossoming, certainly not later than the time of the so-called June drop.   This was only a very short time after application and shows the prompt response obtained from such a quickly available fertilizer. Similar results have attended the spring use of nitrate of soda in many other experiments with apples and pears. Indeed so well is the use of this fertilizer gaining recognition for this purpose that large quantities are now used in commercial orchards to deal with many of the difficulties that formerly were considered pollination problems. Fewer data are available on the influence of quickly available nitrogenous fertilizers on the setting of other deciduous fruits. It is known, however, that such fertilization is beneficial in the case of peaches and of strawberries[188] growing under conditions where the available nitrogen supply is limited. In the case of cherries, even those growing in very nitrogen-deficient soils, but little better fruit setting is obtained from the use of nitrogen-carrying fertilizers.[106] Grapes are comparatively unresponsive in this respect.

Influence of Nitrogen on Size of Fruit.—Since the size the fruit attains is an expression of the plant's vegetative activities it may be supposed that the factors or treatments leading to an increased shoot and leaf development will likewise lead to increased size of fruit. This expectation is justified by the results of many field trials with orchard fertilizers. Representative of many data that might be introduced are those presented in Table 46 for apples. In terms of percentages, the increase in size there reported amounts to 25 or over.

TABLE 46.—SIZE OF APPLES AS INFLUENCED BY NITRATE APPLICATIONS
(*After Lewis and Allen*[185])

Treatment	Per cent. grading		
	175 to 150 per bushel	138 to 112 per bushel	100 per bushel and larger
Check (no fertilizer)....................	22.09	39.76	38.15
Nitrate of soda.........................	2.28	26.91	70.76

Pears from nitrate fertilized trees in the Rogue River valley have been reported to average about 178 to the box, while those from unfertilized plots averaged 225.[245] The graphs in Figs. 25 and 26 indicate in a general way the observations of Stewart in Pennsylvania and Alderman in Virginia on the influence of fertilizer treatments on fruit size, especially as increases in size are correlated with increased or decreased vegetative growth and with increased or decreased yield. In some of the cases reported by Stewart, but not shown in the graphs, fertilizer applications were accompanied by decreased size of fruit. In commenting on his data Stewart[278] says: "In the matter of fruit size, some benefits are indicated . . . but they have proved less as a rule than is commonly supposed. Manure has naturally been most consistent in increasing the average size of the fruit, probably chiefly on account of its mulching effect . . . in general we believe that the plant food influence will always be secondary to moisture conservation and proper thinning, wherever greater fruit size is desired." Alderman[8] in his fertilizer work with peaches found but little increase in size from the use of fertilizers, nitrogen in combination with potash showing slight gains. At the Missouri

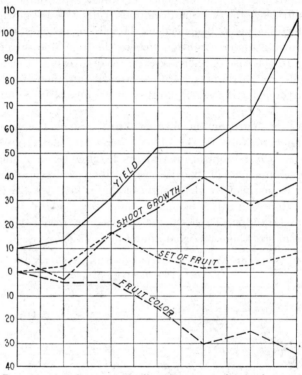

Fig. 25.—Response of apple trees to fertilizer treatments, showing increases or decreases in yield, fruit setting and fruit coloration accompanying increased shoot growth. (*Plotted from data given by Stewart.*[278])

Station it was found that in some cases the fertilization of peaches with nitrogen was attended by a marked decrease in size of fruit, this decrease sometimes amounting to as much as 40 per cent.[318] Cherries are not likely to show much increase in size as a result of fertilizer applications.[106]

One explanation of the frequent failure of the fruit from fertilized trees to show an increase in size over that from unfertilized trees and of occasional decreases in size lies in the fact that much larger crops are borne, owing perhaps to a better setting, and there is a resultant greater competition between the fruits for the products of photosynthesis. Another explanation lies in the increased wood growth and leaf area of the plants and consequently in their increased demand for water. As this increase in leaf surface may sometimes amount to over 100 per cent. it is easy to understand how water may become a limiting factor. Especially is this true when it is remembered that the osmotic concentration of the leaves is greater than that of the developing or maturing fruits and hence in times of stress the fruits may actually lose water to the leaves which supplies their transpiration requirements and keeps them turgid.[52]

This, however, is an indirect effect of nitrogenous fertilizers on size of fruit, occasionally important in orchard practice and suggesting that increased attention should be given to meeting the trees' requirements for moisture when nitrogenous fertilizers are used. It also raises a series of interesting and important, but wholly unanswered, questions as to the relative influence different fertilizers may have on different parts of the tree—for example, roots, leaves, fruit. It is clear that, at present, there are no means of increasing the size of fruit directly through the use of any particular fertilizer. Fertilizers can lead to the production of larger fruit only as they lead to increased vegetative growth and the consequently increased amounts of manufactured foods and as they lead to a greater extension of the root system and to a consequently greater intake of water or in still other indirect ways.

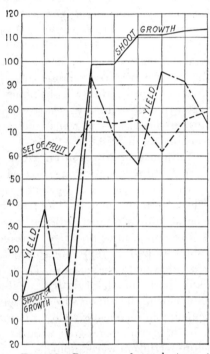

Fig. 26.—Response of peach trees to fertilizer treatments, showing increases or decreases in yield and fruit setting accompanying increased shoot growth. (*Plotted from data given by Alderman.*[8])

Influence of Nitrogen on Color of Fruit.—There has been much discussion in pomological literature concerning the use of fertilizers for aiding the coloration of fruits, and applications of potash and phosphoric acid have been rather generally recommended for this purpose. Hedrick was one of the first to submit experimental data bearing on this question. After a 10-year trial with several varieties in an old New York apple orchard growing in a rather heavy clay he concluded that no influence on color of fruit could be ascribed to the potash or phosphoric acid which had been used.[145] Stewart[278] in summarizing the results of his work with apples in Pennsylvania says: "None of the fertilizer treatments has resulted in any marked improvement in color. Slight and irregular benefits are shown by potash and by some of the phosphate applications, but nothing of any importance. . . . " Some of the graphs in Figs. 25 and 26, plotted from data presented by Stewart, furnish clear evidence in support of his conclusions. Alderman[7] reports a reduction of the red color in peaches accompanying the use of nitrogenous fertilizers and ascribes it to late maturity and to increased density of the foliage. Conversely, some slight increases in color from the use of potash or phosphoric acid he ascribes to the slight checking effect these materials sometimes have on vegetative growth. It is significant that the curves representing average influence of fertilizers on color are almost exactly the reverse of those representing their influence on vegetative growth. In other words, the two phenomena, those of color formation and new vegetative growth, are negatively correlated. This, of course, applies only in those cases in which coloration of the fruit depends on sunlight reaching the fruit itself.

Influence of Nitrogen on Yield.—In general the tendency of nitrogenous fertilizers is to increase vegetative growth, promote the formation of fruit buds, increase the percentage of flowers setting fruit and lead to larger size in the individual fruits. It is inevitable therefore that their general influence must be greatly to increase yields. Many data might be presented in support of this general conclusion. Those given in Tables 47 and 48 represent some of the more striking results that have been obtained; these, however, have been duplicated in orchards in many parts of the country. Table 49 is particularly interesting as emphasizing the importance of nitrogen compared with the other nutrient elements, in increasing yields. Perhaps it should be noted that the trees in both of these orchards were in a rather weak vegetative condition before fertilizers were applied.

TABLE 47.—INFLUENCE OF QUICKLY AVAILABLE NITROGENOUS FERTILIZERS ON YIELD OF APPLES IN THE HOOD RIVER VALLEY
(*After Lewis and Allen*[185])

TREATMENT	AVERAGE YIELD PER TREE (IN LOOSE BOXES)
Check (no fertilizer).............................	0.90
Nitrate of soda...................................	10.01

In contrast to such striking results from the use of fertilizers it should be mentioned that nitrogen, alone and in combination with other nutrients, has been applied to many orchards without resulting in materially increased yields. Thus Hedrick and Anthony[147] summarize the results of a 20-year experiment in a New York orchard as follows: "Adding acid phosphate at the rate of 340 pounds per acre per year has not given a noticeable increase in yield. The addition of 196 pounds of muriate of potash to the 340 pounds of acid phosphate seems to have resulted in an increased yield. The annual application of 50 pounds of readily available nitrogen in addition to the phosphoric acid and potash has caused no increase in yield." Gourley,[116] likewise, working in New Hampshire with a soil of entirely different character, obtained but slightly increased yields from the use of nitrogen alone or in combination over those attending a clean cultivation-cover crop method of soil management without fertilization. The first of these two investigators states, however: "An analysis of the soil before the experiment was begun shows that at that time there was, in the upper foot of soil, enough nitrogen (total)

TABLE 48.—AVERAGE ANNUAL RESULTS FROM ORCHARD FERTILIZERS IN OHIO
(*After Ballou*[23])

Treatment	Average yield per tree (pounds)	Average gain per acre (barrels)	Value of increase per acre	Net increase per acre
Nitrate of soda 5 pounds............	315.6	67.7	$169.25	$163.25
Nitrate of soda 5 pounds, acid phosphate 5 pounds, muriate of potash 2½ pounds.....................	205.8	37.4	93.50	83.50
Tankage 5 pounds, bone 5 pounds, muriate of potash 5 pounds.......	93.8	6.5	16.25	8.25
Nitrate of soda 5 pounds, acid phosphate 5 pounds.................	214.2	39.8	99.50	91.50
Muriate of potash 5 pounds.........	96.0	7.2	18.00	15.50
Stable manure 250 pounds..........	100.1	8.3	20.75	20.75
Checks (no fertilizer).............	69.9			

per acre to last mature apple trees 183 years, of phosphoric acid, 295 years, of potash, 713 years."[146] Evidently amounts of these nutrients sufficient for the trees' growth and production were being made available year after year by various natural agencies. The second of the two investigators, though not reporting on the total nitrogen supply of the soil, presents data to show that the clean cultivation-cover crop method of management made available each season plenty of nitrogen, though after some years there was some evidence that nitrogen applications in the near future would increase yields.[119] In the presence of abundant supplies additional applications gave no increased yields worth mentioning. Interesting in this particular connection are data presented in Table 49 showing the effects of various amounts of nitrogen-carrying fertilizers on yield of pears. The trees were yielding well without fertilizer applications but when small amounts of quickly available nitrogen were applied they at once responded, production apparently reaching a maximum (thinning being practiced) for the size of trees in question. Applications of larger amounts of fertilizer under these conditions resulted in no greater yield. If larger amounts are available they are not taken up or if taken up they are not used in increased fruit production. It is economical for the grower to apply only such fertilizers in such amounts as the tree can use with profit to himself.

The Correlation between Vegetative Growth and Yield.—Bearing directly on the question of the influence of fertilizers, particularly nitrogenous fertilizers, on yield and also on that much disputed question as to whether vegetative growth and fruit production are antagonistic tendencies, are the graphs shown in Figs. 25 and 26, plotted from data on apple yields and growth as influenced by fertilizers in Pennsylvania and from

TABLE 49.—EFFECTS OF VARIOUS AMOUNTS OF NITROGEN-CARRYING FERTILIZERS ON YIELD OF PEARS
(*After Reimer*[245])

1917 treatment	Yield, boxes per tree	1918 treatment	Yield, boxes per tree
Check	12.13	Check	15.00
10 pounds nitrate of lime per tree	15.12	10 pounds nitrate of lime per tree	18.84
10 pounds nitrate of soda per tree	15.45	10 pounds nitrate of soda per tree	18.37
5 pounds nitrate of soda per tree	16.53	5 pounds nitrate of soda and 5 pounds superphosphate per tree	16.63
5 pounds nitrate of soda per tree	17.03	5 pounds nitrate of soda	17.72
5 pounds nitrate of soda per tree	15.06	5 pounds sulphate of ammonia	18.23

data on peach yields and growth in West Virginia. The solid lines in Fig. 25 represent increase in yield (in percentages) resulting from the use of various fertilizer combinations. The dash-dot lines represent increases in vegetative growth, figured in the same way, length of terminal shoots being taken as a measure of vegetative vigor. Both lines represent 10-year averages of a number of experiments on mature apple trees growing under various soil conditions. Though these curves show slight irregularities, those for increases in growth take the same general direction as those for increases in yield. In other words, as vegetative growth has increased, yields have increased, but yields have increased much more rapidly than vegetative growth. This latter fact would seem to prove beyond all question not only that increased vegetative growth due to fertilization is not generally antagonistic to heavier fruit production, but that within limits it actually encourages heavier fruiting. Data recently presented for apple tree growth and yields in Delaware lead to the same general conclusion.[235] Graphs shown in Fig. 26, made from 4-year averages for increases in peach yields in West Virginia through fertilization, show the same relationship between vegetative growth and yield. Here, though yields have not quite kept pace with the increased vegetative growth, the conclusion is obvious that in the peach increased wood growth is associated with increased fruit production.

The same graphs showing the general relationship between vegetative growth and yield also throw some light on the way in which the fertilizers have increased production. Under the conditions of these tests about half of the increased yield was due to the greater wood growth; in other words, to the effect of the fertilizer in producing additional fruit spurs and fruit-bud-bearing shoots. The other half of the increase was due apparently to the greater activity of the old spurs. Presumably increased yield was not obtained in the New York and New Hampshire experiments to which reference has been made because the trees' nutritive requirements for new wood growth were fully met by the supply already available in the soil and because they were already producing heavy crops. That decreased yield sometimes accompanies increased vegetative growth following the use of nitrogenous fertilizers is indicated by results with strawberries in Missouri[51] and with red raspberries in New York.[53]

Influence of Nitrogen on Composition and on Season of Maturity.— The composition of various plant tissues, especially in so far as their mineral constituents are concerned, has been shown to be influenced considerably by the character of the soil in which they grow. Their composition would be expected, therefore, to show the influence of fertilizer application. Some interesting experimental data on this question have been obtained with rye, buckwheat and certain other crops. These crop plants were grown in what were considered normal media and in media possessing excessive amounts of certain nutrients. The following statements from the report on these experiments may be quoted here.[139] "In general it appears as if the nutrients actually required for normal growth of the crops, when there are plenty of other ingredients to furnish the indifferent ash, need not exceed 2.0 per cent. of nitrogen, 1.5 per cent. of potassium oxid, and 0.5 per cent. of phosphoric oxid. . . . In comparing excessive percentages with the foregoing amounts, it may be noticed that in certain instances . . . the percentages have increased to the following high magnitudes: Nitrogen, 3.96 and potassium oxide 5.56 in 1911 in rye; and phosphoric oxide 1.36 in 1916 in buckwheat. Of course, these amounts are much in excess of what was necessary." The olive has been said to have a higher oil content when grown on a limestone soil.[293] Presumably fertilizing the olive orchard heavily with lime would have some influence in the same direction. Strawberries on nitrogen-fertilized plants have been found to wilt more in times of severe drought than those on unfertilized plants.[51] Wickson[319] states: "Puffiness of oranges is clearly due in some cases to excess of nitrogenous manures" and "the effect of excessive use of stable manures, or of other manures very rich in nitrogen, upon the products of the vine has been frequently noted as destructive to bouquet and quality."

There are a number of indirect ways in which fertilization, particularly with nitrogenous fertilizers, influences composition. For example, the use of nitrate of soda in the apple orchard has been shown frequently to result in increased size of fruit; such differences in size are often correlated with differences in texture, in juiciness and in what is generally termed quality. These influences are not well enough understood, however, to make possible definite recommendations for the developing of certain qualities or substances, as sugar or acid or pectins, through the use of fertilizers.

There has been much dispute regarding the influence of fertilizers on the keeping quality of fruit, the general contention being that nitrogenous materials contribute toward a softer texture and a shorter storage period and that potash- and phosphorus-carrying materials have the opposite effect. Recent investigations with apples in Ohio,[118] Washington[196] and West Virginia[172] and with both apples and peaches in Maryland[9,93,312] indicate that any such effects are of such small magnitude as to be of little commercial importance. Even with strawberries, in which the influence on texture is even more pronounced, it is apparently not of great importance.[263] Often resistance or susceptibility to certain diseases is closely correlated with the chemical composition of the tissues subject to invasion, and even a slight change in composition that might be brought about either directly or indirectly through the use of some fertilizer might be of great use in reducing injury from the invading parasite or its toxin.

The effect of nitrogenous fertilizers on season of maturity of the wood has been mentioned. In the section on Temperature Relations it is shown that the breaking of the winter rest period in certain fruits is closely correlated with the time of maturing of the wood in the fall and in turn susceptibility to low temperatures in late winter is associated with the breaking of the rest period. Thus, indirectly, applications of nitrogen may have an important influence on certain forms of winter injury. Indeed the peach and some other fruits are probably grown sometimes under conditions where fertilization with nitrogen-carrying materials may be profitable for this reason if for no other. On the other hand, evidence has been submitted that fertilization with nitrogen alone —fertilization presumably heavy enough to result in an unbalanced nutrient condition—has rendered peach trees in South Carolina more susceptible to various factors which cause death and has markedly increased their mortality—while their fruits have been more susceptible to arsenical injury, sunburn and cracking.[222]

Application of nitrate of soda has delayed the ripening of peaches in West Virginia from 1 week to 10 days, the delay being greater in the later varieties.[7] Observations elsewhere indicate that almost any material carrying quickly available nitrogen has a similar influence on many other fruits. On the other hand, applications of nitrogenous fertilizers to black raspberries have been reported as advancing maturity, at least in the sense of causing a larger percentage of the fruit to ripen during the early part of the harvesting period.[199] Doubtless this is due, at least in part, to the greater amounts of carbohydrates produced by the foliage of the nitrogen-fertilized plants.

In a later chapter it is shown that, within certain limits, the plant shows very much the same response to certain kinds of pruning as it does to applications of nitrogen-carrying fertilizers. In other words it is possible within certain limits to accomplish by proper fertilization results comparable to those produced by pruning. This is true particularly in the effects of these two practices on new shoot and leaf growth, on the better setting of fruit and on the size of fruit. Probably for best results there should be a judicious combination of both practices. For commercial production, however, it will often be found more practicable to reduce the pruning to a minimum and to depend rather on fertilization. Fertilizers are comparatively cheap and they are quickly and easily applied. On the other hand pruning that is properly done requires considerable judgment and skill and is comparatively expensive. To the extent that the same results can be obtained by the two methods, much greater profits will be realized from the investment in fertilizers.

Summary.—In many cases the use of quickly available nitrogenous fertilizers in the orchard has resulted promptly in considerably increased vegetative growth, the response being evident in longer shoots and in greater numbers of leaves that are larger in size and darker in color than those of unfertilized trees. For the most part these responses have been made by trees recently showing a lack of vegetative vigor, trees most likely to be found in sod land or in infertile soils. On the other hand there has been little evidence of increased vegetative growth from the application of such fertilizers to moderately rich soils in which the trees are already making a good growth. In many orchards, therefore nitrogen is not a limiting factor to growth and in those where marked responses are obtained from moderate applications, larger applications often evoke no greater response. Increased blossom bud formation often accompanies the increased vegetative growth that follows the use of nitrogenous fertilizers. Fruit setting in trees showing poor vegetative vigor is greatly increased. The size of the fruit may be decreased or increased by the use of nitrogenous fertilizer depending on whether water is a limiting factor. The correlation between the amount of new vegetative growth and fruit size is generally positive but not high. Yield, which is a product of fruit bud formation, fruit setting and subsequent development, naturally is often increased greatly by nitrogen applications. The development of the red color of many fruits is somewhat checked by the use of nitrogenous fertilizers because of the heavier shade incident to the increased vegetative growth. Within fairly wide limits fruit production is found to increase with an increase in vegetative vigor. The general effect of nitrogenous fertilizers is to delay maturity of both wood and fruit. Though some influence is shown on the composition of the fruit, in most cases this is of secondary importance.

CHAPTER XIII

FERTILIZERS, OTHER THAN NITROGENOUS, IN THE ORCHARD

The conclusion should not be drawn from the statements in preceding chapters that in practice only nitrogenous fertilizers are of value in the deciduous fruit plantation. A single instance in which a favorable response attended the use of some other fertilizer would indicate that the problem should be considered from other points of view; there are many such instances.

The Indirect Effects of Fertilizers.—Repeated reference has been made to the direct and possibly indirect effects of fertilizers on the solubility or availability of other soil ingredients, on soil reaction, or on the plants that constitute the mulch or the cover crop. Without doubt this last mentioned influence is one of the most important, especially in orchards not under clean cultivation. In either a sod- or grass-mulch or a cover-crop method of culture the vegetation produced between the trees is returned to the soil. Only those mineral constituents are returned that are obtained from the soil, but in every case there is added a considerable amount of organic matter which, through its effect on soil texture and water-holding capacity as well as through the chemical effects of its decomposition products, plays a very important part in the general aspect of productivity; with leguminous crops the nitrogen supply is actually augmented. Furthermore the mineral constituents may be so changed in form by these intercrops as to be much more available to the crop plants. It is generally considered that the value of these intercultures is more or less directly proportional to the amounts of vegetation produced and Anthony has presented evidence to show that in the cultivated orchard "cover crop growth is a fairly reliable index to probable tree growth and yields 8 to 10 years later."[17] If this is the case any soil treatment or fertilizer which results in an increased growth of the interculture may be of indirect benefit to the tree. As a rule these crop plants grown between the trees are greatly helped by applications of nitrogen-carrying fertilizers made primarily for the trees' direct and immediate use. Under such circumstances the trees consequently receive a double benefit from their application, an immediate benefit from such portions as they are able to absorb before it leaches away or is used by the other plants and a deferred benefit realized only when these plants decay.

245

Phosphoric Acid.—As already stated, most soils on which fruits are raised already contain sufficient phosphorus in an available form for normal tree growth and production, and its application in fertilizers in order directly to provide a greater supply is unnecessary. Some cases, however, have been reported where fruit plants have made a prompt

TABLE 50.—EFFECTS OF CERTAIN FERTILIZERS ON THE PRODUCTION OF MULCHING MATERIAL
(*After Ballou*[23])

Annual fertilizer treatment per acre	Yield in pounds	Kind of cover crop
Acid phosphate 350 pounds..............	2,716	Red clover
Acid phosphate 350 pounds, muriate of potash 175 pounds....................	2,884	Red clover
Acid phosphate 350 pounds, muriate of potash 175 pounds, nitrate of soda 350 pounds............................	3,458	Timothy, red top, blue grass
Unfertilized........................	840	Poverty grass, weeds

response to its application. Thus Beckwith[27] has found it profitable for cranberries grown on savanna lands in New Jersey, and Chandler[51] for strawberries in southwestern Missouri.

Phosphoric acid is frequently of much indirect benefit to orchard trees. Some measure of this influence may be obtained from data presented in Table 50, for an orchard under the sod-mulch method of management in southern Ohio. Acid phosphate alone increased the yield of mulching material more than threefold and a so-called complete fertilizer increased it over fourfold. Of equal significance was the change effected in the nature of the dominant vegetation. The unfertilized areas are reported as covered with a thin growth of poverty grass and weeds.[23] When these areas were fertilized with nitrate of soda alone or when that material was used in large quantities in combination with other fertilizers, timothy, redtop, bluegrass and orchard grass rapidly took the place of the weeds and poverty grass. When acid phosphate was used alone or in combination with potash, clover came in thickly and crowded out the grasses. The ground was stocked with all of these species before any fertilizer was applied. The effect of the different applications was simply to furnish one group or another with conditions particularly suitable for its growth while the plants of the other group remained small and stunted. This effect is particularly interesting in the case of the acid phosphate, as the clover whose development it made possible is a nitrogen gatherer and thus the application of phosphorus would result ultimately in an increased nitrogen supply for the trees. Probably it would not be safe to recommend generally the maintenance of the nitrogen supply in the orchard through the use of acid phosphate, but there are conditions where such a method of procedure might be entirely practicable and there are probably many other orchards in which it would be desirable to supplement nitrogen-carrying fertilizers with those carrying phosphorus. Attention has already been called to the fact that, in general, the use of phosphatic fertilizers cannot be depended on for heightening the color of fruit or for improving its shipping or storage qualities.

Sulphur.—Similarly there is reason to believe that vegetative growth and production may be increased by the use of sulphur-carrying fertilizers, even though the soil may contain a supply of available sulphur well in excess of the trees' actual requirements. Elsewhere in this section it is stated that in certain fruit-growing sections sulphur is a limiting factor for the growth of leguminous intercultures, especially alfalfa. In such cases the judicious use of sulphur-carrying fertilizers may have a far-reaching influence on the trees, though they themselves may not be able to use any of it. The good results frequently obtained from the use of acid phosphate and credited to the influence of the phosphorus may be due in part to the sulphur carried by that fertilizer. One effect of heavy applications of sulphur is to increase soil acidity, though this usually wears away within a year or two. This action of sulphur has been found to be important enough to warrant its use in certain soils used for pineapple culture in Porto Rico from the standpoint of helping control weeds, mole crickets and nematodes.[149]

This question of the influence of different fertilizer treatments on the nature of the plant population in undisturbed soil has been studied very carefully at the Rothamstead Experimental Station in England. Differences are to be expected with varying soil conditions and without doubt the response in an orchard would be different from that in an open meadow such as that in which the Rothamstead investigations were conducted. Nevertheless the following statement from the summary of this work is very suggestive:

"In the produce grown continuously without manure the average number of species found has been 49. Of these, 17 are grasses, four belong to the order Leguminosæ, and 28 to other orders. The percentage, by weight, of the grasses has averaged about 68, that of the Leguminosæ about nine, and that of species of other orders about 23.

"In the produce of the plot already referred to as the most heavily manured, and yielding the heaviest crops, the average number of species found has been only 19, of which 12 to 13 are grasses, one only (or none) leguminous, and five to six only represent other orders; whilst the average proportions by weight have been—of grasses about 95 per cent., of Leguminosæ less than 0.01 per cent., and of species representing other orders less than 5 per cent.

"On the other hand, a plot receiving annually manures such as are of little avail for gramineous crops grown separately in rotation, but which favor beans or clover so grown, has given, on the average, 43 species. Of these, 17 in number are grasses, four Leguminosæ, and 22 belong to other orders, but by weight, the percentage of grasses has averaged only 65–70, that of the Leguminosæ nearly 20, and that of species belonging to other orders less than 15. . . .

"It is found that there is a considerable difference in the percentage of dry substance in the produce, and very considerable difference in the percentage of mineral matter (ash) in that dry substance. There is still greater difference in the percentage of nitrogen in the dry matter, and, again, a greater difference still in the percentage of individual constituents of the ash. When, indeed, it is remembered that a plot may have from 20 to 50 different species growing upon it, each with its own peculiar habit of growth, and consequent varying range and power of food-collection, it will not appear surprising that different species are developed according to the manure employed; and, this being so, that the character and amount of the constituents taken up from the soil by such a mixed herbage should be found much more directly dependent on the supplies of them by manure than is the case with a crop of a single species growing separately.

"In further illustration it may be mentioned that, not only does the percentage of nitrogen in the dry substance of the produce of the different plots vary considerably, but the average annual amount of it assimilated over a given area is more than three times as much in some cases as in others. Again, the percentage of potash in the dry substance is three times as much in some cases as in others; whilst the difference in the average annual amount of it taken up over a given area is more than five times as much on some plots as on others—dependent on the supplies of it by manure, and the consequent description of plants, and amount, and character, of growth induced. The percentage and acreage amounts of phosphoric acid also vary very strikingly; and so again it is with other mineral constituents, but in a less marked degree."[180]

Potash.—Instances in which the use of potash-carrying fertilizers have failed to give satisfactory returns are far more numerous than those in which positive responses have been obtained. However, cases of the latter sort are not unknown. McClelland has reported increased yields of coffee in Porto Rico from the use of potassium. Indeed it gave more consistent increases than did either nitrogen or phosphorus.[205] Applications of potash have increased the resistance to disease of both banana[239] and pineapple in Porto Rico and have checked the development of mottling[103] or frenching of foliage in a number of deciduous fruits. Evidence has already been presented that the value of potash-carrying fertilizers for promoting fruit coloration and in increasing its shipping and storage qualities has been greatly over-estimated.

Lime.—Calcium has been mentioned as an element practically always present in quantities far greater than orchard trees require. Indeed very large amounts are likely to lead to chlorotic conditions through making the soil reaction alkaline and thus rendering iron unavailable. Nevertheless liming the soil accelerates nitrification and may thus indirectly help the orchard plants to obtain a larger supply of nitrogen. The strawberry has been mentioned particularly as a plant preferring an acid soil and as being actually harmed by applications of lime. Yet it is common experience that strawberries do exceptionally well following clover, though clover is very sensitive to acid soils and usually profits greatly from liming. In this case it is entirely practicable to apply lime to the clover field a year before the sod is turned under for the strawberry plants. The lime stimulates the growth of the clover and its effect on soil reaction will have largely, if not wholly, disappeared by the time the ground is ready for the strawberries. Ultimately the strawberries will profit greatly from the lime applied to the clover that preceded them, though its direct application might result in injury.

Illustrations might be given of other indirect influences of fertilizers, but enough has been said here and at other places in this section to afford some idea of the many ways in which they may affect orchard trees. Enough has been said, also, to make it clear that these indirect are often as important as the direct influences, for there may be no occasion to supply the plant with more nutrients. With our present knowledge it is impossible to predict with certainty all of the effects, direct and indirect, that any particular fertilizer will have in a given orchard.

Plant Nutrient Carriers; Different Forms of Fertilizers.—The necessity that the different plant nutrients be in certain forms if they are to be taken up by the tree has been discussed under the subjects of Solubility and Availability in Chapter VII. This does not mean, however, that fertilizers must contain these elements in these particular forms, for as soon as applied they become subject to numerous changes through the physical, chemical and biological factors always at work in the soil. Nevertheless there are certain advantages and certain disadvantages inherent in different fertilizers because of the form in which they carry the elements for which they are valued. A brief discussion of this matter as it applies to orchard problems is included at this point.

Nitrogen from Inorganic Sources.—The more common of the nitrogen-carrying commercial fertilizers are nitrate of soda, sulphate of ammonia and dried blood. Only the first of these three materials contains nitrogen in a form in which it is used in any considerable amounts by most plants. It is therefore one of the most readily available forms of nitrogen, though the nitrogen of the two other materials soon becomes available. The first two of these fertilizers are readily soluble in water and in the soil solution; dried blood is less soluble. This at once raises the practical question of loss through leaching. Some expression of the differences between these fertilizers in this respect as well as in their rates of availability is obtained from an investigation on a light sandy loam in Florida.[58] The report on this investigation states: "For the period from July 13, 1911, to July 17, 1913, 41 per cent. of the sulphate of ammonia applied to the soil leached thru and was lost in the drainage water; 72.5 per cent. of the nitrate of soda, and 38.3 per cent. of the dried blood were lost. . . . The larger loss of nitrate of soda is explained by the fact that this material is very readily soluble in the soil moisture and that the soil has very little if any power to retain or fix nitrogen in the nitrate form. . . . In its original form the nitrogen of dried blood is not readily soluble in the soil water, and consequently very little is lost in the leaching process until nitrification occurs. In this change the organic nitrogen of the blood is changed first to ammonia, then to the nitrite and finally to the nitrate form, when it becomes as readily soluble as the nitrate of soda and is leached out as readily. Nitrification of the dried blood is a gradual process, extending over a period of time which may be of several weeks' duration, depending on soil conditions. Because of this, some of the nitrogen of dried blood, or for that matter, a number of other materials, will remain in the soil a considerably longer time and be available to the crop over a longer period than nitrate of soda. This is especially true where heavy rains occur after the latter has been applied to the soil. . . . While sulphate of ammonia is readily soluble in the soil water the soil has the power of fixing or absorbing at least a portion of the ammonia, thus preventing it from leaching away. This takes place through chemical means and is common to all soils. Very sandy soils can absorb only a small amount of ammonia; loam and clay soils are able to absorb much larger quantities."

Attention may be called also to the opposite influences of nitrate of soda and sulphate of ammonia on soil reaction. In the former the nitrogen is combined with a basic and in the latter with an acid radical. As the nitrogen is used by the plants the soil is gradually rendered more basic in the first instance and more acid in the second; in the latter case the sulphate generally combines with calcium, resulting ultimately in a loss of this element from the soil through leaching. Collison[58] has found that in some soils this loss of calcium when sulphate of ammonia is used as a fertilizer amounts to over twice that taking place when nitrate of soda is applied. The change in soil reaction occasioned by one or two successive applications of the same material would seldom be large enough to have great practical importance in the orchard, but since the effects are cumulative repeated applications for many years might conceivably result in injury to the trees. The remedy for this situation is the use first of the nitrate of soda and then of the sulphate of ammonia, keeping the soil reaction about as it is at the outset.

Attention should be called to the inconsequential difference obtained in actual field trials from the use of these nitrogen-carrying fertilizers when nitrogen is the limiting factor and when amounts are used carrying approximately the same quantities of nitrogen. During recent years a considerable number of other nitrogen-carrying fertilizers have been available on the market. These include calcium nitrate, calcium cyanamid, urea, calurea, diammophos, nitrophoska and a number of others. Experience with these products is somewhat limited but, on the whole, is satisfactory.

The different influences of these nitrogenous fertilizers on the intercultures in the orchard may be of greater significance than the differences in their direct influence on the trees. The acidic influence of the sulphate of ammonia is likely to increase gradually the growth of certain species like bluegrass, timothy, redtop and orchard grass and to decrease the growth of the clovers and certain other legumes. The basic influence of the nitrate of soda has the opposite effect. This is brought out strikingly by work at the Rothamstead Experimental Station[182] extending over a period of 30 years. Therefore if certain leguminous cover crops are to be grown or more especially if it is desired to keep the orchard in a permanent clover or alfalfa sod, some caution should be exercised in the use of sulphate of ammonia. Sodium, calcium or potassium nitrates could be used more safely.

The results of many investigations[316] with field crops indicate that a given quantity of nitrogen in the form of nitrate of soda has a greater influence than the same amount carried in many other fertilizers. That is, it has more crop-producing power when held in one form than in another. Furthermore this relative efficiency varies with many factors, such as the kind of crop plant and the character of the soil. Presumably this varying crop-producing power is associated with secondary or indirect effects that the fertilizer or its disintegration products may have on the plant through their influence on soil reaction, the availability of other soil constituents and many other soil conditions and processes. Very little is known regarding the varying crop-producing value of nitrogen carried in different fertilizers when they are used on fruits, though, apparently, a pound of nitrogen carried in one of them is worth about as much as a pound carried in any other.

Nitrogen from Organic Sources.—A word should be said regarding the use of certain nitrogen-carrying organic fertilizers. Barnyard compost and green manuring crops have been recommended often as the best sources of nitrogen for the orchard. There can be no doubt but that they are effective fertilizers when nitrogen is a limiting factor, often yielding returns greater than those obtained from commercial fertilizers used in quantities carrying equal amounts of nitrogen. However, a part of their beneficial influence is without doubt due to other nutrients that they carry and to the effects on the physical condition of the soil.

Thus Schreiner and Shorey,[255] in discussing the physical condition of the soil as affected by organic matter, state: "The organic matter may, and in fact generally does, play an intimate part in the behavior of the mineral particles, entering into chemical combination, coating them or cementing them together. The organic matter becomes, therefore, of the greatest importance in its influence on the great controlling factors in crop production, such as the solubility of the soil minerals, the physical structure of the soil granules, and the water-holding power of soils. To illustrate this, there was found in California a soil which could not be properly wetted, either by rain, irrigation, or movement of water from the subsoil, with the result that the land could not be used profitably for agriculture. On investigation it was found that this peculiarity of the soil was due to the organic matter, which when extracted had the properties of a varnish, repelling water to an extreme degree. The soil, once freed of this ingredient, had a high water-holding power."

Some suggestion of the many ways, direct or indirect, in which organic matter affects tree growth and production may be derived from the following statements pertaining to the rosette of pecans: "The experimental and other evidence indicates very strongly that pecan rosette is a sign of a soil deficient in humus, fertility, and moisture supply. . . . The constant addition of large quantities of humus-forming materials, thereby both bettering the physical condition of the soil and increasing its water-holding capacity and fertility, is absolutely necessary to produce healthy trees from those already diseased and to prevent the development of new cases of rosette. . . . some consistent and definite soil-building policy should be adopted in the pecan orchards of the South if rosette is to be overcome and healthy productive orchards maintained. The program of work should involve the growing of one crop, preferably a legume, which may be returned to the soil. . . . In these experiments, heavy applications of stable manure, cottonseed meal and stable manure, and cottonseed meal alone, in connection with legumes, have proved highly beneficial to rosetted trees."[210] Though in cases like this it is impossible at present to distinguish between the influence of the nitrogen and that of the other components of the organic matter there is no reason for minimizing their combined effects or for failing to resort freely to the use of organic fertilizers in orchard practice where observation and experience indicate that they may be of decided benefit. The nitrogen of organic fertilizers is more slowly available than that of the common nitrogenous commercial fertilizers and experience shows that for quick results the commercial sources are more satisfactory. Investigation shows that the nitrogen both of barnyard manure and of green manure crops plowed under in April or May becomes available only gradually for plant growth during the latter half of the growing season.[317]

Phosphorus.—Though experiments have shown little or no direct benefit to deciduous fruits from the application of phosphatic fertilizers these are often useful in stimulating the growth of intercultures or in promoting desirable changes and reactions in the soil.

The leading phosphatic fertilizers available for use in the orchard are rock phosphate or "floats," acid phosphate or superphosphate and ground bone. The phosphorus in raw rock phosphate or "floats" and in ground bone is held in the form of tri-calcium phosphate, which is very nearly insoluble in water or in the soil solution and hence becomes available for plant growth very slowly as it is acted upon gradually by various soil agencies. The phosphorus of acid phosphate or superphosphate is held as mono-calcium phosphate, which is soluble and is the form in which plants are supposed to absorb most of their phosphorus. When added to the soil it unites with more calcium to form di-calcium or "reverted" phosphate which is intermediate in solubility between the mono- and tri-calcium compounds. Gradually this di-calcium phosphate unites with more calcium to form tri-calcium phosphate and it finally exists in the soil in the same form as in raw rock phosphate. For this reason "floats" or raw rock phosphate might be inferred to have equal value with the acid phosphate as a fertilizer. This is not the case, however, since the acid-treated material, being readily soluble, goes down into the soil and becomes fairly evenly distributed throughout the area reached by the roots. Furthermore, the plants are able to obtain considerable quantities before it becomes "reverted" or certainly before it is changed to the very nearly insoluble tri-calcium form. Mention may be made again of the possibility that some of the benefit from acid phosphate is due to the sulphur that it carries as well as to the phosphorus. Unlike nitrogen, phosphorus is not lost from the soil in large quantities through leaching. The reasons for this have been brought out in the preceding discussion. Some indication of the phosphorus fixing power of soil is afforded by an experiment with a light sandy loam in Florida in which it was found that at the end of four years only 0.05 per cent. of the amount applied in fertilizers had been lost through the drainage water.[255]

Potassium.—Though there are a number of different forms in which potassium may be applied, the two most common are the muriate and the sulphate. Where these two forms of potash have been used side by side in the fruit plantation the sulphate has usually, though not always, given more striking results. The suggestion may be repeated that when there is an apparent need of potash fertilizers, as indicated by a material response from the use of the sulphate, the possible need of sulphur be thoroughly investigated. In marked distinction to the case afforded by phosphorus we have but little evidence of an indirect benefit to the trees through any increased growth of the intercultures resulting from the use of potash-carrying fertilizers.

Sulphur.—Too little evidence on the use of sulphur-carrying fertilizers in the orchard is available to warrant an extended discussion of the different forms in which it may be applied. Evidently many different forms are eligible, for it has resulted in increased yields of certain orchard intercultures when used in the form of both potassium sulphate and calcium sulphate (gypsum) and increased grape yields have been reported from the use of both gypsum and flowers of sulphur.[54] Indeed it has been noted that alfalfa and certain other legumes have been greatly benefited from the sulphur contained in the lime-sulphur spray, which had dripped from sprayed trees or had drifted to the ground in the process of spraying.

Lime.—Though calcium is one of the elements essential for the growth of plants, the point has been made that there are but few soils to which its application in fertilizers is desirable for the purpose of supplying the tree directly with additional amounts and though there are indirect ways in which it may frequently benefit orchard trees, there are indirect ways in which it may also injure them. The data that have been presented make it clear, furthermore, that the same plant may be either benefited or injured by liming, according to the condition of the soil. That there are marked differences between species—and even varieties of the same species—in their tolerance of lime or their tolerance of the soil basicity with which it is likely to be associated or in their response to lime applications, should be emphasized. The results of work at the Rhode Island Experiment Station may be cited. Those results have been summarized as follows: "According to experiments made by the Rhode Island Agricultural Experiment Station on acid soils in that State, the plants tested may be classified with regard to their behavior toward lime as follows: Plants benefited by liming: . . . alfalfa, clover (red, white, crimson and alsike) . . . oats, timothy, Kentucky bluegrass, Canada pea, Cuthbert raspberry, gooseberry, currant (white Dutch), Orange quince, cherry, Burbank Japan plum, American linden . . . plants but little benefited by liming . . . rye, . . . Rhode Island bent, and redtop; plants slightly injured by liming . . . Concord grape, peach, apple, and pear; plants distinctly injured by liming . . . velvet bean, . . . blackberry, black-cap raspberry, cranberry, Norway spruce, and American white birch. Other plants said to be injured are the chestnut, azalea, and rhododendron."[315]

Another point that may be mentioned in connection with the application of lime is that there is little occasion to use it in the fruit plantation for flocculation purposes. Soils with a texture so impervious that the flocculating effects of lime are needed to promote drainage and aeration are generally too poorly suited to fruit production, even with the aid of such palliative measures as liming.

Season for Applying Fertilizers.—Comparatively few data are available upon which to base a decision as to the best time for applying fertilizers of different kinds in the orchard. Without doubt many factors have a bearing in this connection. Among the more important may be mentioned: the varying states or conditions of the plant as the season advances, the changing nutrient value of the soil moisture supply including the possibility of losses from leaching and bacterial activities of different kinds. It is only as these are understood and properly evaluated in each individual case that fertilizer applications can be timed to best advantage. When easily soluble nitrogenous fertilizers are required large amounts should not be put on in the fall, during the winter or too early in the spring, on account of the danger of leaching. Indeed, this is always a prime consideration in making nitrogen applications, though relatively unimportant with other fertilizers. On the other hand, fertilizers carrying nitrogen in organic combination must be applied sufficiently early to give disintegration processes time for making the nitrogen available to the plants before it is too late for them to absorb it.

Frequent observation and experience indicate that orchard fruits respond very quickly to easily soluble nitrogenous fertilizers such as nitrate of soda and sulphate of ammonia, when these are made as growth is starting in the spring or later during the growing season. Thus Ballou[23] reports a greatly increased set of fruit in weak, devitalized apple trees when nitrate of soda was applied just before the opening of the flowers. In this case not more than 3 weeks had elapsed before it was clearly evident that the trees were receiving benefit from the application. In fact this immediate effect of quickly available nitrogen has led to the general practice of applying it just as growth is starting and it would seem that experience bears out the wisdom of so timing nitrate applications. On the other hand, when nitrogen is needed, not so much for aiding the setting of fruit or perhaps for increasing the vegetative growth made during the early part of the current season—this latter being an influence which, as yet, has not been very accurately determined—but rather for its effects the following season, through organic products elaborated during the summer and fall months and stored through the winter, the best time for fertilizer applications may be quite different.

Some evidence in support of this last suggestion is furnished by experimental work in England.[154] Applications of quickly available fertilizers to orchard trees of a number of varieties in August, supplemented by applications in the spring at the time of fruit setting, caused trees to bear annual crops. The immediate effect of the midsummer applications is to cause the trees to hold their foliage later in the fall, thus accumulating larger stores of elaborated foods and making possible the formation of stronger, if not more, fruit buds. Experimental studies and large-scale field trials with both apples[157,254] and cherries[106] indicate that fall applications of nitrogenous fertilizers are at least the equal of spring applications of the same size and that in some instances they may prove superior. It is rather important so to time late summer or fall applications that they do not stimulate the trees to put out a second growth that does not have time properly to mature and that is thus subject to winter injury.

The Relation of Seasonal Conditions to Response from Fertilizers.— Many features of environment may be limiting factors to growth. The supply of nutrients in the soil constitutes only one series or group of these factors. With a change in other factors it is to be expected that a definite balance of nutrients in the soil will limit growth in different ways and a corresponding variation is to be expected from the use of a particular fertilizer on a particular soil and for a particular crop, depending on temperature, humidity, rainfall and other factors. Such differences have been studied in certain grain and forage crops. Thus applications of nitrogenous fertilizers to grass land give much more striking results when the season is comparatively dry than when it is wet.[181] Little is known regarding the responses of fruit trees to the same fertilizer with varying seasonal conditions. The great differences found in field crops, however, suggest that some variations may be expected.

Summary.—Potash, phosphoric acid and lime-carrying fertilizers are seldom required by orchard trees, which rarely show a direct response to their application. However, these fertilizers often increase greatly the growth of intercrops or cover crops and when these are used for mulching or green manuring purposes tree growth and production are indirectly increased. This indirect influence is particularly important in case the intercrop is a legume. Nitrate of soda and sulphate of ammonia are the most commonly used nitrogenous fertilizers, though a number of other more recently introduced forms appear to be equally satisfactory. Sodium nitrate tends to leave the soil more basic in reaction and sulphate of ammonia has the opposite effect. These different residual effects may be of considerable importance under some conditions. Phosphorus is generally applied as acid phosphate; potassium, as either muriate or sulphate. Data as to the best time for fertilizer applications are meager. They indicate, however, that for increasing the setting of fruit, quickly available nitrogenous fertilizers should be used just as the trees are starting growth in the spring. The nature and relative magnitude of the response from similar fertilizer applications may be expected to vary considerably with different growing-season conditions.

Suggested Collateral Readings

Bedford, H. A. R. and Pickering, S. U. The Effect of Grass on Trees, etc. Pp. 259–312. Science and Fruit Growing. London, 1919.

Curtis, O. F. The Translocation of Solutes in Plants. (Particularly Chapters 1–4.) New York, 1935.

Jörgensen, I., and Stiles, W. Carbon Assimilation. New Phytologist Reprint No. 10. London, 1917.

Palladin, V. I. Plant Physiology, Edit. by B. E. Livingston. Chapters 3, 4, 5, 7, 8. Pp. 60–117 and 139–212. Philadelphia, 1918.

Russell, E. J. Soil Conditions and Plant Growth. Chapters 2, 6, 7. Pp. 19–51 and 117–152. London, 1915.

Spoehr, H. A. Photosynthesis. (Particularly Chapters 2, 3, 5.) New York, 1926.

Literature Cited

1. Abbott, C. E. Am. Jour. Bot. 22 (4): 476–485. 1935.
2. Abbott, O. Bot. Gaz. 76: 167–184. 1923.
3. Adams, W. R. Vt. Agr. Exp. Sta. Bul. 282. 1928.
4. Addoms, R. M., and Mounce, F. C. N. J. Agr. Exp. Sta. Ann. Rept. p. 43. 1931.
5. Addoms, R. M., and Mounce, F. C. Plant Physiol. 7 (4): 643–656. 1932.
6. Albert, P. Forst. naturwiss. Ztschr. 3: 9. 1894.
7. Alderman, W. H. W. Va. Agr. Exp. Sta. Bul. 150. 1919.
8. Alderman, W. H. Proc. Am. Soc. Hort. Sci. 17: 261–266. 1920.
9. Aldrich, W. W. Md. Agr. Exp. Sta. Bul. 326. 1931.
10. Allison, R. V., Bryan, O. C., and Hunter, J. H. Fla. Agr. Exp. Sta. Bul. 190. 1927.
11. Ames, J. W. Ohio Agr. Exp. Sta. Mo. Bul. 5. 1920.
12. Anderssen, F. G. Jour. Pom. and Hort. Sci. 10 (2): 130–146. 1932.
13. André, G. Compt. rend. 734: 1514. 1903.
14. André, G. Chimie Agricole. 1: 415. Paris, 1914.
15. Ibid. 1: 425.
16. Anon. Exp. Sta. Rec. 58 (1): 20. 1928.
17. Anthony, R. D. Pa. Agr. Exp. Sta. Bul. 261. 1931.
18. Ariz. Agr. Exp. Sta. Ann. Rept. 46: 66. 1935.
19. Atkinson, J. D. N. Zeal. Jour. Sci. Tech. 18: 391–397. 1936.
20. Atkins, W. R. G. Roy. Dublin Soc. Sci. Proc., n. ser. 17: 201–210. 1923.
21. Bain, H. F. Jour. Agr. Res. 55 (11): 811–836. 1937.
22. Ball, E. D., Titus, E. G., and Greaves, J. E. Jour. Ec. Entom. 3: 187–197. 1910.
23. Ballou, F. H. Ohio Agr. Exp. Sta. Bul. 301. 1916.
24. Barnard, C., and Thomas, J. E. Jour. Council for Sci. and Ind. Res. (Australia). 6 (4): 285–296. 1933.
25. Bayer, A. Pflanzenphysiologische Bedeutung der Kupfer. Königsberg, 1902.
26. Beamee-Nieuland, N. Boschbouwk. Tydschr. Tectona. 11 (3): 187–205. 1918. Cited in Exp. Sta. Rec. 43: 320. 1920.
27. Beckwith, C. S. N. Jer. Agr. Exp. Sta. Ann. Rept. Pp. 449–459. 1922.
28. Behrens, J. Gartenflora. 47: 269. 1898.
29. Bennett, J. P. Phytopathology. 17 (10): 745–746. 1927.
30. Bennett, J. P. Cal. Agr. Exp. Sta. Circ. Bul. 231. 1931.
31. Bioletti, F. T. Cal. Agr. Exp. Sta. Bul. 241 (no date).

32. Black, C. A.   N. H. Agr. Exp. Sta. Tech. Bul. 10.   1916.
33. Blackman, F. F.   Ann. Bot.   19: 281–295.   1905.
34. Bose, S. R.   Indian Sci. Cong. Proc. (Calcutta).   13: 212–213.   1926.
35. Bouyoucos, G. J.   Mich. Agr. Exp. Sta. Tech. Bul. 44.   1919.
36. Bradford, F. C.   Ore. Agr. Exp. Sta. Bul. 129.   1915.
37. Breazeale, J. F.   Jour. Agr. Res.   18: 272.   1919.
38. Breazeale, J. F.   Ariz. Agr. Exp. Sta. Tech. Bul. 16.   1927.
39. Brenchley, W. E.   Inorganic Plant Poisons and Stimulants.   Cambr. Agr.
    Monogs.   Cambridge, 1914.
40. Brenchley, W. E., and Warrington, K.   Ann. Bot. (London).   41: 167–187.
    1927.
41. Brown, G. G.   Ore. Agr. Exp. Sta. Bul. 159.   1919.
42. Brown, H. T., and Escombe, F.   Phil. Trans. Roy. Soc. London.   190B: 233–
    291.   1900.
43. Brown, H. T., and Escombe, F.   Proc. Roy. Soc. London.   76B: 29–111.
    1905.
44. Burgess, P. S., and Pohlman, G. G.   Ariz. Agr. Exp. Sta. Bul. 124.   1928.
45. Burns, G. P.   Vt. Agr. Exp. Sta. Bul. 267.   1927.
46. Bushnell, J.   Minn. Agr. Exp. Sta. Tech. Bul. 34.   1925.
47. Butler, O. R., Smith, T. O., Curry, B. E.   N. H. Agr. Exp. Sta. Tech. Bul. 13.
    1917.
48. Caldwell, J. S.   Jour. Agr. Res.   30: 1133–1176.   1925.
49. Cal. Agr. Exp. Sta. Ann. Rept. for 1928–1930.   P. 38.   1930.
50. Cameron, F. K., and Bell, J. M.   U. S. D. A., Bur. Soils Bul. 30.   1905.
51. Chandler, W. H.   Mo. Ag. Exp. Sta. Bul. 113.   1913.
52. Chandler, W. H.   Mo. Agr. Exp. Sta. Res. Bul. 14.   1914.
53. Chandler, W. H.   Proc. Am. Soc. Hort. Sci.   17: 201–204.   1920.
54. Chauzit, J.   Compt. rend. Acad. Agr. France.   5: 835–837.   1919.   Cited in
    Exp. Sta. Rec.   42: 222.   1920.
55. Childers, N. F., and Coward, F. F.   Proc. Am. Soc. Hort. Sci.   32: 160–163.
    1936.
56. Colby, G. E.   Cal. Dept. Agr. Mo. Bul.   10: 35.   1921.
57. Collison, R. C.   N. Y. Agr. Exp. Sta. Bul. 447.   1920.
58. Collison, S. E.   Fla. Agr. Exp. Sta. Bul. 154.   1919.
59. Cook, F. C.   Jour. Agr. Res.   22: 281–287.   1921.
60. Coupin, H.   Compt. rend.   127: 400.   1898.
61. Ibid.   170: 753–754.   1920.
62. Coville, F. V.   U.S.D.A., Bur. Pl. Ind. Bul. 193.   1910.
63. Coville, F. V.   U.S.D.A. Bul. 6.   1913.
64. Cubbon, M. H.   Jour. Am. Soc. Agron.   17: 568–577.   1925.
65. Cummings, M. B., and Jones, C. H.   Vt. Agr. Exp. Sta. Bul. 211.   1919.
66. Curtis, O. F.   Am. Jour. Bot.   7: 101–124.   1920.
67. Czapek, F.   Biochemie der Pflanzen.   2: 156–158.   Jena, 1905.
68. Ibid.   2: 188.
69. Ibid.   2: 198.
70. Ibid.   2: 737.
71. Ibid.   2: 739.
72. Ibid.   2: 740.
73. Ibid.   2: 744.
74. Ibid.   2: 745.
75. Ibid.   2: 764, 765.

76. Ibid.   2: 765.
77. Ibid.   2: 766.
78. Ibid.   2: 769.
79. Ibid.   2: 772.
80. Ibid.   2: 776.
81. Ibid.   2: 795.
82. Ibid.   2: 797.
83. Ibid.   2: 798.
84. Ibid.   2: 800.
85. Ibid.   2: 805.
86. Ibid.   2: 830.
87. Ibid.   2: 868.
88. Daniel, L.   Rev. hort.   10 (N.S.): 102.   1910.
89. Darrow, G. M. and Waldo, G. F.   U.S.D.A., Tech. Bul. 453.   1934.
90. Davidson, O. W. and Shive, J. W.   Soil Science.   37: 357–386.   1934.
91. Davis, M. B.   Jour. Pom. and Hort. Sci.   8 (4): 316–344.   1930.
92. Davis, W. A., Daish, A. J., and Sawyer, G. C.   Jour. Agric. Soc.   6: 406–412. 1914.
93. Degman, E. S.   Proc. Am. Soc. Hort. Sci.   26: 182–186.   1929.
94. Drinkard, A. W.   Va. Agr. Exp. Sta. Ann. Rept.   P. 159.   1909–1910.
95. Dutton, W. C.   Mich. Agr. Exp. Sta. Sp. Bul. 218.   1932.
96. Emmons, E.   Agriculture of New York, Vol. 1.   Albany, 1849.
97. Ewert, A. J.   Proc. Roy. Soc. Victoria.   24 (N.S.): 367–419.   1912.
98. Finch, A. H., and Kinnison, A. F.   Ariz. Agr. Exp. Sta. Tech. Bul. 47.   1933.
99. Fischer, R.   Ernährung der Pflanze.   28: 440.   1932.
100. Floyd, B. F.   Fla. Agr. Exp. Sta. Ann. Rept.   Pp. 35R–46R.   1917.
101. Ibid.   Bul. 140.   1917.
102. Follett-Smith, R. R., and Bourne, C. L. C.   Agr. Jour. Brit. Guiana.   7: 17–20. 1926.
103. Franklin, J. H.   Mass. Agr. Exp. Sta. Bul. 168.   1916.
104. Fred, E. B.   Va. Agr. Exp. Sta. Ann. Rept.   Pp. 132–134.   1908.
105. Ibid.   Pp. 138–142.
106. Gardner, V. R.   Mich. Agr. Exp. Sta. Sp. Bul. 195.   1930.
107. Gardner, V. R.   Jour. Agr. Res.   50 (5): 457–478.   1935.
108. Garner, W. W., and Allard, H. A.   Jour. Agr. Res.   18: 553–606.   1920.
109. Gile, P. L., and Carrero, J. O.   Porto Rico Agr. Exp. Sta. Rept.   Pp. 10–20. 1917.
110. Gile, P. L., and Carrero, J. O.   Jour. Agr. Res.   20: 33–62.   1920.
111. Gladwin, F. E.   N. Y. Agr. Exp. Sta. Bul. 458.   1919.
112. Goff, E. S.   Wis. Agr. Exp. Sta. Ann. Rept.   16: 289.   1899.
113. Ibid.   17: 266.   1900.
114. Ibid.   18: 304.   1901.
115. Gonehalli, V. H.   Bombay Dept. Agr. Bul. 29.   1914.   (Cited by Tottingham, W. E.   Jour. Am. Soc. Agron.   2: 6.   1919.)
116. Gourley, J. H.   N. H. Agr. Exp. Sta. Bul. 168.   1914.
117. Ibid.   Bul. 190.   1919.
118. Gourley, J. H., and Hopkins, E. F.   Proc. Am. Soc. Hort. Sci.   26: 167–173. 1929.
119. Gourley, J. H., and Shunk, V. D.   N. H. Agr. Exp. Sta. Tech. Bul. 11.   1916.
120. Gourley, J. H., and Smock, R. M.   Ohio Agr. Exp. Sta. Bul. 517.   1933.
121. Gracie, D. S., and Trench, A. D. L.   Kenya Colony and Protectorate Dept. Agr. Bul. 7.   1931.

122. Graves, J. E., Carter, E. G., and Goldthorpe, H. C.   Jour. Agr. Res.   16: 107–135.   1919.
123. Gray, J., and Pierce, G. J.   Am. Jour. Bot.   6: 131–155.   1919.
124. Greaves, J. E.   Soil Science.   38 (5): 355–362.   1934.
125. Guyot, A. L.   Prog. agr. et vit.   43: 406–408.   1927.
126. Haas, A. R. C.   Calavo News.   June–July, 1936.
127. Haas, A. R. C.   Calif. Citrogr.   22 (6): 17.   1936.
128. Haas, A. R. C., and Klotz, L. J.   Hilgardia.   5 (8): 175–190.   1931.
129. Haas, A. R. C., and Reed, H. S.   Bot. Gaz.   83: 77–84.   1927.
130. Ibid.   83: 161–171.   1927.
131. Haas, A. R. C., and Thomas, E. E.   Bot. Gaz.   86: 345–354.   1928.
132. Haberlandt, G.   Bot. Ztg.   1877.   (Cited by Albert, P.   Forst. naturwiss. Ztschr.   3: 9.   1894.)
133. Harris, J. E.   Mich. Agr. Exp. Sta. Tech. Bul. 19.   1914.
134. Hart, E. B., and Tottingham, W. E.   Jour. Agr. Res.   5: 223–250.   1915.
135. Hartig, R.   Lehrbuch der Anatomie und Physiologie der Pflanzen.   Berlin.   1891.   P. 178.
136. Harvey, E. M.   Ore. Agr. Exp. Sta. Bul. 215.   1925.
137. Hartwell, B. L.   R. I. Agr. Exp. Sta. Bul. 183.   1920.
138. Hartwell, B. L., and Damon, S. C.   R. I. Agr. Exp. Sta. Bul. 177.   1919.
139. Hartwell, B. L., Pember, F. R., and Merkle, G. E.   R. I. Agr. Exp. Sta. Bul. 176.   1919.
140. Harvey, E. M., and Murneek, A. E.   Ore. Agr. Exp. Sta. Bul. 176.   1921.
141. Hawaii Agr. Exp. Sta. Rept.   P. 44.   1919.
142. Headden, W. P.   Col. Agr. Exp. Sta. Bul. 131.   1908.
143. Ibid.   Bul. 160.   1910.
144. Heck, A. F., Fred, E. B., and Whitson, A. R.   Wis. Agr. Exp. Sta. Bul. 405.   1929.
145. Hedrick, U. P.   N. Y. Agr. Exp. Sta. Bul. 289.   1907.
146. Ibid.   Bul. 339.   1911.
147. Hedrick, U. P., and Anthony, R. D.   N. Y. Agr. Exp. Sta. Bul. 460.   1919.
148. Heinicke, A. J., and Childers, N. F.   Cornell Univ. Agr. Exp. Sta. Mem. 201.   1937.
149. Hendrickson, H. C.   Porto Rico Agr. Exp. Sta. Ann. Rept.   1925.
150. Henrici, M.   Verhandl. Naturf. Ges. Basel.   30: 43–136.   1919.
151. Hill, H. and Davis, M. B.   Can. Dept. Agr. Bul. 110 (n.s.).   1929.
152. Hoagland, D. R., and Chandler, W. H.   Proc. Am. Soc. Hort. Sci.   29: 276–271.   1932.
153. Hoagland, D. R., and Snyder, W. C.   Proc. Am. Soc. Hort. Sci.   30: 288–294.   1933.
154. Hodgsoll, H. E. P.   Jour. Pomol.   1: 217–223.   1920.
155. Hooker, H. D., Jr.   Science.   46 (N.S.): 197–204.   1917.
156. Hooker, H. D., Jr.   Mo. Agr. Exp. Sta. Res. Bul. 40.   1920.
157. Hooker, H. D., Jr.   Proc. Am. Soc. Hort. Sci.   19: 241–243.   1922.
158. Hopkins, C. G., and Aumer, J. P.   Ill. Agr. Exp. Sta. Bul. 182.   1915.
159. Horticulturist.   1: 60.   1846.
160. Howard, A.   Roy. Soc. (London) Proc. Ser. B. 97, No. B.   683: 284–321.   1925.
161. Isbell, C. L.   Ala. Agr. Exp. Sta. Bul. 226.   1928.
162. Johnston, S.   Mich. Agr. Exp. Sta. Sp. Bul. 252.   1934.
163. Jörgensen, I., and Stiles, W.   Carbon Assimilation.   New Phytologist Reprint No. 10.   London, 1917.

164. Jost, L. Pflanzenphysiologie. 3te Auflage. P. 103. Jena, 1913.
165. Kearney, T. H. U.S.D.A., Bur. Pl. Ind. Bul. 125. 1908.
166. Kelley, W. P. Hawaii Agr. Exp. Sta. Bul. 26. 1912.
166a. Kelley, W. P., and Brown, S. M. Hilgardia. 3: 456–457. 1928.
167. Kelley, W. P., and Thomas, E. E. Cal. Agr. Exp. Sta. Bul. 318. 1920.
168. Kiesselbach, T. A. Nebr. Agr. Exp. Sta. Res. Bul. 6. 1916.
169. Kirby, R. S. Ia. Acad. Sci. 25: 265. 1918.
170. Klebs, G. Abh. Naturf. Ges. Halle. 25: 116. 1906.
171. Klebs, G. Proc. Roy. Soc. London. 82: 547–558. 1910.
172. Knowlton, H. E., and Hoffman, M. B. Proc. Am. Soc. Hort. Sci. 27: 28–31. 1930.
173. Korstian, C. F., Hartley, C., Watts, L. F., and Hahn, G. G. Jour. Agr. Res. 21: 153–169. 1921.
174. Kraus, E. J. Bienn. Crop Pest and Hort. Rept. Ore. Agr. Exp. Sta. 1: 71–78. 1911–1912.
175. Kraus, E. J. Ore. Agr. Exp. Sta. Research Bul. 1. Pt. 1. 1913.
176. Kraus, E. J., and Kraybill, H. R. Ore. Agr. Exp. Sta. Bul. 149. 1918.
177. Lagatu, H., and Maume, L. Prog. agr. et vit. 49: 576–581. 1932.
178. Laurent, E. Compt. rend. Soc. roy. bot. Belg. 29 (2): 71–76. 1890.
179. Laurent, E. Bul. Acad. roy. Belg. 32 (3): 815–865. 1896.
180. Lawes, J. B., and Gilbert, J. H. Rothamstead Memoirs. 2: 291–292. 1880.
181. Ibid. 2: 390–405.
182. Lawes, J. B., Gilbert, J. H., and Masters, M. T. Rothamstead Memoirs. 2: 1252–1263. 1882.
183. Leclerc, J. A., and Breazeale, J. F. U.S.D.A. Yearbook. Pp. 389–402. 1908.
184. Leclerc du Sablon. Rev. gén. bot. 16· 341–368; 386–401. 1904. 18: 5–25; 82–96. 1906.
185. Lewis, C. I., and Allen, R. W. Hood River Branch (Ore.) Agr. Exp. Sta. Rept. 1914–1915.
186. Lilleland, O. Better Crops with Plant Food. 20 (10): 17–19. 1936.
187. Loew, O., and May, D. W. U.S.D.A., Bur. Pl. Ind. Bul. 1. 1901.
188. Loree, R. E. Mich. Agr. Exp. Sta. Tech. Bul. 70. 1925.
189. Loughridge, R. H. Cal. Agr. Exp. Sta. Bul. 133. 1901.
190. Lubimenko, V. N. Mem. Acad. Sci. Petrograd. 8: 33. 1916. (Cited in Physiol. Abstr. 4: 413–414. 1919.)
191. Machargue, T. S. Ky. Agr. Exp. Sta. Rept. Pt. 1., Pp. 16–18. 1926.
192. Magistad, O. C., and Breazeale, J. F. Ariz. Agr. Exp. Sta. Tech. Bul. 25. 1929.
193. Magness, J. R. Ore. Agr. Exp. Sta. Bul. 139. 1916.
194. Ibid. Bul. 146. 1917.
195. Magness, J. R., and Furr, J. R. Proc. Am. Soc. Hort. Sci. 27: 207–211. 1930.
196. Magness, J. R., and Overley, F. L. Proc. Am. Soc. Hort. Sci. 26: 180–181. 1929.
197. Maquenne, L., and Demoussey, E. Bul. Soc. Chim. 27: 266–278. 1920.
198. Marcovitch, S. Tenn. Agr. Exp. Sta. Ann. Rept. 42: 33. 1929.
199. Marshall, R. E. Mich. Agr. Exp. Sta. Tech. Bul. 111. 1931.
200. Massey, A. B. Va. Agr. Exp. Sta. Ann. Rept. 1919–1927: 45. 1928.
201. Marsh, R. S. Bot. Gaz. 75: 400–413. 1923.
202. McCleary, F. C. New South Wales Agr. Gaz. 50: 397.–406 1929.
203. Ibid. Pp. 523–524.
204. McClintock, J. A. Ga. Agr. Exp. Sta. Bul. 139. 1921.
205. McClelland, T. B. Porto Rico Agr. Exp. Sta. Rept. 1925.

206. McCool, M. M., and Millar, C. E.   Mich. Agr. Exp. Sta. Tech. Bul. 43.   1918.
207. McCue, C. A.   Trans. Peninsular Hort. Soc.   1915.
208. McGeorge, W. T.   Ariz. Agr. Exp. Sta. Tech. Bul. 60.   1936.
209. McLarty, H. R.   Sci. Agr.   16: 525–533.   1936.
210. McMurran, S. M.   U.S.D.A. Bul. 756.   1919.
211. Mer, E.   Bul. soc. bot.   45: 299.   1898.   d'Arbaumont, J.   Ann. sci. nat. bot.   (8) 13: 319–423; 14: 125–212.   1901.
212. Metzger, W. H., and Janssen, G.   Jour. Agr. Res.   37 (10): 599–628.   1928.
213. Michel Durant, E.   Variation des substances hydrocarboneés dans les feuilles. Dissertation.   Nemours.   1917.
214. Mitchell, H. L., and Frim, R. F.   Black Rock Forest Papers.   1 (2): 6–9. 1935.
215. Molisch, H.   Bot. Ztg.   55: 49–61.   1897.
216. Montemartini, L.   Atti ist. bot. Univ. Pavia.   (2) 15: 1–42.   1918.
217. Morris, L. S., and Crist, J. W.   Mich. Agr. Exp. Sta. Tech. Bul. 77.   1927.
218. Mowry, H., and Camp, A. F.   Fla. Agr. Exp. Sta. Bul. 273.   1934.
219. Munson, W. M.   Me. Agr. Exp. Sta. Bul. 89.   1903.
220. Murneek, A. E.   Plant Physiol.   1: 1–26.   1925.
221. Ibid.   Plant Physiol.   4: 251–264.   1929.
222. Musser, A. M., and Scott, L. E.   S. Car. Agr. Exp. Sta. Ann. Rept.   48: 115.
223. Neubauer, H. G.   Gartenbauwiss.   10: 380–421.   1936.
224. Neubauer, C.   Ann. Oenol.   5: 343–364.   1875.
225. Newton, G. A., and Damlof, K. B.   Soil Sci.   24: 95–102.   1927.
226. Nightengale, G. T. and Blake, M. A.   N. Jer. Agr. Exp. Sta. Bul. 566.   1934.
227. N. Mex. Agr. Exp. Sta. Ann. Rept.   P. 31.   1912–13.
228. N. Y. Agr. Exp. Sta. Ann. Rep.   Pp. 166–168.   1891.
229. Nobbe, F., Baeseler, D., and Will, H.   Landw. Versuchs-Sta.   30: 381–423. 1884.
230. Oddo, B., and Polacci, G.   Gazz. chim. ital.   50 (1): 54–70.
231. Paddock, W., and Whipple, O. B.   Fruit Growing in Arid Regions.   P. 330. New York, 1911.
232. Palladin, V. I.   Plant Physiology.   Edit. by B. E. Livingston.   P. 82.   Philadelphia, 1918.
233. Ibid.   P. 83.
234. Ibid.   P. 254.
235. Partridge, N. L.   Proc. Am. Soc. Hort. Sci.   16: 104–109.   1919.
236. Petit, P.   Compt. rend.   111:975.   1893: Ascoli, Lieb. Physiol. Chem.   28: 426. 1899.
237. Pfeiffer, O.   Ann. Oenol.   5: 271–315.   1875.
238. Pickering, S. U.   Ann. Bot.   31: 183–187.   1917.
239. Porto Rico Agr. Exp. Sta. Rept. for 1927.   P. 7.   1929.
240. Quaintance, A. L.   Ga. Agr. Exp. Sta. Ann. Rept.   13: 350.   1900.
241. Rassiguier.   Prog. agr. et vit.   18 (No. 35): 204–206.   1892.   (Cited by Gile, P. L., and Carrero, J. O.   Jour. Agr. Res.   20: 38.   1920.)
242. Reed, H. S., and Dufrenoy, J.   Hilgardia.   9 (2): 113–135.   1935.
243. Reed, H. S., and Parker, E. A.   Jour. Agr. Res.   53 (5): 395–398.   1936.
244. Reimer, F. C.   Ore. Agr. Exp. Sta. Bul. 163.   1919.
245. Ibid.   Bul. 166.   1920.
246. Richter, L.   Landw. Versuchs-Sta.   73: 457–477.   1910.
247. Ricks, G. L., and Gaston, H. P.   Mich. Agr. Exp. Sta. Sp. Bul. 265.   1935.
248. Ripperton, J. C., Goto, Y. B., and Pahau, R. K.   Hawaii Agr. Exp. Sta. Bul. 75.   1935.

249. Rivera, V. I problemi agrari del mezzogiorno. Mem. R. Staz. Patal. Veg. P. 18. Rome, 1919.
250. Roberts, I. P. Cornell Univ. Agr. Exp. Sta. Bul. 103. 1895.
251. Roberts, R. H. Proc. Am. Soc. Hort. Sci. 14: 105. 1917.
252. Roberts, R. H. Wis. Agr. Exp. Sta. Bul. 317. 1920.
253. Schneiderhan, F. J. Exp. Sta. Rec. 60 (1): 55. 1929.
254. Schrader, A. L., and Auchter, C. E. Proc. Am. Soc. Hort. Sci. 22: 150–161. 1925.
255. Schreiner, O., and Shorey, E. C. U.S.D.A., Bur. Soils Bul. 74. 1910.
256. Schreiner, O., and Skinner, J. J. U.S.D.A., Bur. Soils Bul. 70. 1910.
257. Ibid. Bul. 77. 1911.
258. Ibid. Bul. 87. 1912.
259. Ibid. Bul. 108. 1914.
260. Schreiner, O., Reed, H. S., and Skinner, J. J. U.S.D.A., Bur. Soils Bul. 47. 1907.
261. Shedd, O. M. Ken. Agr. Sta. Bul. 188. 1914.
262. Shibata, K., Shibata, Y., and Kasiwagi, I. Jour. Am. Chem. Soc. 41: 208. 1919.
263. Shoemaker, J. S., and Greve, E. W. Ohio Agr. Exp. Sta. Bul. 466. 1930.
264. Shuhart, D. V. Jour. Agr. Res. 34 (7): 687–696. 1927.
265. Shull, C. A. Science. 52 (N.S.): 376–378. 1920.
266. Sideris, C. P. Hawaii Pineapple Canners' Sta. Bul. 8. 1926.
267. Skinner, J. J. U.S.D.A., Bur. Soils Bul. 83. 1911.
268. Smith, R. E. Cal. Agr. Exp. Sta. Bul. 336. 1921.
269. Snyder, J. C. Bot. Gaz. 94 (4): 771–779. 1933.
270. Sorauer, P. Pflanzenkrankheiten. 3te. Auflage. 1: 289. Berlin, 1909.
271. Ibid. 1: 292.
272. Ibid. 1: 297.
273. Ibid. 1: 305.
274. Ibid. 1: 310.
275. Ibid. 1: 312.
276. Ibid. 1: 391.
277. Spoehr, H. A. Carnegie Inst. Wash. Publ. 287. 1919.
278. Stewart, J. P. Pa. Agr. Exp. Sta. Bul. 153. 1918.
279. Stewart, R. Ill. Agr. Exp. Sta. Bul. 227. 1920.
280. Stewart, R. Ill. Agr. Exp. Sta. Circ. 245. 1920.
281. Storey, H. H., and Leach, R. Ann. App. Biol. 20: 23–56. 1933.
282. Stoykowitch, W. Recherches physiologiques sur la prune. Dissertation. Nancy, 1910.
283. Taubenhaus, J. J., and Roney, J. N. Texas Agr. Exp. Sta. Ann. Rept. 47: 92. 1934.
284. Taylor, R. H. Cal. Agr. Exp. Sta. Bul. 297. 1918.
285. Taylor, T. C., and Nelson, J. M. Jour. Am. Chem. Soc. 42: 1726–1738. 1920.
286. Teodoresco, E. C. Ann. Sci. nat. Bot. (8) 10: 141–164. 1899.
287. Thomas, R. P. Wis. Agr. Exp. Sta. Res. Bul. 105. 1930.
288. Thomas, E. E., and Haas, A. R. C. Bot. Gaz. 86: 355–362. 1928.
289. Thompson, R. C. Ark. Agr. Exp. Sta. Bul. 123. 1916.
290. Tiedjens, V. A. Plant Physiol. 9 (1): 31–58. 1934.
291. Tiedjens, V. A., and Robbins, W. R. N. Jer. Agr. Exp. Sta. Bul. 526. 1931.
292. Tottingham, W. E. Jour. Am. Soc. Agron. 2: 1. 1919.
293. Trabut, W. Cited by Kearney, T. H. U.S.D.A., Bur. Pl. Ind. Bul. 125. 1908.

294. Traub, H. P.   Minn. Agr. Exp. Sta. Tech. Bul. 53.   1927.
295. Truog, E.   Wis. Agr. Exp. Sta. Res. Bul. 41.   1916.
296. Tsuji, T.   La Plante.   60: 413–414.   1918.
297. Turner, L. M.   Ark. Agr. Exp. Sta. Bul. 312.   1934.
298. Valleau, W. D., and Johnson, E. M.   Ky. Agr. Exp. Sta. Res. Bul.   281.   1927.
299. Vandecaveye, S. C., Homer, G. M., and Keaton, C. M.   Soil Sci.   42 (3): 203–215.   1936.
300. Van Slyke, L. L., Taylor, O. M., and Andrews, W. H.   N. Y. Agr. Exp. Sta. Bul. 265.   1905.
301. Vasnievski, S.   Bul. intern. acad. sci. Cracovie B.   Pp. 615–686.   1917.
302. Voechting, H.   Jahrb. wiss. Bot.   25: 149–208.   1893.
303. Waldo, G. F.   Jour. Agr. Res.   40 (5): 393–407.   1930.
304. Ibid.   40 (5): 409–416.   1930.
305. Wallace, T.   Jour. Pom. and Hort. Sci.   7: 172–198.   1928.
306. Walster, H. L.   Bot. Gaz.   69: 97–125.   1920.
307. Waltman, C. S.   Ky. Agr. Exp. Sta. Bul. 321.   1931.
308. Warren, F. G.   N. J. Agr. Exp. Sta. Rept.   P. 199.   1906.
309. Webber, H. J.,   U.S.D.A. Yearbook.   P. 193.   1894.
310. Weber, R.   Landw. Versuchs-Sta.   18: 18–48.   1875.
311. Weber, R.   Forst. naturwiss. Ztschr.   1: 13.   1893.
312. Weinberger, J. H.   Proc. Am. Soc. Hort. Sci.   26: 174–179.   1929.
313. West, E. S., and Barnard, C.   Jour. Council for Sci. and Ind. Res. (Australia).   8: 94–95.   1935.
314. Westgate, J. M.   Hawaii Agr. Exp. Sta. Press Bul. 51.   1916.
315. Wheeler, H. J.   U.S.D.A. Farmers Bul. 77.   1905.
316. Wheeler, H. J.   Manures and Fertilizers.   Pp. 113–124.   New York, 1914.
317. Whiting, A. L., and Schoonover, W. R.   Ill. Agr. Exp. Sta. Bul. 225.   1920.
318. Whitten, J. C., and Wiggins, C. C.   Mo. Agr. Sta. Buls. 131, 141, 147.   1915–1917.
319. Wickson, E. J.   California Fruits.   P. 164.   San Francisco.   1910.
320. Wiegand, K. M.   Bot. Gaz.   41: 373.   1906.
321. Wiesner, J.   Die Entstehung des Chlorophylls.   Vienna, 1877.
322. Wilson, B. D., and Wilson, J. K.   Cornell Univ. Agr. Exp. Sta. Mem. 95.   1925.
323. Woodbury, C. G., Noyes, N. A., and Oskamp, J.   Ind. Agr. Exp. Sta. Bul.   207.   1917.
324. Wright, W. J.   Proc. Am. Soc. Hort. Sci.   11: 9–14.   1912.
325. Young, H. C., and Winter, H. F.   O. Agr. Exp. Sta. Bimonthly Bul.   22: 147–152.   1937.
326. Zaliesski, W.   Die Bedingungen der Eiweissbildung den Pflanzen.   P. 53   Charkow.   1900.
327. Zimmerman, A.   Ztsch. angew. Chem.   6: 426.   1893.

SECTION III
TEMPERATURE RELATIONS
OF FRUIT PLANTS

Of the four great factors of plant environment, moisture, soil, light and temperature, the fruit grower can modify two considerably. He can irrigate or drain, he can fertilize, if necessary; he can, to some extent, modify soil texture; light and temperature he must take as they come. The object of the present section is to indicate how, though temperatures cannot be changed, except in certain minor respects, fruit growing can be modified to capitalize favorable temperatures or to minimize the unfavorable effects. Knowing the various effects of heat or its lack the grower is able to choose fruits best adapted to existing conditions, to avoid attempting the impossible or the very hazardous, to pick favorable sites and so to manipulate his plants that they will have the best possible adjustment to the various temperature conditions of their environment.

Temperatures influence plants in several ways bearing directly on fruit growing: (1) they delimit zones beyond which the growing of specific fruits becomes commercially hazardous because of low winter temperatures; (2) they delimit zones beyond which the growth of certain fruits becomes unprofitable because of high summer temperatures; (3) they make certain areas unprofitable for some fruits because of low summer temperatures; (4) they render much good land of doubtful value for several fruits because of danger from spring frosts; (5) within areas ordinarily safe for growing certain specific fruits an occasional deviation from normal may cause considerable damage; (6) some insects and diseases are more or less dependent on proper temperatures for their optimum development.

Lest this statement should give an unpleasant connotation to temperature relations, it should be stated conversely that these very limitations predicate the presence at some places of temperatures favorable to fruit growing. The existence of fruit growing at all is obvious proof. Unfortunately attention is centered rather on the limitations, so that, though many unfavorable conditions are fairly closely understood, optimum temperatures for the various fruits are not defined so clearly.

Schimper,[205] commenting on the difficulty of temperature investigations, states: the "existence of such action on vegetable organisms is less clearly recognizable than is that of water. We can directly observe the ingress of water into a plant and its egress, we can explain physiologically the effects caused by these, and we can follow the transpiration current along its course, whereas the action of heat is carried on in the molecular region of the protoplasm beyond our ken, and is visible to us only in its final consequences, such as the acceleration, retardation or complete cessation of physiological processes. The œcological phenomena display similar processes. Protective adaptations against a want or superfluity of water are within our power of observation, those against cold and heat are entirely beyond them. We can directly see whether any plant naturally inhabits a dry or a moist station, but not whether it belongs to the flora of a cold or warm climate. Indeed plants from hot deserts frequently have a strong resemblance in habit to those of polar zones."

The metabolism of a plant may be regarded as a complicated set of chemical reactions, subject to several influences. Among the factors governing chemical reactions and vital processes the chemist and the physiologist recognize temperature. There are certain limits, apparently, for all vital reactions, limits wide in some instances, narrow in others. Some plants require a relatively high temperature for setting in motion the processes known as growth; others will carry on similar processes at a lower point. One may go on at a certain temperature in a given plant, while another in the same plant may require more heat. At a low temperature a plant is said to rest; certain processes are in truth suspended, but others are inaugurated. Finally, there is a point so low that the plant cannot exist; it dies apparently from cold. On the other hand, all plants show their maximum growth activity within the limits of a comparatively small range of temperature; above these limits some reactions are retarded or some are so accelerated as to become harmful, or new injurious reactions begin and the net results that are recognized as growth or fruitfulness are diminished; here again the point is finally reached where the equilibrium of reactions is broken and death ensues.

Withal, it must be considered that temperature is only one of the factors affecting plant growth. Even a single plant may be limited at various times by quite different features of its environment.

Investigation has shown that in soy beans in Maryland growth was controlled during one fortnight by temperature, but in the next by the rainfall-evaporation ratio.[158] In Ceylon it has been found that with *Agave* and *Furcræa* temperature is always the limiting factor; with *Dendrocalamus* sometimes it is temperature, sometimes water supply. In January *Vitis* is limited in growth by temperature and in July by the water supply, while with *Capparis* and *Stifftea* the limiting factors are water supply during the day and temperature during the night.[220]

MacDougal[139] shows the operation of limiting factors in his study of the growth of tomato fruits. As the temperature of the fruits increased, growth progressed until the rise caused a loss of water exceeding the gain. The higher temperatures did not accelerate growth unless the relative humidity of the atmosphere was high; a rise in temperature with decreased humidity retarded or stopped growth or even caused an actual diminution of volume.

CHAPTER XIV

GROWING-SEASON TEMPERATURES

Horticulturists, particularly in the Old World, have recognized in a manner the importance of growing-season temperatures to fruit plants. Most of the efforts at precise study of this nature, however, have been made by those particularly interested in phenology.

HEAT UNITS

Various investigators have made efforts to show that, wherever a given plant is grown, to complete its cycle that plant requires a certain amount of heat. When it has received this amount of heat, whether in n days or $n + r$ or $n + s$ days, it will have completed its cycle. The outline of this idea was enunciated first, probably, in 1735 by Reaumur.[1] Numerous writers since that time have attempted to refine the methods used in studies of this sort. Adanson, for example, recognizing that averages which included readings below freezing were misleading, inasmuch as such temperatures do not reverse plant activity but merely suspend it, discarded all such readings. Others have assumed higher temperatures as the zero points for their calculations. Gasparin considered that "effective temperatures" began at 5°C. He also considered a thermometer in full sunshine on sod to show the true temperature of the plant more nearly than one registering air temperature alone and that "the warmth in the sunshine is to the warmth of the air in the shade as though one has been transported in latitude from 3 to 6° farther south."[1] Mason[152] reached the conclusion that the zero point or minimum temperature permitting growth of the date palm lies somewhere between 48° and 50°F. for the actual region of cell division.

DeCandolle[66] believed sunlight in itself to influence vital processes independently of temperature, since several annuals which he had under observation required a greater total of heat degrees for flowering and for ripening in the shade than they received in full sunlight.

The Relative Values of Different Effective Temperatures.—Most investigations in phenology until comparatively recent date have been based on the assumption that, above the basic temperature which initiates plant growth, each degree is of equal value with any other. Lately, however, the principle of Van't Hoff and Arrhenius, namely, "that within limits, the velocity of most chemical reactions doubles or somewhat more than doubles for each rise in temperature of 10°C.," has been shown to have considerable bearing on certain processes in plants. As the Livingstons[133] point out, certain of the purely physical processes involved in growth do not follow this principle and its application to plants is, therefore, qualified. Fully recognizing the numerous limitations inherent in the data at present available, they have, nevertheless, tentatively assigned "efficiency indices" to the various degrees of temperature, reproduced in part in Table 1, and applied them to the temperature data at various points in the United States.

In a subsequent paper Livingston proposes a different system, based on Lehenbauer's studies of root growth in maize.[132]

This system differs from the others in that it is based on observed rates of growth and in taking cognizance of a decreased rate of growth with temperatures above the optimum. A comparison of the values obtained with the three systems is given in Table 1. Livingston evidently regards this work only as a step toward further study, since he states: " . . . these indices are to be regarded as only a first approximation and . . . much more physiological study will be required before they may be taken as generally applicable. In the first place, they are based upon tests of only a single plant species, maize, and there are

TABLE 1.—A COMPARISON OF TEMPERATURE INDEX VALUES, STARTING WITH 40°F. AS UNIT, ACCORDING TO THREE SYSTEMS

Temperature	System		
	Remainder	Exponential	Physiological
40	1	1.0000	1.000
50	11	1.4696	6.333
58	19	2.0000	16.111
68	29	2.9391	46.000
76	37	4.0000	82.333
86	47	5.8782	120.000
94	55	8.0000	103.333
99	60	9.6980	73.111
112	73	16.0000	3.778

probably other plants . . . for which they are not even approximately true. . . . no doubt other phases of growth in the same plant may exhibit other relations between temperature and the rate of shoot elongation. Third, these indices refer to rates of shoot elongation, and there are many other processes involved in plant growth, which may require other indices for their proper interpretation in terms of temperature efficiency. Fourth, they apply strictly only under the moisture, light and chemical conditions that prevailed in Lehenbauer's experiments . . . Fifth, and finally, plants in nature are never subject to any temperature maintained for any considerable period of time. . . . "

Influence of Latitude on Heat Requirements.—Phenological data on any single fruit plant gathered over a wide area are rather scarce at present and those available are not altogether satisfactory. However, in combination with temperature data compiled by the Weather Bureau some of these data are interesting, particularly since, to some extent, they corroborate findings of other investigators.

In the Early Harvest Apple.—Table 2 is compiled from phenological data gathered by Bailey[9] and from daily normal temperatures for the various points,[22] except that the temperature for Columbia, Mo., is joined with the phenological data for Boonville, a short distance away. Some of the phenological data may be open to question, as, for example, the ripening date for Thomasville, Ga., but even with some allowance for errors, there is apparent a general tendency for temperature summations at southern points to exceed those of more northern location. Though

TABLE 2.—HEAT UNITS CALCULATED ON SEVERAL SYSTEMS COMPARED WITH DATES OF BLOSSOMING AND OF RIPENING IN THE EARLY HARVEST APPLE

| Locality | Date | | Normal temperature at average date of blossoming, Fahrenheit | Remainder | | | Exponential Jan. 1 to ripening | Physiological Jan. 1 to ripening |
	Blossoming	Ripening		Jan. 1 to blossoming	Blossom to ripening	Total Jan. 1 to ripening		
Thomasville, Ga....	Mar. 10	July 10	59	933	3,952	4,945	536	8,383
Augusta, Ga.......	Mar. 27	May 30	59	922	1,820	2,742	315	3,455
Atlanta, Ga.......	Apr. 8	July 1	59	819	2,573	3,392	378	5,005
Raleigh, N. C.....	Apr. 6	July 2	56	597	2,560	3,157	366	4,758
Boonville, Mo.....	Apr. 20	June 23	56	347	1,729	2,076	234	2,979
Erie, Pa..........	May 23	Aug. 18	60	558	2,600	3,158	341	2,110
Ithaca, N. Y......	May 10	July 28	55	283	2,102	2,385	261	3,305
Rochester, N. Y...	May 21	Aug. 11	59	476	2,267	2,743	293	1,547

relative positions of certain stations change with different systems of computing the effective temperatures, the same tendency holds throughout and is perhaps most evident with the physiological index summations. If a different zero point—say 50°F.—be assumed, the relative differences are not reduced materially; in fact they are rather intensified, for though northern points would have somewhat lower summation totals, those for Thomasville, Ga., would not be reduced at all, since the normal daily temperature for early January is 50°F.

In the Elberta Peach.—Gould[96] reports ripening dates for the Elberta peach at various points in the United States. Certain of these seem near enough to stations for which Bigelow[22] has computed daily normal temperatures to make comparisons valid. Table 3 shows summations to the date of ripening and for the year at these points, with the proportion which they bear respectively to each other. Linsser[130] has suggested that this ratio should be constant, but the data here presented do not support his suggestion. The same tendency to greater summations in the south than in the north is apparent here. Waugh[243] found heat units for the blossoming of the "American Wild Plum" in 1898 as follows: Stillwater, Okla., 967; Parry, N. J., 909; State College, Pa., 725; Burlington, Vt., 577.

TABLE 3.—HEAT UNITS TO THE DATE OF RIPENING OF ELBERTA PEACH AT VARIOUS POINTS AND TOTAL HEAT UNITS FOR THE YEAR

Locality	Date of ripening	Remainder		Linsser's constant	Exponential index to ripening
		To ripening	For year		
Atmore, Ala.............	July 11	4,654	9,540	48.8	522.9
Plain Dealing, La........	July 10	4,572˙	8,143	56.1	519.2
Van Buren, Ark.........	July 15	3,817	8,006	47.7	432.6
Vacaville, Cal...........	July 6	3,332	7,478	44.6	.....
Manteo, N. C...........	Aug. 10	4,911	8,475	57.9	562.6
Central Ind.............	Sept. 15	4,090	5,346	76.5	499.4
Lewiston, Idaho.........	Aug. 1	3,006	5,260	57.1	334.2
Palisades, Col...........	Aug. 26	4,483	6,001	74.7	500.0
Port Clinton, Ohio.......	Aug. 25	3,639	5,170	70.4	392.8
Freewater, Ore..........	Aug. 17	3,622	5,488	66.2	403.4
Lake region, Mich.......	Sept. 10	3,483	4,292	81.1	374.1
Ipswich, Mass..........	Sept. 17	3,880	4,669	83.1	418.2

In Citrus Fruits and Grapes.—Studies by Hodgson[115] on the factors influencing the ripening period of citrus fruits indicate that "the summation totals of heat units for regions of high summer temperatures are considerably higher than for regions of lower maximum temperatures." This suggests that temperatures above a certain maximum either are not utilized or possibly may even delay the ripening of the fruit and is in line with the observed failure of a number of varieties of the *labrusca* type of grape of northern origin to ripen properly in sections having hot climates.

In Chestnut Blight.—Stevens has made an interesting application of these various constants to studies of the growth of the chestnut blight fungus. Assuming 45°F. as the lowest effective temperature, he compares the summations of temperatures above that point at various localities with the observed growth of the blight cankers and finds that "the temperature summation falls off somewhat more rapidly northward than does the amount of growth." In a later paper he reports that the summations on the "Physiological basis" do not fit the observed growth so well as the summations of remainder or exponential indices.[226,227]

Variations in Heat Requirements from Season to Season.—Sandsten[203] made a study of heat units accumulating at blossom time for the apple and plum during several seasons at Madison, Wis. As appears from Table 4, composed of items taken from his data, he found considerable variation from year to year and from variety to variety. Combining

TABLE 4.—NUMBER OF POSITIVE TEMPERATURE UNITS (ABOVE 32°F.) RECEIVED EACH YEAR FROM JAN. 1 TO THE DATE OF FIRST BLOOM

Variety	1902	1903	1904	1905
Wealthy...................	810.5	837:5	752.0	690.0
Borovinka.................	837.0	810.5	727.0	599.0
Charlamoff................	837.0	928.0	752.5	713.0
Hibernal..................	785.0	837.5	707.0	599.0
Grimes....................	785.0	810.5	752.5	652.0

with these figures the total heat units for the last 6 months of the previous growing season he secured a closer approach to uniformity as expressed in percentage of the smallest yearly total to the greatest yearly totals for any variety (see Table 5). Sandsten interprets his data as showing that other factors besides the heat units from Jan. 1 have a

TABLE 5.—NUMBER OF POSITIVE TEMPERATURE UNITS (ABOVE 32°F.) RECEIVED FROM PRECEDING JULY 1 TO THE DATE OF FIRST BLOOM

Variety	1901–1902	1902–1903	1903–1904	1904–1905
Wealthy.....................	5,106.5	4,827.5	4,601.5	4,801.5
Borovinka...................	5,133.5	4,801.5	4,576.0	4,710.5
Charlamoff..................	5,133.5	4,918.5	4,601.5	4,824.5
Hibernal....................	5,081.5	4,827.5	4,556.0	4,710.5
Grimes......................	5,081.5	4,801.0	4,601.5	4,763.5

bearing on the time of flowering and enumerates as possible factors the stage of advancement of the buds at the time of growth cessation in the fall, the size of the crop borne in the previous year, "soil conditions and the amount of plant food present in the soil; and fifth, the individual characteristics and state of health of the tree or plant." General observation on peach trees shows a sequence in opening blossoms corresponding to the stage of advancement of these buds in the fall, the difference in time of flowering on the same branch amounting sometimes to several days, which would make a difference occasionally of 50 units or more on the Fahrenheit scale. Magness makes an interesting suggestion in this connection which is referred to under Fruit Bud Formation.

Seeley[214] applied the method of temperature summations to the Late Crawford peach, as recorded in the Mikesell data for Wauseon, Ohio.

His summary of results, shown in Table 6, indicates no close agreement from year to year for the same locality. Somewhat closer tallying was secured when maximum figures were used (line 4). Seeley shows that air temperatures as recorded by thermometers in the conventional shelter do not indicate at all closely the actual temperatures of the leaves.

TABLE 6.—THE LEAST AND THE GREATEST TEMPERATURE SUMMATIONS IN THE LIFE PHASE OF THE LATE CRAWFORD PEACH

(*After Seeley*[214])

Summation	Jan. 1 to blossoming	Blossoming to ripening	Jan. 1 to ripening	Ripening to blossoming	Average
Least..................	183	2,776	3,030	486	..
Greatest...............	362	3,991	4,347	1,250	..
Percentage.............	50	70	70	38	61
Maximum (per cent.)......	64	71	72	61	69

Acclimatization to Varying Amounts of Heat.—It is conceivable that through acclimatization plants gradually may require more or less heat for a given function; evidence to this effect is cited by Bailey.[11] Cuttings of Concord grape from Maine, central New York and southern Louisiana planted simultaneously under uniform conditions at Ithaca, N. Y., made in a given time the following respective growths: 2.66 inches, 1.6 inches and 1.3 inches. The seed potato trade of Maine is founded on the quickened response to a given temperature by potatoes grown there. Data already cited in this chapter show a tendency for plants in northern sections to attain a given stage of development with less heat than in southern sections. Elsewhere it is shown that plants accommodate themselves to a wide range of moisture, nutrient and light conditions; therefore it is not surprising that they show a corresponding adaptation to various temperature conditions.

In General.—It is possible that more detailed measurements, taken perhaps on a different basis from that used by climatologists, would secure more uniformity than the figures cited above. Temperatures taken in sunlight would seem to be more reliable expressions of conditions in buds and leaves than those taken in shade. Some writers have suggested maximum temperatures as the basis for calculations. In any case, however, it seems doubtful if temperature alone can be made the index of plant activities.

Schimper[206] aptly points out that "different organs and functions require very different amounts of heat, that unfavorable temperatures cause subsequent inhibition, and that other factors besides heat, especially humidity, cooperate and intervene. We need not, then, be surprised if there is very little accord in phaenological observations, and that the utmost one can do is to admit their having a certain importance for purely descriptive geographical botany in the characterization of certain districts. No importance, on the other hand, need be assigned to the theoretical views, nor to the sum total of temperatures."

OPTIMUM TEMPERATURES

It is well known that some plants grow at lower temperatures than others. The necessity of a certain amount of heat during the growing season is recognized in the statement that in some regions the summers are too cool for certain fruits.

Variation within the Species or Variety.—In considerable areas of north central Europe, peach growing is limited, not by the cold of winter but by the low summer temperature. The same limitation, though less obvious, probably applies to pears, as is indicated by the transition from open exposures in the south of France to the trained and sheltered trees in the north. Among plants of warmer climates the date palm shows a heat requirement that is not satisfied in all sections where the winters are sufficiently mild. The grape is among the plants most frequently cited by phenological workers as showing this same exaction in its requirement. Variety adaptation in apples probably depends on growing-season temperature, among other factors. In addition it seems rather likely that this factor is operative in another way though its effects necessarily are masked by their own results; low summer temperature may delay maturity to such an extent that an ensuing winter of medium intensity is injurious. The obvious and immediate cause of trouble here would be winter injury but the antecedent cause would be the cool summer. Much of the winter injury characteristic of parts of Europe seems to be involved with low summer temperatures.

The effects of temperature alone in certain phases can be compared best, perhaps, in plants of the deserts, since these regions show rather greater uniformity in other conditions than most humid sections. In the date palm temperature assumes considerable importance.

According to Swingle:[231] "The northern limit and the limit of altitude in northwestern Africa at which dates can be grown are set more by the deficient summer heat failing to ripen the fruit than by the cold in winter." Very early ripening dates, he reports, can be grown far to the north where the summers are not warm enough to ripen later varieties. Swingle confirms DeCandolle's calculation of 64.4°F. as the point below which no effect is produced on flowering or fruiting of the date palm. Affirming that under desert conditions temperature summations have considerable significance he states that 2000°C., using 18°C. as the zero point, are necessary to ripen Deglet Noor dates satisfactorily.

Mason[151] cites Caruso as authority for the statement that 51° to 52°F. is zero point for the olive and adds that in California zero may be somewhat higher, probably 55° to 56°F. He assigns a definite number of heat units as necessary for ripening the olive before autumn, but points out that in some localities with low summer temperatures and little or no frost in winter the fruit may remain longer on the trees. In some places the requisite number of heat units is not accumulated until December.

The apple shows some indications of the effects of excessive summer heat at some points in the United States and of deficient summer heat at others. Along the southern limits of its successful culture there is a general tendency to vigorous vegetative growth with little fruit production and much of the fruit that is borne rots on the tree. In that period when apple varieties were being tested and when the varietal composition of the orchard was not determined by market standards of the large cities, the Ribston Pippin attained a much greater popularity in eastern Maine than in any other section of the country then growing apples. Other English varieties were more favorably received there than in any other state. Downing[70] considered that the Ribston attained far better quality along the Penobscot River than in the middle states. Incidentally he mentioned English gooseberries as succeeding better around Bangor, Maine, than elsewhere. It seems probable that the cool summers of that section favored the best development of these fruits.

The converse limitation is less generally understood but it is none the less potent. Most varieties of apple have certain heat requirements for the attainment of their best quality or indeed for their ripening. Cions of the Baldwin, favored by a succession of mild winters in Aroostook County, bore fruit which failed to ripen because it was arrested in its development by cold weather while still green.[34] Shaw[218] found marked differences in Ben Davis grown in various sections, indicating incomplete development in much of the northern apple-growing section. The Jonathan apple probably attains its highest degree of perfection in the warm summers of central and southern Missouri and northern Arkansas and of some of the valleys and table lands of Idaho and Colorado. It likewise does very well in the southern two or three tiers of counties of Michigan where the mean May to September temperature averages 66°F., but a little farther north in the same state, where the mean temperature for the same period is 62° to 64°F., though coloring and ripening properly, the fruit fails to attain satisfactory size. The limits of successful culture of many varieties are conditioned by the minimum winter temperatures, thus rather obscuring the importance of summer heat but, as with other fruits, there seems to be some reason for considering winter hardiness in some cases to be affected by summer temperatures. So far as climatological data show, the minimum winter and average winter temperatures for Boston, Mass., and Columbia, Mo., are almost identical, but their summer temperatures differ considerably. Winesap is considered tender and unsatisfactory in Massachusetts while in Missouri it is one of the best commercial varieties. Apparently the limitation is set by winter temperature in the Mississippi valley and by summer temperature, directly or indirectly, along the Atlantic seaboard. The northern commercial limit of York Imperial crosses the Mississippi near the southern Iowa border and the Atlantic coast in New Jersey.[218] Here again the correspondence between the northern limits east and west is better in summer temperatures than in those of winter. The same control is evident with Rome Beauty.

Shaw[218] concluded after extended study that a certain optimum summer temperature may be assigned to each variety of apple, ranging from 52°F. for Hibernal and Oldenburg to 67°F. for Terry and Yates. As appears from Table 7 the temperature range of the chief commercial varieties is somewhat more narrow. A considerable effect, however, on the limits of commercial cultivation of apple varieties must be assigned to summer temperature.

TABLE 7.—OPTIMUM AVERAGE SUMMER TEMPERATURES FOR LEADING COMMERCIAL VARIETIES

(*After Shaw*[218])

Baldwin	56°F.	Yellow Newtown	60°F.
Rhode Island	56	York Imperial	62
Northern Spy	56	Grimes	62
Wealthy	56	Stayman	63
Jonathan	59	Winesap	64
Delicious	59	Ben Davis	64

In the United States, Lippincott[131] traced isotherms for combined June, July, August and September temperatures and correlated them with the grapes growing in the zones thus marked out. Here a combined selection is exercised by summer and by winter temperatures and in addition, as pointed out elsewhere the summer temperatures doubtless have some influence on the effect of winter cold. However, there can be no doubt that summer temperatures have a direct effect of their own. In favored localities in the zone with a mean of 65°F. he found Clinton and Delaware, with a few other varieties. In the 67°F. zone he included Concord and Hartford Prolific; Isabella, Diana and Rogers' Hybrids he considered to require 70°F. Catawba, Norton's Virginia, Herbemont and Scuppernong were assigned to regions with average summer temperatures of 72° or higher.

In Michigan, Partridge includes those portions of the southern peninsula with an average mean May to September temperature of 66°F. and a mean growing season of 170 days as well suited to the culture of the Concord grape. Areas with a mean summer temperature of 64°F. and a growing season of 157 days are regarded as of doubtful suitability, and areas with a mean summer temperature of 62°F. and a still shorter growing season are classified as entirely unsuited to its culture.[181]

According to Bijhouwer[23] the northern and southern boundaries of the area within which extensive plantations of the mango are found in the Dutch East

Indies coincide approximately with the January and July isotherms of 15°C., respectively.

Differences within the Variety for Separate Processes.—Different processes in the same plant have different optimum temperatures.

Phytolacca decandra at Carmel, Cal., grows well but flowers only under certain conditions as, for example, when prostrate branches receive sufficient additional heat from the soil to enable them to form viable seeds, while the erect stems do not.[134]   In connection with fruit setting it is shown that lower temperatures than usual convert male blossoms of the papaya into perfect flowers.   Schimper points out the difference in the temperature curve for the two forms of gaseous exchange and states that assimilation occurs at lower temperatures than any other function.   He cites evidence of assimilation in *Abies excelsa* and other plants at −40°C. and cites Böhm as finding the optimum for the walnut at 30°C. No distinct respiration could be observed in *Abies* below −10°C.; this function increases, speaking in general terms, with the temperature until the lethal point is approached.   Quoting Schimper[206] again: "There are, however, certain physiological processes for which not only the optima, but also the upper zeros are so low that, as a rule, they can take place only in winter, late autumn, or early spring.   The category of functions that are active at low temperatures only includes among others the obscure processes which are fermentative in nature, according to Sachs' hypothesis, and which awaken into activity hibernating parts of plants; among such processes may be cited the conversion of starch into fatty acids and the reverse. . . .   Lower temperatures exert a favourable influence on the sexual organs and on the parts œcologically connected with them (perianths, inflorescence axes) in many parts of the temperate and frigid zones. The cardinal degrees for the growth—and perhaps for the inception—of the primordia of flowers are often much lower than for the growth of vegetative shoots, so that the former are favoured by a relatively lower temperature, and the latter by a high temperature, during development.   It is well known that *Crocus, Hyacinthus*, and other perennial herbs do not send out flowers or inflorescences at a high temperature, but shoot out luxuriantly into leaf.   Also in the forcing of fruit trees the temperature must be kept moderate before, and especially during, the blossoming period.   For the same reason many temperate plants seldom blossom in the tropics; for example, most of our fruit trees. . . .   Kurz found in the mountains of Burmah that increased coolness due to increased altitude expedited the blossoming of temperate plants such as *Rhododendron* and *Gentiana*, but delayed that of tropical ones."

As Schimper[208] points out, the forcing of fruit under glass is merely a shortening of the dormant season and the period of maturity is advanced only as much as the inception of growth precedes that in the open.   The temperatures found best for the trees indoors are those they receive at corresponding stages out of doors in favorable regions; higher temperatures are not beneficial.

Price[191] reports investigations showing certain temperatures more favorable to the opening of fruit buds than others. With branches of various fruit trees in incubators maintained at different temperatures he found progressive acceleration in the opening of the buds with the higher temperatures. Some of the data he reports are used in compiling Table 8.

TABLE 8.—INFLUENCE OF TEMPERATURE ON OPENING OF FRUIT BUDS

Fruit	Date of beginning	Days to full bloom		
		70°F.	79°F.	88°F.
Abundance plum..................	Jan. 28, 1908	10	8	7
Hale plum.......................	Dec. 3, 1909	12	6	4
Luster peach.....................	Feb. 2, 1909	13	9	8
Kieffer pear.....................	Mar. 7, 1910	13	9	7
Oldenburg apple..................	Apr. 1, 1909	12	11	7
Rome Beauty apple...............	Apr. 22, 1909	8	6	4

Tufts[236] reports interesting indications that very high temperatures may retard the ripening of fruit. "Here," he states, referring to the Winters section in the Sacramento valley, " . . . the apricot ripens some two or three weeks prior to the ripening of the apricot crop in the Santa Clara Valley, although apricot trees in the Santa Clara Valley bloom ten days earlier than they do in the Winters section. Undoubtedly the nearness of the ocean and the influence of the San Francisco Bay profoundly modify the climate of the Santa Clara Valley. The apricot crop in the Winters section is entirely harvested by July 1.

"When it comes time for the prune harvest, however, we find that the Santa Clara Valley is generally pretty well along—about half way through—before the prunes in the Sacramento Valley are ready. The only explanation we have for this apparent inconsistency is the fact that probably the temperatures for the ripening of the apricot crop are optimum in the Winters section. However, after the first of July the weather gets excessively warm, with the result that the prunes are retarded in their development, and the optimum temperatures for the development of the prune crop probably exist in the Santa Clara Valley during the latter part of the growing season."

Schimper,[207] emphasizing that different functions require different temperatures, states: "the œcological optimum temperature does not remain constant during the whole development of a plant, at least in temperate regions, but . . . shows a rise as development proceeds. . . . We learn too from the art of fruit forcing that we must regard the rise not as constant but as oscillating." He cites Pynaert in giving the temperatures shown in Table 9 as most favorable in forcing the peach. At two periods the temperature is lowered. Ward[241] in England and Schneider[209] in northwest Europe differ somewhat in detail from this temperature statement; Schneider indicates a lowering of temperature at the time of stoning.

TABLE 9.—OPTIMUM TEMPERATURES IN FORCING THE PEACH[207]
(Degrees Centigrade)

	Day temperature	Night temperature
First week	9 to 10	5 to 7
Second week	10 to 12	7 to 9
Third week	12 to 15	9 to 11
To flowering	15 to 18	11 to 14
At flowering	8 to 12	6 to 10
After flowering	15 to 18	11 to 14
During stoning	12 to 15	9 to 11
After stoning	16 to 19	12 to 15
At fruit ripening	20 to 22	15 to 17

Variation in Quality with Amount of Summer Heat.—The fruit which has received the most careful study in its relation to temperature conditions is the grape. Blodgett,[27] writing in 1857, when grape growing in America was in an experimental stage, predicted very closely, from climatological data, the geographic distribution of the industry in the United States.

Boussingault[30] early remarked on the variation in yield and quality of wine of a vineyard in Flanders, the variation depending on the temperature of the growing season, and reported data shown in Table 10. Baragiola,[16] taking successive samples of grapes through two autumns, found a striking correspondence between sugar increase and temperature, regardless of the stage of ripening at which the low or high temperatures occurred. A brief period of warm weather late in the season compensates apparently to a considerable degree for earlier deficiencies: a brief period of cool weather at the same stage apparently goes far to nullify previous favorable conditions. Heat requirements for grapes during the growing season can be understood best from European experience since the

TABLE 10.—RELATION OF SUMMER TEMPERATURES TO YIELD AND CHARACTER OF WINE[30]

Year	Mean temperature			Wine, per acre (gallons)	Percentage of alcohol	Alcohol per acre (gallons)
	Growing season, degrees Centigrade	Summer, degrees Centigrade	Beginning of autumn, degrees Centigrade			
1833	14.7	17.3	11.4	311	5.0	11.4
1834	17.3	20.3	17.0	314	11.2	46.3
1835	15.8	19.5	12.3	621	8.1	50.0
1836	15.8	21.5	12.2	544	7.1	38.6
1837	15.2	18.7	11.9	184	7.7	14.0

climatology of this fruit has been studied most extensively there and is to a considerable degree free from the complication of winter temperature limitations. Boussingault[30] considered that the mean temperature of the growing season must be at least 59°F. and of the summer 65° to 67°F. to produce Vinifera grapes satisfactorily. In some of the equatorial table lands of South America, he states, where the mean temperature is 62° to 66°F. with little range, though the vines flourish the grapes never become thoroughly ripe and good wine cannot be made where the constant temperature is not at least 68°F. Besides a warm summer, a mild autumn free from continued low temperature is necessary. Some regions are assured of sufficient heat in every summer; others must have a summer warmer than the average to produce a satisfactory wine. Along the doubtful zone of grape growing the careful selection of site is emphasized.

A somewhat different, but nonetheless important, influence of growing-season temperature on the keeping quality of pears has been pointed out by Magness. In commenting on his data, some of which are condensed in Table 11, he states:[148]

"From a survey of the fruit as grown under the widely varying climatic conditions of the Pacific Coast, it is apparent that a marked relationship exists between the keeping quality of Bartlett pears following their removal from the tree and the summer temperatures under which the fruit is grown. . . . Bartlett pears grown in the Antelope Valley and other very hot districts in California have a widely known reputation for keeping quality. Often the summer temperatures in this region run to 115°F. The upper Sacramento Valley and foothills of the Sierra Nevada Mountains, also having high temperatures during the growing season, produce pears that can be shipped to any point in the United States. . . . Pears from the lower Sacramento Valley, in the region between Sacramento and the mouth of the river, are also very good shippers, although occasional trouble is encountered. This is especially true of fruit from the lower and cooler portion of this region. In this lower valley region fruit is sometimes found breaking down at the core while still sound at the surface, but this tendency is not common in fruit from this section. . . . In the Yakima and Wenatchee districts of Washington very great difficulty has been experienced in shipping fruit through to eastern markets. In former years the losses from fruit breaking down in transit were very heavy. By prompt and very efficient pre-cooling, however, it has been possible to handle the Yakima Valley fruit during recent years without much loss. The Wenatchee Valley, with a somewhat cooler growing season and less cold-storage capacity for pre-cooling, still suffers considerable loss of Bartlett pears on eastern shipments. The temperature in these districts (the Yakima and Wenatchee Valleys) is not markedly lower than that at Sacramento. It is true, however, that during a normal season the peak of the picking season in the former regions is not reached until the first week in September. It will be noted that September temperatures represent a sharp drop below those of July and August. This may account in part for a greater difficulty with this than the records would seem to warrant."

A similar influence of growing-season temperature on the keeping quality of pears is known to extend to other sections and to many other varieties.

Comparatively high summer temperatures have been noted as accentuating a type of flesh injury in the Yellow Newtown apple in California known as "internal browning."[175]

TABLE 11.—RELATION OF GROWING-SEASON TEMPERATURES TO KEEPING QUALITY OF PEARS

(*After Magness*[148])

District and station	June		July		August		September		Remarks
	Max., degrees Fahrenheit	Min., degrees Fahrenheit	Max., degrees Fahrenheit	Min., degrees Fahrenheit	Max., degrees Fahrenheit	Min., degrees Fahrenheit	Max., degrees Fahrenheit	Min., degrees Fahrenheit	
Antelope valley, Cal.[1]......	....	....	....	....	....	....	....	....	Fruit of very highest keeping and shipping quality
Upper Sacramento valley:									
Chico..............	89.3	55.0	98.9	60.2	97.4	58.3	....	....	Fruit of excellent carrying and keeping quality
Red Bluff.............	87.8	61.6	94.7	66.3	95.1	65.1			
Marysville............	87.9	58.0	95.8	60.8	94.6	59.5			
Sierra Nevada foothills:									
Rocklin..............	86.0	52.7	94.7	58.8	94.2	57.3	....	....	Fruit ripens evenly and is of firm texture
Auburn...............	85.1	55.0	91.7	61.1	91.8	60.3			
Lower Sacramento valley[2]:									
Sacramento............	82.3	56.2	88.8	58.2	88.8	57.7	....	....	Occasionally fruit becomes overripe in transit east, particularly from the lower and cooler portions of this region
Yakima, Wash.:									
Moxie.................	80.9	48.0	88.9	53.1	87.4	51.1	77.3	42.4	Great difficulty in shipping, careful precooling necessary
Wenatchee, Wash.:									
Wenatchee............	74.9	49.0	83.7	55.8	81.0	54.6	71.4	47.6	Tendency to break down at core
Santa Clara valley, Cal.:									
San Jose..............	76.9	48.7	80.9	52.0	79.9	51.3	....	....	Fresh eastern shipments practically abandoned because of breaking down in transit
Santa Clara...........	77.0	46.5	82.5	50.6	81.5	49.6			
Sonoma County, Cal.:									
Santa Rosa............	77.9	45.8	82.0	49.1	82.1	47.1	....	....	About the same as Santa Clara Bartletts
Willamette valley, Ore.:									
Salem.................	72.1	49.7	79.6	53.3	80.1	53.1	....	....	Little attempt made to ship to eastern markets. Canneries take total crops

[1] The temperature record is not available, but the summer range is the highest of any place listed.
[2] The main pear district is somewhat cooler than Sacramento. Records are not available.

Variation in Season of Maturity with Amount of Summer Heat.—

The effect of summer temperatures on the time of ripening and on keeping qualities of apples is well known. The Wealthy, a fall or early winter apple in Minnesota, becomes a summer apple in Missouri. The Baldwin loses quality and becomes progressively a poorer keeper toward the south except at higher and cooler altitudes. Sometimes the transition is rather abrupt. The Dudley, a winter apple in Aroostook County, Maine, is a fall apple at Bangor and a summer apple farther south.[34] Apples grown in southern latitudes develop color over a larger part of the surface, but the colors are more intense in the north.

SOIL TEMPERATURES

That the temperature of the soil is not without influence on plant growth is evident from the florist's resort to bottom heat for certain plants and the rather definite heat requirements for the rooting of cuttings. It has been shown that *Opuntia versicolor* can be stimulated to considerable vegetative growth despite unfavorably cool atmosphere by the maintenance in the soil of favorable temperatures for root growth.[40] Lindley[128] stated that a certain variety of *Nelumbium* though in full vegetative vigor was without flowers when the soil temperature was 85°F., but blossomed at 70° to 75°F., while another variety ceased blossoming at this same temperature.

Obvious difficulties are encountered in attempting a determination of suitable temperatures for root growth in trees. Lindley[129] arranged a statement of favorable soil temperatures for various fruits, based on observations in sections where these fruits flourish; the growing-season temperatures thus indicated range from 54°F. for the gooseberry, 59°F. for the apple, and 65°F. for the peach to 85°F. for the mango. Goff[92a] found that root growth begins very early in most fruit plants in Wisconsin, starting in most cases in advance of the buds. When currant buds were but little swollen some of the new roots were 3 inches long. Goff stated, however, that warmer temperatures did not accelerate root growth as much as might be expected from the early start. Comparison of the growth of young apple trees under various systems of culture, with accompanying differences in soil temperature, has shown that the two systems inducing the greatest extremes in temperature resulted in practically the same growth.[173] The extremes, however, were not widely separated and well within the range where normal root activity might be expected. In some soils and in some sections soil temperatures rise to a point where normal growth processes are interfered with. Under such conditions some kind of ground cover will furnish considerable protection. Thus Morris has found that in the centers of the squares between the trees at Yakima, Wash., when temperatures of 107° and 95°F. were recorded at depths of 2 and 6 inches, respectively, in clean cultivated blocks, the corresponding temperatures under an alfalfa sod were 66° and 64°F.[167]

It would seem that in some cases when a choice of stocks is possible the adaptability of the several stocks to soil temperatures should be considered, along with other factors. It appears rather illogical, for example, to plant prune trees on peach roots in a soil so cold that it would not be considered suitable for peaches. An instance of at least partial adaptability to soil temperatures has been reported in Baluchistan, where plums, peaches, etc., on Black Damask and Mazzard roots repeatedly failed to thrive, though the same combinations are satisfactory in Great Britain.[119] Using other stocks such as Mariana, Myrobolan and Mahaleb, that apparently are better adapted to hot, dry soils, much better results were secured.

INDIRECT TEMPERATURE EFFECTS

Finally, another limiting effect of growing-season temperatures should be considered, namely, that on fungous diseases. Apple scab, for example, has a generally northern range, suggesting adaptability to cool summers, while blotch is confined to sections with rather warm summers. Pear blight is distinctly a warm weather disease; brown rot is favored by high temperatures in conjunction with humidity. All these diseases take toll of the fruit grown where they are present; brown rot, in conjunction with curculio, makes plum growing a hazardous occupation in the southeast United States and blight practically prohibits the commercial production of the European pear in the southeast and in the Mississippi valley.

Codling-moth prevalence is more or less directly proportional to growing-season temperatures, especially night temperatures, and the length of the growing season, and control is correspondingly more difficult in the hotter sections. Some spray materials, *e.g.*, many of those containing copper, are much more likely to cause russeting of the fruit and other forms of injury at low than at high temperatures, whereas the reverse is true of certain other classes of spray material, *e.g.*, many of those containing sulphur.[210] These responses of trees to their environment and to the fungicides or insecticides with which they are treated must be given due consideration by the fruit grower.

Summary.—Functional activity and growth of any kind in a plant have definite temperature requirements. Within the limits between which the growth processes can proceed development is slowest near each extreme—that is, close to the lower and close to the upper limit. Growth is most rapid at an optimum temperature somewhere between the two extremes, but usually nearer the upper than the lower limit. Furthermore the optimum for certain growth processes is quite different from that for others within the same plant and the extremes likewise may be different for different activities. Consequently it becomes extremely difficult, if not impossible, to assign definite values to different temperatures in their total growth effects, and the "heat units" necessary for completing certain changes, or carrying the plant through certain aspects of its seasonal life history, vary considerably with conditions. In general fewer heat units are required by a given plant in northern than in southern latitudes. Other conditions being equally favorable, there is the best varietal adaptation in sections where growing-season temperatures most nearly approach the optimum for the variety in question. The importance of summer growing temperatures in determining the commercial limits of fruit varieties is underestimated. Summer temperature likewise exerts an important influence in determining the season of maturity of the fruit and in some instances its size, coloration, quality and keeping quality. Soil temperature is of possible importance in influencing growth and in determining the geographical range of certain varieties. Injurious effects of soil temperatures can be minimized sometimes by the use of stocks of the right kinds. Summer temperatures also have an important indirect effect on orchard plants through their influence on the range or activity of certain parasites.

CHAPTER XV

WINTER KILLING AND HARDINESS

The limits to fruit growing set by low winter temperatures have been indicated. This limitation has been shown to be influenced more or less by other factors, precipitation in some cases, summer temperatures in others. Low winter temperatures are important, however, in other respects than merely marking boundaries separating a section where a given fruit is grown from another section where it is not. Damage by freezing is not confined to any one region; it is as definitely an injurious factor in California and Florida for tender species as it is in Montana or Wisconsin for the more hardy fruits. It is not confined to the borderlands of a fruit zone but in one way or another makes itself felt well within the regions adapted to fruit growing. It is not a simple matter of uniform, predictable reaction to a given temperature but is modified, intensified or palliated by varying factors and is itself probably a group of fatal or damaging reactions assembled for convenience or for want of discriminating classification under the single name of winter killing.

DEATH FROM FREEZING

Several explanations of the actual process of killing of tissue by low temperatures have been made; it seems possible that there may be more than one way by which the killing is brought about. Parenthetically, it should be stated that the original theory and the one still most frequently advanced by practical men, *i.e.*, that death by cold is due to expansion accompanying freezing and a consequent rupture of the cell walls, is not tenable as can be proved mathematically or by microscopic examination. The bursting of trunks and limbs, cited to justify this contention, is considered later. The view held most generally by investigators ascribes death to withdrawal of water from the cell, a process comparable to death by plasmolysis.

Tissue Freezing Is Accompanied by Cell Dehydration.—Numerous investigators have shown that ice is very rarely formed within the cell unless the cooling is very rapid, more rapid, in fact, than would occur in nature. Before freezing begins, since the cell sap contains substances in solution and because of capillary supercooling, most tissues must be at a temperature several degrees below the freezing point. The first evident step in the process of freezing is a contraction of the protoplasm and the

284

appearance of water in the intercellular spaces where it has been forced or drawn from the cell. Ice formation begins at various points in the intercellular spaces, frequently making lens-shaped masses of hexagonal crystals, larger at the side which draws on the greater number of cells. As the growing ice needles deplete the water of the intercellular spaces, more is drawn from the cell contents.[256] The continuance of this process, however, makes the sap remaining within the cells more concentrated and thus increases "the force with which the remaining quantities of water are held."[256] A still stronger force, operating as a reserve, is that known as molecular capillarity, holding with extreme tenacity a certain amount of water of imbibition. Hence, it is with increasing difficulty that ice formation continues and it must cease sooner or later unless the temperature be lowered further. Moreover, the very process of solidi-fication liberates a certain amount of heat. Therefore it is not surprising that, as the temperature falls, the ice formation for each degree becomes progressively less. Müller-Thurgau found, at −4.5°C., 63.8 per cent. of the water of an apple frozen, while at −15.2°C. only 79.2 per cent. had frozen.[256] Wiegand[255] found very little ice in dormant twigs of many species of forest trees at 20°F. At 0°F. ice was plainly visible in buds of 19 species out of the 27 examined; 6 of the remaining 8 showed ice, but in small scattered crystals, at −15°F. These buds "all contained little cell-sap and small cells with rather thick walls."

As the ice crystals increase, the cell walls collapse and become packed together in dense masses. Buds and bark of hardy trees show this condi-tion, as do evergreen leaves, but at suitable temperatures they expand, draw back the water and become normal.

Wiegand[255] reports: "The ice was found to occur always in broad prismatic crystals arranged perpendicular to the excreting surface; and usually formed a single continuous layer throughout the mesophyll of the scale or leaf, to accom-modate which the cells were often separated to a considerable distance. This ice sheet was composed of either one or two layers of the prismatic crystals, depending on the water content of the adjacent surfaces, and was often as thick as the whole normal scale. The cells surrounding the ice, having lost their water content, were in a more or less complete state of collapse, depending upon the resistance of the walls, and often occupied a space smaller than the ice itself. These cells were uninjured, however, and would resume their normal condition on thawing. . . . In young anthers the ice often filled the entire anther cavity and in it the pollen grains were imbedded in a completely collapsed state." At temperatures between −23.5°C. and −18°C. in the apple and pear the tissue was "packed full of ice in shoot and in the mesophyll of the scales." In general, the species in which ice formed most readily had larger cells, a higher water content and a greater proportion of water to cell wall and protoplasm.

"In the twigs," Wiegand states, "ice is also present in very cold weather, where it may be found in three different localities. The largest quantity occurs in the cortex, where the ice crystallizes in prisms arranged in single or double series according to the law of freezing tissues. The ice is more frequently in the form of a continuous ring, or really a cylinder, extending entirely around the twig, prying apart the cells of the cortex in which it lies. The outer cylinder of cortex in such twigs is completely separated from the inner layers when frozen. In a few species instead of the continuous layer, lens-shaped ice masses are interpolated irregularly throughout the cortex. The cortical cells after the withdrawal of water are as completely collapsed as were those in the bud scales, but they also usually regain their normal condition on thawing. In the wood ice rarely forms in large quantities. It is usually confined to small masses in the vessels themselves, or, according to some authors, sometimes extends in radial plates in the pith rays. In sectioning twigs I, myself, have never seen ice in the wood elsewhere than in the vessels or wood cells. In the pith the ice, so far as I have been able to observe, always occurs within the cells and therefore in very small masses." As Wiegand points out, Müller-Thurgau found ice in the large vessels and frequently in the wood cells of pear and most distinctly in the grape.

Frozen twigs of several species were found to expand on thawing, two apple twigs, for example, increasing in diameter from 2.97 millimeters and 3.89 millimeters to 3.03 millimeters and 3.95 millimeters respectively. In the willow, the only species on which this determination was made, more than half the total expansion was in the bark, the percentages being, respectively, 13.5 for the bark and 2.5 for the wood. To explain the contraction of twigs on freezing Wiegand suggests: "When the water is extracted from the walls of the wood-cells, the latter contract to a slight extent just as they do when wood seasons. This accounts for a part of the shrinkage. The rest and greater part occurs in the cortex. Here the intercellular spaces are quite large and numerous and are normally filled with air. When freezing occurs the ice forms in the spaces and the cells collapse while the air is mostly driven completely out of the twig. The contraction in the cortex will be approximately equal to the volume of the air expelled plus that of the air compressed minus the expansion of the ice while freezing." Curiously enough in all cases studied, except in *Populus* and *Acer* and including apple, pear and plums, Wiegand found that buds increased decidedly in size upon freezing. Prillieux[192] demonstrated conclusively a loss of air and of weight in frozen plant tissues.

Freezing, Not Cold, Kills.—Most investigators do not accept the view that, aside from some cases occurring above the freezing point to be discussed later, absolute cold kills any plant, whether by "shock," "cold rigor" or other effects. Again quoting Wiegand: "Most plants are killed by the first ice formation within the tissue. If they survive this, a considerably lower temperature is required to kill them, or they may be capable of enduring any degree of cold. It has been demonstrated . . . that, in the case of delicate tissues at least, death occurs when the ice formation has progressed to a certain extent. . . . Death seems due to the actual withdrawal of water to form ice, not to the cold. The ice formation dries out the cells and the plant suffers therefore from drought conditions. Every cell has its critical point, the withdrawal of water beyond which will cause the death of the cell, whether by ordinary evaporation or by other means. It may be supposed that the delicate structure of the protoplasm necessary to constitute living matter can no longer sustain itself when too many molecules of water are removed from its support. In the great majority of plants this point lies so high in the water content that it is passed very soon after the inception of ice formation, hence the death of many plants at this period. Others may be able to exist with so little water that a very low temperature is necessary before a sufficient quantity is abstracted to cause death. From some plants enough water cannot be abstracted by cold to kill them." Several investigators have shown that certain tissues, cooled to a temperature which is fatal if ice formation occurs, will withstand that same temperature if ice formation does not occur.

After investigating several possible ways in which bud scales and wool packing might serve to protect the embryo flowers and shoots during the winter, Wiegand concluded that their main function is not to shut out cold or even to retard temperature changes (about 10 minutes seemed the limit for the greater part of any change), but rather to retard the loss of moisture and to prevent mechanical injury especially when the buds are frozen. Lilac buds lost in 3 days, at temperatures between −18°C. and −7°C., 2.8 per cent. of water when bud scales were left on; with bud scales removed the loss of water was 39 per cent. Heat absorption due to the color of bud scales in horse-chestnut buds amounted to 15°F. Chandler[48] also found that "scales of peach buds do not serve to protect them from low temperature. Buds frozen in the laboratory with the scales removed were slightly more resistant to low temperature than were buds with the scales not removed."

Freezing and the Deciduous Habit.—The view that death from low temperatures is due to a withdrawal of water is supported by the consideration that the deciduous habit is in most cases essentially a protection against water loss during the winter and that the leaves of evergreen plants are particularly adapted to reduce the rate of transpiration to a minimum.

An interesting and suggestive parallelism exists between the autumnal behavior of trees in temperate regions and the changes in trees in regions subjected to prolonged dry but warm weather. In both cases they assume a distinctly xerophytic character. The most obvious phenomenon accompanying this transition is leaf-fall. Of this Coulter, Barnes and Cowles[56] say: "The leaf behavior of deciduous trees and of tropical evergreens obviously is related to external factors, in the former being associated with climatic periodicity (either of moisture, as in the monsoon forests of India, or of temperature, as in the northern deciduous forests), while in the latter it is associated with uniform moisture and temperature. That the deciduous and the evergreen habits are related to external conditions may be inferred from many trees and shrubs (*e.g.*, poison ivy, Virginia creeper, various oaks) which shed their leaves in regions of cold winters, but retain them in warmer climates; furthermore, various plants (as the grape and the peach) become evergreen in uniform tropical climates, and even those species that remain deciduous (as the persimmon and the mulberry) have much longer periods of leafage.

"The exact factors involved in leaf-fall, that is, in the development of the absciss layer, are imperfectly known. In the monsoon forest and in other regions of periodic drought, it is probable that leaf-fall results directly from the desiccation incident to the increased transpiration and decreased absorption during the dry period. Autumnal leaf-fall in cool climates probably is due to desiccation resulting from continued transpiration at a time when absorption is diminished by reason of low temperature, although desiccation due to dryness in the soil or air may cause the absciss layer to develop in early summer. A severe frost in early autumn may retard leaf-fall through injury to the tissues that develop the absciss layer.

. . . . . .

"The shedding of leaves at the inception of a cool or dry period is of inestimable advantage, especially in trees with delicate leaves, because of the enormously reduced transpiration thus resulting. The leafless tree is one of the most perfectly protected of plant structures, since impervious bud scales and bark cover all exposed portions."

Accompanying leaf-fall the moisture contents of the various tissues change. From summer to early winter there is a considerable lowering of the moisture percentage as shown in Table 12, adapted from data by Baake *et al.*,[8] showing the moisture percentage in twigs of several varieties of apple.

TABLE 12.—PERCENTAGE MOISTURE CONTENT OF APPLE TWIGS

	Dormant	Bud swelling	Blossoming	Summer growth period	Wood ripening
Hibernal...................	42.43	48.65	.....	58.98	.....
Oldenburg.................	45.64	53.31	65.53	60.50	53.67
Wealthy...................	45.04	51.66	62.15	61.11	52.98
Yellow Transparent..........	46.32	52.10	65.57	61.49	55.04
McIntosh..................	46.82	50.52	61.87	57.76	51.88
Red Astrachan.............	47.30	54.86	65.79	60.82	55.31
Jonathan..................	43.52	52.00	62.62	58.77	51.63
Winesap...................	47.58	50.57	64.48	58.67	51.53
Grimes....................	48.23	49.54	65.22	58.95	54.16
Ben Davis.................	47.76	51.94	63.20	59.44	51.09
Average, 17 varieties.......	45.765	52.56	64.19	58.92	52.55

Killing above the Freezing Point.—As already mentioned, a number of plants and plant tissues may be killed by cold above the freezing point. Included here are such staple crops as rice, cotton and peanuts, and such tree fruits as the coffee and mangosteen. Very short exposures to near-freezing temperatures do not prove fatal, but longer exposures do. It has been suggested that in these plants at these low temperatures oxygen absorption proceeds much faster than the elimination of carbon dioxide and that there are other disturbances to a sensitive balance between various vital processes that lead to the accumulation of toxic products within the cells.[165,216]

INCREASING HARDINESS

By Increasing Sap Density.—A logical consequence of the theory of death through withdrawal of water by freezing is the correlation of an increased sap density (molar concentration) with a lower killing temperature for any given species. This has been demonstrated by Gail[87] as characterizing a number of non-deciduous species and is considered by him as a factor of some importance in accounting for their increase in hardiness as winter approaches. Chandler's investigations have likewise demonstrated this for a number of deciduous tree fruits. Sap density was increased by various means, such as withholding water, watering with mineral solutions, inducing absorption of various substances and it was reduced by shading; in each case with greater density there was greater hardiness. Unfortunately, attempts to increase sap density and therefore hardiness, in peach trees, cabbage and tobacco plants, by heavy applications of potash fertilizers were not successful in attaining either object.[48] European writers have claimed increased hardiness from phosphate or potash applications; their evidence, however, is not entirely convincing.

Wilted tissue, presenting another case of increased sap density through withdrawal of water, was tested for hardiness by Chandler with no significant results. This seems entirely consistent since the sap density in this case is the result, not of the addition of substances in solution, but rather of the withdrawal of water and may be closely comparable to the initial stage of freezing itself. When a longer and slower wilting appeared to be induced on dormant peach twigs, possibly resulting in a somewhat more fundamental change in the protoplasm, hardiness seemed increased.

By Increasing Water-retaining Capacity.—Another consequence of the theory that death is due to the withdrawal of water from the cell and later from the tissue, is that resistance to cold must be increased by factors tending to increase the water-retaining capacity of the cells.

Observations on the moisture content of apple twigs reported by Beach and Allen,[19] shown in Table 14, reveal an important relation to hardiness. From July to December there is considerable variation in the moisture content of the several varieties. On Jan. 15, however, following several days of severe cold, the two hardiest varieties, Hibernal and

Wealthy, have a noticeably higher moisture content than the tenderer varieties; furthermore, the loss of water from July to January is very much less in these two hardiest varieties than in the others.

Data of similar purport, drawn on for Table 13, are reported by Strausbaugh[229] in Minnesota. Water losses accompanying markedly cold weather were greater in the less hardy plums. Following a period of relatively warm weather the less hardy varieties showed a marked increase in moisture content, possibly because they were less dormant, possibly because they had lost more.

These observations indicate that the actual moisture content of a tissue at most times has less connection with hardiness than its water-retaining capacity. The water lost is less significant than the water retained. Protection against injury from low temperatures depends on the amount of water the plant can retain at a critical moment against the great force which tends to draw water out of the cells to form ice crystals in the intercellular spaces. This force can be appreciated by the familiar ability of growing ice crystals to split rocks. To hold water against this influence, the protoplasm must have a certain amount of its moisture supply in a form which is not easily frozen. In the section on Water Relations plant tissue is shown to contain, in addition to its free and readily frozen water, water in an adsorbed or colloidal state, which does

TABLE 13.—CHANGES IN WATER CONTENT OF FRUIT BUDS OF SEVERAL VARIETIES
OF PLUMS
(*Arranged from Strausbaugh*[229])

	Stella (semihardy)	Tonka (semihardy)	Assiniboine (hardy)
Nov. 19..........................	50.38	50.51	46.51
Dec. 1............................	43.51	43.93	45.49
Loss............................	6.87	6.58	1.02
Dec. 26..........................	49.30	50.70	46.80
Increase........................	5.79	6.77	0.86
Jan. 16..........................	45.98	44.41	47.36
Jan. 23..........................	44.34	39.16	47.31
Loss............................	1.64	5.25	0.05
Feb. 21..........................	41.98	43.24	46.83
Mar. 5..........................	39.78	40.46	46.16
Loss............................	2.20	2.78	0 67
Loss Nov. 19 to Mar. 5...........	10.60	10.05	0.35

TABLE 14.—MOISTURE CONTENT OF APPLE TWIGS ON DIFFERENT DATES[19]

Variety	July 15	Nov. 15	Dec. 26 to 28	Jan. 15	Decrease July 15 to Jan. 15
Delicious............	60.3	50.5	50.5	42.5	17.8
Gano................	57.2	53.2	51.2	44.3	12.9
Grimes..............	60.7	52.0	57.7	43.6	17.1
Hibernal............	53.5	50.4	52.0	46.8	6.7
Wealthy.............	60.4	50.6	51.0	47.5	9.0

not freeze except at temperatures ranging to $-78°C$. If a plant tissue contains enough adsorbed water, it presumably can withstand any winter temperature. Its free water freezes, but there is enough water which is not readily frozen to maintain the life of the protoplasm.

It seems paradoxical that tender plant tissues usually contain more water than those which are hardier. In fact Johnston found the ratio of water content to dry weight of fruit buds a fairly good index of the relative hardiness of certain peach varieties and similar observations have been made by many other investigators. However, it is shown presently that the development of the water-retaining capacity follows as a reaction to a diminished water supply. Hence, there is a direct relation between the lower total water content of hardy tissues and their greater content of adsorbed water which is not readily frozen. Furthermore, the water-holding capacity operates less effectively in dilute solutions.[201]

Water in the adsorbed or colloidal condition cannot hold materials in solution but may cause higher results in sap density determinations. Since in hardy plants there is a smaller amount of free water which can hold materials in solution, the sap solutes must be held ordinarily in a more concentrated solution than in tender plants. Hence the correlation between sap density and hardiness found by Chandler and confirmed by other investigators; however, since there is no direct causative relation between hardiness and sap density, it sometimes happens that the correlation does not hold. Pantanelli,[180] for example, was unable to find a relation between resistance to cold and molecular concentration (sap density) with wheat or beets, though the correlation held for sunflower, tomato and corn.

Clear distinction is necessary between cell water loss and tissue water loss. Cell water loss is the cause of death by freezing. Tissue water loss must, in many cases, accentuate cell water loss and thus indirectly lead to killing. Though the two forms are distinct, in most cases each promotes the other. It is probable that some plants are retentive of cell water and not of tissue water, hence hardy but not drought resistant; others are presumably retentive of tissue water but not of cell water, hence drought resistant but not hardy. However, there is a strong tendency toward parallelism in drought resistance and cold resistance. The data here presented are based on this parallelism.

Xerophytic adaptations are well known to students of morphology; they serve primarily as protection against tissue loss, but may have an ultimate bearing on cell loss and therefore on hardiness. Strausbaugh[229] shows that the lenticel area on the twigs of a semihardy plum is from three to six times that of a hardy variety. He shows also a greater loss of water from the twigs of a tender than from those of a hardy variety. Thus, occasionally, morphological differences may influence, though indirectly, cell water loss. Rather extensive investigations, however, have failed to establish consistent morphological differences between hardy and tender varieties. Cell water loss, then, must depend on something other than structure.

Water-retaining Capacity Associated with Colloid Content.—Plant tissue which withstands freezing must be supposed to contain or be

TABLE 15.—PENTOSAN CONTENT OF PLANT TISSUES IN TERMS OF FRESH WEIGHT[116]
(1920 *Wood*)

	Nov. 8, 1920		Dec. 2, 1920	
	Bases, per cent.	Tips, per cent.	Bases, per cent.	Tips, per cent.
Wealthy..........................	6.52	5.41	5.99	5.11
Yellow Transparent..............	5.15	3.55	5.89	5.06
Missouri Pippin..................	3.29	4.37	5.01	4.91
Stayman Winesap.................	4.72	3.28	5.26	3.96
Ben Davis (short shoots—mature)...	5.64	5.19	5.59	4.56
Ben Davis (long shoots—immature).	3.90	3.22	4.04	3.79
Currant..........................	4.78	4.44	5.01	3.68
Cuthbert raspberry (mature)........	5.20	3.09	4.28	3.24
Cuthbert raspberry (immature).....	1.61	1.28	killed	killed

able to manufacture substances which will hold water in an adsorbed or colloidal condition. These substances must themselves be colloids, they must have a great water-holding and water-absorbing capacity, they must be known to occur in practically all plants capable of withstanding winter conditions and they must be distributed generally through practically all plant tissues. The compounds which answer best to these specifications are the pentosans, more particularly the water-soluble pentosans. Evidence is presented in the section on Water Relations to show that pentosans of some sort are probably the compounds holding water in an adsorbed or colloidal condition in plant tissues; this is confirmed by determinations of Hooker,[116] given in Table 15, which show a correlation between pentosan content and hardiness.

This evidence supports the idea that pentosans largely determine the water-retaining capacity of plant cells, though the particular compounds concerned remain to be determined.

Water Soluble Pentosans in Particular.—Water soluble pentosans, such as gums or pectins, seem the most likely to act as water-retaining substances. Studies by Rosa indicate that this is the case. Some of his

TABLE 16.—SOLUBLE AND INSOLUBLE PENTOSANS IN CABBAGE AND TOMATO
(*After Rosa*[201])

	Total pentosan	Hot-water-soluble pectin	Insoluble (by difference)
Cabbage:			
Tender......................	0.215	0.075	0.140
Hardy (dry grown).............	0.423	0.292	0.131
Hardy (by exposure)...........	0.530	0.408	0.124
Tomato:			
Tender......................	0.693	0.070	0.623
Dry grown...................	0.720	0.071	0.649
Exposed.....................	0.682	0.071	0.611

data, reported in Table 16, show the tomato to have a higher total pentosan content than the hardier cabbage, but the soluble pentosans are quite differently arranged. The increase of total pentosans in cabbage of differing degrees of hardiness is due entirely to the increase in soluble pentosans; with the tomato, in which no treatment materially increases hardiness, there is no increase in soluble pentosans.

On the other hand, a study of seasonal variations in the hardiness and the pentosan content of certain evergreens has failed to establish any relation between the two,[71] indicating either that variations in sap density, such as were demonstrated by Gail,[87] are a controlling factor in these species or that colloidal substances other than pentosans assume a dominant role in this connection. Investigation is likely to show that a number of other substances exercise important water-retaining properties and, therefore, tend toward hardiness. Fat emulsions conceivably may act in this way.

Whatever the compounds may prove to be, their water-adsorbing power undoubtedly is affected to a marked degree by the factors which generally increase or decrease the water-retaining properties of colloids. The effects of nitrogenous compounds and hydrogen-ion concentration on hardiness have been emphasized by Harvey and may be of a similar nature.

Pentosan Content, Water-retaining Capacity and Hardiness Responsive to Environmental Conditions.—The water-retaining capacity of plant tissues is increased by any condition which limits the water supply without producing actual injury. This is discussed in the section on Water Relations. Rosa presents data, given in Table 17, showing an increase in the pentosan content of plants hardened by exposure to low temperatures in a cold frame. This indicates also that the hardening or maturing of plant tissue by exposure to cold is essentially a reaction to a limited water supply.

TABLE 17.—PENTOSANS OF VEGETABLE PLANTS IN PERCENTAGES OF FRESH WEIGHT
(*After Rosa*[200])

	Cabbage	Leaf lettuce	Cauliflower
Moisture series on greenhouse plants			
1. Tender plants grown in wet soil..........	0.215	0.106	.....
2. Medium hardy plants grown with moderate moisture supply...................	0.320	.....	.....
3. Hardy plants grown in dry soil..........	0.423	0.402	.....
4. Hardy plants, partly wilted for 2 weeks....	0.412	.....	.....
Coldframe series			
1. Tender greenhouse plants..............	0.207	0.126	0.191
2. Hardened 1 week......................	0.413	.....	.....
3. Hardened 2 weeks.....................	0.530	0.230	0.403
4. Hardened 3 weeks.....................	0.604	.....	.....

Rosa shows also that there is a fairly constant increase in the pentosan content of vegetables from early fall until the plants are killed by cold. The data in Table 18 indicate that maturity is associated with increased pentosan content and greater water-retaining capacity.

TABLE 18.—PENTOSAN CONTENT OF GARDEN PLANTS IN PERCENTAGES OF FRESH WEIGHT[201]

Date	Kale	Cabbage	Celery
Oct. 7.........................	0.511	0.289	0.567
Oct. 20.........................	0.528	0.580	0.801
Nov. 3.........................	0.537	0.545	0.793
Nov. 10.........................	0.722	0.621	1.029
Nov. 18.........................	1.064	0.782	.....

Increased Hardiness with Increased Maturity.—The most generally recognized and most potent single factor influencing killing by cold, particularly in tissues withstanding a fair amount of freezing, is the degree of maturity attained at the time of exposure. So widely is this state recognized in field conditions, that experimental evidence on this point, though available, is hardly necessary. Some less known, but widely occurring, phases of immaturity in trees are considered later. The greater susceptibility of immature tissue to injury from cold is due, in part, to the fact that pentosans or other water-retaining substances have not developed; the greater water content of such tissue is evidence of the lack of those drying conditions necessary for the proper development of pentosans and hence of maturity. Chandler found no constant difference in the moisture content of the twig cortex during the winter, though its hardiness varied considerably. With reference to density he states: "It would seem certain then that while a part of the increased hardiness of tree tissue in winter may possibly be accounted for by the greater sap density, not all of it can; certainly not the greater hardiness of December tissue over that of October." The same investigator offers the following suggestion based on experimental evidence; "It would seem highly probable that, except in the case of cambium, the additional hardiness acquired by the different tissues of the trees as they pass into winter, is a change in the protoplasm such that it can withstand the great loss of water rather than a change in the percentage of moisture or in sap density."

RAPID TEMPERATURE CHANGES

Since maturity is a reaction to dry conditions whether produced by exposure to cold or by actual limitation of the water supply, it is logical to expect distinct differences in the amount of injury produced by rapid freezing when no time is allowed for the development of pentosans and by a gradual reduction of temperature permitting an increase in the water-retaining capacity of the tissue to develop.

Killing with Slow and with Rapid Freezing.—The injurious effects of rapid freezing seem to have received little attention until the recent work of Winkler and of Chandler.

Winkler,[259] working with dormant twigs that killed at −22°C. upon rapid freezing, found that by small successive reductions of temperature, at −16°C. for 3 days, at −18°C. for 2 days, at −20°C. for 3 days, at −22°C. for 2 days, at −25°C. for 3 days, the twigs were enabled to withstand 12 hours of freezing at from −30°C. to −32°C. Chandler[48] reports on the results of his work, in part, as follows: "The rate of temperature fall is very important indeed, especially in case of winter buds. In fact apple buds can be frozen in a chamber surrounded by salt and ice rapidly enough that practically all of them will be killed at a temperature of zero F., or slightly below, while it is well known that they may go through a temperature of 20°F. to 30°F. below zero with but slight injury where the temperature fall is not so rapid . . . the killing temperature of rapidly frozen twigs was four and a half degrees higher than that of the more slowly frozen twigs, and even then the buds of the rapidly frozen twigs killed the worst, . . . rapid falling in the early part of the freezing temperature down to −12°C., does more harm than rapid fall in the latter part of the period, from −12°C. to the killing temperature." "Many young fruits and succulent plants were also frozen slowly and rapidly but there was so little apparent difference between the results that the data are not given. The killing temperature lies so near the freezing point that possibly the slowly frozen tissue kills badly because it is exposed to temperatures around the killing point longer." " . . . the rate of temperature fall with winter twigs and buds exerts the greatest influence on the extent of killing at a given temperature of any feature we have so far discussed. And in the case of very forward, rather tender, fruit buds, the rate of temperature fall exerts great influence. Thus on March 24, 1913, when all buds especially the peaches, plums and cherries, had made much growth, a temperature of −11.5°C. killed as many buds with rapid temperature fall as a temperature of −16.5°C. with a slower temperature fall."

A factor involved in very rapid lowering of the temperature is the possibility of ice formation within the cells. Though the rate of temperature fall involved probably does not occur in nature, it may have been produced in some of the experiments just described.

Slow and Rapid Thawing.—Practical men have long held that rapid thawing intensifies damage from low temperatures and many investigators have accepted this view. The fruit grower who heats his orchard during the cold nights of the growing season tries just as carefully to keep the early morning sun from the blossoms; the young florist is taught by older men to supply heat very slowly if accident has lowered the temperature of the greenhouse to a critical point.

Wiegand[256] found that thawing generally occurs at temperatures below 0°C., or about at the freezing point (−3.5°C. to −2.3°C. for buds). Sudden thawing or several rapid alternations of freezing and thawing did not seem injurious.

It has been held that rapid thawing induces excessive transpiration and prevents the return into the cell of the sap withdrawn in freezing. The trend of opinion among recent investigators, however, fails to support this view, it having been found to hold only in a very few cases. As already indicated, it can be shown definitely, sometimes at least, that death occurs before any thawing begins; furthermore, the method used by Sachs and much in vogue among gardeners to induce slow thawing, namely, immersion or sprinkling with water, is in reality a method leading to more rapid thawing than would occur in air. The water causes a coating of ice on the exterior, thus liberating heat to the tissue. Though objections might be adduced to this view, the chief matter of interest here is that investigators have found, in practically all cases, no difference in killing to ensue whether the thawing be rapid or retarded. It should be pointed out, however, that there are no reports of inquiry into the effect of sunlight on frozen tissue. Injuries due to the effect of light on frozen tissue might easily be attributed to rapid thawing. There seems to be enough evidence in field conditions of association of sunlight and injury to warrant careful study, particularly in view of the increased permeability known to accompany increased light.

VARIATION IN CRITICAL TEMPERATURES

Definite evidence, under experimental conditions, has shown that the critical temperature at which killing results is not a definite point for any species, variety or individual plant but is the result of a complex of conditions. It probably depends to a great degree on water-retaining capacity or the amount of water present that is not readily frozen, but other factors may be equally important under certain circumstances and unquestionably there are a number of factors affecting the water-retaining capacity of the cell colloids. All of these may constantly be fluctuating more or less independently of one another and their product, the killing temperature, must therefore assume many different values. This is abundantly borne out in field observations of winter killing.

Summary.—The most tenable of the theories explaining killing from cold ascribes death to dehydration of the cells. Ice formation generally begins in the intercellular spaces and the process draws water from the cells. The water is withdrawn gradually, each decrease in temperature being followed by further water loss from the cells, though the rate of this loss becomes progressively lower. Death occurs when the dehydration proceeds beyond a certain point. The increasing density of the cell sap with continued water loss tends to hold the remaining water more tenaciously and thus protects the cell somewhat against further loss and eventual death. The cell colloids, particularly the water soluble pentosans, operate in the same direction and play a still more important part. These substances (the water soluble pentosans) develop in some plants in response to certain environmental conditions—particularly decreasing temperature and a decreased moisture supply. These facts suggest that certain cultural treatments may be employed to increase the hardiness of plant tissue. Rapid freezing is probably more dangerous than slow freezing to plant tissue because there is not time for the plant to develop a greater water-retaining capacity; consequently it loses a larger percentage of its moisture at a given temperature. Contrary to general belief there is little evidence that rapid thawing is more injurious than slow thawing. However, this should not be taken to mean necessarily that rapid thawing in bright sunshine is not more injurious than slow thawing under cloudy conditions, since the increased permeability accompanying increased light may have an influence. Critical temperatures for a given species will vary considerably with conditions.

CHAPTER XVI

WINTER INJURY

Macoun[146] enumerates ten manifestations of winter injury in orchard fruits, *viz.:* root-killing, bark-splitting, trunk-splitting, sunscald, crotch injury, killing back of branches, black heart, trunk injury, killing of dormant buds and winter-killing of swollen buds. As one form of bark-splitting, Macoun includes a condition considered here as crown rot. These forms may occur singly or in varying combinations; some are products of severe conditions that almost of necessity entail other forms characteristic of less severe freezing; some may be responses of varying plant conditions to the same weather and some may be responses of identical plant conditions to varying weather. Still other manifestations are recorded occasionally.

Conditions Accompanying Winter Injury.—Nine of the ten forms of winter injury distinguished by Macoun[146] appear above ground. This diversity is due probably to a wider range of internal conditions in the tops and to a wider range in above-ground environmental factors. It may be attributed also to the greater facility with which top injuries are studied; were observations of parts below ground more easily made, what is now referred to simply as root injury might be found to consist of several kinds. Above ground so diverse are the manifestations of winter injury that the whole condition seems confusion confounded, abounding in contradictions. Certain trees in an orchard suffer winter injury and others do not. Excess soil moisture causes winter injury in one instance and lack of soil moisture causes it in another. Cold leads directly to winter injury yet sometimes high temperatures induce it hardly less directly. At times young trees suffer more; at others, older trees. Orchards in high wind-swept spots are damaged; again it is the low-lying orchards that are afflicted. Late maturing trees suffer in one locality; somewhere else it is the early maturing trees. Now it is trees weakened by neglect that lack hardiness; again it is the highest cultivated trees that fail. An early winter freeze is the cause at one time; in another case a late winter freeze brings destruction. An early freeze has been known to kill peaches while pecans survived.

Table 19, arranged from data assembled at the New York Agricultural Experiment Station, at Geneva[171] and showing climatic conditions at that point, is designed to show the varying conditions that may induce or

TABLE 19.—SELECTED METEOROLOGICAL DATA FOR GENEVA, N. Y.[171]

	Rainfall (inches)			Mean temperatures (degrees Fahrenheit)							Minimum temperatures (degrees Fahrenheit)				
	Aug.	Sept.	Oct.	Aug.	Sept.	Oct.	Nov.	Dec.	Jan.	Feb.	Oct.	Nov.	Dec.	Jan.	Feb.
1883-4	3.47	2.12	2.10	65.6	56.3	46.6	39.1	27.5	17.6	28.3	25.0	13.0	7.5	−13.0	3.0
1884-5	1.44	3.17	1.67	69.9	65.2	50.2	36.6	27.8	20.6	11.4	23.0	15.0	−15.5	6.0	−11.5
1885-6	5.02	2.11	2.88	65.0	58.3	49.6	39.3	27.8	19.6	22.9	25.5	18.0	4.0	−18.7	−11.0
1886-7	2.86	2.31	1.79	67.5	61.8	49.6	36.8	22.6	19.2	23.2	27.5	17.0	6.0	−8.0	−7.0
1887-8	3.03	0.75	1.74	66.5	57.7	47.0	37.6	27.2	16.4	22.8	21.2	15.0	3.0	−8.0	4.0
1888-9	4.02	2.73	3.47	68.0	62.2	43.9	39.4	29.3	29.1	18.1	29.0	8.0	0.0	6.0	7.0
1889-90	1.98	2.50	3.32	66.0	60.5	44.0	40.3	35.2	31.2	30.9	21.2	17.0	8.0	5.0	9.5
1890-1	4.34	5.81	4.54	67.7	60.1	49.3	37.6	21.4	25.9	28.3	32.0	17.0	8.0	4.0	2.5
1891-2	3.16	1.12	1.34	68.5	66.2	48.3	38.4	35.5	21.4	25.6	33.1	12.0	7.0	−5.0	2.8
1892-3	4.77	2.68	1.59	69.4	61.2	50.0	35.8	25.2	15.5	20.6	33.1	18.0	3.5	6.0	8.5
1893-4	5.38	4.64	3.59	68.8	58.0	52.7	36.0	27.5	29.7	20.6	25.0	12.0	1.5	11.0	8.5
1894-5	1.22	0.94	0.72	66.8	64.9	52.7	36.0	31.5	21.8	16.9	33.0	19.5	0.2	−16.5	14.0
1895-6	2.66	4.27	2.26	71.2	61.7	45.4	42.9	27.1	23.2	24.1	33.0	19.5	2.0	3.5	21.0
1896-7	3.33	2.36	0.73	70.6	60.2	56.5	39.7	29.0	22.0	26.1	28.0	16.0	2.0	4.0	5.5
1897-8	3.27	1.86	3.83	67.6	62.3	52.6	37.0	27.0	22.0	26.8	29.0	25.0	3.0	2.0	8.0
1898-9	3.60	2.23	3.65	71.6	65.6	52.1	38.9	30.0	22.1	20.4	31.0	16.0	1.0	2.0	0.0
1899-00	1.05	0.91	1.35	74.1	60.6	57.9	41.1	28.7	26.1	18.5	26.0	19.0	5.0	14.0	−2.5
1900-1	1.75	2.46	2.32	71.0	64.0	51.4	34.3	27.7	23.7	28.1	28.0	13.0	4.0	2.0	3.0
1901-2	5.52	2.88	4.19	67.6	64.0	52.5	46.3	25.7	18.9	23.1	29.0	22.0	5.0	2.0	4.0
1902-3	2.41	1.30	2.06	65.5	63.6	48.4	36.2	23.3	19.8	23.9	28.0	12.0	4.0	14.0	18.0
1903-4	7.21	3.26	3.69	68.2	61.9	52.4	37.6	32.0	32.5	26.1	20.5	9.0	2.0	2.0	6.0
1904-5	2.56	1.90	3.56	68.7	63.7	51.2	37.9	26.1	24.9	21.3	30.0	16.0	1.0	−18.0	7.0
1905-6	5.44	2.16	2.48	72.8	67.3	47.0	38.7	31.8	24.9	23.6	24.0	22.0	13.5	9.0	−14.0
1906-7	3.68	2.73	2.73	68.4	64.4	52.9	40.0	29.2	27.7	22.6	27.0	18.0	3.0	7.0	1.0
1907-8	1.35	1.66	1.18	68.8	67.0	47.7	44.5	25.7	25.1	22.1	27.0	21.0	−2.5	8.0	3.0
1908-9	1.79	2.22	1.73	70.0	63.5	53.1	35.7	21.5	24.9	21.6	26.0	21.0	3.0	1.0	4.0
1909-10	2.21	3.21	2.37	69.0	63.2	50.7	36.6	35.1	15.9	21.6	33.0	18.0	13.0	12.0	−10.0
1910-11	5.47	5.89	1.42	70.9	62.8	53.5	42.5	35.5	32.7	17.7	31.0	20.0	12.0	8.0	−14.0
1911-12	3.36	1.62	4.03	68.6	68.4	53.0	39.2	33.6	25.4	29.6	26.0	16.0	6.0	9.0	−10.0
1912-3	2.21	1.78	1.55	70.5	61.4	55.4	41.0	28.0	26.5	19.5	29.0	21.0	−6.0	3.0	−8.0
1913-4	1.65	2.15	4.44	67.8	61.4	58.0	45.3	33.0	29.0	29.6	26.0	16.0	4.0	−10.0	8.0
1914-5	6.05	1.78	1.41	73.5	66.0	45.9	35.3	19.5	24.6	20.2	29.0	21.0	−18.0	−10.0	11.0
1915-6	5.90	1.62	4.37	70.5	60.1	52.9	44.0	28.0	26.5	19.5	29.0	21.0	6.0	8.0	8.0
1916-7	3.47	2.15	4.37	73.5	66.0	58.0	45.0	33.0	24.6	20.2	29.0	16.0	4.0	3.0	10.0
1917-8	1.99	1.82	2.50	70.5	60.1	45.9	35.3	19.5	33.3	23.4	26.0	9.0	−18.0	−10.0	11.0
Average	3.30	2.42	2.50	69.1	62.4	50.7	38.6	28.4	24.1	22.7					

accompany winter injury. Unusual climatic features that have, conceivably, a bearing here, are shown in heavy type. The highest and the lowest rainfalls for August, September and October, the highest mean temperatures for August, September and October and the lowest mean temperatures from October to February are thus distinguished and the minimum temperatures for each month indicated. The winters of 1895–1896, 1903–1904 and 1917–1918 may be considered the seasons of greatest winter injury for this section in recent years. It is evident at once that the rainfall preceding the winter of 1895–1896 was the lowest of any season reported; that preceding the 1903–1904 season was the highest and that preceding the 1917–1918 winter was very close to an average. The three destructive winters were, then, preceded by both extremes and an average rainfall. Though the rainfall for the months considered was in 1897 only 0.02 inch more than that of 1896, no serious damage was reported; though the rainfall for these months in 1915 was only 0.58 inch less than that of the same period in 1903–1904, no widespread damage followed.

The seasons with highest average temperatures for the last of the growing season, 1900 and 1906, were not followed by the greatest destruction. The lowest monthly temperatures for October, November, January and February came in years not distinguished for greatest winter-killing. Only in December did the lowest monthly temperature occur in a winter of extensive injury. The absolute minima for October, for November and for January fall outside the years of greatest damage.

Reviewing by seasons: the 1895–1896 winter shows extreme conditions (heavy type) in low rainfall and low late winter temperatures; the most noteworthy divergence of the 1903–1904 winter was the heavy rainfall, while for 1917–1918 the high and low monthly precipitations combined to make an average rainfall and the noteworthy features for that winter were the low temperatures of November and December. Not far from Geneva, at Ithaca, Bailey[10] wrote of the 1895–1896 winter, "the phenomenal injury wrought by last winter was probably not wholly the result of low temperature. The drought of the last summer and fall no doubt augmented the injury." In reviewing the winter of 1903–1904, for states east of the Mississippi, Stockman[228] stated that the severity "was not due to occurrence of very low minimum temperatures but to the number and succession of days whose mean temperatures continued below the normal. . . At only two stations having 25 years or more of records was the record of lowest temperatures broken. No record of minimum temperatures at a regular Weather Bureau station was broken during December and February."

It seems, then, that an extreme of any one feature of the climate is not of itself likely to cause widespread injury, but that injury depends considerably on a combination of accentuated, rather than on isolated extreme, conditions. Thus 1895–1896 may be described as in many ways a characteristic Dakota winter in its drying out effects; in 1903–1904 late maturity with late cold and in 1917–1918 immaturity and early cold are the distinguishing features.

Speculation is uncertain but in this case rather interesting. It cannot, of course, be proved but it seems possible that had the rainfalls of 1895 and 1917 been exchanged the damage would have been less in both cases; or, had the rainfall of 1915 been combined with the August-October temperature of 1900 and the November minimum of 1904, how great might have been the danger! Out of the 35 seasons covered in Table 18, only six have no notable climatic extreme to be recorded.

Winter Injuries Classified.—Winter killing of hardy fruits in temperate regions, then, may depend on: (1) a lack of maturity in tissues, (2) a lack of ability to resist winter drought conditions, (3) too ready response to short periods of warm weather in the winter. These are listed here in the probable order of their relative importance and frequency, though in any given section the sequence may be changed. In the Minnesota-Dakota section, for example, it is probable that winter drought and absolute cold are more frequently the causes of winter killing; in the northeast the lack of maturity of tissues is probably the one dominant factor, while farther south much of the winter killing of buds is the result of the breaking of dormancy by unseasonable warm weather, followed by ordinary cold.

These classes can be recognized in many cases by the form of the resultant injury, though sometimes different causes appear to have nearly identical effects. Crown injury and crotch injury may be related with some certainty to lack of maturity. Killing back of branches results from the same factor, but may be regarded also as a sign of varietal tenderness or it may be caused by winter drought. Killing of apple fruit buds in northern sections appears to be a result of absolute cold, but with peaches in climates such as that of Missouri it is to a considerable extent induced by ready development before cold weather has passed. Winter sunscald is a localized manifestation, ordinarily, of a late winter freezing. Trunk splitting is frequently associated with an immature condition and at times with a sudden and considerable drop in temperature.

The diversity of causes and multiplicity of effects make it quite evident that any attempt at setting definite temperatures as injurious or fatal without regard to other conditions is futile. Though there is a generally accepted belief that $-14°F$. is fatal to peach fruit buds, they have been known to survive $-20°F$. It is not always the coldest winter that does the greatest damage. Much depends on the character of the preceding autumn, whether it induced proper "ripening" of the wood or forced late growth and on the period at which the cold weather occurred;

of course much depends on the treatment accorded any given orchard or tree during the preceding summer and autumn.

INJURIES ASSOCIATED WITH IMMATURITY

Early maturity of wood is of paramount importance in most of the northeastern United States and is by no means a negligible factor outside that region. Most of the injury in Washington state orchards in the disastrous freeze of late November, 1896, can be attributed clearly to immaturity rather than to the actual temperature ($-12°F$.) attained[15] and similarly the widespread damage to fruit trees in the same state following temperatures of 10° to 15°F. during the period of Oct. 31 to Nov. 3, 1935, was associated with immaturity. Any region with a comparatively short growing season and with fairly heavy late summer and autumnal rainfall is subject to winter killing because of immaturity. Other combinations of conditions may produce occasionally the same susceptibility in regions ordinarily free from these dangers. Thus in most irrigated sections climatic conditions are such that injuries of this type are not to be expected; however, they are frequently brought about by the injudicious use of irrigation water early enough in the autumn to prolong growth. In the freeze of 1896, in Washington, most of the orchards that had been irrigated in late summer suffered more than others.[15] Late irrigation should be very late, if immunity to this form of injury is to be insured. Furthermore, it should be borne in mind that maturity is only a relative term, the so-called "maturity" of the Willamette valley, for example, being quite different from the "maturity" of Wisconsin. Therefore, a given temperature, common in Wisconsin but unusual in the Willamette, might be harmless in the one location but very injurious in the other, even to trees of the same variety.

Much of the damage from winter temperatures in England and in northern France and Germany is evidently associated with lack of maturity, since particularly cool summers followed by winters of moderate severity have frequently proved more damaging than colder winters that followed favorable growing seasons. A "cold winter" for England would be considered mild in the northern states or Canada; in England it might cause considerable damage and none in New York or Michigan. The prevalence of "frost cankers" as the chief manifestation of winter injury in England lends weight to this view.

Affecting More or Less the Entire Plant.—Emerson[76] states: "Resistance to cold in trees is due often almost wholly to the habit of early maturity rather than to constitutional hardiness. Black walnut trees at the Experiment Station (Nebraska), grown from northern seed, by virtue of perfect maturity, passed through the extremely severe winter of 1898–1899 without apparent injury while similar black walnut trees from

southern seed, owing to imperfect maturity, have had their new growth
killed back from a few inches to two or three feet for the past six years and
yet notwithstanding this great difference in resistance to cold in winter, a
comparatively light freeze late in the spring of 1903 killed the new growth
of the northern trees just as completely as it did that of the southern ones.
Northern trees are constitutionally no hardier than southern but their
superior resistance to winter cold was due to their habit of ripening their
new growth perfectly in the fall."

Macoun[144] introduces evidence to the same effect: "From the writer's
experience with over 3,000 species and varieties of trees and shrubs,
exclusive of cultivated fruits, from many countries and climates, which
are under his care and observation at the Central Experiment Farm,
Ottawa, we have drawn the following conclusions regarding the hardiness
of trees: A tree or shrub which will withstand a test winter at Ottawa
must be one which ripens its wood early. Trees or shrubs which are
native to places having a longer or much longer growing season than at
Ottawa grow larger than native species or those from a somewhat similar
climate to the native species, and when a test winter comes their wood is
not sufficiently ripened, or winter-resistant, and they are more or less
injured or perish. . . . Another observation regarding tender trees has
been that after a season when the growth has been strong more injury is
likely to occur than in a season when the growth is short . . . the
season of all the hardiest varieties [of apples] is summer or autumn . . .
apples which mature early and are in condition for eating in summer and
autumn are grown on trees which ripen their wood early, and, on the other
hand, an apple which is not ready for use until winter is usually grown
on a tree which does not ripen its wood early."

Attention may be called to the doubtful wisdom of fall planting in
northern regions of trees grown far to the south. These trees, to be
shipped in time for planting in the north, must be dug when they are
still quite immature. They are, if planted in the fall, exposed to cold
winter temperatures and are thus doubly at a disadvantage. It is true,
the digging may in itself induce a degree of maturity through drying out,
but hardly as much as would be attained by trees grown farther north.
The wisdom of delaying digging as long as possible is obvious.

Tender Plants May Be More Resistant than Hardier Plants.—A temperature of 15°F. at South Haven, Mich., on Oct. 10, 1906, uniformly
killed peach trees while pecans, in the same orchards, survived.[234] Here
is undeniable evidence of a tender species being more hardy at that time
because of maturity than a species that is far more hardy in its mature
condition. Similarly, records show that apple trees planted 2 and
3 years in Wyoming were killed by a temperature of 12°F. in September, when they were still in full leaf,[39] though there are numerous instances

of trees surviving approximately equal temperatures without material injury when they were partly leaved out in the spring.

The Effect of Summer Conditions Favorable for Late Growth.—During the winter of 1903–1904 in Ohio, though the chief damage was to trees of low vitality, vigorous trees succumbed in numerous cases. These were almost invariably in "low, moist, rich black soil favoring extreme growth of soft, poorly matured wood, or in orchards in rich soils, receiving late cultivation."[100] Emerson[74] found similar susceptibility in peaches growing in rather moist soils or receiving late cultivation in Nebraska. Zero weather or even 6°F. above is considered more harmful in very early winter in Montana than −30° or −40°F. later.[79]

Selby[215] supplies other interesting cases of injury in Ohio associated with immaturity. In 1880–1881, late cultivation in two orchards, accompanied by heavy August rainfall and normal September rainfall, produced heavy and prolonged growth. Late November brought zero weather; the December minimum was −13°F. These temperatures ordinarily are of no great significance but in this case they caused complete destruction of Baldwin apple trees. On a larger scale and over a wider area, the same climatic conditions, when approximated in the growing season of 1906, were followed by widespread winter injury. In this case the following winter was severe but, as is shown in Table 20, arranged from Selby's data, in no month of this winter did the temperature closely approach recorded minima. It was definitely established that much of the injury was done by a temperature of +18°F. on Oct. 12. The unusual features of these two damaging years were, not the winter temperatures, but the summer and fall temperatures and rainfall.

TABLE 20.—CLIMATIC CONDITIONS ACCOMPANYING WINTER INJURY IN OHIO[215]

| Month | Temperature (degrees Fahrenheit) | | | | | | Rainfall (inches) | | |
| | 1880 | | Average 23 years | | 1906 | | 1880 | Average 23 years | 1906 |
	Mean	Minimum	Mean	Minimum	Mean	Minimum			
May	65.8	35.5	61.2	19	61.3	24	1.24	3.63	2.17
June	63.4	45.5	69.7	29	69.8	34	5.65	3.94	3.41
July	74.5	52.0	73.9	34	72.1	43	6.06	3.37	5.14
August	71.0	48.0	71.5	31	74.6	43	5.03	3.04	4.77
September	64.8	41.5	65.5	23	68.9	36	2.02	2.71	2.92
October	52.3	30.5	53.5	8	52.7	18	2.27	2.13	3.19
November	33.9	−5.0	40.9	−8	41.1	14	2.39	3.05	2.59
December	25.7	−13.0	31.1	−32	32.3	−15	1.06	2.74	3.68
	1881				1907		1881		1907
January	24.2	−2.0	27.8	−34	32.2	−23	1.31	2.70	6.11
February	29.0	−2.5	26.8	−39	26.0	−19	3.25	2.66	0.85
March	35.6	13.0	38.8	−17	45.9	−2	2.75	3.39	5.55

"Second Growth" Particularly Susceptible.—Excessively dry summer weather also, if followed by a fair precipitation in early autumn, may result in immature wood at the entrance into winter.[253] The dry summer may cause a "premature dormancy" followed by second growth. Instances of this are furnished sometimes by the fall blossoming of fruit trees. The severe winter of 1917–1918 resulted in greater damage to old trees in Indiana than to young, and the suggestion is made that this condition "is possibly accounted for by the fact that many old trees made a late second growth while on vigorous young trees the growth was not arrested by dry weather in late summer and they matured normally."[98] It is interesting to contrast this condition with the greater damage to young trees in Ohio following the wet summer of 1906.

Blackheart.—Blackheart has long been recognized as a form of winter injury. It is most frequently found in those sections characterized by other forms of winter injury associated with immaturity and is itself to be regarded as due, at least in part, to lack of maturity of storage and conducting tissues. In its early stages it may be recognized by a slight darkening of the outer layers of wood, followed by progressive color changes until they become dark brown or almost black by the end of the following growing season. In the meantime a new layer of wood may have been formed through the activity of the cambium, more or less completely enclosing the darkened tissue. If fungi causing decay do not gain entrance and spread through the blackhearted tissues and from them to the enveloping layers of healthy wood, and if these new layers are not in turn killed during subsequent periods conducive to injury of this type, the tree may entirely recover. On the other hand, growth following extensive injury of the blackheart type is likely to be weak and consequently subject to further injury, so that a tree once injured is very likely eventually to succumb to a series of increasingly severe injuries of the same kind. What apparently first occurs is a killing of the protoplasts in the parenchyma cells, "followed by an occlusion of the vessels by a substance resembling wound gum. The killed parenchyma cells, and occluded vessels together form what is termed 'blackhearted wood'."[67,225] Not only is this darkened wood no longer able to serve as conducting tissue for water and nutrients, but apparently the food materials that are stored in it are changed in character and rendered unavailable for new tissue formation the following spring, thus explaining the very limited amount of new growth that is usually made following winter injury of the blackheart type.

Conditions and practices that predispose young vigorously growing trees to blackheart injury include late cultivation, too liberal use of nitrogenous fertilizers, late rains and heavy late-summer irrigation. It is an even more common disorder of older trees that are weakened by overbearing, premature defoliation from leaf-destroying fungi or insects or other evidences of lack of proper care. Both the young vigorously growing trees and the weakened older ones are characterized by poorly matured conducting and storage tissues. It is one of the most common forms of winter injury to tree fruits in the northeastern states and is even more serious in its consequences than its prevalence would indicate because in so many instances the orchard owner does not recognize its symptoms, does not suspect its presence and, therefore, does not employ either preventive or remedial measures that reduce the damage.

Preventive Measures.—Unfortunately the weather cannot be predicted reliably far ahead. However, it seems evident that August rainfall frequently is important in the northeast in determining tree maturity in October and that orchard operations in that section should be varied somewhat during August according to the rainfall. A very dry August should be accompanied by late cultivation to lessen the likelihood of second growth; a very wet August would indicate the wisdom of stopping cultivation altogether and sowing a quick-growing, moisture-consuming cover crop. A warm, moist October cannot be foretold, but its effects can be forestalled, at least in part, by a suitable cover crop which will reduce soil moisture. Furthermore, spraying and other measures can be employed to protect the foliage and prevent it from falling prematurely, thus contributing to the better maturity of the woody tissues, and, in the case of trees too heavily loaded, thinning can be practiced to reduce the crop to a size that they can mature without too seriously exhausting the trees' food reserves.

Localized Injuries.—Aside from the occasional serious and widespread damages just mentioned, there are, probably every winter, minor localized injuries. It is impossible, however, to draw any sharp line between what is here termed localized injuries and more general injury. For instance, the killing back of shoots, canes or limbs, if severe, would be considered in the latter class; if it were light it might as readily be considered localized.

Crotch and Crown Injury.—A form of injury, often unnoticed for some time after its occurrence, but with greater potentiality of ultimate serious consequences, is the killing of more or less limited areas of bark on the trunk, particularly at the crown of the tree or at the crotches. Attention may be drawn to the dead area first by its sunken appearance consequent to the growth of the surrounding uninjured tissue or it may become evident through the cracking of the bark at the injured area or sometimes by the loosening of the bark.

Of the apple varieties commonly grown in the regions where this injury has been most studied, Ben Davis seems most susceptible, with Baldwin showing considerable tenderness in this respect. King, though less widely grown, is so notoriously subject to this malady that the injury is sometimes called the "King disease." It seems significant that all of these varieties are late growers. Gravenstein, in Nova Scotia, is also reported as susceptible.[144]

Grossenbacher[101] reports crown rot much more common in cultivated land than in sod and particularly in land formerly in sod but recently plowed. He also reports high, wind-swept situations with thin soils to be more subject, though it seemingly appears in any situation. No one side of the trees is uniformly injured, according to his observations, though all cases occurring at any one time in a given orchard are likely to be confined to some particular exposure. Trees which have made a rather unusually large, or rather late, growth appear more liable to injury.

In the 1913 freeze, in the citrus regions of California, the crotches were the parts of the trunk found most damaged.[246] Crotch injury and those forms of crown rot not due primarily to the attacks of parasitic organisms are probably most frequently associated with early winter injuries associated with immaturity. Consequent to the winter injury, fungus infestation of the dead area may appear but, excepting the fire-blight bacillus, no organism has been shown definitely to be the primary causative agent in producing this disorder.

Localized Injuries and Delayed Maturity.—Chandler[48] states: "The wood at the base of the trunk and at the crotches of all rapidly growing branches seems to reach a condition of maturity in early winter more slowly than does other tissue."

This view corroborates studies by Mer[160] on the duration of cambial activity in various trees, reported in part as follows. "Just as it awakes gradually in the different regions of a tree cambial activity ceases progressively at the end of summer. . . . It disappears from the branches before disappearing from the trunk. In trees that are closely grouped, it leaves first the low branches, less vigorous than those of the top, and the basal and median parts of these branches before their extremity. It is only following this that it leaves the higher shoots. In the large branches of an isolated tree it stops earlier at the tips than at the middle. It is at the level of the basal swelling that it persists the longest. In the trunk it stops first at the top, then at the middle and finally at the base. When growth is not very active it ceases, on the contrary, earlier in the lower region. . . . It is in the portion of the trunk situated immediately below the soil that cambial activity is confined last.

"It is evident that in the regions of the trunk where the vegetative activity is the most pronounced, because they are the youngest or because they are the best nourished, cambial activity awakes first. . . . It is there also, that in general, it stops latest. On the other hand, in all circumstances where growth is slow, we see cambial activity manifesting itself slowly and stopping earlier. . . . Between the length of the cambial activity and its intensity there is, then, a manifest relation."

This statement seems in itself adequate explanation for much of the localization of winter injury associated with immaturity. Field studies in several regions seem to correlate immaturity with this type of injury rather uniformly.

Contributing Factors.—The drying effect of wind should be considered, as also the effect of cold winds on the temperature of the exposed tissues. Winter killing is sometimes more severe in the three or four rows nearest the windward side of the orchard. Many of the older prune orchards in the northern end of the Willamette valley still showed, 15 years later, the marks of the freeze of November, 1896, in the shape of dead areas on the northwest sides of the trunks, corresponding to the direction of the air drift at the time of the freeze. In many cases of this sort the dead tissue ceases abruptly at the point where snow stood at the time of the injury, suggesting at least that the injury was due to the temperature effect of the wind. The effect of snow on soil temperatures will be shown later. This protective influence evidently is not confined to the soil, as data shown in Table 21 clearly indicate.

TABLE 21.—TEMPERATURE UNDER 10-CENTIMETER SNOW COVERING
(*After Goeppert*[223])

Date	Under snow, degrees Centigrade	Air, degrees Centigrade
Feb. 4	−3.0	−12.6
Feb. 5	−4.6	−14.7
Feb. 8	−6.5	−16.7
Feb. 10	−6.0	−14.9
Feb. 11	−5.0	−15.8
Feb. 13	−2.0	− 5.7
Feb. 15	−1.5	− 2.8

Consideration should be given, also, to the unequal maturing of tissues on different sides of the tree trunk. Casual observations in autumn have indicated that maturity may be attained more rapidly on one side of the stem than on another. It would follow, then, that a given temperature in autumn might prove injurious to the tissues of one side and not of the other, without the intervention of other causal agents. Furthermore, it should be considered that the temperature a few inches above the soil may be, on clear cold fall nights, 10° colder than is indicated by a shelter thermometer, so that an official temperature record of 20°F.

may mean that the tissues at the crown were exposed to a temperature of 10°F.

Remedial Measures.—In view of the different circumstances under which this type of injury occurs it is probable that not all the factors mentioned are operative in any given instance and that only one of them, if sufficiently intensified, may produce the injury. The one condition apparently requisite to crown rot and to crotch injury is immaturity in the tissues at the point involved. The prospective grower is safe in utilizing protection, natural or created, from winds, particularly those prevailing in early winter, and the grower whose orchard is on an exposed site should pay careful attention to the attainment of as complete maturity as possible in his trees. Banking, though laborious and expensive, is justified under threatening conditions. For trees already damaged the best treatment is to cut away the injured bark and to cover the exposed surfaces with grafting wax or paint and possibly to bridge-graft.

WINTER INJURY ASSOCIATED WITH DROUGHT

In spite of the great water-retaining capacity of the tissues of the most hardy deciduous fruits in a dormant state, they are not able to withstand an indefinite amount of desiccation. Especially when the evaporating power of the air is high they gradually lose water. This will result eventually in a desiccation that may mean the death of the tissue unless the water lost is replaced promptly. Recovery from winter desiccation, or the ability to withstand long continued hard freezing (physiological drought) or long continued winter drought (atmospheric), depends therefore on a supply of available moisture upon which the roots may draw. In many sections there is seldom, if ever, a winter when soil moisture would be a limiting factor in this connection. In others it is frequently a limiting factor and gives rise to those injuries that are classed here as associated with winter drought.

Fundamentally all injury to dormant tissues from cold is to be regarded as induced by drying out. Paradoxically, it is generally the tissue containing the most moisture that is most subject to damage. The injury, however, comes from immaturity and not from excess moisture. Apparently there is a certain quantum of water, varying with the kind of plant and with conditions, that is essential to protoplasmic life and this is retained more tenaciously by mature tissue. Hence, in considering winter injury a distinction must be drawn between moisture in the plant tissues (water of composition and surplus moisture) and moisture in the environment. Though the two are closely related, freezing (drying out) of immature tissue in a moist environment should be distinguished from freezing (drying out) due to dry environment though the final lethal process is the same.

Immaturity and Winter Drought

Injury from drying out may have certain manifestations in agreement with that from immaturity. It is, however, somewhat more evident in the tops though it may extend to the trunk. Fruit buds in the apple are killed more generally by this type of freezing than through immaturity. Wood formed the previous year suffers heavily; with more extreme conditions the damage extends downward. Injury associated with immaturity may start either on the young twigs or on the trunk. In one case the young twigs suffer because they are immature; in the other because they are the most subject to drying out, just as they would be in excessive growing-season drought. Winter drought injury may discolor wood on older parts of the tree but it does not kill cambium readily.

It should be remarked, also, that in some regions it is quite conceivable that much of the winter killing in the tops may originate primarily as root killing. Conditions there are favorable to root injury and it has been definitely shown many times to occur. Early winter root-killing would be followed by a drying out of the top. The latter symptom naturally would be more evident and would pass as killing of the top, the true cause being obscured. However, the preventives for both classes of injury agree in requiring a high soil moisture content after danger of inducing late growth has passed.

Water Loss from Dormant Tissues

Some measure of the loss of water by dormant trees is afforded by the data presented in Table 22 showing decreases in weight of 8-year old apple trees during two winters in Wisconsin.[202] Obviously these losses are in trees severed from their roots. If the loss in moisture of standing

TABLE 22.—LOSS IN WEIGHT OF APPLE TREES DURING TWO WINTERS[202]
(Weight, pounds)

Date	Tree 1	Tree 2	Tree 3	Tree 4
Dec. 19, 1902	36.6	24.6	35.7	30.4
Feb. 27, 1903	34.7	23.5	34.4	29.0
Apr. 3, 1903	31.4	21.4	31.6	26.5
Loss	5.2	5.2	4.1	3.9
Dec. 5, 1903	26.2	24.2	....	....
Mar. 26, 1904	25.6	23.6	....	....
Loss	0.6	0.6	....	....

trees, where the supply of water would be renewed to some extent, should be determined, it would be considerably greater but the degree of exhaustion would be less because, as has been shown earlier, the loss by evaporation diminishes as the degree of exhaustion increases. If the dry weight of the trees could be deducted, the percentage loss of moisture would be correspondingly increased. Quite noticeable are the differences in moisture losses during the two winters recorded in Table 22. The winter of 1903–1904, though severe, was moist and many cloudy days occurred. There was little winter injury in Wisconsin during that season.

Bailey[12] estimates that a large apple tree loses from 250 to 350 grams of water each day through the winter. Observations on moisture content of apple twigs in Iowa show an actual increase from November to December in many varieties; on Jan. 15, however, following several days of severe cold, there was a very marked decrease, though the respective intervals between observations were 5 weeks and 3 weeks[19] (see Table 14).

Water Conduction in Trees during the Winter

Bailey[12] cites evidence gathered in New York showing loss of moisture in twigs during winter and a higher moisture content during a thaw than during a previous period of cold weather, indicating a conduction of sap during the milder weather. Indeed such a conduction must be conceded else the tree would inevitably dry out. Wiegand[255] showed a conduction of water to *Pinus Laricio* buds at temperatures between $-18°$ and $-6.7°C$. Buds severed from the tree but sealed immediately on the cut surfaces showed an average water content of 41.2 per cent. after 3 days while buds taken fresh from the tree at the end of this time, even though the twigs had been frozen, showed an average content of 47.5 per cent. It is probable that interference with conduction, or an evaporation rate much higher than conduction, is just the condition requisite for winter drought injury.

Relation of Freezing to Water Conduction.—It is well known to every wood-chopper of the northern woods that trees freeze even to the center in prolonged cold weather. Investigations have shown that in trees of 6 to 8 inches diameter the difference in temperature between the center and the outside in the morning is only 1° or 2°R., though in trees 2 feet in diameter it may be on single days 5°, 6° or 7°R.; with air temperatures of $-13°$ to $-15°R.$ the tree temperature was $-12°$ to $-14°R.$; most important, the longer the temperature of the air remains uniform the more the temperature of the tree approaches that of the air.[211] The temperature of the alburnum or sap wood in maple has been shown to follow the air temperatures fairly closely.[123] More detailed figures taken morning, noon and night, at a depth of 8 centimeters in a box elder tree, indicate that tree temperatures follow the trend of the air temperatures very closely, not, however, reaching the full extremes of the outside fluctuations unless these are maintained for some time.[224]   Figure 27, arranged from a part of these figures, shows typical daily fluctuations of air and tree temperatures.   Table 23 shows the averages of the temperatures recorded during January and February.   Observations in Lapland show winter temperatures in live and dead trees to be practically the same.[81]

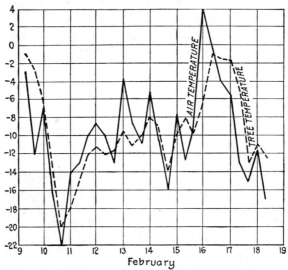

Fig. 27.—Temperature fluctuations in a tree trunk.   (*After Squires*[224])

Grape vines have been grown in a greenhouse, so trained that certain canes passed outside and were then brought back into the house.   The base and the upper parts, inside the greenhouse, opened their buds quickly

TABLE 23.—TREE AND AIR TEMPERATURES
(*After Squires*[224])

	January		February	
	Air, degrees Centigrade	Tree, degrees Centigrade	Air, degrees Centigrade	Tree, degrees Centigrade
6 to 7 a.m.......	−10.84	−9.37	−11.93	−10.46
12 to 1 p.m.......	− 6.60	−8.90	− 4.35	− 7.55
6 to 7 p.m.......	− 9.20	−7.50	− 8.65	− 7.00
Entire day........	− 8.88	−8.57	− 8.31	− 8.34

and continued to grow.   On cold mornings, however, with the outside temperature around −10°C., the leaves on the upper part of the stem were very much wilted, because of the interference with sap conduction in the portion of the stem outside. With rising temperature, however, they recovered.[72]

These considerations make it evident that prolonged cold weather must interfere materially with sap conduction while at the same time the conditions accompanying extreme cold are the very conditions which favor greater drying out. It should be considered, too, that the conductive regions in the tree are near the outside of the stem. Many cases of twig killing must, therefore, be considered as due to drought, short, perhaps, but intense in localized areas. Possibly the greater susceptibility of twigs to this injury is not due entirely to failure in conduction but may be explained in part by the lack of a sufficient amount of sapwood to serve as a local reservoir. Even prolonged cold does not affect the upper part of tall trunks as much as it does the low, smaller branches though conduction from the ground is conceivably as difficult; the tissues on the trunk, however, have both relatively and absolutely a greater amount of sapwood on which presumably they may draw.

Where Winter Drought Conditions Prevail

Winter drought conditions are in a measure independent of soil conditions and may be considered as of possible occurrence over a wide range of territory. The coldest weather in humid sections is accompanied by dry atmospheric conditions; occasionally after a dry summer and fall these sections suffer from winter killing due to desiccation. Long continued severe, though not excessive, cold would induce physiological drought. The winter of 1895, already mentioned, was of this type. It is, however, infinitely more common, in proportion to the amount of fruit grown, in regions of prevailingly dry atmosphere and intense cold. Wyoming, the Dakotas and parts of Minnesota furnish abundant examples. Rainfall is comparatively light in those sections and the soil frequently freezes with a low moisture content. Winter precipitation is less than summer, frequently only a fourth as great and there is much clear, cold weather.

Protection against Winter Drought Injuries

Necessarily protective measures against winter injury associated with drought must be preventive. They must either reduce water loss or increase water supply.

Winter Irrigation.—Buffum[39] advocates in Wyoming thorough irrigation "late in the fall, before the ground has frozen and when growth has ceased. The later this irrigation can be done the better as the object is to store moisture in the soil sufficient for winter . . . where orchards are planted on bottom lands that have a continual supply of moisture fall irrigation may be unnecessary. But on upland it is the surest way to prevent trees from winter killing and when possible irrigations through the winter will be found advantageous." In North Dakota, Waldron[239] writes: "Parts of our own plantation have been cultivated every year until the ground freezes with only the best results . . . the treatment that provides the trees with the greatest amount of soil moisture in the fall will tend to prevent winter killing." Elsewhere the same writer states: "The cause of winter killing in mild weather is the drying up of the twigs. . . . Trees and shrubs that are neglected during the latter part of summer so that the ground becomes hard and dry, ripen their wood prematurely and unless fall rains are abundant the drying process sets in before winter begins, leaving the plant in poor shape to endure further drying. . . . Some of the plants that defer this change (to winter condition) the longest are among the hardiest we have."[240]

Cultivation.—Experimental demonstrations with Wealthy apple trees, on 15 widely separated farms in South Dakota, give quantitative verifica-

TABLE 24.—EFFECT OF CULTURAL CONDITIONS ON WINTER-KILLING IN SOUTH DAKOTA[157]

Lot number	Number trees, 1916	Number trees dead, 1919	Number trees severely injured, 1919	Number healthy trees, 1919	Average growth (inches)	Average percentage of soil moisture, Nov. 15	Average percentage of soil moisture, Feb. 15
1	50	41	7	2	2.0	14.70	14.2
2	50	16	18	16	9.0	17.95	19.2
3	50	22	13	13	6.5	15.50	15.2
4	50	7	11	32	15.0	31.50	33.8

tion of the opinions just quoted (Table 24). Lot 1, showing the lowest moisture content and the greatest injury to trees, was composed of trees planted in prairie sod; Lot 2 was cultivated each 10 days till Aug. 10; Lot 3 was "cultivated each 10 days till July 1, followed by a cover crop of fall rye or buckwheat" and Lot 4, which showed least injury, was cultivated each 10 days until Aug. 10, just as Lot 2, but in addition received a heavy watering just before the ground froze for the winter. The investigator concluded that "summer cultivation is positively needed and in very dry seasons fall watering or irrigation of some sort is not only advantageous but necessary."

Cover Crops.—Another point of interest here is the lower soil moisture in the cover crop lot and the somewhat greater attendant injury, as compared with the clean cultivated lot. Had a winter favorable to root killing intervened, the results in these two plots might have been different. However, the danger from cover crops in this region of light rainfall is apparently more frequently present than the danger from their absence which is discussed presently. This point doubtless has occasionally equal application in dry situations in other regions. Comparison of these results with those of Emerson, reported below, indicates that the best insurance against winter injury in general in this region—and in occasional sites in more humid sections—is a frost-tender cover crop with a heavy late fall irrigation. To be sure, in those districts where irrigation water is not available, the preventive measures against the winter injuries associated with drought must of necessity be incomplete. However, the recognition of the liability of a given site to this form of injury may enable the grower so to shape his cultural practices early in the season as to minimize the danger.

Studies by Emerson[75] in Nebraska show the effect of cover crops of different kinds on the hardiness of young peach trees. The cover crops are considered in two classes, frost-resistant and frost-killed. Table 25, reproduced from Emerson's report, shows the effect of these crops on soil moisture content.

TABLE 25.—EFFECT OF VARIOUS COVER CROPS ON SOIL MOISTURE DURING THE FALL OF 1900[75]

Kind of cover crop	Sept. 20	Oct. 9	Oct. 27	Nov. 7	Nov. 20	Dec. 11
Frost-resistant crops:						
Rye	15.2	11.8	12.1	14.1	15.5	16.0
Oats	15.1	13.3	12.3	14.9	13.9	14.4
Rape	15.8	12.8	11.8	14.4	14.2	14.0
Field peas	19.5	15.8	14.7	17.2	15.0	15.6
Average	16.4	13.4	12.7	15.2	14.7	15.0
Frost-killed crops:						
Millet	16.5	12.6	12.4	19.4	18.9	17.6
Cane	17.3	15.1	13.8	20.0	19.6	17.9
Corn	17.6	13.8	13.5	18.7	19.0	19.7
Average	17.1	13.8	13.2	19.4	19.2	18.4
No crop:						
Few weeds	20.0	18.4	20.3	20.6	19.8	18.1
Few weeds	18.6	17.8	18.2	19.1	18.3	18.5
Average	19.3	18.1	19.3	19.9	19.1	18.3

Figure 28, also from Emerson, a graphic representation of the same figures, shows these effects even more strikingly. Both classes reduced soil moisture sharply in September and October, a very desirable effect when the need for ripening of wood is considered. Early in November, however, the frost-killed crops, no longer growing, ceased to draw on the moisture supply while the frost-resistant crops kept the moisture content low.   When it is recalled that Emerson's earlier work showed 19 dead trees and none uninjured out of 25 in soil with 15.2 per cent. moisture, as here under frost-resistant crops, while soil with 19.8 per cent., the nearest figure to that of the soil under frost-killed crops, showed three dead and 12 uninjured, the importance of this difference is evident.   The graph for the soil with no cover crop shows a somewhat higher moisture content in December than either class of cover crops but it also shows a high moisture content in September and October, suggesting a prolonged growing season and poor maturity in the tops.   This is what actually occurred. Emerson's work emphasizes the importance of a water supply after maturity is attained.

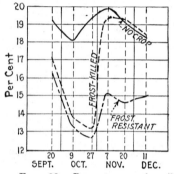

Fig. 28.—Percentages of soil moisture in bare ground and under frost-killed and frost-resistant cover crops. (*After Emerson*[75])

A plentiful supply of available water is an important factor determining the recovery of plant tissues from the effects of low temperatures.   Pantanelli has shown that the activity of the roots is of great importance in determining the recuperative power of the plant after the aerial parts have been exposed to low temperatures and that all those factors that reduce the absorbing capacity of the roots, such as insufficient aeration, salinity, alkalinity and the presence of toxic substances reduce the recuperative power of the plant.

Windbreaks.—The relation to the orchard of shelter belts composed of hardy trees and shrubs has been the subject of much discussion, of some observation but of little precise study.   Variations in local conditions of exposure to prevailing winds and in the character of these prevailing winds, as well as the topography of the orchards themselves, preclude the possibility of windbreaks being universally beneficial or injurious. Their efficacy, when properly placed, in cutting down the windfall loss from summer storms, is not a matter for discussion here.   In the Michigan and New York fruit sections much of the advantage claimed for them is the protection they afford from those types of winter injury that are associated with drying out and they are set usually on a northern boundary of the orchard.

Commenting on the relation of windbreaks to winter injury in the Great Plains region, Baird states[13]: "The fruit garden on the northern Plains will thrive largely in proportion to the extent to which it is protected from wind. . . . One of the most striking things observed in the horticulture of the section is that wherever successful fruit growing is found there is also found adequate protection from wind. If natural protection is not available—and it is not available to the great majority of Plains farmers—shelter belts should be planted and grown to a height of at least 5 or 6 feet before fruit growing is attempted." In some regions windbreaks are probably planted as much for protection against the hot drying winds of summer as for protection against the cold drying winds of winter.

Effect of Wind Velocity.—Of quantitative data on windbreak effects, few are available. The increased snow deposit in places sheltered from the full sweep of the wind is a matter of common observation. After the snow has fallen the windbreak acts to preserve it from evaporation by protecting it from the full force of the wind. Fernow[81] states that snow evaporates ten times as fast in warm wind (velocity not stated)

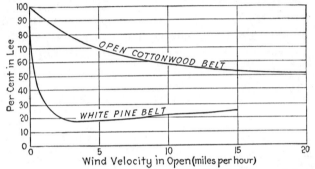

Fig. 29.—Wind at points five times the heights of windbreak to leeward, in terms of wind in open. (*After Bates*[18])

as in calm air. Provided the snow accumulation is not great enough to injure the tops of young trees this effect must be beneficial since data to be introduced show the great power of snow in protecting roots against freezing. How much the windbreak prevents the drying out of the tree tops during the high, desiccating cold winds of winter is a matter which with present data can be only conjectured.

Certain experiments have shown that "with the temperature of the air at 84 and a relative humidity of 50 per cent. evaporation with the wind blowing at 5 miles an hour was 2.2 times greater than in the calm; at 10 miles 3.8; at 15 miles 4.9; at 20 miles 5.7; at 25 miles 6.1 and at 30 miles per hour the wind would evaporate 6.3 times as much water as a calm atmosphere of the same temperature and humidity."[99]

Bates[18] found, in comparing wind movements in the open with those at a leeward point distant from the windbreak five times its height, that "a wind which reaches a velocity of 25 miles per hour in the open will, in the shelter of a good windbreak, have a velocity of . . . only 5 miles per hour."

Combining these sets of figures, the evaporation in this case would be only 39 per cent. of that in the open. Figure 29, reproduced from

Bates' study, shows the percentage of protection to increase with the wind velocity.

Effect on Evaporation.—Card[41] in Nebraska determined the rates of evaporation at different distances from a windbreak 8 rods wide and 25 to 40 feet high. Though these observations were made in summer, they are somewhat indicative of winter conditions and furthermore they have an important bearing on the state of trees as they approach dormancy. If the evaporation on the windward side of the windbreak during all the time that drying winds were blowing be represented by 100, then the evaporation at a point 12 rods distant on the leeward side would be proportionally 83 and at 3 rods distant it would be 55. During a period of high though not particularly dry wind the respective rates were as 100 to 67 to 29. Numerous interesting studies of evaporation rates are reported by Bates, as shown in Table 26, arranged from his data.

Effect on Soil Moisture.—The importance of soil moisture in relation to winter drought has been shown. For this reason, Card's determinations of soil moisture at varying distances on the leeward side of a wind-

TABLE 26.—MEAN EFFICIENCY OF WINDBREAKS IN AREA OF GREATEST
PROTECTION
(*After Bates*[18])

Kind of windbreak	(Area 12 times as wide as height of trees)						
	Width, feet	Height, feet	Moisture saved at different velocities, per cent.				Period of observation
			5	10	15	20	
Cottonwood grove (underplanted)	. . .	75	23.9	31.9	38.7	40.1	July, Sept.
White pine belt.	25	20	31.1	33.3	35.8	. . . .	Nov.
Cottonwood row (natural density)	. . .	50	12.3	18.6	26.6	33.4	June, July, Aug.
Cottonwood belt (no low branches).	100	70	11.7	13.9	15.5	17.0	Aug., Sept.
Cottonwood row (reinforced with ash).	. . .	40	12.8	20.2	23.7	25.8	Sept.
Osage orange hedge (lower branches trimmed)	. . .	23	26.0	27.2	27.2	27.5	June, July, Aug.
Mulberry, single row.	. . .	32	. . . .	28.7	. . . .	. . . .	Aug.

break are of particular interest. Table 27, arranged from his report of determinations made November 5, shows a difference well worth consideration, particularly as they were made at the approach of winter. Assuming, as Card does, that soil moisture up to 10 per cent. is not available for plants, the average available moisture up to a distance of about 7 rods was 2.55 per cent.; beyond that point it was 0.65 per cent.

The area protected by a windbreak is variable. It has been stated that in the Rhone valley each foot in the height of a windbreak protects plants for 11 feet to the leeward.[81] From rather general observations in Iowa and Nebraska it has been estimated that a rod of ground is sheltered for each foot in height of the windbreak, and other estimates state that a windbreak 25 feet in height will protect 10 rods of orchard. Bates found that the area extended on the average not more than 20 times the height of the windbreak; at this distance the wind velocities were found to be almost as great as on the windward side. Card's soil moisture determinations indicate that for this windbreak the effects were not evident beyond 7 rods. Unfortunately these figures were made in an

TABLE 27.—SOIL MOISTURE AT VARYING DISTANCES FROM A WINDBREAK[41]

Distance (rods)	Percentage of moisture	Available for plants
1	14.0	4.0
3	12.6	2.6
5	11.3	1.3
7	12.3	2.3
9	10.7	0.7
11	10.5	0.5
13	10.6	0.6
15	10.8	0.8

open field and there is at present no means of stating just to what extent the orchard will protect itself at points beyond the sheltering effects of the windbreak, though observation indicates that it does to a considerable extent. Injury from cold drying winds in the 1903–1904 winter was found to be more severe in the outside rows of many orchards.

INJURIES CHARACTERISTIC OF LATE WINTER CONDITIONS

Primarily all winter injuries are induced by cold. This fact should be kept in view though for convenience the late winter injuries are treated as due to warm weather. It is not the heat that does the harm but cold weather, even in moderate degree, following warm weather. In one form or another, all fruit growing sections in temperate regions suffer through injuries proceeding from these causes.

The Rest Period

Discussion of the rest period at this point should not be taken to mean that it is regarded among the effects of temperature; it is considered here very briefly because of its relation to them. Periodicity of growth is found in plants wherever they are; equatorial regions with uniform temperatures present the phenomenon of plants in the resting stage while others are in growth. Sometimes on the same tree one branch is resting while others are growing. Other factors than temperature are undoubtedly concerned with the inception and with the end of the rest period.

The dormant season should not be confused with the rest period, though the two overlap more or less; in temperate regions the former may begin after—or before—and generally extends beyond, the latter. In the peach, for example, the rest period may begin to "break" in January though the temperatures prevailing may prolong the dormant season into April. The rest period is not a time of complete cessation of plant activities. The activities commonly recognized as growth are at a standstill, but other functions, undoubtedly of equal necessity to the plant, are active. The beginning and end are probably gradual processes.

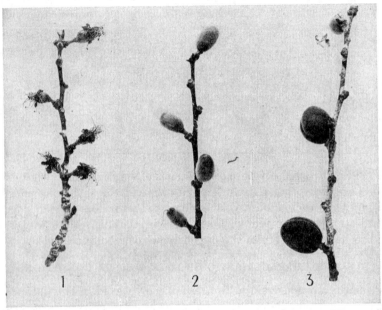

FIG. 30.—Twigs taken from Royal apricot trees on Mar. 30, 1930, at Winters, Calif., showing variation in size of fruit. This variation was caused by greater delay in opening of some buds than of others after a warm winter. (*After Chandler, et al.*[51])

If an attempt is made to force peach trees into growth in a greenhouse during November or early December little success is attained; if the attempt is made in late December less difficulty is encountered while in January there would be still less difficulty. In the first instance the trees are in the rest period; in the second, the rest period is breaking. In the first case, no matter how favorable the environment, there is no response; in the second, the response is rapid whenever the environment is suitable.

It is the duration of the rest period, or, perhaps more accurately, the absence of factors or agencies which bring it to an end, that sets the southern limit to the culture of many fruits. In Cuba,[118] southern Florida[118] and portions of the other Gulf states[248] and southern California[248] deciduous fruits, such as the apple and peach, grow not at all or, if they survive, behave in an erratic manner. The more tropical the climate, the slower are they to leaf out and flower in the spring and the more irregular are their foliation and flowering. One tree in a planting or one branch on a tree may be half leaved out and in full flower when other trees or other branches on the same tree have quarter or even half-grown fruits, and still others may be in a dormant condition. This delay in foliation is likely to be accompanied by more or less heavy shedding of flower buds and a consequent reduction in yield. The same difficulty is experienced along the northern limits of deciduous fruit culture in South Africa.[149] This irregularity in behavior varies greatly with different varieties and is much more accentuated following exceptionally mild winters, such as 1923–1924 in California and 1936–1937 in Georgia. In the latter state, Albany is probably close to the southern limit of commercial peach culture, and even there few varieties other than Hiley Belle can be grown successfully.[138] On the other hand, the mildly retarding effect of a prolonged rest period in areas a little north of those where its influence makes fruit culture hazardous proves advantageous in aiding otherwise early blossoming varieties to escape danger from late spring frosts.[51]

Chandler[46] shows an interesting parallelism between the percentage of buds killed in 1905–1906 and the percentage of buds of the same varieties that could be forced into development early in the following winter. The data are summarized in Table 28, which is arranged from a

TABLE 28.—PERCENTAGE OF BUDS STARTING EARLY AND OF BUDS KILLED[46]

Group	Percentage of buds started Dec. 12, 1906	Percentage of buds started by Dec. 22, 1906	Percentage of buds killed in 1905–1906
Hill's Chili type	3.6	40.7	39.7
Chinese Cling type	0.0	13.0	51.2
Chinese Cling, excluding Elberta, a hybrid	0.0	6.7	44.3
Green Twig varieties	0.0	8.7	50.6
Heath Cling type	27.9	86.7	79.1
Other Persians	12.6	65.7	78.9

more detailed statement in Chandler's report. The relation is close enough to indicate why a given variety, of the Persian type for example, may be tender in the south where its rest period is likely to be broken and still be hardy in the north where cold weather is constant, or why in the same orchard it may be hardy during a winter of steady and fairly severe cold and still be tender during a mild winter.

Recent studies indicate some correlation, even in Minnesota, between hardiness and the intensity of the rest period in certain plums, as shown in Table 29. These suggest that the rest period may be more important in the north than it generally has been considered, though they do not explain observed differences in bud killing early in the winter.

TABLE 29.—TIME REQUIRED FOR BLOOMING UNDER LABORATORY CONDITIONS AT DIFFERENT INTERVALS DURING THE WINTER
(After Strausbaugh[229])

Date collected	Stella (semi-hardy)		Tonka (semi-hardy)		Assiniboine (hardy)	
	Date of bloom	Days required	Date of bloom	Days required	Date of bloom	Days required
Oct. 3...	Oct. 17	15	Oct. 17	15	Did not bloom	..
Nov. 8...	Nov. 22	15	Nov. 22	15	Did not bloom	..
Nov. 19...	Dec. 4	16	Dec. 4	16	Did not bloom	..
Jan. 24...	Feb. 2	10	Feb. 2	10	Feb. 18	26
Feb. 6...	Feb. 15	10	Feb. 15	10	Feb. 23	18
Feb. 21...	Mar. 2	11	Mar. 2	11	Mar. 8	17
Feb. 28...	Mar. 7	9	Mar. 7	9	Mar. 14	16
Mar. 5...	Mar. 13	9	Mar. 13	9	Mar. 19	15

Different plants appear to have rest periods of unequal length; in fact some, such as certain spiraeas, seem to have none. However, the rest period for each plant seems to be fairly constant provided no disturbing influence acts upon the plant. It follows, then, that the earlier the plant enters upon its period of rest the earlier the period is over. This is a matter of some practical import, as appears later.

The rest period can be shortened, or broken, by various treatments. Etherization, light, wounding, desiccation, hot-water baths and exposure to freezing all bring it to an early end. For the forcing of certain flowers, such as lilacs, etherization is sometimes used; the greenhouse man who wishes to force fruits exposes the trees to cold. Northern greenhouses in Europe can force fruit and have it on the markets somewhat in advance of the greenhouse fruit crop from many more southern parts because the trees can be exposed to a freezing temperature earlier in the north and the rest period broken earlier. With most deciduous fruits, however, freezing temperatures are not required to break the rest period. Relatively cool or chilling temperatures are sufficient. According to Chandler and associates,[51] basing their conclusions on orchard observations in California over a considerable period, " . . . temperatures of 33° to 40° Fahrenheit are as good as freezing temperatures, if not better. Exposure of buds to temperatures that average about 48° will break the rest period, but a longer time is required than in colder weather." Darrow[64] has found that with a relatively long day (14 to 16 hours) the rest period of strawberries is broken more readily and at a higher temperature than when growing under shorter day conditions. Yarnell[260] states that a total of 800 to 1,000 hours of lapsed time below 45°F. is effective in breaking the rest period of peaches in Texas. Often the difference in mean temperature between trees partially in the shade and those fully exposed to the sun is sufficient to effect a breaking of the rest period and permit normal foliation of the one lot while the others exhibit delayed and irregular foliation.[51,247] Dormant season spraying with oil emulsions,[24,149] or, better still, with oil emulsions to which some toxicant, such as dinitrocyclohexylphenol,[51] has been added has proven effective in hastening the ending of the rest period and contributed to more normal foliation and flowering to an extent sufficient to make the practice commercially profitable. Apparently the practice in the Philippine Islands of smudging mango trees in order to make them blossom more profusely or, at certain desired periods, so that the flowers may escape injury from those fungi that are particularly serious during the rainy season, is based on more or less of a comparable influence of some of the gaseous constituents of the smudge in breaking the rest period of their flower buds.[29,88,95]

For most deciduous fruit growers, however, the chief interest is in prolonging the rest period; this can be done in some cases, discussed later, by postponing its advent. In northern sections, though the temperatures are undoubtedly severe enough early in the winter to break the rest period, they are low enough to prolong dormancy and the rest period is relatively of less importance there. Farther south, where warm periods come during the winter, it is of much greater significance.

The exact nature of the changes involved in the beginning and the end of the rest period is not known. A puzzling fact is mentioned by Schimper: A low temperature in the growing season will not have the same effect as in the dormant season; the change of starch to sugar in the potato accompanying cold in the winter is not duplicated in the summer. Since ordinary growing temperatures are without effect on the rest period, chemical changes appear not to be the controlling factors. Since time is a recognized factor a physical change is suggested. It seems significant that all processes known to shorten the rest period are known also to increase permeability.

Injuries to Fruit Buds

The killing of fruit buds which have started into activity is more evident in southern sections. Whitten[252] discusses winter killing of the peach in Missouri as of this nature. He states: "The growth of buds during warm weather in winter renders them very susceptible to injury from subsequent freezing. This is the most common cause of winter killing to peach buds in this state. Very often a warm spell as early as February causes peach buds to make considerable growth. If growth starts to any great extent the subsequent cold weather is almost sure to kill the buds." Chandler[48] states that "there has very seldom been a year when buds in the peach section of southern Missouri have not been started sufficiently by Feb. 1 to be killed by a temperature considerably higher than would be required to kill buds in northern Missouri, or certainly in Michigan, New York or New England on the same date."

It is possible that occasionally the injury in these cases of warm weather followed by cold is due merely to the sudden drop in temperature. Indeed, Chandler[48] cites convincing evidence to this effect: "In the year of 1901–1902 all of the buds were killed at the Missouri Experiment Station orchard by a temperature of $-23°F$. on Dec. 20. In 1902–1903 practically all buds were killed by a temperature of $-15°F$. on Feb. 17. In 1903–1904 buds were killed on all varieties except General Lee, Chinese Cling, Thurber, Carman, Gold Drop, Triumph and Lewis by a temperature of $-14°F$. on Jan. 29. During the winter of 1904–1905 nearly all the buds were killed, yet practically all trees had a few left alive and Triumph and Lewis a fair crop following a temperature of $-25°F$. on Feb. 13. . . . on Jan. 12, 1909, practically all the buds were killed except on the most hardy varieties by a temperature of $-11°F$. In fact, fewer peaches were borne at Columbia following the winter of 1908–1909 than following the winter of 1904–1905 when the temperature fell to $-25°F$. on Feb. 13. . . . there was not more warm weather to start the buds preceding the freeze of Jan. 12, 1909, at Columbia . . . than preceding the freeze of Feb. 13, 1905, at Columbia.

"It would hardly seem possible that the buds in either case could have been started into slight growth preceding the freeze. Buds start very slowly even at high temperature early in January. . . . the low temperature of Jan. 12, 1909, came suddenly following high temperature while that of Feb. 13, 1905, came following 42 days of rather low temperature. For 16 days the maximum temperature did not go above the freezing point."

Chandler suggests two possible reasons for buds surviving the colder temperature of the 1904–1905 winter: the long exposure to low temperature which hardened them and the very slow falling of the temperatures.

Changes in Water Content of Buds during Winter.—There is, however, abundant evidence that development in peach buds during warm periods of the winter is frequently a contributing factor in winter injury. Investigations in Maryland show a progressive change which easily may be accelerated by pronounced warm weather.[122] It seems significant that

TABLE 30.—WATER CONTENT OF PEACH FRUIT BUDS
(*After Johnston*[122])

Date of sample	Average green weight (grams)		Average dry weight (grams)		Ratio water content to green weight		Ratio water content to dry weight	
	Elberta	Greens-boro	Elberta	Greens-boro	Elberta	Greens-boro	Elberta	Greens-boro
Nov. 8............	0.124	0.121	0.073	0.073	0.41	0.40	0.69	0.65
Dec. 6............	0.144	0.129	0.079	0.073	0.46	0.43	0.84	0.76
Jan. 7............	0.144	0.123	0.082	0.075	0.43	0.38	0.76	0.62
Feb. 7............	0.164	0.128	0.082	0.075	0.49	0.42	0.99	0.71
Mar. 7............	0.327	0.220	0.115	0.092	0.65	0.58	1.85	1.37
Mar. 28..........	1.050	0.750	0.205	0.180	0.80	0.76	4.12	3.17

the more tender variety of the two studied shows this change in greater degree.

Contributing Factors.—Roberts,[197] in Wisconsin, investigating blossom bud killing in the sour cherry, concluded that susceptibility is in direct relation to the degree of advancement, the more advanced blossoms suffering most. He states: "The amount of injury is in relation to the degree of development of the blossom buds, which, in turn, is usually in [inverse] proportion to the amount of growth the tree is making." These conclusions were reached after microscopic investigation as well as field studies.

The position of the hardiest buds was investigated by Chandler[46] whose report follows, in part: . . . "the hardy buds are those borne at the base of the whips (last year's growth). . . . at the base of the whips on trees not cut back only a slightly larger percentage of buds were killed than were killed at the tips of cut back trees. . . . Now it is possible to head back so severely that no fruit buds will be formed except at the outer end of the branches. This is especially true if the tree has a narrow dense head. . . . If the tree be spreading in form, heading back is not so likely to cause the next season's wood to be in very long whips that either have branches at the basal nodes instead of fruit buds, or have the leaves at these basal nodes killed by the shade before fruit buds can be formed. This is true because the spreading heads would afford room for a larger number of whips to grow and obtain light, and the larger the number of nearly equal growing whips, other conditions of the tree being equal, the shorter necessarily will be the growth in each whip." Data are cited showing a loss of 60.2 per cent. of fruit buds on a large low-growing, spreading Oldmixon as compared with 86.4 per cent. on a tree of the same variety making very large, upright growth and 90.8 per cent. on still another Oldmixon making small upright growth.

Protective Measures.—Late entrance into the resting stage has been said to cause a delay in breaking the rest period. This may be effected in a number of ways.

Pruning.—One of the means of inducing late growth and late entrance into the resting period is pruning heavily enough to stimulate vigorous growth. Chandler[46] reports results of investigations in forcing twigs of a large number of peach varieties which he summarizes as follows:

"Average per cent. started on trees making large growth (cut back)..20.5
"Average per cent. started on trees making small growth (not cut back)..31.2
"Number of varieties in which trees not cut back started first.........20
"Number of varieties in which trees cut back started first............. 3.
"Number in which both started about equally...................... 4.

" . . . If we take the average of buds started on twigs taken December 22, or later, that is, when the resting period is nearly ended, we have;—
"For trees making large growth (cut back) 28.3 per cent. started.
"For trees making smaller growth (not cut back) 48.6 per cent. started.
"Taking only those varieties in which one tree had 60 per cent. of the buds started, and therefore may be considered to have finished its resting period, we have as an average—
"On trees making large growth (cut back) 44.3 per cent. of the buds started;
"On trees making smaller growth (not cut back) 83.4 per cent. of the buds started."

It is apparent that the more favorable the conditions become for breaking of the rest period the more evident becomes the restraining influence of late maturity.

TABLE 31.—BUDS KILLED AT −3°F. ON PRUNED AND UNPRUNED TREES[48]

Variety	Per cent. killed	
	Pruned	Unpruned
Elberta	48.5	67.8
Oldmixon Free	62.9	78.0
Triumph	30.0	59.1
Lewis	16.0	25.7
Early Tillotson	23.9	54.7
Average	36.2	59.8

That this retardation of development by pruning actually results in lessening winter injury of the type under discussion is shown by numerous instances cited by Chandler. After a succession of warm days followed by a fall to −3°F., which would hardly kill any considerable number of buds unless they had started into development, a count was made of dead buds on pruned and unpruned trees. Table 31, arranged from Chandler's data, shows one instance. Even more striking is his enumeration of results at Brandsville, Missouri, following the freeze of Mar. 16, 1911, when 98.08 per cent. of the buds on unpruned trees were killed while only 81.9 per cent. were killed on the severely pruned trees.[48] The killing on the pruned trees seems high but 18.1 per cent. of peach buds may produce a full crop, as they did in this instance, while the unpruned trees bore only a few peaches.

Fertilization and Cultivation.—Nitrogenous fertilizers, stimulating vegetative growth, have much the same effect as pruning, according to Chandler. In one case, at Brandsville, Mar. 16, 1911, unfertilized trees lost 98.4 per cent. of their buds while trees fertilized with ammonium sulfate lost 77.6 per cent. and those which had received nitrate of soda lost 87.1 per cent. In one instance the fertilizer saved enough buds to make a full crop, in the other enough for a fair crop.

Late cultivation has been reported to have the same results in retarding the rest period and increasing hardiness.

Thinning.—Thinning has been observed to have beneficial effects on hardiness. Chandler[46] cites a case in which buds of certain varieties survived a winter that killed those of most varieties. These trees then bore a full crop but in the following winter their fruit buds succumbed while the varieties tender in the previous year survived. To secure experimental data the fruit on half of each of several heavily loaded trees was thinned with the results shown in Table 32. When the experiment

TABLE 32.—EFFECT OF THINNING FRUIT ON HARDINESS OF BUDS[48]

Variety	Percentage of buds killed	
	Thinned	Unthinned
Seedling...............................	18.5	58.9
Elberta Seedling........................	31.6	36.7
Oldmixon Cling.........................	44.5	53.4
Poole's Favorite........................	41.7	52.8
Poole's Favorite No. 2..................	40.9	55.4
Average................................	35.4	51.4

was repeated in 1908,[48] the effects of the freeze of Jan. 12, 1909, following weather such that all buds may be regarded as dormant at the time, were quite different, the unthinned limbs losing 92.5 and the thinned 93.2 per cent. of their buds. Laboratory results are reported as follows:

"These results suggest that thinning has its effect on the rest period rather than on the intrinsic hardiness of the buds. Where the tree is bent under a heavy load and under the strain of bearing a heavy crop, as when it is not thinned, the moisture supply probably being partially shut off, the same condition will prevail, at least to some extent, as when the trees are not cultivated; they will become dormant earlier and end their rest period earlier. Thus thinning, like heavy pruning and fertilizing with nitrogen can be expected to increase the hardiness of peach fruit buds only in climates like that from Central Missouri South, where there is likely to be weather warm enough to start the buds into growth before the effect of the rest period ends."

Whitewashing and Shading.—Sunlight is an important influence in forcing buds.[252] The spraying of peach trees with whitewash resulted in a reduction of heat absorption, with the effects on blossoming shown in Table 33, arranged from a similar table by Whitten. These data

TABLE 33.—BLOSSOMING DATES OF WHITEWASHED PEACH TREES[252]

Variety	First blossoms		Full bloom		Last blossoms	
	White-washed	Not white-washed	White-washed	Not white-washed	White-washed	Not white-washed
Heath Cling....	Apr. 13	Apr. 11	Apr. 21	Apr. 18	Apr. 29	Apr. 27
Wonderful.....	Apr. 14	Apr. 11	Apr. 22	Apr. 18	Apr. 29	Apr. 25
Rivers' Early ..	Apr. 13	Apr. 9	Apr. —	Apr. 21	Apr. 29	Apr. 27
Silver Medal...	Apr. 13	Apr. 7	Apr. 18	Apr. 13	Apr. 28	Apr. 21

do not, however, show the full force of reduced sunlight absorption as its effectiveness would be greatest during the warm periods of winter while atmospheric temperatures are lower and when even slight development may result in winter killing. Somewhat similar results have been obtained with plums in Ontario, but not with the apple,[142] which blossoms much later when the air temperature has greater influence in proportion to heat of insolation than it has earlier in the season. Even farther south, because of the difficulty in keeping trees well covered with whitewash and the consequent expense involved together with the ever-present possibility of conditions that will kill buds despite the covering, this method is little used.

Board shelters have been found even more efficacious than whitewashing but again the expense involved precludes their use.[252] However, a choice tree or two can sometimes be located on the shady side of a building to good effect and sometimes a hill can be of advantage in securing partial shade from the low midwinter sun for a good sized orchard.

In General.—The peach has been used as illustrative matter here, because it has been studied the most thoroughly. More or less similar application may be made to Japanese plums, apricots, almonds and cherries.

Finally it should be emphasized that the breaking of the rest period in the buds is entirely independent of the roots and that efforts to retard blossom development during warm periods in the winter by mulching the ground to keep it frozen or by spreading snow on the ground around the trees are absolutely wasted. Trees open their buds while the soil about the roots is still frozen or after they have been cut away from the roots. Time and again evidence to this effect has been presented and afterward the same useless effort repeated. The winter rest period of buds can be influenced through the roots during the growing season only.

Attention must be called to the greater application of the principles just outlined the farther south the location and their diminished applicability northward. Wiegand[255] reported that in New York fruit buds did not grow from about Nov. 15 until about Mar. 1, when apple and apricot buds began a relatively rapid development culminating in open blossoms 8 and 7 weeks later respectively. Peach buds did not begin their spring growth until Mar. 23 and came into blossom with the apricots on Apr. 23. It appears from these observations that the cooler and shorter growing season in the north, though it stops growth earlier by the calendar, makes the peach buds less advanced at the onset of the dormant period and less easily started into growth, while the colder winters add to this effect.

However, an interesting case is reported by Maynard[153] in Massachusetts. Early in November, 1884, peach buds appeared fully matured. Following warm weather late in the month the stamens and pistils increased measurably in size and the bud scales loosened. The minimum temperature to Dec. 11 was 18°F.; at this time some buds had been killed, but the majority were unhurt and the petals had begun to take on color. Following a minimum of 10°F. on Dec. 19 and 20 all fruit buds were destroyed.

Premature starting from the rest period is, however, a less common occurrence in northern peach regions. The very practices recommended for retarding it, if carried out too thoroughly in northern regions, though they might conceivably benefit the grower once in 20 seasons, would in the other 19 make his trees more liable to injury because immature and he would probably have damaged trees in 10 of these years. The southern grower guarding perhaps once against immaturity would suffer from precocious bud development 10 times. Each grower must determine the danger more commonly met in his orchard and steer wide of this particular rock, hoping he will no more than scrape his keel on the other. At the same time the grower in "southern" regions may be on the northern limit for certain of the southern peach groups and thus in the same orchard he may have to contend with short rest period in one variety and with immaturity in another.

Injuries to Vegetative Tissues

Sunscald is the common name of a late winter injury likely to occur in the north as well as in the south.   It is found on all types of fruit trees, on European chestnut and on various shade and forest trees.   Very small trees are rarely troubled by winter sunscald and trees old enough to develop thick, scaly bark are less subject in the parts so protected. Attention is drawn to the injury by the dead and dry appearance of the bark on the southwest side of the trunk where the sun strikes strongest between noon and 2 o'clock.   Sometimes this area is filled with a fermented fluid and the injury is called "sour sap."   Later the bark may loosen and fall away leaving an exposed area of dead sap-wood.   Many trees pruned to an open center are affected at the crotch or even high on the south side of those scaffold limbs that lean to the north.   In this last position the sun's rays are received nearly at right angles and the injury there is in many cases very severe.

The chief importance of this injury lies in its ultimate effects rather than in its immediate results.   It leads at once, obviously, to partial obstruction of conduction of nutrient and food materials, but of greater moment is the exposure to fungi and borers and the resultant mechanical weakening of the tree.

Distinguished from Summer Sunscald and Injuries Associated with Immaturity.—Distinction between this type and winter killing associated with immaturity on the one hand and between this type and summer sunscald on the other is sometimes difficult.   In fact some writers have denied the existence of sunscald and some have maintained that summer heat never kills bark.   Evidence showing that bark is sometimes killed by high temperatures is easily gathered.   Fisher[84] quotes Vonhausen as finding, between the sapwood and bark, a temperature of 120°F. when the air temperature was 91°F., while in Bavaria, Hartig observed a temperature of 131°F. between the bark and sapwood of some isolated 80-year old spruce trees.   This is a lethal temperature for leaves and herbaceous shoots and is presumably so for cambium cells.   In forests when an opening is made, the standing trees on the north side of the clearing in many cases show the sunscald high on the south side of their trunks.   Young apple trees, set late in the spring in sandy soil and headed back so they had little protecting top, have been observed even in New Hampshire, to show severe sunscald by midsummer.

Caution should be observed, however, in attributing all injuries on the southwest side of the tree to late winter sunscald. Balmer[15] describing the effects of a November freeze in Washington mentions that trees with high trunks, leaning from the afternoon sun, suffered notably. In several cases the bark on the southwest side of the trunks split open. Investigators seem to have overlooked the possible effects of radiation in this connection. It is shown under Frost Injury that the temperature near the soil on a frosty night may be 10° or more lower than that recorded by a sheltered thermometer near by. An October temperature of 20°F. is not uncommon; with suitable radiation conditions the temperature near the soil, if 10° lower, would be 10°F., low enough to cause considerable injury to immature tissues. Since somewhat lower temperatures occur over sod under these conditions than over cultivated ground the occurrence of "sunscald" in sod orchards need not be surprising. Injury of this kind is obviously associated with immaturity. Therefore it is not safe to consider sunscald altogether a late winter injury.

Moisture and Temperature Conditions in the Affected Parts.—The winter sunscald, however, is much more common. It is not induced by simple insolation but by interacting effects on heat and cold. This is quite evidently the malady described by Downing[68] in 1846 as "frozen sap blight" and rather confused with pear blight by many of the early American pomological writers. The description by Downing clearly indicates this form, as he includes *Ailanthus*, Spanish chestnut and catalpa among the plants affected. He attributed the trouble to sudden thawing and proposed as a remedy shading the south side of the trunk and whitewashing. Somewhat later he recorded that on Dec. 19, 1846, a bright mild day, with snow on the ground, a naked thermometer registered 97°F. while one with a whitewashed bulb registered 79°F.[69] Various suggestions as to the way sunscald is brought about have been made, including rapid thawing, increased flow of sap followed by freezing so that the bark is pushed off, breaking of the rest period in the warmed area and alternate freezing and thawing. Müller-Thurgau[85] found in March a water content of 53.8 per cent. in the bark on the south side of a plum tree and 48.5 per cent. on the north while the bark of a tree wrapped with rushes showed moisture percentages of 51.5 and 51.3 on the south and north sides respectively. He considered these figures to corroborate the suggestion that a localized breaking of the rest period subjected the affected areas to injury from subsequent cold.

The most extensive investigation on this phase of winter killing is that of Mix.[164] Particular attention was given to the cambium since this tissue suffers severe injury "and without injury to the cambium and outermost xylem the bark would not separate from the wood." Observations of temperature under the bark on the northeast and southwest sides of apple trunks showed no significant differences on cloudy days but marked variations on bright days, demonstrating the warming effect of the sun's rays. Tables 34 and 35 are selected from data reported by Mix from these observations and are representative of his more extended figures. The temperatures for Mar. 10 are worthy of special attention,

TABLE 34.—TREE TEMPERATURES ON CLOUDY DAYS
(*After Mix*[164])

Date	Hour	Southwest side, degrees Centigrade	Northeast side, degrees Centigrade	Air, degrees Centigrade
Jan. 15	11:00	−6.9	−7.5	−5.5
Jan. 16	1:30	3.3	2.8	2.6
Jan. 17	1:30	−1.9	−3.0	−3.9
Jan. 19	1:00	−3.9	−3.9	−2.5
Jan. 20	11:40	0.0	0.0	1.1
Jan. 21	1:00	0.0	0.0	−2.2
Jan. 23	1:10	−2.2	−2.2	0.0
Jan. 24	1:10	−0.5	−0.5	4.4

TABLE 35.—TREE TEMPERATURES ON SUNNY DAYS
(Data from same tree as Table 34)
(*After Mix*[164])

Date	Hour	Southwest side, degrees Centigrade	Northeast side, degrees Centigrade	Air, degrees Centigrade
Jan. 14	3:00	−2.8	−12.2	−12.2
Jan. 26	3:25	1.1	−2.8	−1.4
Feb. 2	1:30	12.2	−1.1	0.5
Feb. 3	1:35	15.0	2.8	9.4
Feb. 4	1:05	12.8	0.8	1.6
Feb. 8	2:10	−0.5	−4.4	−6.7
Feb. 9	12:50	−4.4	−9.4	−8.3
Feb. 13	1:00	−6.4	−15.0	−11.7
Feb. 15	2:50	3.9	−9.4	−12.2
Feb. 23	1:00	−6.4	−11.4	−14.4
Feb. 24	1:00	−2.8	−16.1	......
Feb. 25	12:55	1.7	−9.7	−5.6
Feb. 26	11:00	−1.9	−10.0	......
Mar. 10	1:30	20.5	0.0	1.1
Mar. 12	12:50	15.0	−3.3	−4.4
Mar. 24	1:15	12.2	1.7	3.9
Mar. 25	1:00	11.1	5.0	8.9

being 32°F. on the northeast side and 69°F. on the southwest side at the same time. On Feb. 10, Mix observed on the southwest side of one tree a fall from 59° to 27°F. between 2 o'clock and 9, the air temperature dropping from 28° to 19°F. in the same time, while on the northeast side the temperature fell from 25° to 19°F. The temperature of the southwest side dropped 32°F. while that of the northeast side fell 6°F. On another tree the temperature on the southwest side fell between 5 o'clock and 6 (sunset at 5:30) from −0.3° to −14.4°C. while on the northeast side it dropped from −9.4° to −18.3°C. This, it should be emphasized, was in 1 hour. By morning the temperatures on both sides were frequently observed to be approximately equal. The southwest side of a tree trunk is evidently subject to wider fluctuations in temperature and to more sudden falling of temperature after the sun's heat is withdrawn at sunset. Even more striking temperature differences may occur occasionally. In fact Mix records a temperature of 92°F. on the southwest side on Feb. 20, while the temperature on the northeast side was 35°F.

The effect of snow in relation to sunscald seems to have escaped the attention of writers on this subject. Sunlight striking snow is to a large extent reflected and a late winter snow is bound to have no little influence in intensifying the heating on the southwest side of tree trunks. If, as frequently happens in late winter in northern latitudes, a snowfall during the night is followed by a clear warm day and a night of considerable cold the change in temperature of the southwest side must be considerable and abrupt.

Similarly, the influence of color of bark in absorbing or reflecting the sun's rays often is of importance in determining temperature of the inner bark and cambium and therefore in minimizing or accentuating sunscald. Brown, black and brownish-red barks have been found to absorb the most heat and maintain the highest temperatures in full sunlight, while white and red barks show temperatures closest to those of the surrounding air.[108] When the air temperature is just below freezing there is repeated freezing and thawing of black or brown bark with every passing cloud, a condition associated with sunscald. On the other hand, bark that reflects the rays of the red end of the spectrum is subject to far less temperature change. This may explain in part the greater susceptibility of the apple over the pear to sunscald.

Rapid freezing, especially during the first part of the temperature fall, has been shown by Chandler[48] to cause killing at a relatively high point. These are the very conditions just recorded and seem adequate to explain killing by sunscald without any assumption that growth has started. Artificial freezings accompanied by microscopic examination of tissues made by Mix showed no difference in hardiness on either side when frozen under identical conditions. Rapid freezing killed at −20°C. while slow freezing caused no injury at $-28°C$. As spring advances these tissues become less hardy, but equally on all sides of the trunk. The conclusion seems inevitable, therefore, that it is rapid freezing after sundown that causes winter sunscald.

Preventive Measures.—Prevention of the rapid fall is best effected by keeping the day temperature down. Anything that will shade the trunk, as a stake or a bundle of corn stalks, will do this well. Whitewash also, because of its low heat absorption, may be used to advantage.

TABLE 36.—TEMPERATURES OF WHITEWASHED, TARRED AND UNTREATED TREES[164]

Date	Air, degrees Centigrade	Untreated		Whitewashed		Tarred	
		Northeast, degrees Centigrade	Southwest, degrees Centigrade	Northeast, degrees Centigrade	Southwest, degrees Centigrade	Northeast, degrees Centigrade	Southwest, degrees Centigrade
Jan. 15........	3.9	1.7	11.1	0.6	2.2	3.3	20.5
Jan. 30........	−5.6	−8.3	−4.4	−8.9	−2.8	−4.9	13.9
Feb. 4........	0.0	−3.3	7.2	−4.1	1.1	−0.6	17.8
Feb. 10.......	−1.7	−3.9	15.0	−6.7	−0.6	−1.1	29.0
Feb. 19.......	3.9	−1.7	17.2	−2.2	5.0	0.0	31.1
Feb. 20.......	6.1	0.0	21.7	−0.6	6.1	1.7	33.3
Average.....	1.1	−2.6	11.3	−3.2	1.8	−0.3	24.3

Table 36, arranged from data reported by Mix, shows the sharp contrast in sunny side temperatures between a whitewashed and an untreated tree, a difference that becomes more marked as the temperatures go higher. The difference appears considerable enough to save treated trees from sunscald in many cases. The same table suggests also a reason why gas tar, occasionally applied as a borer repellant, is said frequently to kill trees. The difference between the temperatures under whitewash and under tar is due apparently to the respective heat absorptive powers of white and black colors, as their minimum early morning temperatures were practically the same.

INJURIES DUE TO SUDDEN COLD

Though some types of injury already discussed as associated with immaturity of tissue might be considered to belong in the category of injuries due to sudden cold, they may be classed more correctly as due to untimely cold. Here, too, probably belongs the type known as winter sunscald which is discussed under late winter injuries but the present section is limited in its application to injuries occasioned by a sudden change from moderate cold to intense cold.

General Effects.—Chandler[48] has been quoted earlier as reporting greater injury to plant tissue attendant upon sudden lowering of temperature. His statement, however, should be reproduced here: "The rate of temperature fall is very important indeed, especially in case of winter buds. In fact, apple buds can be frozen in a chamber surrounded by salt and ice rapidly enough so that practically all of them will be killed at a temperature of 0°F., or slightly below, while it is well known that they may go through a temperature of 20 to 30°F. below zero with but slight injury where the temperature fall is not so rapid. . . . the killing temperature of rapidly frozen twigs was 4.5° higher than those of the more slowly frozen twigs and even then the buds of the rapidly frozen twigs killed the worst." Table 37, chosen from several reported by Chandler, shows the difference vividly.

TABLE 37.—EFFECT OF SLOW AND RAPID TEMPERATURE FALL ON CHERRY FRUIT BUDS[48]

Variety	Manner of freezing	Date	Number of buds	Percentage killed
Montmorency............	Slowly to −20°C.	Mar. 2	163	3.0
Montmorency............	Rapidly to −20°C.	Feb. 29	130	96.0
Early Richmond.........	Slowly to −20°C.	Mar. 9	297	5.0
Early Richmond.........	Rapidly to −20°C.	Mar. 14	263	98.0

However, it should be remembered that Chandler found also a rapid fall to −12°C. more injurious than a rapid fall from −12°C. to the killing temperature. This is shown strikingly in Table 38, adapted from a table by Chandler.

No data bearing on this matter drawn from field observations are available. Fortunately, as Chandler states, "In this investigation it

TABLE 38.—EFFECT OF RAPID FALL EARLY AND LATE IN THE FREEZING[48]

Variety	Manner of freezing	Date	Number of buds	Percentage killed
Elberta peach..............	Slow to −12°; fast −12° to −16°	Dec. 20	135	3.7
Elberta peach..............	Fast to −12°; slow −12° to −16°	Dec. 20	77	71.4
Elberta peach..............	Slow to −17.5°	Dec. 20	129	6.2
Elberta peach..............	Fast to −16.0°	Dec. 8	135	98.5
Montmorency cherry.......	Fast to −12°; slow to −20°	Feb. 24	142	75.0
Montmorency cherry.......	Slow to −12°; fast to −20°	Feb. 27	136	15.4
Montmorency cherry.......	Fast to −20°	Feb. 27	130	96.0
Montmorency cherry.......	Slow to −20°	Mar. 2	163	3.0

was not possible to cause the temperature to fall more slowly than the most rapid fall to be observed naturally in the climate of this station (Missouri)." Hence, the "slow" of Tables 37 and 38 is the "fast" of nature. Seldom, in nature, are temperature changes more rapid or more extreme than the one recorded on New Year's Day, 1864, in the northern Mississippi valley. A drop of 50°F. from temperatures above freezing was registered at many points within a 24-hour period. Yet at places in western Michigan along the lake shore, where such a temperature fall was recorded but where minima were not below −14°F., peach trees bore heavy crops the following summer.[35]

However, it seems quite possible that certain "warm spots" in an orchard may heat considerably during a clear, cold day only to have a very rapid drop in temperature following sunset and that some of the injury attributed to buds "starting growth" during winter is in reality due to a sudden and considerable drop of this kind. Nevertheless, in a large number of cases when wholesale destruction of fruit buds occurs it can be traced to some other cause.

Trunk Splitting.—Trunk splitting is much more common in forest and shade trees and most of the literature on this type of injury deals with these trees. Nevertheless, it is by no means unknown in fruit trees; instances are on record of fruit trees splitting through the trunk.[232]

Close measurements in Europe have shown that temperatures under the freezing point induce a contraction in the trunks of various forest trees which with long continued freezing reaches the magnitude of an annual ring.[86] Deciduous trees react much more readily than evergreen. The generally accepted view is that a rapid fall of temperature induces a considerable contraction of the bark and outer wood while the inner wood, still at a much higher temperature, does not shrink equally; hence the splitting. The cracks start generally at the bark and proceed radially toward the center of the tree or even beyond. Objection has been raised that clefts extending beyond the center could not be caused in this way but if it be assumed that the center of the tree is already frozen, those who have cut frozen wood and know how easily it splits will have little difficulty in believing that an initial cracking at the periphery may be transmitted beyond the center because of the glassy nature of frozen wood and the pull of the contracting bark.

Wind may, as has been suggested,[101] be associated with this type of injury under certain circumstances but there can be no doubt whatever that splitting occurs on absolutely still nights, the sharp, rifle-like report accompanying the fissure being very noticeable under such conditions. Fisher[33] discusses the subject at some length. He reports that most frost cracks occur in cold weather between midnight and morning and may close again with rising temperature; further, that sometimes an internal frost crack occurs, the sap-wood rending while the bark holds intact. Hardwoods with large medullary rays are most liable to this injury, oak, beech, walnut, elm, ash and sweet chestnut being mentioned as specially susceptible in Europe.

The cracks are said to occur most frequently in the lower part of the trunk, especially where growth is uneven, as near roots, at knots or where the stem is eccentric. The south side, the region of most vigorous circumferential growth, suffers most, according to Fisher. Large old trees suffer more than young because under conditions inducing this injury there is in the old trees a greater difference in temperature between center and periphery. Late winter, when the sap has begun to flow, is said to be the most favorable time for developments of this kind. Under normal conditions these cracks close with a rise in temperature and the tissues in time grow together; this spot is weaker, however, and subject to a recurrence of the injury. Repeated splitting and healing may give rise to a lipped callus.

Observations in America agree generally with Fisher's, adding the maple to the list of subject trees and finding perhaps more cracking on long, straight-grained, clear boles. Indeed it seems that the two chief reasons for the comparative resistance of fruit trees lie in their being low headed, with short areas of trunk free from branches and in their smaller trunks. Under cultivation they probably do not mature so early as forest trees and the sappy growth of young trees may be injured in early winter in contrast with late winter for forest trees. It is stated that fruit trees growing late and entering the winter with wood not thoroughly ripened are most subject to frost cracks in Colorado.[63]

On apple limbs an injury similar in appearance, and likely to be confused with this type, sometimes occurs when there is one sided development of the limb so that a heavy load of fruit is borne on one side unbalanced by any considerable load on the other side, resulting in a fracture in a vertical plane. Occasionally after a nearly horizontal limb is headed back to a large branch ascending at about 45° a heavy load on the ascending branch will cause a splitting of the upper part of the limb from the lower, the fracture being in this case horizontal. These injuries obviously occur near harvest and should be differentiated from the true "frost cracks" without difficulty.

The reverse of the conditions described in connection with radial clefts, that is to say, the sudden warming of the outer layers of the trunk while the inside is still cold, is said to produce a different kind of injury, known to foresters as a "cup-shake." Here the cleavage instead of being in a radial direction is along an annual ring, involving a smaller or greater amount of the circumference. This form may possibly occur in fruit trees but in most cases of separation along annual rings in such plants the injury may be traced to direct killing just inside the cambium, discussed under Blackheart. Even under natural conditions the cupshake is far less common than the frost crack.

In connection with trunk splitting, the splitting of the bark while the wood remains intact should be mentioned. As already indicated this is generally in immature tissues, produced possibly at times by the same conditions that induce trunk splitting but more frequently by the conditions commonly associated with crown rot and crotch injury. It should be understood, also, that splitting of the wood sometimes seems to be associated to some extent with immaturity[15] and it may possibly, as for example, when it occurs during protracted and intense cold, be due to drying out.

Summary.—Winter injury takes many different aspects, 10 more or less distinct forms being considered in this discussion. Many different environmental conditions are associated with winter injury, though for convenience these may be grouped in three classes: (1) conditions encouraging immaturity of tissues, (2) conditions leading to winter drought, (3) conditions leading to premature quickening in late winter and early spring. Certain sections or regions are particularly subject to extremes of one kind or another.

Injuries associated with immaturity are especially common in the more humid sections with short growing seasons. Plants adapted to comparatively long growing seasons when taken to sections with shorter growing seasons are particularly subject to injuries of this character. "Second growth" is likely to be immature and subject to winter injury. Cultural practices which encourage late vegetative growth should be avoided in regions where immaturity is a frequent problem. Crown injury and crotch injury are in most cases associated with immaturity of tissues at the affected points. Wind and variation in temperature between different sides of the limb or trunk may be contributing factors. Treatment for these localized injuries should be both preventive and remedial.

Injuries due to winter drought are especially common in sections like the Dakotas and Wyoming where winter precipitation is low, the snow covering scanty and the evaporating power of the air high. The tissues are desiccated by the cold dry winds and recovery of turgidity is difficult or impossible because of low soil moisture, deep soil freezing and the inability of the conducting system to function while frozen. Protective measures include the use of winter irrigation, thorough cultivation, frost-killed cover crops and windbreaks or shelter belts.

Many cases of injury from cold during late winter are associated with a breaking of the rest period, resulting in some resumption of growth and an accompanying decrease in resistance to low temperatures. They are brought on by periods of mild weather during late winter. Fruit buds particularly are susceptible to injury from this cause. Buds in certain positions are especially subject to this form of injury. The ending of the rest period in midwinter or spring is related to some extent to the time of its inception in the fall. Consequently factors or practices which delay its beginning tend to protect against the forms of winter injury incident to its breaking. Among such practices may be mentioned: Moderately late cultivation, reasonably heavy pruning, applications of nitrogenous fertilizers and thinning. The end of the dormant period may be delayed somewhat by whitewashing and shading, which reduce heat absorption.

Most sunscald is attributable to extreme and rapid fluctuations in temperature of the affected tissues. Injuries similar in appearance sometimes are caused by midsummer heat or they may be associated with immaturity coupled with low temperature.

In general, rapid decreases in temperature are more damaging than more gradual decreases to the same or even to a lower point. A special form of injury due to very rapid temperature decline is trunk splitting or frost crack.

CHAPTER XVII

WINTER INJURY TO THE ROOTS

Root killing is very common in sections where winter precipitation is light and it is rather common in humid sections where it is not always recognized. It may occur, regardless of precipitation, at any point where the soil freezes at all deeply (see Table 39); it is characteristically associated with light and dry soils and with scanty snow cover. In orchards on rolling land it is very likely to be localized, due to differences in the depth of snow covering. If no part other than the roots is injured the tree may start growth in the normal way, sending out vegetative shoots and blossoms and perhaps even setting fruit; some time in the summer, usually with the first warm, dry weather, it dies. Felled trees will sometimes start growth in a comparable manner. If only a part of the roots have been injured, the effect is quite likely to be a slowing in top growth. As the damage is below ground, it escapes ordinary observation and the slow growth of the tree may seem quite inexplicable. This condition may last for several years or until the balance between root and top is more nearly restored.

Soil Temperatures in Winter.—For a thorough understanding of the nature of root killing and of the conditions associated with it, some knowledge of soil conditions during the winter and of the distribution of roots in the soil is necessary. Table 40, taken from a report covering 12 years of soil temperature observations at Lincoln, Neb.,[230] shows quantitatively the effect of depth on soil temperatures.

TABLE 39.—MEAN SOIL TEMPERATURES AT 6 INCHES[230]
(Degrees Fahrenheit)

	December	January	February	March
Pennsylvania	34.9	32.0	31.4	32.9
Idaho	35.2	32.1	32.1	32.9
Minnesota	....	23.0	21.0	38.0
Wyoming	24.1	22.2	22.7	31.0
Nebraska	32.0	28.6	27.8	36.6
Michigan	·33.8	32.0	32.0	33.5
Woburn, England	39.5	39.0	39.1	39.9
Colorado	34.0	27.7	30.4	36.3
Illinois	34.9	32.7	31.5	39.3
Alabama	57.0	56.1	57.1	53.4

The Pennsylvania figures are for State College, 1892–1896 inclusive; Idaho, for Moscow, 1903–1904 (Idaho Exp. Sta. *Bul.* **49**); Minnesota, 1889 (a mild winter); Wyoming, averages for Laramie, 1895, 1898, 1899; Nebraska, from Table 39; Michigan, selected as typical, from Mich. Agr. Exp. Sta., *Tech. Bul.* **26**, p. 104; Woburn, England, *2d Rept.*, Woburn Experiment Farms (1900); Colorado, Fort Collins; Illinois (Urbana), (1897–1916); from *Bul.* **208**, Ill. Agr. Exp. Sta.; Alabama, from Ala. Agr. Exp. Sta. *Bul.* **10**.

Table 41 is arranged from the same source and is introduced to show absolute minima at several depths, over a series of years.

TABLE 40.—AVERAGE SOIL TEMPERATURES AT LINCOLN, NEB.[230]
(Degrees Fahrenheit)

Depth	January	February	March	April	May	June
Air...................	25.2	24.2	35.8	52.1	61.9	71.0
6 inches................	28.6	27.8	36.6	53.3	65.1	75.7
12 inches...............	31.2	30.2	35.4	49.3	60.7	69.9
24 inches...............	35.4	33.5	35.4	45.6	56.2	64.6
36 inches...............	38.5	35.5	35.8	43.8	53.5	61.3

Depth	July	August	September	October	November	December
Air...................	76.0	74.5	67.6	55.5	38.7	28.3
6 inches................	81.6	80.1	72.0	57.8	41.5	32.0
12 inches...............	75.7	75.7	69.2	57.8	44.7	35.2
24 inches...............	70.2	72.2	68.7	60.0	49.2	40.1
36 inches...............	67.4	69.8	67.6	61.6	52.2	43.3

TABLE 41.—MINIMUM SOIL TEMPERATURES AT LINCOLN, NEB.[230]
(Degrees Fahrenheit)

Winter	6 inches	12 inches	24 inches	36 inches
1893–1894	19.6	24.5	30.2	34.2
1894–1895	14.9	22.9*	29.2*	29.8
1895–1896	18.0	27.4	35.5	38.0
1896–1897	22.0	27.0	33.0	35.1
1897–1898	20.0	26.5	34.5	36.5
1898–1899	7.0	13.5	24.0	30.5
1899–1900	22.0	28.0	33.0	35.0
1900–1901	24.0	28.0	34.0	36.0
1901–1902	19.0	27.0	33.0	35.0

* Data incomplete.

The maximum depth of frost penetration at the same point has been reported as detailed in Table 42. Recently, however, it has been shown that soil does not freeze until it is cooled several degrees below 32°F.[33] Consequently since these figures were based on the assumption of freezing at 32° the actual frost penetration was not so great as is indicated.

Critical Temperatures for Tree Roots.—In the section on Water Relations the extent and the depth of some fruit tree root systems are

TABLE 42.—MAXIMUM DEPTH OF FROST PENETRATION AT LINCOLN, NEB.[230]

Date	Depth, inches	Date	Depth, inches
Mar. 9, 1891	30.9	Jan. 19, 1897	21.2
Jan. 19, 1892	21.9	Feb. 8, 1898	16.8
Feb. 12, 1893	32.2	Feb. 10 to Mar. 28, 1899	36.0
Feb. 27, 1894	29.0	Feb. 29, 1900	21.6
Feb. 7–27, 1895	36.0*	Feb. 12, 1901	20.0
Jan. 4, 1896	18.4	Feb. 9, 1902	21.6

* Not recorded to maximum penetration.

indicated. The data there given indicate that in the majority of fruit growing regions by far the greater part of the feeding roots is in the surface foot of soil.

The finer roots of beech, oak and ash, trees that are considered at least fairly hardy, die at temperatures between 8.6° to 3.2°F.[237] and the roots of other hardy plants are reported killed at temperatures from 14° to 5°F.[48] Working with apple roots, under laboratory conditions, Chandler found that "the killing temperature varies from −3°C. in summer to about −12°C. [26.6°F. to 10.4°F.] in late winter with rather rapid freezing." He remarks further, "They are still very tender in autumn when tissue above ground has begun to increase rapidly in hardiness . . . as the roots extend away from the crown they become more and more tender and apparently this tenderness is greater on those roots that extend downward into the soil." It may, then, be concluded that the roots of most plants are more tender, at a given temperature, than the parts above ground. Parenthetically, though Chandler's statement as to increasing tenderness with increasing distance from the crown may be accepted, it should be understood that root killing is frequently observed at or near the crown and not elsewhere, probably because this part is nearest the top soil and therefore exposed to colder temperatures, as shown in Table 40.

Carrick[45] found a marked difference in tenderness of roots at different seasons in New York. "The material frozen in October and November," he states, "shows a marked tenderness compared with roots tested in February and March. The period of maximum resistance seems to end somewhat before the last of March, tho the date would, of course, vary with the conditions affecting after-ripening and possibly also with the variety . . . This range of hardiness indicates a difference in resistance of between 3 and 4 Centigrade degrees. These seasonal differences obtain, not only in the apple seedlings, but in all the roots reported in this paper."

Another interesting factor in root injury is reported by Carrick. He finds that, "the resistance is in direct proportion to the diameter of the root," and suggests that this fact accounts for the occasional observation in laboratory freezings of root killing at the tips when the roots near the crown are uninjured.

A study of Table 39, with the killing temperatures given above in mind, shows that the average soil temperatures in the recognized fruit growing sections noted are substantially above the danger point and suggests one reason why fruit growing in certain other sections requires some special precautions. Attention is due, further, to the consideration that these are average figures in which fluctuations to lower points are submerged. In Table 41 the actual seasonal minimum temperatures at one point are segregated. It is particularly significant that the winter of 1898–1899, when the soil temperature at Lincoln, Neb., reached 7°F., was the winter characterized by an extreme amount of root killing in Iowa,[62] Wisconsin[94] and Ontario.[141]

Factors Influencing Frost Penetration.—Temperature alone, or air temperature alone certainly, is not the sole controlling factor in root killing. A temperature of −20°F. maintained for several days has caused extensive root killing in Ontario.[61] Goff[94] in an interesting survey of an extensive area involved in the freeze of February, 1899, found little damage in several regions where the unofficial temperatures went as low as −50° or even −52°F., though in no case where root killing occurred had the temperature gone below −36°F. A report from Waukee, Iowa, indicated root killing with a minimum of −24°F.; other localities suffered severely at −23°F.

Protection Afforded by Snow.—The principal difference lay in the fact that in some sections snow lay on the ground while in others there was none. Goff's analysis showed 34 localities with more or less snow at the time of the freeze; of these, 20 reported definitely that the chief injury was in the tops, three reported roots and tops equally damaged, while in one there was more injury to roots than to tops in apples but more in the tops of cherries and plums than in the roots. Fifty-seven localities were without snow at the time of the freeze; definite statements of comparative injury indicated 43 cases where the principal damage was in the roots, 3 placed it in the tops and 1 reported roots and tops equally damaged.

Similar testimonials concerning the value of a snow covering are common in pomological literature. Quantitative data applicable here are given by Bouyoucos.[31] Table 43, arranged from his figures taken at a depth of 3 inches, shows the temperature differences between ground without snow, ground under compacted snow, under uncompacted snow and under vegetation plus compacted snow.

TABLE 43.—EFFECT OF SNOW COVER ON SOIL TEMPERATURE, JANUARY, 1915[31]
(Degrees Fahrenheit)

Monthly average		Maximum-minimum				Air		
	Bare	Snow, compact	Uncompact	Uncompact + vegetation	Maximum	Minimum	Average
Maximum.................	28.79	29.65	31.51	34.82	.....	.....	.....
Minimum.................	24.95	28.66	31.11	34.55	27.96	13.80	20.64
Range....................	3.84	0.99	0.40	0.27	.....	.....	.....
Jan. 6, { maximum.......	32.30	32.00	32.00	35.70	.....	.....	.....
{ minimum.......	32.10	31.80	32.00	35.50	39.00	33.00	36.00
Jan. 29, { maximum.......	20.00	22.30	29.60	33.00	.....	.....	.....
{ minimum........	14.50	20.80	29.00	32.50	13.00	−13.00	0.00
Jan. 30, { maximum.......	21.20	21.10	28.80	32.80	.....	.....	.....
{ minimum........	7.50	15.60	27.00	32.30	18.00	−13.00	2.00

The minimum for Jan. 30 is certainly at the danger point for tree roots in bare ground, while under compacted snow it is 8.1°F. higher and under vegetation plus compacted snow it is almost 25° higher. The fruit grower cannot induce snowfall at his will but he sometimes has a choice between a slope where snow will remain and one where it will melt away with a little warm weather. He knows that knolls and wind swept spots in general are likely to need special care and that cover crops and windbreaks tend to hold snow that might otherwise blow away.

Different Systems of Soil Management.—A protective covering of vegetation can be provided by the grower with more surety than a snow

TABLE 44.—AVERAGE MINIMUM SOIL TEMPERATURES IN UNCULTIVATED AND CULTIVATED SOIL AND IN SOD[31]
(Degrees Fahrenheit)

Month	Uncultivated (bare)	Cultivated (bare)	Sod
Dec., 1914.........................	31.92	33.26	35.34
Jan., 1915.........................	31.11	32.59	34.55
Feb., 1915.........................	30.70	32.49	33.52

covering. Table 44, arranged from data by Bouyoucos,[31] shows the effect of this covering on minimum soil temperatures at 3 inches depth. The superior protection afforded by cultivated, bare soil as contrasted with compacted soil is worthy of note.

Craig[62] in Iowa reported soil temperature at 6 inches depth on a January day, after hard freezing, two degrees warmer in sod than in cultivated soil.

Depth of freezing is a fairly good indicator, though indirect, of soil temperature. Gourley[97] records observations made in New Hampshire in March when freezing was at its greatest depth for the season; these are shown in Table 45. These figures are of special interest since they show the protective effect of increased cover-crop growth induced by fertilizer. applications. The "cultivated with cover crop" plot had a scanty growth.

TABLE 45.—DEPTH OF FREEZING AS AFFECTED BY SOIL COVERING

Clean cultivated (no cover crop)........................ 16 inches
Cultivated, with cover crop............................. 15 inches
Sod.. 12 inches
Fertilizer, cultivation and cover crop.................... 10 inches
Fertilizer (excess nitrogen) cultivation and cover crop....... 7 inches

Sandsten[202] made measurements of the depth of frost penetration in early February under different crops in Wisconsin. Table 46 shows his

TABLE 46.—FROST PENETRATION UNDER DIFFERENT COVER CROPS[202]

Bluegrass sod... 18.0 inches
Clean cultivation (no cover crop)....................... 16.0 inches
Rape.. 15.0 inches
Oats.. 8.0 inches
Hairy vetch... 7.5 inches

data. He interprets these observations to emphasize the protective value of an uncompacted cover, the bluegrass sod offering little insulation because of the lack of dead air spaces. He also considers the lower amount of moisture in sod land to have an important bearing. In connection with the data here cited from Gourley and from Sandsten it should be recalled that the soil does not freeze until its temperature is several degrees below 32°F.

Oskamp[173] reports soil temperatures observed in Indiana with different soil covers. Table 47 is arranged from his data. It should be noted

TABLE 47.—MONTHLY MINIMUM SOIL TEMPERATURES[173]
(Degrees Fahrenheit)

	Clean cultivation and cover crop	Straw mulch
Jan., 1915....................................	31.0	34.0
Feb., 1915....................................	32.0	34.0
Dec., 1915....................................	32.5	38.0
Jan., 1916....................................	28.5	35.0
Feb., 1916....................................	32.0	35.0
Dec., 1916....................................	33.0	35.0

that this comparison is between straw mulch and land growing a cover crop, which has been shown to have higher minimum temperatures than uncultivated or cultivated bare land or sod. A direct comparison of the extremes is not available, but by comparing minimum temperatures in bare land with those in sod (Tables 44 and 45), then sod with cover crop (Tables 45 and 46) and finally cover crop with straw mulch, some idea of the superior protective qualities of the straw mulch can be formed. As will appear later, the difference between safe and killing temperatures for roots is slight and a few degrees are apparently more important below ground than above.

Soil Type.—Increased injury in sandy soil has been reported so frequently that the precise temperature conditions existing in the lighter soils should be examined carefully. Table 48 shows absolute minimum temperatures for certain months, recorded at a depth of six inches, in soils of different types.

TABLE 48.—ABSOLUTE MINIMUM TEMPERATURES IN DIFFERENT SOILS
(*After Bouyoucos*[31])
(Degrees Fahrenheit)

	Gravel	Sand	Loam	Clay	Peat
Dec., 1912..............	29.0	29.7	30.3	30.2	31.4
Jan., 1913..............	30.8	29.1	30.9	31.2	31.1
Feb., 1913..............	**21.1**	**17.3**	**22 3**	**23.1**	**19.1**
Dec., 1914..............	30.0	25.3	31.5	30.3	32.6
Jan., 1915..............	30.5	27.1	31.4	32.0	32.4
Feb., 1915..............	32.1	32.4	31.3	31.9	32.2
Average.............	28.9	26.8	29.6	29.8	29.8

These figures show a sufficient difference to indicate a possible cause for increased root killing in sandy soils. It should be stated, however, that Bouyoucos records a very marked tendency for all soils to assume a uniform temperature if air temperatures remain stable long. The lower minima in sand are due probably to more rapid conductivity so that a cold spell of short duration, as most cold waves are, would take effect here but be over before it would affect some of the other soils to the same extent. Thus, Bouyoucos states, "The 12-inch depth of gravel and sand froze Feb. 3, that of loam, clay and peat on Feb. 5, or 2 days later; while the 18-inch depth of the various soils froze as follows: gravel, Feb. 6, sand, Feb. 8, clay, Feb. 10, loam, Feb. 11, that of peat did not completely freeze, its temperature remaining a few tenths of a degree above 32°F. throughout the rest of the winter." As to the effect of organic matter in soil, he comments on his investigations as follows:

"The minimum temperature attained was highest in peat, slightly less and about the same in the various soils treated with peat and lowest in the untreated sand." A continued turning under in the spring of cover crops tends to raise the soil content of organic matter. The cover crop protects, then, while above ground by blanketing the soil and when turned under it affords some protection in the following winter through the increased amount of organic matter it has supplied. Thus in Washington, Overholser and Overley[174] found a temperature of 26.5°F. at a depth of 10 inches in a loose orchard soil with no snow covering; under similar conditions, but with the soil packed, the temperature was 19°F. Such differences in texture are due in a large measure to their content of organic matter.

Soil Moisture.—Another factor, possibly of equal importance, affecting root-killing in sandy soils, is the amount of moisture present. No evidence need be introduced here as to the comparatively low moisture content of the average sandy soil. Emerson[74] made some very interesting studies of the effects of moisture on killing, in which lots of 25 young trees each were exposed to a Nebraska winter, in boxes of loam soil with varying degrees of moisture. His tabular statement of results is reproduced here as Table 49.

TABLE 49.—ROOT-KILLING OF APPLE SEEDLINGS AS RELATED TO SOIL MOISTURE

Box	Where kept	Soil cover	Percentage of soil moisture	Number of roots		
				Uninjured	Injured	Dead
1	Outdoors	None	10.4	0	5	20
2	Outdoors	None	15.2	0	6	10
3	Outdoors	None	19.8	12	10	3
4	Outdoors	None	25.6	13	4	8
5	Outdoors	Straw mulch	16.0	18	7	0
6	Outdoors	Snow occasionally	15.8 ·	10	8	7
7	Cool, dry cave	None	10.0	25	0	0

Emerson comments on his results in part as follows: "That the great injury to the seedling roots in the drier soils is not due directly to the dryness alone but to dryness and cold combined, is evident from the fact that the roots were absolutely unhurt in equally dry soil kept in a cool dry cave. . . . That dryness alone was not responsible is shown by the comparatively slight injury to roots in rather dry soil which was protected by a 4-inch mulch of straw, while roots in bare soil of almost the same moisture content were very badly hurt.

"Just why severe freezing should injure roots worse in rather dry than in moist soil is not shown by the test reported above. On further investigation it may be found that roots are simply unable to withstand severe freezing or to recover from it unless surrounded by an abundance of moisture. Be this as it may, it is quite probable that one cause of the great injury in rather dry soil is alternate freezing and thawing . . . the more water a soil contains the less subject it is to frequent alternate freezing and thawing.

"The fact that the apple seedlings were much less seriously injured where protected by a mulch of straw than they were in bare ground is to be explained by the effect of mulches on freezing and thawing of the ground. The latter was tested during the winter of 1901–1902. The mulch protected the soil not only against severe freezing during cold nights, but also against alternate freezing and thawing. The temperature changes observed on February 2, 3 and 4, 1902—a very cold period—are especially interesting. The surface of the bare ground thawed during the middle of the day and froze severely each night. Two inches lower, however, the soil did not thaw out during this very cold weather, though the temperature changes between day and night were great. The temperature of the mulched ground, both at the surface and 2 inches beneath it, remained constantly below the freezing point and, moreover, varied but little during the period."

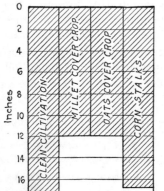

Fig. 31.—Depth of freezing under various covers, in absence of snow. (*After Emerson*[75])

Recent studies by Bouyoucos[32] suggest an interesting possibility in this connection. He shows that in practically all agricultural soils some of the moisture remains unfrozen at ordinary temperatures and, indeed, even at $-78°C$. The amount of unfrozen water varies with the kind of soil, becoming in general greater as the soils vary from the simple and non-colloidal to the complex and colloidal. The amount freezing at $-78°C$. is very little, if any, greater than that freezing at $-4°C$. It seems possible, then, that the increased amount of root injury in sandy soils may be due, in addition to the lower amount of moisture in such soils, as mentioned above, to the extremely small amount of water remaining unfrozen at temperatures only slightly below 0°C. while the finer soils have a reserve of capillary adsorbed unfrozen water under such circumstances.

It should also be recognized that temperatures in the different soils may have been different. In any case, however, the result is the same; damage is greater in soils that are dry at the time of freezing.

Relation of Cover Crops to Root Killing.—The effects of single factors on soil temperatures, and therefore on root killing, have been set forth. The value of a snow cover has been shown; the increase of soil temperatures with transition from bare ground through sod to cover crops has been reviewed; minima varying with the character of the soil have been indicated and finally dryness of soil has been shown to be associated with root killing. In orchard practice, however, these factors are rarely operative singly and some rather complicated interactions may be expected.

Emerson's[75] studies on depth of freezing under two sets of conditions are of great importance since they show the interactions referred to above. Figures 31 and 32, reproduced from his studies, indicate depth of freezing without snow covering and with snow covering respectively. Under both sets of conditions the clean cultivated land froze deepest. More striking, however, is the different position occupied by the corn plot under different conditions. The reason becomes apparent, however, when the depth of snow covering on the several plots is considered. The close relation between depth of snow and depth of freezing, shown in all plots, is of interest.

Emerson's observations furnish more information: "Early in the winter . . . it was noted that soy beans had very few leaves left and that the plants stood perfectly erect, furnishing almost no protection to the soil and that cowpeas, tho they still held their leaves, stood too erect to furnish much protection. The field peas, on the other hand, had held their leaves well and matted down nicely, forming a very good mulch. Corn was also found to have remained very erect as was also the case with cane and millet. Later in winter it was noted that the snow was held very well by corn, cane, millet, soy beans and cowpeas, while field peas and rye, the good covers, laid too flat on the ground to catch the drifting snow. The almost bare stems of such plants as soy beans, which still stood erect, held the snow much better than a plant like field peas which retained its leaves but matted down too close upon the ground. The stalks left standing after a crop of corn grown in the ordinary way has been harvested make a very efficient snow holder but furnish very little protection to the ground at times of intense cold unaccompanied by snow."

The superior snow-retaining qualities mentioned, particularly in the case of corn, are operative mainly when the snow fall is accompanied by wind.

Summarizing the requirements for a cover crop under Nebraska winter conditions, Emerson says: "It should start growth promptly in order to insure an even stand and to choke out weeds. It should grow vigorously to insure a heavy winter cover and to dry the ground in case of late-growing trees so as to hasten their maturity. It should be killed by the early frosts so that it will stop drying the ground after danger of late tree growth is passed and help to conserve our light rains so much needed by the trees in winter. . . . A cover crop should be heavy enough to furnish as good direct protection as possible against freezing and thawing and it should stand sufficiently erect to hold snow against the power of strong winds." Of the crops tried, that which appeared to come nearest meeting these requirements in Nebraska was German millet.

In Michigan, amber sorghum and Sudan grass have been found far more satisfactory cover crops than those that have been in more general use, such as oats, vetch, rape, soy beans and buckwheat, because they produce much larger amounts of organic matter in the short cool growing

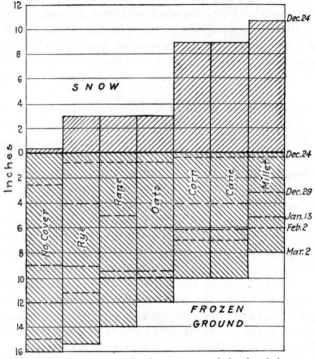

Fig. 32.—Relation of cover crops to depth of snow and depth of frozen soil. (*After Emerson*[75])

seasons of that section.[182]   In order to obtain best results they should be sown in late June or early July instead of in August.

Root Killing in Different Fruits.—There is less latitude in the root hardiness of the various species than in the hardiness of their tops. Nevertheless there are enough differences in many cases to make the choice of root stocks very important.

The Apple.—Carrick[45] found that the majority of dormant apple roots were seriously injured at a temperature of −12°C., with considerable injury at −7°C. He reports the cambium as the most tender tissue, followed closely by the phloem, with the cortex less tender. Under extreme conditions xylem and pith are said to be killed. French-grown stocks were found substantially as hardy as the native-grown seedlings.

In all cases there was a considerable variation, as would be expected among seedling plants. This difference, it may be remarked, is likely to assume considerable importance under field conditions. Furthermore, significant differences in hardiness have been found between the cion roots of some of the hardier apple varieties and that of the French Crab-seedling stocks upon which they are commonly grown,[190] indicating the possibility of the eventual use of hardy stocks that are propagated vegetatively in order to avoid much of the root killing from low temperature. However, as pointed out by Bradford,[35] probably the most practicable method of dealing with root killing in this fruit is through cultural methods after planting rather than avoidance of the difficulty through selection before planting.

The Pear.—Studies on pear roots by the same investigator indicated that Kieffer roots were more resistant than the French stock. A temperature of −11°C. during the dormant period produced extensive injury in both. In April Kieffer showed only slight injury at −9°C. while 2-year French roots were killed. Pear roots seemed to acquire hardiness later than those of the apple and never become quite so hardy. Quince roots, however, are killed at somewhat higher temperatures than are pear roots, and hence dwarf pear trees have been found more susceptible to winter root injury than are standards.[35]

The Peach.—The peach root is relatively hardier in the zone of distribution of this species than is the apple root along the northern border of apple growing. Occasionally, however, root killing in peaches occurs. Goff[94] records that in the freeze of 1899 peach tops suffered more than the roots; Green and Ballou[100] indicate peach root killing in Ohio. Macoun[141] reports similar injury to thousands of peach trees in southern Ontario in the winter of 1898–1899. However, root killing without any appreciable amount of injury to the top, as occurs from time to time in the apple, is extremely rare in the peach; conditions severe enough to injure peach roots generally will work far greater damage to the tops.

Carrick[45] summarizes the results of laboratory freezing of peach roots as follows: "As a general rule the order of resistance of the various tissues in the peach root seems to be as follows: pith, cortex, phloem, cambium, xylem. At −18°C. or below, the xylem was usually killed during the hardiest period. In most cases during February and March the pith is the tissue most easily killed, but in April the cambium is the least resistant.

"It is not so easy, with the data at hand, to assign an arbitrary limit within which the peach root is injured by freezing. This is because of the great variation in the root tissues. The peach cambium certainly is as hardy as the pear cambium, tho less so than the apple. Regardless of the size of the root, most of the peach material tested showed some injury at −10°C., and, except in unusual cases, serious injury occurred at −11°. This would then place the hardiness of the peach root very close to that of either pear seedling."

The Cherry.—Sour cherries frequently suffer from root killing on the northern margin of their range, sometimes under conditions such that the top is uninjured. Hansen[105] states: "One great difficulty in cherry growing in this state is the tender imported Mahaleb and Mazzard stocks upon which we are compelled to bud and graft at present. These root-kill in severe winters." Under some conditions the flower buds of sour cherry may be more resistant than the roots. Craig[61] reported on damage to cherry stocks in Iowa in 1898–1899: "In nursery, the former [Mazzard] was practically a total loss of 2-year-olds and a complete loss of 1-year-old in the region of the severe root killing. Mahaleb suffered less. Morello stock and own-rooted Morello trees generally escaped with slight injury, except in exposed situations. . . . In the college nurseries the practice of root grafting the cherry received commendation by the fact that the only trees which escaped were those which were partly on their own roots." *Prunus pennsylvanica* is reported from several sources to be hardy but is difficult to work commercially.

Carrick[45] places the relative hardiness in cherry stocks in descending order as follows: Mahaleb, *Prunus Besseyi*, *Prunus pennsylvanica*, Mazzard and he finds the Mahaleb generally much hardier than the apple roots investigated. "In large Mahaleb roots during their hardiest period," he states, "little injury is found under −14°C., while at −15° the injury is relatively small. . . . The Mazzard roots in no instance withstood −11°, but the number of tests run at −10° was insufficient to place this as its minimum. From these results the Mazzard cherry stock does not appear hardier than Kieffer pear stock."

The Plum.—Iowa's experience with plums in the winter 1898–1899 is thus stated by Craig.[62] "Plums, native or European, worked on peach or Myrobolan killed, on Marianna badly injured, on Americana slightly injured, but these recovered rapidly except where they were, in a few instances, permanently injured. . . . Americanas worked on peach roots escaped where well rooted from the cion. Sand cherry stock (*Prunus Besseyi*) has been used to some extent in the state. In no case have I found these roots injured in the slightest degree. In passing I may add that experience has not yet developed the ultimate effect of this stock upon the cion. Thus far its dwarfing influence upon varieties of the Americana type is satisfactorily demonstrated. Domestica plums on own roots fared better than the same varieties on peach, Myrobolan or Marianna." Elsewhere: "On the matter of plums the sand cherry (*Prunus Besseyi*) appears to be the hardiest form we know anything about. Native plums in the college orchard on this stock were entirely uninjured last winter, while the same varieties on Americana stocks alongside were injured or killed." Carrick places Myrobolan in the same group as Mazzard cherry and pear for hardiness.

The Grape.—Reports of root killing in grapes are relatively rare. The comparatively deep-rooting habit, combined with sufficient tenderness of tops to discourage grape growing in regions where root killing is common, may account for this apparent resistance. Furthermore, most grapes of American origin are in fact hardy varieties on their own roots and if it be safe to reason from the analogy of cion-rooted trees, the roots should share the hardiness of the tops. Niagara has been reported to be notoriously tender in bud and root.[92] Hansen[105] reports considerable trouble in parts of South Dakota from root killing; the New York vineyards suffered extensive damage in the winter of 1903–1904. Hedrick[113] suggests that the St. George (a variety of *rupestris*) stock used in some experimental work at Geneva, N. Y., may be more hardy than certain others and notes that American varieties on their own roots winter killed extensively.

Carrick made numerous laboratory freezings of six varieties of grapes to compare their relative hardiness. The varieties studied, representing several species, fell readily into two classes, *viz.*, Clinton, Concord and Diamond, "rather resistant to cold" and Cynthiana, Lindley and Norton, "relatively easy to kill by freezing." Within the groups the differences in hardiness are not striking. For the hardier group, "Only scattering injury is recorded at −11°, −12°, and −13°C. At an exposure of −14.5°, 22 out of 27 Concord roots were uninjured, and only a trace of cambium and cortex injury was noted in the remainder. . . . At −18°, however, the cambium, phloem, and cortex tissues were completely injured in all roots, with some xylem injury in the Diamond and the Concord. . . . The limits of this second group (Cynthiana, Lindley and Norton) lie between −10° and −12°C., the roots usually undergoing considerable injury at −11°. In relative hardiness this places these varieties between the Mazzard cherry and the apple. The Clinton, Concord, and Diamond roots, even excluding the influence of size, are considerably more resistant than apple roots, and Concord and Clinton seem equal if not superior to the Mahaleb stock.

" . . . *Vitis æstivalis*, represented by Norton and Cynthiana, is not adapted to severe cold, and this may account for the fact that its range is limited to the South. The tenderness of Lindley is probably due in part to the influence of *Vitis vinifera*, which, as is well known, will not survive the winter in the latitude of New York State without much protection. Concord and Diamond represent *Vitis labrusca*, the Northern Fox grape, which, while restricted in distribution, is found in Maine. *Vitis vulpina*, represented by Clinton—a variety with extremely resistant roots—has the greatest range of any American species of grape, it having been found in Canada north of Quebec."[45]

The Small Fruits.—Among small fruits Carrick found a wide range in hardiness. The blackberry, dewberry and red raspberry roots tested appeared to rank with the Myrobolan plum and the Mazzard cherry. Eldorado seemed the hardiest of the blackberries under observation, but, curiously enough the Lucretia dewberry seemed somewhat more hardy than Eldorado. The roots of the Cuthbert raspberry appeared equal in hardiness to the Eldorado blackberry. None of the varieties studied survived a temperature of $-12°C.$, though many of the larger roots were uninjured at $-11°C.$ On the other hand, currant and gooseberry roots were extremely resistant; a Downing gooseberry root withstanding $-20.5°C.$, though this probably would be the limit of hardiness. On the basis of the material examined Carrick rather provisionally rates the gooseberry roots as slightly more resistant than the currant.

Preventive and Remedial Treatments.—Danger of root injury may be permanent or temporary. If the past history of the locality shows extensive root injury the grower should bear this in mind as a possible threat. If his site is sandy or chronically dry or wind swept in winter he is threatened continually and may be justified in accommodating his orchard practice accordingly. A temporary condition of danger may occur, such as a dry autumn, in orchards ordinarily safe. Early winter cold snaps are most to be feared, because the roots are then tender and there is less likely to be a snow covering. However, it may be February that brings disaster.

Deep Planting and Mulching.—Preventive methods are more efficacious and generally cheaper than palliative measures. Deeper planting than usual, if the winter water table is not too high, may protect the roots, especially in the first winter. Protective soil coverings, either mulches or cover crops, should be used in very dry locations; the advantage of a snow blanket should be remembered in choice of site or in selecting a cover crop.

The tendency of deep planted trees to send out roots from the cion is well known. Some varieties do this more freely than others. These roots when they come from cions of extremely hardy varieties are generally hardier than the stocks commonly used. In those of the northern sections where root killing is most likely there is a tendency to grow trees formed by grafting long cions on short pieces of root for the purpose of inducing cion rooting, thus securing increased hardiness in the roots. No experimental evidence is available to show clearly whether cion roots of hardy apple varieties are hardier than those of tender varieties, but Craig[62] records numerous instances when cion roots proved more hardy than the stocks on which they were worked. Hansen,[106] writing in South Dakota, says: " . . . in ordinary winters the roots emitted by the scions of hardy varieties are sufficiently hardy but . . . they are not proof against such winters as that of 1898–1899."

Use of Hardy Stocks.—Top working on stocks of known hardiness is another method of combating root killing in those sections particularly subject to it. *Pyrus baccata* is said by Hansen to succeed in the Transbaikal section of Siberia where the mean annual temperature is 27°F. and the mean temperature of the coldest month $-18.4°F.$ and where the annual rainfall is 11.42 inches. He reports young seedlings of this species to have wintered perfectly despite a temperature of −40°F. with no snow. The "Virginia crab" is also reported to be more hardy than French crab. However, these have more or less dwarfing effect and do not make an altogether satisfactory union.[145] This method of securing greater hardiness of root apparently offers greater possibilities with plums, cherries and peaches than it does with apples.

Pruning.—After the damage has occurred, there is little that can be done. If the killing is complete or nearly so the trees should be removed. However, many times the root destruction is incomplete; some of the roots that start straight down from the crown on old trees will frequently escape. In many of these cases a heavy pruning back, or, if there is also injury in the top, a moderate pruning back, will enable the tree to survive and still have many years of usefulness. Very young trees that have suffered only partial destruction of the roots can be restored in many instances by banking the trunks with earth, inducing the formation of additional cion roots. If heavy pruning is to be employed on winter-injured trees, however, care should be taken to make sure that the injury is in the roots instead of the tops, for heavy pruning of trees whose tops are seriously injured, especially if the injury is of the black-heart type, is likely to prove fatal.

Handling Nursery Stock in Cold Weather.—One form of root injury likely to be encountered in regions remote from the territory commonly subject to killing of this type is that occurring on nursery trees. Root growth in apple trees in Missouri has been shown to continue long after the top has assumed a completely dormant appearance, in fact until winter has well set in.[254] In a growing state, it will be recalled, roots are damaged by temperatures only a few degrees below freezing and even in a dormant state they will stand only comparatively high temperatures.[48] Chandler states: "In case of 1-year-old roots of the French crab, used as stock by most of the nurserymen, about −5 to −8°C. (23 to 15.8°F.) is as low a temperature as they can be depended upon to withstand with no injury." Fall dug trees, necessarily lifted before the ground freezes and often dug rather early must have very tender roots, so tender in fact that exposure to a slight frost after digging in this stage is likely to have very serious consequences. Extreme care in protecting tree roots against any freezing from the time they are dug until they are planted is amply justified.

Summary.—Root killing is particularly common in sections with low winter temperatures and little snowfall. Minimum soil temperatures of 24° to 25°F. at a depth of 6 inches are very common in deciduous fruit sections and soil temperatures of 7°F. have been recorded in Nebraska. Freezing temperatures are frequently registered to a depth of 2, and occasionally to a depth of 3 feet. The critical temperature for the roots of most hardy species during their dormant season ranges from about 14° to 5°F. During the growing season it is much higher. Minimum soil temperature is influenced greatly by soil covering, being distinctly higher under snow or a mulch formed by some cover crop than under bare ground. Fertilizers may indirectly protect roots against severe freezing by promoting the growth of weeds or of cover crops. Frost penetrates more deeply in light than in heavy soils. Roots are killed more readily in dry than in moist soils. Considerable differences exist in the relative resistance of the roots of different species and varieties. Preventive measures include moderately deep planting, the use of cion-rooted trees or trees on hardy stocks, the choice of locations not unduly exposed to the wind, the use of cover crops to hold the snow and thus both directly and indirectly blanket the soil and in some cases artificial mulching. Remedial treatment consists chiefly in judicious pruning. Care should be taken in handling nursery stock that the roots are not exposed to freezing temperatures in packing, unpacking or heeling in and they should be protected from freezing while in storage or transit.

CHAPTER XVIII

WINTER INJURY IN RELATION TO SPECIFIC FRUITS

The discussion of winter killing to this point has been general. Any species furnishing convenient illustrative material has been drawn on and most of the types considered affect each species more or less; the prevailing conception has been the tree in general rather than any specific kind. There are, however, differences in the problem of hardiness as it relates to the several species and detailed points of adjustment to these differences. These can be considered more conveniently by discussing each fruit singly, evaluating for each the different types of injury to which it is liable and indicating, wherever possible, the best means of minimizing the difficulties.

The Apple.—The apple is the most widely grown fruit in America and is, at one point or another, exposed to practically every form which winter injury can take; it seems, however, practically immune to some of them. Aside from sunscald there is little or no evidence that the apple suffers from those types of injury that are characteristic of late winter, *i.e.*, from warm weather followed by cold. Though killing of fruit buds sometimes occurs it seems hardly probable that this is a killing of buds which have broken the rest period. At the time of the Easter freeze of 1920 in the lower Missouri valley many varieties had pushed their buds so far along that they showed pink. These varieties of course suffered more or less but their killing constitutes a case of damage to succulent tissues rather than of winter injury. Late blossoming varieties, though the buds had swelled noticeably, were not damaged by the drop to 14°F. Though this is not conclusive evidence it is suggestive. A February freeze of −7°F. in Georgia when some Japanese plums were in bloom, worked serious injury to plums and peaches but caused no damage to the apple.[193]

Whipple[251] introduces clear evidence of fruit bud killing in Montana and shows that little readily recognized evidence that the buds have been fruit buds is left after they are killed. If the injury is confined to the floral parts as Whipple has shown to be the case at times, the vegetative parts grow and the casual observer concludes that the tree has failed to form fruit buds and is going through an off year. It is, therefore, possible that this killing may occur at times when it is not recognized. Nevertheless it is safe to assume that fruit bud killing is comparatively rare and that when it does occur it is not necessarily related to the breaking of the rest period.

Injuries Associated with Immaturity.—Difficulties due to prolongation of the growing season are far more common in the apple. Indeed, disregarding the winter drought conditions in the north prairie states, which are not apple growing states in a commercial sense, it is, in one form or another, the prevailing type of injury. A large proportion of recorded cases of winter injury may be traced to immaturity. This probably accounts for the many cases observed in which the wood is killed while the buds are not. The various forms of injury associated with immaturity have been discussed and require no elaboration here.

There remain for consideration, however, some interesting differences between varieties in hardiness. Most European varieties were early found lacking in this respect along the Atlantic coast and the apples developed in the eastern states in turn proved tender when transplanted to the northern prairie states. From available data it is not yet possible to reduce varietal differences from an indefinite empirical status to a basis capable of quantitative expression. Macoun's statement, quoted above under Immaturity, that hardiness is merely an expression of complete maturity, is undoubtedly true in a large measure. The winter apples of southern latitudes are tender at the north though there are exceptions, as Ben Davis which is probably hardier than Baldwin, and the winter apples of the north, hardy there, are summer or fall apples in the south. The summer apple in the north, finishing its active season early, has time to develop maturity such that it withstands the winters;

TABLE 50.—DATE OF FORMING TERMINAL BUDS[19]

Variety	Nursery trees	Orchard trees	Variety	Nursery trees	Orchard trees
Hibernal...........	July 25	July 1	Ben Davis.........	Sept. 27	July 1
Oldenburg.........	Aug. 20	July 1	Gano.............	Sept. 27	July 10
Salome............	Aug. 20	*	Jonathan..........	Sept. 27	July 22
Soulard...........	Aug. 20	*	Patten............	*	July 1
Virginia...........	Aug. 20	*	Grimes............	*	July 15
Wealthy...........	Aug. 20	July 12	Delicious..........	*	July 22
McIntosh..........	Aug. 28	*	Ingram............	*	*
Silken Leaf........	Sept. 1	*	Iowa Blush........	*	*
Winesap...........	Sept. 5	July 22	Lansingburg.......	*	*
Anisim............	Sept. 5	*	Minkler...........	*	*
Black Annette.....	Sept. 20	*	Roman Stem......	*	*

* Terminals not formed at time of first frost, about Oct. 1.

the winter apple must grow longer to complete its cycle and has less opportunity to acquire the condition that makes it hardy. As an index of comparative maturity Beach and Allen[19] report observations on the date of terminal bud formation in several varieties, which are reproduced here, with some change of arrangement, as Table 50. Despite some inconsistencies, as, for example, the relative positions of Winesap, Ben Davis and Delicious, there is a general correspondence between the date of terminal bud formation and the generally accepted relative hardiness of the varieties reported upon.

The water content of most tissues may be taken as an index of maturity, diminishing as this condition is approached; the same is true of other tissues. This being true a study of the moisture contents of different varieties ought to give an index of this relative maturity.

Shutt[219] reports an interesting set of moisture determinations at Ottawa, reproduced here as Table 51. These 10 varieties were arranged by Macoun in groups in decreasing order of hardiness, as follows: Group 1 (hardiest), Oldenburg, Yellow Transparent, McMahon White; Group II, Wealthy, Scott's Winter; Group III, Scarlet Pippin, Walworth Pippin; Group IV (least hardy), Hebble White, Boy's Delight, Blenheim Pippin.

TABLE 51.—PERCENTAGE OF WATER IN APPLE TWIGS JAN. 23, 1903[219]

Variety	Basal portion	Terminal portion	Whole twig
Yellow Transparent................	45.55	45.10	45.30
McMahon White..................	45.45	46.96	46.14
Oldenburg.......................	45.02	47.51	46.15
Walworth Pippin..................	44.72	47.67	46.20
Boy's Delight....................	44.74	44.75	46.25
Wealthy.........................	46.82	48.72	47.70
Scarlet Pippin....................	47.13	49.92	48.58
Hebble White....................	49.09	48.82	48.91
Scott's Winter...................	47.50	50.36	48.98
Blenheim Pippin.................	48.93	51.38	50.24

Comparison of Macoun's arrangement with Shutt's figures, considering in particular the terminal portions of the twigs, shows a correspondence that at least suggests a relationship. Shutt comments on these figures in part as follows: . . . "it would seem, therefore, that we have direct and definite proof that there is a distinct relationship between the moisture content of the twig and its power to resist the action of frost and that those trees whose new growth contains the largest percentage of water, as winter approaches, are in all probability the most tender."

Table 14 shows the moisture content, at different dates, of several varieties of apples. Of these Hibernal and Wealthy are generally recognized as the hardiest. It is significant that these two varieties had the least moisture in July and that in January, after a week of cold weather, including a minimum of −15°F., having lost the smallest amounts of moisture, they had the greatest moisture contents. Winesap, figures for which were not complete, dropped in water content, between July 15 and Dec. 26, from 60.4 to 45.7 per cent., having on that date the lowest water content. It is also the least hardy of the varieties under consideration. The hardier varieties were found to lose less water through the bark in a given time.

Various workers have studied the structure of apple twigs but no one has been able to correlate definitely any structural differences with hardiness or its lack. There seems some tendency for hardier varieties to have somewhat thicker bark and more starch in their tissues but these characters are by no means constant. Were the starch content shown to be correlated, it could hardly be regarded as a causal agent but more likely a product of the conditions that make the variety hardy, through making it mature.

In short, then, the only character that can be linked definitely with hardiness in the apple is maturity. If one variety is hardier than another because it matures better, the cultural practices that make the tender variety mature better make it in effect more hardy. A well matured tree of a tender variety is undoubtedly more hardy than an immature tree of a hardy variety. This accounts for many apparent inconsistencies in field observations.

Control Measures.—Efforts have been made to influence cold resistance by topworking upon stocks of great hardiness. In so far as root killing is prevented this practice has proved beneficial. It is also a wise practice if the growing of varieties notoriously subject to crown rot or crotch injury is to be undertaken. However, that hardiness of stock increases the hardiness of the cion is not shown conclusively by any evidence available. It is conceivable that an early maturing stock might influence the top slightly in the same direction but any influence of this character is comparatively insignificant. Macoun[145] reports top grafting varieties not perfectly hardy on stocks of very hardy varieties at Ottawa, Ontario; among the cions used were Baldwin, Benoni, Esopus, Fallawater, King, Newtown, Northern Spy, Ontario, Rhode Island, Rome Beauty, Sutton, Wagener, Winesap and York Imperial; the stocks used were McMahon, Gideon, Haas and Hibernal. The grafts endured several winters, but "the test winter of 1903–1904 killed practically all of them," though the stocks survived. It is, however, interesting to note that Sorauer[222] considered that grafting of weak growing varieties upon vigorous stocks results in an increased amount of frost canker, characteristic of immature tissues.

There is a limit to the effects that can be induced by cultivation. No amount of cultural manipulations can make a variety mature its fruit and its wood in a situation where it does not receive sufficient heat (where the season is too short). It is not without significance that only one of the important winter apples of the south can be grown to any advantage in the north. Whether the cause be called failure to mature or lack of constitutional hardiness, there is a northern limit to the culture of every variety and that limit is reached more quickly for some varieties than for others.

Varietal Differences.—Out of the vast and costly experiments in hardiness carried on by planting and replanting, the sieve of selection has shown certain varieties to withstand winter cold in average conditions better than others. Since Baldwin is perhaps the best known single variety in most sections where apple hardiness is important it is used as a standard of reference. King and Grimes are of about the same degree of hardiness as Baldwin in trunk, crotch and limb, but distinctly more susceptible to crown or collar injury.[35] If grown in sections where immaturity of wood is likely to be encountered, they should be double-worked on hardier intermediates, such as Northern Spy or Delicious.

Hardier than Baldwin is a quality possessed by but few varieties of extensive commercial possibilities though this statement does not mean that Baldwin is particularly hardy. Rhode Island Greening is apparently as hardy as Baldwin, and Northern Spy, Wagener and Delicious are distinctly hardier. In the list of varieties recommended by Hedrick, Booth and Taylor[109] for the St. Lawrence and Champlain Valleys, where Baldwin does not succeed, are Fameuse, McIntosh, Oldenburg, Wealthy, Blue Permain, Jewett Red, St. Lawrence, Gravenstein, Red Astrachan, Yellow Transparent, Canada Baldwin, Longfield and numerous crab apples. More recent observations in Maine[225] and at the Central Experimental Station at Ottawa, Canada,[25] indicate that Cortland ranks with McIntosh in hardiness and that Melba, Joyce, Lobo and Lawfam are somewhat hardier.

For "the most northerly district" of Quebec, Macoun[145] recommends Tetofski, Blushed Calville, Lowland Raspberry, Duchess, Charlamoff, Antonovka, Wealthy, Hibernal, McMahon, Longfield, Patten Greening, McIntosh, Milwaukee, Winter Rose, Stone, Scott Winter and Malinda. It is stated that the summer and autumn varieties are the hardiest.

At the Northwest Experiment Farm, in Minnesota, where winter conditions are probably as severe as at any point where apples can be expected to grow, the list of approved varieties is limited, aside from certain crab apples, to four: Hibernal, Oldenburg, Okabena and Patten Greening.[217]

If one variety were to be picked as the hardiest of all cultivated varieties of the apple grown in America it would probably be Hibernal.

The Pear.—The pear is like the apple in its reactions to winter conditions. It is somewhat less hardy than the apple. Though apples are grown at points where the mean temperature of December, January and February is 13°F., the northern limit of the pear follows in general the mean temperature line of 20°F.[82] Nevertheless certain varieties possess considerable hardiness. Though evidence as to actual hardiness in the northern Mississippi valley is not available because of the complications introduced by fire blight prevalence, some information may be secured from experience in certain eastern states where blight is not so serious.

Pears suffered extensive injuries in New York during the extremely severe winter of 1903–1904.[80] Young trees, though the bark and wood were discolored, made good recovery, in one case forming a layer of 5 millimeters over the old sap-wood in the first summer. Trees that had been injured by psylla were killed outright in many cases. Dehorning old trees that were injured aggravated their poor condition.

Waite[238] reported extensive damage to pears in the Hudson River valley during the same winter. Pointing out that pear orchards are planted customarily in low rich ground, in other words, on sites more inviting to winter injury than those ordinarily chosen for peaches, he states that pears were as severely injured as peaches and do not possess the recuperative powers of the peach. Elevation made great difference in the amount of damage. "The young pear trees are rather less hurt than the older trees, as in the case of the peach, but it should be noted in this connection that young pear trees having the wood blackened, although they will push out their wood and make a start, are very apt to decline or else maintain their life in a very feeble manner as a result of the dead wood at the heart. They have not the ability to recover by depositing a thrifty layer of sap-wood. Pear trees under 3 or 4 years of age which are badly frozen and which show blackened or discolored wood, even though the bark may look normal from the outside and may appear to be alive and quite fresh when cut into, should be cut off below the snow line and allowed to sprout."

Injury to pears occurred in the localized Michigan freeze of October, 1906.[233] Though peaches were killed, it was only in low places and in vigorously growing trees that pears were seriously injured. Blackening of the wood was found. Apples were very little injured under the same conditions. In parts of Washington an early winter freeze caused splitting of trunks on the south side and blackening in the wood of the fruit spurs down to the limbs, with damage in some sections to the blossom buds.[15] Bailey[10] reports killing of fruit buds at Ithaca, N. Y., with no injury to wood, during a dry cold winter. Injury to wood occurred elsewhere, he states, at the same time, but evidently he does not consider this severe.

The following varieties have been reported suitable for culture in Vermont and hence presumably hardy: Vermont Beauty, Flemish Beauty,

Anjou, Winter Nelis, Onondaga, Tyson, Lawrence and Sheldon.[245]   As "succeeding in many gardens" Angouleme, Bartlett, Buffum, Seckel, Louise Bonne de Jersey are mentioned.   At Orono, Maine, a little beyond the northern limit of the Baldwin apple, the hardier varieties have been found to be Clapp Favorite, Flemish Beauty, Howell, Lawrence, Sheldon and Winter Nelis.[170]

Chandler states that Anjou is one of the hardiest varieties at Ithaca, N. Y., probably a little more so than Clapp Favorite and Sheldon, certainly less than Flemish Beauty.   Bartlett is generally conceded to be rather tender.   Flemish Beauty has proved the hardiest variety of the better class of pears tested at Ottawa, Ont.[140]   Evidence elsewhere corroborates this selection, though even this variety is by no means immune to winter injury in regions of commercial fruit growing.[20]   In Michigan, the Kieffer has been found to be about as hardy as any of the European varieties commonly grown.[35]

Though Winter Nelis is listed as relatively hardy in northern New England, the fact that its fruits do not ripen properly and attain high quality in that and other northern sections illustrates the fact that with some fruits mean growing-season temperatures, rather than winter minima, set the practicable northern limits to their culture.

The Peach.—The difference in the hardiness problem in peaches north and south has been discussed, maturity being stated as the leading factor in the north, the rest period in the south.   Root killing has been shown to be of relatively small importance in the peach, though it is by no means unknown.   Extensive killing occurred in the Michigan peach section in a freeze on Oct. 10, 1906, while the trees were still in full foliage.[233]   At South Haven the temperature fell to 17°F., and some unofficial thermometers registered 6°F.   Cambium and sap-wood injuries extending to the snow line were common.   Frost cankers on peach trunks and crotches are found sometimes, following winters of extreme cold or a late growing season.[121]   "Gum pockets usually form under the flattened areas and the gum often oozes out during periods of wet weather.   The injured area is usually rather indefinite about the margin and the formation of a healthy roll of callus is thereby much retarded."

It has been shown earlier that no stated temperature can be assumed as fatal.   However, fruit buds are generally more tender than wood. When, therefore, there occur cases in which the wood is killed and the buds survive, they may be considered good evidence of lack of maturity. There is hardly a winter without some killing back of young twigs which may be interpreted as indicating a lack of maturity.   The care generally exercised in selecting sites for peach orchards to secure freedom from spring frosts fortunately has another equally desirable, though seldom recognized, effect in that it secures greater maturity.   There is a remarkable uniformity, throughout reports of various freezes in northern states, in locating the greatest injury in trees growing in moist, rich soil and receiving late cultivation. Another point of agreement is the ascribing of great injury to trees low in vitality from various causes such as San Jose scale, leaf curl, low fertility, borers and poor drainage. Green and Ballou[100] mention an orchard in which the San Jose scale spray was omitted in 1902 on three rows running through the middle. In the severe winter of 1903–1904 these three rows were killed while the rest were uninjured. Whether the greater injury to weak trees is actual and due to some specific condition characteristic of weakness or whether it is apparent and due to their inferior recuperative powers is not clear. A given degree of injury would be more evident, certainly, on a weak than on a strong tree.

Waite,[238] reporting on the January, 1904, freeze in New York, distinguished three classes of injury: "(1) In bearing peaches the trees most injured by freezing show the bark entirely blackened and dead, more or less separated from the trunk and the wood turned a very dark brown color. The injury extends far up onto the limbs although the bark usually has not separated on the branches. Such trees are dead beyond all question. The bark on such trees still retained its vitality. Sometimes a rise of 10 or 15 feet resulted in trees being less seriously injured. (2) With many peach trees the bark is lightly separated from the wood which is of a dark-walnut color next to the cambium and brown throughout. Though still alive the bark is somewhat browned and discolored, the youngest or outer layer of wood has been frozen until it is now of a dark-walnut color and the wood is blackened throughout. Many of these trees are of doubtful vitality and will probably succumb. Others have enough vitality to enable them to pull through. Where bark is adhering or only partially separated from the trunk the chances for recovery are good. The tops of such trees are usually found in fair condition, the wood brownish, but the white cambium layer uninjured though lying immediately in contact with brown, dead wood. The twigs, especially the 1-year wood, sometimes have been frozen so badly that they will not be able to push out the leaf buds. In severe cases the leaf buds themselves are killed, but, as a rule, they are still alive. Of course on all such trees the fruit buds are killed. The most injured part is the trunk just above the snow line. . . . (3) The third class, which may be described as the moderately frozen trees, in which the wood above the snow line is blackened but the bark not separated from the wood and with the cambium still apparently alive, although water-soaked and injured, frequently has minute brown streaks in the bark immediately in contact with the cambium. Such trees will almost invariably recover. . . . Nearly every tree in the entire Michigan fruit belt was frozen in

February, 1899, so that the wood was blackened and dead clear to the bark. A new layer of live white wood formed inward from the white bark, the trees made a fairly good growth, having no fruit crop to carry, and bore the year following a record fruit crop."

As in the apple, the bark on the trunk near the ground seems to mature late and is particularly liable to injury. After seasons favoring late growth mounding of earth to cover this region somewhat has been found very profitable insurance. In several instances in Ohio in 1903–1904 a few shovelfuls of earth at the crown made the difference between dead trees and uninjured trees.[100]

Since the practice of treating the crowns of peach trees for borers with paradichlorobenzene has come into use, injury from this fumigant and borer injury itself have sometimes been mistaken for killing due to cold. Moreover, the soil mounds made around the base of the trees incident to this borer treatment are likely to delay the maturity of the wood and bark tissues at that point and lead to collar injury unless the soil is leveled off within two or three weeks after the trees are mounded.

Chandler[49] records an interesting case of mild injury associated with immaturity. After a very rainy August in 1914 the minimum for the winter, $-9°F.$, occurred late in December. In the following spring the blossoms of several varieties were at least three weeks late in opening. Examination disclosed injury to the pith of the bud, extending even as far as the pith of the twig. There was very little injury elsewhere. Usually the flower parts are less resistant than the pith of the bud and of the twig. The temperature evidently was not low enough to kill matured buds but it did damage the immature tissues. The trees in question bore a normal crop that season. Similar cases have been observed at other times.[17]

Treatment of damaged trees consists of the ordinary prophylactic measures and a moderate pruning. Very heavy heading back, or dehorning, has proved decidedly injurious when the bark or the wood is damaged; a fair amount of pruning is, however, beneficial.[102] This should be done before growth starts. There is a general tendency to overestimate damage and immediately after a freeze many orchards have been taken out which would have recovered in time had they been allowed to remain. Trees with any considerable injury to the trunk should by no means be allowed to bear fruit in the season following the injury.[94]

Observations by Mer[161] on oaks may explain the injurious effects of very heavy pruning. Investigating old winter injuries of the "black heart" type, he found considerable starch still in the injured wood but little in the wood subsequently laid down, indicating that the tree was unable to withdraw starch from the injured tissue. This suggests that if the injury is extensive the tree will have difficulty the following spring in securing sufficient carbohydrates to sustain growth until a supply can be secured from the new leaves. If the pruning is heavy enough to remove all the buds which make new growth most readily the difficulty must be increased. If, however, no buds are removed the scanty carbohydrate supply is apportioned to so many growing points that none receives enough to sustain growth until it can become self-supporting and the tree dies of carbohydrate starvation.

Hardiness in wood and in bud are not always combined in the same variety. Elberta, generally considered hardy in wood, seems tender in the fruit buds. Hedrick,[110] reporting a questionnaire of New York and Michigan peach growers, states their selections for wood hardiness as follows: For New York in order named, Crosby, Hill's Chili, Stevens' Rareripe, Gold Drop and Elberta; for Michigan, Hill's Chili, Crosby, Gold Drop, Kalamazoo and Barnard. Jaques Rareripe, Wager, Carman, Belle of Georgia, Hale's Early, Champion and Greensboro are listed as hardier than the average in this respect. Early Crawford, Late Crawford, Chair's Choice, St. John and Niagara are rated as the five most tender in wood of the varieties commonly grown in New York. Salway is listed as tender in Michigan. Among the newer varieties, Rochester and South Haven have proven comparatively hardy in wood. J. H. Hale has similarly been reported as hardier than Elberta in Utah,[2] though in Michigan it is distinctly more tender, particularly at the crown and in the crotches.

In fruit buds, New York growers find greater hardiness in Crosby, Hill's Chili, Triumph, Gold Drop, Stevens' Rareripe and Kalamazoo; Michigan growers find Hill's Chili, Gold Drop, Crosby, Kalamazoo, Barnard, Rochester and South Haven the hardiest. Concerning the five most tender varieties in bud there is entire agreement in New York and Michigan as to the order of their tenderness: Early Crawford, Late Crawford, Chair's Choice, Reeves' Favorite and Elberta. The Peento group is extremely tender.

The Cherry.—Sweet cherries are generally known to be far more tender than the Dukes, Amarelles and Morellos. As outlined by Finch[82] the northern range of cherries is marked by the mean winter temperature of about 16°F. For the three coldest of the pomological districts into which the United States is divided in the fruit catalog of the American Pomological Society only one variety of sweet cherry, Black Tartarian is recommended and that recommendation is confined to one district. For the same districts 13 varieties of Duke and Morello cherries are recommended.[194] Of 26 varieties in the catalog, 13 are recommended for District 1 and of these, 10 evidently are considered worth growing in District 2 which includes most of the northeastern fruit growing sections.

The three leading commercial varieties, Early Richmond, Montmorency and English Morello, are considerably hardier than the Baldwin apple. However, some of the hardiest apples appear to be hardier than the hardiest cherries. Hansen[105] states that root killing is the one great difficulty in cherry growing in South Dakota. Following the February, 1899, freeze, with a minimum of −27.5°F., at Madison, Wis., some root killing was reported, but most varieties brought their fruit buds through, Large Morello, Late Morello, Shadow Amarelle, Dyehouse and Ostheim having over 90 per cent. live buds.[94] Enough Montmorency and Early Richmond buds survived −35°F., registered at a number of points in northern Michigan in February, 1936, to produce good crops the following summer.

Curiously enough many varieties undamaged in the 1899 freeze had their buds killed in the winter of 1896–1897 with a minimum of −23°F. During the summer of 1896 the trees had been in sod and there was much dry weather. Considerable variation in the hardiness of the embryo flowers, not alone between varieties, but on the same tree and even within the same bud, has been reported.[93] Careful study showed a strong inclination toward tenderness in varieties having the greater number of flowers per bud and a similar susceptibility in individual buds within the variety. The periphery of the tree had 39.9 per cent. live buds while the central part had 69.9 per cent. alive. Goff did not regard this difference as due alone to the greater number of flowers in the peripheral buds but suggested that it might be due to the protection afforded by the branches and to conduction of heat along the trunk from the soil. Roberts,[197] also working in Wisconsin, reported that winter injury to cherry buds is frequent in that state and sometimes it is severe enough to affect seriously the yield of fruit. Frequently only one or two of the four or five blossoms within the bud are killed. Studies made in the spring of 1917 are interesting in several respects. All injury had been confined to blossom buds. Older trees showed more injury than young and the exposure appeared to have little relation to the amount of injury during that winter. Trees which had been partly defoliated by the shot hole fungus the previous season received less bud injury than normal trees. The shortest and the longest spurs were less injured than spurs of medium length and on terminal shoots there was less injury in the buds at the base and at the tip than along the central portion of the shoot. Larger buds were most frequently injured.

The injury occurred early in December following a temperature of −12°F. and could not have been due to development excited by warm winter weather. Microscopic study showed that the buds most damaged were the most advanced in their development. Late maturity could not have been the factor involved as the trees and parts of trees growing latest were the least injured. This finding is in agreement with Goff's earlier report of greater tenderness in the winter of 1896–1897 when the trees stood in sod and the weather was dry, both of which conditions favor early formation and rapid development of fruit buds. It appears, then, that cultural practices tending to promote vigorous growth and fairly late maturity would have some effect in reducing injury of this sort, though Roberts states that it could not be eliminated altogether.

Although under "normal" conditions the cherry is not very liable to injuries associated with immaturity, some varieties of sweet cherries were slightly injured in Michigan in October, 1906, when peach trees were killed and pears considerably injured in some places.[233] Moreover, cherries showed considerable injury in Washington in late November, 1896, at a temperature somewhat below 0°F.,[15] and observations in Michigan indicate that winter injury of the blackheart type is an important factor contributing to, if not the direct cause of, the death of more cherry trees, both sweet and sour, than all other factors combined. However, this immaturity is due to the premature defoliation caused by the leaf-spot fungus or by injudicious spraying, rather than to a failure of the trees that hold their foliage normally to ripen their wood properly.

Bessarabian, Brusseler Braun, Lutovka, English Morello and Early Richmond appear, from the scant data available, to be the hardiest of the commonly grown varieties in both wood and bud to midwinter cold.

Only a little less serious than blackheart due to immaturity in the sour cherry is a late winter type of injury to the flower buds, which has been described as a "delayed dormant season" killing.[91] In Michigan this occurs in late March or early April when the buds have swollen slightly, but before they have opened. At this stage the buds of both Montmorency and Early Richmond are relatively much more tender than are those of the sweet cherry varieties and of other deciduous fruits, thus reversing the order of their hardiness a few weeks earlier when in a dormant condition.

The Plum.—Perhaps because of the number of botanical species from which the cultivated varieties have sprung, plums show a wide range in hardiness; though some are more tender than the majority of peaches, others are hardier than the hardiest apples. Hedrick[112] states that the Nigra plums are the hardiest of our tree fruits and are able to resist nearly as much cold as any cultivated plant. Only a little less hardy are the Americanas. The relative hardiness of the other groups is thus summarized by Hedrick: "Insititias as represented by Damsons come next with varieties of Domestica as Arctic, Lombard and Voronesh nearly as hardy. The Domesticas are less hardy than the apple, ranking in this respect with the pear. Of Domesticas the Reine Claude plums are as tender to cold as any though some consider Bradshaw more tender. . . . The Triflora (Japanese) plums vary more in hardiness than any other of the cultivated species. Speaking very generally they are less hardy than Domesticas, the hardiest sorts, Burbank and Abundance, being somewhat hardier than the peach, while the tenderest varieties, of which Kelsey is probably the most tender, are distinctly less hardy than the peach. Of the remaining plums, the Hortulana, Munsoniana and Watsoni groups, there are great diversities in opinion as to hardiness. Probably all the varieties in these last groups are as hardy as the peach with a few sorts in each more hardy than the peach. It is to be expected from the more northern range of the wild prototypes that the Hortulana and Watsoni plums are somewhat hardier than *Prunus Munsoniana.*"

Waugh[244] indicates distinct varietal ranges, within the species: "The tenderness of Bradshaw seems to belong more to the fruit buds than to the wood and correspondents do not seem to agree in their reports; but upon the basis of statistics received, we may trace the northern limit of the Bradshaw . . . which runs from 100 to 300 miles south of the line traced for Lombard. . . . In fact a majority of the standard varieties, such as Coe Golden Drop, Italian Prune, Jefferson, Lincoln, Moore Arctic, Pond, Shippers' Pride and Washington, would probably be found to conform fairly well to the same limits as Lombard." Of the Japanese plums, "Abundance, Chabot (Chase, Yellow Japan), Hale, Red June, Willard and Ogon seem to be about as hardy as Burbank. Satsuma stands about midway between Burbank and Kelsey."

In North Dakota, Waldron[240] states: "Only one species of plum (Americana) can be grown with any success in the State. So far as tried here they are all hardy though some ripen late and most of them are vigorous and productive. . . . All things considered they are the easiest and most profitable fruit to grow in North Dakota. . . . . For general cultivation the following varieties will be likely to succeed: De Soto, Forest Garden, Weaver, Cheney, Wolf, Rolling Stone, and Wyant." In parts of Minnesota Rolling Stone, De Soto, and Surprise are too late in ripening their fruit to be satisfactory in cultivation, though they are not stated to lack hardiness.[52] For the colder parts of Vermont several varieties have been reported to be as hardy as the sugar maple: Stoddard, Hawkeye, Quaker, Aitkin, Surprise, Cheney, De Soto, Forest Garden, Wolf, Wyant and Weaver.[245]

In Wisconsin many varieties have brought their buds through a temperature of $-38°F$. in one winter, though they succumbed to $-23°$ in another,[94] indicating that the condition of the tree makes a considerable difference in the amount of cold that can be endured. Experience in Michigan indicates that with the plum, as with the cherry, winter injury is most likely to be of the blackheart type, associated with immaturity due to very heavy crops or to premature defoliation caused by fungous attack.[35] In view of the work of Chandler with peaches and Roberts with cherries it seems possible that the advancement of the buds when they enter the resting stage may have much to do with their hardiness. No definite data are available, unfortunately, on this point, but the superior hardiness of the Americana group, which is late in maturing, appears to justify investigation. It would seem, since plum blossoms are injured more frequently than the woody parts, that maturity might be delayed safely to some extent without unduly increasing liability to injury in other ways.[229]

Recent investigations in Minnesota indicate that some of the injury to plum blossoms is associated with early breaking of the rest period. Treatment to increase hardiness by retarding blossom formation and development would tend also to delay the breaking of the rest period.

The Apricot.—Though, for the most part, the apricot is grown in sections where winter-killing of wood or dormant buds is not an important limiting factor, the quick response of the buds to growing-season temperatures in the spring, which renders them susceptible to injury from late freezes and frosts, restricts apricot culture to a few rather limited areas. In general, both wood and dormant flower buds of the apricot are more hardy than those of the peach; however, trees of the Jones apricot were killed in the winter of 1926–1927 in Utah where Elberta peach trees survived. Old trees of the Royal apricot were injured less than old trees of the Chinese and Moorpark varieties.[2]

The Grape.—Winter-killing is not so prominent a factor in grape growing as it is with some of the tree fruits. Two reasons may be assigned for this comparative freedom from injury. First, varieties grown commercially in the majority of sections subject to winter-killing are descended, at least in part, from the native species and therefore profit from the adjustment of the native species to their environments. Second, the difficulty of securing satisfactory ripening of the fruit, because of the shorter growing season, tends to limit the northward spread of grape culture to points with winter extremes well within the adaptation of the vine.

Nevertheless, the grape is far from immune to winter injury. Varieties with Vinifera qualities predominating or from species native to regions of mild winters have distinct climatic limitations and even the so-called hardy varieties frequently suffer. There is little evidence to connect winter drought with winter injury except in so far as a dry soil freezes deeper. Heavy winter irrigation has proved of no value with Viniferas in New Mexico.[90] Under very severe conditions root killing may occur; at times the vines are killed to the ground and there are frequent instances of killing of fruit buds because of imperfect maturity. Gladwin[92] records three seasons out of eight at Fredonia, N. Y., when the vines did not reach proper maturity. Sometimes heavy rains late in the growing season bring about this condition; again it may be due to the ripening of a heavy crop. The light crop usually following a heavy fruiting is commonly ascribed to exhaustion of the vines but it may be due also, at least in part, to the killing of a large number of imperfectly matured buds. Since the grape bud is compound and mixed, the primary floral parts may be killed and only the secondary shoot develop the following spring. This tends to obscure the killing and the sterility of the shoot is attributed to exhaustion following the heavy crop of the preceding season. Gladwin shows that the three lightest crops of the period studied followed the seasons when the sugar content of the grapes (an index of maturity) was lowest. However, since vines which have not borne are affected also, much of the immaturity must come from other causes. Indeed, Budd[37] considered immaturity and tenderness to result from the lack of a crop and remarked that the wood of Rogers' hybrids ripened well when bearing a crop, but without a crop did not mature. Much greater injury has been reported in low ground, particularly in ground with poor drainage.

At times very low temperatures, even when the vines are mature, will cause a discoloration of the wood without actually killing the vine.

Anthony[6] reports recent investigations of the practicability of growing certain Vinifera varieties in the eastern United States. When a moderate amount of winter protection is given, by bending the vines down and covering with a few inches of earth, very satisfactory results are obtained. Indeed, with the varieties tested, the limiting factor seemed to be the heat and length of the growing season rather than tenderness to winter cold. Anthony states: "A well matured Vinifera is seldom killed outright by the winter even if given no protection, but the effect of the first winter is usually to decrease the plant's vitality to such an extent that it is unable to reach proper maturity the next season and so is usually killed the second winter."

Mounding has been effective in protecting Vinifera grapes in New Mexico[90] and hardy grapes in Iowa were satisfactorily wintered by a slight mounding about the trunks and a slight covering of the tips of the canes with soil.[37] Straw protection has been less satisfactory on Viniferas in New York than laying the vines down and giving a slight earth covering. Vines treated in this last manner have proved hardy in very trying climates.

Severe freezes in grape-growing regions damage all varieties so that a close estimate of hardiness in such places is difficult. However, as the culture extends into colder regions varietal differences become more evident. The American Pomological Society's catalog highly commends: for Section I, Brighton, Cottage, Diamond, Herbert, Lady, Lindley,

Moore Early, Moyer, Niagara (?), Victor, Winchell (Green Mountain), Woodbury and Worden; for Section II, Janesville and Winchell; for Section XIV, Diamond is the only variety to receive even a qualified recommendation.[194]

For Vermont, Waugh[242] recommends Moore Early, Worden, Moyer, Brighton, Wyoming Red and Green Mountain. The Northwest Minnesota Experiment Station for a more trying situation recommends Beta, Janesville and Campbell Early.[217] Hansen in South Dakota expresses preference for Worden, Concord and Moore Early in favorable situations and for unfavorable locations, Janesville.[105] The difficulty with Concord in Vermont appears to arise not from its lack of hardiness, but rather from the brevity of the growing season.

THE SMALL FRUITS

Though winter-killing in cane fruits is common, more common, perhaps, than it is among tree fruits, conditions of plant and environment favoring or reducing injury are far less understood. This is due, in part to the large number of units involved so that the loss of a few plants is hardly noticed, in part to the short normal life of a cane fruit plantation so that even an extensive loss is not so calamitous as that of an orchard and in part to the quick recovery of the plants from the common forms of winter injury. When a tree trunk is severely injured recovery is a matter of several years, if indeed it is ever complete. Raspberry or blackberry canes, on the other hand, may kill to the ground but only one crop is lost and the following autumn generally finds the plants in as good condition as ever.

The growing of small fruits has, in most of the northern sections, because of these conditions, developed along two lines; in some cases only hardy varieties are grown and no winter protection is given and in others protection is given and desirable varieties grown regardless of their hardiness. Hence inquiry into hardiness as it relates to small fruits generally has taken the form of variety testing for this quality; related experimental data are very meager. Field observations as recorded are frequently contradictory and puzzling. A certain variety, for example, half hardy in New York would be expected to be wholly adapted to Georgia; actually it may prove fully as tender in the south as in the north. The red raspberry as a group is generally conceded in northern regions to be hardier than the blackcap group yet the reverse condition obtains over wide areas.[43] Though loganberry and other western dewberries are very tender, in one winter at Corvallis, Ore., with a minimum of 20°F., when Cuthbert raspberries were killed at the collar, the loganberry was unharmed. Furthermore, cane fruits frequently suffer from drought injury which is doubtless sometimes confused with winter injury and so reported.

Winter injury to cane fruits may take one of several forms. Root killing occasionally occurs, especially in dry, cold climates with little snow. Where this occurs, covering the canes is of no avail unless the roots also are covered. In other cases the canes may kill to the ground, or they may kill part way back, or the laterals may kill. Immature canes appear to kill more easily at the tips and close to the ground and would sometimes be benefited by mounding. The canes may be weakened only and blossom but fail to mature the crop. Under exceptional conditions currant and gooseberry fruit buds may be killed while the stems live.

Immaturity Most Important.—It is a generally accepted principle in the growing of cane fruits that maturity is important to hardiness. Immature tips, laterals on canes pinched back and suckers that develop late are sometimes injured by comparatively mild freezing; a temperature of 12°F. in November has caused extensive damage to raspberry tissues of this sort in Missouri. Even in Virginia caution about late cultivation, inducing an immature and tender growth, appears necessary,[4] and data have been obtained in Missouri indicating that cultural treatments which promote a vigorous late-season growth of cover crops increase the hardiness of blackberry and raspberry canes.[137] In Illinois spraying treatments to control red spider have resulted in a marked increase in hardiness of raspberry canes.[5] This is attributed to the greater maturity resulting from the manufacture and storage of food reserves by leaves that otherwise would fall prematurely.

Relation of Summer Pinching to Maturity.—The effect of pinching on raspberries in northern sections where maturity is clearly a factor with tree fruits is well illustrated by Table 52, which shows the resistance to winter killing of different varieties pinched at 15 to 20 inches and of the same varieties unpruned. It is evident that the lateral growth induced by pinching is not so hardy as the unbranched canes; presumably this is due to immaturity.

A statement of Michigan experience is not without interest.[235] "Hansell, King, Miller [red raspberries] seldom branch and should not be pinched back. When allowed to grow naturally the canes form strong buds from which the fruiting branches will be developed the following season while if the ends are pinched the buds will develop the first year into slender shoots upon which the fruit buds will be weak, . . . [with an] increased tendency toward winter-killing. Hence, for non-branching varieties pinching back is not to be recommended." However, Card[43] reports instances in which canes growing fairly late in the season have been hardier because they were smaller and of more compact growth and in reality better matured. It is worthy of note, also, that it is a common practice among dewberry growers in the South Atlantic states, where winter injury to cane fruits is by no means unknown, to mow all canes after the fruit has been picked; evidently no serious winter killing to the late growing shoots results. Results attending the influence of midsummer or late summer removal of the surplus weak shoots of the bramble fruits on the hardiness of those that remain are conflicting.

TABLE 52.—WINTER RESISTANCE OF PRUNED AND UNPRUNED RASPBERRIES[60]
(10 = no injury)

	Pruned		Unpruned	
	Protected	Unprotected	Protected	Unprotected
Heebner..................	9.0	4.0	10.0	5.0
Springfield...............	9.0	7.0	9.0	7.0
Royal Church............	2.0	2.0	4.0	5.0
Carman..................	7.0	5.0	9.0	8.0
Thompson Early Prolific...	8.0	7.0	9.0	7.0
Herstine.................	7.0	4.0	9.0	6.0
Parnell..................	8.0	4.0	8.0	5.0
Golden Queen............	5.0	5.0	8.0	5.0
Reider..................	8.0	4.0	8.0	4.0
Brandywine.............	8.0	6.0	9.0	7.0
Niagara.................	7.0	4.0	9.0	6.0
Marlboro...............	7.0	4.0	9.0	5.0
Hansell.................	8.0	6.0	10.0	7.0
Clarke..................	7.0	5.0	8.0	5.0
Cuthbert...............	7.0	4.0	9.0	7.0
Turner.................	9.0	6.0	9.0	6.0
Caroline................	8.0	6.0	9.0	7.0
Average.............	7.3	4.9	8.6	6.0

Average pruned,   6.08
Average unpruned, 7.29

Varietal Differences from Year to Year.—Phenological notes on cane fruits are not sufficiently extensive to indicate whether there is any correlation between varietal behavior in regard to maturity and resistance to cold weather. Comparison of the dates of ripening of fruit with the recorded degree of winter-killing fails to establish any connection; the same is true with regard to the date of blossoming. There is, furthermore, some inconsistency in varietal behavior. Table 53, arranged from reports on variety tests of blackberry in Massachusetts, shows a considerable fluctuation in the percentage of canes killed in successive winters, with a considerable difference in varieties. Thus Agawam's record is 30–0–0 while Erie's is 20–20–80. This indicates that more than one factor must be operative in determining hardiness and that though maturity is frequently very important, it is by no means to be considered the sole factor.

TABLE 53.—PERCENTAGE OF BLACKBERRY CANES KILLED IN SUCCESSIVE WINTERS[154]

	1890	1891	1892
Agawam	30	0	0
Early King	10	12	8
Erie	20	20	80
Minnewaski	0	8	5
Snyder	10	0	0
Wachusett	20	0	10
Western Triumph	30	8	3
Wilson	20	5	40

Injuries from Drought Not Uncommon.—Any variety may be weakened from drought or fungous diseases and suffer unduly the following winter. It is well known that large amounts of moisture in the soil induce winter killing and that accumulation of ice on the surface of the soil has the same effect. The relation of winter drought to winter killing is perhaps less appreciated. Some unpublished investigations by Emerson in Nebraska on this matter are of great importance, pointing as they do to the conclusion that "injury to raspberries in that locality was apparently almost wholly a matter of winter drying."[77] Canes coated with paraffin suffered no appreciable injury while untreated canes on the same stools were killed to the ground or to the snow line. Observing that when the snow cover was deep enough to keep the soil from freezing the canes were not injured, even in the parts that projected above the snow, Emerson tried to secure the same results by mulching. Various mulches were tried and the ground was in many cases kept from freezing but the canes were killed down to the mulch. "Temperature readings taken at various depths in the mulch indicated that for a period of some weeks a portion of the mulch was continuously below the freezing point. Of course, the water absorbed by the roots from the unfrozen ground could not pass through the frozen part of the cane. Other studies suggested, though I perhaps did not have sufficient data to prove it, that the canes are not frozen for any length of time when surrounded by snow."[77]

Card[43] remarks that, though in Nebraska covering of raspberries and blackberries is necessary, the same varieties are commonly grown in New York without protection, despite the fact that the winters in Nebraska are no colder. He reports that during one winter in Nebraska when the mercury fell below zero (Fahrenheit) but once, with −5° as the minimum, unprotected canes were killed. Plants in adjoining rows exactly alike, except that they were laid down and covered, were entirely uninjured.   The following winter was much colder but the soil was moist from autumn rains and both raspberries and blackberries came through in good condition without protection.   Growers of raspberries in Wyoming are advised to stop irrigation about Aug. 1 but to give a heavy late fall irrigation, besides covering the plants.[39]   There is general agreement that cane fruits suffer more in seasons and in sections with little snow.

It is possible that much of the benefit attendant upon covering canes comes from the reduced drying out rather than from actual protection from cold.   Even a trivial protection seems sufficient, sometimes just enough to hold the canes down.   Lying prostrate without covering they escape most of the drying effect of the wind; when covered with earth or snow they will resist extreme cold.   Such protection is essential in some sections, in others the profit in the operation depends on the variety grown.   Thus, in some experiments at Ottawa it was found that the increased yield resulting from protection of the hardiest varieties did not repay the cost of the operation, though other less hardy varieties thus treated gave 16 to 22 per cent. greater yields or enough to leave a profit for the work.[59]   Incidentally, it was reported that the plants thus protected ripened their crops 5 to 8 days ahead of those not protected. In Colorado minimum temperatures around zero ordinarily do not necessitate covering raspberry canes;[114] in New York unprotected raspberry plantations stand considerably lower temperatures without material injury.

Group and Varietal Characteristics.—The small fruits as a class exhibit a rather wide range of hardiness.   Currants probably are to be regarded as the hardiest of all cultivated fruits, with gooseberries only slightly less so.   Next in order, in the north at least, come the red raspberries descended from native species—those of Europe are tender— followed by the blackcap raspberries which in turn are hardier than the blackberries.   There is some overlapping; the hardier black raspberries are hardier than the more tender of the red raspberries and some blackberries in turn are hardier than certain of the raspberries.   Least hardy of all are the dewberries, which are really tender though their trailing habit makes possible their culture much farther north than their upright hybrids with the blackberry can be grown without protection.   The dewberry and the blackberry, like the plum, are derived from several native species and their range in hardiness is correspondingly wide.   The loganberry, Phenomenal berry and allied forms are tender to temperatures below 15°F. and the Himalaya and Evergreen blackberries are very little, if any, hardier.   On the one hand, then, is the currant, hardier without protection than the apple or the plum; on the other is the dewberry, rather less hardy than the peach though it is sometimes grown where the peach is not grown, because it is more easily protected.

Among currants the smaller Red Dutch and Raby Castle types are considerably hardier than the large-fruited varieties, the Fay and Cherry types.[147] London Market, Pomona and White Grape have been found relatively hardy at the Great Plains Experimental Station at Mandan, N. D.[13] Gooseberries rarely suffer from winter killing but where comparisons have been possible Houghton seems the hardiest, with Downing and Industry only slightly less resistant. Turner seems for a long time to have been considered generally the hardiest of the older red raspberries; though the newer Sunbeam and Ohta appear even hardier, a large number of varieties, such as Hansell, Marlboro and Herbert, are hardy enough for all but the most trying climates. Hardier than many of the red raspberries, particularly those with European ancestry, are the hardiest blackcaps, including Plum Farmer and Older. Of the blackberries, Snyder is generally the hardiest, with Eldorado and Agawam ranking close to it. Lucretia is perhaps the most widely grown dewberry in the northern states, being grown successfully in Iowa and Minnesota when covered with soil through the winter.

Summary.—Though winter injury from other causes sometimes occurs, both the apple and the pear suffer most from those forms associated with immaturity. Certain cultural practices encourage earlier maturity, but in these fruits protection against winter injury is most readily secured by a judicious selection of varieties. The peach, plum and cherry suffer from injuries associated with immaturity and with an early breaking of the rest period, the latter being the most important with the peach and certain plums and the former with other plum groups and the cherry. Protective measures lie principally in controlling season and degree of maturity, though something can be accomplished by selection of varieties. Grapes suffer mainly from those forms of winter injury associated with immaturity. Varieties show great differences in their hardiness. In addition to the protective measures adapted to the tree fruits protection by artificial covering of the canes during the winter is sometimes practicable with this fruit. The small fruits show a wide range in hardiness, some of them, as the currant and gooseberry, being among the hardiest and others, as the western dewberries, being very tender. The bramble fruits, in addition to being subject to a general killing back, are particularly susceptible to injury at the crown.

CHAPTER XIX

THE OCCURRENCE OF FROST

Though spring and autumn frosts determine the geographic limits of certain fruits less frequently than minimum winter temperatures, they are nevertheless of no small importance in fruit production. There are some whole sections of the country, as for instance the high table lands of eastern Oregon, where fruit growing is very uncertain because frost may occur at almost any time during the growing season. There are many other sections or areas where spring frosts frequently occur so late that certain fruits such as the apricot or the almond cannot be successfully grown, or where autumn frosts are so early that late maturing fruits such as the grape do not ripen properly and consequently are not grown. Furthermore, within regions or sections that are suitable for fruit culture there are many sites or locations which, because of their susceptibility to frost, are unsuited for orchard purposes or where, if fruit is planted, it requires expensive artificial protection from frost. Finally, there come years when untimely frosts levy a heavy toll on the fruit crop in isolated places or over wide areas generally considered to be favorably located for fruit production. Early autumnal frosts seldom cause concern so far as the season's crop is concerned, though in grapes and some of the late maturing or everbearing types of small fruits they may be responsible for considerable damage. On the other hand, comparatively few and exceptionally fortunate are the fruit growers who are entirely free, year after year, from concern about possible spring frosts. The cost of full protection from spring frosts of certain pear orchards in the Rogue River valley has amounted sometimes to $40 per acre. It is quite likely, however, that many crop failures arising from other causes are attributed to frost damage and it is certain that much can be done to lessen this injury by the careful selection of kinds and varieties of fruit adapted to the particular situation or by selecting a situation suitable to the kinds or varieties of fruit that it is desired to grow. Furthermore, under favorable circumstances much can be accomplished by palliative methods, such as heating the orchard.

FROST FORMATION

Though discussion of the nature, occurrence and prediction of frosts belongs properly in treatises on meteorology, a brief outline of the more important facts concerning frost formation, so far as they concern the fruit grower, seems necessary here because this subject is not studied so widely as is warranted. It should be understood, however, that cold weather aside from frosts may damage fruit crops and it is not always necessary that the temperatures go below the freezing point. Dorsey shows that cold weather, though the temperature remains above freezing, immediately following the pollination of certain plum varieties, results in such a slow growth of the pollen tube that abscission of the style often takes place before fertilization, the result being as complete failure to set fruit as though frost had actually occurred during the blossoming period. Low temperatures also prevent the bees from effecting pollination.

Frosts and Freezes Distinguished.—Furthermore, not all freezing temperatures are due to frosts. English writers use the term "frost" to designate freezing temperature of any kind but usage in the United States restricts "frost" to a kind of cooling well recognized and limited in its scope. A "freeze," as distinguished from a frost, is due to the importation of cold air from other regions and may be accompanied by a high wind; a frost is due to a local cooling of air and occurs during calm weather. The depth of the layer of cold air over the land is usually much greater during a freeze than at the time of a frost.

A frost may take the form called a "hoar" frost, with a visible deposit of frozen moisture, or it may be a "dry" or "black frost" with freezing temperatures but with no deposit. Freezing temperatures may accompany snow squalls. All of these may injure orchard fruits. Against freezes the fruit grower is generally unable to contend by palliative methods; against frost much effort has been expended and it is upon frost that much horticultural thought has been centered.

Relation of Radiation to Frost.—Some knowledge of the nature of radiation is necessary to a proper understanding of the nature of frost. It is generally considered by physicists that all substances are constantly receiving and emanating heat. This radiation heat travels in straight lines through ether and through air, being absorbed by them little or none. Striking a solid substance it is in part reflected and in part absorbed, the amounts of reflection and of absorption varying with the substance. During a clear day the heat received by any substance through radiation from the sun and from other substances is in excess of the amount emitted through radiation; during a clear night the heat lost by radiation exceeds that gained. On a cloudy day the sunlight is cut off to a great extent and the substance is warmed less than on a clear day; during a cloudy night much of the heat lost by radiation is reflected by the clouds and the substance is cooled less than on a clear night. Absorption of solar radiation by the atmosphere varies little with the weather, averaging around 20 per cent.[36] In clear weather reflection and scattering to space amount to about 9 per cent. of the original sunshine, in cloudy weather to as much as 58 per cent., with an average for all weathers of about 35 per cent.[36] Thus, even in clear weather, only about 70 per cent. of the original sunshine reaches the earth's surface, and on the average (including cloudy, partly cloudy and clear days) only about 45 per cent. reaches it.[36] Radiant heat from the earth is absorbed by water vapor, carbon dioxide and ozone.

Radiation is proportional to the exposed surface, and the amount of heat stored and available for radiation is to a large extent proportional to the volume of the radiating substance. Therefore vegetation, which has a large surface in proportion to its volume, cools by radiation with relative rapidity.

Though air freely permits the passage of radiation heat, it radiates little itself in comparison with other substances. There is, it is true, an appreciable amount of radiation from the air. The rapid cooling of air after sunset is largely a radiation effect, especially if the air at higher elevations is rather free from water vapor as is usually the case with a high barometer. However, in comparison with radiation from the earth's surface that from the air is small. Coming in contact with radiating and therefore cooler substances, air loses heat to them by conduction and is thereby cooled. If the air is in motion, the cooled air and the warmer air form a mixture which is constantly coming in contact with the radiating substances bringing to them fresh supplies of heat. If, on the other hand, the air is calm, the cooling of the radiating substances and therefore of the adjacent air continues as long as conditions remain stable, frequently till the sun rises.

Temperature Inversion.—Evidently the nocturnal cooling of the air is largely dependent on the cooling of the earth's surface by radiation. The cooling effect is, therefore, most marked near the surface, but since on even the stillest night the air becomes somewhat mixed its temperature may be affected for from 200 to 600 feet above the surface, the effect becoming less with increasing height.[166] During the day the temperature decreases at the normal adiabatic rate with increasing distance from the earth. This relation is unchanged at night except in so far as it is disturbed, as shown above, by radiation up to a height of 200 to 600 feet. There is, then, at night, first an increase in temperature with distance above the earth, followed by the normal adiabatic decrease. This phenomenon is known to meteorologists as the temperature inversion.

The extent of the temperature inversion is indicated by Table 54, showing the averages of observations made throughout the year at varying heights above a thermometer placed on grass and fully exposed to the sky, expressed in relation

TABLE 54.—AVERAGE TEMPERATURES AT DIFFERENT HEIGHTS COMPARED TO THAT IN GRASS[135]

DISTANCE ABOVE GRASS	INCREASE (DEGREES FAHRENHEIT)
1 inch	3
6 inches	6
1 foot	7
12 feet	8
50 feet	10
150 feet	12

to the readings of this thermometer. The steepness of the inversion varies from night to night and it is more marked in some localities than in others but it necessarily exists whenever frost occurs. This temperature inversion causes frost but it also makes possible the combating of frosts by orchard heating as shown later. Humphreys[120] points out another interesting relation of this inversion to frost damage: " . . . it is obvious that the tops of open and sparsely foliaged trees, especially if rather tall, often are less subject to frost and more easily protected than are the lower limbs. On the other hand, when the tree is low and its outer foliage sufficiently dense to produce a protecting canopy over the under and inner branches, as is generally the case with orchard trees, the difference between the free radiation from the exposed fruit and the restricted radiation from that which is covered may usually be sufficient, even when there is a marked temperature inversion, to subject the former and not the latter to the greatest danger from frost and freeze."

Radiation and Thermometer Readings.—The full importance of radiation to the horticulturist needs emphasis. Lack of recognition of this factor has diminished the value of much investigational work. A thermometer exposed to the open air is radiating and receiving heat. During a clear night the outgoing exceeds the incoming heat and the thermometer registers a lower temperature than that of the air. Inside a shelter practically all the outgoing radiation heat is reflected to the thermometer which consequently registers very close to the actual air temperature. During May in cranberry marshes in Wisconsin there were found differences between sheltered and exposed thermometers over bare soil averaging 2.3°F. for all nights of record, including nights not clear. Occasionally the exposed thermometers recorded as much as 5.7 and 6.4° lower than the thermometers in shelters.[57] Inasmuch as these temperatures were taken near the ground it is possible that they represented extreme conditions and would be of direct importance only to the cranberry and strawberry grower. Sheltered and unsheltered thermometers at a height of 5.5 feet from the ground at Williamstown, Mass., showed differences at the time of the minimum temperature averaging 1.6° and a maximum difference of 4°F.[163] It is evident, then, that the exposed and sheltered thermometers do not check and that the differences are not constant.

Radiation and Plant Temperatures.—Plants as well as thermometers lose heat by radiation. Seeley[214] working with strawberries found considerable difference between plant temperatures and air temperatures.

He reports in part on his results as follows: "The plant thermometer readings were usually lower than the air temperature in the early morning, the minimum usually being about 3 or 4°[F]. lower than the air, the difference being greater, of course, when the weather was clear with but little wind velocity. The plant cooled off more rapidly than the air in the early evening so that at 7 p. m. it was usually 3 or 4°[F.] lower in temperature than the surrounding air." At times the temperature of the plant may fall to 8°C. below that of the surrounding air and plants may be frozen stiff though the thermometer indicates one or two degrees above zero (C.),[186] and there are records showing that occasionally plants are cooled by radiation to a temperature 12 to 15°F. below that of the surrounding air.[136] Tomato vines under apple trees sometimes escape frost when those exposed to radiation are killed and the temperature on a lawn under a tree may be 5° higher than in the open.[169]

Observations, predictions and conclusions, then, must be made with three standards in mind: the air temperature, the exposed thermometer temperature and the plant temperature. Though the exposed thermometer doubtless registers closer to the plant temperature than the sheltered thermometer, it must be remembered that predictions are based on and apply to sheltered thermometer readings. The differences between the three temperatures may not be great but they are at times great enough to vitiate conclusions drawn from observations and they may conceivably become at times great enough to have material effects.

Dewpoint and Its Relation to Frost.—Air is commonly known to contain more or less water vapor. Other things equal, the higher its temperature the more vapor it can contain and conversely the lower its temperature the less moisture it can hold. If, therefore, any sample of air be cooled enough it will reach the point where it can no longer hold as vapor all the moisture it contains and some of it is deposited. Obviously the drier the air at a given temperature the farther must its temperature fall before the moisture is condensed. The dewpoint, or temperature at which condensation occurs, varies, then, with the absolute amount of moisture present in the air.

As radiation proceeds from soil, vegetation and other substances it has been shown that the temperature of the air in the immediate neighborhood of these substances falls. In a calm this cooling frequently proceeds to the point at which moisture is condensed; if this point is above the freezing point dew is formed; if below, frost is formed directly. It should be observed that frost is but an index of a low temperature and is not of itself injurious. It should be observed further that radiating substances, particularly in a dry atmosphere, may cool the air several degrees below the freezing point without any deposit of frost. This is the black or dry frost. It is possible, too, for cooling to be extremely localized so that frost forms when the free air temperature is several degrees above freezing; frosts have occurred with a free air temperature of 40°F.

The condensation of moisture from the air sets free a certain amount of heat and retards the further fall in temperature. To that extent dew or even frost formation is beneficial as compared with low temperature without moisture condensation. It was formerly assumed that the liberation of heat from condensation would check any further temperature fall and that because of this the dewpoint as determined the previous evening would forecast the minimum temperature of the night. However, with a change in direction of the wind or in its velocity, there may be a rapid rise or lowering of dewpoint—as much as 20°F. in 3 hours[103] —or clouds may be brought in or carried away and consequently such forecasts are subject to considerable error.

Relation of Clouds and Wind to Frost Occurrence.—Evidently conditions favoring loss of heat by radiation and a calm condition of the air combine to produce dew or frost. Clouds reflect the heat lost by radiation and even radiate some of their own heat so that the passage of a cloud may for a short time raise the temperature a degree or two. Therefore cloudy nights, though still, are not very likely to be frosty. A fair breeze does not prevent radiation but it mixes the air and prevents excessive cooling of any small portion of it; therefore, windy nights are not likely to be frosty. It is the nights which combine good radiation conditions with still air that the fruit grower should watch when his trees are in bloom.

INFLUENCE OF LOCATION ON DANGER FROM FROST

It has been shown that in the northern hemisphere the blossoming of fruit trees begins early in the south and, subject of course to minor differences, moves northward at a rate of 4 or 5 days for each degree of latitude, though somewhat more rapidly to the west of a given point than to the east. If the date of the last killing frost in the spring moved northward at the same rate, the calculation of the chances of a given fruit's escaping frost at any location would be a simple matter. Unfortunately conditions are much more complicated. Dates of blossoming and of last frosts fluctuate from year to year. There are local variations particularly in the occurrence and severity of frosts; these are considered later. The present phase of the discussion is intended to point out that certain regions are more subject, perhaps, to late frosts at critical times for the fruit grower than other localities.

The Blossoming Season and Latitude.—Figure 33 shows the dates of blossoming for the Wildgoose plum at various points in the United States for 1898, a season that was, on the whole, rather earlier than the average.[244] Unfortunately not enough data are available for the construction of a map showing average blossoming seasons for any particular variety of fruit and minor fluctuations due to varying weather in different sections might change in another season the lines shown in the figure. However, the figure shows in a general way the northward progress of the blossoming season.

Unpublished figures compiled by Phillips give average data for several kinds and varieties of fruits and show that the blossoming season moves northward more rapidly in the Mississippi valley than along the Atlantic seaboard (*cf.* Table 55). Phillips finds the rate for each degree of latitude to be: along the Atlantic coast, 5.7 days; in the Mississippi valley,

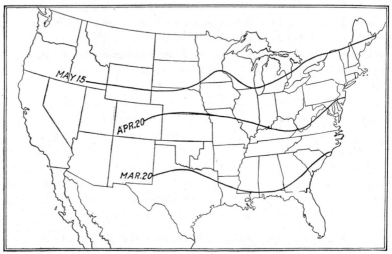

FIG. 33.—The blossoming season of Wildgoose plum for 1898.   (*After Waugh*[244])

4.8 days and for the Pacific region, 3.4 days. Somewhat similar relative progress has been found for certain phases of insect life.[117] These differences between sections assume importance in connection with the dates of the last killing frosts.

TABLE 55.—AVERAGE DATE OF FULL BLOOM FOR SEVERAL FRUITS AT DIFFERENT LATITUDES
(*After Phillips*[188])

Latitude	Pacific section	Mississippi valley	Atlantic section
35°	Mar. 11	Mar. 16	Mar. 19
36°	Mar. 14	Mar. 16	Mar. 24
38°	Mar. 19	Mar. 30	Apr. 10
40°	Mar. 18	Apr. 11	Apr. 19
41°	Mar. 22	Apr. 19	Apr. 26
42°	Mar. 27	Apr. 27	May 5
Average all parallels................	Mar. 19	Apr. 4	Apr. 11

Average Date of Last Spring Frost and Latitude.—The average dates of the last killing spring frosts are shown in Fig. 34. Though there is a general northward recession, local conditions evidently complicate this process in the extreme so that latitude alone is not a safe guide in determining the date of the last frost. The date lines of last frosts are obviously not parallel. As an example, the last-frost date line for June 1 is worth consideration. Barely dipping below the forty-fifth parallel in New England it leaves the United States to reappear in Minnesota where it remains well above the forty-fifth parallel until it leaves the states at the Canadian boundary. Entering the United States again in Montana it moves southward to New Mexico, almost

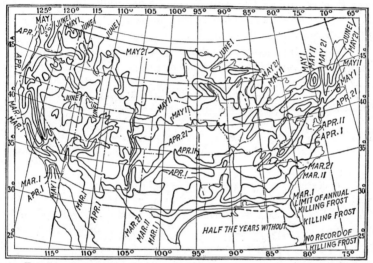

Fig. 34.—Average dates of last killing frost in spring. (*After Reed*[195])

to the thirty-fifth parallel, embracing a wide range of territory until it leaves Idaho, reappearing again in Washington.

Average Dates and Frost Danger.—An average date, if the data on which it is based be sufficient to give it validity, means that approximately 50 per cent. of the occurrences are prior to this date and 50 per cent. follow it. If the average date of blossoming and the average date of the last frost for a given locality coincide there are possible four combinations of events: (1) blossoming before the average and frost before the average, a condition which may or may not be disastrous to fruit at that point; (2) blossoming before the average and frost later than the average, very likely to be a disastrous combination; (3) blossoming after the average date and frost before the average date, a safe condition, and (4) blossoming later than the average and frost after the average, unsafe. In cases 1 and 4 the last frost may or may not precede the blossoming, with chances balancing. Cases 2 and 3 balance each other. It appears, therefore, that locations where the average blossoming date and average last frost date coincide have an even chance of escaping frost, a margin of safety that is rather small for growing of the fruit in question.

Determining Frost Risks in Different Sections and Localities.—Averages, of course, do not indicate the range of the figures that they represent. The range of last frost dates may be considerable at one point and limited at another, with the averages identical. Table 56 shows variations in the last frost dates on record for several stations with identical average date for this event. Such averages have only a limited significance for the fruit grower, unless the fruit he grows generally blossoms considerably later than the average date of the last frost.

The last column in Table 56 records standard deviations from the average date of the last frost, Apr. 15 in each case. This standard deviation means, taking Roseburg for example, that over a considerable

TABLE 56.—SPRING FROST DATA FOR SELECTED STATIONS[196]

Station	Average date	Last in 9 to 10 years	Last in 1895 to 1914	Standard deviation
Keokuk, Iowa............	Apr. 15	Apr. 30	May 4	11.7
Cumberland, Md..........	Apr. 15	May 2	May 12	13.0
New Bedford, Mass........	Apr. 15	Apr. 28	May 2	10.0
Lebanon, Nev............	Apr. 15	Apr. 15	May 1	12.4
Roseburg, Ore...........	Apr. 15	May 10	May 10	19.7

period, in approximately half the years the last frost will occur between 20 days before Apr. 15 and 20 days after, or between Mar. 27 and May 5; in approximately one-fourth of these years it will occur before Mar. 27 and in approximately one-fourth of the years it will occur after May 5. The record shows that the latest date of last frost for this station is May 10. Figure 35 shows the rather considerable range of standard deviations in dates of last frosts at various points in the United States.

Of greater immediate value to the fruit grower is Fig. 36, showing dates "when the chance of killing frost falls to 1 in 10."[195] If the average date of blossoming at a given point is identical with the date of the 1:10 chance for that point the probability of damage is slight, being in fact $\frac{1}{2} \times \frac{1}{10} = \frac{1}{20}$, or one chance in 20. This may happen very frequently in cane fruits and grapes, though in most cases the average date for orchard fruits would precede that of the 1:10 chance. Comparison of such average blossoming dates as are available and of real validity shows that very few orchard fruits have less than one chance in 10 of encountering frost.

The data here presented are introduced as suggestive rather than for their absolute value. As pointed out elsewhere, a frost recorded as "killing," though damaging to tender vegetation, may do little or no damage to fruit blossoms; similar data based on the last occurrence of 30° or 29°F. would be of more direct value to the fruit grower. Neverthe-

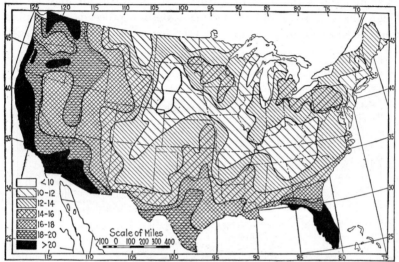

Fig. 35.—Standard deviations of dates of last killing frosts in spring. (*After Reed*[195])

less the general liability of certain regions to frosts damaging to fruits holds true, whatever criterion be adopted, and though it would be hazardous to apply the present data unreservedly to any one point they serve adequately for comparison between different points. Arranged on a slightly different basis and in conjunction with accurate blossoming charts, which are not available, they would have even greater value. At present only generalizations are possible. The tendency of blossoming to advance more rapidly in the central than in the Atlantic states and the irregularity in the recession of last frosts, with a general tendency toward faster recession on the Atlantic seaboard, makes a given fruit more liable to frost damage in the Mississippi valley region than on the Atlantic coast, if local variations do not intervene.

INFLUENCE OF SITE ON MINIMUM TEMPERATURES

The air in the neighborhood of radiating surfaces has been shown to be cooled by conduction and the air temperature on a still night to increase with distance from the surface. As the air in contact with radiating surfaces cools it becomes more dense and tends to sink. It is then replaced by air somewhat warmer, probably for the most part flowing in from the same level, which air in turn cools and sinks. If the supply of relatively warm air be extensive enough and warm enough, the radiating surfaces may be kept from reaching the freezing point. This frequently happens on hillsides where the coolest air is continuously being pushed downward by air nearly as cool and warmer air is flowing in from the side. So much cool air may accumulate, however, that it fills a depression completely and raises the level of warm air. The warm air may be raised so high above a given object that, as radiation proceeds, the replacing air has little heat to give up. It therefore fails to warm the surface

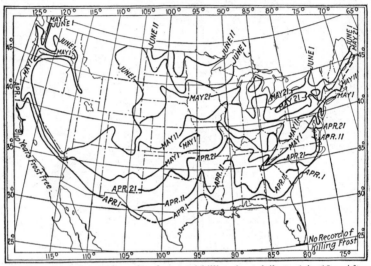

Fig. 36.—Computed dates when the chance of killing frost fails to 1 in 10. After these dates killing frost will occur only 10 years in a century. (*After Reed*[195])

sufficiently to prevent freezing.[150] Little replacement can be expected by warm air from above since it is lighter.

However, other things being equal, the wider a valley the greater its area in proportion to its circumference; consequently the reservoir of free warm air at any level is greater in proportion to the radiating shoreline at that level. The higher levels, in a given valley, therefore, in addition to having better "drainage facilities" for removal of cold air have larger reservoirs of warm air on which they can draw. For the same reasons a slight elevation above a wide valley may be considerably freer from frost than a higher elevation above a more restricted valley.

The term "air drainage," used to signify the resemblance of the flow of cold air to the flow of water, is more or less unscientific and inexact.[150] Nevertheless it is a convenient term; it suffices for practical purposes and doubtless will continue in use. In many cases there is an actual flow of air, closely comparable to the flow of water. This flow of air is frequently the salvation of orchards in narrow valleys which otherwise would fill quickly with cold air.

TABLE 57.—MINIMUM TEMPERATURES AT STATE COLLEGE, N. M.

(After Garcia[89])

(Station *A* 25 feet higher than Station *B*)

Day	March 1912		March 1913		April 1912		April 1913	
	A	B	A	B	A	B	A	B
1	....	....	....	....	32.0	24.5	45.0	42.0
2	....	....	....	....	38.0	26.0	40.0	35.0
3	....	....	....	....	38.0	33.0	40.0	36.5
4	....	....	....	....	49.0	46.5	34.0	31.5
5	....	....	....	....	44.0	45.0	35.0	31.5
6	....	....	....	....	39.0	34.0	51.0	40.0
7	....	....	....	....	39.0	36.0	38.0	36.0
8	....	....	....	....	40.0	37.5	36.0	33.5
9	....	....	....	....	37.0	34.5	33.0	30.5
10	....	....	....	....	52.0	45.0	38.0	36.5
11	....	....	....	....	39.0	34.0	36.0	35.5
12	....	....	....	....	41.0	40.0	29.0	25.5
13	....	....	....	....	36.0	33.0	30.0	27.0
14	....	....	....	....	32.0	29.0	31.0	28.0
15	....	....	....	....	39.0	34.0	39.0	35.0
16	....	....	18.0	13.0	40.0	35.5	38.0	35.0
17	....	....	20.0	16.5	38.0	32.5	44.0	40.0
18	....	....	25.0	20.5	39.0	33.0	49.0	44.0
19	....	....	41.0	35.0	40.0	34.0	39.0	35.0
20	....	....	42.0	38.5	49.0	40.0	59.0	45.0
21	....	....	30.0	27.0	40.0	35.0	46.0	44.0
22	....	....	36.0	31.0	31.0	29.0	53.0	43.5
23	....	....	32.0	26.5	38.0	33.0	43.0	42.0
24	30.0	25.0	19.0	17.0	51.0	45.0	31.0	27.0
25	36.0	33.0	21.0	19.0	43.0	39.0	32.0	29.0
26	45.0	39.0	31.0	26.5	34.0	28.5	36.0	33.0
27	35.0	32.5	35.0	31.5	49.0	40.0	39.0	35.0
28	35.0	29.0	....	....	44.0	39.0	40.0	36.0
29	34.0	29.0	....	....	40.0	35.5	44.0	40.0
30	33.0	26.5	....	....	48.0	39.0	44.0	40.0
31	41.0	30.0	....	....	....	....	....	....
Average..	36.1	30.5	29.1	25.2	40.6	35.7	39.7	35.7

In the discussion of Sites the statement is made that air drainage insuring as much freedom from spring frosts as possible is one of the most important considerations in picking the site for an orchard. It should be stated here conversely that the best method of ensuring against frost and against the continual tax of frost-fighting is the proper selection of a site.   There are certain sections where to secure proper soil or plentiful moisture it becomes necessary for the prospective fruit grower to locate on low sites that are subject to frost.   He should recognize clearly that he is exchanging relative immunity from frost for other advantages; the exchange may be profitable if the frosts are not too numerous and too severe.   Over a large part of the country, however, a considerable latitude in choice is available and intelligent discrimination in the choice of site may very easily make the difference between considerable profit and heavy loss.   The grower who is forced to protect his orchard may make a profit in spite of his heavy overhead expense and annual tax; the grower whose location is such that he is comparatively immune from spring frosts is more likely to be commercially successful.

Sometimes the line that divides desirable and undesirable locations is very finely drawn.   Table 57 shows minimum temperatures during the blossoming season at two locations not far apart and with only 25 feet difference in elevation. The dissimilarities in average minima are at once obvious.

More important, however, is the consideration that Station B during the time covered by these data registered temperatures below freezing 28 times as compared with 13 for Station A; Station B registered temperatures 28°F. or less 14 times while this point was reached at Station A, only five times.   Analyzing the figures in another way: in the spring of 1912 Station B had a minimum of practically 28°F. as late as Apr. 26 though Station A did not reach this figure during the season.   In 1913 the last minimum of 28°F. or less for Station A occurred on Mar. 26 and for Station B the date was Apr. 14.

Similar variations were found in Nevada between two points 190 feet apart and differing in elevation by 13.5 feet.[53]   The average April and May minimum for the higher station was 42.7°F.; for the lower it was 39.5°.   On selected single nights paired observations were 29–22, 34–31, 32–24, 39–31, 37–30.   The diversity in the amount of fruit grown in 2 years on sites such as these, other things being equal, must necessarily be great and the difference in expense of orchard heating in the two cases would be well worth considering.

In some cases this effect is said to be somewhat neutralized by the increased earliness of higher elevations.   As a rule vegetation is later at high altitudes, but this condition is reversed frequently between points differing in altitude only a few hundred feet.   An interval of 2 weeks between the first blossoming dates has been reported at points in Utah 2 miles apart and with 200 feet difference in elevation.[3]   It is not, however, clear that this was due wholly to the elevation since slopes and condition of soil and of trees were not stated and the variations reported are certainly much more marked than is ordinarily the case, making 1 day's difference for each 14 feet in elevation.   Were the air constantly still during the whole season up to blossoming, the moderately high elevations might indeed accumulate enough excess of heat to make considerable difference but in nature this condition obtains only during a very small portion of the time and such differences as do occur generally may be attributed to other effects.

The steepness of slope necessary to effective freedom from frost varies with the local topography. Young[262] states: "From observations in the Pomona Valley, California, it appears that there is little if any advantage to be gained by locating an orchard in the upper portion of a long uniform slope of 150 feet or less to the mile. However, in even slight depressions of whatever shape or direction on this slope the frost hazard is likely to be considerably greater."

MINOR FACTORS AFFECTING TEMPERATURE

Of interest chiefly to growers of strawberries and cranberries are certain differences in narrowly restricted limits, differences usually small but frequently important. Included among these are those due to elevation, to the character of the soil covering and to the state of the soil.

Minor Differences in Elevation.—Observations on three sets of thermometers at several points in Williamstown, Mass., with the upper thermometers exposed at a height of 5.5 feet, the lower at 0.5 foot, show differences tabulated in Table 58, from which it appears that a strawberry plant may be exposed to considerably lower temperatures on a frosty night than the trees above it or than the thermometer in the ordinary shelter. Milham points out that the differences are greatest at the time of the minimum temperature and at the coldest station, in other words when conditions for frost are most favorable. Strawberry growers should bear this in mind in interpreting for their own use forecasts issued by the Weather Bureau.

TABLE 58.—TEMPERATURE DIFFERENCES WITH HEIGHT[163]
(Degrees Fahrenheit)

	Station 1	Station 8 (8 p.m.)	Station 7	Station 1	Station 8 (minimum)	Station 7
Average difference	0.5	1.5	2.1	0.5	2.0	2.9
Largest difference	2.0	4.0	5.0	2.0	4.0	5.0

On the other hand Cox[57] found temperatures at 5 inches above the soil lower than those at the surface, particularly on nights with good radiation conditions.

"The average depression of temperature," he writes, "at the 5-inch height below that at the surface for the season of 1907 (May to October inclusive) was 1°[F]. The average depression on clear cool nights probably reached 4°. There were several instances of differences exceeding 6°." Cox evidently was not entirely satisfied with the possible explanations he advanced for this difference though they doubtless explain it in part. He states, "In a marsh grasses and uprights from the vines interfere slightly with radiation from the thermometers placed on the surface and it is probable that a thermometer or leaf exposed at an elevation above the surface loses its heat more rapidly by radiation than if it rested upon the surface because the upper one is not shielded in any way and while the radiation is going on from the lower one, at the same time heat is being conducted to it from the ground beneath. A thermometer resting upon the surface of the bog becomes a part of the soil or vegetation upon which it rests, as it were, and is benefited by the free conduction of heat to it from the ground, while the conduction to and through the air is very slight in comparison; because of these differences in radiation and conduction, the surface thermometer usually registers a higher temperature than the instrument a few inches above. For the same reason, the temperature of the vegetation at the surface and 5 inches above would vary as these temperatures have varied, especially when the surface vegetation is shielded above. It is a matter of common knowledge that in the bogs the cranberries growing at the tops of the uprights a few inches above the ground are often damaged by frost while those lying on or near the ground escape injury."

Cox reports also two series of observations on temperatures at various heights up to 36 inches above the surface. On the bog the 5-inch height had the lowest average minimum temperature, the surface averaging 1.7° higher than the 5-inch level and 1.4° lower than the 36-inch level. In a garden on upland the differences were less. Cox summarizes his observations on this point as follows: "The temperature at 2.5 inches averaged lowest, 44.5°[F], instead of at 5 inches, as on the bog, but the difference was very slight between these two elevations—0.1°. The surface thermometer averaged highest, 45.5° but there was only 1° difference on an average between the two extremes while the average surface reading was 0.6° higher than at 36 inches. The average for the entire season fairly represents the conditions prevailing each month, the highest in each case occurring at the surface and the lowest at 2.5 inches." Table 59, compiled from Cox's report, shows minima for nights selected because of the low temperatures and indicates no substantial variation from his averages.[57]

TABLE 59.—MINIMUM TEMPERATURES IN OPEN OVER SANDY LOAM
(Degrees Fahrenheit)

Date (1907)	Sur-face	2.5 inches	5 inches	7.5 inches	10 inches	12 inches	15 inches	36 inches
May 20........	24.9	23.7	23.8	24.0	24.8	24.9	25.0	25.9
May 21........	24.9	22.9	23.0	23.1	23.1	23.1	23.0	23.8
June 6........	34.7	31.4	31.5	31.7	31.7	31.7	31.2	31.4
Sept. 22........	28.0	27.8	27.8	28.1	28.3	28.0	28.2	28.6
Sept. 30........	25.0	24.6	24.7	25.0	25.2	25.1	25.2	25.4

It is evident that these differences are not constant. Some light is thrown on the effect of radiation by data compiled from Greenwich observations showing that a thermometer on grass fully exposed to the sky registered lower than a thermometer suspended 4 feet from the ground:[135]

<table>
<tr><td></td><td>DEGREES
FAHRENHEIT</td></tr>
<tr><td>On cloudless nights...</td><td>9.3</td></tr>
<tr><td>Half cloudy..</td><td>7.3</td></tr>
<tr><td>Principally cloudy..</td><td>6.8</td></tr>
<tr><td>Entirely cloudy..</td><td>3.4</td></tr>
</table>

Influence of Soil.—Reference is made again to Cox's work for data concerning the minimum temperatures over two different soils. Table 60 shows minima for selected nights with the average for the month. The difference, striking at the surface, becomes very slight at 3 feet. The differences up to 5 inches are, however, of no little significance to the strawberry grower. They are to be regarded as due to character of the soils, since other conditions were uniform. Incidentally it may be stated that Cox considers it possible for identical atmospheric conditions to cause a light frost in the spring and not in the fall because of the difference in soil temperatures at the two seasons. To the extent that a high day temperature indicates considerable heat furnished the soil, it diminishes

TABLE 60.—MINIMUM TEMPERATURES IN OPEN OVER TWO SOILS[57]
(September, 1906)

Day of month	Over peat			Over sand			Differences between peat and sand		
	Surface	5 inches	36 inches	Surface	5 inches	36 inches	Surface	5 inches	36 inches
5	38.4	33.1	34.8	45.0	35.9	35.9	−6.6	−2.8	−1.1
14	35.6	33.0	34.7	43.9	35.0	35.1	−8.3	−2.0	−0.4
24	35.7	32.5	33.4	41.0	34.0	33.5	−5.3	−1.5	−0.1
27	33.9	31.0	30.4	40.3	30.8	30.3	−6.4	+0.2	+0.1
28	39.8	31.9	35.7	43.0	35.7	36.1	−3.2	−3.8	−0.4
30	34.0	28.8	31.4	39.6	31.0	33.0	−5.6	−2.2	−1.6
Monthly mean..	50.6	47.0	48.7	53.6	48.6	49.0	−3.0	−1.6	−0.3

the probability of frost the following morning. Furthermore Cox states, "It is practically impossible for frost to occur in the bogs on the first cool night following a warm spell, but it is likely, if conditions are favorable, on the second night after the soil has become cold."

The difference in temperature over the two soils is due probably to their difference in radiating and conducting powers. Peat absorbs and radiates heat readily but of course the heat lost by radiation warms the air exceedingly little; peat is a poor conductor and cannot warm the air greatly by conduction. The sand, though not so good an absorber of heat, is a better conductor and warms the air above it at night.

Influence of Soil Covering.—A thick mat of vegetation covering the soil prevents much heating during sunshine. At night, though it prevents conduction of heat from the soil, it radiates heat and thus tends to lower the air temperature further. It is not strange therefore that lower temperatures are found over vegetation than over bare ground. Table

TABLE 61.—TEMPERATURES OVER SOD AND OVER BARE GROUND
(*After Seeley*[213])
(Degrees Fahrenheit)

	p.m.	a.m.	Loss
Surface, bare ground..........................	45.0	27.3	17.7
Surface, sod................................	43.0	23.9	19.1
Half inch below surface, bare ground...........	46.2	30.1	16.1
Half inch below surface, sod..................	43.0	23.9	11.7

61, giving the means of observations on 18 mornings at Peoria, Ill., shows the increase in difference of surface temperatures between sod and bare ground from afternoon to morning. The sod surface is 2° cooler in the afternoon and 3.4° cooler in the morning. Below the surface, however, the sod loses less.

In minimum temperatures 5 inches above the surface on cranberry bogs considerable difference, according to the density of the vegetation, is reported by Cox,[57] from observations made in September, 1906. Table 62, which records his observations for the coldest nights, shows the magnitude of these variations attributable to the difference in the amount of vegetation and the effect it has on soil temperature. Similar inequalities

TABLE 62.—MINIMUM TEMPERATURES WITH THICK AND WITH THIN VEGETATION
(*After Cox*[57])
(Degrees Fahrenheit)

Day of month	Thinly vined	Thickly vined	Difference
5	33.1	28.3	−4.8
14	33.0	28.8	−4.2
24	32.5	28.9	−3.6
27	31.0	24.4	−6.6
28	31.9	28.0	−3.9
30	28.8	23.0	−5.8
Monthly mean......	47.0	43.6	−3.4

may be expected in very weedy and dense strawberry beds. More frost damage has been observed in weed-infested German vineyards than in those kept clean.[169]

The effect of mulching, a common practice in strawberry growing, should be mentioned at this point. As a winter protection the value of a mulch is indubitable. In early spring a mulch tends to retard blossoming, an effect which may or may not be desirable. Once the plants are in blossom, however, a mulch may invite frost damage.

Lazenby[127] reported observations to this effect: "To compare temperatures over mulched and unmulched ground I took 16 observations with a self-registering minimum thermometer daily between May 17 and June 1 of last year. The average minimum over straw was 43.2°; over bare ground 46.4°. The greatest difference was 7°. This year the average minimum over straw was 32.3°; over bare ground 34° with a maximum difference of 3.5°."

This effect is due probably to the exclusion of sunshine from the soil during the day and to increased radiation at night. If the mulch is used to cover the plants during frost, its effect is, of course, totally different.

Influence of Soil Moisture.—Observations on surface temperatures in wet and in dry sanded bogs at Berlin, Wis., in 1906, indicated a consistent, and at times considerable, difference. Table 63, compiled

TABLE 63.—SURFACE MINIMUM TEMPERATURES ON DRY AND ON WET SANDED BOGS
(*Adapted from Cox*[57])
(Degrees Fahrenheit)

Date	Dry sand	Wet sand	Difference
Sept. 14.............................	43.9	37.7	−6.2
Sept. 24.............................	41.0	37.4	−3.6
Sept. 27.............................	40.3	33.1	−7.2
Sept. 28.............................	43.0	38.0	−5.0
Sept. 30.............................	39.6	32.3	−7.3
Oct. 1.............................	35.8	27.3	−8.5
September mean......................	53.6	51.2	−2.4

by the selection of the coldest nights, shows that at the very time when these differences are most important they are greatest. It might be argued that the wet sand was coldest because it had given up more heat; however it is stated that on Oct. 1 cranberries in this bog were frozen, except in the dry sanded section. The lower minimum on the wet sand is attributed to the heat lost in evaporation at the surface.

It should be remarked that irrigation with relatively warm water at the time of frost apparently has proved of considerable value occasionally but irrigation that merely wets the soil and keeps it cold is probably injurious. An experimental investigation in Wisconsin showed very little difference in temperature over irrigated and over unirrigated blocks.

King,[126] commenting on the results, stated: "Not only did frost form after the water was brought to the areas but some of the rape leaves became stiff with streams of water flowing both sides of the row. It is true, however, that a very perceptible difference could be noted in the degree of stiffness which foliage took on above and close to the water, and that which was more distant. For close to the water the leaves did not become so rigid as to break in the hand while at a distance from the water they did.

"It is quite possible that were broad areas irrigated at such times the protection would be more marked, but it does not look very hopeful for the protection against night frosts by this method, especially where the temperature falls 3 or 4° below freezing."

It seems evident from the data above that evaporation does not interfere with radiation sufficiently to offset its cooling effect and that unless the water actually imparts heat it is deleterious. A thoroughly saturated soil is, however, likely to retard frost formation.

Cox[58] states: "The explanation is found in the high specific heat of water. A certain quantity of heat lost during the night time from relatively dry ground and its vegetable cover cools the exposed portions of these poor heat-conducting objects to a very low temperature. An equal loss of heat from the same substances when they are loaded with moisture results in only a small lowering of the temperature not only because the water must now be cooled in addition to the ground and vegetation but, as we know, water requires the removal of considerable heat to cool it slightly. The radiation losses from the saturated surfaces may also be less than from the dry surfaces."

Evidently looseness in application of terms "wet" and "dry" has led to some apparently conflicting results. Petit[184] records observations

TABLE 64.—TEMPERATURES IN MOIST AND DRY SOILS
(*After Petit*[184])
(Degrees Centigrade)

Date and time	Dry soil	Saturated soil
Apr. 23, 4.00 p.m.	29.7	21.6
Apr. 23, 7.15 p.m.	18.5	16.1
Apr. 24, 5.20 p.m.	3.9	6.5

that at first seem contradictory to those of Cox, since they indicate higher temperatures over the wetter soil (*cf.* Tables 64 and 65). Petit states that the chief cooling influence in wet soil, evaporation, is inactive at night, that the moist soil conducts heat more rapidly than the dry and therefore can receive more heat from below; he evidently considers that these factors offset the greater radiation he ascribes to wet soil and the lower heat storage during the day. Curiously enough he finds that dew forms earlier and is more abundant on the moist soil. It is possible, however, that Cox and Petit worked with soils of different texture and moisture content and that their results are not necessarily conflicting.

TABLE 65.—SURFACE TEMPERATURES OVER WET AND OVER DRY SOILS
(*After Petit*[184])
(Degrees Centigrade)

Date	Time	Not watered	Watered
Sept. 23	4.30 p.m.	18.2	15.6
Sept. 23	6.00 p.m.	14.0	12.4
Sept. 23	10.00 p.m.	6.9	7.3
Sept. 24	5.00 a.m.	2.3	3.2
Sept. 28	5.15 p.m.	10.6	10.6
Sept. 28	9.25 p.m.	5.6	6.9
Sept. 29	5.55 a.m.	4.0	5.2

Effect of Cultivation.—In a series of observations on the minimum temperatures over cultivated and uncultivated soils at Peoria, Ill., it was found that cultivation apparently increased the temperature about 2°.[213] Cox states: "It is as important to cultivate as it is to practice drainage," but adds that "it is impossible to determine absolutely the advantage in exact degrees gained by cultivation, draining or sanding." It is evident that his statement refers to any attempt to make the observed differences fit all cases.

Cultivation is said by Petit to increase the loss from the surface of the soil by radiation, diminishing heat conduction from below; tamping the soil is stated to lessen this danger. It should be observed that the temperatures recorded are those of the surface and not of the air above.

TABLE 66.—TEMPERATURES AT SURFACE OF CULTIVATED AND PACKED SOILS
(*After Petit*[184])
(Degrees Centigrade)

Date and time	Packed	Stirred	Lumps
July 15, 1898—4.30 p.m.	....	37.9	37.4
July 15, 1898—8.15 p.m.	....	17.8	15.8
Aug. 4, 1898—8.00 p.m.	16.8	14.2	12.6

Increased surface of the loosened soil would tend to increase the loss of heat by conduction and might easily raise the temperature of the air immediately above it, though the surface itself be cooled.

Significance—Particularly in Small Fruit Culture.—A saving of 2° or 3° may or may not be an important matter according to circumstances and consequently any one of the factors affecting temperature may in itself be important. However, it is frequently the case that several of them are operative at once and their combined effect is likely to be considerable, particularly on nights when these differences are most important.

Cox expresses this aptly: "While there is an average difference of 3.4° . . . between the minimum thermometers in the thinly vined and the heavily vined sections, a difference of 2.4° . . . between the minimum thermometers on peat and sanded bogs, both thinly vined, and a difference of 2.2° between the surface and 5 inches, it is obvious why an average difference of 10° . . . can exist between a minimum thermometer exposed at the most favorable location as far as drainage and sanding and cultivating are concerned and another in a most unfavorable location, an unsanded peat section with a very dense growth of vegetation, and poor drainage. [The greatest difference observed by Cox was 17.1°F.] It is not strange therefore that in a bog where there is a variation in the conditions of sanding, draining, and cultivation, the range in minimum temperatures is considerable, and that a portion of a bog is seriously injured by frost while another portion completely escapes."[57]

These inequalities are extremely localized; probably none of them is effective at the height of trees and they are of little importance to the orchardist. They are, however, of extreme importance to the grower of small fruits. His is the most difficult problem in heating his fruit plantation but, on the other hand, he can do more than any other fruit grower to prevent frost. Generally he has the same freedom as the orchardist in the selection of site; in addition he can take advantage of minor localized variations. In aiming to profit by them he is following cultural practices that are beneficial to his fruit plants in other ways.

Summary.—Spring frost is important in setting geographic limits to the commercial culture of fruits of some kinds and in determining the regularity of crops, yields and profits in practically all deciduous fruit growing sections. Frost formation depends to a considerable extent on the radiation of heat by exposed surfaces during the night. Because of radiation on still clear nights, temperatures close to the earth are lower than those at somewhat greater elevations, giving rise to the condition known as temperature inversion. On account of radiation the real temperatures of plants may be several degrees lower than those registered by sheltered thermometers. When the dewpoint is very low, freezing will occur without frost formation. Clouds and wind both protect against frost, the former by reducing the total effect of radiation, the latter by mixing warm air with that which has been cooled. In a general way both the blossoming dates of fruits and the average dates of the last killing frosts range later with each increase in latitude, though the progress of the two is not always parallel. Study of Weather Bureau records showing average last dates of killing frosts, together with the standard deviations therefrom, will make possible an accurate determination of frost danger beyond any particular date for any given locality, though not for any site. Air drainage secured by suitable elevation is of considerable importance in determining danger from frost in particular sites. Minor differences in temperature within narrow limits in space are occasioned by minor differences in elevation, amount of soil moisture, character of the soil covering, type of soil and system of cultivation. These are seldom important in influencing frost injury to tree fruits; however, they may be of considerable importance in small fruit culture.

CHAPTER XX

PROTECTION AGAINST FROST

The fruit grower should have, not only knowledge of the conditions under which frost occurs, but information as to the exact danger points for his various fruits and as to the value of different protective measures that may be at his disposal.

CRITICAL TEMPERATURES

If heating is to be done it should be delayed until the temperature is near the critical point to save expense and exhaustion of the fuel in the heaters before morning. If it is known that the blossoms of one variety or of one species are more tender than others protective effort may be concentrated more or less on the tender plants. At times it has been assumed arbitrarily that a certain temperature is fatal and that because certain orchards had been exposed to that temperature they would bear no crop. Accordingly the calyx spray was omitted, to save labor and expense, only to have it appear later that a fair crop had survived the freeze but had become thoroughly infested by codling moth, scab and other pests. If, then, there is a certain temperature that is universally fatal to the blossoms of all fruits or of one kind of fruit it should be known.

A compilation of temperatures stated as dangerous to blossoms of various fruits is reproduced here as Table 67.

The considerable difference in the damaging points as stated by these various writers is significant and it seems probable that the range of killing temperatures is as great if not greater than indicated by the table; West and Edlefsen state that there is sometimes a spread of 5°. The variations in temperatures between sheltered thermometers, exposed thermometers and plant tissues make field observations of only limited value. Variations in radiation conditions make the correction of thermometer readings to plant temperatures uncertain. Furthermore, different blossoms must be exposed to radiation in varying degrees because of diversity in their positions in the cluster and on the branch.

Assuming, however, that temperatures can be measured accurately, as doubtless has been done in closely controlled work such as that of Chandler and of West and Edlefsen, the final result is still a complex involving several factors whose separate measurement is difficult. Several blossoms, alike in development, will show differences in their

TABLE 67.—A LIST OF "DANGER POINTS" AS GIVEN BY DIFFERENT AUTHORS
(*After West and Edlefsen,*[249] *with additions*)
DEGREES FAHRENHEIT

Fruits	Closed but showing color	In blossom	Setting	Authority
Apples.................	27	29	30	1
	27	29	30	2
	27	29	30	3
	25	28	28	4
	25	28	28	5
	25	28	29	6
Peaches................	20	25	28	1
	29	30	30	3
	29	30	30	2
	22	28	28	4
	25	27	27	5
	25	26	28	6
Cherries...............	22	28	29	1
	29	30	30	2
	22	28	28	4
	25	28	30	6
Pears..................	27	29	29	1
	29	29	29	2
	28	29	29	3
	25	28	28	4
	25	28	30	6
Plums..................	30	31	31	1
	30	30	31	2
	30	31	31	3
	22	28	28	4
	25	28	30	6
Apricots...............	30	31	32	2
	30	31	32	3
	22	28	28	4
	25	27	30	6
Prunes.................	30	31	31	2
	30	31	31	3
	28	29	30	6
Almonds................	26	27	30	7
Grapes.................	30	31	31	7

Authorities: (1) Wilson, W. M.[258]   (2) O'Gara, P. J.[172]   (3) W. H. Hammon.[89]
(4) Paddock and Whipple.[176]   (5) W. H. Chandler.[48]   (6) Garcia and Rigney.[89]
(7) Young, Floyd D.[261]

resistance to the same freezing; different trees of the same variety will set materially different crops; finally, varieties are unequally susceptible.

It is impossible at present to state to what extent fruit blossoms are or can be supercooled, at what temperature ice formation occurs or at what temperature damage results. General sudden freezing following supercooling is considered in itself injurious.[187] To what extent this applies to fruit blossoms cannot be stated at present. Indeed it is possible that under natural conditions supercooling as ordinarily understood does not occur in fruit blossoms. The influence of capillarity on freezing in these tissues cannot be stated now. It is, however, safe to conclude that critical temperatures as determined by laboratory methods would be somewhat lower than would appear from field observations with ordinary thermometer exposures, because of the differences between air temperatures and plant temperatures under the radiation conditions accompanying most frosts. For the same reason precise determination of killing points would not be of direct application in the orchard. Parenthetically it may be remarked that the insufficient recognition of radiation effects on plant tissues in horticultural investigation may account for many of the conflicting results secured.

However, studies in artificial freezing are interesting, though the high degree of humidity that accompanies them is not invariably present in nature.

On the other hand, studies by Ellison and Close of critical temperatures for apple blossoms have led them to conclude:[73] "Evidence . . . shows unmistakably that the dew point at the time of the frost has a very important bearing on the amount of damage that will be caused by low temperature. When the dew point is 32°F., when the air temperature reaches 32°F. and the dew point falls as the temperature falls, severely low minimum temperatures can be endured with but slight damage, whereas the same temperature conditions with a low dew point will cause very severe damage."

This high humidity may serve conceivably to inoculate the plants with freezing nuclei and cause freezing at higher temperature than would be required in a drier atmosphere. Despite limitations, however, the tests by artificial freezing possess considerable significance. West and Edlefsen have reported some rather extended investigations of this sort.

In part, they summarize their results as follows: "Ben Davis apple buds in full bloom have experienced temperatures of 25, 26, and 27°F. without injury, but 28° usually killed about one-fifth. Twenty-nine degrees or above are safe temperatures. Twenty-five degrees kills about one-half and 22° about nine-tenths. On several occasions, however, apples matured on branches that experienced 20° when the buds were in full bloom.

"With Elberta peach buds in full bloom, 29°F. or above are the safe temperatures, because even though occasionally 26, 27, and 28° do no damage, yet on most occasions 28° will kill from one-fourth to one-half. Twenty-six degrees kills about one-half of them and 22° about nine-tenths. Temperatures as low as 18° have failed to kill all of them.

"With sweet cherry buds in full bloom, 30°F. is the safe temperature; 25, 26, 27, 28° have done no damage, but 29° usually kills about one-fifth. Twenty-five degrees usually kills about one-half, and when the buds were showing color 22° killed only two-fifths of the buds.

"Sour cherries are hardier than the sweet varieties. When the buds were showing color 23°F. did not harm them, and when they were in full bloom 26° killed about one-fifth and 22° only two-fifths of them.

"With apricots, 29°F. is the safe temperature; 26 and 27° killed about one-fifth and 22° killed one-half. . . .

"The foregoing figures refer to the buds when in full bloom. Starting from this stage, the earlier the stage of development the hardier the buds are; and in general, when the fruit is setting the injury is from 5 to 10 per cent. more than when they are in full bloom.

"Sour cherries are the hardiest, and then follow in order apples, peaches, apricots, and sweet cherries."[250]

Field observations sometimes indicate that open peach blossoms are more resistant than apple blossoms at the same stage.

At Different Stages of Blossom Development.—Table 67 indicates that the difference in tenderness of blossoms at various stages in their development is well recognized. Table 68, arranged from a similar table by West and Edlefsen, shows experimental data that are, in general, confirmatory.

TABLE 68.—HARDINESS OF JONATHAN APPLE BUDS TO VARIOUS DEGREES OF ARTIFICIAL COOLING[249]

Date	Stage of blossom	Duration of freezing, minutes	Temperature, degrees Fahrenheit	Percentage damaged
April 25..........	Full bloom	10	24.5	52.0
April 29..........	Full bloom	5	26.5	36.0
April 25..........	Full bloom	45	27.5	54.0
April 29..........	Full bloom	5	28.5	0.0
May 9..........	Fruit setting	25	28.0	46.0
May 9..........	Fruit setting	5	25.5	93.0
May 9..........	Fruit setting	5	26.5	40.0
May 10..........	Fruit setting	20	26.5	22.5
May 10..........	Fruit setting	30	27.5	21.0
May 9..........	Fruit setting	15	27.5	59.0
May 9..........	Fruit setting	5	27.5	62.0

It should be remembered that not all the blossoms on a tree are going through the same stage of development at any given time and the amount of damage done by a light to moderate frost will depend to a considerable extent on the number of opened and of unopened buds.   This is shown in Table 69.

Strawberries that are half grown, however, appear able to stand more freezing than the blossoms.

Coit[54] reports on this fruit: "Blossoms are injured by temperatures below 30° at the ground but young fruit endures temperatures as low as 24° at the ground and 28° in a government shelter without injury and green fruit protected by foliage endures temperatures several degrees below this.   Ripening fruit endures less cold, being injured by temperatures below 25° at the ground.   A good picking was taken from Excelsior plants Dec. 24, 1903, although the mercury had fallen at the ground to 22 to 26° during 10 nights of the month.   Some

TABLE 69.—PERCENTAGE OF OPEN AND OF UNOPENED BLOSSOMS KILLED BY THE FREEZE OF APR. 4, 1908 (24°F.)

(After Chandler[48])

Variety	Buds open	Buds unopened
Oldmixon Free.....................	69.9	36.6
Oldmixon Free.....................	25.4	15.3
Elberta	24.4	7.1
Elberta.........................	51.1	1.1

green fruit well protected with foliage survived January, 1904, the mercury falling to 14 at the ground one night, 16 one night, 17 two nights, 18 one night and 19 three nights; and a few berries ripened during the early part of the month."

According to Darrow and associates,[65] "The deeper the color of a cranberry the more severe the frost it will endure.   An immature green berry will be injured by a temperature of 28°F.; an uncolored (greenish white) one will endure 27°F.; while one of the same variety deeply colored will stand 23°F.   When there is danger of frost at harvest time advantage may be taken of this by picking the areas having the lighter colored fruit first, leaving those with darker colored berries until later if necessary."

Varietal Differences.—Varietal differences in hardiness are sometimes apparent in apples.

In one case in Missouri the greatest injury in Jonathan seemed to be in the stamens while in Oldenburg the pistil was damaged.   It may be suggested that this type of injury might have some interesting bearing on the pollination of mixed orchards.

In Iowa many of the Russian varieties were hardier in blossom than standard varieties in better locations.   Similarly among the native plums a freeze that killed the ovaries of several varieties such as Rollingstone which, incidentally, is very resistant to winter cold, injured only a part of the blossoms of De Soto,

Cheney and other varieties. These in turn were surpassed in resistance by the Russian plums which were said to have been "less exposed than our native plums."[38] The Bosc pear has been reported as more tender in blossom than the other pears.[261] Blake[26] reports that in New Jersey temperatures ranging between 23° and 28°F. the nights of April 16–18, 1928, killed approximately half the flower buds of Maiden Blush, Gravenstein, Rhode Island Greening, McIntosh and Grimes and almost none of those of Stark, Jonathan, Wealthy, Duchess and Stayman, though all were in practically the same stage of development (the so-called pre-pink stage). In these earlier stages of their development flower buds of the Delicious and Winesap apples show relatively the same measure of resistance to injury from cold; at a later stage those of the Delicious are more tender than the Winesap.[73] Chandler states that among peaches "the large flowered varieties seemed uniformly to be the most hardy, probably because the petals remained closed over the pistils longer."[47] This statement was in reference to resistance to frosts at blossoming time; after that period no determining factor could be found. Elberta, tender at some other stages, seemed to resist very late frosts as well as most varieties.

Some varieties of strawberry are more susceptible to frost injury than others because their flower stalks are longer and more inclined to raise the blossoms above the protection of the leaves.[7]

Schuster[212] reports on the Ettersburg No. 121 strawberry: "The first blossoms being below the foliage are quite well protected from ordinary frost. Foliage protection is quite a factor when comparing this variety with other varieties of light foliage, as the primary blossoms are very apt to be fully protected during the frost, while the secondary blossoms that extend beyond the foliage will usually be frosted. Due to the extended blossoming period, it will take repeated frosts to destroy the crop unless there is a heavy freeze."

Some interesting studies have been made in an attempt to correlate varietal morphological peculiarities with differences in hardiness.

Emery,[78] in Montana, found injury in strawberry varieties ranging from 12 per cent. to zero. The date of bloom in this case seems to have had little effect, since Warfield, one of the earliest blossoming of the 58 varieties under observation, escaped all injury. Wilcox[257] at the same station found the anthers of certain varieties injured by frost; the tissue in which the pollen grains were embedded ruptured and a small proportion of the pollen grains were killed. Some injury was observed in styles and stigmas, probably enough to interfere with their functioning. In blossoms which had been fertilized the injury was confined to the akenes; in no case was the receptacle injured. The akenes became discolored rapidly. In resistant varieties they were so deeply imbedded in their pits as to be practically surrounded by the pulp. Tender varieties had their akenes most exposed or in very shallow depressions. Between these extremes there was a regular gradation. It thus seems possible that a variety may be resistant at one stage—before fertilization, for example—and yet be tender at another stage, say, after fertilization.

Vigor and Recuperative Ability.—The vigor of the tree is stated frequently to be a factor in the damage produced by frost. This opinion may be founded on observations of the crop the weak trees bear and in failure to recognize that, frost or no frost, such trees fail often to set a large percentage of fruit. A series of freezings of blossoms from strong and from weak Gano apple trees indicated no superior hardiness in blossoms from the more vigorous; in fact the average of the various tests was very slightly in favor of the weak trees.[48] In herbaceous plants, injury sometimes appears more pronounced in those making a less vigorous growth, but in all probability the observed difference is due to the superior recuperative powers of the more vigorous plants. There is some indication that plants treated with nitrate of soda recover from frost damage better than others. This recovery is, however, in the vegetative portions. There is, occasionally, a fairly large second bloom on apple and pear trees following a frost, but this is the exception and apparently it is not related to vegetative vigor. Recuperative power is of little immediate benefit to the grower once the blossoms are killed.

Weather Conditions before and after Freezing.—The weather preceding and immediately following the freeze may be factors of some little importance.

Pfeffer,[186] speaking of plant tissues in general, says: "The resistance to cold depends to a certain extent upon the present and previous external conditions. Thus Haberlandt found that seedlings grown at 18° to 20°C. froze more readily than those grown at 8°C." Rosa[199] found that cabbage grown in a greenhouse at 20°C. killed when exposed to −4°C. for 1 hour while plants grown in a cold frame were uninjured by exposure to the same temperature for over 2 hours. It seems reasonable to suppose that the same principle applies to fruit blossoms. Garcia[89] records that a temperature of 24.75°F. at 2 a.m. followed by a rise to 31° at 5:30 caused less than 3 per cent. injury to Alexander peach blossoms which were in full bloom at the time, though in other instances considerable damage followed a temperature of 25.5°. It should be recalled that there is practical unanimity among investigators that rapid thawing is not in itself injurious, but there is no evidence as to the effects of light on frozen tissue. Light is known to increase permeability and may well be conceived to prevent the return to the cells of water which has been withdrawn upon freezing, thus causing injury to tissues which otherwise would recover their normal state. The common conviction among practical horticulturists that rapid thawing is injurious may be founded on observations of the effect of light on frozen tissue. Furthermore, the effects of the duration of exposure to a given temperature have not been established definitely.

Signs of Damage.—The thermometer, evidently, frequently fails to give close or reliable indication of the amount of damage a frost has inflicted. A fairly close estimate may be made, ordinarily, late in the forenoon following a freeze, by an examination of the buds themselves.

The pistils are the parts most readily affected in the blossom, becoming, when damaged, wilted and discolored, though the bud may unfold its petals and stamens. Curiously, in April, 1920, at Columbia, Mo., a temperature of 14°F. when Jonathan apple blossoms were fairly well advanced seemed to damage, not the pistils, but the stamens which turned orange in color, and the effects also became evident on the stems near the purse. A similar condition, though less pronounced, has been observed in the Willamette valley in Oregon. Sometimes the petals are dwarfed but the bud otherwise uninjured. In peaches advanced beyond the blossoming stage, Chandler[48] states that the veins surrounding the seed are the most tender, followed in order by the kernel and the flesh. Chandler suggests that the greater tenderness of the seed may be correlated with the difference in sap density. The young seeds of the apple seem particularly tender and after a frost they frequently are brown while the flesh is apparently undamaged.

Paddock and Whipple[178] state that after fertilization has occurred apple blossoms may survive some injury to the seeds, though blossoms of the stone fruits frozen to the extent that the basal part of the pistil is damaged rarely set fruit. When interior apple tissues outside the seed cavities are damaged the fruit does not mature. In this particular case, they say, the injury becomes apparent early, in a yellowing of the tissues around the stem end of the fruit. Seedless apples, particularly of some varieties, frequently develop to maturity but generally are somewhat smaller than those with seeds. The same writers state that the pear will mature fruit after showing still more injury than the apple. In the young fruit they find much the same conditions holding, though the stone fruits are said not to show injury which is confined to the seed cavity until the time of the final swelling just before ripening, when the injured fruit will show gummy exudations and ripen abnormally or it may drop before ripening. When the injury is more extensive they drop shortly after blossoming. Apples and pears survive injury to the seeds alone and in most cases with no other visible evidence of damage. Apples injured outside the seed cavity do not mature but pears so injured develop abnormally through enlargement of what would ordinarily be the neck of the fruit. This enlargement, together with the retarded development of the parts surrounding the core, results in the familiar "bullneck." Injury to pear flesh apparently must extend well away from the core to prevent the development of the fruit, though it conceivably may interfere to some extent with the so-called "secondary effect" of pollination. The younger spur leaves of the apple and pear may be more or less dwarfed and deformed as a result of frost at or just before blossoming time.

Impaired germination of pollen of pear, plum, cherry and peach on exposure for 6 hours to a temperature of $-1.5°C.$ has been reported.[204] Chandler[48] found that pollen of the Jonathan apple after exposure to $-3°C.$ showed a germination of 33 per cent. as compared with 84 per cent. for unfrozen pollen, and pollen of the Cillagos apple frozen for 30 minutes at $-8°C.$ germinated 25 per cent. as compared with 67 per cent. for unfrozen.

Frost Injury and the Size of the Crop.—Finally it must be considered that the damage from a given frost is a varying quantity. Some peach trees on which 1,000 peaches would be a good crop bear 20,000 or more fruit buds. Obviously, with other conditions favorable, a loss of 80 per cent. of the buds would not interfere with the production of a full crop and in a commercial sense this frost would not prove damaging. If, however, the same trees were bearing only 8,000 buds a loss of 80 per cent. might become a serious matter.

It should be apparent that no set rules of procedure as governed by observed temperatures can be given. Probably the safest course for the grower when freezing occurs is to try to keep the temperature above 29°F. if he is heating his orchard and after a frost it is best to proceed on the assumption of a full crop unless the evidence to the contrary is convincing.

AVOIDING FROST THROUGH LATE BLOSSOMING VARIETIES

The relatively wide range in blossoming dates of the many kinds and varieties of fruits is often important in determining the relative danger from frost to an orchard on a given site. Conversely, the blossoming dates should have bearing on the decision as to the type of fruit to be planted. On a very large scale the limiting factor in the growth of apricots and almonds is not their lack of hardiness to winter cold, since some varieties are probably as hardy as, or even hardier than, the peach, but rather their extremely early blooming.

Blossoming Range Varies with Earliness.—The earlier the average date of blossoming in any section the longer is the spread of the ordinary season of bloom. In the north the time between the first peach and the last apple to blossom is frequently shorter than the interval in the south between the first and the last peach. Consequently the relative earliness or lateness in blossoming of a variety may be more important in some regions than in others. Table 70 shows the difference between peaches

TABLE 70.—NUMBER OF HEATINGS NECESSARY TO PROTECT UTAH ORCHARDS
(*After West and Edlefsen*[249])

County	Number of years	Peach	Apple	Apricot	Cherry
Utah (Provo)............	16	93.0	46.0	....	....
Provo Bench...........	16	28.0	13.0	....	....
Box Elder (Corinne)....	14	32.0	8.0	45.0	21.0
Salt Lake (Salt Lake)....	16	36.0	15.0	....	....
Weber................	13	66.0	4.0	....	....
Cache................	16	8.0	3.0	....	....
Totals..............	....	263.0	89.0	45.0	21.0
Average per year.....	....	2.9	0.97	3.2	1.5

and apples in the number of times heating might be necessary at various places in Utah. The difference between a total of 263 heatings for the peaches and 89 for the apples would make a considerable item in the cost of production. In addition, the later blooming fruit is not only likely to encounter fewer frosts but such as it does encounter are likely to be less severe. Finally, it should be recalled that the later stages of a blossom's development are the most tender; for this reason also a given frost is likely to damage the early variety more. This double effect is well shown in Table 71.

TABLE 71.—PERCENTAGE OF PEACH BLOSSOMS KILLED BY TEMPERATURE OF 28°F
(*After Garcia*[89])

Varieties	Fruits just setting	Freshly opened flowers	Buds about to open
Elberta........................	97	..	..
Crothers.......................	95	..	..
Salway.........................	87	..	..
Texas King.....................	86	66	45
Hynes' Surprise.................	91	73	47
Alexander......................	91	72	56

This table shows that for blossoms just setting fruit there was not enough difference to indicate any varietal superiority in hardiness. However, Elberta, Crothers and Salway blossoms were all of the most advanced stage which is very tender. The three other varieties had a considerable number of blossoms less advanced at the time of the freeze so that, despite a rather large percentage of killing, the fruit of these varieties had to be thinned, while the first three varieties bore very little, Elberta in fact bearing none at all.

TABLE 72.—DATE OF FIRST BLOSSOMS RELATIVE TO LAST MINIMUM OF 29°F. AT
WAUSEON, OHIO, FOR 30 YEARS

Blossoming relative to frost	Apple, years	Pear, years	Peach, years	Plum, years	Cherry, years	Grape, years	Strawberry, years	Red raspberry, years
Type variety:								
Before.............	8	11	13	12	14	0	10	0
After...............	22	19	14	17	15	26	16	26
Early variety:								
Before.............	10	13	13	15	15	0	..	0
After..............	20	17	14	14	14	26	..	26
Late variety:								
Before	5	12	12	11	14	0	..	0
After	25	18	15	18	15	26	..	26

Table 72 is based on the Mikesell data,[162] with additions.   Though computed rather arbitrarily it shows in a general way the relative susceptibility to frost at Wauseon of the fruits under observation there (see Type fruits).   In addition an attempt is made to show how earlier or later blossoming varieties of the respective fruits would have been affected.   A somewhat artificial method was necessary.   Taking as guide the average blossoming dates of various fruits at Geneva, N. Y.,[111] the varieties studied in Table 71 were interpolated and the differences between their average dates of blossoming at Geneva and that of the earliest and latest blossoming common varieties grown there were used in the Wauseon figures.   Thus the apple was figured on the basis of Gravenstein being 2 days earlier in blossoming than the type variety (King).   The Bartlett pear was fitted into the New York tables on the assumption that it blossomed with Clapp Favorite and Angouleme; Anjou and Vermont Beauty were the extremes, 2 days earlier and later respectively.   The plum (variety not stated) was placed in the middle of the Domestica group.

The table should not be taken too literally as it is constructed on such arbitrary assumptions (including the temperature selected as injurious).   Nevertheless it shows quite clearly the respective chances of frost damage to different fruits at a given spot in northern latitudes and in a measure the relative importance of early and late blossoming varieties which is much greater in some fruits than in others.   Furthermore, it should be understood clearly that the blossoming dates of all kinds and varieties of fruits have a much wider spread in milder climates than that of the northeast and these differences are much greater and more important in these regions.

Figure 37 shows the blossoming dates of certain fruits in relation to the last spring temperature of 27°F. at a point in southern Utah.   In no year did the apricot or the almond blossom after the last temperature of 27°, and in no case did the Yellow Transparent, generally a rather early blossoming apple, bloom before.   Between these extremes lie the Elberta peach, which blossomed after the last 27° temperature in 2 years out of the 8 represented, and the German prune which preceded it in 1 year out of 6 recorded.   The likelihood of damage or safety from frost in this locality quite evidently depends on the kind of fruit chosen, more so than in sections where the blossoming season has less spread.   At Geneva, N. Y., the average interval from the first peach blossom to the last apple tree's first bloom is 15 days.   However, there are unquestionably years in almost any fruit growing region when the blossoming period actually determines the difference between a full or a partial crop—or a crop failure.

Blossoming Period and Fruit Bud Position.—In addition to varietal difference in blossoming season there is occasionally some diversity within the variety.   There is a tendency, though it is by no means constant, for vigorous trees to blossom somewhat later; sometimes the interval between vigorous and weak trees is 2 to 3 days.   Terminal and lateral fruit buds of apple frequently are several days behind the spur fruit buds in opening; in at least one instance Jonathan trees have lost practically all the spur blossoms from frost and still returning a partial crop from their terminal buds. The outer buds on long twigs and all buds on short twigs in peaches are the first to open and the slight difference in development of these and the basal blossoms on the same trees has made at times a vast difference in the crop borne in respective zones.[48]

Retarding Blossoming.—Attempts at retarding fruit blossoms so they will escape a certain amount of exposure to frost have not proved successful on a commercial scale. Whitewashing the branches to reduce the

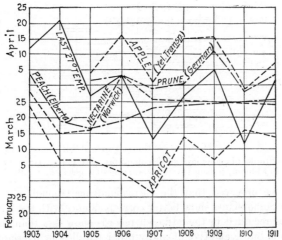

Fig. 37.—Frost susceptibility of several fruits as determined by date of blossoming. (*After Ballantyne*[14])

amount of heat absorbed from sunlight has been discussed previously; shading has been shown to have only a very limited application. Despite abundant evidence to the contrary the notion persists that mulching retards the opening of fruit buds. Except for fruits whose tops are covered, as strawberries, it is of no value.

If late blooming is urgently needed it is best secured by selecting late blossoming varieties, planting them on a north slope and keeping them growing vigorously. The last two measures are effective only within comparatively narrow limits, leaving the first as the best method of evading frost damage. In certain fruits the present varietal range in blossoming season is hardly sufficient to secure protection through the selection of the later blooming sorts, but in others practical immunity from damage may be obtained in that way. There is reason to believe that late blooming varieties of many fruits may be bred and the ultimate solution of the frost problem lies in that direction.

Indices to Blossoming Periods in New Location.—Sometimes in considering locations where fruit has not been grown it is desirable to know at what time the trees may be expected to bloom. It is possible that phenological observations on native plants in different sections would show a degree of correspondence with the various fruits so that certain native plants might serve as indicators of what fruit trees would do in the same locality.

Figure 38, arranged from the Mikesell Records,[162] shows the overlapping of the King apple in the stage from first blossom to full bloom with poison ivy, a fairly common wild plant, in the stage from buds starting to the first fully formed

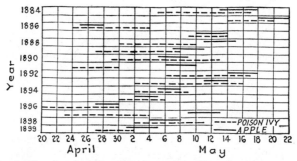

Fig. 38.—Comparable phenological stages in apple and poison ivy. (Apple from first blossom to full bloom; poison ivy from starting of buds to first fully formed leaf.)

leaf. It will be observed that the correspondence, though not invariable, is rather close. Some plants show better correspondence with the King apple than others; several recorded in the Mikesell records show less than the poison ivy. This instance is but suggestive of many other parallels or overlappings in blossoming seasons that may be established—parallels that in many cases would repay careful study.

FROST PREDICTION

It is frequently important to know a few hours in advance whether or not a frost will occur, so that final preparations for protection against its effects may be made. In a general way frost may be looked for on a clear, still night; clear, because it favors radiation, still, because the cooled air is not mixed with the warmer air. These conditions are associated with high barometric pressure. However, they do not always produce frost and a closer estimate is desirable.

Relation of Dewpoint to Minimum Temperature.—Until recently the dewpoint as determined in late afternoon or early evening has been considered to mark the minimum temperature for the following morning. Air contains varying percentages of moisture; the higher the temperature the more it can carry as vapor. If any given sample of air is cooled the point is reached ultimately where some of the moisture is deposited.

This is the dewpoint. The condensation of moisture releases heat to the air and it was thought that the heat thus released was sufficient to prevent any further drop in temperature and that the evening dewpoint therefore marked the minimum for the following morning.

Careful comparison of indicated and actual temperatures has shown, however, that the afternoon or evening dewpoint alone is not a sufficiently reliable indicator to be of any great value in predicting the minimum for the following morning. In fact Cox[57] records a slight degree of frost with the humidity at 100 per cent. Ordinarily, however, it may be assumed that when the evening relative humidity is from 40 to 50 per cent., the ensuing minimum temperature on a characteristic radiation night will be very close to the evening dewpoint; when the evening relative humidity is below 40 per cent. the minimum will average 5° above the evening dewpoint; with evening relative humidities above 50 per cent the minimum temperatures will be below the evening dewpoint.

Little reliance can be placed on the afternoon maximum alone as an indicator unless it is very high indeed. No maximum below 75 or 76°F. should be regarded as a guarantee against frost the following morning.

Weather Bureau Methods.—At present no one method of predicting minimum temperatures is in use by Weather Bureau officials throughout the country. Local conditions apparently make a certain method fit closely at one point while at another point it gives less satisfactory results. It seems probable that observations extending over at least 2 years for each section should be accumulated and the data studied to determine which method will give the closest approximation in future predictions.

Smith[221] has devised several methods and applied them to data from different points. The simplest, perhaps, is the so-called median temperature method. This is based on the assumption that, in weather characteristic of most spring frosts, the "radiation nights," clear and rather still, the temperature falls practically at a uniform rate from a maximum in the afternoon to a minimum in the morning and that the times of maximum and minimum temperatures will be the same for all such days. The average time of the median, half way between the times of the maximum and of the minimum, is ascertained from previous records of the particular station. A thermometer reading at this median time, subtracted from the afternoon maximum, gives, presumably, half the total fall in temperature to be expected. Thus if the maximum were 70°F., the median temperature 50°, the difference, 20°, taken from the median temperature, would indicate the expected minimum to be 30°. Under conditions obtaining at some stations this method seems the most reliable that has been tried. In general it seems to give closer approximations to actual temperatures in regions of very low humidity, not, perhaps, because the method works better there than elsewhere, but possibly because the other methods do not work so well. As indicated by Hallinbeck, with certain precautions in its application it seems to work well at Roswell, New Mexico. Wherever compared with the older method of assuming identity between evening dewpoint and morning minimum it has proved superior.

Still more accurate predictions were found possible in Ohio by Smith, using the equation $y = a + bR$, where R is the evening relative humidity, y the variation of the morning minimum temperature from the evening dewpoint, while a and b are constants derived from previous data accumulated at points with like conditions. This linear equation, when plotted, fitted the Ohio data very satisfactorily, but charts from certain other points were fitted more closely by a parabola whose equation was modified by Smith to read $v = x + by + cz$ in which x, y and z are coefficients to be determined from previous data, b the evening relative humidity, c the square of the relative humidity and v the variation of the minimum temperature of the following morning from the evening dewpoint. The value found for v is added to or subtracted from the evening dewpoint and the minimum temperature indicated.

The method of obtaining the constants is explained in detail in Supplement 16 of the *Monthly Weather Review*. As has been suggested above, the constants vary with the locality. As samples, the following may be cited: for the $y = a + bR$ equation, at Lansing, Mich., $a = -11.2$, $b = 0.727$, at Grand Junction, Col., $a = -7.01$, $b = 0.53$; for the $v = x + cz + by$ equation, Modena, Utah (all nights, radiation or otherwise), $x = 7.3$, $y = 0.18$, $z = 0.0057$; for Montrose, Col., $x = -22.0$, $y = 0.383$, $z = 0.01167$.

The first equation has been found to give satisfactory results at some places, the second has proved preferable at others; as stated above, the median temperature method seems best here and there, while in some cases still other methods are used. Sometimes a mean between results secured by two methods has proved more nearly accurate than either singly. One disadvantage of the median temperature method as compared with the others outlined here lies in the fact that the forecast cannot be made until several hours later than is possible from the methods based on hygrometric data. The fact that different methods fit various places is probably an expression of the differences in topography and in humidity, relation to centers of high pressure and other factors somewhat peculiar to particular localities but all combining in frost production.

It should be borne in mind also that the methods outlined fit only radiation nights and that occasionally fruit blossoms are damaged by cold in other ways such as high cold winds or cold snow squalls. To forecast these, reliance must be placed on the weather map. The problem is, in any case, sufficiently complex to warrant the grower who wishes reliable forecasts in trying to secure them from the nearest station of the Weather Bureau, either directly or by corrections from forecasts made for some nearby point.

Local Interpretation of "Key Station" Predictions.—It will be understood, considering the local differences in temperature, that the general forecast may require correction for the grower's own site. The forecast, as issued, is based upon observations from sheltered instruments at a certain spot; yet it is given out necessarily to cover a wide radius of territory where local differences may be considerable. Districts that are well organized for frost fighting have several "key stations" for which the forecasts are corrected individually. Even in such cases, however, it may be necessary to make discriminating corrections if the probable minimum for a given spot is to be determined.

Table 73 shows minimum temperatures on cold spring mornings at 5.5 feet and 0.5 foot elevations at three spots in the village of Williamstown, Mass. Station *A* is a shelter thermometer and may be considered the "key station." It is of interest to see how predictions for the key station would apply to strawberries at Station 7. As is shown in the last column of the table the difference is variable but always considerable, under conditions favorable to frost. As Milham,[163] from whose data the table is taken, states, it is not a difference due to site alone; in adapting the forecast for Station *A* to vegetation at Station 7 allowances must be made as follows: 2° for the deviation between sheltered and exposed thermometers, 3° for the inequality in height of the two thermometers above ground and 6° for the difference in site. These together indicate a total

TABLE 73.—MINIMUM TEMPERATURES AT WILLIAMSTOWN, MASS.[163]

Date	Station *A* (shelter)	Station 1		Station 8		Station 7		Difference, Station *A* and lower 7
		Upper	Lower	Upper	Lower	Upper	Lower	
1907								
April 27.........	32	..	30	30	27	27	23	9
May 1..........	33	29	28	28	25	25	21	12
May 5	38	36	34	32	32	31	27	11
May 11..........	27	25	24	..	..	18	15	12
May 12..........	42	41	40	39	36	33	31	11
May 20..........	37	35	35	34	32	34	31	6
May 21..........	39	38	38	36	34	36	33	6
May 24..........	33	31	30	..	..	25	20	13
May 28..........	37	36	36	34	32	31	31	6
1908								
April 29.........	40	38	38	37	36	35	34	6
May 1..........	39	37	36	35	32	31	28	11
May 3..........	35	33	33	31	30	31	27	8
May 4..........	42	30	30	28	27	28	24	18
May 5..........	46	45	44	43	39	40	35	11
May 9..........	39	39	39	38	37	38	38	1
May 10..........	42	40	40	38	36	36	34	8
May 14..........	40	39	39	39	37	36	34	6

of 11° which, it is evident from the table, was realized frequently. Though it is unsafe to generalize from a few observations, it is interesting to note that for the lower temperatures at Station *A* the departures for Station 7 averaged greater than they did for the higher temperatures at Station *A*; in other words it would seem that as the temperature at Station *A* came nearer to the freezing point the temperature at Station 7 was in even greater measure more likely to drop below that point. Evidently a strawberry grower at Station 7 should deduct at least 11° from the minimum indicated for Station A to forecast the probable temperature at his own place; if apples were the crop at the same point the deduction would be somewhat less.

Even greater differences are reported by Cox[57] between minima on the bog at Mather, Wis., and the minima at the "key station" La Crosse, 55 miles away. Shelter minimum temperatures on the upland at Mather for May, 1907, averaged 3.8° below those at La Crosse with ranges from −14° to +8°; minima at 5 inches above the bog at Mather averaged −8.5° below those for La Crosse, with ranges from −20° to +5°. Cox states that the average difference when the weather is clear and the pressure high is about 18°, so that in such weather a minimum of 50° for La Crosse signifies a bog minimum at Mather of about 32°.

The grower who wishes to prophesy with accuracy what the minimum will be in his own orchard, bog or field must rely on the Weather Bureau to furnish information as to the probable minimum at some fixed point and he must rely on himself to adapt these indications to the spot where his own crop is located.   To do this it will be necessary to keep accurate records of minima at his own orchard on all clear nights during the spring for 2 or 3 years, to compare them with the records of the Weather Bureau and from these data to determine the probable and the safe corrections to be made.

FROST FIGHTING

The data already discussed show that much can be accomplished in combating frost by selection of site, fruit and variety and in some cases by cultural practices.   All these measures may be regarded as preventive. There remain for consideration the palliative measures.

Smoke Screens to Reduce Radiation.—In view of the emphasis placed on radiation as a factor under frost conditions, efforts to prevent heat loss through radiation might be expected to be fruitful.   In fact it is rather generally assumed that a dense smoke will so retard radiation losses that frost damage will be checked or prevented.   Such cases have been recorded.   However, quantitative data available for comparison of temperatures in smudged areas where the heating factor is eliminated with those in unsmudged and unheated areas do not indicate a sufficient saving of heat to make the smudge in itself of any great value.   Table 74 shows temperatures in a smudged area and in an unsmudged area adjacent, in a German vineyard.   The averages include some figures not presented here.

The differences are at the most too small to be of practical importance.   It was suggested that the small difference was due to air movement and the investigator appears not to have been convinced that greater differences might not be found under other conditions.

Kimball and Young,[125] using a pyrogeometer, measured the radiation in smudged and in unsmudged areas in California and Oregon, finding decreases by smudging from 0.110 and 0.115 calories per minute per square centimeter to averages of 0.098 and 0.103 respectively in California and in Medford, Oregon, from 0.109 to an average of 0.099. Considerable fluctuation under the smoke occurred, the maximum decrease amounting to 28 per cent. with averages respectively of 11, 10 and 9 per cent. They conclude from their investigations that "the retardation of nocturnal radiation by the smoke cloud plays an insignificant part in frost protection."

Similar studies in Maryland are reported by Kimball and MacIntire.[124] White phosphorus was burned on nights favoring frost and temperatures

TABLE 74.—TEMPERATURES IN SMUDGED AND UNSMUDGED AREAS[169]
(Degrees Centigrade)

Hour	Temperature	
	Smudged	Unsmudged
10:30	+2.01	+1.87
11:30	+1.53	+1.40
12:30	+0.78	+0.62
1:30	+0.13	+0.07
2:30	−0.73	−0.50
3:30	−0.90	−0.95
4:30	−1.14	−1.25
5:30	−0.05	−0.03
Average...............	0.098	0.042

were recorded within and outside the area covered by smoke. Though the smoke screen decreased somewhat the rate of cooling of blackened surfaces horizontally exposed, there was only a slight increase in air temperature under and in the smoke and this apparently was due principally to heat imparted by the hot particles of phosphorus pentoxide and metaphosphoric acid.

The reflection of heat from smoke clouds is evidently very small. Müller-Thurgau[169] points out that smoke differs in its composition from clouds. It should be recalled that radiation is constantly occurring, clouds or no clouds, and that they do not prevent radiation but only reflect heat, and since outgoing and incoming heat approach equal value on cloudy nights the net loss by radiation is small. Smoke differs from water vapor in being relatively transparent to long heat waves. There is a relatively large difference in the way violet (or blue) and yellow (or red) are transmitted through dust in the air—for example, the sun is yellow or red at horizon, the short waves not being transmitted so readily as the longer yellow and red waves. The sun looks red through smoke, showing the same effect. The smoke screen appears opaque because the eye uses the shorter waves but it must be very much less opaque to the long waves which the earth radiates.

Covering and Spraying.—The protection of plants from frost by covering them with paper or cloth is of course effected through saving of the heat otherwise lost through radiation. The efficacy of this method is well known though it is not practicable in the orchard.[155]   An experiment in California showed that with an outside minimum of 19° the lowest temperature under a paper covering spread over an almond tree was 24°, a saving equal to the rise in temperature secured in many instances by orchard heating.

The protective effects of water spray were investigated in Utah by keeping a block of apricots under a continuous fine spray during a frost.[249] Ice formed on the blossoms and it finally appeared that only the sprayed trees were damaged. The injury was not a mere failure to set fruit; there was actual killing. In view of the work of Harvey[107] it seems probable that in this case the ice formation on the surfaces of the blossoms inoculated the inside tissues with ice crystals and actually hastened their freezing.

Orchard Heating.—The most successful results so far achieved in preventing low temperatures have been realized by the use of large numbers of small heaters, warming the air itself. This practice has become a settled part of orchard routine in some sections; in others it has been in extensive use but is now almost obsolete. There can be no doubt of its efficacy in some cases. Frequently, however, it has been considered too expensive insurance. The heating capacity of a set of heaters is limited and sometimes in a severe freeze the temperature sinks so low they are unable to maintain a protecting temperature, or in some cases a high cold wind renders them useless. On the other hand, a few degrees of freezing rarely destroys a whole crop. The full value of these heaters is, then, realized only with minima in a certain narrow range; with minima outside, they are either unnecessary or useless.

It is probable that failure to realize these limitations led to the installation, during the greatest vogue, of orchard heating equipment in many places where its true usefulness is rarely available and that failure to realize its limitations at the outset caused unjustifiable expectations of its value. In either case the reaction was bound to cloud the instances and circumstances in which it can be of real worth.

Furthermore, orchard heating has been invoked at times when the difficulty, supposedly frost, was in reality something entirely different. At one time many cherry growers at The Dalles, in Oregon, installed extensive heating equipment to induce a proper setting of fruit when their orchards were of self sterile and inter-sterile varieties and what they actually needed was provision for proper cross pollination. Orchard heating cannot make weak trees set heavy crops. In view of the equal influence of freezing on blossoms of weak and of strong trees, as cited previously in this section, the increases sometimes reported in fruit set after frost on nitrate-fertilized trees may constitute a splendid testimonial for nitrate fertilization but they do not in themselves indicate that orchard heating without fertilization would have been beneficial.

Heat Units in the Fuel.—Limits must be recognized to the amount of actual heating any ordinary equipment can secure.

McAdie[156] indicates this in some interesting calculations. "At the present time," he states, "with a hundred burners to the acre, using a gallon each of oil, something like 15,000,000 British thermal units or 3,760,000 [kilogram] calories would be given off, provided the combustion was perfect, which of course is never true. Now, to raise the temperature of the air 1°F. over an acre to a height of 15 feet is practically heating 653,400 cubic feet of air. In practice it is found that to maintain the temperature on a still night 1° above the freezing temperature requires 0.252 calories per hour per cubic foot. Therefore for a period of 7 hours, which is about the average duration of a low temperature [McAdie wrote in California], although 10 hours is a safer period, there will be required 1,138,200 calories. And if a raise of 5° is required it is evident that more than 5,500,000 calories are needed or more than the full number of heat units in the fuel under perfect combustion."

In practice oil is burned generally at a faster rate than that used in McAdie's calculations, but the published results of careful experiments indicate that the actual heating achieved rarely exceeds 5° and that 4° is a liberal estimate of what may be expected with ordinarily favorable conditions. A breeze of 6 miles an hour materially lowers the net gain of heat; any movement lowers it somewhat and dead calms are rare. According to Young, in the lard-pail type of heaters only about 40 per cent of the heat in the oil is actually realized in combustion and even in the high stack type it is doubtful if more than 70 or 80 per cent of its fuel value is attained. A still further loss is caused by the height of the "ceiling layer" of air which, though variable, permits in any case the accumulation of heat at a height above the trees.

Height of the "Ceiling Layer."—The holding of heated air within a few feet of the ground appears mysterious unless the inversion of temperature be considered. Data introduced previously have shown that the normal adiabatic cooling of the air upward from the earth, characteristic of daytime, is modified during radiation nights and that the air only a few feet above the ground is distinctly warmer than that at or near the surface. It is this layer of warm air, acting as a roof or ceiling, that makes possible the warming of the air at the level of the trees.

As the warmed air ascends from the heaters it mixes with other some-what cooler air and the mixture finally reaches a layer of the same temperature; it then has no impulse to rise farther.

Figure 39, by Humphreys,[120] shows a typical frosty morning temperature gradient and is used by him to indicate how heat may be wasted. He shows that under the given conditions any portion of the surface

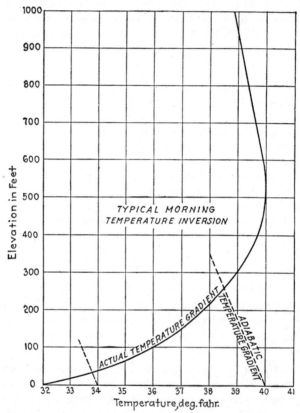

FIG. 39.—Illustrating the physical possibility of protecting outdoors from frost by artificial heating. (*After Humphreys*[120])

air warmed from 32 to 34°F. would rise to about 30 feet only, as shown by the adiabatic curve from 34°, until it would reach the layer of air having a temperature equal to its own. If it were warmed to 40°, however, it must rise over 250 feet, cooling somewhat by diminished pressure, until it reaches air with an equal temperature. Thus in one case the ceiling is about 30 feet high, in the other it is 250 feet high. When the gradient begins at, say, 24° instead of 32°, in other words when the outside unheated surface air is at 24°, whether or not the gradient is affected at 500 feet, the ceiling above the 34° mark is raised, meaning that not only must the air now be heated from 24 to 34°, 10 degrees instead of 2, but a greater amount of air must be heated. The increasing difficulty of heating toward morning is due evidently to other factors besides the heaters themselves.

If a few large fires are employed the body of warmed air rising from them is so great that it does not become mixed readily and rises farther than the heat from the small fires, being thus rendered ineffective in warming the air at lower levels. Large fires of course emit a considerable amount of radiation heat which warms the surfaces exposed, but since the intensity of heating by radiation diminishes as the square of the distance from the source of heat it soon becomes ineffective. In addition the current set up above the large fire draws in the colder surface air to replace the warmed air driven high aloft and it is easy to conceive that it may disturb ceiling layers considerably.

Effect of Wind.—Winds, besides carrying heat away directly, break up the "ceiling layer" of warm air and unless the heated areas are very large and the wind such that the warmed air is "blown down," they make heating efforts of little avail. Windbreaks, therefore, though at times they may invite frost conditions, may render heating more effective, though they cannot preserve the ceiling layer which is necessary for full realization of its possibilities.

Humphreys,[120] assuming a radiation per minute per square centimeter of 0.1 calorie and evidently basing his calculations on soil surface area alone, disregarding vegetative surfaces, concluded that for each plot of ground 10 meters by 10 meters there would be needed per hour 6,000,000 calories, which, assigning a value of 8,500 calories per gram of petroleum, indicates the need of approximately a pint and a half of oil per hour to offset radiation or to hold the temperature from falling. If a moderate air movement occur, new air must be warmed constantly. Humphreys, assuming the dewpoint below 32°, land surface horizontal, temperature of air 32° and a wind of $2\frac{1}{4}$ miles per hour (approximately 1 meter per second), with air weight 1,290 grams per cubic meter, makes an interesting calculation of the amount of heat necessary to warm the entering air 2°C. to an elevation of 12 meters. He states: "Now the specific heat of the atmosphere is very approximately 0.24. Hence to warm 1 cubic meter of the given air 1°C. requires about 310 calories. Hence, to warm the air 2°C. to an elevation of 12 meters, as it enters the given area with the given velocity of 1 meter per second, will require, per linear meter at right angles to its direction, approximately $2 \times 12 \times 310 \times 7{,}440$ calories per second, or the consumption of, roughly, 3.7 liters or 6.5 pints of oil per hour."

A considerable amount of the heat imparted to the air as it enters is retained while the air drifts through the orchard; therefore, though radiation must be fought equally at all points the raising of air temperature itself is more properly done on the windward edge. With the somewhat idealized conditions enumerated above, assuming an orchard 1 kilometer square (about 247 acres) with the breeze at right angles to one side the oil requirements are stated by Humphreys: to counteract radiation 8,600 liters; to warm the entering air 3,700 liters. A rectangular orchard might require more or less oil to warm the entering air, according to the direction of the breeze and if the breeze is quartering two sides must be warmed, but the amount to offset radiation alone is constant. In other words the oil necessary to offset radiation is determined by area alone; the amount necessary to warm entering air is determined by the outline of the orchard and by the direction and velocity of the wind.

Concerning the influence of wind velocity Humphreys says: "Of course a greater wind velocity than $2\frac{1}{4}$ miles per hour, the velocity above assumed, would appear to necessitate a correspondingly larger consumption of fuel for the border or entrance heating. But this, presumably, is not true in practice, since probably even this velocity, certainly a greater one, would considerably mix the surface-cooled air with the warmer air above, and thereby decrease the amount of necessary heating. During a perfect calm the required border heating is zero; it is also zero when there is a fairly good breeze and hence has its maximum value at some quite moderate intermediate velocity."

It should be noted that Humphreys is stating that the higher the velocity of the air movement the higher the air temperature is likely to be. This is quite different from the case of high wind at a dangerous temperature, for here the heating required increases with the wind velocity and too many times becomes impossible.

The choice of heater types depends on the nature of the service required. In some sections where dangerous temperatures are of short duration the simple 1-gallon heaters will be adequate; in other sections longer burning may be required. Young[261] points out that the size of the temperature inversion characteristic of many of the California frosts permits the use of stack heaters which, perhaps, could not be employed in sections where the temperature inversion is weaker. No one type is best for all sections or for all occasions in one section.

Conditions Determining Practicability.—No general discussion can decide the question whether orchard heating is profitable. The continuance of the practice in certain sections over a long period is rather good evidence that with conditions as they are in those sections it is either profitable or necessary or both. The necessity of the practice, if fruit is to be grown in a certain spot, may mean that it is desirable or it may mean that the spot should be devoted to some other crop. If the value per acre of the crop is high, as with oranges, heating may be economically sound; if the value per acre of the crop is low, heating is of doubtful wisdom. If a given spot is exposed to several frosts a year heating is likely to pay as compared with no heating but it may be that fruit growing should be abandoned at that spot. During the decade 1913-1922 unprotected apple orchards in the Pecos valley suffered six total and three partial crop failures because of frost. Protected orchards bore eight full crops during that same period.[103] Obviously heating was very effective in preventing or reducing frost damage but its cost has been too great to enable the producers of that section to compete successfully with those of other areas where heating is unnecessary.

The installation of an orchard heating equipment involves a heavy overhead expense. Each year heaters and fuel must be distributed and made ready. The chief difference in expense between a frosty and a frostless spring so far as heating is concerned is in the oil consumed and a reduction or increase in the labor charge. The profits of the frostless season are taxed only somewhat less than those of the frosty season. Frequently the yearly expense has amounted to $20 per acre; it has reached $40. In many, if not in most, fruit growing sections, $40 per acre added to the initial price of the land will secure sites located advantageously enough to escape this tax.

In many of the citrus orchards of southern California, orchard heating has come to be regarded as more or less of a standard practice. At least they are provided with heaters that may be used whenever occasion requires. On the other hand, in the deciduous fruit growing areas orchard heating is not so common as it was some years ago. Certain sections have abandoned it altogether, in others only a few growers continue it. In some instances too much has been expected of it; in others the falling in fruit prices from an artificial level has been a contributing cause, but probably in the majority of cases it has been abandoned for the excellent reason that it has not paid.

It will be seen from the Wauseon figures that heating at that point would be an expensive insurance considering the number of times it would be useful. If, in addition, the orchards are, as is the case frequently, bearing chiefly in alternate years, the likelihood of heating being profitable over a long term is further reduced. Assuming a damaging frost in half the blossoming seasons, a ratio far greater than that for the largest apple growing sections, and assuming a crop in alternate years, the chance of heating being required to save a crop is $\frac{1}{2} \times \frac{1}{2}$ or 1 in 4. If damaging frost occurs once in 3 years the chance is $\frac{1}{3} \times \frac{1}{2}$ or 1 in 6. At Wauseon, with very liberal allowance, it is, for the King apple, 2 in 15. It is significant that much of the experimental work on orchard heating has been done at temperatures above freezing because there was not enough frosty weather for all the tests. There are, too, in almost all sections, springs when the crop is damaged by high cold winds, under such conditions that heating fails to protect it sufficiently. If a season of this kind is added to seasons when heating is unnecessary the number of years when it really pays is still further reduced.

The fruit grower is forced, sooner or later, consciously or unconsciously, to consider the economic doctrine of marginal utility. This means, as applied to the topic under discussion, that until all the land otherwise well adapted to fruit growing and free from frost danger in a given area is in use for that purpose it is of doubtful expediency to attempt fruit growing on land that will require heating. It means, too, that in seasons when profits in general run low they are, other things equal, wiped out first on the land that requires heating.

In addition to the doctrine of marginal utility the grower should apply to his analysis the law of the minimum. Orchard heating is not likely to be profitable to him if his spraying is defective, his pruning poorly done, his land lacking in drainage or irrigation, his trees weak or if his fruit is not marketed to advantage. When he is satisfied that he has developed these essentials so that none of them is limiting his profits and that frost is the limiting factor he can consider orchard heating. In some cases it will be profitable; in more cases it will not.

FROST EFFECTS

Manifestations of frost injury aside from the dropping of the fruit are sometimes found. The so-called bull-necked pears previously mentioned are rather common and are sometimes confused with seedless fruit, particularly with that arising from late bloom. Russet bands, generally extending more or less completely around the middle of the fruit, though sometimes near the calyx end, occur on pears and occasionally on apples. Similar russeted areas, frequently somewhat raised, but less regular in location, are found on plums. Apples and pears with this form of injury are said to wilt rather rapidly.[177]

In the apple the outside leaves of a cluster sometimes show a form of injury called "frost-blister."[176] As observed in New Hampshire and Missouri, this injury does not appear to reduce the size of the affected leaves which are normally small and it apparently does not extend beyond the first two or three leaves to unfold. The injury evidently may occur when the buds are still very little advanced. The appearance is sufficiently described by the name; the "blisters" are caused by the separation of the upper and the lower surfaces. The leaves tend to curl and in many cases drop off. Inasmuch as those most affected are of doubtful importance to the growing spur this type of injury is probably unimportant.

Another interesting consequence of frost injury is the so-called "secondary bloom." When there is extensive killing of fruit buds the spurs which have bloomed may form new blossoms, which in some cases have been observed to mature fruit, sometimes with and sometimes without seeds. The same phenomenon may occur independently of any frost. It is discussed more fully under Fruiting Habit.

Summary.—The critical temperature for opening flower buds varies greatly with their stage of development and somewhat with species and variety. Some of the fully expanded flowers of many fruit varieties will withstand an apparent temperature of 25°F. without injury, though some will be killed at or above this point. Unopened flower buds are considerably more frost resistant. Plants in a vigorous condition are apparently no more resistant to frost, but they possess greater recuperative ability. Often trees losing a considerable percentage of their blossoms from frost still have enough good buds to bear a full crop. In many cases danger from frost can be avoided to a great extent by the selection of late blossoming varieties. Relatively greater immunity from frost danger can be secured in this way with those fruits and in those sections showing a considerable range in blossoming. The blossoming season of many fruits may be slightly retarded by certain cultural practices, but, except in the case of fruits like the strawberry that can be entirely covered, such methods of frost protection are of secondary importance. In new sections the probable blossoming dates of certain varieties of fruit may be foretold with considerable accuracy by comparison with the blossoming season of native plants. The probability of frost occurring on any particular night can be foretold fairly accurately by the middle of the preceding afternoon. Several methods are employed, some of them being more reliable in certain districts than others. The predictions for regular Weather Bureau "key" stations, corrected to apply to local conditions are of greatest general use. Several distinct methods of preventing frost have been used in fruit growing sections. The use of smoke screens is of little value in checking the radiation of heat at night. Orchard heating is practicable under certain conditions. However, only a limited protection is afforded by orchard heaters, the exact amount depending on the height of the "ceiling layer" of the air, on the number and kind of heaters and on the amount of wind. A protection of 4 or 5°F. on typical frosty nights is all that can be expected under average conditions. Before the installation of orchard heating equipment is warranted there should be reasonable assurance that growing conditions during the average season and the average margin of profit warrant it. Frost occurring after the time of fruit setting may occasionally arrest the further development of seeds and still permit the fleshy tissues to develop and mature, giving rise to fruits abnormal in size and shape. It may also cause the appearance of "frost rings" or bands of russet around the apical end of the fruit. It occasionally leads to certain other pathological conditions in fruit or foliage.

Suggested Collateral Reading

Schimper, A. F. W. Plant Geography upon a Physiological Basis. Pp. 35–51; 241–259. Oxford, 1903.

Wiegand, K. M.   The Biology of Twigs in Winter.   Bot. Gaz.   41: 373.   1906.

LITERATURE CITED

1. Abbe, C.   U. S. D. A., Weather Bur. No. 342: 168.   1905.
2. Abell, T.   Utah Agr. Exp. Sta. Ann. Rept.   1927.
3. Alter, J. C.   U. S. D. A., Mo. Weather Rev.   40: 929.   1912.
4. Alwood, W. B.   Va. Agr. Exp. Sta. Bul. 147.   1903.
5. Anderson, H. W., and Kadow, K. S.   Ill. Agr. Exp. Sta. Ann. Rept.   49: 265.
    1937.
6. Anthony, R. D.   N. Y. Agr. Exp. Sta. Bul. 432.   1917.
7. Augur, P. M.   Proc. Am. Pom. Soc.   P. 54.   1885.
8. Baake, A. L.   Proc. Am. Soc. Hort. Sci.   17: 279.   1920.
9. Bailey, L. H.   Mich. Agr. Exp. Sta. Bul. 40.   1888.
10. Bailey, L. H.   Cornell Univ. Agr. Exp. Sta. Bul. 117.   1896.
11. Bailey, L. H.   Survival of the Unlike.   P. 297.   New York, 1901.
12. Bailey, L. H.   The Principles of Fruit Growing.   P. 11.   New York, 1906.
13. Baird, W. P.   U. S. D. A. Farmers' Bul. 1522.   1927.
14. Ballantyne, A. B.   Utah Agr. Exp. Sta. Bul. 128.   1913.
15. Balmer, J. A.   Wash. Agr. Exp. Sta. Bul. 30.   1897.
16. Baragiola, W. I. and Godet, C.   Landw. Jahrb.   48: 275.   1914.
17. Bartlett, G.   Horticulturist.   1: 549.   1847.
18. Bates, C. G.   U. S. D. A., Forest Service Bul. 86.   1911.
19. Beach, S. A., and Allen, F. W., Jr.   Ia. Agr. Exp. Sta. Res. Bul. 21.   1915.
20. Beach, S. A., and Close, C. P.   N. Y. Agr. Exp. Sta. Ann. Rept.   15: 408.
    1897.
21. Bedford, H. A. R. and Pickering, S. U.   2d Rept. Woburn Exp. Fruit Farm.
    P. 242.   London, 1900.
22. Bigelow, F. H.   U. S. D. A., Weather Bur. Bul. R.   1908.
23. Bijhouwer, A. P. C.   A Contribution to the Knowledge of the Flowering and
    Fruiting Habits of the Mango Tree, Mangifera indica L.   Wageningen
    (Holland).   1937.
24. Black, M. W.   Jour. Pom.   14: 175–202.   1936.
25. Blair, D. S.   Sci. Agr.   16 (1): 8–15.   1935.
26. Blake, M. A.   N. Jer. Agr. Exp. Sta. Ann. Rept.   49: 194.   1928.
27. Blodgett, L.   Climatology of the U. S.   P. 437.   1857.
28. Bonebright, J. E.   Ida. Agr. Exp. Sta. Bul. 35.   1903.
29. Borja, V., and Bautista, B.   Philippine Jour. Agr.   3: 111–143.   1932.
30. Boussingault, J. B.   Rural Economy.   Transl. by Law.   P. 255.   New York,
    1855.
31. Bouyoucos, G. J.   Mich. Agr. Exp. Sta. Tech. Bul. 26.   1916.
32. Ibid.   Tech. Bul. 36.   1917.
33. Bouyoucos, G. J.   J. Agr. Res.   20: 267.   1920.
34. Bradford, F. C.   Thesis Univ. Maine.   1911.
35. Bradford, F. C.   Mich. Agr. Exp. Sta. Sp. Bul. 149.   1926.
36. Brooks, C. F.   Bul. Am. Met. Soc.   13 (2): 217–220.   1932.
37. Budd, J. L.   Ia. Agr. Exp. Sta. Bul. 7.   1889.
38. Ibid.   Bul. 13.   1891.
39. Buffum, B. C.   Wyo. Agr. Exp. Sta. Bul. 34.   1896.
40. Cannon, W. A.   Plant World.   20: 361.   1917.
41. Card, F. W.   Nebr. Agr. Exp. Sta. Bul. 48.   1897.
42. Card, F. W.   Bush Fruits.   P. 24.   New York, 1917.
43. Ibid.   P. 37.

44. Carpenter, L. G.   Col. Agr. Exp. Sta. Ann. Rept.   3: 147.   1890; 4: 75.   1891.
45. Carrick, D. B.   Cornell Univ. Agr. Exp. Sta. Mem. 36.   1920.
46. Chandler, W. H.   Mo. Agr. Exp. Sta. Bul. 74.   1907.
47. Chandler, W. H.   Mo. Agr. Exp. Sta. Cir. 31.   1908.
48. Chandler, W. H.   Mo. Agr. Exp. Sta. Res. Bul. 8.   1913.
49. Chandler, W. H.   Proc. Am. Soc. Hort. Sci.   12: 118.   1915.
50. Chandler, W. H.   Correspondence, 1921.
51. Chandler, W. H., Kimball, M. H., Philip, G. L., Tufts, W. P., and Weldon, G. P. Cal. Agr. Exp. Sta. Bul. 611.   1937.
52. Chapman, H. H.   Minn. Agr. Exp. Sta. Bul. 81.   1903.
53. Church, J. L., Jr., and Ferguson, S. P.   Nev. Agr. Exp. Sta. Bul. 79.   1912.
54. Coit, J. E.   Ariz. Agr. Exp. Sta. Bul. 61.   1909.
55. Conley, J. D., and Ridgaway, C. B.   Wyo. Agr. Exp. Sta. Bul. 23.   1896. Met. Repts.   1898, 1899.
56. Coulter, J. M., Barnes, C. R., and Cowles, H. C.   Textbook of Botany.   2: 585. New York.   1911.
57. Cox, H. J.   U. S. D. A., Weather Bur. Bul. T.   1910.
58. Cox, H. J.   U. S. D. A., Weather Bur. No. 583: 177.   1916.
59. Craig, J.   Cent. (Can.) Exp. Farms Bul. 22.   1895.
60. Craig, J.   Cent. (Can.) Exp. Farms Ann. Rept.   10: 119.   1896.
61. Ibid.   10: 147.   1896.
62. Craig, J.   Ia. Agr. Exp. Sta. Bul. 44.   1900.
63. Crandall, C. S.   Col. Agr. Exp. Sta. Bul. 41.   1898.
64. Darrow, G. M.   Science.   85: 391–392.   1937.
65. Darrow, G. M., Franklin, H. J., and Malde, O. G.   U. S. D. A., Farmers' Bul. 1400.   1924.
66. DeCandolle, A.   Geog. bot. raison.   Paris, 1855.
67. Dorsey, M. J., and Strausbaugh, P. D.   Bot. Gaz.   76: 113–143.   1923.
68. Downing, A. J.   Horticulturist.   1: 58.   1846.
69. Ibid.   2: 339.   1847.
70. Ibid.   2: 416.   1847.
71. Doyle, J., and Clinch, P.   Roy. Dublin Soc. Sci. Proc. n. ser., 18 (24): 265–275. 1926.
72. Ducharte, P.   Compt. rend.   60: 754.   1865.
73. Ellison, E. S., and Close, W. L.   Mo. Weather Rev.   55 (1): 11–18.   1927.
74. Emerson, R. A.   Nebr. Agr. Exp. Sta. Bul. 79.   1903.
75. Ibid.   Bul. 92.   1906.
76. Emerson, R. A.   Nebr. Agr. Exp. Sta. Ann. Rept.   19: 101.   1906.
77. Emerson, R. A.   Correspondence, Dec. 14, 1920.
78. Emery, S. M.   Mont. Agr. Exp. Sta. Bul. 16.   1898.
79. Ibid.   Bul. 24.   1899.
80. Eustace, H. J.   N. Y. Agr. Exp. Sta. Bul. 269.   1905.
81. Fernow, B. E.   U.S.D.A., Forestry Div. Bul. 7.   1893.
82. Finch, V. C., and Baker, D. O.   Geography of the World's Agriculture.   P.77. Washington, 1917.
83. Fisher, W. R.   Schlich's Manual of Forestry.   4: 505.   1907.
84. Ibid.   4: 522.
85. Frank, A. B.   Die Krankheiten der Pflanzen.   2: 204.   Breslau, 1895.
86. Friedrich, J.   Ueber den Einfluss der Witterung auf den Baumwachs.   P. 155. Vienna, 1897.
87. Gail, F. W.   Bot. Gaz.   81: 434–445.   1926.
88. Galang, F. G., and Agati, J. A.   Philippine Jour. Agr.   7 (2): 245–262.   1936.

89. Garcia, F., and Rigney, J. W.   N. Mex. Agr. Exp. Sta. Bul. 89.   1914.
90. Ibid.   Bul. 100.   1916.
91. Gardner, V. R.   Jour. Agr. Res.   50 (6): 563–572.   1935.
92. Gladwin, F. E.   N. Y. Agr. Exp. Sta. Bul. 433.   1917.
92a. Goff, E. S.   Wis. Agr. Exp. Sta. Ann. Rept.   15: 220.   1898.
93. Ibid.   16: 283.   1899.
94. Goff, E. S.   Wis. Agr. Exp. Sta. Bul. 77.   1899.
95. Gonzalez, L. G.   Philippine Agr.   21: 533–540.   1933.
96. Gould, H. P.   Peach Growing.   P. 354.   New York, 1918.
97. Gourley, J. H.   N. H. Agr. Exp. Sta. Tech. Bul. 12.   1917.
98. Greene, L.   Purdue Univ. Agr. Exp. Sta. Ann. Rept.   31: 46.   1918.
99. Green, S. B.   Minn. Agr. Exp. Sta. Bul. 32.   1893.
100. Green, W. J., and Ballou, F. H.   Ohio Agr. Exp. Sta. Bul. 157.   1904.
101. Grossenbacher, J. G.   N. Y. Agr. Exp. Sta. Tech. Bul. 23.   1912.
102. Gunderson, A. J.   Ill. Agr. Exp. Sta. Bul. 218.   1919.
103. Hallenbeck, C.   Mo. Weather Rev.   51: 25.   1923.
104. Hammon, W. H.   Cited by 89.
105. Hansen, N. E.   S. D. Agr. Exp. Sta. Bul. 50.   1897.
106. Ibid.   Bul. 65.   1899.
107. Harvey, R. B.   J. Agr. Res.   15: 2.   1918.
108. Harvey, R. B.   Ecology.   4: 391–394.   1923.
109. Hedrick, U. P., Booth, N. O., and Taylor, O. M.   N. Y. Agr. Exp. Sta. Bul. 275.   1906.
110. Hedrick, U. P.   Hort. Soc. of N. Y. Mem.   2: 119.   1907.
111. Hedrick, U. P.   N. Y. Agr. Exp. Sta. Bul. 299.   1908.
112. Hedrick, U. P.   Plums of New York.   P. 103.   Albany, 1911.
113. Hedrick, U. P.   N. Y. Agr. Exp. Sta. Bul. 355.   1912.
114. Herrick, R. S., and Bennett, E. R.   Col. Agr. Exp. Sta. Bul. 171.   1910.
115. Hodgson, R. W.   Cal. Agr. Exp. Sta. Ann. Rept. for 1928–29.   P. 100.   1930.
116. Hooker, H. D., Jr.   Proc. Am. Soc. Hort. Sci.   17: 204–207.   1920.
117. Hopkins, A. D.   U.S.D.A., Mo. Weather Rev. Sup. 9.   1918.
118. Horne, W. J., Weldon, G. P., and Babcock, E. B.   Jour. Heredity.   17 (3): 99–104.   1926.
119. Howard, A., and Howard, G. L. C.   Sci. Rept. Agr. Inst. Pusa. 48.   1916–1917.
120. Humphreys, W. J.   U.S.D.A., Mo. Weather Rev.   42: 562.   1914.
121. Jehle, R. A.   Cornell Univ. Agr. Exp. Sta. Cir. 26.   1914.
122. Johnston, E. S.   Am. J. Bot.   6: 373–379.   1919.
123. Jones, C. H., Edson, A. W., and Morse, W. J.   Vt. Agr. Exp. Sta. Bul. 103.   1903.
124. Kimball, H. H., and MacIntire, B. G.   Mo. Weather Rev.   51: 396.   1923.
125. Kimball, H. K., and Young, F. D.   U.S.D.A., Mo. Weather Rev.   48: 461.   1920.
126. King, F. H.   Wis. Agr. Exp. Sta. Ann. Rept.   13: 207.   1896.
127. Lazenby, W. R.   Proc. Am. Pom. Soc.   P. 54.   1885.
128. Lindley, J.   The Theory and Practice of Horticulture.   P. 150.   London, 1855.
129. Ibid.   P. 155.
130. Linsser, C.   Cited by Bailey, L. H.   Survival of the Unlike.   P. 292.   New York, 1901.
131. Lippincott, J. B.   U.S.D.A., Ann. Rept.   P. 200.   1862.
132. Livingston, B. E.   Physiol. Res.   1: 8.   1916.
133. Livingston, B. E., and Livingston, G. J.   Bot. Gaz.   56: 5.   1913.

134. Lloyd, F. E.   Plant World.   20: 121.   1917.
135. Loomis, E.   Treatise on Meteorology.   P. 91.   New York, 1892.
136. Ibid.   P. 93.
137. Lott, R. V.   Mo. Agr. Exp. Sta. Res. Bul. 95.   1926.
138. Lutz, H.   Letter to F. C. Bradford, dated Jan. 25, 1937.
139. MacDougal, D. T.   Hydration and Growth.   Carn. Inst. Wash. Publ. 297.
     P. 167.   1920.
140. Macoun, W. T.   Rept. Cent. (Can.) Exp. Farms.   12: 99.   1899.
141. Ibid.   13: 73.   1900.
142. Ibid.   13: 92.   1900.
143. Macoun, W. T.   Cent. (Can.) Exp. Farms Bul. 38.   1901.
144. Macoun, W. T.   Proc. Am. Soc. Hort. Sci.   3: 7.   1906.
145. Macoun, W. T.   Cent. (Can.) Exp. Farms Bul. 38.   2d ed.   1907.
146. Macoun, W. T.   Proc. Am. Soc. Hort. Sci.   6: 15.   1909.
147. Macoun, W. T.   Trans. Mass. Hort. Soc. Pt. 1.   P. 39.   1916.
148. Magness, J. R.   U.S.D.A. Bul. 1072.   1922.
149. Mally, C. W.   So. Africa Union Dept. Agr. Bul. 125.   1934.
150. Marvin, C. F.   U.S.D.A., Mo. Weather Rev.   42: 583.   1914.
151. Mason, S. C.   U.S.D.A., Bur. Pl. Ind. Bul. 192.   1911.
152. Mason, S. C.   Jour. Agr. Res.   31: 401–414.   1925.
153. Maynard, S. T.   Agriculture of Massachusetts.   P. 348.   Boston, 1884.
154. Maynard, S. T.   Mass. Agr. Exp. Sta. Buls. 10.   1890; 15.   1891; 21.   1893.
155. McAdie, G.   U.S.D.A., Mo. Weather Rev.   40: 282.   1912.
156. Ibid.   40: 618.
157. McCall, F. E.   Amer. Fruit Grower.   39: 7.   July, 1920.
158. McLean, F. T.   Physiol. Res.   2: 129.   1917.
159. Mell, P. H.   Ala. Agr. Exp. Sta. Bul. 8.   1890.
160. Mer, E.   Compt. rend.   114: 242.   1892.
161. Ibid.   124: 1111.   1897.
162. Mikesell, T.   U.S.D.A., Mo. Weather Rev. Sup. 2.   1915.
163. Milham, W. I.   U.S.D.A., Mo. Weather Rev.   36: 250.   1908.
164. Mix, A. J.   Cornell Univ. Agr. Exp. Sta. Bul. 382.   1916.
165. Molisch, H.   Sitzber. Akad. Wiss. Wien, Math. Naturw. Kl.   105 (1): 82–95.
     1896.
166. Moore, W. L.   Descriptive Meteorology.   P. 82.   New York, 1911.
167. Morris, O. M.   Wash. Agr. Exp. Sta. Bul. 217.   1927.
168. Mosier, J. G.   Ill. Agr. Exp. Sta. Bul. 208.   1918.
169. Müller-Thurgau, H.   Landw. Jahrb.   45: 453.   1886.
170. Munson, W. M.   Me. Agr. Exp. Sta. Ann. Rept.   7: 96.   1893.
171. N. Y. Agr. Exp. Sta. Ann. Rept.   37: 468.   1919.
172. O'Gara, P. J.   U.S.D.A., Farmers' Bul. 401.   1910.
173. Oskamp, J.   Proc. Am. Soc. Hort. Sci.   14: 118.   1917.
174. Overholser, E. L., and Overley, F. L.   Wash. Agr. Exp. Sta. Ann. Rept. 42.
     1922.
175. Overholser, E. L., Winkler, A. J., and Jacob, H. E.   Cal. Agr. Exp. Sta. Bul. 370.
     1923.
176. Paddock, W., and Whipple, O. B.   Fruit Growing in Arid Regions.   P. 325.
     New York, 1911.
177. Ibid.   P. 326.
178. Ibid.   P. 327.
179. Ibid.   P. 353.

180. Pantanelli, E.   Atti Accad. Lincei.   27(1): 126–130; 148–153.   1918.
181. Partridge, N. L.   Mich. Agr. Exp. Sta. Sp. Bul. 121.   1923.
182. Partridge, N. L., and Toenjes, W.   Mich. Agr. Exp. Sta. Circ. Bul. 163.   1937.
183. Pa. Agr. Exp. Sta. Ann. Repts.   1892, 1893, 1894, 1895, 1896.
184. Petit, A.   Rev. Hort. 13(N.S.): 206.   1913.
185. Pfeffer, W.   Physiology of Plants. Transl. by Ewart.   2: 236.   Oxford, 1903.
186. Ibid.   2: 237.
187. Ibid.   2: 246.
188. Philips, H. A.   Thesis. Cornell Univ.   1920.
189. Porter, E. D.   Minn. Agr. Exp. Sta. Bul. 7.   1889.
190. Potter, G. F.   N. Hamp. Agr. Exp. Sta. Tech. Bul. 27.   1924.
191. Price, H. L.   Va. Agr. Exp. Sta. Ann. Rept.   P. 206.   1909–1910.
192. Prillieux, E.   Compt. rend.   74: 1344.   1872.
193. Quaintance, A. L.   Ga. Agr. Exp. Sta. Ann. Rept.   11: 123.   1899.
194. Ragan, W. H.   U.S.D.A., Div. Pom. Bul. 8.   1899.
195. Reed, W. G.   Proc. 2d Pan-Amer. Sci. Cong.   P. 625.   1917.
196. Reed, W. G., and Tolley, H. R.   U.S.D.A., Mo. Weather Rev.   44: 354.   1916.
197. Roberts, R. H.   Proc. Am. Soc. Hort. Sci.   14: 105.   1917.
198. Roberts, R. H.   Wis. Agr. Exp. Sta. Res. Bul. 52.   1922.
199. Rosa, J. T., Jr.   Proc. Am. Soc. Hort. Sci.   16: 190.   1919.
200. Ibid.   17: 207–210.   1920.
201. Rosa, J. T., Jr.   Mo. Agr. Exp. Sta. Res. Bul. 48.   1921.
202. Sandsten, E. P.   Wis. Agr. Exp. Sta. Ann. Rept.   21: 258.   1904.
203. Sandsten, E. P.   Wis. Agr. Exp. Sta. Bul. 137.   1906.
204. Sandsten, E. P.   Wis. Agr. Exp. Sta. Res. Bul. 4.   1910.
205. Schimper, A. F. W.   Plant Geography upon a Physiological Basis.   P. 34. Oxford, 1903.
206. Ibid.   P. 37.
207. Ibid.   P. 45.
208. Ibid.   P. 47.
209. Schneider, Numa.   Rev. Hort.   11(N.S.): 21.   1911.
210. Schneiderhan, F. J.   Va. Agr. Exp. Sta. Bul. 245.   1926.
211. Schübler, G.   Poggendorf's Annal. Phys. u. Chem.   10: 581.   1827.
212. Schuster, C. E.   Ore. Agr. Exp. Sta. Bien. Crop Pest and Hort. Rept.   3: 44. 1920.
213. Seeley, D. A.   U.S.D.A., Mo. Weather Rev.   36: 259.   1908.
214. Ibid.   45: 354.   1917.
215. Selby, A. D.   Ohio Agr. Exp. Sta. Bul. 192.   1908.
216. Sellschop, J. P. F., and Salmon, S. C.   Jour. Agr. Res. 37 (6): 315–338.   1929.
217. Selvig, C. G.   Rept. Exp. Farm, Crookston, Minn.   1917–18.
218. Shaw, J. K.   Mass. Agr. Exp. Sta. Ann. Rept.   23: 177.   1911.
219. Shutt, F. T.   Trans. Roy. Soc. Can.   (Ser. 2.)   9(4): 149.   1903.
220. Smith, A. M.   Ann. Roy. Bot. Gar. Peradeniya.   (Abs. in Bot. Gaz.   44: 6. 1917.)
221. Smith, J. W.   U.S.D.A., Mo. Weather Rev. Sup. 16.   1920.
222. Sorauer, P.   Schutz der Obstbäume gegen Krankheiten.   P. 42.   Stuttgart, 1900.
223. Ibid.   P. 46.
224. Squires, R. W.   Minn. Bot. Studies.   1: 452.   1894–1898.
225. Steinmetz, F. H., and Hilborn, M. T.   Me. Agr. Exp. Sta. Bul. 388.   1937.

226. Stevens, N. E.   Am. J. Bot.   4: 1.   1917.
227. Ibid.   4: 112.
228. Stockman, W. B.   U.S.D.A., Mo. Weather Rev.   32: 125.   1904.
229. Strausbaugh, P. D.   Bot. Gaz.   71: 337.   1921.
230. Swezey, G. D.   Nebr. Agr. Exp. Sta. Ann. Rept.   16: 95.   1903.
231. Swingle, W. T.   U.S.D.A., Bur. Pl. Ind. Bul. 53.   1904.
232. Taft, L. R.   Mich. Agr. Exp. Sta. Sp. Bul. 11.   1898.
233. Ibid.   Sp. Bul. 40.   1907.
234. Ibid.   Sp. Bul. 46.   1908.
235. Taft, L. R., and Lyon, T. T.   Mich. Agr. Exp. Sta. Bul. 169.   1899.
236. Tufts, W. P.   Correspondence, 1921.
237. Von Mohl, C.   Bot. Ztg.   6: 6.   1848.
238. Waite, M. B.   U.S.D.A., Bur. Pl. Ind. Bul. 51.   1905.
239. Waldron, C. B.   N. D. Agr. Exp. Sta. Bul. 25.   1896.
240. Ibid.   Bul. 49.   1901.
241. Ward, H. W.   The Book of the Peach.   P. 27.   London, 1903.
242. Waugh, F. A.   Vt. Agr. Exp. Sta. Bul. 62.   1898.
243. Waugh, F. A.   Vt. Agr. Exp. Sta. Ann. Rept.   11: 270.   1898.
244. Ibid.   11: 273.
245. Waugh, F. A.   Vt. Agr. Exp. Sta. Bul. 74.   1899.
246. Webber, H. J. *et al.*   Cal. Agr. Exp. Sta. Bul. 304.   1919.
247. Weldon, G. P.   Cal. St. Dept. Agr. Month. Bul.   23 (7–9) 160–181.   1934.
248. Weldon, G. P., and Leslie, J. W.   Cal. Agr. Exp. Sta. Circ. Bul. 328.   1933.
249. West, F. L., and Edlefsen, N. E.   Utah Agr. Exp. Sta. Bul. 151.   1917.
250. West, F. L., and Edlefsen, N. E.   J. Agr. Res.   20: 8.   1921.
251. Whipple, O. B.   Mont. Agr. Exp. Sta. Bul. 91.   1912.
252. Whitten, J. C.   Mo. Agr. Exp. Sta. Bul. 38.   1897.
253. Ibid.   Bul. 49.   1900.
254. Whitten, J. C.   Mo. Agr. Exp. Sta. Res. Bul. 33.   1919.
255. Wiegand, K. M.   Bot. Gaz.   41: 373.   1906.
256. Wiegand, K. M.   Plant World.   9: 2.   1906.
257. Wilcox, E. V.   Mont. Agr. Exp. Sta. Bul. 22.   1899.
258. Wilson, W. M.   Standard Cyclopedia of Horticulture.   3: 1282.   1915.
259. Winkler, H.   Jahrb. f. Wiss. Bot.   52: 467.   1913.
260. Yarnell, S. H.   Tex. Agr. Exp. Sta. Ann. Rept.   48: 25.   1935.
261. Young, F. D.   U.S.D.A., Farmers' Bul. 1096.   1920.
262. Young, F. D.   U.S.D.A., Mo. Weather Rev.   48: 463.   1920.

SECTION IV
PRUNING

Fruit production by the trees, shrubs and vines that yield edible fruits is dependent on (1) the possession of the mechanism or machinery for fruit production that is characteristic of the species or variety in question and (2) its proper and more or less efficient functioning. Thus it is characteristic of most varieties of the brambles to bear fruit clusters terminally on short shoots developing from lateral buds on year-old canes. If the plant is so handled as to prevent or reduce the formation of lateral shoots of this type, fruiting is correspondingly limited. It is characteristic of certain varieties of the walnut to bear terminally only on short shoots developing from subterminal buds on the growth of the previous season. Obviously then the production and preservation of subterminal buds are prerequisites to fruit production in those varieties. The peach bears fruit on shoots of the past season but only at nodes from which no lateral branches arise.

However, some of the lateral buds on last year's raspberry and blackberry canes do not produce fruiting shoots; some of the shoots from subterminal buds of the walnut are barren and many nodes on the unbranched primary peach shoot do not have fruit buds. The framework, the machinery, for fruit bud formation is apparently there, but no fruit buds are formed. The mechanism does not function in the way it is desired. This functioning or non-functioning of the fruiting machinery is to be regarded as a definite response to varying conditions within the tree—primarily conditions of nutrition, which in turn may be influenced by age, vigor, food supply, temperature, humidity and many other factors.

In some cases production is limited by the amount of fruiting machinery, or, as the grower would say, the amount of bearing surface. In others the limiting factor to production is the irregular, imperfect or inefficient functioning of the fruiting mechanism. For the grower the ideal condition is to have the plant well equipped with fruit producing machinery and to have that machinery working efficiently. One or two further parallels may be drawn at this point between the living plant and the hypothetical manufacturing establishment with which it has been compared. Good equipment with fruit producing machinery does not mean the maximum amount that can be crowded into the available room any more than an amount plainly inadequate for the establishment. Too

432

much fruiting wood unduly taxes the tree for its maintenance. On the other hand maximum production cannot be expected from a half-equipped plant. An efficiently working machine is not one that is carrying an overload any more than it is one carrying half or a third of a load. Regular, steady, annual production of large but not maximum amounts is desirable.

Perhaps in certain species the problem of securing heavy and regular fruit production is somewhat simpler than has been indicated. In the jaboticaba whose blossoms and fruits come out indiscriminately anywhere on the bark, from the crown or even exposed roots to the tips of the youngest branches, the question of developing a special fruit producing mechanism never arises. The plant cannot grow without developing its fruit machinery and it is only the proper functioning of this bark that is a limiting factor to production. Certain other tropical and subtropical fruits present other apparent exceptions to the general statements that have been made, but they need not be given serious consideration here, for they do not alter materially the general principles involved or their application in deciduous fruit production.

Therefore it is desirable to determine as nearly as possible the exact nature of the fruiting habits of the different species and the methods by which they can be modified and controlled. What is the fruiting mechanism of the various fruits? What constitutes an adequate equipment for plants of different sizes or ages? How can the amount best be increased or limited? How does it usually function under varying conditions? What methods can be employed to make it work at full efficiency, carry a full load, year after year? How long does the machinery last? What are the best means of getting rid of useless or inefficient machinery and of securing new equipment? When is it best to attempt to repair and speed up equipment that is working poorly and when is it best to discard it and obtain new? The answers to these and many other related questions are of first importance to the grower, for profitable production depends on them to no small degree.

CHAPTER XXI

GROWING AND FRUITING HABITS

Left to themselves the plants of each species, or even of each variety, show more or less distinctive growing and fruiting characteristics. The former are partly under the control of the grower, so that it is possible for him to make plants of quite different growing habits assume a nearly uniform shape in the orchard or to train two of the same kind so that they appear very unlike. His control over bearing habits is less complete though much can be done to modify them in certain directions. Both are influenced directly or indirectly by nearly every cultural practice. Pruning, however, using that term in its broader sense, is the most direct and most important of these practices.

Some growers prune their trees; some do not. Others prune some of their fruit trees, but leave other kinds unpruned. The trees or plants of certain species are generally given some kind of pruning treatment; those of certain other species are almost as generally let alone. In some orchards pruning is a regular annual operation; in others it is done biennially or at long irregular intervals. There is no horticultural practice concerning which there is a greater diversity of opinion or in the application of which there is a greater diversity of procedure. If the average grower is asked why he prunes or why he does not, his answer is likely to be that he believes it is good for the tree or that it is not good for it. Seldom does he give specific objectives that he has in mind or that he believes may be accomplished by means of pruning. If specific objectives are mentioned they are likely to be among the following: (1) to open the tree so that the fruit will color more satisfactorily, (2) to train it to some desired form, (3) to remove dead or diseased limbs, (4) to remove water sprouts, (5) to thin the fruit.

All of these are accomplished by pruning if the work is done properly; nevertheless they are not its primary objects. Fundamentally, pruning, in common with other cultural practices, should be directed to encourage the production of larger quantities of fruit, the production of fruit of better grade, or to lower the cost of production; its value, like that of any other orchard operation, may be determined by the extent to which it contributes in any one or more of these three directions.

Pruning may be considered from many points of view and subdivided in many ways. In the following discussion it is considered briefly as a means of modifying shape and in more detail as it influences development, location and functioning of the fruiting machinery of the tree.

PRUNING FOR FORM—TRAINING

There is frequent failure to distinguish clearly between pruning and training. The two practices are often regarded as one and the same or at least as inseparable. Training concerns form primarily; pruning affects function primarily. Training determines the general character and even the details of the plant's outline and of its branching and framework; pruning is meant to assist more in determining what the tree does in respect to fruiting. Training may be illustrated by reference to what may be done easily with the grape. Without cutting off or cutting back a single cane, it is possible to train a vine on a one-wire trellis, a two-wire trellis, a three-wire vertical trellis, a three-wire horizontal trellis, an arbor, or in any one of a dozen other ways. The training simply gives the vine its form and has comparatively little to do with the number or size of the bunches of fruit it produces. Similarly, fruit trees are made to assume one form or another—for example, high-headed or low-headed, open-centered or closed-centered, flat-topped or pyramidal—and production is influenced comparatively little by these shapes. It is true that the pruning saw and shears are generally used in forcing the trees into the one shape or the other, and hence, perhaps the operation should be spoken of as "pruning for form." Nevertheless the operation affects form principally and consequently is here discussed under the heading of training, even though strictly speaking the use of that term should be limited to such changes in form as are effected without the removal of parts. If parts are removed at such a time and in such a way as to modify materially the functioning of the whole tree or of some of its parts, even though its general shape is left unchanged, the operation should be considered pruning. Many times both shape and function are modified by a single operation, which then is to be regarded as both pruning and training; often, however, it is chiefly one feature of the tree's growth that is influenced.

General Objects.—In general, training has little direct effect on the amount of fruit borne. Some of the pruning practices that accompany certain methods of training may affect yields profoundly, but the training in itself is of only secondary importance in this connection. On the other hand training may be a factor in determining grade, or what is frequently referred to as "quality." Its influence on grade is produced largely through making it difficult or easy to spray thoroughly and consequently in aiding or hindering the control of insects and diseases. Standard control measures for certain pests may lose half of their efficiency if the plants have been untrained or poorly trained. This influence is distinct from and additional to the direct control of certain pests by cutting out and destroying infected parts. In certain fruits the shape and openness of the tree are important in influencing the coloration. Training is important also in reducing certain production costs. Tillage and other soil treatments, spraying, thinning, propping, trellising and harvesting all may be greatly facilitated by proper training.

In a general way training should tend so to distribute the fruiting wood and the fruit that all orchard or vineyard operations may be conducted with greatest facility and lowest cost. It should eliminate or minimize the necessity and cost of trellising, propping, or artificially supporting the plant and its fruit. It should provide the leaves and developing fruits with as nearly as possible optimum conditions for coloration without danger from sunscald and, wherever feasible, it should aim to provide those conditions least favorable for the work of injurious insects and diseases. In view of all these possible effects of training and of the widely varying conditions under which plants of even the same variety are grown, it is evident that the best method of training a plant in one situation may be quite distinct from what is best in another and it often happens that two fruits or two varieties of the same fruit should be trained differently when grown in the same environment.

Since the training of trees presents certain problems distinct from those of pruning it seems desirable to consider them separately from their possible influence on function.

Details in Training.—A comparatively large part of the training that trees are to receive should be given during the first few years of their growth. It is during this period that they are building their framework and taking on the general form that the grower has decided shall be theirs during the rest of their lives. During later years efforts are directed mainly to preserve the form already given the tree and attention is given to its pruning as distinguished from training.

Height of Head.—By height of head is meant the distance from the ground at which the main or scaffold limbs branch from the trunk. Trees in which the scaffold limbs come out within $2\frac{1}{2}$ or 3 feet from the ground are spoken of as low-headed; those in which they come out from the trunk 4 feet or more from the ground are high-headed. The height of head generally is established at the time of setting by the distance from the ground at which the top is cut off, though it is possible to raise the head or sometimes to lower it by later treatment. In the older orchards high-headed trees are the rule. It was thought that high-heading facilitated cultivation and other orchard operations and perhaps was better for the tree. More recent tendencies have been in the direction of lower heads. If properly handled it is no more difficult to cultivate around and under such trees and pruning, spraying, thinning and picking are greatly facilitated. Furthermore, low-headed trees are less subject to sunscald and suffer less from high winds.

Number of Scaffold Limbs.—The number of scaffold limbs found in orchard trees varies from 2 to 15 or 20. Neither extreme is desirable. If there are only two or three main scaffold limbs they are almost certain to form crotches that are likely to split and allow one or both parts to break down. A large percentage of the injury resulting from trees breaking when heavily loaded with fruit or when subjected to severe winds is due indirectly to sharp crotches that could have been avoided by the use of more and better spaced scaffold limbs. Should one limb of a group of three split down, a third of the tree is gone; should one of eight be lost, most of the tree still remains and the injury, which is much less likely to happen, is more readily repaired. On the other hand too many scaffold limbs, as 10 to 12, give rise to thick, brushy tops that make work in them difficult. A moderate number, five to eight, makes a tree that is mechanically strong and at the same time open enough to facilitate necessary orchard operations.

Distribution of Scaffold Limbs.—Of still greater importance than the number of scaffold limbs is their distribution. When they come out from the trunk at points close together, as for instance, when the upper one of five is only 8 or 10 inches above the lowest they form bad crotches much sooner than if they are distributed over a longer distance on the trunk. When they are distributed over $1\frac{1}{2}$ or 2 feet of the trunk each limb has a chance to make more or less "shoulder"; weak crotches with subsequent splitting are avoided. It may require a little attention to select and develop scaffold limbs that are separated well from one another, on account of the tendency of the tree to make its most vigorous growth from buds near the end of the trunk or near the extremities of its branches but it is well worth while. Furthermore, it should be remembered that the distribution of these limbs is determined once and for all by the first two or three prunings and no amount of later work will entirely correct a mistake made then. If a tree is headed at a height of 33 to 36 inches it is possible to have a good number of well-distributed limbs and at the same time have a low-headed tree. One of the main advantages of the "modified leader" type of training is the opportunity for a wide spacing of the scaffold limbs.

Open and Closed-centered Trees.—There has been much discussion over the relative merits of open-centered or vase-shaped and close-centered or leader trees. Both forms have their advocates. Both are extensively used and both are successful—good evidence that the exact form in which trees are trained is a matter of secondary importance from the standpoint of production. Theoretically at least, the open-centered method of training admits more sunlight and thus enables the fruit to attain a higher color than is possible in the closed-centered tree, though in reality the tree that is started with the open center is often allowed to become more thick-topped than many "leader" trees. Obviously, this is a matter that can be of no real importance in fruits where coloration does not depend on the light reaching the fruit itself. From the very nature of the case the central-leader type of tree forms more scaffold limbs than the open-centered tree and consequently it is less likely to split at the crotches. It is often more bushy-topped but this condition is not necessary.

It has become a generally accepted practice to train certain fruits in certain styles. For instance, peaches are almost always grown in the vase form and pears are trained with a central leader. In some cases whole sections use a certain style for practically all their tree fruits. To what extent these practices are based on careful comparisons of different methods of training for the fruit or the locality in question and to what extent they are followed simply because the custom has become established is often difficult to say. A careful study of training methods might lead in many cases to some change that would be of considerable commercial importance to the particular district or for the particular variety.

The general method of procedure in training a tree to the central-leader type is each year to prune back the central and upper shoot or leader less severely than the lateral shoots or limbs surrounding it. If an open-centered tree is desired the opposite method should be followed. It is a mistake in attempting to train a tree to the open-centered type to cut out entirely the interior and central limbs. This merely provokes the production of water sprouts to take their place and more cutting out must be done. By cutting back the interior and upper shoots and limbs more severely than the outer, the former are subordinated and the latter are made the dominant limbs in the tree. In other words, it is easier and better to grow an open-centered tree with a comparatively open center—with only a few, small, subordinate, fruiting branches in the interior—than one with a completely open or hollow center.

A different type of training that is coming into favor is known as the "modified leader." As the name suggests, it is intermediate between the open-centered and the leader tree. It is developed by training to the leader type for the first 4 or 5 years and from then on as an open-centered tree. This results in a tree with a central leader extending some 3 to 5 feet above the point where it was originally headed and then an open center above that. It possesses practically all the advantages of the two other types and few or none of their disadvantages.

Trees of Different Shape.—Less attention need be devoted to the general shape of the tree than to certain other features of its training. Nevertheless, there are occasional arguments for flat-topped or round-topped trees or other forms. In general, little emphasis should be placed on these particular shapes. It is not a bad plan to allow the tree considerable freedom in assuming the general shape that is natural. Training for form should be limited to correcting minor defects rather than altering profoundly the shape.

Lowering the Tops of Trees.—In the course of time the trees of many species become so tall that the added cost of gathering the fruit from the topmost branches reduces the margin of profit to the vanishing point. Furthermore the higher branches shade the lower and reduce their efficiency as fruit producers. The increased difficulty in controlling insects and diseases in the tops of very tall trees, even with the aid of the best of the present power spraying outfits, makes those portions of doubtful value to the grower even though it might be possible to harvest the fruit economically. One investigator sets 25 feet as about the limit in height for profitable apple production[15] and with the smaller spraying outfits the limit is probably well below that figure. The problem of controlling the height of trees and keeping their lower branches actively producing a good grade of fruit is thus very real.

Many growers wait until the trees get much too tall for profit and then "dehorn;" that is, they cut back the limbs severely, leaving large stubs that promptly send out an abundance of strong vigorous watersprouts. Eventually new fruiting wood is developed from this new growth, but in the meantime crowding is likely to force this new growth up, so that by the time the top has been bearing a few years it is too high again and another dehorning becomes necessary.

A much better method of lowering the tops of tall trees is to cut back into 2-, 3-, or 4-year-old wood, always to a lateral branch. The more nearly horizontal this side limb, the better. By thus cutting to a lateral the flow of sap is utilized in a somewhat increased growth and few or no watersprouts develop. A year or two later this lateral can be cut back to one of its side branches, or perhaps the whole structure can be removed, the cut being to a still lower side limb on the main branch that in the meantime has been strengthened by the heading back of the season before.

This, it will be recognized, is a procedure aiming constantly to keep the tree within bounds rather than permitting it first to become far too tall and then greatly reducing its height. To be most successful it should begin when the tree reaches about the desired height and from then on it should constitute a part of the regular pruning treatment that the tree receives. It will not be necessary to lower every part or limb of every tree each year; only the tallest, those getting too high, need be cut back. This practice not only results in the production of fewer watersprouts but it keeps the lower part of the tree in a better producing condition than is possible with occasional dehorning. It is a heading back in name mainly—really resulting in more thinning than cutting back—and is followed by the kind of a response that attends thinning out. A still better plan is so to prune in the earlier life of the tree that resort to the rather drastic measures just described is unnecessary. If the older wood in the lower part of the tree that becomes less and less productive with time is regularly removed, the new growth above it is not forced to grow so high as otherwise it would, and it is promptly bent down by the weight of subsequent crops.[58,59]   It may seem paradoxical to say that the best pruning to keep the tops of trees from growing too high is pruning that is largely limited to their lower limbs, but such is the case.

Eliminating and Subordinating Limbs.—It has just been stated that in the training of open-centered trees it is usually better to suppress or subordinate the interior limbs than to attempt their total elimination. This last can be done by cutting them out and then repeatedly removing watersprouts that take their place, but this involves much labor. If they are subordinated the water sprout problem is largely eliminated and they may serve as fruit-producing branches for many years. In apples, pears and other spur-bearing fruits, their retention may also aid materially in bringing the trees into bearing earlier, because if properly handled they develop fruit spurs and fruit buds freely at a period when heavy pruning back for proper form may prevent to a great extent formation of spurs on the more permanent framework of the tree. Often one of the best ways to subordinate and make fruiting branches from these interior limbs is to let them remain with no heading back at the beginning of their second season. They then produce short vegetative growths from their terminal buds, with few or no lateral shoots but with many lateral spurs. After their second season's growth they are headed back into 2-year old wood. Treated in this way they make but little further shoot growth and little difficulty is experienced in keeping them as subordinate fruit-bearing limbs.

Preventing the Formation of Crotches.—It is a principle of rather general application that the unequal cutting back of two parts in the same tree or plant tends to subordinate that part pruned more severely and to give the advantage to the other. The amounts of new shoot growth developing from the two parts that have been cut back unequally are likely to be closely correlated with the bark areas that are left after pruning.[2] Equal cutting of two shoots or limbs of about the same length results in their equal subsequent development into a fork or crotch that is a point of weakness in the framework of the tree. Crotches can be largely avoided and the framework correspondingly strengthened by pruning with the idea of making one of two equal branches a leader and the other a lateral subordinate to it.

Similarly, as is pointed out by Macdaniels and Curtis,[43] weak crotches can be strengthened by proper pruning. To quote: "The conception that growth of the vascular tissues is so largely determined by the coming together of food from the leaves and nutrients from the roots, and that these substances tend to move in straight lines parallel to the axes of the elements of the vascular tissues, is of value in interpreting the growth response to various cultural practices. For example, on this basis it is apparent that the width of the annual ring in any one section of the branches or the trunk of a fruit tree is dependent on the leaf surface anatomically attached to that section above, and the roots attached below. Thus, if the orchardist desires to build up a branch on the upper side, or promote the filling-in of a narrow crotch, it is important to leave foliage attached to those parts of the branch that are directly above the section to be strengthened."

BEARING HABITS

There is reason to believe that with proper nutritive conditions in the plant, particularly with an accumulation of certain carbohydrates, any partly developed bud may undergo differentiation, form flower parts and develop as a fruit bud. This assumes that other limiting factors, such as moisture and temperature, are favorable. It is conceivable that in the developing buds of some plants a stage is finally reached when such a differentiation cannot take place except by the unfolding of the bud into a leafy structure and the subsequent formation of the fruit bud at a new growing point. In general, though, every bud is to be regarded as a potential flower bud. In every kind of plant, however, most of the flower buds are formed in certain definite positions, probably because it is only in those positions that nutritive and other conditions favorable for flower-bud formation ordinarily occur. It is therefore possible to speak of the bearing or fruiting habit of a plant, though the use of this term does not mean that other types of bearing, other fruiting habits, may not be found on the same plant under unusual conditions. Not infrequently the crop borne from flowers appearing in such an unusual place exceeds that produced by those considered characteristic. For instance, the nectarine would be classed generally as a tree bearing its fruit buds laterally on shoots, but the Stanwick variety is as typical a spur bearer as the Montmorency cherry.

Since all buds are to be regarded as potential flower buds, flowers or inflorescences and hence fruits, may be borne wherever buds are borne— usually (1) terminally on long or short growths, or (2) laterally in the axils of the current or past season's leaves and now and then (3) adventitiously from any point on the exposed bark of limbs, trunks or roots. As a rule the position of the flower or inflorescence on the shoot relative to the growth of the current season is characteristic of the species or variety and is subject to but little change. The inflorescences of the raspberry and blackberry are always terminal to the growth of the current season and the flowers or inflorescences of the persimmon are always lateral.   Flower-bearing shoots may arise from either terminal or lateral buds on either long or short growths (spurs), or they may arise from adventitious buds.   There is often considerable variation within the species, variety, or even individual plant in this respect.

Relation of Growth Habits to Position of Fruit Buds.—Within limits certain habits of growth are necessitated by, or at least are associated with, particular fruiting habits.   In general, plants with terminal fruit buds have a somewhat restricted habit of growth.   Terminal bearing tends to promote greater compactness of tree or plant than bearing from lateral fruit buds, because it forces the development of laterals from below, rather than beyond, the flowers or flower clusters.   Plants whose fruit buds are borne either terminally (apple) or laterally (sweet cherry) on short growths or spurs are generally more compact than those like the peach or grape whose fruit buds are borne on long shoots and the problem of preventing their bearing areas from getting too far away from the trunk or head of the plant is less serious.   If fruit buds are borne later-ally on long shoots there may be a distinct difference in the general man-ner of growth, depending on whether they are found principally on the basal, median or distal portion and the grower will employ a "short," "medium" or "long" pruning system, as the case may be.

Different Kinds of Flower-bearing Shoots.—Regardless of the location of the fruit bud—that is, whether terminal or lateral—when it unfolds it may give rise to any one of three distinct types of flower-bearing struc-tures: (1) it may contain flower parts only and develop a single flower (as in the peach) or a flower cluster (as in the cherry) without leaves, (2) it may be a mixed bud and develop a short or long leafy shoot terminating in an inflorescence (as in the apple), (3) it may be mixed and develop a short or long leafy shoot bearing flowers or flower clusters in some of its leaf axils (as in the persimmon).

A Classification of Plants According to Bearing Habits.—Since the flower bud itself is either terminal or lateral, there are six main types of fruiting, six distinct bearing habits, the classification being based upon the location of the fruit buds and the type of flower-bearing structure to which they give rise.   These six main groups together with the more important of the fruits they include are shown in the accompanying diagram.

There are endless variations within these main groups; certain species or varieties sometimes bear in one way and sometimes in another, or in two or more ways at the same time.

The following discussion points out some of the peculiarities of the more important fruits.   Several special groups also are included to bring together those fruits having in their bearing habits certain peculiarities

CLASSIFICATION OF FRUITS ACCORDING TO FRUITING HABITS

	Fruit buds terminal	Fruit buds lateral
Flower bud containing flower parts only	**I** Loquat Mango	**IV** Peach Plum Apricot Cherry Almond Plumcot Currant Gooseberry Kumquat Northern papaw Walnut (staminate catkins) Hickory (staminate catkins) Pecan (staminate catkins)
Flower bud mixed Flowering shoot with terminal inflorescences	**II** Apple (principally) Pear (principally) Quince Medlar Hawthorn Haw Elder Juneberry Walnut (pistillate flowers) Hickory (pistillate flowers) Pecan (pistillate flowers)	**V** Blackberry Raspberry Dewberry Grape Filbert Blueberry Cranberry (European) Cashew nut Brazil nut Pond-apple (and various other anonaceous fruits) Apple (occasionally) Pear (occasionally)
Flower bud mixed Flowering shoot with lateral inflorescences	**III** Guava Tropical almond Rose-apple (and other species of Eugenia) Olive (partly)	**VI** Persimmon Mulberry Fig Cranberry (American) Chestnut Chinquapin Oak Beech Pistachio Star-apple Jujube Avocado Olive (partly)

that make it desirable to consider them separately from the main groups to which they might be referred.

Group I.—Fruit buds borne terminally, containing flower parts only and giving rise to inflorescences without leaves.

None of the common deciduous fruits has this bearing habit. It is best illustrated perhaps by the loquat and the mango (see Fig. 40). Growth is continued by branches rising from lateral buds below the inflorescence; some of these branches form terminal buds for a succeeding crop. The indications are that in the mango fruit bud differentiation does not take place long before the flowering season and sometimes two, three or even four crops of flowers are formed during the year, though this is not likely if there is a good set of fruit which is carried through to maturity. In case some accident happens to the terminal flower bud of the mango, some of the axillary buds may differentiate flower parts and thus form fruit buds.

Group II.—Fruit buds borne terminally, unfolding to produce leafy shoots that terminate in flower clusters.

This bearing habit is characteristic of most of the pome fruits and is found likewise in a few others of minor economic importance.

In the apple and pear most of the terminal fruit buds are on spurs, (see Fig. 41) though in young vigorous trees of certain varieties many of the long shoots form terminal flower buds. Seldom, however, is any considerable percentage of the crop borne in this latter way. The fruit buds of these plants are mixed and invariably give rise to very short growths with a few short internodes, leaves of ordinary size and a lateral branch (sometimes two or more) arising in the axil of one of the leaves; this branch may bear fruit the following season, though usually fruit bud formation is delayed a year or more. The spur may live a great many years and bear repeatedly. The actual records of individual spurs generally show an irregularly alternate bearing habit. New spurs originate from lateral buds on shoots of the preceding season and occasionally from latent or adventitious buds on the trunk or older limbs. The continued bearing of the individual spurs makes for a comparatively compact type of tree growth.

The juneberry or shadbush (*Amelanchier*) and hawthorn or azarole (*Cratægus*) have bearing habits practically identical with those of the apple and pear just described.

Mention should be made that both the apple and pear occasionally bear lateral fruit buds on long shoots. Certain varieties, like Wagener, are particularly given to this habit. It is found more frequently in young vigorous trees than in those with a settled bearing habit. However, the fact that it may occur on almost any variety and that occasionally a considerable percentage of the crop may be borne in this way, is evidence that this habit is a response to unusual nutritive conditions. The special treatment that should be accorded trees fruiting in this manner is discussed under Pruning of the Apple and Pear.

The bearing habit of the quince and the medlar is similar to that of the apple and pear, except that when the terminal (mixed) fruit bud unfolds it gives rise to a leafy shoot of medium length, with medium long instead of short internodes and the flowers are borne terminally on this shoot. Fruit buds for the following season's production are borne terminally on shoots springing from lateral buds on either flowering or non-flowering shoots, or from terminal buds on older shoots that the year before did not differentiate flower buds. These fruits consequently are not such compact growers as the apple or pear, though the shorter growth of their purely vegetative shoots and the greater tendency for their lateral buds to

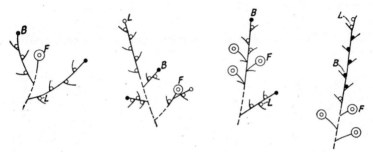

Figs. 40–43.—Diagrams showing (from left to right) bearing habits of loquat, apple, olive and peach. *F* equals fruit; *B* equals flower bud; *L* equals leaf bud. One-year-old wood shown by solid line, two-year-old wood by broken line.

grow rather than remain latent may give them a very thick and brushy appearance.

The haw (*Viburnum*), elder (*Sambucus*), and clove (*Caryophyllus aromaticus*) have bearing habits similar to the quince and medlar, though occasionally they differentiate flower buds terminally, like the apple and pear on short growths, which are essentially spurs. All these fruits are opposite-leaved and it frequently happens that the lateral buds in the axils of the upper leaves differentiate flower parts. This is more likely to happen if the terminal bud is injured or destroyed.

Group III.—Fruit buds borne terminally, unfolding to produce leafy shoots with flowers or flower clusters in the leaf axils.

This might be called an incomplete terminal bearing habit, for the fruit itself is not borne terminally, but is lateral to the growths upon which it appears. However, the flower buds are terminal. The terminal buds of the flowering shoots may differentiate flower parts for the following year's production or new buds may develop from lateral leaf buds.

None of the common deciduous fruits has this bearing habit. It is found in the pomegranate, the tropical almond (*Terminalia catappa*), the guavas (*Psidium* spp.), the olive, and in a number of the species of *Eugenia*. In the pomegranate, guava and in the *Eugenias* the fruit buds are formed on short shoots or spurs and the flowers and fruits in the axils of the outermost leaves. In the olive the inflorescences are generally found in the axils of the shoot's lower leaves and flowering shoots sometimes spring from lateral as well as terminal buds (see Fig. 42). The tropical almond (*Terminalia*) has a somewhat peculiar growing and fruiting habit, the terminal mixed flower buds being formed on the ends of long shoots. When these unfold they give rise to short growths or spurs, in the axils of whose upper leaves flowers and fruits are borne. The long growths or shoots originate from lateral buds.

Group IV.—Fruit buds borne laterally, containing flower parts only and giving rise to inflorescences without leaves or if leaves are present they are much reduced in size.

In the peach, lateral fruit buds are formed on the long shoots (see Fig. 43). Two additional or supernumerary leaves commonly appear

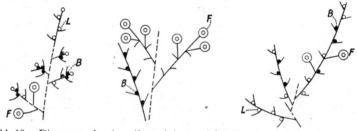

Figs. 44–46.—Diagrams showing (from left to right) bearing habits of sweet cherry, raspberry and grape.

at many nodes as the season progresses and fruit buds develop in their axils. The bud in the axil of the original leaf generally remains a leaf bud; rarely it too differentiates flower parts. This whole structure may possibly be considered a much reduced secondary growth. Often only a single extra leaf develops at the node, in which case only one fruit bud forms at that point, that in the axil of the supernumerary leaf. The peach also forms fruit buds on secondary or even on tertiary lateral branches. As a rule when the fruit buds occur on the upper or outer portions of secondary shoots and sometimes on the primary shoots, they are single, being differentiated from the bud in the axil of the single leaf. They are likely to be in pairs at the more basal nodes. As already stated, the flower buds of the peach are usually produced on what would be called long growths or shoots, though under certain cultural and pruning treatments many varieties form short laterals that are comparable to spurs in every way. The flower bud of the peach produces only one flower. Growth is continued by terminal or by lateral leaf buds.

The sweet cherries and the Domestica and Insititia groups of plums form their flower buds for the most part laterally on spurs (see Fig. 44). These come from lateral buds on the shoots of the preceding season, and their new shoots form both terminal and lateral buds on shoots or on older wood.

The almond, apricot, plumcot, the Japanese and American plums, the sour cherry, the currant and the gooseberry have a fruiting habit which is a combination of that of the peach on the one hand and the sweet cherry on the other. They bear in both ways, though certain varieties may show a greater tendency in the one direction or the other. As a rule, fruit bud production on shoots gradually gives way to production on spurs as the plants become older and less vigorous. Supernumerary fruit buds are produced freely at the nodes of the long vigorous shoots of Japanese and American plums and in the currant and gooseberry.

The kumquat (*Citrus Japonica*) and the northern pawpaw (*Asimina triloba*) differentiate their flower buds in the axils of the leaves on long shoots of the current season and the following season these buds give rise to leafless inflorescences. This bearing habit corresponds to that of the sweet cherry, except that production of the flower buds is on long rather than on short growths.

Group V.—Fruit buds borne laterally, unfolding to produce leafy shoots that terminate in flower clusters.

The blackberry, raspberry, dewberry and their hybrids form fruit buds either on primary shoots that come up from their crowns or roots each year, or on their secondary lateral shoots (see Fig. 45). These flower buds develop into leafy shoots with terminal inflorescences and individual flowers or flower clusters in the leaf axils. In most varieties the entire cane dies after bearing and growth is continued by the formation of new canes springing from the crown or roots.

In the unopened flower bud of the grape (see Fig. 46), the inflorescence is terminal to a leafy shoot also within the bud, like that of the raspberry and blackberry. As the bud opens, however, the bud in the axil of the topmost leaf of this developing shoot unfolds and continues the growth of the shoot. This results in pushing the flower cluster to one side so that the inflorescence appears lateral and opposite a leaf. Several flower clusters are formed terminally at successive intervals on the same shoot and in turn are crowded to one side and hence to apparently lateral positions. As a rule only certain branches or canes of the grape bear lateral buds that differentiate flower parts. These branches or canes usually arise from buds near the base or in the median portion of bearing shoots. What appears to be the bud or "eye" of the grape really consists of two or three buds within the one; a well developed central shoot and one or two less highly developed lateral growing points. In case the central bud develops prematurely and is killed by frost, its place may be taken by another of the group. Occasionally the grape produces flowering shoots from latent or adventitious buds.

In the filbert, which has no true terminal buds, some of the more apical lateral buds develop into short leafy shoots ending in clusters of pistillate flowers (see Fig. 47). Other lateral buds grow out into dwarf shoots, which are without normal-sized leaves, are branched and really constitute the male inflorescences. These remain dormant until winter or early spring when they open to discharge their pollen. At the base they may have resting buds which give rise to vegetative or pistillate flower-bearing shoots the following year.

The cashew nut (*Anacardium*) and the Brazil nut (*Bertholletia*) also bear terminally on shoots from lateral buds.

In the cherimoya, pond-apple, sour-sop, sugar-apple and various other Anonaceous fruits the fruit buds are borne laterally and the inflorescences terminally, with the growth of the flowering shoots proceeding much as in the grape. Here the flowers and fruits appear to be between nodes, or extra-axillary. Not infrequently they develop on short spur-like branches.

In the blueberries the inflorescences develop both terminally and in the axils of leaves on new shoots springing from lateral buds. This bearing habit is a combination of the typical conditions found in Groups V and VI as here classified. Ordinarily there are no true terminal buds in this group but if terminal buds are formed they are usually fruit buds. In *Vaccinium atrococcum* the flowering shoot has no foliage. Fruit bud differentiation apparently takes place in late fall in the axils of leaves near the end of the shoot.

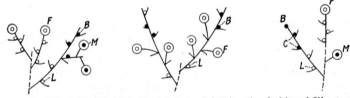

Figs. 47–49.—Diagrams showing (from left to right) bearing habits of filbert, chestnut and walnut. In filbert and walnut *B* equals pistillate flower buds, *C* equals staminate flower buds; *M* equals male catkins.

The European cranberry (*Vaccinium oxycoccus*), litchi (*Nephelium litchi*) and sea-grape (*Coccoloba uvifera*) have similar bearing habits.

Group VI.—Fruit buds borne laterally (or pseudoterminally), unfolding to produce leafy shoots with flower clusters in the leaf axils.

In the persimmon any lateral bud and not infrequently adventitious or dormant buds on 2-year-old or older wood, may become a fruit bud. The following year these unfold and form leafy shoots with solitary pistillate or with clusters of staminate flowers in the axils of the more basal leaves. The male and female flowers may be borne on the same tree or on different trees.

The mulberry has a similar bearing habit, except that both pistillate and staminate flowers are usually borne on the same flowering shoot. The male flowers are formed in the axils of the more basal leaves and the pistillate flowers in the axils of higher leaves.

In the American cranberry (*Vaccinium macrocarpon*) the flowering shoots arise from lateral buds on the creeping vegetative branches. The flowers are borne singly in the leaf axils.

The chestnut, chinquapin, oak and beech have very similar bearing habits (see Fig. 48). The pseudoterminal or more apical lateral buds, when they differentiate flower parts, give rise to shoots in the axils of the leaves. Male catkins appear in the lower axils and female, or mixed male and female, clusters above them. Sometimes dwarf shoots arise from the basal buds in the chestnut and produce male catkins only in the leaf axils. True terminal buds are sometimes formed in the oak and beech and these may be fruit buds. In the beech there are short spur-like growths which have no lateral buds except a single pseudo-terminal bud. This is never a flower bud.

The fig bears lateral fruit buds. Its pseudoterminal bud, which is usually larger than the others, is generally vegetative. Frequently more than one bud is formed in a leaf axil and they appear in pairs, side by side. The fruits are formed singly in the leaf axils. The fig can bear three (or more, according to some authorities) distinct crops in a year.

In the avocado the lateral flower buds give rise to flowering shoots in which the inflorescences are in the axils of the more basal leaves.

The pistachio (*Pistacia vera*) and star apple (*Chrysophyllum*) have a similar bearing habit and the olive, which has been mentioned as belonging in Group III, might as readily be included here, since it produces lateral as well as terminal flower buds.

In the jujube (*Zizyphus jujube*) several flowering branches may arise at a single node. Solitary flowers are borne in the leaf axils of these branches. After the ripening of the fruit the leaves and fruit fall off and finally the entire branch falls. Buds for the following crop are differentiated on strictly vegetative branches. There is thus a definite dimorphism of branches in this species, the fruiting branches being deciduous and not forming a part of the permanent framework of the tree.

Group VII.—Fruit buds borne both terminally and laterally, inflorescences generally terminal. The fruits that are discussed here might be included with those of Groups II and IV for they represent a combination of those two fruiting habits, but for convenience they are considered separately.

In the walnut, hickory and pecan the terminal bud may give rise to a short leafy shoot ending in a female inflorescence (see Fig. 49). The male flowers are borne on leafless inflorescences arising from lateral

buds not far below the terminal.   In the walnut there are two superposed
buds in each leaf axil, the upper being usually the first to open.   At a
single node two male inflorescences may appear simultaneously from the
two buds, or a leafy shoot may come from the upper and an inflorescence
from the lower.   In the hickory the male catkins are sometimes borne
in the axils of the basal leaves on the terminal shoot, resulting in the production of male and female flowers on the same shoot.

Group VIII.—Fruit buds adventitious.   Since adventitious fruit
buds are necessarily lateral, the plants included here might readily be
classed with those of Group IV, V or VI.   However, this bearing habit
is more or less distinct and these fruits may well be placed in a separate
class.

The jaboticaba and cambuca form adventitious flower buds on their trunks,
main and smaller limbs and even on their exposed roots.   These produce no
leaves when they open.

The cacao bears in the same way, though the flower buds appear first on the
trunk and, as the trees grow older, on the whorled branches.

The coffee produces fruiting branches from adventitious buds at the nodes.
The upper bud becomes a horizontal fruit-bearing branch, the lower an upright
vegetative shoot.

Group IX.—There is another group of plants which have fruit buds
in the axils of the leaves and in which these buds unfold and develop
their flowers and fruits very soon after the flower parts are differentiated.
However, it is not possible to draw a clear line between this fruiting
habit and that described for Group IV.

This group includes the passion fruit (*Passiflora*), the papaya (*Carica papaya*)
and many others with a more or less herbaceous type of growth.   In culture,
as well as in growing and fruiting habits, these plants resemble certain vegetables
more closely than deciduous fruits.

The Relation of Fruiting Habit to Alternate Bearing.—Terminal
fruit bud formation often has been regarded as an explanation of the
alternate bearing frequently occurring in species or varieties with this
fruiting habit.   However, not all the terminal buds on shoots and spurs
of plants with a terminal-fruit-bud-bearing habit develop into fruit buds
at one time.   Many are leaf buds and unfold leafy non-flowering shoots
or spurs.   Fruit bud differentiation depends on nutritive conditions in
and about the terminal bud at such time or times when differentiation
can take place.   Terminal bearing involves a definite limitation to shoot
or spur extension in a straight line.   New vegetative extension must be
from lateral buds if all terminals form fruit buds in one season, but this
seldom occurs and those buds that do not become fruit buds one year
may therefore become differentiated into fruit buds the next season.

In this way regular annual bearing is possible if nutritive conditions within the plant remain such that fruit bud differentiation can occur each year. Even if all terminals were to differentiate fruit buds one season and to flower and fruit the next, there would still be opportunity for the formation of another set of fruit buds terminally on the new shoots or new spurs. Therefore regular annual bearing would still be possible provided nutritive conditions were favorable. The terminal fruiting habit does not in itself lead to alternate bearing except in the event that practically every terminal forms a fruit bud one season and sets fruit the next while at the same time growing conditions this second season prevent fruit bud differentiation on the new shoots or spurs developed from lateral buds. When this extreme is encountered it should be handled as a problem in nutritive conditions to be corrected by the control of environmental factors. In other words, though many varieties of plants which bear fruit buds terminally are much inclined to alternate bearing, that tendency is not a necessary product or accompaniment of terminal fruit bud formation.

Obviously the production of fruit buds laterally on either spurs or shoots makes every provision for regular annual bearing, not only of the plant as a whole, but of the individual part, if conditions within the plant are favorable for fruit bud differentiation.

Regularity of bearing, therefore, is a cultural problem, to be dealt with by influencing nutritive conditions. Attention is given to this phase of the question in the section on Nutrition.

Possible Causes of Different Bearing Habits.—Knowledge of bearing habits is decidedly fragmentary and little is known concerning the factors which may control it or influence it in any way. However, it is known that the apple with its characteristic terminal fruit bearing habit stores the bulk of its starch in the pith while the peach with its characteristic lateral fruit bearing habit stores the bulk of its starch in the leaf gaps. Since carbohydrate, and particularly starch, accumulation is so closely associated with fruit bud differentiation, at least in the apple, it is possible that anatomical structure may have much to do with the region of starch storage and that this in its turn may be an important factor determining the bearing habit.

Summary.—The general purpose of all pruning is to increase yields, improve grades and reduce production costs. These objects may be attained either through modifying the form or through influencing the functioning of the tree as a whole or of its individual parts. Pruning for form is essentially training. Training seeks directly to secure the distribution of the fruit bearing parts that is most advantageous for economy of production, disease and insect control, for minimum loss from breaking of limbs and for proper coloration. These ends are furthered by (1) heading the tree properly, (2) providing a reasonable number of well-spaced scaffold limbs, (3) preventing the formation of weak crotches, and (4) keeping the tops of the trees from growing too high or spreading too far. Pursuant to these aims the plants are generally trained in one or another of several standard shapes. Thus training results in a certain degree of uniformity of appearance in the orchard.

The bearing habits of most species and varieties are fairly well fixed, though they are subject to some modification by pruning and other cultural treatment. Fruit buds are differentiated either terminally or laterally and when they open they may give rise to (1) leafless flower clusters, (2) leafy growths with terminal flower clusters, or (3) leafy growths with lateral flower clusters. There are thus six distinct bearing habits and in addition a number of combinations between these types. The more common fruits are classified in respect to their bearing habits. Alternate bearing is not a necessary product of any type of bearing. If nutritive conditions within the tree are favorable fruit buds may be formed every year. Consequently alternate bearing is a problem in nutrition. Different bearing habits are probably associated with different methods or places of food storage.

CHAPTER XXII

PRUNING—THE AMOUNT OR SEVERITY

Pruning can vary in three major respects and in three only. It can vary: (1) in amount or severity, (2) in kind or distribution and (3) in the season at which it is done. Characteristic responses by the plant are to be expected not only as the pruning varies in any of these three respects but according to fruiting habit and as the plant itself varies in age, vigor and nutritive condition. These three major aspects of pruning are discussed in the order in which they have been mentioned.

A search through horticultural literature reveals a great diversity of opinion as to the influence of varying amounts of pruning on growth and productiveness. Some have considered heavy pruning a great stimulant to vegetative growth especially, though perhaps having the opposite effect on fruit production. This idea is reflected in the phrase "prune in the winter for wood." Others have regarded pruning of any kind and more particularly, pruning in any amount, as harmful because it has been thought to check growth. Most of these partly accepted ideas have been based upon theoretical considerations or field observations, of which some have been sound and accurate but many have been either fallacious or inaccurate or have failed to consider other important facts. Not until comparatively recent years have exact and pertinent experimental data been available.

Influence on Size of Tree.—Bedford and Pickering[5] were among the first to make a careful study of the different effects of various amounts of dormant season pruning on the apple. Table 1 shows the mean tree size and weight for all varieties studied and given different pruning treatments covering a period of ten years. The figures for tree size take into consideration spread and height and trunk circumference. Clearly these show that the unpruned tree increases in size and weight more rapidly

TABLE 1.—INFLUENCE OF AMOUNT OF PRUNING ON TREE SIZE IN THE APPLE
(*After Bedford and Pickering*[5])

	VERY LITTLE OR NO PRUNING	MODERATE PRUNING	HARD PRUNING
Tree size relative	106	100	82
Tree weight relative	120	100	84

than the pruned tree and that the heavier the pruning the more pronounced is the check upon growth. In commenting on the somewhat greater influence of pruning on weight than on size revealed by the figures in the table Bedford and Pickering remark, "This increase in weight must be due to an increase in weight of the stem and main branches, for it cannot be accounted for merely by the weight of wood removed during pruning: the prunings would, on an average, have amounted to 27 pounds per tree during the ten years in the case of the moderately pruned trees, whereas these trees at the end of this time showed a deficit of 49 pounds as compared with the unpruned ones." Gardner[26] in Oregon and Alderman and Auchter[1] in West Virginia (see Table 2), both working with young apple trees, obtained results leading to the same conclusions.

TABLE 2.—INFLUENCE OF AMOUNT OF PRUNING ON SIZE OF YOUNG APPLE TREES
(*After Alderman and Auchter*[1])

Variety	Type of pruning	Number of trees	Height (in feet)	Spread (in feet)
Stayman	Heavy	24	7.32	5.29
Stayman	Moderate	19	7.89	5.52
Stayman	Light	19	9.50	5.75
Rome	Heavy	13	7.45	3.68
Rome	Moderate	8	8.18	4.17
Rome	Light	11	9.16	4.23
Gravenstein	Heavy	17	7.43	4.05
Gravenstein	Moderate	7	6.83	4.19
Gravenstein	Light	10	8.94	4.34
Stark	Heavy	19	7.57	5.17
Stark	Light	4	10.79	6.85
York, Grimes and Rome	Heavy	7	9.55	4.83
York, Grimes and Rome	Moderate	5	9.73	6.17
York, Grimes and Rome	Light	6	10.50	7.10

The unpruned tree increases in size more rapidly than the moderately or heavily pruned tree, not because it produces more new shoot growth each year, but because it loses none by pruning. Tufts,[71] in California, studying the influence of varying amounts of pruning on newly set apricots, sweet cherries, peaches, pears and European and Japanese plums found, in every instance, less rapid increases in trunk circumference with each increase in the severity of the pruning (see Table 3). Since he found correlation coefficients ranging from 0.83 to 0.92 for trunk circumferences and weights of top and coefficients ranging from 0.76 to 0.84 for trunk circumferences and weights of root, depending on the species, it is evident that trunk circumferences may be taken, other things equal, as fairly accurate indices to tree size. Consequently his data, together with those of both earlier and more recent investigators, are evidence that, in general, pruning results in a check to increase in size.

TABLE 3.—INCREASE IN TRUNK CIRCUMFERENCE UNDER VARYING PRUNING
TREATMENTS
(*After Tufts*[71])

Kind of fruit	Pruned severely (centimeters)	Pruned moderately (centimeters)	Pruned lightly (centimeters)
Apricot (Royal)..................	11.7	12.6	15.3
Cherry (Napoleon)..............	10.0	11.2	12.3
Peach (Elberta).................	12.0	16.9	19.4
Pear (Bartlett).................	8.7	9.1	9.7
Plum (Climax)..................	6.3	10.4	11.3
Plum (Pond)...................	7.2	8.8	9.4
Prune (French).................	6.2	7.1	8.4
Average.....................	8.9	10.9	12.3

Amount and Character of New Shoot Growth.—The framework of the tree is developed from its shoots of the preceding or earlier years. Since the general influence of pruning is to check increase in size, it might be reasoned that it results in a corresponding decrease in the amount of new shoot growth produced each year. On the other hand it is possible that the check to increase in size might be due largely, or even entirely, to the annual removal of wood. Experimental data on this question were obtained by Bedford and Pickering.[5] They selected a number of shoots in a tree, all as nearly as possible of uniform length (about 36 inches) and thickness. Some were pruned back to a length of 6 inches, some to 12 inches, some to 24 and some had only their terminal buds removed. Table 4 shows the relative numbers, lengths and weights of the new side

TABLE 4.—EFFECTS OF PRUNING BACK INDIVIDUAL SHOOTS VARYING AMOUNTS
(*After Bedford and Pickering*[5])

Length of shoot after pruning, in inches...............	6	12	24	36
Weight of original shoot and laterals (relative).........	100	179	310	562
Thickening of the original shoot (relative).............	100	114	117	129
New shoots formed:				
Number (relative).............................	100	116	198	292
Length (relative).............................	100	113	145	183
Weight (relative).............................	100	108	123	142

shoots that were formed and also the influence of these treatments on the parent branch. Heavy pruning back resulted in fewer side shoots with less total length and less weight than lighter pruning or than none at all. The greatest decrease was in the number of new shoots, from which it may be inferred that individually these shoots were somewhat longer and stronger than those on the lighter pruned limbs.   The difference in weight of old wood after a year's growth is particularly striking, the unpruned trees having over five times the amount of those pruned heavily.   These same investigators found, however, that in mature trees that had been bearing for a number of years heavy pruning resulted in almost twice as much new shoot growth as was produced by unpruned trees.

On the other hand Blake and Connors,[9] in New Jersey, found that pruned peach trees produced in the first year somewhat more new shoot growth than unpruned trees.   The average for the latter in their Vineland experiment was 695 inches and for the pruned trees (all treatments) 753 inches.   In West Virginia, Alderman and Auchter[1] report that heavy pruning of the apple resulted in somewhat greater new shoot growth for the first 2 or 3 years, but that greater shoot development accompanied lighter pruning as the tree became older (see Table 5).   Gardner[27] in Oregon, likewise working with young apple trees, found that different

TABLE 5.—EFFECT OF LIGHT AND HEAVY PRUNING ON NEW SHOOT GROWTH IN
APPLES OF DIFFERENT AGES
(After Alderman and Auchter[1])

Season	Pruned heavily		Pruned lightly		Gain over heavy pruning (feet)
	Average total length, feet	Average total removed, feet	Average total length, feet	Average total removed, feet	
1911	4.41	3.30	5.58	3.44	. . . . .
1912	16.25	12.91	15.51	4.78	−0.74
1913	41.53	33.16	34.33	13.89	−7.20
1914	84.08	49.17	99.39	22.12	15.31
1915	161.74	. . . . .	224.89	. . . . .	63.15

varieties respond in a quite dissimilar manner to pruning of the same severity.   His data, some of which are summarized in Table 6, show that lightly or moderately pruned Grimes produced more shoot growth annually than unpruned trees, but those heavily pruned produced distinctly less than the check trees.   On the other hand the heavily pruned Romes produced more shoot growth annually than those pruned moderately or not at all, while on the whole the severity of annual pruning seemed to make but little difference in the amount of new shoot growth in Gano and Esopus.   At first these data may seem so contradictory that no conclusion or interpretation is possible.   However, attention may be called to the great variations shown by young apple trees of different varieties in their growing habits and to the change in these differences with age.   Thus there is a great dissimilarity between young trees of Rome and Grimes in the number of spurs and the peach usually produces no true spurs. When these peculiarities of age and variety are considered along with the data that follow on the influence of various pruning treatments on fruit spur and fruit bud production the contradictions that have been noted do not appear so puzzling.

TABLE 6.—EFFECT OF LIGHT AND HEAVY PRUNING ON NEW SHOOT GROWTH IN YOUNG APPLES OF DIFFERENT VARIETIES

(After Gardner[27])

Variety	Number of trees averaged	Severity of annual pruning, per cent.	Average 1914 shoot growth, centimeters	Average 1915 shoot growth, centimeters	Average 1916 shoot growth, centimeters	Average number fruit spurs in fall of 1916
Grimes	71	none	492	1762	3852	402
Grimes	38	0–25	675	2251	4713	457
Grimes	55	26–50	714	2401	4913	341
Grimes	75	51–75	378	1339	2818	116
Gano	32	26–50	456	2493	5435	158
Gano	14	51–75	561	2464	5459	111
Rome	28	none	629	2051	3520	142
Rome	36	26–50	508	1973	3634	34
Rome	29	51–75	845	2541	4630	31
Esopus	27	none	583	2121	2287	505
Esopus	56	46–76	453	1736	3077	134

In recapitulation it may be said that different species and varieties show great variations in their response by new shoot production to prunings of like severity. These differences are due primarily to growing and fruiting habits and secondarily to age, vigor and nutritive conditions, as well as to environmental conditions with which they may happen to be associated at the time.

Leaf Surface and Root System.—Any practice that would effect a reduction in the amount of new shoot growth, and perhaps of spurs as well, would be expected to result in a corresponding decrease in leaf area and in root development. Chandler's[14] investigations of the relation of certain pruning practices to subsequent root development show

TABLE 7.—INFLUENCE OF VARYING AMOUNTS OF PRUNING ON SUBSEQUENT LEAF AND ROOT DEVELOPMENT

(After Chandler[14])

Treatment	Number of trees	Average leaf surface before pruning, May 23, 1918 (square inches)	Average leaf surface after pruning, May 23, 1918 (square inches)	Average leaf surface, Sept. 17, 1918 (square inches)	Average root weight May 19, 1919 (grams)	Average top weight, May 19, 1919 including prunings (grams)
Unpruned	41	756.48	756.48	1737.94	208.5	684.0
Little pruning	33	819.14	470.27	1219.80	166.9	558.3
Much pruning	39	775.70	291.61	895.96	126.3	494.3

this reduction. Some of his data are summarized in Tables 7 and 8. In commenting on the data presented in Table 8, Chandler[14] says:

"It will be seen that in all cases the leaf surface has been rather markedly reduced. On the other hand except in case of the summer-pruned trees, when

TABLE 8.—EFFECT OF PRUNING ON LEAF SURFACE AND TOP AND ROOT GROWTH OF PEACH TREES 4 YEARS OLD AT BEGINNING OF EXPERIMENT
(After Chandler[14])

Treatment	Average leaf surface in 1916		Average leaf surface in 1917		Tree, weight, pounds	Weight prunings, pounds	Root weight, pounds
	June, square inches	September, square inches	June, square inches	September, square inches			
Elberta:							
Pruned 1916 and 1917........	14,239	80,659	31,209	59,579	96.3	116.4	27.4
Unpruned.................	24,771	97,850	98,169	116,344	116.3	116.3	37.3
Crawford Early:							
Pruned summer 1916, spring 1917...........	2,202	50,034	18,904	68,070	75.8	97.4	20.9
Unpruned.....	17,886	85,721	74,389	142,920	111.9	111.9	34.6
Pruned spring 1917..........	......	......	40,681	79,563	126.3	134.7	34.9
Unpruned.................	......	......	114,516	144,911	131.7	131.7	44.9

the weight of the prunings has been added to that of the tree, the total weight of pruned and unpruned trees is practically the same. The root growth, however, has been greatly reduced. When it is considered that this reduction in growth has occurred during the last 2 years of the 6 years during which the trees have been in the orchard, it will be realized how striking the reduction is. Thus if at the beginning of 1916 the roots weighed 15 pounds, then the root growth on the unpruned trees since that time has been nearly twice that on the pruned tree. Unfortunately we have no records as to the root weight of trees 4 years old, but it must have been 10 pounds or more, since by records that we have the tops would then have weighed from 30 to 35 pounds. If the root weight at the beginning was 10 pounds, then the root growth in the pruned trees since that time has been but 65 per cent. of that made by the unpruned trees."

In effect the influence of a heavy top pruning on the subsequent development of the tree is more or less comparable to that of a root pruning.

Presumably, pruning practices which do not reduce top growth in trees of other kinds or of greater age than those studied would not have such an influence on root growth; exact data, however, are lacking. It is significant, nevertheless, that in young trees pruning of the top has been found greatly to influence the extent of root development the following season. This suggests one of the indirect ways through which pruning one season may influence growth and development 2 or 3 years later.

Influence on Fruit Spur and Fruit Bud Formation.—In Table 6 are presented data on the influence of varying amounts of pruning on fruit spur formation in young apple trees. The less the pruning the larger is the number of fruit spurs formed. With very severe pruning there is a great reduction, the checking influence differing greatly with the variety, however. Varieties like Esopus and Grimes, that are much inclined to develop spurs at an early age, show a relatively greater check in this respect than those like Rome and Gano that as young trees produce comparatively few spurs. In any case, however, pruning tends to reduce their number. Data are presented showing also that severe pruning acts in a similar manner in decreasing the numbers of fruit buds that form on the spurs.[27] Similar data on fruit bud formation in young apple trees have been obtained in West Virginia[1] and in England.[5] The ratio of flower clusters for the years 1909–1914 obtained by the English investigators in one of their experiments was 52 for hard pruning, 100 for moderate pruning and 180 for no pruning. There were corresponding differences in total yield. All these investigators show that heavily pruned trees may be expected to come into bearing more slowly than those pruned moderately, lightly or not at all. That this influence is as characteristic of evergreen as of deciduous species is indicated by experiments with citrus fruits,[66] olives[8] and coffee.[50] Apparently the time at which fruit bud differentiation takes place is little influenced by pruning practices.[77]

A practice that checks the rate of increase in tree size and that reduces total shoot growth, fruit spur and fruit bud formation would be expected to have a similar influence on yield. That this conclusion is in line with general experience is indicated by studies with apples,[48] peaches,[28] cherries,[25] grapes,[79] oranges,[64] lemons,[65] coffee[50] and some of the brambles.[40,41] Furthermore, the heavier the pruning, the greater is the reduction in yield. On the other hand, heavy pruning does not always result in decreased yields. Data obtained in an experiment with Arkansas and York Imperial apple trees that had been bearing for a number of years and were somewhat lacking in vigor, summarized in

TABLE 9.—INFLUENCE OF PRUNING ON YIELDS IN A DECLINING APPLE ORCHARD
(After Alderman and Auchter[1])

	Arkansas, 1914–1915 crops (bushels per tree)	York, 1914 crop (bushels per tree)
Heavy pruning............................	9.65	14.02
Moderate pruning........................	8.20	11.94
Light pruning............................	7.89	9.15

Table 9, show steady increments in yield with each increase in the severity of the pruning.[1] The heavy pruning must have had the effect of reducing somewhat the total number of fruit spurs, at least in comparison with the trees pruned more lightly. Consequently the increased yields must have been due either to the formation of a larger number of fruit buds or to the better setting of the blossoms. This is an influence not unlike that already pointed out as very frequently attending the judicious use of nitrogenous fertilizers. It is not to be expected that continued heavy pruning of these same trees would result in further increases in yield; nor can pruning be generally recommended to secure benefits that can be obtained more readily by means of soil treatments.

TABLE 10.—THE EFFECT OF PRUNING THE VINIFERA GRAPE ON NUMBER OF LEAVES, ON FRUIT CLUSTERS AND ON BERRY DEVELOPMENT
(*After Winkler*[78])

| Treatment | Leaves to a vine | Crop to a vine, kilos | Clusters | | | Normal berries | | Average weight of all berries, grams |
			Number to a vine	Average weight, grams	Average length, centimeters	Number to a cluster	Per cent. of total berries	
Non-pruned, with flower cluster thinning......	3,400	25.9	58	474	28.0	116	93	4.1
Cane-pruned, with flower cluster thinning......	1,700	15.1	38	430	27.0	124	92	4.2
Normally pruned (crop limited by pruning)...	760	13.7	62	211	20.8	45	68	3.8
Severely pruned (crop reduced by pruning)..	540	8.9	44	200	20.0	35	63	3.1

Influence on Leaf Area and Fruit Size.—When pruning is severe enough materially to stimulate new shoot growth, the individual leaves are likely to average larger than those on unpruned or lightly pruned trees and the trees give the observer the impression of possessing a greater total leaf area. Alderman and Auchter[1] have reported an instance in which the total leaf area of heavily pruned apple trees greatly exceeded that of lightly pruned trees, but the influence of pruning is more likely to be in the opposite direction. Thus Winkler[79] reports that heavy pruning of Vinifera grapevines results in greatly reducing the total leaf area, the difference being very pronounced early in the season when a lack of carbohydrates is likely to be a limiting factor in fruit setting (see Table 10). The almost universal dwarfing effect of heavy pruning on the tree as a whole leads to the conclusion that in general the effective leaf area for the season is substantially reduced. On the other hand there is evidence that there may be considerable defoliation without a corresponding reduction in photosynthesis, owing to increased efficiency of the leaves that are left.[11,33] A pruning, therefore, that reduces leaf area by a third will not reduce carbohydrate manufacture by nearly that amount.

It is the general opinion that pruning almost invariably results in an increase in size of fruit. Perhaps this tendency is most clearly shown in such fruits as the raspberry and blackberry, which, in the absence of pruning, are inclined to set more fruit than they can mature properly. Similarly, apples, pears, peaches and many other fruits frequently set too heavily, and pruning has been rather generally recommended (and practiced) for the purpose of thinning the crop, it being thought that gains in size would compensate for losses in number. The work of Johnston[40] indicates that this may hold for raspberries. It does not hold, however, for most fruits. Thus, in reporting on pruning studies with apple trees in Michigan, Marshall states:[48] "Pruning has often been likened to thinning and recommended as a substitute for it. In reality it is followed by distinctly different results. When a tree is pruned in the conventional way, potentially good and poor fruits are removed; when it is thinned the poorer fruits principally are removed and the larger, more perfect specimens left for maturity. It is not possible, even in 'detail' pruning, to pre-thin fruit as satisfactorily as when the half-grown fruit is on the tree. Fruit thinning may result in both a higher percentage and more bushels of A-grade apples. Pruning effects its improvement in grade largely through a reduction in yield. Pruning cannot be considered a satisfactory substitute for fruit thinning." Later studies[28] show that practically the same situation holds for the peach. However, pruning is one of the most practical means at the growers' disposal for increasing the size of fruits in those species where, for obvious reasons, thinning is impracticable.

Attention should be called to the fact, however, that pruning sometimes results in a decrease in size of fruit. This was found to be true by Winkler with Vinifera grapes,[78] where, presumably, limitation of leaf area was responsible for a carbohydrate deficiency. In the instance cited by Bedford and Pickering,[5] the decreased size of fruit is possibly explained by the increased leaf area of the trees and the consequently greater requirement of this foliage for water—a requirement that under the conditions of the experiment the roots were unable to supply.

Pruning as a Cause of Abnormal Structures.—In the sections on Water Relations and Nutrition attention is directed to certain pathological conditions that may result from extremes of moisture or from an unbalanced nutrient supply. Pruning may disturb both the water and food relations of the plant; hence certain pathological conditions may follow, particularly from heavy pruning. Daniel,[20] who has given this question considerable attention, enumerates a rather large number of monstrosities more or less directly attributable to pruning. Among the more important of these may be mentioned the forcing out of the so-called "second-bloom" from the limbs and trunks of pear trees, marked increases in size and changes in the form of leaves, fasciation and the metamorphosis of the glands of apricot leaves into small leaflets. He considers these abnormalities to be due to an upsetting of the balance normally existing between transpiration and assimilation. It should be remembered, however, that in many instances these abnormal structures arise independent of any pruning.

Amount of Pruning Varying with Fruiting Habit.—The facts just presented on the results to be expected from light, moderate, heavy or no pruning, show clearly that no rigid rules can be stated as to the amount of pruning best suited to orchard trees even of a single age or of a single kind. However, if certain other pertinent facts and principles be considered, the amount to be given orchard trees becomes somewhat more easily determined.

The fruit grower wishes to produce as soon as possible a tree, shrub, or vine sufficiently large to bear crops of at least moderate size. It is necessary, furthermore, that the plant have a strong framework for the support of the smaller branches and their fruiting wood and that it be adequately equipped with the spurs or shoots that bear fruit buds. For the first year or several years, in many species, fruit production is neither expected nor desired. The maturing of fruit and to a certain extent even the formation of fruit buds and potential fruiting wood might tax the energies of the plant so that increase in size would be checked seriously though such evidence as is available indicates that the early bearing associated with light pruning is less likely to reduce later productivity than is the dwarfing due to heavy pruning early in the life of the tree[66] or vine.[79] A little later, however, when the tree approaches such age and size that heavy production may be expected the grower desires it to develop gradually (or sometimes quickly) fruit-producing growth and he wishes to keep this growth actively at work. As the tree becomes still older its natural growing habits are very likely to encumber it with too much fruiting wood, more than its roots and leaves can supply with food materials for heavy and regular production. The grower's aim then should be to get rid of the old unproductive wood or to invigorate it or to limit the formation of new wood. His problem is first that of building the plant; then it is equipping it and providing for such extensions and new equipment as space and conditions permit and finally it becomes a problem of maintenance at maximum efficiency.

When these general principles are considered in their relation to the varying results attending pruning in different amounts, it is evident that, in general, tree, bush and vine fruits should be so pruned when young as to provide a strong, stocky framework with well spaced limbs. As the plant approaches bearing age and size, pruning should be less severe, to permit or encourage the production of fruiting wood. Perhaps in extreme cases it may be desirable at this stage to do no pruning at all. As the plant becomes still older, pruning is again increased in severity, thus limiting or sometimes reducing the amount of fruiting wood and in this way concentrating the energies of the tree upon a better support of what is left. The lower line shown in Fig. 50 gives graphically some

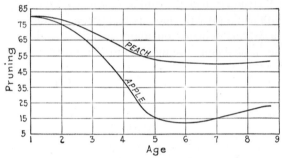

Fig. 50.—Graphs showing relative amounts of pruning required for the peach and apple at different ages.

idea of the manner in which the amount of pruning should vary with age in the average apple, pear, plum or cherry tree which is rather slow growing at first and bears principally on spurs. Of course as the trees vary in vigor, rapidity of growth, fruiting habits and in other respects there should be accompanying changes in the severity of the annual pruning. Thus the peach ordinarily begins bearing at an earlier age than the apple or cherry. Consequently it should be pruned to leave fruiting wood and permit bearing earlier. Furthermore, since it bears fruit only on shoots of the preceding year, regular production depends on annual provision for a good supply of new shoots. If these are to be produced on the lower part of the tree where the weight of the fruit will not place an excessively severe strain upon the crotches somewhat heavier annual pruning is necessary. At no stage in the life of the peach tree is it necessary practically to discontinue pruning in order to develop fruiting wood and bring it into bearing. The upper line in Fig. 50 shows roughly how the amount of pruning desirable for trees of this kind varies with age. Similarly it is possible to draw graphs for the amounts of pruning required by trees of other kinds. It should be emphasized, however, that these will vary in details not only with different kinds of fruits, but with varieties of the same kind and for the same variety from place to place and under varying soil and environmental conditions.

Summary.—By and large, unpruned trees increase in size more rapidly than pruned trees of the same kinds and the dwarfing effect of pruning is more or less directly proportional to its severity. This dwarfing effect is a result not so much of the production of less new shoot growth each year as of the amounts of wood removed. The dwarfing effect of top pruning extends to the root system because of the reduction in total leaf area. Pruning generally results also in a diminution in the number of fruit spurs in spur producing species, though there may or may not be a corresponding reduction in number of fruit buds and in the resulting yield. Within certain limits it tends to increase the size of the fruit. Extremely heavy pruning may occasionally result in different types of abnormal growth, such as fasciation. The severity of pruning that is desirable depends on many conditions, the age of the tree and its bearing habit being among the more important.

CHAPTER XXIII

PRUNING—THE METHOD

It seems strange that a horticultural practice as old as pruning should have come down to the present with so little realization that it includes questions of kind as well as of amount and of season. Nevertheless, most of the literature is silent on this matter, as though all pruning were necessarily the same in kind, except perhaps for the innumerable detailed ways of cutting to certain buds or of leaving certain spurs or shoots for replacement purposes. The fundamental differences between essentially distinct practices have not been generally recognized. Instead, attention has been focused upon the minute and less important details of procedure. Without doubt this lack of realization that pruning may vary greatly in kind and that entirely different results attend distinct kinds or types of pruning has been responsible for much of the confusion and apparent contradiction that is evident on comparison of the reports of various writers and investigators.

Heading Back and Thinning Out.—A number of classifications of pruning as to kind are possible. However, none is more serviceable than one which recognizes the difference between heading back and thinning out. It is difficult, if not impossible, to differentiate absolutely between the two for sometimes the removal of a branch or part of a branch is at the same time a thinning out and a heading back. In general, however, the differences between the two are clear and evident even to a casual observer. Thinning out removes entirely a shoot, spur, cane, branch, limb, or whatever the part may be; heading back removes only a portion, leaving another portion from which new growths can develop.

Influence on New Shoot and New Spur Formation.—Theoretically a heading back that is equal in severity to a certain thinning out removes approximately the same amount of wood and the same number of buds. In practice, however, there is a considerable difference. A thinning out that removes 50 per cent of the shoots, gets rid of just half the amount of wood of the past season and just half of the total number of buds, both lateral and terminal. On the other hand a 50 per cent heading back removes somewhat less than half the weight of woody tissue formed the past season and somewhat more than half the total number of new buds, for it removes an equal number of the lateral buds and all the

465

terminals. A heading back that is equal in severity to a certain thinning out is therefore more severe in one respect and less severe in another. If the pruning is comparatively heavy the difference is slight, but if the pruning is light the difference is correspondingly greater.

Observation shows that when growth begins the terminal and sub-terminal buds are usually the first to start and in the majority of deciduous trees and vines (less frequently in shrubs) they produce the longest

TABLE 11.—INFLUENCE OF HEADING BACK AND THINNING OUT ON SHOOT AND SPUR FORMATION IN YOUNG APPLE TREES

(*After Gardner*[27])

Variety	Number of trees averaged	Severity of pruning (per cent.)	Average 1914 shoot growth (centimeters)	Average 1915 shoot growth (centimeters)	Average number of fruit spurs, 1915	Kind or pruning, 1916	Average 1916 shoot growth (centimeters)	Average number of fruit spurs, 1916
Grimes	32	26–50	697	2297	82	Thinning	4123	360
Grimes	23	26–50	731	2495	83	Heading	5703	322
Grimes	39	51–75	389	1315	22	Thinning	2308	130
Grimes	36	51–75	368	1362	23	Heading	3328	101
Gano	18	26–50	450	2376	15	Thinning	4577	158
Gano	14	26–50	462	2609	14	Heading	6293	158
Gano	4	51–75	560	2493	15	Thinning	5072	110
Gano	10	51–75	562	2435	15	Heading	5846	111
Rome	19	26–50	507	1990	9	Thinning	3352	43
Rome	17	26–50	508	1956	10	Heading	3915	25
Rome	8	51–75	1007	2851	9	Thinning	4785	54
Rome	21	51–75	682	2230	8	Heading	4474	25
Esopus	29	46–76	444	1659	28	Thinning	2122	180
Esopus	27	46–76	461	1813	28	Heading	4031	144

and strongest shoots, though shoots may grow from many of the lower buds. However, seldom do all the lateral buds start and as a rule the largest percentage of those that remain dormant are on the basal portion of the shoot. Those species that bear principally on spurs form these spurs mainly from buds on the median and terminal portions of the shoot. Heading back, therefore, limits fruit-spur formation to a greater extent than a correspondingly heavy thinning out. This is obvious from the data presented in Table 11, showing the amounts of shoot growth and the numbers of spurs formed by vigorous 5-year old apple trees of different varieties that had been headed back or thinned out with equal severity. However, the influence on fruit-spur formation of heading as compared with thinning out is much more pronounced in some varieties than in others. Gano, for instance, showed practically no difference in this respect.

Even more striking than the inequality in numbers of spurs from the two kinds of pruning was that in the amount of new shoot growth. Heading back invariably led to greater shoot production than a corresponding amount of thinning out (see Table 11). In Esopus the amount of new shoot growth was almost double that in the thinned trees. Apparently thinning out some of the shoots in a tree does not result in diverting the same amount of food and moisture they would have used into the

FIG. 51.—Grimes apple tree, showing a typical response to heading back. Compare with FIG. 52.

remaining unpruned shoots. Certainly it does not result in a sufficiently increased new shoot growth from them to compensate for that which would ordinarily have grown from the portion of the top that has been pruned away. It has some stimulating influence of this kind but it also results in a reduction in the total new growth formed. On the other hand heading back has a more stimulating influence and the pruned shoots tend to give rise to as much (often more) new shoot growth as would have arisen from the unpruned tree. This is well illustrated by Figs. 51 and 52 which show the response of two trees of Grimes to the same amount of pruning, the tree in Fig. 51 having been headed back and that in Fig. 52 having been thinned out.

Influence on General Shape and Habit.—Incident to quite different effects of heading and of thinning upon the amount of new shoot growth and the number of new spurs are the influences of these practices on general shape and growth habit. Thinning out places no check on the natural tendency to grow principally from the terminal and subterminal

Fig. 52.—Grimes apple tree, showing a typical response to thinning out. Compare with Fig. 51.

buds. Consequently plants pruned exclusively in this way grow tall and wide spreading and they gradually develop a more open, "rangy" habit than they would otherwise. This may be advantageous or disadvantageous to the grower, depending on a number of conditions. On the other hand constant heading checks this tendency to extend out and up and results in a plant compact in habit and often very dense in growth. The average well kept hedge furnishes an extreme example of the direction in which all heading tends. Indeed much of the usual pruning of the bramble fruits, which consists largely in heading back both leaders and laterals and the pruning that frequently is afforded other deciduous fruits—especially when they are young—results in a type of growth and a condition of tree in many ways closely comparable to that of the privet or osage orange hedge.

Influence on Fruit-bud Formation and Fruitfulness.—The orchard is grown and maintained not primarily for its shoot growth or for its spurs, but for fruit. The grower therefore wishes to know the influence of different pruning practices on fruit-bud formation. It has been shown previously that this occurs at varying times in diverse plants and that different species present entirely unlike fruit bearing habits. That is to say, some bear on spurs, some on shoots; some bear terminally, some laterally. If, then, pruning practices differ greatly in their influences on spur and on shoot formation, corresponding, perhaps greater, differences may be expected in their influences on fruit-bud formation and fruiting. The practice that leads to greater fruitfulness in one species may tend in the opposite direction in another. Thus heading back may be a good practice in growing the peach because it encourages new shoot growth on which the fruit buds are borne and on the other hand, heading back may be a bad practice for the pear, because it generally limits the formation of fruit spurs on which most of the fruit of this species is borne.

In contrast to thinning out, heading back generally tends not only to reduce the number of spurs in spur bearing species but also to lower the percentage that differentiate fruit buds. In these same species, thinning out, though it may reduce somewhat the total number of fruit spurs, has been shown under some conditions to lead to the formation of fruit buds and to the maturing of fruit on a larger percentage of those remaining. Data on this question obtained from pruning experiments with young apple trees in Oregon are furnished in Table 12. The figures presented in the last three columns of this table also show something of the influence of these two pruning practices on fruit-bud formation on shoots. Though the apple is not generally considered a shoot bearer, where this investigation was carried out, two of the varieties studied, Rome and Gano, bear principally on shoots for the first few seasons. Thinning out generally encouraged terminal and lateral fruit-bud formation on shoots more than a corresponding heading back, though there were some exceptions. In commenting on these data Gardner[27] says:

"The moderately thinned Grimes trees were somewhat more than twice as productive of fruit buds as the correspondingly headed trees; the heavily thinned Grimes trees were 10 times as productive of fruit buds as correspondingly headed trees. The moderately thinned Rome trees were nearly twice and the heavily thinned, nearly five times as productive of fruit buds as those correspondingly headed. On the other hand, moderately thinned Gano trees produced but slightly more fruit buds than those moderately headed, and heavily thinned trees of this variety averaged distinctly fewer buds than those heavily headed. The last statement also holds true of the heavily pruned Esopus trees. A more

TABLE 12.—INFLUENCE OF THINNING OUT AND HEADING BACK SHOOTS ON FRUIT-BUD FORMATION IN THE APPLE

(After Gardner[27])

Variety	Kind of pruning	Severity of pruning (per cent.)	Number of trees averaged	Number of fruit spurs, fall of 1916 (average)	Number of fruit spurs flowering 1917 (average)	Number of shoots flowering terminally in 1917 (average)	Number of lateral flower clusters, 1917 (average)	Total number of flower clusters, 1917 (average)
Grimes	No pruning	.....	71	402	29.5	2.7	5.0	37.2
Grimes	Thinning	1–25	38	457	24.8	3.9	4.6	33.3
Grimes	Thinning	26–50	32	360	31.7	2.6	10.0	44.3
Grimes	Heading	26–50	23	322	8.9	7.4	2.2	18.5
Grimes	Thinning	51–75	39	130	18.0	0.9	6.2	25.1
Grimes	Heading	51–75	36	101	0.1	1.3	1.0	2.4
Gano	Thinning	26–50	18	158	12.9	59.3	31.6	103.8
Gano	Heading	26–50	14	158	14.8	65.0	16.4	96.2
Gano	Thinning	51–75	4	110	8.5	43.5	15.0	67.0
Gano	Heading	51–75	10	111	14.6	53.6	13.7	81.9
Rome	No pruning	.....	28	142	31.6	3.5	72.4	107.5
Rome	Thinning	26–50	19	43	5.6	1.3	47.5	54.4
Rome	Heading	26–50	17	25	5.2	5.3	21.9	32.4
Rome	Thinning	51–75	8	54	5.0	2.6	51.7	59.3
Rome	Heading	51–75	21	25	3.5	2.8	6.4	12.7
Esopus	No pruning	.....	27	635	41.9	0.3	10.4	52.6
Esopus	Thinning	41–76	29	180	17.2	0.1	7.2	24.5
Esopus	Heading	41–76	27	144	11.4	2.1	17.6	31.1

detailed study of the table brings out a number of additional points. In the first place, it is noted that thinning, as compared with an equally severe heading, almost invariably led to an increased production of fruit buds upon fruit spurs. The one exception to this statement is furnished by the heavily headed Gano tree, a variety in which severe heading of short shoots in the interior seems often to have the effect of forcing the development of strong fruit spurs from the remaining lateral buds. The short interior shoots of other varieties do not show such a tendency to respond to severe heading in this way. Heading-back was invariably accompanied by a greater development of terminal fruit buds on shoots than thinning out. In the case of a variety like Gano, that when young bears a large percentage of its fruit buds in this way, this effect may be sufficient to give the tree a larger total number of fruit buds than correspondingly thinned trees. Attention is called, however, to the fact that a continuation of the winter heading year after year would remove the fruit buds on all the shoots headed and thus actually result in decreased flower and fruit production as compared with thinning.

"Another point worth noting, but not brought out in the table is the fact that the shoots bearing terminally average much shorter in the thinned than in the headed trees. They are generally so placed, moreover, that in the thinning of shoots they can be left to advantage while sterile ones are taken out.

"Except for Esopus, winter thinning of shoots, as compared with heading, led to greatly increased production of lateral fruit buds on shoots. In the case of the heavily pruned Rome trees, the proportion of such lateral fruit buds was 8 to 1 under the two pruning treatments. Furthermore, the distribution of these lateral fruit buds is such that a given heading-back (for instance, 50 per cent.) would remove a much larger percentage than an equally severe thinning out. This percentage, in the case of Esopus, would be enough greater more than to counterbalance the effect upon total fruit production of larger numbers of such lateral fruit buds.

"Taking all these facts into consideration, it is evident that the effect of thinning-out and likewise of heading back upon fruit-bud formation varies greatly with the variety. The pruning practice that will lead to the largest fruit-bud production in one variety will not necessarily lead to it in another. Thus it becomes important for the grower to become better acquainted with the exact fruiting habits of his varieties under his conditions as well as to the response that these varieties make to various pruning practices."

Thinning and Heading Lead to Different Nutritive Conditions.—The explanation of the varying effects of thinning out and of heading back on fruit-bud formation is not found exclusively in the different fruiting habits of the several species and varieties. New growth early in the season is made chiefly at the expense of stored foods, particularly carbohydrates. In the section on Nutrition, data are presented showing that the younger wood is comparatively richer in food reserves than older tissues. Heading back, therefore, removes a larger amount of the tree reserves than a correspondingly severe thinning out and leaves it less able to recuperate, especially if the pruning has been severe.

Furthermore, analyses[35] show that the new growth from near the cut ends of headed shoots has a higher nitrogen content than the new growth from unpruned shoots, a fact that helps to explain the relatively vigorous growth that results from heading. Spring thinning, on the other hand, tends to conserve both the nitrogen and carbohydrate supplies in the tree. The 2-year old wood retains larger amounts of nitrogen and of carbohydrates the first two weeks after pruning. Thinning produces in the tips of the shoots that are left a condition resembling that brought about by a nitrate application, the amounts of nitrogen, sugar and water being intermediate between those found in the checks and in the fertilized trees. There is one noticeable difference, however. While the fertilizer treatment decreases the nitrogen content of the older wood, the thinning increases it. This may be associated with the development of lateral branches from the thinned shoots.[35]

It is also pointed out in the section on Nutrition that the initiation of the fruitful condition, or in other words fruit-bud formation, is associated with an accumulation of carbohydrates in the regions where fruit buds can be formed. Carbohydrate accumulation in turn depends on carbohydrate manufacture on the one hand and on carbohydrate utilization on the other. When the latter process lags behind the former, opportunity is finally afforded for the laying-down of fruit buds. In the last analysis, therefore, pruning influences fruit-bud formation to the extent that it influences carbohydrate accumulation or carbohydrate utilization or the status of the ever changing ratio between them.

Thinning out not only removes less stored food than a corresponding heading back, but, as just pointed out, it also leads to increased fruit-spur formation and decreased shoot growth. This means decreased carbohydrate utilization and increased carbohydrate manufacture, because spurs are short growths with relatively large leaf surfaces. Their growth is made very early in the season and from then on they are manufacturing and accumulating rather than spending or dissipating organs. On the other hand heading back produces fewer of these short growths and more of the longer and stronger shoots that complete their growth much later. Consequently they more nearly exhaust the plant's reserves than the shoots and spurs of thinned trees and their carbohydrate contributions to the tree as a whole come later and may amount to less.

Furthermore the thinned is more open than the headed tree. Its leaves are better exposed to light and presumably they are for that reason somewhat more effective manufacturing organs. The more common formation of fruit buds in the better exposed parts of the tree is evidence on this point. The rather general production of fewer and smaller leaves on spurs in the interior shaded portions of compact headed trees, in contrast to the larger and more numerous leaves on the spurs of open thinned trees, is another fact pointing to material differences in the rate of carbohydrate accumulation in their fruiting wood.

Still another reason for the difference in response from heading back and from thinning out lies in a disturbance of an equilibrium within the branch itself induced by heading back. Each branch, as it grows, may be regarded as a system in equilibrium, comparable to that in the plant as a whole. That is, there is a balance between part and part. If a portion of the branch is removed this balance is disturbed. Equilibrium is reestablished by regeneration of the part pruned away. Apparently little readjustment is necessary after thinning out, because the equilibrium of the remaining branches is not disturbed. The adjoining parts will function more nearly as they would, had no pruning been done.

The Places of Thinning and of Heading in Pruning Practice.—The preceding discussion shows that no rules can be laid down as to the relative amounts of heading and of thinning that should be given trees of a certain kind or of a certain age. Rather is it necessary to study carefully each problem as it arises, to interpret and to apply the general principles that have been pointed out. In a general way, however, it may be stated that both the development of a more extensive fruiting system and more especially the better and more efficient functioning of that system are favored more by thinning than by heading. There are notable instances of other effects, however, *e.g.*, in the bramble fruits, in which the heading back of the canes or other growth limits the energies of the plant to production on the remaining shoots or spurs and causes them to produce larger, if not more, fruits. In the section on Fruit Setting it is pointed out that pinching back the growing shoots of the grape before blossoming sometimes leads to a better setting. In most species continued thinning out leads eventually to tall or wide spreading and "rangy" plants, plants that require wider spacing in the orchard, that often make undue expense in pruning, spraying and other care and that are unable to mature their crops without a great number of mechanical supports. Judicious heading back corrects these tendencies and promotes a compact type of growth that, in these respects, is much more satisfactory. In fact it may be stated that in general the main purpose of heading back is to control the form of the tree, bush or vine—to train it. In practice this means that while the trees are young they should receive relatively more heading back and less thinning out, because they are then being trained. As they grow older they should receive relatively less heading and more thinning, because they will require less and less training for shape and more attention to the proper functioning of their fruit-producing wood. Species like the peach and grape, which, because of their growing habits, continually require considerable training for compactness and shape, should receive correspondingly more heading when mature than certain other species like the apple or walnut that have entirely different growing habits.

Fine, as Compared with Bulk Pruning.—In pruning practice and in the consideration of pruning problems aside from those dealing with the healing of wounds, pruning is generally regarded as something directly affecting the tree as a whole. It is common to speak of pruning this tree heavily and that one lightly, of heading back one and thinning out another, of winter pruning in one instance and summer pruning in another. A certain tree having been neglected for a number of years is said to require a heavy pruning to bring it back to a vigorous productive condition. Such sweeping statements disregard frequent cases in which though possibly certain parts of the tree should be pruned heavily, certain other parts should be pruned lightly, if at all. If a heavily pruned tree fails to attain quickly a vigorous productive condition there is query why the result has not been satisfactory. When it is decided that another tree requires only a light pruning, only a very few branches are removed. If such pruning is attended by some of the results usually accompanying

heavy pruning there is speculation regarding the reason.   These statements, which will be recognized as based upon very general experience,
show that pruning is regarded somewhat as a bulk problem—as something
which is decided on for the tree as a whole, done to the tree as a whole
and to which the tree as a whole responds.   Yet the results frequently

Fig. 53.—A Bartlett pear tree, three years after a heading back of the main upright
limbs.   Notice that the response to this pruning has been principally close to where the
cuts were made.

obtained indicate nothing more clearly than that pruning is not exactly
a problem of bulk.

Results Following "Dehorning."—The sucker type of growth that
almost invariably follows very severe cutting back or "dehorning" is
well known.   If the dehorning has been done in winter or early spring,
numerous comparatively upright shoots are produced during the following
summer.   The usual practice is to thin these out and head back those

that are left, in order to develop as quickly as possible new fruiting branches. Thus is the tree "rejuvenated." So well is this procedure understood that the question as to when and how to rejuvenate trees has been considered practically settled. However, even a cursory examination of a tree that has recently received such a treatment shows that only a part has responded. Undisturbed branches in the lower part of the dehorned tree usually continue to grow in the ordinary way. Their spurs bear flowers and fruit but little more regularly and yield a product of but little better grade than before. There is nearly the same tendency for their older spurs and smaller fruiting branches to become gradually weaker and die. Apparently neither as whole units nor in their separate parts have these lower branches been accelerated or retarded in growth. In many cases they do not even produce watersprouts, such as develop so abundantly on the dehorned branches above them. In other words, an important portion of the tree apparently has not been affected in any way by the dehorning. This is brought out clearly in Fig. 53. The treatment has resulted merely in the production of new wood to replace a portion of the old top.

Even more striking evidence on this question of the distance to which the influence of pruning extends is furnished by trees that have been partly dehorned, that is, have had a portion of their branches cut back very severely and others of equal size and reaching to an equal height left untouched. In such instances those responses, commonly regarded as characteristic of dehorning, usually are limited to the branches that have been cut back. These branches produce watersprouts in abundance, but the unpruned branch continues to grow and function as though nothing had been done to upset the usual conditions in the tree. Examples of this occur in old trees of many species that are being top-worked, when the process is being distributed over a period of several years. The influence of the heavy pruning, incident to the top working process, usually is not reflected to any appreciable extent in a changed manner of growth in the ungrafted limbs (see Fig. 54).

Results Attending the Removal of a Few Large Limbs.—The entire removal of one or more comparatively large limbs, the majority being left unpruned, is a type of pruning in more or less sharp contrast to the bulk heading back just discussed. It may be considered a kind of bulk thinning. Many fruit growers prune in this manner, which possesses at least the advantage of requiring little labor. Experience shows that when a single large limb is removed from almost any part of a tree, watersprouts develop to take its place and the rest of the top continues to grow as before. The watersprouts arise, for the most part, not from limbs far removed from the pruning wound, but close to the point where the cut was made. There is an unmistakable response to the pruning, but that response is evident within a very limited area.   The tree as a whole does not show it.

Those who, after permitting a leader to develop for a number of years and to form a close centered tree, have finally tried to train to an open center or vase shape can furnish abundant evidence on the question under discussion.   The removal of the central leader from trees of this kind

FIG. 54.—An old Italian prune tree.   All of the main limbs but one were cut back four years before this picture was taken.   The unheaded limb in the center shows little response to the pruning.

(bulk heading back or bulk thinning out, depending on the form of the tree and where the cut is made), is almost always followed by the production of a number of watersprouts that tend to take its place.   The subsequent removal of these watersprouts is followed by the production of still others, nearly always at points near the wound left by the removal of the leader.   The unpruned branches seem little influenced by the cutting out of the leader.

In attempting to train young Yellow Newtown apple or Bartlett or Anjou pear trees to an open center, or the McIntosh apple or Winter

Nelis pear to a closed center, there is difficulty in keeping these trees from growing dense in the center in the first instance and from spreading out or even growing down in the second; though the shoots are cut out or off. Furthermore—a matter of equal or greater importance—there is difficulty in making the other shoots and limbs of these same trees spread out or grow upright, as the case may be and thus profit by the nutrient materials that it is desired to divert from the closely pruned parts. In fact so persistently do the watersprouts tend to replace removed limbs, that the easiest way to develop an open centered tree is not to cut out all of the growth in the center, but rather to suppress it by pruning it a little more severely than the surrounding branches that are desired for the main framework. Even then it is doubtful if the usual characteristic growth of the remaining branches is materially changed. Similarly, when young trees are lightly, or even heavily, headed back new shoots are sent out, but mainly from points where some of them can easily replace the portion removed. It is not common for distant untouched portions of the tree to show a well defined response to pruning.

Results Attending Thin-wood Pruning.—Just as there are differences between fruit-spur and fruit-bud formation on the slender, densely shaded shoots of trees that have been headed back as compared with the stockier, better lighted shoots of trees that have been thinned, so there are differences in the performance of slender and of stocky branches of fruiting age in the same tree or in different trees. Growth-performance records of the fruiting branches on a number of standard apple varieties covering a series of years were obtained by Ricks and Gaston[58] in Michigan (Table 13). They show that the number of apples borne by any individual branch tends to be directly proportional to its diameter. Thus, 4-year old fruiting branches of the Wealthy apple that were $\frac{1}{4}$ inch or less in diameter at the base averaged 3.4 fruits apiece; those of the same age that were $\frac{3}{8}$ inch or more in diameter at the base averaged 10.6 fruits apiece; those intermediate in size averaged 5.8 apiece (Fig. 55). Furthermore, the fruits borne on the slender branches were for the most part small and poorly colored, while those borne on the stocky wood were large and well colored. These differences were great enough to make the monetary value of the fruit produced by a stocky branch 10 times that borne by a slender one of the same age.

These characteristics of fruiting wood of the same age but varying diameter, characteristics found to hold for all varieties studied, led Ricks and Gaston to develop a system of pruning which they have called "thin-wood" pruning and which consists simply in the removal of the weak, slender, relatively unproductive and unprofitable bearing wood from the tree. The stout, stocky bearing wood is left, more or less regardless of how thick and brushy it may leave certain portions of the tops. They call attention to the fact that most of the slender or "thin" wood is found in the lower and interior parts of the tree, while the stocky wood is in the outer and upper portions.   Correlated with this distribution of fruiting wood of different types in the several portions of the tree was the finding that 60 per cent. of the total returns, considering quantities and grades, was obtained from the "top" portion, 33 per cent. from the

FIG. 55.—Typical "thick," "intermediate" and "thin" branches, each with its load of fruit. Note the variation in productive capacity.   (*After Ricks and Gaston*[58])

"outside" and only 7 per cent. from the "interior."   Thin-wood pruning differs rather fundamentally from what has come to be the more or less conventional method of pruning mature apple trees, which consists in removing relatively more of the stocky, productive wood in the top of the tree than of the weak slender wood in the lower and interior portions. Ricks and Gaston report, however, that their thin-wood method of pruning causes only a slight reduction in total yield, while it effects a marked influence on average grade through eliminating the small poorly

TABLE 13.—BRANCH PERFORMANCE RECORDS OF SEVEN STANDARD VARIETIES

(After Ricks and Gaston[58])

Number of branches studied	Diameter, inches	Per cent. of apples in respective size groups						Number of apples per branch	Total weight, ounces	Per cent. of apples in respective color grades			Age	Length, inches	Average annual growth, inches
		Less than 2 inches	2 to 2¼ inches	2¼ to 2½ inches	2½ to 2¾ inches	2¾ to 3 inches	More than 3 inches			U.S. Fancy	U.S. No. 1	U.S. Com'l			
Jonathan:															
104	²⁄₈ −	22	33	33	10	2	..	4.1	12.6	21	38	41	5.3	31.9	6.3
104	²⁴⁰⁰⁄−	6	34	40	17	3	..	7.9	26.8	61	19	20	4.5	59.8	14.3
104	³⁄₈ +	2	27	37	26	7	1	12.1	41.7	76	19	5	5.0	103.7	22.4
McIntosh:															
64	²⁄₈ −	8	21	44	25	2	..	3.4	10.5	1	10	89	5.3	38.9	7.5
64	²⁴⁰⁰⁄−	..	5	38	40	15	2	5.9	22.1	9	16	75	4.2	54.2	12.8
64	³⁄₈ +	..	1	16	48	29	6	10.3	44.1	41	35	24	3.9	82.1	21.4
Duchess:															
57	²⁄₈ −	22	30	29	18	1	..	3.2	8.6	..	11	89	8.2	30.3	3.7
57	²⁴⁰⁰⁄−	7	10	26	45	12	..	6.1	21.8	5	36	59	7.3	49.3	6.8
57	³⁄₈ +	2	3	14	45	36	..	9.3	41.9	23	44	33	4.8	65.0	13.6
Baldwin:															
51	²⁄₈ −	33	35	23	8	1	..	3.9	8.9	7	20	73	10.5	31.6	3.0
51	²⁴⁰⁰⁄−	5	17	38	35	4	1	6.5	21.4	18	22	60	7.2	49.7	6.9
51	³⁄₈ +	2	6	29	49	12	2	12.0	46.1	61	29	10	4.9	55.7	11.9
Northern Spy:															
21	²⁄₈ −	8	47	35	9	1	..	4.7	12.8	8	24	68	8.2	40.4	4.9
21	²⁴⁰⁰⁄−	6	19	32	31	11	1	7.9	26.9	5	20	75	6.6	67.0	10.2
21	³⁄₈ +	..	1	12	40	37	10	11.8	53.8	42	31	27	5.3	92.0	17.4
Grimes:															
115	²⁄₈ −	29	43	23	5	..	..	3.7	8.5	...	...	...	8.3	37.7	4.6
115	²⁴⁰⁰⁄−	9	34	46	11	..	..	6.1	17.0	...	...	...	7.7	58.2	7.6
115	³⁄₈ +	1	18	52	27	2	..	11.8	35.9	...	...	...	5.8	63.8	11.2
Transparent:															
70	²⁄₈ −	61	27	12	..	..	..	3.0	4.3	...	...	...	8.0	33.6	4.2
70	²⁴⁰⁰⁄−	39	32	26	3	..	..	6.0	12.5	...	...	...	7.5	55.7	7.6
70	³⁄₈ +	14	34	44	8	..	..	10.8	28.6	...	...	...	5.6	68.7	12.5

colored fruits and increasing somewhat the amounts of the larger ones with better color. As stocky, productive branches are borne down so that they assume a horizontal or drooping direction their new growth becomes progressively less vigorous and stocky and in time classifies as thin wood and is removed. In thin-wood pruning renewal is from the top rather than the bottom of the tree.

Based on the same differences in fruiting performance of stocky and slender branches these investigators have proposed what they term the "graduated space" method of thinning for apples.[29] This calls for very wide spacing of fruits on the slender branches and close spacing of those on the stocky branches and results in less reduction in total yield and greater improvement in grade than is effected by the more conventional even spacing of fruits in thinning practice.

Results Attending Spur Pruning.—As they become older, some varieties of apple and pear trees develop large numbers of fruit spurs, which often branch and rebranch until they become fruit spur clusters. Usually when there are such large numbers of fruit spurs only a comparatively small percentage can flower and fruit in any single season and the record of any single spur, or even spur cluster, especially in an older part of the tree, would show very irregular fruiting. In such trees, though there is little vegetative growth in the general acceptation of the term, nearly all the energies of the tree are really being absorbed in a slow vegetative growth of the spurs. The recognition of this condition leads the grower to try dehorning or some other type of bulk pruning as a remedial measure. That bulk pruning is only a partial remedy has already been shown. Occasionally a grower tries the removal of a part of the spurs from such trees. As the spurs possess a very large percentage of the growing points and bear practically all of the leaf system of a tree in such condition, a thinning of spurs is in one sense the equivalent of a heavy pruning though the total weight of the wood removed may be negligible. When treated in this way trees produce few or no watersprouts, though the removal of a few large branches with an equivalent number of growing points leads to their formation. However, the remaining spurs grow more vigorously and the new shoots developing from lateral and terminal buds are much larger and stronger. As a net result, though the tree is changed little, if at all, in general form, the rate of growth of nearly all its individual parts is accelerated and the ways in which they function are materially changed. The tree as a whole has been affected because nearly all its individual parts have been affected.

Application to Practice.—A consideration of the points that have been made leads unmistakably to at least one conclusion: namely, that the radius of influence within the tree of any pruning (that is, the cutting out or cutting back of any particular shoot or branch) is comparatively small. Parts close to the pruning wound, or perhaps close to a space left by the removal of a branch, respond to the pruning treatment. Generally speaking, other parts of the tree do not. In other words, pruning does not appreciably affect the tree as an entity; it affects the whole tree only indirectly through its effect on limited portions. To stimulate the formation of fruit spurs pruning must be done close to the point where they are desired and to increase the productivity of spurs already present pruning must be done in their immediate neighborhood. This in turn means light, or rather fine, as opposed to coarse, pruning. It is necessary to avoid bulk pruning and give greater attention to detail. In the young tree pruning should concern itself mainly with shoots and the smaller branches. In older trees it should be limited largely to the removal of the weak, slender, relatively unproductive wood found principally in the lower and interior portions of the tree.

Most of the trouble from fungous or bacterial infection comes from the large wounds, those made in bulk pruning. This is not an important factor in the culture of the bush or vine fruits but it is usually of considerable importance in the tree fruit plantation. Indeed it is not too much to say that the life of the average orchard tree is reduced by one-third through the work of wound fungi and bacteria. Fine, as opposed to coarse or bulk, pruning is the most practicable way of preventing losses of this sort.

Carrying the line of reasoning a step farther it becomes evident that pruning should be regular and frequent. This is a statement which most growers know to be true from observation and experience, though the reasons may not always be clearly understood. However, the points that have been brought out furnish an explanation of some of the characteristic results following irregular pruning. Trees left unpruned for several years usually seem to require the removal of some of the larger branches or limbs. This approaches the bulk type of pruning and stimulates new vegetative growth more than it invigorates the older fruiting wood; new vegetative growth of this sort is as likely to increase as to diminish difficulties.

What has been stated should not be construed as condemnation of occasional heavy pruning, that is, the removal of a considerable amount of growth. Though heavy pruning as commonly done is bulk pruning, it is not necessarily so. It may consist in the removal of a large amount of shoot growth and small branches and instead of giving rise to water-sprouts, it may stimulate the normal vegetative growth and the fruit spur system. The spur pruning to which reference has been made is evidence to this effect.

Even bulk pruning is not always harmful. There are occasions when a growth of strong vigorous shoots or watersprouts is desired in some part of the tree.   Particularly is this true in trees that have suffered from winter injury or some other form of dieback.   Then too, it should be remembered that many species do not bear on fruit spurs or on short growths of any other kind.   Their flower buds are formed freely upon their longest and strongest shoots and bulk pruning which leads to this type of vegetative growth may in no way check fruitfulness.

Root Pruning.—Root pruning has long been a recognized practice among many European fruit growers, particularly those of the British Isles and the adjacent continental countries and for many years it was generally recommended (but rarely done) in the United States.   Though its use has not been limited to trees grown as dwarfs it has been employed much less commonly with standards.   In this country particularly, as the culture of dwarf fruit trees has become relatively less important, root pruning has all but disappeared from the list of cultural operations.   However, a certain amount of root pruning is almost always accomplished in the regular cultivation of standard orchard trees.   For this reason, though tillage is thought to effect a root pruning seldom, some of the more important effects of severing a portion of the tree's roots at different seasons may well be noted.

In the culture of dwarf trees of almost any kind, Rivers,[61] one of the leading exponents of the practice, recommended an annual, or at least a biennial, shortening of all the roots.   In describing the operation he said: "Open a circular trench 18 inches deep around the tree, 18 inches from the stem, and cut off every root and fibre with a sharp knife.   When the roots are so pruned, introduce a spade under one side of the tree, and heave it over so as not to leave a single tap-root; fill in your mould, give a top dressing of manure, and it is finished.   The diameter of your circular trench must be slowly increased as years roll on; for you must, each year, prune to within $1\frac{1}{2}$ or 2 inches of the stumps of the former year.   Your circular mass of fibrous roots will thus slowly increase, your tree will make short and well-ripened shoots, and bear abundantly."   It is generally recommended that this root pruning be done in the late fall.   The major response will then be evident the following spring and summer in a reduced vegetative growth and an increased formation of fruit buds.

Some conception of the dwarfing influence of continued root pruning on apples grown on Paradise stocks is afforded by an investigation conducted at the Woburn Experiment Station in England.   In summarizing their results, Bedford and Pickering[6] state: "In one series the trees were root-pruned every year, in another every other year, and in a third every fourth year; actual lifting from the ground being adopted, till they became too large for this to be done without excessive injury.   The check caused to the growth of the trees was apparent from every point of view, and its extent may be gathered from the weights of the trees when they were ultimately removed. Thus with the Cox, which were removed after 15 years, the weights of those trees which had been root-pruned every fourth year were only 43 per cent of those which had not been root-pruned; where the operation had been performed every other year, the weights were 7 per cent of the non-treated trees, and with the yearly operation, 3 per cent; indeed, in the last case, the trees had scarcely increased in weight since they had been planted, and had been dead for several years before they were removed." These investigators then state that root pruning is followed by increased crop production, though usually this is not evident until the second season after the operation. However, repeated root pruning so weakens the trees that they soon fall behind non-treated trees in yield. Bedford and Pickering conclude that "root-pruning is an operation which should be practiced with extreme moderation, and only in those cases where excessive branch-growth calls for stringent measures." The root-pruning investigations of Drinkard[22] in Virginia led to practically the same conclusions. He reported a greatly reduced shoot growth, with leaf areas on the root-pruned trees only 5 to 20 per cent. of those on the checks. Furthermore the leaves of the treated trees were smaller and paler than those of the untreated trees. This check in vegetative growth was accompanied by an increased formation of fruit buds; these, however, were so weak that comparatively few set fruit and yields were less than those obtained from trees not root-pruned.

The experimental results of these and of other recent investigators do not, on the surface, agree with the opinions of many of the earlier writers regarding the desirability of root pruning. The quotation from Rivers, however, included with the recommendations for annual or biennial root pruning one for liberal applications of manure and a study of the earlier literature dealing with this subject shows that artificial feeding and often artificial watering was assumed for practically all root-pruned trees. The relatively great productivity of the root-pruned dwarfs of European and other gardens therefore should be regarded as due only partly to root pruning, some of the other attendant practices being perhaps more responsible.

Seldom, if ever, would the operations incident to clean culture or any other system of soil management result in a root pruning as severe as that contemplated in the regular practice that goes by that name. Nevertheless the deep plowing of trees growing in a shallow soil or in a soil that compels shallow rooting actually effects a considerable, and occasionally a very severe, root pruning. If this comes just before or during the period of fruit setting, it is likely greatly to interfere with that process and reduce the size of the crop. Teske and Gardner[69] record an instance in which a single deep cultivation of a field of black raspberries reduced yield by a half. On the other hand, moderate or light root pruning may be expected to afford a temporary stimulus to fruit-bud production and at the same time to check vegetative growth more or less, though either or both of these direct effects may be masked by the indirect influence that the tillage exerts.

Special Pruning Practices.—Stripping, notching, ringing and girdling may be considered together as a group of special orchard practices rather closely related to pruning. The names used to designate them are sufficiently descriptive to make unnecessary any further explanation of the procedure involved. They are all performed with the aim of so controlling the translocation of elaborated foods that their accumulation in certain parts may lead to increased fruit-bud formation and hence to greater fruitfulness or to a better setting of the flowers or to a better development of the fruit itself.

The upward movement of water in the tree, of the transpiration stream, is known to occur in the outer layers of the wood. Knowledge of the translocation of elaborated foods is less complete, though it is rather generally agreed that their downward movement is through the phloem. Investigations of Curtis[18] indicate that no appreciable quantities of carbohydrates move upward through the xylem and that such elaborated food materials as are stored in the xylem move only radially in the wood. Their upward transfer is limited mainly to the tissues of the bark, except for a limited translocation by means of diffusion. Consequently those portions of shoots or branches above the point where the flow of elaborated foods has been checked by girdling or ringing depend on their own resources in so far as elaborated foods are concerned. That is, they cannot receive foods manufactured elsewhere in the plant and foods that they manufacture must be stored within their tissues or utilized by them. If the operation is performed during the dormant season or very early during the growing season, vegetative growth above the ringed or girdled point will be checked because of the early exhaustion of the stored carbohydrates and the reduced leaf area will limit the synthesis of a new supply. On the other hand, this new supply that is synthesized cannot be translocated to the roots or other part of the tree and must be stored or utilized in close proximity to its point of manufacture. Girdling or ringing after the first flush would permit a greater amount of growth beyond the point of operation because food stored elsewhere would be to some extent available for this new growth and following the ringing there would be opportunity for a correspondingly greater accumulation of foods. A matter of practical importance in connection with ringing is that when the operation is performed after the middle of June callus growth takes place freely from both edges of the ring, whereas ringing before then results in callus from the upper edges only.[67] Healing of the wound is hastened by sealing with a strip of adhesive tape or similar bandage, but is delayed if it is treated with paint or grafting wax. The general influence of notching and stripping is in the same direction as that of ringing, but is less pronounced because the operations themselves only partly stop translocation through the phloem.

It is evident that the effect of any of these special practices on accumulation and concentration of food materials is almost certain to be more pronounced in the summer than it is during the spring months. This explains why they so often fail to encourage the formation of fruit buds and greater fruitfulness for which they have been so frequently recommended, the period of fruit-bud differentiation having passed before their concentrating effects are realized.

The following quotation from Drinkard's[22] summary of his work in Virginia bears on this point: "Ringing at different seasons when accompanied by or preceded by spring pruning, of the branches produced no noticeable stimulation of fruit bud formation. Ringing at the time growth was resumed in the absence of spring pruning did not stimulate fruit bud formation. The treatment was given too early. Ringing at the time the foliage was fully developed in the absence of spring pruning gave the best results; however, when the treatment was given at the time the fruit buds began to become differentiated there was some stimulation to fruit bud development. Stripping at different seasons when accompanied by or preceded by spring pruning, had no stimulative effect on fruit bud formation. The effects of stripping were offset by those of spring pruning. Stripping at the three seasons already mentioned, in the absence of spring pruning, stimulated fruit bud formation uniformly."

The facts relating to food translocation and manufacture may also partly explain why ringing so frequently results in an increase in size or in some modifications of the texture or composition of the fruit that matures during late summer or in early fall. Thus Daniel[19] reports a marked increase in size of the fruits of the tomato and egg-plant from ringing; Paddock,[51] Bioletti[7] and Husman[38] have reported a similar increase in grapes. On the other hand Howe[37] found no increase in size of fruit in ringed apples, pears, cherries and plums, though he reports other late-season effects in the earlier maturity of fruit and a much earlier dropping of the foliage. Paddock[51] likewise has reported an earlier maturity of grapes borne on ringed shoots, an earliness sometimes amounting to as much as two weeks. It has been noted frequently that grapes borne on ringed shoots contain relatively less sugar and more acid[38] or are somewhat poorer in quality[51] than those borne on untreated shoots.

In the section on Fruit Setting ringed shoots of the grape and of certain other fruits are mentioned as setting in many cases a larger per-

centage of their blossoms than those not treated in this way, if the operation is performed just previous to the opening of the flowers. Seldom is
the difference great enough to make the operation worth while for this
purpose. A few varieties of the grape, however, without such treatment
grow so vigorously that they set but little fruit and with them the operation should be performed annually. Thus in the Fresno (California)
Experiment Vineyard 12-year-old ringed Panariti grafts on 10 different
resistant stocks averaged 7.5 tons per acre during 1917 and 1918, while
unringed vines on the same stocks and under the same conditions averaged 2.3 tons per acre.[38]

From the data presented here and in the section on Nutrition it
is evident that the concentrating influence of ringing, stripping and
related practices depends not alone on their effects on new vegetative
growth, leaf area and food manufacture, but also on food utilization.
In turn the utilization of the elaborated foods that are synthesized in the
shoot beyond the point of ringing depends on the available water and
nutrient supply. If the soil is comparatively dry and low in nitrates, the
effect of ringing or related practices may be quite different than with an
abundant supply of both moisture and nutrients, because the products
of synthesis beyond the ringed point may be utilized in an entirely
different manner. This factor has received very little consideration and
it must be properly evaluated before any ringing operation can be performed with certainty of its effects on either fruit bud formation or on the
development of fruit. Inadequate consideration of this factor has caused
much apparent contradiction and uncertainty in the results attending this
group of practices.

In at least one respect there is general agreement among those who
have employed ringing, stripping or other operations to check the transfer
of food. They all report a tendency to check the growth of the plant during later years and thus have a dwarfing influence. This is proportional
to the degree of starvation of the roots through separation from their supply of elaborated foods and its ultimate effect on growth and development
is in every way comparable to the results attending root pruning. It
should be mentioned also that ringing inflicts mechanical injuries that
sometimes heal slowly and for this reason alone it should be used with
great caution, if at all, on certain fruits like the plum and cherry. Apparently with the grape alone, among the common deciduous fruits, should
this group of practices be a regular cultural treatment and even in the
grape only a very few of the most vigorously growing varieties can be
ringed with profit. Other cultural treatments may be combined and
employed to better advantage to bring about the same conditions that
these special practices induce and with far less danger of undesirable
after-effects.

Summary.—In kind all top pruning may be considered either as heading back or as thinning out. These two kinds produce quite different results, particularly as the pruning increases in severity. In general, thinning out is accompanied by less new shoot growth but more new spur and fruit-bud formation than correspondingly severe heading back. Heading back tends to make trees more, and thinning out less, compact in habit. The different responses from the two methods of pruning are due probably in large part to the distinct nutritive conditions to which the practices give rise. Both methods have their places in orchard management, heading back being more useful in keeping the tree well shaped and thinning out in developing its fruiting wood and in keeping that wood in good working order. As most trees grow older they should receive relatively more thinning out and less heading back.

In kind, pruning may be coarse or fine with essential differences in the attendant responses. Coarse or bulk pruning tends to disturb seriously the equilibrium within the plant and generally results in the production of watersprouts. Careful fine pruning, on the other hand, evokes a much more general response and removes the older fruiting wood as it becomes weaker and less productive.

Root pruning has a dwarfing influence and its greatest use is in the culture of dwarf trees. The supposed influence of root pruning in promoting fruitfulness is due probably in part, if not largely, to other practices such as irrigation and fertilization which generally accompany the culture of dwarfs. That which is done incident to cultivation, especially just before and during the period of fruit setting, is likely to reduce yield.

Girdling, notching, ringing and stripping are special practices, related to pruning, which have for their object the promotion of fruitfulness through interrupting the translocation of foods. Their use is attended by uncertain results and they are not to be recommended under average conditions.

CHAPTER XXIV

PRUNING—THE SEASON

The subject of pruning has been shown to present three major aspects, one of which is a consideration of the varying response from pruning at different seasons. Theoretically at least this involves a study of the different effects from pruning each successive month, or perhaps at more frequent intervals. Practically the question is much less complicated, involving principally a comparison of the effects attending pruning during the growing season with those following winter pruning.

Pruning at Different Times during the Dormant Season.—Pruning at different times during the dormant period may, however, receive brief consideration. Dormant or winter pruning is generally understood to mean late winter or early spring pruning, since it is usually done then. Winter pruning, however, may begin as soon as the plants become more or less dormant in the fall and may continue into the spring until vegetation is starting actively. The supposed advantages and disadvantages of pruning at different times during the dormant period have been long discussed. Apparently so far as any effect on the amount and character of subsequent growth is concerned there is little or no difference. This is brought out clearly by experimental work with apples in England[5] and in Minnesota[10] and with grapes in New York.[31] On the other hand since there is a gradual translocation of food materials from the canes to the trunk and roots of the grape during a 3- or 4-weeks period following leaf fall,[72] pruning before this translocation is complete or after the reverse movement has begun in the spring should result in a somewhat greater check to vigorous growth of the vine than a corresponding pruning during the period between these extremes. This effect has been noted both in France[56] and in California.[7]

In California the time of winter pruning has been found to be important in determining when grape vines of the Vinifera group start growth. Vines pruned immediately after the fall of the leaves started earliest; those pruned in midwinter started about 4 days later and those pruned considerably later, when bleeding commenced, were delayed about 6 days. "Pruning when the terminal buds commenced to swell retarded the lower buds 11 days, and, when the terminal buds had grown 2 or 3 inches, 20 days."[7] In other words the lateness of starting of the buds was in the order of the lateness of the pruning.

In commenting on some of the practical applications of these facts in grape culture in California Bioletti[7] remarks: "The retardation of the starting of the shoots in the spring may be a valuable means of escaping the injurious effects of spring frosts. In one of our tests, the crop on nine rows pruned Mar. 13, was saved, while that of 12 rows pruned Nov. 19, and Dec. 21, was completely ruined by a frost on Apr. 21. Late pruning also retards the blossoming though somewhat less than it does the starting. Pruning as late as March may retard the blossoming 10 days. The time of ripening is also influenced slightly in the same direction. When spring frosts occur, this influence appears to be reversed. The vines pruned early may blossom and ripen their fruit later. This is because the frost having destroyed the first shoots, the only flowers and fruit which appear are on buds which have started after the frost . . .

"Pruning may be done, therefore, in frostless locations and with varieties which set their fruit well, at any time when the vines are without leaves. Where spring frosts are common the pruning should be as near the time of the swelling of the buds as possible. The benefits of late pruning without its inconveniences can be obtained by the system of 'double' or (clean) pruning practiced in some regions. This may be applied in various ways. The simplest is to shear off all the canes to a length of 15 to 18 inches at any time during the winter that is convenient. This permits plowing and other cultural operations, and the final pruning is done in April. A better method is to prune the vine as usual but to leave the spurs with four or five extra buds. These spurs we then shortened back to the proper length as late as practicable. In some cases the method practiced in the Medoc may be used. This consists in leaving a foot or 15 inches of cane beyond the last bud needed and removing all the extra buds at the time of pruning. The base buds are said to be retarded by the length of cane above them the presence of buds on the cane having no effect."

Pruning late in the dormant season is quite likely to be attended by more or less bleeding. Seldom is the amount great enough to be harmful though many growers prefer to avoid any. In a few species, as for example, the English walnut, late pruned trees may bleed very profusely and the moist exposed surfaces offer an excellent opportunity for infection. For this reason, if for no other, fall pruning may occasionally be preferable to spring pruning. When dormant-season pruning is delayed until the buds swell or start to open, there is likely to be more injury to fruit spurs and buds due to breakage as the pruned limbs are pulled out of the tree.

Summer Pruning.—In the discussion of the effects attending various amounts of winter pruning there was shown to be a slower net increase in size with pruned than with unpruned trees and the more severe pruning was shown to have the more pronounced retarding influence. Similar results generally follow summer pruning and for about the same reasons. The real question is whether or not summer pruning has a greater retarding effect than a correspondingly severe winter pruning of the same kind.

Influence on Vegetative Growth.—The new shoots and leaves in the spring are built chiefly at the expense of food materials formed the preceding season and stored through the winter. After the leaves are fully expanded they become manufacturing organs and eventually return to the plant a supply of elaborated foods equal to or in excess of that consumed in their development. At first, however, their growth is in effect parasitic and it is not until they have been active for some time that they have fully replaced the materials used in their growth. Summer pruning removes them after they have levied their tax on the tree's reserve foods and often before they have contributed much to its welfare. It must have, generally, a greater retarding influence on net increase in size than a correspondingly heavy winter pruning. This devitalizing effect of summer pruning has been noted by many observers and recently has been the subject of a number of experimental studies.

Alderman and Auchter[1] found that young summer pruned apple trees averaged only 120 feet of new shoot growth in 1915 while winter pruned trees of the same age and of the same varieties averaged 188 to 216, according to the severity of the pruning. The summer pruned trees increased in spread, height and circumference more rapidly than trees pruned very severely in the winter, but much less rapidly than those pruned moderately or lightly in the winter. Apple trees just coming into bearing produced, after winter pruning, shoots that were 20 to 50 per cent longer and 10 to 20 per cent thicker than those on summer pruned trees. In one orchard under investigation they found that the total leaf area of summer pruned trees averaged only from 299 to 459 square feet, that of trees pruned both summer and winter averaged from 527 to 794 square feet and that of trees pruned only during the winter averaged from 660 to 1,144 square feet. Not only were there fewer leaves on the summer pruned trees, but these leaves averaged smaller in size. The leaves of the summer pruned trees were paler and yellowish, suggesting an additional reduction in their photosynthetic abilities. Arkansas and York Imperial trees in full bearing, on the other hand, showed practically no difference in the responses to summer and to winter pruning. In fact the summer pruned trees of middle age produced more terminal shoot growth than those pruned lightly during the dormant season, though somewhat less than those pruned heavily. Table 14 presents

TABLE 14.—RELATIVE LENGTH OF NEW SHOOTS OF THE PLUM, CUT BACK AT
DIFFERENT DATES
(After Bedford and Pickering[5])

May 27	July 14	Nov. 2	Mar. 16	May 15	July 14	Not cut back
1905	1905	1905	1906	1906	1906	
125	75	100	100	65	18	67

data obtained in England from pruning back weak declining plum trees at various seasons. The figures show the relative lengths of the new shoot growth. In this case the July pruning was little short of disastrous to the trees. Certain experimental results obtained in Virginia from various summer and winter prunings combined with special practices such as ringing, stripping and root pruning, show, despite some apparent inconsistencies, that pruning during the growing season checks new shoot formation and increment in trunk circumference more than does winter pruning.[23] Batchelor and Goodspeed,[4] reporting an experiment with young bearing Jonathan and Gano apple trees in Utah, state that summer pruning caused reduced vitality, though their figures show that the average length of the new shoots under both pruning treatments was practically the same during the 3 years for which the data are given.

Summer pruning, however, does not always retard growth more than winter pruning. Experiments in New Jersey showed that peach trees

TABLE 15.—INFLUENCE OF EARLY SUMMER PRUNING ON SHOOT DEVELOPMENT
IN YOUNG APPLE TREES
(*After Gardner*[26])

Variety	Pruning treatment	Average shoot growth removed by winter pruning, centimeters	Average shoot growth removed by summer pruning, centimeters	Average total shoot growth for season, centimeters	Average net gain of tree in shoot length for season, centimeters
Wagener	Winter pruned only	538	....	2690	2152
Wagener	Winter and summer pruned	533	1611	4250	2106
Yellow Newtown	Unpruned	...	....	2720	2720
Yellow Newtown	Winter pruned only	826	....	3460	2634
Yellow Newtown	Winter and summer pruned	488	1904	4930	2548
Jonathan	Unpruned	...	....	3576	3576
Jonathan	Winter pruned only	967	....	5165	4198
Jonathan	Winter and summer pruned	941	3837	7430	2652
Grimes	Unpruned	...	....	2270	2770
Grimes	Winter pruned only	988	....	2965	1977
Grimes	Winter and summer pruned	501	1603	4360	2256

pruned during the dormant season averaged 3,821 inches of new shoot growth in 1916, while those pruned in the summer averaged 4,227.[9] Though this difference is perhaps not much above experimental error, it at least indicates that summer pruning does not always have a dwarfing influence. In Table 15 are presented data obtained in Oregon showing the influence on shoot development in young apples of rather severe early summer pruning. In kind and in severity the summer pruning treatment was practically identical with that given in the winter. In every instance the summer pruned trees produced more total shoot growth—58 per cent. in the Wagener trees, 44 per cent. in Yellow New-town, 44 per cent. in Jonathan and 47 per cent. in Grimes—than those that were pruned during the dormant season only. A part of this increased growth came before the time of summer pruning (about July 1), but the larger part of it was produced during the summer months follow-ing the pruning. The growth produced before the time of summer prun-ing is to be regarded as the consequence of a summer pruning treatment of the same kind the preceding season; the growth after the pruning was a direct response to that pruning. There was practically no difference between the summer and winter pruned trees in their net increase in size, except in Jonathan. The winter pruned trees of that variety showed a greater net growth, principally on account of the great amount of wood removed by the summer treatment. Vincent[73] in Idaho has reported the 11-year record of an apple orchard of Jonathan, Rome, Grimes and Wage-ner a part of which received only winter pruning from the start while the other part received only summer pruning (Aug. 6 to Sept. 6). In kind and amount the pruning of the two portions was as nearly alike as possi-ble. Table 16 summarizes some of the growth records of these trees. For the most part the average heights, widths and trunk circumferences were slightly greater in the winter pruned than in the summer pruned trees, while the reverse was true in regard to average shoot lengths. In no case, however, were the differences large enough to be significant. Clearly, summer pruning exerted no dwarfing influence in this orchard.

These almost diametrically opposite results attending summer pruning in carefully controlled experimental work can be harmonized. The tree is to be regarded as a system in mobile equilibrium. This equilib-rium involves a condition of balance between part and part and between constituent and constituent within the plant and a condition of adjust-ment to the environment without. Chief among these factors of environ-ment are temperature, light, moisture and food supply. Growth of any kind is a response to the condition of the equilibrium within and of the adjustment without. Pruning, at any time—and more especially summer pruning—disturbs both the adjustment to the environment without and the balance within. The immediate effect on the tree as a whole of any summer pruning is to reduce the carbohydrate supply and the rate of carbohydrate manufacture and at the same time to increase the supply of water and other nutrients, particularly nitrates, that is available to the rest of the plant. The size or amount of this influence depends on: (1) the severity, (2) the kind and (3) the time of the pruning and on (4) the moisture and (5) the nutrient supply available in the soil. Its general effect on growth therefore may be expected to correspond closely to that of fertilization and irrigation at that particular time. If the pruning is not severe enough to reduce carbohydrate supply and carbohydrate manufacture to the point where they limit new

TABLE 16.—GROWTH RECORDS OF SUMMER- AND WINTER-PRUNED APPLE TREES IN IDAHO

(*After Vincent*[73])

Variety	Pruning	Average shoot length eleventh year, inches	Average height eleventh year, feet	Average width eleventh year, feet	Average diameter eleventh year, inches
Jonathan..........	Winter	16.1	17.24	19.51	7.43
Jonathan..........	Summer	18.2	15.98	17.71	7.35
Rome.............	Winter	15.4	15.88	14.35	6.58
Rome.............	Summer	14.8	15.75	13.60	6.56
Grimes...........	Winter	12.7	16.00	15.30	6.71
Grimes...........	Summer	16.2	15.38	14.67	6.32
Wagener..........	Winter	11.9	14.65	12.25	5.82
Wagener..........	Summer	12.4	14.36	12.95	5.61

tissue formation, active growth ensues. This apparently is the explanation of the results obtained with young peach trees in New Jersey[9] and with young apple trees in Oregon.[26] Soil conditions were such and the pruning was such, in time, kind and severity, that a vigorous new vegetative growth was promoted following the pruning and terminal bud formation was completed at a considerably later date. This condition may frequently result in an actual increase of food reserves at the time of leaf abscission, especially in sections with a late growing season, because of the greatly increased leaf surface. On the other hand if the pruning is of such character that carbohydrates and other elaborated foods are removed in considerable quantity and if it is done at a time when soil and tree conditions do not stimulate later growth the same season, there is not only an immediate reduction in size but reserves for the following season are depleted and growth the next year will be correspondingly restricted. Summer pruning under such conditions has a distinct dwarfing influence.

In conclusion, then, it may be stated that summer pruning does not necessarily have either a dwarfing or an invigorating influence. It may have the one or the other, depending on the severity, kind and time of pruning (as related to the state of development of the plant, rather than to the exact date on which the pruning may be done). Environmental conditions also, particularly nutrient supply, soil moisture and light, influence greatly the nature of the response from summer pruning. Consequently it should be employed as an orchard practice only when due consideration is given the several factors on which its results depend. The amateur or the careless grower cannot use it safely. The careful student of fruit growing can often employ it with reasonable certainty of the results and frequently will find it of great value. The results attending summer pruning in some of the best managed cane fruit plantations furnish ample evidence of this effect.

Influence on Production.—The grower, however, is interested particularly in knowing whether or not certain specific objectives can be accomplished—or accomplished more readily—by doing the work at one season rather than at another. This really is the question leading to most of the discussion over summer pruning.

The opinion receiving general acceptance is expressed in the proverb, "prune in winter for wood and in summer for fruit." Quintinye[55] states that summer pruning leads to the formation of fruit buds for the following crop. Hovey,[36] referring particularly to the apple and pear, states that it leads to the formation of fruit spurs and thus indirectly aids in fruit production. Quinn[54] recommends pinching back in summer to promote fruitfulness in the pear and Barry[3] recommends this practice even more generally for the same purpose. Waugh[75] states that summer pruning tends to promote fruit-bud formation. Cole,[17] Downing[21] and many others recommend summer pruning in preference to winter pruning, but because wounds made at that time heal more readily than those made at other seasons. On the other hand Pearson[53] states that summer pruning may either promote or repress fruitfulness, depending on how it is done. The general idea is that fruitfulness is promoted by summer pruning through checking growth or weakening the plant.

Though the majority of the opinions just cited are from American writers, it should perhaps be stated that it is in European countries that the practice is most commonly employed and that it is in those countries that it is generally believed to be of particular value in promoting fruitfulness. In America there is a much greater diversity of opinion. Much of the apparent difference in results attending summer pruning in this country and in Europe is to be explained through the difference in the methods employed. The growers of this country mean by the term summer pruning a pruning similar in kind and in amount to that ordinarily done during the dormant season. On the other hand, summer pruning to the European fruit grower means something entirely different—for the most part a pinching or at least a pruning that can be done largely "with the thumb and forefinger." This type of pruning is employed in America neither in summer nor in winter. As explained later under Pinching the practice of summer pruning commonly employed in Europe is hardly applicable here because of economic considerations and consequently the extensive European literature on summer pruning is only of incidental interest to most American fruit growers.

In the section on Nutrition, data are presented showing that vigor of growth and productiveness are not necessarily antagonistic qualities. Indeed, the largest yields are always obtained from rather vigorous plants. The belief that increased fruitfulness should follow summer pruning as generally practiced in America, is therefore based on two assumptions, both of which are fundamentally wrong. This is shown by some of the more recent investigations in this particular field—notably those in Virginia,[23] West Virginia[1] and Utah.[4] All these showed decreased production of flower clusters or decreased yields of fruit following the summer pruning of young trees just coming into bearing or with their bearing habits not yet well established and all report an accompanying decrease in vegetative growth. In one of the West Virginia experiments the yield of the summer pruned trees averaged barely a third of the yield from those receiving winter pruning. On the other hand Bedford and Pickering[5] in one series of experiments found flower-bud formation following summer pruning greater by 13 to 41 per cent. than following winter pruning, depending on the time of operation. Alderman and Auchter,[1] who found summer pruning a considerable check to fruit production in apple trees just coming into bearing, report no such general influence on mature trees. Table 17 summarizes the yields obtained in Idaho over a 7-year period from winter and from summer pruned plots. In every variety under trial summer pruning resulted in an increased yield.

TABLE 17.—AVERAGE YIELDS IN POUNDS PER TREE FROM WINTER- AND SUMMER-PRUNED TREES

(*After Vincent*[73])

Variety	Pruning	Yields							
		1910, pounds	1911, pounds	1912, pounds	1913, pounds	1914, pounds	1915, pounds	1916, pounds	Total, pounds
Jonathan....	Winter	29.0	35.3	95.5	127.8	257.4	50.3	239.4	834.7
Jonathan....	Summer	33.9	21.3	95.5	144.3	252.1	51.7	272.1	870.9
Rome.......	Winter	13.9	65.2	52.5	58.8	76.8	18.7	105.7	391.6
Rome.......	Summer	13.9	30.0	58.5	85.0	80.0	23.0	160.4	450.8
Grimes......	Winter	13.2	61.0	85.1	101.6	128.7	102.1	197.3	689.0
Grimes......	Summer	20.0	71.0	99.5	195.5	88.5	155.6	108.3	738.4
Wagener....	Winter	29.0	17.2	67.0	22.0	83.7	6.2	177.4	402.5
Wagener....	Summer	54.3	59.4	123.2	50.8	159.0	27.2	215.5	689.4

In commenting on these increases Vincent[73] says: "If the entire orchard had been summer-pruned there would have been an increase per acre during the 7 years as follows: Jonathan, 30.02 boxes or an increase of 4.28 boxes per year; Rome, 49.7 boxes, or an increase of 7.1 boxes per year; Grimes, 50.6 boxes or an increase of 6.07 boxes, per year; Wagener, 240.9 boxes or an increase of 34.4 boxes per year. Summer pruning therefore has increased crop production on all the plats and quite substantially on the Wagener."

In neither the mature West Virginia trees nor the Idaho trees was summer pruning attended by an appreciably decreased vegetative growth.

At first glance these records of yields from summer and winter pruned trees seem contradictory. As is the case with the corresponding records of shoot growth, however, they can be reconciled. It has been pointed out that fruit production depends on (1) the formation of fruit-producing wood and (2) on the proper functioning of that wood. Furthermore, different kinds of fruits have quite unlike fruiting habits and the processes culminating in fruit production may be quite different in one from those in another. The effect of summer pruning on fruitfulness, therefore, is not a simple question, but rather a series of questions each of which must be answered in turn.

Among the major aspects of the summer pruning problem may be stated the following: (1) The concentrating effects of different kinds and amounts of pruning at various times during the growing season. (2) The relation of diverse summer pruning treatments to shoot growth both of the current and of the following season. (3) The influence on new spur formation. (4) The effect on fruit bud formation—on spurs and on shoots. (5) The relation to the intake of nutrients and to the manufacture, translocation, storage and utilization of elaborated foods. (6) The influence on color and size of fruit. These questions are not entirely distinct; they are inter-related and inter-dependent. Since few data are available concerning some of them, any discussion at this time must of necessity be incomplete. It is attempted here on a few aspects only of the general problem, those which have more or less immediate practical bearing and on which the evidence seems reliable.

Summer Pruning to Develop Framework.—Data have been presented concerning the influences of summer pruning on vegetative growth in general and on new shoot formation in particular. No further attention is devoted here to this problem except to indicate a rather special use of early summer pruning in developing the framework of young, strong, vigorously growing trees.

Trees of many kinds growing under favorable conditions often develop shoots 2½ or 3 feet—and sometimes more—in length during their second, third and fourth seasons in the orchard. Occasionally they make such growth their first season and shoots of this character are not at all uncommon as the trees grow older. Ordinarily most of this shoot growth is cut away in the annual dormant season pruning, some being taken out entirely and the terminal half or even three-fourths of each remaining shoot generally being removed. This heavy cutting back is necessary for securing a strong framework and a compact type of growth. The question naturally arises whether these trees can be pruned in midsummer shortly after the shoots have attained a length equaling that to which they would be cut back at the usual winter pruning. This would then be followed by the production of secondary lateral shoots, many of which could be saved with little or no heading back at the following winter pruning. In this way two steps in the construction of the framework of the tree would be taken in one season and theoretically a year would be saved in growing the tree to producing size and in bringing it into bearing. This type of summer pruning, which includes both thinning and heading early in the summer (about July 1) was studied with apples in Oregon.[26] Though such varieties as Jonathan, Grimes, Yellow Newtown and Wagener summer pruned in this way did not make the equivalent of two seasons' ordinary growth in one summer, three successive years of such treatment resulted in trees comparable in size, fruit spur development and productiveness to winter pruned trees a year older. In other words a year had been gained in developing their framework and in bringing them into bearing. Observation led to the belief that this method of pruning is equally valuable in forcing the early development of both pears and sweet cherries. This special pruning practice is desirable with young trees only under favorable growing conditions when they are making new shoots at least $2\frac{1}{2}$ feet in length and where the growing season is long enough to permit a proper maturity of the late secondary shoots.

Summer Pruning as a Conservation Measure.—It has been stated before that the removal of any living portion of the top of a plant at any time deprives the plant of a certain amount of elaborated food material. This is true particularly of pruning in summer when the storage tissues have been depleted for the building of new structures. However, the removal of any portion of the top reduces somewhat the demand on the root system for nutrients and moisture; under certain conditions this reduction may enable the roots to supply the remaining parts with amounts nearer their requirements for growth. In this way pruning can be said to have a stimulating influence. In other words, it may be regarded as a conservation measure, making given amounts of moisture and nutrients go farther; because these larger amounts of materials are available, certain parts may manufacture and store more elaborated foods than they could otherwise. This may be considered a concentration effect. The concentration is limited to certain parts and in some instances other parts may suffer and perhaps the plant as a whole may be weakened. Apparently one of the more important objectives that may be accomplished by pruning during the growing season is due to this influence.

This effect of summer pruning depends on many factors. Among the more important are: (1) the severity of the pruning, (2) its kind, (3) the exact stage of development of the plant at the time the pruning is done and (4) the soil conditions before, at the time of and after the operation.

Independent of the other factors, it is evident that, within certain limits, the more severe the pruning the greater will be its effect in diverting into the remaining parts nutrients and moisture. However, a point is always reached, unless the operation is performed shortly before the beginning of the dormant season, when an increase in the severity of the pruning results in forcing into growth buds that otherwise would remain dormant until the following spring. At this point its general effect changes from conservation to dissipation since the new tissues demand not only soil nutrients and moisture but elaborated foods as well. The branches, canes or shoots remaining and perhaps the whole plant, are left weaker in that they are likely to enter the dormant season less richly supplied with elaborated food materials. In general the conservation effects of any pruning cease when it promotes greater utilization of reserve foods in the building of new tissue. Were these effects (that is, the ratio that they bear to the total effects) of summer pruning plotted in a curve as they vary with the severity of the pruning this curve would start close to the 100 per cent value with very light pruning and fall steadily with each increase in severity until the zero point is reached. Furthermore this general situation would obtain regardless of the kind of the pruning or of the exact time of the operation, though in no two cases could the curves be expected to be exactly parallel.

Closely related to the stimulating effect of varying amounts of summer pruning is the influence of the stage of seasonal development at which it is done. In general a very early summer pruning, particularly if it consists in thinning out, is most effective in diverting the energies of the plant into other developing or already developed tissues. It may lead to greater elongation of shoots, to shorter internodes and more leaves, possibly to the formation of side branches or to several other growth responses or it may simply result in a more efficient functioning of the remaining tissues. This, for instance, is the general effect of the prompt removal of watersprouts, suckers or other shoots just as they are starting. If the pruning is done a little later, during the period of most rapid vegetative growth, it may have a concentrating effect (that is, lead to the greater accumulation of elaborated foods) or it may have the opposite effect and force out a crop of secondary shoots, the kind of the response varying with the severity and kind of the pruning. Pruning late in the growing season, if not too severe, is almost sure to have a concentrating effect (for the particular parts affected), since no new growth will take place to utilize the stored foods and there will be still further accumulations resulting from the increased supply of nutrients and of light.

Of the two kinds of summer pruning, thinning out generally has a much greater concentrating effect than heading back. The latter practice, unless it consists in a mere pinching out of the terminals or unless it comes very late in the season, results immediately in the formation of numerous secondary lateral branches. Their development consumes food materials that have been, or are being, manufactured and results in a shading of leaves lower in the tree and possibly in reduced rates of photosynthesis and of food manufacture. However, a light heading back or pinching of the terminals of the grape early in the season, thus temporarily checking new shoot growth, is said to aid materially the setting of fruit in certain varieties.[7] This is a concentration effect, though the practice is of special rather than general application. On the other hand thinning out has no such tendency to encourage the development of secondary shoots; certainly they are not formed to anything like the same extent as with summer heading. More light is admitted to the interior of the plant which is better supplied with nutrients and moisture and the result is an increased accumulation of elaborated foods. The results attending a well distributed thinning of the shoots and smaller branches would be more pronounced in this direction than those following a coarse or bulk thinning.

When soil conditions, particularly moisture and nutrient supply, encourage new vegetative growth, summer pruning is much less likely to exert concentrating effects than it is when less moisture and less nitrogen are available. Indeed its influence may be the reverse, particularly if the summer pruning has been mainly heading back. Generally speaking, it is easier to secure the concentration effects of summer pruning when the available soil moisture and nitrates are not too high and when atmospheric conditions favor a high transpiration rate. These, it will be recognized, are the conditions under which it has been suggested by Chandler[13] that summer pruning can be employed advantageously as a moisture-conserving measure to prevent the wilting of partly grown fruits on heavily laden and vigorously growing trees. The influence of certain summer pruning practices on the formation of fruit buds, discussed a little later, is probably due to their concentrating effect.

In a general way it may be stated that summer pruning is often very useful because of its influence in diverting the energies of the plant into other channels. In the average plant most of the watersprouts and suckers (except those used for renewal purposes) are worse than useless. They dissipate energies and yield little in return. Their prompt removal is a conservation measure and is particularly important in certain fruits like the grape and in nearly all young trees. The longer the delay in cutting them out the less is gained by removing them. Practically the same statement holds for the early summer removal of a portion of the barren shoots in the grape and certain other plants. Midsummer or late summer pruning may be desirable occasionally, in so far as it reduces transpiration losses and indirectly aids in the sizing and coloration of the fruit.

It should be reiterated that the concentrating effect of pruning does not necessarily invigorate the plant as a whole. In fact it may have exactly the opposite influence, though certain parts are favored by the process. Thus a heavily laden peach tree pruned in late July as a protection against drought is probably weakened by the operation and may show the effects in the new growth put out the following spring, though the pruning operation enabled the fruit to mature properly. The situation is simply another aspect of a problem constantly encountered in pruning practice—that of subordinating or even eliminating one part in the interest of another.

Influence on New Spur Formation.—The influence of summer pruning on new shoot formation and consequently on the fruit-producing wood in plants bearing on shoots or canes has been discussed. There remains consideration of its influence on new spur formation. Spurs are generally formed from lateral buds on the long growths of the current or of the preceding season. Only a certain percentage of these grow out into spurs, the number depending on many factors, among the more important of which are (1) the supply of nutrients and elaborated food materials available for their growth and (2) the relative stage of development or the size of the buds themselves. The influence of summer pruning on the supply of available foods has just been considered under the head of Concentration; consequently that aspect of the question need not be discussed further.

Observation shows that in almost all species there are considerable differences in the size of the lateral buds on the long growths or shoots. Usually those on the basal portion are small and inclined to remain dormant unless stimulated into growth by some special pruning or other treatment; the buds on the median and terminal portions of the shoot are better developed and grow out readily, to form either shoots or spurs. Apparently their greater size and development are due largely to the better light supply and to the more favorable location for food manufacture, of the leaves that subtended them. Obviously almost any pruning and particularly any summer pruning will influence the amount of light reaching the leaves on the remaining shoots. In many fruits summer heading back, unless very light and done comparatively late in the season, encourages the formation of laterals or secondary shoots and consequently produces poorer conditions for photosynthesis in the lower parts of the plant. At the same time, as shown later under Pinching, it results in thickening the bark on the lower portion of the shoot and therefore in different food storage conditions that are associated with the change in the relative proportions of the several tissues. These effects may outweigh in importance those occasioned by greater shading. There is reason to believe that in at least some fruits summer heading acts as a stimulus to fruit-bud formation on the current season's shoots. On the other hand thinning out admits more light to the leaves on the lower part of the shoots and thus encourages the elaboration of foods and the formation of larger and stronger buds. Summer thinning therefore tends to encourage fruit-spur formation. This is in a sense another concentrating effect of summer pruning. It is evident from what has been said that the earlier in the season the pruning is done the greater is its influence in this direction.

Gardner[26] has reported that in young apple trees not yet in bearing greatly increased fruit-spur formation follows early summer pruning in addition to winter pruning. This is not so much because of the better spur production from the buds left on the primary shoots after the summer pruning as because after the pruning many secondary shoots are produced on which the buds grow out readily to form new spurs the following season. In apples nearly all the buds on these late summer secondary shoots enter the winter in practically the same condition as, and are comparable in every way to, the buds on the median and terminal portions of the primary shoots.[45] In fact one of the most useful purposes served by the early summer pruning of young vigorously growing spur bearing trees like the apple is to increase the number of spurs over that secured by winter pruning alone. It is worthy of mention that spurs developing from these secondary late summer shoots are as a rule especially strong, vigorous and likely to produce fruit buds.

Influence on Fruit-bud Formation.—In the section on Nutrition it is shown that, in all cases studied, fruit-bud differentiation is associated with carbohydrate accumulation in the immediate vicinity of the buds concerned. The work of Magness[46] on young apple trees indicates that this accumulation takes place principally where there is the greatest effective leaf area. In other words, within certain limits those spurs that have the largest and best lighted leaves accumulate the largest reserves of carbohydrates and differentiate the most fruit buds. He found that by partial or complete defoliation of spurs well supplied with leaves, fruit-bud formation on these spurs could be entirely prevented, even though adjacent spurs retaining their full complements of leaves formed fruit buds freely. Similarly he found that the formation of lateral fruit buds took place only in the axils of good sized, well lighted leaves.

Magness[46] summarizes his results as follows: "Fruit-bud initiation will not take place, and fruit buds will not form in most varieties in the absence of a fair amount of leaf area in the tree.

"Food material stored in the tree through the dormant season is apparently stored largely in the tissue adjacent to the leaves in which it was manufactured. This is shown by the fact that the defoliated portion does not develop as strongly and well during the spring following the treatment, as does the undefoliated portion.

"Leaf area in one part of the tree will usually not supply food material to the buds in another part to the extent necessary to cause them to become fruit buds. Defoliating one-half of a tree has little influence upon the undefoliated portion, but that part which is defoliated functions as it would if all the leaves had been removed from the whole tree.

"Removing the same number of leaves, without any pruning, has practically the same effect upon the fruit-bud formation for the immediate year following that a summer pruning, removing leaves from the same position, would have.

"Buds on 1-year wood, in areas from which the leaves have been removed are slower in starting out into growth, and make a weaker growth the following spring than do other buds on the same shoots not defoliated. This is more noticeable in some varieties than in others.

"One shoot seems to be very largely independent of other shoots about it so far as fruit-bud formation is concerned. It is apparently largely dependent upon its own leaves for nourishment.

"Removing leaves from individual spurs tends to prevent the formation of fruit buds upon those spurs, although it does not entirely check the development of flower parts.

"On those spurs which form fruit buds, notwithstanding defoliation, the blossoms are, on the average, considerably later in opening in the spring.

"Axillary buds of the Wagener seem to be almost entirely dependent upon the immediate subtending leaf for the carbohydrate supply with which they are nourished. Removing the subtending leaf entirely prevents fruit-bud formation. Buds so treated either remained entirely dormant during the following growing season or pushed out into very weak growth. Very few of them showed a development approaching normal."

Magness' work may explain incidentally why the basal portions of shoots often produce relatively fewer fruit buds than the median and terminal portions. The basal portions are poorly lighted and, assuming leaves of equal size, they would manufacture smaller amounts of elaborated foods. Neither spurs nor shoots can be expected to differentiate fruit buds freely if they are heavily shaded. Summer pruning, however, may admit more light both to the spurs and to the basal portions of the shoots at the same time it concentrates the supply of nutrients. This direct influence on the factors associated with fruit-bud formation could hardly help but influence more or less directly the relative number of fruit buds. Obviously early summer pruning comprising thinning out instead of heading back would have the greatest influence of this kind. No pruning practice after fruit-bud formation for the season is completed could conceivably have any influence in this direction and heading back with the formation of many secondary lateral branches would cause still heavier shading and reduce rather than increase fruit-bud formation. Doubtless many of the cases in which summer pruning has failed to produce an increased number of fruit buds have been due to its consisting mainly in heading back or being done too late to have any important influence in this direction. Experience shows that a light or moderate early summer thinning of the shoots of those trees such as the peach that bear laterally on shoots may aid in the formation of fruit buds on the basal and median portions of those shoots. In general, however, the total number of buds is reduced by the summer pruning, and not infrequently yields also are reduced.[28]

Influence on Fruit Color and Quality.—In the apple, peach and certain other fruits the development of the red colors in the skin of the fruit depends mainly on sunlight. With those fruits summer pruning naturally influences their coloration, particularly if the pruning consists mainly in thinning out. Vincent[73] reports that summer, as compared with winter, pruning the apple in Idaho resulted in an increase of 33 per cent. of extra fancy apples in Jonathan, 32 per cent. in Rome and 5 per cent. in Wagener, the grading being mainly on the basis of standard commercial color requirements. The coloring of certain other fruits, as plums and grapes, does not depend on light reaching the fruit itself, though pigment formation depends on carbohydrate manufacture in near by leaves. Consequently summer pruning is of less direct aid in the coloration of these fruits. Bioletti,[7] however, states that judicious summer pruning may occasionally favor the coloring of the fruit in certain grape varieties. Presumably this influence is exercised through the better lighting of the foliage near the fruit clusters.

Most fruits develop their color late in the growing season or shortly before ripening. Consequently summer pruning to promote a better coloring of the fruit may be done comparatively late. In pruning for this purpose caution should be exercised; too severe or too early summer pruning is likely to result in more or less sunburn of the fruit. The effect of summer pruning on composition of fruit will, likewise, vary with conditions. If it is not so severe that there is ample foliage left for the manufacture of foods for the developing or ripening fruit, quality will not be injured. But where photosynthetic processes are seriously reduced, quality is sure to be impaired. Wellington has reported both delayed maturity and a reduction in sugar content of grapes of as much as 7.6 per cent. attending rather heavy summer pruning.[76]

Summer Pinching.—It is impossible to distinguish clearly between what is termed pinching and what is usually termed topping or heading back. The difference between the operations is simply in the maturity of the tissues at the time the operation is performed and in the relative amount of new growth removed. In some species, as for example the brambles, pinching leads to considerable branching of the pinched shoots; in many others it may be attended by very little branching, one or two of the subterminal buds promptly growing out to replace the leader. Consequently its general effect may be concentration or dissipation and dilution, depending on the species and on conditions. Summer pinching has been much used in European fruit growing and in the growing of fruits under glass. In this country it has been used mainly with the brambles and with grapes, though occasionally it is helpful in checking or directing growth in some of the other fruits.

There seems to be much difference of opinion among growers and investigators as to the wisdom of summer pinching of brambles. Both satisfactory and unsatisfactory results have been reported. Apparently much depends on the time of the operation; furthermore varieties respond quite differently to the same treatment. Macoun[44] has reported that at Ottawa, Canada, red raspberries pinched back in early summer and thus forced to branch, generally yield less than untreated plants. Since Kenyon, Loudon, King, Hansell and Miller (red raspberries) do not branch freely, they should never be summer pinched.[68] The main advantage claimed for summer pinching is that it results in a lower, more compact, bushy plant with mechanically stronger canes than those that are unheaded and unbranched. Consequently they hold up their fruit better and require less trellising. Dewberries which usually require trellising are seldom summer pinched. It is generally agreed that if raspberries or blackberries are to be summer pinched the operation should be performed early, when the shoots are only 18 to 24 inches high or perhaps even before this.[12] Pinching higher or cutting back to this point at a later date is likely to result in weak, late-maturing laterals that are especially subject to winter injury and are less likely to give rise the following year to good fruiting shoots. Blackberries and black raspberries generally respond better than red raspberries to summer pinching. Pinching the ends of the growing shoots just before blossoming has been stated to aid sometimes in the setting of fruit in the grape; it is thus a partial remedy for "coulure."[77] Bioletti[7] mentions pinching as sometimes useful also in protecting grapes from sunburn by causing the shoots, through more rapid lignification, to remain more upright and to furnish more shade for the fruit clusters. But little evidence is available concerning the influence of summer pinching on fruit-bud formation in the grape and at present it cannot be recommended confidently for any effect of this sort.

The early and repeated pinching back of shoots of the apple and pear to stimulate the development of fruit spurs and fruit buds has been discussed freely. Thomas[70] states that "by pinching off the soft ends of the side-shoots after they have made a few inches of growth—the sap immediately accumulates, and the young buds upon the remainder of these shoots, which otherwise would produce leaves, are gradually changed into fruit buds. To prevent the breaking of these buds into new shoots by too great an accumulation of the sap, partial outlet is left for its escape through the leading shoot of the branch, which at the same time is effecting the desired enlargement of the tree. . . . It often happens, and especially when the pinching is done too early, that the new buds send out shoots a second time the same season. When this occurs, these second shoots are to be pinched in the same manner as the first, but shorter; and third ones, should they start, are to be similarly treated." Barry,[3] Rivers[60] and others recommend the same treatment for the same purpose and these early authorities have been followed by many later writers. Recently Ballard and Volck[74] in California have shown that, by two or three repeated summer pinchings, fruit spurs bearing fruit buds can be developed from watersprouts of the apple in one season. They found also that normal shoots throughout the tree respond in the same way to similar treatment. Gaucher[30] recommends early summer pinching in spurs which are growing out into vegetative shoots. He states this pinching usually stops further growth from the terminal bud and forces out at lower points on the spur lateral buds that otherwise would remain latent. These then develop into branch spurs that often form fruit buds the first season. If a single pinching does not result in fruit-spur and fruit-bud formation, a second pinching is recommended.

Goumy[32] studied the influence of summer pinching on the subsequent development of bark and wood; some of his results are summarized in Table 18. Pinching obviously has led to a proportionally greater development of the bark. Goumy found also some difference between the relative amounts of bark and of wood in the spurs on the year old growth of pinched and unpinched spurs. The determination of just what these differences in relative amounts of bark and wood signify in terms of nutritive conditions and food reserves is difficult, but presumably they favor fruit-bud formation in the pinched shoots.

However, summer pinching has been practiced frequently for the purpose of promoting fruit spur and fruit-bud formation and has not secured the expected response. In general it may be stated that, though the practice may produce satisfactory results if followed properly by successive pinching of secondary and tertiary shoots, the amount and kind of labor involved are such as to make it of doubtful value in the commercial fruit plantation in America. When trees are grown as standards other measures or practices that are available will call forth more of a mass response and will provide at much less expense the requisite number of fruit spurs and fruit buds.

TABLE 18.—INFLUENCE OF SUMMER PINCHING ON RELATIVE THICKNESS OF BARK AND WOOD IN THE PINCHED SHOOT OF THE PEAR
(After Goumy[32])

Tissue	Shoot not pinched	Shoot pinched
Pith...............................	2.3	2.8
Wood..............................	5.5	3.7
Bark..............................	2.25	3.4
Bark tissues in particular:		
Epidermis.........................	1.0	1.0
Cortical parenchyma...............	2.2	4.4
Sclerenchyma......................	0.6	0.5
Cortex............................	1.6	3.0
Cambium...........................	0.6	0.6

The early summer pinching of shoots in young trees for the purpose of subordinating those that are not wanted for permanent framework is only occasionally employed but is frequently to be recommended. In newly planted trees the buds within a short distance from the ground often start to grow. Generally the resulting shoots are promptly rubbed off or they are pruned away after they have been allowed to grow a year. In either case the growth of the upper branches is very likely to be checked. If these lower shoots are promptly pinched back so as to leave three or four leaves apiece the upper shoots are not checked in their development, the trunk is shaded and the food materials that their leaves manufacture will be of considerable value in promoting a vigorous growth the following season, after which they can be removed. Similarly in trees, that have been growing in the orchard for 1, 2 or 3 years, are formed many shoots that ordinarily are removed at the following dormant-season pruning. Their growth reduces somewhat the development of those desired for the permanent framework. Pinching them back early in the season suppresses them and the nutrients and moisture are largely diverted into other parts, but at the same time their leaf surface serves to manufacture elaborated foods for the current and the following seasons.

Summary.—On the whole but little difference is likely to result from pruning at different times during the dormant season, though in certain fruits early pruning is followed by earlier foliation in the spring. This is a factor of commercial importance in grape culture. Very late pruning generally leads to more bleeding than earlier pruning. Bleeding from pruning wounds seldom harms the plant.

Summer pruning may have a dwarfing or an invigorating influence (as compared with a corresponding winter pruning), depending on its severity, kind, the stage of development of the plant and on environmental conditions—particularly nutrient supply, soil moisture and light. A light summer thinning encourages fruit-spur formation through favoring the development of larger and stronger lateral buds from which spurs are formed. The same practice promotes fruit-bud formation also if the work is done early enough in the season. Heading back tends to stimulate purely vegetative growth. Judicious summer pruning is more or less a conservation measure. This applies particularly to the removal of watersprouts and other superfluous growth. In very strong vigorously growing trees 2 to 5 years old early summer pruning results in encouraging a late secondary growth and this may be a means of hastening the general development of the tree if there is a long growing season and other conditions are favorable. A light summer pruning may aid materially the coloration of fruit in certain species.

Summer pinching in general encourages the development of secondary shoots. This is often desirable in the culture of the bramble fruits. Pinching may be used also to subordinate individual shoots and, in the spur-bearing species, it may result in their developing into spurs. This practice is of doubtful utility, however, in the culture of standard trees.

CHAPTER XXV

PRUNING WITH SPECIAL REFERENCE TO PARTICULAR FRUITS

In a preceding chapter were discussed some of the more important general or mass effects of pruning. Mention was made also of the more specific influence of certain practices on fruit-spur, shoot or fruit-bud formation in particular parts of the tree, though this concerned the general aspects of those questions rather than the particular applications presented by different fruit plants. Another chapter attempts to explain in some detail the fruit bearing habits of the more common fruits. There remains for discussion the adaptation of pruning practices to plants having these different methods of bearing so that maximum annual production may be obtained along with the form of tree or plant most conducive to long life and economy in production. It should not be inferred, however, that all fruit plants with the same fruiting habit should be pruned alike. Their general growing habits, that is, the amount and character of their new vegetative growth, may be quite different and necessitate equally diverse pruning treatments. Though the Winter Nelis pear has essentially the same bearing habit as the Maiden Blush apple, the two must be pruned differently because they are so unlike in their vegetative growth and the red raspberry with essentially the same fruiting habit as the black raspberry should be pruned more severely because of its great tendency to sucker; many other instances might be cited.

Broadly speaking, pruning may be said to influence fruit-bud and fruit formation—bearing habit—in two ways, directly and indirectly. Its most important direct influence is to thin the crop through the removal of actual or potential fruit-bearing wood. Another rather direct influence is its effect on the location or distribution of fruiting wood, both spurs and shoots. Its indirect influence is effected mainly through changing nutritive conditions within the tree and consequently limiting or encouraging fruit-spur or fruit-bud formation. As these indirect effects have been considered rather fully in the preceding chapters but little attention is given them here. Furthermore no attempt is made to discuss the influence of different pruning treatments on the fruiting habits of any of the tropical or subtropical fruits or of a number of the less important deciduous fruits.

508

Pruning the Apple and the Pear.—As has been pointed out, apple and pear flowers are for the most part borne terminally on short growths springing from terminal buds on other short growths, or spurs. Individual spurs are wont to bear only every other year, though annual bearing spurs are not rare and are common in trees of certain varieties. More frequently, however, individual spurs fail to produce even every other year, bearing perhaps only once in 3 or 4 years, or very irregularly. These spurs may live many years and there is nothing in their manner of growth to necessitate a deterioration in efficiency as they grow older. In reality, however, they flower and, more particularly, set and mature fruit, much less regularly as they increase in age.[80] Without doubt this is due to unfavorable nutritive conditions induced by crowding and competition with other parts of the tree for food, moisture and light. Records show, nevertheless, that even very old spurs may bear good fruits and that when strong and vigorous they are more efficient fruit producers than those that are much younger but lacking in vigor.[80] Roberts[63] has reported a marked correlation between the vigor of spurs, as measured by the length of each year's growth and by the number and area of their leaves and performance in flower-bud formation. Spurs of medium length with relatively large leaf areas and consequently with the means of accumulating reserves of elaborated foods are more likely to form fruit buds.

Heavy annual production, then, would seem among other things to depend on (1) the formation of an adequate supply of fruit spurs, (2) the retention of those already formed and (3) maintaining all of them in a vigorous condition so that they may flower and fruit regularly. These requirements plainly cannot be met or supplied by any single pruning practice or by any combination of pruning practices. They depend on many factors, chief among which are nutritive conditions within the plant, which, in turn, are influenced most readily by fertilizers and various systems of soil management. Pruning, however, is important in this connection.

The Formation of Fruit Spurs.—As pointed out elsewhere, maximum fruit-spur formation is encouraged by leaving the trees unpruned or by pruning them very lightly. Such treatment or lack of treatment leaves the largest possible number of buds from which spurs may develop; consequently an approach to this treatment is recommended to induce bearing in a short time. Formerly the artificial bending of long shoots was quite generally recommended to make them more fruitful through the formation of fruit spurs. However, this practice is of doubtful value and certainly is not to be recommended under average field conditions.[27] When certain shoots are selected for removal in young apple trees, new fruit-spur formation is favored by leaving those that are vigorous and comparatively upright.[24]   As the trees become older and possess fruit spurs in numbers sufficient to provide full crops less attention need be given to obtaining new spurs.   Some of the old spurs die out or are lost through accident but in spite of this the numbers increase as the tree grows older.   Usually more spurs form than the tree can support to advantage and it is only in the tree between 4 and 6 or 8 years of age that there is need of definite effort to encourage their development.

Very rarely do new spurs form directly on the old wood from either latent or adventitious buds.   In case the spurs in the lower-interior part of the tree die out or are destroyed the only way to develop new spurs in that region is to prune back the top of the tree somewhat heavily.   This will force out watersprouts from latent or adventitious buds.   At the same time there should be enough thinning out to permit free access of sunlight and thus promote the development of large leaves and large lateral buds which a year later may develop into fruit spurs.   These watersprouts are then treated in very much the same way as the tops of trees just coming into bearing; the same may be recommended for the strong vigorous growth in trees recently "dehorned" or recently topworked.

Retaining Efficient and Removing Inefficient Fruiting Wood.—As long as fruit spurs and the branches that support them continue to produce reasonable numbers of fruits of good size, color and quality, they should be retained, for they are profitable.   When they cease to do so, they should be removed, unless at the same time those in the same trees that are stout and stocky in character likewise cease to function satisfactorily. In this latter case, general invigoration of the entire tree through fertilizer applications or other soil management practices is suggested.

Summary of Usual Pruning Treatment.—Briefly, the general pruning treatment recommended for the apple and the pear, considering their growing and bearing habits and their responses to different types of pruning, may be stated as follows: During the first few years in the orchard, assuming at least a moderately strong growth, the tree should be pruned rather severely and this should consist in both thinning out and heading back, with the emphasis perhaps on heading back.   This heavy pruning is for the purpose of properly developing the framework of the tree.   If it has made a weak growth, pruning should be correspondingly lighter. As the tree becomes older, pruning gradually decreases in severity until at 6 or 7 years, when it reaches bearing age and size, very little is done. As pruning lessens in severity it gradually changes in kind, consisting less in heading back and more and more in thinning out.   This general procedure develops a fruit-spur system and brings it into bearing.   After the tree is once in bearing, pruning slowly increases in amount but continues to be mainly a thinning out; this thinning should comprise the removal of small, weak limbs in the lower and interior part of the tree rather than the cutting of a few large limbs. When this plan is followed there is some thinning of fruiting wood and of the fruit crop, overbearing is prevented and the general grade of the fruit is improved. The idea so long advanced that considerable pruning is required in mature apple trees from the standpoint of improving size, color and grade is not borne out by the results of experimental studies. It may effect some increase in the percentage of the larger, more merchantable sizes, but this is generally at the expense of a relatively greater reduction in total yield and often in the yield of the larger sizes themselves.[48] Greater increases in size and greater improvement in color can be secured more economically by methods or practices other than pruning. Furthermore, with the advent of modern spraying equipment pruning is no longer necessary in order to secure insect and disease control. Its function in the old tree is primarily that of improving grade through removing the wood that produces most of the small, poorly colored fruit. This means pruning of the thin-wood type.

Special Suggestions for Unusual Fruiting Habits.—Certain varieties of the apple and the pear have been said to bear many fruit buds terminally or laterally on long shoots. This is particularly common during the period when they are just coming into bearing. Under these circumstances greater care must be exercised against the unnecessary removal of any new shoots and heading back should be reduced to a minimum until the trees have a better developed fruit-spur system and are bearing a considerable percentage of their crop on it. The production of lateral fruit buds on long shoots, it should be noted, presents a case similar to that of the peach and consequently the pruning of such trees should resemble that ordinarily given peach trees as much as it does that of the average apple or pear variety. However, most of these lateral fruit buds in the apple are borne on the terminal half or even third of the shoot, while a considerable percentage of those of the peach are found on the basal half. This necessitates much more care in heading back the fruit-bearing shoots in these particular varieties than is requisite in the peach.

Pruning the Peach.—The peach is perhaps the best known representative of that group of fruits which bear lateral fruit buds on long growths or shoots. These buds contain flowers only and with their falling, or with the maturing of the fruits which develop from them, that portion of the branch to which they were attached becomes barren. Neither fruits nor flowers are again borne upon it. New growth develops from the terminal bud or from lateral leaf buds at some of the non-flowering nodes or in some instances from adventitious or latent buds lower in the tree. It is therefore characteristic of the peach to have its fruiting wood carried a foot or two farther out and up each year, leaving long stretches of non-fruiting wood that serves only as a connecting link between the fruiting periphery of the tree and its root system.

Seldom does the peach tree of bearing age fail to differentiate enough fruit buds for a heavy crop.   In fact it commonly produces many more than are desired, so that some pruning is advisable for the purpose of thinning the crop.   Furthermore, since the fruit buds are produced each year on the new wood of the current season there is no danger of rendering the tree unproductive for a period of several years, as in the apple or the pear, by cutting away its fruiting wood.   Therefore the two main problems in pruning this fruit are to thin the crop and to "keep the tree within bounds," that is, to prevent its fruiting wood from developing so far away from the trunk that propping, picking, spraying and fruit thinning involve too much expense.   Almost any kind of pruning serves the former purpose if it is severe enough; on the other hand the location of the new fruiting wood and the distribution of its fruit buds depend very considerably on the type of pruning that is employed.   In fact it would not be far from correct to say that in the bearing peach tree the severity of pruning should be governed largely by the amount of crop thinning required and its kind should be determined by the desired distribution of the following season's fruiting branches and fruit buds.

When and How Severely.—The bearing peach tree should be pruned lightly or heavily, depending on whether it gives promise of bearing just enough or too much, if little or no pruning is done.   It is not desirable, however, to attempt to do all or even a large part of the fruit thinning by means of pruning, as such procedure is likely substantially to reduce yields.[49]   As a rule prospects cannot be estimated accurately until the trees are in bloom or even until the fruit has set, on account of danger from late spring frosts.   Theoretically it is wise to wait until that time and then to prune with the aim of providing as nearly as possible a full crop but still of reducing the labor of fruit thinning to a minimum.   In practice this can seldom be done because it is necessary to utilize labor for other purposes at that time of the year.   If crop prospects are ruined by a late frost the trees can be dehorned advantageously, because this heavy pruning will not result in any loss of fruit and since new growth for the following season's production will be forced to develop from the main scaffold limbs, the bearing surface will be lowered and made more compact.   If midwinter or late winter freezing destroys the fruit buds this same type of pruning can be done earlier.

Pruning to Secure Most Favorable Location of Fruiting Surface.— The usual method of pruning the bearing peach tree comprises such thinning out as seems necessary, this thinning consisting generally in the removal of wood from the center of the tree so as to provide an extreme open center. In fact the average peach tree as found in the commercial orchard illustrates more nearly the vase or goblet shaped form than almost any other species. This thinning out is then followed by as severe heading back of the shoots as is compatible with leaving enough good fruit buds—or flowers if the operation has been delayed until the blooming season—to provide for a full crop. If the number and distribution of buds are such that the heading back can be rather severe the new shoot growth will be forced to come out rather low and the tree will be kept relatively compact, though the fruiting wood of the following season will be necessarily somewhat farther out from the trunk than that of the current season. In the majority of cases, a type of pruning that is essentially a light to moderate thinning and that has sometimes been designated by the term "long" is likely to give the best results with the peach when considered from the standpoint of its influence on both quality and size of fruit.

Pruning the Sweet Cherry.—Typical of that group of fruits whose flower buds are borne laterally on short spurs and give rise to an inflorescence only is the sweet cherry. The terminal of the sweet cherry spur is always a leaf bud by which the growth of the spur is continued each year. New spurs originate from some of the lateral leaf buds on the shoots of the preceding season and new shoot growth proceeds from other lateral buds, from terminal buds on shoots, from latent or adventitious buds on the older wood and occasionally from the terminal buds of spurs. However, comparatively few shoots arise from buds of the last two classes in the sweet cherry. The lateral buds on the year-old shoots of young vigorously growing trees are little inclined to produce spurs, but either grow out into new shoots or remain dormant. Consequently the young trees of this species are thick brushy growers, strongly vegetative in character and often slow in coming into bearing. Old trees of the same species present a rather sharp contrast to this condition. Most of the lateral buds on their shoots produce spurs or remain dormant. Often new shoot growth is produced mainly from the terminal buds of the last year's shoots, the result being a tree that is markedly reproductive and often lacking in vigor.

As the problem in the young tree is first to secure a strong framework and then a good equipment of fruit spurs, much as in the apple and pear and as its shoots and spurs originate from buds in the same locations, its pruning treatment the first few years should correspond closely to that of those fruits. In other words pruning should be fairly heavy at first, gradually decreasing in amount till at 6 or 7 years little is done. At the same time it should change gradually from a treatment which consists largely in heading back to one which consists almost entirely in thinning out.

As the tree becomes older, however, its pruning treatment should diverge gradually from that customarily given the apple or pear. Its natural tendency to produce large numbers of fruit spurs obviates the necessity of employing any treatment to encourage greater spur and fruit bud production. At the same time this growing habit results in a fairly open top in which the foliage is well exposed to light. On the other hand measures should be taken to promote a greater vegetative growth, particularly in those varieties or under those conditions that tend toward the development of new shoots from terminal buds only. Otherwise long pole-like fruiting branches, subject to much injury from the wind when heavily loaded with fruit, will develop. Heading back to promote branching, however, must be done with considerable care. If the heading is into 2-year, 3-year, or older wood, new side branches are not likely to form, and the limbs in question are subordinated to an unimportant position in the tree. Heading back to near the base of the one-year old shoots is much more likely to induce the branching desired, though this alone is often rather ineffective in large trees somewhat lacking in vigor. A certain amount of pruning back to 2-year, 3-year or older laterals is often effective in keeping the tree within bounds and mild dehorning may be resorted to for the same purpose and to encourage the production of strong new vegetative growth. There is little occasion to do much thinning out in the sweet cherry tree that is well in bearing, and the heading back is mainly for the purpose of lowering the top and correcting form. In the case of that portion of the sweet cherry crop that is grown for fresh consumption, as opposed to canning, a considerable premium is paid for size, and size of fruit in turn is usually correlated rather closely with vigor of growth. Now and then considerable pruning is warranted from this standpoint as a supplement to other cultural practices intended to promote vegetative growth.

Pruning the Almond, Apricot, Plum, and Sour Cherry.—As has been stated in the classification of fruiting habits, the almond, apricot, plum and sour cherry form a series intermediate in their habits of bearing between the peach on the one hand and the sweet cherry on the other. That is, all of these fruits bear fruit buds laterally on both long and short growths. Some of them, as certain of the almonds and Japanese plums, approach the peach more closely; others, as the Insititia plums, approach the sweet cherry more closely. The age and vigor of the trees and the cultural conditions under which they are grown influence the relative distribution of fruit buds on spurs and on shoots. Roberts[62] states that weak or moderately vigorous sour cherry trees bear a much larger percentage of their fruit buds on medium to short shoots than do the vigorous trees of the same varieties. The reverse is likely to hold in certain varieties of the Japanese plum.

Since the bearing habits of these fruits are intermediate between those of the peach and of the sweet cherry, it follows that, in general, their pruning treatments should likewise be intermediate between those given typical bearing trees of those species. If the bearing habit is more like that of the peach, the pruning treatment should be correspondingly severe; if it is more like that of the sweet cherry, it should be correspondingly light.

There are, however, numerous exceptions. For instance, the Montmorency cherry forms fruit spurs readily and ordinarily bears half or more of its fruit on them; the English Morello bears its fruit almost exclusively on shoots, like the peach. It might, therefore, be assumed that the Morello should be pruned more severely than the Montmorency. Such is not the case, for, although almost any pruning reduces the yield of both varieties, it has its greatest influence in this direction on the Morello. In the case of the apricot, as with the peach, considerable improvement in size and grade of fruit can be effected by proper pruning. Considerable heading back, as well as a reasonable amount of thinning out, is desirable with this fruit in order both to increase size and to stimulate a vigorous growth of new shoots whose foliage will protect the fruit from sunburn.[57]

In general with these fruits it is usually desirable to employ those cultural and pruning practices that encourage the spur-bearing, rather than the shoot-bearing, habit. The production of fruits on spurs means compactness of trees, less danger from the breaking of limbs and lighter and less expensive pruning. There is not the necessity of so frequent pruning for "renewal" purposes. It has been found, in some varieties of the sour cherry at least, that spur-borne fruit buds are hardier than those borne on shoots.[62]

Pruning the Currant and Gooseberry.—The fruiting habits of the currant and the gooseberry resemble that of the apricot more closely than those of any of the other tree fruits. Within certain limits their pruning treatment should follow closely that found best suited to the apricot. Since the currant and gooseberry are bush, rather than tree, fruits, they have a marked tendency to throw out strong vigorous new shoots from the crown or from the base of the old canes. The growth of this wood, together with fruiting of the older wood, weakens the latter and a point is soon reached where its retention is no longer profitable. Experience has demonstrated that canes more than four years old should be removed to make room for the younger and more vigorous growth. As a rule more new shoots form each season than can be retained without undue crowding. Consequently they are thinned each spring to from 3 to 6 of the strongest and best distributed; these are headed back to a height of 2 or 3 feet to keep the bush more compact. Thus, when the currant or gooseberry plantation once becomes well established, its annual pruning actually comprises a removal of the old canes that are becoming weak and a thinning of the new shoots to make provision for the replacing of the old wood that is discarded. Injured or diseased canes are of course removed and some attention should be devoted to training.

Certain varieties or types that have growing or fruiting habits different from those described as typical should receive a correspondingly different pruning treatment. The wood of the black currant loses its vigor and becomes relatively unproductive at an earlier age than that of the red currant or the gooseberry. Consequently the old canes are removed after they have fruited 1 or 2 years and a correspondingly larger number of new shoots are retained each season for replacement purposes.

Both currants and gooseberries may be trained in either the bush or the tree form. In America the bush form is preferable, both because less labor is required in training and because it lends itself more readily to an economical control of the currant borer.

Pruning the Brambles.—Most of the bramble fruits are perennials, with biennial canes. The dying of the canes at the end of their fruiting season the second year necessitates their removal. From the standpoint of checking the spread of insects and disease, it is good practice to remove the old canes at the close of the fruiting season. On the other hand, if they are allowed to remain until fall or the following spring, they afford a certain amount of mechanical support to the new shoots of the current season and reduce loss from breakage due to wind. This is an important consideration in many locations.

The early spring pruning of this group usually consists in some thinning out of the cane growth that is to bear fruit during the following summer and at the same time a heading back of the main canes or of their laterals, or perhaps of both. This pruning is done almost exclusively for the purpose of thinning the crop. If done properly it reduces the number of fruit buds but results in little or no reduction in the total yield. Naturally its severity varies greatly with variety and with the environmental conditions. The moisture supply during the ripening season limits yield in the bramble fruits probably more frequently than any other single factor. Consequently the severity of the pruning should be influenced by the prospect for available water during and just before harvesting. Under conditions of ample rainfall or abundant irrigation water and of relatively high atmospheric humidity this pruning may be much less severe than when summer drought is likely. The bulk of this spring pruning of dormant or nearly dormant canes should consist in heading back rather than in thinning out, since the entire removal of any except the weakest canes or laterals reduces yield without effecting a compensating improvement in grade. This holds true for both black[40] and red[41,42] raspberries. The laterals from the median and more basal fruit buds generally produce larger clusters and their individual berries are larger than those from the more apical buds. Therefore, rather severe or "short" pruning is recommended for the varieties of this group.[40] Blackberry varieties differ from each other considerably in the distribution of their fruit buds on their main canes and laterals. Varieties like Ward and Lawton that bear a considerable number of fruit buds close to the main cane should be short-pruned; those whose fruit buds are borne farther out on the laterals, like Early King and Taylor, should be headed back less severely.[16] It is a good plan to delay this pruning until the buds are swelling in the spring so that the winter-injured ends of the canes may be removed without extra labor.

The summer pinching of the bramble fruits has been discussed under the heading of Pinching and need not be treated at this point.

Few or no data are available showing the best methods of pruning certain types of the blackberry that have perennial canes. However, observation indicates that they can be handled best by treating them as ordinary varieties with biennial canes. That is, their canes are pruned out as soon as they have fruited once, even though they would bear a second crop were they allowed to remain.

The so-called everbearing or fall-bearing raspberries produce their late summer crop terminally on the main shoot or on sub-terminal laterals of shoots of the current season. The following main-season crop is borne on laterals coming from lower parts of the same canes. They should be winter pruned in the same way as related mid-season varieties.

Pruning the Grape.—More has been written about pruning and training the grape than any other fruit. Many different systems or methods have been worked out and described in detail and an examination of any considerable part of this literature is as likely to be confusing as it is enlightening. This is not because the several practices differ so much in the principles involved, but because there is so great diversity in the methods of their application that the principles themselves are likely to remain hidden.

As pointed out in the classification of bearing habits, the grape produces its fruit buds laterally on shoots, which at the close of the growing season and for a year thereafter are called canes. These fruit buds give rise to flower-bearing or fruiting shoots on which the inflorescences appear to be lateral. However, many shoots form few or no fruit buds, particularly those springing from latent or adventitious buds on 2-year-old or older wood—in other words, those arising from the arms, head, trunk or crown of the plant. Only those shoots (canes, when a year old) coming from lateral buds on the canes of the preceding season are sure to form fruit buds, though under some conditions those coming from the older wood differentiate a limited number.   Furthermore not all buds on shoots springing from the preceding year's canes contain flower parts.   Those at the basal one to four or five nodes, depending largely on variety, seldom do.   Though it is difficult, and often impossible, to distinguish the fruit buds from the leaf or wood buds by their external appearance, their position on the plant offers a rather accurate index to their character and the grower or student, once he becomes well acquainted with the characteristics of the individual variety, will have little difficulty in telling which are of the one kind and which of the other.

Severity of Pruning.—Practically all grape vines differentiate each year more fruit buds than can grow into fruiting shoots and set and mature grapes the following season.   It is therefore unnecessary in pruning the grape to give thought to securing larger numbers of fruit buds. The real problem is that of reducing to just the right number those that are already formed and normally would or could produce fruiting shoots the following season.   Furthermore, this must be done in such a way that the fruit will be well distributed and that the new shoots on which fruit buds for a succeeding crop are differentiated will be so located as to preserve the compactness and established form of the vine.

The reduction of fruit buds to just the right number is often difficult and always requires an accurate knowledge of fruit-bud location in the particular variety and good judgment as to how much fruit the vine should bear.   Overpruning reduces the crop and diverts the energies of the plant into excessive wood growth.   This is well illustrated by the work of Maney[47] in Iowa.   Underpruning permits the plant to overbear, resulting in too many clusters, undersized berries of inferior quality and a weakening of the vine itself so that succeeding crops will be reduced in size and the life of the plant shortened.   These statements, of course, apply to the pruning of many other fruit plants, but not to the same extent that they do to the grape.   In practice perhaps the best way of determining the severity of pruning is, following a suggestion of Hedrick,[34] to figure the problem for each vine on a mathematical basis.   He says in reference to varieties of the Labrusca and Labrusca-hybrid types: "A thrifty grape-vine should yield, let us say, 15 pounds of grapes, a fair average for the mainstay varieties.   Each bunch will weigh from a quarter to a half pound.   To produce 15 pounds on a vine, therefore, will require from 30 to 60 bunches.   As each shoot will bear two or three bunches, from 15 to 30 buds must be left on the canes of the preceding year. . . .   Pruning, then, consists in calculating the number of bunches and buds necessary and removing the remainder."   As some of the fruiting shoots may be broken off incident to the work of cultivation, spraying or other vineyard operations, it may be well to leave a few extra fruit buds; this matter, however, can be overdone easily.

Special mention should be made of the variation in the relative amounts of pruning to be given vines of any given variety, not only with their age and the conditions of soil moisture and fertility but, in grafted vines, with the stocks on which they are grown. Certain stocks have the reputation of producing shy-bearing vines, though actually they are unproductive only when pruned too closely.

Another point already mentioned is the provision that should be made for the production of properly placed new shoots on which fruit buds for the following crop can form. In practice this "proper distribution" generally involves their location as near the head of the vine as possible, so that the fruiting wood is not pushed out unnecessarily each season; thus the plant is kept compact. In many varieties this is secured by retaining the lowest or basal cane (fruiting shoot of the preceding season) on each arm or spur and pruning away those originating farther from the head. In certain other varieties, however, the fruiting shoots develop only from buds at nodes some distance from the base of the canes and the more basal buds remain dormant when the heading back is light enough to permit the development of fruiting shoots. Pruning varieties with such growing and fruiting habits in the way just described would quickly carry the bearing surface of the vine far from its head and necessitate frequent resort to pruning like that called dehorning in tree fruits. The usual method of handling vines of this type is each year to prune lightly or moderately certain canes for fruit production, leaving them with the requisite number of fruit buds and to prune severely other canes so that all their fruit buds are removed and they are forced to develop vegetative shoots from their basal buds. These vegetative shoots then become the fruiting canes of the following year, while those that have borne fruit are entirely removed. These much shortened canes are spoken of as "renewal spurs."

Kind of Pruning.—Pruning the grape, like the pruning of most other fruits, includes some thinning out and some heading back. The relative amounts of these two types desirable in any given case depend largely on the style of training employed. Invariably all the past season's shoots are removed except those retained for their fruit buds or for "renewal" or "replacement." This is a thinning out process. If the style of training calls for pruning to spurs, more of last season's shoots must be retained; consequently there can be less thinning out than if the vines are pruned to canes. As the pruning should leave a fairly definite number of fruit buds, the amount of heading back of the canes left after thinning varies inversely with their number. Thus there is much less severe heading with a two-wire Kniffin system of training than with pruning back to spurs. Little need be said at this point regarding the summer pruning of the grape, as the more important features are discussed in Chap. XXIV.

Methods of Training.—As already indicated, there is almost endless variety in methods of training the vine. A description of each, even of those that are fairly distinct, would require many pages and probably would be of little real use. The fundamental objects of all these methods differ little from those governing the training of other fruit-producing species. Training should increase yields, improve grades or quality and reduce production costs through facilitating other vineyard operations. In this fruit the usual training methods, at least those employed in America, have little influence on total yields.[31] They do, however, affect quality and production costs. No one method of training is necessary for the production of fruit of the highest grade or quality. Thus in New York, vines of the Concord have been found to mature their fruit better when trained to the umbrella Kniffin system than when trained in any of the other ways standard in that state.[31] Husmann and Dearing[39] report that in Muscadine grapes the upright system permits the fruit to ripen more evenly than does the overhead system. Only after a careful study of the growing and fruiting characteristics of the different varieties in various sections and soils and on different stocks can the best system of training be selected and the best system for one variety may not be best for another in the same vineyard.

In general those systems of training in which the new shoots are allowed to droop are much less costly than those in which they are tied in horizontal or vertical positions; consequently it is only under special conditions that these latter methods of training are to be recommended. Along the northern limits of outdoor grape culture some of the low renewal systems of training greatly facilitate the work incident to artificial winter protection and are quite generally employed. Those varieties whose canes bear fruit buds almost to the very base, are naturally better suited to spur renewal than those whose canes habitually form only wood buds in the same regions. With these latter cane renewal or a combination of long and short spur renewal is more practicable. Only those varieties (particularly of the Vinifera group) with comparatively stocky and rigid trunks that require no artificial supports can be trained to the tree form advantageously. Other varieties require trellising.

Suggested Collateral Readings

Chandler, W. H. Fruit Growing. Chapters 15–19. 1925. New York.

Drinkard, A. W. Fruit Bud Formation and Development. Ann. Rept. Va. Agr. Exp. Sta. Pp. 159–205. 1909–1910.

Sorauer, P. A Popular Treatise on the Physiology of Plants. Transl. by F. E. Weiss. Pp. 134–168. London, 1895.

RICKS, G. L., and GASTON, H. P. The Thin Wood Method of Pruning. Mich. Agr. Exp. Sta. Sp. Bul. 265. 1935.

GASTON, H. P., and RICKS, G. L. The Graduated Space Method of Thinning Apples. Mich. Agr. Exp. Sta. Sp. Bul. 281. 1937.

LITERATURE CITED

1. Alderman, W. H., and Auchter, E. C. W. Va. Agr. Exp. Sta. Bul. 158. 1916.
2. Asami, Y. Jour. Sci. Agr. Soc. No. 312. P. 461. 1928.
3. Barry, P. The Fruit Garden. Pp. 94–95. Detroit, 1853.
4. Batchelor, L. D., and Goodspeed, W. E. Utah Agr. Exp. Sta. Bul. 140. 1915.
5. Bedford, H. A. R., and Pickering, S. U. Science and Fruit Growing. Pp. 57–80. London, 1919.
6. Ibid. P. 46.
7. Bioletti, F. T. Cal. Agr. Exp. Sta. Bul. 241. 1913.
8. Ibid. Bul. 348. 1922.
9. Blake, M. A., and Connors, C. H. N. J. Agr. Exp. Sta. Bul. 326. 1917.
10. Brierley, W. G. Proc. Am. Soc. Hort. Sci. 16: 102–104. 1919.
11. Burns, G. P. Vt. Agr. Exp. Sta. Bul. 267. 1927.
12. Card, F. W. Bush Fruits. Pp. 48–51; 70–73. New York, 1917.
13. Chandler, W. H. Mo. Agr. Exp. Sta. Res. Bul. 14. 1914.
14. Chandler, W. H. Proc. Am. Soc. Hort. Sci. 16: 88–101. 1919.
15. Childs, L. Ore. Agr. Exp. Sta. Bul. 171. 1920.
16. Colby, A. S. Proc. Am. Soc. Hort. Sci. 17: 241. 1920.
17. Cole, S. W. The American Fruit Book. P. 57. Boston, 1850.
18. Curtis, O. F. Am. J. Bot. 7: 101–124. 1920.
19. Daniel, L. Compt. rend. 131: 1253–1255. 1900.
20. Daniel, L. Trav. scient. Univ. de Rennes. 6 (2): 22–72. 1907.
21. Downing, A. J. The Fruits and Fruit Trees of America. P. 31. New York, 1856.
22. Drinkard, A. W. Va. Agr. Exp. Sta. Ann. Rept. Pp. 96–120. 1913–1914.
23. Drinkard, A. W. Va. Agr. Exp. Sta. Tech. Bul. 17. 1917.
24. Edminster, A. F. Ore. Agr. Exp. Sta. Bul. 146. 1917.
25. Gardner, V. R. Mich. Agr. Exp. Sta. Sp. Bul. 195. 1930.
26. Gardner, V. R., et al. Ore. Agr. Exp. Sta. Bul. 139. 1916.
27. Gardner, V. R. Ore. Agr. Exp. Sta. Bul. 146. 1917.
28. Gardner, V. R., Marshall, R. E., and Hootman, H. D. Mich. Agr. Exp. Sta. Sp. Bul. 184. 1928.
29. Gaston, H. P., and Ricks, G. L. Mich. Agr. Exp. Sta. Sp. Bul. 281. 1937.
30. Gaucher, N. Handb. der Obstkultur. Pp. 602–644. Berlin, 1902.
31. Gladwin, F. E. N. Y. Agr. Exp. Sta. Bul. 464. 1919.
32. Goumy, E. Thesis Presented to the Faculty of Science of the University of Paris. 1905.
33. Hartig, R. Lehrbuch der Anatomie und Physiologie der Pflanzen. Berlin. 1891. P. 178.
34. Hedrick, U. P. Manual of American Grape Growing. P. 114. New York, 1919.
35. Hooker, H. D. Mo. Agr. Exp. Sta. Res. Bul. 72. 1924.
36. Hovey, C. M. Hovey's Mag. of Hort. 15: 301. 1849.
37. Howe, G. H. N. Y. Agr. Exp. Sta. Bul. 391. 1914.
38. Husmann, G. C. U. S. D. A. Bul. 856. 1920.
39. Husmann, G. C., and Dearing, C. U. S. D. A., Bur. Pl. Ind. Bul. 273. 1913.

40. Johnston, S.   Mich. Agr. Exp. Sta. Sp. Bul. 143.   1925.
41. Johnston, S., and Loree, R. E.   Mich. Agr. Exp. Sta. Sp. Bul. 162.   1927.
42. Lott, R. V.   Col. Agr. Exp. Sta. Bul. 367.   1931.
43. Macdaniels, L. H., and Curtis, O. F.   Cornell Univ. Agr. Exp. Sta. Mem. 133.
    1930.
44. Macoun, W. T.   Can. Dept. Agr. Bul. 56.   1907.
45. Magness, J. R.   Ore. Agr. Exp. Sta. Bul. 139.   1916.
46. Magness, J. R. et al.   Ore. Agr. Exp. Sta. Bul. 146.   1917.
47. Maney, T. J.   Ia. Agr. Exp. Sta. Bul. 160.   1915.
48. Marshall, R. E.   Mich. Agr. Exp. Sta. Sp. Bul. 169.   1928.
49. Marshall, R. E.   Mich. Agr. Exp. Sta. Tech. Bul. 116.   1931.
50. McClelland, T. B.   Porto Rico Agr. Exp. Sta. Bul. 32.   1928.
51. Paddock, W.   N. Y. Agr. Exp. Sta. Bul. 151.   1898.
52. Paddock, W., and Whipple, O. B.   Fruit Growing in Arid Regions.   P. 112.
    New York, 1910.
53. Pearson, A. H.   J. Roy. Hort. Soc.   29: 274.   1896.
54. Quinn, P. T.   Pear Culture for Profit.   P. 72.   New York, 1889.
55. Quintinye, J. de la.   Instructions pour les jardins fruitiers et potagers.   2: 579.
    Paris, 1746.
56. Ravaz, L.   Taille hâtive ou taille tardive.   1912.   (Cited by Bioletti, F. T.
    Cal. Agr. Exp. Sta. Bul. 241.   1913.)
57. Reed, H. S.   Cal. Agr. Exp. Sta. Bul. 574.   1934.
58. Ricks, G. L. and Gaston, H. P.   Mich. Agr. Exp. Sta. Sp. Bul. 265.   1935.
59. Ripperton, J. C., Goto, Y. B., and Pahan, R. K.   Hawaii Agr. Exp. Sta. Bul. 75.
    1935.
60. Rivers, T.   The Miniature Fruit Garden.   P. 8.   New York, 1866.
61. Ibid.   Pp. 12, 82.
62. Roberts, R. H.   Wis. Agr. Exp. Sta. Bul. 298.   1919.
63. Ibid.   Bul. 317.   1920.
64. Shamel, A. D.   Calif. Citrogr.   10 (12): 415.   1925.
65. Shamel, A. D., and Pomeroy, C. S.   Calif. Citrogr.   18: 218.   1933.
66. Shamel, A. D., Pomeroy, C. S., and Caryl, R. E.   U. S. D. A. Farmers' Bul.
    1333.   1923.
67. Swarbrick, T.   Jour. Pom. and Hort. Sci.   6: 1–43.   1927.
68. Taft, L. R., and Lyon, T. T.   Mich. Agr. Exp. Sta. Bul. 169.   1899.
69. Teske, A. H., and Gardner, V. R.   Mich. Agr. Exp. Sta. Sp. Bul. 165.   1927.
70. Thomas, J. J.   American Fruit Culturist.   P. 82.   New York, 1867.
71. Tufts, W. P.   Cal. Agr. Exp. Sta. Bul. 313.   1919.
72. Vidal, J. L.   Rev. de Viticulture.   1: 895–903.   1894.
73. Vincent, C. C.   Ida. Agr. Exp. Sta. Bul. 98.   1917.
74. Volck, W. H.   Mo. Bul. Cal. St. Com. Hort.   6: 80–89.   1917.
75. Waugh, F. A.   The American Apple Orchard.   P. 90.   New York, 1912.
76. Wellington, R.   N. Y. St. Hort. Soc. Proc.   74: 204–207.   1929.
77. Wiggans, C. B.   Jour. Agr. Res. 31: 865–883.   1925.
78. Winkler, A. J.   Hilgardia.   4 (6): 153–173.   1929.
79. Ibid.   1: 525–542.   1926.
80. Yeager, A. F.   Ore. Agr. Exp. Sta. Bul. 139.   1916.

SECTION V
FRUIT SETTING

It is customary to speak of the reproductive activities of the plant as distinct from its vegetative activities. That use of terms is accepted and followed here, though it is not always an easy matter to differentiate between the two. The woody tissues of the shoot and spur may by common consent be considered vegetative in character. Likewise, it is generally agreed that the ovarian tissues of the fruit may be classed as reproductive, being more intimately associated with reproduction than with vegetative growth. On the other hand, there might easily be some difference in opinion regarding the tissues composing the peduncle or central axis of the inflorescence. In many plants these structures differ but little from other stem structures and they are vegetative in character. On the other hand, when these tissues become fleshy and form an integral part of the developing fruit, as they do in the pineapple, fig and many other fruits, they would as naturally be considered along with the ovarian tissues with which they are so closely associated. Mention is made of these points to emphasize the fact that the problem of fruit setting is not necessarily limited to a consideration of strictly reproductive tissues and reproductive activities. Indeed, the formation of an abscission layer at the base of the ovary, the pedicel or the peduncle is a function of the sporophytic tissue at that point. Consequently it is subject to the same influences, though perhaps not to the same extent or in exactly the same way, as abscission layers developed in other places. However, fruit setting and fruit formation depend on the initiation and successful completion of at least some of the reproductory processes. Therefore, the more important of the processes more or less directly concerned with the setting of fruit are outlined briefly.

In the great majority of higher plants, fruit and seed formation are conditioned on the bringing together and fusion of two specialized cells known as gametes. The larger of these cells is called the egg and is borne in the embryo sac. The smaller gametes are formed by a division of the generative nucleus of the pollen grain. The flower is the special organ of the plant for the production of these gametes. More specifically the stamen or microsporangium is the organ for the production of the male gametes and the ovule or macrosporangium the organ for the production of the female gametes. The great diversity in the size, form, color and odor of flowers does not modify the funda-

mental processes which take place, following pollination, in the growth of
the pollen tube or in fertilization. In this discussion, therefore, but
little attention need be given to the structure of the so-called non-essential
flower organs.

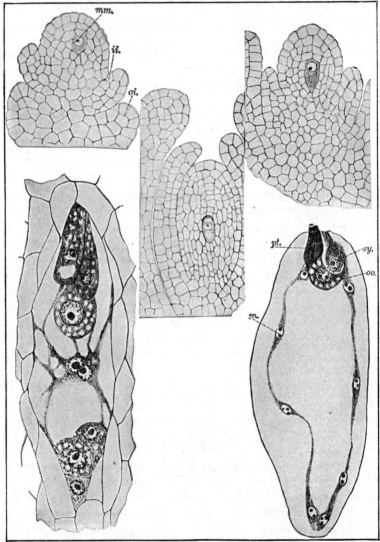

PLATE I.—Successive stages in the development of the ovule of the orange. In Fig.
1, *mm* = macrospore, *ii* = inner integument, and *oi* = outer integument. Figs. 2 and 3,
later stages in which the integument more nearly encloses the nucellus. Fig. 4, the fully
developed embryo sac, showing the egg apparatus at the upper end, the polar bodies near
the center, the antipodals at the bottom. Fig. 5, the embryo sac after fertilization, one
of the synergids (*pt*) disintegrating, the egg cell at *oo*, and 8 endosperm nuclei (*en*). (*After
Osawa*.[170])

CHAPTER XXVI

THE STRUCTURES AND PROCESSES CONCERNED IN FRUIT FORMATION

The entire flower may be regarded as a specialized branch, consisting of a central axis to which are attached several whorls or sets of organs that bear a certain resemblance to leaves. The two outer or lower whorls, the calyx and corolla, take no direct part in reproduction and are spoken of as non-essential organs, though after fertilization the calyx may undergo considerable differentiation and form a considerable part of the mature fruit. As stated before, the stamens bear the male gametes. In the higher plants, exclusive of the gymnosperms, the female gametes are developed inside an enclosed structure, the ovary. This last may consist of a single carpel (or modified leaf, to follow the conception of one school of botanists) or of several that are more or less completely united. In the latter case the ovary, and the fruit which develops from it, may be several-loculed. That portion of the central axis of the flower to which the several sets of floral organs are attached is the receptacle or torus.

A fruit may be defined as a ripened ovary together with whatever may be intimately attached to it at maturity. If it consists of a ripened ovary only, as in the peach or tomato, it is a simple fruit; if it includes additional structures it is spoken of as an accessory fruit. Sometimes the accessory structure may be the torus, as in the apple; sometimes the torus and the calyx, as in the cranberry and sometimes a part of the peduncle or pedicel, as in some varieties of the pear. The developing ovaries of certain fruits grow together and give rise (1) to aggregate fruits, if they all belonged to the same flower, as in the raspberry, or (2) to multiple fruits if they belonged to different flowers, as in the mulberry. In the latter the mature fruit includes ovarian, toral and stem tissues. Not infrequently the ovarian tissues constitute only a small part of the mature fruit and as a rule it is the accessory tissues (when they are present) in which the pomologist is mainly interested, for they are likely to constitute most of its edible portion. However, it is the ovary with its enclosed ovules on which fruit formation depends; consequently a discussion of fruit setting and fruit formation must start with the ovary and its ovules.

The Ovule.—The ovule arises as a protuberance from the inner wall of the ovary. The particular points, lines or surfaces from which it springs are known as the placentæ. Successive stages in the development of a typical ovule are shown in Figs. 1 to 3 of Plate I. The ovules of different species vary greatly in size, shape and degree of development and differentiation. However, practically all differentiate into a central portion and one or two enveloping layers. The central portion is known as the nucellus, the enveloping layers as the outer and inner integuments. These several structures are clearly shown in Figs. 2 and 3 of Plate I. The integuments never completely enclose the nucellus but leave an opening of varying size, the micropyle, through which the pollen tube usually passes to effect fertilization. The stalk or filament by which the ovule is attached to the ovarian wall is known as the funicle. Through it the ovule and later the developing seed receives its supply of food material. In many species the funicle is fused with the outer integument for a short distance, giving rise to a ridge known as the raphe. The point where the nucellar and integumental tissues are continuous and grown together is the chalaza.

The Embryo Sac.—At an early stage in the development of the nucellus, one of its cells becomes differentiated from the others and is known as the macrospore. This cell enlarges and divides first into two and then into four cells forming the axial row. The first division of the macrospore mother cell is the reduction division, which means that the number of chromosomes in the nucleus of each of these four cells is half of the number in the mother cell from which they were derived. Ordinarily only one of these four cells develops and this becomes the embryo sac, shown in Fig. 3 of Plate I. Its nucleus divides into two, then four and finally eight, presenting the condition shown in Fig. 4 of Plate I. At this stage the protoplasm of the embryo sac is highly vacuolated. At one end, three of the nuclei are visible, constituting the egg apparatus. Only one is capable of being fertilized. The other two are called synergids; their exact function is not known. At the opposite end of the embryo sac are three nuclei called antipodals which are separated at an early stage from the rest of the sac contents by the formation of cell walls. These cells do not take any direct part in the process of fertilization and they do not influence the development of the fruit so far as known. Sooner or later they, like the synergids, disintegrate. Near the center of the embryo sac are the other two nuclei called polar bodies because each has come from the group of nuclei at the extreme ends or poles of the embryo sac. These nuclei fuse into one, forming the fusion nucleus, which then divides rapidly to produce the endosperm; in many instances one of the two male gametes unites with the fusion nucleus before its division begins, thus bringing about double fertilization.

Pollen.—Stamens originate as small protuberances at their points of insertion on the axis of the flower. At first these projections consist

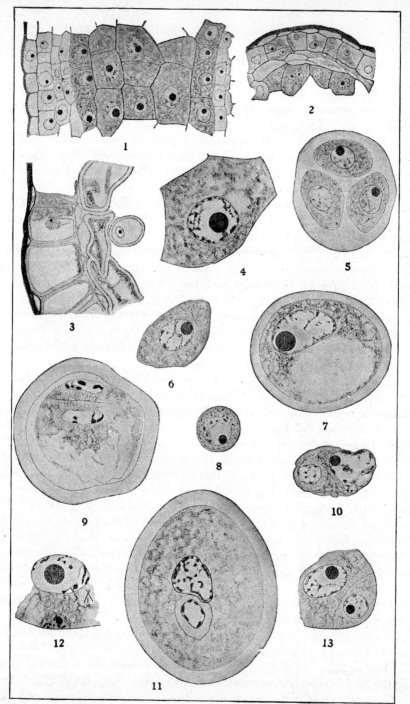

PLATE II.—Successive stages in the development of the pollen grain of the grape. Fig. 1, section of anther showing epidermal, middle, tapetal and mother-cell layers. Figs. 2 and 3, later stages in these same layers. Fig. 4, a pollen-mother-cell. Fig. 5, the tetrad stage in the pollen-mother-cell. Fig. 6, a microspore or pollen grain, before its liberation from the pollen-mother-cell. Fig. 7, a pollen grain of the Concord grape. Fig. 8, the generative cell in a mature pollen grain. Figs. 9–12, various stages in the development of the generative and vegetative nuclei, but in each instance one or both nuclei are undergoing degeneration. Fig. 13, the normal generative cell and vegetative nucleus of a pollen grain. (*After Dorsey*.[60])

of homogeneous tissue, but differentiation soon occurs and it becomes possible to recognize filament and anther. The anther increases in size more rapidly than the filament and gives rise to a structure that is generally grooved longitudinally on the outside and four-loculed in cross section. Figures 1 to 8 of Plate II show successive stages in the development of the male reproductive cell, or pollen grain, from the tissues of the anther in the grape. At a comparatively early stage there is a differentiation between the cells of its outer layers and those in the interior. This differentiation has progressed rather far in the section shown in Fig. 1, Plate II, the epidermal, middle, tapetal and mother-cell layers being clearly distinguishable. Eventually the epidermal and sub-epidermal layers undergo a series of changes which lead to their separation from the sporogenous tissue within and to their assuming the role of a simple protective shell or covering. Some idea of these changes is afforded by Figs. 2 and 3 of Plate II. Figure 4 of Plate II shows a single large pollen-mother-cell just previous to the reduction division, which gives rise to four daughter cells, each of which is surrounded by a membrane or cell wall. This is the so-called tetrad stage, shown in Fig. 5, Plate II, though only three of the four microspores are shown in the plane in which that figure was drawn. Shortly after the formation of these tetrads the mother-cell wall breaks down and liberates the microspores. Figure 6 of Plate II shows one of the microspores of the Brighton grape just previous to its liberation and Fig. 7 of Plate II shows one of the Concord variety a short time after its liberation. Its thick wall, large nucleus and vacuole are prominent. Usually some time before, though sometimes after, the dehiscence of the anther and the dispersal of the pollen there are further changes within the pollen grain. The nucleus divides giving rise to two daughter nuclei. One is called the generative nucleus, because it alone gives rise to the gametes. This generative nucleus becomes surrounded by a cell wall and is then called the generative cell of the pollen grain. The other is called the vegetative nucleus, because its function is more closely associated with germination and because it functions as the nucleus of the pollen tube. Figures 9 and 12 of Plate II show two stages in the development of these two nuclei, though both cases are somewhat abnormal because they show the initial stages of a degeneration that leads to impotency. Figure 13 of Plate II shows the generative cell and vegetative nucleus of a mature pollen grain of the Concord grape before dehiscence of the anther.

Pollination.—In the ordinary course of events the maturing of the ovules and of the pollen grains is followed by a transfer of pollen from stamen to stigma. If the transfer is from stamen to stigma of the same flower or to the stigma of another flower on the same plant, or, in the case of pomological varieties, to the stigma of a flower on any plant of the same variety, the process is self pollination. If the transfer is to the flower of another individual, or, in the case of pomological varieties, to the flower of another variety, the process is cross pollination. When self pollination is effected without the aid of any outside agency, such as wind or insects, the process is known as autogamy. Though this condition has been rather generally assumed by growers to be characteristic of fruit plants bearing perfect flowers, the evidence indicates that it is the exception. Consequently provision must usually be made for pollen transfer with self pollinated as well as with cross pollinated varieties. Many of the peculiarities of form, structure, color and odor of flowers are closely associated with means for securing proper self or cross pollination. Some of the factors which are of importance in aiding or preventing pollination are discussed later.

Germination of the Pollen Grain.—Pollination is usually followed promptly by the germination of the pollen grain. This is brought about by the absorption of water and various substances in the stigmatic fluid. The grain swells and a tube is pushed out through one of the pores in the outer covering or extine. The tube is formed by the intine or inner covering which pushes out through the germ pore. As it elongates it penetrates the tissues of the style by growing between the cells and as it advances toward the ovarian cavity its rate of growth may increase. The styles of the flowers of many species contain rows of cells that may be looked upon as specialized conducting tissue for the purpose of guiding and facilitating the growth of the pollen tubes. In other species there is no evidence of such tissue. For the most part pollen tubes digest their way as they go, by the secretion of a pectin-digesting enzyme. This dissolves the middle lamella which is composed of pectin-like substances that hold adjoining cells together and thus permits the insertion of the pollen tube betweem them.[177] As early as 1894, Green[92] found that the pollen of many kinds of plants contains diastase and some kinds were found to contain invertase as well. Besides these enzymes, Paton[178] reports finding amylase, catalase and reductase in the pollen of Easter lily, red maple, Siberian crab apple, Austrian pine, magnolia, dandelion and a number of other plants, erepsin, pepsin, trypsin and iipase in some, and zymase in the Siberian crab apple. The inability of much of the pollen of certain species of *Cassia* even to germinate unless subjected to the influence of an outside supply of diastase, reported by Tischler[223,224] from Buitenzorg, Java, illustrates a still earlier role of enzymes in the fruit-setting process. During the process of germination these enzymes increase in amount. Presumably they are effective in rendering available, for the nutrition of the pollen tube, food materials stored in either pollen grain or style.   This assumption is supported by work which showed that pollination produces a rapid rise of respiratory activity in the gynaeceum.[247]

In *Pelargonium zonale* the amount of carbon dioxide produced by the pollinated flowers is 5.8 times greater than that produced by the unpollinated flowers, though most other cases studied were somewhat less extreme.   It was also found that in every case pollination resulted in some change in the respiratory coefficient—the ratio of oxygen taken in to the carbon dioxide given off.

Course of the Pollen Tube.—For the most part, the growth of the pollen tube is directed by chemotropic influences supplied by the tissues of

TABLE 1.—THE INFLUENCE OF THE INCLUSION OF THE STIGMA OF A DIFFERENT
VARIETY UPON POLLEN GERMINATION OF PEARS
(Germinated in a 15 per cent. cane sugar solution at a temperature of 16.5° to 18°C.
and reading taken after 24 hours)
(*After Reinecke*[191])

Pollen variety	Stigma variety	Germination, per cent.	Pollen-tube length, microns
Forelle	Without stigma	40	42.6
Forelle	Forelle	45	319.5
Forelle	Kieffer	70	426.0
Forelle	Flemish Beauty	60	71.0
Kieffer	Without stigma	1	71.0
Kieffer	Kieffer	80	639.0
Kieffer	Forelle	85	710.0
Kieffer	Bergamotte	55	284.0
Flemish Beauty	Without stigma	45	142.0
Flemish Beauty	Flemish Beauty	50	248.5
Flemish Beauty	Kieffer	70	305.3
Flemish Beauty	Forelle	85	355.0
Glou Morceau	Glou Morceau	5	35.5
Glou Morceau	Beurre Diel	4	355.0

the ovary, the ovules and by the style and stigma.   Miyoshi[155] sowed pollen grains on agar in which were imbedded pieces of stigma, ovary and ovules of different degrees of development.   The pollen tubes grew toward the pieces from the vicinity of the stigma, but they were attracted most strongly by ovules ready for fertilization, growing into the micropyle in each instance.   In other investigations pieces of stigmatic tissue were observed to influence the direction of pollen tube growth at distances up to 70 times the diameter of the pollen grain.[127]   Recent studies by Reinecke[191] and Johannson[121] indicate that not only is there an influence of stigmatic secretions on pollen germination and rate of pollen tube growth but that a given variety of pollen may be influenced very differently by stigmas of different varieties (see Table 1).

Pollen tubes are especially sensitive to sugar solutions, growing toward them readily. They tend to grow away from dry air and "show a preference for spaces saturated with aqueous vapour to such as are less humid."[127] Investigations of the mode of growth of the pollen tube in *Houstonia* led to the conclusion that the tissues of the style influence its direction only in a passive manner but that "a chemotactic stimulus originating in the egg-apparatus, or the egg itself, is the chief directive influence."[150] Dorsey, however, has found tubes growing in plum styles with aborted ovules; therefore it is possible that growth often depends less on a normal egg-apparatus than the work with *Houstonia* would indicate. Dorsey found also that in the apple the pollen tube may grow beyond the ovule and down into the stem. Kerner and Oliver[127] state that ovules ready for fertilization "attract not only pollen-tubes from pollen of the same species, but of others far removed from it in point of affinity. The delicate hyphae of several mould-fungi are similarly attracted."

In some species the pollen tube does not enter the ovarian cavity and find its way into the ovule through the micropyle. Instead, when it reaches the base of the style, it turns aside and continues its progress through ovarian, placental and funicular tissues, finally penetrating the ovule through the chalaza. This is known as chalazogamic fertilization and is characteristic of the walnut,[17] pecan[1] and filbert.[166]

Time for Pollen Tube Growth.—Ordinarily germination of the pollen grain occurs promptly after pollination, the pollen tube grows fairly rapidly and fertilization occurs within a period of 1 or 2 days, though the time may be expected to vary with temperature and other environmental factors. Under favorable conditions there is an interval of from 9 to 120 hours between pollination and fertilization in apples, plums and cherries.[197,135] In Wisconsin, fertilization of apple blossoms was found to take place in 3 or 4 days less time, following pollination, in strongly vegetative trees, as compared with those that were in a low state of vigor.[194] The very much slower growth of Rome apple pollen tubes in Rome styles as compared with that of the tubes of other apple varieties and of Chojuro pear pollen tubes in Chojuro styles, reported by investigators in West Virginia[135] and Japan,[3] is interesting and may offer an explanation of some cases of self sterility.

A period of from 26 to 41 hours has been reported in the case of certain cucurbitaceous plants,[134] 4 days in one of the species of *Gastrodia*,[141] one month in *Betula*,[11] several months in *Hamamelis*[203] and approximately a year in certain of the oaks.[35] That there may be a great variation in this respect between closely related plants is evident from the behavior of the Satsuma orange in which about 30 hours have been found to elapse between pollination and fertilization,[30] while a corresponding period of 4 weeks has been reported in *Citrus trifoliata*.[170]

Fertilization.—In Fig. 13 of Plate II are shown the vegetative nucleus and the generative cell of the mature pollen grain. During the growth of the pollen tube the nucleus of the generative cell divides, giving rise to two male gametes, each consisting of a nucleus and a small portion of stainable material. The pollen tube, after entering the micropyle, penetrates the intervening tissue of the nucellus and then enters the embryo sac. The following account of fertilization is adapted from Mottier's[157] description of the process: The end of the tube may enter the sac at one side of the synergids, in which case only one of these cells is at once disorganized, the other retaining its normal structure for some time. This condition is illustrated in Fig. 5, Plate I. Often it enters between the two synergids, in which case both cells disintegrate almost immediately. "As soon as the end of the pollen tube enters the embryo-sac it opens, discharging the two male gametes and other contents. One of the male nuclei enters the egg-cell and applies itself to the nucleus of the egg, while the other passes into the cavity of the saç. . . . It is presumably the first male nucleus which escapes from the pollen tube that unites with the nucleus of the egg, but positive proof on this point is wanting. . . . As fusion progresses, the nuclei become quite alike in shape, size and structure. Their membranes gradually disappear at the place of contact, their cavities become one, and the resulting fusion nucleus, which is in the resting condition, can scarcely be distinguished from the nucleus of an unfecundated egg. The nucleoli finally unite also." The fertilized egg cell becomes the embryo cell, the antecedent of the embryo.

Secondary Fertilization.—Attention has been called to the presence of two nuclei, the so-called polar nuclei, near the center of the mature embryo sac. These are shown clearly in Fig. 4 of Plate I. Usually these two fuse with the second sperm nucleus and the nucleus resulting from this triple fusion divides repeatedly giving rise to many daughter nuclei, shown in Fig. 5 of Plate I. Soon these daughter nuclei are separated by the formation of cell walls, the resulting tissue being the antecedent of the seed endosperm.

Sometimes the second sperm nucleus fuses with but one of the polar nuclei[243] and sometimes it degenerates in the cytoplasm of the embryo sac. In the former case, the endosperm is of the same parentage as the embryo beside which it develops; in the latter case it is built from maternal tissue alone. In plants with albuminous seeds, this results in the condition known as xenia.

Development of the Embryo and Endosperm.—Following the process of fertilization the embryo cell "divides by a transverse wall into two cells, one directed towards the micropyle, the other towards the base of the embryo sac. The upper of these two cells stretches, and is repeatedly

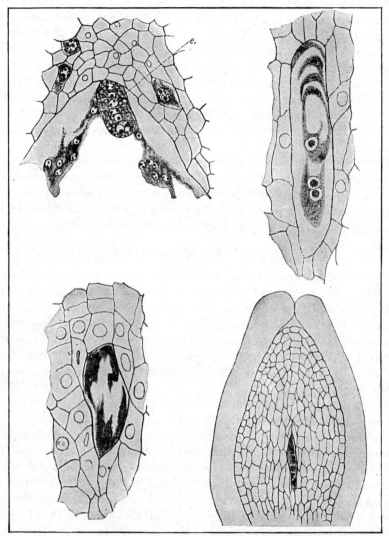

PLATE III.—Fig. 1, an early stage in the development of the normal orange embryo, showing the so-called suspensor. Figs. 2–4, stages in the development of the ovule of the orange showing various degenerative changes which result in embryo abortion; should the fruit mature it would be seedless. (*After Osawa.*[170])

segmented; thus a string of cells is formed, known as the suspensor, bearing at its lower extremity the embryo-cell, which gives rise to the greater portion of the young plant."[131] This stage is shown in Fig. 1, Plate III.

Coordinate with the development of the embryo is that of the endosperm. To be exact, in most developing seeds the growth of the endosperm is at first more rapid than that of the embryo. In many exalbuminous seeds there is a period of very rapid growth of the endosperm during which the young embryo either grows very slowly or persists in a practically resting stage. This is followed by a period of rapid embryo development, which occurs largely at the expense of the materials accumulated in the endosperm. The initiation of this period of rapid growth in the slow growing or resting embryos is apparently one of the "sticking points" in the process of seed formation and in many species it is very important in determining whether or not the fruit shall mature or fall prematurely.

In the developing seeds of most species the tissues of the nucellus disintegrate and their substance is used by the growing endosperm or embryo. In some species, however, the nucellar tissues persist and develop into a storage tissue that can hardly be distinguished from endosperm. Storage tissue of such origin is known as perisperm.

THE SETTING OF THE FRUIT

The fertilization process and the following segmentation and growth of the embryo and endosperm within the ovule are accompanied by changes in the surrounding ovary wall and often in the torus and other adjoining tissues. Most noticeable among these changes are a thickening and an increase in size, perhaps with some change in color, shape and position, so that it is evident very soon after blossoming that the fruit has or has not "set," or that there is or is not a possibility of its maturing properly in due time.

However, some blossoms do not set fruit and sometimes the percentage that sets is extremely small. Nothing is of greater importance to the fruit grower than having a reasonable percentage of the blossoms set. Yield, income and profits are all absolutely dependent on what the tree does in this respect at and just after the time of blossoming. Of course accidents or unfavorable conditions later in the season may injure or destroy the crop, but they are contingencies with which the grower has greater confidence in dealing than the accidents that may befall at the time of fruit setting.

The term "fruit setting" is used here to refer to the initial and appreciable swelling of the ovary occurring shortly after the period of petal fall. It is generally accompanied by some thickening of the pedicel or of the peduncle. Meanwhile, flowers that have not "set" are turning yellow or withering and falling off. After this stage is passed accidents may happen and the "June drop" or some other "drop" or some environmental factor may cause abscission; nevertheless, at least for the time being, it appears as though fertilization had taken place and the chances are good for the fruit maturing.

What Constitutes a Normal Set of Fruit.—It is not to be expected that all the blossoms will set fruit, even though conditions are ideal. In most species and varieties they are produced in such profusion that a total set would be little short of calamitous for the grower. He is more interested in obtaining a reasonable number of fruits of good marketable size than a much larger number of a size for which there is little demand. Furthermore, he prefers a crop such as the trees can mature without undue exhaustion, for then he is surer of crops the following years.

The set that the grower would call perfect varies greatly with species, variety and with conditions. In 1899, Fletcher[75] counted 4,725 blossoms of the apple, pear, plum and apricot; from these 617 fruits developed what was considered a full crop for the branches on which they were borne. It would be called a perfect set by the grower, yet the percentage actually setting was 13. The setting of 20 to 30 per cent. of the blossoms of the Muscadine grape would give a full crop,[117] though with grapes of the Labrusca type a similar set would give rise to loose straggly bunches that would have to be placed in the cull grade. A full-grown avocado tree may produce upwards of a million individual blossoms, there often being several hundred to a cluster, so that the actual fruiting of a fraction of 1 per cent. will provide an abundant crop. If, however, the setting of 10 per cent. of the blossoms provides for a full crop, a 5 per cent. set will provide only half a crop, though proportionally but a few more blossoms drop. In terms of the percentage of blossoms setting, then, a difference of a few per cent. may have a great effect on the size of the crop so that it becomes important to ascertain the causes of these slight differences and the methods of controlling them.

The usual failure of many blossoms to set and mature fruit is due to many factors, the more important of which are discussed later. It should be understood, however, that many cultivated varieties characteristically produce more blossoms than possibly can mature into fruits and that consequently a certain amount of dropping is to be expected. This may be regarded in the same light as the nearly universal abortion of one of the two ovules in the ovaries of most stone fruit varieties or two of the three ovaries in the flower of the date palm—phenomena due to deep-seated hereditary causes that are quite beyond control by any cultural means.

The June Drop and Other Drops.—All of the flowers that fail to mature fruit do not drop at one time and a continuous dropping from the flowering stage up to the time of maturity is not common. Instead there are more or less definite periods or stages when extensive dropping occurs. The loss comes in a series of waves, varying with the different fruits in number and in the length of time between them. There appear to be certain "sticking points," critical periods, through which each fruit must proceed to reach full maturity. When one of these sticking points is safely passed there is comparatively little danger of the fruit falling before the next critical period arrives. Apparently these sticking points for fruit setting are closely correlated with definite changes in the development taking place in the embryo and in the endosperm of the seeds.

Dorsey[61] has made a careful study of dropping of blossoms and newly-set fruits in the plum and the following account, adapted from his report, illustrates the phenomenon as it occurs in fruits in general:

The First Drop.—The first drop takes place very soon after blossoming. Examination of the pistils of the flowers dropping at this time shows that they are defective. In some, pistil abortion has occurred at an earlier stage than in others though the stage at which it occurs is quite constant for each variety. Pistils show all degrees of development, ranging from mere rudiments up to those that are nearly perfectly formed. The more defective pistils drop earliest, but all flowers come into full bloom. Flowers with defective pistils always drop at the pedicel base and neither the calyx tube nor the style is shed by abscission because growth is not carried far enough. The immediate cause of the dropping is the abortion of pistils that are structurally defective and cannot function.

The Second Drop.—"The first drop is followed 2 weeks or so after bloom by another distinct wave of falling pistils. While there are a few intergrading forms between these two drops, certain features of the second drop separate it distinctly from the first. Unlike the pistils of the first drop, those of the second have every external appearance of being normal. Enlargement up to a certain point takes place and in most cases the calyx tube breaks away at least in part even though there is insufficient growth in the young plum to throw it off. The style is not deciduous in the earliest pistils to fall, but, like the calyx tube, drops in those which fall later. . . . Pistils which fall in the second drop, as in the first, absciss at the pedicel base while the pistil is still green, although the pedicel has become light yellow. Yet in the last pistils of the second drop to fall the abscission layer is formed at the base of the ovary and in some instances can be easily broken off at this point. . . .

"Emphasis is placed upon the following points. . . . : (a) the period of abscission of the second drop extended from 17 to 30 days after bloom; (b) beginning with the first pistils to fall, size differences between those persisting and those which fell, gradually increased with time; (c) pistils which fell within the above-mentioned time limit enlarged only up to a certain point; (d) those pistils with the stigmas snipped before pollination, enlarged, before falling, to a size comparable with that of those not so treated; and (e) in each variety there was a gradual increase in the size of the pistils which fell off. . . .

"The condition found in the unfertilized series is in marked contrast with that found when fertilization takes place. As early as 18 days after bloom the embryo sac in which the egg has been fertilized extends the entire length of the nucellus to the chalaza, and a jacket of endosperm, usually only one cell thick, covers the entire area of the 'dumb-bell-shaped' sac. With the completion of these changes in the embryo sac the embryo may be no larger than four cells across. . . .

"It will be seen from the above observations that all the evidence shows that fertilization has not occurred in the pistils which fall at the second drop. . . . Pollination may have taken place, but tube growth was retarded to such an extent that fertilization was prevented probably by the abscission of the style."

The Third Drop or June Drop.—"Following the second drop there is still another—the so-called 'June drop.' In popular usage the term June drop applies primarily to the third drop of large plums because they are much more conspicuous, but does not include the relatively few which fall from time to time, even up to maturity . . . It has been shown that time and size of dropping draw a relatively sharp line between the first and the second waves of dropping. Likewise these two factors separate the second drop from the third. . . . When fertilization does not take place enlargement reaches only a certain point, the maximum recorded being in the 5.6 to 6.0 millimeter class, while the mode is near 3.0 millimeters. Among the last of the second drop an occasional ovule is found with slight embryo development, which shows that there are connecting forms between the second and third drops as well as between the first and second. In approximately one month the second drop is over, and those setting have so increased in size as to place them in a distinct size class from those which have fallen. . . .

"Sections have been made of the embryos of a large number of plums which fell at the June drop. Dissections were also made of ovules at various stages to determine the amount of growth in the embryo. The general condition found may be summarized as follows: (*a*) embryo development started but growth stopped at any time from the stage when the embryo was a few cells across to the time at which it had reached nearly the mature size; (*b*) endosperm had partly formed, but the embryo gained the ascendency to such an extent that it was often found naked in the nucellus; (*c*) enlargement in the seed could reach nearly the mature size when fertilization had once occurred, accompanied by only a slight growth of the embryo. . . .

"The status of development in the ovule in the third drop shows marked differences from that in the second. Firstly, greater size is attained than is ever found in the second drop, and secondly, instead of there being disintegrating nuclei within a slightly elongated embryo sac, tissues cease growing at various stages rather than disintegrating. This latter fact alone suggests an additional stimulus absent in the second drop. . . . "

The sweet cherry, some varieties, at least, of the apple and pear and a number of other fruits have similar periods when their blossoms or developing fruits drop in large numbers. In some instances they occur relatively earlier or later, as the case may be, or there may be only two waves or perhaps only a single wave of dropping, and these waves are not always associated with the same environmental conditions or with the same stages of development of embryo or endosperm. Thus, in the pecan the first, and usually the heaviest, drop of pistillate flowers occurs at or just prior to pollination and is of flowers that never quite reach a stage where pollination and fertilization are possible.[255]

Certain other fruits, such as the currant and the raspberry show quite different characteristics in their fruit setting and fruit dropping. In some, as the strawberry, the flowers either set fruit or fail to set and there is no later dropping or abortion. However, the so-called June drop, which may or may not occur in June and may correspond either to the second or the third drop of the plum, is important in determining the size of the crop with most deciduous tree fruits.

Usually, though not always, the relation between the losses incident to the successive drops varies with the severity of any one of them. Heinicke[100] points out that when the "first" drop in the apple is relatively large the June drop is relatively small; on the other hand the June drop is heavy if a comparatively large proportion of the flowers begin to form fruits. This may vary according to variety or with the conditions under which it is grown. Comparable to this is the condition pointed out by Reed[189] in certain lemon varieties, in which an individual flower bud on a small inflorescence has a greater chance to set and develop into a mature fruit than one on a large inflorescence. Napoleon is an example of a sweet cherry variety that, as grown in the Pacific northwest, almost invariably shows a heavy first drop, a light to heavy second drop, depending on conditions, and an almost negligible June drop. When Llewelling is grown under similar conditions it usually shows a fairly heavy first drop, a light second drop and a very heavy June drop.

It is interesting in this connection that occasionally certain flowers of the cluster do not set well, while others set fruit perfectly. Schuster[198] has called attention to this peculiarity in the flower clusters of Ettersburg 121, a strawberry variety. The primary flowers of the cluster, those coming from the forks, set freely; only a small percentage of the secondaries, those coming from the lateral branches of the peduncle, set fruit. The case is not exactly one of blossom dropping, for the flowers do not drop off; but it is at least in certain respects comparable to the first drop described by Dorsey for the plum, though the pistils do not appear to be defective. Valleau[236] found in some species and in certain varieties of the strawberry that the later flowers to open may have sterile pistils. He ascribes this to a tendency toward diœciousness.

Another interesting case of the June drop or of a phenomenon comparable to it is found in the date palm. Ordinarily by the end of June three partly grown fruits of approximately equal size have developed from the three ovaries of each pistillate flower. If pollination and fertilization have taken place two of these developing fruits drop off, leaving a single one to mature. On the other hand, if the flowers have not been pollinated, all three may persist and continue to grow slowly; they never reach full edible maturity and are without value. They are seedless, closely crowded together and generally somewhat deformed.[219]

Fruit Setting, Fruitfulness and Fertility Distinguished.—In the preceding discussion the term "fruit setting" has been used to refer both to the initial setting of the fruit at or just after the time of blossoming and to its remaining on the plant until maturity. The term is used often in a somewhat narrower sense to indicate whether or not it remains attached to the plant for any considerable time after flowering and whether any enlargement of the ovary takes place. Probably in the case of the plum just described in detail few would regard the fruit as having set if it did not survive the second drop, but many would consider it as having set if it remained through this period, even though abscission took place at the time of the third or June drop. There are reasons for refraining from an attempt to limit too closely the meaning and use of the term. However, it is desirable to be able to refer to definite conditions that are exemplified in many different species. By common consent the term "fruitful" is used to describe the plant that not only blossoms and sets fruit, but carries it through to maturity. The plant that is unable to do this, or that does not do it, is "unfruitful" or "barren." "Fertility" indicates ability not only to set and mature fruit but to develop viable seeds. Inability to do this is described by the terms "infertility" and "sterility." Fruitfulness and fertility are not synonymous, for many fruits, like the banana, mature their fruits though they bear no mature seeds. This should be emphasized because fruitful plants are often spoken of as being fertile, when, as a matter of fact, they may or may not be. Fertile plants are necessarily fruitful. Self fruitfulness, therefore, refers to the ability of the plant to mature fruit without the aid of pollen from some other flower, plant or variety, as the case may be; self fertility indicates a similar ability to mature viable seed without the aid of pollen from some other flower, plant or variety.

Sterility and Unfruitfulness Classified.—In a general way the causes of sterility, unfruitfulness and of the failure of the fruit to set may be grouped in two main classes—those internal to the plant and those external, that concern more directly its environment. Frequently it is difficult, if not impossible, to differentiate between these groups of factors, for they are interdependent to an important extent; nevertheless it is convenient to make such a grouping.

Summary.—The essential organs of the flower as they concern fruit setting and fruit production are the pistils and stamens, though other parts may enter into the structure of the fruit. The changes taking place in the ovule and anther just previous to the time of pollination and fertilization are described in detail.   Pollination is followed by the germination of the pollen grain and the growth of the pollen tube, under the influence of chemotropic factors, down the style.   With the penetration of the nucellus by the pollen tube and the fusion of one of the generative nuclei of the latter with the egg cell, fertilization is complete, though a secondary fertilization of one of the polar nuclei by the second generative nucleus occurs frequently.   The embryo results from the segmentation and growth of the embryo cell and the endosperm is the tissue developing from the polar nuclei.   Fertilization is usually followed by a growth of the surrounding ovarian tissues, resulting in a "setting" of the fruit. As a rule only a small percentage of the flowers of most deciduous fruits "set" and many of those that remain fall before the fruit reaches maturity.   In many fruits there are several distinct periods of dropping, these distinct waves being referred to as the first, second and June drops. These periods of dropping generally are closely associated with definite stages in the development of the tissues of the ovule.   Fruit setting, fruitfulness and fertility are distinguished.   The factors responsible for unfruitfulness may be classified for convenience into those which are external and those which are internal to the plant.

CHAPTER XXVII

UNFRUITFULNESS ASSOCIATED WITH INTERNAL FACTORS

Stout[209] recognizes three types of sterility that are to be attributed mainly to internal factors: (1) sterility from impotence, (2) sterility from incompatibility, (3) sterility from embryo abortion. Sterility from impotence arises when one or both of the sex organs fails to attain full development. This may be complete, in which case either no flowers or no sex organs are formed, or it may be partial, in which case either stamens or pistils are abortive. Sterility from incompatibility arises when, though the sex organs are completely formed, they fail to function properly. In the last type of sterility the gametes are formed and apparently function but abortion of the developing embryo takes place before maturity is reached. The same classification may hold for the externally controlled factors with which unfruitfulness and the failure to set fruit are associated. It may be observed that the sterility due to impotence represents an evolutionary tendency in the group or species—an evolutionary tendency that finds immediate expression in a distribution of the two sexes between different flowers or branches on the same plant or between different plants. The distinction between sterility due to incompatibility and that due to embryo abortion is drawn in recognition of the time or stage of development at which the male and female gametes, both structurally and functionally perfect, show their incompatibility—their inability to unite or develop together to form a mature embryo.

Perhaps a classification of the causes of sterility associated with internal factors and based upon more fundamental processes would recognize: (1) those due to evolutionary tendencies, mentioned above; (2) those due to genetic influences, regardless of the exact time or stage of development when the two kinds of gametes show their mutual aversion and (3) those due to physiological factors, in which case there is not true incompatibility but a failure of the plant to provide nutritive conditions suitable for continued growth. This last type of sterility cannot always be differentiated clearly from that due to environmental factors or to that due to genetic influences, if the evidence of such influences comes after the fertilization process has been completed.

DUE PRINCIPALLY TO EVOLUTIONARY TENDENCIES

In nature the advantage of cross fertilization in maintaining the vigor of the species has resulted in many cases in the development of certain characteristics which make self fertilization difficult, if not impossible. These factors, so favorable to the maintenance of the species, may, in cultivation, limit its usefulness and range. The more important of these characteristics, as they concern the fruit grower, are mentioned here.

Imperfect Flowers: Diœcious and Monœcious Plants.—Most fruit-producing species bear perfect flowers. There are some, however, in which the sexes are separated. In certain species, such as the walnut and pecan, they are found in different flowers on the same tree or plant; in others, such as the papaya and sometimes the strawberry, they are found on different plants.

Similarly, the flowers of some plum varieties produce so little pollen that for all practical purposes they must be classed as unisexual,[121] and they too should be interplanted with good pollen producers. The failure of a number of the ornamental types of pomegranate to set and mature much fruit, though blossoming freely, is likewise due in considerable measure to their flowers being unisexual.[107]

Monœcious plants bear the pistillate and staminate flowers on the same individual and are always fruitful—at least theoretically—and rather frequently they are self fruitful. Certainly the segregation of the sexes to separate flowers of the plant does not in itself interfere with pollination, fruit setting and fruitfulness. Among the more common fruits that are monœcious are the walnut, pecan, filbert, and chestnut. The members of the Cucurbitaceæ also are for most part monœcious.

Probably the strawberry is the most widely grown of the diœcious fruits. A comparatively large percentage of its varieties bear perfect flowers, but some of the best are pistillate. For many years after the strawberry was introduced into cultivation no attention was paid to the matter of planting so as to secure pollination of the pistillate varieties, hence much of the failure of the fruit to set properly in the plantations of a century ago. It was not until the observations of Nicholas Longworth of Cincinnati were brought to the attention of horticulturists generally in the fifties that the unisexuality shown by plants of this species attained recognition and planting practices were modified accordingly. Experience has taught long since that these pistillate sorts should be interplanted with perfect flowering varieties. There are many strawberry varieties classified as perfect flowering that produce only small amounts of pollen. These, as well as the imperfect sorts, should be interplanted with good pollen producers.

The Japanese persimmon or kaki presents a very interesting case of sex distribution. Many of its varieties, such as Tanenashi, Hyakume, Hachiya and Costata, produce only pistillate flowers year after year. These are called "pistillate constants" by Hume.[113] Certain other varieties bear each year pistillate flowers and also some staminate flowers; these he designates as "staminate constants." Still other varieties bear only pistillate flowers some seasons and in other seasons both pistillate and staminate. These are called "staminate sporadics." Hume[114] also records the occasional appearance of perfect flowers on trees that regularly or occasionally bear staminate flowers, though they have not been found on plants of the pistillate constant type. In other words, certain varieties are monœcious, others diœcious; still others vary from the one condition to the other and occasionally a variety becomes temporarily perfect flowering. The study of these flowering characteristics of the persimmon and the classification of the more important of its varieties have done much to explain the rather erratic behavior of this plant in fruit setting and the maturing of seed-bearing or seedless fruits.

Even more variable is the distribution of the sexes between different flowers and different plants in the papaya. Higgins and Holt[106] recognize 13 classes of trees, depending on the combination or separation of stamens and pistils and on form of the flower clusters, corolla and fruit. Independent of the classes based on features other than sex distribution, these types are:

1. Pure pistillate flowering plants.
2. Pure staminate flowering plants.
3. Plants producing both staminate and perfect flowers.
4. Plants producing both staminate and perfect flowers, but with sterile pollen. These might be called pseudo-hermaphrodite plants.
5. Plants producing staminate and perfect flowers in which neither pistils nor pollen are fertile. The plants might be called sterile hermaphrodites.
6. Plants producing staminate, pistillate and perfect flowers.
7. Plants producing pistillate and perfect flowers.
8. Plants producing staminate and pistillate flowers.

Types 2 and 5 are necessarily unfruitful, though type 5 is unfruitful apparently because of incompatibility rather than impotence, for the sex organs are developed but non-functioning. Types 1 and 4 are self unfruitful, though it is possible that 4 is self barren because of incompatibility rather than impotence. The other types are self fruitful; at least fruitfulness is not impossible because of impotence. Some of these self fruitful types are diœcious, some are polygamo-diœcious. Types 1 and 2 are by far the most common; that is, the papaya is for the most part unisexual. Consequently in the average planting of that fruit it is customary to retain a few of the staminate trees in order to insure a good set of fruit on those bearing pistillate flowers. Of course staminate trees remain barren, but if there should be only relatively few of them, they probably would be valued more highly than an equal number of the fruit producers.

The fig shows a distribution of its sexes somewhat less complicated than the papaya; nevertheless this distribution should often be given careful attention at the time of planting. Two kinds of flower clusters are borne by fig trees. Certain trees bear pistillate flowers only. The standard fig varieties include trees of this type exclusively. Certain other trees, called "caprifigs," produce both pistillate and staminate flowers within the same cluster. As a rule, the staminate flowers are borne near the "eye" of the fig and the pistillate flowers near its base. Fig trees may thus be placed in two classes in respect to sex distribution, diœcious or unisexual trees and monœcious trees. The pistillate flowering trees alone produce the figs of commerce. The monœcious trees or caprifigs are planted only for the purpose of furnishing pollen for the pistillate sorts.

Some authorities would take exception to certain of the statements just made about the nature of fig flowers. Eisen[66] states that there are three kinds of flowers on trees of the caprifig class—pistillate, staminate and gall. The gall flower is regarded as a specialized pistillate that can harbor the pollen-carrying *Blastophaga* wasp but cannot develop seed. Rixford,[193] on the other hand, holds that all so-called gall flowers are in reality simple pistillates, not structurally different from other pistillate caprifig flowers that occasionally are pollenized, set fruit and form seed. Usually they do not have the opportunity to set and develop seed because they are not pollinated or because they are stung by the *Blastophaga* and subsequently become galls.

Eisen[66] and many others recognize a third kind of pistillate flower which they call "mule" flowers. These are produced by most of those cultivated varieties which yield seedless fruits. They are held to be somewhat different in structure from the pistillates of such varieties as the Smyrna, that are capable of setting seed. However, Rixford[193] has shown that these so-called mule flowers do set and mature seed when properly pollinated and consequently considers them true pistillates.

Heterostyly.—It has been stated that the flowers of many species present peculiarities of form and structure, the main function of which is to aid in bringing together the male and female gametes so that fertilization may take place and reproduction be insured. However, many of these peculiarities of form and structure are of such a nature as to prevent self pollination and make cross pollination more certain. If cross pollination does not occur, the plant is very likely to remain unfruitful even though perfect sex organs have been developed.

One of these diversities of form is heterostyly, a type of dimorphism in which some of the flowers have short styles and long filaments and other flowers of the same species or variety have long styles and short filaments. The structure and arrangement are such that when these flowers are visited by pollen-carrying insects no self pollination takes place but pollen from short stamens is deposited upon the stigmas of the short pistils and pollen from the long stamens is carried to the stigmas of the long pistils. Cross pollination between two flowers of the same form on a single plant may occur, but the arrangement assures a considerable amount of crossing between plants. It has been shown that when the pistils of heterostyled plants are pollenized with pollen from the same flowers or from other flowers containing stamens of an equal height the union may be fruitful but is likely to be attended by varying degrees of sterility.[45] This, however, introduces the factor of incompatibility, about which more is said later.   Apparently heterostyly is relatively unimportant in determining setting in deciduous fruits.

Dichogamy : Protandry and Protogyny.—It has just been pointed out that in heterostyled plants the sexes are nearly as completely separated and self pollination as completely prevented as in monœcious plants. Likewise there may be more or less separation of the sexes and a prevention of self pollination in perfect flowered plants through the maturing of the two sex elements at different times.   This behavior of the plant is known as dichogamy.   If the stamens ripen before the pistil is ready to receive pollen the flower is protandrous, if the reverse condition holds it is protogynous.   Dichogamy is incomplete when there is an overlapping in the seasons of maturity of the two sex elements; otherwise it is complete.   Complete dichogamy insures pollination with some other flower and perhaps with another plant.   Incomplete dichogamy tends in that direction, but still allows opportunity for a certain amount of selfing.

The frequent occurrence of dichogamy and consequently its importance in influencing the setting of fruit is not generally appreciated. Kerner and Oliver[129] state: ". . . It appears that all species of plants whose hermaphrodite flowers are adapted to cross-fertilization by the relative position of anthers and stigmas are, moreover, dichogamous, although this dichogamy may be of slight duration.   Plants with heterostyled flowers are also dichogamous, since those with short-styled and those with long-styled flowers develop at different times. . . . As far as we can tell at present all monœcious plants are protogynous. . . . Alders and Birches, Walnuts, and Planes, Elms and Oaks, Hazels and Beeches are all markedly protogynous.   In most of these plants . . . the dust-like pollen is not shed from the anthers until the stigmas on the same plant have been matured 2 to 3 days.   Sometimes the interval between the ripening of the sexes is still greater.   The majority of diœcious plants are also protogynous."   In the chestnut there are two distinct groups or series of flowers—one developing on the preceding season's shoot growth and another from the axils of the current season's leaves.   The two groups of catkins mature and shed their pollen at different periods that do not overlap.   The pistillate flowers on the same trees become receptive during the interval between, and at each end slightly overlapping, the periods that the two sets of catkins are shedding their pollen.[185]   The tree is thus, each season, characteristically both protogynous and protandrous in a marked degree.   Both Waugh[239] and Dorsey[61] call attention to the existence of dichogamy in the plum. Pecan varieties have been classified in two main groups, those exhibiting dichogamy and those which mature their stamens and pistils simultaneously.[216] In Oregon, Franquette, the leading variety of English walnut, is protandrous to such a degree that its interplanting with some other variety to ensure pollination has been considered desirable by some growers.[12]

A rather extreme case of periodicity in pistil and pollen maturity is afforded by the avocado. Characteristically the individual flowers of a given variety open for two short periods, separated by a number of hours or by a day, and during these periods all the flowers of the tree (and, therefore, of the variety) that are open are in unison. Pistils are receptive, but no pollen is shed during the first of the two periods; pollen is shed, but no pistils are receptive during the second period. Self pollination is, therefore, impossible, even though the flowers are perfect and pistils are receptive and pollen is being shed every day throughout the blossoming season. Fruit production is possible only when adequate provision is made for cross pollination.[195, 213]

A similar case of dichogamy, but involving interspecific relationships, is described by Wester[246] for Anonas. Flowers of the cherimoya (*Anona cherimolia*) and of the custard apple (*A. reticulata*) were found to shed their pollen in the afternoon from about 3:30 to 6:00. Flowers of the sugar apple (*A. squamosa*) discharge their pollen from sunrise to about 9:00 a. m. A few trees of this latter species were found to shed their pollen in the afternoon and these same trees did not shed any pollen in the morning. Many pollinations were made, the results of all pointing to the same general conclusion. The following account of one of his experiments illustrates the results obtained: " . . . 143 flowers on one sugar apple tree were, in April and May, 1908, pollinated with their own pollen or that of flowers of other plants of the same species, 41 with pollen of the cherimoya, 31 with pollen of the pond apple, and 51 flowers with pollen of the custard apple. In no instance did fruit set where the pollen was applied to the stigma simultaneously with the discharge of its pollen; practically all responded where it was applied 15 to 48 hours previous to this act, though here, as in the case of the cherimoya, the tree shed much of the fruit before it matured owing to its inability to carry it all."

The flower clusters of the caprifig, the monœcious form of the fig tree, afford an extreme and very interesting instance of dichogamy.[66] The stamens and their pollen do not mature until shortly before the ripening of the fig, when the wasps have attained their maturity in the gall flowers of the same flower clusters and are ready to emerge and enter other fruits to which they carry pollen. On the other hand the pistillate flowers of the fig are receptive weeks, or even months, earlier. In this way the wasps, carrying the pollen from one crop (*e.g.*, the profichi) of the fig, enter the flowers of the following crop (mammoni) at a time when their stigmas are receptive. It is possible for self pollination to take place within the tree, but there is at least a crossing between two successive crops of the caprifig and there is often actual cross pollination between trees or varieties.

Commenting on the significance of dichogamy Kerner and Oliver[130] remark: "From these facts we may infer that every dichogamous plant has an opportunity for illegitimate crossing or hybridization at the beginning or end of its flowering, and that dichogamy—especially incomplete dichogamy—is the most important factor in its production. Of course this does not exclude dichogamy from playing an important part in legitimate crossing as well. On the whole, however, we can maintain the view that the separation of the sexes by the maturation of the sexual organs at different times leads to hybridization, while their separation in space promotes legitimate crossing. The fact that the separation of the sexes in time and space usually occurs in conjunction harmonizes with this conclusion, *i.e.*, that the diœcious, monœcious, and pseudo-hermaphrodite flowers, as well as those hermaphrodite flowers whose sexual organs are separated by some little distance, are in addition incompletely dichogamous, because by this contrivance the flowers of any species obtain (1) the possibility of hybridization at the beginning or end of their flowering period, and (2) of legitimate crossing during the rest of that time. This also explains why incomplete dichogamy is so much more frequent than complete dichogamy; why there are no diœcious species of plants with completely dichogamous flowers; and why, if one ever should occur, it would of necessity soon disappear. Let us suppose that somewhere or other there grows a species of Willow with completely protogynous diœcious flowers, that is to say, a species in which the female flowers mature first, and have ceased to be receptive before the male flowers in the same region discharge their pollen. Hybridization only could occur in it, and the young Willow plants resulting from it would all be hybrids whose form would no longer agree absolutely with that of the pistilliferous plant. The species would therefore not be able to reproduce its own kind by its seed, and it would leave no descendants of similar form; in other words, it would die out."

Data are not available as to the exact degree of dichogamy characteristic of all the different species and varieties of fruits; therefore it is impossible to state accurately the extent to which it interferes with their self pollination or to what extent it is a factor in determining their fruit setting. Furthermore, as is shown later, the completeness of dichogamy varies considerably with environmental conditions. There can be no question, however, but that in many varieties it explains the failure of numerous blossoms to set.

Impotence from Abortive Flowers and from Degenerating or Aborted Pistils or Ovules.—It is obvious that, if the setting and maturing of fruit usually depend on the union of two properly formed sex cells, anything which occurs to interfere with the development of the flower or the development and proper functioning of either gamete probably will result in unfruitfulness or at least in sterility. This occurs in the developing flowers, pistils and stamens of many species and is responsible for many failures in fruit setting. Abortion of partially developed flower buds or flowers before reaching the blossoming stage is of rather common occurrence. Woodroof[254] states that in the pecan the terminal portion of the pistillate cluster is almost always defective and is shed at pollination time and that sometimes there is a general shedding of entire clusters before

even the first individuals of the cluster reach maturity, especially following years of heavy cropping.   More or less of a similar situation is found
in the developing flower clusters of certain grape varieties and of the
tomato.   The later flowers of the strawberry cluster are always abortive.
Apparently flower abortion is more common in plants having indeterminate, than in those having determinate, inflorescences, but it is by no
means limited to the former.

Sometimes degeneration takes the form of an abortion of the pistil,
the rest of the flower appearing normal.   This may occur early or comparatively late in the course of its development; consequently in certain
species there are pistils in all stages from those very rudimentary and
plainly not functioning to those that apparently are perfect in structure
and ready for fertilization.   Goff[84] records this condition as very common
in many varieties of our native plums, and Hodgson[107] states that the
same thing is found in the pomegranate.   It occurs more frequently in
the ornamental types of the pomegranate than in those varieties cultivated primarily for their fruit; in either case it is one of the main causes of
the failure of the fruit to set.   Waugh,[239] in a rather extended study of the
occurrence of defective pistils in plums, found striking differences in
various groups.   His findings are summarized in Table 2.

TABLE 2.—PERCENTAGE OF DEFECTIVE PISTILS IN DIFFERENT GROUPS OF PLUMS
(After Waugh[239])

Domestica group	4.3	Wayland group	10.5
Japanese group	11.2	Wildgoose group	19.8
Americana group	21.2	Chicasaw group	10.5
Nigra group	17.0	Hybrids group	18.1
Miner group	1.9		

In a number of species and varieties the pistils attain their usual size
and they contain ovules that to the unaided eye appear entirely normal.
However, examination shows partial or complete degeneration in the
embryo sac just prior to its maturing; therefore fertilization is impossible.
Embryo sacs of the orange showing degeneration at various stages in
their development are pictured in Figs. 2 to 4 of Plate III.   Sometimes
these degenerative processes set in early in the development of the ovules
and their abortion is so complete that it is evident to the unaided eye
at the time for fertilization.   In the Unshu and Washington Navel
oranges, however, the fruits may develop in spite of that defect, though
they are seedless.   Embryo sac abortion thus becomes in certain instances
a cause of seedlessness rather than unfruitfulness.   Pistil abortion,
apparently at a comparatively late stage in development, has been found
to explain the failure of many strawberry blossoms to set fruit and the
production of "nubbins" from many others.[236]   One of the two ovules

in the ovary of the plum[61] and other stone fruits is often much smaller than the other at the time of flowering, showing that at least a part of the almost universal failure of one of the ovules to develop into a seed is due to processes operating before the time of fertilization. It should be noted in this case, as in many other fruits, that the abortion of a part of the ovules of the flower does not lead necessarily to unfruitfulness. The relation of number or proportion of seeds to the holding of the fruit is discussed in another connection.

Impotence of Pollen.—It has long been known that many apparently perfect flowered plants produce only small amounts of pollen and that occasionally a considerable portion of that which is borne is non-viable. In fact it is unusual to find pollen that is 100 per cent. viable. However, until recently there has been little realization of the importance of this factor in determining fruit setting and fruitfulness.

Beach[7,8,9] was one of the first to investigate this subject carefully as it pertains to deciduous fruits. He found that varieties of American grapes fall readily into three classes in respect to fruitfulness when dependent on their own pollen for fertilization. These he called self fertile, self sterile and partly self sterile. The varieties of the partly self sterile group varied from vineyard to vineyard and from season to season in their degree of self sterility, but those of the self fertile group remained completely self fertile; likewise those of the self sterile group remained completely self sterile. Controlled cross pollination experiments led to the conclusion that the partial or complete self sterility of those two groups was not due to any defect in the pistils but to impotence in their pollen, though an abundance of it was formed. The stamens of the self fertile varieties were erect, while those of the self sterile sorts were reflexed. A detailed study of the pollen of these different classes showed marked differences in the shape and appearance of the grains.[15] Those of the self fertile varieties were oblong, blunt at the ends and quite symmetrical and they germinated well; those of self sterile sorts were irregular in shape and did not germinate well. Stamens of the partly self sterile varieties were found to contain some good and some poor pollen.

A little later Reimer and Detjen[190] reported that all the varieties of the Muscadine grape bear reflexed stamens only and that all their pollen is defective. Their flowers are pseudo-hermaphrodites rather than true hermaphrodites. For fruit to set the pistils must receive pollen from male or staminate vines. The plants of this species are essentially diœcious. Failure to recognize this fact has been responsible for much of the unfruitfulness previously encountered in the culture of this group of grapes. Among the plants growing wild about three-fourths are staminate and one-fourth pseudo-hermaphroditic with functional pistils.[117] More recently there have been found[55,116] several plants of this species producing true hermaphrodite flowers; these have afforded a starting point for the breeding of a new and perfect flowered race of Muscadine grapes.

Apparently the failure properly to set and mature fruit occasionally found in European varieties of grapes is likewise due at least partly to defective pollen.[13] This dropping of grape blossoms or of the partly developed berries in those of the Vinifera varieties is commonly known as "coulure."

Dorsey[60] has made a study of the cytological changes within the developing pollen grain of the grape leading to, or associated with, its impotence. Figures 9 to 11 in Plate II show something of the nature of these degenerative changes. He distinguishes between what he terms sterile pollen and aborted pollen. In the former after true pollen grains are formed degeneration occurs in either their generative or vegetative nuclei or in both. Aborted pollen results from the arresting of development at an earlier stage. The following quotation from his report brings out the more important details of his investigations:

"In the formation of the sterile and fertile pollen of the grape the heterotypic and homotypic divisions and the divisions of the microspore nucleus take place normally. Sterile pollen in the grape results from degeneration processes in the generative nucleus or arrested development previous to mitosis in the microspore nucleus. Where degeneration begins early after the division of the microspore nucleus, both the generative and vegetative nucleus may be affected. If the generative cell is well organized before disintegration begins the vegetative nucleus may remain normal. . . .

"Aborted microspores occur in various percentages in the native forms, as well as in the cultivated varieties. While in the end the result is the same, a distinction should be made between *aborted* and *sterile* pollen. The former occurs in both sterile and fertile forms and seems to be due to arrested development soon after being liberated from the tetrad, while the latter results from disintegration processes subsequent to mitosis in the microspore nucleus, and occurs associated with the reflex type of stamen and the absence of the germ pore. . . .

"The amount of aborted pollen which occurs in the grape varies much in different vines. In the 52 cultivated varieties the average per cent. of aborted pollen is 22.83, compared with 4.08 in 121 wild staminate vines of *V. vulpina* and 3.70 in 50 wild pistillate. . . . Of the 52 cultivated varieties only 10 have less than 5 per cent. of aborted pollen. . . .

"The difference between the percentage of aborted pollen in known hybrids and the pure forms, among the cultivated varieties, is only slight. The average per cent. of aborted pollen from 10 vines, of varieties generally regarded to be pure *V. labrusca*, is 23.10, while that for 38 of the hybrid varieties is 24.60. There are some instances, however, among the hybrids, as in Black Eagle, where the amount of aborted pollen is small. . . .

"Since aborted pollen occurs in much the same relative amounts in the self fertile and self sterile varieties, from the standpoint of fertilization and the setting of fruit it would seem that the aborted pollen is unimportant in the grape because in the fertile forms there is still an abundance of potent pollen."[60]

The discussion thus far has been limited to the grape, not because sterility and unfruitfulness due to pollen abortion do not occur in other fruits, but simply because the condition found in the grape was the first to be studied carefully, and it will serve to illustrate what is true in many other fruit groups. Two to 10 per cent. of the pollen of the mango is regularly defective.[184] Dorsey[61] finds pollen abortion common in the plum, noting that in that fruit the disintegration processes usually occur after the liberation of the tetrad from the pollen mother cell. If distinction is to be made between pollen sterility and pollen abortion, in this case as in the grape, the defective pollen of the plum is sterile rather than aborted. In neither the plum nor the mango, however, is the percentage of defective pollen high enough to interfere seriously with the setting of the fruit. Pollen abortion has been reported as a practically constant characteristic of blackberries in New England.[20] Furthermore it has been found to vary greatly with the variety and species. For instance *Rubus allegheniensis* was found to have about 96 per cent., while *R. hispidus* had less than 10 per cent., morphologically perfect pollen. Between these extremes were all gradations. The higher percentages of defectiveness were enough to reduce very materially the set of fruit. Researches by Longley[143] indicate that in this genus pollen sterility is usually associated with a triploid or pentaploid condition of the chromosomes, whereas those forms that produce relatively fertile pollen have the normal (diploid) number. A similar condition is reported in the strawberry.[236]

Characteristically the J. H. Hale[34] and Shanghai[4] varieties of peach produce only abortive pollen and are consequently self barren and some seasons a large percentage of the pollen of a number of other peach varieties is sterile. The Marguerite Marillat pear and several varieties of plum are reported as producing very little pollen, most of which is abortive, in Sweden.[121] Pollen abortion likewise occurs to such an extent in a number of varieties of the sweet cherry[119] and the apple[111] as to render them partially self barren and make them poor pollenizers for other sorts. With the apples, as with blackberries and raspberries, pollen sterility is evidently associated with irregular chromosome behavior.[136,204] Winkler has shown that the pollen germinability of a number of varieties of the European grape is influenced by pruning to great enough an extent to account for the difference between straggly and full, compact clusters.[251,252]

Degeneration occurs in nearly all the pollen mother cells of the Washington Navel orange.[30,170] Consequently practically no mature and perfect pollen grains are formed. In the Unshu variety[170] degeneration is not so general; nevertheless it affects a large number of the pollen mother cells. In these two varieties, as in certain others, pollen abortion is not accompanied by unfruitfulness because the fruits are capable of parthenocarpic development, but it is responsible for partial or complete suppression of their seeds.

DUE PRINCIPALLY TO GENETIC INFLUENCES

The forms of self sterility and self unfruitfulness discussed up to this point are due plainly to factors associated with the fundamental constitution of the protoplasm. It is also clear that sterility due to these factors is inherited, though the underlying causal agents are evolutionary tendencies within the species. Self sterility and self unfruitfulness that are to be attributed more directly to genetic factors, to the inheritance received, are here discussed under the headings of hybridity and incompatibility. However, it is impossible to differentiate sharply between these two types of sterility.

East and Park[65] remark: "Self-sterility is a condition determined by the inheritance received, but can develop to its full perfection only under a favorable environment." In his study of fertility in chicory Stout[210] found that out of a total of 101 plants in one crop which came from three generations of known self sterile ancestry 11 were self fertile and 90 were self sterile. From his data he was able to conclude not only that self sterility is inherited but that in this species narrow breeding is more likely to give rise to self sterile plants than is broad breeding. Detjen[54] concluded from his studies with the southern dewberry (*Rubus trivialis*) that not only is self sterility in that species transmitted to its pure offspring, but frequently to its hybrid progeny.

Sterility and Unfruitfulness Due to Hybridity.—Unfruitfulness and sterility have long been recognized as conditions frequently associated with hybridity. Generally the wider the crossing the greater is the degree of sterility encountered. Many instances might be cited; a few will suffice. Waugh[241] describes a hybrid between the Troth Early peach and the Wildgoose plum that has been named the Mule. It bears an abundance of flowers, but they are without pistils or petals. The stamens are numerous, but malformed, assuming something of the shape and appearance of pistils. The variety is fairly constant in its flower characteristics, completely sterile and also barren. He mentions another peach-plum hybrid, known as the Blackman, with similar characteristics. The Kamdesa, a hybrid between the peach and sand cherry (*Prunus besseyi*) is barren. Its flowers have two to six pistils, which, apparently, are incapable of setting fruit, and its pollen is sterile.[94] A hybrid between the pear and the quince, described under the name Pyronia, flowers and fruits freely but is always seedless.[228] Most of the citranges, hybrids between the sweet orange and *Citrus trifoliata*, produce some fertile pollen but no fertile female gametes.[220] In these cases hybridity is responsible for sterility alone, instead of sterility and barrenness, as in the peach-plum hybrids. The seedlessness of many of the commercial varieties of the banana and pineapple is attributed by Tischler[225] to the hybrid nature of their ancestries, a conclusion supported by later findings of Cheesman and Larter[25] and of Graner[90] as to their chromosome number. The diploid number of most of the fertile varieties was found to be 22, while 81 of 92 seedless varieties studied had 33 diploid chromosomes. The Royal and Paradox walnuts, hybrids between the Persian and the California and Eastern Black respectively, are almost barren. In these cases, as in many other hybrids, barrenness due to hybridity is associated with great vegetative vigor. The high percentage of aborted pollen found in wild and cultivated blackberries in New England is to be attributed mainly to a condition of hybridity.[20]

The sterility of a number of hybrid raspberry forms has been shown to be associated with an unequal distribution of the chromosomes during pollen tetrad formation.[144] A number of hybrids between *Vitis rotundifolia* and various species of the Euvitis group have been found almost completely sterile; this is attributed mainly to their hybrid condition.[57] In describing one of these *V. vinifera* × *V. rotundifolia* seedlings Detjen[57] says:

"Flowers perfect hermaphroditic and imperfect hermaphroditic; stamens upright and pistils medium large in the perfect hermaphroditic; stamens reflexed and pistils well developed in the imperfect hermaphroditic flowers. . . . The pollen in the perfect hermaphroditic flowers is a mixture of shriveled and plump, sterile and fertile grains. The fertility of these plump grains has been demonstrated in actual hand-made cross-pollinations, also by selfing some of the flowers. The pollen in the imperfect hermaphroditic flowers is all shriveled and impotent. The pistils in both types of flowers are mostly sterile, only two from 17 perfect hermaphroditic flower-clusters having developed into berries in 1918. The perfect hermaphroditic flowers are sterile because of hybridization, while the imperfect hermaphroditic flowers are sterile due to the double phenomenon of hybridization and intersexualism with attendant impotence."

However, abortion of pollen and of pistils cannot always or entirely be attributed to hybridity; and, conversely, hybridity is not always a cause of unfruitfulness or even of sterility. Indeed, certain varieties of the date palm (*Phoenix dactylifera*) are said to set fruit better when pollinated with pollen of *P. canariensis* than with pollen from male trees of their own species.[182] Many of the cultivated American varieties of the grape that are probably pure species bear some aborted pollen and, furthermore, many varieties of known hybrid origin are highly self fertile. In discussing this matter Dorsey[60] says: "Since both fertile and sterile hybrids occur among the cultivated varieties of American grapes, hybridity is not necessarily a cause of sterility. The relation of the sterile pollen to the absence of the germ pore, the reflexed type of stamen, and the tendency toward dioeciousness, suggest that pollen sterility in the grape is only a step toward functional dicliny." The same investigator[61] reports somewhat more aborted pollen in some of the hybrid plum varieties than in some of those of pure species and also a tendency for the degeneration processes to start earlier in the hybrids.

All the available evidence warrants the conclusion that the highest fertility is correlated with neither the narrowest nor the broadest breeding possible.

Incompatibility.—One of the most common causes of self unfruitfulness and self sterility is incompatibility between the pollen and the ovules of the same plant or of the same variety. That is, both the ovules and the pollen of the plant are fertile in themselves, but they fail to effect conjugation. Müller found self incompatibility in *Oncidium flexuosum* and a number of other species of orchids.[46] In some instances not only did the pollen fail to impregnate the ovule but its action was injurious or poisonous to the stigmas, causing them to turn brown and to decay prematurely. At the same time unpollinated stigmas remained fresh. Those that were pollinated with pollen from other plants showed no signs of injury; fertilization took place and fruit set; the pollen that acted so injuriously upon the stigmas of its own flowers functioned perfectly on other plants. The same condition has been reported in *Lobelia*[46] and as not uncommon in *Cichorium intybus*.[209]

The self sterility or self unfruitfulness that has been reported in the apple,[142,185] in pears,[76,237] in the sweet cherry,[82,218] in some of the Duke and sour varieties,[67,128] in the plum,[147,239] in dewberries and blackberries,[54] in the almond,[230] the blueberry,[38] cacao,[146] and in certain varieties of the filbert,[122,199] is probably in large part attributable to incompatibility. In practically all of the instances cited the varieties set fruit properly when cross pollinated, showing that the pistils were perfectly developed and functional. Furthermore the pollen from these same varieties proved viable and capable of taking part in the fertilization process and in yielding mature fruits and seeds when it was applied to other varieties of the same species. Nevertheless, barrenness followed self pollination. However, in most cases data are lacking to show whether or not pollination is followed by fertilization. It is known that in some instances fecundation takes place and the immediate cause of the failure of the fruit to set or mature is embryo abortion at a later stage. Though this has been mentioned as a distinct cause of fruit dropping, it is very closely related to, if it is not actually one aspect of, incompatibility. Therefore the self sterility and self unfruitfulness of these common fruits may be considered as due to incompatibility, using that term in its broader sense signifying that the normal processes of fertilization fail somewhere between the production of functional gametes and the fusion of the sex cells.

Presenting an interesting contrast to the many instances of self unfruitfulness and self sterility are a number of cases in which fruit and sometimes seed development follows pollination with pollen of a different species or even genus of plants. Thus the Burbank plum, a Japanese variety which is self unfruitful, sets fruit when pollinated with Reine Claude, one of the European varieties,[152] and *Prunus cerasifera, P. Pissardi* and *P. spinosa* have likewise been found good pollenizers for it.[227] The Victoria pomelo, ordinarily seedless, produces seeds freely when pollinated by certain other citrus species,[256] and pollen of *Petunia violacea* applied to the stigmas of *Nicotiana sp.* flowers lead to the setting and development of fruits—in this case seedless.[256]

Interfruitfulness and Interfertility.—Just as the terms self fruitfulness and self fertility refer to the ability of a plant or a variety to mature fruits or seed with pollen from its own flowers, so interfruitfulness and interfertility indicate the ability of two plants or two varieties to mature fruits and seed with each other's pollen. Varieties that are self unfruitful because of diœcism, such as for instance pistillate flowered strawberries, figs of the Smyrna type and the date palm, have long been known to be interbarren as well. Other fruit varieties, such as many of the grapes, that are self barren, or partly so, because of impotent pollen, have been recognized as interbarren for the same reason.[56] Until comparatively recently, however, it has been the rather general belief that most fruit varieties are interfertile, or at least interfruitful, even though they might be self sterile, provided that they bear good pollen. That is, it was assumed that any variety of apple can successfully pollenize and fecundate any other apple variety, the only precaution necessary in planting being to choose varieties blossoming at approximately the same season. Occasional instances of interunfruitfulness were encountered in experimental studies[185] but later work with the same varieties in the same or in a different place often proved them interfruitful and the first results were regarded as due to accident or experimental error. However, Whitaker and Milton, which are open pollinated seedlings of the Wildgoose plum, have been reported intersterile and though both are fertile when pollinated with Sophie, that variety is sterile to their pollen.[242]

In 1913, Gardner[82] reported the three leading varieties of the sweet cherry grown on the Pacific Coast as intersterile and interunfruitful in Oregon and a little later the same condition was reported for two of these varieties in California.[229] At the same time all three varieties were found to have perfectly good pistils and potent pollen. This is clearly an instance of intersterility due to incompatibility. More recently other varieties of the sweet cherry have been found interunfruitful,[18,119,137,245] and a similar condition has been reported for a number of almond,[230] plum,[105,188,245] pear[148,191] and filbert[122,199] varieties. The evidence relating to cross incompatibility in the apple is conflicting, but apparently under some conditions and with certain varieties there is a marked tendency in this direction.[110,119,172] Apparently the color strains of a number of the standard self-unfruitful varieties are unfruitful when interplanted with each other or with the parent variety.[112,174] Not to be confused for cases of interunfruitfulness due to incompatibility are those in which one of the varieties, such as Baldwin, Rhode Island Greening and Stayman Winesap, is a very poor pollen producer and therefore unable to provide for a setting of fruit on any other variety.[111]

Stout[209] has found cross incompatibility occurring sporadically in his pedigree cultures of chicory and it has been recorded in tobacco.[65] In summarizing their observations on cross incompatibility in tobacco, East and Parks state:[65] "Cross-sterility in its nature identical with self-sterility was found in every population of self-sterile plants tested. The percentage of cross-sterility in different populations, based in each case on numerous cross matings, varied from 2.4 per cent. to 100 per cent."

Cross-sterility is much less common than self-sterility but apparently is to be expected in all those groups in which self-sterility exists. Data are not available to show to what extent, if at all, the degree of interunfruitfulness can be modified by environmental conditions and it is not possible to tell, without trial, which varieties are and which are not interfruitful.

In Reciprocal Crossings.—In the investigations with tobacco to which reference has just been made, there was found a uniformity of behavior between reciprocal crossings.[65] That is, if a certain crossing proved sterile, its reciprocal was likewise sterile and if one variety proved incompatible with two others, those two were likewise sterile to each other. On the other hand, in California, pollen of the Tragedy plum, a European variety, has proved to be an effective pollenizer for several Japanese varieties, but that variety has failed to set fruit when supplied with their pollen.[105] Sweet cherries have been reported as good pollenizers for sour varieties under certain circumstances, though the reciprocal crosses were not successful.[126]

Vitis vinifera, V. bourquiniana, V. labrusca and *V. cordifolia* hybridize freely with *V. rotundifolia* and *V. munsoniana* when the latter two are used as the pollen parent, but they hybridize much less freely when the reciprocal crossing is made.[56] Crane[39] cites an instance of several plum varieties that failed to set fruit when pollinated by certain other varieties of the same group, though their own pollen was effective for pollenizing these other varieties. A similar situation has been noted as characterizing clones of the rubber tree, *Hevea brasiliensis*.[156]

An interesting case of interfruitfulness of a reciprocal crossing but of intersterility when the crossing was made one way and interfertility when made the other appeared in work done at the Georgia Experiment Station.[69] Flowers of the upland cotton, *Gossypium Barbadense*, were crossed with pollen of the okra, *Hibiscus esculentus*. Perfect cotton bolls were produced but the seeds were nonviable. The reciprocal crossing resulted in normal appearing okra fruits and in viable seeds. Wellington[244] secured seedless tomatoes by using pollen of the Jerusalem cherry, *Solanum pseudocapsicum*, but no fruit was formed when the reciprocal crossing was made.

DUE PRINCIPALLY TO PHYSIOLOGICAL INFLUENCES

Besides the effects of evolutionary and genetic influences in limiting the set of fruit there are a number of others that can be conveniently grouped as physiological, though exact demarcation is impossible.

Unfruitfulness Due to Slow Growth of the Pollen Tube.—Closely related to the unfruitfulness and the sterility due to incompatibility is that caused by the very slow growth of the pollen tubes in the style. Indeed, this may be considered one type of incompatibility, due to chemotropic influences.

Darwin[50] made many crossings between different forms of heterostyled dimorphic and trimorphic plants. He found that when pistils were pollinated with pollen from stamens of corresponding height there was a high degree of fertility; when pollinated from stamens of a different height there were varying degrees of sterility. This sterility ranged from slight to absolute. Pollen from stamens of a height corresponding to that of the stigma (legitimate pollination) placed on stigmas 24 hours after pollination from stamens of another height (illegitimate pollination) was found to effect fertilization, the earlier applied pollen still remaining ungerminated. Plants raised from the few seeds obtained from illegitimate pollinations showed many of the characteristics of hybrids between species, being few flowered, weak or perhaps profuse flowered and partly sterile. Practically the same has been found in the heterostyled flowers of buckwheat.[207] In the legitimate pollinations less than 18 hours was required for the growth of the pollen tube and the fusion of its generative cell with the egg cell of the embryo sac. In the illegitimate pollinations more than 72 hours were necessary for the same series of events. Discussing the cause of self-sterility in *Nicotiana* East and Parks say:[65] " . . . The immediate difference between a fertile and a sterile combination is in the rate of pollen tube growth. If at the height of the season a series of self pollinations and a series of cross pollinations are made on a single plant and the pistils fixed, sectioned and stained at intervals of 12 hours, it is found by plotting the average length of the pollen tubes in each pistil against time in 12-hour periods that the growth curve of selfed pollen tubes is a straight line which reaches less than half the distance to the ovary during the life of the flower, while the curve of crossed pollen tubes resembles that of an autocatalysis and reaches the ovary in less than 96 hours." Similar differences have been found in the rate of pollen tube growth in selfed and crossed apples,[37,111,135] pears[5,169,191] and certain citrus fruits.[234]

Obviously, slow pollen tube growth alone cannot be responsible for a failure of the fruit to set, for eventually the tubes would reach the ovules. However, flowers do not remain attached to the flower cluster or to the stem indefinitely when fertilization does not occur. Unless it occurs within a fairly short time, varying with species, variety and environmental conditions, abscission takes place at the base of the style, ovary, pedicel or peduncle and fruit setting is prevented.

The failure of the flowers to set fruit through the retarding of pollen tube growth by low temperature is discussed in another connection.

Premature or Delayed Pollination.—Hartley[95] has found that the flowers of tobacco are very susceptible to injury from premature pollination. When mature pollen grains are applied to immature pistils they germinate, penetrate the styles and enter the ovules and if the ovules are not ready for fertilization the flowers soon fall. In cases of this kind "the separation of the flower from the plant was rapid and complete and not accompanied by any previous wilting of the flower, but invariably occurred at a joint situated at the base of the peduncle." This is somewhat different from the falling of flowers from other causes. Table 3 shows the results of one series of pollinations at various stages of pistil maturity. Hartley did not find any injurious results from pollinating orange blossoms nine days before opening and but little injury from premature pollination in the tomato. To what extent premature pollination interferes with the set of fruit in the orchard is unknown.

TABLE 3.—INFLUENCE OF PREMATURE POLLINATION ON SETTING IN TOBACCO
(*After Hartley*[95])

Number flowers	Time pollinated	Per cent set
20	4 days before opening	5
40	3 days before opening	5
20	2 days before opening	0
40	1 day before opening	77
20	½ day before opening	95
20	When fully receptive	95

It is well known that if pollination is long delayed the blossoms fall without setting. Kusano,[141] working with orchids belonging to the genus *Gastrodia*, found that when pollination was delayed for 2 to 3 days fertilization took place in an almost normal manner. When it was delayed 4 days it was rather ineffective and when it was effective the resulting fruit varied in size "according to the number of embryogenic seeds." He also made the interesting observation that when pollination was delayed 3 to 4 days a comparatively large percentage of the seeds formed were polyembryonic, while seeds resulting from earlier pollination seldom contained more than one embryo.

Nutritive Conditions within the Plant.—There is abundance of both circumstantial and experimental evidence to show that the nutritive conditions within the plant just before, at and just after the time of blossoming are important in determining the percentage of the blossoms that will develop properly and also the percentage that will finally reach maturity.

Effect on Pollen Viability.—Sandsten[197] collected pollen from old apple trees in a poor state of vigor and at the same time from strong young trees of the same varieties in an adjoining orchard. The average percentage germination of the first lot was 39.8 while that of the second lot was 56.5. The average number of hours required for germination of the pollen from the strong trees was 19.8; for that from the weak trees, 28.7. Though these differences may not be great enough under average conditions to account for much failure to set fruit, it is conceivable that they may be of real importance under some conditions. Roberts has reported that in dwarf apple trees fertilization occurred in 3 or 4 days less time on very strongly vegetative trees than on poorly vegetative trees.[194] Furthermore, it is possible that greater differences frequently exist between the pollen of strong and weak blossoms of other varieties and of other fruits.

Effect on Defectiveness of Pistils.—Goff[84] reported the percentage of defective pistils borne by trees of the American varieties of plums and consequently their fruitfulness to be closely correlated with nutritive conditions within the tree. Exhaustion or weakening one season by overbearing, drought or poverty of soil was found to induce the production of many defective pistils the following spring. He suggested thinning as a preventive. Dorsey[61] has observed the same occurrence in the plum group in Minnesota. He mentions two cases in particular: "One variety, Wickson, bore two heavy crops of crossed plums in the greenhouse and the following year all pistils were aborted. In the second instance, Wolf under orchard conditions bore heavily in 1914, and for three consecutive seasons afterward produced less than 1 per cent. of normal pistils." Hendrickson[104] mentions two French prune trees in California, one of which bore a heavy and the other a light crop in 1916. In 1917 the conditions of these two trees were reversed. Paralleling these alternations in crop yields were differences in the actual percentage of blossoms setting and maturing fruit. In each case the light crop was due partly to a poorer setting of the blossoms through exhaustion from heavy bearing the previous season. The pecan, which differentiates its pistillate flower buds in late winter or early spring, may fail to bring these flowers through to a stage where they can be fertilized, even though they are formed in normal numbers, if the tree produced a heavy crop the year before and growing conditions were rather unfavorable.[255]

That carbohydrate deficiency is a common cause of coulure, or blossom abortion and dropping, in *Vitis vinifera* has been demonstrated by Müller-Thurgau[159] and Winkler.[253] The investigations of both of these workers, and later of Partridge[176] with the Campbell Early, a variety containing both *vinifera* and *labrusca* blood, indicate that such pruning and other cultural treatments as lead to a maximum foliage development and, therefore, a maximum carbohydrate manufacture and accumulation early in the season produce the largest and most compact bunches. This is brought out by the data presented in Table 5. Murneek[163] has attributed much of the flower bud and flower abortion that takes place in greenhouse-grown tomatoes to a carbohydrate shortage due to limited light supply, high temperature and the demand of developing fruits for most of the carbohydrate that is being manufactured.

Fruit Setting of Flowers in Different Positions.—Some fruits, like the plum and cherry, bear on both shoots and spurs and it is to be expected that slightly different nutritive conditions obtain in these different tissues. Dorsey[61] studied fruit setting of the plum in these positions and found a distinctly heavier June drop in the shoot-borne fruits. Some of his observations are particularly interesting:

"In the varieties available in this investigation there was a pronounced June drop in the plums borne on the terminal wood. In fact, on the older trees fruit seldom matured in this position. The dropping of fruit from the terminal growths can be partly accounted for on the basis of the competition from a thorn or branch which is developed between the lateral fruit buds on the terminal twigs the second season. This condition occurs over the entire outer area of the tree. . . . Under favorable conditions fruit matures on the terminal shoots, but the percentage to set is small considering the mass of bloom, and even the small setting noted above is far in excess of the usual condition when there is a full crop on the remainder of the tree. It is apparent that in this position competition takes place between fruit and branch as well as between different fruits."[61]

Strong and Weak Spurs.—A number of important correlations have been reported between fruit setting in the apple and nutritive conditions in the spurs or limb upon which the blossoms are borne.[100] As between limbs from the same trees, on those with a light bloom 73.8 per cent. of the spurs set fruit, while on those with a heavy bloom only 14.1 per cent. set fruit. Of the spurs on vigorous limbs with large leaves 41.6 per cent. set fruit; 15.7 per cent. set on weak limbs with small leaves. Spurs that lost all their flowers and fruit at the time of the first drop had the smallest average number of flowers (4.45) and those that finally set had the largest average (5.74). Furthermore, a slightly higher percentage of the flowers borne on spurs with many flowers actually developed into fruits than of those borne on spurs with few flowers. Of 2,066 spurs making more than 1 centimeter growth in length in 1915, 791, or 38.3 per cent., set fruit in 1916; of 3,171 spurs making less than 1 centimeter of growth in length in 1915 only 561, or 17.7 per cent., set fruit in 1916. Five hundred ninety-five flower-bearing spurs of several varieties that set fruit averaged 2.55 grams in weight; 760 flower-bearing non-setting spurs of the same varieties averaged only 1.50 grams in weight. Table 4 shows still more clearly the influence of weight of spur on its fruitfulness. In a series of defoliation experiments Heinicke found that though 50.6 per cent. of the check spurs set fruit, only 47.6 per cent. of those partly defoliated and 20.2 per cent. of those completely defoliated set.

TABLE 4.—WEIGHT OF BALDWIN APPLE SPURS HOLDING FRUITS VARYING LENGTHS OF TIME
(After Heinicke[100])

Time spur held fruit	Number of spurs	Average weight in grams
Until first drop........................	30	2.94
Until June drop........................	28	3.29
After June drop........................	30	4.27

Evidence from Ringing Experiments.—Certain plants which under ordinary circumstances would not set and develop fruit parthenocarpically have been made to do so by ringing or girdling and thus leading to the accumulation of an extra store of food materials above the injury. Instances of this kind have been recorded in the gooseberry[70] and grape.[9] That ringing often does not have such an influence on fruit setting is indicated by certain experiments with Nicotiana.[244] It is probable however that ringing has quite different effects on various plants and broad generalizations cannot be made from the available data.

Evidence from Starvation Experiments.—Kusano[141] produced experimentally a series of extreme nutritive conditions in an orchid belonging to *Gastrodia*, at the time of fertilization and during the period of development of the fruit by partly or completely separating the ovaries from their source of food. Though the results he obtained probably would not apply generally to the developing fruits of other species treated similarly, they are instructive in pointing out some of the relations existing between fruitfulness, sterility and nutritive conditions. The following quotations from Kusano's report summarize his findings:

"Imperfect or almost no fruit, but normal seed with embryo: where the normally fertilized flower is separated from its nutritive connection.

"Imperfect or almost no fruit, and nearly normal but embryoless seed: when the unpollinated flower is parted from its nutritive connection; the number of seeds is exceedingly diminished.

"Imperfect or almost no fruit and seed, but almost normal embryo: when the fertilized flower is subjected to an extremely unfavorable condition of nutrition. In this case the typical integument is quite suppressed in development and the ovular tissue developed previous to the fertilization stage partakes of the formation of the imperfect seed-coat. . . .

"From the above we see that the embryo does not require during its development the accompaniment of the normal development of the ovarial wall and the sporophytic ovular tissue and that the seed-coat alone can develop completely, independent of the formation of the embryo, or of the normal development of the fruit-wall. But it must be remembered that a nutritive condition which renders the development of the fruit-wall unfavorable may bring about a small amount of embryoless seed.

"In the process of fruitification the embryo is placed in the first rank for development; if the nutritive condition is favorable, it accompanies the development of the seed-coat and fruit-wall; if not, only the latter portions are in high degree retarded in development. A similar relation may exist between the fruit-wall and the embryoless seed; under the condition which induces most ovules to develop into embryoless seeds the fruit-wall develops most vigorously; under an insufficient supply of nutritive substances the number of the seed-forming ovules is diminished, and in this case the fruit-wall is sacrificed for development; in the extreme case of an insufficient nutrition both the fruit-wall and a larger number of ovules are suppressed in development, thereby supplying limited nutritive material to a few ovules, enabling them to form seed. . . . The development of the fruit-wall alone under entire suppression of the ovular development is found in some instances of the habitual parthenocarpy."

A case of extreme sensitivity to the more or less constantly changing nutritive conditions within the plant is afforded by the setting and later development of the fruit of greenhouse-grown cucumbers. Tiedjens[222] states: " . . . if a plant is in good health and sets six cucumbers on six succeeding days, they may all start to grow. If something tends to cut down the food supply, four of the cucumbers, depending on time of pollination and position on the plant, may continue to grow uninterruptedly, while the other two stop growing until more food is available. If two of the four cucumbers are picked the remaining two may resume growth. However, the plant is producing new foliage and new flower buds while cucumbers are maturing. If no new pistillate flowers have been formed, the two small cucumbers may grow and form cucumbers the upper half of which will be small, while the tip half will be quite bulgy and will contain a large number of viable seeds. However, if new pistillate flowers have been pollinated on the plant, they may receive the support of the plant and grow while the two small cucumbers either ripen into nubbins with a few viable seeds or become yellow pickles."

A somewhat specialized case of the influence of nutritive conditions within the plant on flower development and fruit setting is afforded by certain instances of changes in sex expression. Thus, Gardner[82a] has reported that normally hermaphrodite strawberry plants will sometimes produce pistillate flowers only when grown under conditions unfavorable for carbohydrate accumulation, and Murneek[164] has noted a rapid change in Cleome from a condition of cyclic sterility to one of complete fruitfulness following the removal of pistils of plants high in nitrogen. He states: "Soon after initiation of depistillation a continuous succession of perfect flowers was produced without the slightest manifestation of the characteristic periodic alternation to maleness.

"Moreover, in fully 50 per cent. of plants in this group complete hermaphroditism and hence fruitfulness was manifested from the very beginning, due to the daily removal of pistils. On these specimens not a single staminate flower was produced throughout their lifetime. Many of these plants were permitted to form over 300 flowers—all hermaphrodites. When fruit was allowed to develop the usual cyclic condition of sterility was readily initiated.

"To make it more certain that variations in sex expression in Cleome is not of genetic but of purely nutritional or correlative character, a certain number of plants of the soil or nitrogen high series were trained to a diaxial type of growth. Such two-stemmed plants are easily secured by an early removal of all axillary growth excepting at two desired points. The main stem is cut off above these side shoots. One of the branches on each plant was left undisturbed producing fruit periodically. Pistils were removed from the second in a manner detailed above. The results in all cases were as if two individual plants had been employed for the experiment. The depistillated half of each plant exhibited the characteristic inhibition of staminate cycle. After a certain time only perfect flowers were formed on the treated branch. During the same period the normal or control branch showed the usual intermittent alternation in sexuality and fruitfulness."

Presumably the developing flowers and fruits of different kinds differ in their sensitiveness to nutritive conditions, and the same variety or tree may vary considerably from time to time. The examples that have just been cited would lead to the inference that, in general, rather small changes in composition are likely to be responsible for marked differences in behavior. This may be the case, though studies with the apple in New York have led Heinicke[101] to conclude that "Nitrogen and carbohydrate apparently may be present in any proportions relative to each other that it is possible to bring about early in spring during the time abscission usually occurs, in trees that produce a satisfactory number of perfectly formed flowers. The developing fruit at that time seems to be able to utilize, adapt itself or remain indifferent to a large excess of either of these materials." This point of view is supported by results obtained in Japan by Asami and Ito[6] on pear and a number of herbaceous crops.

It may be noted in passing that the influences of the nutritive condition of the plant upon fruit setting, fruitfulness and fertility that have been pointed out have been in part upon flower cluster, flower, pistil or pollen abortion and thus more or less indirect and they have been in part direct in apparently affecting the ability of the developing seeds or fruits to complete their maturing processes. No direct or indirect influence on compatibility has been noted. However, experimental studies with chicory have led to the conclusion that, at least in that species, "self-compatibility and self-incompatibility operate independently of the purely nutritive relations of the embryos to their parent plants."[211]

Summary.—The individual plants of many species and likewise many bud-propagated varieties are self unfruitful because their flowers are unisexual and flowers of but one sex occur on a single plant. Among deciduous fruits often self unfruitful from this cause the kaki or Japanese persimmon, the muscadine grape and the strawberry are the most familiar. The fig, date palm and papaya are familiar examples of subtropical and tropical fruits whose plants are unisexual. Of more general occurrence among fruits is dichogamy. Though seldom complete, it accounts for the failure of many individual blossoms to set fruit and emphasizes the importance of planting with cross pollination in mind, even though the varieties in question are partly self fertile. Heterostyly is not important in limiting the "set" of deciduous fruits. Impotence (partial or complete) resulting from the degeneration of pistils or ovules is very common among certain deciduous fruits. Many varieties, particularly of grapes, produce large numbers of impotent pollen grains and they have all the appearance of perfect flowering sorts, though in reality they are pseudo-hermaphrodites. If the embryo sacs degenerate and fruit still forms, seedless specimens are produced. The self sterility of many varieties is associated with the hybrid condition of the plant. Hybrids between rather distantly related forms are likely to be self sterile and often self unfruitful as well. On the other hand, there is some evidence that very narrowly bred varieties or strains are rather inclined to sterility. When sterility is due to hybridity it is likely to be associated with pollen or embryo sac degeneration. Incompatibility is another cause of much self unfruitfulness. This is particularly important in the apple, pear, plum and cherry. Not only are some varieties self unfruitful but incompatibility exists between them and certain other varieties. This characteristic has immediate importance in the sweet cherry, pear and almond. In some cases failure to set fruit properly is due to premature or delayed pollination or to a slow growth of the pollen tube. Unfavorable nutritive conditions within the plant are responsible for much failure in fruit setting. Trees that have been weakened by overbearing or other causes are very likely to produce pistils which are defective or pollen that is low in vitality. There is often considerable difference between flowers borne in various positions, or between those borne on strong and weak limbs, in their abilities to set fruit.

CHAPTER XXVIII

UNFRUITFULNESS ASSOCIATED WITH EXTERNAL FACTORS

Practically every phase of the environment to which the plant is subject just before, at and shortly after the time of blossoming has some effect on fruit setting. The influence may make itself felt through rendering the plant or the variety more or less completely dichogamous, through the production of more or less defective pistils, ovules, embryo sacs or pollen grains, through affecting compatibility, indirectly through aiding or interfering with pollen transfer or in a number of other ways.

Nutrient Supply.—It is often impossible to distinguish clearly between the influence of nutritive conditions within the plant and of conditions of nutrient supply without upon fruit setting, fruitfulness and fertility. Though the nutrient supply available to the plant probably acts upon fruit setting and development largely through first influencing nutritive conditions within, there are so many cases in which the association between the two is so evident that the intervening effect of the environment upon nutritive condition within is overlooked. Furthermore, nutritive conditions within the plant are controlled more readily by affording or withholding certain nutrients than by most other means. It is therefore desirable to give some attention to nutrient supply as it influences fruit setting and fruitfulness.

Darwin[48] states that much manure renders many kinds of plants completely sterile. He cites Gärtner as authority for the statement that sterility from overfeeding is very characteristic in certain families, Gramineæ, Cruciferæ and Leguminosæ being mentioned specially. In India *Agave vivipara* is said invariably to produce bulbs but no seeds when grown in a rich soil, though when it is grown in a poor soil without too much moisture the converse condition holds.[49] Sandsten[196] found that excessive feeding of tomatoes caused abnormal flowers. In some instances the stamens almost aborted; in others the pistils were greatly thickened and overgrown. There was a general tendency for the overfed plants to produce fruits with fewer seeds. Two plants produced seedless fruits of normal size. Though these two plants produced many flowers they set fruit poorly. Analyses are not available, but the presumption is that in all of these instances the tissues of the plants were relatively high in nitrogen and low in carbohydrates.

The Jonathan apple, which is usually self sterile or nearly so on rich land in Victoria (Australia), becomes self fruitful when grown on land of low productivity.[72]   The Hope grape, which is classified as a perfect flowered variety of the Muscadine group, produces true hermaphrodite flowers only when given proper cultivation and care.[55]   Under neglect "its pistils gradually cease to function and the vine assumes the general role of one that is staminate."   This is just the reverse of the condition found in the Hautbois race of strawberries, which is reported as perfect flowered and productive when grown under ordinary culture, though in a rich soil the stamens develop poorly and produce little good pollen, the result being a poor setting of fruit.[23]   Extreme poverty of soil leads to dwarfing and sometimes sterility, certain species of clover being mentioned particularly.[48]

In this connection attention should be called to data presented in Table 69 of the section on Nutrition.   Applications of nitrate of soda to apple trees a week or 10 days before blossoming increased the set of fruit by as much as 300 per cent. in some instances.   Similar results have been obtained with pears.   Many other fruits show a similar, though usually less striking, response to spring applications of quickly available nitrogenous fertilizers, provided the trees are in a weakened condition as a result of starvation.   There is some evidence that a relatively high nitrogen content of the fruit-bearing spur or shoot at the time of blossoming favors the fruit-setting process,[96] and, of course, judicious nitrogen fertilizer applications in the spring tend to bring about such a nutritive condition.   Petri[180] found that olive branches containing as low as 0.7 to 0.9 per cent. nitrogen often flowered freely but failed to set fruit, whereas under similar conditions those containing two or three times as much set fruit freely.   On the other hand it is equally clear that sterility can be induced in the plant by very heavy applications of the same kind. There is some reason to believe, however, that when such fertilizers are used in quantities sufficient to induce barrenness it is because they have promoted so much greater vegetative growth that carbohydrate supplies have been exhausted.   In other words, carbohydrate shortage rather than nitrogen surplus seems to be the immediate cause of the failure of the fruit to set.   Color is lent to this interpretation by data reported by Heinicke[101] showing that apple flowers will set normally within as wide a range in the supply of nitrogen as can be induced by spring fertilizer applications.

Pruning and Grafting.—In the preceding chapter reference was made to the necessity of an abundant carbohydrate supply at blossoming time if *vinifera* grapes are to set and mature large compact clusters, and Table 5 presents data on the importance of pruning in this connection.   Vines that were cane-pruned and then had some of their flower clusters removed produced twice the weight of fruit and 4 times as large clusters as those given the normal severe spur pruning.[253]   Pollen from the spur-pruned vines showed a viability of 11 to 12 per cent., while that from cane-pruned vines had a viability of 37 to 38 per cent. Thus, pinching the growing tips of the shoots of certain European grape varieties when they are 18 to 24 inches long and the blossom bunch is well formed helps materially in the setting of the fruit.[14] Pruning, along with other practices, is reported to be one of the means of keeping the Hope grape (one of the Muscadine group) in a true hermaphroditic condition.[55] If this is neglected the variety tends to sterility through a weakening and an abortion of its pistils.

Investigations in both Oregon[21] and New York[102] indicate that in the case of the Anjou pear not only does comparatively heavy pruning aid in the fruit-setting process, but that a heavy setting is seldom obtained without it and Cooper[36] in Arkansas and Murneek and associates in Missouri[165] report a better setting of apples on trees pruned moderately or heavily than on trees pruned lightly or left unpruned. In general, both thinning out and heading back the canes of red[125] and black[124] raspberries reduce the number of flowers per cane that reach the full blossoming stage and that set and mature fruit, although there is an accompanying increase in the numbers on the individual fruiting laterals. How much of this influence would be classified as being on flower development and how much as being on the fruit-setting process itself it is impossible to state. The situation, however, is comparable to that found in the grape, except that in the latter fruit heavy pruning tends to reduce fruit setting and cluster size whereas in the brambles it has the opposite effect. These strikingly different effects of pruning on fruit setting apparently are associated with differences in growing and flowering habits and also with their varying influence on nutritive conditions within the plant. The change of sex, from staminate to pistillate or to hermaphrodite, sometimes effected in the papaya by heavy pruning affords a rather extreme illustration of the influence of this practice on flower formation, fruit setting and productivity.[118] The varying proportion of staminate and hermaphrodite flowers shown by different Citrus varieties under different conditions is attributed to nutrient supply by Uphof.[233]

The influence of the stock on the growth and productivity of the cion is known sometimes to be very great and it might be expected that in some instances stock would exert considerable influence on fruit setting. This appears to be the case, though there is only a limited amount of evidence bearing directly on the question. *Rosa hugonis* and Paul's Scarlet Climber rose are said to be practically sterile when grown as own-rooted plants, but grafted plants bear seed freely.[167] On the other hand, the grafting of cions of different varieties of potatoes on non-tuber-forming species of *Solanum*, thus presumably effecting an increase in the concentration of elaborated foods in the potato tops, did not lead to the formation of seed balls and seeds.[214]   The Malta orange grafted on rough lemon or "khatti" stock in Baluchistan produces fruits averaging 16 to 17 seeds; when grafted on the sweet lime the fruits of the same variety average but seven seeds.[22]   In this case the trees have remained fruitful, but fecundity has been modified.   Though data on this question as it pertains to deciduous fruits are almost lacking, there is reason to believe that the subject is often of real importance in commercial production.

Locality.—Fruit setting on trees of the same variety is often much better in one locality than in another.   It might be possible to segregate the various factors of soil, temperature, humidity, light, etc., that constitute what is termed locality and to assign to each its portion of the total influence on fruit setting.   This, however, is often difficult and

TABLE 5.—INFLUENCE OF CARBOHYDRATE SUPPLY ON FRUIT SETTING IN GRAPES OF
THE *Vinifera* TYPE
(*After Winkler*[253])

	Non-pruned (some flower clusters removed)	Normally pruned	Severely pruned
Weight of vine after pruning, kilograms.......	39.10	12.70	4.50
Carbohydrates:			
Per cent. in dormant vine................	7.10	6.48	6.22
Weight in dormant vine after pruning, kilograms....................................	2.78	0.82	0.28
Leaves:			
Number per vine......................	3,400.00	760.00	540.00
Weight May 5, kilograms................	3.87	0.18	0.06
Weight June 22, kilograms..............	5.97	1.54	0.85
Weight Oct. 15, kilograms..............	8.80	3.47	3.06
Berries—number per cluster...............	116.00	45.00	35.00

from the grower's standpoint it is only the environmental complex and the plant's response to it that are discernible.   Therefore it is suitable to make some mention of the influence of locality in fruit setting, without attempting a detailed analysis.

The common lilac is said to bear seeds moderately well in England but in parts of Germany its capsules never contain seed.[48]   Stout and Clark[26] cut in halves the tubers of 15 varieties of potatoes.   One set of halves was planted in the New York Botanical Garden and the other at Presque Isle, Maine.   All the varieties bloomed profusely in Maine, while at the New York Botanical Garden only 2 bloomed well, 3 produced a few flowers and 10 produced no flowers that opened.   The America grape has been found self sterile in the Experiment Station grounds at Columbia,

Mo., though it has been reported perfectly self fertile farther south.[248] Since the immediate cause of self sterility in the American varieties of grape is of two general types—pollen abortion and degeneration in the generative nucleus—locality may be considered to have an influence on pollen development. *Acorus calamus,* when grown in certain parts of Europe, becomes sterile through the degeneration of both pollen grains and embryo sacs.[158] The Jonathan apple is often self sterile in Victoria (Australia),[72] though in the United States it is almost invariably self fertile. As self sterility in the apple is due usually to incompatibility or embryo abortion, the conclusion seems warranted that it is in one of these ways that the difference between the localities produces this distinctive effect on fruitfulness. The Bosc pear is self sterile in many sections but has been found to be partly self fruitful in New York, and in the Union of South Africa, is reported as regularly parthenocarpic.[191]

Still another way in which the factors characteristic of locality influence fruitfulness is in the production of defective pistils. Waugh[239] obtained flowers of the Burbank plum from different sources and found the percentages of defective pistils to be as shown in Table 6. He found all the pistils of Rollingstone defective in flowers obtained from Minnesota City, Minn., and none in a lot obtained from Lafayette, Ind. He observed also that in some seasons certain plum varieties were protogynous in one locality and protandrous in another.

TABLE 6.—PERCENTAGE OF DEFECTIVE PISTILS IN BURBANK PLUM
(*After Waugh*[239])

Source of flowers	Per cent. defective	Source of flowers	Per cent. defective
Denison, Tex..............	27	Phoenix, Ariz.............	5
Santa Rosa, Cal............	0	Manhattan, Kan..........	21
Starkville, Miss............	9	Parry, N. J..............	0
Auburn, Ala...............	36		

A case in which self fertility and fruitfulness vary according to locality, apparently through some influence on compatibility, was mentioned by Darwin.[51] He stated that "*Escholtzia* is completely self sterile in the hot climate of Brazil, but is perfectly fertile there with the pollen of any other individual. The offspring of Brazilian plants became in England in a single generation partially self-fertile, and still more so in the second generation. Conversely, the offspring of English plants, after growing for two seasons in Brazil, became in the first generation quite self sterile."

Season.—Just as it is almost impossible to separate the influence on fruit setting of nutritive conditions within the plant from those of nutrient supply without, so it is almost impossible to distinguish the influence of locality from that of season. Seasonal variations at the same place may give rise to practically the same changes in environment as are occasioned by differences in localities during a single season. When this is true approximately the same responses to the changed conditions would be expected. Darwin[46] stated that Kölreuter had several plants of *Verbascum phœniceum* that for 2 years flowered freely and, though self sterile, were interfertile with other plants, but that later "assumed a strangely fluctuating condition, being temporarily sterile on the male or female side, or on both sides, and sometimes fertile on both sides; but two of the plants were perfectly fertile throughout the summer." Trees of the native plum varieties have been found to vary greatly in fertility from season to season,[86] and a plum variety that is protandrous one season may be protogynous the next.[239]

An interesting case of a return of the potato to the fertile condition through seasonal influences has been observed in the Greeley district of Colorado.[74] The Pearl variety as grown in that section usually produces no flowers. During seasons that are unfavorable for the normal development of the plant and its tubers, however, flowers are formed on the late branches. Though ordinarily the blossom buds of the potato fall off, in this case they opened but no pollen was produced. Thus the degeneracy from the standpoint of the potato grower is accompanied by some added development in the direction of fruitfulness. A "bastard" type is described as occurring sometimes in the Greeley fields of this variety; in this there is still further degeneration of the tuber-bearing habit, but an abundance of potent pollen is produced.

End-season Fertility.—End-season fertility of normally self sterile plants is rather common. Whitten[248] reports that, "during 1897, Ideal, a hybrid (grape) variety, proved to be self-impotent early in the season but self-potent later on, the season being favorable to a succession of bloom throughout the summer." He states that since the vine had little fruit to carry, it made a vigorous growth and bore a succession of flowers. The appearance of the self fertile condition late in the season was accompanied by an increasing uprightness of the stamens and presumably with the formation of good instead of sterile pollen. A gradual decrease in the percentage of defective mango pollen has been noted as the season advanced.[184] East and Park[65] found end-season fertility developing in their self sterile *Nicotiana* plants. In this case the immediate cause of the normal self sterility was a slow growth of the pollen tubes, presumably a result of chemotropic influences; the appearance of the self fertile condition followed an acceleration in pollen growth. These investigators remark: "Since we have reason to believe that the difference between a sterile and a fertile combination in these plants is the ability of the pollen grain through something inherent in its constitution to call forth in the tissue of the style in the former and not in the latter case a secretion which accelerates pollen-tube growth, it follows that in weakened style tissue some change has occurred that renders this secretion more easily produced." They report that self sterility can be restored in these weakened plants by allowing them to go through a period of rest and then forcing them into vigorous growth. Their suggestion that "truly self-fertile plants cannot be forced into self sterility by any treatment" obviously holds if self fertility is defined to agree with that concept. However, if that is to be the concept of self fertility it may be questioned whether any of our cultivated fruits be self fertile. In the fruit plantation there are fruit setting, fruitfulness and fecundity conditions which vary with environment.

Contrasting sharply with the end-season fertility that has just been mentioned as sometimes occurring in the grape, mango and tobacco is an end-season sterility found by Valleau[236] to be quite common in the strawberry. Indeed, it is probable that a certain type of end-season sterility is to be expected in the flowers of species that produce an indeterminate type of inflorescence, such as that of the pecan or grape. In the Philippine Islands the flowers of the Washington Navel orange, a parthenocarpic variety that requires no pollination, that open during February and March are said to set fruit much better than those opening during the regular seasons.[226]

A striking example of seasonal influence on fruit setting and fruitfulness occurs in figs of the San Pedro class.[33] In varieties of this group the early crop, or brebas, set freely without pollination, developing seedless fruits. The later main or summer crop will not set and mature without caprification. This, like the strawberry, is particularly interesting both because it is an instance of early season rather than late season fruitfulness and because it is a constant characteristic of these varieties.

Change of Sex with Season.—Related to the influences of season on fruit setting, fruitfulness and fertility, or, more accurately, to be mentioned as the immediate explanation of some of those influences, are the occasional effects of season upon the complete suppression of one or the other of the two sex organs, its effect upon their development when normally they are undeveloped or nonfunctional and its effect upon change of sex. The sweet gale or bog myrtle (*Myrica gale*) is a small shrub which grows abundantly in the swamps of Europe, Asia and North America. It is described by many authorities as strictly diœcious. However, it has been found that intersexes or mixed plants of many gradations are present everywhere in the peat moors of England.[52] Furthermore, a study of individual plants for a series of years showed that changes of sex occurred from year to year. Plants entirely female in 1913 were entirely male in 1914. Plants female in 1913 were mixed in 1914, entirely male or nearly all male in 1915 and again female in 1916. There is a record of a hybrid grape vine (*V. riparia* ×

V. labrusca) which fruited only twice during a 30-year period, "the pistils evidently varying in strength but being generally too weak to produce fruit."[15] Though the date palm is usually diœcious, still a tree that ordinarily produces pistillate flowers only may develop occasionally a cluster of staminate flowers, or perhaps one year produce a few hermaphrodite flowers and never do so again.[182] Certain varieties of the Japanese persimmon show great variation in the kinds of flowers they bear from year to year.[32,113] In some seasons they produce pistillate flowers only and in other seasons they produce a number of staminate flowers along with the pistillates. "Seedling [persimmon] trees are very unreliable in the production of blossoms, bearing male flowers during the first few years, then a small proportion of female flowers, while later the appearance of male flowers is sporadic on some trees and regular on others."[32]

Age and Vigor of Plant.—Practically inseparable from the influences on fruit setting of nutritive conditions within the plant, of nutrient supply without, of locality and of season, is that of age and vigor. The change from the production of staminate flowers only to that of some staminate and some pistillate flowers and later of pistillate flowers only, mentioned in a preceding paragraph as common in seedlings of the Japanese persimmon, is a case in point. Young vigorous apple trees often fail to set fruit under controlled cross pollinations, when old and less vigorous trees of the same varieties set freely.[185] Waugh[239] found on the average a higher percentage of defective pistils in young and vigorous plum trees than in older trees of the same kinds. The Muscat of Alexandria grape is reported to show marked susceptibility to "coulure" or dropping for the year or two after starting to bear, but later this trouble is much less serious.[13] Young grape vines have been found to produce less pollen than mature vines of the same variety.[15]

In the instances cited, age of plant has been the factor apparently associated with the degree or percentage of fruit setting. It is probable, however, that age is effective through its influence on vigor and the internal conditions of nutrition or hybridity with which vigor is associated. It is interesting that Stout found self compatibility in chicory entirely independent of differences in vegetative vigor, thus suggesting that some of the internal factors controlling fruit setting and fertility are not influenced by vigor. As in the cases where fruitfulness is influenced by variations in nutritive conditions, nutrient supply, locality and season, most of the influence of varying age and vigor seems to be through effects on impotence preceding fertilization and embryo abortion at a later stage and not on compatibility, using that term in its narrower sense.

Temperature.—The general effect on the setting of fruit of temperatures slightly below freezing just before, at or shortly after blossoming is well known and in the section on Temperature Relations is a somewhat detailed account of the more important factors in frost occurrence and their bearing upon fruit production. However, temperatures well above the freezing point often are important in determining the setting of fruit. Darwin[49] calls attention to the rather common failure of European vegetables to develop fruits and seeds when grown in India and attributes this failure to the hot climate of that country. Cochran[29] found in New York that at temperatures of 90° to 100°F. no flowers of the common pepper set fruit, though good setting was obtained at temperatures between 60° and 80°F. In some of these instances the influence of temperature may be more directly upon the formation of flower buds and flower parts than upon the processes of fruit setting. In some instances where there is an apparent association between high temperature and dropping of blossoms or partially formed fruit the effect of the high temperature may be registered through its influence on transpiration rate and consequent water deficits within the plant.

Goff[86] has shown that though pollen of most deciduous fruits, like the plum, cherry, apple and pear, germinates freely at temperatures of 50°F. or above, the process is practically inhibited by temperatures of 40°F. or lower. In a number of plums the stigma is receptive for a period of only 4 to 6 days. The abscission of the style occurs in from 8 to 12 days after bloom and it is not influenced to any great extent by temperature.[62] On the other hand, the period required for the germination of the pollen grain and its penetration of the style may depend on temperature and may be as short as 4 days and as long as 12. A period of cool, but frostless, weather during blossoming, therefore, may practically prevent fertilization and thus very materially limit the set of fruit. Presumably similar conditions are found in many other fruits, though the relative importance of this factor varies greatly with different species and varieties.

In this connection mention should be made of the indirect influence of temperature on fruit setting through its effect on the activity of pollen-carrying insects. Evidently the temperature at which bees and other pollen-carrying insects will work depends on conditions, for 40°F. has been given as the lowest temperature at which the honey bee will take flight[62] though normally they do not leave the hive until the temperature reaches about 60°F., except after a considerable period of confinement. Whatever the exact temperature may be, it is evident that should all other conditions be favorable a continued period during blossoming well above freezing but still too low for much activity of the pollen-carrying insects may account for many failures in fruit setting.

An interesting example of the influence of temperature on fruit setting is furnished by the papaya. Though usually a strictly diœcious plant, the "male" form sometimes bears fruit in cool climates. In commenting on the change of sex here involved Higgins and Holt remark:[106] "This 'fruiting of the male papaya' takes place most freely in cool climates outside the tropics or at high altitudes. In Hawaii it may be seen that these trees fruit more abundantly on the mountains than near the sea level. Information received by correspondence with experiment stations and botanic gardens in many parts of the world, in reply to direct inquiry, have confirmed this conclusion. In torrid climates the fruiting of the male is rare. It is to be remembered in this connection that all the staminate flowers of the male trees possess an undeveloped or an abortive pistil. The only change in the cases mentioned consists in the development of this pistil."

Light.—It is doubtful if variations in light supply are important in determining the setting of deciduous fruits. However, it is of some interest that the willow-herb (*Epilobium angustifolium*) develops its flowers normally and sets fruit and seed freely in open sunny situations but when shaded its flower buds abort and fall off before opening.[132] Tomatoes grown in the greenhouse during the short days of winter do not set fruit freely, probably due largely to carbohydrate shortage,[163] and Fauchere is of the opinion that the virescence and abortion of flowers of the coffee plant when grown in partial shade are similarly due to disturbed nutritive conditions.[73] Shading experiments during the blossoming season in Wisconsin have led Bradbury and Roberts[19] to conclude that a limited light supply may be a very important factor in determining the setting of sour cherries, though a similar study by Gray[91] in Michigan did not substantiate that conclusion. Both Darrow[41] and Vaile[235] have reported that the development of stamens and petals in strawberry flowers takes place only when the plants are exposed to rather long photoperiods, and thus plants forced in greenhouses in midwinter tend to develop pistillate flowers. Here again the effect may be causally related to the relatively low carbohydrate-nitrogen ratio reported by Gardner[82a] as leading to the suppression of the male organs in the strawberry, or it may represent a different type of light influence.

Disturbed Water Relations.—In the section on Water Relations it is shown that conditions of low atmospheric humidity, high temperature, exposure to high winds and a limited supply of soil moisture sometimes induce in trees moisture deficits that lead to the formation of an abscission layer and the dropping of the blossoms or fruits. In summarizing the results of his investigations on fruit setting in the apple, Heinicke says: " . . . the influence of extremes in the carbohydrate-nitrogen ratio in the chemical composition of the cluster base or adjoining tissues on the formation of abscission layer in normal flowers or young fruits, seems to be slight as compared with the influence of disturbed water relationships during the early stages of fruit development."[101]

The water loss in developing Washington Navel orange fruits at an early stage of development at and shortly after midday has been shown to be as much as 30 per cent.[31] As the fruits become larger, however, and the ratio of volume to surface increases, such water losses are relatively smaller under similar environmental conditions, and there is a corresponding decrease in the loss of fruit from dropping.[93] This suggests as a preventive measure the employing of cultural methods in the orange grove that promote an early setting of fruit.

Practically the same conditions have been found responsible for much of the shedding of the developing bolls in cotton.[77] Studies of boll abscission in cotton, however, led to the conclusion that the water deficit in the leaves and stems was only indirectly the cause of abscission since the water deficit produced in the tissues a rise in temperature which was "the stimulus which directly leads to abscission."

Discussing the shedding of cotton bolls because of water deficits Floyd explains how a surplus of water may act in the same way. He says:

"If the general conclusion that the grand march of shedding is due to the depletion of moisture in the deeper soil be true, irrigation and better soil manipulation are indicated as remedies. It has been shown experimentally by Barre, in South Carolina, that irrigation has the effect of inhibiting shedding. The observations of Balls that the rise of the water table in Egypt due to the Nile floods, by asphyxiating the deeper roots and so limiting the water supply, causes severe shedding, are quite in harmony with the above findings, since too much water may have quite the same effect as too little, and suitable drainage is thereby indicated as surely as irrigation."[77]

Presumably it is because of more or less severe root pruning and consequent temporary water deficits that deep cultivation during the blossoming and fruit-setting season is often so harmful. A single deep cultivation at this critical period has been known to reduce the crop in a black raspberry plantation by more than a half,[221] and other fruits are known to be especially sensitive to injuries to their root systems at this period. In the Philippines the flowers of the Washington Navel orange that appear during the more humid months of February and March are said to set fruit much better than those that open at the regular seasons,[226] and similarly in Trinidad those flowers of the cacao opening in the wet season (September) adhere better than those opening when the atmosphere is drier (May-June).[186]

The dropping of flowers or partly developed fruits that is due to water deficits is partly under control. Irrigation, tillage, the use of certain cover crops, windbreaks and care to see that the roots are not unduly disturbed during the blossoming and fruit-setting period are among the more important means that tend to lessen the difference between absorption and transpiration in times of stress.

Not only may a water deficit lead to the dropping of flowers and newly set fruits, but it has been shown experimentally that very high atmospheric humidity tends to cause the abscission of partly developed apples,[100] and it is said that irrigation of the olive during the blossoming season often causes its blossoms and young fruit to drop.[40] Some of those cases[81] where moderate desiccation of the soil during the post-blossoming period, as compared with more moist soil conditions, leads to a better setting and fruit development, may be due to water relations directly or possibly to the influence of the soil moisture on growth and carbohydrate accumulation.

Rain at Blossoming.—Rain at blossoming is recognized generally as one of the most important factors limiting the set of fruit.

The following regarding weather conditions at blossoming time in New York verifies this statement:[97] "Wet weather almost wholly prevented the setting of fruit in New York in the years 1881, 1882, 1883, 1886, 1890, 1892 and 1901. Rain is mentioned as one of the causes of a poor setting of fruit in the years 1888, 1889, 1891, 1893, 1894, 1898, 1905. . . . Rain and the cold and wind that usually accompany it at blossoming time cause the loss of more fruit than any other climatal agencies. The damage is done in several ways. The most obvious injury is the washing of the pollen from the anthers. The secretion on the stigmas also is often washed away or becomes so diluted that the pollen does not germinate. It is probable that the chill of rainy weather decreases the vitality of the pollen and an excess of moisture often causes pollen grains to swell and burst."

Experimental evidence on the damaging influence of rain on fruit setting is furnished by an experiment in which a Mount Vernon pear tree was sprayed continuously for 219 hours while in bloom.[71] This tree set very little fruit while a tree of the same variety standing nearby and not subjected to such treatment set a good crop. Similar results were obtained with two Duchess grape vines.

However, plants possess many protective devices which serve to reduce injury to their blossoms from rain. Thus in *Vaccinium* and many other genera the flower is pendent and the essential organs are protected by a bell-shaped corolla; in *Opuntia* and many others the petals close over stamens and stigma during damp weather; the male racemes of the Juglandaceæ and Cupuliferæ are pendulous and shed water almost perfectly when mature and in *Vitis* anthers that have dehisced and shed part of their pollen close and shut out water upon the advent of rain.[128] In the investigation just cited, it was found that pollen of the Duchess grape when examined under the microscope[71] after

11 days of continuous spraying was apparently uninjured. Work with the plum has shown conclusively that after pollination the pollen is washed from the stigmas only with great difficulty and that stigmas will secrete their fluid a second time if rain removes that first secreted.[62] Rain, however, is usually accompanied by temperatures below those characterizing fair weather at the same season. Thus Hedrick in the report just cited states that "rainfall came in periods of prolonged cold weather in the years 1881, 1882, 1883, 1886, 1888, 1889, 1891, 1892, 1894, 1898, 1905. Frosts and cold weather accompanied the rains in 1888, 1889, 1890, 1891, and 1892." In the light of these and many other observations and findings as to the distinctly different effects of low temperature on rate of pollen tube growth and time of style abscission, it may be questioned if rain at blossoming is in itself a very important factor in limiting the set of fruit. Other conditions, particularly lower temperatures, with which rain is generally associated, and interference with the work of pollen-carrying insects, are more important. This statement is not made for the purpose of minimizing the importance of "rainy weather" at blossoming in reducing the fruit crop. It is desirable, however, that there be a correct understanding of the relative importance of the different factors that usually constitute "rainy weather" and that there be a realization that even a hard rain, if of short duration and not accompanied by very low temperatures, is not ordinarily a serious limiting factor in this connection.

Wind.—The average fruit grower regards wind as one of the most important agents in the transfer of pollen from stamen to stigma. Many plants, such as the walnuts, oaks, hickories and hazels, are wind-pollinated and with these a reasonable amount of wind at blossoming is a distinct aid in securing a good set of fruit. However, the majority of the deciduous fruit crops are insect-pollinated. With these, wind hinders rather than helps pollination, since bees and other pollen-carrying insects work most effectively in a still atmosphere and in a strong wind they refuse to work at all. Abundant evidence on this point may be found in orchards with some exposed and some protected situations. Other conditions equal, there will be a much better set of fruit where the trees are protected from the full sweep of the wind and in exposed places there is often a much better set on the leeward than on the windward side of the trees.

In addition to the indirect effect of wind through interfering with the work of pollen-carrying insects, it may operate more directly in whipping about the flowers and causing mechanical injuries. It may also cause the stigmatic fluid to dry prematurely and thus prevent the germination of the pollen grains. In some species at least, the action of wind is more pronounced early in the usual period of pistil maturity than later.[62]

There are many cases in which the protection afforded the fruit plantation at the time of blossoming is of greater importance than any other service rendered by a windbreak.

Insects and Fungous and Bacterial Diseases.—The flowers of many species are subject to the attacks of various fungous and bacterial diseases and often their work at this time is serious enough greatly to reduce the set of fruit. Thus, the pear thrips may infest the blossoms of the pear, apple, prune and other fruits in such numbers as to blast all the flowers on the tree or even in the orchard.[245] Similarly the normal set of the pear may be greatly reduced by an infestation of the pear midge, that of the apple may be reduced by an attack of the bud moth or leaf roller or rosy aphis and that of cherries and plums by the curculio.

Fire blight is generally recognized as one of the most important factors in limiting the set of fruit in pears; the apple and the pear scab are responsible for the falling of many flowers of those fruits at or shortly after blossoming; brown rot attacks the blossoms of practically all the stone fruits; black rot works on grape blossoms, causing many to drop; the flowers of the mango[184] are attacked frequently by an anthracnose; the list might be extended almost indefinitely. Naturally the losses occasioned by these fungous and bacterial attacks at the time of fruit setting vary greatly with locality, variety and seasonal conditions. For instance, there are certain restricted areas where fire blight of the pear and apple is not found, though the disease may levy a very heavy toll on pear blossoms a hundred miles distant. The Grimes apple is but little subject to the scab fungus and ordinarily its setting of fruit will not be materially reduced by it, though a Winesap crop in the same orchard may be practically ruined by its work upon the blossoms. In California brown rot is a serious disease on the blossoms of the apricot only in "regions exposed to ocean influences and does not develop except in times of unusually moist weather."[109] Fungi have been reported as attacking the anthers and stigmas of the loganberry in British Columbia[53] and the newly set fruits of the cranberry in New Jersey.[63] Fortunately most of the fungous and bacterial diseases that attack the blossoms of fruit trees can be controlled by spraying or other preventive measures; consequently losses due to these factors are avoidable in many cases.

Spraying Trees When in Bloom.—Though spraying trees with the proper materials may be effective in preventing the attacks of certain diseases that otherwise would seriously reduce the set of fruit, it is not necessary or desirable to spray during blossoming. Spray applications at that time are seldom recommended and are generally regarded as undesirable. They may reduce the set of fruit either directly through injuring the pollen or stigma or indirectly through interfering with the work of bees and other pollen-carrying insects.

Beach[10] made a number of laboratory cultures of pollen grains in media to which varying amounts of Bordeaux mixture alone and Bordeaux mixture with an arsenical poison had been added. He found that 200 parts of Bordeaux mixture to 10,000 parts of his culture media practically prevented the germination of pollen and that much smaller amounts had a distinct inhibiting influence. On the other hand in one experiment spraying apricots when in bloom with the regular summer strength of the lime-sulphur mixture and with a weak Bordeaux mixture caused no injury to the flowers and no interference with fruit setting.[109] This suggests at least that in actual field practice no great injury in fruit setting is likely to result from the use of fungicides alone when trees are in bloom.

Apparently the indirect effects on fruit setting of spraying with arsenical poisons when trees are in bloom are much more serious. It has been shown that a very small amount of arsenic—less than 0.0000005 gram of arsenious trioxide—is a fatal dose for a bee and most bees die within a few hours after being poisoned.[187] Bees work as freely upon sprayed as upon adjacent unsprayed trees. Price[187] found that the mortality of bees in a check cage was only 19 per cent., as compared with 69 per cent. in a lime-sulphur-arsenate of lead sprayed cage and as compared with 49 per cent. in a sulphur-arsenate of lead dusted cage.

The suggestion is made that if it has been impossible to spray before blossoming for the control of fungi which interfere with fruit setting and such fungi are known to be present to a serious extent, spraying may continue into, or even through, the blossoming season, but a fungicide alone should be used at that time.

Other Factors That Cause the Dropping of Fruit and Flowers.—Many other agencies besides those mentioned may occasionally cause flowers or developing fruits to drop prematurely. Among these may be mentioned the presence of small amounts of illuminating gas in the atmosphere.[87] Spraying with certain materials, independent of any direct effect on the stigma or on pollen-carrying insects, may cause blossoms or partially developed fruit to drop. Dutton[64] has shown that the continued use of lime-sulphur spray may reduce the crop of apples as much as a half, perhaps partly through a more or less direct effect on the blossoms but more especially through its influence on the functioning and premature dropping of the leaves. This influence is apparently cumulative over a period of years. Arsenate of lead, both alone and in combination with various fungicides, has been shown to cause lesions on the pedicels of cherries and prunes that interfere with sap conduction and that lead to dwarfing, shriveling and sometimes dropping of the fruit.[83]

Bushnell[24] has found that fruit setting in certain cucurbitaceous plants is characterized by a distinct periodicity. That is, flowers opening during a 2- or 3-day period may set freely, those opening during the next 2 or 3 days set poorly, then there is another period of good setting and so on.

Summary.—The most important of the direct effects of the environment through the plant itself is in influencing nutritive conditions. Soil type, water supply, fertilizers, cultivation and pruning are important in this connection. Low temperature and rain are the two most important of the environmental factors indirectly affecting fruit setting through affording or preventing the opportunity for pollination, the germination of the pollen grain and fertilization. Wind is an aid to pollination in those species whose pollen is wind-borne, but often a serious limiting factor in those whose pollen is insect-borne. Insect and fungous attack often seriously interferes with the setting of fruit.

It is evident from the subject matter presented in this and the two preceding chapters that the whole subject of fruit setting is complex. In the first place it depends on a number of internal factors, many of which are entirely beyond any direct or indirect control. Secondly, blossoming generally comes at a season when great fluctuations in temperature, humidity and the other features of environment are likely. It is therefore not surprising that the response of the tree to the combination of all these interrelated factors and conditions varies from year to year, from orchard to orchard and even from tree to tree. It is fortunate indeed for the grower that the most important of the limiting factors to fruit setting—both those internal and those external to the plant—are within the grower's control by either direct or indirect means.

CHAPTER XXIX

FACTORS MORE DIRECTLY CONCERNED IN THE DEVELOPMENT OF THE FRUIT

The discussion thus far has been limited mainly to a consideration of the primary results of fertilization. From the grower's standpoint, however, the nature and extent of its indirect effects are often of equal or greater importance.

The immediate or primary result of fertilization is the initiation of the series of changes in the mature embryo sac leading to the development of the embryo and endosperm. The changes subsequently occurring in the ovarian wall and oftentimes in attached tissues result in the setting and development of the fruit. These are the indirect or secondary effects of fertilization.

Stimulating Effects of Pollen on Ovarian and Other Tissues.—Before fertilization takes place, the pollen often has an important influence on the development of ovarian and other tissues connected with the fruit. This effect is independent of the process of fertilization and may be exercised though fertilization never occurs. For example, Wellington[244] secured fruits of the Seckel pear by applying to its stigmas pollen of the Yellow Transparent apple, and Millardet[154] obtained fruits of certain varieties of the European grape by employing pollen of *Ampelopsis hederacea*. Presumably in neither case could fertilization occur, though the pollen tubes may have entered the embryo sacs. Triturated pollen applied to the stigmas of certain curcurbits has induced a partial development of their fruits[149] and fully formed but seedless fruits of certain species have been obtained by applying to their stigmas spores of *Lycopodium*.[80] In both of these cases fruit development must be attributed to the stimulating influence of the pollen or spores. Goodspeed[88] reports that emasculated but unpollinated flowers of the Thompson Seedless grape do not set fruit; however, emasculated and pollinated flowers set freely, though the resulting fruits are seedless because of embryo sac degeneration.

Some of the most interesting, and perhaps among the most striking, cases of response to the stimulus of pollination are found among the orchids.[44] In most species of this family the ovule is in a very rudimentary stage of development at the time of pollination. In some of these if pollination is not effected the ovules never reach the stage at which

581

fertilization can take place, but immediately after pollination the tissues of the ovule proceed to complete their development and finally reach the stage for fertilization.   In many cases several weeks between the time of pollination and fertilization are required for the ovules to reach maturity.

Kusano,[141] who studied the influence of pollination in stimulating the development of the ovary and fruit in *Gastrodia*, found that many fruits would develop in this genus when no pollination occurred.   These parthenocarpic fruits were normal in appearance, though somewhat below the average in size.   Seeds were formed but they were without embryos and the number of these imperfectly formed seeds was usually below that in fruits resulting from ordinary pollination. When *Gastrodia* flowers are pollinated with pollen of *Bletia*, another orchid, fruits likewise developed but they were much larger than the parthenocarpic fruits developing without pollination, though they too were without embryo-containing seeds and presumably no fertilization had occurred.   Fruits of the first category, that is, those developing without the stimulus of pollination, were classed as instances of vegetative or autonomic parthenocarpy; those of the second class were considered instances of stimulative or aitionomic parthenocarpy.   Commenting upon the results of some of his experiments, Kusano[141] remarks: "As regards the parthenocarpic development by the foreign pollen two points may be worthy of consideration.   First, the size of the resulting fruit may depend on the intensity of the stimulus.   This is evidenced by the experiment with the Bletia-pollinium; pollinated the day of bloom, the pollinium sends out massive tubes, leading the fruit to maximal growth, but the delayed pollination brings about a feebler development of the tube, perhaps owing to a certain modified condition of the stigma, and consequently smaller fruits result. Further, the pollinia of other orchids yield smaller fruits than the Bletia-pollinium, in conformity with the feeble development of the pollen-tubes.   Secondly, it may be most probable that the size of the fruit correlates with the duration of the stimulus acted upon.   The product of the normal-sized fruit by crossing Bletia appears to be due to the longevity of activity of the pollen-tube, remaining alive and vigorous far beyond the period of maturation of the fruit, and thus exerting the stimulus unceasingly upon the ovules and ovary throughout the interval of their complete development. . . .   As far as observed in Gastrodia, we are led to the view that the ovarial development is correlated with the embryogenic development of the ovules when the tube of its own pollinium is concerned, but when it is induced by the foreign pollen tube, it is likely comparable to the gall formation by the action of fungi or insects.   So that, though the kind of the stimulus is unknown, whether chemical or mechanical, we may ascribe the resulting effect to an incessant stimulus of sufficient intensity."

The Effect of Certain Stimulating Agents on Fruit Setting.—It has long been known that the fruits of certain species which seldom or never develop parthenocarpically can be made to set occasionally by treating the stigmas with certain stimulating agents other than pollen.   Indeed the use of *Lycopodium* spores, mentioned in a preceding paragraph, may be regarded as a stimulating agent of this character. Hartley[95] secured a partial set of fruit in tobacco by treating receptive stigmas with magnesium sulfate and other chemicals. The seeds of these fruits were poorly developed and without embryos. Wellington,[244] working with the same species, obtained some fruits, likewise without good seeds, by "singeing young buds with a hot platinum wire, by exposure of young plants to chloroform gas, and by cutting away a portion of the pistil and pollinating the stub both with and without the accompaniment of a germinative fluid." The ovaries of certain orchids can be made to develop into fruits by the mechanical irritation of the stigmas.[44]

Closely related to the effects of mechanical irritation and of various chemicals on fruit setting are those of the presence of the stings of certain insects. Müller-Thurgau[160] stated that the presence of a certain gall insect would cause the setting of pear flowers and a brief rapid growth of the fruit, though these insect-infested specimens fell before reaching maturity. Figure 56 shows a flower cluster of the LeBrun pear shortly after petal fall. The outside flowers had been pollinated, had set fruit, and were developing normally; of the two center specimens one had not been pollinated and was about to drop; the other, infested with the gall insect, had not only set but was enlarging much more rapidly than fruits developing normally. Kraus[140] reports that not only fruits but embryo-containing seeds often develop from the flower clusters of self sterile

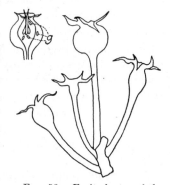

FIG. 56.—Fruit cluster of the LeBrun pear. The central fruit has been parasitized. The outer two have set and are developing normally. The other one is about to fall off. In the cross section, larvae are shown at *g*. (*After Müller-Thurgau.*[160])

and self barren apple varieties when those flower clusters are attacked by aphids. The same development has been recorded in the sweet cherry.[82] In such instances the resulting fruits are generally much dwarfed and malformed and seldom can the seeds be made to germinate; as a rule the fruits contain fewer and smaller seeds than normally developed specimens of the same varieties.[175]

Some observations of Johnson[123] on this point are very interesting. Several species of cacti often retain their fruits long after maturity. They may persist for months or in some cases for years. Johnson, examining a large number of plants of *Opuntia versicolor* in April and May, found only about 25 per cent. bearing persistent fruits. However, about 9 out of 10 of those plants which did bear apparently normal persistent fruits bore also abnormal gall fruits, the result of the stings of one of the gall insects. This led Johnson to suggest, "that the cause of the persistence of the normal fruits may be the same as the cause of the abnormality as well as of the persistence of the far more common gall fruits."

One of the most interesting cases of the influence of the presence of insects, independent of their pollen-carrying activities, on fruit setting is found in the male fig, or caprifig.[33,66,193]   These are not in fact male trees; their flower clusters contain both staminate and pistillate flowers.   Occasionally some of the pistillate flowers of these clusters are pollinated and develop seeds, but as a rule if the *Blastophaga* wasps enter the cluster they oviposit in the pistillate flowers and so-called gall flowers result.   While the larvæ of the *Blastophaga* are developing in the gall flowers the staminate blossoms of the cluster mature so that their pollen is shed when the mature wasps are ready to emerge.   Such flower clusters on the caprifig are known as insectiferous figs.   If, however, the *Blastophaga* wasps do not enter these clusters at the stage when their pistillate flowers are ready for pollination or oviposition, the cluster may or may not persist until its staminate flowers mature their pollen. (From a practical standpoint their remaining and maturing are of no value, since no wasps are in them to emerge and carry pollen to the flowers of pistillate trees.)   Such clusters are known as polliniferous figs. In any case they drop off before the insectiferous figs reach full maturity and the dropping is in a way comparable to the June drop of many other fruits.   Since pollination is unnecessary for the setting and persistence of the insectiferous fig it must be concluded that the mechanical or chemical stimulus resulting from the insect's presence is the real cause of setting.   The growth stimulus changes the twigs and branches[66] bearing insectiferous figs so that they may be told readily from those bearing only polliniferous figs by their thickness, length and general vigorous appearance.   This response, not unlike that frequently attending the injection of some chemical substance into vegetative tissue, is at least suggestive of the complexities involved in fruit setting.

Seedlessness and Parthenocarpy.—Seedless fruits are found in a great many species.[217]   In some cases they are of rather infrequent occurrence, their production apparently depending on unusual conditions of culture or environment.   In others they appear frequently and many seedless strains or varieties have been established and are propagated extensively by vegetative means.   In such cases the seedlessness is due primarily to internal causes that are usually but little influenced by changes in environment.

Investigations with the grape by Stout[212] have led to this conclusion: "The most effective course in breeding for the development of seedless sorts is suggested by the conditions of intersexualism.   Most individuals and varieties producing seedless or near-seedless fruits are strongly staminate. The former can be used as male parents on the latter, which do produce a few viable seeds. Plants strongly male and seedless can be crossed with plants strongly male but weakly female and near-seedless and, also, the self-fertilized progeny of the latter may be obtained. In this way families weak in femaleness may undoubtedly be obtained in which a considerable number of individuals will produce seedless fruits."

Parthenocarpy refers to the ability of a plant to develop its fruit (1) without fertilization or even (2) without the stimulus that comes from pollination. In other words, the growth of the ovarian and other tissues of the fruit can occur without any stimulus from the accompanying development of the ovules into seeds. Parthenocarpic fruits are usually, but not always, seedless. In some species fruits will develop and viable seeds will be formed even if no pollination takes place. Such plants are parthenocarpic and parthenogenetic at the same time. (Parthenogenesis is common in certain strawberry varieties.) Furthermore, many parthenocarpic fruits contain aborted or partly developed seeds, or seeds that, though normal in appearance, are incapable of germination. On the other hand, not all seedless fruits are parthenocarpic. In some cases seedlessness is due to embryo abortion some time after fertilization; unless pollen had been available to furnish the stimulus for fruit setting no later development of the fruit would have been possible.

It is evident therefore that seedlessness and parthenocarpy are rather distinct phenomena though it frequently happens that the two are associated.

Seedlessness of Non-parthenocarpic Fruits.—The immediate cause of seedlessness in fruits that have not developed parthenocarpically is embryo abortion. This in turn may be due either to internal or to external factors. Frost or freezing temperature after the fruit has set is perhaps one of the most common of the environmental factors leading to this condition; it has been observed repeatedly in pears, apples and peaches. The developing embryo of the seed seems for some reason more tender to low temperatures than the ovarian and other tissues surrounding it. Consequently embryo development is arrested; however, if the growth of the fruit has proceeded far enough it will continue through to maturity, though such fruits are often materially smaller than those containing seeds. In many pear varieties, particularly those that normally are either elongated or pyriform, the seedless specimens are generally quite distinct in shape.[21] Each has a shorter transverse diameter through the core, but is much thickened at the basal end. Sandsten[196] has produced seedless tomatoes by excessive feeding. Though no statement is made as to whether or not these fruits developed parthenocarpically, it is presumable that pollination at least and probably fertilization took place and that seedlessness was due to embryo abortion.

In a preceding paragraph it was shown that full maturity of the fruits on a caprifig tree is usually attained only when some of its pistillate flowers are inhabited by the developing *Blastophaga* wasp. Ordinarily these fruits mature no seeds because few or none of the pistillate flowers are pollinated. In this fruit, then, embryo abortion and seedlessness are associated with a stimulus resulting from the attack of a certain insect.

Embryo abortion, resulting in seedlessness, is not, however, always due to external factors. For instance, according to one investigator only about 25 per cent. of the fruits of the Blue Damson plums contained good plump seeds.[147] The remaining 75 per cent. were seedless or their seeds were only half grown and non-viable. Many other plum varieties were found to bear a large percentage of seedless fruits. Nevertheless, none of these varieties developed fruit parthenocarpically and in some of them cross pollination was necessary for any set at all. "The kind of pollen used seems to have had little bearing upon the relationship of fruit production to seed production, as the percentage of seeds developed in any variety seems to be rather constant regardless of the kind of pollen used."[147] The same type of seedlessness has been observed in many sweet cherry varieties, in the May Duke cherry reaching sometimes over 95 per cent. of the fruits. Seedlessness that is not associated with parthenocarpy is likewise frequent in some of the cultivated varieties of the filbert, where it is a serious matter since seeds constitute the crop. A thorough study would undoubtedly show that seedlessness is frequently associated with embryo abortion in the developing seeds of many cultivated fruits. Though in many varieties if seed abortion takes place at any stage the fruit drops prematurely, in many others it can occur at a late, and still others at an early, stage and still the fruit will persist and mature properly. Evidently seedlessness from this cause depends on the varying requirements of the ovarian tissues of different fruits for the stimulus imparted to them by the growth of the partly developed seeds within. Instances of this kind, however, probably always follow fertilization. Perhaps seedlessness may be regarded more or less as the few-seeded condition that we consider normal in many fruits carried a step further. Thus, the ovaries of peaches, plums and other stone fruits contain two ovules. Characteristically one of these aborts, leaving the other to develop. The ovaries of the date and coconut palms each contain three ovules; two abort, leaving only one to develop. Stout[215] finds that ordinarily the fruits of the Delaware grape contain only one or two seeds each, though the ovaries at the time of pollination each contain four ovules that to all appearances are alike, and furthermore "no amount or kind of pollination can increase the number of seeds."

Vegetative and Stimulative Parthenocarpy.—Distinction has been made between vegetative or autonomic and stimulative or aitionomic parthenocarpy. In certain species or varieties parthenocarpic development is vegetative; in other species it is stimulative; in still others both kinds occur. The cases of parthenocarpy that have been reported for a number of species have not been studied carefully enough to make possible their classification. Among the fruits reported as vegetatively parthenocarpic may be mentioned the banana,[2] many varieties of the Japanese persimmon,[113,114] certain mulberries,[27] certain peach varieties,[208] the medlar,[133] the papaya,[106] the egg plant, summer squash and the English cucumber,[161] a number of varieties of the orange[170] and many varieties of the fig.[66] These fruits, or certain of their varieties, either occasionally or regularly set and mature fruit without the stimulus even of pollination. Among those that have been reported parthenocarpic when subjected to certain stimuli, usually the stimulus of pollination, are the pepino,[162] some of the squashes,[68] tobacco,[244] pear[244] and Jerusalem cherry.[244] Reinicke[191] has reported a number of pear varieties that seldom develop fruits parthenocarpically in the United States as regularly parthenocarpic in parts of South Africa, and, furthermore, this parthenocarpy may be either vegetative or aitionomic. This furnishes another illustration of the influence of environmental conditions on parthenocarpic development. Many varieties of Muscadine[190] and of Labrusca and Labrusca-hybrid grapes[8] have been reported as occasionally or sparingly parthenocarpic when subjected to the stimulus of pollination with impotent pollen, and the Thompson Seedless[88] grape is regularly parthenocarpic under similar conditions. The Sultanina, Sultanina Rose and Black Monukka, also seedless varieties, produce many normal embryo sacs and some defective ones; fertilization may or may not take place, but, if it does, embryo abortion promptly follows; in the Black Corinth the embryo sacs abort before the flowers open and no fertilization is possible.[179,215]

Though not exactly classifying as a case of stimulative parthenocarpy, the Citrus group exhibits a closely related condition. Many of their seeds are polyembryonic, the adventive embryos developing from nucellar tissues. However, the stimulus of fertilization is said to be necessary to the development of the apogamic embryos, though the sexual embryos may be eliminated in the course of the development of the seed.[79] On the other hand, the Washington Navel orange normally produces no pollen and requires no pollination in order to set and mature its seedless fruits.[170,226,234]

In discussing the influence of nutritive conditions within the plant on fruit setting attention has been directed to their influence on parthenocarpy. Apparently unusual accumulation of elaborated foods in proximity to flowers in the receptive stage often acts as a stimulus to further growth and development and in this way inhibits the formation of an abscission layer much as would the stimulus occasioned by the stings of certain insects or by developing seeds.

Relation of Anatomical Structure of Fruit to Parthenocarpy.—As has been pointed out, seedlessness is to be expected at least occasionally in almost every species and variety and it is probable that the same may be said of parthenocarpy. It may be noted, however, that it is more frequent in species whose fruits the botanist classifies as inferior, those into whose structure tissues other than the ovary enter. Though this may be a mere coincidence, it at least suggests that the greater stem-like character of such fruits imparts to them a stronger tendency to persist

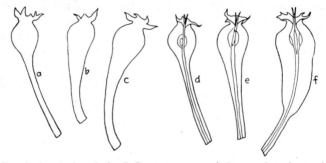

Fig. 57.—Developing fruits of the LeBrun pear; *a* and *d* normal seed-containing fruits *b*, *c*, *e* and *f* seedless. (*After Müller-Thurgau.*[160])

than there is in those whose tissues when mature are entirely carpellary in nature. They seem to be less in need of the stimulus of fertilization. In Fig. 57 are shown pears of the LeBrun variety, one of which is developing as a result of the stimulus afforded by pollination and fertilization. The other two are developing parthenocarpically. The greater development of the stem tissues in the latter case is very suggestive.

Suggestive also in this connection are the following statements by Johnson[123] on the perennation and proliferation of the fruits of *Opuntia fulgida*. "It is true that the vegetative joints and both the fertile and sterile fruits resemble each other greatly in their capacity for proliferation. There seems no adequate reason, however, for assuming that either the proliferating habit or the fundamental structure of the fruit is a secondary thing in the evolution of the opuntias. On the contrary, it is natural that the thick-skinned, water-stored joints of these cacti should have proved capable of persisting on moderately moist soil until rooted deeply enough to secure a water-supply adequate for the starting of a young plant. The fruit being . . . really a stem in organization, up to the latest phase of its development, it is also very naturally capable of proliferation to root and shoot. The capacity of joint and fruit for persistence and proliferation is probably as old as the fleshy character of the family. The persistence of the sterile fruits, at least to maturity, is not a really surprising thing, in view of the preponderatingly vegetative and stem-like character of the bulk of the wall of the ovary. Sterile ovaries occur in many species of angiosperms, but in most of these the carpels constitute the bulk of the fruit. Therefore, when the seeds are wanting in these forms, and the carpels as usual fail to develop, no fruit is formed and the flower bud soon withers and drops off. In *Opuntia*, on the contrary, even if the seeds and carpellary portion of the fruit do fail to develop, the basal stem-like part may go on, practically unhindered in its vegetative growth, and mature quite normally."

Between the conditions represented by autonomic parthenocarpy on the one hand and varietal interunfruitfulness on the other there is a series exhibiting practically all possible expressions of the tendency to set and mature fruit. Only a little less extreme than the tendency to fruitfulness shown by plants vegetatively parthenocarpic is that of plants aitionomically parthenocarpic. Next in the series are the plants that can set and mature fruit if self pollinated and fertilized, though embryo abortion takes place almost at once. These in turn are followed by plants which require varying degrees of development in the seeds that they may properly mature their fruit. Finally there are those that require the maturing of viable seeds along with the development of their fruits else premature dropping will occur.

The Value of Seedless and Parthenocarpic Fruits.—Seedlessness in edible fruits is generally regarded as a valuable variety characteristic for commercial purposes. In many cases at least the market is willing to pay a premium for it. Mention of the regard in which seedless grapes and oranges are held is ample evidence. Bananas and pineapples containing seeds would probably find a very limited market. Even a material reduction in the number of seeds would be a great asset in the blueberry, the blackberry, the watermelon, the sugar apple and in many other fruits. On the other hand, in many fruits seedlessness would not be an asset. There would be little advantage in seedless apples or pears, if the carpels remained. It has been pointed out that many fruits of our ordinary plum and cherry varieties are seedless, but this condition is not generally known or even suspected because the bony endocarp (stone) remains unchanged.

For the grower, parthenocarpy probably is a more valuable variety characteristic than seedlessness. If his fruits are parthenocarpic he is insured against crop failure from self and cross unfruitfulness and, if their parthenocarpy is autonomic, through failures resulting from lack of pollinating agents or pollinating weather, his setting of fruit is more or less guaranteed. It should not be inferred, however, that all the flowers of parthenocarpic varieties set fruit and that all these fruits mature. Mention has been made of the relation of water deficiencies at blossoming or shortly thereafter to dropping in the Washington Navel orange.[31] Many other agencies that limit fruit setting in non-parthenocarpic varieties cause the dropping of those varieties that develop parthenocarpically.   In other words, the parthenocarpic condition is only a partial and not a complete insurance against crop failure from premature dropping.

From a practical standpoint seedlessness and parthenocarpy are to be considered more as varietal characteristics to be sought when breeding or originating new varieties or strains, rather than as conditions to be produced by cultural means.

The Relation of Seed Formation to Fruit Development.—It has just been pointed out that in some species or varieties ovarian and other tissues of the fruit may develop independently of those of the enclosed ovules.   This condition, however, is by no means universal and such parthenocarpic fruits are usually somewhat different in size, shape or other characteristics from seed-containing specimens of the same kinds. Furthermore, in the seed-containing specimens important differences in development are often associated with varying seed number and distribution.

Structure of Fruit.—Evidence that certain tissues of the pear undergo a proportionally greater development in seedless than in seed-containing specimens is presented in Fig. 57.   That this is very common in other fruits is indicated by the work of many investigators.   Thus in seedless eggplants, the outer portions of the fruit grow more rapidly than the inner portions, "the placentæ evidently requiring the stimulus of the growing ovules to induce development."[161]   In seedless fruits of the eggplant and in those in which the development of the ovary is arrested at an early stage there is sometimes a very marked and abnormal development of the subtending calyx.   "Usually the most prominent indication that impregnation has taken place, in the eggplant, is the rapid growth of the calyx.   Many times, however, the calyx becomes much enlarged while for some reason the ovary fails to develop.   I have frequently seen examples of this, in which the calyx was fully 6 inches long."[161] Ewert[70] studied the structure of seedless and seed-bearing gooseberry fruits and found striking differences in their cell size and structure.   The cells of the placentæ and inner ovarian wall of seed-containing fruits averaged 45–90$\mu\mu$ in diameter, while many of those in the seedless specimens were seven or eight times as large.

Form.—The pears shown in Fig. 57 are illustrations of changes in form accompanying changes in internal structure due to seedlessness.   Munson[161] observed that the parthenocarpic seedless fruits of English cucumbers were cylindrical in shape, but that when they were pollinated and seeds developed the apical one-third of each fruit was much enlarged, owing to the location of the seeds in that end and not in the basal portion. Seedless or nearly seedless specimens of Taber No. 129, a variety of Japanese persimmon, are almost conical and distinctly pointed, while seed-bearing specimens of the same variety are oblate. Furthermore, "Taber No. 23 when seedy is oblate-rounded, but when seedless it assumes an almost quadrangular form with very blunt or rounded corners. Zengi is oblate-rounded when seedy, but approximates a truncated cone in shape, or is distinctly oblong when seedless."[113]

Size.—Perhaps an even more striking influence of seed formation on the development of the fruit is in size. Seedless grapes are much smaller than seed-containing berries of the same variety and berries containing aborted seeds are intermediate between those that are seed-containing and those that are seedless.[9] Seed-containing gooseberries have been found to average 5 grams in weight, while seedless berries of the same variety averaged only 3 grams.[70] Seedless apples and pears are often, though not always, smaller than seed-containing specimens. In the date palm the seedless fruits maturing from unpollinated flowers are only one-third to half the size of normal seed-containing fruits of the same varieties.[183]

Furthermore in fruits normally containing a number of seeds considerable correlation is likely between the size of the fruit and the number of seeds developing. Munson[161] found this true in the tomato and he observed that the locules were well developed only on the side of the fruit containing a considerable number of good seed. The influence of seed

TABLE 7.—NUMBER OF SEEDS IN FRUITS THAT DROP AND IN FRUITS THAT REMAIN
(ON THE APPLE TREE)
(*After Heinicke*[100])

Number of seeds to the fruit	Baldwin		Rhode Island		Maiden Blush	
	Attached fruit	Drop fruit	Attached fruit	Drop fruit	Attached fruit	Drop fruit
1	..	2	..	6	1	3
2	5	16	..	13	4	17
3	9	12	4	18	9	17
4	9	7	1	9	7	8
5	14	4	5	15	4	6
6	6	6	5	2	10	7
7	3	..	5	1	10	3
8	1	1	6	2	11	4
9	..	..	1	..	6	..
10	..	..	1	..	2	..
11	..	..	1	..	..	..
12	..	..	..	..	1	..
13	..	..	..	..	1	..

number on the premature dropping of apples is shown by data summarized in Table 7. Though the possession of a certain number of developing seeds did not insure the fruit against dropping and though some of the few-seeded fruits persisted and matured, there was a well-marked tendency for the latter to fall prematurely and an equally distinct tendency for the several-seeded fruits to persist. In a previous paragraph it was pointed out that the setting and maturing of apples are favored by the size, strength and vigor of the limbs and spurs on which they are borne. Table 8 presents further data which show the varying seed numbers in fruits of approximately the same size but borne on spurs of varying weights. It is noticeable that with fruit weights remaining constant the number of seeds they contain varies inversely as the weights of the spurs. In other words, the poorer development of fruit generally found on weak spurs is offset if the fruits have enough seeds. This has led to the suggestion that developing seeds have a pulling power for water and sap, enabling the fruits of which they form a part to develop more or less at the expense of other fruits with presumably smaller food-attracting abilities.[100]

TABLE 8.—SEED NUMBER COMPENSATING FOR SPUR WEIGHT IN THE APPLE
(After Heinicke[100])
(Weight of fruit constant, number of seeds and weight of spurs varying)

Lot	Variety	Fruit weight (grams)	Number of seeds per fruit	Spur weight (grams)
1	Tompkins King..................	14.95	2	5.54
		14.72	4	5.05
		14.86	6	2.31
		13.30	7	1.98
2	Tompkins King..................	16.05	2	3.97
		16.96	6	1.45
3	Tompkins King..................	30.96	3	6.09
		31.68	6	3.75
4	Tompkins King..................	95.90	2	5.05
		97.10	4	2.40
5	Rhode Island....................	25.58	3	4.86
		25.31	8	2.28
6	Westfield.......................	21.64	5	2.33
		21.87	8	1.31

Experimental evidence in corroboration of this suggestion was obtained by coating with vaseline partly grown apples on spurs removed from trees and exposed to a drying atmosphere. It was found that the leaves on the spurs were able to withdraw less water from many-seeded than from few-seeded fruits and more from the side of a fruit having no seeds than from the side where the locules contained a number.[100]

Müller-Thurgau[160] found a similar correlation between fruit size and number of seeds in grapes, as is shown in Table 9, and Valleau[236] found the size of strawberry fruits closely correlated with the number of their akenes.

TABLE 9.—RELATION OF SEED NUMBER TO FRUIT SIZE IN GRAPES
(*After Müller-Thurgau*[160])

Variety	Seedless	1 seed		2 seeds		3 seeds		4 seeds	
	Flesh, grams	Flesh, grams	Seeds, grams	Flesh, grams	Seeds, grams	Flesh, grams	Seeds, grams	Flesh, grams	Seeds, grams
Riesling.............	25.0	58.2	2.1	77.2	3.9	89.0	5.2	112.0	6.0
Early Burgundy.......	27.9	52.9	1.8	92.4	3.7	110.5	5.2	140.0	7.3
Portugieser..........	23.7	81.6	2.14	116.7	4.12	140.8	5.9	155.8	6.9
White Gutedel........	58.7	135.8	2.4	196.6	5.0	232.7	7.4	.....	.....
Orleans.............	60.3	112.6	3.1	202.0	7.4	244.4	10.9	258.8	14.9

It should not be inferred, however, that seedless fruits are always smaller than seed-containing fruits of the same varieties or that fruits containing many seeds are larger than those containing but few. For instance, in his pollination work with plums, Marshall[147] found that many varieties mature a large percentage of seedless fruits. These cannot be distinguished from those containing seeds by their size or any other external characteristic. The same is true of fruits of the sweet cherry. Furthermore it has been found that seed-bearing fruits of the Japanese persimmon are uniformly smaller than seedless specimens of the same varieties.[113]

Composition and Quality.—Associated usually with differences in the structure of fruits are variations in composition and quality. This holds true for the structural changes associated with varying seed number, and indeed the differences in composition are often greater than would be expected from observation of the variations in structure. Table 10 shows the sugar content and acidity of seedless and normal pears and Table 11 shows differences in composition between caprified and uncaprified figs of several varieties. The difference in acidity between the seedless and seed-containing pears is striking and is sufficient to make a considerable variation in quality. Though the distinctions between the caprified and the uncaprified figs are on the whole less prominent they are great enough to be of commercial importance in such varieties as the Dottato. There are differences also in color of flesh between caprified and uncaprified figs of the same variety.[193]

Perhaps the most striking dissimilarities in composition and quality between seedless and seed-bearing fruits are found in certain varieties of the kaki or Japanese persimmon. Zengi, Hyakume and certain other sorts are always solid, dark fleshed when they have a good supply of seeds, or when there are only three or four seeds and these are well distributed.[113]   When there is only a single seed, or two or three seeds in adjacent locules, the flesh surrounding these is dark while that some

TABLE 10.—INFLUENCE OF SEED NUMBER ON SUGAR CONTENT AND ACIDITY IN
PEARS
(*After Ewert*[70])

	Grams of reducing sugar in 100 cubic centimeters of sap	Grams of acid, calculated as malic acid, in 1000 cubic centimeters of sap
Fruits seedless............	5.81	0.98
Fruits 1-seeded...........	8.33	1.61
Fruits 2-seeded..........	9.26	1.79

distance away is light colored.   When these varieties produce seedless fruits all of their flesh is light colored.   Okame and Yemon, possessing full complements of seeds, have dark colored flesh immediately surround-

TABLE 11.—ANALYSES OF CAPRIFIED AND UNCAPRIFIED FIGS
(*After Condit*[33])

Variety	Analysis by	Per cent water	Per cent sugar
Fig d'Or, caprified......................	Du Sablon	80.00	11.20
Fig d'Or, uncaprified....................	Du Sablon	74.00	12.60
Fig Datte, caprified.....................	Du Sablon	71.00	14.30
Fig Datte, uncaprified..................	Du Sablon	71.00	18.70
Bourjassotte, caprified...................	Du Sablon	70.00	3.50
Bourjassotte, uncaprified................	Du Sablon	76.00	6.20
Adriatic, caprified.......................	W. V. Cruess	.....	19.05
Adriatic, uncaprified....................	W. V. Cruess	.....	18.00
Dottato, caprified (Kadota)...............	W. V. Cruess	.....	35.20
Dottato, uncaprified (Kadota).............	W. V. Cruess	.....	28.40
Dottato (dried), caprified................	F. W. Albro	22.57	75.36
Dottato (dried), uncaprified..............	F. W. Albro	25.75	68.16
Adriatic (half dried), caprified	F. E. Twinning	27.05	34.80
Adriatic (half dried), uncaprified	F. E. Twinning	28.70	35.50
Adriatic (fresh), uncaprified..............	M. E. Jaffa	70.70	18.78
Adriatic (fresh), caprified................	M. E. Jaffa	74.70	13.00
Adriatic (dry), uncaprified...............	M. E. Jaffa	18.00	51.50
Adriatic (dry), caprified.................	M. E. Jaffa	16.00	48.50

ing the seeds, but light colored flesh next to the skin.   Tsuru, Costata, Triumph and some others are light fleshed whether seeds are present or not.   The dark flesh of persimmons is edible while still hard and firm, but the light flesh remains astringent until it softens.   Hume[113] states that no variety is known which is dark fleshed when seedless, but Condit[32] reports an apparent exception to this rule.

Variation in seed number is accompanied by differences in composition in many other fruits. In most grape varieties, for instance, seedless fruits are much sweeter than seed-containing berries of the same kinds. On the other hand, the differences in composition are often negligible. There is no general rule that can be laid down stating that seedlessness tends either to improve or to detract from quality.

Season of Maturity.—There is often a considerable difference in the time intervals between fruit setting and maturing of seedless and seed-containing fruits of the same variety. As a rule the parthenocarpic or seedless fruits are slower in reaching maturity than the seed-bearing specimens. Munson[161] mentions several instances in which flowers of the cucumber, pumpkin and summer squash were induced to set fruit by applying to their stigmas pollen of certain other species of cucurbits. The resulting fruits which were seedless required over 2 months longer for maturity in some cases and in all cases a somewhat longer period than was necessary for the development of normal fruits from intra-specific pollination. The so-called "second bloom" fruits of the apple and pear that set 2 to 4 weeks after the usual blossoming period and are very often seedless frequently never mature properly and such maturity as they do attain is reached only after they have persisted on the trees much longer than the extra 2 to 4 weeks that would compensate for their late setting. Caprified figs of the Smyrna type drop from the trees at full maturity; uncaprified figs tend to persist and usually must be cut or pulled from the trees, as they will fall only when past their prime.[66] In the Japanese persimmon seed-containing fruits usually ripen earlier. Zengi commonly matures its seed-bearing fruits in late July, while its seedless fruits may not be ready for harvest until December.[113] In other varieties there may be less difference in ripening periods, though they are often quite distinct. Fruits bearing only one or two seeds show a tendency to ripen with the seedless, while those with a greater number show a tendency to ripen with the normal fruits.[113]

In California, where the Bartlett pear is self fruitful to a considerable degree, Overholser and Latimer[173] found that " . . . crossed Bartletts colored and ripened in storage before the selfed. The first pickings of crossed pears kept better than the first picking of selfed, because the former were nearer the proper stage of maturity while the latter were immature. . . . With fruit picked relatively late, however, the self-pollinated pears had an optimum date two weeks later and a maximum date two months later. . . . A difference in methods of spoiling was noted. The breakdown in selfed pears, which were removed from storage and ripened, was characterized by a browning and softening of the tissue commencing at the surface of the fruit and progressing inwardly until the entire specimen was spoiled. The cross-pollinated specimens broke down at the core first, and the browning and softening of the tissue progressed outwardly." In almost all cases the relation of seed number to season of maturity is of very secondary importance.

Specific Influence of Pollen on Resulting Fruit.—Much has been said on the supposed specific influence of the pollen on the characteristics of the fruit resulting from the pollination. For instance, it has been claimed that the red color of striped apple varieties is intensified after pollenizing with a dark red sort. The pollination of varieties with an acid flesh with pollen from a sweet or subacid variety has been said to result in fruit less acid in character. Early maturing sorts are claimed to mature their fruits somewhat later if pollinated by late ripening kinds. These conceptions are based on a misunderstanding of the processes actually involved in pollination, fertilization and fruit development, or on faulty observations, or on a wrong interpretation of field observations that may have been accurate.

There is little evidence to indicate any immediate influence of pollen on the color of the resulting fruit, or any direct effect on its composition, flavor, quality, shape, season of maturity or keeping quality. This statement is borne out by a number of extensive cross and self pollination experiments[162,250] as well as by a theoretical consideration of the nature of the tissues and processes involved in fruit setting and maturing. Of course if in a series of pollination experiments some pollen is used on a certain variety and normal seed-containing fruits result and then pollen of some other kind is used on other flowers stimulating them to set and mature seedless fruit, differences in size, shape, composition and season of maturity may be obtained. However, these are diversities associated more directly with the relationship existing between seed formation and fruit development and not directly between kind of pollen and fruit development. In the same way the pollination of pistils of a given sort with pollen of half a dozen other varieties with which it is inter-fruitful may result in one crossing in fruits averaging say two seeds, in another crossing in fruits averaging four seeds, and so on. Under these conditions minor differences in size, composition, shape and even flesh color and season of maturity may follow. Differences of this kind probably account for such inequalities in fruit size in the pear as were found by Waite[237] when he used pollen of several kinds on Bartlett or Kieffer pistils (see Table 12).

The limited data available indicate that with most fruits these variations are relatively unimportant except in comparing cross pollinations with self pollinations. That is to say, many varieties that will set and mature fruit when self pollinated will set and mature distinctly larger fruits when cross pollinated, regardless of the kind of pollen used if only it is from a compatible variety. The explanation of the smaller fruits resulting from self pollination is that though selfing often results in fruitfulness the fruits bear few or no perfect seeds, while the cross pollinated fruits have the usual number of good seeds. In other words, it is crossing so as to secure a good complement of seeds, rather than crossing with some particular variety, that is responsible for the difference in size and is consequently important in the orchard. Investigations conducted with many fruits indicate that the number or percentage of seeds developing in the fruits of different kinds is to a considerable extent a varietal characteristic or at least it is more dependent on the variety and the

TABLE 12.—INFLUENCE OF KIND OF POLLEN ON FRUIT SIZE AND SEED WEIGHT
IN PEARS
(*After Waite*[237])

Cross	Average weight of fruit, grams	Average weight of seeds, grams
Bartlett × Bartlett...............	100.4	0.07
Bartlett × Anjou.................	116.1	0.38
Bartlett × Easter................	167.7	0.38
Bartlett × Angouleme.............	133.6	0.30
Bartlett × White Doyenne.........	89.4	0.27
Bartlett × Clapp Favorite........	114.2	0.32

condition of the tree or plant than on the kind of pollen, assuming that an adequate supply of good pollen is available. There is a limited amount of data that indicate that pears developing as a result of cross pollination mature somewhat earlier and do not keep quite so long in storage as those resulting from selfing.[173]

Kraus[139] has pointed out that the occasional striping of self colored fruits of the apple, so often cited as proof of an immediate influence of the pollen on the character of the resulting fruit, is in reality a special form of bud mutation. Bud mutations of this kind may in many cases be propagated vegetatively and striped varieties obtained.

What appears at first as an exception to some of the preceding statements has been recorded for the developing fruits of the vanilla. McClelland[151] crossed two types of this plant—*Vanilla planifolia* and the "vanillon" type. "The typical well-developed fruit of *V. planifolia* from a close-fertilized blossom is a long slender capsule tapering at the stem end but carrying its fullness well down toward the blossom end. It contains thousands of tiny, oily, black seeds. . . . The fruits [of the vanillon type] are much thicker and shorter . . . and differ in being of a more uniform thickness near the two ends, the blossom end frequently being rather tapering. Where to either the *V. planifolia* or the vanillon stigma pollen of the other has been applied a very marked modification in the form of the fruit has resulted." These differences in shape apparently are associated with the location within the capsule of the ovules that were fertilized and develop into seeds. When *V. planifolia* pollen is used on vanillon stigmas, fertilization takes place mainly toward the apical end of the ovary and not toward the basal end, while in self pollenized vanillon stigmas fertilization occurs clear to the bottom of the ovarian cavity. On the other hand, the pollen tubes of the vanillon type seek the basal ovules in the ovaries of the *V. planifolia* type when that crossing is made. In reality, instead of being an exception to the statement that crossing with a particular kind of pollen affords no direct influence on the character of the resulting fruit, this is but another instance of an indirect effect on shape, the direct relationship being between kind of pollen and seed number in the one case and seed number and location and shape of fruit in the other.

That in some instances, however, certain kinds of pollen may have a specific influence on the developing fruits of certain other varieties, independent of its influence on seed number, is indicated by the observations of Nixon.[168] He has found that the fruit of the Deglet Noor and certain other varieties of the date palm average a third to a half larger and mature either earlier or later, as the case may be, when the blossoms have been pollenized by the pollen of certain staminate trees than when pollenized with pollen from certain other trees. Correlated with these differences in maturing season were certain differences in composition and quality of flesh, which, however, were attributed more to temperature and humidity conditions prevailing just previous to ripening than to any direct effect of the specific staminate plant furnishing the pollen. These direct effects of pollen on the developing fruit have been spoken of as instances of metaxenia.

Summary.—Ordinarily the development of the carpellary and other tissues of the fruit depends on fertilization and the consequent development of seeds from the ovules. In some cases, however, the development of the fruit may proceed without an accompanying growth of seeds, or even without the stimulus of fertilization. In still other cases development may occur in the absence of pollination. Parthenocarpy is a term used to cover those cases of fruit development in the absence of fertilization. Parthenocarpic fruits are usually seedless, though seeds may develop in them parthenogenetically. Some seedlessness is due to embryo abortion after fertilization and therefore is not associated with parthenocarpy. Fruits which the botanist classifies as accessory are somewhat more inclined to parthenocarpic development than those consisting of ovarian tissues only. Parthenocarpy is no insurance, however, against loss of crop from excessive dropping of blossoms under certain conditions. In general, seedlessness is valuable from the commercial standpoint. In most instances there is a distinct correlation between the formation of seeds and the development of the fleshy tissues of the fruit— the greater the seed number, the larger the fruit. Other limiting factors, however, may destroy this correlation. Between seed-containing and seedless fruit of the same varieties, there are often distinct differences in form, composition and ripening period. However, there is no good evidence that the specific qualities or characteristics of the pollen variety are in any way stamped upon the resulting fruit.

CHAPTER XXX

FRUIT SETTING AS AN ORCHARD PROBLEM

The preceding discussion has shown that certain fruit varieties are completely self fruitful, others are partly self fruitful and still others are self barren. With varieties definitely known to be self fruitful it is safe to plant solid blocks to a single variety without making any provision for cross pollination. The heavy production that characterizes large plantations of the Concord grape, the Baldwin apple, the Montmorency cherry, the Cuthbert raspberry and many other fruits is sufficient evidence on this point. On the other hand many varieties that are often considered self fruitful because in the average season they set a full crop without the aid of any foreign pollen, are often greatly benefited by cross pollination. Thus though the French prune is generally considered self fruitful and there are many large orchards consisting exclusively of that variety, a higher percentage of its blossoms set when cross pollinated with Imperial than when selfed.[104] In general it is good practice always to make provision for cross pollination when planting the orchard, unless there is definite knowledge that this is not needed for the variety when grown under the conditions in question. Even though a variety is entirely self fruitful under a given set of conditions the evidence shows that in many cases the increase in the size of fruit resulting from the stimulus of cross fertilization is sufficient to warrant planting together two or more varieties which bloom at the same time.

Fortunately the selection of varieties to secure effective cross pollination does not usually add many complications to the problem of variety selection. In most fruits the grower prefers to raise two or more varieties rather than a single sort. By choosing those that ripen at different seasons the harvesting problem is usually greatly simplified and often problems of tillage and spraying as well. When the orchard is to be planted to two or more varieties for reasons other than cross pollination, it is necessary only to make a selection such that their blossoming seasons overlap to a considerable extent. When it seems best to have as large a part of the orchard as possible consist of a single variety, the problem of selecting one for cross pollination purposes is not materially different than before. First and foremost, its blossoming season should overlap that of the main sort. Then, questions of its maturing season, productiveness, market value and so on, should receive due consideration.

Another point that should receive attention in the selection of a pollenizer to be planted in limited numbers for the benefit of a main sort is its pollen-bearing qualities. Some varieties are heavy pollen producers; others bear only limited amounts. Thus Meylan is one of the best varieties of the English walnut and Glen Mary one of the poorest strawberries to plant for pollinating other varieties.

The Number of Pollenizers.—The question often is raised as to the number or percentage of pollenizers necessary when business considerations make it desirable to limit them as much as possible. No very definite rule can be given. In most deciduous tree fruits every third tree in every third row will furnish all the pollen necessary for the remaining 89 per cent. This proportion, however, would not be practicable in the strawberry plantation when it is desired to grow pistillate varieties mainly. Much depends on the provision for cross pollinating agents. If it is an insect-pollinated plant and pollen-carrying insects are numerous (say amounting to one colony of bees for each 1 or 2 acres of fruit trees) fewer trees of the less valuable pollenizers are necessary than if the bees are few.

In cases where large blocks of a single self unfruitful variety have been planted and the trees have been in the orchard for a number of years much quicker results can be obtained by grafting over some of them than by removal and replanting. Occasionally growers solve the difficulty by grafting over a limb or two in each tree, but this usually complicates the problem of harvesting and from an economic standpoint is less satisfactory than changing the entire tops of certain trees.

Temporary Expedients.—Immediate results are often obtainable in self unfruitful orchards through securing from trees of other varieties large branches containing numerous flower buds and placing them here and there in the self barren orchard. This permits pollen-carrying insects to effect a transfer of pollen from these branches to the pistils of the orchard trees. Such branches should be cut just as their flowers are starting to open and stood in buckets of water so that they will keep fresh while their flowers are opening and shedding pollen. This is only a temporary expedient, for it is troublesome and often rather expensive; however, it has been the means of insuring a good set of fruit in many cases when there would have been a crop failure otherwise. It really is a kind of artificial pollination, comparable to practices in vogue for thousands of years in the production of dates and many varieties of figs.

Pollinating Agents.—Wind and insects have been mentioned as the chief pollen-carrying agencies for deciduous fruits. Of the two, insects are by far the more important except in some of the nut crops. In fact the amount of cross pollination effected through the agency of the wind in apples, pears, peaches and other insect-pollinated fruits is practically negligible. This has been shown experimentally for the plum by Waugh[241] and for other fruits by other investigators. Among pollen-carrying insects the common honey bee is probably the most important for the fruit grower. Its importance is such that the presence of an ample number should be insured during the blossoming season. In many sections growers make a practice of securing colonies of bees from apiarists to place in their orchards during blossoming and they find that the rental they pay yields them a higher rate of interest on their investment than any other item in their cost of production. No hard and fast rules can be laid down regarding the number of colonies necessary for effective pollination in an orchard of a given size. Much depends on the size of the trees, their profusion of bloom and the number of hours of favorable weather for pollination during their flowering season and the presence or absence of other pollen-carrying agents. Ordinarily one colony of bees to each 1 or 2 acres of orchard, depending on conditions, will produce satisfactory results and sometimes they will take care of a considerably larger acreage.

It is often assumed that perfect flowered and self fruitful varieties require no outside agent for the transfer of pollen from stamen to stigma. In other words, the self fruitful variety is assumed to be autogamous. This is often the case, at least to a certain extent. However, it has been found in California that Imperial prune trees from which bees were excluded during the blossoming season set only 0.34 per cent. of their blossoms, while trees of the same variety accessible to bees but protected from cross pollination from other varieties set 3.02 per cent.[104] In the French prune 19 per cent. of the blossoms matured fruit where bees visited them, while only 0.43 per cent. matured fruit where the bees were excluded. Similar conditions have been found to obtain with many other kinds of fruit. In the absence of definite knowledge that the varieties he is growing are both self fruitful and autogamous the grower should make adequate provision for pollen transfer.

The Fruit-setting Habits of Different Fruits.—In the preceding discussion of the factors influencing the setting of fruit most deciduous fruit species have been mentioned along with certain others. Following are summarized statements of the more important fruit-setting characteristics of the common fruits.

Apple.—The flowers of the apple are true hermaphrodites. Occasionally defective pistils are found and generally a portion of the pollen grains are defective, though apparently all varieties mature a certain amount of good pollen.[16] The percentage, however, varies with environmental conditions and in the case of a few varieties, such as Winesap and Rhode Island Greening, the percentage of good pollen is so small that they should not be used for pollination purposes. Many varieties are self fruitful, many others are self barren or partly so. Lewis and Vincent[142] reported about 70 per cent. of the varieties studied as self barren in Oregon; Gowen[89] found about 63 per cent. completely self barren and only 13 per cent. completely self fruitful in Maine and Hooper[108] reported about two-thirds of the varieties he worked with in England to be self sterile. A number of recent studies show that in many cases self sterility is associated with a deviation from the normal diploid chromosome number ($2N$ in the apple $= 34$) and that both self fertility and good pollen production are most likely to be found in the normal diploid varieties. There are, however, many exceptions. The degree of self fruitfulness in the apple varies greatly with the age and vigor of the trees, the season, locality and many other factors. Thus the Jonathan, which is self fruitful in many parts of the United States, is self fruitful in Victoria (Australia) when grown on soils of medium productivity, but self barren when grown on rich soils.[72] Among the prominent commercial varieties that are classed as comparatively self fruitful, at least in a number of sections, are: Baldwin, Ben Davis, Gano, Jonathan, Oldenburg, Yellow Newtown, Grimes, Wagener, Yellow Transparent, Willow Twig, Esopus, Stark. On the other hand, nearly all of these varieties have been reported partly or completely self barren in certain localities or at certain times. Among those classed as partly or completely self barren are: Arkansas Black, Gravenstein, King, Arkansas, Maiden Blush, Missouri Pippin, Rome, Ralls, Rhode Island, Salome, Tolman, Wealthy, Winesap and York. These varieties, however, may frequently prove self fruitful.

Young vigorous trees just coming into bearing have been observed repeatedly to be much more likely to drop their fruit than trees of the same varieties somewhat older and having the bearing habit well established. On the other hand, old weak trees frequently bloom very heavily but set little or no fruit. Often this situation can be remedied by liberal applications of nitrate of soda or some other quickly available nitrogenous fertilizer shortly before blossoming.

Apple scab and fire blight frequently attack the blossoms or the newly set fruits and are responsible for much dropping at an early stage. These diseases can be controlled by proper spraying and sanitary measures respectively.

Interunfruitfulness has been reported for a few varieties,[89,119] particularly some of those of the Winesap group; but a large body of data indicates that cross sterility is of comparatively little importance in apple production. However, the color strains of a number of varieties that have originated as bud mutations have been found interunfruitful with each other and with the parent forms where the parent forms themselves are self unfruitful.[112,172,174]

Parthenocarpy occurs rather frequently, but true parthenocarpic varieties are rare.

Pear.—The flowers of the pear, like those of the apple, are true hermaphrodites. So far as known, all varieties produce at least a certain amount of good pollen. However, many pear varieties are self barren because of self incompatibility. Waite[237] reported 22 out of 36 varieties as self unfruitful. Among the more prominent of this group are: Anjou, Bartlett, Clairgeau, Clapp Favorite, Columbia, Easter, Howell, Louise and Winter Nelis. Among the more important of the self fruitful varieties are: Angouleme, Bosc, Flemish Beauty, Kieffer, LeConte, Seckel, Tyson and White Doyenne. However, Kieffer has been reported practically self sterile in Virginia[76] and Bartlett has been found partly self fruitful in certain localities in California.[231] It has been found that most sparingly self fruitful pear varieties generally mature fruits with few or no good seeds and that these fruits are distinctly inferior in size to those of seed-bearing fruits of the same varieties resulting from cross pollination. Pears generally should be so planted as to secure the benefits from crossing.

Bartlett and Seckel are the only two of the more common varieties that have been found to be cross incompatible,[148] though this condition has been reported for certain other varieties.[126] Though parthenocarpy is not uncommon in pears, and none of the varieties of commercial importance is parthenocarpic regularly in America, some of these same varieties are reported as "exhibiting this phenomenon annually on a very generous scale" in parts of South Africa.[191]

Quince.—Circumstantial evidence points clearly to the conclusion that the commonly cultivated varieties of the quince are self fruitful. This is supported by the results of investigations of Dorsey in New York (data unpublished).

Peach.—Experimental work with the peach at the Missouri,[249] Delaware,[28] and Virginia[76] Stations indicates that practically all the commonly grown varieties are self fruitful. The J. H. Hale is the one exception of importance in America, that variety producing abortive pollen and requiring cross pollination by some other variety producing fertile pollen.[34] A number of other less common varieties, however, have been reported as being self barren from the same cause.[4,34,245] Except for these few varieties, the grower is safe in planting entire orchards to a single variety.

Almond.—The work of Tufts[230] has shown that all almond varieties that were tested are generally self sterile under California conditions, though in occasional seasons certain varieties will set a fairly good crop with their own pollen. This self unfruitfulness is due to incompatibility rather than to imperfect pollen, for the pollen proves satisfactory on the pistils of certain other varieties. Certain varieties were found also to be interbarren; I.X.L. and Nonpareil will set practically no fruit when interplanted and the same is true for plantings of Languedoc and Texas. Lutri[145] in southern Italy has found some varieties self fertile and others self sterile.

Plum.—Plum varieties vary greatly in their abilities to mature fruit without the aid of cross pollination. Waugh[239,240,241,242] reported practically all the commonly cultivated varieties of the Japanese and American species to be self sterile; this has been confirmed by the investigations of others.[85,99,103,147,238] More recently, Beauty and Climax have been reported partially self fruitful, but benefited by cross pollination.[245]

A considerable number of European varieties, including Giant, Green Gage, Italian, French and Blue Damson have been found partly or completely self fruitful in Oregon,[147] and Sutton[218] reported 18 out of 39 varieties to be fully self fruitful and five more partly self fruitful in England. Florin has reported several varieties of this group as more or less self unfruitful because of the fact that they produce little or no good pollen, their stamens being replaced by petaloid scales.[78]

Hendrickson[103] and Marshall[147] reported all Japanese varieties tested as interfruitful, but later researches have disclosed a number of cases of cross incompatibility in the Japanese group. Thus, Formosa and Gaviota are reported as reciprocally incompatible, and Formosa pollinated with El Dorado gives a good set, whereas the reciprocal cross is a failure.[245] Dickson[59] reports that in Canada the Shiro remains barren when interplanted with Burbank, though when its flowers are hand pollinated with Burbank pollen, a reasonable percentage set and mature fruit.

Waugh[240] found American varieties generally interfertile. Some exceptions, however, have been recorded. Thus Whitaker and Milton, both seedlings of Wildgoose, are interbarren and, curiously enough, both are fertile with Sophie; however, Sophie used as the pistil parent is fertile with neither.[242] Marshall,[147] working with varieties of *P. domestica*, found any one combination to give as good set of fruit as any other; Sutton,[218] working with other varieties of the same species, reached the same conclusion, except that intersterility appeared in three varieties. However, two of these three varieties originated as bud sports from the third. A few other instances of cross incompatibility in the *Domestica* group have been reported.[39,188] The European plums are not interfruitful to any considerable degree with those of either the Japanese or American groups, though both Tragedy[105] and Reine Claude[152] have been reported as satisfactory pollenizers for certain Japanese sorts. Dorsey[61] obtained only eight mature fruits from 1,327 flowers of the Compass pollinated with Yellow Egg, while 114 flowers set and matured fruit when pollinated with Burbank. Though both crosses evidently may be classed as interfertile, there is a great difference in the degree of fertility exhibited.

Except for certain varieties of the several European groups known to be self fruitful, plums always should be planted so they will secure the advantages of cross pollination.

Apparently both self and cross unfruitfulness in the plum is due principally to incompatibilities and not to degeneration of the pollen or of the embryo sacs.

Investigations conducted at the California Experiment station[232] indicate that the varieties commonly grown in that state are fully self fertile, though Kostina[138] reports some of the Crimean varieties as self barren.

Cherry.—Until comparatively recently cherries have been assumed to be self fruitful. In 1913, Gardner[82] reported several varieties of the sweet cherry, all that were tested, as self unfruitful under Oregon conditions and a little later Tufts[229] reported a number of the same varieties self barren in California.

More recent tests in many parts of the world[18,39,119,126,138,200,218] indicate that self barrenness is practically universal in this group. There are many instances where what have been regarded as solid blocks of a single variety have fruited heavily and regularly but investigation has shown that there were scattered through the planting a number of seedling trees, perhaps of the Mazzard type, or trees closely resembling but nevertheless distinct from the variety in question that have been propagated and distributed under a common varietal name.[82,202]   Reports on the sour and Duke types are conflicting.   Under both Michigan[148] and New York[98] conditions the common sour varieties—Montmorency, Early Richmond and English Morello—have been found completely self fertile; but the Ohio station has reported improved setting from cross pollination,[205] and in Oregon[201] a considerable number of the sour varieties have been found almost completely self barren.   Crane[39] in England has reported the several varieties tested as self compatible, but Kostina[138] has reported 19 out of 29 varieties as self barren in Crimea and the remaining 10 as only partially self fruitful.   Sutton[218] has found Late Duke fully self fertile in England, but May Duke and Archduke only partially so.   Investigations in Oregon[82] and Ohio[205] indicate that, in general, varieties of the Duke group set better when cross pollinated than when self pollinated and that perhaps even better results will be obtained when they are pollinated by pollen of either the sour or sweet varieties. Shoemaker[205] has suggested the sweet varieties as pollenizers for the early blooming Dukes and the sour varieties for those that blossom late.

Interunfruitfulness has been found among some of the varieties of the sweet cherry—notably Napoleon, Lambert and Bing—in both Oregon[82] and California,[229] and more recently other instances have been recorded.[18,39,61,119,126,245] Sweet and sour cherries are interfruitful to some degree, though sour varieties are apparently less satisfactory as pollenizers for the sweet group than is true of the reciprocal combination.[126,205]

Self unfruitfulness and cross unfruitfulness in the cherry are due to incompatibilities rather than to any structural defects of pollen or ovules, though most of the Duke varieties are characterized by a rather large percentage of imperfect pollen.[205]

Grape.—As mentioned already, conditions in the grape range all the way from complete self fruitfulness to complete barrenness. Varieties of hybrid origin particularly are likely to be self barren, though this condition is found in many varieties descended from a single species.[57,60] Among some of the more common self fruitful varieties may be mentioned: Clinton, Champion, Concord, Isabella, Moore Early, Niagara, Worden, Agawam, Catawba, Delaware, Diamond and Norton. Among those that are self unfruitful are: Salem, Barry, Brighton and the following are among those often at least partly self fruitful: Lindley, Vergennes, Wyoming.[8]

Practically all the varieties of the Muscadine group bear pseudohermaphroditic flowers and should have staminate vines interplanted with them.

The immediate factor responsible for self barrenness in the grape is the production of impotent or sterile pollen which is incapable of fertilizing the ovules of the same or of any other variety.[15,60] Consequently self barren varieties are interbarren and partly self barren sorts are partly interbarren. Self fertile varieties should be interplanted with the self barren or partly self barren kinds. The production of impotent or sterile pollen is associated almost invariably with curved or reflexed stamens; good pollen is produced in erect stamens. This flower character therefore affords an accurate index to the degree of self fruitfulness that may be anticipated, except in the comparatively few parthenocarpic varieties.

Many grape varieties occasionally produce a few seedless berries when not pollinated or when pollinated with impotent pollen. This characteristic apparently is aided by certain practices such as ringing or girdling. In a few varieties, such as Thompson's Seedless, this occurs regularly.[88] According to Stout,[212] seedless American grape varieties generally produce good pollen, but since their "femaleness" is not strongly developed they are not able to mature good seeds. Carbohydrate deficiency, often a consequence of very heavy pruning, has been shown to be a common cause of the failure to set properly in the case of certain varieties of Vinifera grapes.[252]

Strawberry.—Strawberry varieties are generally classed as pistillate flowering and perfect flowering. Apparently all the perfect flowering sorts produce good pollen and all are self fruitful and apparently any perfect flowering variety may be planted with any pistillate flowering sort for purposes of cross pollination. Since, however, some of the perfect flowering varieties produce only small amounts of pollen, they are not ideal pollenizers for pistillate sorts. In general the later maturing flowers of the inflorescence, particularly in the perfect flowering varieties, are less fertile than earlier flowers of the same cluster and this pistil sterility is "expressed in the production of irregularly shaped berries or entirely sterile flowers."[236]

Currant and Gooseberry.—Few exact data are available on the pollination requirements of the currant and the gooseberry. However, field observation indicates clearly that the varieties commonly grown in this country are self fruitful and hence no provision need be made for cross pollination. Hooper[108] has reported all the varieties of the English gooseberry which he tested to be self fertile.

The Brambles.—Until comparatively recent date the bramble fruits have generally been considered self fruitful. Hooper,[108] working with a number of varieties of the raspberry and with the loganberry in England, found all that he tested self fertile but reported some increase in size of fruit resulting from cross pollination. In North Carolina 11 out of 15 varieties of dewberries were found self barren and 12 out of 16 varieties of blackberries self fruitful. The varieties of *Rubus villosus* generally were self fruitful, those of *R. trivialis* self barren. There was no increase in size of fruit from cross pollination in those varieties maturing fruit when selfed. The Vineland (Ontario) Horticultural Experiment Station[192] has reported that a number of the seedlings of the raspberry which they have obtained in their breeding work are self sterile. Others are self fruitful or partly so. A number of the blackberry-dewberry hybrid varieties are partly or wholly self barren. Apparently sterility in this group is closely associated with the formation of imperfect pollen and this condition in turn appears to be due in large part to hybrid ancestry and irregularities in chromosome number, *i.e.*, deviations from the normal diploid number.[43,144]

The Cranberry and Blueberry.—The cranberry is reported as being practically self fertile under Wisconsin conditions.[42] In New Jersey the cultivated varieties of the high-bush blueberry have been reported as self sterile or as only producing undersized, late-maturing berries when pollinated with their own pollen.[38] In Michigan, however, these same varieties were found to be completely self fruitful.[153]

The Nuts.—The walnut, pecan, hickory, chestnut and filbert are all monoecious, and a large number of their varieties are characterized by partial dichogamy. In some varieties, especially of the pecan,[1,216] the dichogamy is almost complete, rendering the tree or variety self unfruitful to a marked degree. The common varieties of the filbert not only show partial dichogamy but are self incompatible as well,[120,200] and a few instances of cross incompatibility have been reported.[199]

Persimmon.—The kaki, or Japanese persimmon, includes varieties bearing pistillate flowers only and those bearing both pistillate and staminate flowers. Of the varieties in the latter class some bear staminate flowers regularly, others bear them sporadically. The names pistillate constants, staminate constants and staminate sporadics have been applied to these several groups.

Some varieties set fruit freely without pollination and they mature seedless fruits. Others require pollination and their fruits usually contain one or more seeds. Apparently pollination is not so essential to the securing of a good persimmon crop in California as in Florida.[32]

The differences in the size, shape, color, flavor and season of maturity of seed-bearing and seedless persimmons have been discussed previously.

There is reason to believe that most pistillate flowers of the native American persimmon (*Diospyros virginiana*) require pollination from staminate trees of the same species in order to set and mature a good crop. The Japanese and American varieties of persimmon are not interfruitful.[115]

Summary.—In the absence of definite knowledge that the variety being planted is self fruitful under local conditions provision should always be made for cross pollination. Even when varieties are self fruitful the increase in size often obtained as a result of cross pollination warrants the use of other pollenizers. In most tree fruits one of the pollenizing variety is sufficient for 8 or 10 trees of the leading sort. Top grafting and the use of flowering branches of other varieties at the blossoming season are the most satisfactory methods of providing for cross pollination in established self unfruitful or inter-unfruitful orchards. Insects, particularly the honey bee, are the most effective pollinating agents in the deciduous fruit plantation. There should be ample provision for pollen transfer, even in orchards of self fruitful varieties. The fruit-setting habits and pollination requirements of different deciduous fruits are discussed.

Suggested Collateral Readings

Eisen, G.   The Fig.   U. S. D. A. Div. Pom., Bul. 9.   Pp. 74–128.   1901.

Literature Cited

1. Adriance, G. W.   Bot. Gaz.   91: 144–166.   1931.
2. d'Angremond, A.   Flora.   107: 57.   1914.

3. Asami, Y.   Tokyo Imp. Univ. Inst. Hort. Rept.   1926.   P. 139.
4. Asami, Y.   Jour. Sci. Agr. Soc. (Tokyo, Japan).   1927.   Pp. 364–367.
5. Asami, Y., and Hayami, F.   Jour. Hort. Assoc. Japan.   5 (2): 222–232.   1934.
6. Asami, Y., and Ito, H.   Jour. Hort. Assoc. Japan.   8 (2): 337–346.   1937.
7. Beach, S. A.   N. Y. Agr. Exp. Sta. Bul. 157.   1898.
8. Ibid.   Bul. 169.   1900.
9. Ibid.   Bul. 223.   1902.
10. Beach, S. A.   Proc. Am. Pom. Soc.   P. 72.   1901.
11. Benson, M. F.   Trans. Linn. Soc. II.   Bot. 3: 409–424.   1894.
12. Better Fruit.   24 (Oct.): 1929.
13. Bioletti, F. T.   Cal. Agr. Exp. Sta. Bul. 197.   1908.   (P. Viala and P. Pacottel cited as authority.)
14. Bioletti, F. T.   Cal. Agr. Exp. Sta. Cir. 191.   1918.
15. Booth, N. O.   N. Y. Agr. Exp. Sta. Bul. 224.   1902.
16. Booth, N. O.   Proc. Am. Soc. Hort. Sci.   P. 25.   1906.
17. Bower, F. O.   Botany of the Living Plant.   London.   1919.   P. 270.
18. Bowman, F. T.   New South Wales Dept. Agr. Sci. Bul. 55.   1937.
19. Bradbury, D. and Roberts, R. H.   Wis. Agr. Exp. Sta. Bul. 410.   1930.
20. Brainerd, E., and Peitersen, A. K.   Vt. Agr. Exp. Sta. Bul. 217.   1920.
21. Brown, F. R.   First Bienn. Crop Pest and Hort. Rept. Ore. Agr. Exp. Sta.   Pp. 41–43.   1911–12.
22. Brown, W. R.   Agr. Res. Inst. Pusa Bul. 93.   1920.
23. Burbidge, F. W.   Cultivated Plants; Their Propagation and Improvement.   P. 472.   Edinburgh and London, 1877.
24. Bushnell, J. W.   Proc. Am. Soc. Hort. Sci.   17: 47–52.   1920.
25. Cheesman, E. F., and Larter, L. N. H.   Jour. Genet.   30 (1): 31–52.   1935.
26. Clark, C. F.   Mem. Hort. Soc. N. Y.   3: 289–294.   1927.
27. Claypole, E. W.   Rept. U. S. Com. Agr.   Pp. 318–321.   1887.
28. Close, C. P.   Del. Agr. Exp. Sta. Rept.   14: 99–102.   1902.
29. Cochran, H. L.   Cornell Univ. Agr. Exp. Sta. Mem. 190.   1936.
30. Coit, J. E.   Cal. Agr. Exp. Sta. Ann. Rept.   P. 105.   1914.
31. Coit, J. E., and Hodgson, R. W.   Cal. Agr. Exp. Sta. Bul. 290.   1918.
32. Condit, I. J.   Cal. Agr. Exp. Sta. Bul. 316.   1919.
33. Ibid.   Bul. 319.   1920.
34. Connors, C. H.   Proc. Am. Soc. Hort. Sci.   19: 147–151.   1922.
35. Conrad, A. H.   Bot. Gaz.   24: 408–418.   1900.
36. Cooper, J. R.   Ark. Agr. Exp. Sta. Bul. 227.   1928.
37. Cooper, J. R., and Wiggins, C. B.   Ark. Agr. Exp. Sta. Bul. 312.   1934.
38. Coville, F. V.   U. S. D. A. Bul. 974.   1921.
39. Crane, M. B.   Mem. Hort. Soc. N. Y.   3: 119–133.   1927.
40. Crider, F. J.   Ariz. Agr. Exp. Sta. Bul. 94.   1922.
41. Darrow, G. M.   Jour. Agr. Res.   34: 403.   1927.
42. Darrow, G. M., Franklin, H. J., and Malde, O. G.   U. S. D. A. Farmers' Bul. 1400.   1924.
43. Darrow, G. M., and Longley, A. E.   Jour. Agr. Res.   47 (5): 315–330.   1933.
44. Darwin, C.   The Variation of Animals and Plants under Domestication.   2d Edition.   1: 434.   New York, 1894.
45. Ibid.   2: 113.   (Cited on authority of Hildebrand.)
46. Ibid.   2: 115–117.
47. Ibid.   2: 119.
48. Ibid.   2: 147.

49. Ibid. 2: 152–153.
50. Ibid. 2: 165–169.
51. Darwin, C. Cross and Self Fertilization in the Vegetable Kingdom. Pp. 343–344. 1895.
52. Davey, A. J., and Gibson, C. M. New Phytol. 16: 147–151. 1917.
53. Dearness, J., and Foster, W. R. Canad. Jour. Res. 9: 43–48. 1933.
54. Detjen, L. R. N. C. Agr. Exp. Sta. Tech. Bul. 11. 1916.
55. Ibid. Tech. Bul. 12. 1917.
56. Ibid. Tech. Bul. 17. 1919.
57. Ibid. Tech. Bul. 18. 1919.
58. Detjen, L. R. Del. Agr. Exp. Sta. Bul. 143. 1926.
59. Dickson, G. H. Sci. Agr. 17 (12): 727. 1937.
60. Dorsey, M. J. Minn. Agr. Exp. Sta. Bul. 144. 1914.
61. Dorsey, M. J. Genetics. 4: 417–488. 1919.
62. Dorsey, M. J. Jour. Agr. Res. 17: 103–126. 1919.
63. Driggers, B. F. N. J. Agr. Exp. Sta. Bul. 450. 1927.
64. Dutton, W. C. Mich. Agr. Exp. Sta. Sp. Bul. 219. 1932.
65. East, E. M., and Park, J. B. Genetics. 2: 505–609. 1917.
66. Eisen, G. U. S. D. A., Div. Pom. Bul. 9. 1901.
67. Eisnet, O. N. Y. Agr. Exp. Sta. Bul. 617. 1932.
68. Erwin, A. T. and Haber, E. S. Ia. Agr. Exp. Sta. Bul. 263. 1929.
69. Exp. Sta. Rec. 3: 135. 1892.
70. Ewert, R. Landw. Jahrb. 39: 463–470. 1910.
71. Fairchild, D. G., and Beach, S. A. N. Y. Agr. Exp. Sta. Rept. 11: 607–611. 1892.
72. Farrell, J. Jour. Agr. Victoria. 15: 142. 1917.
73. Fauchere, A. Jour. Agr. Trop. 10: 99. 1910.
74. Fitch, C. L. Proc. Am. Soc. Hort. Sci. 11: 100. 1913.
75. Fletcher, S. W. Cornell Univ. Agr. Exp. Sta. Bul. 181. 1900.
76. Fletcher, S. W. Va. Agr. Exp. Sta. Rept. Pp. 213–224. 1909–1910.
77. Floyd, F. E. Trans. Roy. Soc. Canada. (Ser. 3) 10: (Sec. 4) 55–61. 1916.
78. Florin, E. H. Contrib. from the Perm. Com. on Orch. Res. No. 12. 1927. (Stockholm).
79. Frost, H. B. Hilgardia. 1: 365–402. 1926.
80. Gaertner, K. F. Versuche und Beobachtungen über die Bastardzeugung im Pflanzenreich. Stuttgart. 1849.
81. Gagnepain, F. Mem. Hort. Soc. N. Y. 3: 373–376. 1927.
82. Gardner, V. R. Ore. Agr. Exp. Sta. Bul. 116. 1913.
82a. Gardner, V. R. Mo. Agr. Exp. Sta. Res. Bul. 57. 1923.
83. Gloyer, W. O. N. Y. Agr. Exp. Sta. Bul. 540. 1926.
84. Goff, E. S. Wis. Agr. Exp. Sta. Bul. 63. 1897.
85. Ibid. Bul. 87. 1901.
86. Goff, E. S. Wis. Agr. Exp. Sta. Ann. Rept. 18: 289–303. 1901.
87. Goodspeed, T. H., McGee, J. M., and Hodgson, R. W. Univ. Cal. Publ. Bot. 5: 439–450. 1918.
88. Goodspeed, T. H. Address before General Session Bot. Soc. Am. Chicago, Dec. 28, 1920.
89. Gowen, J. W. Me. Agr. Exp. Sta. Bul. 287. 1920.
90. Graner, E. A. Rev. Agr. (Brazil). 9 (7–8): 333–340. 1934.
91. Gray, G. P. Mich. Agr. Exp. Sta. Tech. Bul. 136. 1934.
92. Green, J. R. Phil. Trans. Roy. Soc. 185 B: 385–409. 1894.

93. Haas, A. R. C.   Bot. Gaz.   83: 312.   1927.
94. Hansen, N. E.   S. Dak. Agr. Exp. Sta. Bul. 237.   1929.
95. Hartley, C. P.   U. S. D. A., Bur. Pl. Ind. Bul. 22.   1902.
96. Harvey, E. M., and Murneek, A. E.   Ore. Agr. Exp. Sta. Bul. 176.   1921.
97. Hedrick, U. P.   N. Y. Agr. Exp. Sta. Bul. 299.   1908.
98. Hedrick, U. P.   Cherries of New York.   P. 83.   Albany, 1915.
99. Heideman, C. W. H.   Ann. Rept. Minn. State Hort. Soc.   23: 187–195.   1895.
100. Heinicke, A. J.   Cornell Univ. Agr. Exp. Sta.   Bul. 393.   1917.
101. Heinicke, A. J.   Proc. Am. Soc. Hort. Sci.   20: 19–25.   1923.
102. Heinicke, A. J.   Mem. Hort. Soc. N. Y.   3: 135–138.   1927.
103. Hendrickson, A. H.   Cal. Agr. Exp. Sta. Ann. Rept.   P. 45.   1916.
104. Hendrickson, A. H.   Cal. Agr. Exp. Sta. Bul. 291.   1918.
105. Ibid.   Bul. 352.   1922.
106. Higgins, J. E., and Holt, V. S.   Hawaii Agr. Exp. Sta. Bul. 32.   1914.
107. Hodgson, R. W.   Cal. Exp. Sta. Bul. 276.   1917.
108. Hooper, C. H.   Jour. Royal Hort. Soc.   37: 531–535.   1912.
109. Howard, W. L., and Horne, W. T.   Cal. Agr. Exp. Sta. Bul. 326.   1921.
110. Howlett, F. S.   O. Agr. Exp. Sta. Bul. 402.   1927.
111. Ibid.   Bul. 404.   1927.
112. Howlett, F. S.   Jour. Agr. Res.   47 (7): 523–537.   1933.
113. Hume, H. H.   Proc. Am. Soc. Hort. Sci.   Pp. 88–93.   1913.
114. Hume, H. H.   Trans. St. Louis Acad. Sci.   22: 125–135.   1913.
115. Hume, H. H.   Jour. Heredity.   5: 131.   1914.
116. Husmann, G. C., and Dearing, C.   U. S. D. A., Bur. Pl. Ind. Bul. 273.   1913.
117. Husmann, G. C., and Dearing, C.   U. S. D. A. Farmers' Bul. 709.   1916.
118. Iyengar, B.   Jour. Mysore Agr. and Exp. Union.   15 (4): 156.   1936.
119. Johannson, E.   Meddel. Perm. Kom. Fruklodlingsförsök (Sweden).   No. 7.   1926.
120. Johannson, E.   Meddel. Perm. Kom. Fruklodlingsförsök (Sweden).   No. 11.   1927.
121. Johannson, E.   Swedish Perm. Com. on Orch. Res. (Stockholm).   Bul. 16.   1929.
122. Johannson, E.   Swedish Perm. Com. on Orch. Res. (Stockholm).   Contrib. No. 35.   1935.
123. Johnson, D. S.   Carnegie Inst. of Wash. Pub. 269.   1918.
124. Johnston, S.   Mich. Agr. Exp. Sta. Sp. Bul. 143.   1925.
125. Johnston, S., and Loree, R. E.   Mich. Agr. Exp. Sta. Sp. Bul. 162.   1927.
126. Kamlah, H.   (Cited in Exp. Sta. Rec. 60: 233.   1929.)
127. Kerner, A., and Oliver, F. W.   Natural History of Plants.   2(1): 407–414.   New York, 1895.
128. Ibid.   Pp. 104–129.
129. Ibid.   Pp. 312–313.
130. Ibid.   P. 317.
131. Ibid.   P. 420.
132. Ibid.   P. 453.
133. Kirchner, O.   Jahreshefte Ver. f. vaterl. Naturk. in Würtemburg.   1900.
134. Kirkwood, J. E.   Torrey Bul.   33: 327–341.   1906.
135. Knight, L. I.   Proc. Am. Soc. Hort. Sci.   14: 101–105.   1917.
136. Kobel, F.   Landw. Jahrb. Schweiz.   40: 441–462.   1926.
137. Kobel, F., and Steinegger, P.   Landw. Jahr. Schweiz.   973–1018.   1933.
138. Kostina, K. F.   Jour. Gov't. Bot. Gard. (Nikita, Yalta, Crimea).   10 (1): 78.   1928.

139. Kraus, E. J. Bienn. Crop Pest and Hort. Rept. Ore. Agr. Exp. Sta. 1: 71–78. 1913.
140. Kraus, E. J. Jour. Heredity. 6: 549–557. 1915.
141. Kusano, S. Jour. Coll. Agr. Imp. Univ. Tokio. 6: 7–120. 1915.
142. Lewis, C. I., and Vincent, C. C. Ore. Agr. Exp. Sta. Bul. 104. 1909.
143. Longley, A. E. Mem. Hort. Soc. N. Y. 3: 15–17. 1927.
144. Longley, A. E., and Darrow, G. M. Jour. Agr. Res. 27: 737–748. 1924.
145. Lutri, I. Ital. Agr. 72: 139–155. 1935.
146. Marshall, J. Imp. Coll. Trop. Agr., Trinidad. Cacao Res. Ann. Rept. 3: 34. 1933.
147. Marshall, R. E. Proc. Am. Soc. Hort. Sci. 16: 42–49. 1919.
148. Marshall, R. E., Johnston, S., Hootman, H. D., and Wells, H. M. Mich. Agr. Exp. Sta. Sp. Bul. 188. 1929.
149. Massart, J. Bul. Jard. Bot. Brux. 1: 85–95. 1902.
150. Mathewson, C. A. Torrey Bul. 33: 487–493. 1906.
151. McClelland. Jour. Agr. Res. 16: 245–251. 1919.
152. Macdaniels, L. H. Proc. Am. Soc. Hort. Sci. 20: 123–127. 1923.
153. Merrill, T. A. Mich. Agr. Exp. Sta. Tech. Bul. 151. 1936.
154. Millardet, A. Rev. de Viticulture. 16: 677–680. 1901.
155. Miyoshi, M. Bot. Zeit. 52: 1–28. 1894.
156. Morris, L. E. Rubber Res. Inst. Malaya Quart. Jour. 1: 121–131. 1929.
157. Mottier, D. M. Carnegie Inst. Wash. Pub. 15: 174–180. 1904.
158. Mücke, M. Bot. Ztg. 66: 1–23. 1908.
159. Müller-Thurgau, H. Landw. Jahrb. Schweiz. 12: 135–203. 1898.
160. Ibid. 22: 564–597. 1908.
161. Munson, W. M. Me. Agr. Exp. Sta. Ann. Rept. Pp. 29–58. 1892.
162. Ibid. Pp. 218–229. 1898.
163. Murneek, A. E. Plant Physiology. 1: 1–34. 1925.
164. Murneek, A. E. Mem. Hort. Soc. N. Y. 3: 65–72. 1927.
165. Murneek, A. E., Yokum, W. W., and Cubbin, E. N. Mo. Agr. Exp. Sta. Res. Bul. 138. 1930.
166. Nawaschin, S. Bot. Centralbl. 63: 104–106. 1895.
167. Nicolas, J. H. Mem. Hort. Soc. N. Y. 3: 55–57. 1927.
168. Nixon, R. W. Jour. Agr. Res. 36: 126. 1928.
169. Ore. Agr. Exp. Sta. Bien. Rept. 1921–1922: 66–72.
170. Osawa, I. Jour. Coll. Agr. Imp. Univ. Tokio. 4: 83–116. 1912.
171. Ibid. 4: 237–264. 1913.
172. Overholser, E. L. Cal. Agr. Exp. Sta. Bul. 426. 1927.
173. Overholser, E. L., and Latimer, L. P. Cal. Agr. Exp. Sta. Bul. 377. 1924.
174. Overholser, E. L., Overley, F. L., and Claypool, L. L. Wash. Agr. Exp. Sta. Ann. Rept. for 1931. P. 43.
175. Parrott, P. J., Hodgkiss, H. E., and Hartzell, F. Z. N. Y. Agr. Exp. Sta. Tech. Bul. 66. 1919.
176. Partridge, N. L. Mich. Agr. Exp. Sta. Tech. Bul. 106. 1930.
177. Paton, J. B. Doctor's Dissertation. Yale University. 1920.
178. Paton, J. B. Proc. Soc. Exp. Biol. Med. 17: 60–61. 1919.
179. Pearson, H. M. Science. 76: 594. 1932.
180. Petri, L. Atti r. Accad. Econ. Agr. Georg., Firenze. 5: 138–147. 1916.
181. Pope, W. T. Hawaii Agr. Exp. Sta. Bul. 55. 1926.
182. Popenoe, P. B. Date Growing. P. 113. Altadena, Cal. 1913.
183. Ibid. P. 105.
184. Popenoe, W. U. S. D. A. Bul. 542. 1917.

185. Powell, G. H.   Del. Agr. Exp. Sta. Ann. Rept.   12: 109–139.   1900.
186. Pound, F. J.   Cacao Res. I. C. T. A. (Trinidad).   Ann. Rept. 2: 29–36.   1933.
187. Price, W. A.   Purdue Univ. Agr. Exp. Sta. Bul. 247.   1920.
188. Rawes, A. N.   Jour. Roy. Hort. Soc.   46: 353–356.   1921.
189. Reed, H. S.   Jour. Agr. Res.   17: 153–165.   1919.
190. Reimer, F. C., and Detjen, L. R.   N. C. Agr. Exp. Sta. Bul. 209.   1910.
191. Reinicke, O. S. H.   Un. S. Afr. Dept. Agr. Sci. Bul. 90.   1930.
192. Rept. Vineland (Ont.) Hort. Exp. Sta.   P. 17.   1919.
193. Rixford, G. P.   U. S. D. A. Bul. 732.   1918.
194. Roberts, R. H.   Wis. Agr. Exp. Sta. Bul. 352.   1923.
195. Robinson, T. R., and Savage, E. M.   U. S. D. A. Dept. Circ. 387.   1926.
196. Sandsten, E. P.   Wis. Agr. Exp. Sta. Ann. Rept.   22: 300–314.   1905.
197. Sandsten, E. P.   Wis. Agr. Exp. Sta. Res. Bul. 4.   1909.
198. Schuster, C. E.   Bienn. Crop Pest and Hort. Rept. Ore. Agr. Exp. Sta.   3:44–46.
       1921.
199. Schuster, C. E.   The Oregon Grower.   3 (6): 5.   1922.
200. Schuster, C. E.   Ore. Agr. Exp. Sta. Bien. Rept.   66–72: 1921–1922.
201. Schuster, C. E.   Ore. Agr. Exp. Sta. Bul. 212.   1925.
202. Schuster, C. E.   Better Fruit.   19 (5): 1924.
203. Shoemaker, D. M.   Johns Hopkins Univ. Circ.   21: 86–87.   1902.
204. Shoemaker, J. S.   Bot. Gaz.   81: 148–171.   1926.
205. Shoemaker, J. S.   O. Agr. Exp. Sta. Bul. 422.   1928.
206. Sirks, M. J.   Arch. Néerland. Sci. Ex. et Nat. (Ser. B).   3: 205–234.   1917.
207. Stevens, N. E.   Bot. Gaz.   53: 277–308.   1912.
208. Stewart, F. C., and Eustace, H. J.   N. Y. Agr. Exp. Sta. Bul. 200.   1901.
209. Stout, A. B.   Mem. N. Y. Bot. Garden.   6: 333–454.   1916.
210. Stout, A. B.   Am. Jour. Bot.   4: 375–395.   1917.
211. Stout, A. B.   Jour. Genetics.   7: 71–103.   1918.
212. Stout, A. B.   N. Y. Agr. Exp. Sta. Tech. Bul. 82.   1921.
213. Stout, A. B.   Contrib. N. Y. Bot. Gard. Pub. No. 251.   1923.
214. Stout, A. B.   U. S. D. A. Bul. 1195.   1924.
215. Stout, A. B.   N. Y. Agr. Exp. Sta. Tech. Bul. 238.   1936.
216. Stuckey, H. P.   Ga. Agr. Exp. Sta. Bul. 124.   1916.
217. Sturtevant, E. L.   Mass. Hort. Soc. Trans.   1880.   Pp. 132–161.
218. Sutton, I.   Jour. Genetics.   7: 281–300.   1917–1918.
219. Swingle, W. T.   U. S. D. A., Bur. Pl. Ind. Bul. 53.   1904.
220. Swingle, W. T.   Mem. Hort. Soc. N. Y.   3: 19–21.   1927.
221. Teske, A. H., and Gardner, V. R.   Mich. Agr. Exp. Sta. Sp. Bul. 165.   1927.
222. Tiedjens, V. A.   Mass. Agr. Exp. Sta. Bul. 225.   1925.
223. Tischler, G.   Jahrb. Wiss. Bot.   47: 219–242.   1910.
224. Tischler, G.   Zeitsch. Bot.   9: 417–488.   1917.
225. Tischler, G.   Mem. Hort. Soc. N. Y.   3: 9–13.   1927.
226. Torres, J. P.   Philippine Jour. Agr.   3 (3): 217–229.   1932.
227. Tosti-Croce, E.   Ital. Agr.   71: 575–580.   1934.
228. Trabut, L.   Jour. Heredity.   7: 416.   1916.
229. Tufts, W. P.   Cal. Agr. Exp. Sta. Ann. Rept.   P. 46.   1916.
230. Tufts, W. P.   Cal. Agr. Exp. Sta. Bul. 306.   1919.
231. Ibid.   Bul. 307.   1919.
232. Tufts, W. P., Hendrickson, A. H., and Philp, G. L.   Mem. Hort. Soc. N. Y.
       3: 171–174.   1927.
233. Uphof, J. C. T.   Gartenbauwissenschaft.   7: 121–142.   1932.

234. Ibid. 8: 394–410. 1934.
235. Vaile, J. E. Doctor's Dissertation. Univ. of Ill. 1933.
236. Valleau, W. D. Jour. Agr. Res. 12: 613–670. 1918.
237. Waite, M. B. U. S. D. A., Div. Pom. Bul. 5. 1895.
238. Waite, M. B. Amer. Agric. 75: 112. 1905.
239. Waugh, F. A. Vt. Agr. Exp. Sta. Ann. Rept. 10: 87–93. 1896–1897.
240. Ibid. 11: 245. 1897–1898.
241. Ibid. 13: 358. 1899–1900.
242. Waugh, F. A. Plums and Plum Culture. Pp. 282–307. New York, 1901.
243. Webber, H. J. U. S. D. A., Div. Veg. Phys. and Path. Bul. 22. 1900.
244. Wellington, R. Am. Nat. 47: 279–306. 1913.
245. Wellington, R., Stout, A. B., Eisnet, O., and Van Alstyne, L. M. N. Y. Agr. Exp. Sta. Bul. 577. 1929.
246. Wester, P. J. Torrey Bul. 37: 529–539. 1910.
247. White, J. Ann. Bot. 21: 487–499. 1907.
248. Whitten, J. C. Mo. Agr. Exp. Sta. Bul. 46. 1899.
249. Ibid. Bul. 117. 1914.
250. Wicks, W. H. Ark. Agr. Exp. Sta. Bul. 143. 1918.
251. Winkler, A. J. Hilgardia. 1: 539–542. 1926.
252. Ibid. 2: 107–124. 1926.
253. Ibid. 4: 153–173. 1929.
254. Woodroof, J. G., and Woodroof, N. C. Jour. Agr. Res. 33: 677–685. 1926.
255. Woodroof, J. G., Woodroof, N. C., and Bailey, J. E. Ga. Agr. Exp. Sta. Bul. 148. 1928.
256. Yasuda, S. Agric. and Hort. 9: 647–656. 1934. (Abstracted in Jour. Roy. Hort. Soc. 59 (2): 320. 1934.)

SECTION VI
PROPAGATION

The universality of variation in plants when propagated sexually is well known. Comparatively few are the fruit plants which reproduce their like by seed with any great degree of certainty. Though this condition has certain disadvantages it is, on the whole, fortunate. The animal breeder or the breeder of seed propagated plants, when he has obtained a desirable individual, confronts the problem of reproducing its like, of fixing the strain. The propagator of fruit plants facing the same problem has a different solution; from the parent plant he cuts pieces each of which produces a plant practically the same as the original. The problem of propagation of fruit plants is essentially making these pieces of the parent plant live. Sometimes they grow if thrust into earth; hence, propagation by cuttings. Again, they must be placed on rooted plants with which they can unite; hence, budding and grafting, which are in reality the placing of cuttings in another medium.

Though the conception is simple, actual practice involves a seemingly interminable variety of refinements and detail, varying with the climate, the species, even the variety and with economic conditions. The mere feasibility of a given process does not demonstrate its expediency and though the process is expedient it does not necessarily follow that the product is of lasting value. A certain stock may be desirable to the nurseryman because it is cheapest, or most easily worked or makes the best initial growth and still it may not be well suited to the orchard. This condition may be reversed. Again, a given stock may be entirely satisfactory if the trees are planted in one section or in one soil and totally unsuited to another section or to another soil.

Though the art of grafting (the term as used in this discussion includes budding) apparently antedates the art of writing, many questions growing out of its application are far from answered, at least so far as American practice is concerned. In the early days of standardized apple production, when the seedling orchards were newly topworked to named varieties, there was much discussion of the effect of stock on cion and of related questions, but attention was soon diverted to the protection of fruit and trees from pests and for many years little notice has been given the underground parts of the trees, except when it was forced upon growers in some sections. With the rise of commercial nurseries the newer generation of fruit growers know little about the propagation of the trees they grow; many do not know on what stocks their trees have been worked.

Similarly, until comparatively recently scientific investigation has devoted little attention to these matters, being concerned with perhaps more pressing problems. For most of the precise study in this field indebtedness must be acknowledged to European workers.

CHAPTER XXXI

THE RECIPROCAL INFLUENCES OF STOCK AND CION

The normal condition of growth for any plant is for it to have roots, stem and leaves developed from a single seed or, in the case of a plant propagated by a cutting, to have these several parts developed from tissues that originally came from a single seed. In other words all of its parts belong to one and the same individual. In the plant propagated by budding or grafting the root system and perhaps the stem is that of one individual; the leaf system is that of another. The stock must supply the cion with its mineral nutrients; the cion must supply the stock with its elaborated foods, both perhaps somewhat different in kind, in total amount and in proportions of different constituents than would be the case were the cion on its own roots or were the stock possessed of its own top. Furthermore, between the two is the graft union, a connecting tissue that may not function exactly the same as a corresponding amount of conducting tissue of either stock or cion. Thus there are two factors, graft union and stock, that may cause the cion to grow and function somewhat differently than if it were on its own roots, and, similarly, graft union and cion may exert a corresponding influence on the stock.

NATURE OF THE GRAFT UNION

A graft union is essentially a healed wound. If, on many trees, while the bark is slipping freshly, a rectangle is cut in the bark, the piece lifted and immediately returned to its original position and bound securely against the wood surface, it unites readily, through dovetailing of parenchymatous callus cells arising from the inner surface of the bark and the outer surface of the wood. Only let, for the piece of bark originally removed, a similar piece taken from another branch, tree or variety and bearing a bud capable of further growth, be substituted, the same healing process occurs, and the result is in essentials what is called "budding." If, while or shortly before the cambium is active, an apple shoot is slit longitudinally for one or two inches at some point below the tip and then bound securely so as to press the severed portions firmly together, they unite in the course of a few weeks; in this case the union occurs only through the dovetailing of callus cells pushed out from the cut edges of the wood and the phloem. Though the tissues

618

that were cut never unite, the new tissues soon form a continuous layer so perfect that in many, if not most, cases the microscope does not reveal the exact point of union. If, instead of binding the two halves together directly, we interpose between them a shoot taken from another branch, tree or variety and so cut that its exposed cambium surfaces can be brought into line with those of the split branch, and then tie the whole together firmly, the same union processes occur, along two lines this time instead of one. This is grafting.

As growth continues this new callus-derived cambium functions just like the cambium of the stock below or of the cion above, and the new layers of wood and of bark are continuous from stock, through callus and on into the cion. In the earlier stages parenchyma only is differentiated, and evidence obtained by Ohmann[231] indicates that at least a fair amount of conduction takes place through it. Then as the need arises, depending on species, age of cion, kind of graft, etc., tracheids and other conductive tissues are formed.[231] According to Herse,[152] the order of reappearance of woody elements in the vicinity of the graft union is the same as it is in the healing of ordinary wounds through callus formation. The typical percentage relationship of the tissues is restored or approached before the normal length of the elements is attained. In the formation of new tissues following the establishment of cambial continuity, it appears that differentiation of the cells of the cion is influenced by the cells of the stock adjacent to the cion cambium. Thus cambium cells of the cion differentiate medullary ray tissue where in contact with ray cells of the stock, etc.[239] When stock and cion are thoroughly congenial, the graft union soon becomes so perfect that the microscope does not reveal the exact point of contact any more than it does in quickly healed wounds.

Graft unions sometimes develop wholly unaided by man; they have been noted on branches of many species; excavation of root systems of mature apple, maple, chestnut and many coniferous trees reveals many of them. Grafting, then, despite much of the atmosphere of sorcery that has been breathed over it and much of the anathema that has fallen upon it, is a natural process. One of Shakespeare's characters terminates a brief dissertation on grafting by saying:

> " . . . nature is made better by no mean
> But nature makes that mean. . . .
> The art itself is nature."

It is highly probable that Shakespeare borrowed this thought from della Porta, an Italian polymath and playwright, but it has not been better expressed.

Natural as the process is, some plants do not graft readily by practicable methods. In some cases growth of callus is so slow or meager that the cion perishes before union adequate to its support can be established; in some cases tylosis formation, a reaction incident to cutting of the wood, must retard the flow of water and nutrients to the cion. Both of these difficulties are apparent in the walnut, and tylosis formation must be restrictive in the grape. In some plants, as in peach, cherry and plum in various degrees, any cut penetrating the xylem induces copious gum flow which must restrict sap flow and probably interferes with callus formation; in these trees budding that does not involve cutting the xylem is generally more successful than grafting. In all these cases, though failures may be numerous, the successful unions are likely to endure for the span of life natural to the tree.

Man sometimes attempts the use of a natural process to produce unnatural combinations. In grafts involving widely unrelated plants, failure is prompt and complete. Cleft grafts of apple on oak, made at East Lansing, Mich., and callused in soil to prevent drying of the cion, showed abundant callus in the apple and very little in the oak, but in both cases the callus was covered with a distinct periderm, of a type formed in bark as protection against unfavorable external conditions; each plant was isolating itself from the other. In view of the specificity of proteins in plants, such results are not surprising when tissues from wholly unrelated plants are brought into juxtaposition.

In some cases the initial union is rather easily secured, but its duration may be brief or it may persist for many years without becoming complete. Peach buds take readily on the Marianna plum, but the plants thus formed die suddenly in the nursery row, apparently because of failure of the root system.[310] Similarly peach on another American plum has been reported to live only so long as shoots from the roots are retained. These cases suggest the failure of the stock to receive some essential elaborated food from the cion imposed upon it and do not necessitate any supposition of the failure being due to the graft union.

In other cases, however, the graft itself appears to be the principal factor in dwarfing and in the comparatively short life of the synthesized tree. The dwarf pear tree, produced by working a pear cion on a quince root, is an excellent illustration. The dwarfing effect thus produced has been generally attributed to the restrictions imposed by the limited range of the quince root. If this view were entirely correct, the quince should reach unnaturally great size when worked on pear roots. Actually working of quince on pear in a nursery at East Lansing, Mich., repeatedly produced trees which made miserable growth and were mostly short-lived; the "vigorous" pear stocks dwarfed the quince cion much more than the quince stocks dwarfed the pear cion. Examination of the pear-quince union under the microscope shows a rather normal initial union followed by interruption, at first temporarily, later tending to be prolonged, of continuity in cambium and phloem tissues and, ultimately, of course, in the xylem itself.[48]   The breaks apparently occur in late summer, and the most plausible explanation   to be earlier cessation of xylem formation (with continued   .ormation) in the quince than in the pear.   The effect :   tree so constituted is continuously self ringing; hence   precocity in fruiting and its small stature. The root system   dwarfed, and it in turn dwarfs the top.   Several combinations of the stone fruits, as apricot on some plums and on peach, appear to present the same phenomenon, since they break readily at the graft union and the fractures reveal the same lack of tissue continuity as is found in the pear-quince union.

What has been described under the name "xyloporosis"[33] as a disease sometimes attacking budded lime trees is apparently a manifestation of uncongeniality between stock and cion of the type associated with a poor graft union.   "External symptoms are in the form of pores in the wood and corresponding pegs in the bark. Internal symptoms are cessation of growth of cambium and, therefore, of the annual rings at the xylem, occurring largely at the junction of stock and cion."[33] Though it has been suggested that it is caused by a stoppage of the descending sap at the point of union of stock and cion, it seems more probable that the break in continuity of the cambium comes first, and that leads to a stoppage in water and food transport.

Congeniality of Grafts.—Distinction should be made between congeniality and adaptability.   The former term refers to the degree of success of the union between stock and cion, the latter term to the relation of the combined parts to environment, most often to soil and climate. Husmann's conception of perfect congeniality in grapes is a condition in which "a variety grafted on another behaves as if the stock were grafted with a scion of itself, the union being perfect and the behavior of the vine the same as that of an entire ungrafted plant."[167]   He states also, "When both stock and scion are suited to the conditions, but will not thrive when grafted, congeniality is lacking."   Further: "The adaptability of varieties to soil, climates and other conditions can often be closely forecasted, but congeniality has to be determined by actual test."

Congeniality, or its lack, seems to exist in about four degrees.   First, is entire lack of ability to unite, as in apple on oak, cherry on poplar, ash on mountain ash.   Here too belong some of the grafts mentioned by Vergil, who was a poet and not a farmer, and the "charlatan" grafts, exhibited at various periods in Europe, produced by means such as leading a grape vine up through the hollow trunk of a cherry tree.   The second degree of congeniality involves combinations such as peach on some American plums (already mentioned), pear on apple and the reverse, and pear on American mountain ash (*Sorbus americana*). These combinations may unite readily but are usually short-lived, particularly if all the foliage is supplied by the cion.

Budding Hale's Early peach buds set on a clonal plum stock (Damas A) resulted in a perfect stand of buds, but every whip died in its first season, while on another plum stock (Damas D) the failures in budding

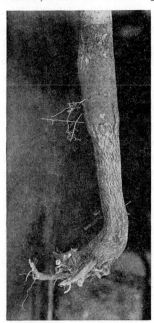

amounted to 27 per cent., but all the successful buddings grew and all the trees planted were alive after four years in the orchard.[310] The third degree involves combinations more lasting than the second, but not so enduring as the normal life of a tree of the cion variety. Here belong the dwarf pear, cherry on Mahaleb cherry, sweet cherry on *Prunus pennsylvanica*. In the last-mentioned combination the tree reaches perhaps half the normal cherry stature and then begins to die back from the branch tips. Heavy pruning may keep it alive for some time, while unpruned specimens die or blow over, but the combination cannot be considered successful. In this case the root system appears to be unable to develop beyond a definite size and a marked overgrowth of the cion occurs. Pear trees on commercial seedlings of *Pyrus calleryana* and of wild types of *Pyrus ussuriensis* have shown a similar tendency at South Haven[175] and at East Lansing, Mich. The fourth class comprises cases of perfect congeniality, as already defined.

Fig. 58.—A graft showing early manifestation of incompatibility. Old Home pear grafted on *P. ussuriensis* stock. It died in the summer of 1932. Photographed in May, 1933. Note the development of a few cion roots.

In the Apple.—The various species of apple seem, in general, to have considerable tolerance for one another. Disparity in growth is in some cases so great that one symbiont frequently outgrows the other very markedly, as in the common apple on many crab apples, with ultimately disastrous effects, but cases of early death or fractures at the graft union are comparatively rare. Some varieties occasionally split at the union with some of the dwarfing stocks; a clonally propagated seedling of Northern Spy dies within a year when budded to certain varieties and some verbal reports hint a physiological incompatibility of Wealthy on Northern Spy.

American experience with cultivated apples on crab apple stocks has been confined chiefly to the north central states. The published reports of this experience are confusing because of lack of clear statement as to type or species of crab apple stock used and because of lack of clearness in differentiating between incompatibility and impracticability. In addition, some of the native stocks transplant poorly; this may have given erroneous impressions of their congeniality to cultivated apple cions.[206] One report of emergency pioneer use of a "wild crab" near Kalamazoo, Mich., indicated death of the cions in three years.[218] *Malus coronaria* has frequently accepted grafts of apple;[56,209] the only available explicit statement dealing expressly with union on *coronaria* states[270] that "apples generally have not made good unions." Grafts on Soulard crab, supposedly a hybrid between *M. iœnsis* and the cultivated apple, grow readily; the ultimate results are rather uniformly unfavorable from a practical point of view,[172] but whether incompatibility, in the narrower sense, is involved, is not clear, since the grafts sometimes bear well for a time at least.[171]

It is perhaps significant that the ornamental American forms of apple are reported to be shorter lived on seedlings of common apple than on some of the native crabs.[288] Grafts of apple on *M. baccata* and some of its local forms are used regularly to some extent in the north central states and in Manchuria;[233] they exert a dwarfing effect and seem to be preferred only where root freezing precludes use of the usual stocks.[270] Hybrids of *M. baccata* with common apple, as Transcendent and Whitney 20, seem to form rather lasting, although frequently swollen, unions with the cultivated apple; many varieties overgrow these hybrid stocks, but when fractures develop they seem to occur at the crotches rather more frequently than at the union.

Malus prunifolia has been recommended as a dwarfing stock in dry soils in cold regions,[194,204] but adverse reports are not lacking.[242] A form of *prunifolia*, var. *ringo*, is extensively used in Japan[9] as a preferred stock for European apples, on account of its complete immunity from woolly aphis; and *M. Sieboldii* (*Pyrus toringo*) is similarly used in that country. Some years ago it was reported[56] to be in common use as a dwarfing stock for apples in Bessarabia and the section north of the Black Sea. Seedlings of *M. Sargentii*, considered by Asami to be a botanical variety of *Sieboldii*, are now under test as dwarfing stocks for apple in Iowa.

On the pear, apple grafts are generally short-lived. An unidentified apple dwarfing stock produced two crops of fruit on a seedling of *Pyrus ussuriensis* at East Lansing, Mich., before the stock died, apparently from starvation. Apple cions have been reported[210,267] as growing on the "apple-quince," but not reassuringly. In France apple shoots reached a growth of 6 feet on an unidentified quince in 2 years;[216] in another case,[186] a growth of 3 feet was made in 1 year, but subsequent growth languished. According to one report,[67] the apple has been rather freely grown on quince in Turkey. On a related form, the Japanese quince (*Chaenomeles*) fruiting of apple has been recorded,[216] and the reciprocal combination grows fairly well, for a time at least.

On *Crataegus mollis* the apple is reported to make poor unions.[270] Cions have made at least some growth on mountain-ash[271] and have fruited on the small *Aronia* (*Pyrus arbutifolia*).[297] On *Amelanchier* the take of cions is poor and the initial growth poor.[28,227]

In the Pear.—Since, with the exception of Kieffer, which is a hybrid with *Pyrus serotina*, the important varieties of pear belong to the species *P. communis*, the usual propagation on seedlings of this species has seemed simple. When, however, to secure resistance to disease or to produce dwarf trees, other stocks of different species or genera are used, complications involving some degree of uncongeniality, sometimes differing with the variety, arise. *P. betulaefolia* was highly endorsed as a pear stock, particularly for light soils, at the Arnold Arboretum many years ago, but scarcity of seed has prevented general trials. At Geneva, N. Y., seedling stocks of this species have produced outstanding trees of Bartlett, Seckel and Kieffer, but poor trees of Anjou, in the nursery and in the first 2 years in the orchard.[285] *P. serotina* produced large vigorous trees of Kieffer, which is half *serotina*, but weak trees of Bartlett and Seckel. *P. ussuriensis* has produced vigorous trees of Kieffer but has produced less satisfactory trees of Bartlett and Seckel. On *P. calleryana*, at Geneva, Kieffer, as well as Bartlett and Seckel, have made weak trees. Kieffer generally grows vigorously in the nursery on seedlings of *P. communis* and is not conspicuously uncongenial to this species, but orchard trees on *communis* roots are less vigorous than own-rooted trees.[282] Le Conte, another hybrid of nature similar to Kieffer, is reported in Texas to manifest similar uncongeniality with *communis* stocks.[54]

Dwarf pear trees, produced by working on quince stocks, were rather numerous in Italy in 1589.[236] In the ensuing years experience has sorted out varieties as successful or not successful on quince, rather well-defined categories being established. Primarily the distinction seems based on growth habit, varieties that are inherently weak growers being generally unsuited to culture on quince. Compatibility of union is, however, important in that some varieties, as Bartlett, Bosc and Clairgeau, whose culture as dwarfs is desirable in some regions, form poor unions with the quince stock, while others, as Duchesse d'Angoulême, Hardy, Winkfield (Curé of Europe) and Amanlis make very good unions with this stock. Consequently the three last-named are sometimes used as interstocks, being grafted on the quince and in return receiving grafts of the desirable but refractory varieties.

The "quince root" is not uniform. As early as 1828 note was made that certain pear varieties failed very soon on the pear-shaped quince (Malling G).[45] In 1845[29] the differences in quince stocks received mention in America and preference for the Angers has been expressed freely.[84] In recent years, comprehensive studies of several quince stocks at the East Malling Research Station in England have shown that most of the types take the pear bud readily, but that when the bud grows out marked differences appear[5] and certain pear varieties (Durondeau, Pitmaston) grow very poorly and have high mortality on certain quince stocks (as Fontenay and Portugal), though a few varieties, as Conference, grow fairly well on these same stocks; on the other hand, the variety Dr. Jules Guyot does not grow well on the Angers and similar stocks which suit most varieties. One clonal selection of layered pear stock "has for some years shown symptoms which suggest delayed incompatibility." A variety known as Collins was said to kill trees on which it was topworked.[309] It should be noted that these peculiarities are varietal; all the pears are of one botanical species, all the quinces are likewise varieties of one species.

The pear seems to have varietal peculiarities which extend to and are perhaps matched by individual peculiarities of still other stocks with which it is generally uncongenial. The Seckel pear has been frequently mentioned as enduring longer grafted on apple than other varieties tried; conversely, the Tolman Sweet has been mentioned as a better stock for pears than most apples, though it has not proved particularly compatible with pear at East Lansing, Mich. Individual, varietal and specific idiosyncrasies must play a part in the diverse and contradictory results secured from grafting pear on hawthorn (*Crataegus*). In the middle of the seventeenth century, Austen wrote: "As for a Peare upon a Thorne . . . most commonly they dye in two, or three years."[10] Since that time, in various countries, numerous unfavorable reports and an occasional favorable report have appeared.

From 1860 to 1880, numerous trials were made in the eastern and central states, with generally unfavorable results. Nevertheless, remarkable specimens are claimed, such as a 94-year old pear grafted on *Crataegus mollis*, with a circumference of 8 feet and an occasional yield of 30 bushels,[125] and it was claimed in 1860 that many trees worked on native swamp white hawthorn during the French occupation of the lower Mississippi still persisted.[2] It is reported[212] that only a few varieties, notably Flemish Beauty, succeed on the vigorous *C. coccinea; C. tomentosa* is reported as more dwarfing than *C. coccinea*. Another report[173] states that in eastern Massachusetts pear outgrows the *coccinea* stock, and the trees are short-lived. In England, Hogg[157] reported that only a few varieties succeed upon White Thorn (presumably *C. oxyacantha*); Reine des Poires, however, "succeeds admirably"; a tree 25 or 30 years old is mentioned, while at East Malling one lot of pears on *C. oxyacantha* are reported as making "exceptionally vigorous growth" for 9 years. But results with other selections of this species were less favorable, Reine des Poires being "completely incompatible."[5]

In France, the American *Crataegus coccinea* has been reported as a more promising stock for pears than *C. oxyacantha*.[149]   Another report states that only vigorous varieties succeed on *Crataegus*, and these usually last only 10 to 12 years.[34]   The Baltet nurseries, for a time, looked with favor on the use of the Portugal quince as an intermediate stock between pear and hawthorn.[27]   In Palestine, it is stated, *C. azarolus* is a good stock for early varieties of pear;[1] whether its unsuitability for late varieties is due to incompatibility is not reported.

The whole record, too extensive for reproduction here, is so full of contradictions that, after allowance is made for mistaken identification of *Crataegus* species and for differences in location, there seems to be some basis for belief that occasional combinations of stock and cion may have a rather high degree of compatibility.

Experience with pear on mountain ash (*Sorbus*) has been as diverse.   Simultaneous death of pear top and *Sorbus* stock as far as the ground, when 2 or 3 years old (whether from climatic factors or from incompatibility is not clear), has been reported in Iowa.[212]   In Germany grafts on *Sorbus aucuparia* united well and grew well for 2 years, slowed perceptibly in the third year and were all dead in 10 years,[191] but the same report mentions a pear bearing every year on mountain ash.   In Maine, it was reported that budding pear on young trees of *Sorbus aucuparia* produced good whips of Winkfield and Glou Morceau, while other varieties grew poorly and some not at all.[122]   Later the same writer summarized his rather extensive work:[123] " . . . although some ten years ago I worked several thousand in this way (in nursery) and with 20 or 30 different varieties, I got no trees to succeed for any length of time nor to come into good bearing at all; while by grafting the limbs of grown trees (of *Sorbus americana*) 10 or 15 feet high and three to six inches in diameter I have seen them loaded with bushels of fine fruit for several years in succession; but even such trees may not be expected to succeed for any long term; a few years of bearing is all that can be expected.   As with the quince, some varieties succeed well, others but poorly, and others not at all upon the Mountain Ash.   The best I have proved are Flemish Beauty, Fulton and Belle Lucrative.   The Bartlett has also done well."[123]

Some midwestern nurseries were growing pears on mountain ash as early as 1848[102] and both the European and American species were tried in several states. Flemish Beauty, Howell and Bartlett were reported to grow best on these stocks, while Louise Bonne de Jersey grew less vigorously than on quince.   The greater hardiness of *Sorbus americana* made it preferable in Minnesota.[220]   In recent experiments at the East Malling Research Station, the Fertility pear produced excellent 1-year trees on *S. aucuparia*, but in nine years in the orchard growth was "stunted" and less vigorous than that on *Crataegus oxyacantha*.[5]   These citations and others not presented here indicate that in general the *Sorbus* species are less congenial to pears than are some forms of *Crataegus*, but they show the same diversity, suggesting varietal preferences in cion and in stock.

Pear grows for a time on the service berry or shadbush (*Amelanchier*); printed experience indicates variable results with it, mostly unsatisfactory,[123] though pears have been produced on it.[297]   In France, it was reported that pear grew on *Cotoneaster affinis*, but not on the evergreen species *C. buxifolia* and *C. micro-*

phylla.[6]   Varieties with thin wood are said to succeed better than coarse-growing varieties on *C. vulgaris* and *C. parviflora.*[192]

Some of these cases of uncongeniality are recognizable readily in distinctly poor growth or in graft unions whose fracture reveals considerable lack of connection between stock and cion, or in both.   Other cases are less obvious and are recognizable only when comparison with better combinations of stock and cion is possible.

Sometimes appearance or behavior suggests an uncongeniality that does not exist.   Marked disparity in diameter of stock and cion does not necessarily signify uncongeniality, at least of any practical importance. Many old apple orchards reveal such cases which have existed for decades without apparent effect on performance.[230]   Some of the more uncongenial grafts may produce no swelling at all.[48]   A tree of slender-growing variety topworked in the branches to a coarse-growing variety (as Rhode Island Greening apple on Duchess) may develop mechanical difficulties, but the fracture is more likely to occur at the crotches than at the graft union, and the union should not be considered uncongenial in the sense employed here.   Likewise the repeated failure of dwarf pears in the north central states is attributable primarily to the tenderness of the quince root to winter freezing rather than to uncongeniality.

In the Plums.—The plums grown in the United States belong in several distinct species, the Europeans (*Prunus domestica*), the Damsons (*P. insititia*), the Japanese (*P. salicina*) and varieties of several native species including *P. hortulana, P. munsoniana, P. americana, P. angustifolia.*   When it is considered that, in addition, hybrids between some of these species are cultivated and that some of the stocks used belong to still other species, it is not remarkable that some incompatibilities are found.

In a comparative trial at Geneva, N. Y.,[144] trees of the three varieties of Japanese and of the *domestica* and *insititia* plums grew best on Myrobolan seedlings and poorly on *americana* seedlings.   The varieties belonging to *P. munsoniana* grew equally well on Marianna, Myrobalan, peach, and rather poorly on *americana* roots.   Since in some of these tests the trees on their own roots grew very poorly the growth differences cannot with certainty be attributed to incompatibility; in fact, the general behavior shows a rather remarkable picture of compatibility.

The experiment at Geneva, in conformity with American usage, embraced seedling stocks and the results represent the performance of average seedlings.   Some of the stocks commonly used, however, are rather variable as seedlings.   The wide range of variation in Myrobalan seedlings has been noted on both sides of the Atlantic.[16,179,135]   Multiplication of seedlings, by asexual methods, into clons brings out some interesting individual peculiarities in compatibility, which indicate what must happen to some degree when a large group of seedlings is budded.

Considerable information on the nature of individual idiosyncrasies, if not on their proportion to a whole population of seedlings, is afforded by studies at the East Malling Research Station.[5] In these experiments, cions of some varieties of plum have been grown on clonal stocks of several types in common use in Europe and of certain selections made at East Malling, and, in a few instances, on seedlings. One of the notable features of these studies is the lack of close relationship between initial "take" of buds and the subsequent manifestations of incompatibility. This is not surprising to those who have done budding on any range of material and observed the marked differences among stocks in responsiveness to environmental conditions. The take of sweet cherry buds, for example, is almost invariably greater on Mahaleb stocks than it is on sweet cherry seedlings, the so-called Mazzards of the nursery trade. At East Malling, however, the take of Damson varieties was consistently low on Brussels and Common Plum stocks, and no trees survived more than 2 years. At East Malling, of the buds of Czar plums set on Kroosgespruim, 83 per cent. took, but mortality, due apparently to incompatibility, reduced the stand as 1-year old trees to 30 per cent., and in another year to 13 per cent. The same variety took to the extent of 81 per cent. on Common Plum, and the stand of 2-year old trees was 70 per cent. On Marianna the take was only 58 per cent., but the final stand was 41 per cent. Since the figures reported for stand of trees seem to have been computed on the basis of total buds set, the percentage stand computed on the basis of take would be somewhat different, amounting in the respective cases to 16, 86 and 71 per cent. Comparison on a similar basis of results with similar combinations secured by grafting shows respective stands after 2 years of 55, 81 and 64 per cent.; though the apparent incompatibility with the Kroosgespruim stocks is reduced in this case, it is still too great for practical purposes. A clonal selection (G) of St. Julien, whose seedlings are generally given a high rating for stock value in the United States, showed consistently low compatibility for Czar cions.

In marked contrast to the results with the Czar plum, which seems unusually exacting in its requirements, are the results secured with the Victoria plum on the same stocks. With this variety the percentages of survival of grafts which took on Myrobalan B, Common Plum, Brussels, Marianna and St. Julien G were, respectively 98, 96, 100 and 98, as compared with 89, 81, 27, 64 and 17 for Czar.

In the orchard, mortality connected apparently with incompatibility was particularly high with Czar on Brussels and Marianna and with

President on Brussels and Common Plum, the respective mortalities with the latter variety being 64 and 62 per cent. in 12 years.

The Japanese varieties of plums have been worked on peach stocks more consistently than any other types, perhaps because they are as a group no hardier than the peaches and are not ordinarily planted where the peach root would be affected by adverse environment. Japanese varieties, except Climax, seem to take well when topworked on peach.[151] In Texas it has been reported that most of the Japanese varieties, particularly Burbank and Satsuma, thrive on the Marianna stock.[222] Japanese varieties tend to overgrow *americana*[79] or other American stocks,[287] and they appear to fail on *Prunus spinosa*.[224]

Experience with European varieties of plum on American stocks has been variable but generally unfavorable. Lombard has been described as overgrowing wild (probably *americana*) stocks and being short-lived, but Miner was reported to be a good stock for Lombard.[170] *Domesticas* in general seem to overgrow *americana* stocks.[79] The Marianna stock seems compatible to more varieties of European type than most American forms of plum, but seems incompatible to some varieties. President appears to suffer on this stock.[75] Its behavior under Victoria and Czar cions is mentioned elsewhere.

Varietal differences in stock and in cion seem to affect the compatibility of plum on almond; a case is reported in California[151] of Sugar prune cions dying within 3 years when topworked on I. X. L., Peerless, Drake and Nonpareil almonds and being in good condition after 7 years on Eureka and Ne Plus Ultra. Some Japanese plum varieties, as Apex, Duarte and Formosa, and some European varieties, as Agen, Hungarian and President, are reported to be compatible with almond. Similarly some plum varieties "make excellent unions when topworked on apricot, while others seem to possess no affinity for it."

On Japanese apricot (*Prunus mume*) Wickson and Santa Rosa form defective unions, but use of the Manchurian apricot as an interstock seems to obviate this difficulty;[268] *domestica* varieties in general seem to form rather doubtful unions with this stock, though Sugar and Clyman seem to make smooth unions, for a few years at least. Several possible interstocks, of various types, as Methley plum (*P. salicina* × Myrobalan), a sand-cherry hybrid, and Clyman, a *domestica*, are under test in California.

Domestica plums and prunes have been rather commonly grown on peach seedlings. Reports have been rather frequent that Lombard does not grow well on peach,[235] and occasional reports have been made that other varieties of European type, as Reine Claude and McLaughlin,[217] Smith's Orleans and Washington, fail on this stock. The Robe de

Sergeant prune is reported in New South Wales as not budding well on peach; in this case the Agen prune seemed to function satisfactorily as an interstock.[75] In California,[251] Yellow Egg, Jefferson and Washington plums and Robe de Sergeant, Imperial Epineuse and Sugar prunes have been said to lack affinity for the peach root. Diamond and Grand Duke are similarly reported. In Vermont, the Newman plum seemed to have much greater affinity for peach roots than did Green Gage, Stoddard, Chabot or Milton; in fact, the last three did very poorly on peach stock.[273]

Most of the experience involving native plums as cion has been accumulated in sections where environmental factors, such as drought, root freezing or nematodes, affect results with many stocks to a degree that makes evaluation of compatibility alone very difficult. After considerable experimentation, an Iowa nurseryman[313] concluded that Myrobalan and St. Julien stocks were uncongenial to native varieties and that Marianna stocks were not entirely congenial to them. Wild Goose and Miner have been reported as growing well on peach roots where these are not affected by cold or by heavy soils,[160] but *americanas* in general seem to form defective unions with this stock.[245] In Georgia, many native plums have been reported to be as long-lived on peach seedlings as on Marianna plum, though they make stronger growth on the latter.[179] In Maryland, J. W. Kerr[179] considered Marianna the best general stock, though he noted that some European types do not succeed on it. In Texas, Marianna stocks were much more successful for *americana*, Chickasaw and European varieties than was the peach, but adaptability here clouded compatibility. A variety of the Beach plum (*Prunus maritima*) seemed to succeed on Wild Goose, Chickasaw (*P. angustifolia*) and *P. domestica*.[16] Bailey reported that many of the *hortulanas* grow well on peach and on Marianna.[16] De Soto, an *americana* variety, has been found unsatisfactory on roots of Miner, a subspecies of *hortulana*.[241] The Chickasaw varieties seem to grow well on Marianna[222,302] and, where conditions are favorable, on peach.[16] Apricot stocks do not make permanent unions with American varieties of plum.[126]

Waugh states that buds of plum take on the common chokecherry, but that he never heard of a tree coming to maturity on this stock. Buds of plum have grown 2 years on the wild black cherry (*Prunus serotina*), but they do not live long.[300] On the sand cherry (*P. besseyi*), plums of European, Japanese and the several American species take readily; the trees are dwarfed and tend to be spreading in habit, perhaps from early and heavy bearing.[130]

In the Peach.—In the United States the use of peach seedlings as stocks for peach has been so general that some books on peach culture have mentioned no other stock,[113] and in 1925 peach stocks were used for 97 per cent. of the peach trees produced in American nurseries.[150] In Europe, however, the use of plum stocks has been rather general, the only points of difference being in the type of plum favored. Special conditions of environment have sometimes led to recourse to almond and to apricot.

An early European writer[187] seems to have placed plum stock below apricot and peach as stocks for peach.   By 1757, the Mussel stock was in common use in England, but seedlings of the Green Gage plum were recommended.[153]   About the same time the St. Julien stock was receiving use in France.[38]   By the middle of the nineteenth century varietal differences in peach compatibility with Mussel plum stocks were reported,[311] some varieties apparently growing better on the Pear plum, and Damson stocks and almond stocks were finding advocates.[38]   The Mussel was, however, the most common stock, though some nectarines were noted as unthrifty on it,[157] the Brompton stock was under debate and the Pear plum had produced short-lived trees.   The Black Damson plum was reported as overgrown by peach tops;[247] the same was reported for Brussels plum.[4]

In northern Germany, differentiation among plum stocks was noted rather early, and by 1873 some strains of Damson (Black, Red Early, Red Doveheart) were reported suitable; stocks derived from prunes were considered doubtful and the Myrobalan was being rather widely used.[185] Burbidge[66] specified certain French peaches as succeeding only on the Pear plum, whereas the Brompton was said to suit nearly all varieties equally well.   By 1885 the Croux nurseries, in France, were using the Damas de Toulouse as preferable to the old St. Julien.[177]   At this time the almond was the leading peach stock in southern France, with a few seedling peaches in use, while in the north the Black Damson and St. Julien dominated.[148]   In comparatively recent years the St. Julien stock seems to be well regarded in Germany.[8]   In England, at present, peaches are commonly worked on the Mussels and Brompton layered stocks and on seedling St. Julien and Damson stocks.[5]   For high standards the *domestica* variety Schöne von Löwen (Belle de Louvain) has been recommended as an interstock.[7]

As early as 1862,[121] the Myrobalan was described as "the worst stock for the peach," and subsequent reports have been uniformly of the same tenor.   The few favorable reports on this stock have come mostly from portions of Germany and Switzerland,[112,119] where soil and climate are apparently unfavorable to other stocks.   American experience has been rather generally unfavorable from Massachusetts[272] to Alabama.[146] According to a report[120] which seems typical, the first year's growth from the bud is rather good, but whether trees are planted in the orchard or left undisturbed in the nursery, poor growth, yellowish foliage and premature defoliation are characteristic of the second year. In Australia, peach trees on Myrobalan are reported to have lived only a year or two.[111]

Variability in Myrobalan seedlings has been noted,[162] and indications of possibility of selection of Myrobalan types for peach have been observed in California.[164] Investigations at East Malling have similarly shown considerable variability among St. Julien seedlings in their compatibility to peach; of five clonal selections of this stock tested, three have consistently produced good trees, and two have invariably failed completely;[5] and of two Myrobalan selections tested, one failed, whereas the other produced good trees. Brussels and Common Plum stocks "have always failed completely. . . . Although the buds often start to grow they are invariably dead by the end of the season." Brompton, three Mussel stocks, Pershore, Kroosgespruim and St. Julien de Toulouse stocks always produced 1-year trees rather well, but signs of incompatibility developed in a few years in the peach trees worked on St. Julien de Toulouse.

The Marianna plum, which grows readily from cuttings, has received a uniform series of adverse reports. In 1892, Bailey[16] quoted Onderdonk as reporting the Marianna a failure as a peach stock in Texas; in 1894, Berckmans[37] reported in Georgia that peach on Marianna makes a most vigorous growth in the first year from the bud, "but they soon fail and seldom survive the first year's production of fruit," and in 1895, it was reported in Germany that recourse to an interstock was necessary if peaches were to be grown on Marianna stocks.[286] In 1896 T. V. Munson, who had been hopeful of the Marianna as a peach stock in 1887 and was still finding it useful for plums, reported that peach on this stock dies invariably in from 1 to 3 years. In more recent experiments,[164,205] many trees die suddenly in the middle of the first season, after making growths of 4 to 6 feet. The roots seem to die first. In England, Marianna is reported to give consistently a "goodly proportion" of 1-year old trees.[5]

Peach buds have grown rather well on young stocks of Wild Goose, Miner and other Chickasaw varieties.[158,146] At one time some New York nurseries grew, experimentally, peach on seedlings of "wild, or Canada plum,"[78] and this was endorsed by J. J. Thomas[279] as next in value to the peach stock, but for reasons not now apparent the practice did not continue long. The sand cherry (*Prunus besseyi*) has been used with success as a dwarfing stock for peach.[130]

On apricot stocks the peach tends to break at the point of union,[151] but frequently this combination produces rather long lived and productive trees.[98] Double working with almond or with Sugar prune has been suggested in California.[162] On the Japanese apricot (*Prunus mume*) peaches tend to overgrow the stock; some varietal differences exist, Muir being abnormal almost from the start, while Lovell seems to make an unusually smooth union.[268]

Prunus spinosa (the sloe) has been used occasionally over a long period as a dwarfing stock for peach, with apparently satisfactory results. At South Haven, Mich., *P. mexicana*, which is said to be practically immune to borer attack, exerts a dwarfing influence on the peach, which considerably overgrew the stock, and the combination proved short-lived.[176]

In Iowa it was reported that Russian apricot was short-lived on the roots of certain plums.[59] Some of the trees died without breaking off, death being due to the failure of the roots to receive enough elaborated food from above, though the tops seemed to suffer greatly until the root systems failed.

On the "Karoo" soils of South Africa the peach-almond has found favor as a stock for the peach because of its resistance to soil alkali.[96]

In the Cherries.—In the ordinary course of propagation of cherries few or no well defined cases of incompatibility arise. It is altogether possible that the commonly used Mahaleb stock is mildly incompatible to species grown for fruit; cases have been reported of trees breaking at the graft union, and trees on Mahaleb frequently have a marked "shelf" at the union. But in proportion to the number of trees grown the more striking manifestations of incompatibility are few. English Morello and several sour varieties with red juice have been reported to form defective unions, which seem to become evident more rapidly in dry weather.[60] The considerable variation in sweet cherry varieties and apparent variation in Mahaleb,[127,145] a matter but little investigated as yet, suggest that differing degrees of compatibility may exist and that careful selection in Mahaleb stocks may isolate forms which will retain the several undoubted advantages of this stock and increase average compatibility. Considering the wide range in fruiting types of cherry cultivated it would not be strange if careful study revealed incompatibilities. Withal, the stocks available being what they are, it is probable that, except for a few favored regions, adaptability is a more important consideration than compatibility in the choice of a cherry stock.

On the pin cherry (*Prunus pennsylvanica*) buds of sweet cherry grow readily,[154,296,306] but, as observed in Michigan, sweet cherries on this stock grow to a diameter of perhaps 8 inches, as the stock fails by a wide margin to keep pace and the trees begin to die back in the tops. It has been reported that Duke and Morello cions remain smaller than the pin-cherry stocks[117] and Early Richmond and Dyehouse trees on this stock seem to have been in good condition for 12 years.[16] Most reports are, however, unfavorable.[313] On *P. virginiana* (choke cherry) and *P. serotina* (wild black cherry) failure is usually prompt.[110,143,154]

The sand cherry, which, though classed taxonomically among cherries, shows close grafting affinities to plum and peach, has not proved of any value as a stock for cherries.[270,312] On *Prunus americana* and *Amygdalus davidiana* failure was general.   Grafts of Early Richmond and Montmorency have been reported as growing vigorously early in the season on Miner plum, but the stock died before autumn.[55]   Buds of Royal Amarelle on *P. insititia* (Damson) made rather short growths, bore fruit in the second year and died down as soon as the fruit was ripe.[118]   Grafting cherry on St. Julien plum is reported in France[100] but seems to have excited little comment there or elsewhere.

On cherry laurel (*Prunus laurocerasus*), Leroy[193] reported, after many attempts, inability to secure long existence of cherry cions or even fruiting. Grafts of sour cherry on this stock seem to have fruited well for 5 or 6 years at least.[69]

The Nanking cherry (*Prunus tomentosa*), likewise assigned by taxonomists to the cherries, also grafts better on peaches and plums than on cherry.   In China, its home, it is customarily worked on a peach (*P. davidiana*).[215]   Some union has been secured on *P. pumila* and *P. besseyi*, and St. Julien, Myrobalan, *hortulana* plums, *P. mexicana*, Sapa and Tokeya plums.   On *P. munsoniana*, the Nanking cherry grew well for three years, but the union proved defective.[275]

In the Apricot.—The apricot is commonly budded on seedlings of the apricot or peach, though a survey of California nurseries in 1919 showed that nearly 24 per cent. of their nursery trees at that time were on Myrobalan plum,[163] that stock being used to adapt the trees to soils too heavy or too wet for the apricot or peach.   In England, various plum stocks, especially Mussel and Common Plum, have long been favorites.[199] With all of these stocks good unions are made, except for some varieties on certain of the plums.[101]   The almond has been widely tried as a stock for the apricot.   The young trees grow vigorously but the union is short-lived;[101,307] however, a type known as the "peach-almond," which shows greater compatibility, has found favor on the "Karoo" soils of South Africa, because of its tolerance of soil alkali.[95]

In the Grape.—The development of stocks for European grapes (*Vitis vinifera*) is one of the greatest achievements in horticultural history. Prior to 1870, simple rooted cuttings were used, but the spread of the root louse (*Phylloxera*), to which *V. vinifera* is fatally susceptible, forced recourse to grafting on stocks of resistant American grapes.   These, in turn, presented difficulties, most of them would not grow in the chalky soils which prevail in some of the important areas, and those which showed adaptibility to these soils were not readily propagated or showed lack of congeniality with the desired European varieties.   Hybrids between various American species, particularly *V. riparia* and *V. rupestris*, and the European grapes produced a series of stocks with adaptability to various soil conditions, resistance to phylloxera and ease of propagation.   From these "Franco-Americans" has been selected a series of stocks, each rather well classified for a particular set of conditions, with due regard to the cion to be used.   No one stock is best for all locations.

The European grape (*V. vinifera*) as cion unites with various forms of the Muscadine grape (*V. rotundifolia*) but dies in a few years; its behavior is similar on *Ampelopsis* and *Cissus*.[291] On *Riparias* it shows less, but still noticeable, incompatibility; on *V. labrusca, V. berlandieri* and *V. cordifolia* it seems compatible. Berckmanns[36] reported that Labrusca and Aestivalis grapes interworked readily but that, apparently because of the difference in the texture of the wood, Labrusca varieties would not take on Vulpina. Bioletti[40] recognizes certain of the Vinifera group of grapes as having "defective affinity" in that they do not unite at all well with the stocks in common use; he recommends a special stock for these varieties because it makes an excellent union with them. Among these varieties he lists Emperor, Ferrara, Cornichon, Muscat, Mataro, Folle Blanche, Pinot, Gamay, Gutedel; the stock recommended for them is known as 1202.

Congeniality of Reciprocal Grafts.—Reciprocal or inverse grafts are not always equally successful. This may be due in part to lack of adaptability rather than to a lack of affinity, but there appears at times to be a real lack of congeniality in a graft whose opposite is congenial. In some of Daniel's work the grafts of pimento on tomato seemed rather less successful than those of tomato on pimento.[93] Sahut[255] states that the Mahaleb succeeds as a cion on no other cherry though it is the standard stock for the sour cherry in America and that the pear does better on the apple than the apple on the pear. Baltet states that medlar does well on quince, but the quince fails on medlar; the same holds true with quince on hawthorn and *vice versa*. Sweet cheery on sour cherry is more successful than the reverse combination.[195]

Tufts states: " . . . it has been the experience of certain growers in the Vacaville section, California, that practically all the varieties of Japanese plums will work satisfactorily with *domestica* varieties. However . . . the insertion of European plum scions on Japanese plums does not always result in a satisfactory union. It has been found that plum orchards, where worked over to Japanese varieties, could not be worked back to European varieties unless all the Japanese wood was taken from the tree."[281]

Similar contrasts in reciprocal grafts occur in the combination of various evergreen on deciduous plants. There are numerous instances of at least passable success in grafts of this sort, but the inverse combination, deciduous on evergreen, is almost invariably a failure.

Congeniality and Adaptability.—Congeniality and adaptability are sometimes differentiated only with difficulty, as is shown by the following quotation from Blunno:[44] "In France, however, it was found that the yield of the French vines grafted on *du Lot* was low; our experience is exactly the same at the Viticultural Station, Howlong [New South

Wales]—the wine-grape varieties grafted on this stock are the poorest croppers of all.   In Sicily, however, the affinity between the native European vines and the Rupestris du Lot seems to be perfect and the yield is

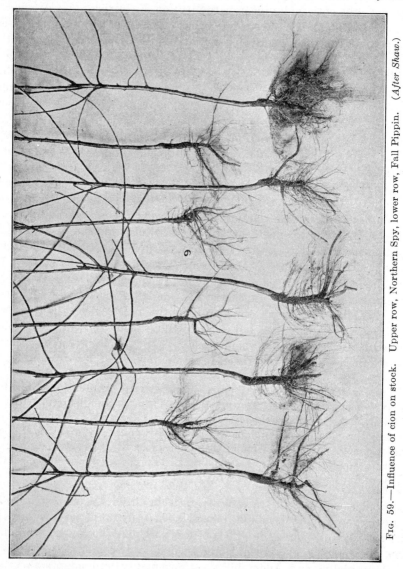

Fig. 59.—Influence of cion on stock.   Upper row, Northern Spy, lower row, Fall Pippin.   (*After Shaw.*)

heavy.   In this state the principal wine-grapes are French varieties and this explains how our experience with vines on Rupestris du Lot as poor croppers is similar to that in France."

The most congenial combination is not necessarily the most successful, as is shown by an experience in New York, cited by Bailey.[17] Plum and peach stocks failed to make satisfactory unions with the apricot and sometimes the trees were broken at the union by high winds. Worked on apricot roots, the apricot made a better union and few trees were lost through breaking off; nevertheless in spite of the congeniality of this combination, the death rate of these trees was higher than that of apricots on other stocks. This evidently is a case of a lack of adaptability being the limiting factor.

Reactions to freezing may dictate the choice of stocks. In the more northern of the prairie states some nurseries work apples on roots of the Siberian crab, despite its disadvantages, because its greater hardiness makes it safer than ordinary seedlings in many locations where winters are intense and snowfall generally light. Even in the recognized fruit-growing areas of the northeastern states, the sensitivity of the quince stock to winter temperatures is one of the factors operative against the use of dwarf trees. The Marianna plum stock is of doubtful value for regions where soil temperatures may run low in occasional winters. The Mazzard cherry, in early days a principal cherry stock in the middle west, was once abandoned completely because of its tenderness to freezing. However well suited the peach stock may be to certain hardy plums, its use in regions where the peach tree is tender, unless snow covering is guaranteed, would be unwise. Working a hardy top on a tender stock does not necessarily make that stock more resistant to cold.

Similarly, there is no evidence that soil requirements are changed by the top, and peach roots under plum tops seem no more able to thrive in heavy, moist soils than they do under peach tops.

From India is reported an interesting case. Brown,[53] trying numerous stocks for Malta and Satsuma oranges, found extraordinary differences in the behavior of the same variety on different stocks and of the same stock worked to different varieties. For the Malta orange the "rough lemon" gave greatest vigor and fruitfulness, the "sweet lime" was suitable only to amateur growing, producing a small tree with a few oranges of high quality, while the citron and sour orange were unsuitable. On the other hand the Satsuma orange gave best results on the sweet lime; the rough lemon and citron proved unsuitable. Figures 59, 60 and 61 show clearly differences associated with the influence of stock on cion and of cion on stock. It is noted by Brown that his results are not in accord with American experience, particularly in the poor growth with the sour orange as a stock for the Malta orange. The Satsuma on the same stock was satisfactory, completely reversing the results obtained in California.

This situation seems analogous to that just outlined for grapes and suggests that adaptability and possibly congeniality may be operative in producing these striking differences and contradictions.

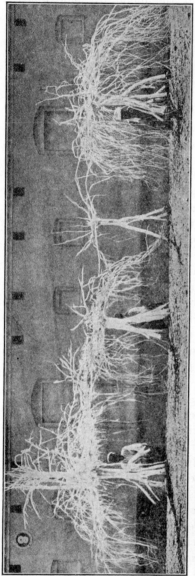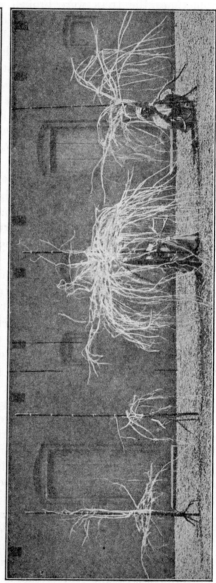

Fig. 60.—Influence of cion on stock in citrus in India. Top, various roots with heads of Sangtara (*Citrus nobilis,* Lour.); lower, same roots with heads of Malta (*C. Chinensis,* Osbeck). From left to right in each picture: (1) "sour orange" or "khatta" (*C. Aurantium,* Linn.), (2) citron or "galgal" (*C. Medica,* Linn.), (3) "rough lemon" "khatti" or "kharna" (*C. Limonum,* Osbeck), (4) "sweet lime" "mitha" or "sharbete" (*C. Limonum*). (*After W. Robertson Brown.*[53])

THE INFLUENCE OF STOCK ON CION

Consideration of the importance of adaptability and of obvious cases of incompatibility, with the possibility that other incompatibilities, less apparent, may exist and be effective though not fatal, leads to the question whether, were these effects fully understood, the effect of stock on cion would not be fully explained. Certainly the cion is not entirely passive in its relationships with the stock; in some cases of dwarfing the relationship is reciprocal or cyclic, each symbiont dwarfing and being dwarfed. On the other hand, some of the rather consistently occurring cases in which a variety appears to grow better on roots other than its own are difficult to explain on the basis of either compatibility or adaptability. Grape growing affords some instances of this sort.

The dwarfing effect of Oldenburg roots on other apple varieties noted by Bailey[20] seemed to extend even to Oldenburg tops, as observed in a limited number of trees at East Lansing, Mich. Budded on seedling

Fig. 61.—Influence of stock on cion. Left, "Malta" orange on *C. Aurantium*, sour orange ("khatta" of India); right, same on *C. Limonum*, rough lemon ("kharna" of India). Twenty-seven months planted. (*After W. Robertson Brown.*[53])

roots Oldenburg is a rather vigorous grower in the nursery and only when fruiting begins does it lag behind in growth.

It seems plausible, therefore, that a given tree or vine may have foliage and branches capable of greater growth than its own roots permit, that the belowground and aboveground parts are not balanced as to potentialities. The explanation does not lie wholly in absorption by the roots or digestion by the leaves or in transport; some stems differ in their ability to utilize the same materials. When Whitney 20 is budded on a nursery tree of Rhode Island Greening and is in turn budded to Rhode Island Greening, both Greening portions outgrow the Whitney segment standing between them. If upward movement were seriously affected, the Greening top would suffer; if downward movement were retarded, the lower Greening portion would be dwarfed. Apparently the Whitney, even with the same water, nutrient and food supply, is unable to make the diameter increase that characterizes Rhode Island Greening. On the other hand, as was reported in 1665,[240] interposition of a segment of one of the Paradise dwarfing stocks between the seedling root and the fruiting top, reduces the growth of the top. Recently it has been shown that certain of these dwarfing stocks, particularly Malling V, even when used as intermediates, do not conduct potassium in quantities sufficient for the well-being of the fruiting top.[295]

Stature.—In general the top of a grafted tree tends to assume a size equal to that of the top which the stock would have formed if ungrafted. There are, however, exceptions and qualifications. Northern Spy, itself a vigorous grower, tends somewhat to dwarf many other varieties worked on its roots.[263] Some varieties of apple form characteristically small trees, while others assume large stature, both worked on similar stock. Certain dwarf varieties of peach remain dwarfed regardless of the stock on which they are worked.

The sour orange is a thrifty vigorous-growing stock, and many orange varieties are regularly budded on it, but the Satsuma, which makes a standard tree on a number of stocks, is very much dwarfed when grown on sour orange roots.[276] In limited trials conducted by Cummings in Vermont,[82] Mazzard cherry budded on Mahaleb stock made much greater growth than it did on its own roots.

It is stated that Grimes and Winesap apples increase in vigor when worked on vigorous stocks.[223] A similar influence is exercised by American persimmon on Japanese persimmon cions.[166] *Prunus pumila* (sand cherry) makes an increased growth on plum stock.[90] Among growers of Vinifera grapes the Rupestris St. George (du Lot) stock is generally known to induce unusually vigorous growth in varieties worked upon it and skilful vignerons recognize the difference when pruning.

Hedrick[140] reports an experiment in which a number of grape varieties more or less grown in the grape regions of New York were studied on three stocks; Clevener, a Labrusca-Riparia hybrid, grown in New York as a direct producing wine grape, Rupestris St. George (or du Lot), a stock obtained through California from France and Riparia Gloire, also a repatriated American. It should be borne in mind that all the cion varieties are commonly grown in this section as direct producers, *i.e.*, on their own roots. In almost every case at least one of the stocks used caused a marked increase in vigor over that of the cion variety on its own roots. Table 1, condensed from Hedrick's data, shows the growth ratings of several varieties as direct producers and on the various stocks. This growth rating should be distinguished from total growth since Hedrick states distinctly that the grafted made less wood growth than the ungrafted vines.

In general, when a symbiotic relation between stock and cion exists at all, there is apparently a tendency toward a balance between the two. The influence is relative. A dwarfing stock is dwarfing because of the limitations on its development relative to the top. There is nothing inherent which impels it to dwarf all tops worked on it. As an example

TABLE 1.—RELATIVE GROWTH RATING OF GRAPE VARIETIES ON DIFFERENT STOCKS
IN 1910
(*After Hedrick*[140])

Variety	Own roots	St. George	Gloire	Clevener
Brighton.................	55.0	56.0	73.7	75.0
Campbell.................	17.3	62.1	54.6	35.0
Catawba.................	40.0	74.0	70.0	81.6
Concord.................	46.0	94.0	90.7	....
Delaware.................	46.0	60.0	68.7	81.6
Herbert.................	64.6	87.5	87.1	....
Iona...................	26.8	45.6	43.0	....
Niagara.................	53.9	84.5	57.5	56.4
Vergennes................	44.1	77.8	69.2	90.3
Worden.................	26.1	36.0	61.6	38.1
Average 20 varieties.....	40.0	63.2	65.2	67.9

the quince may be considered. It obviously dwarfs pears in general, yet it is said to increase the vigor of *Cratægus glabra* Thunb.,[256] while its dwarfing effect on the loquat is slight or absent.[74]

Parenthetically it may be stated that much of the conflicting evidence concerning quince stock is due to the different kinds of quince used. Barry, as early as 1848, noted a mixing of quince stocks as received from French nurseries.[29] Apparently in England until recently the situation has been very much confused.[134]

Form.—Closely related to vigor of growth, possibly interwoven with it, is form or habit of growth. According to Loudon,[202] "*Cerasus canadensis*," naturally a rambling shrub, assumes an upright habit when grafted on the common plum, while *Tecoma radicans* on catalpa forms a round head with pendent branches. *Garrya elliptica*, Sahut states,[258] grafted on *Aucuba* branches less. *Chamæcyparis obtusa pygmæa*, according to Burbidge,[64] worked on *C. Boursieri*, grows erect, while on *Biota* or *Thuya*, or if grown from cuttings, it spreads horizontally on the ground. The same writer quotes Briot to the effect that the *Libocedrus tetragona* is changed from a narrow cylindrical column to a wide-spreading form by working on *Saxegothœa*.

Among fruit plants, the apple, plum, peach and the citrus fruits have been cited as showing in the habit of their tops the influence of the stocks on which they are growing.

Knight[182] described this influence: "The form and habit which a peach tree of any given variety is disposed to assume, I find to be very much influenced by the kind of stock on which it has been budded; if upon a plum or apricot stock, its stem will increase in size considerably, as its base approaches the stock, and it will be much disposed to emit many lateral shoots, as always occurs in trees whose stem tapers considerably upwards: and, consequently, such a tree will be more disposed to spread itself horizontally, than to ascend to the top of the wall, even when a single stem is suffered to stand perpendicularly upwards. When on the contrary, a peach is budded upon the stock of a cultivated variety of its own species, the stock and the budded stem remain very nearly of the same size at, as well as above and below, the point of their junction. No obstacle is presented to the ascent, or descent, of the sap, which appears to ascend more abundantly to the summit of the tree. It also appears to flow more freely into the slender branches, which have been the bearing wood of preceding years; and these extend themselves very widely, comparatively with the bulk of the stock and large branches."

Comparing the growth of the Milton plum on various stocks, Waugh[299] reported: "The trees of this variety growing on Wayland roots are upright narrowly vase-form, with relatively few large branches. They are almost as narrow headed as typical trees of Abundance or Chabot. On Marianna roots, in the very next row, the trees of Milton are low, round-headed, bushy, with thick-spreading, drooping tops, much like trees of Marianna. If anything, they exaggerate the typical character of the Marianna head. Moreover, the leaves are several shades darker and glossier and the twigs are dark red instead of being green as in trees of the same variety growing on Wayland roots. On Americana Milton has almost the same characters as on Wayland."

Somewhat later Stuart,[273] describing these same trees, wrote: "At the present time the differences in color of foliage and bark of young twigs are not noticeable, neither is the 'upright narrowly vase-form' head of Milton on Wayland anywhere near so pronounced. Notwithstanding these modifications, however, there is still a marked difference in the habit of growth of the trees upon Wayland and Marianna stocks. On Wayland the habit of growth is more or less upright, whereas on Marianna the head is low, bushy and spreading. Doubtless, as the trees grow older, these differences will tend to become less marked." On *Prunus besseyi* stocks the peach is dwarfed and assumes a spreading, bushy habit.[130] According to Hatton[136] the Jaune de Metz (Malling apple stock No. 9), which is itself a spreading grower, tends to make varieties budded upon it very spreading in habit. On the other hand, Malling types 12 and 13, which are upright-pyramidal in habit, tend to "close up" the tops of other varieties grown upon them.

Rough lemon stock is said to produce tall upright trees of the varieties worked on it.[46]

Seasonal Changes.—In the orchard or vineyard, cultural practices have, in the majority of cases, no very obvious influence on the time of starting growth, but the effect on ripening and maturity is more marked. The classical experiment of introducing a vine or a branch of a tree into a warmed room during the winter, keeping its connection with the parent stock and observing it start growth while the remainder of the plant is still dormant, would lead to the inference that the cion is practically independent of the stock in the spring flush or growth. So it proves in most cases.

End-season Effects. Ripening of Fruit.—Concerning effects at the other end of the growing season there is some conflict of evidence. It is rather well known that some of the annual species of Convolvulaceæ become perennial when grafted on perennial species.[65] Daniel reports that by grafting the annual parts of certain perennials on certain other perennial plants he has succeeded in prolonging the life of the cions.[87] Conversely, in some instances, cions of perennials grafted on annual stocks have died at the usual time for the stocks, though Lindemuth[197] has shown a case where the plant lived longer. Such instances as these are more striking than those observed in fruit plants, where the possibility of change is necessarily more limited. It is sometimes claimed that grafting in itself hastens maturity in grapes by a few days. Cole[73] states that several growers in Victoria claim a few days earlier ripening in peaches worked on almond than on peach stock, while in France Sahut[258] claims that the Myrobalan plum induces earlier ripening in peaches than does almond stock. Sahut states also that cherries ripen earlier on *Laurocerasus* than on ordinary cherry seedlings and the Reine Claude plum on Damas is said to be somewhat earlier than on St. Julien. Cole reports that heavy autumnal rains in Victoria are not so likely to induce second growth or fall blossoming in plums worked on Marianna roots as in those worked on Myrobalan and attributes this to the early dormancy of the former stock.

In America topworked trees were more common formerly, proportionately at least, than they are now and discussions of mutual influences were correspondingly more frequent. These discussions show a surprising variety of experience and opinion, particularly in the effect of the stock on the time of ripening of fruit in the autumn. Diametrically opposite results apparently come from identical combinations of stock and cion. Hovey recounted extensive combinations of early pears on late and *vice versa* in Massachusetts, without any change from the usual season of ripening. There was, however, rather good evidence that plums on Myrobalan ripened earlier than on late plums. In apples,

Shaw states that "particularly with Rhode Island Greening the season of ripening is influenced by the stock."[266]

The trifoliate stock is generally conceded to secure early ripening in oranges. Florida experience seems to indicate that oranges on rough lemon stock cannot be held on the trees so long as when grafted on sour orange.[294]

The grape, however, supplies the best examples of stock influence on fruit ripening. Wickson states that the Riparias Gloire and Grand Glabre induce ripening one to two weeks ahead of Rupestris St. George. Hedrick found that many American grapes on Gloire and Clevener stocks consistently ripen their fruit ahead of the same varieties on their own roots. In the St. George there was less uniformity of effect; in fact this stock seemed to retard the ripening of some varieties. This difference of a few days is likely to assume considerable practical importance with late varieties in regions where autumnal frosts come early or where autumnal rains are frequent.

Husmann[167] considers that the degree of congeniality between cion and stock influences the time of ripening. From this point of view it may be inferred that the same stock may have a retarding effect on one variety and hasten the ripening of another. Much conflicting evidence, in other fruits besides grapes, may be reconciled in this way.

Table 2, including data taken more or less at random from Husmann's figures, indicates that this possibility may be realized. Taking Lenoir as the standard, grapes on St. George have ripened, in one case 4 days ahead, in another case 9 days after, Lenoir. Dog Ridge has ripened fruit on its cion varieties 2 days ahead and 13 days after the same varieties on Lenoir.

Data introduced later to show differences in the composition of fruit on several stocks may be anticipated here. Those differences that are

TABLE 2.—RIPENING DATES OF GRAPE VARIETIES ON DIFFERENT STOCKS
(After Husmann[167])

Variety	Stock		
	Dog Ridge	Lenoir	Rupestris St. George
Aramon..................	Sept. 29	Sept. 27	Sept. 28
Bastardo.................	Sept. 23	Sept. 20	Sept. 25
Beclan...................	Sept. 28	Sept. 28	Sept. 26
Bicane...................	Sept. 23	Sept. 23	Sept. 24
Blauer Portugieser.........	Sept. 23	Sept. 10	Sept. 15
Boal de Maderc...........	Sept. 28	Sept. 15	Sept. 24
Bolynino.................	Sept. 26	Sept. 28	Sept. 24

found can be considered to represent such as might occur in separate specimens on the same tree or vine. Much of the available data is from European sources, or, if from America, it concerns such plants as are shown elsewhere to be rather sensitive to temperature conditions during the growing season. In other words, nearly all the available data concern plants or situations such that the difference between heat required and heat available is small. The grape in the northeastern states is near the limit of its summer heat requirements; the pear and the apple are not.

The evident readiness of European authorities to recognize small differences in ripening according to the stocks used and the preponderance of American opinion—aside from a few instances—to the contrary can be reconciled if the climatic differences are considered. Just as a few days of unusual heat in the spring will force into simultaneous bloom varieties that blossom at different times in a cooler season, the greater heat at harvest in America probably obscures small differences that would be apparent in a cool region or in a cool season.

End-season Effects. Maturity of Wood.—Evidence of the effect of the stock on the maturity of the wood, on the contrary, seems brought out more clearly in America than in Europe because of the different winter climates and the intimate relation of maturity to hardiness. There is, however, some mention of these effects in parts of France. Baco reports considerable difference in the time of ripening of the wood in grapes, stating: "In recapitulation, the grafted vines ripened their canes less than vines on their own roots. In this respect many grafts have appeared to us to be influenced by the stock about as they would be by nitrogenous fertilizers or by a mellow deep and fertile soil if one had not grafted them."[13] Since these differences have most intimate relation to hardiness, they are discussed under the effects of the stock on hardiness.

The fall of leaves from a deciduous stock does not cause the fall of leaves on an evergreen cion. Though the trifoliate orange is deciduous, other varieties worked on it are not; though the quince is deciduous, a grafted loquat top is evergreen. This holds true in other cases. However, despite this retention of foliage, it is probable that the deciduous stock has some effect tending toward a partial dormancy. Evidence of this lies in the smaller injury at a given temperature to orange on trifoliate than on evergreen stocks and in the possibility of transplanting the loquat on quince without "balling" of the roots, provided the leaves are stripped, though this cannot be done if it is on its own roots.

Spring Effects.—Returning, for the sake of completeness, to the effect of stock on spring growth, the behavior of cherries on Chickasaw plum may be cited as typical. The stock starts much earlier and throws out leaves and shoots while the cherry grafts remain dormant until their customary season of growth."[132]   However, Brown[52] recognizes a delay in blossoming of plums and almonds on certain varieties of plums.   He states: "Blossoms appear on plums from 1 to 2 weeks later than the almond.   Where the plum stock has been tried the delay has been about one-half the difference between the two blooming periods."   It seems quite possible that this difference can exist in one climate and not in another.   A retarded entrance into the rest period in the autumn is shown elsewhere to delay the opening of peach blossoms in the spring.   If the plum stock prolongs growth in the fall, it will evidently have a retarding effect on blossoming in the spring.   However, the rest period is a retarding factor only in climates with mild winters and early springs and it is only in such climates that the retarding influence of plum stocks would become obvious.   In the north the rest period ends before the dormant period and no retarding influence from the stock would be expected.

In New York, sweet cherries and the Dukes have been reported as blossoming somewhat earlier when grown on Mahaleb than when grown on Mazzard stocks, though this influence was not found to extend to the maturing season, nor was it evident in sour cherries.[165]   In England, apples grown on some of the Malling stocks have been found to show differences of as much as 7 days in date of first bloom and 3 days in date of full bloom as compared with blooming dates of the same varieties grown on other stocks.[137]

Baco[11] recorded considerably more copious bleeding in Baroque and Tannat grapes grafted on various American and hybrid stocks than on their own roots.   He also reported differences in the time of breaking of the buds; those on the own-rooted vines opened much more regularly and somewhat earlier than those on the grafted vines.   As a rule the vines on hybrid stocks blossomed later and more irregularly.[12]

Here again, as in the ripening of fruits, it is in Europe and particularly with grapes that more attention is given to slight differences due to stocks and here again climatic factors explain the few differences observed.

Several European commentators are inclined to emphasize the need of substantially the same seasons of growth inception in stock and cion to insure compatibility.   Lindemuth states that his investigations have led him to the same conclusion in this respect as that of Lucas, to wit: a graft of an early starting kind on a late starting kind is never successful: " . . . late starting kinds grafted on early starting stocks, very frequently become sick, since they are not able to take up the quantity of sap which the early-starting seedling offers.   Canker injuries at the point of grafting are very often the consequences of defective grafts of this kind.   Less easily does the early starting cion become sick on late starting sorts.   The more nearly equal in time and strength the growth of the cion and stock are, the better, according to the opinion of Dr. Lucas, is the success of the graft."[203]

An expression of the same influence in the apple in Brittany is furnished by Duplessix;[107] " . . . if one inserts a cion of Doux Normandie [blossoming in June] on a stock from seed of Launette [blossoming late in April], the sap will ascend in the trunk 6 weeks before the graft is ready to receive it. The tree may die. If it lives the sap will accumulate in the swelling at the base of the graft and this swelling . . . can become in its turn a cause of death. . . . If the reverse be tried, the cion of Launette will require sap when the Doux Normandie trunk is not ready to provide it and the cion of Launette will perish or it will grow slowly for want of feeding at a useful time.

" . . . A stock starting earlier than the graft is preferable to one starting later."

Though these two views differ in details, they agree in the general harmfulness of great differences in the starting season between stock and cion. The very fact that these differences can become harmful is evidence against any considerable modification of either stock or cion in season of growth inception.

In brief, then, the influence of the stock on the season of the cion may be stated, for spring manifestations, in Knight's words: "The graft, or bud, whenever it has become firmly united to the stock, wholly regulates the season and temperature, in which the sap is to be put in motion, in perfect independence of the habits of the stock, whether these be late or early." Concerning the effects on autumnal processes, it may be said that some influences exist but may be obscured by the climate and that they are not necessarily parallel to the nature of the stock.

Hardiness.—As to the effects of the stock on the hardiness of the cion there is considerable conflict of evidence, due in part, perhaps, to lack of precise definitions. It is frequently stated in European pomological literature that pears on quince stock are much freer from canker than on pear stock. Elsewhere in this work rather strong evidence is cited to show that the common frost canker of Europe is associated with lack of maturity. Field surveys in Oregon have shown that the common European varieties of pear are more subject to winter injury in the trunk when grown on Japanese pear (*Pyrus serotina*) seedlings than when propagated on the ordinary *P. communis* seedlings.[68] Evidence presented earlier in this section suggests that certain stocks may affect the season of maturity of the tops.

Hardiness has been shown to be involved to a great extent with water-retaining capacity which in turn appears to depend in no little degree on maturity. It may be affected by cultural practices and in some cases, apparently, by the stocks used. The stock may, to this extent, be considered to induce hardiness in the top.   If, however, the conception of hardiness be that of a specific property which is present or absent there is no evidence that it is transmitted from stock to cion.   It is conceivable that a stock may in itself be hardy but through the congeniality of the graft it may actually diminish the hardiness of the cion.

Fruit growers of the upper Mississippi Valley have a well defined belief that such varieties as Jonathan and Grimes are rendered hardier by topworking on Haas, Oldenburg and similar hardy varieties.   It seems plausible that with some varieties there is a certain increase in hardiness due to a slightly earlier maturity; more important, however, is the consideration that the cases under examination are not so much cases of increasing hardiness as they are of substituting a hardy variety in those parts of the tree that are particularly susceptible to winter injury. Even though the hardiness of the cion were not increased in the least, a tree of Jonathan topworked into Oldenburg framework could not help but be hardier, though only within limits.   Macoun,[208] in Canada, top-working such varieties as Baldwin into hardy stocks, was unable to increase the hardiness sufficiently to stand a test winter.

Hedrick[143] reports that Mahaleb stock makes hardier tops in cherries, both in nursery and in orchard, because of the earlier ripening of the wood. *Prunus lusitanica* is said to ripen its wood earlier on *Prunus Padus* stock than on its own roots and to withstand cold weather better, probably on that account.[77]   Budd[55] reports the Jonathan apple ripening its terminal shoots better on Gros Pommier "than on its own roots" and states that "the hardiness of a variety is increased by the influence of a stock with a determinate habit of growth. . . .   In our own State [Iowa] we have evidence that by the selection of proper stock we can grow Jonathan or Dominie on low, wet soils where they would not reach bearing size, root-grafted . . . the main utility with us of top-working on such prepotent stocks as Gros Pommier, Duchess, Wealthy, Wolf River, etc., is in the way of fitting the less hardy scion for enduring the tempera-ture of our test winters."

Experience with grafted grapes in regions where winter killing is important was more extensive in an earlier generation than in the present. The literature of the times shows a tendency to agreement in the increased hardiness of certain varieties such as Iona and Adirondac on hardy stocks such as Concord.   Precise observations as to the reason for this were not common, but the suggestion was made that Iona roots were tender.[237] The increased hardiness was secured, if this be true, by the substitution of a hardy variety in a tender part and not by changing the nature of the cion.   Here again, roots inducing early maturity appear to increase hardiness.   Nicholas Longworth,[159] after extensive trials, reported,

"Foreign vines grafted on our natives are equally tender as on their own stock and are, with me, often killed down to the native stock."

It is not, it should be noted, invariably the stocks inducing early maturity that are hardiest. St. George stocks, as reported by Hedrick, induced late growing in many cases; however, they suffered rather less from winter killing than the other stocks tested. Hedrick suggested that the deep rooting habit of this variety may be connected with its hardiness.

Onderdonk[232] and Vosbury[294] reported that in the Gulf States the trifoliate orange increased the hardiness of the varieties worked upon it and attributed the hardiness to the deciduous habit of the trifoliate, inducing a degree of dormancy in the cion varieties and thereby making them more cold resistant. In the freeze of 1913 in California lemons worked on orange trunks proved more hardy than those in their own trunks, hardier not only in the orange trunks but in the lemon tops. It was suggested[304] that in some way the trunks of the trees modified the dormancy of the tops. This condition was more apparent in young trees than in those in bearing age. As in the Gulf States, trees on trifoliate were somewhat hardier than those on other stocks. In cases of severe injury, however, when the entire top has been killed, the trifoliate is unable to send up any sprouts and dies, though it has not itself suffered any direct injury from the cold weather.

Disease Resistance.—Cole[73] recommends the "Kentish sucker as a cherry stock for fruit growers in Victoria because many varieties are less likely to gum when worked upon this stock than on Mazzard seedlings." Presumably the gumming to which Cole refers is the physiological type. Barss,[32] in Oregon, recommends the genuine Mazzard stock as freer from bacterial gumming than miscellaneous seedlings from the ordinary sweet varieties. This, however, is another case of substitution in part of the tree rather than of change in the part grafted in, since to secure the greater freedon from the disease it is necessary to grow the tree two or three seasons in the nursery or the orchard and then graft it over in the limbs.

Sometimes increased resistance to fungous diseases is claimed from top working, as in the gooseberry on *Ribes aureum*, but no evidence is available of any direct influence. In the case just cited any increased resistance is due probably to the changed habit of the plant, the increased height securing better aeration.

In California the black walnut is used as a stock for the English walnut (*Juglans regia*), in large part because of its resistance to a soil fungus, the mushroom root rot (*Armillaria mellea*), to which the English walnut roots are very susceptible. This is, again, a case of substitution and not an influence of stock on cion.

The claim is sometimes made that certain stocks make the top more or less resistant to insect or fungous attack. Since vigorously growing trees are more subject to aphis or to fire blight and perhaps less subject to certain cankers, it is quite conceivable that a stock affecting growth may indirectly have such an influence. The same effect, however, can be secured by cultural practice and no available evidence indicates any modification of a specific nature in the cion by the stock making it more or less liable to insect or fungous attack.

Virus Diseases.—Diseases of a mosaic nature are, of course, transmitted in either direction by grafting. Since John Lawrence,[189] in 1717, noted the transmission from the cion to the stock of variegation in leaves, this fact and its converse have been cited as standard evidence of the influence of stock on cion or of cion on stock or both. Numerous instances of such transmission are easily found, but have lost much of their significance through the view that in many cases variegation is a pathological condition and that grafting is in such a case also an inoculation. Daniel[91] states that some cases of *court noué* in the grape can be traced to grafting and expresses the belief that it is due to "a kind of physiological trouble induced by osmotic changes caused by the union of plants of different chemical functional capacities." Daniel's statement that the characteristic shortened internode appears also on shoots from the stock suggests a condition similar to the transmission of pathological variegation rather than a specific change due to grafting. Variegation arising from other than pathological causes seems not to be transmitted from stock to cion or from cion to stock.

Physiological Diseases.—Differing somewhat in kind from disorders due to fungous or bacterial attack or to the presence of a virus are those grouped for convenience under the name "physiological." These are associated with disturbances in the intake, translocation and utilization of water and the various mineral elements, the synthesis, accumulation and utilization of various organic substances or with customary and orderly sequence of a number of life processes. A number of these disorders have been described and the circumstances attending their appearance discussed in the sections on Water Relations and Nutrition. Some of the influences of various stock-cion relationships to their occurrence and severity are pointed out here.

Although, in general, water, mineral nutrients and elaborated foods pass through the graft union freely, the evidence indicates that in some instances the union constitutes a barrier that entirely prevents the passage of certain substances, whereas in others it slows down their translocation very considerably. In brief it effects a selective action upon translocation comparable to selective absorption by roots. Hofmann[156] grafted the dark reddish purple Refugee bean on the white Navy bean and found that its anthocyanin pigment, a soluble glucoside, did not cross the union, whichever one was used as the stock.   Similarly Guignard[128] found that a cyanophoric glucoside did not traverse the graft union when either an herbaceous or woody plant elaborating this material was intergrafted with one which does not produce it.

In reciprocal grafts of the red beet and sugar beet the red pigment does not cross the line of union,[39] and, according to Roach,[249] molybdenum is absorbed in limited quantities by Malling apple stock No. 9 but is not translocated up into the tops of certain apple varieties grafted upon it. On the other hand, Daniel[86] has found that atropine passes readily from *Atropa belladonna* cions into potato stocks.   As instances where translocation is accelerated or retarded by the graft union, Eaton and Blair[109] report the boron content of the leaves of a number of different kinds of trees and herbaceous plants varying with the stocks upon which they are grown.   Haas and Halma[129] found that when the lemon is budded on to either sweet orange or grapefruit, the stocks showed a lower magnesium content than when left unbudded.   On the other hand, with sweet orange or grapefruit as the cion variety and sour orange as the rootstock, soluble-magnesium content was higher in the rootstock than where the lemon was used for the top.

Colby[72] has found that certain Malling apple stocks permit the ready downward passage of elaborated foods but seriously interfere with their movement in the other direction.   This is in contrast to the more usual influence of certain graft unions in checking the downward translocation of carbohydrates to the roots[174,190] and thus promoting fruitfulness.

These changes in the composition of different tissues above and below the graft union, to say nothing of alterations in the rapidity and sequence of various processes, doubtless account for greater resistance or susceptibility to certain physiological disorders.   For instance, it has been reported from California[35] that pear trees grafted on Japanese pear or quince stocks develop chlorosis on high-lime soils much more quickly and severely than do those on French stocks.   Similarly, stone fruits on Myrobalan stocks generally show little or no chlorosis, while peaches and apricots on peach stocks may suffer severely.   Presumably these influences are due to differences in the ability of the several stocks to obtain iron from the soil.   Daniel states that grafted beans grown in nutrient solution were free from chlorosis longer than check plants which had absorbed more of the solution.   "Since the chlorosis could not be attributed," he states, "to anything but the presence of an excess of a salt (carbonate of lime, or another), it is necessary to admit that this salt has passed in less quantity because of the different osmosis and because of its utilization at the graft union to neutralize the acidity of the wound surface.   In a word, these results show very clearly that the graft, considered by itself, modifies the regimen of water and of soluble salts, that is to say, of the functional capacities of the grafted plants."

In support of this view he cites Viala and Ravaz to the effect that the Herbemont grape was free from chlorosis on Clairette; likewise Merlot on Viala. It seems possible that these last instances may be due to a high degree of congeniality between the varieties mentioned. Blunno[44] states that many resistant stocks are without chlorosis until they are grafted, but become so afterward, explaining this through the weakening of the plants by grafting. Susceptibility is greater, he reports, when the graft is not well healed and any weakening influence such as a fungus or insect pest, even on a resistant variety, favors infestation by phylloxera.

Yield.—Some commentators are disposed to believe that grafting *per se* disposes the plant to fruitfulness. This is well expressed in this statement: "Seedling apples, especially those which are of a vigorous nature, run to wood and produce few fruits, or begin very late to produce them. Grafted apples, on the contrary, begin earlier to fruit."[106] . . . Undoubtedly early bearing is favored by grafts which have not united perfectly, just as it is by ringing or by any influence obstructing translocation. Comparatively few exact data are available indicating whether or not grafts which unite readily have the same effect. However, Hodgson and Cameron,[155] reporting on their propagation studies with Citrus in southern California state that five rootstocks, namely, sour, sweet and trifoliate oranges, grapefruit and rough lemon, came into bearing two seasons earlier when budded to themselves than when unbudded. This difference was not associated with any dwarfing influence, as the trees were of essentially the same size. The mere presence of the graft union thus caused the trees to fruit earlier than naturally.

Precocity of bearing is necessary to the success of any variety in cultivation; deficiency in this respect is the chief objection to the Northern Spy apple and the chief reason that it is now so little planted. Naturally, then, grafted trees of cultivated varieties tend to come into bearing early; otherwise the varieties would not be in cultivation. Some varieties come into bearing at an earlier age than others, though all are grafted presumably on the same stocks. This time can be hastened or retarded by cultural means. Vigorous seedlings are late in bearing; so are vigorous grafted trees.

The influence of different stocks on the functioning of the cion is shown neatly by experiments such as those of Lindemuth[198] on potatoes. This investigator found that the potato on *Datura*, a vigorous growing stock, forms aerial stolons freely. The combination plant grows vigorously and manufactures much starch which cannot go into tuber formation as it would in an ordinary potato plant. It is, therefore, because of the vigor of the stock, utilized in the conversion of the potato stolons into leafy shoots.   On a weakly growing stock, however, such as *Capsicum annuum*, starch accumulation exceeds utilization and tuber formation ensues from the buds which on *Datura* stocks give rise to shoots.

Fruit-bud Formation.—Voechting[293] "has shown that buds which grew from the base of the inflorescence of a beet in the second year came out as leafy shoots supplied with large leaves, if they were grafted on a 1-year beet; on the contrary, they infloresced if they were placed on a stock already in its second year."

Leclerc du Sablon[190] shows differences in total carbohydrates in the tops of Angoulême 2 years grafted on pear and on quince stocks. Except in May the carbohydrate content of the pear on quince is higher than that of the pear on pear.   In view of the importance of carbohydrate content to fruitfulness this difference seems of possible significance, though it is comparatively slight at the ordinary time of fruit-bud formation.

TABLE 3.—TOTAL CARBOHYDRATES IN TOPS OF ANGOULÊME PEARS GRAFTED ON PEAR AND ON QUINCE

(After Leclerc du Sablon[190])

(Per cent. on dry weight basis)

	ON PEAR	ON QUINCE
Jan. 19	23.7	25.9
Feb. 26	21.7	25.4
Mar. 28	24.3	27.9
May 9	21.6	21.3
June 17	22.2	22.6
July 22	22.6	22.9
Sept. 7	24.5	25.8
Oct. 16	23.4	25.4
Nov. 22	23.4	25.3
Dec. 26	23.4	25.5

Specific citations are hardly necessary to show the influence of certain stocks on fruit-bud formation.   The dwarfing stocks, through limiting growth and therefore carbohydrate utilization, have a general tendency to permit sufficient carbohydrate accumulation for free formation of fruit buds.   European and Japanese chestnuts, for example, worked into chinquapin, bear in 1 or 2 years.[76]   The kumquat is said to bear heavy crops while still a mere bush when budded on trifoliate orange stock.[276]   It should be remembered, however, that the total framework on which fruit buds can be formed is smaller and the total production of fruit buds on a given area of ground is not necessarily greater and may even be smaller, when dwarfing stocks are used.   In some cases certain stocks not dwarfing in themselves make poor unions with cions set in them and exercise a dwarfing effect.   Some Wildgoose plums are said to be more fruitful on peach roots.[131]

These instances are introduced here, not as showing a general tendency toward any marked influence of stock on cion, but rather the dearth of more positive evidence. Considering the amount of topworking that has been done, little evidence of a change of practical importance has been accumulated. There has been a general tendency to assume that if there is any influence on the size of fruit the dwarfing stocks tend to produce larger fruit. Most of the instances just cited fail to bear out this idea.

In Victoria Cole[73] reports that many varieties of plums which are shy bearers on Myrobalan stock are prolific on Marianna. "Although some varieties . . . somewhat overgrow this stock it is no great fault but an improvement—it influences the bearing qualities of varieties so inclined to overgrow."

In France some years ago, according to Pepin,[234] there was a dwarfing apple stock, neither Paradise nor Doucin, known as the Pommier hybride or bâtard; grafts on this grew vigorously but bore little fruit and that little was inferior.

Bioletti,[41] reporting on the St. George grape stock, states: "In some cases the vines grow well but the crops are unsatisfactory. This has

TABLE 4.—PRODUCT OF PANARITI GRAPES ON DIFFERENT STOCKS AT FRESNO, CAL.
(*After Husmann*[168])

Stock	Yield (in pounds per vine)		Sugar content (Balling scale)		Acid as tartaric (grams per 100 cubic centimeters)	
	1917	1918	1917	1918	1917	1918
Adobe Giant.............	7.5	7.5	30.5	27.0	0.9675	0.8770
Aramon × Rupestris Ganzin No. 1..............	21.0	11.0	28.0	26.0	0.7650	0.8255
Dog Ridge..............	3.0	3.0	26.5	28.0	0.8300	0.8250
Lenoir.................	1.5	2.0	28.0	26.0	0.6450	0.7500
Mourvedre × Rupestris No. 1202..............	8.0	1.5	23.5	28.0	0.8700	0.7575
Riparia Gloire...........	5.0	2.0	23.5	30.0	0.8850	0.9450
Riparia × Rupestris No. 3309.................	17.0	20.0	28.5	26.0	0.8650	0.8250
Rupestris St. George......	6.5	2.0	28.5	26.0	0.7800	0.8550
Salt Creek..............	8.0	1.5	28.0	26.0	0.7800	0.8175
Solonis × Riparia No. 1616.................	24.5	19.0	29.0	26.0	0.6900	0.8325
Average..............	10.2	6.95	27.4	26.9	0.80775	0.8310

been noted only in rich valley soil of the coast counties and only with certain varieties.   A similar condition has often been noted in Europe, but it is usually easily overcome by longer pruning and diminishes with age."

Husmann[168] shows very striking differences in the product of the Panariti or currant grape on various stocks in California, as shown in Table 4.

Rolfs[254] suggests a difference in the value of different stocks for the mango.   The kumquat on sour orange roots grows a vigorous tree but it is practically barren.

Fruit Setting.—A casual survey of European literature shows a considerable body of opinion to the effect that the setting of fruit is influenced sometimes by the stock on which the fruiting wood is worked.   Particularly does this appear in grapes.   Ravaz is quoted to the effect that in sandy soils strong growing stocks fail to set fruit and for this reason many of the Riparia and Rupestris hybrids are not well suited to such soils.[292] Baco[12] found the short and reflexed stamens characteristic of many hybrid stocks, but very rare in the pure Vinifera, produced in Baroque grafted on 1202.   These characters have been shown in the section on Fruit Setting to be associated with lack of viability in the pollen.   Though it is not clear from Baco's account whether this condition was universal on this stock, he recorded it on other stocks also, including the Rupestris du Lot (St. George).   Consequent upon this condition was a considerable amount of *coulure* and of *millerandage*.   Nevertheless, he recorded a general increase in production on these same stocks.[15]

Rupestris du Lot stock is reported to cause poor setting of fruit in many Victorian vineyards;[44] the vigorous growth of this same stock produces coulure in some varieties in California.[308]   Odart, writing before the days of phylloxera in Europe, stated that the Raisin des Dames set fruit much better when grafted on the common white Muscat;[158] Burbidge[61] cites similar cases from the experience of forcing house grape growers.   Baltet[25] states that the Cabernet grape when grafted is exempt from coulure beside own-rooted plants that are badly affected and quotes Hardy: "Graft the Chasselas Gros-Coulard, even on itself, and you will be resisting coulure."   In Australia when the Kieffer pear is grown on wet soils better setting occurs if quince roots are used.[73]   Sahut[258] states that *Chionanthus virginica*, grafted on ash, flowers abundantly but never fruits, while as a seedling it bears.

Size of Fruit.—So many factors affect the size of fruit that often it is difficult or impossible to determine from the evidence how much influence may be attributed to stock.   Stuckey, however, reports that, though the pecan grows well when grafted on hickory (*Hicoria alba*) stocks, 13 varieties averaged 109 nuts to the pound, compared to 51 to the pound when grown on pecan roots.[274] Sometimes grape growers imagine an increase in the size of the individual berries when certain stocks are used. Burbidge,[62] for example, cited an instance in which the Gros Guillaume grape was considered to form larger berries on Muscat of Alexandria than on Black Hamburg. Pepin[234] stated that certain almonds grafted on bitter almond or on St. Julien plum stocks bore smaller fruit. His statement of a stock which produced small fruit in the apple has been mentioned earlier. Daniel[93] found that tomato grafts on pimento produced less fruit than on their own roots and that the fruit was generally smaller. The Golden Pippin in England when worked on free growing stock was said to be larger, mealy and poorer in keeping quality than on less vigorous stock.[211] In America some of the older generation of pear growers thought that small fruited varieties, such as Dana's Hovey, bore larger fruits when worked on vigorously growing stocks. The sand cherry has been said to produce larger fruits on *Prunus americana* than on its own roots.[130] Many California growers believe that peach roots induce larger fruit in both European and Japanese plums than plum or almond roots.[281] Hedrick,[142] however, reported no difference in numerous varieties of apples grown on Doucin, Paradise and standard stocks.

TABLE 5.—AVERAGE YIELD PER VINE OF OWN ROOT AND GRAFTED GRAPE VARIETIES,
1911
(*After Hedrick*[140])

Variety	Own roots, pounds	St. George, pounds	Gloire, pounds	Clevener, pounds
Campbell.................	16.00	23.69	20.41	18.35
Concord.................	16.20	16.93	.16.95	....
Vergennes...............	17.36	22.13	24.52	21.17
Herbert.................	12.21	11.89	14.95	....
Iona....................	15.17	16.42	17.68	....
Niagara.................	20.51	22.55	24.57	21.79
Catawba.................	15.37	12.95	16.41	21.94
Delaware................	12.75	24.25	14.25	17.75
Brighton................	14.43	15.56	13.06	17.40
Worden..................	10.37	16.47	15.95	15.71

Reference has been made to the greater growth of American grapes on certain stocks in an experimental planting in New York.[140] The same investigation showed much greater productivity in the grafted vines. Typical comparisons are shown in Table 5, condensed from Hedrick's results. Summarizing, on an acre-yield basis, the results for all varieties, including many not listed in the table just given, the yields by stocks for that year were, in tons per acre: on own roots, 4.39; on St. George,

5.36; on Gloire, 5.32 and on Clevener, 5.62.   Averages for 3 years were in the same order of magnitude.

"The crop on the grafted vines was increased," Hedrick states, "through the setting of more bunches and the growth of larger bunches and berries.   The increase in the number of bunches was easily determined by actual count but for the statement regarding size we have only the fact that the proportion of unmarketable grapes was greater on the ungrafted than on the topworked vines.   The greater fertility of the varieties on other than their own roots cannot be ascribed to larger vines. No data are available as to size of vines but judging by the eye alone the grafted vines do not make as much wood as do the varieties on their own roots."

It should be stated that there is by no means a unanimity of opinion as to the effect of dwarfing stocks on the size of the individual fruit, even in Europe.

Quality.—Practically all the older authorities were agreed that in some cases the stock influences the quality of the fruit borne by the cion; as to the extent of this influence there was more diversity of opinion.

Downing,[103] writing in 1845, stated: "A slight effect is sometimes produced by the stock on the quality of the fruit.   A few sorts of pear are superior in flavour but many are also inferiour, when grafted on the Quince, while they are more gritty on the thorn.   The Green Gage, a plum of great delicacy of flavour varies considerably upon different stocks; and Apples raised on the crab, and Pears on the Mountain Ash, are said to keep longer than when grown on their own roots."

Barry[30] spoke of the Beurre Diel pear as, "Sometimes gritty at the core on pear stock; invariably first rate on the quince."   Again, of the Glou Morceau: "like the Duchesse d'Angouleme, Louise Bonne and some others, it is decidedly superior on the quince."[31]

Lindley[200] wrote: "It is not merely upon the productiveness or vigour of the scion that the stock exercises an influence; its effects have been found to extend to the quality of the fruit.   This may be conceived to happen in two ways— either by the ascending sap carrying up with it into the scion a part of the secretions of the stock, or by the difference induced in the general health of a scion by the manner in which the flow of ascending and descending sap is promoted or retarded by the stock.   In the Pear, the fruit becomes higher coloured and smaller on the Quince stock than on the wild Pear, still more so on the Medlar. . . . Mr. Knight mentions such differences in the quality of his Peaches. . . . Since the quality of fruit is thus affected by the stock, it seems allowable to infer that the goodness of cultivated fruits is deteriorated by their being uniformly worked upon stocks whose fruit is worthless; for example, the Almond or the austere Plum can only injure the Peaches they are made to bear, the Crab the Apple, and so on."   Lindley cites with apparent approval numerous other instances of the sort.

A generation later the grape growers of France were forced by the ravages of the phylloxera to confront this question in connection with the grafting of their Vinifera varieties on American vines whose fruit was, at the best, of indifferent quality. Much misgiving was felt lest the quality of the wines made from the new combination plants should be inferior to that of the older vines on their own roots. This great experiment, one of the greatest pomological experiments the world has seen, has failed to show any consistent deterioration in the quality of the product that could be attributed to the use of American stocks. In fact, at times wine from grafted vines has brought higher prices than that from the same varieties on their own roots.[26]

Sahut cites among instances where the quality is not injured by the stock, Vinifera grapes on American stocks, cherry on Mahaleb, almond on bitter almond, apricot on the common plum. In some cases, he states, more, larger and better fruits are secured by particular stocks, as in pears on the quince, apples on the Paradise, peach on the almond. The loquat on hawthorn, he states, is more perfumed and less acid than on its own or on quince roots, while of pears on hawthorn some retain and some lose their quality.

Some years ago California citrus growers hesitated to use sour orange stock through fear of spoiling the quality of their fruit, but extensive tests have shown no differences induced by either sour or sweet stock.[219]

Swingle[276] reports that the Satsuma orange on sweet orange stock bears fruit that is coarse, dry and insipid, as well as being later in ripening than on trifoliate stock, while on the latter the fruit is much improved in quality. Elsewhere the incompatibility between this orange and all stocks except trifoliate is discussed.

In Pomaceous Fruits.—Riviére and Bailhache[248] present 3 years' average analyses of Triomphe de Jodoigne pears from trees of equal age, standing side by side, one on quince, the other on pear roots. The fruits on the standard tree averaged 280 grams in weight, those on the dwarf, 406 grams; total sugars per liter of juice: in the standard, 93.4 grams, in the dwarf, 102.3 grams. The investigators calculate that a crop of 300 fruits would produce on the standard tree 7 kilograms of sugar and on the dwarf, 11. Two years' investigations on Doyenné d'hiver showed: On quince stocks, average weight of fruit, 435 grams, sugar percentage in juice, 11.59; on standard, average weight of fruit, 230 grams, sugar percentage in juice, 9.04.

Commenting on some experimental tests of dwarf apples in New York, Hedrick[142] states: "It is a common claim that dwarf apple trees produce larger, handsomer and better flavored fruits than standard trees. There is little in these three orchards to substantiate these claims. There are differences between trees on the three stocks but they are as often as not in favor of standards as of dwarfs."

In Stone Fruits.—For the stone fruits Knight[183] may be quoted: "But I have subsequently planted two trees (of Moorpark apricot) growing upon plum stocks, and two upon apricot stocks, upon the same aspects, and in a similar soil, giving those upon the plum stocks the advantage of some superiority in age, and I have found the produce of the apricot stocks to be in every respect greatly the best. It is much more succulent and melting, and differs so widely from the fruit of the other trees that I have heard many gardeners, who were not acquainted with the circumstances under which the fruit was produced, contend against the identity of the variety. The buds were, however, taken from the same tree.

. . . . . .

"I have also some reasons for believing that the quality of the fruit of the peach tree is, in some cases at least, much deteriorated by the operation of the plum stock."

In Grapes.—Curtel[83] reported a difference in must from Pinot grapes on their own roots and on Riparia roots. More careful studies in 1903 are recorded in Table 6. In his discussion Curtel stated that there were differences according to the variety and the stock and that since the amount of organic nitrogen was thought to explain the observed differences in susceptibility to wild yeasts the matter might assume considerable practical importance.

TABLE 6.—ANALYSES OF JUICE EXTRACTED FROM GRAPES
(After Curtel[83])
(Parts in 1000)

	Pinot on Riparia	Pinot on own roots	Gamay on Solonis	Gamay on own roots
Dextrose	87.30	81.07	153.50	158.70
Levulose	102.05	98.05	. . . . . .	. . . . . .
Total acidity	9.20	8.54	10.43	8.60
Bitartrate of potassium	8.47	8.51	9.41	10.43
Phosphoric acid	0.46	0.61	. . . . . .	. . . . . .
Organic nitrogen	4.02	3.17	. . . . . .	. . . . . .
Ash	5.15	5.45	. . . . . .	. . . . . .
Tannin	1.05	1.85	1.04	1.10
Coloring matter	100.00	126.00	100.00	106.00

Bioletti compares grapes grown on certain stocks:[40] "The quality of the grapes was in nearly all cases, where a comparison was possible, better on *Riparia* stock than on St. George. The grapes were larger and sweeter. The higher sugar content was, moreover, usually accom-

panied by higher acidity, showing that the grapes were better developed."
Quantitative data are shown in Table 7.

Husmann[167] uses sugar and acid determinations of grapes as a test of
the congeniality of the graft. Extensive determinations were made to
test the effects of various stocks on the quality of the fruit. "These
tests," Husmann states, "have yielded very interesting and suggestive

TABLE 7.—COMPARISON OF COMPOSITION OF GRAPES ON RIPARIA AND ON ST. GEORGE
(*After Bioletti*[40])

Variety	Stock					
	Riparia Gloire		Riparia Grande Glabre		St. George	
	Sugar	Acid	Sugar	Acid	Sugar	Acid
Valdepenas............	27.5	0.65	....	....	23.5	0.56
Zinfandel...............	26.5	0.92	....	....	24.0	0.85
Gros Mansene...........	24.1	1.20	26.7	1.12	....	....
Fresa..................	25.6	0.92	24.0	0.83	....	....
Vernaccia..............	27.5	0.84	27.6	0.92	24.2	0.61
Marsanne..............	23.3	0.50	25.0	0.67	21.6	0.62
Chardonay.............	25.0	0.60	22.8	0.87	....	....
Sultana................	24.0	0.75	....	....	24.7	0.75
Cornichon.............	....	....	20.3	0.77	18.4	0.65
Mean.................	25.4	0.80	24.4	0.86	22.7	0.67

data which, when contrasted with the growth ratings of the same vines
based on observations and measurements of growth during the same
growing seasons, indicate that there is a close correspondence between
these important chemical constituents of the fruit and the congeniality
of graft and stock as determined by observation of growth. Similar ratings of the growth of a variety grafted on various stocks are found to be
accompanied by fairly definite percentages of sugar and acid. Under
like conditions of growth the sweetness and acidity of the fruit, as well as
its time of ripening, are evidently materially influenced by the congeniality of the graft and stock."

This is of considerable importance. It indicates that the congeniality
of the graft is influential rather than the stock and that the same stock
may with one variety increase the sugar content and with another decrease
it.

Qualitative Differences and Quantitative Variations.—Since composition, ripening and keeping quality of fruits are more or less related,

an effect produced on one of these implies an effect on the others.   It was stated, many years ago, that there was a month's difference in the keeping quality of Hubbardston apples grown on Hightop Sweet and on Roxbury Russet in the same soil and with the same culture.   Rhode Island Greening on Hightop Sweet was said to be only a fall variety.   The crab stock of England made the Golden Pippin keep longer than did the free stock.   Daniel,[92] who states that Labrusca stock has a rather unfavorable action on the table and wine qualities of certain white grapes, does not specify the nature of the action.

These differences are quantitative rather than qualitative.   No evidence is available showing a qualitative change in fruits, in the sense of an introduction or a manufacture of entirely different compounds, emanating from the stocks used.   Furthermore, accepting all the cases alleged, there is still no clear evidence of any change beyond such differences as could be effected by changes in maturity.   A reference to Ravaz appears to show a possible relation of the stock to quality in fruit.   It is stated[308] that, "to secure high gravity must in his opinion it is stocks with Riparia-like behavior which should be selected—one requires vines with slow and regular vegetation, the activity of which ceases early in the season.   In a word, the vines should behave in as nearly as possible the same way as though they were growing on a dry hillside."

Apparently, then, the nature of the fruit the stock bears is a matter of indifference; the two possibly important factors are (1) the vegetative habits of the stock, (2) the congeniality of stock and cion.   In the light of present knowledge of the formation and ripening of fruit, it would be difficult to arrive at any other conclusion.   An apple is sweet or sour according as it contains more or less sugar; the acid content is fairly uniform.   This is determined largely in the spur or the neighboring branch; the trunk or roots cannot have much effect on it.   The roots may keep the tree growing late and so influence the ripening, but the quality of the fruit the stock bears cannot be expected to influence the top.   A stock with good fruit but unsuitable vegetative habits might influence the cion to produce inferior fruit and *vice versa;* a stock of a sweet variety may make the fruit of a cion sweeter or more acid.

Longevity.—In Michigan[48] and New York,[144] plum trees budded on peach roots are likely to be short-lived, not because their tops are any more tender to cold than those of trees growing on plum roots, but because the peach roots themselves are more subject to winter injury.   Similarly, in the colder sections cherry trees are likely to be short-lived if grown on Mazzard roots.[48]   These, however, are instances of a lack of adaptability of the stock to its environment rather than of any direct effect on the cion.

There are, however, numerous instances of shortened life on the part of the cion associated with a lack of compatibility with its rootstock.

The high mortality rate in peach trees budded on Myrobalan or Marianna plum stocks,[164] after making a vigorous growth on them for a year or two, is a case in point.   The rather sudden decline of lemon trees 12 to 20 years old budded on sour orange stock in southern California is similarly attributed by Newman[226] to a lack of congeniality.   In Michigan, sweet cherry budded on *Prunus pennsylvanica* has been found to behave in the same way.[253]   It is the generally accepted view that processes greatly increasing fruitfulness tend to hasten the ultimate death of the plant. This opinion has ample corroboration in the dwarf apples and pears and in recent years has been a very real problem to grape growers.   Blunno[44] mentions some instances that have a bearing here.

"The Riparias, which are considered excellent stocks for loose, rich, deep soils such as are found on river flats, have given some disappointment in a few places in Sicily and Algiers," he states.   "For the first few years vines grafted on them are loaded with fruit, which over-production seems to exhaust the plant. . . .

"Similarly the Riparia × Rupestris No. 3306, which is generally planted in practically the same classes of soil as the Riparias and the R × R No. 3309, in soils a little stiffer, have gradually given signs of exhaustion in various localities. . . .   Wherever the Riparia and Riparia × Rupestris hybrids failed it was always noticed that the exhaustion followed several years of very heavy crops; those vignerons who managed, by a skilful pruning, to keep the vines from yielding so heavily, have these vines still in bearing."

Sometimes grafting has opposite effects.   Without specifying as to the effect on fruitfulness, Jost records that *Pistacia vera* (the pistachio nut) as a seedling lives at the most 150 years, on *P. lentiscus* only 40, while on *P. terebenthinus* it reaches 200 years.

General Influence of Stock on Cion.—Such evidence as is available on the influence of stock on cion has been presented.   This influence wherever it is positive, is, almost without exception, quantitative.   There is no doubt of the influence of stock on vigor and form of growth; there seems little reason to doubt some influence of the stock on the termination of the growing season, which is, after all, only a phase of vigor.   If, now, the effect of stock on vigor be accepted, most other influences of stock on cion can be explained through that one influence.   Few of these influences differ from effects that might be secured from so manipulating cultural conditions as to modify vigor.   Cultural conditions can be changed to induce early fruiting or late growth or earlier ripening or hardiness or disease resistance or increased fruit-bud formation or better setting of fruit or larger or better ripened fruits.   Girdling the grape will increase the sugar content and size of the fruit.   The dwarfed trees of China that bear inferior undeveloped fruit are on their own roots;[201]

the inferiority of the fruit is brought about by manipulation, not by any influence of stock on cion.

The influence of the stock on cion is not to be minimized; much harm has come from ignoring it. Frequently it is of extreme importance. However, it is important to the cion mainly as its vigor is important to the cion and as the graft union is satisfactory; the cion, for adjustment to one locality or purpose, may require a vigorous stock; for adjustment to another locality or purpose it may require a less vigorous stock or one that thrives in a soil of peculiar character. Adjustment of stock to cion, then, should be made with these factors in mind. In addition, the choice of stock should, where choice is possible, be made with soil, pests and cultural practices in view; conversely these should be considered in their relation to the stock as well as to the top.

INFLUENCE OF CION ON STOCK

Instances of apparent influence of cion on stock are more striking in plants other than those grown for their fruit, possibly because the interest of the fruit grower is centered chiefly in the cion and minor influences on the stock are less likely to attract attention. Furthermore, an influence of cion on stock might involve a reaction on the cion and so be attributed to the effect of stock on cion. However, a few cases, some undoubted and some less clearly defined, are available for consideration.

Just as among the influences of the stock on the cion, the effect on vigor and form of the cion is the most obvious, possibly because most readily observed, so among the effects of the cion on the stock those on vigor and form of the stock are most conspicuous.

Size and Number of Roots.—Daniel,[85] working with various Cruciferæ, found that in some cases when the cion belonged to a species of greater height than that of the stock it accelerated the growth of the latter and that, when conditions were reversed, an inhibiting effect was exercised. Sahut[259] stated: "If the cion belongs to a more vigorous species or variety it stimulates the vigor of the stock. The common hawthorn, grafted with hawthorn bearing double pink flowers, with *Sorbier des oiseleurs*, *Azerolier d'Italie* and the common *Robinia* grafted with *R. decaisneana*, develops much more rapidly. It is the same with the majority of European vines [grapes] when grafted on American York Madeira or Rupestris stocks which are less vigorous. If the cion is less vigorous it restrains the vegetation of the stock. The Dwarf peach of Orleans, grafted on peach or almond, and Chinese plums on Damascene or St. Julien [are examples]. It is the same with the majority of European grapes on Riparia or Jacquez."

Instances drawn from American experience are not lacking. Swingle[276] states: "Although the Trifoliate is naturally a small tree and of slow growth, when used as a stock its growth is so stimulated that its diameter always continues greater than that of the scion. . . . This form of union wherein the stock slightly outgrows the scion has been noticed also in the case of the loquat grafted on the quince growing at Eustis, Fla. In this case, also, the variety so grafted began to bear when still very young and has borne abundant crops since." Bonns[46] confirms the large growth of the trifoliate stock, even while it is exercising a dwarfing effect on the lemon tops worked on it.

Brown[51] states that the Myrobalan root system is larger than usual if it is worked with peach tops.

Bioletti and dal Piaz[43] compare Zinfandel and Tokay grapes growing on Rupestris St. George stocks. Here the stocks are cuttings and therefore even more comparable than most seedling stocks. The greater growth of the Zinfandel top is balanced by a corresponding development of the root system.

Whether the cause be incompatibility, poor graft union or something else, there is apparently sufficient evidence to warrant the statement that in some cases the cion does influence the stock. Since pruning the top of any tree, regardless of the stock, tends to reduce the root system and since some dwarf trees are kept so only by heading back, the necessity for seeking a mysterious influence is not apparent. A top which will not grow vigorously may be expected to act on the stock as would a heavy pruning; a top which is able to supply the roots with abundant food may be expected to increase their growth. Nevertheless, caution should be exercised against ascribing too much to this effect. Some grape stocks cannot grow fast enough to supply some cions; the sand cherry cannot be developed by a vigorous top to the size necessary for the successful support of a rapidly growing plum. If the implied effect of stock on cion be admitted, limitation in that of cion on stock is obvious.

Distribution and Character of Roots.—Possibly because the root systems of nursery plants come under observation much more than those of the same plants once they are set in orchard or vineyard, there is considerable evidence of an effect of cion on stock in young fruit plants. Nurserymen frequently identify certain pear or apple trees by their root systems, though all are on seedling stocks. Hovey,[211] however, himself a nurseryman, indicated that this could not be done in all cases; some strong growing varieties, he stated, would have strong, and weak growers such as Winter Nelis would have correspondingly weak, root systems. It is stated that the roots of trees grafted with Siberian Crab "generally run down more than those of other trees."[211]

Murneek[223] states: "Upright growing varieties of apples of the Russian type, for instance, will form a correspondingly deep growing root system while those of the Winesap type will be flat and shallow. This can be extended even to particular varieties. The Red Astrachan, Oldenburg, Fameuse, for example, form each a characteristic root system of its own. In this connection, Shaw believes 'that the size or stoutness of the main branches is positively correlated with the size of the main roots and angle of the branch with the angle of the main roots and the axis of the tree. In many individual cases this correlation is obscure, yet careful observations with large numbers of trees will reveal it.'" Bailey[18] stated that Northern Spy and Whitney tops make the roots of the stock grow deeper than usual. In England, it has been reported that when the Lord Derby and Beauty of Bath varieties are grown on Malling apple stock No. 6, nearly 60 per cent. of the roots are fine and fibrous, but with Grenadier and Newton Wonder tops, less than 40 per cent. of the roots are fibrous.[138]

Waugh,[298] discussing plum propagation, reported: " . . . Stoddard tops seem to give some of the curved tap-root character of the Americanas to all the stocks on which they grow. . . . One interesting point was in the way in which Stoddard tops induced a conspicuous branching of the root system when worked on peach. With other varieties the peach gave almost always a clean, unbranched tap-root. The weak growth of Green Gage naturally served to induce only a weak growth in most of the stocks on which it was worked; while the rampant growth of Chabot had exactly the opposite effect. The strongly branching root systems found on Chabot trees were probably due in part to the energetic way in which the foliage acted during the growing season. Marianna stocks, which seemed to be uncongenial to Milton, giving only a poor union, made very little growth when grafted with Milton scions. No other case was observed in which Milton appeared to have any influence on its stock. Newman seemed to influence all stocks in the way of giving off more secondary roots. Nearly all stocks when grafted with Newman gave a strong, vigorous growth, considerably above the average, tending at the same time to produce more both of secondary roots and of fibers." In the following year he reported: "No case was observed this year in which the scion showed any marked effect on the stock."[299]

Baco[14] cites numerous grape stocks in which the roots grow more spreading when grafted with Baroque; among these are: Riparia Gloire, Rupestris du Lot and Riparia × Rupestris 3306. On the other hand, Chasselas × Berlandieri 41 B becomes deeper rooted when grafted with the same cion variety. This last stock, it is said, succeeds best in warm, dry seasons and the deeper penetration of the roots is held to be disadvantageous in many locations and seasons.

Longevity, Growing Season and Hardiness.—Some rather spectacular instances of modification in growing habits of stocks are reported.

Lindemuth[198] grafted an *Abutilon* cion on the roots of an annual plant, *Modiola caroliniana*, and thereby kept the combination plant alive 3 years and 5 months. *Althœa narbonnensis* has tops which die to the ground every winter. Grafted with *Abutilon Thompsoni*, a plant of *Althœa* with no other top could not secure the proper materials for forming winter buds and died. Another specimen, similarly grafted, but sending out a sucker from the root, lived and kept the cion living over a year. Daniel[87] obtained similar results with *Solanum pubigerum* on Giant tobacco, which is an annual in Brittany.

Sahut[259] cites numerous instances of evergreen cions, as *Cratœgus glabra* and *Raphiolepis* on the common quince, etc., succeeding on deciduous stocks. However, these cases lose some of their significance in the light of present knowledge of winter processes in deciduous plants. The same writer states that when the late opening St. Jean walnut is grafted on the common walnut the stock "is obliged to hold back a month or more. Deciduous cherries," he states, "on the Laurier-Amande (evergreen) make the stock rest almost absolutely. The varieties of grape which push out late, Carignane, for example, grafted on Riparia or other American species which start sensibly earlier, hold the stock back. The European early starting grapes, as Aramon, when on late American stocks, as York Madeira, force the stock to earlier growth."

Perhaps more definite information may be secured from certain instances where the cion appears to have an effect on hardiness. Since this is in many cases a matter of maturity the effects recorded may be considered equally as effects on maturity.

Vard[289] in an extensive survey following the severe winter of 1890–1891 in France found that rose stocks which had supported cions of Tea and Bourbon roses had not only lost their cions but were themselves killed back to the ground. Unbudded stocks or those which had supported hardy varieties suffered little.

Following the cold winter of 1913 in California Webber and others found some apparent cases of "a definite influence of the tops upon the stocks. In one case," they report, "in the spring of 1912 a nursery of sour seedlings was budded to Eureka lemons. Many of these buds did not take, so that during the freeze of January, 1913, there were in this nursery, at the same elevation and under the same conditions, yearling lemon tops on sour stock (buds had been inserted several inches above the ground) alongside of sour seedlings. While a slight injury to the foliage was the only harm experienced by the latter, the lemon tops were killed, and the frozen wood extended 3 to 4 inches down on the sour stock. Similar conditions were found on pomelo stock while the pomelo seedlings were scarcely touched."[304]

Other Influences.—Sahut states that quince roots topworked to pear are more particular in their soil requirements than those not worked over; they require a more fertile soil. However, as he indicates, the general rule is to the contrary; otherwise the selection of lime resistant, drought resistant and moisture resistant stocks would be to no point. The cion itself does not render the stock subject to phylloxera or immune to woolly aphis, though a lack of congeniality may induce weakness and hence a lack of recuperative power. The transmission from cion to stock of variegation has been discussed previously; it cannot be regarded as an instance of true influence exerted on the stock by the cion.

In General.—Just as in the case of stock on cion, in considering the influence of cion on stock it is seldom necessary, so far as fruit plants are concerned, to predicate any direct effect other than on vigor. Every other influence that has been established or attributed can be explained as exercised indirectly through vigor and can be placed on a quantitative basis. This action on vigor may be direct when the two parts to the graft are congenial and make a good union, or it may be indirect when there is apparent uncongeniality and the union is poor. Qualitative influences, such as the passage of alkaloids across the graft, or the barring of inulin by the graft, are not necessary to explain any observed phenomena resulting from grafting in fruit plants.

CHAPTER XXXII

THE ROOT SYSTEMS OF FRUIT PLANTS

The choice of stocks for the various fruits, where any considerable latitude is possible, is frequently rather complex. First, two economic interests are concerned, the grower's and the nurseryman's; second, several natural factors, the congeniality of the union involved, the relation of the stock to the soil, to the climate and to the variety. Rarely is it possible to secure a stock that meets all requirements in all situations; the result is generally a compromise.

CONFLICTING INTERESTS OF NURSERYMAN AND FRUIT GROWER

The nursery business, like most businesses, is competitive. The individual nurseryman is, therefore, sometimes compelled to adopt certain alternative choices which may not be to the best interest of the grower or, ultimately, of the nursery business itself. The responsibility for this situation rests not with the nurseryman alone, for as long as growers will buy cheap trees, ignoring their real value for the conditions under which they are to be grown, all nurseries are more or less forced to offer cheap trees and often find difficulty in selling better. The nurseryman's immediate interest, then, rests in securing stock that is cheap, that makes a good union, with a high percentage of successful grafts, and that makes a marketable tree quickly.

The plums, with the multiplicity of species cultivated for fruit and of species available for stocks, serve as an excellent illustration of conflicting interests and factors. Some years ago it became evident that for successful plum culture in the north central states a very hardy stock was necessary. The Americana stocks met the growers' requirements very well in nearly all respects. However, seed for growing the stocks in large quantities was not readily available. The Marianna stock, rooting readily from cuttings in the south, was much cheaper. Trees on Marianna roots could be produced at little expense and were sold at a price which virtually precluded competition from the better suited, but higher priced, trees on Americana roots. Want of discrimination on the part of buyers of nursery stock made this situation possible. Waugh furnishes another illustration. The St. Julien plum, he states, is the best stock for Domestica plums, making "a better, stronger, longer-lived tree than Myrobalan." He proceeds to quote a nurseryman's letter,

in part, as follows: "St. Julien stocks are much preferred by the orchard-
ists in this locality, because trees certainly do better in every way on that
stock.   They sprout less from the root, are longer-lived, and generally
more vigorous than when on Myrobalan stocks.   We occasionally plant
some St. Julien seedlings, but do not make a practice of it, because in
the first place St. Julien seedlings cost more than double the price of
Myrobalans, and they are not as thrifty the first year they are transplanted.   They also are attacked by a fungus which causes them to lose
their leaves early in the summer, thus preventing the budding of the
stocks altogether, or a partial failure in the buds when this leaf fungus is
not corrected.   Of course, when taken in time we can in a large measure
prevent this falling of the leaves by spraying with Bordeaux mixture, but
taking all things into consideration, it is quite a bit more expensive to
raise plums on St. Julien stock, and we find that we cannot get any more
for them in the open market, so that we have become discouraged growing
stocks on the St. Julien root."   Hedrick quotes J. W. Kerr of Maryland
to the effect that though for that section he prefers the peach as a stock
for the Domestica plums, there are many varieties of this species that
will not form a good union with the peach and in these cases he is forced
to use Marianna or Myrobalan stock.

Growers of Vinifera grapes have found that no one stock is suitable
to all conditions.   Cuttings of a given species may not root freely and
it is eliminated from the list of available stocks, no matter how resistant
it may be to phylloxera or how desirable in other respects.   Another
species or variety may not give a large percentage of successes in bench
grafting and the establishment of a vineyard on this stock becomes a
matter of more labor and greater expense.

Dawson[97] gives the scarcity of seed as the chief reason against the
employment of *Pyrus betulæfolia* which he states would be a very satisfactory stock for pears on dry soil.

The Mazzard stock for cherries is preferred by growers in some sections, but nurserymen have rather forced the use of Mahaleb. . The
Mazzard has several features which make it rather unsatisfactory for the
nurseryman; one of these is its sensitiveness to weather conditions in
the nursery row so that though buds may take readily one season the
following year may give entirely unsatisfactory results, or the budding
season may close abruptly before the work is complete.[124]

Enough evidence has been introduced to show that the best stock for
the nurseryman, under existing circumstances, is not always best for the
grower.   The responsibility, however, rests with the grower.   When he
is so convinced of the superiority of a given stock that he is willing to pay
the price for it, the nurseryman will produce trees on that stock.   Until
the grower realizes that the best stock in the orchard may not be the

best stock in the nursery or *vice versa* the nurseryman can do only as he has been doing.

ADAPTATION OF STOCKS TO PARTICULAR CONDITIONS

Further, it must be remembered that a plant that is valuable to the grower in one location may prove otherwise in another. Climatic conditions may simplify the choice for a certain grower by eliminating all but the most hardy stocks, but they may complicate matters for the nurseryman who is selling to a wide territory.

Adaptation to Soil Temperatures.—A grower ordering stock from a nursery in a milder climate should consider that he may be getting trees with stocks not adapted to his conditions. A northern grower, for example, securing plum trees from the south, would do well to make sure that they are not on peach or Marianna roots, though some of the leading nurseries no longer use these stocks. The southern grower may be more interested in securing a stock that will not sucker or in extreme cases, as cited by the Howards,[161] he may even require a stock that is able to endure high soil temperature. These investigators found that in Baluchistan the peach and plum stocks commonly used in Great Britain would not succeed, but by using stocks which they considered better adapted to hot, dry soils, such as Marianna, Myrobalan and Mahaleb, they secured much better results.

Adaptation to Soil Texture and Composition.—Prune trees in the Pacific northwest have been planted in many cases without much regard to the stock on which they were worked. In numerous instances prunes with peach roots have been planted in rather heavy, poorly drained land in which the planting of peach trees would not be considered.

French horticulturists had not solved the problem presented by phylloxera when they had isolated certain varieties of American grapes that were resistant to this pest, that lent themselves to making good cuttings and satisfactory graft unions with the Vinifera cions. Many of the French vineyard soils are strongly calcareous; in these soils only comparatively few of the American vines flourish. Hence, ability to withstand calcareous soils must be considered in any choice of stocks for rather wide use in France. When California vineyards were invaded by phylloxera the stocks tried and approved in France were naturally given early consideration. However, lime tolerance is not so important in California since comparatively little vineyard soil is calcareous; of much greater importance, in some localities in this state, is ability to withstand drought, in others ability to flourish in soils with a high water table for part of the year. Rupestris St. George (du Lot), because of its deep roots, withstands drought better but suffers severely when the water table stands near the surface for long; the shallow rooted Riparia Gloire and certain

Berlandieri hybrids meet requirements here. Most Vinifera-American hybrids adapt themselves to these conditions. The Muscadine grapes also are adapted to moist soils and hot climates.[225] In California, as in France, ignorance of local conditions and of the stocks suited to them may indeed lead to utter failure.

Other plants than the grape prove refractory on calcareous soils in France and in many cases recourse to a lime resistant stock has proved successful. Dental[99] furnishes an instance in the Australian *Acacia dealbata* which grows freely in calcareous soils on *A. floribunda* though on its own roots it will not grow in such soils. A similar expedient is necessary for the growth of certain pines in these soils. Some Australian experience seems to indicate that sour orange is the best stock for orange and lemon in sections where the irrigation water is likely to contain alkali in considerable quantities.[292] California experience indicates that lemon is unusually susceptible to alkali.[178] On the other hand, lemon roots are stated to be the best foragers in poor soils in this section. *Prunus davidiana* is now under trial in California as an almond stock; the particular quality commending it is its ability to grow in more alkaline soils than other commonly used almond stocks.[278] Two successive plantings of peaches in one California orchard were killed by alkali; following this peaches on Davidiana roots have proved successful in the same soil.[281] Cock[70] states that the trifoliate orange, though it is too dwarfing in its effects to be a commercial success, may be used to advantage in very wet soils. In the Gulf States the trifoliate succeeds in rich, moist soils and is unsuited to light, dry soil.[294] Pomelo in California appears to suffer most from drought.[46] Sahut[258] states that in wet soils the peach and apricot grow better on plum roots than on their own or on almond roots and that the cherry on Mahaleb grows in poor soils where it would not grow on its own roots. Myrobalan roots are reported from California as being more tolerant to wet soils than most other plum stocks.[290]

The degree of refinement to which adaptation of stocks can be carried is shown by Bioletti's tentative recommendations of stocks for Vinifera grapes in California:[40]

"The Rupestris St. George has given its best results in the hot, dry interior on deep soils. . . .

"For a great majority of our soils and varieties the two Riparia × Rupestris hybrids 3306 and 3309 promise to be superior in every way to the St. George. The former for the moister soils and the latter for the drier. . . .

"For the wettest locations in which vines are planted—in places where the water stands for many weeks during the winter, or where the bottom water rises too near the surface during the summer—the most promising stock is Solonis × Riparia 1616.

"For moist, rich, deep, well-drained soils, especially in the coast counties and on northerly slopes, the St. George is utterly unsuited. The crops on this stock, in such locations, are apt to be small, and the sugar content of the grapes defective. In these locations the Riparia Gloire is much to be preferred, and will undoubtedly give larger crops of better ripened grapes.

"None of the above stocks give good results, as a rule, in very compact soils. For such soils the most promising varieties are 106[18] in the drier and Aramon ✕ Rupestris No. 1 or 202[13] in the wetter locations. In dry, shallow soils 420A and 157[22] give promise of being excellent stocks."

Some stocks show such catholicity in taste that it is safe to grow trees on them for planting in all locations that are at all suited. The California black walnut, for example, adapts itself to so many soils that it is almost universally used in California as stock for the English (or Persian) walnut, though its resistance to root rot (*Armillaria mellea*) is also an important factor.

Sorauer[269] quotes Lieb to the effect that *Pyrus malus prunifolia major* and *P. m. baccata cerasiformis* have been found valuable as stocks for apple in very exposed or dry positions.

Immunity or Resistance to Soil Parasites.—Adaptation to soil must be paralleled at times by adjustment to diseases. The Damson plum seems rather resistant to crown gall and in special cases might be given preference for this reason. Shaw has found that cion-rooted apple trees show crown gall in different forms according to variety. "Thus," he states, "the Jewett apple shows usually if not always the hard form of the gall, the Red Astrachan the simple form of the hairy root and the Oldenburg the woolly knot form with many soft fleshy root growths. Other varieties show the brown root form and still others often the aerial form. . . .

"Some varieties on their own roots seem to be largely if not entirely immune to this disease. If this proves to be really the case, here may lie the solution of the problem of the prevention of crown gall. . . . Probably the economic advantage would warrant the extra effort necessary to propagate such trees, only under conditions where the crown gall was especially troublesome.

"There are other root diseases which are injurious, especially through the southern part of the apple belt, that might possibly be avoided in a similar fashion."[264]

The pear affords an interesting example. The so-called Japanese pear (*Pyrus serotina*) is more resistant to blight than the French stock, but seems rather susceptible to mushroom root rot and is sensitive to soil moisture. In Oregon, standard varieties propagated on it are reported[68] as being more susceptible to winter injury in the trunk and its fruits as more susceptible to "black end," both disorders being associated with unsatisfactory water relations at certain seasons. Choice between the two may at times involve nice discrimination. In some soils the lemon suffers from root rot to such an extent that other stocks are substituted. In Florida the sweet orange roots formerly used as stocks were so badly attacked by root rot that this stock has been superseded. Similar susceptibility is found in California. In regions subject to pear blight the displacement of French seedling pear stock by other stocks, such as *Pyrus serotina, P. ussuriensis* and *P. calleryana,* that are resistant or immune can be forecasted, except as other troubles may develop.

PROPAGATION BY CUTTINGS

Under this head are considered the various forms of cuttings, layers, stools and the like which depend on the formation of roots from the wood of the variety to be cultivated, without the intervention of grafting or budding. All plants thus propagated are on their own roots. The list of fruit plants so propagated commonly includes the fig, olive, grape, currant, gooseberry, mulberry, filbert and pomegranate from hardwood cuttings; the various dwarfing apple stocks and quince from mound layers or stools; the strawberry by rooted "runners;" the black raspberry, loganberry and dewberry by rooted tips of canes, the red raspberry and blackberry by suckers; the cranberry and blueberry by hard or soft wood cuttings or by "tubering" or "stumping" as the case may be. If pomological literature be searched at all carefully there appear some rather surprising additions to the list of plants that can be propagated by cuttings, particularly by hardwood cuttings, including frequently the citrus fruits, plums, pears and apples.

"Some of the plums grow well from cuttings. This is especially true of Marianna, and millions of Marianna cuttings are made every year in this country, mostly for stocks. . . . The St. Julien plum grows fairly well from cuttings, and nearly all the Myrobalan varieties may be propagated this way. Some of the Japanese varieties, especially Satsuma, have been grown from cuttings in the southern states. Practically, however, propagation by cuttings is confined to the Marianna."[300]

That the apple may be propagated by cuttings is indicated by quotations from Knight, though possibly he is describing what is now known to be a rather common pathological condition in the apple.

"There are several varieties of apple tree, the trunks and branches of which are almost covered with rough excrescences, formed by congeries of points which would have become roots under favorable circumstances; and such varieties are always very readily propagated by cuttings."[181] The Paradise and Doucin stocks root more or less readily from cuttings.

Darwin[94] cites Tennent as saying, "in the Botanic Gardens of Ceylon the apple tree sends out numerous underground runners which continually rise into small stems, and form a growth around the parent tree."

Ribston Pippin is said in England to grow readily from cuttings.

Again quoting Knight: "Peach and Nectarine trees, particularly of those varieties which have been recently obtained from seed, may be propagated readily by layers, either of the summer or older wood; and even from cuttings, without artificial heat; for such strike root freely."[184]

Advantages and Disadvantages.—Propagation by cuttings may or may not be advantageous; there is nothing in the process itself that makes it one or the other. When it is readily accomplished it is obviously the cheapest process, but the plant may do better on some other roots than its own. Many varieties of roses are budded on Manetti or other stocks rather than being grown from cuttings in order to obtain a more thrifty vigorous growth.

The lemon is reported in Australia[73] as inferior on its own roots, being more susceptible to unfavorable soil moisture conditions. The Vinifera grapes root readily from cuttings but the roots so formed are subject to phylloxera infestation; recourse is therefore made to grafting these grapes on resistant stocks which in turn are grown from cuttings. The Oldenburg apple on its own roots appears decidedly inferior,[263] though McIntosh and Stayman make notably fine growth on their own roots. Sometimes when it would be desirable to have trees on their roots their failure to root readily from cuttings makes the process impracticable. Many of the apples and plums that are extremely resistant to cold winter weather form, if set deeply, roots from the cion that are much hardier than those of the stocks commonly supplied. A method of ready propagation by cuttings in such cases would be of great advantage. To meet this difficulty special methods have been devised; these are discussed presently. To take advantage of the relative immunity of Northern Spy roots to the woolly aphis, Australian growers have, since about 1870,[280] taken considerable pains to develop these roots, either by layering, stooling or grafting with a "starter," and upon the Spy stock work the variety they wish to grow. In some cases, then, fruit plants which grow readily from cuttings are grafted on other stocks at greater expense; in other cases, plants which do not form their own roots readily are induced to do so, though such plants are more expensive.

Objection is sometimes made to plants propagated by cuttings as compared with those developed on seedlings, because of certain supposed shortcomings. They are occasionally said to be shallow rooted; Hatton,[133] however, states, regarding dwarf apple stocks: "We have found it just as possible to raise stocks of deep anchorage by layers and other vegetative methods as it is easy to find shallow-rooted ones in any collection of free stocks raised from pips." This supposed shallowness of the root system was turned to account by the early Spanish settlers of Louisiana, who propagated the peach by layering to suit it to alluvial

lands where the water table is high.[238]   Cock,[71] writing on citrus fruits in
Victoria, states that layers and cuttings are always weak and more liable
to disease than seedlings.   Macdonald,[207] also in Victoria, writing of the
olive, states: "It is possible that, in poor soils or trying situations, the
seedling may be the more thrifty and long-lived tree, but experience in
this country has not gone to prove that this is the case.   Many of the
oldest trees in Australia were raised from truncheons and are still doing
well.   However, their age is comparative youth in the life of the olive
tree, and perhaps it is as well to accept the opinion of continental writers
on the greater longevity of seedling trees until there is greater evidence
at hand to the contrary."

In New South Wales seedling plums are considered to make better
root systems than cuttings.[3] Grapes, gooseberries and currants have
passed through many generations of cuttings, without perceptible
diminution in vigor.   The process, therefore, apparently is not *per se*
devitalizing.   It has, moreover, certain marked advantages, one of
which is uniformity of the roots.

This uniformity in the roots frequently is of considerable importance.
The constant tendency to variation in seedlings is not confined to quality,
color and size of the fruit but extends to every character of the plant.
They may vary in vigor of growth as much as in the color of the fruit;
the quality of fruit varies no more than the stature; the depth of rooting,
resistance to cold, to drought, to moisture, to alkali, all are variable
characteristics.   Hatton[133] states: "Free stock is a comprehensive term,
meaning no more than seedlings which include dwarf stocks both fibrous
and stump-rooted, as well as vigorous ones resulting from a well-balanced
root system."   The seedling root, then, is in a measure an unknown
quantity.   The tree planted in the orchard is standardized above ground,
uncertain below ground.   The stock for any individual tree may be more
vigorous or more hardy or more resistant than the average; it is just as
likely to be less so.   In France the prospective grape grower whose soil is
strong in lime knows that certain stocks do not thrive on those soils; he is
able to pick a lime-enduring stock, for grape root stocks have been standardized through growth from cuttings.   If, however, he has a rocky,
thin soil in a hot, dry exposure, he can select another stock, known to be
the best for such locations.   Were he to rely on seedlings he would be
indulging in a lottery whose results could be told only after a year or more.
To replace those which failed he would use more unknown quantities.

Grapes in Particular.—Varietal differences in the character of root
systems produced from cuttings are recognized in grapes.   Bioletti and
dal Piaz[43] explain the susceptibility of Riparia and the immunity of
Rupestris stocks to drought by the shallow roots of the former and
the deeply penetrating roots of the latter.   In poorly drained soils and

in soils with the water table high for any length of time, these same peculiarities tend to reverse the order of suitability. Hedrick suggests that the small amount of winter killing of grapes on Rupestris St. George stock as compared with that on other stocks in an experimental vineyard in New York may have been due to its deep rooting habit.[140] The advantage of having stocks of known performance is obvious.

Apples and Pears in Particular.—Fortunately apple and pear stocks are fairly adaptable. They seem so, certainly—perhaps because there is no standard with which to compare them. However, every careful grower recognizes that some of his trees consistently bear more or less than others. This raggedness may be attributed to minor variations in soil and doubtless correctly so in many cases; it is sometimes attributed to bud variation, though the work of Crandall[80] suggests the doubtful importance of this source of variation. The unevenness in a seedling orchard strongly suggests that were the tops all removed and grafts of one variety inserted on the roots the resulting trees would show considerable differences in vigor and productiveness. Mention is made elsewhere of results in Missouri showing considerable variation in seedling apples.

Hatton[133] states, in the course of a comparison of Paradise, free and crab stocks: "We are faced, then, with two converging series quite arbitrarily divided, the one ranging from dwarfness to vigour and the other from vigour to dwarfness; the only real distinction being that the Paradise series has been raised vegetatively, and any particular member of the series can be reproduced by that method again and again, whilst the free series has been raised from seed, and as long as this method is employed infinite variety and inequality will continue, except in rare cases.

"It is often argued that 'true crabs' are less variable than 'ordinary free stocks' but I cannot learn what the trade distinction stands for. If free stocks are the chance children of cider fruits, crabs (commercial not botanical) are the chance progeny of wildings; but every district has many, many so-called crabs varying in vigour and character. I have seen them strong and clean; dwarfing and root knotted, whilst the types of fruit are various. I do not pretend to assert that free stocks from particular sources may not be more even than from other sources. That simply depends on the chance crosses, on the varieties mixed or cross pollinated, which in some cases may be more advantageous than in others; but I do say that stocks raised from pips will always be variable, and therefore incompletely satisfactory, except for the purpose of raising new types of stock for subsequent vegetative propagation, if we find degeneration or imperfection in the existing types."

Examination of an orchard, injured here and there by root killing, forces belief in the variation shown by the seedling roots and an appreciation of the desirability of a stock that is uniformly hardy. If a vigorous, hardy, resistant stock could be isolated and propagated, much of the unevenness in yield and uncertainty in hardiness would be eliminated.

Furthermore, the importance to the experimenter of having each tree on its own roots should be emphasized. The lack of uniformity in yields of trees in the same plot in fertilizer, cultural or pruning experiments has done much to invalidate results and more definite conclusions might well be expected if the root systems as well as the tops of the trees were identical.

Vegetative propagation of apple stocks seems not only of probable value but worthy of study as a real possibility. Hatton[133] in a paper of great importance reports that in the investigations of Paradise apple stock at East Malling one type was isolated which is free growing, not in the least dwarfing in its effects; this stock is propagated readily by vegetative methods. Further study of this type and search for others like it seem of great importance. The great amount of variation found by Hatton gives promise of isolating stocks which will show particular adaptabilities to different conditions in a manner comparable to those now catalogued for grapes and of making possible much finer fitting of trees to environment.

Propagating Apples and Pears by Layerage and Hardwood Cuttings.— Investigation of propagation of apples and pears by hardwood cuttings seems of possible value as well. These cuttings root readily in the tropics and in some of the southern states, such as Florida, Mississippi and Texas, and could perhaps be rooted elsewhere if proper soil temperatures were provided. Kieffer and LeConte among pears and Northern Spy among apples seem to root especially well, though this ability is possessed by other varieties. Similar cases have been reported in England.

Warcollier in France is reported to have had mediocre results with cuttings of 30 to 50 centimeters of the previous season, well ripened; success was possible only with soft wooded varieties. Others in France reported very satisfactory results using branches of 3 or 4 years' growth, with side growths removed, plunged into the soil to a depth of 10 to 25 centimeters. Varieties of moderate or feeble vigor, particularly one known as "Petit doux," gave the best results.[108]

The propagation of the Northern Spy stocks used for all apples in Victoria is chiefly from layers and stools. The parent Spy stocks are planted 2 feet apart in rows 4 or 5 feet distant in June (autumn in Australia). The processes followed are described by Cole:[73] "In August cut back to within an inch of the ground level, so as to get a supply of buds to or below the soil to push out. The following August cut back to two buds any weak or light growth, pegging down the stronger parallel with the row or other planted stocks. The buds upon the pegged-down growths, being now brought into a vertical position, will send up a sufficient supply of shoots for working upon sound lines. About November, mould them up lightly by removing some of the higher soil from the middle of the rows. During the following winter remove soil about the layers and cut away any light shoots that may have rooted hardening back others close to the main layer.

"The propagator should not be too eager in removing rooted shoots from the main layers until after the fourth season, but will be repaid by cutting hard back, forming good, well-rooted crowns for future use.   From now out the operator will require to use his own judgment regarding the growths he cuts hard back and those he leaves for pegging down after removing any that may be rooted.   In the winter mould up after cutting away any rooted stocks and the pegging down is finished, and again in November or December.   Deep or over moulding should be avoided.

"*Stooling.*—This method is somewhat similar to that of layering, but instead of pegging down the unrooted shoots they are cut hard back each year, so as to encourage as many as possible to show out.   The second season from planting, and after the shoots have been cut back to within an inch or so of the stool, mould lightly, and again in November or December.   If the shoots do not root, this moulding will cause them to become bleached close to the crown of the stool. Upon being hardened back, shoots that give the best results will be formed. When removing rooted shoots in the winter, leave any that are very small for the following year; also any that are weak and spindly. . . .

"The cooler and moister districts are the best adapted for the raising of Spy stocks by these two methods (layering and stooling), as the rooting of the shoots is controlled by even moisture during late summer and early autumn.   From healthy, old, and well established stools, and those putting up medium and not over-strong shoots, the best results are obtained.   The writer advises that layering and stooling should be worked conjointly."

The use of Northern Spy stock is mentioned by Wickson[307] in California. Paul C. Stark, however, states that Northern Spy has not proved satisfactory in the central states, as a stock, forming knots on the roots and rooting with some difficulty.

In the northern central states where seedling roots have proved tender in the cold winters recourse has long been made to an indirect method of securing trees on their own roots.   Long cions are whip grafted on small pieces of seedling roots and planted deep.   Roots are formed more or less freely from the underground portion of the cion; since the varieties grown are necessarily hardy the roots seem to share in this hardiness and have proved actually hardier than the average seedling roots.   In a short time these cion roots generally outgrow the seedling starter which becomes much reduced in proportion and plays an insignificant part in the mature tree.

Varietal Differences and Contributing Factors.—Varieties differ in the readiness with which they emit roots in this way.   Shaw[265] found that some varieties root readily, others only in very niggardly fashion; Baldwin, for example, showing 32 per cent., Ben Davis 51, Sweet Bough 98, Delicious 22, McIntosh 74, Jonathan 11, Grimes 41, Gravenstein 55, Northern Spy 58, Oldenburg 25, Tolman 3, Winesap 34, Wolf River 71,

Yellow Bellflower 3, Yellow Transparent 26. He found also that the same variety performs differently from year to year, possibly from internal conditions, possibly from external. Stark reports that Delicious forms cion roots very readily and the roots are aphis resistant. Moore[221] reports on similar work in Wisconsin. Of the varieties tested Livland Raspberry, Hyslop, McMahon, Pewaukee and Transcendent showed cion roots on 50 per cent. of the trees studied, in the third year. Cion roots are formed more readily in moist soil and, because of this, Moore concludes that grafts planted deep form roots more readily. Table 8, reproduced from Moore's report, shows the difference in cion root formation in moist and in dry soil. At East Lansing, Mich., Red Astrachan and Fameuse were notable for abundant cion root formation; these varieties have a pronounced tendency to form roots in clusters immediately below the bud, while in Northern Spy the roots have a more diffused origin.

Recent investigations in Iowa show that the formation of cion roots is much accelerated by winding the point of grafting tightly with a copper wire.[169]

TABLE 8.—CION ROOTS PRODUCED IN APPLE UNDER DIFFERENT SOIL MOISTURE CONDITIONS

(*After Moore*[221])

Variety	Trees observed		Cion-rooted		Strong cion-rooted	
	Moist	Dry	Moist, per cent.	Dry, per cent.	Moist, per cent.	Dry, per cent.
Peerless............	263	311	42.6	31.4	6.1	5.8
Northwestern......	142	328	63.4	24.1	18.3	2.7
McIntosh.........	94	110	56.4	29.1	21.3	1.8
Hyslop............	40	98	100.0	50.0	100.0	23.5
McMahon.........	31	103	87.1	32.0	58.0	10.7

Maynard[214] mentions the use of short pieces of apple roots as nurse grafts for refractory quince cuttings. "The apple root," he states, "supplies moisture and a little food material until roots are formed on the cion, when it fails to grow more, and we have the quince on its own root."

Another method of propagating trees on their own roots is the planting of own-rooted trees secured as just described and taking cuttings from the roots they form. This depends on the formation of adventitious buds on the roots which some species and some varieties accomplish readily while others apparently do not.

Finally should be mentioned propagation of fruit trees, especially some of the plums and some varieties of apple, from sprouts arising on the roots.   This method is perhaps more common in some sections of Europe than in the United States, partly because the varieties grown lend themselves to this treatment and partly because of the very positive, if somewhat exaggerated, prejudice in the United States against root stocks which sprout freely.

SOURCES OF NURSERY STOCK

With certain reservations it may be said that the proximity of the source of nursery stock is unimportant.   Apple trees grown in Maryland nurseries and then set in Minnesota were found to be as hardy and to grow as well as trees of the same varieties raised in Minnesota.[50]   If the stock is healthy, well developed and well matured, it will grow.   Some of the ornamentals, grown from seed, tend to mature earlier if from northern seed than if from southern and there may be temporarily a somewhat readier response to climatic changes in vegetatively propagated plants from one section than from another but, if there is, it quickly disappears and there is little or no evidence that it is of any practical importance.

It should, however, be realized that different stocks are used in growing certain fruits by nurseries in different parts of the country and that this may be of extreme importance.   The northern plum grower, for example, is more likely to get hardy plum roots from a nursery near home than he is from a nursery whose chief clientage is in a section with milder winters.

For fall planting, northern growers will be more likely to get well ripened trees from northern sources where the trees naturally mature earlier.   That this may assume importance is shown in the section on Temperature Relations.

Withal the mere mailing of an order to a local nursery is not always a guarantee that the stock sent to fill the order is of local origin.   Many nurseries buy much of their stock from distant points.   However, if the stock is good and, in cases where a difference in roots is important, if the roots are of the right kind, the grower need not concern himself greatly about its origin.

GRADES OF NURSERY STOCK

Fruit trees are offered for sale by nurseries in several grades, which are based on size as measured by either height or diameter or both.   Since the largest trees cost the most, the question whether there is any ultimate advantage in them is of practical importance.

The very fact of the grading shows the difference between individuals. If this is a temporary matter, due to better immediate environment of one tree in the nursery row there will be no final difference in the growth and performance of these trees. The rather extensive studies of Tukey and Brase in New York[283] indicate that a considerable part of the variation in size of seedlings upon which apple and cherry trees are ordinarily propagated is due to spacing and other factors of environment and a relatively large proportion of the small seedlings will produce medium to large nursery trees upon being budded or grafted over. If, however, the variation be an expression of inherent differences, the planting of lower grade stock may have serious consequences.

Since relative uniformity of tops may be presumed in vegetatively propagated varieties, stock influences must be the cause of any consistent differences in later growth and performance between the small and large nursery tree. Most of the stocks used are seedlings and therefore more variable than the vegetatively propagated stocks, some kinds more than others. Some of this variation is undoubtedly temporary, but there are good reasons for thinking some of it is more deeply seated.

Webber[303] reports investigations with citrus fruits that bring out these inherent differences in seedling stocks very strikingly.

He summarizes his investigations in part as follows:

"Nursery trees even when grown from selected buds taken from selected trees differ greatly in size when they reach transplanting age. Commonly the large trees are sold first and the small trees later when they reach the required size.

"Large, medium and small nursery trees of Washington Navel and Valencia oranges and Marsh grapefruit grown in comparative tests show that after $2\frac{1}{2}$ years in the orchard the large trees remain large, the intermediate trees remain intermediate and the small remain small. The evidence indicates that this condition is inherent in the trees and that in planting orchards only the large nursery trees should be used.

"An examination of sweet and sour orange seedling stock, such as is used for budding, showed the presence of many widely different types. Some of these types were propagated and the trees at the end of the $4\frac{1}{2}$ years still show the same marked difference. Some are fully five times as large as others. Yet all such types are used as stocks."

A later report[305] by the same investigator shows that these differences in size in citrus seedlings and the nursery trees propagated on them continue and become even more pronounced in later years in the orchard. The nursery dwarf or "runt" is almost certain to prove entirely worthless. Webber[305] attributes most of the dwarf-type individuals appearing among citrus seedlings as being due to the development of embryos from fertilized egg cells, while the better grade, comparatively uniform seedlings from which normally vigorous trees are grown are derived from the apogamic embryos of polyembryonic seeds. These "normal" stocks, therefore, though grown from seeds, are comparable to stocks of other species grown from cuttings or layers.

These differences between seedlings probably hold for a number of other fruits. Similarly differences in seedling size and in size of the resulting nursery trees propagated upon them may be permanent. A seedling apple orchard seven years planted, at the Missouri Station, contains trees ranging in circumference from one inch to sixteen. It is not likely that if these seedling roots had been topworked to the same variety they would all have made equally good trees. From all appearances, they have maintained or increased—but not changed—their relative differences in size; the trees that are largest have made good growth each year, while those that are now inferior appear to have been inferior continuously.

In Maine, Sax and Gowen[260] found a high degree of correlation between rate of growth the first few years in the orchard and later growth and similar correlations in yield, though it is a well-known fact that many early differences in tree size and productivity tend to disappear with age. Bioletti[42] reports that in grapes they are far more likely to disappear than to remain.

It should, however, be recalled that there are cases of a delayed effect in dwarfing. Plums worked on sand cherry frequently make vigorous growth in the first year, greater in fact than on other stocks which ultimately grow the larger trees.

Gravenstein, on the Paradise apple in Germany is said to grow very vigorously at first, but to grow very little after bearing.[229] Chester Pearmain and other varieties behave similarly.[195] Like effects have been recorded with *Castanea vulgaris* grafted on *Quercus sessiliflora* in an attempt to grow chestnut in soils strong in lime; growth was very vigorous the first year, but few grafts lived till the third year. Even shorter was the success of Vinifera grapes on *Cissus orientalis* Lamarck.[255] Hatton[133] may be quoted on this point: "It is often denied that this inequality in the stocks shows itself in the worked trees. Although it is true that a strong-growing variety, such as Bramley's Seedling, may largely obliterate this inequality in the maiden, differences again become apparent in the second and third years." To this extent, then, the grower buying 2-year old graded stocks of some trees may perhaps be a little surer of having runts weeded out. At present, however, the extent to which this delayed effect is operative in common fruits cannot be stated.

Briefly, in buying nursery stock, the grower who gets trees of good size for their age, other things equal, is more nearly sure of getting trees that will do well in his orchard. Buying the smaller grades he is buying uncertain plants. They may be stunted only and may ultimately make good trees. They may, however, be composed of runts which are inherently incapable of being anything else. In practice the inferior grades probably contain some stunted and some "runt" trees. The only sure way of differentiating between them is the test of time which is likely to prove more costly to the grower than the difference in price. The inferior grades, therefore, should be regarded with suspicion.

On the other hand, the extremely large tree is open to objections, serious in some cases. If the tree is large only because it is older, only because it has—as often happens—stood in the nursery an extra year or two, it carries no guarantee of inherent good growth; on the contrary, the presumption is against it. It may be only an older runt.

Gardeners know well that the smaller the plant the less disturbance it suffers in transplanting and the more readily it reestablishes itself. A large proportion of the root system of the larger trees is cut off in digging. Data gathered in California show that the largest trees made the smallest percentage diameter increase during the first year in the orchard, indicating a slowness in adjusting themselves to the new location.[147] Furthermore, trees of unduly large size, produced sometimes by over irrigation or heavy fertilization, are more liable to winter injury when planted in the autumn.

Other objections to the larger trees are voiced by Hendrickson:[147] "Branches are often produced the first year in the nursery row. If these branches could be utilized they would be a distinct advantage but they are often broken or injured in the process of packing and must be cut off when the tree is planted. In other cases the branching does not begin near the bottom of the tree or the bottom branches have been shaded out, and hence it is difficult to secure a low-headed tree by using the branches produced in the nursery. Furthermore, the buds on the lower portion are far apart and the tree has a tendency to grow from the top buds. . . .

"The small 1-year old tree as a rule, depending on the kind, produces few or no side branches. Consequently the buds, instead of growing into branches in the nursery, remain dormant until the following year. They are also less liable to injury in packing. Consequently the small tree within a few weeks after the beginning of the growing season is covered from top to bottom with leaves and small branches. The growth is generally more evenly distributed among the several growing points, than in the case of the overgrown tree."

Withal, "large" and "small" sizes, or even grades based on definite measurements, are relative only. Different nursery fields, or the same fields in different years, produce trees varying considerably in size. Varieties differ more or less in their characteristic growths. Consequently even among trees of the same age any grading must be on a relative basis; a certain caliper measurement may denote small trees in one case and medium sized trees in another.

Definite, though not invariable, objections have been shown to both extreme grades in nursery stock, on the one hand practical and on the other hand primarily theoretical but none the less real. The logical consequence is the approval of the medium grades. Experience usually justifies this course.

Selection of Seedling Stocks.—For good or evil, seedling stocks will continue in use, for some fruits, indefinitely. It is likely, however, that at no distant time the sources of seedling stock will receive closer scrutiny than has been given. Indeed a rough selection has been exercised for many years in some cases. Nurserymen generally discard the weakest seedlings because they are more difficult to bud or graft and because it has been found that in many cases the trees grown on them are small sized and, therefore, salable only at low prices. The striking results obtained by Webber[305] and others in their studies of citrus stocks doubtless will lead to a still more general discarding of dwarf and semidwarf seedlings as understocks for the fruits of this group.

In the case of peaches feral stock from Tennessee has been used to a considerable extent and is generally regarded as the best, though with the rise of canneries, peach stones have been available at little cost to growers of nursery stocks and have been widely used.

The variation in seedlings has been mentioned. It is probable, however, that investigation will show certain varieties to produce larger proportions of good seedlings than others. Commercial varieties of fruit are not grown for the value of the seedling stocks they produce. Doubtless some of them will prove of value for this purpose; others will not.

Roeding[252] says: "For several years I have been carrying on experiments with different varieties [of peaches] to determine their value from a standpoint of growth and general freedom from crown gall, and taking it all in all, the Salway comes first, and the trees produced from Lovell and Muir seed next. Within the last few years I have been carrying on experiments with Tennessee natural pits and am already convinced of their value as to the vigor of growth. If the root system is found to be healthy and of a fibrous character, this stock will be given the preference."

In all probability the same statements may be applied to the use of pits of the sweet cherry varieties obtained from the canneries in place of true Mazzard stock.

The so-called Vermont crab stock for apples, in reality grown from cider mill pomace and tracing ultimately in many cases to seedling apples, sometimes has been preferred to crab stock. Gradually, however, imported French seedlings have been used increasingly for apple stocks, because they were cheaper than native grown stock.

Apple seedlings from different parentage will probably, in some cases, show differences worthy of consideration. Data from an orchard of seedlings of known parentage at the Missouri Experiment Station[47] show a marked tendency to inferior growth in all seedlings of Ralls (Geniton) parentage. Similarly, studies at the New York and Michigan stations have shown that seedlings of Baldwin and a number of other triploid varieties are characteristically weak and give rise to poor nursery and orchard trees of other varieties budded on them, whereas seedlings of many other varieties, such as McIntosh and Delicious, are more vigorous and make much better understocks.

The desirability of care in the selection of the source of seedling stocks has received attention in Europe.

Duplessix,[105] writing on apple growing in Brittany, states: "The choice of apple trees furnishing seeds for sowing is very important, for the tree coming from the seed will generally have the principal characters of that tree which supplied the seed. But there are numerous varieties whose wood has a slow, twisting growth, without vigor, and these varieties are not suitable for generating good stocks, which ought to be straight and of a vigorous and rapid growth. Other varieties, as most of the Reinettes and Calvilles, are very subject to canker; . . .

"It is necessary then to extract the seeds from fruits from trees whose wood is healthy and of a very vigorous growth. Right here is a difficulty for cultivators, for the wood varieties generally used by nurserymen, such as the Frequin de Chartres, Noire de Vitry, Gènèreuse de Vitry, Maman Lily, yield few fruits or fruits of second quality and, for this reason, are almost unknown in our orchards."

The same writer carries the matter of selection still further and advocates growing stock from seed of trees corresponding in season of growth inception with those whose grafts they are destined to bear. That nurserymen generally will go to such extreme lengths in the selection of stocks is not to be expected. If, however, experimenters can find certain stocks that possess great merit, adequate sources of supply will probably be developed.

Grafted or Budded Trees.—Certain fruits such as cherries and peaches are propagated customarily by budding and no question is raised as to the value of trees produced in this manner. Some others, as the apple, are readily propagated either by budding or by grafting and the question of preference between trees grown by these methods has been raised frequently. There may be a difference in the adaptability to a given locality of budded or grafted trees, but it rests on a basis other than that usually discussed.

Much of the alleged superiority of budded trees rests on the use of a whole root in budding while in bench grafting one root may be cut to serve three or four cions. It is argued that this cutting down of the root system produces a tree that is permanently inferior to the budded tree. Budding frequently produces a larger tree in a given time in the nursery than grafting, but there is no positive evidence of any permanent difference in trees raised by the two methods and there is much negative evidence that points to the absence of any difference due to the process used *per se* or the amount of root used *per se.*

The real difference between budded trees and grafted trees has been appreciated only in certain sections where the difference was brought out occasionally by the death of one class and the survival of the other. Trees grafted with long cions and short pieces of root and set deep in the nursery tend to throw out roots from the cion, while the seedling root becomes unimportant or dies, as explained elsewhere. Experience has indicated that cion roots arising from wood of varieties that are hardy are themselves more uniformly hardy than the roots on which they are grafted. Such trees are therefore better adapted to localities where root killing is likely. It is regrettable that in recent years so many budded trees have been set in northern fruit growing sections where root grafted, cion rooted trees provide an insurance well worth consideration.

Cion rooted trees may prove superior in other localities because of their persistence or spread or depth or other qualities. If experience with grapes is a valid analogy, considerable difference between varieties in these qualities would appear upon investigation, some cion roots proving superior and others inferior.   In the one case, then, root grafted trees would be superior, in the other, budded trees, since the seedling roots would average better than the cion roots.   In sections with cold winters, particularly sections with scanty snowfall, root grafted trees should be used.

Double Worked Trees.—There are several possible reasons for double working: (1) a lack of congeniality between stock and cion, (2) need of a trunk and scaffold limbs that are mechanically stronger, (3) the top may be subject to disease or winter injury that is more or less characteristic of the trunk.

Certain varieties of the pear unite poorly with quince stock though they unite well with pear.   Therefore, on the quince is worked a variety that does unite well and into this as a stock is budded the desired variety. Beurré Hardy is used by many nurserymen as the linking variety. Bailey[19] recommends Angoulême for the same purpose; Rivers,[246] in England, found a number of varieties useful, including Beurré d'Amanlis. Clairgeau and Seckel are among the varieties said to thrive better when double worked. In California double working is favored for Bartlett on quince roots.[225]

Burbidge[63] mentions another combination in double working: "In soils which do not suit the Quince, but in which the Pear luxuriates, this order may often be reversed by using some good-constituted Pear as the root stock on which to graft the Quince, which again in its turn is worked the following year with the kind of Pear desired to form a fruiting specimen." He also quotes Parkinson (1629) for another interesting example: "Speaking of the red Nectarine, then the rarest and dearest of all fruit trees, he remarks: 'The other two sorts of red Nectarines must not be immediately grafted on the Plum stock, but upon a branch of an Apricock that hath been formerly grafted on a Plum stock.' "

The apricot as described by Baltet[23] is adjusted to dry sites along the Mediterranean by almond roots. Since the grafts do not take well in direct contact, double working is invoked, using a vigorous peach as the connecting link. The same author states that the Damask plum is sometimes used in France as intermediary between the peach top and Myrobalan roots.[22]

Certain varieties of apples are notoriously subject to collar rot. To escape this difficulty they may be worked on another variety that is noted for its resistance. Grimes double worked on Delicious in the nursery is now available. Delicious is said to induce vigorous growth, transforming Bechtel Crab, for example, into a much more satisfactory tree than the ordinary seedling stocks develop. In Michigan, Red Canada (Steele Red) is much preferred as a double-worked tree, usually with Delicious as the intermediate stock, than when propagated in the usual manner by root grafting or budding directly on seedling roots. Thus propagated, it makes a larger and more productive orchard tree. It is probable that more of this kind of double working will be employed in the future.

Blight-resistant kinds of pear are coming into use as stock on which the more susceptible but better flavored pears are worked. The "Japanese" pear has been used for this purpose, with results varying because several species have been imported under this name. Some are comparatively tender, others are uninjured by a temperature of $-40°F$. or even lower; some are comparatively susceptible to blight, others practically immune. Among the more promising of these stocks are *Pyrus ussuriensis, P. ovoidea* and *P. calleryana*[243] but selection of special strains or types to avoid overgrowth by *communis* tops will be necessary before they are commercially valuable. The first of these is extremely hardy; the last is comparatively hardy and is able to thrive in very wet soils. Old Home, a very blight-resistant variety of *P. communis* and likewise a vigorous grower, is also finding favor as an intermediate for topworking pears.[175,244]

There is no doubt that working of dessert varieties in limbs of these trees will greatly decrease the labor and cost of fighting pear blight.

Top working to insure hardiness in the trunk is discussed elsewhere. It may be mentioned here, however, that the use of Rome Beauty trunks for Gravenstein, the leading apple variety in the Sebastopol apple section of California, has prevented the "sour-sap," which has been exceedingly troublesome there.[281]

An interesting possibility in the future of fruit growing in America is top working for the development of a better framework. Increasing competition will ultimately tend toward the use of fruit of high quality. Heretofore, varieties with good quality in fruit but weak growing habits have been discarded; enhanced appreciation of quality is likely to force the fruit grower to use such varieties whether he likes the tree or not. With weak growing varieties he will likely resort to top working on frames formed by more sturdy varieties. For this reason it is interesting to note that in growing certain choice dessert varieties many European growers have followed this practice for a long time. Certain plums, as Petit Mirabelle, which are weak growers, are worked into a sturdy intermediary such as Quetsche, Reine Claude de Bavay, St. Catherine, Krasensky or Andre Leroy.[24] In Algeria the Japanese plums grow better when top worked into peach limbs. The same process is followed with several pears. Growers of choice apples appear to resort to similar devices for Baltet lists numerous varieties as suitable intermediaries and states that nurserymen grow certain varieties especially for this purpose.

According to Lindemuth double worked apple trees have been in great favor in Holland. A variety called "Sweet Pippin" is grafted into seedling stocks close to the ground and on this intermediary the fruiting variety is worked at the height of the head. The sole reason for this preference, it is said, is the thick trunk formed by the Sweet Pippin, obviating the necessity of supporting the young tree during its first few years by a stake. Since apple trees in northern Europe are grown commonly with much higher heads than in the United States this precise quality would be more important there.

Maynard[213] recommends working Bosc, a notoriously poor growing pear, into tops of strong growing varieties such as Ansault, Clapp or Flemish Beauty. In sections particularly subject to pear blight, however, these particular frame stocks would not be advisable. Maynard stated in 1909 that Kieffer had been recommended for this purpose but had "not been successfully tried in the eastern states."

It should be recorded, perhaps, that double working was advocated many years ago, for increasing the quantity and quality of fruit. Grafting in itself was supposed to have this effect and it was thought as voiced by Noisette,[228] that the more the operation was repeated the greater would be the improvement. More commonly it has been utilized for the hardiness or disease resistance or other specific qualities of the intermediate piece or for the adjustment that the intermediate brings about between a top and a root that are uncongenial.

Some evidence has been obtained from recent investigations to show that under certain circumstances an intermediate stock used in double working may exert an influence upon top or upon root very different from that which the stock beneath it would otherwise have on the top or that the top above would otherwise have on the roots. In other words, it more or less dominates the whole tree. Thus Malling apple stock No. 9, which is itself a rather dwarf type, making a limited root and limited top growth, not only dwarfs any top budded or grafted directly upon it but, similarly, dwarfs both top and roots when used as an intermediate.[284] This seems to imply interference with translocation, either by the graft unions or by the intermediate itself. In the case of the Catillac pear, a normally vigorous growing variety, dwarfing Dr. Jules, another vigorous grower, when used as an intermediate under the latter,[180] the interference with transport or other dwarfing influence would seem to be localized in the graft unions.

Possibly the influences of intermediate stocks on character of root systems reported by Roberts in Wisconsin[250] are to be explained as rather specific "stem effects"; possibly they are more comparable to the effects of starvation seen on infertile sandy soils in many places along the eastern shore of Lake Michigan where normally upright or round-topped trees produce very spreading flat tops, in the case of the double-worked trees brought about by the presence of graft unions that have a selective action on translocation of mineral nutrients or elaborated foods. This concept is in line with the interpretation of Tukey and Brase.[284] In either case, however, it is unlikely that double working will be at all commonly employed as a means of securing this type of "intermediate" effect.

INTRA-VARIETY STRAINS AND PEDIGREED TREES

Observation commonly shows much individual variation between the trees in an orchard that has been planted and tended with the purpose of providing conditions as uniform as possible. Furthermore, these differences extend to practically every feature of the tree growth and they are often extreme. Naturally this has suggested the possibility of perpetuating by vegetative propagation the favorable variations. There has been much discussion on this question and on the value of the so-called "pedigreed" trees that are grown from cions cut from individuals of unusual excellence. In many cases very little actual evidence has been available and opinions have been based on an assumed analogy between a vegetatively propagated tree and a sexually reproduced animal or on theoretical considerations.

Some Results with Citrus Fruits.—Shamel and some of his associates have clearly demonstrated that in a number of the varieties of citrus fruits there is a large amount of bud variation that is of real significance. A number of intra-variety strains have been isolated, propagated and have "bred true," if such an expression can be used for the vegetative propagation employed in the citrus fruits.

The following quotations from the reports of Shamel and his associates will make clear the results of their investigation: "Thirteen important strains [of Washington Navel orange] have been found in the investigational performance record plots."[261]

"Twelve important strains of the Valencia variety have been found and described:"[262] "The lowest percentage of off type tree, *i.e.*, marked variations from the best or Washington strain, found in commercial orchards have been about 10 per cent., and the highest about 75 per cent., of the total number of trees in the orchard."[261] "Tree-census observations in Navel orange orchards in California show a general average of about 25 per cent. of trees of diverse strains, most of which are inferior to the Washington as regards both the amount and the commercial quality of the fruit."

"Occasional limbs have been found in such trees [Washington strain] producing typical Golden Nugget fruits consistently from year to year during the entire period of observation. . . . The variation in the amount of annual crops produced by a given series of individual Washington Navel orange trees is relatively uniform throughout the series each year. That is, the highest producing trees in any one year are in general the highest producing ones each year, and the lowest ones remain at the bottom of the list continually. Individual trees are relatively very stable over a series of years in the character and the amount of their production. . . . Suckers, or unusually vigorous nonbearing branches have been used almost universally for this purpose. This practice has led to the propagation of a continually increasing proportion of trees of those strains producing the largest amount of sucker growth. Inasmuch as such trees are usually light bearers and produce inferior fruits this practice has been unfortunate and is the direct cause of the presence of the large proportion of unproductive trees found in many orchards. Fruit bearing bud wood has been selected from limb variations occurring in trees of the Washington or other strains and in several hundred cases where the growth from these buds has fruited every selection has come true."[261]

With such fruits pedigreed is to be preferred to common stock for it represents definite types or strains that run true, when there is considerable uncertainty as to what to expect from the general run of unselected stock. Perhaps "pedigreed" is an unfortunate term to apply to such selected stock; it is rather "improved" stock. Nursery catalogs and the current horticultural magazines commonly refer to such stock as being grown from "selected" buds.

Some Results with Apples.—Hedrick[141] represents fairly well one school of opinion when he says, concerning "pedigreed" apples:

"At the very outset it must be pointed out that the seeming analogy between plants propagated from buds and cions and those grown from seeds has given a false simplicity to the fact and has led many astray. Analogy is the most treacherous kind of reasoning. We have here a case in which the similarity of properties is suggested but the two things are wholly different upon close analysis. In the case of seeds there is a combination of definite characters, in the offspring from two parents. Since the combinations of characters handed down from parents to children are never the same, individual seedlings from the same two plants may vary greatly. On the other hand, a graft is literally a 'chip of the old block' and while plants grown from buds may vary because of environment they do not often vary through heredity. . . The Geneva Station has an experiment which gives precise evidences upon this question of pedigreed stock. Sixteen years ago a fertilizer experiment was started with 60 Rome trees propagated from buds taken from one branch of a Rome tree. Quite as much variation can be found in these trees from selected buds as could be found in an orchard of Romes propagated indiscriminately and growing under similar condition. Data showing the variations in diameter of tree and in productiveness . . . will go far to convince anyone that uniformity of behavior as regards vigor and productiveness of tree and size and color of fruit cannot be perpetuated."

In 1895 the Missouri Station propagated from the highest and from the lowest yielding trees in an orchard of over 200 Ben Davis then in full bearing. The resulting trees were planted alternately in orchard rows and individual yield records were kept from 1912 to 1918 inclusive. Though there was a difference in size and finish of the fruit in the original trees there was none in the fruit borne by their offspring.[115] Investigations in Vermont, reported by Cummings,[81] show no consistent superiority in cions from superior trees of several varieties of apple.

On the other hand, many all-red strains of striped varieties of apples have been discovered as limb or whole-tree sports and are being propagated and distributed by the nurseries. Some are given entirely new names, and they are recognized as new varieties. Others are grown and recognized simply as strains of the old varieties. They differ from the strains of citrus varieties only in that color, rather than other features of tree or fruit, are involved. More recent investigations at the Michigan Experiment Station[104,116] show that variations occur in other important characters of the plant and that considerable improvement can be effected through selection of cion wood to eliminate "off types" and perpetuate desirable mutants. This is distinct from what might be termed the "mass-selection" type of improvement which simply utilizes for propagation what appears to be the best stock, regardless of whether its superiority is due to somatic mutation or to environment, and which, for the most part, yields negative results.

The statement has often been made that cion wood taken from certain parts of the tree gives rise to trees that are better than those propagated from less carefully selected wood. Crandall[80] has given this matter thorough investigation in the apple and reports the following conclusions:

"Summarized data giving comparisons between trees propagated from large buds and those propagated from small buds, together with the aggregate of impressions derived from careful inspections of trees of all groups, admit but one conclusion, namely, that there are no differences, for purposes of propagation, between buds of large size and those of small size.

"Growth curves of trees propagated from buds of different situations on the trees so closely approximate as to leave no basis for assuming that it makes any difference from what situation on the tree the buds are taken.

"All buds from healthy shoots are of equal value for purposes of propagation, at least so far as growth of tree is concerned.

"Fluctuations in growth of individuals within particular groups are decided, often extreme. In general, differences become less with increase in age, provided the trees remain healthy.

"There is no tangible basis upon which to establish the assumption that robust scions are superior to scions of small diameter for purposes of propagation."

These conclusions apparently differ from those of Shamel, Scott and Pomeroy working with citrus fruits. However, it should be noted that sucker growth was found in great abundance only in citrus trees that were "off type" individuals and it was to trees from such parentage that these workers particularly referred. In other words it was only because excessive sucker growth was correlated with a certain type of degeneration that propagation from wood of that kind yielded unsatisfactory results in practice. The evidence seems to warrant the conclusion that normal buds, whether borne on slow or rapid growing shoots or on suckers, are satisfactory for propagation, provided they are healthy and do not come from limbs that are bud mutations. Furthermore, it justifies the nurseryman in propagating from the nursery row, *i.e.*, from young trees, provided there is no question of identity. On the other hand, it is recognized that in species showing more or less dimorphism in their vegetative parts some attention must be given to selection of cion wood. Thus "only terminal branches should be used for scions in budding or grafting the coffee plant, for if budded or grafted with a horizontal scion the resulting plant always develops a low spreading bush and never produces vertical growth."[114]

In General.—Considering the present state of knowledge the prospective purchaser should ascertain accurately just what is meant by the term "pedigreed" or "selected" stock in each case, the extent to which such nursery stock differs from the ordinary in its source and in its later performance record. Not until then can he tell how to reckon its comparative value.

There is no doubt that occasional variations occur and can be perpetuated, but there is also no doubt that much of the variation between trees in the same orchard is due to soil variations or to differences in stocks and that these variations are not perpetuated. The fact that stock is propagated from a superior individual indicates a bare possibility that it is superior but it does not establish a probability that it is, much less a certainty.

Suggested Collateral Reading

Priestley, J. H., and Swingle, C. F. Vegetative Propagation from the Standpoint of Plant Anatomy. U. S. D. A. Tech. Bul. 151. 1929.

Amos, J., Hoblyn, T. N., Garner, R. J., and Witt, A. W. Studies in Incompatibility of Stock and Scion. I. Information Accumulated during Twenty Years of Testing Fruit Tree Rootstocks with Various Scion Varieties at East Malling. East Malling Res. Sta. Ann. Rept. for 1935: 81–189. 1936.

Chang, W. Studies in Incompatibility between Stock and Scion, with Special Reference to Certain Deciduous Fruit Trees. Jour. Pom. and Hort. Sci. 15 (4): 267–325. 1938.

Literature Cited

1. Aaronsohn, A. U. S. D. A., Bur. Pl. Ind. Bul. 180. 1910.
2. Affleck, T. Gardener's Monthly (Meehan's). 2: 177–179. 1860.
3. Allen, W. J. New South Wales Dept. Agr. Farmers' Bul. 86. 1914.
4. Am. Jour. Hort. 9: 301. 1871.
5. Amos, J., Hoblyn, T. N., Garner, R. J., and Witt, A. W. Ann. Rept. East Malling Res. Sta. for 1935, A 19: 81–99. 1936.
6. Andre, E. L'Illustration horticole. 22: 54. 1875.
7. Arendts, C. Möller's Deutsche Gärten Zeit. 13: 249–251. 1898.
8. Ibid. 13: 308–309. 1898.
9. Asami, Y. The Crab-Apples and Nectarines of Japan. Pp. 18, 44. Tokyo. 1927.
10. Austen, R. Observations on Sir Francis Bacon's Naturall History. P. 15. Oxford. 1658.
11. Baco, F. Trav. sci. Univ. Rennes. 10 (2): 88–90. 1911.
12. Ibid. 10 (2): 97.
13. Ibid. 10 (2): 152.
14. Ibid. 10 (2): 158.
15. Ibid. 10 (2): 175.
16. Bailey, L. H. Cornell Univ. Agr. Exp. Sta. Bul. 38. 1892.
17. Ibid. Bul. 71. 1894.
18. Bailey, L. H. Stand. Cycl. Hort. 3: 1363. New York, 1917.
19. Bailey, L. H. Nursery Manual. P. 167. New York, 1920.
20. Bailey, J. S. Mass. Agr. Exp. Sta. Bul. 226. 1926.
21. Baltet, C. L'Art de Greffer. P. 7. Paris, 1902.
22. Ibid. P. 119.
23. Ibid. P. 211.
24. Ibid. P. 369.

25. Ibid.   P. 415.
26. Ibid.   P. 453.
27. Baltet, E.   Jour. d'hort. prat. de Belg.   4 (n.s.): 180.   1860.
28. Barron, A. F.   Jour. Roy. Hort. Soc.   3 (n.s.): 1–4.   1872.
29. Barry, P.   Horticulturist.   3: 136.   1848.
30. Barry, P.   The Fruit Garden.   P. 303.   Detroit, 1853.
31. Ibid.   P. 310.
32. Barss, H. P.   Ore. Agr. Exp. Sta. Bienn. Crop Pest and Hort. Rept. 1: 213.
    1913.
33. Baumgart, S.   Hadar.   9: 71–74.   1936.   (Cited in Horticultural Abstracts.
    6 (2): 133.   1936.)
34. Bellair, G.   Rev. hort.   72: 210–212.   1900.
35. Bennett, J. P.   Cal. Agr. Exp. Sta. Circ. Bul. 321.   1931.
36. Berckmanns, P. J.   Proc. Am. Pom. Soc.   P. 70.   1881.
37. Berckmanns, P. J.   Rural New Yorker.   53: 472.   1894.
38. Le Berryais.   Traité des jardins, ou nouveau de la Quintinye.   Pt. I.   P. 262.
    Paris.   1775.
39. Biffen, R. H.   Ann. Bot., Lond.   16: 174–176.   1902.
40. Bioletti, F. T.   Cal. Agr. Exp. Sta. Bul. 197.   1908.
41. Ibid.   Bul. 180.   1906.
42. Bioletti, F. T.   Hilgardia.   2 (1): 1–23.   1926.
43. Bioletti, F. T., and dal Piaz, A. M.   Cal. Agr. Exp. Sta. Bul. 127.   1900.
44. Blunno, M.   New South Wales Dept. Agr. Farmers' Bul. 80.   1914.
45. B. N. A.   Gardener's Mag. (London).   3: 380.   1828.
46. Bonns, W. W., and Mertz, W. M.   Cal. Agr. Exp. Sta. Bul 267.   1916.
47. Bradford, F. C.   Nat. Nurseryman.   29: 152.   1921.
48. Bradford, F. C., and Sitton, B. G.   Mich. Agr. Exp. Sta. Tech. Bul. 99.   1929.
49. Bridgeman, T.   The Fruit Cultivator's Manual.   Pp. 99–104.   New York.
    1857.
50. Brierley, W. G.   Minn. Hort.   55: 129–134.   1927.
51. Brown, B. S.   Modern Propagation of Tree Fruits.   P. 157.   New York, 1916.
52. Ibid.   P. 160.
53. Brown, W. R.   Agr. Res. Inst. Pusa Bul. 93.   1920.
54. Brunk, T. L.   Country Gentleman.   55: 188.
55. Budd, J. L.   Ia. St. Hort. Soc. Trans.   21 (1886): 101–102.   1887.
56. Budd, J. L.   Am. Garden.   8: 314.   1887.
57. Budd, J. L.   Ia. St. Hort. Soc. Trans.   14 (1879): 432.   1880.
58. Budd, J. L.   Mich. Farmer.   Sept. 21, 1889.
59. Budd, J. L.   Ia. Agr. Exp. Sta. Bul. 10.   1890.
60. Budd, J. L.   Ia. St. Hort. Soc. Trans.   25 (1891): 77–89.   1892.
61. Burbidge, F. W.   Propagation and Improvement of Cultivated Plants.   P. 59.
    London, 1877.
62. Ibid.   P. 60.
63. Ibid.   P. 69.
64. Ibid.   P. 264.
65. Ibid.   P. 267.
66. Ibid.   P. 459.
67. Carrière, E. A.   Rev. hort.   56: 336.   1884.
68. Childs, L. and Brown, G. G.   Ore. Agr. Exp. Sta. Circ. Bul. 103.   1931.
69. Clos, D.   Rev. hort.   4 ser.   V: 342–343.   1856.
70. Cock, S. A.   Jour. Dept. Agr. Victoria.   11: 372.   1913.

THE ROOT SYSTEMS OF FRUIT PLANTS 695

71. Ibid. 11: 714.
72. Colby, H. L. Plant Physiology. 10: 483–498. 1935.
73. Cole, C. F. Jour. Dept. Agr. Victoria. 9. 1911.
74. Condit, I. J. Cal. Agr. Exp. Sta. Bul. 250. 1915.
75. Cooke, W. W. Agr. Gaz. New South Wales. 39 (2): 854–856. 1928.
76. Corsa, W. P. Nut Culture in the United States. P. 80. Washington, 1896.
77. Coulter, J. L., Barnes, C. R. and Cowles, H. C. Text Book of Botany. 2: 779. New York, 1911.
78. Country Gentleman. 23: 78. 1864.
79. Craig, J. Amer. Gardening. 20: 720–721. 1899.
80. Crandall, C. S. Ill. Agr. Exp. Sta. Bul. 211. 1918.
81. Cummings, M. B. Vt. Agr. Exp. Sta. Bul. 221. 1921.
82. Cummings, M. B., Jenkins, E. W., and Dunning, R. G. Vt. Agr. Exp. Sta. Bul. 352. 1933.
83. Curtel, G. Compt. rend. 139: 491. 1904.
84. The Cultivator. 2 (ser. 3): 59. 1854.
85. Daniel, L. Compt. rend. 114: 1294. 1892.
86. Daniel, L. Rev. gén. bot. 6: 5–21. 1894.
87. Daniel, L. Compt. rend. 136: 1157. 1903.
88. Daniel, L. Trav. sci. Univ. Rennes. 2: 73. 1903.
89. Ibid. 2: 173.
90. Ibid. 2: 210.
91. Daniel, L. Rev. hort. 10 (N.S.): 469. 1910.
92. Ibid. 13 (N.S.): 348. 1913.
93. Ibid. 14 (N.S.): 135. 1914.
94. Darwin, C. Animals and Plants under Domestication. 2: 266. New York. 1894.
95. Davis, R. A. Fruit Growing in South Africa. P. 166. 1928.
96. Ibid. P. 194.
97. Dawson, J. Mass. Hort. Soc. Trans. P. 123. 1895.
98. Delabarriere. Rev. hort. 62: 182–183. 1890.
99. Dental, J. B. Rev. hort. 16 (N.S.): 47. 1916.
100. Dervaux, G. La culture des arbres fruitiers. P. 159. Paris. 1924.
101. Despeissis, A. Handbook of Horticulture and Viticulture of Western Australia. P. 95. Perth. 1903.
102. Douglas, R. Ill. Hort. Soc. Trans. 1871: 181–183.
103. Downing, A. J. Fruits and Fruit Trees of America. P. 25. New York, 1856.
104. Drain, B. D. Mich. Agr. Exp. Sta. Tech. Bul. 130. 1932.
105. Duplessix. Trav. sci. Univ. Rennes. 10 (2): 5. 1911.
106. Ibid. 10 (2): 18.
107. Ibid. 10 (2): 38.
108. Ibid. 10 (2): 192.
109. Eaton, F. M. and Blair, G. Y. Plant Physiology. 10: 411–424. 1935.
110. Elliott, F. R. Gardener's Monthly. 12: 214. 1870.
111. Fowler, R. Jour. Dept. Agr. So. Australia. 37: 383–393. 1933.
112. Frank, C. Wiener Obst. u. Garten Zeit. I: 521. 1876.
113. Fuller, A. S. The Propagation of Plants. New York. 1894. Pp. 222–248.
114. Galang, F. G. Philippine Agr. Rev. 21: 362. 1928.
115. Gardner, V. R. Mo. Agr. Exp. Sta. Res. Bul. 39. 1920.
116. Gardner, V. R. Jour. Agr. Res. 50 (5): 457–478. 1935.
117. Gaston, A. H. Ill. St. Hort. Soc. Trans. 23 (n.s.): 240–241. 1889.

118. Gillemot, G. L.   Wiener Obst. u. Garten Zeit.   I: 121–122.   1876.
119. Ibid.   P. 148.
120. Gitton.   Rev. hort.   59: 413.   1887.
121. Glady, E.   Rev. hort.   34: 392–393.   1862.
122. Goodale, S. L.   Horticulturist.   4: 180–182.   1849.
123. Goodale, S. L.   Agr. Maine.   1863: 133–271.
124. Gould, H. P.   U. S. D. A. Farmers' Bul. 776.   1916.
125. Graham, M. J.   Ia. St. Hort. Soc. Rept. (1903): 96–100.   1904.
126. Green, S. B.   Popular Fruit Growing.   P. 180.   St. Paul.   1909.
127. Grubb, N. H., Painter, A. C. and Worwald, H. E.   E. Malling Res. Sta. Ann.
     Rept. (1931): 57–60.   1932.
128. Guignard, L.   Ann. sci. nat., bot. 6: 261–305.   1907.
129. Haas, A. R. C. and Halma, F. F.   Plant Physiology.   4: 113–121.   1929.
130. Hansen, N. E.   S. D. Agr. Exp. Sta. Bul. 87.   1904.
131. Ibid.   Bul. 93.   1905.
132. Harwell, R.   Horticulturist.   5: 257.   1850.
133. Hatton, R. G.   Jour. Roy. Hort. Soc.   45 (2): 257.   1919–1920.
134. Ibid. 45 (2).   269.
135. Hatton, R. G.   Jour. Pom. and Hort. Sci.   2: 1–37.   1921.
136. Hatton, R. G.   Fruit Grower, Fruiterer, Florist and Market Gardener.   Oct. 18
     and 25, and Nov. 1, 1923.
137. Hatton, R. G., and Grubb, N. H.   E. Malling Res. Sta. Ann. Rept.   Pp. 81–86.
     1925.
138. Hatton, R. G., Grubb, N. H., and Amos, J. E.   E. Malling Res. Sta. Ann. Rept.
     P. 112.   1923.
139. Hedrick, U. P.   Plums of New York.   P. 115.   Albany, 1911.
140. Hedrick, U. P.   N. Y. Agr. Exp. Sta. Bul. 355.   1912.
141. Hedrick, U. P.   N. Y. Agr. Exp. Sta. Circ. 18.   1912.
142. Hedrick, U. P.   N. Y. Agr. Exp. Sta. Bul. 406.   1915
143. Hedrick, U. P.   Cherries of New York.   P. 72.   Albany, 1919.
144. Hedrick, U. P.   N. Y. Agr. Exp. Sta. Bul. 498.   1923.
145. Heimann, O. R.   Obst. u. Gemüsebau.   78: 138–141.   1932.
146. Heikes, W. F.   Gardener's Monthly.   24: 110.   1882.
147. Hendrickson, A. H.   Cal. Sta. Dept. Agr. Mo. Bul. 4: 171–174.   1918.
148. Henry, L.   Bul. d'Arboriculture.   Pp. 77–81.   1886.
149. Henry, L.   Le Jardin.   P. 9.   1898.
150. Heppner, M. J.   Am. Fruit Grower.   45: 5, 24.   1925.
151. Heppner, M. J., and McCallum, R. D.   Cal. Agr. Exp. Sta. Bul. 438.   1927.
152. Herse, F.   Landw. Jahrb.   37 (Ergzbd. 4.): 77–136.   1908.
153. Hill, J.   Eden or a Compleat Body of Gardening.   P. 82.   London.   1757.
154. Hill, O. V.   New Eng. Farmer.   10: 490.   1858.
155. Hodgson, R. W., and Cameron, S. H.   Calif. Citrogr.   20 (12): 370.   1935.
156. Hofmann, F. W.   Jour. Agr. Res.   34: 673–676.   1927.
157. Hogg, J.   Mag. of Hort. (Hovey's).   28: 107–113.   1861.
158. Horticulturist.   6: 337.   1851.
159. Ibid.   6: 374.
160. Ibid.   28: 54.   1873.
161. Howard, A., and Howard, G. L. C.   Sci. Rept. Agr. Inst. Pusa.   P. 48.   1916–
     1917.
162. Howard, W. L.   Ia. St. Hort. Soc. Trans.   57: 177–180.   1922.
163. Howard, W. L.   Cal. Agr. Exp. Sta. Circ. Bul. 238.   1922.

164. Howard, W. L., and Heppner, M. J.   Am. Soc. Hort. Sci. Proc.   25 (1928): 178–180.   1929.
165. Howe, G. H.   N. Y. Agr. Exp. Sta. Bul. 544.   1927.
166. Hume, H. H.   Fla. Agr. Exp. Sta. Bul. 71.   1904.
167. Husmann, G. C.   U. S. D. A., Bur. Pl. Ind. Bul. 172.   1910.
168. Husmann, G. C.   U. S. D. A., Bul. 856.   1920.
169. Ia. Agr. Exp. Sta. Ann. Rept.   P. 33.   1919.
170. Ia. St. Hort. Soc. Trans.   (1879): 184.   1880.
171. Ibid.   25: 7–9.   1891.
172. Ill. St. Hort. Soc. Trans.   7 (N.S.): 291.   1874.
173. Jack, J. G.   Garden and Forest.   3: 53–55.   1890.
174. Jensen, C. A., Wilcox, L. V., and Foot, F. J.   Calif. Citrogr.   12: 266–268. 1927.
175. Johnston, S.   Mich. Agr. Exp. Sta. Quart. Bul. 13 (2): 67–68.   1930.
176. Ibid.   Bul. 21 (1): 17–18.   1938.
177. Jour. soc. nat. et cent. d'Hort. de Fr.   3 ser.   7: 428.   1885.
178. Kelley, W. P., and Thomas, E. E.   Cal. Agr. Exp. Sta. Bul. 318.   1920.
179. Kerr, W. S.   Rural New Yorker, 55: 50.   1896.
180. Knight, R. C.   Kent Inc. Soc. for Promoting Experiments in Hort. Ann. Rept. 11: 13.   1927.
181. Knight, T. A.   Phys. and Hort. Papers.   P. 155.   London, 1841.
182. Ibid.   P. 223.
183. Ibid.   P. 273.
184. Ibid.   P. 274.
185. Koch, A.   Illustr. Garten-Zeit.   (Stuttgart.)   17: 11–14.   1873.
186. Lanjoulet.   Rev. hort.   33: 411.   1861.
187. L(aurent), J.   Abrégé pour arbres nains.   Pp. 11–34.   Paris.   1675.
188. Laurent, C.   Trav. sci. Univ. Rennes.   8: 37.   1909.
189. Lawrence, J.   Clergyman's Recreation.   P. 64.   London, 1717.
190. Leclerc du Sablon.   Compt. rend.   136: 623.   1903.
191. Lehmann.   Allg. teut. Gart. Mag.   3: 24–26.   1806.
192. Leroy, A.   Jour. soc. Imp. et Cent. d'hort.   5: 622–623.   1860.
193. Leroy, A.   Dictionnaire de Pomologie.   V: 133.   Paris, 1877.
194. Lieb, E.   Pomol. Monatshefte.   5: 130–136.   1879.
195. Lindemuth, H.   Landw. Jahrb.   7: 909.   1878.
196. Ibid.   7: 912.
197. Lindemuth, H.   Ber. Bot. Gesel.   19: 515.   1901.
198. Ibid.   19: 527.
199. Lindley, J.   A Guide to the Orchard and Kitchen Garden.   P. 137.   London. 1831.
200. Lindley, J.   Theory and Practice of Horticulture.   P. 355.   London, 1855.
201. Livingstone, J.   Trans. Hort. Soc. London.   4: 231.   1822.
202. Loudon, J. C.   The Horticulturist.   P. 283.   London, 1860.
203. Lucas, E.   Die Lehre vom Baumschnitt.   P. 37.   Ravensburg, 1874.   Cited in Lindemuth, H.   Landw. Jahrb.   7: 911.   1878.
204. L(ucas), E.   Pomol. Monatshefte.   5: 116.   1879.
205. McClintock, J. A.   Am. Soc. Hort. Soc. Proc.   23 (1925): 231–232.   1926.
206. Ibid.   27 (1930): 124–127.   1931.
207. Macdonald, L.   Jour. Dept. Agr. Victoria.   10: 69.   1912.
208. Macoun, W. T.   Cent. (Can.) Exp. Farms. Bul. 38.   1907.
209. "Maple Dell."   Gardener's Monthly (Meehan's).   III: 329.   1861.

210. Markscheffel.   Allg. deut. Gartenzeit.   5: 89–91.   1827.
211. Mass. Hort. Soc. Trans.   Pp. 6–43.   1879.
212. Mathews, J.   Ia. St. Hort. Soc. Rept.   (1875): 213–227.   1876.
213. Maynard, S. T.   Successful Fruit Culture.   P. 74.   New York, 1909.
214. Ibid.   P. 197.
215. Meyer, F. N.   Mass. Hort. Soc. Trans.   1916.   Pt. I: 125–130.
216. Michelin.   Jour. soc. cent. d'Hort. de Fr.   3 ser.   5: 321–327.   1883.
217. Mich. Farmer.   22: 14.   1891.
218. Mich. St. Hort. Soc. Proc.   1881.   P. 137.
219. Mills, J. W.   Cal. Agr. Exp. Sta. Bul. 138.   1902.
220. Minn. St. Hort. Soc. Trans.   1881: 71–72.
221. Moore, J. G.   Proc. Am. Soc. Hort. Sci.   16: 84.   1919.
222. Munson, T. V.   Rural New Yorker.   55: 50.   1896.
223. Murneek, A. L.   Better Fruit.   15: No. 7.   1921.
224. Naudin, C.   Rev. hort.   75: 38–41.   1903.
225. Neer, F. E.   Correspondence.   1921.
226. Newman, C. V.   Calif. Citrogr.   11: 375, 405–407.   1926.
227. Neilson, J. A.   Thesis.   Ia. St. Coll.   1921.
228. Noisette, L.   Vollstand. Handb. der Gartenkunst.   Uebersetzt von Sigwart.
        Stuttgart.   1826.
229. Oberdieck.   Illus. Monatshefte für Obst- und Weinbau.   P. 44.   1873.   Cited
        by Lindemuth, H.   Landw. Jahrb.   7: 909.   1878.
230. Der Obst. u. Gemüsebau.   84: 1: Frontispiece.   1938.
231. Ohmann, M.   Centrbl. für Bakt.   21: 232–256, 318–329.   1908.
232. Onderdonk, G.   Proc. Am. Pom. Soc.   P. 92.   1901.
233. Otuka, Y.   Res. Bul. 5, Agr. Exp. Sta.   Manchuria Ry. Co.   1–11.   1931.
234. Pepin.   Rev. hort.   Ser. 3.   2: 183.   1848.
235. Phoenix, F. K.   Horticulturist.   28: 54.   1873.
236. Porta, G. della.   Natural Magic.   III: XI.   81–82.   London.   1658.
237. Proc. Am. Pom. Soc.   1881.
238. Proc. Am. Pom. Soc.   P. 128.   1889.
239. Proebsting, E. L.   Bot. Gaz.   86: 82–92.   1928.
240. Rea, J.   Flora, seu de florum cultura.   Pp. 203–209.   London.   1665.
241. Reeves, E.   Ia. St. Hort. Soc. Ann. Rept.   27 (1892): 279–281.   1893.
242. R(egel), E.   Gartenflora.   17: 125.   1868.
243. Reimer, F. C.   Ann. Rept. Pac. Coast Assoc. Nurserymen.   1916.
244. (Reimer, F. C.)   Ore. Agr. Exp. Sta. Bien. Rept. for 1928–1930.   P. 135.
        1930.
245. Rice, G. G.   Ia. St. Hort. Soc. Ann. Rept.   31 (1896): 49.   1897.
246. Rivers, T.   The Miniature Fruit Garden.   P. 103.   New York, 1866.
247. Rivers, T.   Proc. Roy. Hort. Soc.   N.S. II.   P. XCIV.   1870.
248. Riviere, G. et Bailhache, G.   Compt. rend.   124: 477.   1897.
249. Roach, W. A.   Ann. Rept. E. Malling Res. Sta.   1928–30, II.   Supplement,
        1931, pp. 101–104.
250. Roberts, R. H.   Wis. Agr. Exp. Sta. Res. Bul. 94.   1929.
251. Roeding, G. C.   Fruit Growers' Guide.   P. 18.   Fresno, 1919.
252. Ibid.   P. 26.
253. Rogers, A. J.   Mich. Agr. Exp. Sta. Sp. Bul. 166.   1927.
254. Rolfs, P. H.   Fla. Agr. Exp. Sta. Bul. 127.   1915.
255. Sahut, F.   Rev. hort.   57: 149.   1885.
256. Ibid.   57: 201.

257. Ibid.   57: 258.
258. Ibid.   57: 305.
259. Ibid.   57: 398.
260. Sax, K. and Gowen, J. W.   Genetics.   8: 458–465.   1923.
261. Shamel, A. D. *et al.*   U. S. D. A. Bul. 623.   1918.
262. Ibid.   Bul. 624.   1918.
263. Shaw, J. K.   Proc. Am. Soc. Hort. Sci.   14: 64.   1917.
264. Shaw, J. K.   Science.   45 (N.S.); 461.   1917.
265. Shaw, J. K.   Mass. Agr. Exp. Sta. Bul. 190.   1919.
266. Shaw, J. K.   Correspondence.   1921.
267. Sickler, (J. V.)   Allgem. teut. Gart. Mag.   7: 142–144.   1810.
268. Smith, C. O.   Proc. Am. Soc. Hort. Sci.   25: 183–187.   1928.
269. Sorauer, P.   Manual of Plant Diseases.   3d ed. (transl.)   1: 841.   Wilkes-Barré, Pa.   1920.
270. Stephens, J. M.   U. S. D. A. Dept. Bul. 1301.   1925.
271. Storrs, O. D.   Minn. St. Hort. Soc. Trans.   Pp. 129–130.   1879.
272. Strong, W. C.   Gardener's Monthly.   24: 14.   1882.
273. Stuart, W.   Vt. Agr. Exp. Sta. Ann. Rept.   18: 300.   1905.
274. Stuckey, H. P.   Ga. Agr. Exp. St. Bul. 116.   1915.
275. Swingle, C. F.   Am. Soc. Hort. Soc. Proc.   26 (1929): 77–79.   1930.
276. Swingle, W. T.   U. S. D. A., Bur. Pl. Ind. Cir. 46.   1909.
277. Talbot, J.   Mass. Hort. Soc. Trans.   P. 6.   1879.
278. Taylor, R. H.   Cal. Agr. Exp. Sta. Bul.   297.   1918.
279. Thomas, J. J.   Country Gentleman.   17: 22.   1861.
280. Treen, W. H.   Gardener's Chronicle.   Aug. 19, 1871.   P. 1065.
281. Tufts, W. P.   Correspondence.   1921.
282. Tukey, H. B.   Jour. Heredity.   19: 113–114.   1928.
283. Tukey, H. B., and Brase, K. D.   N. Y. Agr. Exp. Sta. Tech. Bul. 185.   1931.
284. Ibid.   Tech. Bul. 218.   1933.
285. Tukey, H. B., and Brase, K. D.   Am. Soc. Hort. Sci. Proc.   30 (1933): 361–364.   1934.
286. Uhink, G. W.   Möller's deutsche Garten Zeit.   10: 15.   1895.
287. Van Deman, H. E.   Rural New Yorker.   71: (March 13), 1912.
288. Van Eseltine, G. P.   N. Y. Agr. Exp. Sta. Tech. Bul. 208.   1933.
289. Vard, E.   Rev. hort.   63: 514.   1891.
290. Veihmeyer, F. J.   Hilgardia.   2: 196.   1927.
291. Viala, P. and Ravaz, L.   Les Vignes Americaines.   P. 240.   Paris.   1892.
292. Victoria Jour. Dept. Agr.   14: 6.   1916.
293. Voechting, H.   Cited by Lindemuth, H.   Ber. Bot. Gesel.   19: 515.   1901.
294. Vosbury, E. D.   U. S. D. A. Farmers' Bul. 1122.   1920.
295. Wallace, T.   Agric. Progr. (London.)   7: 61–71.   1930.
296. W(aring), W. H.   Country Gentleman.   40: 534.   1875.
297. Ibid.   45: 742.   1880.
298. Waugh, F. A.   Vt. Agr. Exp. Sta. Ann. Rept.   13: 333.   1900.
299. Ibid.   Ann. Rept.   14: 259.   1901.
300. Waugh, F. A.   Plums and Plum Culture.   P. 238.   New York.   1901.
301. Waugh, F. A.   Mass. Agr. Exp. Sta. Tech. Bul. 2.   1904.
302. Watrous, C.   Ia. St. Hort. Soc. Ann. Rept.   (1894): 81–86.   1895.
303. Webber, H. J.   Cal. Agr. Exp. Sta. Bul. 317.   1920.
304. Webber, H. J. *et al.*   Cal. Agr. Exp. Sta. Bul. 304.   1919.
305. Webber, H. J.   Hilgardia.   7 (1): 1–79.   1932.

306. Whittemore, H. C.   Country Gentleman.   12: 351.   1858.
307. Wickson, E. J.   California Fruits.   P. 246.   San Francisco.   1910.
308. Ibid.   P. 345.
309. Wilder, M. P.   Gardener's Monthly (Meehan's) Suppl.   P. 4.   1860.
310. Witt, A. W., and Garner, R. J.   Ann. Rept.   E. Malling Res. Sta. II. Suppl.
      Pp. 22–31.   1931.
311. Wood, J. F.   The Midland Florist.   1: 185–189.   1847.
312. Wragg, M. J.   Ia. St. Hort. Soc. Rept.   30 (1895): 49.   1896.
313. Ibid.   Rept. 32 (1897): 164–167.   1898.

SECTION VII

GEOGRAPHIC INFLUENCES IN FRUIT PRODUCTION

Perseverance has not only developed fruits with qualities superior to those of the wild; it has extended their growth into regions to which they are not native. The two most important orchard fruits of the United States are not indigenous. Social and economic conditions have played no unimportant parts in developing fruit growing or in preventing its development. Transportation facilities or neighboring markets are of utmost importance. Necessary as these all are, however, they can not establish a fruit growing industry unless its development is possible under the complex of natural influences which are grouped conveniently under the term geographic. Though complete analysis of this complex is impossible, since one factor's influence may be modified by that of another factor, some general statements can be made with safety.

A knowledge of the conditions which favor, interfere with or prevent fruit growing at various points may be of considerable value for local application, since it may suggest the capitalization of certain features of the local climate through the growing of fruits best suited to those conditions or it may indicate certain departures of the local climate from the best conditions for a given fruit, necessitating particular care in some phase of management. Furthermore, it may suggest to the plant breeder definite aims in improvement to secure adaptation or possibly it may indicate sources of material with which he can work most profitably. Plant improvement for one section may be quite different from the amelioration necessary in the same fruit for another.

CHAPTER XXXIII

THE GEOGRAPHY OF FRUIT GROWING

Certain fruits like the apple are grown throughout most of the temperate regions of both hemispheres, the industry in the case of the apple reaching its height in the northern half of the United States and Europe and in the southern part of Australia, Tasmania and New Zealand. The pear is cultivated throughout practically the same range; its quantity production is much more localized. Sweet cherry production is developed mainly in the western nations of Europe and the western states of North America. None of these fruits is of great importance in South America, though the grape, which is grown along with the apple and pear in North America, Europe, Asia and Australia is an extremely important fruit on that continent. On the other hand, certain fruits have very restricted geographic ranges. The date is grown mainly in countries bordering the Mediterranean, the jaboticaba in parts of Brazil, the jujube in central China, the pecan in the southeastern United States, the loganberry in Washington, Oregon and California. The accompanying maps (Figs. 62 to 69) present graphically a few interesting facts regarding the geographic distribution of certain of the more common fruits.

Incidentally Figs. 64–66, representing peach trees of bearing age in 1930 and increases and decreases in peach-tree number during the preceding decade, afford some idea of the changes in centers of production that take place, sometimes within relatively short periods.

"The number of peach trees of all ages more than doubled in Illinois between 1920 and 1930, and increased materially in Indiana, Michigan, and the Carolinas; also in north-central Georgia, in northeastern and southwestern Arkansas, and in the Sacramento and lower San Joaquin Valleys in California, western Colorado, and in the Yakima Valley of Washington. . . . There was a notable decrease in number in eastern Texas and south-central Georgia, in the northern Virginia and Maryland area, in New Jersey and eastern Pennsylvania, in western New York, and the northern portion of the peach belt in Michigan, in the Ozark area, and in southern California.

"During the 1930–35 period the number of peach trees in the country as a whole continued to decline, but in a few districts the increase was notable. The major increases were in Howard, Pike, Hempstead, and St. Francis Counties, Arkansas; Meriwether County, Ga.; Spartansburg County, S. C.; Scotland, Richmond, Moore, and Montgomery Counties, N. C.; and Adams and Franklin Counties, Pa. Smaller increases occurred in many counties of eastern Texas,

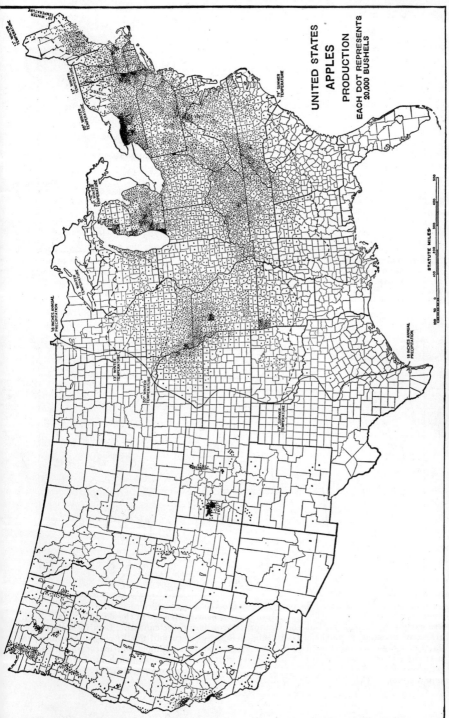

FIG. 62.—Distribution of apple production in the United States. The map is based on the census statistics for 1909, which make no distinction between the production of farm orchards and that of commercial orchards. (*After Finch and Baker.*[9])

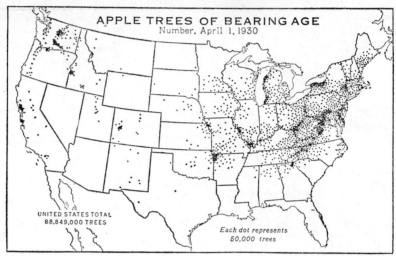

FIG. 63.—Most of the apple trees in the East are located in the Appalachian Mountain and Piedmont region, and around the shores of the Great Lakes where spring frosts are less injurious than in the interior, because of the lake influence or mountain air-drainage protection. The southern limit of the apple region extends only a little beyond the northern limit of cotton, and the western or moisture limit is about the same as that of timothy. Most of the apple trees of the West are in irrigated valleys. (*After Baker and Genung.*[2])

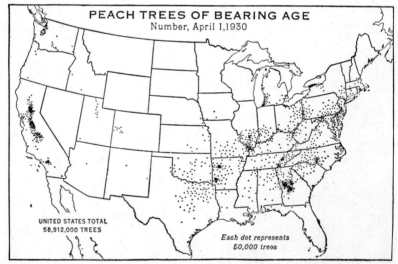

FIG. 64.—The two leading peach areas are the great valley of California and central Georgia. Nearly one-third of the peach trees of bearing age are in these two States. Both are early-peach districts, but the California crop is mostly canned. Less important districts are located in southern California, in southwestern and northwestern Arkansas, in eastern Tennessee, south-central North Carolina, southern Illinois, southwestern Michigan, and the Ontario shore of New York. Cold, dry winters prevent peach production northwest of a line drawn from Chicago to Omaha and thence to Amarillo, Tex. (*After Baker and Genung.*[2])

Mississippi, Alabama, Ohio, Michigan, Iowa, and the Ozark area. (However), the 1930–35 period. . . . included two or three seasons of extremely low and discouraging returns for their fruit. In the second place, it included the winter of 1933–34, one of record severity, which killed thousands of fruit trees both young and old throughout the East. The chief areas of decline in number of peach trees were in Georgia, eastern Tennessee, southern Illinois, the southern Ozarks, and California."[2]

The distribution of individual varieties is equally interesting. For instance the Fameuse apple is of great importance in the St. Lawrence river region, the Yellow Bellflower in parts of California, the Huntsman in Missouri; Yellow Newtown is important in New York, Virginia, Washington, Oregon, California, Tasmania and New South Wales.

It is one thing to construct a map which shows the geographic distribution of various fruits; it is quite another to find the exact reasons for this distribution. Without doubt many factors are operative. Some are of relatively great, others of much less, importance. A single factor may be decisive with one fruit, an entirely different factor with another and a group of several factors may be of almost equal importance in a third case.

LIFE ZONES, CROP ZONES AND FRUIT ZONES

In a broad way the fruit zones of the world coincide more or less closely with the general life zones and crop zones, though the pomologist may use other names to designate them than the biological cartographer does. These general life zones as determined for the United States, southern Canada and northern Mexico by the Bureau of Biological Survey of the United States Department of Agriculture, are shown in Fig. 70.

The Boreal Zone.—As here outlined, the Boreal zone or region includes all of Canada except a portion of Nova Scotia, a strip along the St. Lawrence River and running west through Ontario to Lake Huron and Georgian Bay, southern Saskatchewan and limited areas in southern Manitoba, Alberta and British Columbia. Its southern boundary dips down into the United States so as to include parts of northern New England, northern Michigan, a small strip of northeastern Wisconsin and a considerable part of Minnesota and North Dakota. Irregularly shaped areas characterized by the life of the Boreal region are found here and there in New York and Pennsylvania and at some of the higher elevations of the Allegheny Mountains as far south as southern Tennessee. In the western parts of the United States there are finger-like projections of this region and isolated areas with its characteristic fauna and flora extending as far south as the state of Zacatecas in Mexico. For the most part these extreme southern extensions are limited to the higher elevations of the Rocky, Sierra Nevada, Cascade and Coast mountain ranges. Its

southern limit is marked by the isotherm of 18°C. (64.4°F.) for the six
hottest consecutive weeks of midsummer.[49]   On the whole this region

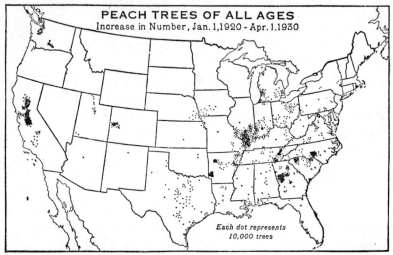

FIG. 65.—Comparison of this figure with Figs. 64 and 66 affords some idea of the changes
in centers of production that sometimes take place within a short period.   The increases
in tree number shown on this map reflect the relatively high prices and profits obtained
from peaches during the early part of this decade from the limited plantings in the areas
in question.   (*After Baker and Genung.*[2])

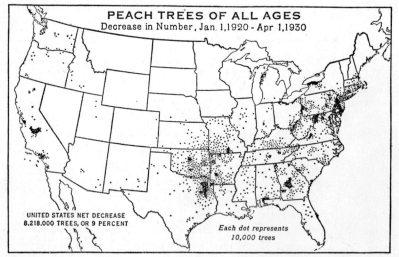

FIG. 66.—The decreases in peach tree population shown on this map were due in part
to injuries from unfavorable extremes of temperature and in part to market conditions.
(*After Baker and Genung.*[2])

is not suited to fruit growing; nevertheless a number of fruits are thoroughly at home and indeed reach their best development along its

southern borders. Among these are the cranberry, blueberry, currant and gooseberry.

The Tropical Zone.—Only a very small part of the continental United States is included within the Tropical region or zone. To be exact, there are three widely separated areas where tropical conditions prevail and tropical vegetation abounds—one in southern Florida, one in extreme southeastern Texas, and one along the California-Arizona line, extending as far north as southern Nevada. Within these areas are such fruits as the banana, pineapple, mango, date palm, cocoanut, papaya and cherimoya. This region is never visited by frosts or freezing temperatures and many of the fruits grown in it are said to be seriously injured by temperatures even closely approaching the freezing point. To the pomologist, as to the biologist, this region is known as the Tropical zone. It is characterized by having more than 14,400°C. (26,000°F.) of heat during the year—degrees of normal mean daily heat in excess of a minimum of 6°C. (43°F.),[49] which is rather arbitrarily assumed as marking the inception of physiological activity in plants.

Austral or Temperate Zone.—Between the Boreal region on the north and the Tropical region on the south and embracing most of the area of the United States, is a region designated as Austral on the maps of biological surveys and designated as the Temperate zone by the pomologist. Frosts and freezes are likely to occur throughout most of this region, but minimum winter temperatures seldom go below −30°F. at the north and the mean temperature of midwinter months even of the more northern sections is well above zero.

Transition Zone.—Biologists recognize three transcontinental life zones within this region, a so-called Transition zone to the north and an Upper Austral and Lower Austral zone to the south. Some of the more hardy fruits, as the apple, pear, red raspberry and the Nigra and European groups of plums find their most congenial home in the Transition zone. In the east this zone includes most of those portions of New England, New York, Pennsylvania and Michigan and in the middle west most of those portions of Wisconsin, Minnesota and the Dakotas not included in the Boreal region; in the west it includes many irregularly shaped areas from the Canadian border to Mexico, and even in Mexico, where elevation causes comparatively low temperatures. "Transition zone species," Merriam states, "require a total quantity of heat of at least 5500°C. (10,000°F.) but can not endure a summer temperature the mean of which for the six hottest weeks exceeds 22°C. (71.6°F.) The northern boundary of the Transition zone, therefore, is marked by the isotherm showing a sum of normal positive temperatures of 5500°C. (10,000°F.), while its southern boundary is coincident with the isotherm of 22°C. (71.6°F.) for the six hottest consecutive weeks."[49]

This Transition zone is in turn divided into three areas by lines having a general north and south direction, areas that differ from one another primarily in rainfall and atmospheric humidity. The eastern area, known as the Alleghanian, extends from the Atlantic seaboard approximately to the 100° meridian, which runs through central North and South Dakota, Nebraska and Texas. To the west of this is a central arid area extending to the Sierra Nevada-Cascade mountain range. West of this is the Pacific coast humid area, very humid at the north but toward the south gradually merging into the conditions presented by the central

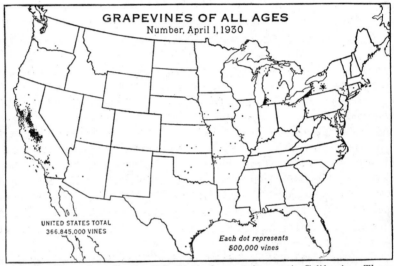

GRAPEVINES OF ALL AGES
Number, April 1, 1930

UNITED STATES TOTAL
366,845,000 VINES

Each dot represents
500,000 vines

FIG. 67.—About three-fourths of the Nation's grapevines are in California. The raisin district centers around Fresno where the sunshine is almost continuous. Wine grapes are more widely distributed, many being grown in the San Francisco Bay counties. Table grapes are grown in both the San Joaquin and Sacramento Valleys, and in southern California. In the East the principal grape districts are in western New York, and extend along the southern shore of Lake Erie. Minor centers are located in the southwest corner of Michigan, in northwestern Arkansas, and in southwestern Missouri. (*After Baker and Genung.*[2])

arid area. Generally speaking, the same fruit species thrive in all of these areas, though they cannot be grown without irrigation in the central arid section. However, though the same fruit species are grown in all three areas the same varieties are not equally successful; consequently each area has a more or less distinctive variety flora.

Upper Austral Zone.—The Upper Austral region includes a comparatively narrow belt of territory in the central Atlantic States but widens out to include a comparatively large part of the corn belt area in the middle west and like the Boreal and Transition regions it includes many irregularly shaped areas from the Canadian line to far below the Mexican border. According to Merriam: "Upper Austral species require a total

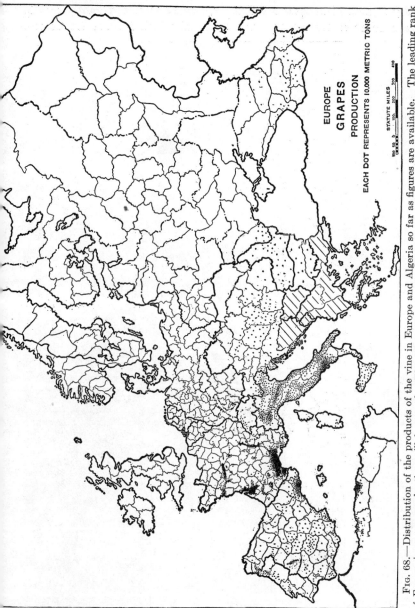

EUROPE
GRAPES
PRODUCTION

EACH DOT REPRESENTS 10,000 METRIC TONS

STATUTE MILES

FIG. 68.—Distribution of the products of the vine in Europe and Algeria so far as figures are available. The leading rank of France in grape production will be noted. The greatest production of wine in France is along the Mediterranean coast near Montpellier. The better known wines, however, come from the Bordeaux region on the Garonne River, from the banks of the Rhone, and from the province of Champagne. The principal centers of wine production in Italy are near Naples and along the slopes of the Apennines in northern Italy. (*After Finch and Baker.*[9])

quantity of heat of at least 6,400°C. (11,500°F.), but apparently cannot endure a summer temperature the mean of which for the six hottest

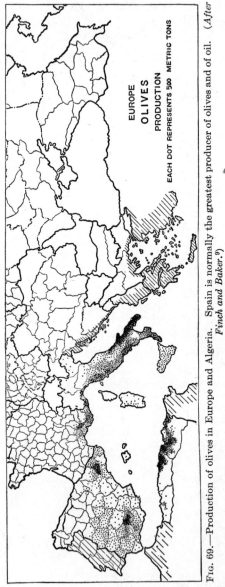

Fig. 69.—Production of olives in Europe and Algeria. Spain is normally the greatest producer of olives and of oil. (After Finch and Baker.[9])

consecutive weeks exceeds 26°C. (78.8°F.). The northern boundary of the Upper Austral zone, therefore, is marked by the isotherm showing a sum of normal positive temperatures of 6400°C. (11,511°F.) while its southern boundary agrees very closely with the isotherm of 26°C.

(78.8°F.) for the six hottest weeks."[49] The eastern half of this zone, known as the Carolinian area, has a humid climate; the western half, known as the Upper Sonoran area, is comparatively arid. The walnut, hickory, sassafras, sycamore, red bud and papaw are typical native trees of the Carolinian area; the sage brush, greasewood and juniper characterize the Upper Sonoran. Within this zone the peach, the Japanese plum, the persimmon and many varieties of the apple, pear, cherry and grape attain their highest development.

Lower Austral or Subtropic Zone.—The Lower Austral zone lies between the Upper Austral and Tropical regions. On the east it includes most of the south Atlantic seaboard and in the Mississippi valley it extends north into southern Missouri, Illinois and Indiana; in the west it includes most of southern California and much of the Sacramento and San Joaquin valleys. Merriam states: "Lower Austral species require a total quantity of heat of at least 10,000°C. (18,000°F.)."[49] Like the Upper Austral zone, its eastern half has a humid and its western half an arid climate. The eastern half is known as the Austroriparian area, the western half as the Lower Sonoran. The former is characterized by such native vegetation as the long-leaf and loblolly pines, the magnolia, the live oak and the pecan. It is a rich agricultural area producing cotton, rice, sugar cane and many other warm season crops. The distinctive fruits of its more northern reaches are the pecan, the muscadine grapes and pears of the oriental hybrid class. The Lower Sonoran area is characterized by many cacti, yuccas, agaves, mesquites and other desert plants. It produces plums, prunes, peaches, cherries, apricots, almonds, grapes and many other fruits in great quantities where irrigation water is available. The southern part of the Lower Austral zone is known to the pomologist as the Subtropic zone. Horticulturally it is one of the most important in the United States. Within it are produced citrus fruits, figs, avocados, loquats, Japanese persimmons and many other less known fruits.

Attention may be directed to the fact that the boundaries of the pomological districts of the United States, as they have been mapped by the American Pomological Society do not coincide exactly with those of the life zones that have been discussed, though the two maps have many features in common.

GEOGRAPHY OF FRUIT PRODUCTION AS INFLUENCED BY TEMPERATURE

It will be noted that these life zones or crop zones include areas characterized by a certain uniformity of climate and that, of all the features that constitute climate, temperature is given first consideration. Indeed the boundaries of the different regions and zones are for the most part isothermals, and the main reason for such irregular outlines, especially in the mountainous districts, is the influence of altitude upon temperature.

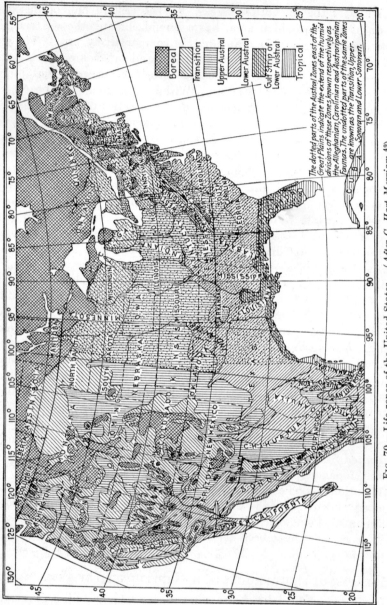

The dotted parts of the Austral Zones east of the Great Plains indicate the extend of the humid divisions of these Zones, known respectively as the Alleghanian, Carolinian and Austroriparian Faunas. The unadotted parts of the same Zones are known as the Transition, Upper-Sonoran and Lower Sonoran.

Boreal
Transition
Upper Austral
Lower Austral
Gulf Strip of Lower Austral
Tropical

Fig. 70.—Life zones of the United States.   (After C. Hart Merriam.[49])

High altitude through its accompaniment low temperature, accounts for the island-like areas of the Boreal or Transition zones in latitudes generally dominated by the life of the Austral. Generally there is a lowering of about 4°F. in mean temperature for each increase in elevation of 1,000 feet. Even at the equator frost will occur at an elevation of about 18,000 feet; on the island of Hawaii, at a latitude of 20° North, frost occurs at an altitude of 4,500 feet or above.[71]

Students of plant geography have used various standards to account for the natural distribution of plants. Many of these have more or less applicability, but none fits all cases completely. Obviously, winter temperatures set a limit on the poleward distribution of all plants sooner or later, but not every species fills out its space limitations thus set. A species such as the cherry, which ripens its fruit early in the season, would in nature be likely to spread poleward until it reached the limit set by low winter temperature, but species such as the persimmon or the pecan, which ripen their fruits late, are likely to reach their natural limits through inability to perpetuate themselves by seed rather than through inability to withstand winter temperatures. Trees of both these species planted at East Lansing, Mich., are perfectly hardy, but never ripen seed. No single temperature standard, then, is likely to measure the distribution of woody perennial plants.

Rainfall is obviously a limiting factor, but its relation to plant life cannot be measured by any single numerical quantity. Regions with identical annual rainfall may vary widely in their native flora because of a difference in the seasonal distribution of the rains or because of differences in the evaporating power of the air. The difference between the free growth of coniferous trees in the northeastern states and the precarious existence of most planted specimens in Missouri, where the rainfall is greater than that of the northeast, is probably due in large measure to the difference in the evaporating power of the air.

Both temperature and rainfall affect fruit growing, but the influences are exercised in ways differing somewhat from those exerted on natural distribution. Since fruit trees are planted, natural reproduction is not of itself a factor in fruit growing, and New York, where seedling apple trees grow wild, has its keenest competition in the apple market from parts of Washington where the natural rainfall supports but a few semi-desert plants. It is true that the area that can be brought under irrigation in the arid regions is limited, but this particular limitation will not affect fruit growing for some time to come. Lack of rain does undoubtedly limit fruit growing in some areas, but not to the extent that it does natural distribution of plants.

Fruit growing is conducted, however, for fruit production, generally for profit, and the mere existence of the trees is not sufficient for this. If spring frosts or winter freezes destroy many crops, profit disappears though the trees remain. If fungus diseases or insect pests are too virulent, excellent trees are only an expense; in many cases their virulence is related to temperature or rainfall or to both. Color, finish, quality or season of ripening may be affected by one of these factors to an extent which becomes important or even limiting commercially. Temperature and moisture effects, as limiting factors, have been considered in earlier pages; at this point they are considered only as they occur in regions where fruit growing is actually carried on commercially and their relation to economic forces is considered more fully.

Peach Growing as Influenced by Temperature.—The varying influences of temperature on the geographic range of fruits are shown clearly by the peach, if comparison be made between Europe and the United States. Table 1 shows mean monthly temperatures at selected points. Bordeaux, Perpignan, Montpellier and Lyons in France may be considered to have temperatures favorable to peach growing. Roscoff, in Brittany, Plymouth, England, and Bergen, Norway, are in regions where few or no peaches are grown, though they are warmer in winter than Rochester, N. Y., which is typical of much of the peach-growing area in the northeastern states. The difference between the points named where peach growing is successful and those where it is not lies in the summer temperatures. So far as winter temperature is concerned peaches apparently could be grown in Berufjord, Iceland; deficiency in summer temperatures seems the limiting factor in a considerable part of Europe.

Between Nashua and Concord, in New Hampshire, about 35 miles apart, runs the northern limit of commercial peach growing in that section. Examination of the table shows only small differences in mean monthly temperatures; the absolute minima for the two stations are, respectively, $-25°F.$ and $-35°F.$ Near the one point commercial peach growing is profitable; a few miles away it becomes unprofitable. The July temperature for Concord is identical with that for Fitchburg, Mass. (*cf.* Table 3), well within the zone of peach growing, and greater than that of Roseburg, Ore. Apparently, then, for conditions obtaining in southern New Hampshire, the northern limit of commercial peach production is set by winter temperatures averaging between those for the two stations given.

Pierre, S. D., has summer temperatures as high as or higher than many sections where the peach grows readily, but its winter temperatures are too low. Near Portland, Maine, the peach reaches its limit in ordinary cultivation and is subject to winter injury. Portland, Ore., with a summer temperature slightly lower, provides, through milder winters, conditions such that the peach grows fairly well. Near Lincoln, Neb., the peach grows about as at Portland, Maine; though the winter temperature averages a shade lower, the summer is warmer, suggesting a greater maturity in the fall with consequent ability better to withstand the winter. This, however, is the only way in which summer temperature may be considered to influence peach growing in any large area of the United States. The chief limiting temperature factor here comes in the winter. Nevertheless the factor of summer temperature or the length of the growing season may become important in isolated areas along the northern border of peach growing.

The southern limits of peach culture, on the other hand, are set by high winter temperatures. Thus at Thomasville, Ga., there is not enough cold weather during the average winter to break the rest period and insure prompt and even foliation and flowering in the spring, Albany being probably close to the southern limit of peach culture in that state.[45] Yarnell[75] reports that in Texas a total of 800 to 1,000 hours of lapsed time below 45°F. is required to break the rest period of most peach varieties.

Grape Growing as Influenced by Temperature.—The northern limit of grape culture, as with the peach, is set by summer temperatures at some points and by winter temperatures at others. Its course in Europe has been defined as extending "from somewhat north of the mouth of the Loire, where the Marne empties into the Seine, to the junction of the Aar and the Rhine, north of the Erzgebirge, to about the 52° of latitude, descends along the Carpathians to the 49°, extends on this parallel eastward, and near the Volga turns southward to its mouth, in the Caspian Sea."[12]

Wine in considerable quantities was made north of this line, in England, and even in Zeeland, in former times. This fact, sometimes cited as proving a change in climate, probably proves no more than a change in taste. "It must be taken for granted that in those times when there was no communication over long distances they were not very exacting in regard to wine, particularly as the best wines were unknown, as must have been the case in northern Germany, the Netherlands and England. If the wine was harsh and sour, it was still wine. . . . With the present facilities for communication and the competition in the wine business resulting therefrom; vine culture is no longer profitable in many places where 30 years ago it was so. . . ."

The boundary thus set, therefore, is not necessarily the limit of the ability of the grape to grow; it does, however, mark the limit of its ability to ripen sufficiently for wine making. This line in western Europe is set by summer temperatures. In eastern Europe it is set by winter temperatures and does represent approximately the real limit of culture of the vine.

Table 2 shows the mean monthly temperatures for a number of selected European stations. Some of these, for example, Bordeaux in France, Florence in Italy, Patras in Greece and Odessa in Russia, are either centers of important viticultural industries or they fairly represent such districts. Others, like Bergen in Norway, Plymouth in England and Roscoff in Brittany are places where outdoor grape culture for wine is impracticable. Yet these latter points have mean winter temperatures

TABLE 1.—MEAN MONTHLY TEMPERATURES IN RELATION TO PEACH GROWING
(Degrees Fahrenheit)

	January	February	March	April	May	June	July	August	September	October	November	December
Bordeaux, France (1)	41	43	47	53	58	64	68	68	64	55	47	41
Perpignan, France (1)..............	41	46	50	56	61	68	73	72	67	58	51	45
Montpellier, France (1)	41	44	48	55	61	68	73	72	65	57	48	42
Roscoff, France (1)................	45	45	46	50	53	58	61	62	59	55	49	46
Plymouth, England (1)	42	43	44	48	53	58	61	61	58	51	47	43
Bergen, Norway (1)	34	34	35	42	45	55	58	58	53	45	38	35
Lyons, France (1)	36	40	46	54	60	66	70	69	63	53	44	37
Berufjord, Iceland (1)	30	29	29	34	39	44	47	47	44	38	34	30
Concord, N. H. (2)................	21	23	32	44	57	65	70	67	60	49	37	26
Nashua, N. H. (2)	23	25	34	46	58	67	71	68	61	49	38	28
Rochester, N. Y. (3)..............	24	24	31	44	57	66	70	68	62	51	38	29
Portland, Maine (3)	22	24	32	43	54	63	68	66	60	49	38	27
Portland, Ore. (3)	39	41	46	51	57	61	66	66	61	53	46	41
Pierre, S. D. (3)	14	17	30	46	59	69	75	73	63	49	32	20
Lincoln, Neb. (3)..................	21	25	36	51	63	72	76	74	65	53	38	27

1. Hann. J., Handb. der Klimatologie, Stuttgart (1911).
2. United States Department Agriculture, Weather Bureau, *Bul. Q.* (1906).
3. United States Department Agriculture, Weather Bureau, *Bul. R.* (1908).

above those of some of the grape growing districts and their absolute minimum temperatures are likewise higher. However, their mean summer temperatures are comparatively low—too low for the grape to mature its fruit and wood properly; consequently the industry does not flourish there.

In the Mississippi valley, the northern limit to the successful culture of the *labrusca* grapes is set by minimum winter temperatures which result in winter-killing of canes and roots; in its central and southern parts by a combination of the mean and mean maximum temperatures of July and August which prevent the fruit from maturing properly. This latter influence is possibly brought about through the acceleration of respiration without a corresponding increase in photosynthesis, thus interfering with carbohydrate accumulation. In Michigan, New York and New England, on the other hand, the northern limits for these same varieties is set by a combination of the mean and mean minimum summer temperatures, just as is true of the *vinifera* varieties in northern Europe.

As between different varieties, there are considerable differences in the maximum and minimum temperatures that they will endure and the mean temperatures under which they will thrive. Thus the Beta will endure considerably lower winter temperatures than the Concord and Delaware; the Fredonia will mature and attain high quality with a mean July–August temperature several degrees lower than that required for Concord, while the Catawba requires one that is several degrees higher still.

Temperature and the Geographic Range of Apple Varieties.—Low winter temperatures preclude extensive commercial apple production in a few states, such as the Dakotas, Wyoming and portions of Montana, and limit seriously the choice of varieties in others, as in Minnesota, Wisconsin, Vermont, New Hampshire and Maine. It is probable, however, that the area from which apple production is limited by summer heat is as great, if not greater, embracing virtually all the Gulf coastal plain, Florida, most of Georgia and much of the South Atlantic coastal plain, as well as considerable areas in California, Arizona and New Mexico. In Arkansas, Georgia and South Carolina, as well as in California and New Mexico, apple production is localized in the cooler portions of the respective states. Information on the southern limits of apple-tree growth is too inexact to permit definite statement as to whether physiological reaction or parasitic infestation, both of which play a part, is the primary limiting factor. Within the limits of tree growth, however, a southerly limit of practical culture is set by failure of fruit to mature or by its dropping before maturity or by light yields or by excessive parasitism, which is the case particularly in warm humid regions. The same general principles operate to establish limits for the profitable culture of different varieties of the apple. Thus, winter temperatures at Eastport, Maine, are higher than those at Lewiston, in the same state. The Baldwin apple grows very well around Lewiston but not at Eastport. The difference in suitability of the two places lies evidently in the summer temperatures. Madison, Wis., has evidently sufficient summer heat to satisfy the Baldwin's requirements; the difficulty in growing Baldwin at this last point is known to be winter temperature. So far as apple growing in the United States is concerned, then, there are along the northern limit, two different factors operating, summer temperature and winter temperature; the effects of the one sometimes mask those of the other. However, there appear to be very few places listed in the table where the Baldwin apple would suffer from lack of summer heat. Data are presented in Tables 3 and 4 showing the mean monthly temperatures throughout the year and the minimum temperatures for the six winter months at a number of stations in the United States. Except for the California and Alaska points, each station included in the tables may be taken as representing fairly well a commercial apple producing section. The figures afford an idea of the range in mean and minimum temperatures within which apple growing is profitable and by inference, an idea of the temperature limits for the commercial varieties.   A comparison of these data with the records of the leading varieties in the several districts represented, likewise affords a fairly accurate measure of their particular temperature requirements and this, in turn, may be used as a basis for judging their probable suitability for sections where they have not been tried but where temperature records are available.

Averages are treacherous at times and caution should be observed in their interpretation.   Lewiston, Maine, shows the lowest mean winter temperatures of any of the apple sections represented in Table 3.   Nevertheless this region grows successfully several apple varieties which cannot be grown in the Bitter Root valley, as represented by Missoula.   Reference to Table 4 shows that the mean temperatures for Missoula conceal a November minimum of $-20°$F. as compared with plus $2°$F. for Lewiston and a January minimum of $-42°$F. for Missoula as compared with $-24°$F. for Lewiston.   Over a long period the amount of winter killing around Lewiston is probably no greater than that around Spokane, Wash., though Lewiston averages $8°$ colder in January and $10°$ colder in February.   The October and November means, however, are only $1°$ apart. Absolute minima for Lewiston in October, November and January are actually higher than those for Spokane ($6°$, $15°$ and $6°$F. respectively). The November temperatures, mean and minimum, seem particularly important in relation to winter injury along the northern border of apple growing.

The total effective growing temperatures at Portland, Ore., and Portland, Maine, are practically the same and the same varieties of apples attain an almost equal development in the two places.   Apparently in this case neither maximum nor mean summer temperatures in Oregon nor minimum winter temperatures in Maine are limiting factors in the growth of the varieties in question.   Mean temperature during the growing season, therefore, in this case becomes an accurate index of adaptation to climate.

On the other hand, the loganberry and sweet cherry which thrive so well in the vicinity of Portland, Ore., cannot be grown profitably near Portland, Maine, because minimum winter temperature is a limiting factor.   The blueberry, which grows so luxuriantly near Portland, Maine, fails to grow near Portland, Ore., not because temperature is a limiting factor but presumably because it does not find a congenial soil.   Failure to recognize the limitations imposed by growing-season temperature upon the successful culture of different fruits and to adjust the orchard enterprise to existing conditions by selection of suitable varieties has probably led to more failures than has ignorance regarding pollination requirements or pruning practices.   This is evidenced by the almost universal planting of the Delicious variety, when, as a matter of fact, it reaches perfection only where there is a relatively long and warm growing season—almost as long and warm as that required for Winesap. Hundreds of thousands of Jonathan trees have been planted in portions of Michigan, New York and New England where the summers are too cool for them and hundreds of thousands of Baldwin, Northern Spy and McIntosh have been planted in New Jersey, Pennsylvania, Ohio, Indiana, Illinois and other states where the summers are too warm for them. In none of these cases does the fruit reach a high degree of perfection, and the producers suffer the consequent losses in financial returns.

Investigations in fruit growing at Sitka, Alaska, show interesting effects of a rather unusual climate. From November to March inclusive the mean temperatures are higher than those of Lewiston, Maine; they exceed those of Rochester, N. Y., for nearly the same period and for December to February they are somewhat higher than those of Martinsburg, W. Va. Zero temperatures are very rare; nevertheless winter killing is common. Records of the Alaska Agricultural Experiment Stations show that such hardy plums as De Soto and Rollingstone, numerous apple varieties selected for hardiness, the sand cherry and blackberries have suffered considerable injury.

The causes of this condition are indicated in the following quotations from reports of the station:

"Only early maturing sorts will succeed. Varieties which are summer apples in the States will be fall apples in Alaska, and those which are fall apples in the States will not mature at all in Alaska. The summer heat is not great enough. In the coast region the season between frosts is long—longer, indeed, by at least two months than in the northern tier of states.

"In the larger portion of the coast region there is little, if any, damaging frost between May 1 and October 1, and some seasons damaging frosts do not occur until the end of October. The drawback to the climate in this region lies not in too great cold, but, anomalous as the statement seems, in the lack of summer heat. . . . The maximum temperature is more generally between 60° and 70°, and some summers it will not go much above 60°. In the interior, on the other hand, the summers are warm enough, at least in places but the season is too short to hope to mature any but the earliest sorts and there is considerable doubt if they will succeed."[14]

"The excessive rainfall and continuous mild weather prolongs the growing season until long into October. The young wood is soft and succulent, and moderately cold weather the following winter kills it.[15]

"The winter of 1908–1909 was quite severe for this part of the coast region. The temperature fell to 2° above zero and 3° above zero in January and February, respectively, and the cold period was protracted over many weeks. As a consequence, the young growth produced in the season of 1908 was partly killed in most cases, and in some cases entirely."[17]

"Blackberries and dewberries cannot be grown successfully in any part of Alaska. They have been tried repeatedly at the Sitka Experiment Station and

TABLE 2.—MEAN MONTHLY TEMPERATURE AT SELECTED EUROPEAN STATIONS
(*Compiled from Hann*[19])
(In degrees Fahrenheit)

	January	February	March	April	May	June	July	August	September	October	November	December
Bordeaux, France	40.6	42.9	46.9	53.0	58.3	64.2	68.2	68.2	63.7	55.4	46.9	41.2
Budapest, Hungary	28.2	31.4	39.9	51.1	60.1	66.7	70.5	68.7	61.1	51.1	40.2	30.6
Patras, Greece	51.1	53.0	56.1	61.1	67.8	74.5	80.8	80.6	76.6	69.8	61.1	53.6
Bremen, Germany	33.6	34.7	38.1	46.0	54.1	60.3	63.1	61.7	56.5	48.4	39.4	35.1
Plymouth, England	42.1	42.8	43.8	48.0	52.9	58.4	61.0	61.0	57.6	51.1	46.8	43.2
Lemburg, Austria	24.3	25.7	31.1	46.2	57.0	64.3	66.4	65.0	57.0	47.3	34.7	27.2
Roscoff, France	45.0	44.8	46.2	50.0	53.4	57.7	61.3	62.1	59.4	55.2	49.3	45.8
Bergen, Norway	34.2	33.6	42.1	48.9	55.1	55.2	55.7	55.6	50.7	45.2	38.5	34.7
Florence, Italy	40.7	42.1	48.9	56.1	63.1	70.7	76.1	74.8	68.6	58.8	49.3	42.6
Nantes, France	40.1	41.9	45.2	51.3	56.3	62.2	65.7	65.0	60.4	52.9	45.3	40.6
Odessa, Russia	25.3	27.7	34.9	47.5	59.2	68.0	72.5	70.9	62.1	51.8	41.0	30.2

TABLE 3.—MEAN TEMPERATURES OF SELECTED STATIONS
(*Compiled from United States Weather Bureau Bul. Q*)
(Degrees Fahrenheit)

	December	January	February	March	April	May	June	July	August	September	October	November
Lewiston, Maine	23	18	20	30	42	54	64	69	66	59	47	36
Fitchburg, Mass.	28	24	25	32	46	57	66	70	68	61	49	39
Rochester, N. Y.	29	24	24	31	45	57	66	71	69	63	51	39
Albany, N. Y.	28	23	24	33	46	59	68	73	71	64	51	39
Vineland, N. J.	34	32	33	40	51	62	72	76	74	67	56	44
Charlottesville, Va.	35	35	37	46	56	66	73	76	75	67	58	47
Martinsburg, W. Va.	34	31	31	40	51	62	72	75	74	67	55	43
Waynesville, N. C.	38	37	36	48	52	62	68	70	70	64	54	46
Clayton, Ga.	40	40	39	50	56	66	72	75	74	68	57	48
Marietta, Ohio	34	32	31	42	53	63	70	74	72	65	53	43
Griggsville, Ill.	32	28	27	40	55	65	73	77	75	68	57	42
Springfield, Mo.	37	34	33	44	57	65	73	77	76	69	58	45
Montrose, Colo.	28	23	31	39	48	57	66	72	69	62	49	36
Provo, Utah	29	27	30	39	49	58	64	74	71	60	49	39
Missoula, Mont.	25	21	25	34	45	54	60	67	66	55	45	32
Payette, Idaho	32	30	34	42	52	60	67	74	73	62	52	42
The Dalles, Ore.	36	32	37	45	53	60	66	71	70	62	52	42
Albany, Ore.	41	39	42	46	51	57	62	67	67	60	53	46
Roseburg, Ore.	42	41	43	47	51	57	61	66	66	61	54	46
Spokane, Wash.	32	26	30	40	48	56	62	69	68	58	48	37
Moxee Wells, Wash.	31	30	35	42	50	58	65	71	70	59	50	39
Walla Walla, Wash.	37	33	37	45	53	60	66	74	74	64	54	43
Sacramento, Cal.	47	46	50	54	58	64	70	74	73	70	62	54
Fresno, Cal.	46	45	51	54	60	67	75	82	81	74	64	55
Los Angeles, Cal.	56	54	55	57	60	63	67	71	72	70	64	60
Roswell, N. M.	40	40	42	52	60	68	76	77	77	71	59	48
Sitka, Alaska	36	31	36	38	41	48	52	55	55	52	47	39

the attempt has always resulted in failure. The summer is not warm enough to develop the fruit and the plants usually winterkill even in mild winters, probably due to the late succulent growth resulting from the abundance of moisture."[17]

Phenological data taken at Sitka are interesting. Apples are recorded as leafing out June 1; Early Richmond cherry in blossom June 15, the Whitney apple on June 20. Early Richmond cherries and Champion gooseberries were ripe August 15; the Cuthbert raspberry usually ripens during the last of August. These dates explain the ability of only a few apple varieties to mature fruit there, the most satisfactory being Yellow Transparent and Livland Raspberry. Patten Greening has set good crops but failed to ripen its fruit.

On the other hand, gooseberries, currants and red raspberries thrive at this point and bear heavily. At the Kenai Station, where repeated efforts failed to produce grain crops because of the cool summers, these fruits were satisfactory.[16] Evidently then, though these fruits endure less heat and drought than grain

TABLE 4.—ABSOLUTE MINIMUM TEMPERATURES OF SELECTED STATIONS
(Compiled from United States Weather Bureau Bul. Q)
(To 1906, Degrees Fahrenheit)

	October	November	December	January	February	March
Lewiston, Maine.....	18	2	−21	−24	−24	− 4
Fitchburg, Mass......	22	5	−14	−14	−16	− 4
Rochester, N. Y......	19	1	−11	−12	−12	− 7
Albany, N. Y........	23	−10	−17	−24	−18	− 8
Vineland, N. J........	22	14	− 5	−11	−13	10
Charlottesville, Va....	26	15	4	− 1	− 9	10
Martinsburg, W. Va..	23	15	− 2	− 2	−13	− 1
Waynesville, N. C....	16	9	− 4	−12	−10	−2
Clayton, Ga.........	24	14	2	− 1	− 5	8
Marietta, Ohio.......	19	15	− 4	− 8	−22	2
Griggsville, Ill.......	20	2	−16	−20	−22	− 2
Springfield, Mo......	21	6	−11	−17	−29	3
Montrose, Colo......	19	−18	−17	−20	−13	− 2
Provo, Utah.........	12	3	− 6	− 7	−18	7
Missoula, Mont......	7	−20	−23	−42	−36	−18
Payette, Idaho.......	16	− 6	− 6	−13	−15	12
The Dalles, Ore......	20	− 2	−18	−13	−19	− 1
Albany, Ore.........	29	23	18	10	11	9
Roseburg, Ore.......	22	14	7	− 6	3	18
Spokane, Wash.......	12	−13	−18	−30	−23	−10
Moxee Wells, Wash...	13	−22	− 8	−15	−22	2
Walla Walla, Wash...	24	− 9	− 2	−17	−15	2
Sacramento, Cal.....	36	27	24	19	21	29
Fresno, Cal..........	36	27	23	20	24	28
Los Angeles, Cal.....	40	34	30	30	28	31
Roswell, N. M........	19	10	− 3	− 4	−14	14

they endure more rain and low growing-season temperatures. Their growing-season requirements appear to resemble those of cabbage and potatoes.

The Effect of Bodies of Water on Temperature.—Large bodies of water have been said to retard temperature changes, making conditions in their vicinity rather more favorable for fruit growing. Table 5 assembles data showing mean monthly temperatures for stations selected

TABLE 5.—MONTHLY MEAN TEMPERATURES AT COASTAL AND AT INLAND POINTS
(*Compiled from Bigelow*[4])
(Degrees Fahrenheit)

	January	February	March	April	May	June	July	August	September	October	November	December
1. Grand Haven, Mich.............	24.5	24.2	30.8	44.0	54.8	64.7	69.7	67.8	61.1	50.2	38.0	30.1
2. Grand Rapids, Mich.............	23.8	25.5	33.0	46.2	59.0	68.1	72.6	70.0	61.8	50.1	38.1	28.8
3. Buffalo, N. Y...................	24.7	24.0	31.2	42.3	54.5	65.1	70.2	68.8	62.9	51.5	39.3	30.1
4. Syracuse, N. Y.................	23.0	23.8	31.4	44.4	57.3	66.9	70.8	68.6	61.6	51.0	38.7	28.3
5. Milwaukee, Wis.................	19.8	21.9	30.9	41.8	53.6	63.5	69.7	68.7	61.5	50.2	36.1	26.0
6. Madison, Wis..................	16.5	19.6	30.1	44.5	57.6	67.3	72.4	69.6	61.1	48.8	34.2	22.7
7. Eastport, Maine...............	20.1	21.4	28.9	38.3	46.9	54.4	59.8	59.7	55.2	46.6	36.8	25.3
8. Northfield, Vt.................	15.1	17.2	26.2	40.2	53.5	62.7	66.6	62.9	54.6	43.6	32.0	20.5
9. Erie, Pa......................	26.5	26.1	33.1	44.7	57.3	67.0	71.8	69.9	63.9	53.1	41.1	31.7
10. Scranton, Pa.................	25.5	26.9	34.9	47.1	58.8	67.2	71.8	69.3	62.2	51.4	39.1	29.8
11. Charles City, Iowa...... ..	11.4	15.1	28.4	46.3	59.5	68.8	73.5	70.7	61.7	48.2	33.0	19.0
12. Dubuque, Iowa	18.3	21.6	33.2	48.9	60.8	69.6	74.7	72.0	63.6	52.0	36.0	24.5

to illustrate this influence. With the exception of the Iowa points, the stations are arranged in contrasting pairs, the odd-numbered stations being located close to considerable bodies of water. In practically every case these stations show higher January means and lower July means than the respective stations with which they are contrasted. In every case the April temperature for the inland station is higher and November temperature lower than at the points near water. The Iowa stations of

TABLE 6.—DATES WHEN NORMAL TEMPERATURE CROSSES 40°F.
(*Compiled from Bigelow*[4])

1. Grand Haven, Mich.........................	Apr. 7	Nov. 8
2. Grand Rapids, Mich........................	Apr. 3	Nov. 9
3. Buffalo, N. Y.............................	Apr. 11	Nov. 12
4. Syracuse, N. Y...........................	Apr. 7	Nov. 11
5. Milwaukee, Wis...........................	Apr. 12	Nov. 5
6. Madison, Wis.............................	Apr. 7	Nov. 2
7. Eastport, Maine...........................	Apr. 23	Nov. 5
8. Northfield, Vt............................	Apr. 16	Oct. 25
9. Erie, Pa.................................	Apr. 5	Nov. 17
10. Scranton, Pa.............................	Mar. 30	Nov. 12
11. Charles City, Iowa........................	Apr. 4	Nov. 2
12. Dubuque, Iowa...........................	Mar. 31	Nov. 7

approximately the same latitude as the majority of the more eastern points show intensification in all these differences. Milwaukee and Grand Haven, at almost opposite points on Lake Michigan, show the influence of the lake on the prevailing winds blowing over it. That the retardation for these stations is generally somewhat greater in the spring than in the fall is shown by Table 6.

Attention may be called to some of the northern finger-like extensions of the Lower Austral zone into latitudes that for the most part belong in the Transition zone. Those along the eastern shore of Lakes Michigan and Huron, the southern shores of Lakes Erie and Ontario and the eastern

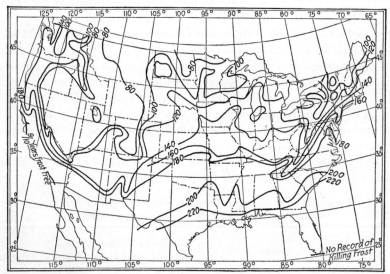

Fig. 71.—Computed length of available growing season 4 years in 5. (*After Reed.*)

shore of Lake Champlain are cases in point and illustrate the extent to which climate is tempered and consequently life zones are modified through the influence of large bodies of water. Lippincott gives one concrete illustration of this influence.[43] On Jan. 1, 1864, a cold wave swept over the north central part of the United States. Many Minnesota points registered temperatures as low as −38°F.; at Milwaukee the thermometer went to −30°F.; yet at Holland, Mich., across Lake Michigan from Milwaukee −8°F. was the lowest temperature recorded. Further inland, at Lansing, Mich., however, −22°F. was experienced. Peach buds were uninjured in a narrow belt along the eastern shore of the lake but were killed at distant points. The data for Milwaukee and Grand Haven in Table 5 show that this influence is constant. In the upper peninsula of Michigan on the southern shore of Lake Superior at Grand Marais, there is an average frost-free growing season of 144 days.

At Seney, 20 miles inland and at practically the same elevation, the frost-free period of summer is only 42 days. Here only a few of the short-season, frost-resistant fruits, such as the low-bush blueberry, can be successfully grown, and with them there are frequent crop failures because of frost injury. At Grand Marais, on the other hand, many kinds of fruit that are hardy to low winter temperatures and that are suited to a cool summer climate may be grown.

Influence of Altitude on Air and Soil Temperatures.—It is well known that an increase in altitude is accompanied by many of the same changes as an increase in latitude, the most important being one in temperature. It is true also that an increase in altitude is accompanied by certain changes in physical environment that are not found at correspondingly higher latitudes. Thus Kerner and Oliver report that in the Tyrolese Alps at an altitude of 2,600 meters the chemical activity of the sun's rays is 11 per cent. greater than at sea level. This alone may account for some of the peculiarities of plant associations noted at different altitudes and possibly may go far toward explaining the more brilliant and intense coloring of certain fruits and their better finish at high altitudes. The same authors report a different ratio between mean soil and air temperatures at high as compared with low elevations (see Table 7) and this too may either intensify or suppress, as the case may be, the differences associated with variations in air temperature only.

TABLE 7.—INCREASE OF MEAN SOIL TEMPERATURE OVER MEAN AIR TEMPERATURE WITH INCREASED ALTITUDE IN TYROLESE ALPS[40]

Elevation, meters	Excess of mean soil temperature over mean air temperature, degrees Centigrade
1000	1.5
1300	1.7
1600	2.4
1900	3.0
2200	3.6

GEOGRAPHY OF FRUIT PRODUCTION AS INFLUENCED BY RAINFALL AND HUMIDITY

Of hardly less significance than temperature is the influence of humidity in determining the limits of life and crop zones and in the geography of fruit growing. By humidity is meant here total rainfall, distribution throughout the season, availability for plant growth and atmospheric humidity. Only in countries or districts where the topography leads to marked differences in rainfall between points close together and enjoying practically the same temperatures are the full effects of humidity strikingly brought out. Thus " . . . at one of the substations of the United States Experiment Station on the Island of Hawaii, a rainfall of 360 inches was recorded for 1 year, while at a point 28 miles away the annual rainfall for the same year was 6 inches. It is possible . . . in the space of an hour's ride to pass from a desert covered with cacti and other drought-resistant plants into a dense tropical jungle reeking with moisture."[71]

For the most part, fruit trees thrive better in a fairly humid climate, a fact shown by the natural distribution of their undomesticated relatives, though many species, like the date palm and olive, succeed in a very arid climate. The spots where total rainfall is too copious for fruit growing constitute an insignificant portion of the area of the United States; on the other hand, irrigation overcomes deficiencies in water supply, and fruit growing is, to a considerable degree, independent of rainfall. Total rainfall is, therefore, of comparatively small significance in determining the distribution of fruit growing. Its distribution, however, though perhaps of minor importance in determining the ability of fruit trees to live, is in some cases the dominant factor in determining the profitable production of fruit.

The whole Pacific coast of North America has a type of rainfall distribution characterized by a rainy winter and a dry summer. At Sitka, October is the rainiest month, but from Seattle to San Diego December registers the heaviest precipitation. The annual total decreases from north to south. Compared to Europe, the rainfall regime of the Oregon and Washington coast resembles that of the coast of north-west Europe, but with a drier summer. The California rainfall pattern (*e.g.*, Sacramento) strongly resembles that of the Mediterranean but does not have the separate high peaks in autumn and spring which characterize the latter region. This distribution covers the interior of California and is continued in the pattern characterizing much of the intermountain area, as represented by Payette, Idaho, and Provo, Utah; here too, winter is the rainy season, but the heaviest rainfall comes somewhat later, and rains fall in spring and early summer. The plains area, extending from Dakota and Montana through western Texas, presents a characteristically continental-climate rainfall pattern in that the maximum rainfall comes in June and the greater portion of the annual precipitation occurs during the growing season. The Gulf States have much heavier precipitation than the plains states in winter, with a maximum in late summer. Most of the middle west states combine the plains tendency toward early summer maximum rainfall, but influenced by the Gulf type enough to have a heavy winter rainfall tending eastward toward the plains type. Eastern New York and most of New England have an unusual pattern in that rainfall varies very little from month to month.

Winter rainfall, where soil is frozen, tends to relatively high run-off losses, and, where soil is rarely frozen, to relatively high percolation losses. Summer rainfall is subject to high evaporation losses but probably comes closer to complete availability for plants. Indeed, were the rainfall in the plains states to come in winter, rather than summer, crop production would be limited very seriously. So far as tree fruit production is concerned, however, there are many advantages in light summer rainfall, provided irrigation water is available. Fungous diseases, notably brown rot of stone fruits and scab in apples and pears, and some insect pests, as apple maggot, are notably less troublesome in dry summers or dry climates. On the other hand, some insects, such as codling moth, are more troublesome under these same conditions.

TABLE 8.—MEAN RAINFALL OF SELECTED STATIONS
(*Compiled Chiefly from United States Weather Bureau Bul. Q*)
(Inches)

	March	April	May	June	July	August	September	October	Total growing season	Total ann.
Rumford Falls, Maine ...	4.1	3.0	3.7	3.8	4.5	3.2	3.0	3.0	28.3	42.1
Fitchburg, Mass.........	4.0	3.3	3.6	3.0	2.9	4.4	3.4	4.0	28.6	45.4
Rochester, N. Y.........	3.1	2.4	3.0	3.1	3.1	2.9	2.3	2.8	22.7	34.5
Albany, N. Y...........	2.8	2.4	3.0	3.7	3.9	4.0	3.2	3.1	26.1	36.9
Vineland, N. J..........	4.3	3.3	3.7	3.6	4.6	4.8	3.8	3.6	31.7	47.3
Martinsburg, W. Va......	3.1	3.2	4.2	3.6	3.7	3.2	2.5	1.6	25.1	35.2
Charlottesville, Va......	3.6	3.4	5.1	5.5	5.7	5.0	5.2	3.5	37.0	49.8
Waynesville, N. C.......	6.4	4.1	3.7	4.4	4.6	4.5	2.4	2.1	32.2	47.7
Clayton, Ga............	7.8	6.3	3.2	5.3	7.0	7.2	4.9	4.0	45.7	68.5
Marietta, O............	3.2	3.3	4.0	4.5	4.4	3.9	3.0	2.9	29.2	42.1
Griggsville, Ill..........	3.2	3.3	5.3	4.5	3.7	2.7	4.0	1.9	28.6	37.0
Springfield, Mo.........	3.9	3.8	5.9	4.8	4.2	3.9	3.8	2.9	33.2	43.6
Montrose, Colo.........	0.8	1.0	0.7	0.2	0.8	1.2	1.0	0.8	6.5	9.3
Provo, Utah...........	1.3	1.1	1.5	0.5	0.2	0.2	0.4	0.8	6.0	10.9
Missoula, Mont.........	1.0	1.0	2.2	2.1	1.0	0.7	1.2	1.2	10.4	15.5
Payette, Idaho.........	0.9	1.0	1.4	0.6	0.4	0.3	0.5	1.0	6.1	12.1
The Dalles, Ore.........	1.3	0.7	0.6	0.6	0.1	0.2	0.6	1.3	5.4	15.4
Albany, Ore............	4.7	3.6	2.6	1.3	0.3	0.4	2.0	3.4	18.3	44.2
Roseburg, Ore.........	3.7	2.5	2.0	1.2	0.4	0.4	1.1	2.6	13.9	34.9
Spokane, Wash.........	1.4	1.3	1.4	1.5	0.7	0.5	1.0	1.4	9.2	18.3
Moxee Wells, Wash......	0.5	0.6	0.9	0.4	0.1	0.2	0.4	0.5	3.6	8.9
Walla Walla, Wash.......	1.7	1.8	1.7	1.1	0.4	0.4	1.0	1.5	9.6	17.7
Sacramento, Cal.........	2.8	2.0	1.0	0.2	T	T	0.3	1.1	7.4	19.9
Fresno, Cal............	1.5	0.6	0.5	0.1	T	T	0.3	0.6	3.6	9.2
Los Angeles, Cal.........	2.7	1.1	0.5	0.1	T	T	0.8	1.5	6.7	15.6
Roswell, N. M..........	0.2	0.4	1.2	2.0	3.4	2.2	2.0	1.6	13.0	15.6
Sitka, Alaska...........	5.8	6.3	3.5	2.8	4.2	6.7	10.7	12.1	52.1	82.3
Lincoln, Neb...........	1.3	2.8	4.3	4.3	3.8	3.7	2.6	1.8	24.6	27.5

The reciprocal of rainfall, *i.e.*, sunshine, is of transcendent importance in ripening fruit and coloring it; this generally increases as rainfall decreases.

The proportion between rainfall and evaporation is a better guide to the suitability of a given region to many plants. Lawton, Okla., for example, has an April-September rainfall equal to that of Boston, Mass. (Table 9), but the evaporation at Lawton is nearly twice as great. The April-September rainfalls at Amarillo, Tex., and at Gardiner, Maine, do not differ greatly, but the evaporation and the flora do. For critical shorter periods the differences are still more pronounced.

Differences such as these are bound to have much effect on the actual possibility of growing certain fruits and on the emphasis necessary on many orchard operations. In the Texas panhandle, for example, flooding with irrigation water will not keep red raspberries from drying out. Fitchburg, Mass. has a mean annual rainfall of 45.4 inches, 28.6 coming during the growing months, while Missoula, Mont., has a total precipitation of only 15.5 inches, of which 10.4 comes during the growing months; yet both are apple growing centers and McIntosh is one of the most satisfactory varieties in both places. Irrigation, however, is employed in Montana. Vineland, N. J., has an annual rainfall of 47.3 inches, three-fourths of which falls during the growing season; yet The Dalles, Ore., with less than one-third of that total rainfall and with only one-sixth as much falling during the growing season as comes during the corresponding period in New Jersey, produces peaches and other stone fruits with success and without the aid of irrigation. A season with a summer rainfall as low as that of The Dalles, would involve considerable loss in New Jersey. The summer temperatures of the two locations are very much alike, as shown in Table 3. Irrigation is considered an absolute necessity in many localities with higher yearly and growing season rainfalls than those of The Dalles. The explanation of the ability of the Oregon section to produce fruit successfully and with such a limited water supply lies in the depth and character of its soil and in the methods of soil management employed.

Often different varieties of the same kind of fruit vary considerably in water requirements. The Yellow Transparent apple will thrive and produce good fruit on less water than the Winesap or York. Certain varieties or types of dates are grown at Alexandria, Egypt, where the mean atmospheric humidity is from 64 to 72 per cent., whereas certain other varieties are grown in some of the desert oases having an atmospheric humidity of only 34 per cent. Those varieties that thrive under the one set of conditions, however, cannot be grown successfully in the other environment.[47] As these humidity requirements of different fruits become known, it is possible to draw, more or less accurately, iso-hyetal lines setting approximate boundaries for districts in which they may be expected to reach a high degree of development.

TABLE 9.—RAINFALL—EVAPORATION RATIO (APR. 1–SEPT. 30) AT VARIOUS POINTS
IN THE UNITED STATES
(Rainfall data from Bul. W. U. S. D. A.; evaporation from Atlas of American Agriculture)

	Rainfall, inches	Evaporation, inches
Indio, Cal.................................	0.52	86.50
Brawley, Cal.............................	1.26	73.80
Hermiston, Ore..........................	2.73	36.65
Walla Walla, Wash......................	6.17	37.93
Roosevelt, Ariz..........................	7.13	68.23
Amarillo, Tex............................	15.50	52.71
North Platte, Neb.......................	14.81	43.65
Fort Collins, Colo.......................	10.79	29.30
Lawton, Okla....:.......................	20.81	45.56
Manhattan, Kans........................	23.30	43.55
Lincoln, Neb.............................	21.72	34.80
Boston, Mass............................	20.04	25.80
Columbia, Mo...........................	24.45	31.00
Wooster, Ohio...........................	22.06	27.96
Gardiner, Maine.........................	16.88	20.35

OTHER FACTORS INFLUENCING THE GEOGRAPHIC DISTRIBUTION OF FRUITS

Sunshine.—The amount of sunshine to which the trees are exposed during their growing season is perhaps of secondary importance in deter-

TABLE 10.—HOURS OF SUNSHINE FOR SELECTED STATIONS
(Compiled from United States Weather Bureau Bul. Q)

	March	April	May	June	July	August	September	October
Boston, Mass..........	195	213	258	274	276	258	232	185
Albany, N. Y..........	186	240	279	300	279	248	240	186
Rochester, N. Y........	171	225	266	290	296	258	223	158
Erie, Pa...............	152	221	263	287	318	269	213	157
Raleigh, N. C..........	198	250	284	293	299	271	271	220
Atlanta, Ga............	197	255	312	303	274	253	250	235
St. Paul, Minn.........	178	236	244	275	312	256	235	176
Omaha, Neb...........	199	240	267	295	341	290	250	202
Kansas City, Mo.......	192	204	232	261	291	279	252	236
Parkersburg, W. Va....	128	181	224	240	279	240	199	159
Boise, Idaho...........	196	222	294	354	405	354	298	216
Salt Lake City, Utah...	193	236	288	355	370	329	296	236
Grand Junction, Colo ..	252	279	337	369	370	317	312	265
Spokane, Wash........	194	235	286	330	372	310	226	160
Portland, Ore..........	166	200	230	329	268	183	148	64
Fresno, Cal............	241	324	370	404	429	400	336	290
Los Angeles, Cal.......	255	275	259	289	341	328	282	263

mining the character of the fruit industry that may develop in different sections, since it nowhere becomes so reduced as to be permanently a limiting factor. However it is often decisive in determining the varieties that can be grown to advantage. This is true at least in the apple in which coloration depends directly on the relative amount of sunshine that reaches the fruit during the ripening season. Thus the data in Table 10 suggest why it is practicable to grow varieties like Winesap at Grand Junction, Col. and in eastern Washington, but not in the vicinity of Portland, Ore.

Parasites.—The prevalence of certain parasites is another factor of no mean importance in determining the geographic distribution of fruit growing—at least in determining what kinds of fruit shall be grown in different districts. For instance, European grapes are not grown in the southeastern United States on account of the prevalence there of the grapevine phylloxera and the downy mildew. European plums are commercially unimportant in the Middle West on account of the brown rot and the black knot. Perhaps in the last analysis certain insects and diseases are particularly troublesome in certain districts because they find there temperature and humidity conditions that are especially favorable for their development and spread; hence fundamentally it is temperature or humidity that really sets limits for these fruits. Nevertheless the immediate factor responsible for limitation of the industry is a parasite.

In some instances, the presence or absence of one of the alternative hosts of a parasite determines where a fruit can or cannot be grown successfully. Thus, culture of the apple is impracticable in areas where there are many red cedar trees, the cedars furnishing a source of infection for a rust which cannot be satisfactorily controlled on the apple by spraying. On the other hand, the presence of gooseberries and black currants in close proximity to stands of the white pine is regarded as a menace because they serve as a host for one of the generations of the white pine blister rust. Certain virus diseases of the peach that are readily recognized in peach trees and that may be kept under control by prompt destruction of trees showing symptoms are also harbored by plum trees. However, their presence in plum trees is not easily detected. The result is that the plums may serve as unsuspected carriers or sources of infection, and there is reason to believe that in some areas culture of the two fruits on the same farm or even in the same community or district is inadvisable.

Wind.—Wind is often considered important in determining whether fruits can or cannot be grown successfully in certain sections. It is to be doubted if wind alone is of great significance over any wide areas. On the other hand, extreme heat or dryness accompanied by winds may cause much damage and practically prevent the culture of certain fruits

in large areas where they frequently occur.   Actually in such cases it is
the combination of high temperature or low humidity—or both—with the
wind that is the real factor.   Data presented in Table 9 are pertinent in
this connection.

Native Range of Parent Species.—The native range of the parent
species without doubt furnishes some indication of the probable geographic range of the forms that are brought under cultivation; nevertheless it is doubtful if it is an index with most fruits of the extent to which
they may be grown for commercial production.   For instance, the common European plum (*Prunus domestica*) is native to central and southeastern Europe.   Its cultivation extends to practically all of Europe
and to much of temperate North America and it is grown to a limited
extent in many other parts of the world.   Though the native home
of the peach is supposed to be China, it reaches its greatest commercial
importance in Europe, North America and southern Africa.   The
Evergreen blackberry (*Rubus laciniatus*) apparently is not cultivated in
southwestern Europe where it is found wild, but is of considerable importance in the Pacific Northwest 6,000 miles from its native home.   On
the other hand the culture of the North American plum (*Prunus americana*) is restricted to an area considerably less than the native range of
the parent species and the litchi (*Nephelium litchi*) is not grown commercially outside China.

Length of Time in Cultivation.—The length of time a species has been
under cultivation naturally has some influence on the amount of territory
over which it extends.   Fruits of recent introduction, such as the pecan,
the blueberry and the loganberry have not had time to become dissemin-
ated widely and tried thoroughly in many sections.   On the other hand,
though the Chinese jujube probably has been in cultivation as long as
the peach, its present geographic range is very small as compared with
that of its sister fruit coming from the same general region.   Some
species, such as the fox grape (*Vitis labrusca*), are cultivated over a very
wide range of territory though they have been in cultivation only a few
decades.

Uses and Quality of Product.—The variety of uses that the fruit and
the plant producing it serve has been doubtless an important factor in
making the cocoanut palm one of the most widely distributed fruits in
cultivation.   For many tropical peoples it is the one most important
plant and there has thus been every encouragement to disseminate it
widely.   The same may be said of the banana.   On the other hand,
though the date palm and the fig are hardly less important, their actual
cultural range is much more restricted.

Quality of product is certainly relatively unimportant in determining
geographic distribution.   Best evidence on this point is obtained by a

comparison of varieties within a group, for it is hardly fair to compare the quality of one group, for example the orange, with that of another, for example the raspberry. Though Elberta is admittedly a second rate peach in quality, it dominates the peach industry of America. The Kieffer pear and the Ben Davis apple occupy similar, though perhaps not quite so prominent, positions in their respective groups.

Relation to Consuming Centers and Transportation Facilities.—The location of large consuming centers and their relation to efficient systems of transportation is very important in determining where many fruits, particularly those of a more perishable character, are grown in quantity. For instance a map showing the distribution of the strawberry industry of North America indicates production centers close to nearly all the larger markets; those production centers distantly located from large markets are connected with them by good transportation systems. The same statements hold for raspberry, blackberry and dewberry production and to a certain extent for fruits like the peach, cherry and plum. For many years "good transportation facilities" were synonymous with ready access to railway or water transport. More recently, the auto-truck has in large part taken the place of the freight car for delivering to markets within a 200- to 500-mile radius of the point of production and close proximity of farm to market or railway shipping point is of secondary importance. The general effect of this change in transportation methods is to favor production where conditions are most favorable for actual growing of the crop rather than in areas or locations less favorable to the crop but with more ready access to the markets. Furthermore, it has favored the culture of varieties of better appearance and higher dessert quality in place of those whose principal merit, perhaps, was their ability to withstand successfully the hardships of cruder transportation and handling methods. Sometimes the location of a fruit-processing establishment makes possible the development of an extensive industry where conditions of environment are favorable but transportation of the fresh product by either rail or truck would be impracticable.

Sometimes factors that are more or less artificial operate, at least for a time, in determining the development of large fruit industries. For instance a large fruit product establishment may be located at some point —its exact location being determined largely by considerations quite distinct from those concerned with fruit production. Within a short time a large fruit industry develops in the vicinity of this plant to supply it with fresh fruit. Had this plant been located a hundred miles away, the first place would have raised no fruit commercially but the industry would have developed around the other. It often happens that a pioneer in some branch of horticulture makes a marked success of growing some particular kind of fruit.   His neighbors promptly follow him in the business and soon a whole community or a whole section becomes famous for its Cuthbert raspberries, or McIntosh apples, or Evergreen blackberries or Neunan strawberries.   In the long run, however, a specialized industry develops and remains chiefly in those sections or districts where factors governing production, harvesting, distribution and marketing are most favorable.   In other words, the present geographic distribution of the different fruit industries represents the result of a struggle for existence, a real natural selection.

Summary.—The most important environmental factor determining the geographic range of cultivated fruits is temperature, though rainfall and humidity act as important limiting factors within the wider limits set by temperature.   The boundary lines of fruit zones follow rather closely those of the life zones recognized by the biologist.   Apparently, minimum winter temperatures are most important in setting the northern limits (in the Northern Hemisphere) to the geographic range of species and varieties and mean summer temperature during the hottest 6 weeks in setting their southern bounds.   With some kinds, however, northern limits are set by the low mean summer temperatures, and with others, southern limits by the high mean winter temperatures.   The limiting effects of natural rainfall are often alleviated by the use of irrigation water or by other cultural practices and also by the selection of drought resistant varieties.   Sunshine, wind and the presence of certain parasites are often important factors in determining the range of particular varieties.   There is no very close relation between the length of time a species or variety has been in cultivation or between the natural range of related forms and its range in cultivation.   Artificial factors, such as nearness to large centers of population, transportation and storage facilities, and temporary market demands, often are of considerable importance in determining the approximate range of a variety or of a fruit and in determining its relative importance within different portions of its range.

CHAPTER XXXIV

ORCHARD LOCATIONS AND SITES

The production of fruit on a scale sufficient to meet the needs of the home at least partly has a general appeal. Indeed it is exceptional to find the farm or even the suburban lot that is without trace of fruit tree, shrub or vine. Such planting of a few fruit-producing plants is often done as much for the pleasure derived from their culture as for the monetary returns. On the other hand, commercial fruit production is a business and appeals to only a comparatively small percentage of the population—even of the farming population. Perhaps this is because it is generally considered an exacting business, requiring special training or special aptitude, or perhaps it is due to other reasons. Whatever the reason, the commercial fruit growers are few in comparison with other classes of farmers. Nevertheless there are frequent recurring waves of interest in commercial fruit production, bringing to those already engaged in some line of farming the question whether or not it would be desirable for them to set a part of their acreage to fruit, or raising in the minds of those who are not engaged in agriculture the question whether they might not raise fruit with profit. In either case a number of matters concerning the establishment of an orchard should be considered before any definite decision is made. These questions are much the same fundamentally for the one group of prospective growers as for the other, though the points of view may be somewhat different. In the one case the problem is to determine what fruits can be grown to best advantage in some particular field, farm or locality; in the other it may take the form of first deciding on what kinds to grow and then in finding the proper place to grow them.

Orcharding in or outside of an Established Fruit Growing Section.— Incidental to the discussion of the geography of fruit growing some of the factors influencing the choice of a location for certain fruits or of fruits for certain locations are mentioned. An intelligent selection in either case depends on a detailed knowledge of the geographic distribution of the industries concerned. Obviously there would be considerable risk in the commercial culture of some fruit in a section where it is not being grown— where it has never been tried or where its cultivation has been discontinued. Thus it would not seem wise to attempt commercial filbert culture in New York or Pennsylvania, or to make other than experimental plantings of the jaboticaba in southern Florida. It would be safer to undertake the commercial production of any fruit where an industry in that particular fruit is already established.

One great advantage in producing fruit of a kind that is well and favorably known and in a section where it is extensively grown is that the marketing problem usually presents fewer difficulties.   The reputation attracts buyers and the fact that growers have been established there often means that efficient selling organizations have been formed.   However, such marketing advantages are often over-emphasized.   In years of heavy production, the apple grower in western New York may wish his orchard were in Indiana or Nebraska.   Moreover, land prices are likely to be high in sections with established reputations; this means a permanently large overhead charge in the cost of production.   If fruit is to be grown under these conditions, the choice of kinds and varieties and the methods of culture must be such as will yield large returns. The usual advantages of production where little fruit is raised are cheap land and good local markets.   However, isolation may mean difficulty in getting in contact with buyers, trouble in securing supplies and no possibility of cooperative effort.   Probably much would depend on the scale of operations contemplated. The small grower can often produce to better advantage in the less developed sections, though conditions favorable to developing a large enterprise are more likely to be found where an industry of some size is already established.

Land Values.—Among the important factors determining the desirability of a piece of land for fruit growing are: land values, the availability of transportation and storage facilities, of fruit products establishments, of labor supply, the social conditions and the educational advantages. Locations only a few miles apart may vary greatly in respect to one or all of these factors.

Perhaps the price paid for land or its valuation has nothing to do with the grade or quantity of fruit that can be produced on a given area and the question of conditions favorable for production can possibly be considered entirely aside from it.   Nevertheless it should be realized that successful orcharding is a question not only of production, but even more of economical production.   This means that there must be a reasonably large margin between production costs and selling prices. Both production costs and selling prices for fruit fluctuate from year to year and the difference between them will likewise vary, but interest on investment constitutes a fixed and important part of the overhead charges figured into the cost of production.   This charge must be discounted every year, crop or no crop.   For instance, if the orchard at bearing age represents an investment of $300 per acre and it yields an average crop of 300 bushels per acre the interest charge against each bushel is about

6 cents; if, however, the orchard represents an investment of $1,000 per acre, a crop of the same size would represent an interest charge of 20 cents per bushel. Of course, if a bumper crop were harvested in the latter case—a crop say of 600 bushels per acre—the interest charge per bushel would be only 10 cents; but on the other hand if a light crop, say 100 bushels, is harvested, the interest charge per bushel would be 60 cents. It is not the intent here to recommend cheap land for growing fruit; such land may prove the most expensive in the end. On the other hand the purchaser or owner of high priced land should figure out before planting the probable charges per bushel, pound, barrel or other unit of fruit produced, that the cost of land contributes toward cost of production.

Transportation Facilities.—Formerly, when fruit moved from farm to railway siding or dock or, in some cases, direct to market by horse-drawn vehicles, location within a few miles of shipping point or consuming center was a matter of great importance. With the autotruck replacing the wagon and the general improvement in both trunk line and country highways, a trip of 50 miles is now made as quickly and at less cost per bushel or crate that is hauled than one of 5 miles by the old methods. This, however, is not without its disadvantages since many producers that formerly had certain markets pretty much to themselves are now finding those markets supplied by distant growers. The market has been widened but competition has been increased. However, in successfully meeting this competition, location is still important. Proximity to a large consuming center, such as New York City or Philadelphia, or to a large wholesale market, such as Benton Harbor, Mich., practically assures any grower an outlet for whatever he raises at a price in line with conditions of the moment and at a very low transportation and marketing cost. Long hauls to these same or other markets entail added transportation expense, besides resulting in more bruising and deterioration of fruit. It is pretty much a case of the advantages formerly possessed by those within 3 to 5 miles of market or shipping point now belonging to those within 30 to 50 miles and restricting the disadvantages of those formerly more than 5 miles away to those more than 50 miles distant.

Location where there is access to a processing plant may make possible salvaging something from the lower grades that otherwise would return no income, or it may afford a steady outlet for certain varieties whose fresh fruit market value is rather low. Location on a heavily traveled highway may enable the producer to build up a profitable roadside market business. In some locations a more expensive package and method of packing must be employed than in others, though the product is eventually retailed at the same price as one that is less expensively packaged. Any one of these items may be important in determining the commercial success of an orchard enterprise, and the subject calls for careful consideration on the part of the producer.

The general trend in the purchasing power of fruits, *i.e.*, the prices received for them in terms of what those amounts will buy of standard commodities, during the past half century or more has been about stationary.[51] There seems little likelihood that it will rise.   Since frequently a third to a half of the total cost to the grower of the fruit as he sells it is represented in package, packing, transportation and other handling charges, it is greatly to his advantage to reduce them to a minimum since, in many instances, that is his most practicable way of widening his margin of profit, and one of the most effective ways of reducing these costs—and that for the life of the orchard—is through his choice of location.

SLOPE OR ASPECT

Many advantages have been claimed for certain slopes—advantages so great that prospective fruit growers are sometimes led to believe that success is practically guaranteed if the land but slopes in a certain direction and that failure is almost equally certain if it slopes the opposite way.   Southern are generally warmer and earlier than northern slopes because they receive the more direct rays of the sun.   Shreve,[57] who has studied the effect of varying physical environment on vegetation in mountain regions, summarizes some of the more important influences as follows: "Two slopes of the same inclination, which lie in opposed positions so that one faces north and the other south, will present to plants two environments differing in almost every essential physical feature.   The temperature of the air on two such slopes might be identical as determined by the thermometer of a carefully established meteorological station, but they are distinctly different as they affect vegetation, for the plants receive very different amounts of heat through diurnal terrestrial radiation.   This circumstance is of small importance to full-grown trees and large plants, but is of great importance to young plants and seedlings.   The soil temperatures of opposed slopes are also widely unlike, even in the presence of the undisturbed cover of natural vegetation.   The two opposed slopes would in all likelihood receive the same rainfall, although this is not necessarily the case.   An equal amount of rain might effect an equal elevation of the soil moisture on the two slopes, and to the same depth, but the soil evaporation of the south slope would greatly exceed that of the north slope, and a lower moisture would soon prevail in the soil of the former.   Greater or less differences may thus be shown to obtain between the opposed slopes with respect to the most vital features of plant environment."

Influence on Soil Temperatures and on the Plant.—Table 11 affords a quantitative expression of the influence of slope on mean soil temperature. Even more significant are the differences in the temperatures of the plants themselves on different slopes. Table 12 shows the mean temperatures one inch beneath the surface of the bark on the north and south sides of tree trunks at the summit of a hill and on its north and south slopes during the winter months in Wisconsin. As would be

TABLE 11.—MEAN SOIL TEMPERATURES (CENTIGRADE) AT A DEPTH OF 80 CENTI-
METERS FOR 3 YEARS ON DIFFERENT SLOPES OF AN ISOLATED CONICAL
SANDHILL AT INNSBRUCK, TYROL

(After Kerner and Oliver[40])

N.	N.E.	E.	S. E.	S.	S.W.	W.	N. W.
15.3°	17.0°	18.7°	20.0°	19.3°	18.3°	18.5°	15.0°

expected, the trees on the south slope show higher midday and afternoon temperatures than those on the northern slope. They also show rather surprisingly lower early morning temperatures. This means that they are exposed to greater extremes and more rapid temperature changes. The relation of such conditions to certain forms of winter injury is pointed out in the section on Temperature Relations. The tendency of the north side of the trunk on the north slope to be colder than the south side in the early morning while on the south slope the reverse condition holds is due probably to the stronger radiation of heat from the ground on the uphill side against the trunk.

Specific Influence on Fruit Growing.—These data indicate that southern and eastern slopes are preferable for the production of fruits for the early markets or for any fruit or variety with which hastened maturity is an important consideration. Thus in New England there are many locations where certain varieties of grapes can be ripened properly only when grown in sheltered spots with a southern exposure. Often there is a difference of a week or more in the maturing seasons of the same variety on the northern and southern sides of the same hill, equivalent to a location many miles southward or northward. On the other hand northern and western slopes are preferable when delayed maturity is the object. Fruits of certain species like the apple and peach are likely to be somewhat higher colored on southern than on northern slopes. It should be noted that late spring and early fall frosts are no more likely to occur on one slope than on another and that consequently more trouble from spring frosts at least will be encountered on southern than on northern slopes because vegetation starts earlier on the former. It is probably on this account mainly that, for general fruit growing, a northern exposure is preferred by most growers. Areas with eastern and western exposures are intermediate in the qualities mentioned between those with northern and southern exposures. Western and southwestern slopes

TABLE 12.—MEAN TREE TEMPERATURES (FAHRENHEIT) ON NORTH AND SOUTH SLOPES DURING WINTER MONTHS
(After King[41])

| | South slope | | | | Summit | | | | North slope | | | |
| | South side of tree | | North side of tree | | South side of tree | | North side of tree | | South side of tree | | North side of tree | |
	7 a.m.	1 p.m.	7 a.m.	1 p.m.	7 a.m.	1 p.m.	7 a.m.	1 p.m.	7 a.m.	1 p.m.	7 a.m.	1 p.m.
December	27.99	42.98	28.60	32.76	29.25	39.79	28.38	32.57	28.78	36.72	28.42	32.99
January	7.57	31.28	9.03	18.59	8.35	26.60	8.37	16.12	7.93	23.11	8.17	15.39
February	8.73	37.15	8.67	20.55	8.92	33.58	9.08	17.47	9.63	28.27	8.73	16.57
March	27.68	47.91	28.13	35.28	27.68	45.12	28.44	29.82	27.55	41.04	27.79	33.39
Mean	17.99	39.83	18.61	26.80	18.54	36.28	18.57	24.00	18.47	32.29	18.28	24.58

TABLE 13.—AIR TEMPERATURE, ATMOSPHERIC HUMIDITIES AND DEWPOINTS FOR POINTS VARYING DISTANCES FROM LARGE BODIES OF WATER

(After Lippincott[43])

Stations	7 a.m.		2 p.m.		9 p.m.		Means		Maximum Temperature	Minimum Temperature
	Temperature	Humidity	Temperature	Humidity	Temperature	Humidity	Temperature	Humidity		
July										
Vineland..........	74.7	89.8	90.1	48.3	73.7	79.5	79.5	72.5	101.5	60.0
Haddonfield......	73.5	70.8	87.3	43.9	75.0	68.6	78.6	61.1	102.0	61.5
Greenwich........	72.5	94.4	83.0	71.9	76.1	86.7	77.2	84.3	94.0	62.0
Kelley's Island...	74.9	88.6	83.2	80.8	74.5	90.2	77.6	86.5	93.0	64.0
August										
Vineland..........	67.3	79.2	83.4	50.0	67.0	83.5	72.6	70.9	91.0	52.0
Haddonfield......	65.0	73.3	76.9	58.8	67.7	75.9	69.9	69.3	88.0	55.0
Greenwich........	65.3	94.5	75.5	75.8	68.9	86.8	69.9	85.7	83.0	55.0
Kelley's Island...	65.8	87.1	73.8	80.1	67.4	87.4	69.0	84.9	85.0	55.0

are perhaps least desirable under average conditions and with most fruits because of the action of the sun and of temperature in causing sunscald on the west and southwest sides of the trunk.

Without doubt too much importance is attached by many to the advantages or disadvantages offered by particular exposures—at least as these exposures have a direct bearing on tree and fruit through a modification of temperature and light conditions. In the great majority of cases the grower can raise fruit successfully on any and all slopes, provided they are not unreasonably steep and have suitable soils. It may be, and often is, desirable to plant certain slopes with fruits of one kind or one variety and other slopes with other kinds or other varieties, so that the advantages offered by the different exposures may be fully utilized. Thus early strawberries might be grown on the south and east sides of a hill and midseason and late varieties on its west and north sides and the harvesting season thereby lengthened a week at each end. The idea that one slope is always best for a certain fruit or a certain variety is erroneous. Much depends on where and for what special purpose that variety is grown.

Indirect Effects.—There are certain indirect influences of slope or exposure on the growth of trees and their maturing of a crop that are of importance equal to, or greater than, that of the more direct influences. Southern and western slopes dry out more rapidly and are more subject to drought than others. Fruit grown on northern or eastern slopes therefore tends to average somewhat larger in size than that produced on a southern or western exposure. In some sections the soil on many southern slopes is much thinner than that on northern, eastern or western exposures and in such instances a particular slope is to be avoided, not because of the slope itself but because of the factors with which it is associated. In much the same way certain slopes are to be avoided in certain sections because of their exposure to prevailing winds. When land slopes away from the direction of the prevailing wind considerable protection is afforded the trees by the contour of the ground, but when it slopes in the direction of the prevailing wind much more trouble is likely.

Abruptness of Slope.—According to Partridge and Veatch,[53,66] who made detailed surveys of soils and sites in the leading fruit-producing areas of Michigan, "the best orchard sites, where profits are most likely to be obtained, are those on broad ridges or upland plains bordering depressions." In other words comparatively level land is preferable to that which is sloping, provided soil and air drainage are satisfactory, and gentle slopes are preferable to those that are abrupt. This is not so much because level land or that which slopes gently is better *per se* than that which slopes more steeply, but because of its smaller susceptibility to erosion. The amount of soil loss from erosion that occurs within a given time on a slope of a certain degree will vary with total precipitation, its distribution throughout the year, the kind of soil, the nature of its vegetative cover and many other factors. In general, however, slopes of more than 8 or 10 degrees are likely to erode badly if cultivated and probably should be maintained under some kind of permanent sod or artificial mulch system of soil management. Many orchards on much steeper hillsides have proven profitable, especially when kept in sod, but production costs are likely to be somewhat higher than on more nearly level land of the same character. This is due not only to the smaller tree growth and yields where the surface soil is thinner because of erosion but to greater difficulty in spraying, removal of fruit and other orchard operations, though different environmental conditions in the two locations may reverse the situation. Thus, in the Piedmont section of Virginia where the orchards are planted on steep hillsides and where it is necessary to spray five to seven times, apples are produced at a lower cost than in the Shenandoah valley where less spraying is required. As a rule it is best to limit orchard planting to slopes so gradual that cultivation may be practiced without great danger from erosion and over which spraying machinery and other equipment may be hauled without serious difficulty. The necessity of gentle slopes is still greater in sections where irrigation is practiced.

AIR DRAINAGE

Fruit growing, more than almost any other branch of agriculture, requires comparative freedom from untimely late spring and early fall frosts; in turn the occurrence of frosts within certain limits is determined largely by what is commonly known as "air drainage," the settling of cold air to lower levels. This is discussed in some detail in the section on Temperature Relations.

Influence of Elevation.—Many factors influence air drainage, some to a very marked extent and others only to a comparatively small degree. Probably the most important single factor in air drainage is elevation. Height above adjoining land or fields usually is of greater significance than absolute elevation above sea level. Frost is as likely to occur during the danger period at the high elevations found in some of the intermountain fruit growing districts as at the low elevations of the seaboard. Portions of the Ozarks with an elevation of over 1,000 feet are as frosty as the Hudson River valley, which lies only a little above sea level. However, as a rule, low lying land is more subject to frost than that somewhat elevated above surrounding or adjoining fields, though there are certain exceptions which are discussed later.

The difference in temperature between two points, one of which is 50 or 100 feet above the other, of course depends on many factors, such

as general lay of land, relative areas of the land having the respective
elevations and proximity to bodies of water.   However, the inequality
in temperature, particularly on quiet nights, in spring and fall when
there is greatest danger from frost, between points only a few dozen feet
apart in elevation is often considerable—often enough to make the
difference between no frost or a very light frost and a killing frost.   Figure 72 shows graphically the diversity in minimum temperature that
sometimes occurs with variations in elevation of 25, 50 and 225 feet.
In this case a disparity of only 25 feet in elevation was accompanied

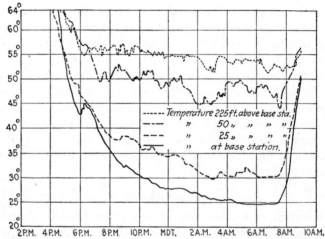

Fig. 72.—Continuous records of the temperature from 4 p.m. to 9 a.m. at the base and
at different heights above the base of a steep hillside, showing the great differences in
temperature that sometimes develop on a clear, still night.   Although the temperature at
the base was low enough to cause considerable damage to fruit, the lowest temperature
225 feet above on the slope was only 51°F.   Note that the duration of the lowest temperature was much shorter on the hillside than at the base.   (*After Batchelor and West.*[3])

by a difference of approximately 5°F. between 8:00 p.m. and 8:00 a.m.
and an inequality of 50 feet was accompanied by a variation of 15°
to 20°F.   At greater elevations the temperature was still higher, though
its rise was not proportional to the increase in height.

This suggests that extreme divergencies in altitude, therefore, are
likely to afford much greater security from frost than moderate differences;
very slight inequalities, even of only a few feet, often are associated with
a sufficient variance in temperature to result in crop safety or crop loss.
Perhaps more nearly average differences in minimum temperature due
to elevation are shown in Fig. 73.   These graphs represent temperature
variations on comparatively still, clear nights at stations in a mountain
valley during the blossoming period of fruits.   Though the minimum
temperature was not invariably recorded at the lowest elevations, on

each of the four nights when there was danger from frost the higher elevations registered temperatures above the probable danger point and a fruit crop on the lower levels probably would have been destroyed. "The minimum temperatures experienced by the bench lands and upper slopes of the tillable area in a mountain valley average from 6 to 10°F.

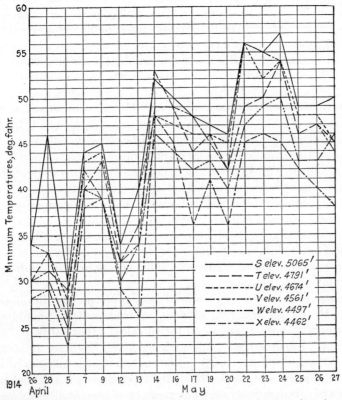

Fig. 73.—The daily minimum temperatures for stations of different elevations extending from the high agricultural land to the lowest agricultural land of the valley. (*After Batchelor and West.*[3])

warmer than the valley bottoms due to the drainage of cold air to the low areas during the typical clear, calm, frosty nights."[3] On calm but cloudy nights the variation in minimum temperatures between high and low points in this valley is reduced to about 40 per cent. of that on calm, clear nights and during windy weather there is very little difference in their minimum temperatures.

The point should be emphasized that the amount of air drainage secured by selecting a site somewhat above the adjoining fields depends not alone on the amount of elevation, but also on the area from which the cold air drains in comparison with the extent of that to which it may settle. If the low ground upon which the cold air may sink is limited in extent and has little outlet while the area to be drained is large, this depression will soon be filled with cold air and the slope above will be afforded no further protection. The case is comparable with a large watershed supplied with an inadequate drainage system. An elevation of 20 or 25 feet above a wide valley may thus afford better air drainage for one orchard than an elevation of 50 feet above a narrow valley affords another. In many cases a ravine or narrow draw along one side of an orchard will afford a given site better air drainage than an adjoining low-lying field covering many acres, provided the draw or ravine is deep, has a good outlet and is not clogged with brush and timber that interferes with free movement of the air. In other words, of two areas having the same elevation one may enjoy much better air drainage and greater freedom from frost because of differences in the contour and topography of the land that borders them.

The graphs in Fig. 73 show the maximum variations in temperatures during the night between stations at different elevations on a hillside. Though day temperatures are not given there is the suggestion that they approximate rather closely. Available data show that such inequalities in elevation as are normally found within single fruit growing districts are responsible for but small differences in maximum day temperatures.[3] In other words, elevation materially influences minimum and average, but not maximum, temperatures.

Thermal Belts.—The influence of elevation on air drainage and consequently on the selection of sites for fruit growing should not be passed over without a reference to the so-called "thermal belts," "thermal zones," "frostless belts" or "verdant zones," as they are variously called. They are comparatively frost-free belts along hillsides or mountain ranges, below and above which frost occurrence is not uncommon. The limits of comparatively few such zones have been accurately mapped; consequently the fruit industry has developed more or less independently of them. However, their occurrence presents an interesting phenomenon and it is desirable to recognize and, if possible, make use of the obvious advantages they provide, for without doubt the fruit growing districts of the country include many such zones that are not being utilized for fruit production.

The following quotations from an article by Abbe[1] will point out more exactly the conditions characteristic of thermal belts:

"Prof. J. W. Chickering, Jr., in the *Bulletin* of the Philosophical Society of Washington, March, 1883, and in the American Meteorological *Journal*, Vol. I, describes the following thermal belt: 'In Polk County, North Carolina, along the eastern slope of the Tryon Mountain range, in latitude north 35°, the thermal belt begins at the base of the mountain, at an elevation of 1200 feet. It is about 8 miles long, and is distinguished by magnificent flora, such as would be characteristic of a point 3° south of the actual latitude.'

"Prof. John Leconte, of Berkeley, California, in *Science*, Vol. I, p. 278, states that at Flat Rock, near Hendersonville, Henderson County, North Carolina, on the flank of the mountain spur adjacent to the valleys of the Blue Ridge, he also observed a frostless zone. The valley is about 2200 feet above sea level, and the thermal belt is 200 to 300 feet above the valley.

"J. W. Pike, of Vineland, N. J., states that among the mountains of California he has discovered that during the night the cold is much greater in the valleys than on the terraces several hundred feet above, due to the settling of the cold air, so that a thermal belt is formed at that height separating the frosty valleys from the colder highlands.

"In the *Tennessee Journal of Meteorology* for January, 1894, published by the State Weather Service, the author describes a thermal belt between Los Angeles and the Pacific Coast. It traverses the foothills of the Cahuenga range, and has an elevation of between 200 and 400 feet and a breadth of about 3 miles. It occupies the midway region of the range.

"In the *American Meteorological Journal*, Vol. I, S. Alexander describes a thermal belt in which the peach tree flourishes in the southeastern portion of Michigan. He shows that the cold island discovered by Winchell in that region is really the bottom of a topographical depression into which the cold air settles. It is a long valley surrounded by a belt of elevated country from 50 to 600 feet above Lakes Michigan and Huron. The valley and the isotherms trend northeast and southwest from Huron County through Sanilac, Lapeer, Oakland, Livingston, and Washtenaw to Hillsdale Counties. The highlands of this region are all much freer from frost than the lowlands, and all much more favorable for early vegetation. He does not state that any point is high enough to be above the thermal belt, but that, in general, two equal parallel thermal belts inclose the cold island between them.

"It is generally conceded that these thermal belts depend both upon the drainage of cold air downward into the lower valleys and the freedom of radiation from the surface of the ground to the clear sky overhead. During a still night, when frosts occur, the surface of the hillside cools by radiation, and hence cools the air in contact with it; the latter flows downward as long as its cooling by radiation and conduction exceeds its warming by compression. Inasmuch as its cooling depends on contact with a still colder soil or plant, it soon accumulates in the lowlands as a layer of cold air, which grows thicker during the night by the steady addition of the thin layer of descending air in contact with the ground on the hillsides. The warmer air, which has not yet had an opportunity to cool by contact with the ground, floats on top of the cold mass; it spreads out toward the hills, and is continuously furnishing its heat to the adjacent hillsides as fast as it comes in contact with them before it also cools and descends. The formation of the thermal belt seems to depend largely upon this gentle circulation during the night time. The lower limit of the belt is defined by the depth of the accumulation of cold air in the confined valley and rises higher in proportion as the night is clearer and longer, and also in proportion as the valley is more or less perfectly inclosed. The upper limit of the thermal belt may depend upon the strength of the wind, and the general temperature of the air. But if there be no wind, then it depends equally on the freedom of radiation to the clear sky and on the above-described circulation of air."

Influence of Bodies of Water.—After elevation, probably the next most important factor influencing air temperature and drainage is proximity to bodies of water. The specific heat of water is high; it absorbs heat slowly and gives it up slowly. Consequently in the spring a large body of water warms more slowly and in the fall it cools more slowly than the surface of the adjacent land or than nearby vegetation. It is slower even than the atmosphere in responding to changes in temperature. Relatively the air shows a great variation in temperature between night and day, while a body of water of considerable size shows no appreciable change. The air warmed during the day, coming in contact with the surface of a body of water, is cooled; consequently the air in close proximity to such a body is cooler than it would be otherwise. On the other hand, at night air cooled to a temperature below that of the water, is warmed by contact with its surface and in turn gives up that heat to vegetation and other bodies with which it comes in contact. Consequently points close to bodies of water are frequently somewhat cooler during the day and warmer at night than corresponding inland points and are freer from frosts, while blossoming is at the same time retarded in their proximity.

Influence of Distance from Water.—Some measure of this influence may be obtained from data presented in Table 13 showing the air temperatures, atmospheric humidity and dewpoints for three stations in New Jersey and one on Kelley's Island in Lake Erie for the months of July and August, 1866. Vineland is about 30, Haddonfield, 50 and Greenwich 5 miles from the ocean, or from wide ocean tributaries, while Kelley's Island, as the name indicates, is surrounded by water. The daily range of temperature is higher the farther the station is removed from the influence of water and also the more remote the station the lower is its mean atmospheric humidity and the lower its mean dewpoint. In other words, those stations close to large bodies of water enjoy a climate more equable in temperature and consequently less subject to frost injury.

The interchange of heat and equalization of temperature in the vicinity of bodies of water is favored by a gentle breeze but it will occur to a certain extent when there is practically no air stirring at inland points. The water is itself responsible for a certain amount of air movement and the attendant air drainage. It is almost needless to state that the larger the body of water the greater is its influence on air movement and air temperature. Much, too, depends on the topography in the immediate vicinity of the body of water. For instance, the so-called "fruit belt" on the eastern shore of Lake Michigan varies in width from less than 2 to over 20 miles (Fig. 74). The lake is as wide where the belt is narrow as where the belt is wide, but the lay of the land is quite

Fig. 74.—Approximate frequency of years having injuriously low temperatures during the period 1920–1921 to 1929–1930. Owing to differences between the records of neighboring stations, the differentiation of clear cut areas cannot be made with absolute accuracy, but the map illustrates the general distribution of areas more or less subject to injuriously cold winters. (*After Partridge and Veatch.*[53])

different. As a rule but little influence of the water is felt back of the crest of the slope toward the lake, bay or river and frequently its influence does not extend to the crest of the slope. Naturally, if the slope is gradual the influence is likely to be felt farther back than if it is abrupt.

Influence of Size and Shape of Body of Water.—Something of the relation between the size of the body of water and that of the area influenced by it may be understood by comparing the width of the fruit belts bordering Lake Michigan or Lake Ontario with those bordering Lake Seneca or Canandaigua in New York. As already stated, the Michigan fruit belt is from 2 to 20 miles wide. The fruit belt along Lake Ontario is of equal width. Lakes Seneca and Canandaigua, themselves only about 4 miles wide at the most, have distinct fruit belts only a quarter of a mile to 2 miles in width. A deep body of water has a much greater influence on the climate of the adjoining land than one which is shallow. The water is in effect a heat sponge, absorbing heat whenever air temperatures rise above the mean and liberating heat whenever they fall below it. Naturally, then, the larger this sponge the greater is its absorbing and liberating capacity. This is particularly important in the case of bodies of water so deep that they seldom freeze over or remain frozen for only a short time, as it relates to their modifying influence on midwinter minimum temperatures. On the other hand many lakes as wide as the finger lakes of central New York, because they are very shallow, furnish little protection to the neighboring slopes. Protection is likely in the vicinity of large rivers, especially if they are deep. Their currents, which delay or prevent their freezing over, may partly compensate for their lack of depth; a river 10 to 20 feet deep and a quarter of a mile wide may afford as much protection to orchards along its course as a lake twice that depth and of the same width. Indeed it is likely to afford greater protection because of its channel down which the cold air may continue to drain indefinitely.

Indirect Temperature Effects.—Bodies of water influence temperatures in their vicinities in other ways than through promoting air drainage. There are certain favored spots where the increased atmospheric humidity due to proximity of water leads to the frequent formation of fog during periods when dangerously low temperatures occur at nearby points and a very effective check is thus placed on loss of heat by radiation. Kelley's Island in Lake Erie has been noted as a place thus rendered especially suited to the culture of comparatively tender long-season fruits and without doubt this is one of the chief factors in making possible the successful culture of European plums in the vicinity of Ste. Anne de Beaupré in Quebec, 200 miles north of the general northern limit for the same varieties.

Probably it would be difficult to separate entirely the different influences of bodies of water upon climate, assigning to air drainage or to increased atmospheric humidity exact figures representing their protective effects. The fact, however, that these other protective influences are at work does not lessen in importance the air drainage that is associated with water surfaces.

Minor Temperature Effects.—Even small bodies of water have measurable, though slight, influences on temperature. Observations of minimum temperatures near a stream 40 feet wide in England, summarized in Table 14, show that the extent of the influence varies.

TABLE 14.—AVERAGE MINIMUM TEMPERATURES (CENTIGRADE) AT AND NEAR RIVER BANK[67]
(Six inches above ground)

	Station 6, 196 feet from river, degrees	Station 8, on river bank (straight part), degrees	Station 7, on river bank (confluence of river and ditch), degrees
Minimum all nights........	2.2	3.0	3.3
Excess on river banks......	...	0.8	1.1
Minimum still nights.......	0.0	0.9	1.4
Excess on river banks......	...	0.9	1.4
Minimum nights with south or southeast wind........	3.5	4.4	5.4
Excess on river banks......	...	0.9	1.9
Minimum nights with north or northeast wind........	1.6	2.0	2.5
Excess on river bank.......	...	0.4	0.9

Importance during the Winter.—Attention has been called particularly to the effects of air drainage on temperature during the spring and fall months and its bearing on the occurrence of frosts. It should not be inferred, however, that air drainage does not take place during other seasons where elevation and topography make it possible. Figures 75 and 76 show differences in minimum temperatures during some of the winter months between stations at unequal elevations in a mountain valley in Utah. These range between 2° and 8°F. on the coldest nights for stations having 64 feet disparity in elevation and are about 10° for stations having 350 feet variance in altitude. Such differences in minimum temperatures during midwinter may often influence the amount of certain kinds of winter injury or winter killing experienced. Air drainage, therefore, is sometimes of as great importance in preventing winter injury as it is in warding off injury from late spring or early fall frosts. Indeed, there are certain sections in which and certain fruits with which elevation to secure air drainage is of greater importance in dealing with midwinter freezing than with spring frost. The bark and trunk splitting occasionally accompanying sudden midwinter drops in temperature in the comparatively mild climate of the Willamette valley is a case in point.

Obstructions.—Air drainage is often impeded more or less seriously by obstructions of one kind or another, such as a stone wall, a hedge or a

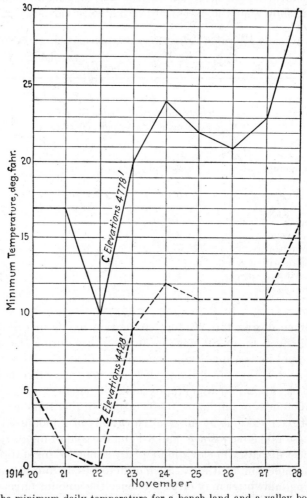

Fig. 75.—The minimum daily temperature for a bench land and a valley bottom station during 9 clear, autumn nights. (*After Batchelor and West.*[3])

high board fence, a mass or belt of shrubbery. Thus it happens that a natural or artificial planting sometimes serving admirably as a wind break and protecting the orchard at certain seasons, hinders air movement on calm nights to such an extent that little of the frost protection naturally expected from the orchard's elevation is actually obtained. No rules can be given for dealing effectively with these hindrances to air drainage, but the whole question should be considered on the ground when selecting an orchard site.

LOCAL VARIATIONS AND THEIR SIGNIFICANCE

Data have been presented showing that points only a few miles apart sometimes, because of topographic peculiarities, present climatic

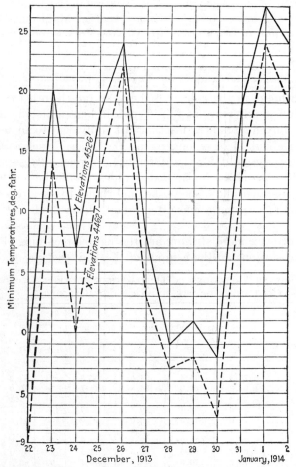

Fig. 76.—Minimum temperatures for stations of different elevations during 12 clear, calm, winter nights. (*After Batchelor and West.*[3])

differences great enough to be of considerable importance in fruit growing. The magnitude of such disparities, often found between points on the same farm and occupying positions differing little in elevation or exposure, is not appreciated. Their influence is often subtle, but nevertheless real.

They may make the difference between the necessity of one or of three applications of a fungicide, an interval of a week in the time of particular spray applications, or of a week in the blossoming or maturing seasons of a fruit.

Temperature.—It is not the intention in this discussion to present further data on the influence of a certain number of "heat-units" in bringing to particular stages of maturity plants of different kinds. However, mention may be made of the variation in the mean temperature between stations only a short distance apart. MacDougal[46] presents data showing that, of two stations in the New York Botanic Garden only a few hundred yards apart and presenting no great difference in elevation, one received 78,836 hour-degrees of heat in 1 year and the other only 68,596. One of these points registered a temperature below freezing during 1,478 hours in the course of the year and the other during 1,736 hours. Here is a difference of 13 per cent. in heat units; in other words, one station enjoyed a temperature that was equivalent to an active growing season of about 11 days longer than the other. Such a disparity is large enough to account for the difference between success and failure with many fruit crops, as for instance grapes, along the northern limits of their cultural range and it shows the importance to the grower of studying carefully the local variations often found within the limits of a single farm.

Equally or even more striking are the figures recording the temperatures of two stations on the campus of the University of California at

TABLE 15.—SHOWING VARIATIONS IN TEMPERATURE BETWEEN TWO STATIONS ON THE CAMPUS OF THE UNIVERSITY OF CALIFORNIA[7]

Month	Mean monthly maximum		Mean monthly minimum		Maximum		Minimum	
	A	B	A	B	A	B	A	B
September, 1902	79.3	71.4	54.5	55.8	94	83.2	48	49.0
April, 1903	62.3	62.0	36.8	44.7	74	70.0	32	36.6
May, 1903	70.8	66.9	43.1	48.3	84	79.1	34	42.6
June, 1903	74.5	73.4	49.7	52.3	108	101.1	36	42.4
July, 1903	75.6	70.0	50.0	52.0	100	94.0	44	46.8
August, 1903	77.4	69.6	48.2	51.9	86	78.9	44	49.0
September 1903	76.6	70.2	48.3	52.2	102	91.7	44	46.0
April, 1904	66.7	64.5	42.5	46.5	88	82.9	34	37.2
May, 1904	76.2	70.0	45.8	49.4	92	85.3	38	40.6
June, 1904	80.5	71.7	47.9	51.3	98	92.8	42	48.2
Average	73.4	69.0	46.7	50.4	92.6	85.9	39.6	43.8

Berkeley, presented in Table 15. Though these stations were 120 feet apart in elevation, elevation alone cannot be held responsible for the differences recorded, for, as mentioned elsewhere, the influence of elevation on mean temperature amounts to only 4°F. for each 1,000 feet. Without doubt many factors contribute to these local variations in temperature, some being more important in one case and others in another. It is not so important that all these factors be known and exactly evaluated in every instance as it is that their combined effect be recognized and properly utilized.

Evaporation, Rainfall and Other Factors.—It is generally recognized that some spots or some locations are more subject than others to the drying action of the wind; however, the extent and importance of differences in this respect are not generally recognized. Gager[13] records results of evaporimeter experiments in the New York Botanic Garden in 1907 that are particularly interesting. Three specially constructed evaporimeters were placed at several points in the garden; one was on a dry rocky knoll partly shaded by trees; a second was on low, poorly drained, marshy ground, also partly shaded and the third was in the open on well drained ground with sod on the one side and cultivated ground on the other. The evaporation losses from these different instruments between June 3 and October 14 were equivalent to 8.47, 4.84 and 12.10 inches, respectively. The precipitation during the same period was 9.32 inches. At the first station precipitation exceeded evaporation loss by only 0.85 inch, at the second station by 4.48 inches, while at the third station the evaporation loss exceeded precipitation by 2.78 inches. In commenting on these data, Gager says: "It should be kept in mind that the loss of water from the evaporimeters is not a measure of the amount of water lost by the soil through evaporation, but it is only an index of the evaporating power of the air for the given station. For the same locality the rate of evaporation from soil and from evaporimeter will materially differ, being less from soil and varying with its nature and condition, as well as with the surroundings above the soil surface." Nevertheless at one station the evaporation losses were between two and three times those at one of the others and such a difference may often be enough to have a great influence on plant growth and crop yield.

Local variations in rainfall are likely to be especially large in sections showing considerable difference in elevation, but they are often important where the elevations are substantially the same. Thus at Davis, California, when the annual rainfall was 16 inches, it was about 25 inches at a point ten miles to the west and having the same elevation. Thirty miles still farther west, but in the foothills of the Coast Range, it was over 50 inches.

With the local variations in temperature and humidity there are often important differences in the prevalence of insects and diseases that, independent of direct influence of the environment on the plant, may set definite limits to the profitable culture of certain fruit varieties.

There may be also minor local variations in their life histories which modify the effectiveness of spraying treatments. The best time for a certain spray in one neighborhood may differ several days from that for another neighborhood not far away.

Summary.—The selection of a location for fruit production, or of kinds and varieties of fruit to be grown in a particular location, involves a consideration and application of the same general principles. The more important economic considerations are the cost of land and the nearness and character of transportation facilities. The overhead charge due to cost of land should never exceed 10 per cent. of the value of the product at the orchard and should not amount to more than half that figure. The cost of hauling to the local market or to a shipping station should levy no greater tax against the total income. Other factors, such as fruit product establishments and coöperative shipping organizations affecting the ability to dispose of products quickly and advantageously are important in commercial production.

Different slopes offer quite distinct environmental conditions for the growth of the plant and certain slopes may be much preferred to others for certain fruits when grown in some sections, though the reverse condition may hold for the same varieties in another section. These environmental differences can be profitably capitalized in many cases if kinds and varieties are selected so as to obtain the closest adaptation to the particular farm or parts of the farm. The same may be said of minor inequalities in temperature, rainfall and evaporation between nearby points that possess nearly the same elevation and exposure.

Factors of great importance in determining danger from late spring and early fall frosts are the air drainage incident to unequal elevation and the proximity to bodies of water. Often comparatively small disparities in elevation (25 to 50 feet) make a considerable difference in danger from frost injury. This influence is important also in determining the amount of damage from midwinter freezing. Proximity to large bodies of water, particularly on their windward side, affords considerable protection from extremes of climate. The range of influence of such bodies of water varies with their size and depth and with the topography of the adjoining slopes.

CHAPTER XXXV

ORCHARD SOILS

All field crops are influenced more or less by the kind of soil in which they are grown. The same may be said of all fruit crops. Just as some land is classed as good for general crops so some may be classed as good for orchard fruits, and just as some is considered good for wheat but poor for alfalfa, so some may be good for pears but poor for strawberries. In a way the factors that are important in determining the value of a particular soil for field crops are also important in determining its value for fruit production. However, were the judging of soils for general farming purposes and for orcharding to be placed on a score-card basis the cards would differ considerably in a number of respects.

For field crops, both surface soil and subsoil are important in determining relative value of the land but the surface soil is generally regarded as of far greater importance. For fruit crops in general they are of more nearly equal significance. Indeed there are many conditions presented in which there is little doubt but that the nature of the subsoil is more significant than that of the surface soil. For field crops physical and chemical conditions are generally considered of substantially equal importance in determining productivity and suitability to individual crops. Though chemical composition is likewise important in the production of trees and other fruit plants, physical condition is a first consideration. The fact that certain fruits, such as the apple, are grown with equal success in some of the heavy clay loams of western New York, the light sandy loams of New Jersey, the loess bordering the Missouri River, the adobes of the Rogue River valley, Oregon and the volcanic ash of the Hood River section of Oregon appears to contradict this; nevertheless closer analysis reveals certain common characteristics of their physical condition—a similarity much greater than is shown in a comparison of their chemical composition.

CONSIDERED FROM THE STANDPOINT OF PHYSICAL CONDITION

Chief among the physical characteristics desirable in an orchard soil are porosity and thorough aeration, coupled, if possible, with depth. The loess soils of the Mississippi, Missouri, Rhine and Hoang-ho valleys are among the best in the world for the fruits that will grow in the climates of these respective regions because they are extremely deep, drainage is practically perfect (the water table often being 50 or more feet below the surface) and they are so well aerated that tree roots often penetrate to a depth of 20 feet and ordinarily to depths of 6, 8 or 10. In the Rhine valley grape roots have been traced to a depth of 15 meters. Similar conditions exist in some of the volcanic ash soils of the Pacific Northwest and the alluvial soils and bench lands of many river valleys in Washington, Idaho, Oregon and California. One of the main reasons certain of the arid soils of California have proved so well suited to fruit growing is that the surface soil grades insensibly into the subsoil and that the latter is well drained and thoroughly aerated; hence roots penetrate to great depths and sustain the plant when the surface soil may become too dry.[28] That good drainage and its corollary good aeration are associated with this condition is indicated by Hilgard[29] when he states that with the rise of the water table in such soils through injudicious irrigation trees that had thrived may actually suffer, much as those planted in shallow soil or soil underlaid with an impervious hardpan and from practically the same causes.

The extent to which the success of the fruit plantation depends on these two factors, drainage and aeration, is not generally realized. In speaking of the soil requirements of the papaya Higgins[25] says: "There are few, if any, soils in which the papaya will not grow if aeration and drainage are adequately supplied. Most of the plantings of this Station are upon soils regarded as unsuitable for other fruit trees, and upon which the avocado is a failure. . . . They are very porous, permitting a perfect drainage and aeration." The same writer goes so far as to say, "There are two essential features of a good banana soil. The first is abundant moisture, the second, good drainage."[24] In speaking of the soil requirements of forest trees one authority maintains that almost any soil is capable of producing any kind of timber if the moisture requirements are satisfied.[23] Even the blueberry, which is often classed as a semiaquatic or bog plant, requires a well aerated medium for its roots and does not, contrary to appearances, send them down into the water or into waterlogged soil[8] though the water table should not be more than 18 to 24 inches below the surface.[36] Obviously, certain shallow rooted species such as the strawberry do not require and could not make full use of a soil of the depth best suited to one of the tree fruits, but even the strawberry will do much better in a soil that is moderately deep (say, two and one half to three feet) and well drained than in one that is shallow or poorly drained and poorly aerated.

Requirements of Different Crops.—However, there are marked differences between species and even between varieties of the same species in their preferences for soils of unlike textures. The peach and almond flourish only in soils of a comparatively light porous texture, while the pear and quince prefer at least moderately heavy soils and will often do well in extremely heavy soils. The pomegranate is reported as doing fairly well in soils ranging from almost pure sand to heavy clay, but it does its best only in those that are fairly heavy and well drained; however, it will endure a wet, poorly aerated soil much better than most fruit plants.[30] Probably nowhere in the world does the pineapple do better than along the east coast of Florida, between Fort Pierce and Lake Worth, where the soil is almost a pure white sand (containing actually upwards of 98 per cent sand, gravel and silt);[70] nevertheless they are grown very successfully on some of the heavy soils of the Hawaiian Islands. It is generally recognized, however, that the soil that may be best for a particular fruit or some particular variety in one section may not be best in another section with different climate and distinct environmental conditions. Thus in New York the Concord grape grows on a wide variety of soils but seems to prefer a fairly strong loam with considerable clay; in western Washington the same variety can be grown successfully only in light sandy or sandy loam soils that tend to hasten maturity of fruit and vine. In general, the more favorable the texture of the soil for both the lateral and vertical development of the root system, the better.

Requirements as to Depth.—Theoretically, a soil need be only half as rich as another in order to support equally well a certain amount of vegetative growth if it is of such a character that roots penetrate twice as deep. Furthermore, since water is a limiting factor as often as plant nutrients, a tree with the deeper root system, though in poorer soil, is really in a better position than one growing in a richer, but shallower, medium. Only under very special conditions should ordinary deciduous tree fruits be planted in a soil in which the roots cannot penetrate freely to a depth of $2\frac{1}{2}$ to 3 feet in humid regions and to a depth of 5 to 10 feet in arid and semi-arid regions; soils that will permit greater penetration are preferable. Shallowness of soil, hardpan or plowsole close to the surface, impervious subsoil and poor drainage are interrelated factors which check vegetative growth, reduce yields and the size, quality and grade of the fruit, favor irregular bearing and lead to numerous physiological troubles, the treatment of which is difficult.

Classification of Soils According to Size of Soil Particles.—Since there is occasion repeatedly to refer to soils of different physical structure, a classification based on mechanical analysis, as used by the Bureau of Soils of the Federal Department of Agriculture, is presented here[60] (see Table 16).

It should be noted in connection with this classification that no account is taken of gravel or stones above 2 millimeters in diameter. Many soils contain rock particles larger than this maximum and not infrequently these constitute a large proportion of the soil volume. Accordingly a soil that in this scheme would be classified as a silt or even a clay might in fact be gravelly or rocky or stony in character. Though these larger components may have a relatively unimportant bearing on water holding capacity, aeration, root penetration and related features, they do influence it materially in its relation to tillage practices and they often prove a limiting factor in determining the kind of crop that can be grown in it advantageously, or the kind of orchard culture that must be practiced. Thus of two soils whose so-called "fine earth" might analyze the same, one might be suitable to the strawberry and the other quite unsuited because of the presence or absence of large quantities of rocks and coarse gravel. It is interesting to compare the mechanical analyses of several soils used for fruit production.

TABLE 16.—SCHEME OF SOIL CLASSIFICATION, BASED ON THE MECHANICAL COMPOSITION OF SOILS

	(1), (2) 2–0.5 milli- meters, per cent.	(1), (2), (3) 2–0.25 milli- meters, per cent.	(6) 0.05–0.005 milli- meters, per cent.	(7) Less than 0.005 milli- meters, per cent.	(6), (7) Less than 0.05 milli- meters, per cent.
Coarse sand............	>25	>50	0–15	0–10	<20
Medium sand..........	<25	>20	0–15	0–10	<20
Fine sand..............	....	<20	0–15	0–10	<20
Sandy loam............	....	>20	10–35	5–15	>20<50
Fine sandy loam........	....	<20	10–35	5–15	>20<50
Loam..................	....	....	<55	15–25	>50
Silt loam..............	....	....	>55	<25	....
Clay loam.............	....	....	25–55	25–35	>60
Sandy clay............	....	....	<25	>20	<60
Silty clay.............	....	....	>55	25–35	....
Clay..................	....	....	.....	>35	>60

(1) "Fine gravel," 2–1 millimeters. (2) "Coarse sand," 1–0.5 millimeter. (3) "Medium sand," 0.5–0.25 millimeter. (6) "Silt," 0.05–0.005 millimeter. (7) "Clay," less than 0.005 millimeter. The residue is composed of "fine sand," 0.25–0.1 millimeter and "very fine sand," 0.1–0.05 millimeter.

Mechanical Analyses of Various Fruit Soils.—Soils A and C with their subsoils B and D (Table 17) are fairly typical of the western New York fruit district, one of the leading apple producing sections of the world. Soil A, the Dunkirk sandy loam, contains 64 per cent. of medium and coarse sand in the surface and slightly more in the subsoil and only about 5 per cent. of clay in both surface and subsoil, while soil C, the

Dunkirk loam, contains only about 30 per cent. of medium and coarse sand in the surface soil and a little more than half that amount in the subsoil, but approximately twice as much of the finer materials—clay and silt. Here, indeed, are marked differences in the average size of soil particles, yet there are but slight differences in the way apple trees grow in these soils. Soil *E*, a fairly typical loess of Nebraska, contains no medium or coarse sand and comparatively large amounts of silt and clay, yet it furnishes excellent drainage and is eminently suited to the production of fruit, particularly apples. Though probably the Billings clay loam (Soil *M*), with its 47 per cent. clay and 91 per cent. of clay and silt combined is not an ideal soil for apples, it is a characteristic soil of the Grand Junction section of Colorado and where the topography permits reasonably good drainage, apple production is profitable. This particular soil serves to illustrate the point that the mechanical analysis of a soil is not always an accurate index to its possibilities for fruit growing. Though this analysis suggests very poor drainage and consequently a lack of suitability for fruit crops, some of this land is fairly well drained and does produce good fruit crops. However, it is but proper to state that the majority of the Grand Junction orchards are on soils of a somewhat lighter character. The Maricopa gravelly sand of California is, as the name suggests, comparatively light and open in character, containing 57 per cent. fine, medium and coarse sand and 11 per cent. fine gravel. It is considered very good for grapes; yet the Alamo clay adobe with 95 per cent. of clay and fine silt is said to be fairly suitable for grapes where the topography is such that drainage is not particularly poor.[65] Probably the gray-brown clay of Sonoma, California, whose mechanical analysis is shown in column *O* in the table, represents more nearly average soil conditions for the grape. Certainly it produces some of the best wine grapes of the country.[46] Citrus fruits likewise thrive on soils ranging from heavy adobes to gravelly loams and gravelly sands. It is interesting to note the texture of one of the pineapple soils of the Florida coast (Soil *H* in the table)—over 98 per cent. fine, medium and coarse sand.

The mechanical analyses of many other fruit soils which might be included would furnish little information, beyond that already given, as to the actual soil requirements of the different fruits. It is evident that the mechanical analysis of a soil carries some suggestion as to its suitability for fruit crops of different kinds but it is an index only in so far as it is an index of texture, drainage and aeration; these qualities depend to a considerable extent on such factors as topography, hardpan, chemical composition, rainfall and the movement of underground water. In other words, it is hardly practicable to attempt exact definition, in terms of soil particle measurements, of the soil requirements for distinct varieties of the same fruit or even of different fruits.

CONSIDERED FROM THE STANDPOINT OF CHEMICAL COMPOSITION

The statement has been made that, broadly speaking, the physical condition of the soil is more important in fruit production than is its chemical composition. However, it should not be inferred that chemical composition is of little significance, or that poor soils are preferable to good soils for orchard purposes. On the contrary, the richer the soil the better, though productivity as it concerns the orchardist, may be quite different from productivity as it concerns the man growing cereals or fiber plants and a soil that is productive in pineapple cultivation may be unproductive in avocado or prune cultivation. The only satisfactory measure of soil productivity is in terms of crop production of the specific plant under consideration. Hardly an orchard of commercial size anywhere fails to show differences in individual tree growth and production due apparently to variation in soil. However, thorough examination would show that many such differences are related to variations in texture or in water-holding capacity rather than in chemical composition. Often the great inequalities between the size, longevity or productivity of trees in various fruit producing sections may be regarded as due largely to chemical composition. The average differences between the apple orchards of western New York and southern Ohio is a case in point—a fact emphasized by the response of the orchards of the latter section to proper fertilizer applications.

Requirements of Different Crops.—It should be recognized, too, that certain fruits are particularly favored by the presence of some element or compound in the soil. For instance, a high lime content is said to be particularly favorable for oil production in the olive.[37] The cherry likewise seems to respond favorably to lime. *Vitis berlandieri* flourishes in, even prefers, a limestone soil; but *V. labrusca* is intolerant of lime.[20] The chestnut has been shown to be subject to chlorosis on soils containing upwards of 3 per cent. lime[10] and pears are reported as frequently chlorotic on calcareous soils.[55] Many crop plants are known to prefer a nearly neutral soil reaction and it has consequently been assumed that most fruit plants do; some, however, as the strawberry, thrive only in an acid medium and the blueberry demands a markedly acid soil.[8] Certain fruits like the grape are very tolerant toward "alkali;" others, like the mulberry, are very sensitive to it. The pineapple is intolerant of manganese.[35] These and the many other peculiarities of a fruit must be kept in mind and soils selected accordingly or, conversely, the soil's peculiarities must be ascertained and the fruit species or varieties selected accordingly.

Much can be done toward adapting a number of fruits to an uncongenial soil by growing them on a stock suited to the soil in question. This matter is discussed in some detail in the section on Propagation.

TABLE 17.—MECHANICAL ANALYSES OF VARIOUS FRUIT SOILS

	A	B	C	D	E	F	G	H	I	J	K	L	M	N	O
Fine gravel, per cent	....	....	....	....	....	3.9	6.7	0.23	0.06	8.91	0.3	....	0.1	11.44	0.6
Coarse sand, per cent	11.7	9.0	4.4	0.3	....	11.4	19.0	3.03	3.08	8.50	0.6	3.42	0.3	16.1	1.7
Medium sand, per cent	52.3	60.5	26.2	15.6	....	13.1	21.1	61.11	57.50	9.51	0.4	1.98	0.2	12.3	1.3
Fine sand, per cent	3.6	9.7	9.7	21.5	0.10	16.4	27.6	33.76	37.78	14.64	1.1	5.86	1.7	28.6	11.0
Very fine sand, per cent	11.1	8.4	30.0	27.9	25.83	11.9	6.9	0.54	0.59	34.45	3.0	10.40	6.2	16.7	13.6
Silt, per cent	15.5	....	19.1	29.0	57.00	33.4	14.6	0.28	0.20	16.22	41.4	50.34	43.8	10.9	52.2
Clay, per cent	5.6	5.1	10.6	5.5	9.49	9.5	4.9	0.50	0.52	5.46	53.5	23.12	47.4	4.0	19.1

Column key:

A — Dunkirk sandy loam, New York,[21] Surface 9 inches.
B — Dunkirk sandy loam, New York,[21] Subsoil.
C — Dunkirk loam, New York,[21] Surface 9 inches.
D — Dunkirk loam, New York,[21] Subsoil.
E — Loess subsoil, Nemaha County, Nebraska.[60]
F — Sandy loam, New Hampshire, Surface 7 inches.
G — Sandy loam, New Hampshire, Subsoil from 7 inches to 3 feet.
H — Pineapple soil, Florida coast,[70] Surface soil.
I — Pineapple soil, Florida coast,[70] Subsoil.
J — Maricopa gravelly loam, Arizona.[61]
K — Alamo clay adobe, California.[65]
L — San Joaquin black adobe, California.[62] Surface foot.
M — Billings clay loam, Colorado.[64]
N — Maricopa gravelly sand, California.[63]
O — Gray-brown loam, Sonoma, California.[33] Surface foot.

TABLE 18.—CHEMICAL ANALYSES OF AVERAGE SOILS OF HUMID AND ARID REGIONS AND OF CERTAIN ORCHARD SOILS IN ASIA MINOR AND CALIFORNIA

	A, average of analyses of 313 soils of arid regions,[27] per cent	B, average of analyses of 466 soils of humid regions,[27] per cent	C, soil from Erbelli, Asia Minor (noted for fig production),[34] per cent	D, Mesa loam from near Riverside, California,[26] per cent
Coarse materials...............	......	....	1.00	25.00
Fine earth......................	......	....	99.00	75.00
Analysis of fine earth:				
Insoluble matter..............	70.565	84.031	76.33	63.67
Soluble silica (SiO₂)...........	7.266	4.213	5.35	13.70
Potash (K₂O).................	0.729	0.216	1.09	0.73
Soda (Na₂O)..................	0.264	0.091	0.19	0.36
Lime (CaO)....................	1.362	0.108	1.96	1.58
Magnesia (MgO)..............	1.411	0.225	1.56	1.85
Manganese oxid (Mn₃O₄).......	0.059	0.133	0.01	0.03
Ferric oxid (Fe₂O₃)............	5.752	3.131	6.49	10.02
Alumina (Al₂O₃)...............	7.888	4.296	3.25	5.06
Phosphorus pentoxid (P₂O₅).....	0.117	0.113	0.29	0.07
Sulfur trioxid (SO₃)...........	0.041	0.052	0.06	0.01
Carbonic acid (CO₂)...........	1.316	....	1.00	....
Water and organic matter.......	4.945	3.644	2.29	2.74
Totals...................	101.715	100.253	99.87	99.82
Humus.......................	0.750	2.700	0.27	0.20
Nitrogen, per cent in humus.......	15.870	5.450	.....	....
Nitrogen, per cent in soil.........	0.101	0.122	.....	....

TABLE 19.—CHEMICAL ANALYSES OF TYPICAL FRUIT SOILS OF WASHINGTON[59]

	A, upper bench land, Wenatchee, per cent	B, volcanic ash, Walla Walla, per cent	C, Kennewick sand, Kennewick, per cent	D, sandy soil, Vashon Island, per cent	E, sandy soil, Vashon Island, per cent
Insoluble silica..............	81.632	77.772	84.402	76.652	72.297
Hydrated silica..............	2.498	5.464	3.332	8.572	8.646
Soluble silica (SiO₂).........	0.316	0.543	0.265	0.348	0.062
Potash (K₂O)................	0.518	0.328	0.312	0.126	0.157
Soda (Na₂O).................	0.233	0.238	0.416	0.106	0.167
Lime (CaO).................	0.714	0.659	0.944	0.615	0.693
Magnesia (MgO)............	0.186	0.104	0.650	0.807	0.548
Manganese dioxid (Mn₃O₄)...	.....	.....	trace	.....	.....
Iron oxid (Fe₂O₃)............	4.760	4.601	4.505	3.064	3.023
Alumina (Al₂O₃).............	6.145	3.925	5.889	4.852	7.634
Phosphorus pentoxide (P₂O₅).	0.225	0.037	0.140	0.044	0.073
Sulfur trioxid (SO₃)..........	.....	.....	0.018	.....	.....
Carbon dioxid (CO₂).........	.....	.....	.....	.....	.....
Volatile and organic matter...	2.969	5.580	1.219	4.467	6.075
Total...................	100.176	99.251	100.040	99.653	100.275
Humus.....................	1.942	1.400	0.465	1.870	3.100
Total nitrogen (N)..........	0.061	0.055	0.035	0.077	0.174

Chemical Analyses of Various Fruit Soils.—In the accompanying tables (18 to 23) are presented chemical analyses of certain typical soils that are more or less noted for fruit production, together with the analyses

TABLE 20.—CHEMICAL ANALYSES OF CERTAIN OREGON SOILS[56]

	"Redhill" land, Salem, per cent	White land, Benton County, per cent	Adobe soil, Benton County, per cent	Sandy loam, Wasco County, per cent	"Shot" land, Multnomah County, per cent
Character of soil:					
Coarse material..........	28.88	16.50	2.25	25.50	34.00
Fine earth...............	71.12	83.50	97.75	74.50	66.00
Analysis of fine earths:					
Insoluble matter..........	68.48	70.26	38.91	63.65	67.40
Soluble silica (SiO₂).......	4.38	5.53	16.74	12.65	5.18
Potash (K₂O)............	0.47	0.06	0.11	0.12	0.28
Soda (Na₂O).............	0.33	0.07	0.03	0.16	0.05
Lime (CaO)..............	0.40	0.66	1.60	1.41	1.35
Magnesia (MgO).........	0.96	.....	1.78	1.10	0.90
Manganese (Mn₃O₄)......	.....	0.04	0.08	.....	0.40
Iron (Fe₂O₃).............	14.78	13.51	23.21	9.23	17.67
Alumina (Al₂O₃).........	.....	.....	.....	.....	.....
Sulfuric acid (SO₃).......	.....	0.05	.....	.....	0.82
Phosphoric acid (P₂O₅).....	0.63	0.03	0.01	0.28	0.34
Water and organic matter..	10.19	10.13	17.44	11.81	7.98
Total...............	99.72	100.34	100.00	100.41	100.07
Humus....................	0.52	1.22	1.80	4.42	1.76

TABLE 21.—CHEMICAL ANALYSES OF CERTAIN FLORIDA SOILS

	A, surface soil, West Palm Beach[50] (pine-apple land), per cent	B, subsoil, West Palm Beach[50] (pine-apple land), per cent	C, surface soil Volusia County[54] (orange land), per cent	D, surface soil, muck land[54] (fruit and truck), per cent
Silica (SiO₂) insoluble............	99.3070	99.5840	96.0852	53.5900
Silica (SiO₂) soluble..............	0.0147	0.0197	....	....
Lime (CaO).....................	0.0037	0.0000	0.0526	trace
Magnesia (MgO).................	0.0000	0.0000	0.0145	trace
Potash (K₂O)...................	0.0048	0.0126	0.0208	0.1500
Iron and alumina (Fe₂O₃ and Al₂O₃).	0.2210	0.2400	1.1726	10.0100
Phosphorus pentoxid (P₂O₅).......	0.0100	0.0087	0.1600	trace
Sulfur trioxid (SO₃)..............	0.0038	0.0038	0.0096	0.0500
Volatile matter..................	0.4860	0.1620	....	....
Humus.........................	0.2000	0.0675	....	....
Nitrogen (N)....................	0.0100	0.0045	0.0890	1.500
Chlorin.........................	....	....	trace	0.0200
Water and organic matter.........	....	....	2.3910	34.9700

of certain other soils that have unknown value for fruit production or that are definitely known to be unsuitable. Comparison may thus be made between "fruit" soils and soils in general and between good and poor fruit land.

TABLE 22.—CHEMICAL ANALYSES OF MANGANIFEROUS AND NORMAL SOILS OF OAHU[39]

Constituents	Manganiferous soil		Normal soil	
	Soil	Subsoil	Soil	Subsoil
Insoluble matter.................	33.46	36.06	40.89	39.25
Potash (K_2O)....................	0.83	0.74	0.51	0.60
Soda (Na_2O)....................	0.40	0.42	0.21	0.32
Lime (CaO).......................	1.39	0.86	0.51	0.66
Magnesia (MgO).................	0.55	0.43	0.37	0.38
Manganese oxid (Mn_3O_4)..........	9.74	8.76	0.22	0.06
Ferric oxid (Fe_2O_3)...............	19.65	21.51	35.72	33.28
Alumina (Al_2O_3)..................	15.50	15.74	3.58	8.66
Phosphorus pentoxid (P_2O_5)........	0.21	0.16	0.07	0.08
Sulfur trioxid (SO_3)...............	0.16	0.09	0.09	0.07
Titanic oxid (TiO_3)...............	0.73	1.09	3.83	2.74
Loss on ignition..................	19.93	14.45	14.22	13.99
Total........................	100.35	100.31	100.22	100.09
Nitrogen (N)....................	0.39	0.23	0.34	0.25

TABLE 23.—CHEMICAL ANALYSES OF MISCELLANEOUS SOILS

	A, Maricopa gravelly loam Arizona,[11] per cent	B, Peach belt soil, South Haven, Mich.,[38] per cent	C, Olive orchard soil, Ventura, Cal.,[6] per cent	D, Slate colored upland adobe, Alameda, Cal.,[5] per cent	E, Loess soil, Kansas City, Mo.,[31] per cent
Insoluble silica (SiO_2)........	72.35	87.23	82.11	64.790	34.98
Soluble silica (SiO_2)..........	10.29	.....	6.88	16.564	.....
Lime (CaO).................	2.07	0.51	0.67	0.868	1.70
Magnesia (MgO)............	1.36	0.46	0.57	0.978	1.12
Potash (K_2O)..............	0.66	0.83	0.47	0.579	1.84
Soda (Na_2O)...............	0.28	0.34	0.42	0.100	1.06
Ferric oxid (Fe_2O_3)..........	4.41	1.52	5.26	3.791	2.36
Alumina (Al_2O_3)............	4.94	2.87	1.30	7.718	6.49
Phosphorus pentoxid (P_2O_5)..	0.09	0.13	0.21	0.143	0.09
Sulfur trioxid (SO_3).........	0.03	0.20	0.09	0.006	0.02
Carbon dioxid (CO_2)........	0.87	.....	......	......	.....
Chlorine..................	0.03	.....	......	......	.....
Water and organic matter....	.....	5.64	2.23	4.601	.....
Humus....................	0.51	.....	0.78	0.697	.....
Nitrogen (N)..............	0.04	0.07	0.074	......	.....

Probably the most striking fact brought out in a study of the chemical analyses of fruit soils (Tables 18 to 23) is their extreme variability and their frequent wide divergence from the averages of the soils of either the humid or arid sections. It is impossible to associate certain extreme soil types with special crops. For instance a single fruit crop would hardly be expected to do equally well on soil like that shown in columns *A* and *B* of Table 20 and those shown in Table 22. The Oahu soils contain seven to 20 times as much phosphorus, 50 to 80 times as much potash and 30 to 40 times as much nitrogen as those of the Florida coast; the difference in some of the other constituents is as great or greater. Yet these soils are almost equally well suited to the pineapple, though their fertilizer requirements are somewhat different. The two Hawaiian soils shown in Table 22 resemble each other closely, much more closely than they resemble the Florida soil, but they show a marked disparity in their suitability for fruit culture and the soil that is the richer in the nutrient elements, nitrogen, potash and phosphoric acid, is the poorer when measured in terms of pineapple production. Though the first three soils from Washington whose analyses are given in Table 19 show marked differences in composition, especially in their phosphorus and nitrogen content, all are noted for their fruit production and proof that even a single fruit, as the apple, reaches a higher stage of perfection in one than in the others is difficult. The soil designated in Table 20 as "White land" does not differ greatly in its analysis from the "Redhill" or the "Shot" land, except that it contains less potash and phosphoric acid. These elements are present, however, in larger amounts than in some of the other fruit soils whose analyses are given. Yet this "White Land" is not suited to fruit production and the "Redhill" land and the "Shot" land are among the best fruit soils of the state. The factor determining the difference between them is drainage. The analyses shown in columns *D* and *E* of Table 19 are particularly interesting in that both soils are from nearby fields on Vashon Island, Wash. The differences in composition as shown by the analyses are comparatively small; both are considered well suited to strawberry culture and the average variety does well upon both soils. Yet the Clark variety is reported as thriving only on the one and as failing to produce satisfactorily on the other.[59]

Evidently the relation of the chemical composition of the soil to suitability for fruit growing is far from well established, much less understood. Without doubt different fruits and possibly distinct varieties of the same fruit require, or at least grow better in, soils of somewhat dissimilar chemical composition. However, since present methods of analysis do not differentiate clearly between those requirements they do not actually measure soil productivity as it is expressed in terms of fruit production and they do not afford a very accurate index to fruit crop adaptation.

Evidence on Soil Requirements from Fertilizer Experiments.—Point is lent the last statement by data presented in Table 24 assembled by Stewart, showing the response to fertilizer applications of trees growing in soils of varying productivity.   In commenting on these data Stewart[58] remarks: "These figures show that the correlation between soil composition, as determined by the methods of soil sampling and analysis above specified, and the actual response of the associated trees to additional fertilization is either exceedingly slight or absent entirely.   One would naturally expect that the largest response would appear where the chemical fertility of the soil was lowest, and *vice versa*.   This evidently has not occurred.   In fact, the least response to practically all types of fertiliza-

TABLE 24.—RELATION OF SOIL COMPOSITION TO FERTILIZER RESPONSE
(*After Stewart*[58])

Soil type	Nitrogen Per cent. (total)	Phosphorus (P$_2$O$_5$) Per cent. (total)	Per cent. (available)	Potash (K$_2$O) Per cent. (total)	Per cent. (available)	Response to fertilization. (Per cent increase in yield) N	P	K	CF[1]	M[2]
Porters................	0.132	0.093	0.017	2.35	0.020	24	1	33	43	20
Montalto	0.071	0.029	0.009	0.66	0.010	3	5	1	29	30
DeKalb.................	0.118	0.087	0.002	1.81	0.029	148	27	23	181	294
Chester.................	0.158	0.116	0.012	2.23	0.040	15	4	3	24	46
Volusia.................	0.163	0.132	0.007	1.69	0.045	94	23	9	93	117
Lackawanna.............	0.300	0.233	0.043	1.78	0.051	27 CF[3]	3 M[3]	69	144	200
Frankstown.............	0.244	0.161	0.032	1.27	0.026	16	21	..	75	86
Chenango...............	0.183	0.315	0.122	1.55	0.145	24	26	..	26	24
Hagerstown.............	0.123	0.135	0.006	1.97	0.042	9	9	..	92	83

[1] Complete fertilizer.   [2] Manure.   [3] Per cent. increase in growth, instead of yield.

tion has occurred in the soil analyzing poorest of all, and some of the largest responses have appeared in the chemically richest soils.   The ordinary methods of soil analysis are not yet adequate to furnish a reliable indication of the fertility needs of an orchard.   Trees on chemically rich soils will not of necessity prove unresponsive to additional fertilization, nor will trees on chemically poor soils always prove responsive.   In other words, some other indicator than the chemical composition of the soil, as here determined, must be relied upon to determine the real need of additional fertility in an orchard.   At present, therefore, the surest and most delicate test yet devised for determining the fertility needs of an orchard soil is the actual respose of the living tree in the soil concerned to appropriate fertility additions."

The soil is a very complex substance and the soil solution likewise; apparently absolute amounts of certain elements or compounds that it contains are not so important as the state of balance or equilibrium existing between them. No better evidence to this effect is needed than some of the facts brought out by the analyses of the Florida and Hawaiian pineapple soils that have been mentioned. Certainly it would not be suspected from these analyses that in the Hawaiian soils with their 20 to 35 per cent. of iron (indeed there is one local pineapple district in the Hawaiian Islands where the soil contains 85 per cent. iron and titanium[72]) the plants often show symptoms of iron starvation and that iron sulphate is their most valuable fertilizer, though less than three-tenths of 1 per cent. of iron furnishes an ample supply in the Florida sands. The relationship between soil and crop is more than that existing between the different factors in a problem in addition and subtraction. Other aspects of this general question are discussed in the sections on Water Relations and Nutrition.

VEGETATION AS AN INDEX TO CROP ADAPTATION

Though at present no single feature of the chemical or mechanical composition of the soil can be designated the chief cause for the way some fruit crops grow on it, soil differences, even slight differences, may be of great significance to the fruit grower. His study of soils should include more than the features brought into contrast by chemical and mechanical analyses. The types of the native vegetation may serve as very useful indices of probable productivity when planted to cultivated crop plants belonging to the same or a closely related genus or family; knowledge of plant ecology may make it possible to predict with accuracy the way some entirely unrelated plant will behave on the soil in question. For instance, in Ohio, land upon which the sugar maple, beech, oak, or chestnut thrive naturally is likely to be well suited to the apple, but land on which the elm is native is seldom desirable for that fruit.[18] In western Oregon and western Washington, hill land supporting a vigorous growth of the native "brake" or fern (*Pteridium aquilinum pubescens*) is characteristically good for prunes. In the Ozarks "post-oak" land is good for grape culture. In Florida "all things considered the best soil (for the pecan) is probably one which has previously supported a growth of holly, willow-leaved oak, dogwood, hickory and those other trees usually found associated with them."[32]

Ney[52] has pointed out that the kinds of forest trees growing on land often form something of an index of its chemical condition. He says, "As regards the chemical composition of the soil, even slightly sour marshy soils are unfavorable to all species of trees except alder, birch, and spruce; whilst sour soils, liable to dry up at certain seasons, are unsuited to all except birch, spruce, Scots and Weymouth pines." Ash, maple, sycamore, and elm require a moderate quantity of lime and beech, hornbeam, oak, as also larch and Austrian pine, thrive best on soils that have at least some lime in their composition.   The hardwoods—oak, ash, maple, sycamore, elm, chestnut, beech and hornbeam—also appear to demand the presence of a considerable quantity of potash, while on the other hand, spruce, silver fir and especially Scotch pine and birch thrive on soils rich in neither lime nor potash.   In Florida a dense growth of palmettos is likely to indicate an undesirable hardpan or subsoil; such soils should be avoided in citrus fruit plantings.

Not only are the kinds of native trees or plants useful in determining the value of a soil for fruit growing, but the type of growth that these species make is of equal significance.   Thus Vosbury[68] states, "Most of the recent citrus plantings in Florida have been made on high pinelands. Three grades of high pineland are recognized.   The best grade is characterized by large straight-growing pines with occasional oaks, hickories, or other hardwood trees.   The soil is a sandy loam, fairly rich in humus, and is underlaid with a clay subsoil at a depth of 6 feet or less.   In second-grade pinelands the pine trees are smaller and there are few or no hardwoods, while the subsoil is further from the surface.   In the third or poorer grade the pines are still smaller and scrubbier and the clay subsoil far below the surface soil."

The soils picked as especially suited to certain field crops in some sections are less likely to furnish a reliable guide to their suitability to certain fruits.   In New England apples will generally do well in those soils considered best suited to corn, for only the lighter earlier soils are able properly to mature that crop in that section, but in Illinois the best corn land is quite different in character and the best apple land is outside the corn belt.

ADAPTATION OF VARIETIES TO PARTICULAR SOILS

In addition to the more or less general soil requirements for different kinds of fruits that have been mentioned, particular varieties or groups exhibit certain soil preferences.

For instance, in speaking of soil adaptations of plums, Hedrick[22] states that the Domesticas and Insititias grow most satisfactorily on rich clay loams, while the Trifloras, Hortulanas and Munsonianas give best results on light soils.   These group names, however, represent distinct species and consequently differences greater than those usual between varieties of the same kind of fruit.

Wilder,[73] who has made a special study of the fruit soils of southern New England, makes the following statements regarding the special soil requirements of certain well known apple varieties: "Soils grading from medium to semi-light fulfill the best requirements of the Baldwin.   This grouping would include the medium to light loams, the heavy sandy loams, and also the medium sandy loams, provided they were underlaid by soil material not lighter than a medium loam nor heavier than a light or medium clay loam of friable structure." From this broad generalization it will be seen that the surface soil should contain an appreciable amount of sand. The sands, moreover, should not be all of one grade, that is, a high percentage of coarse sand would give a poor soil, whereas a moderate admixture of it with the finer grades of sand, together with sufficient clay and silt, would work no harm.

"A surface soil of heavy, silty loam or light, silty, clay loam underlain by silty clay loam excels for the 'green' Rhode Island Greening. Such soil will retain sufficient moisture to be classed as a moist soil, yet it is not so heavy as ever to be ill drained if surface drainage is inadequate. The soil should be moderately rich in organic matter, decidedly more so than for the Baldwin. Such soil conditions maintain a long seasonal growth under uniform conditions of moisture, and thus produce the firm yet crisp texture, the remarkable juiciness and the high flavor for which this variety is noted when at its best. If grown on a soil too sandy, the Rhode Island Greening lacks fineness of grain, flavor and the juicy quality in greater or lesser degree, depending on the extent of the departure from those soil characteristics which contribute to its production.

"This variety [Northern Spy] is one of the most exacting in soil requirements. To obtain good quality of fruit, i.e., fine texture, juiciness and high flavor, the soil must be moderately heavy, and for the first two qualities alone the Rhode Island Greening soil would be admirable. The fact that the Northern Spy is a red apple, however, makes it imperative that the color be well developed and the skin free from the greasy tendency. This necessitates a fine adjustment of soil conditions, for the heaviest of the soils adapted to the Rhode Island Greening produces Northern Spies with greasy skins and usually of inferior color. Its tendency to grow upright seems to be accentuated by too clayey soils, if well enriched and such soils tend to promote growth faster than the tree is able to mature well. On the other hand, sandy soils, while producing good color and clear skins, fail to bring fruit satisfactory in quality with respect to texture and flavor. The keeping quality, too, is inferior to that of the Spy grown on heavier soils in the same district. Hence the soil requirements of this variety are decidedly exacting, and are best supplied apparently by a medium loam underlain by a heavy loam or light clay loam. It should not be planted on a soil lighter than a very heavy, fine, sandy, loam, underlain by a light clay loam, or possibly a heavy loam. On light soils the Northern Spy very often yields less per acre than the Baldwin.

"Both Ben Davis and Gano show less effect from variation in the soils upon which they are grown than any others observed."

In speaking of the special soil requirements of peach varieties the same author has this to say:

"Judging from the experience of a very large number of growers in Connecticut and in other States, combined with field observations, it seems evident that the Champion peach is especially sensitive to any condition of subsoil which hinders the ready movement of moisture within a probable depth of as much as 4 feet from the surface. Carman and Mountain Rose are not quite so dependent as the Champion on soils that drain out hastily, and while they succeed best on soils of a little greater moisture-holding capacity than the Champion, they nevertheless give the best results on deep and well-drained soils. The Elberta and the Belle thrive on well-drained soils that are somewhat stronger than the varieties previously mentioned."[74]

There is some reason to believe that the importance of these variety preferences is often over-emphasized. For instance, to assert that the Yellow Newtown (Albemarle Pippin) apple will do well only on the so-called "pippin" soils of Virginia and North Carolina is to misstate the facts, except perhaps for the soils of those particular states. The variety does equally well on quite different soils in the Hudson River, Hood River and Rogue River valleys and in New South Wales, though on these other soils it may develop a slightly different but in no way inferior, shape, color or flavor. Some of the variation in the chemical composition of fruits is without doubt due to diversities in soil and in some parts of the world these differences are regarded as of considerable importance in the production of grapes for wine; however, much of the variation in composition is due to other factors of environment, such as temperature, sunlight and humidity. Their influence must be subtracted before it can be said that the difference in the quality of fruit from two different sections, or even orchards, is due to soil variation. Nevertheless, the ways in which soil influences the development of individual varieties may well be studied, for often the information gained can be of much use in actual fruit production. For instance, if a piece of land that is to be planted to apple trees includes some light and some heavy soil and two varieties, one a red and the other a yellow apple, are to be set, it will generally be wise to plant the red variety on the lighter soil and the yellow variety on the heavier, so far as possible. Though soil probably exerts very little, if any, direct influence on pigment production in the fruit, the type of vegetative growth obtained on the lighter soil is likely to permit and encourage higher coloration of the fruit than that obtained on the finer textured land.

It is easier to modify through treatment the chemical condition of the soil than its physical condition and obviously, it is generally easier to modify surface soil than subsoil. The subsoil must be taken largely as it is found. Consequently in selecting a piece of land for fruit growing the subsoil should be given specially careful consideration, particularly as regards its physical condition. Both physical and chemical condition of the surface soil may be modified materially, but to effect any considerable change, particularly in physical character, is expensive. The grower should never forget that the business must yield a fair return on the investment.

Summary.—In general, fruit crops demand the same qualities in a soil as cereal or forage plants. On account of their growing habits, however, depth of soil, character of subsoil and general physical condition are of relatively greater importance to the former. Different fruit crops show varying adaptation to soils of quite dissimilar textures. Practically all, however, are alike in requiring considerable depth, thorough aeration and freedom from hardpan, plowsole or other impervious strata. It is impracticable at present to attempt a definition of the soil requirements of different fruit plants in terms of mechanical analysis.

Soils that are unproductive from the standpoint of cereal crops are often productive from the standpoint of fruit production and the reverse situation often occurs. It is even more impracticable to attempt a definition of the soil requirements of different fruits in terms of chemical composition, than in terms of mechanical analysis. The character of the vegetation growing naturally on a soil furnishes one of the best indices to the kinds of fruit that may be expected to thrive on it. Though there are indications of marked adaptation of particular varieties to certain soil types, the importance of such special adaptations is often exaggerated.

Suggested Collateral Readings

Wickson, E. J. California Fruits: How to Grow Them. Pp. 27–37. San Francisco, 1910.

Bowman, I. Forest Physiography. Pp. 27–40, 107–126. New York, 1914.

Russell, E. J. Soil Conditions and Plant Growth. Chapters 3 and 8. Pp. 52–79; 153–169. London, 1915.

Literature Cited

1. Abbe, C. U. S. D. A., Mo. Weather Rev. 21. 1893. Cited by Garriot, E. B. U. S. D. A. Farmers' Bul. 104. 1899.
2. Baker, O. E., and Genung, A. B. U. S. D. A. Misc. Pub. 267. 1938.
3. Batchelor, L. D., and West, F. L. Utah Agr. Exp. Sta. Bul. 141. 1915.
4. Bigelow, F. H. U. S. D. A., Weather Bur. Bul. R. 1908.
5. Cal. Agr. Exp. Sta. Bul. 25. 1884.
6. Cal. Agr. Exp. Sta. Rept. for 1894–1895. P. 15. 1896.
7. Cal. Agr. Exp. Sta. Ann. Rept. 1903–1904.
8. Coville, F. V. U. S. D. A., Bur. Pl. Ind. Bul. 193. 1910.
9. Finch, C., and Baker, D. O. Geography of the World's Agriculture. U. S. D. A., Office Farm Management. 1917.
10. Fliche, P., and Grandeau, L. Ann. Chim. et Phys., ser. 5. 2: 354–379. 1874.
11. Forbes, R. H. Ariz. Agr. Exp. Sta. Bul. 28. 1897.
12. Fritz, H. Intern. wissensch. Bibliothek, Band 68. Leipzig, 1889. Cited by Abbe, C. U. S. D. A., Weather Bur. Bul. 36. 1905.
13. Gager, C. S. J. N. Y. Bot. Garden 8. 1909. Cited in U. S. D. A., Mo. Weather Rev. 36: 63. 1908.
14. Georgeson, C. C. Alaska Agr. Exp. Sta. Ann. Rept. P. 9. 1906.
15. Ibid. P. 21. 1907.
16. Ibid. P. 20. 1908.
17. Ibid. Pp. 8, 9. 1909.
18. Green, W. J. Ohio Agr. Exp. Sta. Bul. 137. 1903.
19. Hann, J. Handbuch der Klimatologie. Stuttgart, 1911.

20. Hedrick, U. P.   Grapes of New York.   Pp. 131, 152.   Albany, 1908.
21. Hedrick, U. P.   N. Y. Agr. Exp. Sta. Bul. 314.   1909.
22. Hedrick, U. P.   Plums of New York.   P. 113.   Albany, 1911.
23. Heyer, G.   Forstl. Bodenk. u. Klimatol.   P. 488.   1856.   Cited in Nisbet, J. Studies in Forestry.   P. 53.   Oxford, 1894.
24. Higgins, J. E.   Hawaii Agr. Exp. Sta. Bul. 7.   1904.
25. Higgins, J. E., and Holt, V. S.   Hawaii Agr. Exp. Sta. Bul. 32.   1914.
26. Hilgard, E. W.   Cal. Agr. Exp. Sta. Rept. for 1890.   P. 41.   1891.
27. Ibid.   Rept. for 1892–1893.   P. 328.   1894.
28. Ibid.   Rept. for 1897–1898.   P. 41.
29. Hilgard, E. W.   Soils, 6th ed.   P. 182.   1914.
30. Hodgson, R. W.   Cal. Agr. Exp. Sta. Bul. 276.   1917.
31. Hopkins, C. G.   Soil Fertility and Permanent Agriculture.   P. 69.   1910. (Computed from his data.)
32. Hume, H. H.   Fla. Agr. Exp. Sta. Bul. 85.   1906.
33. Husmann, G. C.   U. S. D. A., Bur. Pl. Ind. Bul. 172.   1910.
34. Jaffa, M. E.   Cal. Agr. Exp. Sta. Rept. for 1892–3.   P. 238.   1894.
35. Johnson, M. O.   Hawaii Agr. Exp. Sta. Press Bul. 51.   1916.
36. Johnston, S.   Mich. Agr. Exp. Sta. Sp. Bul. 252.   1934.
37. Kearney, T. H.   U. S. D. A., Bur. Pl. Ind. Bul. 125.   1908.
38. Kedzie, R. C.   Mich. Agr. Exp. Sta. Bul. 99.   1893.
39. Kelley, W. P.   Hawaii Agr. Exp. Sta. Bul. 26.   1912.
40. Kerner, A., and Oliver, F. W.   Natural History of Plants.   1 (2): 528.   New York, 1895.
41. King, F. A.   Wis. Agr. Exp. Sta. Ann. Rept. 12: 268–272.   1895.
42. Kinman, C. F.   Porto Rico Agr. Exp. Sta. Bul. 24.   1918.
43. Lippincott, J. S.   U. S. Rept. Com. Agr.   Pp. 137–190.   1866.
44. Loughridge, R. H.   Cal. Agr. Exp. Sta. Bul. 133.   1901.
45. Lutz, H.   Letter to F. C. Bradford, dated Jan. 25, 1937.
46. Mac Dougal, D. T.   Mem. Hort. Soc. N. Y.   2: 3–22.   1907.
47. Mason, S. C.   U. S. D. A. Bul. 271.   1915.
48. Mass. St. Board of Agr., Ann. Rept.   59: 14–15.   1911.
49. Merriam, C. H.   U. S. D. A., Div. of Biol. Surv. Bul. 10.   1898.
50. Miller, H. K., and Hume, H. H.   Fla. Agr. Exp. Sta. Bul. 68.   1903.
51. Motts, G. N.   Mich. Agr. Exp. Sta. Tech. Bul. 120.   1931.
52. Ney. Lehre von Waldbau.   P. 64.   1885.   Cited in Nisbet, J.   Studies in Forestry.   Oxford, 1894.
53. Partridge, N. L., and Veatch, J. O.   Mich. Agr. Exp. Sta. Circ. Bul. 155.   1936.
54. Persons, A. A.   Fla. Agr. Exp. Sta. Bul. 43.   1897.
55. Riviere, G., and Bailhache, G.   Prog. Agr. et Vit.   53 (15): 453–454.   1910.
56. Shaw, G. W.   Ore. Agr. Exp. Sta. Bul. 50.   1898.
57. Shreve, F.   Carn. Inst. Wash. Pub. 217.   1915.
58. Stewart, J. P.   Pa. Agr. Exp. Sta. Bul. 153.   1918.
59. Thatcher, R. W.   Wash. Agr. Exp. Sta. Bul. 85.   1908.
60. U. S. D. A., Bur. Soils, Bul. 5.   1896.
61. U. S. D. A., Operations Div. Soils for 1900.   P. 303.   1901.
62. Ibid. for 1901.   P. 464.   1902.
63. Ibid. for 1904.   P. 1127.   1905.
64. Ibid. for 1905.   P. 959.   1907.
65. Ibid. for 1909.   P. 1721.   1921.
66. Veatch, J. O., and Partridge, N. L.   Mich. Agr. Exp. Sta. Sp. Bul. 257.   1934.

67. Vinson, R. S., and Russell, E. J.   J. Agr. Sci.   2: 225.   1907.
68. Vosbury, E. D.   U. S. D. A. Farmers' Bul. 1122.   1920.
69. Wheeler, H. J.   U. S. D. A. Farmers' Bul. 77.   1905.
70. Whitney, M.   U. S. D. A., Bur. Soils, Bul. 13.   1898.
71. Wilcox, E. V.   Tropical Agriculture.   Pp. 2, 5.   1916.
72. Ibid.   P. 19.   1916.
73. Wilder, H. J.   Mass. St. Board Agr. Ann. Rept.   59: 13–23.   1911.
74. Wilder, H. J.   U. S. D. A. Bul. 140.   1915.
75. Yarnell, S. H.   Tex. Agr. Exp. Sta. Ann. Rept.   48: 25.   1935.

GLOSSARY

Absorption.—The process of taking up water and holding it in pores or open spaces, as a sponge.

Adiabatic.—A curve exhibiting variations of pressure and volume of a fluid when it expands without receiving or losing heat.

Adsorption.—The adhesion of molecules of gases or dissolved substance to the surfaces of solid particles; distinguished from absorption, which is not a surface phenomenon.

Aitionomic.—As referred to parthenocarpy, the ability to develop parthenocarpic fruits only in response to some stimulus external to the ovary.

Akene.—Dry, unilocular, indehiscent fruit, seed-like in appearance, as in the strawberry.

Alkali.—(1) In chemistry, a base; (2) as applied to soils, salts present in amounts harmful to plants, chiefly sodium chloride, sodium sulphate and sodium carbonate.

Anaheim Disease.—A disorder of grapes, associated with drought and overbearing, characterized by more or less dieback of vines and failure on the part of the fruit to mature properly, so called because at one time it was very serious in the vicinity of Anaheim, Cal. More recently thought to be due to virus infection.

Antagonism.—Of salts, a mutual counteraction of their influence on cell permeability.

Arginine.—A basic amino-acid which is a product of protein digestion.

Autocatalysis.—A process of catalysis where the catalytic agent is an end product of the reaction catalyzed.

Autogamy.—When a flower is fertilized by its own pollen.

Autonomic.—As referred to parthenocarpy, the ability to set fruit without the stimulus resulting from pollination.

Barren.—Unproductive.

Black End.—A disorder of certain fruits, especially pears, in which the apical fleshy tissues dry out, turn black and become hard and woody. Usually associated with drought in some form.

Blackheart.—A diseased condition of the woody tissues in which the inner layers become darkened in color, impregnated with certain substances and lose their ability to serve as conducting and storage tissues. Apparently caused by low winter temperatures.

Black Measles.—Another name for the Anaheim disease (which see).

Breba.—One of the crops of the pistillate fig tree, the first to mature in the spring.

Caprifig.—The wild or "male" fig, the uncultivated form.

Chemotropism.—A bending or turning in response to a chemical stimulus.

Chlorosis.—A diseased condition shown by loss of green color.

Choline.—An amine arising as one of the products of lecithin decomposition.

Colloid.—A state of a substance where the units are very large molecules or molecule complexes. Colloids diffuse slowly or not at all through plant or animal membranes.

Compatibility.—(1) Of sex cells, the ability to unite and form a fertilized egg that can grow to maturity. (2) Congeniality as determined by the degree of success of the union between stock and cion.

Corky Core.—A disorder in which the tissues around the core turn brown and become more or less corky, usually accompanied by the development of a bitter taste.

Coulure.—The failure of blossoms to set, resulting in a premature drop. *Cf.* millerandage.

Court-noué.—A physiological disturbance of the grape manifested by short internodes.

Crazy Top.—A disorder of citrus trees associated with an alkaline soil reaction and resulting in a peculiar type of growth.

Creatine.—A nitrogenous compound readily converted into creatinine.

Creatinine.—A basic nitrogenous compound occurring naturally in muscle tissue and urine.

Crinkle.—A disorder of apples in which the surface of the fruit becomes roughened. Supposed to be a form of drought injury.

Cumarine.—An organic compound with vanilla-like odor known as tonka bean camphor.

Dichogamy.—Insuring cross fertilization by the sexes being developed at different times.

Dicliny.—Male and female organs separate and in different flowers.

Dieback.—A disorder of tree, bush and vine fruits characterized by killing back of the younger growth.

Dihydroxy-stearic Acid.—A double hydroxide of a common fatty acid.

Dimorphism.—Presenting two forms, as long and short growths or permanent and deciduous branches.

Diœcious.—Unisexual, the male and female elements in different individuals.

Disaccharide.—A compound sugar yielding two simple sugars on hydrolysis.

Dormant.—Applied to buds when they are not actively growing and to plants when they are not in leaf.

Drought Spot.—A bit of tissue, usually dark in color and more or less dry, near the surface or deeply embedded in the flesh, not caused by parasites but associated with drought.

Emasculation.—The artificial removal of the stamens from the flower before they dehisce.

Embryogenic.—Pertaining to the development of the embryo.

Embryo Sac.—The cell in the ovule in which the embryo is formed.

Endocarp.—The inner layer of the wall of a fructified ovary.

Endosperm.—The nutritive material stored within a seed, originally deposited within the embryo sac.

Exanthema.—A disorder, particularly of citrus fruits, characterized by more or less killing back of the younger wood.

Exocarp.—The outer layer of the wall of a fructified ovary.

Extine.—The outer coat of a pollen grain.

Fasciation.—A deformity in which the stem becomes much flattened as a result of multiple terminal buds arranged in a single plane.

Fecundation.—The fusion of two gametes to form a new cell.

Fecundity.—The ability of flowers to produce seeds that will germinate.

Fertility.—(1) Of flowers, the capacity of producing seeds that will germinate; (2) of soils, the crop producing power.

Fertilization.—(1) The fusion of two gametes to form a new cell; (2) the application of fertilizers.

Frenching.—A disease characterized by loss of color in leaves between the veins.

Fruitfulness.—The capacity of producing fruit.

Fruit Pit.—A disorder, more especially of apples, in which bits of fruit tissue, either at the surface or more or less deeply embedded, become darkened in color, dry out and usually become bitter.

Fruit Setting.—A development of the ovary and adjacent tissues following the blossoming period.

Fruit Spot.—A general term referring to any surface blemish or lesion embedded in the flesh of the fruit and including such disorders as fruit pit and drought spot as well as those due to fungus or bacterial infection.

Gamete.—A unisexual cell which must fuse with another gamete to produce a new individual.

Glucosides.—Compounds that yield sugar and some other substance, usually aromatic, on hydrolysis.

Guanine.—A basic nitrogenous compound related to uric acid; one of the purines.

Gummosis.—A disorder, particularly of stone and citrus fruits, in which there are copious exudations or deposits of gum.

Gum Spot.—A disorder of stone, citrus and certain other fruits in which there are small local deposits of gum in the tissues of fruit, shoot or other organ.

Gynaeceum.—The pistil or pistils of a flower.

Hermaphrodite.—A flower with both stamens and pistils.

Heterostyly.—The presence of styles of two or more forms or two or more lengths.

Heterotypic.—Reduction division of a cell.

Histidine.—A basic amino-acid which is a product of protein digestion.

Homotypic.—As applied to cell division, involving the usual process of karyokinesis.

Hydrolysis.—Chemical splitting by taking up the elements of water.

Hydrophyte.—A plant that naturally grows in the water.

Hygroscopic Coefficient.—The percentage of soil water retained in contact with a saturated atmosphere and in the absence of any other source of moisture.

Hypoxanthine.—A basic nitrogenous compound related to uric acid; one of the purines.

Imbibition.—The process of absorption, usually by a solid.

Imperfect.—In flowers, unisexual.

Impotence.—Inability to produce functional gametes of the one sex or the other; sometimes used in a more general sense to denote sterility.

Incompatibility.—Of sex cells, the inability to unite and form a fertilized egg that can grow to maturity.

Interfertility.—The ability of one variety to set fruit and produce seeds that will germinate when pollenized by another variety.

Interfruitfulness.—The ability of one variety to set and mature seed-containing or seedless fruit when pollenized by another variety.

Intersexualism.—Sex intergrades; a term referring to the varying degrees of development of the two sex organs in the same plant; relative maleness or femaleness of the plant.

Intersterility.—Inability of one variety when pollenized by another variety to set fruit and produce seeds that will germinate.

Intine.—The inner coat of a pollen grain.

Intumescence.—A swelling or enlargement; a tumor.

June Drop.—The abscission of partly developed fruit (often occurring in June).

Latent Bud.—A bud, usually concealed, more than one year old, which may remain dormant indefinitely or may develop under certain conditions.

Lecithin.—A fat-soluble compound containing nitrogen and phosphorus.

Locule.—The cavity of an anther or ovary.

Mamme.—One of the crops of the caprifig or "male" fig, the first to mature in the spring. The fruits of this crop winter over as comparatively large specimens.

Mammoni.—One of the crops of the caprifig or "male" fig, which sets in June and matures in late summer.

Measles.—A disorder of apple trees characterized by a roughening of the bark on twigs and the younger branches.

Mesophyll.—The inner or middle, spongy portion of the leaf.

Mesophyte.—A plant that grows naturally under conditions of moderate humidity, that neither requires nor will survive culture in water or extreme drought.

Metaxenia.—The supposed direct influence of the pollen or pollen parent on the characteristics of the developing fruit.

Millerandage.—A condition in the grape where the ovary persists but the seeds remain small or do not attain usual size; produced by conditions similar to those that lead to coulure.

Monoecious.—The stamens and pistils in separate flowers but borne on the same individual.

Nucleic Acid.—Phosphorus-containing acids, usually combined with protein in all cell nuclei.

Nucleins.—Phosphorus-containing compounds of nucleic acid with protein.

Œdema.—A more or less localized, swollen condition of certain tissues.

Osmosis.—Diffusion through a membrane.

Parenchymatosis.—A disorder in which there is a localized proliferation or expansion of parenchyma tissue.

Parthenocarpy.—The production of fruit without true fertilization.

Parthenogenesis.—The development of the unfertilized egg into the usual product of fertilization without a preceding union of gametes.

Pedicel.—The support of a single flower of an inflorescence.

Peduncle.—The support of an inflorescence or a flower stalk.

Pentosan.—A polysaccharide that yields five-carbon sugars on hydrolysis.

Perennation.—A lasting state, referring particularly to the persistence of fruit long after its usual season of maturity.

Perfect.—Hermaphrodite flowers.

Phyllody.—A disorder in which a shoot or branch develops a much larger number of leaves than is normal.

Picoline.—A basic derivative of pyridine.

Pollination.—The placing of pollen on the stigmatic surface.

Pollinium.—A pollen mass consisting of all the pollen grains of an anther locule.

Polyembryony.—The production of more than one embryo in an ovule.

Polygamo-dioecious.—With hermaphrodite and unisexual flowers on different individuals of the same species.

Polygamous.—With hermaphrodite and unisexual flowers.

Polysaccharide.—A carbohydrate which yields a large but indefinite number of simple sugars on hydrolysis; usually colloids.

Polyterpenes.—Compounds which yield an indefinite number of simple hemiterpene units on distillation; ex. caoutchouc, balata.

Profichi.—One of the crops of the caprifig or "male" fig, the second to mature in the spring. The fruits of this crop appear as small buttons in the late fall or early winter.

Proliferation.—A rapid and repeated production of new parts, as the formation of leafy parts from floral parts.

Protandry.—The pollen being discharged before the pistils are receptive.

Protogyny.—The pistils receptive before the anthers have ripe pollen.

Pseudo-hermaphrodite.—Functional unisexuality in the presence of apparently well developed stamens and pistils.

Purines.—A group of nitrogenous organic compounds such as uric acid, xanthine and caffein.

Pyridine.—A nitrogenous base which is the nucleus of many organic compounds, for example, nicotine.

Pyrimidines.—A group of basic nitrogenous compounds related to the purines and found as products of nucleic acid cleavage.

Quinone.—An oxidation product of benzene.

Respiration.—Gaseous exchange by which the plant absorbs oxygen and gives off carbon dioxide.

Respiratory Coefficient.—The amount of carbon dioxide given off divided by the amount of oxygen used in respiration.

Ring Neck.—A disorder of the avocado in which there is a drying out and shriveling of surface areas on the fruit pedicels.

Rosette.—A condition in which the internodes are much shortened, giving the leaves a bunched or clustered appearance.

Salicylic Aldehyde.—An oxidation product of salicin giving the fragrance to meadow-sweet.

Sod Culture.—A method of orchard soil management in which a permanent perennial crop is grown between the trees, mowed once or twice during the growing season and then allowed to remain on the ground. A limited area around the trees is hoed, spaded or otherwise tilled.

Sod Mulch.—A method of orchard soil management in which a permanent perennial crop is grown between the trees, mowed once or twice during the growing season and then allowed to remain on the ground.

Somaplasm.—The protoplasm other than the germplasm.

Sour Sap.—A sour or fermented condition of the sap, often associated with a high water table or other root disturbance and usually followed by the death of the tree.

Sporogenous.—Producing spores.

Sporophyte.—The plant in the alternating life cycle arising from a fertilized egg and producing spores.

Sterility.—The inability to produce seeds that will germinate.

Stippen.—A disorder closely related to fruit pit, which see.

Supercooling.—Cooling below the freezing point without solidification.

Temperature Inversion.—A rise in temperature with increasing distance from the ground, up to a certain height.

Tetrad.—A group of four cells such as the pollen grains derived from one spore mother cell.

Torus.—(1) The receptacle of a flower, part of the axis on which the flower parts are inserted; (2) the thickening in the center of the membrane in bordered pits.

Trimorphism.—Heterogamy, or with long-, short-, and mid-styled flowers.

Vacuole.—In cells, the cell sap surrounded by protoplasm.

Vanillin.—An aromatic compound, the fragrant constituent of vanilla.

Virescence.—A disorder in which certain vegetative or floral structures become and remain abnormally vegetative and green.

Water Berries.—A disorder of the grape in which the fruits are watery and fail to ripen properly.

Watercore.—A disorder, especially of apples, in which the fleshy tissues, either around the core or near the surface, become watery, hard and glassy.

Wilting Coefficient.—The percentage of moisture in the soil when permanent wilting of plants takes place.

Windburn.—A disorder of the leaves in which first their edges and later perhaps the entire leaf dries out and presents a scorched appearance.

Witches Broom.—A disorder of the stem or its branches in which there is an extreme amount of branching, resulting in a very brushy condition. Sometimes caused by fungus attack.

Xanthine.—A basic nitrogenous compound related to uric acid; one of the purines.

Xenia.—The direct influence of foreign pollen on the part of the mother plant that develops into endosperm.

Xerophyte.—A plant that can endure extreme drought.

Xyloporosis.—A disorder, associated with lack of compatibility between stock and cion, characterized by pores or pits in the wood and corresponding pegs in the bark.

INDEX

(Principal discussions are in **bold face** type)